Advanced **Windows**®

Third Edition

Jeffrey Richter

Microsoft®Press

PUBLISHED BY
Microsoft Press
A Division of Microsoft Corporation
One Microsoft Way
Redmond, Washington 98052-6399

Library of Congress Cataloging-in-Publication Data
Richter, Jeffrey.
    Advanced Windows / Jeffrey Richter. -- 3rd ed.
        p.   cm.
    Includes index.
    ISBN 1-57231-548-2
    1. Microsoft Windows (Computer file)   I. Title.
QA76.76.W56R518   1996
005.26--dc20   96-36633
                                                               CIP

Printed and bound in the United States of America.

 2 3 4 5 6 7 8 9   QMQM   2 1 0 9 8 7

Distributed to the book trade in Canada by Macmillan of Canada, a division of Canada
Publishing Corporation.

A CIP catalogue record for this book is available from the British Library.

Microsoft Press books are available through booksellers and distributors worldwide. For further
information about international editions, contact your local Microsoft Corporation office. Or
contact Microsoft Press International directly at fax (206) 936-7329.

Acquisitions Editor: Eric Stroo
Project Editor: Sally Stickney
Technical Editor: Jim Fuchs

To my mother, Arlene, for her bravery and courage
through the most difficult and trying of times.
Your love and support have shaped me into
the person I am. You're with me wherever I go.
—With all my love, Jeff

To Susan "Q-bert" Ramee, for showing me that
computers are not at the center of the universe,
with all of the planets circling around.
—J "BBB" R

CONTENTS SUMMARY

CHAPTER ONE

THE WIN32 API AND PLATFORMS THAT SUPPORT IT **1**

▶ This chapter explains Microsoft's various APIs and operating system platforms; clarifies the latest catchwords (Win32, Win32s, Windows CE, Windows 95, and Windows NT); and discusses Microsoft's goals for each API. By the end of the chapter, you will understand why I believe this is a very exciting time for software developers and why the Win32 API is the area in which software engineers should be concentrating their development efforts.

CHAPTER TWO

KERNEL OBJECTS **9**

▶ To work effectively with Win32 system services, you must have a solid understanding of kernel objects and the handles that represent them. This chapter explains the theory behind creating, opening, and closing various kernel objects. Issues concerning robustness and security are also discussed. This chapter also shows the three methods for sharing kernel objects across process boundaries: handle inheritance, opening object handles, and duplicating object handles.

CHAPTER THREE

PROCESSES **33**

▶ Under Windows 95 and Windows NT, an instance of an executing application is a process. This chapter explains how a new process is invoked, how it initializes, and how it is destroyed. Various attributes associated with a process are also explained. For example, in Win32 each process has its own address space, which means that one process cannot adversely affect another process—this is not true in 16-bit

Windows. This chapter also introduces Win32 kernel objects, which are the basis for all kernel-related tasks in both Windows 95 and Windows NT. A solid understanding of kernel objects is required for any serious Win32 developer.

CHAPTER FOUR

▶ Threads are at the heart of the multitasking abilities of Windows 95 and Windows NT. For a Win32 process actually to do anything, it must have threads that execute the code and manipulate the data contained in the process. All Win32 processes contain at least one thread, but both Windows 95 and Windows NT allow a process to contain several threads that are scheduled and preemptively multitasked by the operating system. This chapter explains how threads are created, scheduled, and destroyed.

▶ Advanced operating systems such as Windows 95 and Windows NT require sophisticated memory architectures. This chapter explains how the system manages the computer's RAM and paging files on the hard disk to give each process a full 4 GB of virtual address space. The chapter also covers how each process's address space is partitioned and discusses the implementation differences between Windows 95 and Windows NT. One of the features that makes the Win32 memory architecture unique is that Win32 separates the task of reserving regions of address space from the task of committing physical storage to these regions. This chapter explains how these two tasks are accomplished as well as how protection attributes can be assigned to pages of committed physical storage.

▶ This chapter builds on the information presented in Chapter 5. The chapter introduces various Win32 functions that allow you to explore the system's memory configuration and the contents (code and data) of a process's address space.

CHAPTER SEVEN

USING VIRTUAL MEMORY IN YOUR OWN APPLICATIONS 191

▶ This chapter shows how to use virtual memory management techniques in your own applications. Topics include how to reserve regions in a process's address space and techniques for knowing when to commit physical storage to these regions. These techniques allow an application to use physical storage more efficiently than it could under most other operating systems.

CHAPTER EIGHT

MEMORY-MAPPED FILES 233

▶ Windows 95 and Windows NT use memory-mapped files to implement virtual memory management. All of a process's code and data are backed by a file on disk—a memory-mapped file. This chapter shows how memory-mapped files make it almost trivially simple to manipulate disk files. The chapter also shows how to use memory-mapped files to share code and data among multiple processes.

CHAPTER NINE

HEAPS 289

▶ Heaps are the third and last memory management technique offered by the Win32 API. This chapter shows how to create multiple heaps within a single process and explains why a developer might want to do this. This chapter also discusses how the 16-bit Windows heap functions are emulated by the Win32 API under Windows 95 and Windows NT to make it easier for developers to port existing 16-bit Windows source code.

CHAPTER TEN

THREAD SYNCHRONIZATION 313

▶ Whenever multiple threads are executing simultaneously or are being preemptively interrupted, an application will often need to suspend a thread to prevent data corruption. Windows 95 and Windows NT offer several objects for performing thread synchronization; this chapter discusses these objects and describes techniques for using them.

CHAPTER ELEVEN

▶ One of the biggest problems with 16-bit Windows is that it is too easy for a single application to hang all running applications. Robust operating systems such as Windows 95 and Windows NT do not allow applications to compromise the smooth execution of other processes in the system. To create a robust environment, window messages and hardware input are handled differently in Win32 than in 16-bit Windows. These changes may break some source code originally written for 16-bit Windows. This chapter explains how window messages are processed in both Windows 95 and Windows NT.

CHAPTER TWELVE

▶ Dynamic-link libraries (DLLs) have always been the cornerstone of all Windows applications—and they continue to be in Windows 95 and Windows NT. However, DLLs are managed quite differently under Win32 than under 16-bit Windows. This chapter explains how a DLL is mapped into a process's address space and how to appropriately initialize a DLL. In addition, this chapter demonstrates how a DLL can be used to export both functions and data.

▶ In an environment in which multiple threads are running concurrently, it's important to associate data objects and variables with the individual threads of a process. This chapter describes how to use both dynamic and static thread-local storage techniques to associate data with specific threads.

▶ This chapter discusses how an application can manipulate the various file systems offered by Windows 95 and Windows NT: FAT, CDFS, and NTFS. It also covers how to create, remove, and walk directories.

The chapter then shows how to move, delete, and examine the attributes of files in the file system. Finally, this chapter demonstrates how to write an application that gets notified when changes to the file system occur.

▶ This chapter examines how to perform device I/O in Win32. Device I/O includes reading and writing to files as well as to other devices such as mailslots, pipes, serial ports, and sockets. Specifically, this chapter demonstrates how to perform synchronous I/O and various forms of asynchronous I/O techniques including alertable I/O and I/O completion ports.

▶ Structured exception handling (SEH) is a mechanism that allows application developers to write more robust and reliable applications. SEH consists of two components that work together: exception handling and termination handling. Exception handling is a mechanism that allows an application to catch both hardware and software exceptions (for example, invalid memory accesses). Termination handling guarantees that clean-up tasks are performed even if an exception occurs.

▶ Software developers are finding a huge potential for software distribution in international markets. To help developers, Microsoft built full Unicode support into Windows NT and limited Unicode support into Windows 95. Unicode is a 16-bit character set that lets developers easily manipulate characters and strings for different languages and writing systems. This chapter discusses how you can best take advantage of Win32's Unicode facilities to help localize your development projects.

CHAPTER EIGHTEEN

BREAKING THROUGH PROCESS BOUNDARY WALLS

▶ The robust nature of the Windows 95 and Windows NT environments makes it much more difficult to manipulate other processes in the system. Although it is not normal for processes to alter one another, some processes, such as debuggers and other tools, require intimate knowledge of other processes in order to be useful to the software developer. This chapter demonstrates three techniques that allow a process to inject a DLL into another process's address space. These techniques require a knowledge of processes, threads, virtual memory, thread synchronization, window messages, DLLs, structured exception handling, and Unicode.

APPENDIX A

FIBERS

▶ Fibers are lightweight threads that have been added to Win32 to make it easier for software developers to port existing UNIX-based applications to Win32. This appendix explains what fibers are and how to take advantage of them. Designing new applications to take full advantage of the capabilities of fibers is also covered.

APPENDIX B

MESSAGE CRACKERS

▶ Most Windows programmers have never heard of message crackers, even though these programming aids exist for both 16-bit Windows and Win32. This appendix explains how to use message crackers to help you write, read, and maintain your source code. In addition, message crackers make it much easier to port 16-bit Windows source code to Win32 and vice versa.

APPENDIX C

THE BUILD ENVIRONMENT

▶ This appendix explains the CMNHDR.H header file included in all the sample applications presented in this book. This header file contains a number of #*defines*, #*pragmas*, and linker directives. Appendix C also discusses how various compiler and linker switches have been set in each sample application's project make file.

TABLE OF CONTENTS

CHAPTER NINE

HEAPS **289**

CHAPTER TEN

THREAD SYNCHRONIZATION **313**

CHAPTER ELEVEN

WINDOW MESSAGES AND ASYNCHRONOUS INPUT **461**

CHAPTER TWELVE

DYNAMIC-LINK LIBRARIES **529**

CHAPTER SIXTEEN

STRUCTURED EXCEPTION HANDLING **773**

CHAPTER SEVENTEEN

UNICODE **873**

CHAPTER EIGHTEEN

BREAKING THROUGH PROCESS BOUNDARY WALLS **899**

ACKNOWLEDGMENTS

Although my name appears alone on the cover of this book, many people have contributed in some form or another to the book's creation. In many cases, these people are good friends of mine (that is, we occasionally go to movies or out to dinner together); and in other cases, I have never met the individuals and have conversed with them only on the phone or by electronic mail. I could not have completed this book without the assistance or support of each of the following—I thank you all.

Susan "Q" Ramee gave me her love and support throughout the entire process. Sue also proofread chapters and helped me come up with some ideas for the sample programs. And, of course, it would not be right to thank Sue without also thanking her two cats, Natt and Cato. Often, late at night, when I could not sleep and decided to write, Natt and Cato would keep me company. They would frequently shed on my notes and walk across the keyboard as I typed. Any typos you sea in thid boot are duw too Natt amd Cato, knot me, I assure you.

Jim Harkins is one of my best friends. Whenever I think of Jim, I can hear him saying, "When was the last time you put chlorine in the Jacuzzi?" And, although it's not publicly known, Jim is the creator of the very popular and hilariously outrageous game "Guess What The Plant Said?" His direct contribution to this book can be found in the Directory Walker, Alertable File I/O, and File Change sample programs. In addition, Jim also helped me think through many of the thread synchronization issues in the book and the CPU-independent version of *InjectLib*.

Scott Ludwig and Valerie Horvath have become my closest friends. Our favorite pastime is going to movies that have lots of explosions and destruction in them. Scott and Valerie have also been initiating me into the world of professional basketball. (You mean the Harlem Globetrotters?) Scott was a lead developer at Microsoft for the first version of Windows NT. When I was writing the first edition of this book, Scott was extremely patient with me and answered all of my questions. Through the discussions we have had, Scott has earned my utmost respect and admiration.

Lucy Gooding added spice and spices (mostly garlic) to my life. She deserves a medal for putting up with my busy schedule. Now that the book is done, we can spend more time with Me-yow-zer and Chirrp-per.

Jonathan Locke and I share a common interest in music, but for some reason, he prefers 386/25MHz machines to MIPS machines. Jonathan helped with proofing many of the chapters and made several recommendations to mangle my text and alter its meaning. Many of his suggestions opened up either a ball of worms or a can of wax. However, we managed to incorporate them into the book before it went to press.

Keith Pleas and I lead parallel lives and have become extremely good friends over the past few years. We both purchased Ping Pong tables on the same day and have the same cordless headset phone. These days, we mostly talk about "Scent of a Woman."

Jeff Cooperstein is a friend with a keen sense of how to muck with a system and make it do things that it was specifically designed *not* to do. Jeff devised several ways to circumvent Windows NT security (all of which were fixed in Windows NT 3.5) and was also about to start work on his Virus Developer's Kit (VDK). He is also known for saying, "Just disconnect the network cable, the machine won't receive the broadcast packet, plug the cable back in and you're set!"

To all the beautiful women at Class A Travel: Norma Coote, Jenifer Harpster, Nouk Inthaxai, and Jodi Small. Because of all the traveling I do, all of you have become good friends offering advice that usually only the best of money can buy. I have learned to never make a move without consulting all of you first. Their deepest desire is to send me on a pleasure trip instead of a business trip—I promise more pleasure trips in the future.

Lou Perazzoli, Steve Wood, and Marc Lucovsky of the Windows NT development team reviewed a number of chapters and answered many questions related to threads and memory management.

Brian Smith, Jon Thomason, and Michael Toutonghi of the Microsoft Windows 95 development team answered several questions having to do with Windows 95 memory and thread management.

Asmus Freytag (aka Dr. Unicode) reviewed the Unicode chapter and gave me some last-minute suggestions over dinner at Red Robin one very rainy Seattle evening.

Dave Hart of the Windows NT NTVDM development team spent a lot of time with me in person and via e-mail while I asked numerous questions about running 16-bit MS-DOS and Windows applications under Windows NT's NTVDM layer. Although very little of this information appears in the book, Dave gave me a good deal more insight into the workings of Windows NT.

Chuck Mitchell, Steve Salisbury, and Jonathan Mark of the Win32 Visual C++ team answered my questions about structured exception handling, thread-local storage, the C run-time library, and linking.

I would also like to thank/mention Mark Durley and Cezary Marcjan, who found bugs in the first edition and provided me with numerous ideas and stimulating conversations about Win32 programming.

I would also like to thank/mention several additional developers on the Visual C++ team I had the opportunity to work with: Byron Dazey, Eric Lang ("Do they sell milk at the Crest of London?"), Dan Spalding, Matthew Tebbs ("Thanks for brunch!"), Bruce Johnson, Jon Jorstad ("How's this for a better thing to say?"), Dave Henderson, and T.K. Brackman.

Bernie McIlroy helped me test the sample applications on a DEC Alpha machine. Bernie thinks that all introductions should begin with "In the beginning…" and is also well known for his philosophy on life: "Life is a heck of a thing."

Sally Stickney was my editor at Microsoft Press for the third edition of the book. Her untiring effort allowed us to get this book edited in record time. This was especially difficult since I went to Italy just a few weeks before the book went to print.

Jim Fuchs was my technical editor at Microsoft Press for the second and third editions. Jim worked incredibly hard on proofing my source code and resource files. He was absolutely indefatigable while dealing with code changes as he and I worked on the source code at the same time.

Rebecca Gleason was my editor at Microsoft Press for the second edition of the book. I still owe her a big favor for putting all the RC files back into the book at the last moment. Rebecca was on top of everything and always had an answer to my questions—even though her answer was frequently, "It's a style thing." I'm still trying to recover from the 10-alarm barbecue lunch we had from Dixie's BBQ/Porter's Automotive Service shop.

Nancy Siadek, my editor for the first edition of this book, deserves an award for the amount of effort and dedication she gave to me. I'm sure she had no idea what she was getting into. Nancy taught me more about writing in the short time I spent with her than I learned in all my years.

I also want to thank the rest of the Microsoft Press team. Many of them I have never met, but I do appreciate all their efforts. For the third edition: Eric Stroo; Philip Borgnes; artist Travis Beaven; compositors

Peggy Herman, Jeffrey Brendecke, Susan Prettyman, Linda Robinson, Elisabeth Thébaud Pong, and Paul Vautier; proofreaders Richard Carey, Ron Drummond, Patrick Forgette, Teri Kieffer, Roger LeBlanc, Patricia Masserman, Devon Musgrave, Cheryl Penner, and Paula Thurman. For the second edition: Shawn Peck, John Sugg, Jim Kramer, Michael Victor, Kim Eggleston, David Holter, Penelope West, Richard Carter, Elisabeth Thébaud Pong, Peggy Herman, and Barbara Remmele. And those of the first edition: Erin O'Connor, Laura Sackerman, Deborah Long, Peggy Herman, Lisa Iversen, and Barb Runyan.

Thanks also to:

Dan Horn at Borland International, for his suggestions and comments on several chapters and for giving an apple to the teacher.

Jim Lane, Tom Van Baak, Rich Peterson, and Bill Baxter, for their assistance with the DEC Alpha compiler.

Dean Holmes, acquisitions director at Microsoft Press, for signing me and for putting up with delays in the first edition while I purchased my new house.

Gretchen Bilson and everyone at *Microsoft Systems Journal,* for encouraging me to continue writing.

Charles Petzold, for introducing me to Microsoft Press and hot and sour soup.

Carlos Richardson, for helping me get TJ-Net (my home network) up and running in my new house.

Donna Murray, for her love, support, and friendship over the years. I admire you for always pursuing your dreams.

My brother, Ron, for trying to find me a copy of Patrick Moraz's "Salamander." Even though you never found it, I know you tried. I'll ask Peter Gabriel to autograph your golf clubs the next time he's in town. Here's hoping you win the contest and that we and Velveeta-Clear–loving Maria take a trip to Bath, England.

My mom and dad, Arlene and Sylvan, for their love and support over the years. Both of you are welcome to visit me anytime you want. I'll keep the Jacuzzi hot and a bag of popcorn by the TV, and I'll order another set of contour pillows.

INTRODUCTION

I have really enjoyed writing this book. There is nothing I like more than being at the forefront of technology and learning new things. Microsoft Windows 95 and Microsoft Windows NT are definitely at the forefront of technology, and boy, is there a lot of new stuff to learn. But don't let the amount of new stuff scare you.

If you are already a 16-bit Windows programmer, you will find that you can start writing Win32 applications after learning just a few simple techniques for porting your existing code. However, these ported programs will not be taking advantage of the powerful and exciting features that the Win32 environments of Windows 95 and Windows NT now offer.

If you are moving from other operating systems (such as UNIX) to Windows NT, this book will explain how you can best take advantage of the features offered by this rich operating system. It is one thing to make an existing application work on Windows NT; it is another thing to create a native version of your application designed specifically for Windows NT. Windows NT has a lot to offer. If you simply make your existing application run on Windows NT, you will not be in a strong competitive position. However, if you rework some of your application to really benefit from Windows NT's features, you'll probably find that you can delete a lot of your existing code and reduce your application's memory requirements while making your application run faster.

After you have started working with Win32, you can begin incorporating more and more of its features into your applications. Many of the Win32 features make it much easier to write programs. And, as I soon discovered when porting some of my own code, I was able to delete large sections of code from my existing programs and replace them with calls to facilities offered by Win32.

These features are such a pleasure to use and work with that I now do Win32 programming exclusively and frequently speak at companies and conferences explaining how to develop effective Win32 applications. This book should help you get ready for developing applications for an environment that is destined to be the industry standard.

About the Sample Applications

The purpose of the sample applications is to demonstrate with real code how to use the advanced features of Win32. You could never read enough text to replace the knowledge and experience that you gain by writing your own applications. This has certainly been true of my experience with Win32. Many of the sample applications presented throughout this book are direct descendants of experimental programs that I created in an effort to understand how the Win32 functions behave.

Programs Written in C

When it came time to decide on a language for the sample applications, I was torn between C and C++. For large projects, I always use C++—but the fact of the matter is that most Windows programmers are not using C++ yet, and I didn't want to alienate my largest potential audience. So as you'll see, the sample applications are written in C.

Message Cracker Macros

If you are not writing your Win32 application using C++ and a Windows class library (such as Microsoft's Foundation Classes), I highly recommend that you use the message cracker macros defined in the WINDOWSX.H header file. These macros make your programs easier to write, read, and maintain. I feel so strongly about the message cracker macros that I have included Appendix B in this book to explain why message crackers exist and how to use them effectively.

Knowledge of 16-Bit Windows Programming

None of the programs presented in this book rely on extensive knowledge of 16-bit Windows programs, although experience with 16-bit Windows programming is definitely a plus. The sample programs do assume that you are familiar with the creation and manipulation of dialog boxes and their child controls. Very little knowledge of GDI and Kernel functions is required.

When presenting various topics in this book, I do make behavior comparisons between 16-bit Windows and Win32. If you already understand how 16-bit Windows behaves, you should have an easier time understanding how behaviors have changed in Win32.

Running the Sample Applications Under Windows 95

Windows 95 is targeted to run on machines that have only 4 MB of RAM. To accomplish this, Microsoft had to cut some corners when creating Windows 95. For the software developer, this means that some Win32 functions do not have full implementations on Windows 95. With respect to my sample applications, this means that some of the applications have additional functionality when run under Windows NT.

Because of limitations in Windows 95, the following programs run only under Windows NT: ALERTIO.EXE (Chapter 15), IOCMPPRT-.EXE (Chapter 15), TINJLIB.EXE (Chapter 18), and COUNTER.EXE (Appendix A). I explain the reasons for doing this when I introduce these programs in their respective chapters.

Unrelated Code

I wanted to remove any code from the sample programs that was not directly related to the techniques I wanted to demonstrate. Unfortunately, this is not possible when writing any Windows program. For example, most Windows programming books repeat the code for registering window classes in every application presented in the book. I have done my best to reduce this type of nonrelevant code.

One way that I reduce nonrelevant code is by using techniques that are not always obvious to Windows programmers. For example, the user interface for most of the sample programs is a dialog box. In fact, most of the sample programs have a single line of code in *WinMain* that simply calls the *DialogBox* function. As a result, none of the sample programs initialize a WNDCLASS structure or call the *RegisterClass* function. In addition, only two sample applications—FileChng in Chapter 14 and Counter in Appendix A—have message loops in them.

Independent Sample Applications

I have tried to keep the sample applications independent from one another. For example, the memory-mapped files chapter (Chapter 8) is the only chapter containing memory-mapped file sample programs. Because I have structured the sample programs to be independent, feel free to skip earlier chapters and proceed to later chapters.

Occasionally you'll find a sample program that uses techniques or information presented in earlier chapters. For example, the SEHExcpt sample application, presented in the structured exception handling chapter (Chapter 16), demonstrates how to manipulate virtual memory.

I decided to mix these two topics in a single sample program because structured exception handling is a very useful mechanism for manipulating virtual memory. To fully understand this sample application, you should read Chapters 5, 6, and 7 before you examine the SEHExcpt sample application.

One sample application, however, has a little bit of everything: TInjLib, presented in Chapter 18. To fully understand this application, you must have a good understanding of kernel objects, virtual memory, processes, threads, thread synchronization, dynamic-link libraries, structured exception handling, and Unicode. I would say that understanding the TInjLib application qualifies you to go on an interview and say that you really understand Win32 programming.

STRICT Compliance

All the sample programs have been compiled with the STRICT identifier defined, which catches frequent coding errors. For example, with the STRICT identifier defined, the passing of an incorrect handle type to a function is caught during compilation instead of at run time. For more information about using the STRICT identifier, refer to the *Programming Techniques* documentation included in the Win32 SDK.

Error Checking

Error checking should be an integral part of any software project. Unfortunately, proper error checking can make the size and complexity of a software project grow exponentially. To make the sample applications more understandable and less cluttered, I have not put much error-checking code into them. If you use any of my code fragments and incorporate them into your own production code, I strongly encourage you to examine my code closely and add any appropriate error checking.

Bug Free

I would love to say that all the sample programs in this book are bug free. But, as with all software, it's only bug free until someone finds a bug. Of course, I have given my own code several walk-throughs in the hope of catching everything. If you do find a bug, I would appreciate your reporting it to me via my Internet address: *v-jeffrr@microsoft.com*.

Tested Platforms and Environments

The bulk of my research and development for this book has been on a machine with two Intel Pentium CPUs. I have also recompiled and tested all the sample programs on a MIPS machine, a DEC Alpha machine, and a PowerPC machine, using the compilers and linkers that come with Microsoft Visual C++ 4.0 for these platforms. All the programs have been tested under both Windows 95 and Windows NT.

Important

Some of the applications use functions that are new to Windows NT 4. Since Visual C++ 4.*x* shipped prior to Windows NT 4, the Visual C++ header files are missing some of the new function prototypes. This will prevent some of the sample applications from building successfully. To resolve this problem, you must replace the header files that ship with Visual C++ with the header files that ship with the Win32 SDK.

For most of the sample programs, I use no vendor-specific compiler extensions. These programs should compile and link regardless of the machine on which you are running and regardless of which tools you are using to compile and link the sample programs.

However, several of the sample programs do take advantage of some compiler-specific features:

- Named data sections using the following syntax:

  ```
  #pragma data_seg (…)
  ```

- Static thread-local storage using the following syntax:

  ```
  __declspec(thread)
  ```

- Structured exception handling using the following keywords:

  ```
  __try, __leave, __finally, and __except
  ```

  Because most compiler vendors will be modifying their compilers to recognize these four keywords, it is unlikely that you will have to modify the structured exception handling sample programs at all.

- Compiler-assisted function importing and exporting using the following syntax:

  ```
  __declspec(dllimport) and __declspec(dllexport)
  ```

If you are using tools other than those included in Visual C++ 4.0, you will need to discover how your vendor exposes these features and modify the sample programs accordingly.

Unicode

Originally I wrote all the sample programs so that they could compile natively using the ANSI character set only. Then, when I started writing the Unicode chapter, I became a very strong believer in Unicode and tried desperately to come up with a sample program for the Unicode chapter. Then the answer came to me: convert all the sample applications in the book so that they demonstrate Unicode. This conversion effort took only four hours and allows you to compile all the sample applications natively for both ANSI and Unicode.

The disadvantage of doing this is that you might see calls to unfamiliar functions that manipulate characters and strings within the sample applications. For the most part, you should be able to guess what that function does if you are familiar with the standard C run-time library functions for manipulating characters and strings. However, if you get stuck, you should refer to the Unicode chapter (Chapter 17). This chapter explains in much greater detail what I have done in the sample programs. It is my hope that you not be confused by the new character and string functions and that you see how easy it is to write your application code using Unicode.

Installing the Sample Programs

The companion CD-ROM contains the source code for all the sample applications presented throughout this book. In addition, the EXE and DLL files for the x86, MIPS, Alpha AXP, and PowerPC versions of the sample programs are included. Because none of the files on the CD-ROM are compressed, you can simply insert the CD-ROM and load the source code files; you can also run the sample applications directly from the CD-ROM.

On the CD-ROM, the root directory contains the installation software and the CMNHDR.H header file discussed in Appendix C. The root directory also contains several subdirectories. Four of these subdirectories are called X86.BIN, MIPS.BIN, ALPHA.BIN, and POWER-PC.BIN. These subdirectories contain the EXE and the DLL files for their respective CPU platforms. If you are running Windows NT on a platform other than an *x*86, MIPS, Alpha, or PowerPC, you can still access the source code files, but you will not be able to execute any of the sample applications without building them yourself. This means you will need to install the source code files on your hard disk yourself.

The remaining subdirectories contain the source code files for the sample applications. Each sample application is in its own subdirectory. The eight-letter name of each subdirectory contains the name of the sample program.

If you are interested only in examining the source code or running the sample applications, you do not have to copy anything to your hard disk. However, if you want to modify, compile, or debug the sample applications, you will need to copy the files to your hard disk. The next section explains how to access the sample application files depending on whether you are running Windows 95 or Windows NT.

The Accompanying CD-ROM Disc

On Windows NT 4 and Windows 95, inserting the CD-ROM into a drive causes the disc's Welcome application to run automatically. This application allows you to explore the contents of the CD-ROM.

Using the application, you can select any of the buttons described in the following table:

Button	Description
Introduction	Have me explain what the book is about.
Video demos	Play AVI files, in which I explain what each sample application demonstrates and how to use each sample application.
Setup	Copy the source code files and the appropriate executable files to your hard disk.
Explorer	Opens an Explorer window containing the executable files. You can run any of the sample applications from this window.
Credits	See a list of people that helped me produce this book.
Training	A shameless self-promotional video for my seminars.

Under Windows NT 3.51 and earlier, you must manually invoke the Welcome application by running the Welcome.bat file contained in the root directory of the CD-ROM.

CHAPTER ONE

THE WIN32 API
AND PLATFORMS
THAT SUPPORT IT

I am a frequent speaker at industry events, where I am often asked, "What is the difference between Win32, Win32s, Windows NT, Windows 95, and Windows CE?" In this chapter, I will attempt to clarify the differences once and for all. I will also explain why I chose to focus exclusively on Windows 95 and Windows NT when writing this book.

To Dream: The Win32 API

Win32 is the name of an application programming interface (API), that's all—no more, no less. So a set of functions that are available to call from your source code is contained in the Win32 API. When you write a Win32 program, you are calling functions in the Win32 API.

The Win32 API defines a set of functions that an application may call and also defines how these functions behave. Some of the areas covered by the API's functions are listed in Figure 1-1 on the next page.

The Win32 API is implemented on four platforms: Win32s,[1] Windows NT, Windows 95, and Windows CE. Microsoft's plan is to have *all* the Win32 functions implemented in *every* platform that supports the Win32 API. This is a major win for software developers like you and me, as well as for Microsoft. For us, it means we can write the code for our application just once and then package it for the different platforms and

---

1. It is unfortunate that the Win32s platform has *Win32* in its name, because this only adds to the confusion.

ship it to our customers. For Microsoft, it means existing applications can run on all its operating system platforms.

Atoms	Networks
Child controls	Pipes and mailslots
Clipboard manipulations	Printing
Communications	Processes and threads
Consoles	Registry database manipulation
Debugging	Resources
Dynamic-link libraries	Security
Event logging	Services
Files	Structured exception handling
Graphics drawing primitives	System information
Keyboard and mouse input	Tape backup
Memory management	Time
Multimedia services	Window management

Figure 1-1.
Some areas covered by the Win32 API.

Of course, you may be asking yourself, Why do we need different Win32 platforms? Wouldn't it make more sense to have a single Win32 platform and make this one platform pervasive?

Well, if this were a perfect world, the answer to the second question would be "yes." However, this is the real world—and in the real world, one Win32 platform just doesn't cut it. I'll explain why in the next four sections, which introduce the four Win32 platforms and describe where each one fits into Microsoft's operating system strategy.

Win32s

The Win32s platform was the very first shipping platform capable of running Win32 applications. Win32s consists of a set of dynamic-link libraries (DLLs) and a virtual-device driver that add the Win32 API to the 16-bit Windows 3.*x* system. Win32s is not much more than a 32-bit to 16-bit mapping layer sitting on top of 16-bit Windows 3.*x*. This mapping layer uses thunking to convert the 32-bit function parameters to 16-bit parameters and to call the corresponding 16-bit Windows function.

Because Win32s does not extend the operating system's capabilities, most Win32 functions are implemented as small stub functions that simply return, indicating failure. For example, because 16-bit Windows does not support threads, the *CreateThread* function does nothing but return a NULL handle. All the Win32 functions that create kernel objects such as mutexes and events return NULL handles. The Win32s platform does add a few new capabilities, however, such as structured exception handling and limited implementations of memory-mapped files.

Microsoft created Win32s to allow developers to begin writing 32-bit code before the other Win32 platforms became available. Microsoft hoped this would help spark interest in Win32 programming so that when Windows NT shipped, some 32-bit applications would already be available. Unfortunately, Win32s did not take off too well, and I personally know of very few software development efforts that have specifically targeted the Win32s platform.

Windows NT

Windows NT, Microsoft's high-end operating system, is the second Win32 platform to ship from the company. Windows NT is a relatively new operating system that has no MS-DOS heritage. Microsoft expects this design and architecture to take the company's operating systems into the future. However, Windows NT requires substantial memory and hard disk space. This means that the average end user will probably need to purchase additional memory and hard disk space to run the system. As many software companies have discovered over the years, getting users to buy hardware to run software is very difficult. In addition, Windows NT 4.0 has dropped support for 80386 machines and now requires an 80486 or better processor to run.

Windows NT is also a robust operating system that is designed to prevent an ill-behaved application from bringing down the system. By ill-behaved, I mean an application that directly accesses the computer's hardware, such as reading and writing to I/O ports. Unfortunately, a lot of MS-DOS and 16-bit Windows applications are ill-behaved. When you run these applications on Windows NT, the system terminates them when they attempt to access hardware.

For the two reasons just mentioned (required resources and backward compatibility), Windows NT has had less than spectacular sales. But in my opinion, we will all be running Windows NT someday—it just may take a few more years. Why is Windows NT the operating system of the future? I'm glad you asked. I'll explain in detail right now.

First, Windows NT native applications are Win32 applications, giving them the power, robustness, and speed provided by the Win32 API. In addition, Windows NT is capable of running several different types of applications simultaneously. For example, Windows NT can run OS/2 1.*x* character applications, POSIX applications, Presentation Manager 2.*x* applications, MS-DOS applications, and 16-bit Windows applications.

Second, Windows NT is a portable operating system. This means that Windows NT is capable of running on machines that have different CPUs. Most of Windows NT itself is written in C or C++. So if Microsoft wants Windows NT to run on a MIPS R4000, a DEC Alpha, or Motorola's PowerPC, Microsoft needs only to recompile the operating system source code using the target CPU's native compiler and voilà—a version of Windows NT for another platform. Of course, porting the operating system to another CPU architecture is not quite this easy. Two very low-level components of the Windows NT Executive, called the Kernel and the Hardware Abstraction Layer (HAL), need to be written to support the target architecture. Much of the Kernel and the HAL is written in native assembly language and is quite specific to the target machine architecture.

After Microsoft finishes porting Windows NT to a new architecture, all you need to do is recompile your Win32 application and voilà again—your application now runs on a new machine architecture. This actually *is* as simple as it sounds! I have compiled and tested all the sample applications in this book for the following four Windows NT CPU platforms: *x*86, MIPS, Alpha, and PowerPC. The first time I did this, I was amazed at how simple it was. Now I just take it for granted.

You should note that Windows NT is the first Win32 platform for machine architectures based on CPUs other than the *x*86. In other words, if you want to run Win32 applications on a MIPS, Alpha, or PowerPC machine, you will have to use the Windows NT platform. If you have an *x*86 machine, you can choose from three platforms: Win32s, Windows NT, or Windows 95. Windows NT is the most competent of these operating systems, but it does require additional hardware.

The third big feature of Windows NT is that it supports machines with multiple CPUs. So if you are running Windows NT on a machine that contains four CPUs, the operating system is capable of letting four threads run simultaneously. This means the machine can perform four tasks in the time that it takes to perform one task on a machine with a single CPU. This is an incredibly powerful capability, but as you might expect, a machine with several CPUs costs significantly more than one with a single CPU.

Windows 95

Until Windows NT catches more momentum, Windows 95 is Microsoft's Win32 platform for the masses and the long-awaited successor to 16-bit Windows 3.*x*. Because Windows 95 replaces Windows 3.*x*, the Win32s platform is now considered obsolete. So this leaves three Win32 platforms worthy of your consideration: Windows NT, Windows 95, and Windows CE.

Windows 95 is a much better implementation of the Win32 API than its predecessor, Win32s. However, Windows 95 does not contain the full implementation of the Win32 API as found in Windows NT. Windows 95 fills a very large and strategic marketing gap: users with 386 (or better) machines with 4 MB (or more) of RAM. The number of machines that fall into this category is staggering—and it's expected to grow significantly over the next couple of years. Because the Windows NT hardware requirements are too demanding to address this market, Microsoft produced the Windows 95 platform.

In order for Windows 95 to fit in a 4-MB machine, Microsoft was forced to cut back on some of the Win32 API's functionality. As a result, Windows 95 does not fully support some of Win32's asynchronous file I/O functions, debugging functions, registry functions, security functions, and event logging functions (just to name a few)—the functions exist, but they have restricted implementations. Surprisingly, however, Microsoft was able to shoehorn quite a bit of the Win32 API set into Windows 95, making it a very feasible and powerful operating system.

Windows CE

Windows CE is Microsoft's most recent Win32 platform. This new operating system was created to fit the needs of new hardware devices. Specifically, Windows CE was developed for handheld computing devices. These devices are usually battery powered and do not contain floppy or hard disk drives. Most of these machines have 2 MB or 4 MB of RAM, but because they have no disk storage, there is no paging file to provide additional storage. Because of this hardware's severe restrictions, Microsoft was forced to create a new operating system that had a smaller footprint than that of either Windows NT or Windows 95.

Amazingly enough, however, Windows CE is much more powerful than MS-DOS and Windows 3.1. It supports memory-mapped files, structured exception handling, dynamic-link libraries, the registry, preemptive scheduling of threads, and much more. Each process's address space is also protected from other running processes. In addition, Windows CE is a portable operating system that currently runs on MIPS, SH3, and *x*86 processors.

Although I will not specifically cover Windows CE in this book, almost all the Win32 concepts discussed throughout apply to this platform. Of course, where differences do exist it is usually because Windows CE has limitations on the various functions. Rarely does Windows CE add capabilites to the functions and concepts covered in this book. However, Windows CE does offer new Win32 features that are not yet available on any other Win32 platform. These features include user notifications, command bars, file filters, and simple database management. I will not attempt to discuss these new features in this book, but I do plan to address them in future books and articles. The material presented in this book should be thought of as a companion to any additional information regarding Windows CE.

The Reality: The Win32 API

The Win32s, Windows NT, and Windows 95 platforms all contain implementations of all the Win32 functions, which means you can call any of the functions in the Win32 API regardless of which platform you are running on. However, there is implementation and there is *implementation*. When Microsoft says that every Win32 function will be implemented on every platform, what it really means is that every Win32 function will *exist* on every platform. For example, the *CreateRemoteThread* function exists on three platforms: Win32s, Windows NT, and Windows 95. However, the function doesn't actually create a remote thread unless the application calling the function is running on the Windows NT platform. If a process running on Win32s or Windows 95 calls *CreateRemoteThread*, the function does nothing and simply returns NULL, indicating that a new thread of execution could not be created.

The reason for this limitation on Win32s is that Win32s is really just an extension to 16-bit Windows 3.*x* that implements most of the Win32 API by thunking calls to 16-bit Windows functions. Because 16-bit Windows does not support the creation of new threads of execution, Win32s does not support this feature. But remember, Win32s implements all of the Win32 functions, although some of the implementations are limited. On Windows 95, the *CreateRemoteThread* function is not fully implemented. Microsoft didn't feel that the function was useful enough to warrant the additional memory overhead it would need, given that Windows 95 is required to run on a 4-MB machine.

You'll notice that I didn't mention Windows CE in the above discussion. Because of the size restrictions of Windows CE, Microsoft was forced to leave functions out of the OS. For example, the function *CreateMutex* doesn't exist because Windows CE doesn't support mutexes. When you compile your source code for Windows CE, the compiler will give you an error indicating that the function does not exist.

Because this is a Win32 programming book, you should, in theory, expect that you could compile all the sample programs you found here and run them on all Win32 platforms. If it weren't for all the restrictions mentioned above, you could; however, most of the features discussed in this book (for example, multithreaded programming, virtual memory, and memory-mapped files) have full implementations on the Windows 95 and Windows NT platforms, useful implementation on the Windows CE platform, but very limited implementations on the Win32s platform. Because of these limitations, you must run the sample programs under the Windows 95 or the Windows NT platform to see them in all their glory.

In fact, because the Win32s platform has such limited capabilities, I have given no thought whatsoever to it in this book. Everything I have written applies to the Windows 95 and Windows NT platforms only—if something I say happens to be true for the Win32s platform, I assure you it is purely coincidental.

Finally, while writing this book I have tried to pay particular attention to differences between the Windows 95 and Windows NT implementations of the Win32 API. Where appropriate, I have placed boxes with icons, as shown below, in the text to draw attention to implementation details specific to one platform or the other.

This is an implementation detail specific to the Windows 95 platform.

This is an implementation detail specific to the Windows NT platform.

I have also used boxes with icons to include information helpful to programmers porting from 16-bit Windows to Win32, and for important notes—both shown on the next page.

This is important information to help programmers porting from 16-bit Windows to Win32.

 This is an important note.

KERNEL OBJECTS

We begin our understanding of the Win32 API by examining kernel objects and their handles. This chapter covers concepts that are relatively abstract; that is, we're not going to discuss the particulars of any specific kernel object—instead, we're going to discuss features that apply to all kernel objects.

I would have preferred to start off with a more concrete topic, but a solid understanding of kernel objects is critical to becoming a proficient Win32 software developer. Kernel objects are used by the system and the applications we write to manage numerous resources such as processes, threads, and files (to name just a few). The concepts presented in this chapter will occur throughout all the remaining chapters in this book. However, I do realize that some of the material covered in this chapter won't sink in until you start manipulating kernel objects using actual functions. So, as you read various other chapters in this book, you'll probably want to refer back to this chapter from time to time.

What Is a Kernel Object?

As a Win32 software developer, you will be creating, opening, and manipulating kernel objects regularly. The system creates and manipulates several types of kernel objects, including the following:

Event objects	Mailslot objects	Process objects
File-mapping objects	Mutex objects	Semaphore objects
File objects	Pipe objects	Thread objects

These objects are created by calling various Win32 functions. For example, the *CreateFileMapping* function causes the system to create a file-mapping object. Each kernel object is really just a memory block allocated by the kernel and is accessible only by the kernel. This memory block is a data structure whose members maintain information about the object. Some members (object name, security descriptor, usage count, and so on) are the same across all object types, but most are specific to a particular object type. For example, a process object has a process ID, base priority, and an exit code, whereas a file object has a byte offset, a sharing mode, and an open mode.

Because the kernel object data structures are accessible only by the kernel, it is impossible for an application to locate these data structures in memory and alter their contents directly. Microsoft enforces this restriction deliberately to ensure that the kernel object structures maintain a consistent state. This restriction also allows Microsoft to add, remove, or change the members in these structures without breaking any applications.

If we cannot alter these structures directly, then how do our applications manipulate these kernel objects? The answer is that the Win32 API offers a set of functions that manipulate these structures in well-defined ways. Our access to these kernel objects is always via these functions. When you call a function that creates a kernel object, the function returns a handle that identifies the object. Think of this handle as an opaque 32-bit value that can be used by any thread in your process. You pass this handle to the various Win32 functions so that the system knows which kernel object you want to manipulate. We'll talk a lot more about these handles later in this chapter.

To make the operating system robust, these handle values are process-relative. So if you were to pass this handle value (using some form of interprocess communication) to a thread in another process, the calls that this other process would make using your process's handle value would fail. At the end of this chapter, we'll look at three mechanisms that allow multiple processes to successfully share a single kernel object.

Usage Counting

Kernel objects are owned by the kernel, not by a process. In other words, if your process calls a function that creates a kernel object and then your process terminates, the kernel object is not *necessarily* destroyed. Under most circumstances, the object will be destroyed; but if another process is using the kernel object your process created, the kernel knows not to destroy the object until the other process has stopped using it.

The kernel knows how many processes are using a particular kernel object because each object contains a usage count. The usage count is one of the data members common to all kernel object types. When an object is first created, its usage count is set to 1. Then when another process gains access to an existing kernel object, the usage count is incremented. When a process terminates, the kernel automatically decrements the usage count for all the kernel objects the process is still using. If the object's usage count goes to 0, the kernel destroys the object.

Security

Kernel objects can be protected with a security descriptor. A security descriptor describes who created an object, who can gain access to or use the object, and who is denied access to the object. Security descriptors are usually used when writing server applications, and you can ignore this feature of kernel objects if you are writing client-side applications. In fact, the security features were dropped from Microsoft Windows 95 because Windows 95 is not designed to be an operating system that runs server-side software.

Windows 95 does not offer complete security support. However, you should still be aware of security issues and use the proper access information when implementing your application to ensure that it runs correctly on Microsoft Windows NT.

Almost all functions that create kernel objects have a pointer to a SECURITY_ATTRIBUTES structure as an argument, as shown with the *CreateFileMapping* function here:

```
HANDLE CreateFileMapping(HANDLE hFile,
    LPSECURITY_ATTRIBUTES lpFileMappingAttributes, DWORD flProtect,
    DWORD dwMaximumSizeHigh, DWORD dwMaximumSizeLow, LPCTSTR lpName);
```

Most applications will simply pass NULL for this argument so that the object is created with default security. Default security means that the administrator and the creator of the object have full access to the object; all others are denied access. However, you can allocate a SECURITY_ATTRIBUTES structure, initialize it, and pass the address of the structure for this parameter. A SECURITY_ATTRIBUTES structure looks like this:

```
typedef struct _SECURITY_ATTRIBUTES {
    DWORD  nLength;
    LPVOID lpSecurityDescriptor;
    BOOL   bInheritHandle;
} SECURITY_ATTRIBUTES;
```

11

Even though this structure is called SECURITY_ATTRIBUTES, it really includes only one member that has anything to do with security: *lpSecurityDescriptor*. If you want to restrict access to a kernel object you create, you must create a security descriptor and initialize the SECURITY-_ATTRIBUTES structure as follows:

```
SECURITY_ATTRIBUTES sa;
sa.nLength = sizeof(sa);          // Used for versioning
sa.lpSecurityDescriptor = pSD;    // Address of an initialized SD
sa.bInheritHandle = FALSE;        // Discussed later
HANDLE hFileMapping = CreateFileMapping((HANDLE) 0xffffffff, &sa,
   PAGE_READWRITE, 0, 1024, "MyFileMapping");
   :
   :
```

I'm going to postpone discussing the *bInheritHandle* member until the section on inheritance later in this chapter since this member has nothing to do with security.

When you want to gain access to an existing kernel object (rather than to create a new one), you must specify the operations you intend to perform on the object. For example, if I wanted to gain access to an existing file-mapping kernel object so that I could read data from it, I would call *OpenFileMapping* as follows:

```
HANDLE hFileMapping = OpenFileMapping(FILE_MAP_READ, FALSE,
   "MyFileMapping");
```

By passing FILE_MAP_READ as the first parameter to *OpenFileMapping*, I am indicating that I intend to read from this file mapping after I gain access to it. The *OpenFileMapping* function performs a security check first, before it returns a valid handle value. If I (the logged-on user) am allowed access to the existing file-mapping kernel object, then *OpenFile-Mapping* returns a valid handle. However, if I am denied this access, *OpenFileMapping* returns NULL, and a call to *GetLastError* will return a value of 5 or (ERROR_ACCESS_DENIED). Again, most applications do not use security, and Windows 95 doesn't support it at all, so I won't go into this issue any further.

In addition to kernel objects, your application might use other types of objects, such as menus, windows, mouse cursors, brushes, and fonts. These objects are User or Graphics Device Interface (GDI) objects, not kernel objects. When you first start programming for Win32, you might be confused when you're trying to differentiate a User or GDI object from a kernel object. For example, is an icon a User object or a kernel object? The easiest way to determine whether an object is a kernel object is to examine the Win32 function that creates the object. Almost all functions that create kernel objects have a parameter that allows you to specify security attribute information, as did the *CreateFileMapping* function shown earlier.

None of the functions that create User or GDI functions have an LPSECURITY_ATTRIBUTES parameter like the *CreateIcon* function shown here:

```
HICON CreateIcon(HINSTANCE hinst, int nWidth, int nHeight,
   BYTE cPlanes, BYTE cBitsPixel,
   CONST BYTE *lpbANDbits, CONST BYTE *lpbXORbits);
```

A Process's Kernel Object Handle Table

When a process is initialized, the system allocates a handle table for this process. This handle table is used only for kernel objects, not for User or GDI objects. The details of how the handle table is structured and managed are undocumented. Usually, I would refrain from discussing undocumented parts of the operating system. In this case, however, I'm making an exception because I feel that a competent Win32 programmer must understand how a process's handle table is managed. Because this information is undocumented, I will not have all of the details completely correct, and the internal implementation is certainly different among Windows NT, Windows 95, Win32s, and Windows CE. So read the following discussion to improve your understanding, not to learn how the system really does it.

Figure 2-1 shows what a process's handle table looks like. As you can see, it is simply an array of data structures. Each structure contains a 32-bit pointer to a kernel object, an access mask, and some flags.

Index	Pointer to Kernel Object Memory Block	Access Mask (DWORD of Flag Bits)	Flags (DWORD of Flag Bits)
1	0x????????	0x????????	0x????????
2	0x????????	0x????????	0x????????
...	...	...	...

Figure 2-1.
The structure of a process's handle table.

Creating a Kernel Object

When a process first initializes, this handle table is empty. Then when a thread in the process calls a function that creates a kernel object, such as *CreateFileMapping*, the kernel allocates a block of memory for the object, and initializes it; then the kernel scans the process's handle table for an empty entry. Because the handle table in Figure 2-1 is empty, the kernel finds the structure at index 1 and initializes it. The pointer member will be set to the internal memory address of the kernel object's data structure, the access mask will be set to full access, and the flags will be set. (We'll discuss the flags in the inheritance section later in this chapter.)

Here are some of the functions that create kernel objects (this is in no way a complete list):

```
HANDLE CreateThread(LPSECURITY_ATTRIBUTES lpThreadAttributes,
    DWORD dwStackSize, LPTHREAD_START_ROUTINE lpStartAddress,
    LPVOID lpParameter, DWORD dwCreationFlags, LPDWORD lpThreadId);

HANDLE CreateFile(LPCTSTR lpFileName, DWORD dwDesiredAccess,
    DWORD dwShareMode, LPSECURITY_ATTRIBUTES lpSecurityAttributes,
    DWORD dwCreationDistribution, DWORD dwFlagsAndAttributes,
    HANDLE hTemplateFile);

HANDLE CreateFileMapping(HANDLE hFile,
    LPSECURITY_ATTRIBUTES lpFileMappingAttributes, DWORD flProtect,
    DWORD dwMaximumSizeHigh, DWORD dwMaximumSizeLow, LPCTSTR lpName);

HANDLE CreateSemaphore(LPSECURITY_ATTRIBUTES lpSemaphoreAttributes,
    LONG lInitialCount, LONG lMaximumCount, LPCTSTR lpName);
```

All functions that create kernel objects return process-relative handles that can be used successfully by any and all threads that are running in the same process. This handle value is actually the index into the process's handle table that identifies where the kernel object's information got stored. So when you debug an application and examine the actual value of a kernel object handle, you'll see small values like 1, 2, and so on. Remember, the meaning of the handle is undocumented and is subject to change. In fact, on Windows NT the value returned identifies the number of bytes into the process's handle table for the object rather than the index number itself.

Whenever you call a Win32 function that accepts a kernel object handle as an argument, you pass the value returned by one of the *Create** functions. Internally, the function looks in your process's handle table to get the address of the kernel object you want to manipulate and then manipulates the object's data structure in a well-defined fashion.

If you pass an invalid index (handle), the function returns failure and *GetLastError* returns 6 (ERROR_INVALID_HANDLE). It is because handle values are actually indexes into the process's handle table that these handles are process-relative and cannot be used successfully from other processes.

If, when you call a function to create a kernel object, the call fails, the handle value returned is usually 0 (NULL). The system would have to be very low on memory or encountering a security problem for this to happen. Unfortunately, a few functions return a handle value of −1 (INVALID_HANDLE_VALUE) when they fail. For example, if *CreateFile* fails to open the specified file, it returns INVALID_HANDLE_VALUE instead of NULL. You must be very careful when checking the return value of a function that creates a kernel object. Specifically, you can compare the value with INVALID_HANDLE_VALUE only when you call *CreateFile*. The following code is incorrect:

```
HANDLE hMutex = CreateMutex(…);
if (hMutex == INVALID_HANDLE_VALUE) {
    // We will never execute this code because
    // CreateMutex returns NULL if it fails.
}
```

Closing a Kernel Object

Regardless of how you create a kernel object, you indicate to the system that you are done manipulating the object by calling *CloseHandle*:

```
BOOL CloseHandle(HANDLE hobj);
```

This function first checks the calling process's handle table to ensure that the index (handle) passed to it identifies an object that the process does in fact have access to. If an invalid handle is passed, the function returns FALSE and *GetLastError* returns ERROR_INVALID_HANDLE. If the index is valid, however, the system gets the address of the kernel object's data structure and decrements the usage count member in the structure; if the count is zero, the kernel destroys the kernel object from memory.

Just before *CloseHandle* returns, it clears out the entry in the process's handle table—this handle is now invalid for your process, and you should not attempt to use it. The clearing happens whether or not the kernel object has been destroyed! After you call *CloseHandle*, you will no longer have access to the kernel object; however, if the object's count did not decrement to zero, the object has not been destroyed. This is OK; it just means that one or more other processes are still using the object. When the other processes stop using the object (they call *CloseHandle*), the object will be destroyed.

Let's say that you forget to call *CloseHandle*—will there be a memory leak? Well, yes and no. It is possible for a process to leak resources (such as kernel objects) while the process runs. However, when the process terminates, the operating system ensures that any and all resources used by the process are freed—this is guaranteed. For kernel objects, the system performs the following: When your process terminates, the system automatically scans the process's handle table. If the table has any valid entries (objects that you didn't close before terminating), the system closes these object handles for you. If the usage count of any of these objects goes to zero, the kernel destroys the object.

Sharing Kernel Objects Across Process Boundaries

Frequently, threads running in different processes need to share kernel objects. Here are some of the reasons why:

- File-mapping objects allow you to share blocks of data between two processes running on a single machine.

- Mailslots and named pipes allow applications to send blocks of data between processes running on different machines connected to the network.

- Mutexes, semaphores, and events allow threads in different processes to synchronize their continued execution, such as an application that needs to notify another application when it has completed some task.

But because kernel object handles are process-relative, Win32 makes these tasks difficult. Microsoft had several good reasons for designing the handles to be process-relative, however, and the most important reason was robustness. If kernel object handles were systemwide values, one process could easily obtain the handle to an object that another process was using and wreak havoc on that process. Another reason was for security. Kernel objects are protected with security, and a process must request permission to manipulate an object before attempting to manipulate it.

The creator of the object can prevent an unauthorized user from touching the object simply by denying access to it.

In the following section, we'll look at the three different mechanisms that allow processes to share kernel objects.

Object Handle Inheritance

Object handle inheritance can be used only when processes have a parent-child relationship. In this scenario, one or more kernel object handles are available to the parent process, and the parent decides to spawn a child process, giving the child access to the parent's kernel objects. For this type of inheritance to work, the parent process must perform several steps.

First, when the parent process creates a kernel object, the parent must indicate to the system that it wants the object's handle to be inheritable. Keep in mind that although kernel object *handles* are inheritable, kernel objects themselves are not.

To create an inheritable handle, the parent process must allocate and initialize a SECURITY_ATTRIBUTES structure and pass the structure's address to the specific *Create*∗ function. The following code creates a mutex object and returns an inheritable handle to it:

```
SECURITY_ATTRIBUTES sa;
sa.nLength = sizeof(sa);
sa.lpSecurityDescriptor = NULL;
sa.bInheritHandle = TRUE;

HANDLE hMutex = CreateMutex(&sa, FALSE, NULL);
:
:
```

This code initializes a SECURITY_ATTRIBUTES structure indicating that the object should be created using default security (ignored on Windows 95) and that the returned handle should be inheritable.

Even though Windows 95 does not have complete security support, it does support inheritance; therefore, the value of the *bInheritHandle* member is used correctly by Windows 95.

Now we come to the flags that are stored in a process's handle table entry. Each handle table entry has a flag bit indicating whether or not the handle is inheritable. If you pass NULL as the LPSECURITY-_ATTRIBUTES parameter when you create a kernel object, the handle returned is not inheritable and this bit is zero. Setting the *bInheritHandle* member to TRUE causes this flag bit to be set to 1.

Imagine a process's handle table that looks like the one shown in Figure 2-2.

Index	Pointer to Kernel Object Memory Block	Access Mask (DWORD of Flag Bits)	Flags (DWORD of Flag Bits)
1	0xF0000000	0x????????	0x00000000
2	0x00000000	(N/A)	(N/A)
3	0xF0000010	0x????????	0x00000001

Figure 2-2.
A process's handle table containing two valid entries.

The table in Figure 2-2 indicates that this process has access to two kernel objects (handles 1 and 3). Handle 1 is noninheritable, and handle 3 is inheritable.

The next step to perform when using object handle inheritance is for the parent process to spawn the child process. This is done using the *CreateProcess* function:

```
BOOL CreateProcess(LPCTSTR lpApplicationName, LPTSTR lpCommandLine,
    LPSECURITY_ATTRIBUTES lpProcessAttributes,
    LPSECURITY_ATTRIBUTES lpThreadAttributes, BOOL bInheritHandles,
    DWORD dwCreationFlags, LPVOID lpEnvironment,
    LPCTSTR lpCurrentDirectory, LPSTARTUPINFO lpStartupInfo,
    LPPROCESS_INFORMATION lpProcessInformation);
```

We'll examine this function in detail in Chapter 3, but for now I want to draw your attention to the *bInheritHandles* parameter. Usually, when you spawn a process, you will pass FALSE for this parameter. This value tells the system that you do not want the child process to inherit the inheritable handles that are in the parent process's handle table.

If you pass TRUE for this parameter, however, the child will inherit the parent's inheritable handle values. When you pass TRUE for this parameter, the operating system creates the new child process but does not allow the child process to begin executing its code right away. Of course, the system creates a new, empty process handle table for the child process just like it would for any new process. But because you passed TRUE to *CreateProcess*'s *bInheritHandles* parameter, the system does one more thing: it walks the parent process's handle table, and for each entry it finds that contains a valid inheritable handle, the system copies the entry exactly into the child process's handle table. The entry is copied to the exact same position in the child process's handle table as in the parent's handle table. This fact is important because it means that the handle value that identifies a kernel object is identical in both the parent and the child processes.

In addition to copying the handle table entry, the system increments the usage count of the kernel object because two processes are now using the object. For the kernel object to be destroyed, both the parent process and the child process must call *CloseHandle* on the object or terminate. The child does not have to terminate first—but neither does the parent. In fact, the parent process can close its handle to the object immediately after the *CreateProcess* function returns, without affecting the child's ability to manipulate the object.

Figure 2-3 shows the child process's handle table just before the process is allowed to begin execution. You can see that entries 1 and 2 are not initialized and are therefore invalid handles for the child process to use. However, index 3 does identify a kernel object. In fact, it identifies the kernel object at address 0xF00000010, the same object as in the parent process's handle table. The access mask is identical to the mask in the parent, and the flags are also identical. This means that if the child process were to spawn its own child process (a grandchild process of the parent), this grandchild process would also inherit this kernel object handle with the same handle value, same access, and same flags, and the usage count on the object would again be incremented.

Index	Pointer to Kernel Object Memory Block	Access Mask (DWORD of Flag Bits)	Flags (DWORD of Flag Bits)
1	0x00000000	(N/A)	(N/A)
2	0x00000000	(N/A)	(N/A)
3	0xF0000010	0x????????	0x00000001

Figure 2-3.
A child process's handle table after inheriting the parent process's inheritable handle.

Be aware that object handle inheritance applies only at the time the child process is spawned. If the parent process were to create any new kernel objects with inheritable handles, these new handles would not be inherited by an already-running child process.

Object handle inheritance has one very strange characteristic: when you use it, the child has no idea that it has inherited any handles. Kernel object handle inheritance is useful only when the child process documents the fact that it expects to be given access to a kernel object when spawned from another process. Usually, the parent and child applications are written by the same company; however, a different company can write the child application if it documents what it expects.

By far the most common way for a child process to determine the handle value of the kernel object it's expecting is to have the handle value passed as a command-line argument to the child process. The child process's initialization code parses the command line (usually by calling *sscanf*) and extracts the handle value. Once the child has the handle value, it has unlimited access to the object. Note that the only reason handle inheritance works is because the handle value of the shared kernel object is identical in both the parent process and the child process; this is why the parent is able to pass the handle value as a command-line argument.

Of course, you can use other forms of interprocess communication to transfer an inherited kernel object handle value from the parent process into the child process. One technique is for the parent to wait for the child to complete initialization (using the *WaitForInputIdle* function discussed in Chapter 11); then the parent can send or post a message to a window created by a thread in the child process.

Another technique is for the parent process to add an environment variable to its environment block. The variable's name would be something that the child process knows to look for, and the variable's value would be the handle value of the kernel object to be inherited. Then when the parent spawns the child process, the child process inherits the parent's environment variables and can easily call *GetEnvironmentVariable* to obtain the inherited object's handle value. This approach is excellent if the child process is going to spawn another child process because the environment variables can be inherited again.

Changing the Handles Flags

Occasionally, you might encounter a situation in which a parent process creates a kernel object retrieving an inheritable handle and then spawns two child processes. The parent process wants only one child to inherit the kernel object handle. In other words, you may at times want to control which child processes inherit kernel object handles. To alter the inheritance flag of a kernel object handle, you can call the *SetHandle-Information* function:

```
BOOL SetHandleInformation(HANDLE hObject, DWORD dwMask,
  DWORD dwFlags);
```

As you can see, this function takes three parameters. The first, *hObject*, identifies a valid handle. The second parameter, *dwMask*, tells the function which flag or flags you want to change. Currently, two flags are associated with each handle:

```
#define HANDLE_FLAG_INHERIT             0x00000001
#define HANDLE_FLAG_PROTECT_FROM_CLOSE  0x00000002
```

You can bitwise OR both of these flags together if you want to change both of the object's flags simultaneously. *SetHandleInformation*'s third parameter, *dwFlags*, indicates what you want to set the flags to. For example, to turn on the inheritance flag for a kernel object handle, do the following:

```
SetHandleInformation(hobj, HANDLE_FLAG_INHERIT, HANDLE_FLAG_INHERIT);
```

To turn off this flag, do this:

```
SetHandleInformation(hobj, HANDLE_FLAG_INHERIT, 0 );
```

The HANDLE_FLAG_PROTECT_FROM_CLOSE flag tells the system that this handle should not be allowed to close:

```
SetHandleInformation(hobj, HANDLE_FLAG_PROTECT_FROM_CLOSE,
  HANDLE_FLAG_PROTECT_FROM_CLOSE);
CloseHandle(hobj);     // Exception is raised
```

If a thread attempts to close a protected handle, *CloseHandle* raises an exception. You would rarely want to protect a handle from being closed. However, this flag might be useful if you had a process that spawned a child that in turn spawned a grandchild process. The parent process might be expecting the grandchild to inherit the object handle given to the immediate child. However, it is possible that the immediate child might close the handle before spawning the grandchild. If this were to happen, the parent might not be able to communicate with the grandchild because the grandchild did not inherit the kernel object. By marking the handle as "protected from close," the grandchild will inherit the object.

This approach has one flaw, however; the immediate child process might call

```
SetHandleInformation(hobj, HANDLE_FLAG_PROTECT_FROM_CLOSE, 0);
CloseHandle(hobj);
```

to turn off the HANDLE_FLAG_PROTECT_FROM_CLOSE flag and then close the handle. The parent process is gambling that the child process will not execute this code. Of course, the parent is also gambling that the child process will spawn the grandchild, so this bet is not that risky.

For the sake of completeness, I'll also mention the *GetHandleInformation* function:

```
BOOL GetHandleInformation(HANDLE hObj, LPDWORD lpdwFlags);
```

This function returns the current flag settings for the specified handle in the DWORD pointed to by *lpdwFlags*. To see if a handle is inhertible, do the following:

```
DWORD dwFlags;
GetHandleInformation(hObj, &dwFlags);
BOOL fHandleIsInheritable =
    (0 != (dwFlags & HANDLE_FLAG_INHERITABLE));
```

Named Objects

The second method available for sharing kernel objects across process boundaries is to name the objects. Many, though not all, kernel objects can be named. For example, all of the following functions create named kernel objects:

```
HANDLE CreateMutex(LPSECURITY_ATTRIBUTES lpMutexAttributes,
    BOOL bInitialOwner, LPCTSTR lpszName);

HANDLE CreateEvent(LPSECURITY_ATTRIBUTES lpEventAttributes,
    BOOL bManualReset, BOOL bInitialState, LPCTSTR lpszName);

HANDLE CreateSemaphore(LPSECURITY_ATTRIBUTES lpSemaphoreAttributes,
    LONG lInitialCount, LONG lMaximumCount, LPCTSTR lpszName);

HANDLE CreateWaitableTimer(LPSECURITY_ATTRIBUTES lpTimerAttributes,
    BOOL bManualReset, LPCTSTR lpszName);

HANDLE CreateFileMapping(HANDLE hFile,
    LPSECURITY_ATTRIBUTES lpFileMappingAttributes, DWORD flProtect,
    DWORD dwMaximumSizeHigh, DWORD dwMaximumSizeLow, LPCTSTR lpszName);
```

All of these functions have their first and last parameters in common. We have already discussed the first parameter, so we will focus on the last parameter, *lpszName*. When you pass NULL for this parameter, you are indicating to the system that you want to create an unnamed kernel object. When you create an unnamed object, you can share the object across processes using either inheritance (as discussed above) or *DuplicateHandle* (discussed in the next section). To share an object by name, you must give the object a name.

If you don't pass NULL for the *lpszName* parameter, you should pass the address of a zero-terminated string name. This name can be up to MAX_PATH (defined as 260) characters long and must not contain the backslash character ('\'). Unfortunately, Microsoft offers no guidance for assigning names to kernel objects. For example, if you attempt to create an object called "JeffObj," there's no guarantee that an object called "JeffObj" doesn't already exist. To make matters worse, mutexes, events, semaphores, file mappings, and waitable timers all share a single name-space. Because of this, the following call to *CreateSemaphore* will always return NULL:

```
HANDLE hMutex = CreateMutex(NULL, FALSE, "JeffObj");
HANDLE hSem = CreateSemaphore(NULL, 1, 1, "JeffObj");
DWORD dwErrorCode = GetLastError();
```

If you examine the value of *dwErrorCode* after executing the code above, you'll see a return code of 6 (ERROR_INVALID_HANDLE). This error code is not very descriptive, but what can you do?

Now that you know how to name an object, let's see how to share objects this way. Let's say that Process A starts up and calls the following function:

```
HANDLE hMutexProcessA = CreateMutex(NULL, FALSE, "JeffMutex");
```

This function call creates a brand new mutex kernel object and assigns it the name "JeffMutex". Notice that in Process A's handle, *hMutexProcessA* is not an inheritable handle—and it doesn't have to be when you're just naming objects.

Some time later, some process spawns Process B. Process B does not have to be a child of Process A; it might be spawned from the Explorer or any other application. That process B need not be a child of process A is an advantage of using named objects instead of inheritance. When Process B starts executing, it executes the following code:

```
HANDLE hMutexProcessB = CreateMutex(NULL, FALSE, "JeffMutex");
```

When Process B's call to *CreateMutex* is made, the system first checks to find out whether a kernel object with the name "JeffMutex" already exists. Because an object with this name does exist, the kernel then checks the object type. Since we are attempting to create a mutex and the object with the name "JeffMutex" is also a mutex, the system considers this call to *CreateMutex* successful. By that I mean that the system locates an empty entry in Process B's handle table and initializes the entry to point to the existing kernel object.

But even though Process B has called *CreateMutex*, a mutex was not actually created. Instead, Process B was simply assigned a process-relative handle value that identifies the existing mutex object in the kernel. Of course, because a new handle table entry identifies this object, the mutex object's usage count is incremented; the object will not be destroyed until both Process A and Process B have closed their handles to the object. Notice that the handle values in the two processes are most likely going to be different values. This is OK: Process A will use its handle value, and Process B will use its own handle value to manipulate the one mutex kernel object.

Important

You need to be aware of an extremely important concern when having kernel objects share names. When Process B calls *CreateMutex*, it passes security attribute information and a second parameter to the function. These parameters are ignored if an object with the specified name already exists! An application can determine if it did, in fact, create a new kernel object versus simply open an existing object by calling *GetLastError* immediately after the call to the *Create** function:

```
HANDLE hMutex = CreateMutex(NULL, FALSE, "JeffObj");
if (GetLastError() == ERROR_ALREADY_EXISTS) {
    // Opened a handle to an existing object
} else {
    // Created a brand new object
}
```

An alternate method exists for sharing objects by name. Instead of calling a *Create** function, a process can call one of the *Open** functions shown here:

```
HANDLE OpenMutex(DWORD dwDesiredAccess, BOOL bInheritHandle,
    LPCTSTR lpszName);
```

```
HANDLE OpenEvent(DWORD dwDesiredAccess, BOOL bInheritHandle,
    LPCTSTR lpszName);
```

```
HANDLE OpenSemaphore(DWORD dwDesiredAccess, BOOL bInheritHandle,
    LPCTSTR lpszName);
```

```
HANDLE OpenWaitableTimer(DWORD dwDesiredAccess, BOOL bInheritHandle,
   LPCTSTR lpszName);

HANDLE OpenFileMapping(DWORD dwDesiredAccess, BOOL bInheritHandle,
   LPCTSTR lpszName);
```

Notice that all of these functions have the same prototype. The last parameter, *lpszName*, indicates the name of a kernel object. You cannot pass NULL for this parameter; you must pass the address of a zero-terminated string. These functions search the single name-space of kernel objects attempting to find a match. If no kernel object with the specified name exists, the functions return NULL and *GetLastError* returns 2 (ERROR_FILE_NOT_FOUND). However, if a kernel object with the specified name does exist, and if it is the same type of object, the system then checks to see if the access requested (via the *dwDesiredAccess* parameter) is allowed; if it is, the calling process's handle table is updated and the object's usage count is incremented. The returned handle will be inheritable if you pass TRUE for the *bInheritHandle* parameter.

The main difference between calling a *Create*∗ function versus an *Open*∗ function is that if the object doesn't already exist, the *Create*∗ function will create it whereas the *Open*∗ function will simply fail.

Duplicating Object Handles

The last technique for sharing kernel objects across process boundaries requires the use of the *DuplicateHandle* function:

```
BOOL DuplicateHandle(
   HANDLE hSourceProcessHandle, HANDLE hSourceHandle,
   HANDLE hTargetProcessHandle, LPHANDLE lpTargetHandle,
   DWORD dwDesiredAccess, BOOL bInheritHandle, DWORD dwOptions);
```

Simply stated, this function takes an entry in one process's handle table and makes a copy of the entry into another process's handle table. *DuplicateHandle* takes several parameters but is actually quite straightforward. The most general usage of the *DuplicateHandle* function involves three different processes that are running in the system.

When you call *DuplicateHandle*, the first and third parameters, *hSourceProcessHandle* and *hTargetProcessHandle*, are kernel object handles. The handles themselves must be relative to the process that is calling the *DuplicateHandle* function. In addition, these two parameters must identify process kernel objects; the function fails if you pass handles to any other type of kernel object. We'll discuss process kernel objects in more detail in Chapter 3; for now, all you need to know is that a process kernel object is created whenever a new process is invoked in the system.

The second parameter, *hSourceHandle*, is a handle to any type of kernel object. However, the handle value is not relative to the process that is calling *DuplicateHandle*. Instead, this handle must be relative to the process identified by the *hSourceProcessHandle* handle. The fourth parameter, *lpTargetHandle*, is the address of a HANDLE variable that will receive the index of the entry that gets the copy of the source's handle information. The handle value that comes back is relative to the process identified by the *hTargetProcessHandle*.

DuplicateHandle's last three parameters allow you to indicate the value of the access mask and the inheritance flag that should be used in the target's entry for this kernel object handle. The *dwOptions* parameter can be 0 (zero) or any combination of the following two flags: DUPLICATE_SAME_ACCESS and DUPLICATE_CLOSE_SOURCE.

Specifying DUPLICATE_SAME_ACCESS tells *DuplicateHandle* that you want the target's handle to have the same access mask as the source process's handle. Using this flag causes *DuplicateHandle* to ignore its *dwDesiredAccess* parameter.

Specifying the DUPLICATE_CLOSE_SOURCE has the effect of closing the handle in the source process. This flag makes it easy for one process to hand a kernel object over to another process. When this flag is used, the usage count of the kernel object is not affected. I have never had a need to use this flag.

Microsoft is aware of a bug in Windows 95 with respect to the DUPLI-CATE_CLOSE_SOURCE flag. If the calling process is not the source process, the handle is not closed.

An example will demonstrate how DuplicateHandle works. Process X's handle table (Figure 2-4) contains two handle values, 1 and 2. Handle value 1 identifies Process S's process kernel object, and handle value 2 identifies Process T's process kernel object.

Figure 2-5 shows Process S's handle table, which contains a single entry with a handle value of 2. This handle can identify any type of kernel object—it does not have to be a process kernel object.

Index	Pointer to Kernel Object Memory Block	Access Mask (DWORD of Flag Bits)	Flags (DWORD of Flag Bits)
1	0xF0000000 (Process S's kernel object)	0x????????	0x00000000
2	0xF0000010 (Process T's kernel object)	0x????????	0x00000000

Figure 2-4.
Process X's handle table.

Index	Pointer to Kernel Object Memory Block	Access Mask (DWORD of Flag Bits)	Flags (DWORD of Flag Bits)
1	0x00000000	(N/A)	(N/A)
2	0xF0000020 (any kernel object)	0x????????	0x00000000

Figure 2-5.
Process S's handle table.

Figure 2-6 shows what Process T's handle table contains before Process X calls the *DuplicateHandle* function. As you can see, Process T's handle table contains just a single entry with a handle value of 2, and handle entry 1 is currently available.

Index	Pointer to Kernel Object Memory Block	Access Mask (DWORD of Flag Bits)	Flags (DWORD of Flag Bits)
1	0x00000000	(N/A)	(N/A)
2	0xF0000030 (any kernel object)	0x????????	0x00000000

Figure 2-6.
Process T's handle table before calling DuplicateHandle.

If Process X now calls *DuplicateHandle* using

```
DuplicateHandle(1, 2, 2, &hObj, 0, TRUE, DUPLICATE_SAME_ACCESS);
```

then, after this call, only Process T's handle table has changed, as shown in Figure 2-7.

Index	Pointer to Kernel Object Memory Block	Access Mask (DWORD of Flag Bits)	Flags (DWORD of Flag Bits)
1	0xF0000020	0x????????	0x00000001
2	0xF0000030 (any kernel object)	0x????????	0x00000000

Figure 2-7.
Process T's handle table after calling DuplicateHandle.

The second entry in Process S's handle table has been copied to the first entry in Process T's handle table. *DuplicateHandle* has also filled in Process X's *hObj* variable with a value of 1, which is the index in process T's handle table where the new entry got placed.

Because the DUPLICATE_SAME_ACCESS flag was passed to *DuplicateHandle,* the access mask for this handle in Process T's table is identical to the access mask in Process S's table entry. Also, passing the DUPLICATE_SAME_ACCESS flag causes *DuplicateHandle* to ignore its *dwDesiredAccess* parameter. Finally, notice that the inheritance bit flag has been turned on because TRUE was passed for *DuplicateHandle*'s *bInherit-Handle* parameter.

Obviously, you would never call *DuplicateHandle* passing in hard-coded numeric values as I have done in this example. I have used hard-coded numbers only to demonstrate how the function operates. In real applications, you would have the various handle values in variables and you would pass the variables as arguments to the function.

Like inheritance, one of the odd things about the *DuplicateHandle* function is that the target process is not given any notification that a new kernel object is now accessible to it. So, Process X must somehow notify Process T that it now has access to a kernel object and must use some form of interprocess communication to pass the handle value in *hObj* to Process T. Obviously, using a command-line argument or changing Process T's environment variables is out of the question since the process is already up and running. A Windows message or some other IPC mechanism must be used.

What I have just explained is the most general usage of *Duplicate-Handle*. As you can see, it is a very flexible function. However, it is rarely used with three different processes being involved. Usually, it is called when just two processes are involved. Imagine a situation in which one process has access to an object that another process wants access to, or a case in which one process wants to give access of a kernel object to another process. For example, let's say that Process A has access to a kernel object and wants to give Process B access to this object. To do this, you would call *DuplicateHandle* as follows:

```
// All of the following code is executed by Process A.

// Create a mutex object accessible by Process A.
HANDLE hObjProcessA = CreateMutex(NULL, FALSE, NULL);

// Open a handle to Process B's kernel object.
HANDLE hProcessB = OpenProcess(PROCESS_ALL_ACCESS, FALSE,
   dwProcessIdB);

HANDLE hObjProcessB;   // An uninitialized handle
                       // relative to Process B

// Give Process B access to the mutex object.
DuplicateHandle(GetCurrentProcess(), hObjProcessA, hProcessB,
   &hObjProcessB, 0, FALSE, DUPLICATE_SAME_ACCESS;

// Use some IPC mechanism to get the handle
// value in hObjProcessB into Process B.
   :
   :

// We no longer need to communicate with Process B.
CloseHandle(hProcessB);
   :
   :

// When Process A no longer needs to use the mutex, it should close it.
CloseHandle(hObjProcessA);
```

The call to *GetCurrentProcess* returns a pseudo-handle that always identifies the calling process, Process A in this example. Once *Duplicate-Handle* returns, *hObjProcessB* is a handle relative to Process B that identifies the same object that *hObjProcessA*'s handle does when referenced by code in Process A. Process A should never execute the following code:

```
// Process A should never execute attempt to close the
// duplicated handle.
CloseHandle(hObjProcessB);
```

If Process A were to execute this code, the call might or might not fail. The call would succeed if Process A happened to have access to a kernel object with the handle value as *hObjProcessB*. This call would have the effect of closing some object so that Process A no longer had access to it, which would certainly cause the application to behave undesirably (to put it nicely).

Here is another way to use *DuplicateHandle*: Suppose that a process has access to a mutex object. A thread in this process spawns another thread. These two threads are going to access the mutex object. Because Windows is a preemptive multithreaded system, we can't know for sure which of these two threads will complete its task first. However, when both threads have finished using the mutex, the mutex object is no longer needed and should be destroyed. One way to elegantly destroy the mutex object is to let the system keep track of the mutex's usage by calling *DuplicateHandle* to artificially increment the object's usage count. The following code demonstrates:

```
int WINAPI WinMain(HINSTANCE hinstExe, HINSTANCE hinstExePrev,
    LPSTR szCmdLine, int nCmdShow) {

    HANDLE hThread;  // We're going to create a worker thread.
    DWORD dwThreadId;

    // Create a brand new mutex object.
    HANDLE hMutex = CreateMutex(NULL, FALSE, NULL);

    // This process is going to have two different
    // handles to a single mutex object.
    HANDLE hMutexWorker;

    // Increment the usage count of the mutex object, and
    // give this process another handle to it.
    DuplicateHandle(GetCurrentProcess(), hMutex,
        GetCurrentProcess(), &hMutexWorker,
        0, FALSE, DUPLICATE_SAME_ACCESS);

    // Create a worker thread, and pass
    // it the second handle to the mutex.
    hThread = CreateThread(NULL, 0, ThreadFunc,
        (LPVOID) hMutexWorker, 0, &dwThreadId);

    // This thread keeps running and manipulates
    // the mutex via the handle in hMutex.
    :
    :
```

```
        // When this thread is finished using the mutex, it closes it.
        // If the count is zero, the object is destroyed.
        CloseHandle(hMutex);

        // Wait for the worker thread to terminate.
        WaitForSingleObject(hThread, INFINITE);

        // Close the handle to the worker thread kernel object.
        CloseHandle(hThread);

        return(0);
}


DWORD WINAPI ThreadFunc(PVOID pvParam) {
        // A handle to the mutex is
        // passed in the pvParam argument.
        HANDLE hMutex = (HANDLE)pvParam;

        // This thread keeps running and manipulates the
        // mutex via the handle in the local hMutex variable.
        :
        :

        // When this thread is finished using the mutex, it closes it.
        // If the count is zero, the object is destroyed.
        CloseHandle(hMutex);

        return(0);
}
```

PROCESSES

This chapter discusses how the system manages all of the running applications. I'll begin by defining what a process is and explaining how the system creates a process kernel object to manage each process. I'll then show how to manipulate a process using its associated kernel object. Following that, I'll discuss the various attributes, or properties, of a process as well as several functions that are available for querying and changing these properties. I'll also examine the functions that allow you to create or spawn additional processes in the system. And, of course, no discussion of processes would be complete without an in-depth look at how they terminate. OK, let's begin.

A process is usually defined as an instance of a running program. In Win32, a process owns a 4-GB address space. Unlike their counterparts in MS-DOS and 16-bit Windows operating systems, Win32 processes are inert; that is, a Win32 process executes nothing—it simply owns a 4-GB address space that contains the code and data for an application's EXE file. Any DLLs required by the EXE also have their code and data loaded into the process's address space. In addition to an address space, a process owns certain resources such as files, dynamic memory allocations, and threads. The various resources created during a process's life are destroyed when the process is terminated—*guaranteed*.

As I said, processes are inert. For a process to accomplish anything, the process must own a thread; it is this thread that is responsible for executing the code contained in the process's address space. In fact, a single process might contain several threads, all of them executing code "simultaneously" in the process's address space. To do this, each thread has its very own set of CPU registers and its own stack. Every process has at least one thread that executes code contained in the process's address space. If there were no threads executing code in the process's address space, there would be no reason for the process to continue to exist, and the system would automatically destroy the process and its address space.

For all of these threads to run, the operating system schedules some CPU time for each individual thread. The operating system gives the illusion that all the threads are running concurrently by offering time slices (called *quantums*) to the threads in a round-robin fashion, as shown in Figure 3-1.

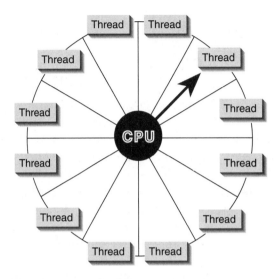

Figure 3-1.
Individual threads are scheduled time quantums by the operating system in a round-robin fashion.

When a Win32 process is created, its first thread, called the primary thread, is automatically created by the system. This primary thread can then create additional threads, and these additional threads can create even more threads.

Windows NT is capable of utilizing machines that contain several CPUs. For example, the machine I am using to write this manuscript contains two Pentium 90-MHz processors. Windows NT is able to assign a CPU to each thread so that two threads are running simultaneously. The Windows NT Kernel handles all the management and scheduling of threads on this type of system. You do not need to do anything special in your code to gain the advantages offered by a multiprocessor machine.

Windows 95 can take advantage of only a single processor. Even if the machine running Windows 95 contains more than one processor, Windows 95 can schedule only a single thread at a time; the other processor(s) sit dormant.

Writing Your First Win32 Application

Win32 supports two types of applications: graphical user interface–based (GUI) and console-based (CUI). A GUI-based application has a graphical front end. GUI applications create windows, have menus, interact with the user via dialog boxes, and use all the standard "Windowsy" stuff. Almost all the accessory applications that ship with Windows (Notepad, Calculator, and Wordpad, for instance) are typical examples of GUI-based applications. Console-based applications more closely resemble MS-DOS text applications: their output is text-based, they don't create windows or process messages, and they don't require a graphical user interface. Although CUI-based applications are contained within a window on the screen, the window contains only text. The command shells—CMD.EXE (for Windows NT) and COMMAND.COM (for Windows 95)—are typical examples of CUI-based applications.

The line between these two types of applications is very fuzzy. It is possible to create CUI-based applications that display dialog boxes. For example, the command shell could have a special command that causes it to display a graphical dialog box, allowing you to select the command you want to execute instead of having to remember the various commands supported by the shell. You could also create a GUI-based application that outputs text strings to a console window. I have frequently created a GUI-based application that creates a console window where I can send debugging information as the application executes. Of the two application types, you are certainly encouraged to use a graphical user interface in your applications instead of the old-fashioned character interface. It has been proven time and time again that GUI-based applications are much more user-friendly.

The only part of the operating system that cares whether an application is CUI- or GUI-based is the system's loader. When the loader loads an application, a subsystem value stored inside the EXE file indicates whether the application is CUI or GUI. If the value indicates a CUI-based application, the loader automatically ensures that a text console window is created for the application. If the value indicates a GUI-based application, the loader doesn't create the console window and just loads the application.

When you create a C/C++ CUI project, Visual C++ sets a linker switch so that the subsystem value in the EXE will be set to CUI, and the C run-time's startup code wants to call a main function that you must write. When you create a C/C++ GUI project, Visual C++ sets a linker switch indicating a GUI subsystem, and the C run-time's startup code wants to call a WinMain function that you must write.

In this chapter, my discussion of the mechanics of creating processes applies to both GUI- and CUI-based applications, but I emphasize GUI-based applications and don't discuss some of the finer details of creating CUI-based ones. If you want more information on creating CUI-based applications, please refer to the *Microsoft Win32 Programmer's Reference.*

All Win32 GUI-based applications must have a *WinMain* function that you implement in your source code. The function must have the following prototype:

```
int WINAPI WinMain(HINSTANCE hinstExe, HINSTANCE hinstExePrev,
    LPSTR lpszCmdLine, int nCmdShow);
```

This function is not actually called by the operating system. Instead, the operating system calls the C/C++ run-time's startup function. The Visual C++ linker knows that the name of this function is *_WinMainCRTStartup*, but you can override the name of the startup function by using the linker's /ENTRY switch. The *_WinMainCRTStartup* function is responsible for performing the following actions[1]:

1. Retrieves a pointer to the new process's full command line.

2. Retrieves a pointer to the new process's environment variables.

3. Initializes the C run-time's global variables accessible from your code by including STDLIB.H. Figure 3-2 shows the list of variables available.

4. Initializes the heap used by the C run-time memory allocation functions (that is, *malloc* and *calloc*) and other low-level input/output routines.

---

1. Visual C++ ships with the source code to the C run-time library. You can find the code for *WinMainCRTStartup* inside the CRt0.C file.

Variable Name	Type	Description
_osver	unsigned int	Build version of the operating system. For example, Windows NT 4.0 was build 1381. Thus _osver has a value of 1381.
_winmajor	unsigned int	Major version of Windows in hexadecimal notation. For Windows NT 4.0, the value is 4.
_winminor	unsigned int	Minor version of Windows in hexadecimal notation. For Windows NT 4.0, the value is 0.
_winver	unsigned int	(_winmajor << 8) + _winminor
__argc	unsigned int	The number of arguments passed on the command line.
__argv	char **	An array of __argc pointers to ANSI strings. Each array entry points to a command-line argument.
_environ	char **	An array of pointers to ANSI strings. Each array entry points to an environment string.

Figure 3-2.
The C run-time global variables available to your programs.

5. Calls your *WinMain* function as follows:

```
GetStartupInfoA(&StartupInfo);

int nMainRetVal = WinMain(GetModuleHandle(NULL), NULL,
   lpszCommandLine,
   (StartupInfo.dwFlags & STARTF_USESHOWWINDOW)  ?
      StartupInfo.wShowWindow : SW_SHOWDEFAULT);
```

6. When *WinMain* returns, the startup code calls the C run-time's *exit* function, passing it *WinMain*'s return value (*nMainRetVal*). The *exit* function performs some cleanup and then calls the Win32 *ExitProcess* function, passing it *WinMain*'s return value.

The remainder of this section discusses the various attributes that are "bestowed" upon a new process.

A Process's Instance Handle

Every EXE or DLL file loaded into a process's address space is assigned a unique *instance handle*. Your EXE file's instance is passed as *WinMain*'s first parameter, *hinstExe*. The handle's value is typically needed for calls that load resources. For example, to load an icon resource from the EXE file's image, you will need to call

```
HICON LoadIcon(HINSTANCE hinst, LPCTSTR lpszIcon);
```

The first parameter to *LoadIcon* indicates which file (EXE or DLL) contains the resource you want to load. Many applications save *WinMain*'s *hinstExe* parameter in a global variable so that it is easily accessible to all the EXE file's code.

The Win32 documentation states that some Win32 functions require a parameter of the type HMODULE. An example is the *GetModuleFileName* function, shown here:

```
DWORD GetModuleFileName(HMODULE hinstModule, LPTSTR lpszPath,
    DWORD cchPath);
```

However, the Win32 API makes no distinction between a process's HMODULE and HINSTANCE values—they are one and the same. Wherever the Win32 documentation for a function indicates that HMODULE is required, you can pass HINSTANCE, and vice versa.

The actual value of *WinMain*'s *hinstExe* parameter is the base memory address indicating where the system loaded the EXE file's image into the process's address space. For example, if the system opens the executable file and loads its contents at address 0x00400000, *WinMain*'s *hinstExe* parameter will have a value of 0x00400000.

The base address where an application loads is determined by the linker. Different linkers can use different default base addresses. The Visual C++ linker uses a default base address of 0x00400000 because this is the lowest address an executable file image can load to when you are running Windows 95. Some older linkers use a default base address of 0x00010000 because this is the lowest address an executable file image can load to when running under Windows NT. You can change the base address that your application loads to by using the /BASE: *address* linker switch for Microsoft's linker.

If you attempt to load an executable that has a base address below 0x00400000 on Windows 95, the Windows 95 loader must relocate the executable to a different address. This relocation increases the loading time of the application, but at least the application can run. If you are developing an application intended to run on both Windows 95 and Windows NT, you should make sure that the application's base address is at 0x00400000 or above.

The *GetModuleHandle* function

```
HMODULE GetModuleHandle(LPCTSTR lpszModule);
```

returns the handle/base address indicating where an EXE or DLL file is loaded in the process's address space. When calling this function, you pass a zero-terminated string that specifies the name of an EXE or DLL file loaded into the calling process's address space. If the system finds the specified EXE or DLL name, *GetModuleHandle* returns the base address at which that EXE or DLL's file image is loaded. The system returns NULL if it cannot find the specified file. You can also call *GetModule-Handle*, passing NULL for the *lpszModule* parameter. When you do this, *GetModuleHandle* returns the EXE file's base address. This is what the C run-time startup code does when it calls your *WinMain* function, as discussed in step 5 on page 37.

Keep in mind two important characteristics of the *GetModuleHandle* function. First, *GetModuleHandle* examines only the calling process's address space. If the calling process does not use any GDI functions, calling *GetModuleHandle* and passing it "GDI32" will cause NULL to be returned even though GDI32.DLL is probably loaded into other processes' address spaces. Second, calling *GetModuleHandle* and passing a value of NULL returns the base address of the EXE file in the process's address space. So even if you call *GetModuleHandle(NULL)* from code that is contained inside a DLL, the value returned is the EXE file's base address—not the DLL file's base address. This is different from how the *GetModuleHandle* function works under 16-bit Windows.

In 16-bit Windows, a task's *hModule* indicates the module database (a block of information used internally by the system to manage the module) for an EXE or a DLL. Even if 200 instances of Notepad are running, there is only one module database for Notepad and therefore only one *hmodExe* value shared by all the instances. One and only one instance of a DLL can be loaded in 16-bit Windows, so only one *hmodExe* value exists for each loaded DLL.

(continued)

(continued)

In 16-bit Windows, each running instance of a task receives its very own *hinstExe* value. This value identifies the task's default data segment. If 200 instances of Notepad are running, there are 200 *hinstExe* values—one for each running instance. Because DLLs also have a default data segment, each loaded DLL also receives its very own *hinstExe* value. You might think that because a DLL can be loaded only once, 16-bit Windows could use the same value for a DLL's *hmodExe* and *hinstExe*. This is not the case, however, because *hmodExe* identifies the DLL's module database, while *hinstExe* identifies the DLL's default data segment.

In Win32, each process gets its own address space, which means that each process thinks it is the only process running in the system. One process cannot easily see another process. For this reason, no distinction is made between a process's *hinstExe* and its *hmodExe*—they are one and the same. For historical reasons, the two terms continue to exist throughout the Win32 documentation.

As stated in the previous section, an application's *hinstExe* identifies the base memory address where the system loaded the EXE file's code into the process's address space. Because of this, it is extremely likely that many processes will have the same *hinstExe* value. For example, invoking NOTEPAD.EXE causes the system to create a 4-GB process address space and load Notepad's code and data into this address space. The code and data might load at memory address 0x00400000. If we now invoke a second instance of NOTEPAD.EXE, the system will create a new 4-GB address space for this process and again load Notepad's code and data at memory address 0x00400000. Because an application's *hinstExe* value is the same as the base memory address where the system loaded the EXE's code, the *hinstExe* value for both of these processes is 0x00400000.

In 16-bit Windows, it is possible to call the *DialogBox* function and pass it an *hinstExe* value that belongs to a task other than your own:

```
int DialogBox(HINSTANCE hInstance, LPCTSTR lpszTemplate,
   HWND hwndOwner, DLGPROC dlgprc);
```

This causes 16-bit Windows to load the dialog box template from the other application's resources. Of course, such an action is questionable anyway—but in Win32 it's no longer possible. When you make a call to a function that expects a *hinstExe* value, Win32 interprets the call to mean that you are requesting information from the EXE or DLL loaded into your own process's address space at the address indicated by the *hinstExe* parameter.

A Process's Previous Instance Handle

As noted earlier, the C run-time's startup code always passes NULL to *WinMain*'s *hinstExePrev* parameter. This parameter exists for backward compatibility and has no meaning to Win32 applications.

In a 16-bit Windows application, the *hinstEXEPrev* parameter specifies the handle of another instance of the same application. If no other instances of the application are running, *hinstEXEPrev* is passed as NULL. A 16-bit Windows application frequently examines this value for two reasons:

1. To determine whether another instance of the same application is already running and, if so, to terminate the newly invoked instance. This termination occurs if a program such as the Print Manager wants to allow only a single instance of itself to run at a time.

2. To determine whether window classes need to be registered. In 16-bit Windows, window classes need to be registered only once per module. These classes are then shared among all instances of the same application. If a second instance attempts to register the same window classes a second time, the call to *RegisterClass* fails. In Win32, each instance of an application must register its own window classes because window classes aren't shared among all instances of the same application.

To ease the porting of a 16-bit Windows application to the Win32 API, Microsoft decided always to pass NULL in the *hinstEXEPrev* parameter of *WinMain*. Because many 16-bit Windows applications examine this parameter when registering window classes, all instances see that *hinstEXEPrev* is NULL and automatically reregister their window classes.

Although this decision eases the job of porting your applications, it also means that applications cannot use the value of *hinstEXEPrev* to prevent a second instance from running. An application must use alternative methods to determine whether other instances of itself are already running. In one method, the application calls *FindWindow* and looks for a particular window class or caption that uniquely identifies that application. If *FindWindow* returns NULL, the application knows that it is the only instance of itself running. In Chapter 12, I present another method for determining whether multiple instances of an application are running.

A Process's Command Line

When a new process is created, it is passed a command line. The command line is almost never blank; at the very least, the name of the executable file used to create the new process is the first token on the command line. However, as you'll see later when we discuss the *Create-Process* function, it is possible that a process can receive a command line that consists of a single character: the string-terminating zero. When the C run-time's startup code begins executing, it retrieves the process's command line, skips over the executable file's name, and passes a pointer to the remainder of the command line to *WinMain*'s *lpszCmdLine* parameter.

It's important to note that the *lpszCmdLine* parameter always points to an ANSI string. Because the system doesn't know whether you are interested in using ANSI or Unicode, Microsoft chose always to pass an ANSI string. Microsoft chose ANSI to help with porting 16-bit Windows code to Win32, because 16-bit Windows applications expect an ANSI string. I discuss Unicode in detail in Chapter 17.

An application can parse and interpret the ANSI string any way it chooses. Because the *lpszCmdLine* is an LPSTR instead of an LPCSTR, feel free to write to the buffer that it points to—but you should not, under any circumstances, write beyond the end of the buffer. Personally, I always consider this a read-only buffer. If I want to make changes to the command line, I first copy the command-line buffer to a local buffer in my application; then I modify my local buffer.

You can also obtain a pointer to your process's complete command line by calling the *GetCommandLine* function:

```
LPTSTR GetCommandLine(VOID);
```

This function returns a pointer to a buffer containing the full command line, including the full pathname of the executed file. Probably the most compelling reason to use the *GetCommandLine* function instead of the *lpszCmdLine* parameter is that both Unicode and ANSI versions of *Get-CommandLine* exist in the Win32 API, whereas the *lpszCmdLine* parameter always points to a buffer containing an ANSI character string.

Many applications would prefer to have the command line parsed into its separate tokens. An application can gain access to the command line's individual components by using the global *__argc* and *__argv* variables. But again, the *__argv* variable is an array of character pointers to

ANSI strings, not Unicode strings. Win32 offers a function that separates any string into its separate tokens, *CommandLineToArgvW*[2]:

```
LPWSTR *CommandLineToArgvW(LPWSTR lpCmdLine, LPINT pArgc);
```

As the *W* at the end of the function name implies, this function exists in a Unicode version only. (The *W* stands for *wide*.) The first parameter, *lpCmdLine*, points to a command-line string. This is usually the return value from an earlier call to *GetCommandLine*. The *pArgc* parameter is the address of an integer; the integer will be set to the number of arguments that are in the command line. *CommandLineToArgvW* returns the address to an array of Unicode string pointers.

CommandLineToArgvW allocates memory internally. Most applications will not free this memory and will count on the operating system to free it when the process terminates. This is totally acceptable. However, if you wish to free the memory yourself, the proper way to do this is by calling *HeapFree* as follows:

```
int nArgc;
LPWSTR *ppArgv = CommandLineToArgvW(GetCommandLineW(), &nArgc);

// Use the arguments…
if (*ppArgv[1] == L'x') {
 .
 .

// Free the memory block
HeapFree(GetProcessHeap(), 0, ppArgv);
```

A Process's Environment Variables

Every process has an environment block associated with it. An environment block is a block of memory allocated within the process's address space. Each block contains a set of strings with the following appearance:

```
VarName1=VarValue1\0
VarName2=VarValue2\0
VarName3=VarValue3\0
 .
 .

VarNameX=VarValueX\0
\0
```

---

2. This function was added in Windows NT 3.5; it does not exist in Windows NT 3.1.

The first part of each string is the name of an environment variable. This name is followed by an equal sign, which is followed by the value you want to assign to the variable. All strings in the environment block must be sorted alphabetically by environment variable name.

Because the equal sign is used to separate the name from the value, an equal sign cannot be part of the name. Also, spaces are significant. For example, if you declare these two variables:

```
XYZ= Win32          (Notice the space after the equal sign.)
ABC=Win32
```

and then compare the value of *XYZ* with the value of *ABC*, the system will report that the two variables are different. This is because any white space that appears immediately before or after the equal sign is taken into account. For example, if you were to add the two strings,

```
XYZ =Home           (Notice the space before the equal sign.)
XYZ=Work
```

to the environment block, the environment variable "*XYZ*" would contain "*Home*" and another environment variable "*XYZ*" would contain "*Work*." Finally, an additional 0 character must be placed at the end of all the environment variables to mark the end of the block.

To create an initial set of environment variables for Windows 95, you must modify the system's AUTOEXEC.BAT file by placing a series of SET lines in the file. Each line must be of the following form:

```
SET VarName=VarValue
```

When you reboot your system, the contents of the AUTOEXEC .BAT file are parsed, and any environment variables you have set will be available to any processes you invoke during your Windows 95 session.

When a user logs on to Windows NT, the system creates the shell process and associates a set of environment strings with it. The system obtains the initial set of environment strings by examining two keys in the Registry. The first key,

```
HKEY_LOCAL_MACHINE\SYSTEM\CurrentControlSet\Control\
   SessionManager\Environment
```

contains the list of all environment variables that apply to the system. The second key,

(continued)

(continued)

`HKEY_CURRENT_USER\Environment`

contains the list of all environment variables that apply to the user currently logged on.

A user may add, delete, or change any of these entries by double-clicking on the System option in the Control Panel and then selecting the Environment tab. This presents the following dialog box:

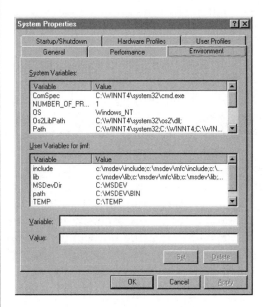

Only a user who has administrator privileges can alter the variables contained in the System Variables list.

Your application can use the various Registry functions to modify these Registry entries as well. However, for the changes to take effect for all applications, the user must log off and then log back on. Some applications, such as Explorer, Task Manager, and the Control Panel, can update their environment block with the new Registry entries when their main windows receive a WM_WININICHANGE message. For example, if you update the Registry entries and want to have the interested applications update their environment blocks, you can make the following call:

```
SendMessage(HWND_BROADCAST, WM_WININICHANGE,
    0L, (LPARAM) "Environment");
```

Normally, a child process inherits a set of environment variables that are exactly the same as those of its parent process. However, the parent process can control what environment variables a child inherits, as I'll show later when we discuss the *CreateProcess* function. By inherit, I mean that the child process gets its own copy of the parent's environment block, not that the child and parent share the same block. This means that a child process can add, delete, or modify a variable in its block and the change will not be reflected in the parent's block.

Environment variables are usually used by applications to allow the user to fine-tune the application's behavior. The user creates an environment variable and initializes it. Then, when the user invokes the application, the application examines the environment block for the variable. If the application finds the variable, the application parses the value of the variable and adjusts its behavior.

The problem with environment variables is that they are not easily set or understood by users. Users need to spell variable names correctly, and they must also know the exact syntax expected of the variable's value. Most (if not all) graphical applications, on the other hand, allow users to fine-tune an application's behavior using dialog boxes. This approach is far more user-friendly and is very strongly encouraged.

If you still wish to continue using environment variables, Win32 offers a few functions that your applications can call. The *GetEnvironmentVariable* function allows you to determine the existence and value of an environment variable:

```
DWORD GetEnvironmentVariable(LPCTSTR lpszName,
    LPTSTR lpszValue, DWORD cchValue);
```

When calling *GetEnvironmentVariable*, *lpszName* points to the desired variable name, *lpszValue* points to the buffer that will hold the variable's value, and *cchValue* indicates the size of this buffer in characters. The function returns either the number of characters copied into the buffer or 0 if the variable name cannot be found in the environment.

The *SetEnvironmentVariable* function allows you to add a variable, delete a variable, or modify a variable's value:

```
BOOL SetEnvironmentVariable(LPCTSTR lpszName, LPCTSTR lpszValue);
```

This function sets the variable identified by the *lpszName* parameter to the value identified by the *lpszValue* parameter. If a variable with the specified name already exists, *SetEnvironmentVariable* modifies the value. If the specified variable doesn't exist, the variable is added and, if *lpszValue* is NULL, the variable is deleted from the environment block.

You should always use these functions for manipulating your process's environment block. As I said at the beginning of this section, the strings in an environment block must be sorted alphabetically by variable name. When these strings are alphabetized, *GetEnvironment-Variable* can locate them faster and the *SetEnvironmentVariable* function is smart enough to keep the environment variables in sorted order.

A Process's Error Mode

Associated with each process is a set of flags that tells the system how the process should respond to serious errors. Serious errors include disk media failures, unhandled exceptions, file-find failures, and data misalignment. A process can tell the system how to handle each of these errors by calling the *SetErrorMode* function:

```
UINT SetErrorMode(UINT fuErrorMode);
```

The *fuErrorMode* parameter is a combination of any of the flags in the following table bitwise ORed together:

Flag	Description
SEM_FAILCRITICALERRORS	The system does not display the critical-error-handler message box and returns the error to the calling process.
SEM_NOGPFAULTERRORBOX	The system does not display the general-protection-fault message box. This flag should be set only by debugging applications that handle general protection (GP) faults themselves with an exception handler.
SEM_NOOPENFILEERRORBOX	The system does not display a message box when it fails to find a file.
SEM_NOALIGNMENTFAULTEXCEPT	The system automatically fixes memory alignment faults and makes them invisible to the application. This flag has no effect on *x*86 or Alpha processors.

By default, a child process inherits the error mode flags of its parent. In other words, if a process currently has the SEM_NOGPFAULT-ERRORBOX flag turned on and then spawns a child process, the child process will also have this flag turned on. However, the child process is not notified of this and might not have been written to handle GP fault errors itself. If a GP fault does occur in one of the child's threads, the child application might terminate without notifying the user. A parent process can prevent a child process from inheriting the parent's error mode by specifying the CREATE_DEFAULT_ERROR_MODE flag when calling *CreateProcess*. (*CreateProcess* is discussed later in this chapter.)

A Process's Current Drive and Directory

The current directory of the current drive is where the various Win32 functions look for files and directories when full pathnames are not supplied. For example, if a thread in a process calls *CreateFile* to open a file (without specifying a full pathname), the system will look for the file in the current drive and directory.

The system keeps track of a process's current drive and directory internally. Because this information is maintained on a per-process basis, a thread in the process that changes the current drive or directory changes this information for all the threads in the process.

A thread can obtain and set its process's current drive and directory by calling the following two functions:

```
DWORD GetCurrentDirectory(DWORD cchCurDir, LPTSTR lpszCurDir);
BOOL SetCurrentDirectory(LPCTSTR lpszCurDir);
```

These functions are covered in more detail in Chapter 14.

A Process's Current Directories

The system keeps track of the process's current drive and directory, but it does *not* keep track of the current directory for each and every drive. However, there is some operating system support for handling current directories for multiple drives. This support is offered by using the process's environment strings. For example, a process can have two environment variables, as shown here:

```
=C:=C:\Utility\Bin
=D:=D:\Program Files
```

These variables indicate that the process's current directory for drive C is \Utility\Bin and that its current directory for drive D is \Program Files.

If you call a Win32 function, passing a drive-qualified name indicating a drive that is not the current drive, the system looks in the process's environment block for the variable associated with the specified drive letter. If the variable for the drive exists, the system uses the variable's value as the current directory. If the variable does not exist, the system assumes that the current directory for the specified drive is its root directory.

For example, if your process's current directory is C:\Utility\ Bin, and you call *CreateFile* to open D:ReadMe.Txt, the system looks up the environment variable =D:. Because the =D: variable exists, the system attempts to open the ReadMe.Txt file from the D:\Program Files directory. If the =D: variable did not exist, the system would attempt to open the ReadMe.Txt file from the root directory of drive D. The Win32 file functions never add or change a drive-letter environment variable— they only read the variables.

Important

You can use the C run-time function *_chdir* instead of the Win32 *SetCurrentDirectory* function to change the current directory. The *_chdir* function calls *SetCurrentDirectory* internally, but *_chdir* also adds or modifies the environment variables so that the current directory of different drives is preserved.

If a parent process creates an environment block that it wants to pass to a child process, the child's environment block will *not* automatically inherit the parent process's current directories. Instead, the child process's current directories will default to the root directory of every drive. If you want the child process to inherit the parent's current directories, the parent process must create these drive-letter environment variables and add them to the environment block before spawning the child process. The parent process can obtain its current directories by calling *GetFullPathName*:

```
DWORD GetFullPathName(LPCTSTR lpszFile, DWORD cchPath,
    LPTSTR lpszPath, LPTSTR *ppszFilePart);
```

For example, to get the current directory for drive C, you would call *GetFullPathName* as follows:

```
TCHAR szCurDir[MAX_PATH];
DWORD GetFullPathName(__TEXT("C:"), MAX_PATH, szCurDir, NULL);
```

Keep in mind that a process's environment variables must always be kept in alphabetical order. Because of this necessity, the drive letter environment variables will usually need to be placed at the beginning of the environment block.

The System Version

Frequently, an application needs to determine which version of Windows the user is running the application on. For example, an application might take advantage of security features by calling the Win32 security functions. However, these functions are fully implemented only on Windows NT.

For as long as I can remember, the Windows API has had a *GetVersion* function:

```
DWORD GetVersion(VOID);
```

This simple function has quite a history behind it. It was first designed for 16-bit Windows. The idea was a simple one: return the MS-DOS version number in the high-word and return the Windows version number in the low-word. For each word, the high-byte would represent the major version number and the low-byte would represent the minor version number.

Unfortunately, the programmer who wrote this code made a small mistake, coding the function so that the Windows version numbers were reversed—the major version number was in the low-byte and the minor number was in the high-byte. Since many programmers had already started using this function, Microsoft was forced to leave the function as is and change the documentation to reflect the mistake.

Because of all the confusion surrounding *GetVersion*, Microsoft added a new function to the Win32 API, *GetVersionEx*:

```
BOOL GetVersionEx(LPOSVERSIONINFO lpVersionInformation);
```

This function requires you to allocate an OSVERSIONINFO structure in your application and pass the structure's address to *GetVersionEx*. The OSVERSIONINFO structure is shown here:

```
typedef struct {
    DWORD dwOSVersionInfoSize;
    DWORD dwMajorVersion;
    DWORD dwMinorVersion;
    DWORD dwBuildNumber;
    DWORD dwPlatformId;
    TCHAR szCSDVersion[128];
} OSVERSIONINFO, *LPOSVERSIONINFO;
```

Notice that the structure has different members for each individual component of the system's version number. This was done purposely so programmers would not have to bother with extracting low-words, high-words, low-bytes, and high-bytes; it should make things much easier for applications to compare their expected version number with the host system's version number. The following table describes the OSVERSION-INFO structure's members.

Member	Description
dwOSVersionInfoSize	Must be set to *sizeof(OSVERSIONINFO)* prior to calling the *GetVersionEx* function.
dwMajorVersion	Major version number of the host system.
dwMinorVersion	Minor version number of the host system.
dwBuildNumber	Build number of the current system.
dwPlatformId	Identifies the platform supported by the current system. This can be VER_PLATFORM_WIN32s (Win32s), VER_PLATFORM_WIN32_WINDOWS (Windows 95), VER_PLATFORM_WIN32_NT (Windows NT), or VER_PLATFORM_WIN32_HH[3] (Windows CE).
szCSDVersion	This field contains additional text that provides further information about the installed operating system.

The *CreateProcess* Function

A process is created when your application calls the *CreateProcess* function:

```
BOOL CreateProcess(
    LPCTSTR lpszApplicationName,
    LPCTSTR lpszCommandLine,
    LPSECURITY_ATTRIBUTES lpsaProcess,
    LPSECURITY_ATTRIBUTES lpsaThread,
    BOOL fInheritHandles,
    DWORD fdwCreate,
    LPVOID lpvEnvironment,
    LPTSTR lpszCurDir,
    LPSTARTUPINFO lpsiStartInfo,
    LPPROCESS_INFORMATION lppiProcInfo);
```

---

3. The "HH" stands for handheld.

When a thread in your application calls *CreateProcess*, the system creates a process kernel object with an initial usage count of 1. This process kernel object is not the process itself but rather a small data structure that the operating system uses to manage the process—think of the process kernel object as a small data structure that consists of statistical information about the process. The system then creates a virtual 4-GB address space for the new process and loads the code and data for the executable file and any required DLLs into the process's 4-GB address space.

The system then creates a thread kernel object (with a usage count of 1) for the new process's primary thread. Like the process kernel object, the thread kernel object is a small data structure that the operating system uses to manage the thread. This primary thread will begin by executing the C run-time startup code, which will eventually call your *WinMain* function (or *main* function if your application is CUI-based). If the system successfully creates the new process and primary thread, *CreateProcess* returns TRUE.

OK, that's the broad overview. The following sections dissect each of *CreateProcess*'s parameters.

If you are familiar with the two 16-bit Windows functions for creating a process, *WinExec* and *LoadModule,* you can see by comparing the number of parameters for these two functions with the new *CreateProcess* function that *CreateProcess* offers much more control over process creation. Both the *WinExec* and *LoadModule* functions are implemented internally as calls to the *CreateProcess* function. And because these functions are supplied only for backward compatibility with 16-bit Windows, no Unicode versions of these functions exist—you can call these functions only by passing ANSI strings.

lpszApplicationName and *lpszCommandLine*

The *lpszApplicationName* and *lpszCommandLine* parameters specify both the name of the executable file the new process will use and the command-line string that will be passed to the new process. Let's talk about the *lpszCommandLine* parameter first.

The *lpszCommandLine* parameter allows you to specify a complete command line that *CreateProcess* uses to create the new process. When

CreateProcess parses the *lpszCommandLine* string, it examines the first token in the string and assumes that this token is the name of the executable file you want to run. If the executable file's name does not have an
extension, an EXE extension is assumed. *CreateProcess* will also search for
the executable in the following order:

1. The directory containing the EXE file of the calling process

2. The current directory of the calling process

3. The Windows system directory

4. The Windows directory

5. The directories listed in the PATH environment variable

Of course, if the filename includes a full path, the system looks for
the executable using the full path and does not search the directories.
If the system finds the executable file, it creates a new process and maps
the executable's code and data into the new process's address space. The
system then calls the C run-time startup routine. As noted earlier in this
chapter, the C run-time startup routine examines the process's command line and passes the address to the first argument after the executable file's name as *WinMain*'s *lpszCmdLine* parameter.

What I have just described is what happens as long as the
lpszApplicationName parameter is NULL (which should be the case 99%
of the time). Instead of passing NULL, you can pass the address to a
string containing the name of the executable file you want to run in the
lpszApplicationName parameter. Note that you must specify the file's extension; the system will not automatically assume that the filename ends
with an EXE extension. *CreateProcess* assumes the file is in the current directory unless a path is specified preceding the filename. If the file can't
be found in the current directory, *CreateProcess* doesn't look for the file
in any other directory—*CreateProcess* simply fails.

Even if you specify a filename in the *lpszApplicationName* parameter,
however, *CreateProcess* passes the contents of the *lpszCommandLine* parameter to the new process as its command line. For example, say that you
call *CreateProcess* like this:

```
CreateProcess("C:\\WINNT\\SYSTEM32\\NOTEPAD.EXE",
    "WORDPAD README.TXT",…);
```

The system invokes the Notepad application; but Notepad's command
line is "WORDPAD README.TXT". This quirk is certainly a little

strange, but that's how *CreateProcess* works. This capability provided by the *lpszApplicationName* parameter was really added to *CreateProcess* to support Windows NT's POSIX subsystem.

lpsaProcess, *lpsaThread*, and *fInheritHandles*

To create a new process, the system must create a process kernel object and a thread kernel object (for the process's primary thread). Because these are kernel objects, the parent process gets the opportunity to associate security attributes with these two objects. The *lpsaProcess* and *lpsaThread* parameters allow you to specify the desired security for the process object and the thread object, respectively. You can pass NULL for these parameters, in which case the system gives these objects default security descriptors. Or you can allocate and initialize two SECURITY-_ATTRIBUTES structures to create and assign your own security privileges to the process and thread objects.

Another reason to use SECURITY_ATTRIBUTES structures for the *lpsaProcess* and *lpsaThread* parameters is if you want either of these two object handles to be inheritable by any child processes spawned in the future by this parent process. (The theory behind kernel object handle inheritance is discussed in Chapter 2.)

Figure 3-3 is a short program that demonstrates kernel object handle inheritance in actual practice. Let's say that Process A creates Process B by calling *CreateProcess* and passing the address of a SECURITY-_ATTRIBUTES structure for the *lpsaProcess* parameter in which the *bInheritHandle* member is set to TRUE. In this same call, the *lpsaThread* parameter points to another SECURITY_ATTRIBUTES structure in which its *bInheritHandle* member is set to FALSE.

When the system creates Process B, it allocates both a process kernel object and a thread kernel object and returns handles back to Process A in the structure pointed to by the *lppiProcInfo* parameter (discussed shortly). Process A can now manipulate the newly created process object and thread object by using these handles.

Now let's say that Process A is going to call *CreateProcess* a second time to create Process C. Process A can decide whether to grant Process C the ability to manipulate some of the kernel objects that Process A has access to. The *fInheritHandles* parameter is used for this purpose. If *fInheritHandles* is set to TRUE, the system causes Process C to inherit any inheritable handles in Process A. In this case, the handle to Process B's process object is inheritable. The handle to Process B's primary thread object is not inherited no matter what the value of the *fInheritHandles* parameter to *CreateProcess* is. Also, if Process A calls *CreateProcess*, passing FALSE for the *fInheritHandles* parameter, Process C will not inherit any of the handles currently being used by Process A.

INHERIT.C

```
/**************************************************************
Module name: Inherit.C
Notices: Copyright (c) 1995-1997 Jeffrey Richter
**************************************************************/


#include <windows.h>


int WINAPI WinMain (HINSTANCE hinstExe, HINSTANCE hinstPrev,
    LPSTR lpszCmdLine, int nCmdShow) {

    STARTUPINFO si;
    SECURITY_ATTRIBUTES saProcess, saThread;
    PROCESS_INFORMATION piProcessB, piProcessC;

    // Prepare a STARTUPINFO structure for spawning processes.
    ZeroMemory(&si, sizeof(si));
    si.cb = sizeof(si);

    // Prepare to spawn Process B from Process A.
    // The handle identifying the new process
    // object should be inheritable.
    saProcess.nLength = sizeof(saProcess);
    saProcess.lpSecurityDescriptor = NULL;
    saProcess.bInheritHandle = TRUE;

    // The handle identifying the new thread
    // object should NOT be inheritable.
    saThread.nLength = sizeof(saThread);
    saThread.lpSecurityDescriptor = NULL;
    saThread.bInheritHandle = FALSE;

    // Spawn Process B
    CreateProcess(NULL, "ProcessB", &saProcess, &saThread,
        FALSE, 0, NULL, NULL, &si, &piProcessB);
```

Figure 3-3. *(continued)*
An example of kernel object handle inheritance.

55

Figure 3-3. *(continued)*

```
// The pi structure contains two handles
// relative to Process A:
// hProcess, which identifies Process B's process
// object and is inheritable; and hThread, which identifies
// Process B's primary thread object and is NOT inheritable.

// Prepare to spawn Process C from Process A.
// Since NULL is passed for the lpsaProcess and lpsaThread
// parameters, the handles to Process C's process and
// primary thread objects default to "noninheritable."

// If Process A were to spawn another process, this new
// process would NOT inherit handles to Process C's process
// and thread objects.

// Because TRUE is passed for the fInheritHandles parameter,
// Process C will inherit the handle that identifies Process
// B's process object but will not inherit a handle to
// Process B's primary thread object.
CreateProcess(NULL, "ProcessC", NULL, NULL,
    TRUE, 0, NULL, NULL, &si, &piProcessC);

return(0);
}
```

fdwCreate

The *fdwCreate* parameter identifies flags that affect how the new process is created. Multiple flags can be specified when combined with the Boolean OR operator.

The DEBUG_PROCESS flag tells the system that the parent process wants to debug the child process and any processes spawned by the child process in the future. This flag instructs the system to notify the parent process (now the debugger) when certain events occur in any of the child processes (debuggees).

The DEBUG_ONLY_THIS_PROCESS flag is similar to the DEBUG-_PROCESS flag except that the debugger is notified of special events occurring only in the immediate child process. If the child process spawns any additional processes, the debugger is not notified of events in these additional processes.

The CREATE_SUSPENDED flag causes the new process to be created, but its primary thread is suspended. A debugger provides a good example for using this flag. When a debugger is told to load a debuggee, it must have the system initialize the process and primary thread; but the debugger does not want to allow the primary thread to begin execution yet. Using this flag, the user debugging the application can set various breakpoints throughout the program in case there are special events that need trapping. Once all the breakpoints have been set, the user can tell the debugger that the primary thread can begin execution.

The DETACHED_PROCESS flag blocks a CUI-based process's access to its parent's console window and tells the system to send its output to a new console window. If a CUI-based process is created by another CUI-based process, the new process will, by default, use the parent's console window. (When you run the C compiler from the command shell, a new console window isn't created; the output is simply appended to the bottom of the existing console window.) By specifying this flag, the new process will send its output to a new console window.

The CREATE_NEW_CONSOLE flag tells the system to create a new console window for the new process. It is an error to specify both the CREATE_NEW_CONSOLE and DETACHED_PROCESS flags.

The CREATE_NO_WINDOW flag tells the system not to create any console window for the application. This flag allows you to execute a console application without any user interface.

The CREATE_NEW_PROCESS_GROUP flag is used to modify the list of processes that get notified when the user presses the Ctrl+C or Ctrl+Break keys. If you have several CUI-based processes running when the user presses one of these key combinations, the system notifies all the processes in a process group that the user wants to break out of the current operation. By specifying this flag when creating a new CUI-based process, you are creating a new process group. If the user presses Ctrl+C or Ctrl+Break while a process in this new process group is active, the system notifies only processes in this group of the user's request.

The CREATE_DEFAULT_ERROR_MODE flag tells the system that the new process is not to inherit the error mode used by the parent process. (See the *SetErrorMode* function discussed earlier in this chapter.)

The CREATE_SEPARATE_WOW_VDM flag is useful only when you are invoking a 16-bit Windows application on Windows NT. If the flag is specified, the system will create a separate Virtual DOS Machine (VDM) and run the 16-bit Windows application in this VDM. By default, all 16-bit Windows applications execute in a single, shared VDM. The advantage of running an application in a separate VDM is that if the application crashes it kills only the single VDM; any other programs running in distinct VDMs continue to function normally. Also, 16-bit Windows applications that are run in separate VDMs have separate input queues. That means that if one application hangs momentarily, applications in separate VDMs continue to receive input. The disadvantage of running multiple VDMs is that each VDM consumes a significant amount of physical storage. Windows 95 runs all 16-bit Windows applications in a single virtual machine—there is no way to override this.

The CREATE_SHARED_WOW_VDM flag is useful only when invoking a 16-bit Windows application on Windows NT. By default, each 16-bit Windows application runs in a single VDM unless the CREATE-_SEPARATE_WOW_VDM flag is specified. However, this default behavior can be overridden if the DefaultSeparateVDM value in the registry under HKEY_LOCAL_MACHINE\System\CurrentControlSet\Control\WOW is "yes". If this value is "yes", the CREATE_SHARED_WOW_VDM flag overrides this value and runs the 16-bit Windows application in the system's shared VDM. Note that you must reboot after changing this registry setting.

The CREATE_UNICODE_ENVIRONMENT flag tells the system that the child process's environment block should contain Unicode characters. By default, a process's environment block contains ANSI strings.

You can also specify a priority class when you're creating a new process. However, you don't have to specify a priority class, and for most applications it is recommended that you don't; the system will assign a default priority class to the new process. The following table shows the possible priority classes.

Priority Class	Flag Identifier
Idle	IDLE_PRIORITY_CLASS
Normal	NORMAL_PRIORITY_CLASS
High	HIGH_PRIORITY_CLASS
Realtime	REALTIME_PRIORITY_CLASS

These priority classes affect how the threads contained within the process are scheduled with respect to other processes' threads. See the section "How the System Schedules Threads" in Chapter 4 for more information.

lpvEnvironment

The *lpvEnvironment* parameter points to a block of memory that contains environment strings that the new process will use. Most of the time NULL is passed for this parameter, causing the child process to inherit the set of environment strings that its parent is using. Or you can use the *GetEnvironmentStrings* function:

```
LPVOID GetEnvironmentStrings(VOID);
```

This function gets the address of the environment string data block that the calling process is using. You can use the address returned by this function as the *lpvEnvironment* parameter of *CreateProcess*. This is exactly what *CreateProcess* does if you pass NULL for the *lpvEnvironment* parameter.

lpszCurDir

The *lpszCurDir* parameter allows the parent process to set the child process's current drive and directory. If this parameter is NULL, the new process's working directory will be the same as that of the application spawning the new process. If this parameter is not NULL, *lpszCurDir* must point to a zero-terminated string containing the desired working drive and directory. Notice that you must specify a drive letter in the path.

lpsiStartInfo

The *lpsiStartInfo* parameter points to a STARTUPINFO structure:

```
typedef struct _STARTUPINFO {
    DWORD   cb;
    LPSTR   lpReserved;
    LPSTR   lpDesktop;
    LPSTR   lpTitle;
    DWORD   dwX;
    DWORD   dwY;
    DWORD   dwXSize;
    DWORD   dwYSize;
    DWORD   dwXCountChars;
    DWORD   dwYCountChars;
    DWORD   dwFillAttribute;
    DWORD   dwFlags;
    WORD    wShowWindow;
    WORD    cbReserved2;
    LPBYTE  lpReserved2;
    HANDLE  hStdInput;
    HANDLE  hStdOutput;
    HANDLE  hStdError;
} STARTUPINFO, *LPSTARTUPINFO;
```

Win32 uses the members of this structure when it creates the new process. Most applications will want the spawned application simply to use default values. At a minimum, you should initialize all the members in this structure to zero and then set the *cb* member to the size of the structure:

```
STARTUPINFO si;
ZeroMemory(&si, sizeof(si));
si.cb = sizeof(si);
CreateProcess(…, &si, …);
```

Failing to zero the contents of the structure before calling *CreateProcess* is one of the most common mistakes I see developers make. Now if you want to initialize some of the members of the structure, just do so before the call to *CreateProcess*.

We'll discuss each member in turn. Some members are meaningful only if the child application creates an overlapped window, whereas others are meaningful only if the child performs CUI-based input and output. Figure 3-4 indicates the usefulness of each member.

Member	Window, Console, or Both	Purpose
cb	Both	Contains the number of bytes in the STARTUPINFO structure. Acts as a version control in case Microsoft expands this structure in a future version of Win32. Your application must initialize *cb* to *sizeof(STARTUPINFO)*.
lpReserved	Both	Reserved. Must be initialized to NULL.
lpDesktop	Both	Identifies the name of the desktop in which to start the application. If the desktop exists, the new process is associated with the specified desktop. If the desktop does not exist, a desktop with default attributes will be created with the specified name for the new process. If *lpDesktop* is NULL (which is most common), the process is associated with the current desktop.

Figure 3-4. *(continued)*

The members of the STARTUPINFO structure.

Figure 3-4. *continued*

Member	Window, Console, or Both	Purpose
lpTitle	Console	Specifies the window title for a console window. If *lpTitle* is NULL, the name of the executable file is used as the window title.
dwX *dwY*	Both	Specify the *x*- and *y*-coordinates (in pixels) of the location where the application's window should be placed on the screen. These coordinates are used only if the child process creates its first overlapped window with CW_USEDEFAULT as the *x* parameter of *CreateWindow*. For applications that create console windows, these members indicate the upper left corner of the console window.
dwXSize *dwYSize*	Both	Specify the width and height (in pixels) of an application's window. These values are used only if the child process creates its first overlapped window with CW_USEDEFAULT as the *nWidth* parameter of *CreateWindow*. For applications that create console windows, these members indicate the width and height of the console window.
dwXCountChars *dwYCountChars*	Console	Specify the width and height (in characters) of a child's console windows.
dwFillAttribute	Console	Specifies the text and background colors used by a child's console window.
dwFlags	Both	See below and the table on page 62.
wShowWindow	Window	Specifies how the child's first overlapped window should appear if the application's first call to *ShowWindow* passes SW_SHOW-DEFAULT as the *nCmdShow* parameter. This member can be any of the SW_* identifiers normally used with the *ShowWindow* function.
cbReserved2	Both	Reserved. Must be initialized to 0.
lpReserved2	Both	Reserved. Must be initialized to NULL.

(continued)

Figure 3-4. *continued*

Member	Window, Console, or Both	Purpose
hStdInput *hStdOutput* *hStdError*	Console	Specify handles to buffers for console input and output. By default, the *hStdInput* identifies a keyboard buffer, whereas *hStdOutput* and *hStdError* identify a console window's buffer.

Now, as promised, I'll discuss the *dwFlags* member. This member contains a set of flags that modify how the child process is to be created. Most of the flags simply tell *CreateProcess* whether other members of the STARTUPINFO structure contain useful information, or whether some of the members should be ignored. The following table shows the list of possible flags and their meanings.

Flag	Meaning
STARTF_USESIZE	Use the *dwXSize* and *dwYSize* members.
STARTF_USESHOWWINDOW	Use the *wShowWindow* member.
STARTF_USEPOSITION	Use the *dwX* and *dwY* members.
STARTF_USECOUNTCHARS	Use the *dwXCountChars* and *dwYCountChars* members.
STARTF_USEFILLATTRIBUTE	Use the *dwFillAttribute* member.
STARTF_USESTDHANDLES	Use the *hStdInput*, *hStdOutput*, and *hStdError* members.

Two additional flags, STARTF_FORCEONFEEDBACK and STARTF_FORCEOFFFEEDBACK, give you control over the mouse cursor when invoking a new process. Because Windows 95 and Windows NT support true preemptive multitasking, it is possible to invoke an application and, while the process is initializing, use another program. To give visual feedback to the user, *CreateProcess* temporarily changes the system's mouse cursor to a new cursor called a start glass:

This cursor indicates that you can wait for something to happen or you can continue to use the system. In the very early beta releases of Windows NT, this cursor didn't exist—*CreateProcess* did not change the appearance of the cursor at all. This was confusing; often, when I ran a program from the Program Manager, the program's windows would not appear immediately and the cursor would still appear as the normal arrow. So I would click on the program icon again in the Program Manager, which I thought wasn't acknowledging my request. Soon the program I wanted would pop up on the screen, followed by another, and another, and another. Now I had to close all the additional instances of the program. It is amazing how big a difference changing the cursor can make. The problem was compounded, of course, because 16-bit Windows does change the cursor to an hourglass when an application is being initialized. Because I was expecting this, I thought that Windows NT wasn't working properly. Old habits are hard to break.

The *CreateProcess* function gives you more control over the cursor when invoking another process. When you specify the STARTF_FORCE-OFFFEEDBACK flag, *CreateProcess* does not change the cursor into the start glass, leaving it as the normal arrow.

Specifying STARTF_FORCEONFEEDBACK causes *CreateProcess* to monitor the new process's initialization and to alter the cursor based on the result. When *CreateProcess* is called with this flag, the cursor changes into the start glass. If, after 2 seconds, the new process does not make a GUI call, *CreateProcess* resets the cursor to an arrow.

If the process does make a GUI call within 2 seconds, *CreateProcess* waits for the application to show a window. This must occur within 5 seconds after the process makes the GUI call. If a window is not displayed, *CreateProcess* resets the cursor. If a window is displayed, *CreateProcess* keeps the start glass cursor on for another 5 seconds. If at any time the application calls the *GetMessage* function, indicating that it is finished initializing, *CreateProcess* immediately resets the cursor and stops monitoring the new process.

The final flag to discuss is STARTF_SCREENSAVER. This flag tells the system that the application is a screen-saver application, which causes the system to initialize the application in a very special way. When the process begins executing, the system allows the process to initialize at the foreground priority of the class that was specified in the call to *CreateProcess*. As soon as the process makes a call to either *GetMessage* or *PeekMessage*, the system automatically changes the process's priority to the idle priority class.

If the screen-saver application is active and the user presses a key or moves the mouse, the system automatically boosts the priority class of the screen-saver application back to the foreground priority of the class flag passed to *CreateProcess.*

To start a screen-saver application, you should call *CreateProcess* using the NORMAL_PRIORITY_CLASS flag. Doing so has the following two effects:

1. The system allows the screen-saver application to initialize before making it run idle. If the screen-saver application ran 100 percent of its time at idle priority, normal and realtime processes would preempt it, and the screen-saver application would never get a chance to initialize.

2. The system allows the screen-saver application to terminate. Usually a screen saver terminates because the user starts using an application. This application is probably running at normal priority, which would cause the threads in the screen-saver application to be preempted again, and the screen saver would never be able to terminate.

Before leaving this section, I'd like to say a word about START-UPINFO's *wShowWindow* member. You initialize this member to the value that is passed to *WinMain*'s last parameter, *nCmdShow*. This value indicates how you would like the main window of your application shown. The value is one of the identifiers that can be passed to the *ShowWindow* function. Usually, *nCmdShow*'s value is either SW_SHOWNORMAL or SW_SHOWMINNOACTIVE. However, the value can sometimes be SW-_SHOWDEFAULT.

When you invoke an application from the Explorer by double-clicking, the application's *WinMain* function is called with SW_SHOW-NORMAL passed as the *nCmdShow* parameter. If you hold down the Shift key while double-clicking, your application is invoked passing SW_SHOW-MINNOACTIVE as the *nCmdShow* parameter. In this way, the user can easily start an application with its main window showing in either the normal state or the minimized state.

Finally, an application can call

```
VOID GetStartupInfo (LPSTARTUPINFO lpStartupInfo);
```

in order to obtain a copy of the STARTUPINFO structure that was initialized by the parent process. The child process can examine this structure and alter its behavior based on the values of the structure's members.

Although the Win32 documentation does not explicitly say so, you should initialilze the *cb* member of the structure before calling *GetStartupInfo* as follows:

```
STARTUPINFO si;
si.cb = sizeof(si);
GetStartupInfo(&si);
    .
    .
    .
```

lppiProcInfo

The *lppiProcInfo* parameter points to a PROCESS_INFORMATION structure that you must allocate; *CreateProcess* will initialize the members of this structure before it returns. The structure appears as follows:

```
typedef struct _PROCESS_INFORMATION {
    HANDLE hProcess;
    HANDLE hThread;
    DWORD  dwProcessId;
    DWORD  dwThreadId;
} PROCESS_INFORMATION;
```

As already mentioned, creating a new process causes the system to create a process kernel object and a thread kernel object. At creation time, the system gives each object an initial usage count of 1. Then, just before *CreateProcess* returns, the function opens the process object and the thread object and places the process-relative handles for each in the *hProcess* and *hThread* members of the PROCESS_INFORMATION structure. When *CreateProcess* internally opens these objects, the usage count for each increments to 2.

This means that before the system can free the process object, the process must terminate (decrementing the usage count to 1) and the parent process must call *CloseHandle* (decrementing the usage count to 0). Similarly, to free the thread object, the thread must terminate and the parent process must close the handle to the thread object. See the "Child Processes" section at the end of this chapter for more information about freeing thread objects.

Important

Don't forget to close these handles. Failure to close handles is one of the most common mistakes developers make and results in a system memory leak until the process that called *CreateProcess* terminates.

When a process is created, the system assigns the process a unique identifier; no other process running in the system will have the same ID number. The same is true for threads. When a thread is created, the thread is also assigned a unique, systemwide ID number. Before *Create-Process* returns, it fills the *dwProcessId* and *dwThreadId* members of the PROCESS_INFORMATION structure with these IDs. The parent process can use these two IDs to communicate with the child process.

It is extremely important to know that the system reuses process and thread IDs. For example, let's say that when a process is created, the system allocates a process object and assigns it the ID value 0x22222222. If a new process object is created, the system doesn't assign the same ID number. However, if the first process object is freed, the system might assign 0x22222222 to the next process object created.

Keep this in mind so that you avoid writing code that references an incorrect process object (or thread). It's easy to acquire a process ID and save the ID; but the next thing you know, the process identified by the ID is freed and a new process is created and given the same ID. When you use the saved process ID, you end up manipulating the new process, not the process you originally acquired the handle to.

You can easily guarantee this doesn't happen by making sure you have an outstanding lock on the process object. In other words, make sure that you have incremented the usage count for the process object. The system will never free the process object while it has a usage count greater than 0. In most situations, you will already have incremented the usage count. For example, the call to *CreateProcess* returns after incrementing the usage count for the process object.

With the usage count incremented, you can use the process ID to your heart's content. When you no longer need the process ID, call *CloseHandle* to decrement the process object's usage count. Simply make sure that you don't use that process ID after you have called *CloseHandle*.

Terminating a Process

A process can be terminated in three ways:

1. One thread in the process calls the *ExitProcess* function. (This is the most common method.)

2. A thread in another process calls the *TerminateProcess* function. (This should be avoided.)

3. All the threads in the process just die on their own. (This rarely happens.)

This section discusses all three methods for terminating a process and describes what actually happens when a process ends.

The *ExitProcess* Function

A process terminates when one of the threads in the process calls *ExitProcess*:

```
VOID ExitProcess(UINT fuExitCode);
```

This function terminates the process and sets the exit code of the process to *fuExitCode. ExitProcess* doesn't return a value because the process has terminated. If you include any code following the call to the *ExitProcess* function, that code will never execute.

This is the most common method for terminating a process because *ExitProcess* is called when *WinMain* returns to the C run-time's startup code. The startup code calls *ExitProcess*, passing it the value returned from *WinMain.* Any other threads running in the process terminate along with the process.

The Win32 documentation states that a process does not terminate until all its threads terminate. As far as the operating system goes, this statement is true. However, the C run-time imposes a different policy on an application: the C run-time's startup code ensures that the process terminates when your application's primary thread returns from *Win-Main* whether or not other threads are running in the process by calling *ExitProcess*. However, if you call *ExitThread* in your *WinMain* function instead of calling *ExitProcess* or simply returning, the primary thread for your application will stop executing, but the process will not terminate if at least one other thread in the process is still running.

The *TerminateProcess* Function

A call to *TerminateProcess* also ends a process:

```
BOOL TerminateProcess(HANDLE hProcess, UINT fuExitCode);
```

This function is different from *ExitProcess* in one major way: any thread can call *TerminateProcess* to terminate another process or its own process. The *hProcess* parameter identifies the handle of the process to be terminated. When the process terminates, its exit code becomes the value you passed as the *fuExitCode* parameter.

Using *TerminateProcess* is discouraged; use it only if you can't force a process to exit by using another method. Normally, when a process ends, the system notifies any DLLs attached to the process that the process is ending. If you call *TerminateProcess*, however, the system doesn't notify any DLLs attached to the process, which can mean that the process won't get the opportunity to close down correctly. For example, a DLL might be written to flush data to a disk file when the process detaches from the DLL. Detachment usually occurs when an application unloads the DLL by calling *FreeLibrary*. Because the DLL isn't notified about the detachment when you use *TerminateProcess*, the DLL can't perform its normal cleanup. The system does notify the DLL when a process ends normally or when *ExitProcess* is called. (See Chapter 12 for more information about DLLs.)

Although it's possible that the DLL won't have a chance to clean up its data, the system guarantees that all allocated memory is freed, all opened files are closed, all kernel objects have their usage counts decremented, and all User or GDI objects are freed regardless of how the process terminates.

All the Threads in the Process Die

If all the threads in a process die (either because they've all called *ExitThread* or because they've been terminated with *TerminateThread*), the operating system assumes that there is no reason to keep the process's address space around. This is a fair assumption to make since there are no more threads executing any code in the address space. When the system detects that no threads are running anymore, the system terminates the process. When this happens, the process's exit code is set to the same exit code as the last thread that died.

What Happens When a Process Terminates

When a process terminates, the following actions are set in motion:

1. Any remaining threads in the process are halted.

2. All the User and GDI objects allocated by the process are freed, and all the kernel objects are closed.

3. The process kernel object status becomes signaled. (See Chapter 10 for more information about signaling.) Other threads in the system can suspend themselves until the process is terminated.

4. The process's exit code changes from STILL_ACTIVE to the code passed to *ExitProcess* or *TerminateProcess.*

5. The process kernel object's usage count is decremented by 1.

When a process terminates, its associated process kernel object isn't freed until all outstanding references to the object are closed. Also, terminating a process does not cause any of its child processes to terminate.

When a process terminates, the code for the process and any resources that the process allocated are removed from memory. However, the private memory that the system allocated for the process kernel object is not freed until the process object's usage count reaches 0. This can happen only if all other processes that have created or opened handles to the now-defunct process notify the system that they no longer need to reference the process. These processes notify the system by calling *CloseHandle.*

After a process is no longer running, the parent process can't do much with the process handle. However, it can call *GetExitCodeProcess* to check whether the process identified by *hProcess* has terminated and, if so, determine its exit code.

```
BOOL GetExitCodeProcess(HANDLE hProcess, LPDWORD lpdwExitCode);
```

The exit code value is returned in the DWORD pointed to by *lpdwExitCode.* If the process hasn't terminated when *GetExitCodeProcess* is called, the function fills the DWORD with the STILL_ACTIVE identifier (defined as 0x103). If the function is successful, TRUE is returned. Using the child process's handle to determine when the child process has terminated is discussed further in Chapter 10.

Child Processes

When you design an application, situations in which you want another block of code to perform work might arise. You assign work like this all the time by calling functions or subroutines. When you call a function, your code cannot continue processing until the function has returned. And in many situations, this single-tasking synchronization is needed.

An alternative way to have another block of code perform work is to create a new thread within your process and have it help with the processing. This allows your code to continue processing while the other thread performs the work you requested. This technique is useful, but it creates synchronization problems when your thread needs to see the results of the new thread.

Another approach is to spawn off a new process—a child process—to help with the work. Let's say that the work you need to do is pretty complex. To process the work, you simply decide to create a new thread within the same process. You write some code, test it, and get some incorrect results. You might have an error in your algorithm, or maybe you dereferenced something incorrectly and accidentally overwrote something important in your address space. One way to protect your address space while having the work processed is to have a new process perform the work. You could then wait for the new process to terminate before continuing on with your own work, or you could continue working while the new process works.

Unfortunately, the new process probably would need to perform operations on data contained in your address space. In this case, it might be a good idea to have the process run in its own address space and simply give it access to the relevant data contained in the parent process's address space, thus protecting all the data not relevant to the job. Win32 gives you several different methods for transferring data between different processes: Dynamic Data Exchange (DDE), OLE, Pipes, MailSlots, and so on. One of the most convenient ways to share the data is to use memory-mapped files. (See Chapter 8 for a detailed discussion of memory-mapped files.)

If you want to create a new process, have it do some work, and wait for the result, you can use code similar to the following:

```
PROCESS_INFORMATION pi;
DWORD dwExitCode;

BOOL fSuccess = CreateProcess(…, &pi);
if (fSuccess) {

    // Close the thread handle as soon as it is no longer needed!
    CloseHandle(pi.hThread);

    WaitForSingleObject(pi.hProcess, INFINITE);
    // The process terminated.
    GetExitCodeProcess(pi.hProcess, &dwExitCode);

    // Close the process handle as soon as it is no longer needed.
    CloseHandle(pi.hProcess);
}
```

In the code fragment above you create the new process and, if successful, call the *WaitForSingleObject* function:

```
DWORD WaitForSingleObject(HANDLE hObject, DWORD dwTimeout);
```

We'll discuss the *WaitForSingleObject* function exhaustively in Chapter 10. For now, all you need to know is that it waits until the object identified by the *hObject* parameter becomes *signaled*. Process objects become signaled when they terminate. So the call to *WaitForSingleObject* suspends the parent's thread until the child process terminates. After *WaitForSingleObject* returns, you can get the exit code of the child process by calling *GetExitCodeProcess*.

The calls to *CloseHandle* in the code fragment above cause the system to decrement the usage count for the thread and process objects to 0, allowing the objects' memory to be freed.

You'll notice that in the code fragment I close the handle to the child process's primary thread kernel object immediately after *CreateProcess* returns. This does *not* cause the child's primary thread to terminate—it simply decrements the usage count of the child's primary thread object. Here's why this practice is a good idea: Suppose that the child process's primary thread spawns off another thread and then the primary thread terminates. At this point, the system can free the child's primary thread object from its memory if the parent process doesn't have an outstanding handle to this thread object. But if the parent process does have a handle to the child's thread object, the system can't free the object until the parent process closes the handle.

Running Detached Child Processes

Most of the time, an application starts another process as a *detached process*. This means that after the process is created and executing, the parent process doesn't need to communicate with the new process or doesn't require the child process to complete its work before the parent process continues. This is how the Explorer works. After the Explorer creates a new process for the user, it doesn't care whether that process continues to live or whether the user terminates it.

To give up all ties to the child process, the Explorer must close its handles to the new process and its primary thread by calling *CloseHandle*. The code sample on the next page shows how to create a new process and how to let it run detached.

```
PROCESS_INFORMATION pi;
BOOL fSuccess = CreateProcess(…, &pi;
if (fSuccess) {
    CloseHandle(pi.hThread);
    CloseHandle(pi.hProcess);
}
```

CHAPTER FOUR

THREADS

In this chapter, I'll discuss the concept of a thread and describe how the system uses threads to execute your application's code. Like processes, threads have properties associated with them, and I'll discuss some of the functions available for querying and changing these properties. I'll also examine the functions that allow you to create or spawn additional threads in the system. And finally, I'll discuss how threads terminate.

When to Create a Thread

A thread describes a path of execution within a process. Every time a process is initialized, the system creates a primary thread. This thread starts at the C run-time's startup code, which in turn calls your *WinMain* function and continues executing until the *WinMain* function returns and the C run-time's startup code calls *ExitProcess*. For many applications, this primary thread is the only thread the application requires. However, processes can create additional threads to help them do their work. The whole idea behind creating additional threads is to utilize as much of the CPU's time as possible.

For example, a spreadsheet program needs to perform recalculations as the user changes data entries in the cells. Because recalculations of a complex spreadsheet might require several seconds to complete, a well-designed application should not recalculate the spreadsheet after each change the user makes. Instead, the spreadsheet's recalculation function should be executed as a separate thread with a lower priority than that of the primary thread. This way, if the user is typing, the primary thread is running, which means that the system won't schedule any time to the recalculation thread. When the user stops typing, the primary thread is suspended, waiting for input, and the recalculation thread is scheduled time. As soon as the user starts typing again, the primary thread, having a higher priority, preempts the recalculation thread. Creating an additional thread makes the program very responsive to the user. It is also fairly easy to implement this type of design.

In a similar example, you can create an additional thread for a repagination function in a word processor that needs to repaginate the document as the user enters text into the document. Microsoft Word for Windows, for example, must simulate multithreaded behavior in 16-bit Windows but could easily spawn a thread dedicated to repaginating the document for the Win32 version. The primary thread would be responsible for processing the user's input, and a background thread would be responsible for locating the page breaks.

It's also useful to create a separate thread to handle any printing tasks in an application. In this way, the user can continue to use the application while it's printing. In addition, when performing a long task, many applications display a dialog box that allows the user to abort the task. For example, when the Explorer copies files, it displays a dialog box that, besides showing the progress of the copy operation, also contains a Cancel button. If you click on the Cancel button while the files are being copied, you abort the operation.

In 16-bit Windows, implementing this type of functionality requires periodic calls to *PeekMessage* inside the File Copy loop. And calls to *PeekMessage* can be made only between file reading and writing. If a large data block is being read, the response to the button click doesn't occur until after the block has been read. If the file is being read from a floppy disk, this can take several seconds. Because the response is so sluggish, I have frequently clicked on the button several times, thinking that the system didn't know I'd canceled the operation.

By putting the File Copy code in a different thread, you don't need to sprinkle calls to the *PeekMessage* function throughout your code—your user interface thread operates independently. This means that a click on the Cancel button results in an immediate response.

You can also use threads for creating applications that simulate real-world events. In Chapter 10, I show a simulation of a supermarket. Because each shopper is represented by his or her own thread, theoretically each shopper is independent of any other shopper and can enter, shop, check out, and exit as he or she sees fit. The simulation can monitor these activities to determine how well the supermarket functions.

Although simulations can be performed, potential problems lurk. First, you would ideally want each shopper thread to be executed by its very own CPU. Because it is not practical to expect a CPU for every shopper thread, the solution is to incur a time overhead when the operating system preempts one thread and schedules another. For example, if your simulation has two threads and your machine has eight CPUs, the system can assign one thread to each CPU. However, if your simulation has 1000 threads, the system will have to assign and reassign the 1000 threads among the eight CPUs over and over again. And some overhead results when the operating system schedules a large number of threads among a few CPUs. If your simulation lasts a long time, this overhead has a relatively small impact on the simulation. However, if the simulation is short, the overhead of the operating system can take a larger percentage of the simulation's total execution time.

Second, the system itself requires threads to run while other processes might be executing. All these processes' threads need to be scheduled for CPU time as well, which almost certainly affects the outcome of the simulation.

And third, the simulation is useful only if you keep track of its progress. For example, the supermarket simulation in Chapter 10 adds entries to a list box as the shoppers progress through the store; adding entries to the list box takes time away from the simulation. The Heisenberg Uncertainty Principle states that a more accurate determination of one quantity results in a less precise measurement of the other.[1] This principle is most definitely true here.

When Not to Create a Thread

The first time many programmers are given access to an environment that supports multiple threads, they're ecstatic. If only they had had threads sooner, their applications would have been so simple to write. And, for some unknown reason, these programmers start dividing an application into individual pieces, each of which can execute as its own thread. This is not the way to go about developing an application.

Threads are incredibly useful and have a place, but when you use threads you can potentially create new problems while trying to solve the old ones. For example, let's say you're developing a word processing application and want to allow the printing function to run as its own thread. This sounds like a good idea because the user can immediately go back and start editing the document while it's printing. But wait—this means that the data in the document might be changed *while* the document is printing. This brings up a whole new type of problem you'll need to address. Maybe it would be best not to have the printing take place in

---

1. Werner Heisenberg actually developed the theory with respect to quantum mechanics, not computer science.

its own thread; but this "solution" seems a bit drastic. How about if you let the user edit another document but lock the printing document so that it can't be modified until the printing has been completed? Or here's a third idea: copy the document to a temporary file, print the contents of the temporary file, and let the user modify the original. When the temporary file containing the document has finished printing, delete the temporary file.

As you can see, threads help solve some problems at the risk of creating new ones. Another common misuse of threads can arise in the development of an application's user interface. In most applications, all the user interface components (windows) should be sharing the same thread. If you're producing a dialog box, for example, it wouldn't make much sense for a list box to be created by one thread and a button to be created by another.

Let's take this a step further and say that you have your own list box control that sorts data every time an element is added or deleted. The sorting operation might take several seconds, so you decide to assign this control to its very own thread. In this way, the user can continue to work with other controls while the list box control's thread continues sorting.

Doing this wouldn't be a very good idea, however. First, every thread that creates a window must also contain a *GetMessage* loop. Second, because the list box thread contains its own *GetMessage* loop, you could open yourself up to some synchronization problems among the threads. You can solve these problems by assigning to the list box control a dedicated thread whose sole purpose is to sort elements in the background.

Now, having said all this, let me take back some of it. In rare situations, assigning individual threads to user interface objects is useful. In the system, each process has its own separate thread controlling its own user interface. For example, the Calculator application has one thread that creates and manipulates all the application's windows, and the Paint application has its own thread that creates and manipulates Paint's own windows. These separate threads were assigned for protection and robustness. If Calculator's thread enters an infinite loop, the resulting problem has no effect on Paint's thread. This behavior is quite different from that we see in 16-bit Windows. In 16-bit Windows, if one application hangs, the entire system hangs. The Win32-based systems allow you to switch away from Calculator (even though it is hung) and start using Paint. See Chapter 11 for more details.

Perhaps the best example of an application that creates windows on multiple threads is the Explorer. If the user is working with one Explorer window, say drive C:\, and the thread for this window enters an infinite loop, the user cannot use this drive C:\ window anymore but can still use other Explorer windows. As you can see, this feature is great because users hate it when the operating system shell stops responding.

Another use for multiple threads in GUI components is in multiple document interface (MDI) applications in which each MDI child window is running on its own thread. If one of the MDI child threads enters an infinite loop or starts a time-consuming procedure, the user can switch to another MDI child window and begin working with it while the other MDI child thread continues to chug along. This can be so useful, in fact, that Win32 offers a special function, shown below, whose result is similar to creating an MDI child window by sending the WM_MDICREATE message to an MDIClient window.

```
HWND CreateMDIWindow(LPTSTR lpszClassName, LPTSTR lpszWindowName,
    DWORD dwStyle, int x, int y, int nWidth, int nHeight,
    HWND hwndParent, HINSTANCE hinst, LONG lParam);
```

The only difference is that the *CreateMDIWindow* function allows the MDI child to be created with its own thread.

The moral of this story is that you should use multiple threads judiciously. Don't use them just because you can. You can still write many useful and powerful applications using nothing more than the primary thread assigned to the process. If after reading all this you're convinced you have a valid need for threads, read on.

Writing Your First Thread Function

All threads begin executing at a function that you must specify. The function must have the following prototype:

```
DWORD WINAPI YourThreadFunc(LPVOID lpvThreadParm);
```

Like *WinMain*, this function is not actually called by the operating system. Instead, the operating system calls an internal function, not part of the C run-time, contained in KERNEL32.DLL. I call this function *StartOfThread*; the actual internal name is not important. Here is what *StartOfThread* looks like:

```
void StartOfThread (LPTHREAD_START_ROUTINE lpStartAddr,
    LPVOID lpvThreadParm) {

    __try {
        DWORD dwThreadExitCode = lpStartAddr(lpvThreadParm);
        ExitThread(dwThreadExitCode);
    }
    __except(UnhandledExceptionFilter(GetExceptionInformation())) {
        ExitProcess(GetExceptionCode());
    }
}
```

77

The *StartOfThread* function sets into motion the following actions:

1. A structured exception handling (SEH) frame is set up around your thread function so that any exceptions raised while your thread executes will get some default handling by the system. See Chapter 16 for more information about structured exception handling.

2. The system calls your thread function, passing it the 32-bit *lpvThreadParm* parameter that you passed to the *CreateThread* function (discussed shortly).

3. When your thread function returns, the *StartOfThread* function calls *ExitThread*, passing it your thread function's return value. The thread kernel object's usage count is decremented, and the thread stops executing.

4. If your thread raises an exception that is not handled, the SEH frame set up by the *StartOfThread* function will handle the exception. Usually, this means that a message box is presented to the user and that when the user dismisses the message box, *StartOfThread* calls *ExitProcess* to terminate the entire process, not just the offending thread.

Although I left it out of the earlier discussion, a process's primary thread actually begins by executing the system's *StartOfThread* function. The *StartOfThread* function then calls the C run-time's startup code, which calls your *WinMain* function. The C run-time's startup code, however, does not ever return back to the *StartOfThread* function because the startup code explicitly calls *ExitProcess*.

The remainder of this section discusses the various attributes that are "bestowed" upon a new thread.

A Thread's Stack

Each thread is allocated its very own stack from the owning process's 4-GB address space. When you use static and global variables, multiple threads can access the variables at the same time, potentially corrupting the variables' contents. However, local and automatic variables are created on the thread's stack and are therefore far less likely to be corrupted by another thread. For this reason, you should always try to use local or automatic variables when writing your functions and avoid the use of static and global variables.

The size of a thread's stack, and how the operating system and compiler manage the stack, are very complex subjects—I postpone discussing these details until Chapter 7.

A Thread's CONTEXT Structure

Each thread has its own set of CPU registers, called the thread's *context*. This CONTEXT structure reflects the state of the thread's CPU registers when the thread was last executing. The CONTEXT structure is the only CPU-specific Win32 data structure. In fact, the Win32 help file doesn't show the contents of this structure. If you want to see the members of this structure, you must look in the WINNT.H file, where you will find this structure defined several times: once for *x*86, once for MIPS, once for Alpha, and once for PowerPC. The compiler selects the appropriate version of this structure depending on the target CPU type for your EXE or DLL.

When a thread is scheduled CPU time, the system initializes the CPU's registers with the thread's context. Of course, one of the CPU registers is an instruction pointer that identifies the address of the next CPU instruction for the thread to execute. The CPU registers also include a stack pointer that identifies the address of the thread's stack.

A Thread's Execution Times

In a multithreaded environment, it becomes much more difficult to time how long it takes your process to perform various tasks. This is because your process might have a thread that is busy recalculating some complex algorithm while threads in other processes are all competing for the same CPU. Since your recalc thread is constantly being preempted, you can't simply write code to time your algorithm as shown here:

```
DWORD dwStartTime = GetTickCount();
// Perform complex algorithm.
DWORD dwElapsedTime = GetTickCount() - dwStartTime;
```

What is needed here is a function that returns the amount of time that the CPU has been assigned to this thread. Fortunately, in Win32 there is a function that returns this information:

```
BOOL GetThreadTimes(HANDLE hThread, LPFILETIME lpCreationTime,
    LPFILETIME lpExitTime, LPFILETIME lpKernelTime,
    LPFILETIME lpUserTime);
```

GetThreadTimes returns four different time values, as shown in the following table:

Time Value	Meaning
Creation time	The time when the thread was created.
Exit time	The time when the thread exited. If the thread is still running, the exit time is undefined.
Kernel time	The amount of time that the thread has spent executing operating system code.
User time	The amount of time that the thread has spent executing application code.

Using this function, you can determine the amount of time necessary to execute a complex algorithm by using code such as this:

```
__int64 FileTimeToQuadWord (PFILETIME pFileTime) {
   __int64 qw;
   qw = pFileTime->dwHighDateTime;
   qw <<= 32;
   qw |= pFileTime->dwLowDateTime;
   return(qw);
}

PFILETIME QuadWordToFileTime (__int64 qw, PFILETIME pFileTime) {
   pFileTime->dwHighDateTime = (DWORD) (qw >> 32);
   pFileTime->dwLowDateTime  = (DWORD) (qw & 0xFFFFFFFF);
   return(pFileTime);
}


void Recalc () {
   FILETIME ftKernelTimeStart, ftKernelTimeEnd;
   FILETIME ftUserTimeStart, ftUserTimeEnd;
   FILETIME ftDummy, ftTotalTimeElapsed;
   __int64 qwKernelTimeElapsed, qwUserTimeElapsed,
     qwTotalTimeElapsed;

   // Get starting times.
   GetThreadTimes(GetCurrentThread(), &ftDummy, &ftDummy,
     &ftKernelTimeStart, &ftUserTimeStart);

   // Perform complex algorithm here.
   :
   :
```

```
// Get ending times.
GetThreadTimes(GetCurrentThread(), &ftDummy, &ftDummy,
    &ftKernelTimeEnd, &ftUserTimeEnd);

// Get the elapsed kernel and user times by converting the start
// and end times from FILETIMEs to quad words, and then subtract
// the start times from the end times.
qwKernelTimeElapsed = FileTimeToQuadWord(&ftKernelTimeEnd) -
    FileTimeToQuadWord(&ftKernelTimeStart);
qwUserTimeElapsed = FileTimeToQuadWord(&ftUserTimeEnd) -
    FileTimeToQuadWord(&ftUserTimeStart);

// Get total time duration by adding the kernel and user times.
qwTotalTimeElapsed = qwKernelTimeElapsed + qwUserTimeElapsed;

// Convert resultant quad word to FILETIME.
QuadWordToFileTime(qwTotalTimeElapsed, &ftTotalTimeElapsed);

// The total elapsed time is in qwTotalElapsedTime and in
// ftTotalTimeElapsed. You can use either form.
    :
    :

}
```

Let me also point out here that there is a function similar to *Get-ThreadTimes* that applies to all of the threads in a process:

```
BOOL GetProcessTimes (HANDLE hProcess, LPFILETIME lpCreationTime,
    LPFILETIME lpExitTime, LPFILETIME lpKernelTime,
    LPFILETIME lpUserTime);
```

GetProcessTimes returns times that apply to all the threads in a specified process. For example, the kernel time returned will be the sum of all the elapsed times that all of the process's threads have spent in kernel code.

Unfortunately, the *GetThreadTimes* and *GetProcessTimes* functions are not functional in Microsoft Windows 95. If you call either of these functions in Windows 95, they return FALSE. A subsequent call to *GetLastError* returns a value of 120 (ERROR_CALL_NOT_IMPLEMENTED), which indicates that these functions are valid only in Microsoft Windows NT.

There is no reliable mechanism for an application to determine how much CPU time a thread or process has used under Windows 95.

The *CreateThread* Function

We've already discussed how a process's primary thread comes into being when *CreateProcess* is called. However, if you want a primary thread to create additional threads, you can have it call *CreateThread*:

```
HANDLE CreateThread(
    LPSECURITY_ATTRIBUTES lpsa,
    DWORD cbStack,
    LPTHREAD_START_ROUTINE lpStartAddr,
    LPVOID lpvThreadParm,
    DWORD fdwCreate,
    LPDWORD lpIDThread);
```

For every call to *CreateThread*, the system must perform the following steps:

1. Allocate a thread kernel object to identify and manage the newly created thread. This object holds much of the system information to manage the thread. A handle to this object is the value returned from the *CreateThread* function.

2. Initialize the thread's exit code (maintained in the thread kernel object) to STILL_ACTIVE and set the thread's suspend count (also maintained in the thread kernel object) to 1.

3. Allocate a CONTEXT structure for the new thread.

4. Prepare the thread's stack by reserving a region of address space, committing 2 pages of physical storage to the region, setting the protection of the committed storage to PAGE_READWRITE, and setting the PAGE_GUARD attribute on the second-to-top page. See Chapter 7 for more information about a thread's stack.

5. The *lpStartAddr* and *lpvThread* values are placed on the top of the stack so that they look like parameters passed to the *StartOfThread* function.

6. Initialize the stack pointer register in the thread's CONTEXT structure to point to the values placed on the stack in step 5; initialize the instruction pointer register to point to the internal *StartOfThread* function.

OK, that's the broad overview. The following sections dissect each of *CreateThread*'s parameters.

lpsa

The *lpsa* parameter is a pointer to a SECURITY_ATTRIBUTES structure. You can also pass NULL if you want the default security attributes for the object. If you want any child processes to be able to inherit a handle to this thread object, you must specify a SECURITY_ATTRIBUTES structure whose *bInheritHandle* member is initialized to TRUE.

cbStack

The *cbStack* parameter specifies how much address space the thread is allowed to use for its own stack. Every thread owns its very own stack. When *CreateProcess* starts an application, it calls *CreateThread* to initialize the process's primary thread. For the *cbStack* parameter, *CreateProcess* uses the value stored inside the executable file. You can control this value using the linker's /STACK switch:

```
/STACK:[reserve] [,commit]
```

The *reserve* argument sets the amount of address space the system should reserve for the thread's stack. The default is 1 MB. The *commit* argument specifies the amount of physical storage that should be initially committed to the stack's reserved region. The default is one page. (See Chapter 7 for a discussion of reserving and committing memory.) As the code in your thread executes, it is quite possible that you'll require more than one page of storage. When your thread overflows its stack, an exception is generated. (See Chapter 16 for detailed information about handling exceptions.) The system catches the exception and commits another page (or whatever you specified for the *commit* argument) to the reserved space, which allows your thread's stacks to grow dynamically as needed.

When calling *CreateThread*, you can pass 0 to the *cbStack* parameter. In this case, *CreateThread* creates a stack for the new thread using the *commit* argument embedded in the EXE file by the linker. The amount of reserved space is always 1 MB. The system sets a limit of 1 MB to stop functions that recurse endlessly.

For example, let's say that you are writing a function that calls itself recursively. This function also has a bug that causes endless recursion. Every time the function calls itself, a new stack frame is created on the stack. If the system didn't set a maximum limit on the stack size, the recursive function would never stop calling itself. All of the process's address space would be allocated, and enormous amounts of physical storage would be committed to the stack. By setting a stack limit, you prevent your application from using up enormous amounts of physical storage, and you'll also know much sooner when a bug exists in your program. The SEHSum sample application in Chapter 16 shows how you can trap and handle stack overflows in your application.

lpStartAddr and lpvThreadParm

The *lpStartAddr* parameter indicates the address of the thread function that you want the new thread to execute. It is perfectly legal and actually quite useful to create multiple threads that all have the same function address as their starting point. For example, you might create an MDI application in which all the child windows behave similarly but each operates on its own thread. The thread function you write must have the same function prototype as this function:

```
DWORD WINAPI ThreadFunc(LPVOID lpvThreadParm) {
   DWORD dwResult = 0;
   :
   :

   return(dwResult);
}
```

The thread function's *lpvThreadParm* parameter is the same as the *lpvThreadParm* parameter that you originally passed to *CreateThread*. *CreateThread* does nothing with this parameter except pass it on to the thread function when the thread starts executing. This parameter provides a way to pass an initialization value to the thread function. This initialization data can be either a 32-bit value or a 32-bit pointer to a data structure that contains additional information.

fdwCreate

The *fdwCreate* parameter specifies additional flags that control the creation of the thread. It can be one of two values. If the value is 0, the thread starts executing immediately. If the value is CREATE_SUSPENDED, the system creates the thread, creates the thread's stack, initializes the CPU register members in the thread's CONTEXT structure, and gets ready to execute the first instruction of the thread function but suspends the thread so that it doesn't start executing.

Immediately before *CreateThread* returns, and while the thread that called it continues to execute, the new thread is also executing—that is, as long as the CREATE_SUSPENDED flag wasn't specified.[2] Because the new thread is running simultaneously, problems can occur. Watch out for code like this:

```
DWORD WINAPI FirstThread(LPVOID lpvThreadParm) {
    int x = 0;
    DWORD dwResult = 0, dwThreadId;
    HANDLE hThread;

    hThread = CreateThread(NULL, 0, SecondThread, (LPVOID) &x,
        0, &dwThreadId);
    CloseHandle(hThread);

    return(dwResult);
}


DWORD WINAPI SecondThread(LPVOID lpvThreadParm) {
    DWORD dwResult = 0;

    // Do some lengthy processing here.
    :
    :
    * ((int *) lpvThreadParm) = 5;
    :
    :
    return(dwResult);
}
```

In the code above, it is very likely that *FirstThread* will finish its work before *SecondThread* assigns 5 to *FirstThread*'s *x*. If this happens, *Second-Thread* won't know that *FirstThread* no longer exists and will attempt to change the contents of what is now an invalid address. This is certain to cause *SecondThread* to raise an access violation because *FirstThread*'s stack is destroyed when *FirstThread* terminates. One way to solve the problem is to declare *x* as a static variable. In this way, the compiler will create a storage area for *x* in the application's data section rather than on the stack.

However, this makes the function nonreentrant. In other words, you couldn't create two threads that execute the same function because the static variable would be shared between the two threads.

---

2. Actually, on a single-CPU machine threads execute one at a time, but it's best to think of them as all executing simultaneously. Also, the new thread's execution is subject to the priority levels of all other threads.

Another way to solve this problem, as well as its more complex variations, is to use synchronization objects, which are discussed in Chapter 10.

lpIDThread

The last parameter of *CreateThread*, *lpIDThread*, must be a valid address of a DWORD in which *CreateThread* will store the ID that the system assigns to the new thread.

Under Windows 95, passing NULL for this parameter causes the function to fail. Under Windows NT prior to version 4, this parameter could not be NULL or the system would attempt to write the thread ID value to address 0x00000000, causing an access violation to occur. Starting with Windows NT 4, Microsoft now allows you to pass NULL if you're not interested in getting the thread's ID.

Important

Of course, this inconsistency between Windows 95 and Windows NT can cause problems for software developers. For example, let's say you develop and test an application on Windows NT 4 that takes advantage of the fact that *CreateThread* will accept NULL for the *lpIDThread* parameter. Now, when you later run your application on Windows 95, your program will fail. You *must* thoroughly test your applications on both Windows 95 and Windows NT, and even in various versions of these systems.

Terminating a Thread

Like a process, a thread can be terminated in three ways:

1. The thread kills itself by calling the *ExitThread* function. (This is the most common method.)

2. A thread in the same or in another process calls the *Terminate-Thread* function. (Avoid this method.)

3. The process containing the thread terminates.

This section discusses all three methods for terminating a thread and describes what happens when a thread ends.

The *ExitThread* Function

A thread terminates when it calls *ExitThread*:

```
VOID ExitThread(UINT fuExitCode);
```

This function terminates the thread and sets the thread's exit code to *fuExitCode*. The *ExitThread* function does not return a value, because the thread has terminated.

This method is the most common because *ExitThread* is called when the thread function returns to the system's internal *StartOfThread* function. The *StartOfThread* function calls *ExitThread*, passing it the value returned from your thread function.

The *TerminateThread* Function

A call to *TerminateThread* also ends a thread:

```
BOOL TerminateThread(HANDLE hThread, DWORD dwExitCode);
```

The function ends the thread identified by the *hThread* parameter and sets its exit code to *dwExitCode*. The *TerminateThread* function exists so that you can terminate a thread when it no longer responds. You should use it only as a last resort.

Important

When a thread dies by calling *ExitThread*, the stack for the thread is destroyed. However, if the thread is terminated by *TerminateThread*, the system does not destroy the stack until the process that owns the thread terminates, because other threads might still be using pointers that reference data contained on the terminated thread's stack. If these other threads attempted to access the stack, an access violation would occur.

When a thread ends, the system notifies any DLLs attached to the process owning the thread that the thread is ending. If you call *TerminateThread*, however, the system doesn't notify any DLLs attached to the process, which can mean that the process won't be closed down correctly. For example, a DLL might be written to flush data to a disk file when the thread detaches from the DLL. Because the DLL isn't notified about the detachment when you use *TerminateThread*, the DLL cannot perform its normal cleanup.

The Process Terminates

The *ExitProcess* and *TerminateProcess* functions discussed in Chapter 3 also terminate threads. The difference is that these functions terminate all the threads contained in the process being terminated.

What Happens When a Thread Terminates

The following actions occur when a thread terminates:

1. All User object handles owned by the thread are freed. In Win32, most objects are owned by the process containing the thread that creates the objects. However, two User objects can be owned by a thread: windows and hooks. When the threads that create these objects die, the system automatically destroys the objects. Other objects are destroyed only when the owning process terminates.

2. The state of the thread kernel object becomes signaled.

3. The thread's exit code changes from STILL_ACTIVE to the code passed to *ExitThread* or *TerminateThread*.

4. If the thread is the last active thread in the process, the process ends.

5. The thread kernel object's usage count is decremented by 1.

When a thread terminates, its associated thread kernel object doesn't automatically become freed until all the outstanding references to the object are closed.

Once a thread is no longer running, there isn't much any other thread in the system can do with the thread's handle. However, these other threads can call *GetExitCodeThread* to check whether the thread identified by *hThread* has terminated and, if it has, determine its exit code.

```
BOOL GetExitCodeThread(HANDLE hThread, LPDWORD lpdwExitCode);
```

The exit code value is returned in the DWORD pointed to by *lpdwExitCode*. If the thread hasn't terminated when *GetExitCodeThread* is called, the function fills the DWORD with the STILL_ACTIVE identifier (defined as 0x103). If the function is successful, TRUE is returned. Using the thread's handle to determine when the thread has terminated is discussed further in Chapter 10.

Gaining a Sense of One's Own Identity

Several Win32 functions require a process handle as a parameter. A thread can get the handle of the process it is running in by calling *GetCurrentProcess*:

```
HANDLE GetCurrentProcess(VOID);
```

This function returns a pseudo-handle to the process; it doesn't create a new handle, and it doesn't increment the process object's usage count. If you call *CloseHandle* and pass this pseudo-handle as the parameter, *CloseHandle* simply ignores the call and does nothing but return.

You can use pseudo-handles in calls to functions that require a process handle. For example, the following line changes the priority class of the calling process to HIGH_PRIORITY_CLASS:

```
SetPriorityClass(GetCurrentProcess(), HIGH_PRIORITY_CLASS);
```

The Win32 API also includes a few functions that require a process ID. A thread can acquire the ID of the process it is running in by calling *GetCurrentProcessId*:

```
DWORD GetCurrentProcessId(VOID);
```

This function returns the unique, systemwide ID that identifies the process.

When you call *CreateThread*, the handle of the newly created thread is returned to the thread making the call, but the new thread does not know what its own handle is. For a thread to acquire a handle to itself, it must call

```
HANDLE GetCurrentThread(VOID);
```

Like *GetCurrentProcess*, *GetCurrentThread* returns a pseudo-handle that is meaningful only when used in the context of the current thread. The thread object's usage count is not incremented, and calls to *CloseHandle* passing the pseudo-handle have no effect.

A thread acquires its ID by calling

```
DWORD GetCurrentThreadId(VOID);
```

Sometimes you might need to acquire a "real" handle to a thread instead of a pseudo-handle. By "real," I mean a handle that unambiguously identifies a unique thread. Examine the code on the next page.

```
DWORD WINAPI ParentThread(LPVOID lpvThreadParm) {
   DWORD IDThread;
   HANDLE hThreadParent = GetCurrentThread();
   CreateThread(NULL, 0, ChildThread, (LPVOID) hThreadParent, 0,
      &IDThread);
   // Function continues...
}

DWORD WINAPI ChildThread(LPVOID lpvThreadParm) {
   HANDLE hThreadParent = (HANDLE) lpvThreadParm;
   SetThreadPriority(hThreadParent, THREAD_PRIORITY_NORMAL);
   // Function continues...
}
```

Can you see the problem with this code fragment? The idea is to have the parent thread pass to the child thread a thread handle that identifies the parent thread. However, the parent thread is passing a pseudo-handle, not a "real" handle. When the child thread begins execution, it passes the pseudo-handle to the *SetThreadPriority* function, which causes the child thread—not the parent thread—to change priority. This happens because a thread pseudo-handle is a handle to the current thread—that is, a handle to whichever thread is making the function call.

To fix this code, we must turn the pseudo-handle into a "real" handle. This transformation can be done by using the *DuplicateHandle* function:

```
BOOL DuplicateHandle(
   HANDLE hSourceProcess,
   HANDLE hSource,
   HANDLE hTargetProcess,
   LPHANDLE lphTarget,
   DWORD fdwAccess,
   BOOL fInherit,
   DWORD fdwOptions);
```

Usually this function is used to create a new process-relative handle from a kernel object handle that is relative to another process (as discussed in Chapter 2). However, we can use the *DuplicateHandle* function in an unusual way to correct the code fragment discussed earlier. The corrected code fragment is as follows:

```
DWORD WINAPI ParentThread(LPVOID lpvThreadParm) {
   DWORD IDThread;
   HANDLE hThreadParent;
```

```
DuplicateHandle(
    GetCurrentProcess(),      // Handle of process that thread
                              // pseudo-handle is relative to
    GetCurrentThread(),       // Parent thread's pseudo-handle
    GetCurrentProcess(),      // Handle of process that the new,
                              // "real," thread handle is
                              // relative to
    &hThreadParent            // Will receive the new,
                              // "real," handle identifying
                              // the parent thread
    0,                        // Ignored because of
                              // DUPLICATE_SAME_ACCESS
    FALSE,                    // New thread handle is not
                              // inheritable
    DUPLICATE_SAME_ACCESS);   // New thread handle has same
                              // access as pseudo-handle

    CreateThread(NULL, 0, ChildThread, (LPVOID) hThreadParent, 0,
        &IDThread);
    // Function continues...
}

DWORD WINAPI ChildThread(LPVOID lpvThreadParm) {
    HANDLE hThreadParent = (HANDLE) lpvThreadParm;
    SetThreadPriority(hThreadParent, THREAD_PRIORITY_NORMAL);
    CloseHandle(hThreadParent);
    // Function continues...
}
```

Now when the parent thread executes, it converts the ambiguous pseudo-handle identifying the parent thread to a new, "real" handle that unambiguously identifies the parent thread, and it passes this "real" handle to *CreateThread*. When the child thread starts executing, its *lpvThreadParm* parameter contains the "real" thread handle. Any calls to functions, passing this handle, will now affect the parent thread, not the child thread.

Because *DuplicateHandle* does increment the usage count of the specified kernel object, it is very important to remember to decrement the object's usage count by passing the target handle to *CloseHandle* when you are finished using the duplicated object handle. This is demonstrated in the code fragment above. Immediately after the call to *SetThreadPriority*, the child thread calls *CloseHandle* to decrement the parent thread object's usage count. In the previous code fragment, I assumed that the child thread would not call any other functions using this handle. If other functions are to be called passing the parent thread's handle, the call to *CloseHandle* should not be made until the handle is no longer required by the child thread.

I should also point out that the *DuplicateHandle* function can be used to convert a pseudo-handle for a process to a "real" process handle as follows:

```
HANDLE hProcess;
DuplicateHandle(
    GetCurrentProcess(),       // Handle of process that the process
                               // pseudo-handle is relative to
    GetCurrentProcess(),       // Process's pseudo-handle
    GetCurrentProcess(),       // Handle of process that the new,
                               // "real" process handle is
                               // relative to
    &hProcess,                 // Will receive the new, "real"
                               // handle identifying the process
    0,                         // Ignored because of
                               // DUPLICATE_SAME_ACCESS
    FALSE,                     // New thread handle is not
                               // inheritable
    DUPLICATE_SAME_ACCESS);    // New process handle has same
                               // access as pseudo-handle
    :
    :
```

How the System Schedules Threads

A preemptive operating system must use some algorithm to determine which threads should be scheduled when and for how long. In this section, we look at the algorithms used by Windows NT and Windows 95.

Important

This section discusses the overall algorithm used by Win32 operating systems to schedule threads. Be aware that Microsoft reserves the right to alter this algorithm in subtle ways. In fact, Microsoft has exercised this right, and the algorithm is slightly different among Windows 95, Windows NT 3.5, and Windows NT 4. Microsoft alters this algorithm when it feels that applications would perform better using the new algorithm. The information presented in this section should be thought of as a rule of thumb, and you must be aware that some things will change as time marches on.

The system schedules all active threads based on their priority levels. Each thread in the system is assigned a priority level. Priority levels range from 0, the lowest, through 31, the highest. Priority level 0 is assigned to a special thread in the system called the *zero page* thread. The zero page thread is responsible for zeroing any free pages in the system when there are no other threads that need to perform work in the system. It is not possible for any other thread to have a priority level of 0.

When the system assigns a CPU to a thread, it treats all threads of the same priority as equal; that is, the system simply assigns the first thread of priority 31 to a CPU, and after that thread's time slice is finished, the system assigns the next priority 31 thread to the CPU. When all the priority 31 threads have had a time slice, the system assigns the first priority 31 thread back to the CPU. Note that if you always have at least one priority 31 thread for each CPU, other threads having priorities less than 31 will never be assigned to a CPU and will therefore never execute. This condition is called *starvation*. Starvation occurs when some threads use so much of the CPU's time that other threads will never execute.

When no priority 31 threads need to run, the system will begin assigning the CPU to priority 30 threads. When no priority 31 and no priority 30 threads need to run, the system assigns the CPU to priority 29 threads, and so on.

At first, you might think that low-priority threads (like the zero page thread) will never get a chance to run in a system designed like this. But as it turns out, threads frequently do not have a reason to run. For example, if your process's primary thread calls *GetMessage* and the system sees that no messages are pending, the system suspends your process's thread, relinquishes the remainder of the thread's time slice, and immediately assigns the CPU to another, waiting, thread.

If no messages show up for *GetMessage* to retrieve, the process's thread stays suspended and the CPU is never assigned to it. However, when a message is placed in the thread's queue, the system knows that the thread should no longer be suspended and will assign the CPU to the thread as long as no higher-priority threads need to execute.

Let me point out another issue here. If a priority 5 thread is running and the system determines that a higher-priority thread is ready to run, the system will immediately suspend the lower-priority thread (even if it's in the middle of its time slice) and assign the CPU to the higher-priority thread, which gets a full time slice. Higher-priority threads always preempt lower-priority threads, regardless of what the lower-priority threads are executing.

How Priority Levels Are Assigned Using the Win32 API

When you create threads, you don't assign them priority levels using numbers. Instead, the system determines the thread's priority level using a two-step process. The first step is to assign a priority class to a process. A process's priority class tells the system the priority required by the process compared to other running processes. The second step is to assign relative priority levels to threads owned by the process. The following sections discuss both steps.

Process Priority Classes

Win32 supports four different priority classes: idle, normal, high, and realtime. You assign a priority class to a process by ORing one of the *CreateProcess* flags listed in the following table with the other *fdwCreate* flags when calling *CreateProcess*. This table shows the priority level associated with each priority class:

Class	*CreateProcess* Flag	Level
Idle	IDLE_PRIORITY_CLASS	4
Normal	NORMAL_PRIORITY_CLASS	8
High	HIGH_PRIORITY_CLASS	13
Realtime	REALTIME_PRIORITY_CLASS	24

This means that any thread created in a process whose priority class is normal has the priority level 8.

I can't stress enough how important it is to select a priority class for your process carefully. When calling *CreateProcess*, most applications should either not specify a priority class or use the NORMAL_PRIOR-ITY_CLASS flag. When you don't specify a priority class, the system assumes normal priority class unless the parent process has an idle priority class. In this case, the child process is also of the idle priority class.

Processes of the normal priority class behave a little differently than do processes using other priority classes. Most applications a user runs are of the normal priority class. When the user is working with a process, that process is said to be the foreground process and all other processes are called background processes.

On Windows NT, when a normal process is brought to the foreground, the system increases the time quantum given to all threads running within the process. For example, let's say that threads are usually given a 15-millisecond time quantum whenever they are scheduled. When the system schedules a thread that is running in a foreground, normal process, however, the system will increase the thread's time quantum by a factor of 3 so that the thread will now receive a time quantum of 45 milliseconds.

On Windows 95, when a normal process is brought to the foreground, the system increases the thread's priority by 1. So, a thread with normal relative thread priority running in a normal priority class process will have a priority level of 9 instead of 8. When the process is moved to the background, the system automatically decrements the thread's priority.

The reason for this change to foreground processes is to make them react faster to the user's input. If the process's threads weren't changed, a normal process printing in the background and a normal process accepting user input in the foreground would be competing equally for the CPU's time. The user, of course, would see that text was not appearing smoothly in the foreground application. But because the system alters the foreground process's threads, the foreground process's threads can process the user's input more responsively.

When running Windows NT, the user can control the system's boosting of normal foreground processes by double-clicking on the System option in the Control Panel and then clicking on the Performance tab. This presents the dialog box on the following page.

(continued)

(continued)

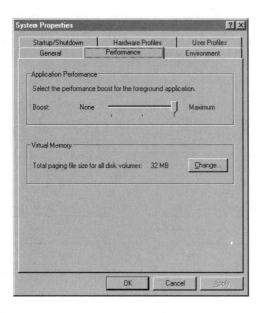

The "Boost" slider indicates how much the foreground thread's time quantum should be boosted. If the slider is at None, the thread's quantum is multiplied by 1; if the slider is at Maximum, the time quantum is multiplied by 3; and if the slider is in the middle, the quantum is multiplied by 2.

The ability to alter the amount of boosting for threads in normal, foreground processes is not offered in Windows 95 because Windows 95 is not designed to be run on a dedicated server machine. Windows NT server machines are frequently installed in a room where no user will operate them directly. When Windows NT machines are set up as dedicated servers, the administrator should select a boost of None so that all threads are scheduled equal time quantums.

Idle priority is perfect for system-monitoring applications. For example, you might write an application that periodically displays the amount of free RAM in the system. Because you would not want this application to interfere with the performance of other applications, you would set this process's priority class to IDLE_PRIORITY_CLASS.

Another good example of an application that can use idle priority is a screen saver. Most of the time a screen saver simply monitors actions from the user. When the user is idle for a specified period of time, the screen saver activates itself. There is no reason to have the screen saver monitoring the user's actions at a very high priority, so the perfect priority for this process is idle.

High priority class should be used only when absolutely necessary. You might not guess this, but the Explorer runs at high priority. Most of the time the Explorer's threads are suspended, waiting to be awakened when the user presses a key or clicks the mouse. While the Explorer's threads are suspended, the system doesn't assign a CPU to its threads, which allows lower-priority threads to execute. However, once the user does press a key, such as Ctrl+Esc, the system wakes up the Explorer's thread. (The Start menu also appears when the user presses Ctrl+Esc.) If any lower-priority threads are executing, the system preempts those threads immediately and allows the Explorer's thread to run. Microsoft designed the Explorer this way because users expect the Shell to be extremely responsive, regardless of what else is going on in the system. In fact, the Explorer's windows can be displayed even when lower-priority threads are hung in infinite loops. Because the Explorer's threads have higher priority levels, the thread executing the infinite loop is preempted and the Explorer allows the user to terminate the hung process.

The Explorer is very well behaved. Most of the time it simply sits idle, not requiring any CPU time. If this were not the case, the whole system would perform much more slowly and many applications would not respond.

The fourth priority flag, REALTIME_PRIORITY_CLASS, should almost never be used. In fact, earlier betas of the Win32 API did not expose this priority class to applications even though the operating system supported it. Realtime priority is extremely high, and because most threads in the system (including system management threads) execute at a lower priority, they will be affected by a process of this class. In fact, the threads in the system that control the mouse and the keyboard, background disk flushing, and Ctrl+Alt+Del trapping all operate at a lower priority class than realtime priority. If the user is moving the mouse, the thread responding to the mouse's movement will be preempted by a realtime thread. This affects the movement of the mouse, causing it to move jerkily rather than smoothly. Even more serious consequences can occur, such as loss of data.

You might use the realtime priority class if you are writing an application that talks directly to hardware, or if you need to perform some short-lived task and want to be pretty sure it will not be interrupted.

A process cannot run in the realtime priority class unless the user logged on to the system has the Increase Scheduling Priority privilege. Any user designated an administrator or a power user has this privilege by default. You can give this privilege to other users and groups by using the Windows NT User Manager application.

Altering a Process's Priority Class

It might seem odd to you that the process that creates a child process chooses the priority class at which the child process runs. Let's consider the Explorer as an example. When you use the Explorer to run an application, the new process runs at normal priority. The Explorer has no idea what the process does or how often its threads need to be scheduled. However, once the child process is running, it can change its own priority class by calling *SetPriorityClass*:

```
BOOL SetPriorityClass(HANDLE hProcess, DWORD fdwPriority);
```

This function changes the priority class identified by *hProcess* to the value specified in the *fdwPriority* parameter. The *fdwPriority* parameter can be one of the following: IDLE_PRIORITY_CLASS, NORMAL-_PRIORITY_CLASS, HIGH_PRIORITY_CLASS, or REALTIME_PRI-ORITY_CLASS. If the function succeeds, the return value is TRUE; otherwise, it is FALSE. Because this function takes a process handle, you can alter the priority class of any process running in the system as long as you have a handle to it and ample access.

The complementary function used to retrieve the priority class of a process is

```
DWORD GetPriorityClass(HANDLE hProcess);
```

As you might expect, this function returns one of the *CreateProcess* flags listed previously.

When you invoke a program using the command shell, the program's starting priority is normal. However, if you invoke the program using the START command, you can use a switch to specify the starting priority of the application. For example, the following command entered at the command shell causes the system to invoke the Calculator and initially run it at low priority:

```
C:\>START /LOW CALC.EXE
```

The START command also recognizes the /NORMAL, /HIGH, and /REALTIME switches to start executing an application at normal priority (also the default), high priority, and realtime priority, respectively. Of course, once an application starts executing, it can call *SetPriorityClass* to alter its own priority to whatever it chooses.

The Windows 95 START command does not support the /LOW, /NORMAL, /HIGH, and /REALTIME switches. Processes started from the Windows 95 command shell always run using the normal priority class.

Setting a Thread's Relative Priority

When a thread is first created, its priority level is that of the process's priority class. For example, the primary thread of a HIGH_PRIORITY-_CLASS process is assigned an initial priority level value of 13. However, it is possible to raise or lower the priority of an individual thread. A thread's priority is always relative to the priority class of the process that owns it.

You can change a thread's relative priority within a single process by calling *SetThreadPriority*:

```
BOOL SetThreadPriority(HANDLE hThread, int nPriority);
```

The first parameter, *hThread*, is the handle to the thread whose priority class you're changing. The *nPriority* parameter can be one of the values shown in the table on the next page.

When a thread is first created, its initial relative priority value is THREAD_PRIORITY_NORMAL. The rules for threads within a process are similar to the rules for threads across processes. You should set a thread's priority to THREAD_PRIORITY_HIGHEST only when it is absolutely necessary in order for the thread to execute correctly. The scheduler will starve lower-priority threads if higher-priority threads require execution.

In addition to the flags listed in the table, two special flags can be passed to *SetThreadPriority*: THREAD_PRIORITY_IDLE and THREAD-_PRIORITY_TIME_CRITICAL. Specifying THREAD_PRIORITY_IDLE causes the thread's priority level to be set to 1 regardless of whether the priority class for the process is idle, normal, or high. However, if the priority class for the process is realtime, THREAD_PRIORITY_IDLE sets the thread's priority level to 16. Specifying THREAD_PRIORITY-_TIME_CRITICAL causes the thread's priority level to be set to 15 regardless of whether the priority class for the process is idle, normal,

Identifier	Meaning
THREAD_PRIORITY_LOWEST	The thread's priority should be two less than the process's priority class.
THREAD_PRIORITY_BELOW_NORMAL	The thread's priority should be one less than the process's priority class.
THREAD_PRIORITY_NORMAL	The thread's priority should be the same as the process's priority class.
THREAD_PRIORITY_ABOVE_NORMAL	The thread's priority should be one more than the process's priority class.
THREAD_PRIORITY_HIGHEST	The thread's priority should be two more than the process's priority class.

or high. However, if the priority class for the process is realtime, THREAD_PRIORITY_TIME_CRITICAL sets the thread's priority level to 31. Figure 4-1 shows how the system combines a process's priority class with a thread's relative priority to determine a thread's base priority level.

Relative Thread Priority	Process Priority Class			
	Idle	Normal	High	Realtime
Time critical	15	15	15	31
Highest	6	10	15	26
Above normal	5	9	14	25
Normal	4	8	13	24
Below normal	3	7	12	23
Lowest	2	6	11	22
Idle	1	1	1	16

Figure 4-1.
How the system determines a thread's base priority level.

Important

The chart in Figure 4-1 shows the thread priorities for normal priority class processes running in the background. For Windows NT, these priorities do not change when the process is moved to the foreground; only the time quantums of the threads change. However, Windows 95 increases the priority of the lowest, below normal, normal, above normal, and highest threads by 1 when the process is moved to the foreground; the idle and time critical threads do not have their priorities boosted.

The complementary function to *SetThreadPriority*, *GetThreadPriority*, can be used to query a thread's relative priority:

```
int GetThreadPriority(HANDLE hThread);
```

The return value is one of the identifiers listed in the table above or THREAD_PRIORITY_ERROR_RETURN if an error occurs.

Changing a process's priority class has no effect on any of its threads' relative priorities. Also note that the effects of calling *SetThreadPriority* are not cumulative. For example, if a thread is created in a process of the high priority class and you execute the two lines

```
SetThreadPriority(hThread, THREAD_PRIORITY_LOWEST);
SetThreadPriority(hThread, THREAD_PRIORITY_LOWEST);
```

the thread will have a priority level of 11, not a priority level of 9.

Important

No Win32 function returns the priority level of a thread. By this I mean that there is no function that takes a thread handle and returns that the thread has a priority level of 8, for example. This omission is on purpose. Remember that the scheduling algorithm is a rule of thumb, and Microsoft reserves the right to change it at any time. You should not design an application that requires specific knowledge of the scheduling algorithm. If you stick with process priority classes and relative thread priorities, you should be OK.

Dynamic Boosting of Thread Priority Levels

The priority level determined by combining a thread's relative priority with the priority class of the process containing the thread is called a thread's *base priority level*. Occasionally, the system boosts the priority level of a thread. This usually happens in response to some I/O event such as a window message or a disk read. For example, a thread having a relative priority of normal and running in a high priority class process has a base priority of 13.

If the user presses a key, the system places a WM_KEYDOWN message in the thread's queue. Because a message has appeared in the thread's queue, the system temporarily assigns the CPU to the thread so that the thread can process the message. The system also temporarily boosts the priority level of the thread from 13 to 15. (The actual value may vary.) This new thread priority level is called a thread's *dynamic priority*. The CPU executes the thread for a complete time slice, and when the time slice is over, the system reduces the thread's priority by one so that it is now 14. The CPU is again assigned to the thread for another time slice, and at the end of this time slice, the system again reduces the thread's priority by one. The thread's dynamic priority is now back to the thread's base priority level. The system never allows a thread's dynamic priority to drop below the thread's base priority level.

Microsoft is always fine-tuning the dynamic boosts of the system to determine the best overall results. All of this is in an effort to keep the system behaving very responsively to the end user. By the way, threads that have a base priority level in the realtime range (between 16 and 31) are never boosted by the system. The system boosts only threads that are in the dynamic range. In addition, the system will never boost a thread's priority into the realtime range (greater than 15).

Windows NT 4 adds two new functions that allow you to disable the system's automatic boosting of thread priorities:

```
BOOL SetProcessPriorityBoost(HANDLE hProcess,
    BOOL DisablePriorityBoost);
```

```
BOOL SetThreadPriorityBoost(HANDLE hThread,
    BOOL DisablePriorityBoost);
```

SetProcessPriorityBoost tells the system to enable or disable priority boosting for all threads within a process, whereas *SetThreadPriorityBoost* allows you to enable or disable priority boosting for individual threads. These two functions have counterparts that allow you to determine whether priority boosting is enabled or disabled:

```
BOOL GetProcessPriorityBoost(HANDLE hProcess,
    PBOOL pDisablePriorityBoost);
```

```
BOOL GetThreadPriorityBoost(HANDLE hThread,
   PBOOL pDisablePriorityBoost);
```

To each of these functions, you pass the handle of the process or thread that you want to query and the address of a BOOL that will be set by the function.

Windows 95 does not have any implementation for these four functions. If you write an application that calls any of these functions, your application will not be able to load on Windows 95.

Suspending and Resuming Threads

Earlier I mentioned that a thread can be created in a suspended state (by passing the CREATE_SUSPENDED flag to *CreateProcess* or *CreateThread*). When you do this, the system creates the kernel object identifying the thread, creates the thread's stack, and initializes the thread's CPU register members in the CONTEXT structure. However, the thread object is given an initial suspend count of 1, which means the system will never assign a CPU to execute the thread. To allow the thread to begin execution, another thread must call *ResumeThread* and pass it the thread handle returned by the call to *CreateThread* (or the thread handle from the structure pointed to by the *lppiProcInfo* parameter passed to *CreateProcess*):

```
DWORD ResumeThread(HANDLE hThread);
```

If *ResumeThread* is successful, it returns the thread's previous suspend count; otherwise, it returns 0xFFFFFFFF.

A single thread can be suspended several times. If a thread is suspended three times, the thread must be resumed three times before it is eligible for assignment to a CPU. Aside from using the CREATE_SUS-PENDED flag when creating a thread, you can suspend a thread by calling *SuspendThread*:

```
DWORD SuspendThread(HANDLE hThread);
```

Any thread can call this function to suspend another thread. It goes without saying (but I'll say it anyway) that a thread can suspend itself but cannot resume itself. Like *ResumeThread*, *SuspendThread* returns the thread's previous suspend count. A thread can be suspended as many as MAXIMUM_SUSPEND_COUNT times (defined as 127 in WINNT.H).

What's Going On in the System

You can use a utility that ships with Visual C++—PSTAT.EXE—to find out which processes are loaded in the system and which threads exist in each process. Unfortunately, this tool does not run under Windows 95, but Windows 95 comes with a PView95 utility that works similarly. Figure 4-2 shows a dump from the PSTAT.EXE application. It lists all the processes and threads currently running in the system. The *pid* field shows the process ID for each process. For example, the process ID for the Explorer (EXPLORER.EXE) is 0x74. The *pri* field to the right of the process ID shows the priority class value for the process. The Explorer's priority value is 13, indicating that it has high priority. The *HandleCount* field indicates the number of entries currently used in the process's kernel object handle table.

Under each process is a list of threads owned by that process. The Explorer has four threads. For each thread, the *tid* field shows the ID of the thread. The *pri* field indicates the priority number of the thread. The *cs* field shows the number of context switches for the thread. The status of the thread is shown at the end of the line. The word *Wait* indicates that the thread is suspended and is waiting for an event to occur before it can resume execution. The reason for the wait is also included.

```
Pstat version 0.2:  memory: 32176 kb  uptime:  0  6:50:37.687

PageFile: \??\D:\pagefile.sys
   Current Size:  44032 kb  Total Used:  10392 kb    Peak Used
  17888 kb

pid:  0 pri: 0 HandleCount:     0 (null)
    tid:  0 pri:16 cs: 564389 Running
    tid:  0 pri:16 cs: 510456 Running

pid:  2 pri: 8 HandleCount:    89 System
    tid:  1 pri: 0 cs:    3730 Ready
    tid:  3 pri:16 cs:   10128 Wait:EventPairLow
    tid:  4 pri:16 cs:    8928 Wait:EventPairLow
    tid:  5 pri:16 cs:   15450 Wait:EventPairLow
    tid:  6 pri:12 cs:   40614 Wait:EventPairLow
    tid:  7 pri:12 cs:     313 Wait:EventPairLow
    tid:  8 pri:12 cs:   19352 Wait:EventPairLow
    tid:  9 pri:15 cs:     607 Wait:EventPairLow
```

Figure 4-2.
Output from the PSTAT.EXE application.

(continued)

Figure 4-2. *continued*

```
      tid:  a pri:18 cs:    1300 Wait:VirtualMemory
      tid:  b pri:17 cs:    1113 Wait:FreePage
      tid:  c pri:16 cs:   26658 Wait:Executive
      tid:  d pri:23 cs:    9986 Wait:Executive
      tid:  e pri: 8 cs:       1 Wait:EventPairLow
      tid:  f pri:14 cs:       8 Wait:LpcReceive
      tid: 18 pri:17 cs:       1 Wait:VirtualMemory
      tid: 21 pri:19 cs:  268710 Wait:UserRequest
      tid: 22 pri:16 cs:    8279 Wait:UserRequest
      tid: 26 pri:16 cs:   10272 Wait:UserRequest
      tid: 3d pri: 8 cs:       3 Wait:Executive
      tid: 56 pri: 6 cs:       3 Wait:UserRequest
      tid: 5a pri:16 cs:      45 Wait:Executive
      tid: 58 pri: 9 cs:      78 Wait:EventPairLow
      tid: 5b pri: 9 cs:       4 Wait:EventPairLow
      tid: 60 pri: 9 cs:     111 Wait:EventPairLow

pid: 11 pri:11 HandleCount:   29 smss.exe
      tid: 10 pri:14 cs:     819 Wait:UserRequest
      tid: 12 pri:14 cs:       6 Wait:LpcReceive
      tid: 13 pri:11 cs:       3 Wait:LpcReceive
      tid: 19 pri:14 cs:     192 Wait:LpcReceive
      tid: 1a pri:12 cs:     101 Wait:LpcReceive
      tid: 1b pri:11 cs:       1 Wait:LpcReceive

pid: 1d pri:13 HandleCount:  183 csrss.exe
      tid: 1e pri:13 cs:      39 Wait:UserRequest
      tid: 14 pri:14 cs:   48245 Wait:LpcReceive
      tid: 15 pri:14 cs:     115 Wait:LpcReceive
      tid: 16 pri:14 cs:       4 Wait:LpcReceive
      tid: 20 pri:15 cs:   48293 Wait:LpcReceive
      tid: 6f pri:14 cs:   48131 Wait:LpcReceive
      tid: 8b pri:14 cs:     447 Wait:UserRequest

pid: 1f pri:13 HandleCount:   43 winlogon.exe
      tid: 17 pri:15 cs:    8375 Wait:UserRequest
      tid: 23 pri:13 cs:       6 Wait:UserRequest

pid: 25 pri: 9 HandleCount:  174 services.exe
      tid: 37 pri:14 cs:      34 Wait:UserRequest
      tid: 39 pri: 9 cs:      23 Wait:Executive
      tid: 3c pri: 9 cs:       2 Wait:LpcReceive
      tid: 45 pri: 9 cs:     213 Wait:UserRequest
```

(continued)

Figure 4-2. *continued*

```
        tid: 47 pri: 9 cs:       18 Wait:UserRequest
        tid: 6d pri: 9 cs:        4 Wait:Executive
        tid: 6e pri: 9 cs:       20 Wait:UserRequest
        tid: 6b pri:11 cs:      445 Wait:UserRequest
        tid: 6c pri:11 cs:      413 Wait:UserRequest
        tid: 46 pri:14 cs:        4 Wait:UserRequest
        tid: 3b pri:15 cs:      909 Wait:UserRequest
        tid: 72 pri:10 cs:        4 Wait:LpcReceive

pid: 28 pri: 9 HandleCount:      87 lsass.exe
        tid: 2a pri:10 cs:        4 Wait:LpcReceive
        tid: 2c pri:14 cs:       10 Wait:UserRequest
        tid: 2d pri:10 cs:       13 Wait:LpcReceive
        tid: 2e pri:10 cs:       15 Wait:LpcReceive
        tid: 2f pri:10 cs:        7 Wait:LpcReceive
        tid: 30 pri:10 cs:        8 Wait:LpcReceive
        tid: 31 pri:10 cs:        5 Wait:LpcReceive
        tid: 32 pri:14 cs:        6 Wait:LpcReceive
        tid: 33 pri: 9 cs:       12 Wait:LpcReceive
        tid: 34 pri: 9 cs:        9 Wait:Executive
        tid: 2b pri: 9 cs:       85 Wait:UserRequest

pid: 27 pri: 8 HandleCount:      83 SPOOLSS.EXE
        tid: 3e pri:14 cs:       16 Wait:Executive
        tid: 3f pri: 8 cs:        2 Wait:UserRequest
        tid: 41 pri:14 cs:       94 Wait:UserRequest
        tid: 42 pri: 8 cs:      137 Wait:Executive
        tid: 55 pri: 8 cs:        7 Wait:UserRequest
        tid: 57 pri: 8 cs:        2 Wait:UserRequest
        tid: 76 pri:11 cs:      236 Wait:LpcReceive
        tid: 71 pri: 8 cs:      134 Wait:Executive

pid: 49 pri: 8 HandleCount:      70 rpcss.exe
        tid: 48 pri:14 cs:       24 Wait:Executive
        tid: 4b pri: 8 cs:      421 Wait:DelayExecution
        tid: 4c pri:14 cs:      232 Wait:LpcReceive
        tid: 4d pri: 8 cs:        2 Wait:LpcReceive
        tid: 5d pri:10 cs:        6 Wait:UserRequest
        tid: 80 pri:15 cs:      294 Wait:LpcReceive
        tid: 61 pri: 8 cs:      495 Wait:DelayExecution

pid: 3a pri: 8 HandleCount:      74 tapisrv.exe
        tid: 4e pri:14 cs:       18 Wait:Executive
        tid: 4f pri: 8 cs:       13 Wait:UserRequest
        tid: 50 pri: 9 cs:        3 Wait:UserRequest
```

(continued)

Figure 4-2. *continued*

```
        tid: 51 pri: 8 cs:       2 Wait:UserRequest
        tid: 52 pri:14 cs:     311 Wait:LpcReceive
        tid: 5f pri:14 cs:       6 Wait:LpcReceive
        tid: 63 pri: 9 cs:       2 Wait:EventPairLow
        tid: 64 pri: 9 cs:       3 Wait:UserRequest
        tid: 65 pri: 9 cs:       3 Wait:EventPairLow
        tid: 66 pri: 9 cs:       3 Wait:EventPairLow

pid: 54 pri: 8 HandleCount:   121 RASMAN.EXE
        tid: 53 pri: 8 cs:      18 Wait:Executive
        tid: 59 pri:14 cs:      65 Wait:UserRequest
        tid: 5e pri:14 cs:      22 Wait:UserRequest
        tid: 67 pri: 8 cs:       2 Wait:UserRequest
        tid: 68 pri: 9 cs:    1053 Wait:UserRequest
        tid: 69 pri: 8 cs:      24 Wait:UserRequest
        tid: 7c pri: 9 cs:      51 Wait:UserRequest
        tid: 5c pri:14 cs:      30 Wait:UserRequest
        tid: 83 pri: 9 cs:       2 Wait:UserRequest
        tid: 85 pri:14 cs:      88 Wait:UserRequest
        tid: 88 pri: 9 cs:       4 Wait:UserRequest
        tid: 89 pri: 8 cs:       3 Wait:UserRequest
        tid: 8a pri:10 cs:    1991 Wait:DelayExecution

pid: 29 pri: 8 HandleCount:    16 nddeagnt.exe
        tid: 6a pri:14 cs:      78 Wait:UserRequest

pid: 74 pri:13 HandleCount:    69 explorer.exe
        tid: 73 pri:15 cs:  230614 Wait:UserRequest
        tid: 7e pri:13 cs:     324 Wait:UserRequest
        tid: 81 pri:13 cs:       1 Wait:LpcReceive
        tid: 9e pri:13 cs:      29 Wait:LpcReceive

pid: 7f pri:13 HandleCount:    31 taskmgr.exe
        tid: 24 pri:14 cs:  265873 Wait:UserRequest
        tid: 84 pri:15 cs:   58241 Wait:UserRequest
        tid: 86 pri:14 cs:   86841 Wait:UserRequest

pid: 70 pri: 8 HandleCount:    94 WINWORD.EXE
        tid: 4a pri: 8 cs:  263093 Running
        tid: 8e pri: 8 cs:       2 Wait:LpcReceive
        tid: ad pri: 8 cs:       1 Wait:LpcReceive

pid: 93 pri: 8 HandleCount:    48 ntvdm.exe
        tid: 96 pri:14 cs:    1074 Wait:UserRequest
        tid: 90 pri:15 cs:    1125 Wait:UserRequest
```

(continued)

Figure 4-2. *continued*

```
pid: a3 pri: 8 HandleCount:   25 rundll32.exe
    tid: a2 pri:14 cs:     468 Wait:UserRequest

pid: 7b pri: 8 HandleCount:   22 cmd.exe
    tid: aa pri:15 cs:     190 Wait:UserRequest

pid: a8 pri: 8 HandleCount:   14 pstat.exe
    tid: a5 pri:14 cs:       9 Running
```

Processes, Threads, and the C Run-Time Library

Microsoft ships six C run-time libraries with Visual C++ 4.*x*. The following table lists the names of the libraries and their descriptions.

Library Name	Description
LIBC.LIB	Statically linked library for single-threaded applications.
LIBCD.LIB	Statically linked debug version of the library for single-threaded applications.
LIBCMT.LIB	Statically linked release version of the library for multi-threaded applications.
LIBCMTD.LIB	Statically linked debug version of the library for multi-threaded applications.
MSVCRT.LIB	Import library for dynamically linking the release version of the MSVCRT40.DLL library. This library supports both single-threaded and multithreaded applications.
MSVCRTD.LIB	Import library for dynamically linking the debug version of the MSVCRT40.DLL library. The library supports both single-threaded and multithreaded applications.

The first question you're probably asking yourself is, "Why do I need one library for single-threaded applications and an additional library for multithreaded applications?" The reason is that the standard C run-time library was invented around 1970, long before threads became available. The inventors of the library didn't consider the problems of using the C run-time library with multithreaded applications.

Consider, for example, the standard C run-time global variable *errno*. Some functions set this variable when an error occurs. Let's say you have the following code fragment:

```
BOOL fFailure = (system("NOTEPAD.EXE README.TXT") == -1);

if (fFailure) {
   switch (errno) {
   case E2BIG:    // Argument list or environment too big
      break;

   case ENOENT:   // Command interpreter cannot be found
      break;

   case ENOEXEC:  // Command interpreter has bad format
      break;

   case ENOMEM:   // Insufficient memory to run command
      break;
   }
}
```

Now let's imagine that the thread executing the code above is interrupted after the call to the *system* function and before the *if* statement. Let's further imagine that the thread is being interrupted to allow a second thread in the same process to execute and that this new thread will execute another C run-time function that sets the global variable *errno*. When the CPU is later assigned back to the first thread, the value of *errno* no longer reflects the proper error code for the call to *system* in the code above. To solve this problem, you need to assign each thread its very own *errno* variable.

This is only one example of how the standard C run-time library was not designed for multithreaded applications. Some of the C run-time variables and functions that have problems in multithreaded environments are *errno, _doserrno, strtok, _wcstok, strerror, _strerror, tmpnam, tmpfile, asctime, _wasctime, gmtime, _ecvt,* and *_fcvt*—to name just a few.

For multithreaded C and C++ programs that use the C run-time library to work properly, a data structure must be created and associated with each thread that uses C run-time library functions. To do this, you create threads using the C run-time's *_beginthreadex* function instead of the Win32 *CreateThread* function:

```
unsigned long _beginthreadex(void *security, unsigned stack_size,
   unsigned (*start_address)(void *), void *arglist,
   unsigned initflag, unsigned *thrdaddr);
```

Parameterwise, *_beginthreadex* has the same parameter list as the *CreateThread* function, although the parameter names and types are not exactly the same. This is because Microsoft's C run-time group feels that

C run-time functions should not have any dependencies on Win32 data types. The _beginthreadex_ function also returns the handle of the newly created thread just like _CreateThread_. However, if you define STRICT when you compile the Windows.H file, you will need to do a lot of casting to make the compiler happy.

When you call _beginthreadex_, it performs the following actions:

1. Allocates an undocumented, internal data structure that contains the per-thread instance data. For example, the single thread's _errno_ variable and a pointer to the thread's _strtok_ buffer are maintained in this data structure. This data structure also contains two members that are initialized to contain the _start_address_ and _arglist_ parameters that you passed to _beginthreadex_.

2. Calls the Win32 _CreateThread_ function to create the new thread. _CreateThread_ is called as follows:

```
hThread = CreateThread(security, stack_size, _threadstart,
    &PerThreadData, initflag, thrdaddr);
```

3. Returns the handle of the newly created thread, or returns 0 if an error occurred.

You'll notice that the new thread is instructed to start at a function called _threadstart_ instead of at the function that you passed to _beginthreadex_. The _threadstart_ function is a function inside the C run-time library that performs the following tasks:

1. Associates the memory address of the per-thread instance data block with the thread using dynamic thread-local storage. (For more information on thread-local storage, see Chapter 13.) The _threadstart_ function is passed this data block's address as its parameter.

2. Initializes the C run-time's floating-point support for the new thread.

3. Enters a structured exception handling frame in order to support the C run-time's _signal_ function.

4. Retrieves the address of your thread function and the parameter you want passed to it from the per-thread instance data block members. The _threadstart_ function then uses these values to call your thread function, passing it the 32-bit value you want.

5. Calls another C run-time function named *_endthreadex* when your thread function returns; passes *_endthreadex* the value that your thread function returns.

The *_endthreadex* function then terminates a thread created by the *_beginthreadex* function; its prototype is

```
void _endthreadex(unsigned retval);
```

The *retval* parameter is the thread's exit code. The *_endthreadex* function performs the following actions:

1. Terminates floating-point support for the thread.

2. Gets the address of the per-thread instance data block associated with the thread.

3. Frees the per-thread instance data block.

4. Terminates the thread by calling the Win32 *ExitThread* function, passing it the value that was passed as *_endthreadex*'s *retval* parameter.

Note that you can call the *_endthreadex* function explicitly if you want. Just be aware that if your thread function returns, the C run-time's *_threadstart* function calls *_endthreadex* on your behalf.

By now you should understand why the C run-time library's functions need a separate data block for each thread created, and you should also see how calling *_beginthreadex* allocates, initializes, and associates this data block with the newly created thread. You should also be able to see how the *_endthreadex* function frees the data block when the thread terminates.

Once this data block is initialized and associated with the thread, any C run-time library functions the thread calls that require per-thread instance data can easily retrieve the address to the calling thread's data block and manipulate the thread's data. This is fine for functions, but you might be wondering how this works for a global variable such as *errno*. Well, *errno* is defined in the standard C headers like this:

```
#if defined(_MT) || defined(_DLL)
extern int * __cdecl _errno(void);
#define errno    (*_errno())
#else    /* ndef _MT && ndef _DLL */
extern int errno;
#endif    /* _MT || _DLL */
```

If you're creating a multithreaded application, you'll need to specify the /MT (multithreaded application) or /MD (multithreaded DLL) switch on the compiler's command line. This causes the compiler to define the _MT identifier. Then, whenever you reference *errno*, you are actually making a call to the internal C run-time library function *_errno*. This function returns the address to the *errno* data member in the calling thread's associated data block. You'll notice that the *errno* macro is defined as taking the contents of this address. This definition is necessary because it's possible to write code like this:

```
int *p = &errno;
if (*p == ENOMEM) {
    :
    :
}
```

If the internal *_errno* function simply returned the value of *errno*, the above code wouldn't compile.

The multithreaded version of the C run-time library also places synchronization primitives around certain functions. For example, if two threads simultaneously call *malloc*, the heap could possibly become corrupted. The multithreaded version of the C run-time library prevents two threads from allocating memory from the heap at the same time. It does this by making the second thread wait until the first has returned from *malloc*. Then the second thread is allowed to enter. Thread synchronization is discussed in more detail in Chapter 10.

Obviously, the performance of the multithreaded version of the C run-time library is impacted by all this additional work. This is why Microsoft supplies the single-threaded version of the statically linked C run-time library in addition to the multithreaded version.

The dynamically linked version of the C run-time library was written to be generic so that it could be shared by any and all running applications and DLLs using the C run-time library functions. For this reason, the library exists only in a multithreaded version. Because the C run-time library is supplied in a DLL, applications (EXE files) and DLLs don't need to include the code for the C run-time library function and are smaller as a result. Also, if Microsoft fixes a bug in the C run-time library DLL, applications will automatically gain the fix as well.

You might be wondering what would happen if you created your new threads by calling the Win32 *CreateThread* function instead of the C run-time's *_beginthreadex* function. Well, here is what happens if a thread created with *CreateThread* calls a C run-time library function that requires the per-thread instance data block:

1. The C run-time function first attempts to get the address of the thread's data block.

2. If the address is NULL, the C run-time library allocates a data block for the thread, initializes, and then associates the block's address with the thread using thread-local storage. (See Chapter 13 for more information on thread-local storage.)

3. The function can now execute successfully because it has the address of the thread's data block.

A couple of problems result, however. First, if the thread uses the C run-time's *signal* function, the entire process will terminate because the structured exception handling frame has not been prepared. Second, if the thread terminates without calling *_endthreadex*, the data block cannot be destroyed and a memory leak occurs. This second problem has a caveat: if the application is using the dynamic-link library version of the C run-time library, the DLL is notified when the thread terminates and the DLL will destroy the thread's data block. Only if the application uses the static-link versions of the C run-time library does this memory leak occur. As a rule, you should always use the C run-time's *_beginthreadex/_endthreadex* functions instead of the Win32 *CreateThread/ExitThread* functions.

As you might expect, the C run-time library's startup code allocates and initializes a data block for your application's primary thread. This allows the primary thread to safely call any of the C run-time functions. When your primary thread returns from *WinMain*, the C run-time library frees the associated data block. In addition, the startup code sets up the proper structured exception handling code so that the primary thread can successfully call the C run-time's *signal* function.

C Run-Time Functions to Avoid

The C run-time library also contains two other functions:

```
unsigned long _beginthread(void (__cdecl *start_address)(void *),
    unsigned stack_size, void *arglist);
```

and

```
void _endthread(void);
```

These two functions were originally created to do the work of the new _beginthreadex_ and _endthreadex_ functions, respectively. However, as you can see, the _beginthread_ function has fewer parameters and is therefore more limited than the full-featured _beginthreadex_ function. For example, if you use _beginthread_, you cannot create the new thread with security attributes, you cannot create the thread suspended, and you cannot obtain the thread's ID value. The _endthread_ function has a similar story: it takes no parameters, which means you cannot give your thread an exit value when it terminates.

The _endthread_ function has a significant problem that you can't see, however. Just before _endthread_ calls *ExitThread*, it calls *CloseHandle*, passing the handle of the new thread. To see why this is a problem, examine the following code:

```
DWORD dwExitCode;
HANDLE hThread = _beginthread(…);
GetExitCodeThread(hThread, &dwExitCode);
CloseHandle(hThread);
```

It is quite possible that the newly created thread will execute, return, and terminate before the first thread can call *GetExitCodeThread*. If this happens, the value in *hThread* is invalid because _endthread_ has closed the new thread's handle. Needless to say, the call to *CloseHandle* will also fail for the same reason.

The new _endthreadex_ function does *not* close the thread's handle, and therefore the code fragment above will work correctly if we replace the call to _beginthread_ with a call to _beginthreadex_. Remember that when your thread function returns, _beginthreadex_ calls _endthreadex_, whereas _beginthread_ calls _endthread_.

WIN32 MEMORY ARCHITECTURE

The memory architecture used by an operating system is the most important key to understanding how the operating system does what it does. When you start working with a new operating system, many questions come to mind: "How do I share data between two applications?" "Where does the system store the information I'm looking for?" and "How can I make my program run more efficiently?" are just a few.

I have found that, more often than not, a good understanding of how the system manages memory can help determine the answers to these questions quickly and accurately. So this chapter explores the memory architecture used by the various implementations of Win32.

A Virtual Address Space

In Win32, every process's virtual address space is 4 GB. A 32-bit pointer can have any value from 0x00000000 through 0xFFFFFFFF. This allows a pointer to have one of 4,294,967,296 values, which covers a process's 4-GB range.

In MS-DOS and 16-bit Windows, all processes share a single address space. This means that any process can read from and write to memory belonging to any other process, including the operating system itself. Of course, this capability leaves every process at the mercy of every other running process. If Process A accidentally overwrites data belonging to Process B, Process B may become very unstable and will probably crash. A robust operating system and environment should not allow situations like this to occur.

In the Win32 environment, this problem is solved because each Win32 process is given its own private address space. When a thread in a process is running, that thread can access only memory that belongs to its process. The memory that belongs to all other processes is hidden and inaccessible to the running thread.

Important

In Windows NT, the memory belonging to the operating system itself is also hidden from the running thread, which means that the operating system's data cannot be accessed accidentally by the thread. In Windows 95, the memory belonging to the operating system is not hidden from the running thread. Therefore, the running thread could accidentally access the operating system's data and corrupt the operating system. It is *not* possible in Windows 95 for one process's thread to access memory belonging to another process. This restriction makes the operating system much more robust than 16-bit versions of Windows but still leaves it open to potential crashes.

As I said, every process has its own private address space. Process A can have a data structure stored in its address space at address 0x12345678, while Process B can have a totally different data structure stored in *its* address space—at address 0x12345678. When threads running in Process A access memory at address 0x12345678, these threads are accessing Process A's data structure. When threads running in Process B access memory at address 0x12345678, these threads are accessing Process B's data structure. Threads running in Process A cannot access the data structure in Process B's address space, and vice versa.

Now, before you get all excited about having so much address space for your application, keep in mind that this is *virtual* address space—not physical storage. This address space is simply a range of memory addresses. Physical storage needs to be assigned or mapped to portions of the address space before you can successfully access data without raising access violations. We will discuss how this is done later in this chapter.

Different implementations of Win32 partition a process's 4-GB virtual address space in slightly different ways. The next two sections describe how Windows 95 and Windows NT partition a process's address space.

How Windows 95 Partitions a Process's Address Space

Figure 5-1 shows how the Windows 95 implementation of Win32 partitions a process's address space.

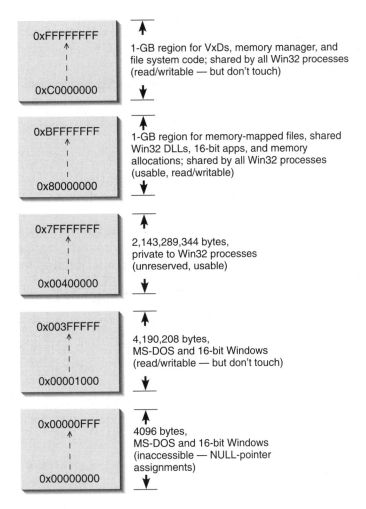

Figure 5-1.
Win32 partitions in Windows 95.

The Partition from 0x00000000 through 0x003FFFFF

This 4-MB region at the bottom of the process's address space is required by Windows 95 in order to maintain compatibility with MS-DOS and 16-bit Windows. From our Win32 applications, we should not attempt to read from or write to this region. Ideally, the CPU should raise an access violation if a thread in our process touches this memory, but for technical reasons, Microsoft was unable to guard this 4 MB of address space. However, Microsoft was able to guard the bottom 4 KB. If a thread in your process attempts to read or write to a memory address between

0x00000000 and 0x00000FFF, the CPU will raise an access violation. Protecting this 4-KB region is incredibly useful in helping to detect NULL-pointer assignments.

Error checking is often not performed religiously in C programs. For example, the following code performs no error checking:

```
int* pnSomeInteger;
pnSomeInteger = (int*)malloc(sizeof(int));
*pnSomeInteger = 5;
```

If *malloc* cannot find enough memory to satisfy the request, it returns NULL. However, this code doesn't check for this possibility—it assumes that the allocation was successful and proceeds to access memory at address 0x00000000. Because the bottom 4 KB of the address space is off-limits, a memory access violation occurs and the process is terminated. This feature helps developers find bugs in their applications.

The Partition from 0x00400000 through 0x7FFFFFFF

This 2,143,289,344-byte (2 GB minus 4 MB) partition is where the process's private (unshared) address space resides. One Win32 process cannot read from, write to, or in any way access another process's data residing in this partition.[1] For all Win32 applications, this partition is where the bulk of the process's data is maintained. Because each process gets its own private, unshared partition for data, Win32 applications are far less likely to be corrupted by other applications, making the whole system more robust.

The Partition from 0x80000000 through 0xBFFFFFFF

This 1-GB partition is where the system stores data that is shared among all Win32 processes. For example, the system dynamic-link libraries, KERNEL32.DLL, USER32.DLL, GDI32.DLL, and ADVAPI32.DLL, are all loaded in this address space partition. This makes these four DLLs easily available to all Win32 processes simultaneously. It also means that these DLLs are loaded at the same memory address for every Win32 process. The system also maps all memory-mapped files in this partition. Memory-mapped files are discussed in more detail in Chapter 8.

---

1. Win32 does offer special functions (*ReadProcessMemory* and *WriteProcessMemory*) that do allow one process to read from or write to data in another process's address space, but these functions are usually called by debuggers.

The Partition from 0xC0000000 through 0xFFFFFFFF

This 1-GB partition is where the operating system's code is located, including the system's virtual device drivers (VxDs), low-level memory management code, and file system code. As with the preceding partition, all the code in this partition is shared among all Win32 processes. Unfortunately, the data in this partition is not protected—any Win32 application may read from or write to this section, potentially corrupting the operating system.

How Windows NT Partitions a Process's Address Space

Figure 5-2 on the following page shows how the Windows NT implementation of Win32 partitions a process's address space.

The Partition from 0x00000000 through 0x0000FFFF

This 64-KB range at the bottom of the process's address space is set aside by Windows NT to help programmers catch NULL-pointer assignments—just like the bottommost 4 KB under Windows 95. Any attempts to read from or write to memory addresses in this partition cause an access violation.

The Partition from 0x00010000 through 0x7FFEFFFF

This 2,147,352,576-byte (2 GB minus 64 KB minus 64 KB) partition is where the process's private (unshared) address space resides. This partition is like the 0x00400000 through 0x7FFFFFFF partition under Windows 95.

When a Win32 process loads, it will require access to the system dynamic-link libraries, KERNEL32.DLL, USER32.DLL, GDI32.DLL, and ADVAPI32.DLL. The code for these DLLs as well as for any other DLLs is loaded into this partition. Each process may load these DLLs at a different address within this partition (although this is very unlikely). The system also maps all memory-mapped files accessible to this process within this partition.

The Partition from 0x7FFF0000 through 0x7FFFFFFF

This 64-KB partition just below the 2-GB line is similar to the 0x00000000 through 0x0000FFFF partition; that is, this partition is off-limits, and any attempt to access memory in this partition causes an access violation. Microsoft reserves this partition to make the implementation of the

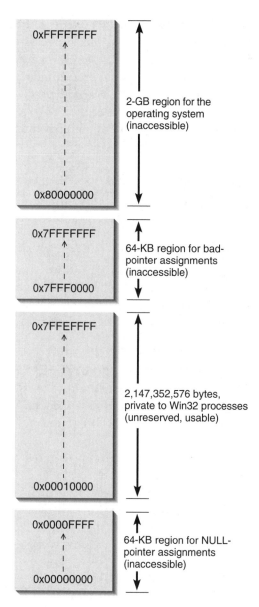

0xFFFFFFFF

2-GB region for the
operating system
(inaccessible)

0x80000000

0x7FFFFFFF

64-KB region for bad-
pointer assignments
(inaccessible)

0x7FFF0000

0x7FFEFFFF

2,147,352,576 bytes,
private to Win32 processes
(unreserved, usable)

0x00010000

0x0000FFFF

64-KB region for NULL-
pointer assignments
(inaccessible)

0x00000000

Figure 5-2.
Win32 partitions in Windows NT.

operating system easier. When you pass the address of a block of memory
and its length to a Win32 API function, the function validates the memory
block before performing its operation. You could easily imagine code
like this:

```
BYTE bBuf[70000];
DWORD dwNumBytesWritten;
BOOL WriteProcessMemory(hProcess, 0x7FFEEE90, bBuf,
   sizeof(bBuf), &dwNumBytesWritten);
```

For a function like *WriteProcessMemory*, the memory region being written to is validated by kernel-mode code, which can successfully access the memory region above 0x80000000. If there is memory at the 0x80000000 address, the call above will succeed in writing data to memory that should be accessible only by kernel-mode code. To prevent this while making the validation of such memory regions fast, Microsoft chose to keep this partition always off limits so that any attempt to read from or write to memory in this region will always cause an access violation.

The Partition from 0x80000000 through 0xFFFFFFFF

This 2-GB partition is where the Windows NT Executive, Kernel, and device drivers are loaded. Unlike with Windows 95, the Windows NT operating system components are completely protected. If you attempt to access memory addresses in this partition, your thread will cause an access violation, causing the system to display a message box to the user and causing Windows NT to terminate your application. See Chapter 16 for more information about access violations and how to handle them.

You're probably thinking that it seems a little unreasonable that Windows NT should steal 2 GB of your address space, and I'd have to agree. However, the MIPS R4000 CPUs require that this range be reserved. Microsoft could have implemented the Windows NT version of Win32 differently on different CPU platforms but decided that developers could port their applications more easily if the top 2 GB were reserved on every Windows NT implementation of Win32.

Regions in an Address Space

When a process is created and given its address space, the bulk of this usable address space is *free,* or unallocated. To use portions of this address space, you must allocate regions within it by calling the Win32 *VirtualAlloc* function (discussed in Chapter 7). The act of allocating a region is called *reserving*.

Whenever you reserve a region of address space, the system ensures that the region begins on an even *allocation granularity* boundary. The allocation granularity may vary from one CPU platform to another. However, as of this writing, all the CPU platforms (*x*86, MIPS, Alpha, and

PowerPC) use the same allocation granularity of 64 KB. The system uses the allocation granularity to more easily manage its internal record keeping of the reserved regions in your address space and to reduce the amount of address space region fragmentation that can occur in your address space.

When you reserve a region of address space, the system ensures that the size of the region is an even multiple of the system's *page* size. A page is a unit of memory that the system uses in managing memory. Like the allocation granularity, the page size can vary from one CPU to another. The *x*86, MIPS, and PowerPC implementations of Win32 use a 4-KB page size, whereas the DEC Alpha implementation uses an 8-KB page size.

If you attempt to reserve a 10-KB region of address space, the system will automatically round up your request and reserve a region whose size is an even multiple of the page size. This means that on an *x*86, a MIPS, or a PowerPC, the system will reserve a region that is 12 KB, and on an Alpha, the system will reserve a 16-KB region.

When your program's algorithms no longer need to access a reserved region of address space, the region should be freed. This process is called *releasing* the region of address space and is accomplished by calling the *VirtualFree* function.

Important

> Sometimes the system reserves regions of address space on behalf of your process. For example, the system allocates a region of address space to store a *process environment block* (PEB). A PEB is a small data structure created, manipulated, and destroyed entirely by the system. When a process is created, the system allocates a region of address space for the PEB.
>
> The system also needs to create *thread environment blocks* (TEBs) to help manage all the threads that currently exist in the process. The regions for these TEBs will be reserved and released as threads in the process are created and destroyed.
>
> Although the system demands that any of your requests to reserve address space regions begin on an even allocation granularity boundary (64 KB), the system itself is not subjected to the same limitation. It is extremely likely that the region reserved for your process's PEB and TEBs will not start on an even 64-KB boundary. However, these reserved regions will still have to be an even multiple of the CPU's page size.

Committing Physical Storage Within a Region

To use a reserved region of address space, you must allocate physical storage and then map this storage to the reserved region. This process is called *committing* physical storage. Physical storage is always committed in pages. To commit physical storage to a reserved region, you again call the *VirtualAlloc* function.

When you commit physical storage to regions, you do not have to commit physical storage to the entire region. For example, you can reserve a region that is 64 KB and then commit physical storage to the second and fourth pages within the region. Figure 5-3 on the following page shows what a process's address space might look like. Notice that the address space is different depending on which CPU platform you're running on. The address space on the left shows what happens on an *x*86, a MIPS, or a PowerPC machine (all of which have 4-KB pages), and the address space on the right shows what happens on a DEC Alpha machine (which has 8-KB pages).

When your program's algorithms no longer need to access committed physical storage in the reserved region, the physical storage should be freed. This process is called *decommitting* the physical storage and is accomplished by calling the *VirtualFree* function.

Physical Storage

In 16-bit Windows 3.1, physical storage was considered to be the amount of RAM that you had in your machine. In other words, if you had 16 MB of RAM in your machine, you could load and run applications that used up to 16 MB of RAM. To help conserve memory, 16-bit Windows had lots of memory optimizations. For example, if you wanted to run two or more instances of an application, 16-bit Windows created a new data segment for each instance but all instances shared the program's code. This significantly reduced the amount of RAM needed to run multiple instances of an application.

Also, in 16-bit Windows 3.1, Microsoft added support for virtual memory in the form of hard disk swap files. But an operating system can use swap files only if the CPU directly supports them. For this reason, 16-bit Windows was able to use swap files only when running on a computer driven by a 386 or later CPU. From an application's perspective, a swap file transparently increases the amount of RAM (or storage) that the

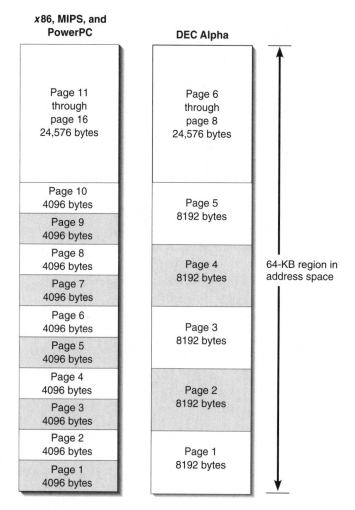

Figure 5-3.
Example process address spaces for different CPUs.

application can use. If you have 16 MB of RAM in your machine and also have a 20-MB swap file on your hard disk, the applications you're running believe that your machine has a grand total of 36 MB of RAM.

Of course, you don't actually have 36 MB of RAM. Instead, the operating system, in coordination with the CPU, saves portions of RAM to the swap file and loads portions of the swap file back into RAM as the running applications need them. Because a swap file increases the apparent amount of RAM available for applications, the use of a swap file in 16-bit Windows is optional. If you don't have a swap file, the system just thinks that there is less RAM available for applications to use.

The Windows 95 and Windows NT implementations of memory management are drastically different from the Windows 3.1 implementation. In these Win32 systems, the amount of RAM in the computer is completely managed by the operating system, and no application has any direct control over this memory.

With Win32 systems, it is best to think of physical storage as data stored in a paging file on a disk drive (usually a hard disk drive). So when an application commits physical storage to a region of address space by calling the *VirtualAlloc* function, space is actually allocated from a file on the hard disk. The size of the system's paging file is the most important factor in determining how much physical storage is available to applications; the amount of RAM you have has very little effect.

Now, when a thread in your process attempts to access a block of data in the process's address space, one of two things can happen, as shown in the flowchart in Figure 5-4 on the following page.

In the first possibility, the data that the thread is attempting to access is in RAM. In this case, the CPU maps the data's virtual memory address to the physical address in memory, and then the desired access is performed.

In the second possibility, the data that the thread is attempting to access is not in RAM but is contained somewhere in the paging file. In this case, the attempted access is called a page fault and the CPU notifies the operating system of the attempted access. The operating system then locates a free page of memory in RAM; if a free page cannot be found, the system must free one. If a page has not been modified, the system can simply free the page. But if the system needs to free a page that was modified, it must first copy the page from RAM to the paging file. Next the system goes to the paging file, locates the block of data that needs to be accessed, and loads the data into the free page of memory. The operating system then maps the data's virtual memory address to the appropriate physical memory address in RAM.

The more often the system needs to copy pages of memory to the paging file and vice versa, the more your hard disk thrashes and the slower the system runs. (*Thrashing* means that the operating system spends all its time swapping pages in and out of memory instead of running programs.) So by adding more RAM to your computer, you reduce the amount of thrashing necessary to run your applications, which will, of course, greatly improve the system's performance.

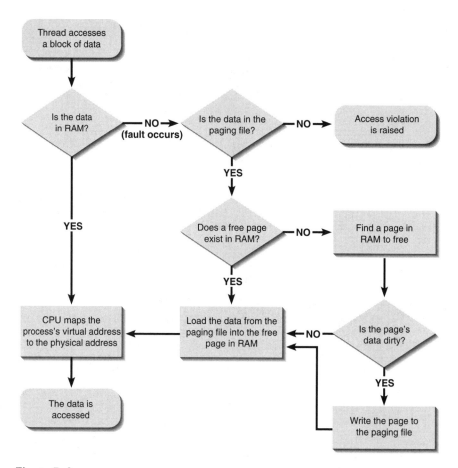

Figure 5-4.
How data is accessed.

Windows NT is capable of using multiple paging files. If multiple paging files exist on different physical hard drives, the system can perform much faster because it can write to the multiple drives simultaneously. You can add and remove paging files by opening the Control Panel, double-clicking on the System icon, selecting the Performance tab, and then choosing the Change button in the Virtual Memory section.

Physical Storage Not Maintained in the Paging File

After reading the previous section, you must be thinking that the paging file can get pretty large if many programs are all running at once—especially if you're thinking that every time you run a program the system must reserve regions of address space for the process's code and data, commit physical storage to these regions, and then copy the code and data from the program's file on the hard disk to the committed physical storage in the paging file.

The system does not do what I just described; if it did, it would take a very long time to load a program and start it running. Instead, when you invoke an application, the system opens the application's EXE file and determines the size of the application's code and data. Then the system reserves a region of address space and notes that the physical storage associated with this region is the EXE file itself. That's right—instead of allocating space from the paging file, the system uses the actual contents, or *image,* of the EXE file as the program's reserved region of address space. This, of course, makes loading an application very fast and reduces the size of the paging file.

When a program's file image (that is, an EXE or a DLL file) on the hard disk is used as the physical storage for a region of address space, it is called a *memory-mapped file.* When an EXE or a DLL is loaded, the system automatically reserves a region of address space and maps the file's image to this region. However, the system also offers a set of Win32 API functions that allow you to map data files to a region of address space. We will talk about memory-mapped files much more in Chapter 8.

Important

When an EXE or a DLL file is loaded from a floppy disk, both Windows 95 and Windows NT allocate storage for the entire file from the system's paging file. The system then copies the file from the floppy into the system's RAM and the system's paging file; the paging file is said to *back* the RAM. Setup programs operate in this way.

Often a setup program begins with one floppy, which the user removes from the drive to insert another floppy. If the system needs to go back to the first floppy to load some of the EXE's or the DLL's code, it is of course no longer in the floppy drive. However, because the system copied the file to RAM and the paging file, it will have no trouble accessing the setup program. When the setup program terminates, the system frees the RAM and the storage in the paging file.

The system does not copy to RAM image files on other removeable media such as CD-ROM or network drives unless the image is linked using the /SWAPRUN:CD or /SWAPRUN:NET switches.

Protection Attributes

Individual pages of physical storage allocated by the *VirtualAlloc* function can be assigned different protection attributes. The Win32 protection attributes are shown in the following table.

Protection Attribute	Description
PAGE_NOACCESS	Attempts to read from, write to, or execute code in memory in this region cause an access violation.
PAGE_READONLY	Attempts to write to or execute code in memory in this region cause an access violation.
PAGE_READWRITE	Attempts to execute code in memory in this region cause an access violation.
PAGE_EXECUTE	Attempts to read or write memory in this region cause an access violation.
PAGE_EXECUTE_READ	Attempts to write to memory in this region cause an access violation.
PAGE_EXECUTE_READWRITE	There is nothing you can do to this region to cause an access violation.
PAGE_WRITECOPY	Attempts to execute code in memory in this region cause an access violation. Attempts to write to memory in this region cause the system to give the process its own private copy of the page of physical storage.
PAGE_EXECUTE_WRITECOPY	There is nothing you can do to this region to cause an access violation. Attempts to write to memory in this region cause the system to give the process its own private copy of the page of physical storage.

The *x*86, MIPS, PowerPC, and Alpha platforms do not support the execute protection attribute, although the Win32 operating system software does support this attribute. These hardware platforms treat read access as execute access. This means that if you assign PAGE_EXECUTE protection to memory, that memory will also have read privileges. Of course, you should not rely on this behavior because Windows NT implementations on other CPUs may very well treat execute protection as execute-only protection.

Windows 95 assigns only the PAGE_NOACCESS, PAGE_READONLY, and PAGE_READWRITE protection attributes to pages of physical storage.

Copy-On-Write Access

The protection attributes listed in the table on the previous page should all be fairly self-explanatory except the last two: PAGE_WRITECOPY and PAGE_EXECUTE_WRITECOPY. These attributes exist to conserve RAM usage and space in the paging file. Win32 supports a mechanism that allows two or more processes to share a single block of data. There is usually no problem doing this as long as the processes all consider the block of data to be read-only or execute-only and do not attempt to write to it. If threads in different processes all wrote to the same block of data, there would be total chaos.

To prevent this chaos, *copy-on-write* protection is assigned to shared data by the operating system. When a thread in one process attempts to write to a shared block of data, the system intervenes and performs the following actions:

1. The system allocates a page of physical storage from the paging file.

2. The system finds a free page of memory in RAM.

3. The system copies the page containing the data that the thread attempted to write to a shared block of data to the free page of RAM obtained in step 2.

4. The system then maps the process's virtual memory address for this page to the new page of RAM.

After the system has performed these steps, the process is able to access its very own private instance of this page of data. In Chapter 8, sharing memory and copy-on-write protection are covered in much more detail.

In addition, you should not pass either PAGE_WRITECOPY or PAGE_EXECUTE_WRITECOPY when you are reserving address space or committing physical storage using the *VirtualAlloc* function. Doing so will cause the call to *VirtualAlloc* to fail; calling *GetLastError* returns ERROR_INVALID_PARAMETER. These two attributes are used by the operating system when it maps EXE and DLL file images.

Windows 95 does not support copy-on-write protection. When Windows 95 sees that copy-on-write protection has been requested, it immediately makes copies of the data instead of waiting for the attempted memory write.

Special Access Protection Attribute Flags

In addition to the protection attributes already discussed, there are two protection attribute flags: PAGE_NOCACHE and PAGE_GUARD. You use these two flags by bitwise ORing them with any of the protection attributes except PAGE_NOACCESS.

The first of these protection attribute flags, PAGE_NOCACHE, disables caching of the committed pages. This flag is not recommended for general use; it exists mostly for hardware device driver developers who need to manipulate memory buffers.

The second of these protection attribute flags, PAGE_GUARD, is also not recommended for general use. Windows NT uses this flag when it creates a thread's stack. See the section "A Thread's Stack" in Chapter 7 for more information about this flag.

Windows 95 ignores the PAGE_NOCACHE and PAGE_GUARD protection attribute flags.

Bringing It All Home

In this section, we'll bring address spaces, partitions, regions, blocks, and pages all together. The best way to start is by examining a virtual memory map that shows all the regions of address space within a single process. The process happens to be the VMMAP.EXE sample application, presented in Chapter 6. To fully understand the process's address space, we'll begin by discussing the address space as it appears when VMMap is running under Windows NT. A sample address space map is shown in Figure 5-5. Later I'll discuss the differences between the Windows NT and Windows 95 address spaces.

Base Address	Type	Size	Blocks	Protection Attribute(s)	Description
00000000	Free	65536			
00010000	Private	4096	1	-RW-	
00011000	Free	61440			
00020000	Private	4096	1	-RW-	
00021000	Free	61440			
00030000	Private	1048576	3	-RW-	Thread Stack
00130000	Private	4096	1	-RW-	
00131000	Free	61440			
00140000	Private	1048576	2	-RW-	Default Process Heap
00240000	Mapped	65536	2	-RW-	
00250000	Mapped	36864	1	-R--	
00259000	Free	28672			
00260000	Mapped	139264	1	-R--	
00282000	Free	57344			
00290000	Mapped	266240	1	-R--	
002D1000	Free	61440			
002E0000	Mapped	12288	1	-R--	
002E3000	Free	53248			
002F0000	Mapped	819200	4	ER--	
003B8000	Free	32768			
003C0000	Mapped	143360	1	-R--	
003E3000	Free	118784			
00400000	Image	36864	5	ERWC	C:\AdvWin\VMMAP.06\Dbg_x86\VMMAP.exe
00409000	Free	28672			
00410000	Mapped	3145728	2	ER--	
00710000	Private	4096	1	-RW-	
00711000	Free	61440			
00720000	Private	4096	1	-RW-	
00721000	Free	61440			
00730000	Private	4096	1	-RW-	
00731000	Free	61440			
00740000	Private	131072	2	-RW-	
00760000	Private	65536	2	-RW-	
00770000	Free	1999110144			
779F0000	Image	˙ 98304	5	ERWC	D:\WINNT\System32\MSVCRT40.dll
77A08000	Free	32768			
77A10000	Image	253952	5	ERWC	D:\WINNT\system32\msvcrt.dll
77A4E000	Free	3612672			
77DC0000	Image	249856	6	ERWC	D:\WINNT\system32\ADVAPI32.dll
77DFD000	Free	143360			

Figure 5-5. (continued)

A sample address space map showing regions under Windows NT.

Figure 5-5. *continued*

Base Address	Type	Size	Blocks	Protection Attribute(s)	Description
77E20000	Image	299008	5	ERWC	D:\WINNT\system32\RPCRT4.dll
77E69000	Free	28672			
77E70000	Image	335872	5	ERWC	D:\WINNT\system32\USER32.dll
77EC2000	Free	57344			
77ED0000	Image	176128	5	ERWC	D:\WINNT\system32\GDI32.dll
77EFB000	Free	20480			
77F00000	Image	372736	5	ERWC	D:\WINNT\system32\KERNEL32.dll
77F5B000	Free	20480			
77F60000	Image	372736	8	ERWC	D:\WINNT\System32\ntdll.dll
77FBB000	Free	123949056			
7F5F0000	Mapped	2097152	3	ER--	
7F7F0000	Free	8126464			
7FFB0000	Mapped	147456	1	-R--	
7FFD4000	Free	40960			
7FFDE000	Private	4096	1	ERW-	
7FFDF000	Private	4096	1	ERW-	
7FFE0000	Private	65536	2	-R--	

The address space map in Figure 5-5 shows the various regions in the process's address space. There is one region shown per line, and each line contains six fields.

The first, or leftmost, field shows the region's base address. You'll notice that we start walking the process's address space with the region at address 0x00000000 and ending with the last region of usable address space, which begins at address 0x7FFE0000. All regions are contiguous. You'll also notice that almost all of the base addresses for nonfree regions start on an even multiple of 64 KB. This is because of the allocation granularity of address space reservation imposed by the system. A region that does not start on an even allocation granularity boundary represents a region that was allocated by operating system code on your process's behalf.

The second field shows the region's type, which is one of the four values—free, private, image, or mapped—described in the following table.

Type	Description
Free	The region of address space is not reserved, and the application may reserve a region either at the shown base address or anywhere within the free region.
Private	The region contains physical storage residing in the system's paging file.
Image	The region contains physical storage residing in a memory-mapped EXE or DLL file.
Mapped	The region contains physical storage residing in a memory-mapped data file.

The way that my VMMap application calculates this field may lead to misleading results. When the region is not free, the VMMAP.EXE sample application guesses at which of the three remaining values applies—there is no Win32 API function we can call to request this region's exact usage. The way that I calculate this field's value is by scanning all of the blocks within the region and taking an educated guess. You should examine my code in Chapter 6 to better understand the way I calculate a field's value.

The third field shows the number of bytes that were reserved for the region. For example, the system mapped the image of USER32.DLL at memory address 0x77E70000. When the system reserved address space for this image, it needed to reserve 335,872 bytes. The number in the third field will always be an even multiple of the CPU's page size (4096 bytes for an *x*86).

The fourth field shows the number of blocks within the reserved region. A block is a set of contiguous pages that all have the same protection attributes and that are all backed by the same type of physical storage—I'll talk more about this in the next section of this chapter. For free regions, this value will always be 0 because no physical storage can be committed within a free region. (Nothing is displayed in the third column for a free region.) For the nonfree regions, this value can be anywhere from 1 to a maximum number of (region size/page size). For example, the region that begins at memory address 0x77E70000 has a region size of 335,872 bytes. Because this process is running on an *x*86

CPU, for which the page size is 4096 bytes, the maximum number of different committed blocks is 82 (335,872/4096); the map shows that there are 5 blocks in the region.

The fifth field on the line shows the region's protection attributes. The individual letters represent the following: E = execute, R = read, W = write, C = copy-on-write. If the region does not show any of these protection attributes, the region has no access protection. The free regions show no protection attributes because unreserved regions do not have protection attributes associated with them. Neither the guard protection attribute flag nor the no-cache protection attribute flag will ever appear here; these flags have meaning only when associated with physical storage, not reserved address space. Protection attributes are given to a region for the sake of efficiency only and are always overridden by protection attributes assigned to physical storage.

The sixth and last field shows a text description of what's in the region. For free regions, this field will always be blank; for private regions, it will usually be blank because VMMAP.EXE has no way of knowing why the application reserved this private region of address space. However, VMMAP.EXE can identify two types of private regions: thread stacks and the process's default heap. VMMAP.EXE can usually detect thread stacks because they will commonly have a block of physical storage within them with the guard protection attribute. However, when a thread's stack is full it will not have a block with the guard protection attribute, and VMMAP.EXE will be unable to detect it. VMMAP.EXE can detect the process's default heap (discussed in Chapter 9) by obtaining the region's base address and comparing it with the value returned by the *GetProcess-Heap* function.

For image regions, you can display the full pathname of the file that is mapped into the region. VMMAP.EXE obtains this information by calling *GetModuleFileName*. For mapped regions, nothing is displayed because VMMAP.EXE has no way of determining what data file the process has mapped to the region.

Inside the Regions

It is possible to break down the regions even further than shown in Figure 5-5. Figure 5-6 shows the same address space map as Figure 5-5, but the blocks contained inside each region are also displayed.

Base Address	Type	Size	Blocks	Protection Attribute(s)	Description
00000000	Free	65536			
00010000	Private	4096	1	-RW-	
00010000	Private	4096		-RW- --	
00011000	Free	61440			
00020000	Private	4096	1	-RW-	
00020000	Private	4096		-RW- --	
00021000	Free	61440			
00030000	Private	1048576	3	-RW-	Thread Stack
00030000	Reserve	1036288		-RW- --	
0012D000	Private	4096		-RW- G-	
0012E000	Private	8192		-RW- --	
00130000	Private	4096	1	-RW-	
00130000	Private	4096		-RW- --	
00131000	Free	61440			
00140000	Private	1048576	2	-RW-	Default Process Heap
00140000	Private	12288		-RW- --	
00143000	Reserve	1036288		-RW- --	
00240000	Mapped	65536	2	-RW-	
00240000	Mapped	4096		-RW- --	
00241000	Reserve	61440		-RW- --	
00250000	Mapped	36864	1	-R--	
00250000	Mapped	36864		-R-- --	
00259000	Free	28672			
00260000	Mapped	139264	1	-R--	
00260000	Mapped	139264		-R-- --	
00282000	Free	57344			
00290000	Mapped	266240	1	-R--	
00290000	Mapped	266240		-R-- --	
002D1000	Free	61440			
002E0000	Mapped	12288	1	-R--	
002E0000	Mapped	12288		-R-- --	
002E3000	Free	53248			
002F0000	Mapped	819200	4	ER--	
002F0000	Mapped	12288		ER-- --	
002F3000	Reserve	774144		ER-- --	
003B0000	Mapped	4096		ER-- --	
003B1000	Reserve	28672		ER-- --	
003B8000	Free	32768			
003C0000	Mapped	143360	1	-R--	
003C0000	Mapped	143360		-R-- --	
003E3000	Free	118784			
00400000	Image	36864	5	ERWC	C:\AdvWin\VMMAP.06\Dbg_x86\VMMAP.exe
00400000	Image	4096		-R-- --	
00401000	Image	12288		ER-- --	
00404000	Image	4096		-R-- --	
00405000	Image	8192		-RW- --	
00407000	Image	8192		-R-- --	
00409000	Free	28672			
00410000	Mapped	3145728	2	ER--	
00410000	Mapped	512000		ER-- --	
0048D000	Reserve	2633728		ER-- --	

Figure 5-6.

(continued)

A sample address space map showing blocks within regions under Windows NT.

Figure 5-6. *continued*

Base Address	Type	Size	Blocks	Protection Attribute(s)	Description
00710000	Private	4096		-RW- --	
00711000	Free	61440			
00720000	Private	4096	1	-RW-	
00720000	Private	4096		-RW- --	
00721000	Free	61440			
00730000	Private	4096	1	-RW-	
00730000	Private	4096		-RW- --	
00731000	Free	61440			
00740000	Private	131072	2	-RW-	
00740000	Private	4096		-RW- --	
00741000	Reserve	126976		-RW- --	
00760000	Private	65536	2	-RW-	
00760000	Private	8192		-RW- --	
00762000	Reserve	57344		-RW- --	
00770000	Free	1999110144			
779F0000	Image	98304	5	ERWC	D:\WINNT\System32\MSVCRT40.dll
779F0000	Image	4096		-R-- --	
779F1000	Image	32768		ER-- --	
779F9000	Image	49152		-R-- --	
77A05000	Image	4096		-RW- --	
77A06000	Image	8192		-R-- --	
77A08000	Free	32768			
77A10000	Image	253952	5	ERWC	D:\WINNT\system32\msvcrt.dll
77A10000	Image	4096		-R-- --	
77A11000	Image	184320		ER-- --	
77A3E000	Image	28672		-R-- --	
77A45000	Image	20480		-RW- --	
77A4A000	Image	16384		-R-- --	
77A4E000	Free	3612672			
77DC0000	Image	249856	6	ERWC	D:\WINNT\system32\ADVAPI32.dll
77DC0000	Image	4096		-R-- --	
77DC1000	Image	172032		ER-- --	
77DEB000	Image	36864		-R-- --	
77DF4000	Image	16384		-RWC --	
77DF8000	Image	4096		-RW- --	
77DF9000	Image	16384		-R-- --	
77DFD000	Free	143360			
77E20000	Image	299008	5	ERWC	D:\WINNT\system32\RPCRT4.dll
77E20000	Image	4096		-R-- --	
77E21000	Image	241664		ER-- --	
77E5C000	Image	16384		-R-- --	
77E60000	Image	4096		-RW- --	
77E61000	Image	32768		-R-- --	
77E69000	Free	28672			
77E70000	Image	335872	5	ERWC	D:\WINNT\system32\USER32.dll
77E70000	Image	4096		-R-- --	
77E71000	Image	258048		ER-- --	
77EB0000	Image	32768		-R-- --	
77EB8000	Image	4096		-RW- --	
77EB9000	Image	36864		-R-- --	
77EC2000	Free	57344			
77ED0000	Image	176128	5	ERWC	D:\WINNT\system32\GDI32.dll
77ED0000	Image	4096		-R-- --	
77ED1000	Image	143360		ER-- --	
77EF4000	Image	4096		-R-- --	

(continued)

Figure 5-6. *continued*

Base Address	Type	Size	Blocks	Protection Attribute(s)	Description
77EF5000	Image	4096		-RW- --	
77EF6000	Image	20480		-R-- --	
77EFB000	Free	20480			
77F00000	Image	372736	5	ERWC	D:\WINNT\system32\KERNEL32.dll
77F00000	Image	4096		-R-- --	
77F01000	Image	237568		ER-- --	
77F3B000	Image	36864		-R-- --	
77F44000	Image	8192		-RW- --	
77F46000	Image	86016		-R-- --	
77F5B000	Free	20480			
77F60000	Image	372736	8	ERWC	D:\WINNT\System32\ntdll.dll
77F60000	Image	4096		-R-- --	
77F61000	Image	233472		ER-- --	
77F9A000	Image	32768		-R-- --	
77FA2000	Image	4096		-RW- --	
77FA3000	Image	4096		-RWC --	
77FA4000	Image	8192		-RW- --	
77FA6000	Image	4096		-RWC --	
77FA7000	Image	81920		-R-- --	
77FBB000	Free	123949056			
7F5F0000	Mapped	2097152	3	ER--	
7F5F0000	Reserve	1048576		ER-- --	
7F6F0000	Mapped	28672		ER-- --	
7F6F7000	Reserve	1019904		ER-- --	
7F7F0000	Free	8126464			
7FFB0000	Mapped	147456	1	-R--	
7FFB0000	Mapped	147456		-R-- --	
7FFD4000	Free	40960			
7FFDE000	Private	4096	1	ERW-	
7FFDE000	Private	4096		ERW- --	
7FFDF000	Private	4096	1	ERW-	
7FFDF000	Private	4096		ERW- --	
7FFE0000	Private	65536	2	-R--	
7FFE0000	Private	4096		-R-- --	
7FFE1000	Reserve	61440		-R-- --	

Of course, free regions do not expand at all because they have no committed pages of storage within them. Each block line shows four fields, which are explained below.

The first field shows the address of a set of pages all having the same state and protection attributes. For example, a single page (4096 bytes) of memory with read protection is committed at address 0x779F0000. At address 0x779F1000, there is a block of 8 pages (32,768 bytes) of committed storage that has execute and read protection. If both of these blocks had the same protection attributes, the two would be combined and would appear as a single 9-page (36,864-byte) entry in the memory map.

The second field shows what type of physical storage is backing the block within the reserved region. One of five possible values can appear in this field: free, private, mapped, image, or reserve. A value of free, private, mapped, or image indicates that the block is backed by physical storage in the paging file, a data file, or a loaded EXE or DLL file, respectively. If the value is reserve, the block is not backed by any physical storage at all, but physical storage may be committed to it later.

For the most part, all the committed blocks within a single region are backed by the same type of physical storage. However, it is possible for different committed blocks within a single region to be backed by different types of physical storage. For example, a memory-mapped file image will be backed by an EXE or a DLL file. If you were to write to a single page in this region that had PAGE_WRITECOPY or PAGE_EXECUTE-_WRITECOPY, the system would make your process a private copy of the page backed by the paging file instead of the file image. This new page would have the same attributes as the original page without the copy-on-write protection attribute.

The third field shows the size of the block. All blocks are contiguous within a region—there will not be any gaps.

The fourth field shows the protection attributes and protection attribute flags of the block. A block's protection attributes override the protection attributes of the region that contains the block. The possible protection attributes are identical to those that can be specified for a region; however, the two protection attribute flags, PAGE_GUARD and PAGE_NOCACHE, which are never associated with a region, may be associated with a block.

Address Space Differences for Windows 95

Figure 5-7 shows the address space map when the same VMMAP.EXE program is executed under Windows 95.

Base Address	Type	Size	Blocks	Protection Attribute(s)	Description
00000000	Free	4194304			
00400000	Private	65536	4	- - - -	C:\ADVWIN3\REL_X86\VMMAP.EXE
00400000	Private	12288		-R-- --	
00403000	Private	8192		-RW- --	
00405000	Private	8192		-R-- --	
00407000	Reserve	36864		- - - - --	
00410000	Private	1114112	4	- - - -	Default Process Heap
00410000	Private	4096		-RW- --	
00411000	Reserve	1044480		- - - - --	
00510000	Private	4096		-RW- --	
00511000	Reserve	61440		- - - - --	
00520000	Private	65536	2	-RW-	
00520000	Private	4096		-RW- --	
00521000	Reserve	61440		-RW- --	
00530000	Private	1179648	6	- - - -	Thread Stack
00530000	Reserve	1077248		- - - - --	
00637000	Private	4096		-RW- --	
00638000	Reserve	24576		- - - - --	
0063E000	Private	4096		- - - - --	
0063F000	Private	4096		-RW- --	
00640000	Reserve	65536		- - - - --	
00650000	Private	1114112	4	- - - -	
00650000	Private	4096		-RW- --	
00651000	Reserve	1044480		- - - - --	
00750000	Private	4096		-RW- --	
00751000	Reserve	61440		- - - - --	
00760000	Private	4194304	2	-RW-	
00760000	Private	65536		-RW- --	
00770000	Reserve	4128768		-RW- --	
00B60000	Free	2001338368			
78000000	Private	327680	4	- - - -	C:\WINDOWS\SYSTEM\MSVCRT.DLL
78000000	Private	241664		-R-- --	
7803B000	Private	28672		-RW- --	
78042000	Private	16384		-R-- --	
78046000	Reserve	40960		- - - - --	
78050000	Free	133890048			
80000000	Private	4096	1	- - - -	
80000000	Reserve	4096		- - - - --	
80001000	Private	4096	1	- - - -	
80001000	Private	4096		-RW- --	

Figure 5-7. *(continued)*

A sample address space map showing blocks within regions under Windows 95.

Figure 5-7. *continued*

Base Address	Type	Size	Blocks	Protection Attribute(s)	Description
80002000	Private	4096	1	- - - -	
80002000	Private	4096		-RW- - -	
80003000	Private	12288	1	- - - -	
80003000	Private	12288		-RW- - -	
80006000	Private	8192	1	- - - -	
80006000	Private	8192		-RW- - -	
80008000	Private	589824	1	- - - -	
80008000	Private	589824		-RW- - -	
80098000	Private	65536	2	- - - -	
80098000	Private	12288		-RW- - -	
8009B000	Reserve	53248		- - - - - -	
800A8000	Private	4096	1	- - - -	
800A8000	Private	4096		-RW- - -	
800A9000	Private	454656	1	- - - -	
800A9000	Private	454656		-RW- - -	
80118000	Private	196608	1	- - - -	
80118000	Private	196608		-RW- - -	
80148000	Private	20971520	6	- - - -	
80148000	Private	331776		-RW- - -	
80199000	Reserve	20480		- - - - - -	
8019E000	Private	16384		-RW- - -	
801A2000	Reserve	4096		- - - - - -	
801A3000	Private	393216		-RW- - -	
80203000	Reserve	20205568		- - - - - -	
81548000	Private	139264	3	- - - -	
81548000	Reserve	65536		- - - - - -	
81558000	Private	8192		-RW- - -	
8155A000	Reserve	65536		- - - - - -	
8156A000	Private	1048576	3	- - - -	
8156A000	Private	53248		-RW- - -	
81577000	Reserve	991232		- - - - - -	
81669000	Private	4096		-RW- - -	
8166A000	Private	4194304	3	- - - -	
8166A000	Private	4096		-RW- - -	
8166B000	Reserve	4186112		- - - - - -	
81A69000	Private	4096		-RW- - -	
81A6A000	Private	16384	2	-RW-	
81A6A000	Private	4096		-RW- - -	
81A6B000	Reserve	12288		-RW- - -	

(continued)

Figure 5-7. *continued*

Base Address	Type	Size	Blocks	Protection Attribute(s)	Description
81A6E000	Private	16384	3	- - - -	
81A6E000	Private	4096		-RW- --	
81A6F000	Reserve	8192		- - - - --	
81A71000	Private	4096		-RW- --	
81A72000	Private	12288	1	- - - -	
81A72000	Private	12288		-R-- --	
81A75000	Private	12288	1	- - - -	
81A75000	Private	12288		-R-- --	
81A78000	Private	131072	1	- - - -	
81A78000	Private	131072		-R-- --	
81A98000	Private	36864	1	- - - -	
81A98000	Private	36864		-R-- --	
81AA1000	Private	4096	1	- - - -	
81AA1000	Private	4096		-RW- --	
81AA2000	Private	2228224	5	-RW-	
81AA2000	Private	69632		-RW- --	
81AB3000	Reserve	61440		-RW- --	
81AC2000	Private	12288		-RW- --	
81AC5000	Reserve	2080768		-RW- --	
81CC1000	Private	4096		-RW- --	
81CC2000	Private	4096	1	- - - -	
81CC2000	Private	4096		-RW- --	
81CC3000	Private	524288	3	- - - -	
81CC3000	Private	8192		-RW- --	
81CC5000	Reserve	512000		- - - - --	
81D42000	Private	4096		-RW- --	
81D43000	Private	4096	1	- - - -	
81D43000	Private	4096		-RW- --	
81D44000	Private	4096	1	- - - -	
81D44000	Private	4096		-RW- --	
81D45000	Private	4096	1	- - - -	
81D45000	Private	4096		-RW- --	
81D46000	Private	4096	1	- - - -	
81D46000	Private	4096		-RW- --	
81D47000	Private	2228224	5	-RW-	
81D47000	Private	69632		-RW- --	
81D58000	Reserve	61440		-RW- --	
81D67000	Private	12288		-RW- --	
81D6A000	Reserve	2080768		-RW- --	
81F66000	Private	4096		-RW- --	

(continued)

Figure 5-7. *continued*

Base Address	Type	Size	Blocks	Protection Attribute(s)	Description
81F67000	Private	2162688	5	-RW-	
81F67000	Private	4096		-RW- --	
81F68000	Reserve	61440		-RW- --	
81F77000	Private	20480		-RW- --	
81F7C000	Reserve	2072576		-RW- --	
82176000	Private	4096		-RW- --	
82177000	Private	4096	1	----	
82177000	Private	4096		-RW- --	
82178000	Private	20480	1	----	
82178000	Private	20480		-R-- --	
8217D000	Private	4096	1	----	
8217D000	Private	4096		-RW- --	
8217E000	Private	4096	1	----	
8217E000	Private	4096		-RW- --	
8217F000	Private	2097152	3	----	
8217F000	Private	4096		-RW- --	
82180000	Reserve	2088960		---- --	
8237E000	Private	4096		-RW- --	
8237F000	Private	4096	1	----	
8237F000	Private	4096		-RW- --	
82380000	Private	4096	1	----	
82380000	Private	4096		-RW- --	
82381000	Private	4096	1	----	
82381000	Private	4096		-RW- --	
82382000	Private	4096	1	----	
82382000	Private	4096		-RW- --	
82383000	Private	4096	1	----	
82383000	Private	4096		-RW- --	
82384000	Free	16384			
82388000	Private	4096	1	----	
82388000	Private	4096		-RW- --	
82389000	Free	172032			
823B3000	Private	4096	1	----	
823B3000	Private	4096		-RW- --	
823B4000	Private	1048576	3	----	
823B4000	Private	28672		-RW- --	
823BB000	Reserve	1015808		---- --	
824B3000	Private	4096		-RW- --	

(continued)

Figure 5-7. *continued*

Base Address	Type	Size	Blocks	Protection Attribute(s)	Description
824B4000	Private	1056768	3	- - - -	
824B4000	Private	4096		-RW- --	
824B5000	Reserve	1048576		- - - - --	
825B5000	Private	4096		-RW- --	
825B6000	Free	1030004736			
BFC00000	Private	393216	5	- - - -	
BFC00000	Private	249856		-R-- --	
BFC3D000	Private	4096		-RW- --	
BFC3E000	Private	12288		-R-- --	
BFC41000	Private	4096		-RW- --	
BFC42000	Private	122880		-R-- --	
BFC60000	Free	2031616			
BFE50000	Private	45056	5	- - - -	
BFE50000	Private	24576		-R-- --	
BFE56000	Private	4096		-RW- --	
BFE57000	Private	4096		-R-- --	
BFE58000	Private	4096		-RW- --	
BFE59000	Private	8192		-R-- --	
BFE5B000	Free	20480			
BFE60000	Private	65536	3	- - - -	
BFE60000	Private	40960		-R-- --	
BFE6A000	Private	8192		-RW- --	
BFE6C000	Private	16384		-R-- --	
BFE70000	Free	393216			
BFED0000	Private	57344	3	- - - -	C:\WINDOWS\SYSTEM\ADVAPI32.DLL
BFED0000	Private	40960		-R-- --	
BFEDA000	Private	8192		-RW- --	
BFEDC000	Private	8192		-R-- --	
BFEDE000	Free	335872			
BFF30000	Private	151552	5	- - - -	C:\WINDOWS\SYSTEM\GDI32.DLL
BFF30000	Private	110592		-R-- --	
BFF4B000	Private	12288		-RW- --	
BFF4E000	Private	12288		-R-- --	
BFF51000	Private	4096		-RW- --	
BFF52000	Private	12288		-R-- --	
BFF55000	Free	45056			
BFF60000	Private	61440	3	- - - -	C:\WINDOWS\SYSTEM\USER32.DLL
BFF60000	Private	28672		-R-- --	
BFF67000	Private	4096		-RW- --	
BFF68000	Private	28672		-R-- --	

(continued)

Figure 5-7. *continued*

Base Address	Type	Size	Blocks	Protection Attribute(s)	Description
BFF6F000	Free	4096			
BFF70000	Private	585728	5	----	C:\WINDOWS\SYSTEM\KERNEL32.DLL
BFF70000	Private	303104		-R-- --	
BFFBA000	Reserve	8192		---- --	
BFFBC000	Private	16384		-RW- --	
BFFC0000	Private	98304		-R-- --	
BFFD8000	Reserve	159744		---- --	
BFFFF000	Free	4096			

The biggest difference between the two address space maps is the lack of information offered under Windows 95. For example, each region and block will reflect whether the area of address space is free, reserve, or private. You will never see the words *mapped* or *image* because Windows 95 does not offer the additional information indicating whether the physical storage backing the region is a memory-mapped file or is contained in an EXE or a DLL's file image.

You'll notice that most of the region sizes are exact multiples of the allocation granularity (64 KB). If the sizes of the blocks contained within a region do not add up to a multiple of the allocation granularity, there is frequently a block of reserved address space at the end of the region. This block is whatever size is necessary to bring the region to an even 64 KB. For example, the region starting at address 0x00520000 consists of 2 blocks: a 4-KB committed block of storage and a reserved block that occupies a 60-KB range of memory addresses.

Finally, the protection flags never reflect execute or copy-on-write access because Windows 95 does not support these flags. The two protection attribute flags, no cache and guard, are also not supported. Because the guard flag is not supported, VMMAP.EXE uses a more complicated technique to determine whether a region of address space is reserved for a thread's stack.

You will notice that, unlike under Windows NT, under Windows 95 the region of address space between 0x80000000 and 0xBFFFFFFF can be examined. This is the partition that contains the address space shared by all Win32 applications. As you can see, the four system DLLs are loaded into this region of address space and are therefore available to all Win32 processes.

CHAPTER SIX

EXPLORING VIRTUAL MEMORY

In the last chapter, we discussed how the system manages virtual memory, how each process receives its own private address space, and what a process's address space looks like. In this chapter, we move away from the abstract and examine some of the Win32 functions that give us information about the system's memory management and about the virtual address space in a process.

System Information

To understand how Win32 uses virtual memory, you need to know how the current Win32 implementation works. The *GetSystemInfo* function retrieves information (including virtual memory information) about the current Win32 implementation:

```
VOID GetSystemInfo (LPSYSTEM_INFO lpSystemInfo);
```

You must pass the address of a **SYSTEM_INFO** structure to this function. The function will initialize the structure's members and return. Here is what the SYSTEM_INFO data structure looks like:

```
typedef struct _SYSTEM_INFO {
   union {
      DWORD dwOemId;                // Obsolete field...do not use
      struct {
         WORD wProcessorArchitecture;
         WORD wReserved;
      };
   };
   DWORD dwPageSize;
   LPVOID lpMinimumApplicationAddress;
   LPVOID lpMaximumApplicationAddress;
   DWORD dwActiveProcessorMask;
```

```
    DWORD dwNumberOfProcessors;
    DWORD dwProcessorType;
    DWORD dwAllocationGranularity;
    WORD wProcessorLevel;
    WORD wProcessorRevision;
} SYSTEM_INFO, *LPSYSTEM_INFO;
```

When the system boots, it determines what the values of these members should be; for a given system, the values will always be the same. *GetSystemInfo* exists so that an application can query these values at run time. Of all the members in the structure, only four of them have anything to do with memory. These four members are explained in the following table:

Member Name	Description
dwPageSize	Shows the size of a memory page. On *x*86, MIPS, and PowerPC CPUs, this value is 4096 bytes. On Alpha CPUs, this value is 8192 bytes.
lpMinimumApplicationAddress	Gives the minimum memory address of every process's usable address space. On Microsoft Windows 95, this value is 4,194,304, or 0x00400000, because the bottom 4 MB of every process's address space is inaccessible. On Microsoft Windows NT, this value is 65,536, or 0x00010000, because the first 64 KB of every process's address space is reserved.
lpMaximumApplicationAddress	Gives the maximum memory address of every process's usable private address space. On Windows 95, this address is 2,147,483,647, or 0x7FFFFFFF, because the shared memory-mapped file region and the shared operating system code are contained in the top 2-GB partition. On Windows NT, this address is 2,147,418,111, or 0x7FFEFFFF, because unusable address space begins just 64 KB below the 2-GB line and extends to the end of the process's address space.
dwAllocationGranularity	Shows the granularity of a reserved region of address space. As of this writing, this value is 65,536 because all implementations of Win32 reserve address space on even 64-KB boundaries.

The System Information Sample Application

The SysInfo application (SYSINFO.EXE), listed in Figure 6-1 beginning on page 152, is a very simple program that calls *GetSystemInfo* and displays the information returned in the SYSTEM_INFO structure. The source code and resource files for the application are in the SYSINFO directory on the companion disc. The following dialog boxes show the results of running the SysInfo application on several different platforms.

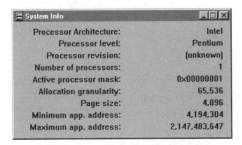

Windows 95 on Intel x86.

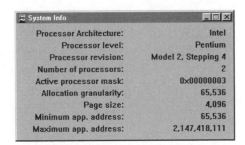

Windows NT on Intel x86.

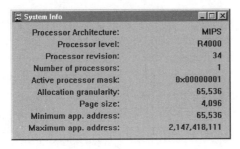

Windows NT on MIPS R4000.

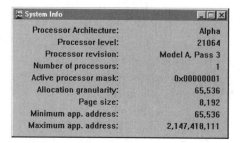

Windows NT on DEC Alpha.

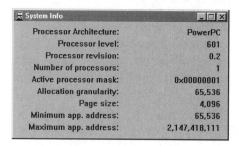

Windows NT on PowerPC.

SysInfo.ico

SYSINFO.C

```
/*********************************************************
Module name: SysInfo.C
Notices: Copyright (c) 1995-1997 Jeffrey Richter
*********************************************************/


#include "..\CmnHdr.H"                    /* See Appendix C. */
#include <windows.h>
#include <windowsx.h>
#include <tchar.h>
#include <stdio.h>
#include "Resource.H"



///////////////////////////////////////////////////////////



// Set to TRUE if the app is running on Windows 95.
BOOL g_fWin95IsHost = FALSE;
```

Figure 6-1.
The SysInfo application.

(continued)

Figure 6-1. *continued*

```
////////////////////////////////////////////////////////////


// This function accepts a number and converts it to a
// string, inserting commas where appropriate.
LPTSTR BigNumToString (LONG lNum, LPTSTR szBuf) {
   WORD wNumDigits = 0, wNumChars = 0;

   do {
      // Put the last digit of the string
      // in the character buffer.
      szBuf[wNumChars++] = (TCHAR) (lNum % 10 + __TEXT('0'));

      // Increment the number of digits
      // that we put in the string.
      wNumDigits++;

      // For every three digits put in
      // the string, add a comma (,).
      if (wNumDigits % 3 == 0)
         szBuf[wNumChars++] = __TEXT(',');

      // Divide the number by 10, and repeat the process.
      lNum /= 10;

      // Continue adding digits to the
      // string until the number is zero.
   } while (lNum != 0);

   // If the last character added to
   // the string was a comma, truncate it.
   if (szBuf[wNumChars - 1] == __TEXT(','))
      szBuf[wNumChars - 1] = 0;

   // Ensure that the string is zero-terminated.
   szBuf[wNumChars] = 0;

   // We added all the characters to the string in
   // reverse order. We must reverse the contents
   // of the string.
   _tcsrev(szBuf);

   // Returns the address of the string.  This is the same
   // value that was passed to us initially.  Returning it
```

(continued)

149

Figure 6-1. *continued*

```
    // here makes it easier for the calling function to
    // use the string.
    return(szBuf);
}


///////////////////////////////////////////////////////////////


void ShowCPUInfo (HWND hwnd,
    WORD wProcessorArchitecture, WORD wProcessorLevel,
    WORD wProcessorRevision) {

    TCHAR szCPUArch[64];
    TCHAR szCPULevel[64];
    TCHAR szCPURev[64];
    szCPULevel[0] = 0;
    szCPURev[0] = 0;

    switch (wProcessorArchitecture) {
        case PROCESSOR_ARCHITECTURE_INTEL:
            lstrcpy(szCPUArch, __TEXT("Intel"));
            switch (wProcessorLevel) {
            case 3: case 4:
                wsprintf(szCPULevel, __TEXT("80%c86"),
                    wProcessorLevel + '0');
                if (!g_fWin95IsHost)
                    wsprintf(szCPURev, __TEXT("%c%d"),
                        HIBYTE(wProcessorRevision) + __TEXT('A'),
                        LOBYTE(wProcessorRevision));
                else
                    lstrcpy(szCPURev, __TEXT("(unknown)"));
                break;
            case 5:
                wsprintf(szCPULevel, __TEXT("Pentium"));
                if (!g_fWin95IsHost)
                    wsprintf(szCPURev,
                        __TEXT("Model %d, Stepping %d"),
                        HIBYTE(wProcessorRevision),
                        LOBYTE(wProcessorRevision));
                else
                    lstrcpy(szCPURev, __TEXT("(unknown)"));
                break;
            }
            break;
```

(continued)

Figure 6-1. *continued*

```
      case PROCESSOR_ARCHITECTURE_MIPS:
         lstrcpy(szCPUArch, __TEXT("MIPS"));
         wsprintf(szCPULevel, __TEXT("R%04d"),
            LOBYTE(wProcessorLevel) * 1000);
         wsprintf(szCPURev, __TEXT("%d"),
            LOBYTE(wProcessorRevision));
         break;

      case PROCESSOR_ARCHITECTURE_ALPHA:
         lstrcpy(szCPUArch, __TEXT("Alpha"));
         wsprintf(szCPULevel, __TEXT("%d"), wProcessorLevel);
         wsprintf(szCPURev, __TEXT("Model %c, Pass %d"),
            HIBYTE(wProcessorRevision) + __TEXT('A'),
            LOBYTE(wProcessorRevision));
         break;

      case PROCESSOR_ARCHITECTURE_PPC:
         lstrcpy(szCPUArch, __TEXT("PowerPC"));
         switch (wProcessorLevel) {
         case 1: case 3: case 4: case 20:
            wsprintf(szCPULevel, __TEXT("%d"),
               600 + wProcessorLevel);
            break;
         case 6:
            wsprintf(szCPULevel, __TEXT("603+"),
               wProcessorLevel);
            break;
         case 9:
            wsprintf(szCPULevel, __TEXT("604+"),
               wProcessorLevel);
            break;
         }
         wsprintf(szCPURev, __TEXT("%d.%d"),
            HIBYTE(wProcessorRevision),
            LOBYTE(wProcessorRevision));
         break;

      case PROCESSOR_ARCHITECTURE_UNKNOWN:
      default:
         wsprintf(szCPUArch, __TEXT("Unknown"));
         break;
   }
   SetDlgItemText(hwnd, IDC_PROCARCH,  szCPUArch);
   SetDlgItemText(hwnd, IDC_PROCLEVEL, szCPULevel);
```

(continued)

Figure 6-1. *continued*

```
   SetDlgItemText(hwnd, IDC_PROCREV,   szCPURev);
}


///////////////////////////////////////////////////////////


BOOL Dlg_OnInitDialog (HWND hwnd, HWND hwndFocus,
  LPARAM lParam) {

  TCHAR szBuf[50];
  SYSTEM_INFO sinf;

  // Associate an icon with the dialog box.
  chSETDLGICONS(hwnd, IDI_SYSINFO, IDI_SYSINFO);

  GetSystemInfo(&sinf);

  if (g_fWin95IsHost) {
     sinf.wProcessorLevel = (WORD)
        (sinf.dwProcessorType / 100);
  }

  ShowCPUInfo(hwnd, sinf.wProcessorArchitecture,
     sinf.wProcessorLevel, sinf.wProcessorRevision);

  SetDlgItemText(hwnd, IDC_PAGESIZE,
     BigNumToString(sinf.dwPageSize, szBuf));

  SetDlgItemText(hwnd, IDC_MINAPPADDR,
     BigNumToString((LONG) sinf.lpMinimumApplicationAddress,
     szBuf));

  SetDlgItemText(hwnd, IDC_MAXAPPADDR,
     BigNumToString((LONG) sinf.lpMaximumApplicationAddress,
     szBuf));

  _stprintf(szBuf, __TEXT("0x%08X"),
     sinf.dwActiveProcessorMask);
  SetDlgItemText(hwnd, IDC_ACTIVEPROCMASK, szBuf);

  SetDlgItemText(hwnd, IDC_NUMOFPROCS,
     BigNumToString(sinf.dwNumberOfProcessors, szBuf));
```

(continued)

Figure 6-1. *continued*

```
   SetDlgItemText(hwnd, IDC_ALLOCGRAN,
      BigNumToString(sinf.dwAllocationGranularity, szBuf));

   return(TRUE);
}


///////////////////////////////////////////////////////////////


void Dlg_OnCommand (HWND hwnd, int id, HWND hwndCtl,
   UINT codeNotify) {

   switch (id) {
      case IDCANCEL:
         EndDialog(hwnd, id);
         break;
   }
}


///////////////////////////////////////////////////////////////


BOOL CALLBACK Dlg_Proc (HWND hDlg, UINT uMsg,
   WPARAM wParam, LPARAM lParam) {

   BOOL fProcessed = TRUE;

   switch (uMsg) {
      chHANDLE_DLGMSG(hDlg, WM_INITDIALOG, Dlg_OnInitDialog);
      chHANDLE_DLGMSG(hDlg, WM_COMMAND, Dlg_OnCommand);

      default:
         fProcessed = FALSE;
         break;
   }
   return(fProcessed);
}


///////////////////////////////////////////////////////////////
```

(continued)

Figure 6-1. *continued*

```
int WINAPI _tWinMain (HINSTANCE hinstExe,
   HINSTANCE hinstPrev, LPTSTR pszCmdLine, int nCmdShow) {

   OSVERSIONINFO osvi;

   chWARNIFUNICODEUNDERWIN95();

   osvi.dwOSVersionInfoSize = sizeof(osvi);
   GetVersionEx(&osvi);
   g_fWin95IsHost =
      (osvi.dwPlatformId == VER_PLATFORM_WIN32_WINDOWS);

   DialogBox(hinstExe, MAKEINTRESOURCE(IDD_SYSINFO),
      NULL, Dlg_Proc);

   return(0);
}


/////////////////////// End Of File ///////////////////////
```

SYSINFO.RC

```
//Microsoft Developer Studio generated resource script.
//
#include "Resource.h"

#define APSTUDIO_READONLY_SYMBOLS
/////////////////////////////////////////////////////////////
//
// Generated from the TEXTINCLUDE 2 resource.
//
#include "afxres.h"


/////////////////////////////////////////////////////////////
#undef APSTUDIO_READONLY_SYMBOLS


/////////////////////////////////////////////////////////////
// English (U.S.) resources

#if !defined(AFX_RESOURCE_DLL) || defined(AFX_TARG_ENU)
#ifdef _WIN32
LANGUAGE LANG_ENGLISH, SUBLANG_ENGLISH_US
```

(continued)

Figure 6-1. *continued*

```
#pragma code_page(1252)
#endif //_WIN32

#ifdef APSTUDIO_INVOKED
/////////////////////////////////////////////////////////////
//
// TEXTINCLUDE
//

1 TEXTINCLUDE DISCARDABLE
BEGIN
    "Resource.h\0"
END

2 TEXTINCLUDE DISCARDABLE
BEGIN
    "#include ""afxres.h""\r\n"
    "\0"
END

3 TEXTINCLUDE DISCARDABLE
BEGIN
    "\r\n"
    "\0"
END

#endif    // APSTUDIO_INVOKED


/////////////////////////////////////////////////////////////
//
// Dialog
//

IDD_SYSINFO DIALOG DISCARDABLE  18, 18, 186, 97
STYLE WS_MINIMIZEBOX | WS_POPUP | WS_VISIBLE | WS_CAPTION
    | WS_SYSMENU
CAPTION "System Info"
FONT 8, "System"
BEGIN
    RTEXT           "Processor Architecture:",IDC_STATIC,
                    4,4,88,8,SS_NOPREFIX
    RTEXT           "ID_PROCARCH",IDC_PROCARCH,96,4,84,8,
                    SS_NOPREFIX
```

(continued)

Figure 6-1. *continued*

```
    RTEXT           "Processor level:",IDC_STATIC,4,14,88,
                    8,SS_NOPREFIX
    RTEXT           "ID_PROCLEVEL",IDC_PROCLEVEL,96,14,84,
                    8,SS_NOPREFIX
    RTEXT           "Processor revision:",IDC_STATIC,4,24,
                    88,8,SS_NOPREFIX
    RTEXT           "ID_PROCREV",IDC_PROCREV,96,24,84,8,
                    SS_NOPREFIX
    RTEXT           "Number of processors:",IDC_STATIC,4,
                    34,88,8,SS_NOPREFIX
    RTEXT           "ID_NUMOFPROCS",IDC_NUMOFPROCS,96,34,
                    84,8,SS_NOPREFIX
    RTEXT           "Active processor mask:",IDC_STATIC,
                    4,44,88,8,SS_NOPREFIX
    RTEXT           "ID_ACTIVEPROCMASK",IDC_ACTIVEPROCMASK,
                    96,44,84,8,SS_NOPREFIX
    RTEXT           "Allocation granularity:",IDC_STATIC,
                    4,54,88,8,SS_NOPREFIX
    RTEXT           "ID_ALLOCGRAN",IDC_ALLOCGRAN,96,54,
                    84,8,SS_NOPREFIX
    RTEXT           "Page size:",IDC_STATIC,4,64,88,8,
                    SS_NOPREFIX
    RTEXT           "ID_PAGESIZE",IDC_PAGESIZE,96,64,84,
                    8,SS_NOPREFIX
    RTEXT           "Minimum app. address:",IDC_STATIC,
                    4,74,88,8,SS_NOPREFIX
    RTEXT           "ID_MINAPPADDR",IDC_MINAPPADDR,96,74,
                    84,8,SS_NOPREFIX
    RTEXT           "Maximum app. address:",IDC_STATIC,4,
                    84,88,8,SS_NOPREFIX
    RTEXT           "ID_MAXAPPADDR",IDC_MAXAPPADDR,96,84,
                    84,8,SS_NOPREFIX
END


/////////////////////////////////////////////////////////
//
// Icon
//

// Icon with lowest ID value placed first to ensure
// application icon remains consistent on all systems.
IDI_SYSINFO         ICON   DISCARDABLE    "SysInfo.Ico"
```

(continued)

Figure 6-1. *continued*

```
/////////////////////////////////////////////////////////////
//
// DESIGNINFO
//

#ifdef APSTUDIO_INVOKED
GUIDELINES DESIGNINFO DISCARDABLE
BEGIN
    IDD_SYSINFO, DIALOG
    BEGIN
        RIGHTMARGIN, 170
        BOTTOMMARGIN, 77
    END
END
#endif    // APSTUDIO_INVOKED

#endif    // English (U.S.) resources
/////////////////////////////////////////////////////////////



#ifndef APSTUDIO_INVOKED
/////////////////////////////////////////////////////////////
//
// Generated from the TEXTINCLUDE 3 resource.
//



/////////////////////////////////////////////////////////////
#endif    // not APSTUDIO_INVOKED
```

Virtual Memory Status

A Win32 function called *GlobalMemoryStatus* retrieves dynamic information about the current state of memory:

```
VOID GlobalMemoryStatus (LPMEMORYSTATUS lpmstMemStat);
```

I think that this function is very poorly named—*GlobalMemory-
Status* implies that the function is somehow related to the global heaps
in 16-bit Windows. Win32 does not have a global heap but does offer
the old global heap functions such as *GlobalAlloc* purely to ease the burden of porting a 16-bit Windows application to Win32. I think that
GlobalMemoryStatus should have been called something like *VirtualMem-
oryStatus* instead.

When you call *GlobalMemoryStatus*, you must pass the address of a MEMORYSTATUS structure. Here is what the MEMORYSTATUS data structure looks like:

```
typedef struct _MEMORYSTATUS {
    DWORD dwLength;
    DWORD dwMemoryLoad;
    DWORD dwTotalPhys;
    DWORD dwAvailPhys;
    DWORD dwTotalPageFile;
    DWORD dwAvailPageFile;
    DWORD dwTotalVirtual;
    DWORD dwAvailVirtual;
} MEMORYSTATUS, *LPMEMORYSTATUS;
```

Before calling *GlobalMemoryStatus*, you must initialize the *dwLength* member to the size of the structure in bytes—that is, sizeof(MEMO-RYSTATUS). This initialization allows Microsoft to add members to this structure in future versions of the Win32 API without breaking existing applications. When you call *GlobalMemoryStatus*, it will initialize the remainder of the structure's members and return. The VMStat sample application in the next section describes the various members and their meanings.

The Virtual Memory Status Sample Application

The VMStat application (VMSTAT.EXE), listed in Figure 6-2 beginning on page 160, displays a simple dialog box that lists the results of a call to *GlobalMemoryStatus*. The information inside the dialog box is updated once every second, so you may want to keep the application running while you work with other processes on your system. The source code and resource files for the application are in the VMSTAT directory on the companion disc. Below is the result of running this program on Windows NT using a 32-MB Intel Pentium machine:

VMStat	
Memory load:	83
TotalPhys:	32,956,416
AvailPhys:	1,142,784
TotalPageFile:	57,503,744
AvailPageFile:	33,816,576
TotalVirtual:	2,147,352,576
AvailVirtual:	2,131,615,744

The *dwMemoryLoad* member (shown as Memory Load) gives a rough estimate of how busy the memory management system is. This number can be anywhere from 0 to 100. The exact algorithm used to calculate this value varies between Windows 95 and Windows NT. In addition, the algorithm is subject to change in future versions of the operating system. In practice, the value reported by this member variable is all but useless.

The *dwTotalPhys* member (shown as TotalPhys) indicates the total number of bytes of physical memory (RAM) that exist. On this 32-MB Pentium machine, this value is 32,956,416, which is just 598,016 bytes under 32 MB. The reason that *GlobalMemoryStatus* does not report the full 32 MB is because the system reserves some storage as a nonpaged pool during the boot process. This memory is not even considered available to the kernel. The *dwAvailPhys* member (shown as AvailPhys) indicates the total number of bytes of physical memory available for allocation.

The *dwTotalPageFile* member (shown as TotalPageFile) indicates the maximum number of bytes that can be contained in the paging file(s) on your hard disk(s). Although VMStat reported that the paging file is currently 57,503,744 bytes, the system can expand and shrink the paging file as it sees fit. The *dwAvailPageFile* member (shown as AvailPageFile) indicates that 33,816,576 bytes in the paging file(s) are not committed to any process and are currently available should a process decide to commit any private storage.

The *dwTotalVirtual* member (shown as TotalVirtual) indicates the total number of bytes that are private in each process's address space. The value 2,147,352,576 is 128 KB short of being exactly 2 GB. The two partitions from 0x00000000 through 0x0000FFFF and from 0x7FFF0000 through 0x7FFFFFFF of inaccessible address space account for the 128-KB difference. If you run VMStat under Windows 95, you'll see that *dwTotalVirtual* comes back with a value of 2,143,289,344, which is just 4-MB short of being exactly 2 GB. The 4-MB difference exists because the system never lets an application gain access to the 4-MB partition from 0x00000000 through 0x003FFFFF.

The last member, *dwAvailVirtual* (shown as AvailVirtual), is the only member of the structure specific to the process calling *GlobalMemoryStatus*—all the other members apply to the system and would be the same regardless of which process was calling *GlobalMemoryStatus*. To calculate this value, *GlobalMemoryStatus* adds up all of the free regions in the calling process's address space. The *dwAvailVirtual* value 2,131,615,744 indicates the amount of free address space that is available for VMStat to do with what it wants. If you subtract the *dwAvailVirtual* member from the *dwTotalVirtual* member, you'll see that VMStat has 15,736,832 bytes reserved in its virtual address space.

There is no member that indicates the amount of physical storage currently in use by the process.

VMStat.ico

VMSTAT.C

```
/***************************************************************
Module name: VMStat.C
Notices: Copyright (c) 1995-1997 Jeffrey Richter
***************************************************************/


#include "..\CmnHdr.H"                    /* See Appendix C. */
#include <windows.h>
#include <windowsx.h>
#include <tchar.h>
#include "Resource.H"


///////////////////////////////////////////////////////////////


// The update timer's ID
#define IDT_UPDATE    1


///////////////////////////////////////////////////////////////


// This function accepts a number and converts it to a string,
// inserting commas where appropriate.
LPTSTR WINAPI BigNumToString (LONG lNum, LPTSTR szBuf) {
   WORD wNumDigits = 0, wNumChars = 0;

   do {
      // Put the last digit of the string
      // in the character buffer.
      szBuf[wNumChars++] = (TCHAR) (lNum % 10 + __TEXT('0'));

      // Increment the number of digits
      // that we put in the string.
      wNumDigits++;
```

Figure 6-2.

The VMStat application.

(continued)

Figure 6-2. *continued*

```
      // For every three digits put in
      // the string, add a comma (,).
      if (wNumDigits % 3 == 0)
         szBuf[wNumChars++] = __TEXT(',');

      // Divide the number by 10, and repeat the process.
      lNum /= 10;

      // Continue adding digits to
      // the string until the number is zero.
   } while (lNum != 0);

   // If the last character added to
   // the string was a comma, truncate it.
   if (szBuf[wNumChars - 1] == __TEXT(','))
      szBuf[wNumChars - 1] = 0;

   // Ensure that the string is zero-terminated.
   szBuf[wNumChars] = 0;

   // We added all the characters to the string in reverse
   // order. We must reverse the contents of the string.
   _tcsrev(szBuf);

   // Returns the address of the string.  This is the same
   // value that was passed to us initially.  Returning it
   // here makes it easier for the calling function
   // to use the string.
   return(szBuf);
}


////////////////////////////////////////////////////////////////


BOOL Dlg_OnInitDialog (HWND hwnd, HWND hwndFocus,
   LPARAM lParam) {

   // Associate an icon with the dialog box.
   chSETDLGICONS(hwnd, IDI_VMSTAT, IDI_VMSTAT);

   // Set a timer so that the information updates periodically.
   SetTimer(hwnd, IDT_UPDATE, 1 * 1000, NULL);
```

(continued)

Figure 6-2. *continued*

```
    // Force a timer message for the initial update.
    FORWARD_WM_TIMER(hwnd, IDT_UPDATE, SendMessage);

    return(TRUE);
}


//////////////////////////////////////////////////////////////


void Dlg_OnTimer(HWND hwnd, UINT id) {

    TCHAR szBuf[50];
    MEMORYSTATUS ms;

    // Initialize the structure length before
    // calling GlobalMemoryStatus.
    ms.dwLength = sizeof(ms);
    GlobalMemoryStatus(&ms);

    // Fill the static controls in the
    // list box with the appropriate number.
    SetDlgItemText(hwnd, IDC_MEMLOAD,
        BigNumToString(ms.dwMemoryLoad, szBuf));

    SetDlgItemText(hwnd, IDC_TOTALPHYS,
        BigNumToString(ms.dwTotalPhys, szBuf));

    SetDlgItemText(hwnd, IDC_AVAILPHYS,
        BigNumToString(ms.dwAvailPhys, szBuf));

    SetDlgItemText(hwnd, IDC_TOTALPAGEFILE,
        BigNumToString(ms.dwTotalPageFile, szBuf));

    SetDlgItemText(hwnd, IDC_AVAILPAGEFILE,
        BigNumToString(ms.dwAvailPageFile, szBuf));

    SetDlgItemText(hwnd, IDC_TOTALVIRTUAL,
        BigNumToString(ms.dwTotalVirtual, szBuf));

    SetDlgItemText(hwnd, IDC_AVAILVIRTUAL,
        BigNumToString(ms.dwAvailVirtual, szBuf));
}
```

(continued)

Figure 6-2. *continued*

```
///////////////////////////////////////////////////////////////


void Dlg_OnCommand (HWND hwnd, int id, HWND hwndCtl,
  UINT codeNotify) {

  switch (id) {
    case IDCANCEL:
       KillTimer(hwnd, IDT_UPDATE);
       EndDialog(hwnd, id);
       break;
  }
}


///////////////////////////////////////////////////////////////


BOOL CALLBACK Dlg_Proc (HWND hwnd, UINT uMsg,
  WPARAM wParam, LPARAM lParam) {

  switch (uMsg) {
     chHANDLE_DLGMSG(hwnd, WM_INITDIALOG, Dlg_OnInitDialog);
     chHANDLE_DLGMSG(hwnd, WM_COMMAND,    Dlg_OnCommand);
     chHANDLE_DLGMSG(hwnd, WM_TIMER,      Dlg_OnTimer);
  }
  return(FALSE);
}


///////////////////////////////////////////////////////////////


int WINAPI _tWinMain (HINSTANCE hinstExe,
  HINSTANCE hinstPrev, LPTSTR pszCmdLine, int nCmdShow) {

  chWARNIFUNICODEUNDERWIN95();
  DialogBox(hinstExe, MAKEINTRESOURCE(IDD_VMSTAT),
    NULL, Dlg_Proc);

  return(0);
}


//////////////////////// End Of File ////////////////////////
```

(continued)

163

Figure 6-2. *continued*

VMSTAT.RC

```
//Microsoft Developer Studio generated resource script.
//
#include "Resource.h"

#define APSTUDIO_READONLY_SYMBOLS
/////////////////////////////////////////////////////////////
//
// Generated from the TEXTINCLUDE 2 resource.
//
#include "afxres.h"


/////////////////////////////////////////////////////////////
#undef APSTUDIO_READONLY_SYMBOLS


/////////////////////////////////////////////////////////////
// English (U.S.) resources

#if !defined(AFX_RESOURCE_DLL) || defined(AFX_TARG_ENU)
#ifdef _WIN32
LANGUAGE LANG_ENGLISH, SUBLANG_ENGLISH_US
#pragma code_page(1252)
#endif //_WIN32

#ifdef APSTUDIO_INVOKED
/////////////////////////////////////////////////////////////
//
// TEXTINCLUDE
//

1 TEXTINCLUDE DISCARDABLE
BEGIN
    "Resource.h\0"
END

2 TEXTINCLUDE DISCARDABLE
BEGIN
    "#include ""afxres.h""\r\n"
    "\0"
END

3 TEXTINCLUDE DISCARDABLE
BEGIN
    "\r\n"
    "\0"
END
```

(continued)

Figure 6-2. *continued*

```
#endif    // APSTUDIO_INVOKED
///////////////////////////////////////////////////////////
//
// Dialog
//

IDD_VMSTAT DIALOG DISCARDABLE  60, 60, 104, 82
STYLE WS_MINIMIZEBOX | WS_POPUP | WS_VISIBLE | WS_CAPTION
    | WS_SYSMENU
CAPTION "VMStat"
FONT 8, "Arial"
BEGIN
    LTEXT          "Memory load:",IDC_STATIC,2,0,51,8
    RTEXT          "Text",IDC_MEMLOAD,52,0,48,8
    LTEXT          "TotalPhys:",IDC_STATIC,2,12,51,8
    RTEXT          "Text",IDC_TOTALPHYS,52,12,48,8
    LTEXT          "AvailPhys:",IDC_STATIC,2,24,51,8
    RTEXT          "Text",IDC_AVAILPHYS,52,24,48,8
    LTEXT          "TotalPageFile:",IDC_STATIC,2,36,51,8
    RTEXT          "Text",IDC_TOTALPAGEFILE,52,36,48,8
    LTEXT          "AvailPageFile:",IDC_STATIC,2,48,51,8
    RTEXT          "Text",IDC_AVAILPAGEFILE,52,48,48,8
    LTEXT          "TotalVirtual:",IDC_STATIC,2,60,51,8
    RTEXT          "Text",IDC_TOTALVIRTUAL,52,60,48,8
    LTEXT          "AvailVirtual:",IDC_STATIC,2,72,51,8
    RTEXT          "Text",IDC_AVAILVIRTUAL,52,72,48,8
END


///////////////////////////////////////////////////////////
//
// Icon
//

// Icon with lowest ID value placed first to ensure
// application icon remains consistent on all systems.
IDI_VMSTAT              ICON    DISCARDABLE    "VMStat.Ico"
#endif    // English (U.S.) resources
///////////////////////////////////////////////////////////


#ifndef APSTUDIO_INVOKED
///////////////////////////////////////////////////////////
//
```

(continued)

Figure 6-2. *continued*

```
// Generated from the TEXTINCLUDE 3 resource.
//


/////////////////////////////////////////////////////////////////
#endif    // not APSTUDIO_INVOKED
```

Determining the State of an Address Space

Win32 offers a function that lets you query certain information (for example, size, storage type, and protection attributes) about a memory address in your address space. In fact, the VMMap sample application shown later in this chapter uses this function to produce the virtual memory map dumps that appeared in Chapter 5. This Win32 function is called *VirtualQuery*:

```
DWORD VirtualQuery(LPVOID lpAddress,
    PMEMORY_BASIC_INFORMATION lpBuffer,
    DWORD dwLength);
```

When you call *VirtualQuery*, the first parameter, *lpAddress*, must contain the virtual memory address that you want information about. The *lpBuffer* parameter is the address to a MEMORY_BASIC_INFORMATION structure that you must allocate. This structure is defined in WINNT.H as follows:

```
typedef struct _MEMORY_BASIC_INFORMATION {
    PVOID BaseAddress;
    PVOID AllocationBase;
    DWORD AllocationProtect;
    DWORD RegionSize;
    DWORD State;
    DWORD Protect;
    DWORD Type;
} MEMORY_BASIC_INFORMATION, *PMEMORY_BASIC_INFORMATION;
```

The last parameter, *dwLength*, specifies the size of a MEMORY_BASIC_INFORMATION structure. *VirtualQuery* returns the number of bytes copied into the buffer.

Based on the address that you pass in the *lpAddress* parameter, *VirtualQuery* fills the MEMORY_BASIC_INFORMATION structure with information about the range of adjoining pages that share the same state, protection attributes, and type. See the following table for a description of the structure's members.

Member Name	Description
BaseAddress	This is the same value as the *lpAddress* parameter rounded down to an even page boundary.
AllocationBase	Identifies the base address of the region containing the address specified in the *lpAddress* parameter.
AllocationProtect	Identifies the protection attribute assigned to the region when it was initially reserved.
RegionSize	Identifies the size, in bytes, for all pages starting at *BaseAddress* that have the same protection attributes, state, and type as the page containing the address specified in the *lpAddress* parameter.
State	Identifies the state (MEM_FREE, MEM_RESERVE, or MEM_COMMIT) for all adjoining pages that have the same protection attributes, state, and type as the page containing the address specified in the *lpAddress* parameter. If the state is free, the *AllocationBase*, *AllocationProtect*, *Protect*, and *Type* members are undefined. If the state is reserve, the *Protect* member is undefined.
Protect	Identifies the protection attribute (PAGE_*) for all adjoining pages that have the same protection attributes, state, and type as the page containing the address specified in the *lpAddress* parameter.
Type	Identifies the type of physical storage (MEM_IMAGE, MEM_MAPPED, or MEM_PRIVATE) that is backing all adjoining pages that have the same protection attributes, state, and type as the page containing the address specified in the *lpAddress* parameter. For Windows 95, this member will always indicate MEM_PRIVATE.

The *VMQuery* Function

When I was first learning about how the Win32 memory architecture is designed, I used *VirtualQuery* as my guide. In fact, if you examine the first edition of this book, you'll see that the VMMAP.exe program was much simpler than the new version I present in the next section. In the old version, I had a very simple loop that called *VirtualQuery* repeatedly, and for each call, I simply constructed a single line containing the members of the MEMORY_BASIC_INFORMATION structure. I studied this dump and tried to piece the Win32 memory management architecture together while referring to the Windows NT 3.1 SDK documentation (which was rather poor at the time). Well, I've come a long way,

baby—I now know that the *VirtualQuery* function and the MEMORY-
_BASIC_INFORMATION structure are not good for creating a
process's virtual address space memory map.

The problem is that the MEMORY_BASIC_INFORMATION structure does not return all of the information that the system has stored
internally. If you have a memory address and want to obtain some simple
information about it, *VirtualQuery* is great. If you just want to know
whether there is committed physical storage to an address or whether a
memory address can be read from or written to, *VirtualQuery* works fine.
But if you want to know the total size of a reserved region or the number
of blocks in a region, or whether a region contains a thread's stack, a
single call to *VirtualQuery* is just not going to give you the information
you're looking for.

To obtain much more complete memory information, I have created my own function, named *VMQuery*:

```
BOOL VMQuery (PVOID pvAddress, PVMQUERY pVMQ);
```

This function is similar to *VirtualQuery* in that it takes a memory address
specified by the *pvAddress* parameter and a pointer to a structure that is
to be filled, specified by the *pVMQ* parameter. This structure is a
VMQUERY structure that I have also defined:

```
typedef struct {
   // Region information
   PVOID pvRgnBaseAddress;
   DWORD dwRgnProtection;    // PAGE_*
   DWORD dwRgnSize;
   DWORD dwRgnStorage;       // MEM_*: Free, Image,
                             //        Mapped, Private
   DWORD dwRgnBlocks;
   DWORD dwRgnGuardBlks;     // If > 0, region contains thread stack
   BOOL  fRgnIsAStack;       // TRUE if region contains thread stack

   // Block information
   PVOID pvBlkBaseAddress;
   DWORD dwBlkProtection;    // PAGE_*
   DWORD dwBlkSize;
   DWORD dwBlkStorage;       // MEM_*: Free, Reserve, Image,
                             //        Mapped, Private
} VMQUERY, *PVMQUERY;
```

As you can see from just a quick glance, my **VMQUERY** structure
contains much more information than *VirtualQuery*'s MEMORY_BASIC-
_INFORMATION structure. My structure is divided into two distinct

parts: region information and block information. The region portion describes information about the region, and the block portion includes information about the block containing the address specified by the *pvAddress* parameter. The following table describes all the members:

Member Name	Description
pvRgnBaseAddress	Identifies the base address of the virtual address space region containing the address specified in the *pvAddress* parameter.
dwRgnProtection	Identifies the protection attribute that was assigned to the region of address space when it was initially reserved.
dwRgnSize	Identifies the size, in bytes, of the region that was reserved.
dwRgnStorage	Identifies the type of physical storage that is used for the bulk of the blocks in the region. The value is one of the following: MEM_FREE, MEM_IMAGE, MEM-_MAPPED, or MEM_PRIVATE. Windows 95 doesn't distinguish between different storage types, so this member will always be MEM_FREE or MEM_PRIVATE under Windows 95.
dwRgnBlocks	Identifies the number of blocks contained within the region.
dwRgnGuardBlks	Identifies the number of blocks that have the PAGE-_GUARD protection attribute flag turned on. This value will usually be either 0 or 1. If it's 1, that's a good indicator that the region was reserved to contain a thread's stack. Under Windows 95, this member will always be 0.
fRgnIsAStack	Identifies whether the region contains a thread's stack. This value is determined by taking a "best guess" because it is impossible to be 100 percent sure whether a region contains a stack.
pvBlkBaseAddress	Identifies the base address of the block that contains the address specified in the *pvAddress* parameter.
dwBlkProtection	Identifies the protection attribute for the block that contains the address specified in the *pvAddress* parameter.
dwBlkSize	Identifies the size, in bytes, of the block that contains the address specified in the *pvAddress* parameter.

(continued)

continued

Member Name	Description
dwBlkStorage	Identifies the content of the block that contains the address specified in the *pvAddress* parameter. The value is one of the following: MEM_FREE, MEM_RESERVE, MEM_IMAGE, MEM_MAPPED, or MEM_PRIVATE. Under Windows 95, this member will never be MEM_IMAGE or MEM_MAPPED.

There is no doubt that *VMQuery* must do a significant amount of processing, including many calls to *VirtualQuery*, in order to obtain all this information—which means it executes much more slowly than *VirtualQuery*. For this reason, you should think carefully when deciding which of these two functions to call. If you do not need the extra information obtained by *VMQuery*, call *VirtualQuery*.

The VMQUERY.C file, listed in Figure 6-3, shows how I obtain and massage all the information needed to set the members of the VMQUERY structure. The VMQUERY.C and VMQUERY.H files are in the VMMAP directory on the companion disc. Rather than go into detail in the text about how I process this data, I'll let my comments (sprinkled liberally throughout the code) speak for themselves.

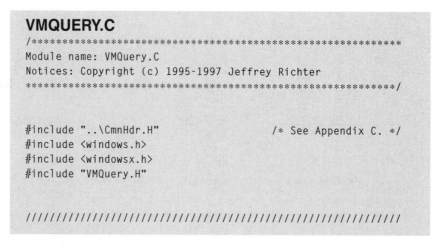

```
VMQUERY.C
/****************************************************************
Module name: VMQuery.C
Notices: Copyright (c) 1995-1997 Jeffrey Richter
****************************************************************/


#include "..\CmnHdr.H"                          /* See Appendix C. */
#include <windows.h>
#include <windowsx.h>
#include "VMQuery.H"


/////////////////////////////////////////////////////////////////
```

Figure 6-3.
The VMQuery listings.

(continued)

Figure 6-3. *continued*

```
typedef struct {
  DWORD dwRgnSize;
  DWORD dwRgnStorage;        // MEM_*: Free, Image,
                            //        Mapped, Private
  DWORD dwRgnBlocks;
  DWORD dwRgnGuardBlks;      // If > 0, region contains
                            // thread stack
  BOOL  fRgnIsAStack;        // TRUE if region contains
                            // thread stack
} VMQUERY_HELP;


// Global-static variable that holds the
// allocation granularity value for this CPU platform. This
// variable is initialized the first time VMQuery is called.
static DWORD gs_dwAllocGran = 0;


////////////////////////////////////////////////////////////


// When NTBUG_VIRTUALQUERY is defined, the code below
// compensates for a bug in Windows NT's implementation of
// the VirtualQuery function.
#define NTBUG_VIRTUALQUERY

#ifdef NTBUG_VIRTUALQUERY
DWORD NTBug_VirtualQuery (LPVOID lpvAddress,
  PMEMORY_BASIC_INFORMATION pmbiBuffer, DWORD cbLength) {

  DWORD dwRetVal = VirtualQuery(lpvAddress,
    pmbiBuffer, cbLength);

  if (dwRetVal == cbLength) {
    // If successful, correct the MBI structure's values.

    if (((DWORD) pmbiBuffer->AllocationBase % 0x1000)
      == 0xFFF) {
      // If the AllocationBase member ends with 0xFFF,
      // the address is 1 byte off.
      pmbiBuffer->AllocationBase = (PVOID)
        ((PBYTE) pmbiBuffer->AllocationBase + 1);
    }
```

(continued)

171

Figure 6-3. *continued*

```
    if ((pmbiBuffer->RegionSize % 0x1000) == 0xFFF) {
        // If the RegionSize member ends with 0xFFF,
        // the size is 1 byte off.
        pmbiBuffer->RegionSize++;
    }

    if ((pmbiBuffer->State != MEM_FREE) &&
        (pmbiBuffer->AllocationProtect == 0)) {
        // If the region is not free and the
        // AllocationProtect member is 0, AllocationProtect
        // should be PAGE_READONLY.
        pmbiBuffer->AllocationProtect = PAGE_READONLY;
    }
}


    return(dwRetVal);
}


#define VirtualQuery NTBug_VirtualQuery
#endif


///////////////////////////////////////////////////////////////////


// This function iterates through all the blocks in a
// region and initializes a structure with its findings.
static BOOL VMQueryHelp (PVOID pvAddress,
    VMQUERY_HELP *pVMQHelp) {

    MEMORY_BASIC_INFORMATION MBI;
    PVOID pvRgnBaseAddress, pvAddressBlk;
    BOOL fOk;
    DWORD dwProtectBlock[4] = { 0 };
        // 0 = reserved, PAGE_NOACCESS, PAGE_READWRITE

    // Zero the contents of the structure.
    chINITSTRUCT(*pVMQHelp, FALSE);

    // From the passed memory address, obtain the
    // base address of the region that contains it.
    fOk = (VirtualQuery(pvAddress,
        &MBI, sizeof(MBI)) == sizeof(MBI));
```

(continued)

Figure 6-3. *continued*

```
if (!fOk) {
    // If we can't get any information about the passed
    // address, return FALSE, indicating an error.
    // GetLastError() will report the actual problem.
    return(fOk);
}


// pvRgnBaseAddress identifies the region's
// base address and will never change.
pvRgnBaseAddress = MBI.AllocationBase;

// pvAddress identifies the address of the first block
// and will change as we iterate through the blocks.
pvAddressBlk = pvRgnBaseAddress;

// Save the memory type of the physical storage block.
pVMQHelp->dwRgnStorage = MBI.Type;

for (;;) {
    // Get info about the current block.
    fOk = VirtualQuery(pvAddressBlk, &MBI, sizeof(MBI));
    if (!fOk) {
        // Couldn't get the information, end loop.
        break;
    }

    // Check to see whether the block we got info for is
    // contained in the requested region.
    if (MBI.AllocationBase != pvRgnBaseAddress) {
        // Found a block in the next region; end loop.
        break;
    }


    // We have found a block contained
    // in the requested region.


    // The following if statement is for detecting stacks in
    // Windows 95. Windows 95 stacks are in a region wherein
    // the last 4 blocks have the following attributes:
    // reserved block, PAGE_NOACCESS, PAGE_READWRITE,
    // and another reserved block.
```

(continued)

173

Figure 6-3. *continued*

```
        if (pVMQHelp->dwRgnBlocks < 4) {
           // If this is the 0th through 3rd block, make
           // a note of the block's protection in our array.
           dwProtectBlock[pVMQHelp->dwRgnBlocks] =
              (MBI.State == MEM_RESERVE) ? 0 : MBI.Protect;
        } else {
           // We have already seen 4 blocks in this region.
           // Shift the protection values down in the array.
           MoveMemory(&dwProtectBlock[0], &dwProtectBlock[1],
              sizeof(dwProtectBlock) - sizeof(DWORD));

           // Add the new protection value to the end
           // of the array.
           dwProtectBlock[3] =
              (MBI.State == MEM_RESERVE) ? 0 : MBI.Protect;
        }


        // Add 1 to the number of blocks in the region.
        pVMQHelp->dwRgnBlocks++;

        // Add the block's size to the reserved region size.
        pVMQHelp->dwRgnSize += MBI.RegionSize;

        // If the block has the PAGE_GUARD protection attribute
        // flag, add 1 to the number of blocks with this flag.
        if (MBI.Protect & PAGE_GUARD) {
           pVMQHelp->dwRgnGuardBlks++;
        }


        // Take a best guess as to the type of physical storage
        // committed to the block. This is a guess because some
        // blocks can convert from MEM_IMAGE to MEM_PRIVATE or
        // from MEM_MAPPED to MEM_PRIVATE; MEM_PRIVATE can
        // always be overridden by MEM_IMAGE or MEM_MAPPED.
        if (pVMQHelp->dwRgnStorage == MEM_PRIVATE) {
           pVMQHelp->dwRgnStorage = MBI.Type;
        }


        // Get the address of the next block.
        pvAddressBlk = (PVOID)
           ((PBYTE) pvAddressBlk + MBI.RegionSize);
     }
```

(continued)

Figure 6-3. *continued*

```
    // After examining the region, check to see whether it is
    // a thread stack.
    // Windows NT: Assume a thread stack if the region contains
    //             at least 1 block with the PAGE_GUARD flag.
    // Windows 95: Assume a thread stack if the region contains
    //             at least 4 blocks wherein the last 4 blocks
    //             have the following attributes:
    //             3rd block from end: reserved
    //             2nd block from end: PAGE_NOACCESS
    //             1st block from end: PAGE_READWRITE
    //             block at end: another reserved block.
    pVMQHelp->fRgnIsAStack =
       (pVMQHelp->dwRgnGuardBlks > 0) ||
       ((pVMQHelp->dwRgnBlocks >= 4) &&
       (dwProtectBlock[0] == 0) &&
       (dwProtectBlock[1] == PAGE_NOACCESS) &&
       (dwProtectBlock[2] == PAGE_READWRITE) &&
       (dwProtectBlock[3] == 0));

    // Return that the function completed successfully.
    return(TRUE);
}


///////////////////////////////////////////////////////////////


BOOL VMQuery (PVOID pvAddress, PVMQUERY pVMQ) {

    MEMORY_BASIC_INFORMATION MBI;
    VMQUERY_HELP VMQHelp;
    BOOL fOk;

    if (gs_dwAllocGran == 0) {
       // If this is the very first time a thread in this
       // application is calling us, we must obtain the size
       // of a page used on this system and save this value
       // in a global-static variable.
       SYSTEM_INFO SI;
       GetSystemInfo(&SI);
       gs_dwAllocGran = SI.dwAllocationGranularity;
    }

    // Zero the contents of the structure.
    chINITSTRUCT(*pVMQ, FALSE);
```

(continued)

Figure 6-3. *continued*

```
// Get the MEMORY_BASIC_INFORMATION for the passed address.
fOk = VirtualQuery(pvAddress,
    &MBI, sizeof(MBI)) == sizeof(MBI);

if (!fOk) {
    // If we can't get any information about the passed
    // address, return FALSE, indicating an error.
    // GetLastError() will report the actual problem.
    return(fOk);
}

// The MEMORY_BASIC_INFORMATION structure contains valid
// information. Time to start setting the members
// of our own VMQUERY structure.


// First, fill in the block members. We'll get the
// data for the region containing the block later.
switch (MBI.State) {
    case MEM_FREE:
        // We have a block of free address space that
        // has not been reserved.
        pVMQ->pvBlkBaseAddress = NULL;
        pVMQ->dwBlkSize = 0;
        pVMQ->dwBlkProtection = 0;
        pVMQ->dwBlkStorage = MEM_FREE;
        break;

    case MEM_RESERVE:
        // We have a block of reserved address space that
        // does NOT have physical storage committed to it.
        pVMQ->pvBlkBaseAddress = MBI.BaseAddress;
        pVMQ->dwBlkSize = MBI.RegionSize;

        // For an uncommitted block, MBI.Protect is invalid.
        // So we will show that the reserved block inherits
        // the protection attribute of the region in which it
        // is contained.
        pVMQ->dwBlkProtection = MBI.AllocationProtect;
        pVMQ->dwBlkStorage = MEM_RESERVE;
        break;

    case MEM_COMMIT:
        // We have a block of reserved address space that
        // DOES have physical storage committed to it.
```

(continued)

Figure 6-3. *continued*

```
        pVMQ->pvBlkBaseAddress = MBI.BaseAddress;
        pVMQ->dwBlkSize = MBI.RegionSize;
        pVMQ->dwBlkProtection = MBI.Protect;
        pVMQ->dwBlkStorage = MBI.Type;
        break;
}


// Second, fill in the region members now that we have
// used the MBI data obtained from the first call to
// VirtualQuery. We might have to call VirtualQuery again
// to obtain complete region information.
switch (MBI.State) {
    case MEM_FREE:
        // We have a block of address space
        // that has not been reserved.
        pVMQ->pvRgnBaseAddress = MBI.BaseAddress;
        pVMQ->dwRgnProtection = MBI.AllocationProtect;
        pVMQ->dwRgnSize = MBI.RegionSize;
        pVMQ->dwRgnStorage = MEM_FREE;
        pVMQ->dwRgnBlocks = 0;
        pVMQ->dwRgnGuardBlks = 0;
        pVMQ->fRgnIsAStack = FALSE;
        break;

    case MEM_RESERVE:
        // We have a reserved region that does NOT have
        // physical storage committed to it.
        pVMQ->pvRgnBaseAddress = MBI.AllocationBase;
        pVMQ->dwRgnProtection = MBI.AllocationProtect;

        // To get complete information about the region, we
        // must iterate through all the region's blocks.
        VMQueryHelp(pvAddress, &VMQHelp);

        pVMQ->dwRgnSize = VMQHelp.dwRgnSize;
        pVMQ->dwRgnStorage = VMQHelp.dwRgnStorage;
        pVMQ->dwRgnBlocks = VMQHelp.dwRgnBlocks;
        pVMQ->dwRgnGuardBlks = VMQHelp.dwRgnGuardBlks;
        pVMQ->fRgnIsAStack = VMQHelp.fRgnIsAStack;
        break;

    case MEM_COMMIT:
        // We have a reserved region that DOES have
        // physical storage committed to it.
```

(continued)

Figure 6-3. *continued*

```
                pVMQ->pvRgnBaseAddress = MBI.AllocationBase;
                pVMQ->dwRgnProtection = MBI.AllocationProtect;

                // To get complete information on the region, we
                // must iterate through all the region's blocks.
                VMQueryHelp(pvAddress, &VMQHelp);

                pVMQ->dwRgnSize = VMQHelp.dwRgnSize;
                pVMQ->dwRgnStorage = VMQHelp.dwRgnStorage;
                pVMQ->dwRgnBlocks = VMQHelp.dwRgnBlocks;
                pVMQ->dwRgnGuardBlks = VMQHelp.dwRgnGuardBlks;
                pVMQ->fRgnIsAStack = VMQHelp.fRgnIsAStack;
                break;
        }

        // Return that the function completed successfully.
        return(fOk);
}


//////////////////////// End Of File ////////////////////////
```

VMQUERY.H

```
/*****************************************************************
Module name: VMQuery.H
Notices: Copyright (c) 1995-1997 Jeffrey Richter
*****************************************************************/


typedef struct {
    // Region information
    PVOID pvRgnBaseAddress;
    DWORD dwRgnProtection;    // PAGE_*
    DWORD dwRgnSize;
    DWORD dwRgnStorage;       // MEM_*: Free, Image,
                              //        Mapped, Private
    DWORD dwRgnBlocks;
    DWORD dwRgnGuardBlks;     // If > 0, region contains
                              // thread stack
    BOOL  fRgnIsAStack;       // TRUE if region contains
                              // thread stack
```

(continued)

Figure 6-3. *continued*

```
    // Block information
    PVOID pvBlkBaseAddress;
    DWORD dwBlkProtection;   // PAGE_*
    DWORD dwBlkSize;
    DWORD dwBlkStorage;      // MEM_*: Free, Reserve, Image,
                             //        Mapped, Private
} VMQUERY, *PVMQUERY;



////////////////////////////////////////////////////////////



BOOL VMQuery (PVOID pvAddress, PVMQUERY pVMQ);



////////////////////////////////////////////////////////////
```

The Virtual Memory Map Sample Application

The VMMap application (VMMAP.EXE), listed in Figure 6-4 beginning
on page 181, walks its own address space and shows the regions and the
blocks within regions. The source code and resource files for the application are in the VMMAP directory on the companion disc. When you
start the program, the following window appears:

```
Virtual Memory Map                                          _ □ ×
00000000    Free        65536
00010000    Private      4096     1   -RW-
  00010000  Private      4096         -RW- --
00011000    Free        61440
00020000    Private      4096     1   -RW-
  00020000  Private      4096         -RW- --
00021000    Free        61440
00030000    Private   1048576     3   -RW-       Thread Stack
  00030000  Reserve   1036288         -RW- --
  0012D000  Private      4096         -RW- G-
  0012E000  Private      8192         -RW- --
00130000    Private      4096     1   -RW-
  00130000  Private      4096         -RW- --
00131000    Free        61440
00140000    Private   1048576     2   -RW-       Default Process Heap
  00140000  Private     12288         -RW- --
  00143000  Reserve   1036288         -RW- --
00240000    Mapped      65536     2   -RW-
  00240000  Mapped       4096         -RW- --
  00241000  Reserve     61440         -RW- --
00250000    Mapped      90112     1   -R--
  00250000  Mapped      90112         -R-- --
00266000    Free        40960
00270000    Mapped     147456     1   -R--
```

The contents of this application's list box were used to produce the
virtual memory map dumps presented in Figure 5-5 on page 131, Figure
5-6 on page 135, and Figure 5-7 on page 139 in Chapter 5.

Each entry in the list box shows the result of information obtained by calling my *VMQuery* function. The main loop looks like this:

```
PVOID pvAddress = 0x00000000;
BOOL fOk = TRUE;
VMQUERY VMQ;
  .
  .
  .
   while (fOk) {
      fOk = VMQuery(pvAddress, &VMQ);

      if (fOk) {
         // Construct the line to be displayed, and
         // add it to the list box.
         ConstructRgnInfoLine(&VMQ, szLine, sizeof(szLine));
         ListBox_AddString(hWndLB, szLine);

#if 1
         // Change the 1 above to a 0 if you do not want
         // to see the blocks contained within the region.

         for (dwBlock = 0; fOk && (dwBlock < VMQ.dwRgnBlocks);
            dwBlock++) {

            ConstructBlkInfoLine(&VMQ, szLine, sizeof(szLine));
            ListBox_AddString(hWndLB, szLine);

            // Get the address of the next region to test.
            pvAddress = ((BYTE *) pvAddress + VMQ.dwBlkSize);
            if (dwBlock < VMQ.dwRgnBlocks - 1) {
               // Don't query the memory info after
               // the last block.
               fOk = VMQuery(pvAddress, &VMQ);
            }
         }
#endif

         // Get the address of the next region to test.
         pvAddress = ((BYTE *) VMQ.pvRgnBaseAddress +
            VMQ.dwRgnSize);
      }
   }
```

This loop starts walking from virtual address 0x00000000 and ends when *VMQuery* returns FALSE, indicating that it can no longer walk the process's address space. With each iteration of the loop, there is a call to

ConstructRgnInfoLine; this function fills a character buffer with information about the region. Then this information is appended to the list.

Within this main loop is a nested loop that iterates through each block in the region. Each iteration of this loop calls *ConstructBlkInfoLine* to fill a character buffer with information about the region's blocks. Then the information is appended to the list box. It's very easy to walk the process's address space using the *VMQuery* function.

VMMap.ico

VMMAP.C

```
/************************************************************
Module name: VMMap.C
Notices: Copyright (c) 1995-1997 Jeffrey Richter
************************************************************/


#include "..\CmnHdr.H"              /* See Appendix C. */
#include <windows.h>
#include <windowsx.h>
#include <tchar.h>
#include <stdio.h>                  // For sprintf
#include <string.h>                 // For strchr
#include "Resource.H"
#include "VMQuery.H"



///////////////////////////////////////////////////////////////


// Set COPYTOCLIPBOARD to TRUE if you want the
// memory map to be copied to the clipboard.
#define COPYTOCLIPBOARD    TRUE//FALSE


#if COPYTOCLIPBOARD
// Function to copy the contents of a list box to the clipboard.
// I used this function to obtain the memory map dumps
// for the figures in this book.


void CopyControlToClipboard (HWND hwnd) {
    int nCount, nNum;
    TCHAR szClipData[20000] = { 0 };
    HGLOBAL hClipData;
```

Figure 6-4.   *(continued)*
The VMMap application.

Figure 6-4. *continued*

```
   LPTSTR lpClipData;
   BOOL fOk;

   nCount = ListBox_GetCount(hwnd);
   for (nNum = 0; nNum < nCount; nNum++) {
      TCHAR szLine[1000];
      ListBox_GetText(hwnd, nNum, szLine);
      _tcscat(szClipData, szLine);
      _tcscat(szClipData, __TEXT("\r\n"));
   }

   OpenClipboard(NULL);
   EmptyClipboard();

   // Clipboard accepts only data that is in a block allocated
   // with GlobalAlloc using the GMEM_MOVEABLE and
   // GMEM_DDESHARE flags.
   hClipData = GlobalAlloc(GMEM_MOVEABLE | GMEM_DDESHARE,
      sizeof(TCHAR) * (_tcslen(szClipData) + 1));
   lpClipData = (LPTSTR) GlobalLock(hClipData);

   _tcscpy(lpClipData, szClipData);

#ifdef UNICODE
   fOk = (SetClipboardData(CF_UNICODETEXT, hClipData)
      == hClipData);
#else
   fOk = (SetClipboardData(CF_TEXT, hClipData) == hClipData);
#endif
   CloseClipboard();

   if (!fOk) {
      GlobalFree(hClipData);
      MessageBox(GetFocus(),
         __TEXT("Error putting text on the clipboard"),
         NULL, MB_OK | MB_ICONINFORMATION);
   }
}

#endif


/////////////////////////////////////////////////////////////////
```

(continued)

Figure 6-4. *continued*

```
LPCTSTR GetMemStorageText (DWORD dwStorage) {
   LPCTSTR p = __TEXT("Unknown");
   switch (dwStorage) {
      case MEM_FREE:    p = __TEXT("Free   "); break;
      case MEM_RESERVE: p = __TEXT("Reserve"); break;
      case MEM_IMAGE:   p = __TEXT("Image  "); break;
      case MEM_MAPPED:  p = __TEXT("Mapped "); break;
      case MEM_PRIVATE: p = __TEXT("Private"); break;
   }
   return(p);
}


/////////////////////////////////////////////////////////////////


LPTSTR GetProtectText (DWORD dwProtect, LPTSTR szBuf,
   BOOL fShowFlags) {
   LPCTSTR p = __TEXT("Unknown");
   switch (dwProtect & ~(PAGE_GUARD | PAGE_NOCACHE)) {
      case PAGE_READONLY:          p = __TEXT("-R--"); break;
      case PAGE_READWRITE:         p = __TEXT("-RW-"); break;
      case PAGE_WRITECOPY:         p = __TEXT("-RWC"); break;
      case PAGE_EXECUTE:           p = __TEXT("E---"); break;
      case PAGE_EXECUTE_READ:      p = __TEXT("ER--"); break;
      case PAGE_EXECUTE_READWRITE: p = __TEXT("ERW-"); break;
      case PAGE_EXECUTE_WRITECOPY: p = __TEXT("ERWC"); break;
      case PAGE_NOACCESS:          p = __TEXT("----"); break;
   }
   _tcscpy(szBuf, p);
   if (fShowFlags) {
      _tcscat(szBuf, __TEXT(" "));
      _tcscat(szBuf, (dwProtect & PAGE_GUARD)   ?
         __TEXT("G") : __TEXT("-"));
      _tcscat(szBuf, (dwProtect & PAGE_NOCACHE) ?
         __TEXT("N") : __TEXT("-"));
   }
   return(szBuf);
}


/////////////////////////////////////////////////////////////////
```

(continued)

Figure 6-4. *continued*

```
void ConstructRgnInfoLine (PVMQUERY pVMQ,
    LPTSTR szLine, int nMaxLen) {

    int nLen;

    _stprintf(szLine, __TEXT("%08X    %s  %10u  "),
        pVMQ->pvRgnBaseAddress,
        GetMemStorageText(pVMQ->dwRgnStorage),
        pVMQ->dwRgnSize);

    if (pVMQ->dwRgnStorage != MEM_FREE) {
        _stprintf(_tcschr(szLine, 0), __TEXT("%5u  "),
            pVMQ->dwRgnBlocks);
        GetProtectText(pVMQ->dwRgnProtection,
            _tcschr(szLine, 0), FALSE);
    }

    _tcscat(szLine, __TEXT("     "));

    // Try to obtain the module pathname for this region.
    nLen = _tcslen(szLine);
    if (pVMQ->pvRgnBaseAddress != NULL)
        GetModuleFileName((HINSTANCE) pVMQ->pvRgnBaseAddress,
            szLine + nLen, nMaxLen - nLen);

    if (pVMQ->pvRgnBaseAddress == GetProcessHeap()) {
        _tcscat(szLine, __TEXT("Default Process Heap"));
    }

    if (pVMQ->fRgnIsAStack) {
        _tcscat(szLine, __TEXT("Thread Stack"));
    }
}


//////////////////////////////////////////////////////////////


void ConstructBlkInfoLine (PVMQUERY pVMQ,
    LPTSTR szLine, int nMaxLen) {

    _stprintf(szLine, __TEXT("  %08X %s %10u          "),
        pVMQ->pvBlkBaseAddress,
        GetMemStorageText(pVMQ->dwBlkStorage),
        pVMQ->dwBlkSize);
```

(continued)

Figure 6-4. *continued*

```
    if (pVMQ->dwBlkStorage != MEM_FREE) {
        GetProtectText(pVMQ->dwBlkProtection,
            _tcschr(szLine, 0), TRUE);
    }
}


///////////////////////////////////////////////////////////////


void Dlg_OnSize (HWND hwnd, UINT state, int cx, int cy) {
    SetWindowPos(GetDlgItem(hwnd, IDC_LISTBOX), NULL, 0, 0,
        cx, cy, SWP_NOZORDER);
}


///////////////////////////////////////////////////////////////


BOOL Dlg_OnInitDialog (HWND hwnd, HWND hwndFocus,
    LPARAM lParam) {

    HWND hWndLB = GetDlgItem(hwnd, IDC_LISTBOX);
    PVOID pvAddress = 0x00000000;
    TCHAR szLine[200];
    RECT rc;
    DWORD dwBlock;
    VMQUERY VMQ;
    BOOL fOk = TRUE;

    // Associate an icon with the dialog box.
    chSETDLGICONS(hwnd, IDI_VMMAP, IDI_VMMAP);

    // Make a horizontal scroll bar appear in the list box.
    ListBox_SetHorizontalExtent(hWndLB,
        150 * LOWORD(GetDialogBaseUnits()));

    // The list box must be sized first because the system
    // doesn't send a WM_SIZE message to the dialog box when
    // it's first created.
    GetClientRect(hwnd, &rc);
    SetWindowPos(hWndLB, NULL, 0, 0, rc.right, rc.bottom,
        SWP_NOZORDER);
```

(continued)

Figure 6-4. *continued*

```
        // Walk the virtual address space, adding
        // entries to the list box.
        while (fOk) {
            fOk = VMQuery(pvAddress, &VMQ);

            if (fOk) {
                // Construct the line to be displayed, and
                // add it to the list box.
                ConstructRgnInfoLine(&VMQ, szLine, sizeof(szLine));
                ListBox_AddString(hWndLB, szLine);

#if 1

                // Change the 1 above to a 0 if you do not want
                // to see the blocks contained within the region.

                for (dwBlock = 0; fOk && (dwBlock < VMQ.dwRgnBlocks);
                    dwBlock++) {

                    ConstructBlkInfoLine(&VMQ, szLine, sizeof(szLine));
                    ListBox_AddString(hWndLB, szLine);

                    // Get the address of the next region to test.
                    pvAddress = ((BYTE *) pvAddress + VMQ.dwBlkSize);
                    if (dwBlock < VMQ.dwRgnBlocks - 1) {
                        // Don't query the memory info after
                        // the last block.
                        fOk = VMQuery(pvAddress, &VMQ);
                    }
                }
#endif

                // Get the address of the next region to test.
                pvAddress = ((BYTE *) VMQ.pvRgnBaseAddress +
                    VMQ.dwRgnSize);
            }
        }

#if COPYTOCLIPBOARD
        CopyControlToClipboard(hWndLB);
#endif
        return(TRUE);
}
```

(continued)

Figure 6-4. *continued*

```
////////////////////////////////////////////////////////////


void Dlg_OnCommand (HWND hwnd, int id, HWND hwndCtl,
   UINT codeNotify) {

   switch (id) {
      case IDCANCEL:
         EndDialog(hwnd, id);
         break;
   }
}



////////////////////////////////////////////////////////////


BOOL CALLBACK Dlg_Proc (HWND hwnd, UINT uMsg,
   WPARAM wParam, LPARAM lParam) {

   switch (uMsg) {
      chHANDLE_DLGMSG(hwnd, WM_INITDIALOG, Dlg_OnInitDialog);
      chHANDLE_DLGMSG(hwnd, WM_COMMAND, Dlg_OnCommand);
      chHANDLE_DLGMSG(hwnd, WM_SIZE, Dlg_OnSize);
   }
   return(FALSE);
}



////////////////////////////////////////////////////////////


int WINAPI _tWinMain (HINSTANCE hinstExe,
   HINSTANCE hinstPrev, LPTSTR pszCmdLine, int nCmdShow) {

   chWARNIFUNICODEUNDERWIN95();
   DialogBox(hinstExe, MAKEINTRESOURCE(IDD_VMMAP),
      NULL, Dlg_Proc);

   return(0);
}


////////////////////////// End Of File //////////////////////////
```

(continued)

Figure 6-4. *continued*

VMMAP.RC

```
//Microsoft Developer Studio generated resource script.
//
#include "Resource.h"

#define APSTUDIO_READONLY_SYMBOLS
/////////////////////////////////////////////////////////////////
//
// Generated from the TEXTINCLUDE 2 resource.
//
#include "afxres.h"


/////////////////////////////////////////////////////////////////
#undef APSTUDIO_READONLY_SYMBOLS


/////////////////////////////////////////////////////////////////
// English (U.S.) resources

#if !defined(AFX_RESOURCE_DLL) || defined(AFX_TARG_ENU)
#ifdef _WIN32
LANGUAGE LANG_ENGLISH, SUBLANG_ENGLISH_US
#pragma code_page(1252)
#endif //_WIN32


#ifdef APSTUDIO_INVOKED
/////////////////////////////////////////////////////////////////
//
// TEXTINCLUDE
//

1 TEXTINCLUDE DISCARDABLE
BEGIN
    "Resource.h\0"
END

2 TEXTINCLUDE DISCARDABLE
BEGIN
    "#include ""afxres.h""\r\n"
    "\0"
END
```

(continued)

Figure 6-4. *continued*

```
3 TEXTINCLUDE DISCARDABLE
BEGIN
    "\r\n"
    "\0"
END


#endif    // APSTUDIO_INVOKED


/////////////////////////////////////////////////////////////
//
// Dialog
//

IDD_VMMAP DIALOG DISCARDABLE  10, 18, 250, 250
STYLE WS_MINIMIZEBOX | WS_MAXIMIZEBOX | WS_POPUP
   | WS_VISIBLE | WS_CAPTION | WS_SYSMENU | WS_THICKFRAME
CAPTION "Virtual Memory Map"
FONT 8, "Courier"
BEGIN
    LISTBOX           IDC_LISTBOX,0,0,0,0,NOT LBS_NOTIFY |
                      LBS_NOINTEGRALHEIGHT | NOT WS_BORDER |
                      WS_VSCROLL | WS_HSCROLL | WS_GROUP |
                      WS_TABSTOP
END


/////////////////////////////////////////////////////////////
//
// Icon
//

// Icon with lowest ID value placed first to ensure
// application icon remains consistent on all systems.
IDI_VMMAP              ICON    DISCARDABLE    "VMMap.Ico"
#endif    // English (U.S.) resources
/////////////////////////////////////////////////////////////
```

(continued)

Figure 6-4. *continued*

```
#ifndef APSTUDIO_INVOKED
/////////////////////////////////////////////////////////////
//
// Generated from the TEXTINCLUDE 3 resource.
//


/////////////////////////////////////////////////////////////
#endif    // not APSTUDIO_INVOKED
```

USING VIRTUAL MEMORY IN YOUR OWN APPLICATIONS

Win32 offers the following three mechanisms for manipulating memory:

- Virtual memory, which is best for managing large arrays of objects or structures

- Memory-mapped files, which are best for managing large streams of data (usually from files) and for sharing data between multiple processes

- Heaps, which are best for managing large numbers of small objects

In this chapter we discuss the first method, virtual memory. The other two methods, memory-mapped files and heaps, are discussed in Chapter 8 and Chapter 9, respectively.

The Win32 functions for manipulating virtual memory allow you to directly reserve a region of address space, commit physical storage (from the paging file) to the region, and set your own protection attributes.

Reserving a Region in an Address Space

You reserve a region in your process's address space by calling *VirtualAlloc*:

```
LPVOID VirtualAlloc(LPVOID lpAddress, DWORD cbSize,
    DWORD fdwAllocationType, DWORD fdwProtect);
```

The first parameter, *lpAddress*, contains a memory address specifying where you would like the system to reserve the address space. Most of the time, you'll pass NULL as the *lpAddress* parameter. This tells

VirtualAlloc that the system, which keeps a record of free address ranges, should reserve the region wherever it sees fit. The system can reserve a region from anywhere in your process's address space—there are no guarantees that the system will allocate regions from the bottom of your address space up or vice versa. However, you can have some say over this allocation by using the MEM_TOP_DOWN flag, discussed later.

For most programmers, the ability to choose a specific memory address where a region will be reserved is a new concept. When you allocated memory in the past, the operating system simply found a block of memory large enough to satisfy the request, allocated the block, and returned its address. But because each Win32 process has its own address space, you can specify the base memory address where you would like the operating system to reserve the region.

For example, say that you want to allocate a region starting 50 MB into your process's address space. In this case, you will pass 52,428,800 ($50 \times 1024 \times 1024$) as the *lpAddress* parameter. If this memory address has a free region large enough to satisfy your request, the system will reserve the desired region and return. If a free region does not exist at the specified address, or if the free region is not large enough, the system cannot satisfy your request and *VirtualAlloc* returns NULL.

Under Windows 95, you can attempt to reserve a region only in the 0x00400000 through 0x7FFFFFFF partition of a process's address space. An attempt to reserve a region in any other partition will fail, causing *VirtualAlloc* to return NULL.

Under Windows NT, you can attempt to reserve a region only in the 0x00010000 through 0x7FFEFFFF partition of a process's address space. An attempt to reserve a region in any other partition will fail, causing *VirtualAlloc* to return NULL.

As mentioned in Chapter 5, regions are always reserved on an allocation granularity boundary (64 KB for all implementations of Win32 to date). So if you attempt to reserve a region starting at address 19,668,992 ($300 \times 65,536 + 8192$) in your process's address space, the system rounds that address down to an even multiple of 64 KB and will reserve the region starting at address 19,660,800 (300 × 65,536).

If *VirtualAlloc* can satisfy your request, it returns a value indicating the base address of the reserved region. If you passed a specific address as *VirtualAlloc*'s *lpAddress* parameter, this return value is the same value that you passed to *VirtualAlloc* rounded down (if necessary) to an even 64-KB boundary.

VirtualAlloc's second parameter, *cbSize*, specifies the size of the region you want to reserve in bytes. Because the system must always reserve regions in multiples of the CPU's page size, an attempt to reserve a region that spans 79 KB will result in reserving a region that spans 80 KB on machines that use either 4-KB or 8-KB pages.

VirtualAlloc's third parameter, *fdwAllocationType*, tells the system whether you want to reserve a region or commit physical storage. (This distinction is necessary because *VirtualAlloc* is also used to commit physical storage.) To reserve a region of address space, you must pass the MEM_RESERVE identifier as the value for the *fdwAllocationType* parameter.

If you're going to reserve a region that you don't expect to release for a long time, you might want to reserve the region at the highest memory address possible. That way, the region does not get reserved from the middle of your process's address space, where it can potentially cause fragmentation. If you want the system to reserve a region at the highest possible memory address, you must pass NULL for the *lpAddress* parameter and you must also bitwise OR the MEM_TOP_DOWN flag with the MEM_RESERVE flag when calling *VirtualAlloc*.

Under Windows 95, the MEM_TOP_DOWN flag is ignored.

The last parameter, *fdwProtect*, indicates the protection attribute that should be assigned to the region. The protection attribute associated with the region has no effect on the committed storage mapped to the region. Regardless of the protection attribute assigned to a region, if no physical storage is committed, any attempt to access a memory address in the range will cause the thread to raise an access violation. This is identical to what happens if you reserve and commit storage to a region using the PAGE_NOACCESS flag.

When reserving a region, assign the protection attribute that will be used most often with the storage committed to the region. For example, if you intend to commit physical storage with a protection attribute of PAGE_READWRITE, you should reserve the region with PAGE_READ-WRITE. The internal record keeping of the system behaves more efficiently when the region's protection attribute matches the committed storage's protection attribute.

You can use any of the following protection attributes: PAGE-_NOACCESS, PAGE_READWRITE, PAGE_READONLY, PAGE_EXE-CUTE, PAGE_EXECUTE_READ, or PAGE_EXECUTE_READWRITE. However, you cannot specify either the PAGE_WRITECOPY or the PAGE-_EXECUTE_WRITECOPY attribute. If you do so, *VirtualAlloc* will not reserve the region and will return NULL. Also, you cannot use either of the protection attribute flags PAGE_GUARD or PAGE_NOCACHE when reserving regions—they can be used only with committed storage.

Windows 95 supports only the PAGE_NOACCESS, PAGE_READONLY, and PAGE_READWRITE protection attributes. Attempting to reserve a region using PAGE_EXECUTE or PAGE_EXECUTE_READ results in a region with PAGE_READONLY protection. Likewise, reserving a region using PAGE_EXECUTE_READWRITE results in a region with PAGE-_READWRITE protection.

Committing Storage in a Reserved Region

After you have reserved a region, you will need to commit physical storage to the region before you can access the memory addresses contained within it. The system allocates physical storage committed to a region from the system's paging file on your hard disk. Physical storage is committed on page boundaries and in page-size chunks.

To commit physical storage, you must call *VirtualAlloc* again. This time, however, you'll pass the MEM_COMMIT identifier instead of the MEM_RESERVE identifier for the *fdwAllocationType* parameter. You usually pass the same page protection attribute that was used when *VirtualAlloc* was called to reserve the region, although you can specify a different protection attribute.

From within the reserved region, you must tell *VirtualAlloc* where you want to commit physical storage and how much physical storage to commit. You do this by specifying the desired memory address in the *lpAddress* parameter and the amount of physical storage, in bytes, in the *cbSize* parameter. Note that you don't have to commit physical storage to the entire region at one time.

Let's look at an example of how to commit storage. Say your application is running on an Intel *x*86 CPU and the application reserves a 512-KB region starting at address 5,242,880. You would like your application to commit storage to the 6-KB portion of the reserved region starting 2 KB into the reserved region's address space. To do this, call *VirtualAlloc* using the MEM_COMMIT flag as follows:

```
VirtualAlloc((PVOID) (5242880 + (2 * 1024)), 6 * 1024,
   MEM_COMMIT, PAGE_READWRITE);
```

In this case, the system must commit 8 KB of physical storage, spanning the address range 5,242,880 through 5,251,072 (5,242,880 + 8 KB). Both of these committed pages have a protection attribute of PAGE-_READWRITE. Protection attributes are assigned on a whole-page basis only. It is not possible to use different protection attributes for portions of the same page of storage. However, it is possible for one page in a region to have one protection attribute (such as PAGE_READWRITE) and for another page in the same region to have a different protection attribute (such as PAGE_READONLY).

Reserving a Region and Committing Storage Simultaneously

At times, you'll want to reserve a region and commit storage to it simultaneously. You can do this by placing a single call to *VirtualAlloc* as follows:

```
PVOID pvMem = VirtualAlloc(NULL, 99 * 1024,
   MEM_RESERVE | MEM_COMMIT, PAGE_READWRITE);
```

This call is a request to reserve a 99-KB region and commit 99 KB of physical storage to the region. When the system processes this call, it first searches your process's address space to find a contiguous area of unreserved address space large enough to hold 100 KB (on a 4-KB page machine) or 104 KB (on an 8-KB page machine).

The system searches the address space because you specified NULL as the *lpAddress* parameter. If you had specified a memory address for *lpAddress*, the system would see whether there was enough unreserved address space at that memory address. If the system could not find enough unreserved address space, *VirtualAlloc* would return NULL.

If a suitable region can be reserved, the system then commits 100 KB (on a 4-KB page machine) or 104 KB (on an 8-KB page machine) of physical storage to the region. Both the region and the committed storage will be assigned PAGE_READWRITE protection.

Finally, *VirtualAlloc* returns the virtual address of the reserved and committed region, which is then saved in the *pvMem* variable. If the system couldn't find a large enough address space or commit the physical storage, *VirtualAlloc* returns NULL.

It is certainly possible when reserving a region and committing physical storage this way to pass a specific address as the *lpvAddress* parameter to *VirtualAlloc*. Or you might need to have the system select a suitable region toward the top of your process's address space by ORing the MEM_TOP_DOWN flag to the *fdwAllocationType* parameter and passing NULL for the *lpAddress* parameter.

When to Commit Physical Storage

Let's pretend you're implementing a spreadsheet application that supports 200 rows by 256 columns. For each cell, you need a CELLDATA structure that describes the contents of the cell. The easiest way for you to manipulate the two-dimensional matrix of cells would be to declare the following variable in your application:

```
CELLDATA CellData[200][256];
```

If the size of a CELLDATA structure were 128 bytes, it would require 6,553,600 (200 × 256 × 128) bytes of physical storage. That's a lot of physical storage to allocate from the paging file right up front for a spreadsheet, especially when you consider that most users put information into only a few spreadsheet cells, leaving the majority unused. The memory usage would be very inefficient.

So, historically, spreadsheets have been implemented using other data structure techniques, such as linked lists. With the linked-list approach, CELLDATA structures have to be created only for the cells in the spreadsheet that actually contain data. Since most cells in a spreadsheet go unused, this method saves a tremendous amount of storage. However, this technique makes it much more difficult to obtain the contents of a cell. If you want to know the contents of the cell in row 5, column 10, you must walk through linked lists in order to find the desired cell, which makes the linked-list method slower than the declared-matrix method.

Virtual memory offers a compromise between declaring the two-dimensional matrix up front and implementing linked lists. With virtual memory, you get the fast, easy access offered by the declared-matrix technique combined with the superior storage savings offered by the linked-list technique.

For you to obtain the advantages of the virtual memory technique, your program needs to do the following:

1. Reserve a region large enough to contain the entire matrix of CELLDATA structures. Reserving a region requires no physical storage at all.

2. When the user enters data into a cell, locate the memory address in the reserved region where the CELLDATA structure should go. Of course, no physical storage is mapped to this address yet, so any attempts to access memory at this address will raise an access violation.

3. Commit just enough physical storage to the memory address located in step 2 for a CELLDATA structure. (You can tell the system to commit physical storage to specific parts of the reserved region—a region can contain both parts that are mapped to physical storage and parts that are not.)

4. Set the members of the new CELLDATA structure.

Now that physical storage is mapped to the proper location, your program can access the storage without raising an access violation. This virtual memory technique is excellent because physical storage is committed only as the user enters data into the spreadsheet's cells. Because most of the cells in a spreadsheet are empty, most of the reserved region will not have physical storage committed to it.

The one problem with the virtual memory technique is that you must determine when physical storage needs to be committed. If the user enters data into a cell and then simply edits or changes that data, there is no need to commit physical storage—the storage for the cell's CELLDATA structure was committed the first time data was entered.

Also, the system always commits physical storage with page granularity (4 KB on x86, MIPS, and PowerPC; 8 KB on Alpha). So when you

197

attempt to commit physical storage for a single CELLDATA structure (as in step 2 on the previous page), the system is actually committing a full page of storage. This is not as wasteful as it sounds: committing storage for a single CELLDATA structure has the effect of committing storage for other nearby CELLDATA structures. If the user then enters data into a neighboring cell, which is frequently the case, you might not need to commit additional physical storage.

There are four methods for determining whether to commit physical storage to a portion of a region:

■ Always attempt to commit physical storage. Instead of checking to see whether physical storage is mapped to a portion of the region, have your program try to commit storage every time it calls *VirtualAlloc*. The system first checks to see whether storage has already been committed and, if so, does not commit additional physical storage. This approach is the easiest but has the disadvantage of making an additional function call every time a CELLDATA structure is altered, which makes your program perform more slowly.

■ Determine (using the *VirtualQuery* function) whether physical storage has already been committed to the address space containing the CELLDATA structure. If it has, do nothing else; if it hasn't, call *VirtualAlloc* to commit the memory. This method is actually worse than the first one; it both increases the size of your code and slows down your program because of the additional call to *VirtualQuery*.

■ Keep a record of which pages have been committed and which haven't. Doing so makes your application run faster: you avoid the call to *VirtualAlloc*, and your code can determine more quickly than the system whether storage has already been committed. The disadvantage is that you must keep track of the page commit information somehow, which could be either very simple or very difficult depending on your specific situation.

■ The best method takes advantage of structured exception handling (SEH). SEH is a Win32 feature that causes the system to notify your application when certain situations occur. Essentially, you set up your application with an exception handler, and then, whenever an attempt is made to access uncommitted memory, the system notifies your application of the problem. Your application then commits the memory and tells the system to retry the instruction that caused the exception. This time, the memory access succeeds, and the program continues running as though there had never been a problem. This method is the best because it requires the least amount of work from you (meaning less code) and because your program will run at full speed. A complete discussion of the SEH mechanism is saved for Chapter 16 in this book.

Decommitting Physical Storage and Releasing a Region

To decommit physical storage mapped to a region or release an entire region of address space, call the *VirtualFree* function:

```
BOOL VirtualFree(LPVOID lpAddress, DWORD cbSize,
    DWORD fdwFreeType);
```

Let's examine the simple case of calling *VirtualFree* first to release a reserved region. When your process will no longer be accessing the physical storage within a region, you can release the reserved region, and all the physical storage committed to the region, by making a single call to *VirtualFree*.

For this call, the *lpAddress* parameter must be the base address of the region. This address would be the same address that *VirtualAlloc* returned when the region was reserved. The system knows the size of the region at the specified memory address, so you can pass 0 for the *cbSize* parameter. In fact, you must pass 0 for the *cbSize* parameter, or the call to *VirtualFree* will fail. For the third parameter, *fdwFreeType*, you must pass MEM_RELEASE to tell the system to decommit all physical storage mapped to the region and to release the region. When releasing a region, you must release all the address space that was reserved by the region. For example, you cannot reserve a 500-MB region and then decide to release only 200 MB of it. You must release all 500 MB.

When you want to decommit some physical storage from the region without releasing the region, you also call *VirtualFree*. To decommit some physical storage, you must pass the memory address that identifies the first page to be decommitted in *VirtualFree*'s *lpAddress* parameter. You must also specify the number of bytes to free in the *cbSize* parameter and the MEM_DECOMMIT identifier in the *fdwFreeType* parameter.

Like committing, decommitting is done with page granularity; that is, specifying a memory address in the middle of a page decommits the entire page. And, of course, if *lpAddress* + *cbSize* falls in the middle of a page, the whole page that contains this address is decommitted as well. So all pages that fall within the range of *lpAddress* to *lpAddress* + *cbSize* are decommitted.

If *cbSize* is 0 and *lpAddress* is the base address for the allocated region, *VirtualFree* will decommit the complete range of allocated pages. After the pages of physical storage have been decommitted, the freed physical storage is available to any other process in the system; any attempt to access the decommitted memory results in an access violation.

When to Decommit Physical Storage

In practice, knowing when it's OK to decommit memory is very tricky. Consider the spreadsheet example again. If your application is running on an Intel *x*86 machine, each page of storage is 4 KB and can hold 32 (4096 / 128) CELLDATA structures. If the user deletes the contents of *CellData[0][1]*, you might be able to decommit the page of storage as long as cells *CellData[0][0]* through *CellData[0][31]* are also not in use. But how do you know? You can tackle this problem in different ways.

- Without a doubt, the easiest solution is to design a CELLDATA structure that is exactly 1 page in size. Then, because there is always one structure per page, you can simply decommit the page of physical storage when you don't need the data in the structure any longer. Even if your data structures were multiples of a page, say, 8 KB or 12 KB for Intel CPUs (these would be unusually large structures), decommitting memory would still be pretty easy. Of course, to use this method you must define your data structures to meet the page size of the CPU you're targeting—not how we usually write our programs.

- A more practical solution is to keep a record of which structures are in use. To save memory, you might use a bitmap. So if you have an array of 100 structures, you also maintain an array of 100 bits. Initially, all the bits are set to 0, indicating that no structures are in use. As you use the structures, you set the corresponding bits to 1. Then, whenever you don't need a structure and you change its bit back to 0, you check the bits of the adjacent structures that fall into the same page of memory. If none of the adjacent structures is in use, you can decommit the page.

■ The last solution implements a garbage collection function. This scheme relies on the fact that the system sets all the bytes in a page to 0 when physical storage is first committed. To use this scheme, you must first set aside a BOOL (perhaps called *fInUse*) in your structure. Then, every time you put a structure in committed memory, you need to ensure that *fInUse* is set to TRUE.

As your application runs, you'll want to call the garbage collection function periodically. This function should traverse all the potential data structures. For each structure, the function first determines whether storage is committed for the structure; if so, the function checks the *fInUse* member to see whether it is 0. A value of 0 means that the structure is not in use, whereas a value of TRUE means that it is in use. After the garbage collection function has checked all the structures that fall within a given page, it calls *VirtualFree* to decommit the storage if all the structures are not in use.

You can call the garbage collection function immediately after a structure is no longer considered to be in use, but doing so might take more time than you want to spend because the function cycles through all the possible structures. An excellent way to implement this function is to have it run as part of a lower-priority thread. In this way, you don't take time away from the thread executing the main application. Whenever the main application is idle or the main application's thread is performing file I/O, the system can schedule time to the garbage collection function.

Of all the methods listed above, the first two are my personal favorites. However, if your structures are not big (less than a page), I recommend using the last method.

The Virtual Memory Allocation Sample Application

The VMAlloc application (VMALLOC.EXE), listed in Figure 7-1 beginning on page 205, demonstrates how to use virtual memory techniques for manipulating an array of structures. The source code and resource files for the application are in the VMALLOC directory on the companion disc. When you start the program, the following window appears:

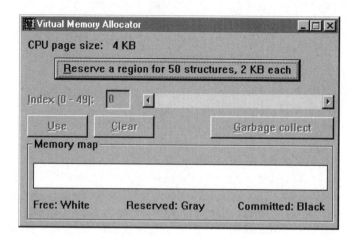

Initially, no region of address space has been reserved for the array, and all the address space that would be reserved for it is free, as shown by the memory map. When you click the Reserve A Region For 50 Structures, 2 KB Each button, VMAlloc calls *VirtualAlloc* to reserve the region, and the memory map is updated to reflect this. After *VirtualAlloc* reserves the region, the remaining buttons become active.

You can now type an index into the edit control or use the scroll bar to select an index, and then click on the Use button. This has the effect of committing physical storage to the memory address where the array element is to be placed. When a page of storage is committed, the memory map is redrawn to reflect the state of the reserved region for the entire array. So if after reserving the region, you use the Use button to mark array elements 7 and 46 as *in use*, the window will look like the window on the facing page (when you are running the program on a 4-KB page machine).

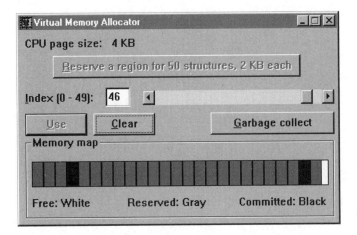

Any element that is marked as *in use* can be cleared by clicking on the Clear button. But doing so does not decommit the physical storage mapped to the array element, because each page contains room for multiple structures—just because one is clear doesn't mean the others are too. If the memory was decommitted, the data in the other structures would be lost. Because selecting Clear doesn't affect the region's physical storage, the memory map is not updated when an array element is cleared.

However, when a structure is cleared, its *fInUse* member is set to FALSE. This setting is necessary so the garbage collection routine can make its pass over all the structures and decommit storage that's no longer in use. If you haven't guessed it by now, the Garbage Collect button tells VMAlloc to execute its garbage collection routine. To keep things simple, I have not implemented the garbage collection function as its own thread.

To demonstrate the garbage collection function, clear the array element at index 46. Notice that the memory map does not change. Now click on the Garbage Collect button. The program decommits the page of storage containing element 46, and the memory map is updated to reflect this, as shown in the window at the top of page 204.

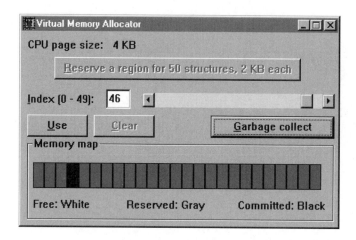

Finally, even though there is no visual display to inform you, all the committed memory is decommitted and the reserved region is freed when the window is destroyed.

This program contains another element that I haven't described yet. The program needs to determine the state of memory in the region's address space in three places:

■ After changing the index, the program needs to enable the Use button and disable the Clear button or vice versa.

■ In the garbage collection function, the program needs to see whether storage is committed before actually testing to see whether the *fInUse* flag is set.

■ When updating the memory map, the program needs to know which pages are free, reserved, and committed.

VMAlloc performs all these tests by calling the *VirtualQuery* function, discussed in the previous chapter.

VMAlloc.ico

VMALLOC.C

```c
/*************************************************************
Module name: VMAlloc.C
Notices: Copyright (c) 1995-1997 Jeffrey Richter
*************************************************************/


#include "..\CmnHdr.H"                      /* See Appendix C. */
#include <windows.h>
#include <windowsx.h>
#include <tchar.h>
#include <stdio.h>                 // For sprintf
#include "Resource.H"


///////////////////////////////////////////////////////////////


UINT g_uPageSize = 0;

typedef struct {
   BOOL fAllocated;
   BYTE bOtherData[2048 - sizeof(BOOL)];
} SOMEDATA, *PSOMEDATA;

#define MAX_SOMEDATA   (50)
PSOMEDATA g_pSomeData = NULL;

RECT g_rcMemMap;


///////////////////////////////////////////////////////////////


BOOL Dlg_OnInitDialog (HWND hwnd, HWND hwndFocus,
   LPARAM lParam) {

   TCHAR szBuf[10];

   // Associate an icon with the dialog box.
   chSETDLGICONS(hwnd, IDI_VMALLOC, IDI_VMALLOC);

   // Initialize the dialog box by disabling all
   // the nonsetup controls.
```

Figure 7-1.
The VMAlloc sample application.

(continued)

Figure 7-1. *continued*

```
    EnableWindow(GetDlgItem(hwnd, IDC_INDEXTEXT), FALSE);
    EnableWindow(GetDlgItem(hwnd, IDC_INDEX), FALSE);
    ScrollBar_SetRange(GetDlgItem(hwnd, IDC_INDEXSCRL),
       0, MAX_SOMEDATA - 1, FALSE);
    ScrollBar_SetPos(GetDlgItem(hwnd, IDC_INDEXSCRL), 0,TRUE);
    EnableWindow(GetDlgItem(hwnd, IDC_INDEXSCRL), FALSE);
    EnableWindow(GetDlgItem(hwnd, IDC_USE), FALSE);
    EnableWindow(GetDlgItem(hwnd, IDC_CLEAR), FALSE);
    EnableWindow(GetDlgItem(hwnd, IDC_GARBAGECOLLECT), FALSE);

    // Get the coordinates of the memory map display.
    GetWindowRect(GetDlgItem(hwnd, IDC_MEMMAP), &g_rcMemMap);
    MapWindowPoints(NULL, hwnd, (LPPOINT) &g_rcMemMap, 2);

    // Destroy the temporary window that identifies the
    // location of the memory map display.
    DestroyWindow(GetDlgItem(hwnd, IDC_MEMMAP));

    // Put the page size in the dialog box just
    // for the user's information.
    _stprintf(szBuf, __TEXT("%d KB"), g_uPageSize / 1024);
    SetDlgItemText(hwnd, IDC_PAGESIZE, szBuf);

    // Initialize the edit control.
    SetDlgItemInt(hwnd, IDC_INDEX, 0, FALSE);

    return(TRUE);
}


///////////////////////////////////////////////////////////////


void Dlg_OnDestroy (HWND hwnd) {
   if (g_pSomeData != NULL)
      VirtualFree(g_pSomeData, 0, MEM_RELEASE);
}


///////////////////////////////////////////////////////////////


void Dlg_OnCommand (HWND hwnd, int id, HWND hwndCtl,
   UINT codeNotify) {
```

(continued)

Figure 7-1. *continued*

```
UINT uIndex, uIndexLast, uPage, uMaxPages;
BOOL fTranslated, fOk, fAnyAllocs;
MEMORY_BASIC_INFORMATION MemoryBasicInfo;

switch (id) {
   case IDC_RESERVE:
      // Reserve enough address space to hold MAX_SOMEDATA
      // SOMEDATA structures.
      g_pSomeData = (PSOMEDATA) VirtualAlloc(NULL,
         MAX_SOMEDATA * sizeof(SOMEDATA), MEM_RESERVE,
         PAGE_READWRITE);

      // Disable the Reserve button and
      // enable all the other controls.
      EnableWindow(GetDlgItem(hwnd, IDC_RESERVE), FALSE);
      EnableWindow(GetDlgItem(hwnd, IDC_INDEXTEXT), TRUE);
      EnableWindow(GetDlgItem(hwnd, IDC_INDEX), TRUE);
      EnableWindow(GetDlgItem(hwnd, IDC_INDEXSCRL), TRUE);
      EnableWindow(GetDlgItem(hwnd, IDC_USE), TRUE);
      EnableWindow(GetDlgItem(hwnd, IDC_GARBAGECOLLECT),
         TRUE);

      // Force the index edit control to have the focus.
      SetFocus(GetDlgItem(hwnd, IDC_INDEX));

      // Invalidate the memory map display.
      InvalidateRect(hwnd, &g_rcMemMap, FALSE);
      break;

   case IDC_INDEX:
      if (codeNotify != EN_CHANGE)
         break;

      uIndex = GetDlgItemInt(hwnd, id, &fTranslated,
         FALSE);
      if ((g_pSomeData == NULL) ||
          (uIndex >= MAX_SOMEDATA)) {
         // If the index is out of range, assume the
         // translation was unsuccessful.
         fTranslated = FALSE;
      }
```

(continued)

Figure 7-1. *continued*

```
        if (fTranslated) {
            VirtualQuery(&g_pSomeData[uIndex],
                &MemoryBasicInfo, sizeof(MemoryBasicInfo));
            fOk = (MemoryBasicInfo.State == MEM_COMMIT);
            if (fOk)
                fOk = g_pSomeData[uIndex].fAllocated;

            EnableWindow(GetDlgItem(hwnd, IDC_USE), !fOk);
            EnableWindow(GetDlgItem(hwnd, IDC_CLEAR), fOk);
            ScrollBar_SetPos(GetDlgItem(hwnd, IDC_INDEXSCRL),
                uIndex, TRUE);

        } else {
            EnableWindow(GetDlgItem(hwnd, IDC_USE),   FALSE);
            EnableWindow(GetDlgItem(hwnd, IDC_CLEAR), FALSE);
        }
        break;


    case IDC_USE:
        uIndex = GetDlgItemInt(hwnd, IDC_INDEX, &fTranslated,
            FALSE);

        if (uIndex >= MAX_SOMEDATA) {
            // If the index is out of range, assume the
            // translation was unsuccessful.
            fTranslated = FALSE;
        }

        if (fTranslated) {
            VirtualAlloc(&g_pSomeData[uIndex],
                sizeof(SOMEDATA), MEM_COMMIT, PAGE_READWRITE);

            // When pages are committed, Windows NT ensures
            // that they are zeroed.
            g_pSomeData[uIndex].fAllocated = TRUE;

            EnableWindow(GetDlgItem(hwnd, IDC_USE),   FALSE);
            EnableWindow(GetDlgItem(hwnd, IDC_CLEAR), TRUE);

            // Force the Clear button control to
            // have the focus.
            SetFocus(GetDlgItem(hwnd, IDC_CLEAR));
```

(continued)

Figure 7-1. *continued*

```
                // Invalidate the memory map display.
                InvalidateRect(hwnd, &g_rcMemMap, FALSE);
            }
            break;

        case IDC_CLEAR:
            uIndex = GetDlgItemInt(hwnd, IDC_INDEX, &fTranslated,
                FALSE);

            if (uIndex >= MAX_SOMEDATA) {
                // If the index is out of range, assume the
                // translation was unsuccessful.
                fTranslated = FALSE;
            }

            if (fTranslated) {
                g_pSomeData[uIndex].fAllocated = FALSE;
                EnableWindow(GetDlgItem(hwnd, IDC_USE),   TRUE);
                EnableWindow(GetDlgItem(hwnd, IDC_CLEAR), FALSE);

                // Force the Use button control to have the focus.
                SetFocus(GetDlgItem(hwnd, IDC_USE));
            }
            break;

        case IDC_GARBAGECOLLECT:
            uMaxPages = MAX_SOMEDATA * sizeof(SOMEDATA) /
                g_uPageSize;

            for (uPage = 0; uPage < uMaxPages; uPage++) {
                fAnyAllocs = FALSE;

                uIndex = uPage * g_uPageSize / sizeof(SOMEDATA);

                uIndexLast = uIndex + g_uPageSize /
                    sizeof(SOMEDATA);

                for (; uIndex < uIndexLast; uIndex++) {
                    VirtualQuery(&g_pSomeData[uIndex],
                        &MemoryBasicInfo, sizeof(MemoryBasicInfo));

                    if ((MemoryBasicInfo.State == MEM_COMMIT) &&
                        g_pSomeData[uIndex].fAllocated) {
```

(continued)

Figure 7-1. *continued*

```
                    fAnyAllocs = TRUE;
                    break;
                 }
              }

              if (!fAnyAllocs) {
                 // No allocated structures exist in the page.
                 // We can safely decommit it.
                 VirtualFree(&g_pSomeData[uIndexLast - 1],
                    sizeof(SOMEDATA), MEM_DECOMMIT);
              }
           }

           // Invalidate the memory map display.
           InvalidateRect(hwnd, &g_rcMemMap, FALSE);
           break;

        case IDCANCEL:
           EndDialog(hwnd, id);
           break;
     }
  }


///////////////////////////////////////////////////////////////

void Dlg_OnHScroll (HWND hwnd, HWND hwndCtl,
   UINT code, int pos) {

   INT nScrlPos;
   if (hwndCtl != GetDlgItem(hwnd, IDC_INDEXSCRL))
      return;

   nScrlPos = ScrollBar_GetPos(hwndCtl);
   switch (code) {
      case SB_LINELEFT:
         nScrlPos--;
         break;

      case SB_LINERIGHT:
         nScrlPos++;
         break;
```

(continued)

Figure 7-1. *continued*

```
      case SB_PAGELEFT:
         nScrlPos -= g_uPageSize / sizeof(SOMEDATA);
         break;

      case SB_PAGERIGHT:
         nScrlPos += g_uPageSize / sizeof(SOMEDATA);
         break;

      case SB_THUMBTRACK:
         nScrlPos = pos;
         break;

      case SB_LEFT:
         nScrlPos = 0;
         break;

      case SB_RIGHT:
         nScrlPos = MAX_SOMEDATA - 1;
         break;
   }

   if (nScrlPos < 0)
      nScrlPos = 0;

   if (nScrlPos >= MAX_SOMEDATA)
      nScrlPos = MAX_SOMEDATA - 1;

   ScrollBar_SetPos(hwndCtl, nScrlPos, TRUE);
   SetDlgItemInt(hwnd, IDC_INDEX, nScrlPos, TRUE);
}


///////////////////////////////////////////////////////////////


void Dlg_OnPaint (HWND hwnd) {
   UINT uPage, uIndex, uIndexLast, uMemMapWidth;
   UINT uMaxPages = MAX_SOMEDATA * sizeof(SOMEDATA) /
      g_uPageSize;

   MEMORY_BASIC_INFORMATION MemoryBasicInfo;
   PAINTSTRUCT ps;

   BeginPaint(hwnd, &ps);
```

(continued)

Figure 7-1. *continued*

```
if (g_pSomeData == NULL) {
   // The memory has yet to be reserved.
   Rectangle(ps.hdc, g_rcMemMap.left, g_rcMemMap.top,
      g_rcMemMap.right, g_rcMemMap.bottom);
}

// Walk the virtual address space, adding
// entries to the list box.
uPage = 0;
while ((g_pSomeData != NULL) && uPage < uMaxPages) {

   uIndex = uPage * g_uPageSize / sizeof(SOMEDATA);

   uIndexLast = uIndex + g_uPageSize / sizeof(SOMEDATA);

   for (; uIndex < uIndexLast; uIndex++) {

      VirtualQuery(&g_pSomeData[uIndex], &MemoryBasicInfo,
         sizeof(MemoryBasicInfo));

      switch (MemoryBasicInfo.State) {
         case MEM_FREE:
            SelectObject(ps.hdc,
               GetStockObject(WHITE_BRUSH));
            break;

         case MEM_RESERVE:
            SelectObject(ps.hdc,
               GetStockObject(GRAY_BRUSH));
            break;

         case MEM_COMMIT:
            SelectObject(ps.hdc,
               GetStockObject(BLACK_BRUSH));
            break;
      }

      uMemMapWidth = g_rcMemMap.right - g_rcMemMap.left;
      Rectangle(ps.hdc,
         g_rcMemMap.left +
            uMemMapWidth / uMaxPages * uPage,
         g_rcMemMap.top,
         g_rcMemMap.left +
```

(continued)

Figure 7-1. *continued*

```
                uMemMapWidth / uMaxPages * (uPage + 1),
            g_rcMemMap.bottom);

      }

      uPage++;
   }

   EndPaint(hwnd, &ps);
}


///////////////////////////////////////////////////////////////


BOOL CALLBACK Dlg_Proc (HWND hwnd, UINT uMsg,
   WPARAM wParam, LPARAM lParam) {

   switch (uMsg) {
      chHANDLE_DLGMSG(hwnd, WM_INITDIALOG,  Dlg_OnInitDialog);
      chHANDLE_DLGMSG(hwnd, WM_COMMAND,  Dlg_OnCommand);
      chHANDLE_DLGMSG(hwnd, WM_HSCROLL,  Dlg_OnHScroll);
      chHANDLE_DLGMSG(hwnd, WM_PAINT,    Dlg_OnPaint);
      chHANDLE_DLGMSG(hwnd, WM_DESTROY,  Dlg_OnDestroy);
   }
   return(FALSE);
}


///////////////////////////////////////////////////////////////


int WINAPI _tWinMain (HINSTANCE hinstExe,
   HINSTANCE hinstPrev, LPTSTR pszCmdLine, int nCmdShow) {

   SYSTEM_INFO SystemInfo;

   chWARNIFUNICODEUNDERWIN95();

   // Get the page size used on this CPU.
   GetSystemInfo(&SystemInfo);
   g_uPageSize = SystemInfo.dwPageSize;
```

(continued)

Figure 7-1. *continued*

```
    DialogBox(hinstExe, MAKEINTRESOURCE(IDD_VMALLOC),
        NULL, Dlg_Proc);
    return(0);
}



/////////////////////// End Of File ///////////////////////
```

VMALLOC.RC

```
//Microsoft Developer Studio generated resource script.
//
#include "Resource.h"

#define APSTUDIO_READONLY_SYMBOLS
/////////////////////////////////////////////////////////////////
//
// Generated from the TEXTINCLUDE 2 resource.
//
#include "afxres.h"


/////////////////////////////////////////////////////////////////
#undef APSTUDIO_READONLY_SYMBOLS


/////////////////////////////////////////////////////////////////
// English (U.S.) resources

#if !defined(AFX_RESOURCE_DLL) || defined(AFX_TARG_ENU)
#ifdef _WIN32
LANGUAGE LANG_ENGLISH, SUBLANG_ENGLISH_US
#pragma code_page(1252)
#endif //_WIN32


#ifdef APSTUDIO_INVOKED
/////////////////////////////////////////////////////////////////
//
// TEXTINCLUDE
//

1 TEXTINCLUDE DISCARDABLE
BEGIN
    "Resource.h\0"
END
```

(continued)

Figure 7-1. *continued*

```
2 TEXTINCLUDE DISCARDABLE
BEGIN
    "#include ""afxres.h""\r\n"
    "\0"
END

3 TEXTINCLUDE DISCARDABLE
BEGIN
    "\r\n"
    "\0"
END

#endif    // APSTUDIO_INVOKED


/////////////////////////////////////////////////////////////
//
// Dialog
//

IDD_VMALLOC DIALOG DISCARDABLE  15, 24, 206, 121
STYLE WS_MINIMIZEBOX | WS_POPUP | WS_VISIBLE | WS_CAPTION |
    WS_SYSMENU
CAPTION "Virtual Memory Allocator"
FONT 8, "System"
BEGIN
    LTEXT           "CPU page size:",IDC_STATIC,4,4,51,8
    CONTROL         "16 KB",IDC_PAGESIZE,"Static",
                    SS_LEFTNOWORDWRAP | SS_NOPREFIX |
                    WS_GROUP,60,4,32,8
    DEFPUSHBUTTON   "&Reserve a region for 50 structures,\
 2 KB each",
                    IDC_RESERVE,22,16,160,14,WS_GROUP
    LTEXT           "&Index (0 - 49):",IDC_INDEXTEXT,4,38,
                    45,8
    EDITTEXT        IDC_INDEX,56,36,16,12
    SCROLLBAR       IDC_INDEXSCRL,80,38,124,9,WS_TABSTOP
    PUSHBUTTON      "&Use",IDC_USE,4,52,40,14
    PUSHBUTTON      "&Clear",IDC_CLEAR,48,52,40,14
    PUSHBUTTON      "&Garbage collect",IDC_GARBAGECOLLECT,
                    124,52,80,14
    GROUPBOX        "Memory map",IDC_STATIC,4,66,200,52
    CONTROL         "",IDC_MEMMAP,"Static",SS_BLACKRECT,8,
                    82,192,16
```

(continued)

Figure 7-1. *continued*

```
     LTEXT          "Free: White",IDC_STATIC,8,104,39,8
     CTEXT          "Reserved: Gray",IDC_STATIC,69,104,52,8
     RTEXT          "Committed: Black",IDC_STATIC,140,
                    104,58,8
END


/////////////////////////////////////////////////////////////
//
// Icon
//

// Icon with lowest ID value placed first to ensure
// application icon remains consistent on all systems.
IDI_VMALLOC            ICON    DISCARDABLE      "VMAlloc.Ico"
#endif    // English (U.S.) resources
/////////////////////////////////////////////////////////////


#ifndef APSTUDIO_INVOKED
/////////////////////////////////////////////////////////////
//
// Generated from the TEXTINCLUDE 3 resource.
//


/////////////////////////////////////////////////////////////
#endif    // not APSTUDIO_INVOKED
```

Changing Protection Attributes

Although the practice is very uncommon, it is possible to change the protection attributes associated with a page or pages of committed physical storage. For example, say you've developed code to manage a linked list, the nodes of which you are keeping in a reserved region. You could design the functions that process the linked list so that they change the protection attributes of the committed storage to PAGE_READWRITE at the start of each function and then back to PAGE_NOACCESS just before each function terminates.

By doing this, you protect your linked-list data from other bugs hiding in your program. If any other code in your process has a stray pointer

216

that attempts to access your linked-list data, an access violation is raised. This can be incredibly useful when you're trying to locate hard-to-find bugs in your application.

You can alter the protection rights of a page of memory by calling *VirtualProtect*:

```
BOOL VirtualProtect(LPVOID lpAddress, DWORD dwSize,
   DWORD flNewProtect, PDWORD lpflOldProtect);
```

Here, *lpAddress* points to the base address of the memory, *dwSize* indicates the number of bytes for which you want to change the protection attribute, and *flNewProtect* can represent any one of the PAGE_* protection attribute identifiers except for PAGE_WRITECOPY and PAGE_EXECUTE_WRITECOPY.

The last parameter, *lpflOldProtect*, is the address of a DWORD that *VirtualProtect* will fill in with the old protection attributes for the storage. You must pass a valid address for this parameter, or the function will raise an access violation. If you are changing the protection attribute of more than one page, the DWORD pointed to by *lpflOldProtect* will receive the old protection attribute for the first page only. *VirtualProtect* returns TRUE if it is successful.

Of course, protection attributes are associated with entire pages of storage and cannot be assigned to individual bytes. So if you were to call *VirtualProtect* on a 4-KB page machine using

```
VirtualProtect(lpRgnBase + (3 * 1024), 2 * 1024,
   PAGE_NOACCESS, &flOldProtect);
```

you would end up assigning the PAGE_NOACCESS protection attribute to 2 pages of storage.

The TInjLib sample application, shown in Chapter 18, demonstrates how to use *VirtualProtect* to alter protection attributes on committed storage.

Windows 95 supports only the PAGE_NOACCESS, PAGE_READONLY, and PAGE_READWRITE protection attributes. If you attempt to change a page's protection to PAGE_EXECUTE or PAGE_EXECUTE_READ, the page receives PAGE_READONLY protection. Likewise, if you change a page's protection to PAGE_EXECUTE_READWRITE, the page receives PAGE_READWRITE protection.

Locking Physical Storage in RAM

Remember that committing physical storage is really a matter of allocating space from the system's paging file. However, for your program to access its data, the system must locate your program's physical storage in the paging file and load it into RAM. The system has been finely tuned and optimized to perform this page swapping so that applications run very efficiently. However, two Win32 functions allow you to override this process: *VirtualLock* and *VirtualUnlock*.

The *VirtualLock* function tells the system that you want to lock a set of pages in RAM. However, the system guarantees that the pages are locked in RAM only while a thread in your process is running. When the system preempts all the threads in your process, the system is free to unlock the pages and swap them to the physical storage in the paging file. When the system is ready to reschedule a thread in your process, it loads all of the pages that you wanted locked back into RAM. When the locked pages are back in RAM, the system allows the rescheduled thread to continue executing. In this situation, your process takes an immediate performance hit whenever a thread is being rescheduled.

When the system is not running any threads in your process, it does not immediately swap the locked pages to the paging file. Instead, the system tries to keep locked pages in RAM as long as possible. If threads in another process do not make heavy use of the RAM, the system will not need to swap your process's locked pages. In this case, when the system reschedules threads in your process, the locked pages will already be loaded in RAM and the system will not have to access the paging file.

Important

The locking of physical storage into RAM is a feature that Win32 offers for special purposes. For example, many device drivers must respond to events very quickly and cannot afford to wait for the system's paging mechanism to load the physical storage on demand. You are much better off allowing the system to perform the page swapping rather than getting involved with it yourself. After all, only the operating system knows how other applications are behaving and what toll they are taking on the system's memory. The operating system's memory management routines have been fine-tuned for this—let them do their job.

(continued)

Important
(continued)

In addition, the locking of physical storage into RAM cannot be used to make your application "realtime" in any way because you cannot lock down all the pages—for system DLLs, device drivers, stack pages, heaps, and so forth—that the system might access while your thread is running. If the system is doing any paging at all, having your process lock down some of the pages that it knows about will probably make your application *less* realtime by forcing pages of storage that might be accessed even more often out of RAM.

If you still want to lock physical storage in RAM, you need to call *VirtualLock*:

```
BOOL VirtualLock(LPVOID lpvMem, DWORD cbMem);
```

This function locks the *cbMem* bytes starting at address *lpvMem* in RAM. If it is successful, TRUE is returned. Keep in mind that all the pages you attempt to lock must be committed physical storage. In addition, *VirtualLock* cannot be used to lock memory allocated with a PAGE_NOACCESS protection attribute. Also, the system will not allow a single process to lock more than approximately 30 pages of storage. This number may seem rather small to you—on an *x86*, this comes to only 122,880 bytes. The reason for this small number is to prevent a single process from greatly affecting the overall performance of the system.

When it is no longer necessary for your application to keep the memory locked, you can unlock it with *VirtualUnlock*:

```
BOOL VirtualUnlock(LPVOID lpvMem, DWORD cbMem);
```

This function unlocks the *cbMem* bytes of memory starting at address *lpvMem*. When you're unlocking memory, it is not necessary to unlock the exact amount that was locked with *VirtualLock*. If the range of memory is unlocked successfully, *VirtualUnlock* returns TRUE.

As with all the virtual functions, operations are performed on a page basis. So if you lock a range of bytes that straddles a series of pages, all pages affected by the range are locked or unlocked.

Under Windows 95, the *VirtualLock* and *VirtualUnlock* functions have no useful implementation and simply return TRUE; calling *GetLastError* returns the value ERROR_CALL_NOT_IMPLEMENTED.

Under Windows NT, you can call *VirtualUnlock* without first calling *VirtualLock*. When you do this, Windows NT removes the specified pages from the process's working set, reducing the memory load on the system. If in your code you know that you will not be accessing certain functions or data for a while, it would be a good idea to call *VirtualUnlock*.

Resetting the Contents of Physical Storage

When you modify the contents of various pages of physical storage, the system tries to keep the changes in RAM as long as possible. However, while applications are running, a demand may be placed on your system's RAM as pages are being loaded from EXE files, DLL files, and/or the paging file. As the system looks for pages of RAM to satisfy recent load requests, the system will have to swap modified pages of RAM to the system's paging file.

Windows NT 4 introduces a new feature that allows an application to improve its performance. This feature is the resetting of physical storage. Resetting storage means that you are telling the system that the data on one or more pages of storage is not modified. The reason to reset storage is to reduce potential reading and writing of pages to the system's paging file.

The following code demonstrates the resetting of physical storage:

```
int WINAPI WinMain (HINSTANCE hinstExe,
    HINSTANCE hinstPrev, LPSTR pszCmdLine, int nCmdShow) {

    const char szAppName[]  = "MEM_RESET tester";
    const char szTestData[] = "Some text data";
    PVOID pvData, pvDummy;
    MEMORYSTATUS mst;
    MEMORY_BASIC_INFORMATION mbi;

    // Commit a page of storage and modify its contents.
    pvData = VirtualAlloc(NULL, 1024,
        MEM_RESERVE | MEM_COMMIT, PAGE_READWRITE);
    strcpy(pvData, szTestData);

    if (MessageBox(NULL, "Do you want to access this data later?",
        szAppName, MB_YESNO) == IDNO) {

        // We want to keep this page of physical storage in our
        // process but the data is not important to us anymore.
```

```
            // Tell the system that the data is not modified.

            // Note: Because MEM_RESET destroys data, VirtualAlloc rounds
            // the base address and size parameters to their safest range.
            // Here is an example:
            //    VirtualAlloc(pvData, 5000, MEM_RESET, PAGE_READWRITE)
            // resets 0 pages on a DEC Alpha (1 page=8KB) and resets one
            // page on other CPU platforms (1 page=4KB).
            // So that our call to VirtualAlloc to reset memory below
            // always succeeds, VirtualQuery is called first to get the
            // exact region size.
            VirtualQuery(pvData, &mbi, sizeof(mbi));
            VirtualAlloc(pvData, mbi.RegionSize, MEM_RESET,
                PAGE_READWRITE);
        }


    // Commit as much storage as there is physical RAM.
    GlobalMemoryStatus(&mst);
    pvDummy = VirtualAlloc(NULL, mst.dwTotalPhys,
        MEM_RESERVE | MEM_COMMIT, PAGE_READWRITE);

    // Touch all the pages in the dummy region so that any
    // modified pages in RAM are written to the paging file.
    ZeroMemory(pvDummy, mst.dwTotalPhys);

    // Compare our data page with what we originally wrote there.
    if (strcmp(pvData, szTestData) == 0) {

        // The data pointed to by pvData matches what we expect.
        // FillMemory forced the modified page at pvData to be
        // written to the paging file.
        MessageBox(NULL,
            "Modified data page was saved.", szAppName, MB_OK);
    } else {

        // The page pointed to by pvData does not match what we
        // expect. FillMemory did not cause the modified page
        // to be written to the paging file because it was reset
        MessageBox(NULL,
            "Modified data page was NOT saved.", szAppName, MB_OK);
    }

    return(0);
}
```

The first thing that the code above does is reserve and commit a region of physical storage. Since the size passed to *VirtualAlloc* is 1024, the system will automatically round this value up to the system's page size

(4 KB on *x86*, MIPS, and PowerPC; 8 KB on DEC Alpha). Now a string is copied into this buffer using *strcpy*. This causes the contents of the page to be modified. If the system later decides it needs the page of RAM occupied by our data page, the system will first write the data that is in our page to the system's paging file. When our application later attempts to access this data, the system will automatically reload the page from the paging file into another page of RAM so that we can access the data successfully.

After writing the string to the page of storage, the code on pages 214–215 presents the user with a message box asking whether the data needs to be accessed at a later time. If the user responds by selecting the No button, the code forces the operating system to believe that the data in the page is not modified. This is done by calling *VirtualAlloc* passing the MEM_RESET flag.

If the pages referenced in the call to *VirtualAlloc* are in the paging file, the system discards them. The next time the application accesses the storage, new RAM pages that are first initialized to zeroes are used. If you reset pages that are currently in RAM, they are marked as not modified so that they will never be written to the paging file. Note that the contents of the RAM page is *not* zeroed, but you should not continue to read from this page of storage. If the system doesn't need the page of RAM, it will contain the original contents; however, if the system needs the page of RAM, it may take it and then, when you attempt to access the contents of it, give you a new page that has been zeroed. Since you have no control over this, you must assume that the contents of the page is garbage after you reset it.

Keep in mind a couple of additional things when resetting storage. First, you'll notice that I call *VirtualQuery* prior to calling *VirtualAlloc*. Usually, when you call *VirtualAlloc*, it rounds the base address down to an even page boundary and then rounds the number of bytes up to an even number of pages. This would be very dangerous to do when resetting storage; therefore, *VirtualAlloc* rounds these values in the opposite direction when you pass MEM_RESET. For example, let's say that you had the following code:

```
PINT pnData = (PINT) VirtualAlloc(NULL, 1024,
    MEM_RESERVE | MEM_COMMIT, PAGE_READWRITE);
pn[0] = 100;
pn[1] = 200;
VirtualAlloc((PVOID) pnData, sizeof(int), MEM_RESET,
    PAGE_READWRITE);
```

This code commits one page of storage and then says that the first 4 bytes *(sizeof(int))* are no longer necessary and can be reset. However, as with all storage operations, everything must be done on page boundaries and in page increments. As it turns out, the call to reset the storage above fails *(VirtualAlloc* returns 0). Here is why: when you pass MEM-_RESET to *VirtualAlloc,* the base address you pass to the function is rounded up to a page boundary and the number of bytes is rounded down to an even number of pages. This happens to ensure that important data is not thrown away. In the example above, rounding the number of bytes down makes it 0, and it is illegal to reset 0 bytes.

The second thing to remember about resetting storage is that the MEM_RESET flag must always be used by itself and cannot be ORed with any other flags. The following call fails and returns NULL:

```
PVOID pv = VirtualAlloc(NULL, 1024,
  MEM_RESERVE | MEM_COMMIT | MEM_RESET, PAGE_READWRITE);
```

It really doesn't make any sense to combine the MEM_RESET flag with any other flag anyway.

Finally, note that calling *VirtualAlloc* with MEM_RESET causes the page protection parameter to be validated; however, the function does not actually use the specified page protection value.

Now, let's get back to the code fragment above. To demonstrate that the storage has been reset, we need to force a heavy demand on the system's RAM. We do this using the following three-step process:

1. *GlobalMemoryStatus* is called to get the total amount of RAM in the machine.

2. *VirtualAlloc* is called to commit this amount of storage. This operation is very fast because the system doesn't actually allocate RAM for the storage until the process attempts to touch the pages.

3. *ZeroMemory* is called so that the newly committed pages are touched. This will place a heavy burden on the system's RAM, causing some pages that are currently in RAM to be written to the paging file.

If the user has indicated that he or she wants to access the data later, then the data was not reset and will be swapped back into RAM later when we attempt to access it. However, if the user has indicated not to access the data later, we have already reset the data and the system will not write it out to the paging file, thereby improving our application's performance.

After *ZeroMemory* returns, I then compare the contents of the data page with the string originally written to it. If the data wasn't reset, the contents is guaranteed to be the same. If the data page was reset, the contents may or may not be the same. In my code fragment, the contents will never be the same because I'm forcing all pages in RAM to be written to the paging file. However, if my dummy region were smaller than the total amount of RAM in the machine, it is possible that the original contents would still be in RAM—as I've pointed out earlier, be careful about this!

A Thread's Stack

Sometimes the system reserves regions in your own process's address space. I mentioned that this happened for process and thread environment blocks in Chapter 5. Another time that the system does this is for a thread's stack.

Whenever a thread is created in your process, the system reserves a region of address space for the thread's stack (each thread gets its very own stack) and also commits some physical storage to this reserved region. By default, the system reserves 1 MB of address space and commits 2 pages of storage. However, these defaults can be changed by specifying the /STACK option to the linker when you link your application:

```
/STACK:reserve[,commit]
```

When a thread's stack is created, the system reserves a region of address space indicated by the linker's /STACK switch. However, you can override the amount of storage that is initially committed when you call the *CreateThread* or the *_beginthreadex* function. Both functions have a parameter that allows you to override the storage that is initially committed to the stack's address space region. If you specify 0 for this parameter, the system uses the commit size indicated by the /STACK switch. For the remainder of this discussion, I will assume we're using the default stack sizes: 1 MB of reserved region with storage committed in single pages.

Figure 7-2 shows what a stack region (reserved starting at address 0x08000000) might look like on a machine whose page size is 4 KB. The stack's region and all of the physical storage committed to it have a page protection of PAGE_READWRITE.

After reserving this region, the system commits physical storage to the top two pages of the region. Just before allowing the thread to begin execution, the system sets the thread's stack pointer register to point to

Memory Address	State of Page
0x080FF000	Top of stack: committed page
0x080FE000	Committed page with guard protection attribute flag
0x080FD000	Reserved page
0x08003000	Reserved page
0x08002000	Reserved page
0x08001000	Reserved page
0x08000000	Bottom of stack: reserved page

Figure 7-2.
What a thread's stack region looks like when it is first created.

the end of the top page of the stack region (an address very close to 0x08100000). This page is where the thread will begin using its stack. The second page from the top is called the *guard page*. As the thread increases its call tree by calling more functions, the thread needs more stack space.

Whenever the thread attempts to access storage in the guard page, the system is notified. In response, the system commits another page of storage just below the guard page. Then the system removes the guard page protection flag from the current guard page and assigns it to the newly committed page of storage. This technique allows the stack storage to increase only as the thread requires it. Eventually, if the thread's call tree continues to expand, the stack region will look like Figure 7-3 on the following page.

Referring to Figure 7-3, assume that the thread's call tree is very deep and that the stack pointer CPU register points to the stack memory address 0x08003004. Now, when the thread calls another function, the

Memory Address	State of Page
0x080FF000	Top of stack: committed page
0x080FE000	Committed page
0x080FD000	Committed page
0x08003000	Committed page
0x08002000	Committed page with guard protection attribute flag
0x08001000	Reserved page
0x08000000	Bottom of stack: reserved page

Figure 7-3.
A nearly full thread's stack region.

system has to commit more physical storage. However, when the system commits physical storage to the page at address 0x08001000, it does not do exactly what it did when committing physical storage to the rest of the stack's memory region. Figure 7-4 shows what the stack's reserved memory region looks like.

As you'd expect, the page starting at address 0x08002000 has the guard attribute removed, and physical storage is committed to the page starting at 0x08001000. The difference is that the system does not apply the guard attribute to the new page of physical storage (0x08001000). This means that the stack's reserved address space region contains all the physical storage that it can ever contain. The bottommost page is always reserved and never gets committed. I will explain the reason for this shortly.

The system performs one more action when it commits physical storage to the page at address 0x08001000—it raises an EXCEPTION-_STACK_OVERFLOW exception (defined as 0xC00000FD in WINNT.H). By using Win32 structured exception handling (SEH), your program

Memory Address	State of Page
0x080FF000	Top of stack: committed page
0x080FE000	Committed page
0x080FD000	Committed page
0x08003000	Committed page
0x08002000	Committed page
0x08001000	Committed page
0x08000000	Bottom of stack: reserved page

Figure 7-4.
A full thread stack region.

will be notified of this condition and can recover gracefully. For more information on SEH, see Chapter 16, including the SEHSum application.

If the thread continues to use the stack after the stack overflow exception is raised, all the memory in the page at 0x08001000 will be used and the thread will attempt to access memory in the page starting at 0x08000000. When the thread attempts to access this reserved (uncommitted) memory, the system raises an access violation exception. If this access violation exception is raised while the thread is attempting to access the stack, the thread is in very deep trouble. The system takes control at this point and terminates the process—not just the thread, but the whole process. The system doesn't even show a message box to the user; the whole process just disappears!

Now I will explain why the bottommost page of a stack's region is always reserved. Doing so protects against accidental overwriting of other data being used by the process. You see, it's possible that at address 0x07FFF000 (one page below 0x08000000), another region of address space has committed physical storage. If the page at 0x08000000 contained physical storage, the system would not catch attempts by the thread to access the reserved stack region. If the stack were to dip below the reserved stack region, the code in your thread would overwrite other data in your process's address space—a very, very difficult bug to catch.

A Thread's Stack Under Windows 95

Under Windows 95, stacks behave similarly to their Windows NT counterparts. However, there are some significant differences.

Figure 7-5 shows what a stack region (reserved starting at address 0x00530000) might look like for a 1-MB stack when running under Windows 95.

Memory Address	Size	State of Page
0x00640000	16 pages (65,536 bytes)	Top of stack: reserved for stack underflow
0x0063F000	1 page (4096 bytes)	Committed page with PAGE_READWRITE protection; stack in use
0x0063E000	1 page (4096 bytes)	PAGE_NOACCESS page to simulate PAGE_GUARD flag
0x00638000	6 pages (24,576 bytes)	Reserved pages for stack overflow
0x00637000	1 page (4096 bytes)	Committed page with PAGE_READWRITE protection for 16-bit component compatibility
0x00540000	247 pages (1,011,712 bytes)	Reserved pages to allow stack to grow
0x00530000	16 pages (65,536 bytes)	Bottom of stack: reserved for stack overflow

Figure 7-5.
What a thread's stack region looks like when it is first created under Windows 95.

First, notice that the region is actually 1 MB plus 128 KB in size, even though we wanted only to create a stack that was up to 1 MB in size. In Windows 95, whenever a region is reserved for a stack, the system actually reserves a region that is 128 KB larger than the requested size. The stack is in the middle of this region, with a 64-KB block before the stack and another 64-KB block after the stack.

The 64 KB at the beginning of the stack are there to catch stack overflow conditions, while the 64 KB at the end of the stack are there to catch stack underflow conditions. To see why stack underflow detection is useful, examine the following code fragment:

```
int WINAPI WinMain (HINSTANCE hinstExe, HINSTANCE hinstPrev,
   LPSTR lpszCmdLine, int nCmdShow) {

   char szBuf[100];
   szBuf[10000] = 0;     // Stack underflow

   return(0);
}
```

When this function's assignment statement is executed, an attempt is made to access beyond the end of the thread's stack. Of course, the compiler and the linker will not catch the bug in the code above, but if your application is running under Windows 95, an access violation will be raised when the statement executes. This is a nice feature of Windows 95 that is not offered by Windows NT. On Windows NT, it is possible to have another region immediately after your thread's stack. If this happens and you attempt to access memory beyond your stack, you might corrupt memory related to another part of your process—and the system will *not* detect this corruption.

Second, note that no pages have the PAGE_GUARD protection attribute flag. Because Windows 95 does not support this flag, it uses a slightly different technique to expand a thread's stack. Windows 95 marks the committed page immediately below the stack with the PAGE_NOACCESS protection attribute (address 0x0063E000 in Figure 7-5). Then, when the thread touches the page below the read/write pages, an access violation occurs. The system catches this, changes the no access page to a read/write page, and commits a new "guard" page just below the previous guard page.

Third, notice the single page of PAGE_READWRITE storage at address 0x00637000 in Figure 7-5. This page exists for 16-bit Windows compatibility. Although Microsoft never documented it, developers found out that the 16 bytes at the beginning of a 16-bit application's stack segment contain information about the 16-bit application's stack, local heap, and local atom table. Because Win32 applications running on Windows 95 frequently call 16-bit DLL components, and some of these 16-bit components assume that this information is available at the beginning of the stack segment, Microsoft was forced to simulate these bytes in Windows 95. When 32-bit code thunks to 16-bit code, Windows 95 maps a 16-bit CPU selector to the 32-bit stack and sets the stack segment (SS) register to point to the page at address 0x00637000. The 16-bit code can now access the 16 bytes at the beginning of the stack segment and continue executing without any problems.

Now, as Windows 95 grows the thread's stack, it continues to grow the block at address 0x0063F000; it also keeps moving the guard page down until 1 MB of stack storage is committed, and then the guard page disappears, just as it does under Windows NT. The system also continues to move the page for 16-bit Windows component compatibility down, and eventually this page goes into the 64-KB block at the beginning of the stack region. So a fully committed stack on Windows 95 looks like Figure 7-6.

Memory Address	Size	State of Page
0x00640000	16 pages (65,536 bytes)	Top of stack: reserved for stack underflow
0x00540000	256 pages (1 MB)	Committed pages with PAGE_READWRITE protection; stack in use
0x00539000	7 pages (28,672 bytes)	Reserved pages for stack overflow
0x00538000	1 page (4096 bytes)	Committed page with PAGE_READWRITE protection for 16-bit component compatibility
0x00530000	8 pages (32,768 bytes)	Bottom of stack: reserved for stack overflow

Figure 7-6.
A full thread stack region under Windows 95.

The C Run-Time Library's Stack Checking Function

MS-DOS and 16-bit Windows applications run in a system that doesn't take advantage of the CPU's ability to assign memory protections to regions of memory. So when your application uses its stack, the CPU can't detect when a stack overflow occurs. Because this bug can be very difficult to detect in these 16-bit environments, many C/C++ compiler vendors offer a compiler switch that causes the compiler to add a call to an internal function (provided in the C run-time library) that verifies the stack hasn't overflowed. This compiler switch is optional because adding the call to the stack checking function both increases the size of your EXE file and makes your application run more slowly.

In the Win32 environment, the CPU can automatically detect when a thread overflows its stack, so there's no need for additional function calls that would make your code bigger and slower.

The 32-bit C/C++ compilers still offer a stack checking function, but the purpose of the function has changed totally. Now the 32-bit stack checking function makes sure that pages are committed to your thread's stack appropriately. Let's look at an example. Here's a small function that requires a lot of memory for its local variables:

```
void SomeFunction () {
   int nValues[4000];

   // Do some processing with the array.
   nValues[0] = 0;      // Some assignment
}
```

This function will require at least 16,000 bytes (4000 × sizeof(int); each integer is 4 bytes) of stack space to accommodate the array of integers. Usually, the code a compiler generates to allocate this stack space simply decrements the CPU's stack pointer by 16,000 bytes. However, the system does not commit physical storage to this lower area of the stack's region until an attempt is made to access the memory address.

On a system with a 4-KB or 8-KB page size, this limitation could cause a problem. If the first access to the stack is at an address that is below the guard page (as shown on the assignment line in the code above), the thread will be accessing reserved memory and the system will raise an access violation. To ensure that you can successfully write functions like the one shown above, the compiler inserts calls to the C run-time library's stack checking function.

When compiling your program, the compiler knows the page size for the CPU system you are targeting. If you are compiling your application for the *x*86, MIPS, or PowerPC, the *x*86, MIPS, and PowerPC compilers all know that the page size for these platforms is 4 KB. If you are compiling for the Alpha, the Alpha compiler knows that the page size is 8 KB. As the compiler encounters each function in your program, it determines the amount of stack space required for the function; if the function requires more stack space than the target system's page size, the compiler inserts a call to the C run-time library's stack checking function. You do not need to specify any compiler switches—the compiler inserts this function automatically as needed.

The pseudo-code on the next page shows what the stack checking function does. I say *pseudo-code* because this function is usually implemented in assembly language by the compiler vendors.

```
// The C run-time library knows the page size for the target system.
#ifdef _M_ALPHA
#define PAGESIZE    (8 * 1024)    // 8-KB page
#else
#define PAGESIZE    (4 * 1024)    // 4-KB page
#endif


void StackCheck (int nBytesNeededFromStack) {
    // Get the stack pointer position.
    // At this point, the stack pointer has NOT been decremented
    // to account for the function's local variables.
    PBYTE pbStackPtr = (CPU's stack pointer);

    while (nBytesNeededFromStack >= PAGESIZE) {
        // Move down a page on the stack--should be a guard page.
        pbStackPtr -= PAGESIZE;

        // Access a byte on the guard page--forces new page to be
        // committed and guard page to move down a page.
        pbStackPtr[0] = 0;

        // Reduce the number of bytes needed from the stack.
        nBytesNeededFromStack -= PAGESIZE;
    }

    // Before returning, the StackCheck function sets the CPU's
    // stack pointer to the address below the function's
    // local variables.
}
```

Visual C++ does offer a compiler switch that allows you to control the page-size threshold that the compiler uses to determine when to add the automatic call to *StackCheck*. You should use this compiler switch only if you know exactly what you are doing and have a special need for it. For 99.99999 percent of all applications and DLLs written, this switch should not be used.

CHAPTER EIGHT

MEMORY-MAPPED FILES

Working with files is something almost every application must do, and it's always a hassle. Should your application open the file, read it, and close the file, or should it open the file and use a buffering algorithm to read from and write to different portions of the file? Win32 offers the best of both worlds: memory-mapped files.

Like virtual memory, memory-mapped files allow you to reserve a region of address space and commit physical storage to the region. The difference is that the physical storage comes from a file that is already on the disk instead of the system's paging file. Once the file has been mapped, you can access it as if the whole file were loaded in memory.

Memory-mapped files are used for three different purposes:

- The system uses memory-mapped files to load and execute EXE and DLL files. This greatly conserves both paging file space and the time required for an application to begin executing.

- You can use memory-mapped files to access a data file on disk. This shelters you from performing file I/O operations on the file and from buffering the file's contents.

- You can use memory-mapped files to allow multiple processes running on the same machine to share data with each other. (Win32 does offer other methods for communicating data among processes—but these other methods are implemented using memory-mapped files.)

In this chapter, we will examine each of these uses for memory-mapped files.

Memory-Mapped EXEs and DLLs

When a thread calls *CreateProcess*, the system performs the following steps:

1. The system locates the EXE file specified in the call to *Create-Process*. If the EXE file cannot be found, the process is not created and *CreateProcess* returns FALSE.

2. The system creates a new process kernel object.

3. The system creates a 4-GB address space for this new process.

4. The system reserves a region of address space large enough to contain the EXE file. The desired location of this region is specified inside the EXE file itself. By default, an EXE file's base address is 0x00400000. However, you can override this when you create your application's EXE file by using the linker's /BASE option when you link your application.

5. The system notes that the physical storage backing the reserved region is in the EXE file on disk instead of the system's paging file.

After the EXE file has been mapped into the process's address space, the system accesses a section of the EXE file that lists the DLLs containing functions that the code in the EXE calls. The system then calls *LoadLibrary* for each of these DLLs, and if any of the DLLs require additional DLLs, the system calls *LoadLibrary* to load those DLLs as well. Every time *LoadLibrary* is called to load a DLL, the system performs steps similar to steps 4 and 5 above:

1. The system reserves a region of address space large enough to contain the DLL file. The desired location of this region is specified inside the DLL file itself. By default, Visual C++ makes the DLL's base address 0x10000000. However, you can override this when you build your DLL by using the linker's /BASE option. All the standard system DLLs that ship with Windows NT and Windows 95 have different base addresses.

2. If the system is unable to reserve a region at the DLL's preferred base address, either because the region is occupied by another DLL or EXE or because the region just isn't big enough, the system will then try to find another region of address space to reserve for the DLL. It is unfortunate when a DLL cannot load at its preferred base address, for two reasons. First, the

system might not be able to load the DLL if it does not have fixup information. (You can remove fixup information from a DLL when it is created by using the linker's /FIXED switch. This makes the DLL file smaller, but it also means that the DLL *must* load at its preferred address.) Second, the system must perform some relocations within the DLL. On Windows 95, the system can fix the relocations as pages are swapped into RAM. On Windows NT, these relocations require additional storage from the system's paging file; they also increase the amount of time needed to load the DLL.

3. The system notes that the physical storage backing the reserved region is in the DLL file on disk instead of in the system's paging file. If Windows NT has to perform relocations because the DLL could not load at its preferred base address, the system also notes that some of the physical storage for the DLL is mapped to the paging file.

If for some reason the system is unable to map the EXE and all the required DLLs, the system displays a message box to the user and frees the process's address space and the process object. *CreateProcess* will return FALSE to its caller; the caller can call *GetLastError* to get a better idea of why the process could not be created.

After all the EXE and DLL files have been mapped into the process's address space, the system can begin executing the EXE file's startup code. After the EXE file has been mapped, the system takes care of all the paging, buffering, and caching. For example, if code in the EXE causes it to jump to the address of an instruction that isn't loaded into memory, a fault will occur. The system detects the fault and automatically loads the page of code from the file's image into a page of RAM. Then the system maps the page of RAM to the proper location in the process's address space and allows the thread to continue executing as though the page of code were loaded all along. Of course, all this is invisible to the application. This process is repeated each time any thread in the process attempts to access code or data that is not loaded into RAM.

Static Data Is Not Shared by Multiple Instances of an EXE or a DLL

When you create a new process for an application that is already running, the system simply opens another memory-mapped view of the file-mapping object that identifies the executable file's image and creates a new process object and a new thread object (for the primary thread). The system also assigns new process and thread IDs to these objects. By using memory-mapped files, multiple running instances of the same application can share the same code and data in RAM.

Note one small problem here. Win32 processes use a flat, 4-GB address space. When you compile and link your program, all the code and data are thrown together as one large entity. The data is separated from the code but only to the extent that it follows the code in the EXE file.[1] The following illustration shows a simplified view of how the code and data for an application are loaded into virtual memory and then mapped into an application's address space:

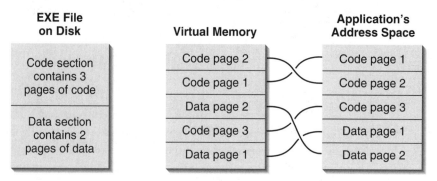

As an example, let's say that a second instance of an application is run. The system simply maps the pages of virtual memory containing the file's code and data into the second application's address space, as shown here:

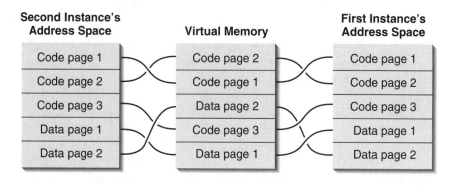

1. Actually, the contents of a file are broken down into sections. The code is in one section, and the global variables are in another. Sections are aligned on page boundaries. Pages are 4 KB on x86, MIPS, and PowerPC CPUs, and 8 KB on the DEC Alpha CPU. An application can determine the page size being used by calling *GetSystemInfo*. In the EXE or DLL file, the code section usually precedes the data section.

236

If one instance of the application alters some global variables residing in a data page, the memory contents for all instances of the application change. This type of change could cause disastrous effects and must not be allowed.

The system prohibits this by using the copy-on-write feature of the memory management system. Any time an application attempts to write to its memory-mapped file, the system catches the attempt, allocates a new block of memory for the page containing the memory the application is trying to write to, copies the contents of the page, and allows the application to write to this newly allocated memory block. As a result, no other instances of the same application are affected. The following illustration shows what happens when the first instance of an application attempts to change a global variable in data page 2:

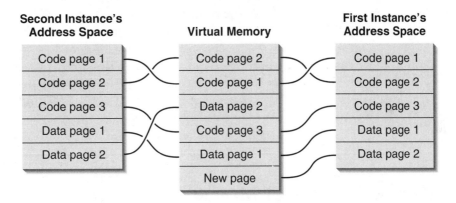

The system allocated a new page of virtual memory and copied the contents of data page 2 into it. The first instance's address space is changed so that the new data page is mapped into the address space at the same location as the original address page. Now the system can let the process alter the global variable without fear of altering the data for another instance of the same application.

A similar sequence of events occurs when an application is being debugged. Let's say that you're running multiple instances of an application and want to debug only one instance. You access your debugger and set a breakpoint in a line of source code. The debugger modifies your code by changing one of your assembly language instructions to an instruction that causes the debugger to activate itself. So we have the same problem again. When the debugger modifies the code, it causes all instances of the application to activate the debugger when the changed assembly instruction is executed. To fix this situation, the system again uses copy-on-write memory. When the system senses that the debugger is attempting to change the code, it allocates a new block of memory, copies the page containing the instruction into the new page, and allows the debugger to modify the code in the page copy.[2]

When a process is loaded, the system examines all the file image's pages. The system commits storage in the page file immediately for those pages that would normally be protected with the copy-on-write attribute. These pages are simply committed; they are not touched in any way. When a page in the file image is accessed, the system loads the appropriate page. If that page is never modified, it can be discarded from memory and reloaded when necessary. If the file's page is modified, however, the system swaps the modified page to one of the previously committed pages in the paging file.

The only difference in behavior between Windows NT and Windows 95 occurs when you have two copies of a module loaded and the writable data hasn't been modified. In this case, processes running under Windows NT share the data, while under Windows 95 each process receives its own copy of the data. Windows NT and Windows 95 behave exactly the same if only one copy of the module is loaded or if the writable data has been modified (which is normally the case).

Memory-Mapped Data Files

The operating system automatically uses the technique described in the previous section whenever an EXE or a DLL file is loaded. However, it is also possible to memory map a data file into your process's address space. This makes it very convenient to manipulate large streams of data.

To understand the power of using memory-mapped files this way, let's look at four possible methods of implementing a program to reverse the order of all the bytes in a file.

---

2. You can create global variables in an EXE or a DLL file and share them among all instances of the file. Briefly, this method requires placing the variables you want to share in their own section by using the *#pragma data_seg()* compiler directive. Then you must use the */SECTION:name, attributes* switch to tell the linker that you want the data in the section to be shared for all instances or mappings of the file. The *name* argument identifies the name of the section containing the data variables you want to share, and the *attributes* argument specifies the attributes of data in this section. To share variables, you'll need to use RSW for read, shared, and write. See Chapter 12 for more information about sharing global variables among multiple instances of a DLL.

Method 1: One File, One Buffer

The first and theoretically simplest method involves allocating a block of memory large enough to hold the entire file. The file is opened, its contents are read into the memory block, and the file is closed. With the contents in memory, we can now reverse all the bytes by swapping the first byte with the last, the second byte with the second-to-last, and so on. This swapping continues until you swap the two middle bytes in the file. After all the bytes have been swapped, you reopen the file and overwrite its contents with the contents of the memory block.

This method is pretty easy to implement but has two major drawbacks. First, a memory block the size of the file must be allocated. This might not be too bad if the file is small, but if the file is huge—say, 2 GB—the system will not allow the application to commit a block of physical storage that large. Large files require a different method.

Second, if the process is interrupted in the middle, while the reversed bytes are being written back out to the file, the contents of the file will be corrupted. The simplest way to guard against this is to make a copy of the original file before reversing its contents. If the whole process succeeds, you can delete the copy of the file. Unfortunately, this safeguard requires additional disk space.

Method 2: Two Files, One Buffer

In the second method, you open the existing file and create a new file of 0 length on the disk. Then you allocate a small internal buffer—say, 8 KB. You seek to the end of the original file minus 8 KB, read the last 8 KB into the buffer, reverse the bytes, and write the buffer's contents to the newly created file. The process of seeking, reading, reversing, and writing repeats until you reach the beginning of the original file. Some special handling is required if the file's length is not an exact multiple of 8 KB, but it's not extensive. After the original file is fully processed, both files are closed and the original file is deleted.

This method is a bit more complicated to implement than the first one. It uses memory much more efficiently because only an 8-KB chunk is ever allocated, but it has two big problems. First, the processing is slower than in the first method because on each iteration you must perform a seek on the original file before performing a read. Second, this method can potentially use an enormous amount of hard disk space. If the original file is 400 MB, the new file will grow to be 400 MB as the process continues. Just before the original file is deleted, the two files will occupy 800 MB of disk space. This is 400 MB more than should be required—which leads us to the next method.

Method 3: One File, Two Buffers

For this method, let's say the program initializes by allocating two separate 8-KB buffers. The program reads the first 8 KB of the file into one buffer and the last 8 KB of the file into the other buffer. The process then reverses the contents of both buffers and writes the contents of the first buffer back to the end of the file, and the contents of the second buffer back to the beginning of the same file. Each iteration continues by moving blocks from the front and back of the file in 8-KB chunks. Some special handling is required if the file's length is not an exact multiple of 16 KB and the two 8-KB chunks overlap. This special handling is more complex than the special handling in the previous method, but it's nothing that should scare off a seasoned programmer.

Compared with the previous two methods, this method is better at conserving hard disk space. Because everything is read from and written to the same file, no additional disk space is required. As for memory use, this method is also not too bad, using only 16 KB. Of course, this method is probably the most difficult to implement. Like the first method, this method can result in corruption of the data file if the process is somehow interrupted.

Now let's take a look at how this process might be accomplished using memory-mapped files.

Method 4: One File, Zero Buffers

When using memory-mapped files to reverse the contents of a file, you open the file and then tell the system to reserve a region of virtual address space. You tell the system to map the first byte of the file to the first byte of this reserved region. You can then access the region of virtual memory as though it actually contained the file. In fact, if there were a single 0 byte at the end of the file, you could simply call the C run-time function _strrev to reverse the data in the file.

This method's great advantage is that the system manages all the file caching for you. You don't have to allocate any memory, load file data into memory, write data back to the file, or free any memory blocks. Unfortunately, the possibility that an interruption such as a power failure could corrupt data still exists with memory-mapped files.

Using Memory-Mapped Files

To use a memory-mapped file, you must perform three steps:

1. Create or open a file kernel object that identifies the file on disk that you want to use as a memory-mapped file.

2. Create a file-mapping kernel object that tells the system the size of the file and how you intend to access the file.

3. Tell the system to map all or part of the file-mapping object into your process's address space.

When you are finished using the memory-mapped file, you must perform three steps to clean up:

1. Tell the system to unmap the file-mapping kernel object from your process's address space.

2. Close the file-mapping kernel object.

3. Close the file kernel object.

The next five sections discuss all these steps in more detail.

Step 1: Creating or Opening a File Kernel Object

To create or open a file kernel object, you always call the *CreateFile* function:

```
HANDLE CreateFile(LPCSTR lpFileName, DWORD dwDesiredAccess,
    DWORD dwShareMode, LPSECURITY_ATTRIBUTES lpSecurityAttributes,
    DWORD dwCreationDisposition, DWORD dwFlagsAndAttributes,
    HANDLE hTemplateFile);
```

Although its name does not suggest it, *CreateFile* is also the function you should use to open an existing file. The 16-bit Windows *OpenFile* function still exists in the Win32 API, but it is supplied for backward compatibility only. New applications should avoid the *OpenFile* function and always use the new *CreateFile* function.

The *CreateFile* function takes quite a few parameters. For this discussion, I'll concentrate only on the first three: *lpFileName*, *dwDesiredAccess*, and *dwShareMode*. *CreateFile* is discussed in more detail in Chapter 15 of this book.

As you might guess, the first parameter, *lpFileName*, identifies the name (including an optional path) of the file that you want to create or

241

open. The second parameter, *dwDesiredAccess*, specifies how you intend to access the contents of the file. You can specify one of the four following values here:

Value	Meaning
0	You cannot read from or write to the file's contents. Specify 0 when you just want to get a file's attributes.
GENERIC_READ	You can read from the file.
GENERIC_WRITE	You can write to the file.
GENERIC_READ | GENERIC_WRITE	You can read from the file and write to the file.

When creating or opening a file for use as a memory-mapped file, select the access flag or flags that make the most sense for how you intend to access the file's data. For memory-mapped files, you must open the file for read-only access or read-write access, so you'll want to specify either GENERIC_READ or GENERIC_READ | GENERIC_WRITE, respectively.

The third parameter, *dwShareMode*, tells the system how you want to share this file. You can specify one of the four following values for *dwShareMode*:

Value	Meaning
0	Any other attempts to open the file fail.
FILE_SHARE_READ	Other attempts to open the file using GENERIC_WRITE fail.
FILE_SHARE_WRITE	Other attempts to open the file using GENERIC_READ fail.
FILE_SHARE_READ | FILE_SHARE_WRITE	Other attempts to open the file succeed.

If *CreateFile* successfully creates or opens the specified file, a file handle is returned; otherwise, INVALID_HANDLE_VALUE is returned.

Important

> Most Win32 functions that return a handle return NULL when they are unsuccessful. *CreateFile*, however, returns INVALID_HANDLE_VALUE, which is defined as 0xFFFFFFFF.

Step 2: Creating a File-Mapping Kernel Object

Calling *CreateFile* tells the operating system the location of the file mapping's physical storage. The pathname that you pass indicates the exact location on the disk, on the network, on the CD-ROM disc, and so on, of the physical storage that is backing the file mapping. Now, you must tell the system how much physical storage is required by the file-mapping object. You do this by calling *CreateFile Mapping*:

```
HANDLE CreateFileMapping(HANDLE hFile, LPSECURITY_ATTRIBUTES lpsa,
    DWORD fdwProtect, DWORD dwMaximumSizeHigh,
    DWORD dwMaximumSizeLow, LPSTR lpszMapName);
```

The first parameter, *hFile*, identifies the handle of the file you want mapped into the process's address space. This handle is returned by the previous call to *CreateFile*. The *lpsa* parameter is a pointer to a SECURITY_ATTRIBUTES structure for the file-mapping kernel object; usually, NULL is passed for default security.

As I pointed out at the beginning of this chapter, creating a memory-mapped file is just like reserving a region of address space and then committing physical storage to the region. It's just that the physical storage for a memory-mapped file comes from a file on a disk rather than from space allocated from the system's paging file. When you create a file-mapping object, the system does not reserve a region of address space and map the file's storage to the region. (I'll describe how to do this in the next section.) However, when the system does map the storage to the process's address space, the system must know what protection attribute to assign to the pages of physical storage. *CreateFileMapping*'s *fdwProtect* parameter allows you to specify the protection attributes. Most of the time, you will specify one of the three protection attributes listed in the table on the top of the following page.

Protection Attribute	Meaning
PAGE_READONLY	When the file-mapping object is mapped, you can read the file's data. You must have passed GENERIC_READ to *CreateFile*.
PAGE_READWRITE	When the file-mapping object is mapped, you can read and write the file's data. You must have passed GENERIC_READ | GENERIC_WRITE to *CreateFile*.
PAGE_WRITECOPY	When the file-mapping object is mapped, you can read and write the file's data. Writing causes a private copy of the page to be created. You must have passed either GENERIC_READ or GENERIC_READ | GENERIC_WRITE to *CreateFile*.

Under Windows 95, you can pass the **PAGE_WRITECOPY** flag to *CreateFileMapping*; this tells the system to commit storage from the paging file. This paging file storage is reserved for a copy of the data file's data; only modified pages are actually written to the paging file. Any changes you make to the file's data are not propagated back to the original data file. The end result is that the **PAGE_WRITECOPY** flag has the same effect on both Windows NT and Windows 95.

In addition to the above page protections, there are four section attributes that you may bitwise **OR** in the *CreateFileMapping* function's *fdwProtect* parameter. A section is just another word for a memory mapping.

The first of these attributes, SEC_NOCACHE, tells the system that none of the file's memory-mapped pages are to be cached. So as you write data to the file, the system will update the file's data on the disk more often than it normally would. This flag, like the PAGE_NOCACHE protection attribute, exists for the device driver developer and is not usually used by applications.

Windows 95 ignores the SEC_NOCACHE flag.

The second section attribute, SEC_IMAGE, tells the system that the file you are mapping is a Win32 portable executable (PE) file. When the system maps this file into your process's address space, the system examines the file's contents to determine which protection attributes to assign to the various pages of the mapped image. For example, a PE file's code section is usually mapped with PAGE_EXECUTE_READ attributes, whereas the PE file's data is usually mapped with PAGE_READWRITE attributes. Specifying the SEC_IMAGE attribute tells the system to map the file's image and to set the appropriate page protections.

Windows 95 ignores the SEC_IMAGE flag.

The last two attributes, SEC_RESERVE and SEC_COMMIT, are mutually exclusive and do not apply when you are using a memory-mapped data file. These two flags will be discussed in the section "Using Memory-Mapped Files to Share Data Among Processes" later in this chapter. When creating a memory-mapped data file, you should not specify either of these flags. *CreateFileMapping* will ignore them.

CreateFileMapping's next two parameters, *dwMaximumSizeHigh* and *dwMaximumSizeLow*, are the most important parameters. The main purpose of the *CreateFileMapping* function is to ensure that enough physical storage is available for the file-mapping object. These two parameters tell the system the maximum size of the file in bytes. Two 32-bit values are required because Win32 supports file sizes that can be expressed using a 64-bit value; the *dwMaximumSizeHigh* parameter specifies the high 32 bits, and the *dwMaximumSizeLow* parameter specifies the low 32 bits. For files that are 4 GB or less, *dwMaximumSizeHigh* will always be 0.

Using a 64-bit value means that Win32 can process files as large as 18 exabytes. (An exabyte, which is abbreviated EB, is 1 quintillion, or 1,152,921,504,606,846,976 bytes.) If you want to create the file-mapping object so that it reflects the current size of the file, you can pass 0 for both parameters. If you intend only to read from the file or to access the file without changing its size, this is what you should do. If you intend to append data to the file, you will want to choose a maximum file size that leaves you some breathing room.

If you have been paying attention so far, you must be thinking that something is terribly wrong here. It's nice that Win32 supports files and file-mapping objects that can be anywhere up to 18 EB, but how are you ever going to map a file that big into your process's address space, which has a maximum limit of 4 GB (only 2 GB of which is usable)? I'll explain how you can accomplish this in the next section.

To really understand how *CreateFile* and *CreateFileMapping* work, I suggest you try the following experiment. Take the code below, build it, and then run it in a debugger. As you single-step through each statement, jump to a command shell and do a directory of "C:\". Notice the changes that are appearing in the directory as you execute each statement in the debugger.

```
int WINAPI WinMain(HINSTANCE hinstExe, HINSTANCE hinstExePrev,
   LPSTR pszCmdLine, int nCmdShow) {

   // Before executing the line below, C:\ does not have
   // a file called "MMFTest.Dat."
   HANDLE hfile = CreateFile("C:\\MMFTest.dat",
      GENERIC_READ | GENERIC_WRITE,
      FILE_SHARE_READ | FILE_SHARE_WRITE, NULL, CREATE_ALWAYS,
      FILE_ATTRIBUTE_NORMAL, NULL);

   // Before executing the line below, the MMFTest.Dat
   // file does exist but has a file size of 0 bytes.
   HANDLE hfilemap = CreateFileMapping(hfile, NULL, PAGE_READWRITE,
      0, 100, NULL);

   // After executing the line above, the MMFTest.Dat
   // file has a size of 100 bytes.

   // Cleanup
   CloseHandle(hfilemap);
   CloseHandle(hfile);

   // When the process terminates, MMFTest.Dat remains
   // on the disk with a size of 100 bytes.
   return(0);
}
```

If you call *CreateFileMapping*, passing the PAGE_READWRITE flag, the system will check to make sure that the associated data file on the disk is at least the same size as the size specified in the *dwMaximumSizeHigh* and *dwMaximumSizeLow* parameters. If the file is smaller than the specified size, *CreateFileMapping* will make the file on the disk larger by extending its size. This enlargement is required so that the physical storage will already exist when the file is used as a memory-mapped file later. If the file-mapping object is being created with the PAGE_READONLY or the PAGE_WRITECOPY flag, the size specified to *CreateFileMapping* must be no larger than the physical size of the disk file. This is because you will not be able to append any data to the file.

The last parameter of *CreateFileMapping*, *lpszMapName*, is a zero-terminated string that assigns a name to this file-mapping object. The name is used to share the object with another process and is discussed later in this chapter. (Chapter 2 also discusses kernel object sharing, but from a more abstract view.) A memory-mapped data file usually doesn't need to be shared; therefore, this parameter is usually NULL.

The system creates the file-mapping object and returns a handle identifying the object back to the calling thread. If the system cannot create the file-mapping object, a NULL handle value is returned. Again, please remember that this is different from *CreateFile*'s invalid handle value of INVALID_HANDLE_VALUE (defined as 0xFFFFFFFF).

Step 3: Mapping the File's Data into the Process's Address Space

After you have created a file-mapping object, you still need to have the system reserve a region of address space for the file's data and commit the file's data as the physical storage that is mapped to the region. You do this by calling *MapViewOfFile*:

```
LPVOID MapViewOfFile(HANDLE hFileMappingObject,
   DWORD dwDesiredAccess, DWORD dwFileOffsetHigh,
   DWORD dwFileOffsetLow, DWORD dwNumberOfBytesToMap);
```

The *hFileMappingObject* parameter identifies the handle of the file-mapping object, which was returned by the previous call to either *CreateFileMapping* or *OpenFileMapping* (discussed later in this chapter). The *dwDesiredAccess* parameter identifies how the data can be accessed. That's right, we must again specify how we intend to access the file's data. You can specify one of four possible values:

Value	Meaning
FILE_MAP_WRITE	You can read and write file data. *CreateFileMapping* had to be called by passing PAGE_READWRITE.
FILE_MAP_READ	You can read file data. *CreateFileMapping* could be called with any of the protection attributes: PAGE_READONLY, PAGE_READWRITE, or PAGE_WRITECOPY.
FILE_MAP_ALL_ACCESS	Same as FILE_MAP_WRITE.
FILE_MAP_COPY	You can read and write file data. Writing causes a private copy of the page to be created. *CreateFileMapping* could be called with any of the protection attributes: PAGE_READONLY, PAGE_READWRITE, or PAGE_WRITECOPY.

It certainly seems strange and annoying that Win32 requires all these protection attributes to be set over and over again. I assume this was done to give an application as much control as possible over data protection.

The remaining three parameters have to do with reserving the region of address space and mapping the physical storage to the region. When you map a file into your process's address space, you do not have to map the entire file at once. Instead, you can map only a small portion of the file into the address space. A portion of a file that is mapped to your process's address space is called a *view*, which explains how *MapViewOfFile* got its name.

When you map a view of a file into your process's address space, you must specify two things. First, you must tell the system which byte in the data file should be mapped as the first byte in the view. You do this using the *dwFileOffsetHigh* and *dwFileOffsetLow* parameters. Because Win32 supports files that can be up to 18 EB, you must specify this byte-offset using a 64-bit value of which the high 32 bits are passed in the *dwFileOffsetHigh* parameter and the low 32 bits are passed in the *dwFileOffsetLow* parameter. Note that the offset in the file must be an even multiple of the system's allocation granularity. (To date, all implementations of Win32 have an allocation granularity of 64 KB.) The section "System Information" in Chapter 6 shows how to obtain the allocation granularity value for a given system.

Second, you must tell the system how much of the data file to map into the address space. This is the same thing as specifying how large a region of address space to reserve. You specify this size using the *dwNumberOfBytesToMap* parameter. You'll notice that this parameter is a single 32-bit value because it could never be larger than 4 GB. If you specify a size of 0, the system will attempt to map a view starting with the specified offset within the file to the end of the entire file.

Under Windows 95, if *MapViewOfFile* cannot find a region large enough to contain the entire file-mapping object, *MapViewOfFile* returns NULL regardless of the size of the view requested.

Under Windows NT, *MapViewOfFile* needs only to find a region large enough for the view requested, regardless of the size of the entire file-mapping object.

If you specify the FILE_MAP_COPY flag when calling *MapViewOf-File*, the system commits physical storage from the system's paging file. The amount of space committed is determined by the *dwNumberOfBytes-ToMap* parameter. As long as you do nothing more than read from the file's mapped view, the system will never use these committed pages in the paging file. However, the first time any thread in your process writes to any memory address within the file's mapped view, the system will grab one of the committed pages from the paging file, copy the page of original data to this paging-file page, and then map this copied page into your process's address space. From this point on, the threads in your process are accessing a local copy of the data and cannot read or modify the original data.

When the system makes the copy of the original page, the system changes the protection of the page from PAGE_WRITECOPY to PAGE-_READWRITE. The following code fragment explains it all:

```
HANDLE hFile, hFileMapping;
BYTE bSomeByte, *pbFile;
    :
    :

// Open the file that we want to map.
hFile = CreateFile(lpszName, GENERIC_READ | GENERIC_WRITE, 0, NULL,
    OPEN_ALWAYS, FILE_ATTRIBUTE_NORMAL, NULL);

// Create a file-mapping object for the file.
hFileMapping = CreateFileMapping(hFile, NULL, PAGE_WRITECOPY,
    0, 0, NULL);
// Map a copy-on-write view of the file; the system will commit
// enough physical storage from the paging file to accommodate
// the entire file. All pages in the view will initially have
// PAGE_WRITECOPY access.
pbFile = (PBYTE) MapViewOfFile(hFileMapping, FILE_MAP_COPY,
    0, 0, 0);

// Read a byte from the mapped view.
bSomeByte = pbFile[0];
// When reading, the system does not touch the committed pages in
// the paging file. The page keeps its PAGE_WRITECOPY attribute.

// Write a byte to the mapped view.
pbFile[0] = 0;
// When writing for the first time, the system grabs a committed
// page from the paging file, copies the original contents of the
// page at the accessed memory address, and maps the new page
// (the copy) into the process's address space. The new page has
// a PAGE_READWRITE attribute.
```

```
// Write another byte to the mapped view.
pbFile[1] = 0;
// Because this byte is now in a PAGE_READWRITE page, the system
// simply writes the byte to the page (backed by the paging file).

// When finished using the file's mapped view, unmap it.
// UnmapViewOfFile is discussed in the next section.
UnmapViewOfFile(pbFile);
// The system decommits the physical storage from the paging file.
// Any writes to the pages are lost.

// Clean up after ourselves.
CloseHandle(hFileMapping);
CloseHandle(hFile);
```

As mentioned earlier, Windows 95 must commit storage in the paging file for the memory-mapped file up front. However, it will write modified pages to the paging file only as necessary.

Step 4: Unmapping the File's Data from the Process's Address Space

When you no longer need to keep a file's data mapped to a region of your process's address space, you can release the region by calling

```
BOOL UnmapViewOfFile(LPVOID lpBaseAddress);
```

The only parameter, *lpBaseAddress*, specifies the base address of the re-turned region. This value must be the same value returned from a call to *MapViewOfFile*. You must remember to call *UnmapViewOfFile*. If you do not call this function, the reserved region won't be released until your process terminates. Whenever you call *MapViewOfFile*, the system always reserves a new region within your process's address space—any previously reserved regions are *not* released.

In the interest of speed, the system buffers the pages of the file's data and doesn't update the disk image of the file immediately while working with the file's mapped view. However, when you are finished with the view and call *UnmapViewOfFile*, the system forces all the modified data in memory to be written back to the disk image. If you need to ensure that your updates have been written to disk, you can force the system to write all the modified data back to the disk image by calling *FlushViewOfFile*:

```
BOOL FlushViewOfFile(LPVOID lpBaseAddress,
   DWORD dwNumberOfBytesToFlush);
```

This function requires the address of the mapped view as returned by the previous call to *MapViewOfFile* and also requires the number of bytes you want to write to disk. If you call *FlushViewOfFile* and none of the data has been changed, the function simply returns without writing anything to the disk.

For a memory-mapped file whose storage is over a network, *FlushViewOfFile* guarantees that the file's data has been written from the workstation. However, *FlushViewOfFile* cannot guarantee that the server machine that is sharing the file has written the data to the remote disk drive because the server might be caching the file's data. To ensure that the server writes the file's data, you should pass the FILE_FLAG_WRITE_THROUGH flag to the *CreateFile* function whenever you create a file-mapping object for the file and then map the view of the file-mapping object. If the file is opened using this flag, *FlushViewOfFile* will return when all of the file's data has been stored on the server's disk drive.

Keep in mind one special characteristic of the *UnmapViewOfFile* function. If the view was originally mapped using the FILE_MAP_COPY flag, any changes you made to the file's data were actually made to a copy of the file's data stored in the system's paging file. In this case, if you call *UnmapViewOfFile*, the function has nothing to update on the disk file and simply causes the pages in the paging file to be decommitted. The data contained in the pages is lost.

If you want to preserve the changed data, you must take additional measures yourself. For example, you might want to create another file-mapping object (using PAGE_READWRITE) from the same file and map this new file-mapping object into your process's address space using the FILE_MAP_WRITE flag. Then you could scan the first view looking for pages with the PAGE_READWRITE protection attribute. Whenever you found a page with this attribute, you could examine its contents and decide whether to write the changed data to the file. If you do not want to update the file with the new data, keep scanning the remaining pages in the view until you reach the end. If you do want to save the changed page of data, however, just call *MoveMemory* to copy the page of data from the first view to the second view. Because the second view is mapped with PAGE_READWRITE protection, the *MoveMemory* function will be updating the actual contents of the file on the disk. You can use this method to determine changes and preserve your file's data.

Windows 95 does not support the copy-on-write protection attribute, so you cannot test for pages marked with the PAGE_READWRITE flag when scanning the first view of the memory-mapped file. You will have to devise a method of your own for determining which pages in the first view you have actually modified.

Steps 5 and 6: Closing the File-Mapping Object and the File Object

It goes without saying that you should always close any kernel objects you open. Forgetting to do so will cause a resource leak in your process. Of course, when your process terminates, the system automatically closes any objects your process opened but forgot to close. But if your process does not terminate for a while, you will accumulate resource handles. You should always write clean, "proper" code that closes any objects you have opened. To close the file-mapping object and the file object, you simply need to call the *CloseHandle* function twice—once for each handle.

Let's look at this a little closer. The following pseudo-code shows an example of memory-mapping a file:

```
HANDLE hFile, hFileMapping;
PVOID pFile;

hFile = CreateFile(...);
hFileMapping = CreateFileMapping(hFile, ...);
pFile = MapViewOfFile(hFileMapping, ...);

// Use the memory-mapped file.

UnmapViewOfFile(pFile);
CloseHandle(hFileMapping);
CloseHandle(hFile);
```

The above code shows the "expected" method for manipulating memory-mapped files. However, what it does not show is that the system increments the usage counts of the file object and the file-mapping object when you call *MapViewOfFile*. This side effect is significant because it means that we could rewrite the code fragment above as follows:

```
HANDLE hFile, hFileMapping;
PVOID pFile;

hFile = CreateFile(...);
hFileMapping = CreateFileMapping(hFile, ...);
```

```
CloseHandle(hFile);
pFile = MapViewOfFile(hFileMapping, ...);
CloseHandle(hFileMapping);

// Use the memory-mapped file.

UnmapViewOfFile(pFile);
```

In working with memory-mapped files, it is quite common to open the file, create the file-mapping object, and then use the file-mapping object to map a view of the file's data into the process's address space. Because the system increments the internal usage counts of the file object and the file-mapping object, you can close these objects at the beginning of your code and eliminate potential resource leaks.

If you will be creating additional file-mapping objects from the same file or mapping multiple views of the same file-mapping object, you cannot call *CloseHandle* early—you'll need the handles later to make the additional calls to *CreateFileMapping* and *MapViewOfFile*, respectively.

Processing a Big File Using Memory-Mapped Files

In an earlier section, I said I would tell you how to map an 18-EB file into a 4-GB address space. Well, you can't. Instead, you must map a view of the file that contains only a small portion of the file's data. You should start by mapping a view of the very beginning of the file. When you've finished accessing the first view of the file, you can unmap it and then map a new view starting at an offset deeper within the file. You'll need to repeat this process until you access the complete file. This certainly makes dealing with large memory-mapped files less convenient, but, fortunately, most files are well under 4 GB in size.

Let's look at an example using an 8-GB file. Here is a routine that counts all the *J* characters (one of my favorites) in this ASCII file in several steps:

```
__int64 WINAPI CountJs (void) {

   HANDLE hFile, hFileMapping;
   PBYTE pbFile;
   SYSTEM_INFO si;
   __int64 qwFileSize, qwFileOffset = 0, qwNumOfJs = 0;
   DWORD dwFileSizeHigh;
   DWORD dwByte, dwBytesInBlock;
   DWORD dwErr;
```

(continued)

```
// We need the allocation granularity value for this system
// because views must always begin with an offset in the data
// file that is a multiple of the allocation granularity value.
GetSystemInfo(&si);

// Open the data file.
hFile = CreateFile("c:\\HugeFile.Big", GENERIC_READ,
   FILE_SHARE_READ, NULL, OPEN_EXISTING,
   FILE_FLAG_SEQUENTIAL_SCAN, NULL);

if (hFile == INVALID_HANDLE_VALUE)
   return(0);

// Create the file-mapping object.
hFileMapping = CreateFileMapping(hFile, NULL, PAGE_READONLY,
   0, 0, NULL);

// We no longer need access to the file object's handle.
CloseHandle(hFile);

if (hFileMapping == NULL) {
   return(0);
}

qwFileSize = GetFileSize(hFile, &dwFileSizeHigh);
qwFileSize += (((__int64) dwFileSizeHigh) << 32);

while (qwFileSize > 0) {

   // Determine the number of bytes to be mapped.
   if (qwFileSize < si.dwAllocationGranularity)
      dwBytesInBlock = (DWORD) qwFileSize;
   else
      dwBytesInBlock = si.dwAllocationGranularity;

   pbFile = MapViewOfFile(hFileMapping,
      FILE_MAP_READ,                          // Desired access
      (DWORD) (qwFileOffset >> 32),           // Starting byte
      (DWORD) (qwFileOffset & 0xFFFFFFFF),//    in file
      dwBytesInBlock);                        // # of bytes to map

   // Count the number of Js in this block.
   for (dwByte = 0; dwByte < dwBytesInBlock; dwByte++) {
      if (pbFile[dwByte] == 'J')
         qwNumOfJs++;
   }
```

```
        // Unmap the view so that we don't get multiple
        // views in our address space.
        UnmapViewOfFile(pbFile);

        // Skip to the next set of bytes in the file.
        qwFileOffset += dwBytesInBlock;
        qwFileSize -= dwBytesInBlock;
    }

    CloseHandle(hFileMapping);
    return(qwNumOfJs);
}
```

This algorithm maps views of 64 KB (the allocation granularity size) or less. Also, remember that *MapViewOfFile* requires that the file offset parameters be an even multiple of the allocation granularity size. As each view is mapped into the address space, the scanning for *J*s continues. After each 64-KB chunk of the file has been mapped and scanned, it's time to tidy up by closing the file-mapping object.

Memory-Mapped Files and Coherence

The system allows you to map multiple views of the same data of a file. For example, you can map the first 10 KB of a file into a view and then map the first 4 KB of that same file into a separate view. As long as you are mapping the same file-mapping object, the system ensures that the viewed data is *coherent*. For example, if your application alters the contents of the file in one view, all other views are updated to reflect the changes. This is because even though the page is mapped into the process's virtual address space more than once, the system really has the data in only a single page of RAM. If multiple processes are mapping views of a single data file, the data is still coherent because there is still only one instance of each page of RAM within the data file—it's just that the pages of RAM are mapped into multiple process address spaces.

Important

Win32 allows you to create several file-mapping objects that are backed by a single data file. Win32 does *not* guarantee that views of these different file-mapping objects will be coherent. It guarantees only that multiple views of a single file-mapping object will be coherent.

When we're working with files, however, there is no reason why another application can't call *CreateFile* to open the same file that another process has mapped. This new process can then read from and write to the file using the *ReadFile* and *WriteFile* functions. Of course, whenever a process makes these calls, it must be either reading file data from or writing file data to a memory buffer. This memory buffer must be one the process itself created, *not* the memory that is being used by the mapped files. Problems can arise when two applications have opened the same file: one process can call *ReadFile* to read a portion of a file, modify the data, and write it back out using *WriteFile* without the file-mapping object of the second process being aware of the first process's actions. For this reason, it is recommended that when you call *CreateFile* for files that will be memory mapped, you specify 0 as the value of the *fdwShareMode* parameter. Doing so tells the system that you want exclusive access to the file and that no other process can open it.

Windows 95 is not able to maintain file coherence as well as Windows NT. For example, examine the following code fragment:

```
BYTE bBuf[1];
DWORD dwNumBytesRead;
HANDLE hFile = CreateFile(...);
HANDLE hFileMap = CreateFileMapping(hFile, ...);
PBYTE pbData = MapViewOfFile(hFileMap, ...);

// Change first byte of file to a capital "X."
pbData[0] = 'X';

// Read the first byte of the file into a buffer.
ReadFile(hFile, bBuf, 1, &dwNumBytesRead, NULL);

// Test to see whether the first byte of the file
// matches the byte read into the buffer.
if (pbData[0] == bBuf[0]) {
   // OS may or may not be Windows 95.
} else {
   // OS is Windows 95.
}
```

This code fragment modifies the first byte of the memory-mapped file and then reads the supposedly modified byte back into a buffer. Windows NT guarantees that the file is coherent, whereas Windows 95 does

(continued)

256

(continued)

not. For this reason, you should not write to a file using both memory-mapped file techniques and buffer write techniques. Of course, if the file is opened in read-only mode, you'll have no problem accessing it using either technique. The problem occurs only if you attempt to write to the file.

By the way, when the file above is closed, Windows NT guarantees that the *X* will be the first byte of the file, whereas Windows 95 does not.

Read-only files do not have coherence problems, which makes them good candidates for memory-mapped files. Memory-mapped files should never be used to share writable files over a network because the system cannot guarantee coherent views of the data. If someone's computer updates the contents of the file, someone else's computer with the original data in memory will not know that the information has changed.

The File Reverse Sample Application

The FileRev application (FILEREV.EXE), listed in Figure 8-1 beginning on page 260, demonstrates how to use memory-mapped files to reverse the contents of an ANSI or a Unicode text file. The source code and resource files for the application are in the FILEREV directory on the companion disc. When you start the program, the following window appears:

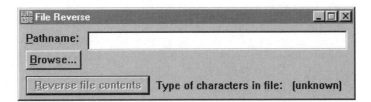

FileRev first allows you to select a file and then, when you click the Reverse File Contents button, the function reverses all of the characters contained within the file. The program will work correctly only on text files; it will not work correctly on binary files. FileRev determines whether the text file is ANSI or Unicode by calling the *IsTextUnicode* function (discussed in Chapter 17).

Under Windows 95, the *IsTextUnicode* function has no useful implementation and simply returns FALSE; calling *GetLastError* returns ERROR-_CALL_NOT_IMPLEMENTED. This means that the FileRev sample application always thinks that it is manipulating an ANSI text file when it is run under Windows 95.

When you click the Reverse File Contents button, FileRev makes a copy of the specified file called FILEREV.DAT. It does this so that the original file won't become unusable because its contents have been reversed. Next FileRev calls the *FileReverse* function, which is responsible for reversing the file, *FileReverse* calls the *CreateFile* function, opening FILEREV.DAT for reading and writing.

As I said earlier, the easiest way to reverse the contents of the file is to call the C run-time function _strrev. As with all C strings, the last character of the string must be a zero terminator. Because text files do not end with a zero character, FileRev must append one to the file. It does so by first calling *GetFileSize*:

```
dwFileSize = GetFileSize(hFile, NULL);
```

Now that you're armed with the length of the file, you can create the file-mapping object by calling *CreateFileMapping*. The file-mapping object is created with a length of *dwFileSize* plus the size of a wide character (for the zero character). If there is a bug in FileRev that overwrites the address space occupied by the file-mapping object, an access violation will occur. After the file-mapping object is created, a view of the object is mapped into FileRev's address space. The *lpvFile* variable contains the return value from *MapViewOfFile* and points to the first byte of the text file.

The next step is to write a zero character at the end of the file and to reverse the string:

```
((LPSTR) lpvFile)[dwFileSize / sizeof(CHAR)] = 0;
_strrev(lpvFile);
```

In a text file, every line is terminated by a return character ('\r') followed by a newline character ('\n'). Unfortunately, when we call _strrev to reverse the file, these characters also get reversed. So that the reversed text file can be loaded into a text editor, every occurrence of the "\n\r" pair needs to be converted back to its original "\r\n" order. This is the job of the following loop:

```
// Find first occurrence of '\n'.
lpch = strchr(lpvFile, '\n');

while (lpch != NULL) {
   *lpch++ = '\r';   // Change the '\n' to '\r'.
   *lpch++ = '\n';   // Change the '\r' to '\n'.

   // Find the next occurrence.
   lpch = strchr(lpch, '\n');
}
```

When you examine simple code like this, it is easy to forget that you are actually manipulating the contents of a file on the hard disk, which shows you how powerful memory-mapped files are.

After the file has been adjusted, FileRev must clean up by unmapping the view of the file-mapping object and closing all the kernel object handles. In addition, FileRev must also remove the zero character added to the end of the file (remember that _strrev_ doesn't reverse the position of the terminating zero character). If you don't remove the zero character, the reversed file would be 1 character larger, and calling FileRev again would not reverse the file back to its original form. To remove the trailing zero character, you need to drop back a level and use the file-management functions instead of manipulating the file through memory mapping.

Forcing the reversed file to end at a specific location requires positioning the file pointer at the desired location (the end of the original file) and calling the *SetEndOfFile* function:

```
SetFilePointer(hFile, dwFileSize, NULL, FILE_BEGIN);
SetEndOfFile(hFile);
```

Important

> *SetEndOfFile* must be called after the view is unmapped and the file-mapping object is closed; otherwise, an ERROR_USER_MAPPED_FILE will occur. This error indicates that the end-of-file operation cannot be performed on a file that is associated with a file-mapping object.

The last thing FileRev does is spawn an instance of Notepad so that you can look at the reversed file. The window at the top of the next page is the result of running FileRev on its own FILEREV.C file.

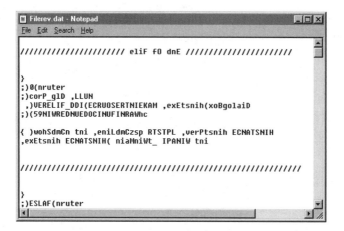

FileRev.ico

FILEREV.C

```
/**************************************************************
Module name: FileRev.C
Notices: Copyright (c) 1995-1997 Jeffrey Richter
**************************************************************/


#include "..\CmnHdr.H"                      /* See Appendix C. */
#include <windows.h>
#include <windowsx.h>
#include <tchar.h>
#include <string.h>               // For _strrev
#include "Resource.H"



///////////////////////////////////////////////////////////////



#define FILENAME   __TEXT("FILEREV.DAT")



///////////////////////////////////////////////////////////////



BOOL FileReverse (LPCTSTR pszPathname, PBOOL pfIsTextUnicode) {

   HANDLE hFile, hFileMap;
   LPVOID lpvFile;
```

Figure 8-1.   *(continued)*
The FileRev Application.

Figure 8-1. *continued*

```
LPSTR lpchANSI;        // Always ANSI
LPWSTR lpchUnicode;   // Always Unicode
DWORD dwFileSize;
int iUnicodeTestFlags = -1;   // Try all tests

// Assume that the text is Unicode.
*pfIsTextUnicode = FALSE;

// Open the file for reading and writing.
hFile = CreateFile(pszPathname, GENERIC_WRITE | GENERIC_READ,
   0, NULL, OPEN_EXISTING, FILE_ATTRIBUTE_NORMAL, NULL);

if (hFile == INVALID_HANDLE_VALUE) {
   // File open failed.
   chMB(__TEXT("File could not be opened."));
   return(FALSE);
}

// Get the size of the file. I am assuming here
// that the file is smaller than 4 GB.
dwFileSize = GetFileSize(hFile, NULL);

// Create the file-mapping object. The file-mapping object
// is 1 character bigger than the file size so that a zero
// character can be placed at the end of the file to terminate
// the string (file). Because I don't yet know if the file
// contains ANSI or Unicode characters, I assume worst case
// and add the size of a WCHAR instead of CHAR.
hFileMap = CreateFileMapping(hFile, NULL, PAGE_READWRITE,
   0, dwFileSize + sizeof(WCHAR), NULL);

if (hFileMap == NULL) {
   // File-Mapping open failed.
   chMB(__TEXT("File map could not be opened."));
   CloseHandle(hFile);
   return(FALSE);
}

// Get the address where the first byte of the file
// is mapped into memory.
lpvFile = MapViewOfFile(hFileMap, FILE_MAP_WRITE, 0, 0, 0);

if (lpvFile == NULL) {
   // Map view of file failed.
   chMB(__TEXT("Could not map view of file."));
```

(continued)

Figure 8-1. *continued*

```
      CloseHandle(hFileMap);
      CloseHandle(hFile);
      return(FALSE);
   }


   // Take an educated guess as to whether the text file
   // contains ANSI or Unicode characters.
   *pfIsTextUnicode = IsTextUnicode(lpvFile,
      dwFileSize, &iUnicodeTestFlags);

   if (!*pfIsTextUnicode) {
      // For all the file manipulations below, we explicitly
      // use ANSI functions instead of Unicode functions
      // because, although the application can be ANSI or
      // Unicode, it is processing an ANSI file.

      // Put a zero character at the very end of the file.
      lpchANSI = (LPSTR) lpvFile;
      lpchANSI[dwFileSize / sizeof(CHAR)] = 0;

      // Reverse the contents of the file.
      _strrev(lpchANSI);

      // Convert all "\n\r" combinations back to "\r\n" to
      // preserve the normal end-of-line sequence.
      lpchANSI = strchr(lpchANSI, '\n'); // Find first '\n'.

      while (lpchANSI != NULL) {
         // We have found an occurrence....
         *lpchANSI++ = '\r';    // Change '\n' to '\r'.
         *lpchANSI++ = '\n';    // Change '\r' to '\n'.
         lpchANSI = strchr(lpchANSI, '\n'); // Find the next
                                            // occurrence.
      }

   } else {
      // For all the file manipulations below, we explicitly
      // use Unicode functions instead of ANSI functions
      // because, although the application can be ANSI or
      // Unicode, it is processing a Unicode file.

      // Put a zero character at the very end of the file.
      lpchUnicode = (LPWSTR) lpvFile;
      lpchUnicode[dwFileSize / sizeof(WCHAR)] = 0;
```

(continued)

Figure 8-1. *continued*

```
        if ((iUnicodeTestFlags & IS_TEXT_UNICODE_SIGNATURE) != 0)
{

            // If the first character is the Unicode BOM
            // (byte-order-mark), 0xFEFF, keep this character
            // at the beginning of the file.
            lpchUnicode++;
        }

        // Reverse the contents of the file.
        _wcsrev(lpchUnicode);

        // Convert all "\n\r" combinations back to "\r\n" to
        // preserve the normal end-of-line sequence.
        lpchUnicode = wcschr(lpchUnicode, L'\n'); // Find first
                                                  // '\n'.

        while (lpchUnicode != NULL) {
            // We have found an occurrence....
            *lpchUnicode++ = L'\r';    // Change '\n' to '\r'.
            *lpchUnicode++ = L'\n';    // Change '\r' to '\n'.
            lpchUnicode =
                wcschr(lpchUnicode, L'\n'); // Find the next
                                            // occurrence.

        }
    }


    // Clean up everything before exiting.
    UnmapViewOfFile(lpvFile);
    CloseHandle(hFileMap);

    // Remove the trailing zero byte added earlier by
    // positioning the file pointer at the end of the file,
    // not including the zero byte, and setting
    // the end-of-file.
    SetFilePointer(hFile, dwFileSize, NULL, FILE_BEGIN);

    // SetEndOfFile must be called after the
    // file-mapping kernel object is closed.
    SetEndOfFile(hFile);
    CloseHandle(hFile);

    return(TRUE);
}
```

(continued)

Figure 8-1. *continued*

```
///////////////////////////////////////////////////////////


BOOL Dlg_OnInitDialog (HWND hwnd, HWND hwndFocus,
  LPARAM lParam) {

  // Associate an icon with the dialog box.
  chSETDLGICONS(hwnd, IDI_FILEREV, IDI_FILEREV);

  // Initialize the dialog box by disabling all
  // the nonsetup controls.
  EnableWindow(GetDlgItem(hwnd, IDC_REVERSE), FALSE);

  return(TRUE);
}




///////////////////////////////////////////////////////////


void Dlg_OnCommand (HWND hwnd, int id, HWND hwndCtl,
  UINT codeNotify) {

  TCHAR szPathname[_MAX_PATH];
  OPENFILENAME ofn;
  BOOL fIsTextUnicode;
  STARTUPINFO si;
  PROCESS_INFORMATION pi;

  switch (id) {
    case IDC_FILENAME:
      EnableWindow(GetDlgItem(hwnd, IDC_REVERSE),
        Edit_GetTextLength(hwndCtl) > 0);
      break;

    case IDC_FILESELECT:
      chINITSTRUCT(ofn, TRUE);
      ofn.hwndOwner = hwnd;
      ofn.lpstrFile = szPathname;
      ofn.lpstrFile[0] = 0;
      ofn.nMaxFile = chDIMOF(szPathname);
      ofn.lpstrTitle = __TEXT("Select file for reversing");
      ofn.Flags = OFN_EXPLORER | OFN_FILEMUSTEXIST;
```

(continued)

Figure 8-1. *continued*

```
        GetOpenFileName(&ofn);
        SetDlgItemText(hwnd, IDC_FILENAME, ofn.lpstrFile);
        SetFocus(GetDlgItem(hwnd, IDC_REVERSE));
        break;

    case IDC_REVERSE:
        GetDlgItemText(hwnd, IDC_FILENAME, szPathname,
            chDIMOF(szPathname));

        // Copy input file to FILEREV.DAT so that
        // the original is not destroyed.
        if (!CopyFile(szPathname, FILENAME, FALSE)) {
            // Copy failed.
            chMB(__TEXT("New file could not be created."));
            break;
        }

        if (FileReverse(FILENAME, &fIsTextUnicode)) {
            // Indicate whether we reversed a file containing
            // Unicode or ANSI characters.
            SetDlgItemText(hwnd, IDC_TEXTTYPE,
                fIsTextUnicode
                    ? __TEXT("Unicode") : __TEXT("ANSI"));

            // Spawn Notepad to see the fruits of our labors.
            chINITSTRUCT(si, TRUE);
            //si.wShowWindow = SW_SHOW;
            //si.dwFlags = STARTF_USESHOWWINDOW;
            if (CreateProcess(NULL,
                __TEXT("NOTEPAD.EXE ") FILENAME, NULL, NULL,
                FALSE, 0, NULL, NULL, &si, &pi)) {

                CloseHandle(pi.hThread);
                CloseHandle(pi.hProcess);
            }
        }
        break;

    case IDCANCEL:
        EndDialog(hwnd, id);
        break;
    }
}
```

(continued)

Figure 8-1. *continued*

```
//////////////////////////////////////////////////////////////


BOOL CALLBACK Dlg_Proc (HWND hwnd, UINT uMsg,
   WPARAM wParam, LPARAM lParam) {

   switch (uMsg) {
      chHANDLE_DLGMSG(hwnd, WM_INITDIALOG,  Dlg_OnInitDialog);
      chHANDLE_DLGMSG(hwnd, WM_COMMAND,  Dlg_OnCommand);
   }
   return(FALSE);
}



//////////////////////////////////////////////////////////////


int WINAPI _tWinMain (HINSTANCE hinstExe,
   HINSTANCE hinstPrev, LPTSTR pszCmdLine, int nCmdShow) {

   chWARNIFUNICODEUNDERWIN95();
   DialogBox(hinstExe, MAKEINTRESOURCE(IDD_FILEREV),
      NULL, Dlg_Proc);
   return(0);
}


////////////////////// End Of File //////////////////////
```

FILEREV.RC

```
//Microsoft Developer Studio generated resource script.
//
#include "Resource.h"

#define APSTUDIO_READONLY_SYMBOLS
//////////////////////////////////////////////////////////////
//
// Generated from the TEXTINCLUDE 2 resource.
//
#include "afxres.h"
```

(continued)

Figure 8-1. *continued*

```
////////////////////////////////////////////////////////////////
#undef APSTUDIO_READONLY_SYMBOLS

////////////////////////////////////////////////////////////////
// English (U.S.) resources

#if !defined(AFX_RESOURCE_DLL) || defined(AFX_TARG_ENU)
#ifdef _WIN32
LANGUAGE LANG_ENGLISH, SUBLANG_ENGLISH_US
#pragma code_page(1252)
#endif //_WIN32


////////////////////////////////////////////////////////////////
//
// Icon
//

// Icon with lowest ID value placed first to ensure application
// icon remains consistent on all systems.
IDI_FILEREV             ICON    DISCARDABLE     "FileRev.Ico"


#ifdef APSTUDIO_INVOKED
////////////////////////////////////////////////////////////////
//
// TEXTINCLUDE
//

1 TEXTINCLUDE DISCARDABLE
BEGIN
    "Resource.h\0"
END

2 TEXTINCLUDE DISCARDABLE
BEGIN
    "#include ""afxres.h""\r\n"
    "\0"
END

3 TEXTINCLUDE DISCARDABLE
BEGIN
    "\r\n"
    "\0"
END
```

(continued)

Figure 8-1. *continued*

```
#endif    // APSTUDIO_INVOKED


/////////////////////////////////////////////////////////////////
//
// Dialog
//


IDD_FILEREV DIALOG DISCARDABLE  15, 24, 216, 46
STYLE WS_MINIMIZEBOX | WS_POPUP | WS_VISIBLE | WS_CAPTION |
    WS_SYSMENU
CAPTION "File Reverse"
FONT 8, "System"
BEGIN
    LTEXT         "&Pathname:",IDC_STATIC,4,4,35,8
    EDITTEXT      IDC_FILENAME,44,4,168,12,ES_AUTOHSCROLL
    PUSHBUTTON    "&Browse...",IDC_FILESELECT,4,16,36,12,WS_GROUP
    DEFPUSHBUTTON "&Reverse file contents",IDC_REVERSE,4,32,80,12
    LTEXT         "Type of characters in file:",
                  IDC_STATIC,88,34,87,8
    LTEXT         "(unknown)",IDC_TEXTTYPE,176,34,34,8
END


/////////////////////////////////////////////////////////////////
//
// DESIGNINFO
//


#ifdef APSTUDIO_INVOKED
GUIDELINES DESIGNINFO DISCARDABLE
BEGIN
    IDD_FILEREV, DIALOG
    BEGIN
        RIGHTMARGIN, 192
        BOTTOMMARGIN, 42
    END
END
#endif    // APSTUDIO_INVOKED

#endif    // English (U.S.) resources
/////////////////////////////////////////////////////////////////
```

(continued)

Figure 8-1. *continued*

```
#ifndef APSTUDIO_INVOKED
/////////////////////////////////////////////////////////////////////
//
// Generated from the TEXTINCLUDE 3 resource.
//


/////////////////////////////////////////////////////////////////////
#endif    // not APSTUDIO_INVOKED
```

Specifying the Base Address of a Memory-Mapped File

Just as you can use the *VirtualAlloc* function to suggest an initial address to reserve address space, you can also use the *MapViewOfFileEx* function instead of the *MapViewOfFile* function to suggest that a file be mapped into a particular address.

```
LPVOID MapViewOfFileEx(HANDLE hFileMappingObject,
   DWORD dwDesiredAccess, DWORD dwFileOffsetHigh,
   DWORD dwFileOffsetLow, DWORD dwNumberOfBytesToMap,
   LPVOID lpBaseAddress);
```

All the parameters and the return value for this function are identical to those of the *MapViewOfFile* function with the single exception of the last parameter, *lpBaseAddress*. In this parameter, you specify a target address for the file you're mapping. As with *VirtualAlloc*, the target address you specify should be on an even allocation granularity boundary (usually 64 KB); otherwise, *MapViewOfFileEx* returns NULL, indicating an error.

Under Windows NT, specifying an address that is not a multiple of the allocation granularity causes the function to fail, and *GetLastError* will return 1132 (ERROR_MAPPED_ALIGNMENT). On Windows 95, the address will be rounded down to an even allocation granularity boundary.

If the system can't map the file at this location (usually because the file is too large and would overlap another reserved address space), the function fails and returns NULL. *MapViewOfFileEx* does not attempt to locate another address space that can accommodate the file. Of course, you can specify NULL as the *lpBaseAddress* parameter, in which case *MapViewOfFileEx* behaves exactly the same as *MapViewOfFile*.

MapViewOfFileEx is useful when you're using memory-mapped files to share data with other processes. As an example, you might need a memory-mapped file at a particular address when two or more applications are sharing a group of data structures containing pointers to other data structures. A linked list is a perfect example. In a linked list, each node, or element, of the list contains the memory address of another element in the list. To walk the list, you must know the address of the first element and then reference the member of the element that contains the address of the next element. This can be a problem when you're using memory-mapped files.

If one process prepares the linked list in a memory-mapped file and then shares this file with another process, it is possible that the other process will map the file into a completely different location in its address space. When the second process attempts to walk the linked list, it looks at the first element of the list, retrieves the memory address of the next element, and then tries to reference this next element. However, the address of the next element in the first node will be incorrect for this second process.

You can solve this problem in two ways. First, the second process can simply call *MapViewOfFileEx* instead of *MapViewOfFile* when it maps the memory-mapped file containing the linked list into its own address space. Of course, this method requires that the second process know where the first process originally mapped the file when constructing the linked list. When the two applications have been designed to interact with each other—which is most likely the case—this isn't a problem: the address can be hard-coded into both, or one process can notify the other process using another form of interprocess communication, such as sending a message to a window.

The second method for solving the problem is for the process that creates the linked list to store in each node the offset from within the address space where the next node is located. This requires that the application add the offset to the base address of the memory-mapped file in order to access each node. This method is not great: it can be slow, it makes the program bigger (because of the additional code the compiler generates to perform all the calculations), and it can be quite error prone. However, it is certainly a viable method, and the Microsoft compiler offers assistance for based-pointers using the __based keyword.

When calling *MapViewOfFileEx*, you must specify an address that is between 0x80000000 and 0xBFFFFFFF, or *MapViewOfFileEx* will return NULL.

When calling *MapViewOfFileEx*, you must specify an address that is between 0x00010000 and 0x7FFEFFFF, or *MapViewOfFileEx* will return NULL.

Memory-Mapped Files and Win32 Implementations

Windows 95 and Windows NT implement memory-mapped files differently. You need to be aware of these differences because they can affect the way you write your code and the robustness of your data.

Under Windows 95, a view is always mapped in the address space partition that ranges from 0x80000000 to 0xBFFFFFFF. Because of this, all successful calls to *MapViewOfFile* return an address within this range. You might recall that the data in this partition is shared by all Win32 processes. This means that if a process maps a view of a file-mapping object, the data of the file-mapping object is physically accessible to all Win32 processes whether or not they have mapped a view of the file-mapping object. If another process calls *MapViewOfFile* using the same file-mapping object, Windows 95 will return the same memory address to the second process that it did to the first process. The two processes are accessing the same data, and the views are coherent.

In Windows 95, it is possible for one process to call *MapViewOfFile* and pass the returned memory address to another process's thread using some form of interprocess communication. Once this thread has received the memory address, there is nothing to stop the thread from successfully accessing the same view of the file-mapping object. However, you should not do this for two reasons:

- Your application will not run under Windows NT, for reasons I'll describe shortly.

- If the first process calls *UnmapViewOfFile*, the address space region will revert to the free state; this means that the second process's thread will raise an access violation when it attempts to access the memory where the view once was.

271

For the second process to access the view of the memory-mapped file, a thread in the second process should call *MapViewOfFile* on its own behalf. When the second process does this, the system increments a usage count for the memory-mapped view. So if the first process calls *UnmapViewOfFile*, the system will not release the region of address space occupied by the view until the second process also calls *UnmapViewOfFile*.

When the second process calls *MapViewOfFile*, the address returned will be the same address that was returned to the first process. This averts the need for the first process to send the memory address to the second process using interprocess communication.

The Windows NT implementation of memory-mapped files is better than the Windows 95 implementation because Windows NT *requires* a process to call *MapViewOfFile* before the file's data is accessible in the process's address space. If one process calls *MapViewOfFile*, the system reserves a region of address space for the view in the calling process's address space—no other process can see the view. If another process wants to access the data in the same file-mapping object, a thread in the second process must call *MapViewOfFile*, and the system will reserve a region for the view in the second process's address space.

Keep in mind this very important note: the memory address returned by the first process's call to *MapViewOfFile* will most likely *not* be the same memory address returned by the second process's call to *MapViewOfFile*. This is true even though both processes are mapping a view of the same file-mapping object. In Windows 95, the memory addresses returned from *MapViewOfFile* are the same—but you should absolutely not *count* on them being the same if you want your application to run under Windows NT!

Let's look at another implementation difference. Here is a small program that maps two views of a single file-mapping object:

```
#define STRICT
#include <Windows.h>

int WINAPI WinMain (HINSTANCE hinstExe, HINSTANCE hinstPrev,
   LPSTR lpCmdLine, int nCmdShow) {

   HANDLE hFile, hFileMapping;
   BYTE *pbFile, *pbFile2;

   // Open an existing file--it must be bigger than 64 KB.
   hFile = CreateFile(lpCmdLine, GENERIC_READ | GENERIC_WRITE, 0,
      NULL, OPEN_ALWAYS, FILE_ATTRIBUTE_NORMAL, NULL);
```

```
// Create a file-mapping object backed by the data file.
hFileMapping = CreateFileMapping(hFile, NULL, PAGE_READWRITE,
   0, 0, NULL);

// Starting at offset 0, map a view of the file
// into the process's address space.
pbFile = (PBYTE) MapViewOfFile(hFileMapping, FILE_MAP_WRITE,
   0, 0, 0);

// Starting at offset 65536, map another view of the file
// into the process's address space.
pbFile2 = (PBYTE) MapViewOfFile(hFileMapping, FILE_MAP_WRITE,
   0, 65536, 0);

if (pbFile + 65536 == pbFile2) {
   // If the addresses overlap, there is one address
   // space region for both views: this must be Windows 95.
   MessageBox(NULL, "We are running under Windows 95",
      NULL, MB_OK);
} else {
   // If the addresses do not overlap, each view has its own
   // address space region: this must be Windows NT.
   MessageBox(NULL, "We are running under Windows NT",
      NULL, MB_OK);
}


UnmapViewOfFile(pbFile2);
UnmapViewOfFile(pbFile);
CloseHandle(hFileMapping);
CloseHandle(hFile);

return(0);
}
```

Under Windows 95, when a view of a file-mapping object is mapped, the system reserves enough address space for the entire file-mapping object. This happens even if *MapViewOfFile* is called with parameters that indicate that you want the system to map only a small portion of the file-mapping object. This means that you can't map a 1-GB file-mapping object to a view even if you specify that only a 64-KB portion of the object be mapped.

Whenever any process calls *MapViewOfFile*, the function returns an address within the address space region that was reserved for the *entire* file-mapping object. So in the code above, the first call to *MapViewOfFile* returns the base address of the region that contains the entire mapped file. The second call to *MapViewOfFile* returns an address that is 64 KB into the same address space region.

The Windows NT implementation is again quite different. The two calls to *MapViewOfFile* in the code above cause Windows NT to reserve two different address space regions. The size of the first region is the size of the file-mapping object, and the size of the second region is the size of the file-mapping object minus 64 KB. Even though there are two different regions, the data is guaranteed to be coherent because both views are made from the same file-mapping object. Under Windows 95, the views are coherent because it *is* the same memory.

Using Memory-Mapped Files to Share Data Among Processes

The ability to share data and information quickly and easily among processes is one of the most compelling reasons to use a Microsoft Windows environment over more restrictive environments such as MS-DOS. Win32 and 16-bit Windows both handle these sharing tasks in a number of ways. In 16-bit Windows, for example, there are several methods for sharing data. Probably the most common method is to call either *SendMessage* or *PostMessage* using a window belonging to another process. Unfortunately, in 16-bit Windows, *SendMessage* and *PostMessage* allow only one 16-bit value and one 32-bit value to be passed to another process. You can also allocate a block of global memory (using the GMEM_SHARE flag) and then pass the handle (as the *wParam* or *lParam* parameter) in a call to *SendMessage* or *PostMessage*. The receiver of this message then calls *GlobalLock* to get an address to the memory block and reads or writes the data.

This method doesn't work in Win32, however, because each process has its own address space and one process cannot easily probe the data in another process's address space. In 16-bit Windows, it's almost too easy to share data—applications frequently manipulate data that doesn't belong to them, causing other applications to crash.

The Win32 system, on the other hand, allows multiple applications (running on the same machine) to share data using memory-mapped files. Memory-mapped files are, in fact, the only mechanism that offers this capability in the Win32 environment. Other techniques for sharing and transferring data, such as using *PostMessage* or *SendMessage* (including using *SendMessage* passing the new Win32 WM_COPYDATA window message), all use memory-mapped files internally.

This data sharing is accomplished by having two or more processes map views of the same file-mapping object, which means they are sharing the same pages of physical storage. As a result, when one process writes to data in a view of a shared file-mapping object, the other processes see the change instantly in their views. Note that for multiple processes to share a single file-mapping object, all processes must use exactly the same name for the file-mapping object.

Let's look at an example: starting an application. When an application starts, the system calls *CreateFile* to open the EXE file on the disk. Then the system calls *CreateFileMapping* to create a file-mapping object. Finally, the system calls *MapViewOfFileEx* on behalf of the newly created process so that the EXE file is mapped into the process's address space. *MapViewOfFileEx* is called instead of *MapViewOfFile* so that the file's image is mapped to the base address stored in the EXE file's image. The system creates the process's initial thread, puts the address of the first byte of executable code of this mapped view in the thread's instruction pointer, and then lets the CPU start executing the code.

If the user runs a second instance of the same application, the system sees that a file-mapping object already exists for the desired EXE file and doesn't create a new file object or file-mapping object. Instead, the system maps a view of the file a second time, this time in the context of the newly created process's address space. What the system has done is map the identical file into two address spaces simultaneously. Obviously, this is a more efficient use of memory because both processes are sharing the same pages of physical storage containing portions of the code that are executing.

The next two sections discuss various techniques for sharing a file-mapping object among multiple processes.

CreateFileMapping and OpenFileMapping

Let's begin by again looking at the *CreateFileMapping* function:

```
HANDLE CreateFileMapping(HANDLE hFile, LPSECURITY_ATTRIBUTES lpsa,
    DWORD fdwProtect, DWORD dwMaximumSizeHigh,
    DWORD dwMaximumSizeLow, LPSTR lpName);
```

When you call this function to create a file-mapping object, you can give the object a name by passing a zero-terminated string as the *lpName* parameter. For example, one process might create a file-mapping object and assign it the name *MyFileMapObj*:

```
HANDLE hFileMap = CreateFileMapping(..., "MyFileMapObj");
```

When the code above executes, *CreateFileMapping* creates the file-mapping object and, if another file-mapping object with the specified name doesn't exist, stores the name with the new file-mapping object.

If a file-mapping object *does* exist with the specified name, however, *CreateFileMapping* does not create a new object. Instead, it increments the usage count for the object and returns a process-relative handle identifying the existing file-mapping object. Note that the system does not change the size of the existing file-mapping object.

You can determine whether a new file-mapping object was created by calling *GetLastError*. Usually, you would call *GetLastError* to determine why a function failed. However, in the case of *CreateFileMapping*, you can call *GetLastError* if the function is successful. If *GetLastError* returns ERROR_ALREADY_EXISTS, *CreateFileMapping* has returned a handle to a previously existing object. If you don't want to use this existing object, you need to close the handle. The following code fragment guarantees that *CreateFileMapping* will create a new object or none at all:

```
HANDLE hFileMap = CreateFileMapping(...);
if ((hFileMap != NULL) &&
    (GetLastError() == ERROR_ALREADY_EXISTS)) {
    CloseHandle(hFileMap);
    hFileMap = NULL;
}
return(hFileMap);
```

Another way that multiple processes can share a file-mapping object is by calling *OpenFileMapping*:

```
HANDLE OpenFileMapping(DWORD dwDesiredAccess,
    BOOL bInheritHandle, LPSTR lpName);
```

This function is similar to *CreateFileMapping* except that it assumes that a file-mapping object already exists—and if the object does not exist, *OpenFileMapping* will not create a new one. So to share a file-mapping object using *OpenFileMapping*, one process must first create the object using *CreateFileMapping*; then the other processes can open the file-mapping object using *OpenFileMapping*. In keeping with my example, all processes but the first open the file-mapping object by calling *OpenFileMapping* and passing a zero-terminated string as the *lpName* parameter:

```
HANDLE hFileMap = OpenFileMapping(..., "MyFileMapObj");
```

OpenFileMapping's first parameter, *dwDesiredAccess*, specifies access rights, such as FILE_MAP_READ, FILE_MAP_WRITE, FILE_MAP_ALL_ACCESS, or FILE_MAP_COPY. The second parameter, *bInheritHandle*, indicates whether child processes should automatically inherit the handle to this file-mapping object. The handle that *OpenFileMapping* returns identifies the process-relative handle to the file-mapping object created by the first process.

If *OpenFileMapping* cannot find a file-mapping object that has the passed name, NULL is returned. If a valid handle is returned, mapping the data into a process's own address space is simply a matter of calling *MapViewOfFile* or *MapViewOfFileEx*. Don't forget to call *CloseHandle* when you have finished using the opened file-mapping object.

Inheritance

A great way for two processes to share a file-mapping object is for one process to create an inheritable file-mapping object handle; the process then spawns a new child process that inherits the parent's file-mapping object handle. The child process's handle value to the file-mapping object will be exactly the same as the parent's handle value.

To create an inheritable file-mapping object handle, you must call *CreateFileMapping* and pass it the address of a SECURITY_ATTRIBUTES structure that is initialized as follows:

```
SECURITY_ATTRIBUTES sa;
sa.nLength = sizeof(sa);
sa.lpSecurityDescriptor = NULL;
sa.bInheritHandle = TRUE;
hFileMap = CreateFileMapping(hFile, &sa, ...);
```

(Alternatively, if the parent process is sharing a file-mapping object created by another process, the parent process can call *OpenFileMapping* and simply pass TRUE for the *bInheritHandle* parameter.)

Then, when the parent process is ready to create the child process, the parent must call the *CreateProcess* function and pass TRUE for the *fInheritHandle* parameter:

```
BOOL CreateProcess(LPCTSTR lpszImageName, LPCTSTR lpszCommandLine,
    LPSECURITY_ATTRIBUTES lpsaProcess,
    LPSECURITY_ATTRIBUTES lpsaThread,
    BOOL fInheritHandles, DWORD fdwCreate, LPVOID lpvEnvironment,
    LPCTSTR lpszCurDir, LPSTARTUPINFO lpsiStartInfo,
    LPPROCESS_INFORMATION lppiProcInfo);
```

This causes the usage count of the file-mapping object to increment; the new child process will be able to use the handle to the file-mapping object, but it will not know what the value of the handle is. You must have some other technique for passing the value of the handle to the child. You can do this by passing a command-line parameter to the child or by sending or posting a message to a window created by the child process.

Whatever method you use (and others exist), the child is responsible for closing its handle to the file-mapping object. Only after all the processes have closed their handles to the file-mapping object does the system delete the object and all of the physical storage that was committed from the paging file for the object.

Memory-Mapped Files Backed by the Paging File

So far I've been discussing techniques that allow you to map a view of a file that resides on a disk drive. Many applications create some data while they run and need to transfer the data or share it with another process. It would be terribly inconvenient if the applications had to create a data file on a disk drive and store the data there in order to share it.

Microsoft realized this and added the ability to create memory-mapped files that are backed by the system's paging file rather than a dedicated hard disk file. This method is almost identical to the method for creating a memory-mapped disk file except that it's even easier. First, there is no need to call *CreateFile* since you will not be creating or opening a dedicated file. Instead, you simply call *CreateFileMapping* as you would normally and pass (HANDLE) 0xFFFFFFFF as the *hFile* parameter. This tells the system that you are not creating a file-mapping object whose physical storage resides in a file on the disk; instead, you want the system to commit physical storage from the system's paging file. The amount of storage allocated is determined by *CreateFileMapping*'s *dwMaximumSizeHigh* and *dwMaximumSizeLow* parameters.

After you have created this file-mapping object and mapped a view of it into your process's address space, you can use it as you would any region of memory. If you want to share this data with other processes, call *CreateFileMapping* and pass a zero-terminated string as the *lpName* parameter. Then other processes that want to access the storage can call *CreateFileMapping* or *OpenFileMapping* and pass the same name.

When a process no longer needs access to the file-mapping object, that process should call *CloseHandle*. When all the handles are closed, the system will reclaim the committed storage from the system's paging file.

Important

Here is an interesting problem that has caught unsuspecting programmers by surprise. Can you guess what is wrong with the following code fragment?

```
HANDLE hFile = CreateFile(...);
HANDLE hMap = CreateFileMapping(hFile, ...);
if (hMap == NULL)
    return(GetLastError());
  :
  :
```

(continued)

Important

(continued)

If the call to *CreateFile* above fails, it returns 0xFFFFFFFF (INVALID-_HANDLE_VALUE). However, the unsuspecting programmer who wrote this code didn't test to check whether the file was created successfully. When *CreateFileMapping* is called, 0xFFFFFFFF is passed in the *hFile* parameter, which causes the system to create a file mapping using storage from the paging file instead of the intended disk file. Any additional code that uses the memory-mapped file will work correctly. However, when the file-mapping object is destroyed, all data that was written to the file-mapping storage (the paging file) will be destroyed by the system. At this point, the developer sits and scratches his or her head, wondering what went wrong!

The Memory-Mapped File Sharing Sample Application

The MMFShare application (MMFSHARE.EXE), listed in Figure 8-2 beginning on page 280, demonstrates how to use memory-mapped files to transfer data among two or more separate processes. The source code and resource files for the application are in the MMFSHARE directory on the companion disc.

You're going to need to execute at least two instances of the MMFSHARE.EXE program. Each instance creates its own dialog box, shown here:

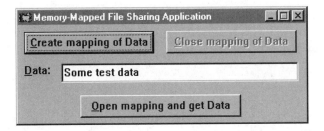

To transfer data from one instance of MMFShare to another, type the data to be transferred into the Data edit field. Then click on the Create Mapping Of Data button. When you do, MMFShare calls *CreateFileMapping* to create a 4-KB memory-mapped file object backed by the system's paging file and names the object *MMFSharedData*. If MMFShare sees that a file-mapping object with this name already exists, it displays a message box notifying you that it could not create the object. If, on the other hand, MMFShare succeeds in creating the object, it proceeds to map a view of the file into the process's address space and copies the data from the edit control into the memory-mapped file.

After the data has been copied, MMFShare unmaps the view of the file, disables the Create Mapping Of Data button, and enables the Close Mapping Of Data button. At this point, a memory-mapped file named *MMFSharedData* is just sitting somewhere in the system. No processes have mapped a view to the data contained in the file.

If you now go to another instance of MMFShare and click on this instance's Open Mapping And Get Data button, MMFShare attempts to locate a file-mapping object called *MMFSharedData* by calling *OpenFileMapping*. If an object of this name cannot be found, MMFShare displays another message box notifying you. If MMFShare finds the object, it maps a view of the object into its process's address space and copies the data from the memory-mapped file into the edit control of the dialog box. Voilà! You have transferred data from one process to another.

The Close Mapping Of Data button in the dialog box is used to close the file-mapping object, which frees up the storage in the paging file. If no file-mapping object exists, no other instance of MMFShare will be able to open one and get data from it. Also, if one instance has created a memory-mapped file, no other instance is allowed to create one and overwrite the data contained within the file.

MMFShare.ico

MMFSHARE.C

```
/*********************************************************
Module name: MMFShare.C
Notices: Copyright (c) 1995-1997 Jeffrey Richter
*********************************************************/


#include "..\CmnHdr.H"                    /* See Appendix C. */
#include <windows.h>
#include <windowsx.h>
#include <tchar.h>
#include "Resource.H"



///////////////////////////////////////////////////////////////////////


BOOL Dlg_OnInitDialog (HWND hwnd, HWND hwndFocus,
   LPARAM lParam) {

   // Associate an icon with the dialog box.
   chSETDLGICONS(hwnd, IDI_MMFSHARE, IDI_MMFSHARE);
```

Figure 8-2. *(continued)*
The MMFShare application.

Figure 8-2. *continued*

```
    // Initialize the edit control with some test data.
    Edit_SetText(GetDlgItem(hwnd, IDC_DATA),
        __TEXT("Some test data"));

    // Disable the Close button because the file can't
    // be closed if it was never created or opened.
    Button_Enable(GetDlgItem(hwnd, IDC_CLOSEFILE), FALSE);
    return(TRUE);
}


///////////////////////////////////////////////////////////////////


void Dlg_OnCommand (HWND hwnd, int id, HWND hwndCtl,
    UINT codeNotify) {

    // Handle of the open memory-mapped file
    static HANDLE s_hFileMap = NULL;
    HANDLE hFileMapT;

    switch (id) {
        case IDC_CREATEFILE:
            if (codeNotify != BN_CLICKED)
                break;

            // Create an in-memory memory-mapped file that
            // contains the contents of the edit control. The
            // file is 4 KB at most and is named MMFSharedData.
            s_hFileMap = CreateFileMapping((HANDLE) 0xFFFFFFFF,
                NULL, PAGE_READWRITE, 0, 4 * 1024,
                __TEXT("MMFSharedData"));

            if (s_hFileMap != NULL) {

                if (GetLastError() == ERROR_ALREADY_EXISTS) {
            chMB(__TEXT("Mapping already exists - not created."));
                    CloseHandle(s_hFileMap);

                } else {

                    // File mapping created successfully.
                    // Map a view of the file
                    // into the address space.
```

(continued)

Figure 8-2. *continued*

```
              LPVOID lpView = MapViewOfFile(s_hFileMap,
                 FILE_MAP_READ | FILE_MAP_WRITE, 0, 0, 0);

              if ((BYTE *) lpView != NULL) {
                 // View mapped successfully; put contents
                 // of edit control into the memory-mapped
                 // file.
                 Edit_GetText(GetDlgItem(hwnd, IDC_DATA),
                    (LPTSTR) lpView, 4 * 1024);

                 // Unmap the view. This protects the
                 // data from wayward pointers.
                 UnmapViewOfFile((LPVOID) lpView);

                 // The user can't create
                 // another file right now.
                 Button_Enable(hwndCtl, FALSE);

                 // The user closed the file.
                 Button_Enable(GetDlgItem(hwnd,
                    IDC_CLOSEFILE), TRUE);

              } else {
                 chMB(__TEXT("Can't map view of file."));
              }
           }

        } else {
           chMB(__TEXT("Can't create file mapping."));
        }
        break;

     case IDC_CLOSEFILE:
        if (codeNotify != BN_CLICKED)
           break;

        if (CloseHandle(s_hFileMap)) {
           // User closed the file. A new file can be
           // created, but the new file can't be closed.
           Button_Enable(GetDlgItem(hwnd, IDC_CREATEFILE),
              TRUE);
           Button_Enable(hwndCtl, FALSE);
        }
        break;
```

(continued)

Figure 8-2. *continued*

```
        case IDC_OPENFILE:
            if (codeNotify != BN_CLICKED)
                break;

            // See if a memory-mapped file named
            // MMFSharedData already exists.
            hFileMapT = OpenFileMapping(
                FILE_MAP_READ | FILE_MAP_WRITE,
                FALSE, __TEXT("MMFSharedData"));

            if (hFileMapT != NULL) {
                // Memory-mapped file does exist.  Map a view
                // of it into the process's address space.
                LPVOID lpView = MapViewOfFile(hFileMapT,
                    FILE_MAP_READ | FILE_MAP_WRITE, 0, 0, 0);

                if ((BYTE *) lpView != NULL) {

                    // Put the contents of the
                    // file into the edit control.
                    Edit_SetText(GetDlgItem(hwnd, IDC_DATA),
                        (LPTSTR) lpView);
                    UnmapViewOfFile((LPVOID) lpView);

                } else {
                    chMB(__TEXT("Can't map view."));
                }

                CloseHandle(hFileMapT);

            } else {
                chMB(__TEXT("Can't open mapping."));
            }
            break;

        case IDCANCEL:
            EndDialog(hwnd, id);
            break;
    }
}


//////////////////////////////////////////////////////////////////
```

(continued)

Figure 8-2. *continued*

```
BOOL CALLBACK Dlg_Proc (HWND hwnd, UINT uMsg,
   WPARAM wParam, LPARAM lParam) {

   switch (uMsg) {
      chHANDLE_DLGMSG(hwnd, WM_INITDIALOG, Dlg_OnInitDialog);
      chHANDLE_DLGMSG(hwnd, WM_COMMAND, Dlg_OnCommand);
   }
   return(FALSE);
}


///////////////////////////////////////////////////////////////////


int WINAPI _tWinMain (HINSTANCE hinstExe,
   HINSTANCE hinstPrev, LPTSTR pszCmdLine, int nCmdShow) {

   chWARNIFUNICODEUNDERWIN95();
   DialogBox(hinstExe, MAKEINTRESOURCE(IDD_MMFSHARE),
      NULL, Dlg_Proc);

   return(0);
}


//////////////////////// End Of File ////////////////////////
```

```
MMFSHARE.RC
//Microsoft Developer Studio generated resource script.
//
#include "Resource.h"

#define APSTUDIO_READONLY_SYMBOLS
/////////////////////////////////////////////////////////////////
//
// Generated from the TEXTINCLUDE 2 resource.
//
#include "afxres.h"


/////////////////////////////////////////////////////////////////
#undef APSTUDIO_READONLY_SYMBOLS
```

(continued)

Figure 8-2. *continued*

```
/////////////////////////////////////////////////////////////////
// English (U.S.) resources

#if !defined(AFX_RESOURCE_DLL) || defined(AFX_TARG_ENU)
#ifdef _WIN32
LANGUAGE LANG_ENGLISH, SUBLANG_ENGLISH_US
#pragma code_page(1252)
#endif //_WIN32


/////////////////////////////////////////////////////////////////
//
// Dialog
//

IDD_MMFSHARE DIALOG DISCARDABLE  38, 36, 186, 61
STYLE WS_MINIMIZEBOX | WS_POPUP | WS_VISIBLE | WS_CAPTION |
    WS_SYSMENU
CAPTION "Memory-Mapped File Sharing Application"
FONT 8, "System"
BEGIN
    PUSHBUTTON          "&Create mapping of Data",
                        IDC_CREATEFILE,4,4,84,14,
                        WS_GROUP
    PUSHBUTTON          "&Close mapping of Data",
                        IDC_CLOSEFILE,96,4,84,14
    LTEXT               "&Data:",IDC_STATIC,4,24,18,8
    EDITTEXT            IDC_DATA,28,24,153,12
    PUSHBUTTON          "&Open mapping and get Data",
                        IDC_OPENFILE,40,44,104,14,
                        WS_GROUP
END


/////////////////////////////////////////////////////////////////
//
// Icon
//

// Icon with lowest ID value placed first to ensure application
// icon remains consistent on all systems.
IDI_MMFSHARE            ICON    DISCARDABLE       "MMFShare.Ico"
```

(continued)

Figure 8-2. *continued*

```
#ifdef APSTUDIO_INVOKED
/////////////////////////////////////////////////////////////////////////
//
// TEXTINCLUDE
//

1 TEXTINCLUDE DISCARDABLE
BEGIN
    "Resource.h\0"
END

2 TEXTINCLUDE DISCARDABLE
BEGIN
    "#include ""afxres.h""\r\n"
    "\0"
END

3 TEXTINCLUDE DISCARDABLE
BEGIN
    "\r\n"
    "\0"
END

#endif    // APSTUDIO_INVOKED

#endif    // English (U.S.) resources
/////////////////////////////////////////////////////////////////////////


#ifndef APSTUDIO_INVOKED
/////////////////////////////////////////////////////////////////////////
//
// Generated from the TEXTINCLUDE 3 resource.
//


/////////////////////////////////////////////////////////////////////////
#endif    // not APSTUDIO_INVOKED
```

Sparsely Committed Memory-Mapped Files

In all the discussion of memory-mapped files so far, we see that the system requires that all storage for the memory-mapped file be committed either in the data file on disk or in the paging file. This means that we can't use storage as efficiently as we might like. Let's return to the discussion of the spreadsheet from the section "When to Commit Physical Storage" in Chapter 7. Let's say that you want to share the entire spreadsheet with another process. If we were to use memory-mapped files, we would need to commit the physical storage for the entire spreadsheet:

```
CELLDATA CellData[200][256];
```

If a CELLDATA structure is 128 bytes, this array requires 6,553,600 ($200 \times 256 \times 128$) bytes of physical storage. As I said in Chapter 7, "That's a lot of physical storage to allocate from the paging file right up front for a spreadsheet, especially when you consider that most users put information into only a few spreadsheet cells, leaving the majority unused."

It should be obvious that we would prefer to share the spreadsheet as a file-mapping object without having to commit all of the physical storage up front. *CreateFileMapping* offers a way to do this by specifying either the SEC_RESERVE or the SEC_COMMIT flag in the *fdwProtect* parameter.

These flags are meaningful only if you're creating a file-mapping object that is backed by the system's paging file. The SEC_COMMIT flag causes *CreateFileMapping* to commit storage from the system's paging file. This is also the result if you specify neither flag.

When you call *CreateFileMapping* and pass the SEC_RESERVE flag, the system does not commit physical storage from the system's paging file; it just returns a handle to the file-mapping object. You can now call *MapViewOfFile* or *MapViewOfFileEx* to create a view of this file-mapping object. *MapViewOfFile* and *MapViewOfFileEx* will reserve a region of address space and will not commit any physical storage to back the region. Any attempts to access a memory address in the reserved region will cause the thread to raise an access violation.

What we have here is a region of reserved address space and a handle to a file-mapping object that identifies the region. Other processes can use the same file-mapping object to map a view of the same region of address space. Physical storage is still not committed to the region, and if threads in other processes attempt to access a memory address of the view in their regions, these threads will raise access violations.

Now, here is where things get exciting. To commit physical storage to the shared region, all a thread has to do is call *VirtualAlloc*:

```
LPVOID VirtualAlloc(LPVOID lpvAddress, DWORD cbSize,
    DWORD fdwAllocationType, DWORD fdwProtect);
```

We already discussed this function in great detail in Chapter 7. Calling *VirtualAlloc* to commit physical storage to the memory-mapped view region is just like calling *VirtualAlloc* to commit storage to a region initially reserved by a simple call to *VirtualAlloc* using the MEM_RESERVE flag. And just as you can commit storage sparsely in a region reserved with *VirtualAlloc*, you can also commit storage sparsely within a region reserved by *MapViewOfFile* or *MapViewOfFileEx*. However, when you commit storage to a region reserved by *MapViewOfFile* or *MapViewOfFileEx*, all the processes that have mapped a view of the same file-mapping object can now successfully access the committed pages.

Using the SEC_RESERVE flag and *VirtualAlloc*, we can successfully share the spreadsheet application's *CellData* matrix with other processes—and use physical storage very efficiently.

Normally, *VirtualAlloc* will fail when you pass it a memory address outside 0x00400000 through 0x7FFFFFFF. However, when committing physical storage to a memory-mapped file created using the SEC_RESERVE flag, you have to call *VirtualAlloc*, passing a memory address that is between 0x80000000 and 0xBFFFFFFF. Windows 95 knows that you are committing storage to a reserved memory-mapped file and allows the call to succeed.

Important

Under Windows NT, you cannot use the *VirtualFree* function to decommit storage from a memory-mapped file that was reserved with the SEC_RESERVE flag. However, Windows 95 does allow you to call *VirtualFree* to decommit storage in this case.

CHAPTER NINE

HEAPS

The third and last mechanism for manipulating memory in Win32 is the use of heaps. Heaps are great for allocating lots of small blocks of data. For example, linked lists and trees are best managed using heaps rather than the virtual memory techniques discussed in Chapter 7 or the memory-mapped file techniques discussed in Chapter 8.

If you are coming from a 16-bit Windows programming background, you are familiar with the two different types of heaps: the local heap and the global heap. Each process and DLL in 16-bit Windows receives its very own local heap, and all processes share a single global heap.

In Win32, heap management is vastly different. Here is a list of some of the differences:

- There is just one type of heap. (It has no special name like "local" or "global" because there is only one type.)

- Heaps are always local to a process; the contents of a process's heap cannot be accessed by a thread in another process. Because many 16-bit Windows applications use the global heap as a method for sharing data between processes, this change to heaps is frequently the source of problems encountered in porting from 16-bit Windows to Win32.

- A single process can create several heaps within its address space and manipulate all of them.

- A DLL does not get its own heap; it uses heaps that are part of the process's address space. However, a DLL can create a heap in the process's address space for the DLL's own purposes. Because many 16-bit DLLs share data between processes using the DLLs' local heap, this change is also a frequent source of porting problems.

This chapter discusses Win32 heaps and the functions that are available to create them, manipulate them, and destroy them. For all new Win32 applications, these are the functions that you should be using. At the end of this chapter, I present a section that describes how Win32 implements the 16-bit Windows heap functions. Take note that the 16-bit Windows heap functions exist in the Win32 API for backward compatibility only. The functions are implemented on top of the new heap functions; they perform slowly and require additional memory. Use the 16-bit Windows global and local heap functions only if you must.

What Is a Win32 Heap?

A Win32 heap is a region of reserved address space. Initially, most of the pages within the reserved region are not committed with physical storage. As you make more allocations from the heap, the heap manager commits more physical storage to the heap. As allocations in the heap are freed, the heap manager decommits physical storage from the heap. Physical storage is committed to the heap in pages.

Every now and then someone asks me for the exact rules that the heap manager uses to decide when to commit or decommit physical storage. Different implementations and different versions of the Win32 API use slightly different rules. Microsoft is constantly performing stress tests and running different scenarios to determine the rules that work best most of the time. As applications and the hardware that runs them change, these rules will change. If this knowledge is critical to your application, don't use heaps. Instead, use the virtual memory functions (that is, *VirtualAlloc* and *VirtualFree*) so you can control these rules yourself.

A Process's Default Heap

When a Win32 process is initialized, the system creates a heap in the process's address space. This heap is called the process's *default heap*. By default, this heap's region of address space is 1 MB in size. However, the system can grow a process's default heap so that it becomes larger than this. You can change the default region size of 1 MB using the /HEAP linker switch when you create an application. Because a DLL does not have a heap associated with it, you should not use the /HEAP switch when you are linking a DLL. The heap switch has the following syntax:

```
/HEAP:reserve[,commit]
```

The process's default heap is required by many Win32 functions. For example, the core functions in Windows NT perform all of their operations using Unicode characters and strings. If you call an ANSI version of a Win32 function, this ANSI version must convert the ANSI strings to Unicode strings and then call the Unicode version of the same function. To convert the strings, the ANSI function needs to allocate a block of memory to hold the Unicode version of the string. This block of memory is allocated from your process's default heap. Many other Win32 functions require the use of temporary memory blocks; these blocks are allocated from the process's default heap. Also, the 16-bit Windows global and local heap functions make their memory allocations from the process's default heap.

Because the process's default heap is used by many of the Win32 functions and because your application has many threads calling the various Win32 functions simultaneously, access to the default heap is serialized. In other words, the system guarantees that only one thread at a time may allocate or free blocks of memory in the default heap at any given time. If two threads attempt to allocate a block of memory in the default heap simultaneously, only one thread will be able to allocate a block, and the other thread will be forced to wait until the first thread's block is allocated. Once the first thread's block is allocated, the heap functions will allow the second thread to allocate a block. This serialized access causes a small performance hit. If your application has only one thread and you want to have the fastest possible access to a heap, you should create your own separate heap and not use the process's default heap. Unfortunately, you cannot tell the Win32 functions not to use the default heap, so their accesses to the heap are always serialized.

As I mentioned at the beginning of this chapter, a single process can have several heaps at once. These heaps can be created and destroyed during the lifetime of the process. The default heap, however, is created before the process begins execution and is destroyed automatically when the process terminates. You cannot destroy the process's default heap. Each heap is identified by its own heap handle, and all of the Win32 heap functions that allocate and free blocks within a heap require this heap handle as a parameter.

You can obtain the handle to your process's default heap by calling *GetProcessHeap*:

```
HANDLE GetProcessHeap(VOID);
```

Creating Your Own Win32 Heaps

In addition to the process's default heap, you can create additional heaps in your process's address space. Basically, you would want to create additional heaps in your own applications for three main reasons:

- Component protection
- More efficient memory management
- Local access

Let's examine each reason in detail.

Component Protection

For this discussion, imagine that your application needs to process two components: a linked list of NODE structures and a binary tree of BRANCH structures. You have two C files: LNKLST.C, which contains the functions that process the linked list of NODEs, and BINTREE.C, which contains the functions that process the binary tree of BRANCHes.

If the NODEs and the BRANCHes are stored together in a single heap, the combined heap might look like Figure 9-1.

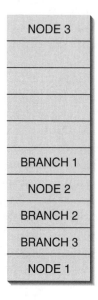

Figure 9-1.
A single heap that stores NODEs and BRANCHes together.

Now let's say that a bug in the linked-list code causes the 8 bytes after NODE 1 to be accidentally overwritten, which causes the data in BRANCH 3 to be corrupted. When the code in BINTREE.C later attempts to traverse the binary tree, it will probably fail because of this memory corruption. This will, of course, lead you to believe that there is a bug in your binary-tree code when, in fact, the bug exists in the linked-list code. Because the different types of objects are mixed together in a single heap, it becomes significantly more difficult to track down and isolate bugs.

By creating two separate heaps, one for NODEs and the other for BRANCHes, you localize your problems. A small bug in your linked-list code does not compromise the integrity of your binary tree, and vice versa. It is still possible to have a bug in your code that causes a wild memory write to another heap, but this is far less likely to happen.

Efficient Memory Management

Heaps can be managed more efficiently by allocating objects of the same size within them. For example, let's say that every NODE structure requires 24 bytes and every BRANCH structure requires 32 bytes. All of these objects are allocated from a single heap. Figure 9-2 shows a fully occupied single heap with several NODE and BRANCH objects allocated

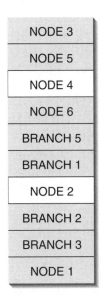

Figure 9-2.
A single fragmented heap that contains several NODE and BRANCH objects.

within it. If NODE 2 and NODE 4 are freed, memory in the heap becomes fragmented. If you then attempt to allocate a BRANCH structure, the allocation will fail even though 48 bytes are available and a BRANCH needs only 32 bytes.

If each heap consisted only of objects that were the same size, freeing an object would guarantee that another object would fit perfectly into the freed object's space.

Local Access

The last reason to use separate heaps in your application is to provide local access. Giving applications a 4-GB address space when you're using a machine containing far less than 4 GB of physical memory requires that the operating system and the CPU work together. When the system swaps a page of RAM out to its paging file, it takes a performance hit. By the same token, another performance hit is taken when the system needs to swap a page of data back from the paging file into RAM. If you keep accesses to memory localized to a small range of addresses, it is less likely that the system will need to swap pages between RAM and the paging file.

So, in designing an application, it's a good idea to allocate things that will be accessed together close to each other. Returning to our linked list and binary tree example, traversing the linked list is not related in any way to traversing the binary tree. By keeping all the NODEs close together (in one heap), you can keep the NODEs in adjoining pages; in fact, it's likely that several NODEs will fit within a single page of physical memory. Traversing the linked list will not require that the CPU refer to several different pages of memory for each NODE access.

If you were to allocate both NODEs and BRANCHes in a single heap, the NODEs would not necessarily be close together. In the worst-case situation, you might be able to have one NODE only per page of memory, with the remainder of each page occupied by BRANCHes. In this case, traversing the linked list could cause page faults for each NODE, which would make the process extremely slow.

Creating Another Win32 Heap

You can create additional heaps in your process by having a thread call *HeapCreate*:

```
HANDLE HeapCreate(DWORD flOptions, DWORD dwInitialSize,
    DWORD cbMaximumSize);
```

The first parameter, *flOptions*, modifies how operations are performed on the heap. You can specify 0, HEAP_NO_SERIALIZE, HEAP-_GENERATE_EXCEPTIONS, or a combination of the two flags.

By default, a heap will serialize access to itself so that multiple threads can allocate and free blocks from the heap without the danger of corrupting the heap. When an attempt is made to allocate a block of memory from the heap, the *HeapAlloc* function (discussed later) must do the following:

1. Traverse the linked list of allocated and freed memory blocks

2. Find the address of a free block

3. Allocate the new block by marking the free block as allocated

4. Add a new entry into the linked list of memory blocks

To illustrate how you might use the HEAP_NO_SERIALIZE flag, let's say that two threads are attempting to allocate blocks of memory from the same heap at the same time. The first thread executes steps 1 and 2 above and gets the address of a free memory block. However, before this thread can execute step 3, the thread is preempted and the second thread gets a chance to execute steps 1 and 2. Because the first thread has not executed step 3 yet, the second thread finds the address to the same free memory block.

With both threads having found what they believe to be a free memory block in the heap, Thread 1 updates the linked list, marking the new block as allocated. Thread 2 then also updates the linked list, marking the *same* block as allocated. Neither thread has detected a problem so far, but both threads receive an address to the exact same block of memory.

This type of bug can be very difficult to track down because it usually doesn't manifest itself immediately. Instead, the bug waits in the background until the most inopportune moment. The potential problems are listed here:

■ The linked list of memory blocks has been corrupted. This problem will not be discovered until an attempt to allocate or free a block is made.

■ Both threads are sharing the same memory block. Thread 1 and Thread 2 might both write information to the same block. When Thread 1 examines the contents of the block, it will not recognize the data introduced by Thread 2.

■ One thread might proceed to use the block and free it, causing the other thread to overwrite unallocated memory. This will corrupt the heap.

The solution to these problems is to allow a single thread exclusive access to the heap and its linked list until the thread has performed all the operations it needs to on the heap. The absence of the HEAP-_NO_SERIALIZE flag does exactly this. It is safe to use the HEAP_NO-_SERIALIZE flag only if one or more of the following conditions are true for your process:

■ Your process uses only a single thread.

■ Your process uses multiple threads, but the heap is accessed by only a single thread.

■ Your process uses multiple threads but manages access to the heap itself by using other forms of mutual exclusion, such as mutexes and semaphores, as discussed in Chapter 10.

If you're not sure whether to use the HEAP_NO_SERIALIZE flag, don't use it. Not using it will cause your threads to take a slight performance hit whenever a heap manipulation function is called, but you won't risk corrupting your heap and its data.

The other flag, HEAP_GENERATE_EXCEPTIONS, causes the system to raise an exception whenever an attempt to allocate or reallocate a block of memory in the heap fails. An exception is just another way for the system to notify your application that an error has occurred. Sometimes it's easier to design your application to look for exceptions rather than to check for return values. Exceptions are discussed in Chapter 16.

The second parameter of *HeapCreate*, *dwInitialSize*, indicates the number of bytes initially committed to the heap. *HeapCreate* rounds this value up to an even multiple of the CPU's page size if necessary. The final parameter, *dwMaximumSize*, indicates the maximum size to which the heap can expand (the maximum amount of address space the system can reserve for the heap). If *dwMaximumSize* is 0, the system reserves a region (size determined by the system) for the heap and expands the region as needed until the region has reached its maximum size. If the heap is created successfully, *HeapCreate* returns a handle identifying the new heap. This handle is used by the other heap functions.

Allocating a Block of Memory from a Heap

Allocating a block of memory from a heap is simply a matter of calling *HeapAlloc*:

```
LPVOID HeapAlloc(HANDLE hHeap, DWORD dwFlags, DWORD dwBytes);
```

The first parameter, *hHeap*, identifies the handle of the heap from which an allocation should be made. This handle must be a handle that was returned by an earlier call to *HeapCreate* or *GetProcessHeap*. The *dwBytes* parameter specifies the number of bytes that are to be allocated from the heap. The middle parameter, *dwFlags*, allows you to specify flags that affect the allocation. Currently only three flags are supported: HEAP_ZERO_MEMORY, HEAP_GENERATE_EXCEPTIONS, and HEAP_NO_SERIALIZE.

The purpose of the HEAP_ZERO_MEMORY flag should be fairly obvious. This flag causes the contents of the block to be filled with zeros before *HeapAlloc* returns. The second flag, HEAP_GENERATE_EXCEPTIONS, causes the *HeapAlloc* function to raise a software exception if insufficient memory is available in the heap to satisfy the request. When creating a heap with *HeapCreate*, you can specify the HEAP_GENERATE_EXCEPTIONS flag, which tells the heap that an exception should be raised when a block cannot be allocated. If you specify this flag when calling *HeapCreate*, you don't need to specify it when calling *HeapAlloc*. On the other hand, you might want to create the heap without using this flag. In this case, specifying this flag to *HeapAlloc* affects only the single call to *HeapAlloc*, not every call to this function.

If *HeapAlloc* fails and then raises an exception, the exception raised will be one of the two shown in the following table:

Identifier	Meaning
STATUS_NO_MEMORY	The allocation attempt failed because of insufficient memory.
STATUS_ACCESS_VIOLATION	The allocation attempt failed because of heap corruption or improper function parameters.

A block allocated with *HeapAlloc* is fixed and nondiscardable, so it is quite possible for the heap to become fragmented as the application allocates and frees various memory blocks. If the block has been successfully allocated, *HeapAlloc* returns the address of the block. If the memory could not be allocated and HEAP_GENERATE_EXCEPTIONS was not specified, *HeapAlloc* returns NULL.

The last flag, HEAP_NO_SERIALIZE, allows you to force this individual call to *HeapAlloc* to not be serialized with other threads that are accessing the same heap. You should use this flag with extreme caution because the heap could become corrupted if other threads are manipulating the heap at the same time.

Changing the Size of a Block

Often it's necessary to alter the size of a memory block. Some applications initially allocate a larger than necessary block and then, after all the data has been placed into the block, resize the block to a smaller size. Some applications begin by allocating a small block of memory and then attempting to enlarge the block when more data needs to be copied into it. Resizing a memory block is accomplished by calling the *HeapReAlloc* function:

```
LPVOID HeapReAlloc(HANDLE hHeap, DWORD dwFlags,
    LPVOID lpMem, DWORD dwBytes);
```

As always, the *hHeap* parameter indicates the heap that contains the block you want to resize. The *dwFlags* parameter specifies the flags that *HeapReAlloc* should use when attempting to resize the block. Only the following four flags are available: HEAP_GENERATE_EXCEPTIONS, HEAP_NO_SERIALIZE, HEAP_ZERO_MEMORY, and HEAP_RE-ALLOC_IN_PLACE_ONLY.

The first two flags have the same meaning as when they are used with *HeapAlloc*. The HEAP_ZERO_MEMORY flag is useful only when you are resizing a block to make it larger. In this case, the additional bytes in the block will be zeroed. This flag has no effect if the block is being reduced.

The HEAP_REALLOC_IN_PLACE_ONLY flag tells *HeapReAlloc* that it is not allowed to move the memory block within the heap, which *HeapReAlloc* might attempt to do if the memory block were growing. If *HeapReAlloc* is able to enlarge the memory block without moving it, it will do so and return the original address of the memory block. On the other hand, if *HeapReAlloc* must move the contents of the block, the address of the new, larger block is returned. If the block is made smaller, *HeapReAlloc* returns the original address of the memory block. You would want to specify the HEAP_REALLOC_IN_PLACE_ONLY flag if the block were part of a linked list or tree. In this case, other nodes in the list or tree might have pointers to this node and relocating the node in the heap would corrupt the integrity of the linked list.

The remaining two parameters, *lpMem* and *dwBytes*, specify the current address of the block that you want to resize and the new size—in bytes—of the block. *HeapReAlloc* returns either the address of the new, resized block or NULL if the block cannot be resized.

Obtaining the Size of a Block

After a memory block has been allocated, the *HeapSize* function can be called to retrieve the actual size of the block:

```
DWORD HeapSize(HANDLE hHeap, DWORD dwFlags, LPCVOID lpMem);
```

The *hHeap* parameter (returned from an earlier call to either *HeapCreate* or *GetProcessHeap*) identifies the heap, and the *lpMem* parameter (returned from an earlier call to *HeapAlloc* or *HeapReAlloc*) indicates the address of the block. The *dwFlags* parameter can be either 0 or HEAP_NO_SERIALIZE.

Freeing a Block

When you no longer need the memory block, you can free it by calling *HeapFree*:

```
BOOL HeapFree(HANDLE hHeap, DWORD dwFlags, LPVOID lpMem);
```

HeapFree frees the memory block and returns TRUE if successful. The *dwFlags* parameter can be either 0 or HEAP_NO_SERIALIZE. Calling this function may cause the heap manager to decommit some physical storage, but there are no guarantees.

Destroying a Win32 Heap

If your application no longer needs a heap that it created, you can destroy the heap by calling *HeapDestroy*:

```
BOOL HeapDestroy(HANDLE hHeap);
```

Calling *HeapDestroy* causes all the memory blocks contained within the heap to be freed and causes the physical storage and reserved address space region occupied by the heap to be released back to the system. If the function is successful, *HeapDestroy* returns TRUE. If you don't explicitly destroy the heap before your process terminates, the system will destroy it for you. However, a heap is destroyed only when a process terminates. If a thread creates a heap, the heap won't be destroyed when the thread terminates.

The system will not allow the process's default heap to be destroyed until the process completely terminates. If you pass the handle to the process's default heap to *HeapDestroy*, the system simply ignores the call.

Using Heaps with C++

One of the best ways to take advantage of Win32 heaps is to incorporate them into your existing C++ programs. In C++, class-object allocation is performed by calling the *new* operator instead of the normal C run-time routine *malloc*. Then, when we no longer need the class object, the *delete* operator is called instead of the normal C run-time routine *free*. For example, let's say we have a class called CSomeClass and we want to allocate an instance of this class. To do this, we would use syntax similar to the following:

```
CSomeClass* pCSomeClass = new CSomeClass;
```

When the C++ compiler examines this line, it first checks whether the CSomeClass class contains a member function for the *new* operator; if it does, the compiler generates code to call this function. If the compiler doesn't find a function overloading the *new* operator, the compiler generates code to call the standard C++ *new* operator function.

After you're done using the allocated object, you can destroy it by calling the *delete* operator:

```
delete pCSomeClass;
```

By overloading the *new* and *delete* operators for our C++ class, we can easily take advantage of the Win32 heap functions. To do this, let's define our CSomeClass class in a header file like this:

```
class CSomeClass {
   private:

   static HHEAP s_hHeap;
   static UINT s_uNumAllocsInHeap;

   // Other private data and member functions
   :
   :
   public:
   void* operator new (size_t size);
   void operator delete (void* p);
   // Other public data and member functions
   :
   :
};
```

In this code fragment, I've declared two member variables, *s_hHeap* and *s_uNumAllocsInHeap*, as static variables. Because they are static, C++ will make all instances of CSomeClass share the same variables; that is, C++ will *not* allocate separate *s_hHeap* and *s_uNumAllocsInHeap* variables for each instance of the class that is created. This fact is very important to us because we want all of our instances of CSomeClass to be allocated within the same heap.

The *s_hHeap* variable will contain the handle to the heap within which CSomeClass objects should be allocated. The *s_uNumAllocsInHeap* variable is simply a counter of how many CSomeClass objects have been allocated within the heap. Every time a new CSomeClass object is allocated in the heap, *s_uNumAllocsInHeap* is incremented, and every time a CSomeClass object is destroyed, *s_uNumAllocsInHeap* is decremented. When *s_uNumAllocsInHeap* reaches 0, the heap is no longer necessary and is freed. The code to manipulate the heap should be included in a CPP file that looks like this:

```
HHEAP CSomeClass::s_hHeap = NULL;
UINT CSomeClass::s_uNumAllocsInHeap = 0;

void* CSomeClass::operator new (size_t size) {
   if (s_hHeap == NULL) {
      // Heap does not exist; create it.
      s_hHeap = HeapCreate(HEAP_NO_SERIALIZE, 0, 0);

      if (s_hHeap == NULL)
         return(NULL);
   }
   // The heap exists for CSomeClass objects.
   void* p;
   while ((p = (void *) HeapAlloc(s_hHeap, 0, size)) == NULL) {
      // A CSomeClass object could not be allocated from the heap.
      if (_new_handler != NULL) {
         // Call the application-defined handler.
         (*_new_handler)();
      } else {
         // No application-defined handler exists; just return.
         break;
      }
   }

   if (p != NULL) {
      // Memory was allocated successfully; increment
      // the count of CSomeClass objects in the heap.
```

(continued)

```
        s_uNumAllocsInHeap++;
    }

    // Return the address of the allocated CSomeClass object.
    return(p);
}
```

Notice that I first defined the two static member variables, *s_hHeap* and *s_uNumAllocsInHeap*, at the top and initialized them as NULL and 0, respectively.

The C++ *new* operator receives one parameter—*size*. This parameter indicates the number of bytes required to hold a CSomeClass object. The first task for our *new* operator function is to create a heap if one hasn't been created already. This is simply a matter of checking the *s_hHeap* variable to see whether it is NULL. If it is, a new heap is created by calling *HeapCreate*, and the handle that *HeapCreate* returns is saved in *s_hHeap* so that the next call to the *new* operator will not create another heap but rather will use the heap we have just created.

When I called the *HeapCreate* function above, I used the HEAP-_NO_SERIALIZE flag because the remainder of the sample code is not multithread safe. In Chapter 10, I discuss features of Win32 that can be incorporated into the above code to make it multithread safe. The other two parameters in the call to *HeapCreate* indicate the initial size and the maximum size of the heap, respectively. I chose 0 and 0 here. The first 0 means that the heap has no initial size, whereas the second 0 means that the heap starts out small and expands as needed. You might want to change either or both of these values depending on your needs.

You might think it would be worthwhile to pass the *size* parameter to the *new* operator function as the second parameter to *HeapCreate*. In this way, you could initialize the heap so that it is large enough to contain one instance of the class. Then, the first time that *HeapAlloc* is called, it will execute faster because the heap won't have to resize itself to hold the class instance. Unfortunately, things don't always work the way you want them to. Because each allocated memory block within the heap has an overhead associated with it, the call to *HeapAlloc* will still have to resize the heap so that it is large enough to contain the one class instance and its associated overhead.

Once the heap has been created, new CSomeClass objects can be allocated from it using *HeapAlloc*. The first parameter is the handle to the heap, and the second parameter is the size of the CSomeClass object. *HeapAlloc* returns the address to the allocated block.

Once the allocation is performed successfully, I increment the *s_uNumAllocsInHeap* variable so that I know there is one more allocation in the heap. The last thing the *new* operator does is return the address of the newly allocated CSomeClass object.

Well, that's it for creating a new CSomeClass object. Let's turn our attention now to destroying one when our application no longer needs it. This is the responsibility of the *delete* operator function, coded as follows:

```
void CSomeClass::operator delete (void* p) {
   if (HeapFree(s_hHeap, 0, p)) {
      // Object was deleted successfully.
      s_uNumAllocsInHeap--;
   }

   if (s_uNumAllocsInHeap == 0) {
      // If there are no more objects in the heap,
      // destroy the heap.
      if (HeapDestroy(s_hHeap)) {
         // Set the heap handle to NULL so that the new operator
         // will know to create a new heap if a new CSomeClass
         // object is created.
         s_hHeap = NULL;
      }
   }
}
```

The *delete* operator function receives only one parameter: the address of the object being deleted. The first thing the function does is call *HeapFree*, passing it the handle of the heap and the address of the object to be freed. If the object is freed successfully, *s_uNumAllocsInHeap* is decremented, indicating that one fewer CSomeClass object is in the heap. Next the function checks whether *s_uNumAllocsInHeap* is 0, and, if it is, the function calls *HeapDestroy*, passing it the heap handle. If the heap is destroyed successfully, *s_hHeap* is set to NULL. This is extremely important because our program might attempt to allocate another CSomeClass object sometime in the future. When it does, the *new* operator will be called and will examine the *s_hHeap* variable to determine whether it should use an existing heap or create a new one.

This example demonstrates a very convenient scheme for using multiple heaps. It is easy to set up and can be incorporated into several of your classes. You will probably want to give some thought to inheritance, however. If you derive a new class using CSomeClass as a base class, the new class will inherit CSomeClass's *new* and *delete* operators. The new class will also inherit CSomeClass's heap, which means that when the *new* operator is applied to the derived class, the memory for the derived class object will be allocated from the same heap that CSomeClass is using. Depending on your situation, this may or may not be what you want. If the objects are very different in size, you might be setting yourself up for a situation in which the heap might fragment badly. You might also be making it harder to track down bugs in your code, as mentioned in the "Component Protection" and "Efficient Memory Management" sections earlier in this chapter.

If you want to use a separate heap for derived classes, all you need to do is duplicate what I did in the CSomeClass class. More specifically, include another set of *s_hHeap* and *s_uNumAllocsInHeap* variables, and copy the code over for the *new* and *delete* operators. When you compile, the compiler will see that you have overloaded the *new* and *delete* operators for the derived class and will make calls to those functions instead of to the ones in the base class.

The only advantage to not creating a heap for each class is that you won't need to devote overhead and memory to each heap. However, the amount of overhead and memory the heaps tie up is not great and is probably worth the potential gains. The compromise might be to have each class use its own heap and to let derived classes share the base class's heap when your application has been well tested and is close to shipping. But be aware that fragmentation might still be a problem.

Miscellaneous Heap Functions

In addition to the Heap functions already mentioned, Windows NT offers several more. In this section, I'll just briefly mention these functions. Keep in mind that Windows 95 does not offer these functions.

Since a process can have multiple heaps within its address space the *GetProcessHeaps* function,

```
DWORD GetProcessHeaps(DWORD NumberOfHeaps, PHANDLE ProcessHeaps);
```

allows you to get the handles of the existing heaps. To call the function, you must first allocate an array of HANDLES and then call the function as follows:

```
HANDLE hHeaps[25];
DWORD dwHeaps = GetProcessHeaps(25, hHeaps);
if (dwHeaps > 25) {
   // More heaps are in this process than we expected.
} else {
   // hHeaps[0] through hHeap[dwHeaps - 1]
   // identify the existing heaps.
}
```

Note that the handle of your process's default heap is also included in the array of heap handles when this function returns.

The *HeapValidate* function,

```
BOOL HeapValidate(HANDLE hHeap, DWORD dwFlags, LPCVOID lpMem);
```

validates the integrity of a heap. You will usually call this function passing a heap handle, a flag of 0 (the only other legal flag is HEAP_NO-_SERIALIZE), and NULL for *lpMem*. This function will then walk the blocks within the heap, making sure that no blocks are corrupt.

To make the function execute faster, you may want to pass the address of a specific block for the *lpMem* parameter. Doing so causes the function to check the validity of only the single block.

Unlike 16-bit Windows, blocks of memory in a Win32 process's heap are not compacted or discarded. However, there is a function called *HeapCompact*:

```
UINT HeapCompact(HANDLE hHeap, DWORD dwFlags);
```

For you 16-bit Windows programmers out there, this function does not do what functions like *GlobalCompact* and *LocalCompact* do. *HeapCompact* scans the specified heap and simply coalesces free blocks together and also decommits any pages of storage that do not contain any allocated heap blocks within them. Normally, you'll pass 0 for the *dwFlags* parameter, but you may also pass HEAP_NO_SERIALIZE.

The next two functions, which are named *HeapLock* and *HeapUnlock*, are used together:

```
BOOL HeapLock(HANDLE hHeap);
BOOL HeapUnlock(HANDLE hHeap);
```

Again, these functions do not have any similarity to the 16-bit Windows heap functions like *GlobalLock*, *LocalLock*, *GlobalUnlock*, and *LocalUnlock*. These functions are for thread synchronization purposes. When you call *HeapLock*, the calling thread becomes the owner of the specified heap. If any other thread calls a heap function (specifying the same heap handle), the system will suspend the calling thread and not allow it to wake until the heap is unlocked by calling *HeapUnlock*).

Functions such as *HeapAlloc*, *HeapSize*, *HeapFree*, and so on call *HeapLock* and *HeapUnlock* internally to make sure that access to the heap is serialized. It would be unusual for you ever to have to call these functions yourself.

The final heap function is *HeapWalk*:

```
BOOL HeapWalk(HANDLE hHeap, LPPROCESS_HEAP_ENTRY lpEntry);
```

This function is useful for debugging purposes only. The function allows you to walk the contents of a heap. You will call this function multiple times. Each time, you'll pass in the address of a PROCESS_HEAP-_ENTRY structure that you must allocate and initialize:

```
typedef struct _PROCESS_HEAP_ENTRY {
    PVOID lpData;
    DWORD cbData;
    BYTE cbOverhead;
    BYTE iRegionIndex;
    WORD wFlags;
    union {
        struct {
            HANDLE hMem;
            DWORD dwReserved[ 3 ];
        } Block;
        struct {
            DWORD dwCommittedSize;
            DWORD dwUnCommittedSize;
            LPVOID lpFirstBlock;
            LPVOID lpLastBlock;
        } Region;
    };
} PROCESS_HEAP_ENTRY, *LPPROCESS_HEAP_ENTRY, *PPROCESS_HEAP_ENTRY;
```

When you start enumerating the blocks in the heap, you'll have to set the *lpData* member to NULL. This tells *HeapWalk* to initialize the members inside the structure. You can examine the members of the structure after each successful call to *HeapWalk*. To get to the next block in the heap, you just call *HeapWalk* again, passing the same heap handle and the address of the PROCESS_HEAP_ENTRY structure you passed on the previous call. When *HeapWalk* returns FALSE, there are no more blocks in the heap. See the Win32 SDK documentation for a description of the members in the structure.

You will probably want to use the *HeapLock* and *HeapUnlock* functions around your *HeapWalk* loop so that other threads cannot allocate and free blocks of memory inside the heap while you're walking it.

The 16-Bit Windows Heap Functions

In this section, I'll discuss how the 16-bit Windows heap functions are implemented in the Win32 API. I'll cover all the global and local heap memory management functions, but I won't offer techniques for using them because I'm assuming that you're already familiar with 16-bit Windows programming techniques and because these functions should be avoided in new Win32 applications. Win32 supports the 16-bit Windows memory management functions solely for easy porting from one environment to another. If you are developing a new 32-bit application, and if you do not intend to compile the application natively for 16-bit Windows, I recommend that you don't use the global and local memory functions—they're slower and have more overhead than do the new Win32 heap functions.

To support the 16-bit Windows local and global heap functions, every Win32 process receives its very own default process heap and its very own handle table when initialized. The default process heap has already been discussed earlier in this chapter. This default heap is where the global and local memory allocations will be made.

The handle table exists so that Win32 can manage the local and global allocations. The handle table is an array of structures; each entry in the array points to a block of memory allocated from the default heap. When you call *GlobalAlloc*, the Win32 system allocates a block of memory from the process's default heap and locates an unused entry in the process's handle table. Then the system saves the address of the allocated block in the handle table and returns the address of the entry in the handle table. This returned value is the handle of the memory block. When you call *GlobalLock*, the system looks at the handle table and simply returns the address of the allocated block of memory in the default heap.

Initially, Win32 allocates a small amount of storage to hold only a small number of handle table entries. As the application continues to make allocations from the handle table, additional handles might become necessary. When this happens, Win32 can increase the amount of storage used by the handle table, allowing additional handles to be allocated.

Because of this additional work required by the system to manage this handle table, it is easy to see why the new Win32 heap functions should be used instead of the old 16-bit Windows functions. However, if you want to continue to use the 16-bit Windows functions so that you can write code that can be natively compiled for both 16-bit Windows and Win32, or if you want to port your application to Win32 quickly, you should know that not all of the 16-bit Windows heap functions perform exactly as they did in 16-bit Windows. The remaining sections in this chapter explain what the 16-bit heap functions do in a Win32 environment.

16-Bit Windows Functions That Port to Win32

Figure 9-3 shows what the 16-bit Windows memory management functions do in Win32. For each entry, the two functions listed perform identical tasks on the heap. (Note that in Win32, both HGLOBAL and HLOCAL are typedefed as HANDLE.)

16-Bit Windows Memory Function	Meaning in Win32
HGLOBAL GlobalAlloc(UINT fuAlloc, DWORD cbAlloc); HLOCAL LocalAlloc(UINT fuAlloc, UINT cbAlloc);	Allocate a memory block.
HGLOBAL GlobalDiscard(HGLOBAL hglb); HLOCAL LocalDiscard(HLOCAL hlcl);	Discard a memory block. Macros defined as: GlobalReAlloc((hglb), 0, GMEM_MOVEABLE); LocalReAlloc((hglb), 0, LMEM_MOVEABLE);
UINT GlobalFlags(HGLOBAL hglb); UINT LocalFlags(HLOCAL hlcl);	Return flag information about a memory block.
HGLOBAL GlobalFree(HGLOBAL hglb); HLOCAL LocalFree(HLOCAL hlcl);	Free a memory block.
LPVOID GlobalLock(HGLOBAL hglb); LPVOID LocalLock(HLOCAL hlcl);	Lock a memory block.
BOOL GlobalUnlock(HGLOBAL hglb); BOOL LocalUnlock(HLOCAL hlcl);	Unlock a memory block.
HGLOBAL GlobalReAlloc(HGLOBAL hglb, DWORD cbNewSize, UINT fuAlloc); HLOCAL LocalReAlloc(HLOCAL hlcl, UINT cbAlloc, UINT fuAlloc);	Change the size and/or flags of a memory block.
DWORD GlobalSize(HGLOBAL hglb); UINT LocalSize(HLOCAL hlcl);	Return the size of a memory block.
HGLOBAL GlobalHandle(LPVOID lpvMem); HLOCAL LocalHandle(LPVOID lpvMem);	Return the handle of the memory block containing the passed address.

Figure 9-3.
Memory functions ported from 16-bit Windows to Win32.

Of all the functions listed in Figure 9-3, only a few had semantic changes when they were ported to Win32. The following section covers these changes.

Functions with Semantic Changes

Whenever an application calls *GlobalAlloc* or *LocalAlloc* to allocate non-fixed memory, the Win32 system must allocate a handle for the data as well as memory space for the data. When *GlobalAlloc* or *LocalAlloc* returns, it returns a handle—the address of an entry in the handle table. For example, let's say that these lines of code are executed:

```
HGLOBAL hglb = GlobalAlloc(GMEM_MOVEABLE, 10);
LPVOID lpv = GlobalLock(hglb);
```

The variable *hglb* is an address to a structure in the handle table. When *GlobalLock* is called, the entry in the handle table is examined to determine the address of the memory block. *GlobalLock* then returns this address.

Both *GlobalLock* and *LocalLock* return the address to the memory block that was allocated. Immediately preceding this block in memory is an internal data structure. This data structure contains some internal management information, such as the size of the allocated block and the handle of the block. When allocating fixed memory blocks, the system does not need to allocate a handle from the handle table. Instead, the system simply allocates the memory block and returns the address to this block when *GlobalAlloc* or *LocalAlloc* returns.

For *GlobalAlloc* and *LocalAlloc*, some of the flags' meanings have changed. Figure 9-4 shows all of the possible flags and what they mean in Win32.

Flag	Meaning in Win32
GHND	Defined as (GMEM_MOVEABLE | GMEM_ZEROINIT).
LHND	Defined as (LMEM_MOVEABLE | LMEM_ZEROINIT).
GPTR	Defined as (GMEM_FIXED | GMEM_ZEROINIT).
LPTR	Defined as (LMEM_FIXED | LMEM_ZEROINIT).
GMEM_DDESHARE, GMEM_SHARE	Win32 does not allow memory to be shared in this way. However, this flag may be used as a hint to the system about how to share memory in the future.

Figure 9-4.
Memory flags and their meanings in Win32.

(continued)

Figure 9-4. *continued*

Flag	Meaning in Win32
GMEM_DISCARDABLE, LMEM_DISCARDABLE	Allocate block as discardable. Win32 ignores these flags.
GMEM_FIXED, LMEM_FIXED	Allocate block as fixed.
GMEM_LOWER, GMEM_NOT_BANKED, GMEM_NOCOMPACT, LMEM_NOCOMPACT, GMEM_NODISCARD, LMEM_NODISCARD, GMEM_NOTIFY, LMEM_NOTIFY	Ignored.
GMEM_MOVEABLE, LMEM_MOVEABLE	Allocate block as movable.
GMEM_ZEROINIT, LMEM_ZEROINIT	Zero contents of block after allocation.
NONZEROLHND	Defined as (LMEM_MOVEABLE).
NONZEROLPTR	Defined as (LMEM_FIXED).

It is incorrect to call *GlobalReAlloc* or *LocalReAlloc* specifying the GMEM_DISCARDABLE or LMEM_DISCARDABLE flag without also including the GMEM_MODIFY or LMEM_MODIFY flag.[1]

Functions That Should Be Avoided in Win32

Figure 9-5 shows 16-bit Windows memory allocation functions that have been kept in Win32 for easier porting between 16-bit Windows and Win32 applications but that are obsolete and should be avoided. Each of the functions existed for one or more of the following reasons:

■ To allow applications to manipulate the shared global heap. In Win32, each application has its own address space and this type of functionality is no longer possible.

---

1. The GMEM_MODIFY flag and the LMEM_MODIFY flag do not appear in Figure 9-4 because they are used only in conjunction with the *GlobalReAlloc* and *LocalReAlloc* functions.

16-Bit Windows Memory Function	Meaning in Win32
BOOL DefineHandleTable(WORD w);	Macro defined as ((w), TRUE)
DWORD GetFreeSpace(UINT u);	Macro defined as (0x100000L)
DWORD GlobalCompact(DWORD);	Always returns 0x100000
void GlobalFix(HGLOBAL);	Same as calling GlobalLock
HGLOBAL GlobalLRUNewest (HGLOBAL h);	Macro defined as (HANDLE)(h)
HGLOBAL GlobalLRUOldest (HGLOBAL h);	Macro defined as (HANDLE)(h)
void GlobalUnfix(HGLOBAL);	Same as calling GlobalUnlock
BOOL GlobalUnWire(HGLOBAL);	Same as calling GlobalUnlock
void *GlobalWire(HGLOBAL);	Same as calling GlobalLock
void LimitEmsPages(DWORD);	Macro defined as nothing
UINT LocalCompact(UINT);	Always returns 0x100000
UINT LocalShrink (HLOCAL, UINT);	Always returns 0x100000
HGLOBAL LockSegment(UINT w);	Macro defined as GlobalFix((HANDLE)(w))
LONG SetSwapAreaSize (UINT w);	Macro defined as (w)
void UnlockSegment(UINT w);	Macro defined as GlobalUnfix((HANDLE)(w))

Figure 9-5.
These 16-bit Windows memory functions should be avoided in Win32.

- To help manage discardable memory. In Win32, memory blocks are never discarded by the system. They can be discarded if an application explicitly calls *GlobalDiscard* or *LocalDiscard*. Both functions really resize the blocks to 0 bytes anyway.

- To help manage movable memory. In Win32, memory blocks are never moved or compacted by the system.

Functions That Have Been Removed from Win32

The following list shows 16-bit Windows memory functions that have been removed from the Win32 API, mainly because they were Intel processor–specific functions. Win32 is a portable API designed to offer all of its functions on any and all CPU platforms to which Win32 is ported. Calling the following functions results in a compiler error because no prototype or macro exists for them:

AllocDStoCSAlias	*GlobalNotify*
AllocSelector	*GlobalPageLock*
ChangeSelector	*GlobalPageUnlock*
FreeSelector	*LocalInit*
GetCodeInfo	*SwitchStackBack*
GlobalDOSAlloc	*SwitchStackTo*
GlobalDOSFree	

CHAPTER TEN

THREAD SYNCHRONIZATION

In an environment in which several threads are running concurrently, it becomes important to be able to synchronize the activities of various threads. The Microsoft Win32-based operating systems provide several synchronization objects that allow threads to synchronize their actions with one another. In this chapter, I'll concentrate on the five main synchronization objects: critical sections, mutexes, semaphores, events, and waitable timers. Other objects also exist for synchronization, and some of them are discussed and demonstrated in other chapters in this book.

This chapter offers numerous techniques for using the five main synchronization objects. For the most part, all the synchronization objects behave similarly. Their differences, however, often make one type of object more suitable for a particular task than another.

Of these five types of synchronization objects, all are kernel objects except critical sections. A critical section is not managed by the low-level components of the operating system and is not manipulated using handles. Because a critical section is the easiest synchronization object to use and understand, we'll discuss it first.

Before we turn to critical sections, however, let's discuss the general concept of thread synchronization.

Thread Synchronization in a Nutshell

In general, a thread synchronizes itself with another thread by putting itself to sleep. When the thread is sleeping, the operating system no longer schedules CPU time for it, and it therefore stops executing. Just before the thread puts itself to sleep, however, it tells the operating system what "special event" has to occur for the thread to resume execution.

The operating system remains aware of the thread's request and watches to see whether and when this special event occurs. When it does

313

occur, the thread is again eligible to be scheduled to a CPU. Eventually the thread will be scheduled and will continue its execution—the thread has now synchronized its execution with the occurrence of the special event.

As we discuss the various synchronization objects throughout this chapter, I'll show you how to specify a special event and how to put your thread to sleep after notifying the system to watch for the special event on your thread's behalf.

The Worst Thing You Can Do

Without synchronization objects and the operating system's ability to watch for special events, a thread would be forced to synchronize itself with special events by using the technique that I am about to demonstrate. However, because the operating system has built-in support for thread synchronization, you should *never* use this technique.

In this technique, one thread synchronizes itself with the completion of a task in another thread by continuously polling the state of a variable that is shared by or accessible to multiple threads. The following code fragment illustrates:

```
BOOL g_fFinishedCalculation = FALSE;

int WINAPI WinMain (...) {
   CreateThread(..., RecalcFunc, ...);
      :
      :
   // Wait for the recalculation to complete.
   while (!g_fFinishedCalculation)
      ;
      :
      :
}

DWORD WINAPI RecalcFunc (LPVOID lpvThreadParm) {
   // Perform the recalculation.
      :
   g_fFinishedCalculation = TRUE;
   return(0);
}
```

As you can see, the primary thread (executing *WinMain*) doesn't put itself to sleep when it needs to synchronize itself with the completion of the *RecalcFunc* function. Because the primary thread does not sleep, it is being scheduled CPU time by the operating system. This takes precious time cycles away from other threads that could be executing code that does something more useful.

Another problem with the polling method as used in the previous code fragment is that the Boolean variable *g_fFinishedCalculation* might never be set to TRUE. This could happen if the primary thread has a higher priority than the thread executing the *RecalcFunc* function. In this case, the system never assigns any time slices to the *RecalcFunc* thread, which will never execute the statement that sets *g_fFinishedCalculation* to TRUE. If the thread executing the *WinMain* function were put to sleep instead of polling, it would not be scheduled time, and the system would have an opportunity to schedule time to lower-priority threads, such as the *RecalcFunc* thread, allowing them to execute.

I can't be any clearer than this: synchronize threads by putting them to sleep. Do *not* synchronize threads by having them continuously poll for special events.

Critical Sections

A critical section is a small section of code that requires exclusive access to some shared data before the code can execute. Of all the synchronization objects, critical sections are the simplest to use, but they can be used to synchronize threads only within a single process. Critical sections allow only one thread at a time to gain access to a region of data. Examine the following code fragment:

```
int    g_nIndex = 0;
const int MAX_TIMES = 1000;
DWORD g_dwTimes[MAX_TIMES];

DWORD WINAPI FirstThread (LPVOID lpvThreadParm) {
   BOOL fDone = FALSE;

   while (!fDone) {
      if (g_nIndex >= MAX_TIMES) {
         fDone = TRUE;
      } else {
         g_dwTimes[g_nIndex] = GetTickCount();
         g_nIndex++;
      }
   }
   return(0);
}
```

(continued)

```
DWORD WINAPI SecondThread (LPVOID lpvThreadParm) {
   BOOL fDone = FALSE;

   while (!fDone) {
      if (g_nIndex >= MAX_TIMES) {
         fDone = TRUE;
      } else {
         g_nIndex++;
         g_dwTimes[g_nIndex - 1] = GetTickCount();
      }
   }
   return(0);
}
```

Both of the thread functions here are supposed to produce the same result, although each is coded a bit differently. If the *FirstThread* function were running by itself, it would fill the *g_dwTimes* array with ascending values. The same thing would happen if we were to run the *SecondThread* function by itself. Ideally, we would like to have both threads running concurrently and still have the *g_dwTimes* array produce ascending values. However, the code above has a problem: the *g_dwTimes* array won't be filled properly because the two thread functions are accessing the same global variables simultaneously. Here is an example of how this could happen.

Let's say that we have just started executing both threads on a system with one CPU. The operating system starts running *SecondThread* first (which could very well happen), and right after *SecondThread* increments *g_nIndex* to 1, the system preempts the thread and allows *FirstThread* to run. *FirstThread* then sets *g_dwTimes[1]* to the system time, and the system preempts the thread and gives time back to *SecondThread*. *SecondThread* now sets *g_dwTimes[1 − 1]* to the new system time. Because this operation occurred later, the new system time is a higher value than that of the time placed into *FirstThread*'s array. Also notice that index 1 of *g_dwTimes* was filled in before index 0. The data in the array is corrupted.

I'll admit that this example is a bit contrived. It's difficult to come up with a real-life example that doesn't require several pages of source code. However, you can easily see how this problem could extend itself to real-life examples. Consider the case of managing a linked list of objects. If access to the linked list was not synchronized, one thread could be adding an item to the list while another thread was simultaneously trying to search for an item in the list. The situation could become more chaotic if the two threads were adding items to the list at the same time.

By using critical sections, you can ensure that access to the data structures is coordinated among threads.

Creating a Critical Section

To create a critical section, you must first allocate a CRITICAL_SECTION data structure in your own process. The allocation of the critical section structure must be global so that different threads can gain access to it. Usually, critical sections are simply global variables. Although the CRITICAL_SECTION structure and its members appear in WINNT.H,[1] you should think of the members of this structure as being off-limits. The Win32 functions that manipulate critical sections initialize and maintain all the members in the structure for you. You should not access or modify any of the members yourself.

After we've added critical sections to our example program, the code looks like this:

```
int    g_nIndex = 0;
const int MAX_TIMES = 1000;
DWORD g_dwTimes[MAX_TIMES];
CRITICAL_SECTION g_CriticalSection;

int WINAPI WinMain (...) {
   HANDLE hThreads[2];

   // Initialize the critical section before the threads so
   // that it is ready when the threads execute.
   InitializeCriticalSection(&g_CriticalSection);

   hThreads[0] = CreateThread(..., FirstThread ...);
   hThreads[1] = CreateThread(..., SecondThread ...);

   // Wait for both threads to terminate.
   // Don't worry about this line; it will be explained shortly.
   WaitForMultipleObjects(2, hThreads, TRUE, INFINITE);

   // Close the thread handles.
   CloseHandle(hThreads[0]);
   CloseHandle(hThreads[1]);

   // Delete the critical section.
   DeleteCriticalSection(&g_CriticalSection);
}
```

(continued)

---

1. CRITICAL_SECTION itself is in WINBASE.H as RTL_CRITICAL_SECTION. The RTL_CRITICAL_SECTION structure is typedefed in WINNT.H.

```
DWORD WINAPI FirstThread (LPVOID lpvThreadParm) {
   BOOL fDone = FALSE;

   while (!fDone) {
      EnterCriticalSection(&g_CriticalSection);
      if (g_nIndex >= MAX_TIMES) {
         fDone = TRUE;
      } else {
         g_dwTimes[g_nIndex] = GetTickCount();
         g_nIndex++;
      }
      LeaveCriticalSection(&g_CriticalSection);
   }
   return(0);
}

DWORD WINAPI SecondThread (LPVOID lpvThreadParm) {
   BOOL fDone = FALSE;

   while (!fDone) {
      EnterCriticalSection(&g_CriticalSection);
      if (g_nIndex >= MAX_TIMES) {
         fDone = TRUE;
      } else {
         g_nIndex++;
         g_dwTimes[g_nIndex - 1] = GetTickCount();
      }
      LeaveCriticalSection(&g_CriticalSection);
   }
   return(0);
}
```

Using a Critical Section

Before you can synchronize threads with a critical section, you must initialize the critical section by calling *InitializeCriticalSection,* passing the address to the CRITICAL_SECTION structure as the *lpCriticalSection* parameter:

```
VOID InitializeCriticalSection
   (LPCRITICAL_SECTION lpCriticalSection);
```

This initializes the members of the structure and must be done before *EnterCriticalSection* is called. The code above shows the critical section being initialized in *WinMain.* Both thread functions are expecting that the *g_CriticalSection* structure variable has been initialized by calling

InitializeCriticalSection before they begin executing. Let's see what happens next.

Referring again to our code example on the preceding pages, let's say that *SecondThread* executes first. It calls *EnterCriticalSection*, passing it the address to the *g_CriticalSection* structure variable:

```
VOID EnterCriticalSection(LPCRITICAL_SECTION lpCriticalSection);
```

EnterCriticalSection sees that this is the first time that *EnterCriticalSection* has been called for the *g_CriticalSection* variable, changes some members in the data structure, and lets the *g_nIndex++;* line execute. After this line executes, the system might preempt *SecondThread* and assign processor time to *FirstThread*. *FirstThread* calls *EnterCriticalSection*, passing the address of the same object that *SecondThread* used. This time, *EnterCriticalSection* sees that the *g_CriticalSection* structure variable is in use and puts *FirstThread* to sleep. Because *FirstThread* is asleep, the system can assign the remainder of its time slice to another thread. The system will stop trying to assign time slices to *FirstThread* until *FirstThread* is awakened.

Eventually *SecondThread* will be assigned another time slice. Then it will execute the following statement:

```
g_dwTimes[g_nIndex - 1] = GetTickCount();
```

This causes *g_dwTimes[0]* to be assigned the current system time. This scenario differs from our first one, in which *g_dwTimes[1]* was assigned a lesser value than *g_dwTimes[0]*. At this point, if the system wants to preempt *SecondThread,* it can do so; but it can't assign time to *FirstThread* because *FirstThread* is still waiting for the critical section to become available. Eventually *SecondThread* will be assigned a time slice again and will execute the following statement:

```
LeaveCriticalSection(&g_CriticalSection);
```

After this line executes, the *g_CriticalSection* variable indicates that the shared data structures are no longer protected and are available to any other thread that wants access to them. *FirstThread* was waiting on *g_CriticalSection*, so it can now be awakened. *FirstThread*'s call to *EnterCriticalSection* sets ownership of *g_CriticalSection* to *FirstThread*, and then *EnterCriticalSection* returns so that *FirstThread* can continue execution.

As you can see, using critical sections allows access of data to only one thread at a time. In some cases, however, it is possible to have more than two threads requiring access to the same data at the same time.

When this happens, each thread must call *EnterCriticalSection* before it attempts to manipulate the data. If one of the threads already has ownership of the critical section, any thread waiting to gain access is put to sleep. When a thread relinquishes ownership by calling *LeaveCriticalSection*, the system wakes up only one of the waiting threads and gives that thread ownership. All the other sleeping threads continue to sleep.

Note that it is legal—and even useful—for a single thread to own a critical section several times. This can happen because calls to *EnterCriticalSection* from the thread owning the critical section increment a reference count. Before another thread can own the critical section, the thread currently owning it must call *LeaveCriticalSection* enough times so that the reference count drops back to 0. Let's see how this works using the following example:

```
int g_nNums[100];
CRITICAL_SECTION g_CriticalSection;
  :
  :

DWORD WINAPI Thread (LPVOID lpvParam) {
   int nIndex = (int) lpvParam;
   EnterCriticalSection(&g_CriticalSection);

   if (g_nNums[nIndex] < MIN_VAL)
      IncrementNum(nIndex);
   else
      g_nNums[nIndex] = MIN_VAL;

   LeaveCriticalSection(&g_CriticalSection);
   return(0);
}

void IncrementNum (int nIndex) {
   EnterCriticalSection(&g_CriticalSection);
   g_nNums[nIndex]++;
   LeaveCriticalSection(&g_CriticalSection);
}
```

In this code fragment, the *Thread* function acquires ownership of the critical section when it first begins executing. In this way, it can test *g_nNums[nIndex]*, knowing that no other thread can change *g_nNums[nIndex]* during the test. Then, if *g_nNums[nIndex]* contains a value less than MIN_VAL, the *IncrementNum* function is called.

IncrementNum is an independent function. It is implemented without any knowledge of what functions call it. Because the function will alter the *g_nNums* array, it requests access to the array by calling *EnterCriticalSection*. Because *IncrementNum* is executing under the thread that already owns the critical section, *EnterCriticalSection* increments only the reference count of the critical section and allows the thread to continue execution. If *IncrementNum* were called from another thread, the call to *EnterCriticalSection* would put that thread to sleep until the thread executing the *Thread* function called *LeaveCriticalSection*.

If you have several unrelated data structures in your application, you would create CRITICAL_SECTION variables for each of the data structures. Then your code would first have to call *InitializeCriticalSection* once for each CRITICAL_SECTION variable. Your threads would also need to call *EnterCriticalSection*, passing the address of the CRITICAL_SECTION variable that applies to the data structure(s) to which the thread wants access. Examine this code fragment:

```
int g_nNum[100];
char g_cChars[100];
CRITICAL_SECTION g_CriticalSection;
  .
  .
  .
DWORD WINAPI ThreadFunc (LPVOID lpvParam) {
   int x;

   EnterCriticalSection(&g_CriticalSection);

   for (x = 0; x < 100; x++) {
      g_nNums[x] = 0;
      g_cChars[x] = 'X';
   }

   LeaveCriticalSection(&g_CriticalSection);
   return(0);
}
```

In this case, you enter a single critical section whose job it is to protect both the *g_nNums* array and the *g_cChars* array while they are being initialized. But the two arrays have nothing to do with one another. While this loop executes, no thread can gain access to either array. If the *ThreadFunc* function is implemented as shown at the top of the next page, the two arrays are initialized separately.

```
DWORD WINAPI ThreadFunc (LPVOID lpvParam) {
   int x;

   EnterCriticalSection(&g_CriticalSection);

   for (x = 0; x < 100; x++)
      g_nNums[x] = 0;

   for (x = 0; x < 100; x++)
      g_cChars[x] = 'X';

   LeaveCriticalSection(&g_CriticalSection);
   return(0);
}
```

So, theoretically, after the *g_nNums* array has been initialized, a different thread that needs access only to the *g_nNums* array and not to the *g_cChars* array can begin executing while *ThreadFunc* continues to initialize the *g_cChars* array. But alas, this is not possible because both data structures are being protected by a single critical section. To fix this, you can create two critical sections, as follows:

```
int g_nNums[100];
char g_cChars[100];
CRITICAL_SECTION g_CriticalSectionForNums;
CRITICAL_SECTION g_CriticalSectionForChars;
   :
   :

DWORD WINAPI ThreadFunc (LPVOID lpvParam) {
   int x;

   EnterCriticalSection(&g_CriticalSectionForNums);

   for (x = 0; x < 100; x++)
      g_nNums[x] = 0;

   LeaveCriticalSection(&g_CriticalSectionForNums);


   EnterCriticalSection(&g_CriticalSectionForChars);

   for (x = 0; x < 100; x++)
      g_cChars[x] = 'X';

   LeaveCriticalSection(&g_CriticalSectionForChars);
   return(0);
}
```

With this implementation another thread can start using the *g_nNums* array as soon as *ThreadFunc* has finished initializing it.

Sometimes you will need to access two data structures simultaneously. If this were a requirement of *ThreadFunc,* it would be implemented like this:

```
DWORD WINAPI ThreadFunc (LPVOID lpvParam) {
   int x;

   EnterCriticalSection(&g_CriticalSectionForNums);
   EnterCriticalSection(&g_CriticalSectionForChars);

   for (x = 0; x < 100; x++)
      g_nNums[x] = 0;

   for (x = 0; x < 100; x++)
      g_cChars[x] = 'X';

   LeaveCriticalSection(&g_CriticalSectionForChars);
   LeaveCriticalSection(&g_CriticalSectionForNums);
   return(0);
}
```

Suppose another thread in the process, written as follows, also requires access to the two arrays:

```
DWORD WINAPI OtherThreadFunc (LPVOID lpvParam) {
   int x;

   EnterCriticalSection(&g_CriticalSectionForChars);
   EnterCriticalSection(&g_CriticalSectionForNums);

   for (x = 0; x < 100; x++)
      g_nNums[x] = 0;

   for (x = 0; x < 100; x++)
      g_cChars[x] = 'X';

   LeaveCriticalSection(&g_CriticalSectionForNums);
   LeaveCriticalSection(&g_CriticalSectionForChars);
   return(0);
}
```

All I did in the function above was switch the order of the calls to *EnterCriticalSection* and *LeaveCriticalSection.* But because the two functions are written the way they are, there's a chance for *deadlock* to occur. Deadlock occurs when a thread will never execute because the resource or resources it is waiting for (the critical sections, in this example) will never be available.

Suppose that *ThreadFunc* begins executing and gains ownership of the *g_CriticalSectionForNums* critical section. Then the thread executing the *OtherThreadFunc* function is given some CPU time and gains ownership of the *g_CriticalSectionForChars* critical section. Now you have a deadlock situation. When either *ThreadFunc* or *OtherThreadFunc* tries to continue executing, neither function will ever be able to gain ownership of the other critical section it requires.

In the example on the previous page, you can easily fix the problem by writing the functions so that they call *EnterCriticalSection* in the same order. This will keep one thread from locking the other one out of a needed resource.

Here is a technique you can use to minimize the time spent inside a critical section. The following code prevents other threads from changing the value in *g_nNums[3]* before the WM_SOMEMSG is sent to a window:

```
int g_nNums[100];
CRITICAL_SECTION g_CriticalSection;

DWORD WINAPI SomeThread (LPVOID lpvParam) {
    EnterCriticalSection(&g_CriticalSection);

    // Send a message to a window.
    SendMessage(hwndSomeWnd, WM_SOMEMSG, g_nNums[3], 0);

    LeaveCriticalSection(&g_CriticalSection);
    return(0);
}
```

It's impossible to tell how much time the window procedure requires to process the WM_SOMEMSG message—it could take a few microseconds or a few years.[2] During that time, no other threads can gain access to the *g_nNums* array. It would be much better to write the code as follows:

```
int g_nNums[100];
CRITICAL_SECTION g_CriticalSection;

DWORD WINAPI SomeThread (LPVOID lpvParam) {
    int nTemp;

    EnterCriticalSection(&g_CriticalSection);
```

---

2. Ideally, the window procedure is written a bit more efficiently than I suggest here and, at most, will not require more than a couple of seconds to run.

```
nTemp = g_nNums[3];

LeaveCriticalSection(&g_CriticalSection);

// Send a message to a window.
SendMessage(hwndSomeWnd, WM_SOMEMSG, nTemp, 0);
return(0);
}
```

This code saves the value in *g_nNums[3]* in a temporary integer variable *nTemp*. You can probably guess how long the CPU requires to execute this line—only a few CPU cycles. Immediately after saving the temporary variable, *LeaveCriticalSection* is called because the array no longer needs to be protected. This second implementation is much better than the first because other threads are stopped from using the *g_nNums* array for only a few CPU cycles instead of for an unknown amount of time.

When an application terminates, all the CRITICAL_SECTION variables should be cleaned up by calling *DeleteCriticalSection*:

```
VOID DeleteCriticalSection(LPCRITICAL_SECTION lpCriticalSection);
```

This function releases all the resources owned by the critical section. Naturally, you should not call *EnterCriticalSection* or *LeaveCriticalSection* using a deleted CRITICAL_SECTION variable unless it has been initialized again with *InitializeCriticalSection*. Also, be sure that you don't delete a critical section if a thread is waiting on a call to *EnterCriticalSection*.

Microsoft Windows NT 4 introduces a new critical section function:

```
BOOL TryEnterCriticalSection(LPCRITICAL_SECTION lpCriticalSection);
```

If, when a thread calls this function, the specified critical section is not owned by any thread (or not already owned by the calling thread), the function gives the calling thread ownership of the critical section and returns TRUE. However, if the critical section is owned by another thread, the function returns immediately with a value of FALSE. The difference between *TryEnterCriticalSection* and *EnterCriticalSection* is that *TryEnterCriticalSection* never suspends a thread.

Microsoft Windows 95 does not have any implementation for the *TryEnterCriticalSection* function. If you write an application that calls this function, your application will not be able to load on Windows 95.

The Critical Sections Sample Application

The CritSecs (CRITSECS.EXE) application, listed in Figure 10-1 beginning on page 330, demonstrates the importance of using critical sections in a multithreaded application. The source code and resource files for the application are in the CRITSECS directory on the companion disc.

When the program starts, *WinMain* invokes a modal dialog box. This dialog box serves as the interface to the application. When the dialog box function receives the WM_INITDIALOG message, the *Dlg_On-InitDialog* function initializes a global CRITICAL_SECTION structure, initializes all the child controls in the dialog box, and creates two threads—*CounterThread* and *DisplayThread*. At this point, three threads are running in this process: the primary thread that's handling the input to the dialog box and its controls, *CounterThread*, and *DisplayThread*.

Toward the top of CRITSECS.C, the following variable appears:

```
// The data that needs protecting
TCHAR g_szNumber[10] = __TEXT("0");
```

This is a character array that is initialized to a string containing the number 0. *CounterThread* converts the number in this character array to an integer, increments the integer by 1, and converts the integer back to a character array so that it can be stored in the *g_szNumber* array. *Display-Thread* reads the number in the *g_szNumber* array and appends the number to a list box control in the dialog box.

When CritSecs is invoked, its list box starts filling with numbers. The Critical Section Test Application dialog box appears as follows:

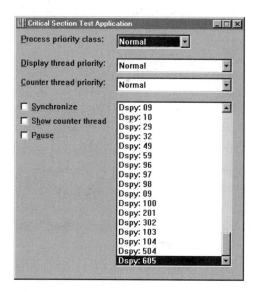

You might notice that the numbers in the list box don't appear in ascending order because CritSecs, by default, does not synchronize access to the *g_szNumber* array. While *CounterThread* is converting the array to an integer, incrementing it, and copying the number back, *DisplayThread* is reading the *g_szNumber* array and adding its contents to the list box.

To see what a big difference the critical sections make, click on the Synchronize check box. CritSecs immediately starts using the *g_Critical-Section* variable that guards access to the *g_szNumber* array. As a result, the list box now shows numbers that are always in ascending order:

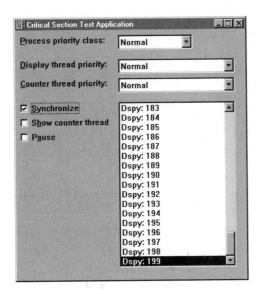

I have added a few other capabilities to CritSecs. The Process Priority Class, Display Thread Priority, and Counter Thread Priority combo boxes let you fiddle with the priority class of the whole CritSecs application as well as the relative priorities of the two threads executing the *DisplayThread* and *CounterThread* functions.

The Pause check box demonstrates how to suspend the threads executing *CounterThread* and *DisplayThread* by calling the *SuspendThread* and *ResumeThread* functions.

The Show Counter Thread check box causes *CounterThread* to append the following line to the list box every time it completes its increment of the number and stores the digits of the number back in the *g_szNumber* array:

```
Cntr: Increment
```

When this check box is on, the list box appears as follows:

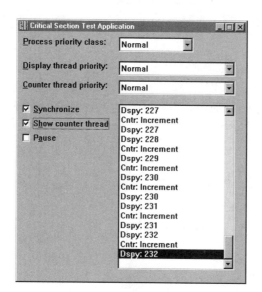

You can see that each iteration of *DisplayThread*'s loop executes faster than each iteration of *CounterThread*'s loop. In some cases, *Display-Thread*'s loop completes two iterations for just one iteration of *Counter-Thread*'s loop. This shows why you should get into the habit of anticipating how the system schedules time to threads. By altering the relative priorities of the two threads, you can alter the order and frequency of this behavior.

CritSecs might produce different results on your computer system depending on certain considerations, such as the following:

- The number of CPUs in your system (if you're running Windows NT)

- The speed of your system

- The number of threads created by other processes also running

- The priority class of other processes running

- The relative priorities of the threads running in these other processes

Two more features of the CritSecs program are worth noting. First, *CounterThread* calls the Win32 *Sleep* function after it stores the number back into the *g_szNumber* array. The prototype for the *Sleep* function is shown here:

```
VOID Sleep(DWORD cMilliseconds);
```

When a thread calls *Sleep*, it tells the system that it doesn't need any CPU time for the number of milliseconds specified by the *cMilliseconds* parameter. *CounterThread* calls *Sleep*, passing a value of 0 for *cMilliseconds*. This tells the system that the thread doesn't need any CPU time for the next 0 milliseconds. This might seem like a useless thing to do, but a side effect of the *Sleep* function exaggerates the results of CritSecs; *Sleep* also tells the system that the thread would like to voluntarily give up the remainder of its time slice. I put the call to *Sleep(0)* in *CounterThread* to dramatize the effect of unsynchronized threads in CritSecs. Without the call to *Sleep(0)*, CritSecs would still behave improperly and not synchronize the threads, but the problem would not be as pronounced.

The second interesting feature of the CritSecs application is how it turns synchronization on and off. You'll see the following line at the beginning of both *CounterThread*'s and *DisplayThread*'s loop:

```
fSyncChecked = IsDlgButtonChecked(g_hwnd, ID_SYNCHRONIZE);
```

This line retrieves and saves the status of the Synchronize check box at the beginning of each loop's iteration. Elsewhere in the loop, I included code such as the following:

```
if (fSyncChecked) {
    EnterCriticalSection(&g_CriticalSection);
}
    .
    .
    .
if (fSyncChecked) {
    LeaveCriticalSection(&g_CriticalSection);
}
```

When I first developed CritSecs, the code above originally looked like this:

```
if (IsDlgButtonChecked(g_hwnd, ID_SYNCHRONIZE)) {
    EnterCriticalSection(&g_CriticalSection);
}
    .
    .
    .
if (IsDlgButtonChecked(g_hwnd, ID_SYNCHRONIZE)) {
    LeaveCriticalSection(&g_CriticalSection);
}
```

When CritSecs used the latter code fragment, a subtle bug was introduced that made some of the threads hang sometimes—but not every time. The *CounterThread* loop would start and see that the Synchronize check box was on. So *CounterThread* would call *EnterCriticalSection*. Then *DisplayThread*, seeing that the Synchronize check box was on, would also call *EnterCriticalSection*. But the system would not let *DisplayThread*'s call to *EnterCriticalSection* return because *CounterThread* currently had ownership of the critical section. While *CounterThread* was reading the number, I would turn off the Synchronize check box. When *CounterThread* made its call to *IsDlgButtonChecked*, it saw that the check box was off and would not call *LeaveCriticalSection*. As long as the check box remained off, *CounterThread* would never release the critical section and *DisplayThread* would stay forever hung, waiting for the critical section.

By saving the state of the check box in a variable and testing the variable before calling *EnterCriticalSection* or *LeaveCriticalSection*, I removed the possibility of executing unmatched *EnterCriticalSection* and *LeaveCriticalSection* calls. As you can see, you must be very careful when designing and implementing multithreaded applications.

CritSecs.ico

CRITSECS.C

```
/**********************************************************************
Module name: CritSecs.C
Notices: Copyright (c) 1995-1997 Jeffrey Richter
**********************************************************************/


#include "..\CmnHdr.H"                    /* See Appendix C. */
#include <windows.h>
#include <windowsx.h>
#include <tchar.h>
#include <stdio.h>                // For sprintf
#include <process.h>             // For _beginthreadex
#include "Resource.H"



///////////////////////////////////////////////////////////////////////


// Global variables
// g_fTerminate is set to TRUE when the dialog box is
// dismissed. It indicates to the worker threads that they
// need to terminate. It is volatile because it can change
// at any time.
```

Figure 10-1.
The CritSecs application.

(continued)

Figure 10-1. *continued*

```
volatile BOOL  g_fTerminate = FALSE;

HWND      g_hwnd;
HANDLE    g_hThread[2];   // Counter[0] & Display[1] threads


// The data that needs protecting
TCHAR     g_szNumber[10] = __TEXT("0");

// The critical section used to protect the data
CRITICAL_SECTION g_CriticalSection;


///////////////////////////////////////////////////////////////////


// Add a string to a list box.
void AddToListBox (LPCTSTR szBuffer) {
   HWND hwndDataBox = GetDlgItem(g_hwnd, IDC_DATABOX);

   int x = ListBox_AddString(hwndDataBox, szBuffer);
   ListBox_SetCurSel(hwndDataBox, x);

   if (ListBox_GetCount(hwndDataBox) > 100)
      ListBox_DeleteString(hwndDataBox, 0);
}


///////////////////////////////////////////////////////////////////


// Thread to increment the protected counter data
DWORD WINAPI CounterThread (LPVOID lpThreadParameter) {
   unsigned int nNumber, nDigit;
   BOOL fSyncChecked;

   while (!g_fTerminate) {
      // Get the status of the Synchronize check box
      // and save it.
      fSyncChecked =
         IsDlgButtonChecked(g_hwnd, IDC_SYNCHRONIZE);

      if (fSyncChecked) {
         // If the user wants us synchronized, do it.
         EnterCriticalSection(&g_CriticalSection);
      }
```

(continued)

Figure 10-1. *continued*

```
// Convert the string number to an integer and add 1.
_stscanf(g_szNumber, __TEXT("%d"), &nNumber);
nNumber++;

// Convert the new integer back to a string.
nDigit = 0;
while (nNumber != 0) {
   // Put a digit into the string.
   g_szNumber[nDigit++] = (TCHAR)
(__TEXT('0') + (nNumber % 10));

   // A call to Sleep here tells the system that we want
   // to relinquish the remainder of our time slice to
   // another thread.  This call is needed for
   // single-CPU systems so that the results of the
   // synchronization or lack thereof are obvious.
   // Normally, your programs would NOT call Sleep here.
   Sleep(0);

   // Get ready to get the next digit.
   nNumber /= 10;
}

// All digits converted to characters.
// Terminate the string.
g_szNumber[nDigit] = 0;

// Characters were generated in reverse order;
// reverse the string.
// Call _strrev if ANSI, Call _wcsrev if Unicode.
_tcsrev(g_szNumber);

if (fSyncChecked) {
   // If the user wants synchronization, do it.
   // In earlier versions of this program, I was calling
   // IsDlgButtonChecked as I did earlier instead of
   // using the fSyncChecked variable. This caused
   // problems because the user could check or uncheck
   // the Synchronize check box in between the calls to
   // EnterCriticalSection and LeaveCriticalSection.
   // This meant that my thread was sometimes leaving a
   // critical section that it had never entered. And my
```

(continued)

Figure 10-1. *continued*

```
                // thread was sometimes entering a critical section
                // that it had never left.
                LeaveCriticalSection(&g_CriticalSection);
            }
            // If the user wants to display something
            // after each iteration, do it.
            if (IsDlgButtonChecked(g_hwnd, IDC_SHOWCNTRTHRD))
                AddToListBox(__TEXT("Cntr: Increment"));
    }
    return(0);  // We get here when the window is dismissed.
}


///////////////////////////////////////////////////////////////////


// Thread to add the current value of
// the counter (data) to the list box
DWORD WINAPI DisplayThread (LPVOID lpThreadParameter) {
    BOOL fSyncChecked;
    TCHAR szBuffer[50];

    while (!g_fTerminate) {

        // Determine whether the user wants the threads
        // to be synchronized.
        fSyncChecked =
            IsDlgButtonChecked(g_hwnd, IDC_SYNCHRONIZE);

        if (fSyncChecked)
            EnterCriticalSection(&g_CriticalSection);

        // Construct a string with the string form of the number.
        _stprintf(szBuffer, __TEXT("Dspy: %s"), g_szNumber);

        if (fSyncChecked)
            LeaveCriticalSection(&g_CriticalSection);

        // Add the string form of the number to the list box.
        AddToListBox(szBuffer);
    }
    return(0);  // We get here when the window is dismissed.
}
```

(continued)

Figure 10-1. *continued*

```
/////////////////////////////////////////////////////////////////

BOOL Dlg_OnInitDialog (HWND hwnd, HWND hwndFocus,
    LPARAM lParam) {
    HWND hWndCtl;
    DWORD dwThreadID;

    // Associate an icon with the dialog box.
    chSETDLGICONS(hwnd, IDI_CRITSECS, IDI_CRITSECS);

    // Save the handle of the dialog box in a global so that
    // the threads can easily gain access to it.  This must be
    // done before creating the threads.
    g_hwnd = hwnd;

    // Initialize the critical section.  This must also be
    // done before any threads try to use it.
    InitializeCriticalSection(&g_CriticalSection);

    // Create our counter thread and let it start running.
    g_hThread[0] = chBEGINTHREADEX(NULL, 0,
        CounterThread, NULL, 0, &dwThreadID);

    // Create our display thread and let it start running.
    g_hThread[1] = chBEGINTHREADEX(NULL, 0,
        DisplayThread, NULL, 0, &dwThreadID);


    // Fill the Process Priority Class combo box and select
    // Normal.
    hWndCtl = GetDlgItem(hwnd, IDC_PRIORITYCLASS);
    ComboBox_AddString(hWndCtl, __TEXT("Idle"));
    ComboBox_AddString(hWndCtl, __TEXT("Normal"));
    ComboBox_AddString(hWndCtl, __TEXT("High"));
    ComboBox_AddString(hWndCtl, __TEXT("Realtime"));
    ComboBox_SetCurSel(hWndCtl, 1);  // Normal

    // Fill the Display Thread Priority
    // combo box and select Normal.
    hWndCtl = GetDlgItem(hwnd, IDC_DSPYTHRDPRIORITY);
    ComboBox_AddString(hWndCtl, __TEXT("Idle"));
    ComboBox_AddString(hWndCtl, __TEXT("Lowest"));
    ComboBox_AddString(hWndCtl, __TEXT("Below normal"));
    ComboBox_AddString(hWndCtl, __TEXT("Normal"));
    ComboBox_AddString(hWndCtl, __TEXT("Above normal"));
```

(continued)

Figure 10-1. *continued*

```
    ComboBox_AddString(hWndCtl, __TEXT("Highest"));
    ComboBox_AddString(hWndCtl, __TEXT("Timecritical"));
    ComboBox_SetCurSel(hWndCtl, 3);   // Normal

    // Fill the Counter Thread Priority
    // combo box and select Normal.
    hWndCtl = GetDlgItem(hwnd, IDC_CNTRTHRDPRIORITY);
    ComboBox_AddString(hWndCtl, __TEXT("Idle"));
    ComboBox_AddString(hWndCtl, __TEXT("Lowest"));
    ComboBox_AddString(hWndCtl, __TEXT("Below normal"));
    ComboBox_AddString(hWndCtl, __TEXT("Normal"));
    ComboBox_AddString(hWndCtl, __TEXT("Above normal"));
    ComboBox_AddString(hWndCtl, __TEXT("Highest"));
    ComboBox_AddString(hWndCtl, __TEXT("Timecritical"));
    ComboBox_SetCurSel(hWndCtl, 3);   // Normal

    return(TRUE);
}


///////////////////////////////////////////////////////////////


void Dlg_OnDestroy (HWND hwnd) {
    // When the dialog box is destroyed, signal the worker
    // threads to terminate.
    g_fTerminate = TRUE;

    // Resume the worker threads in case they're paused.
    ResumeThread(g_hThread[0]);
    ResumeThread(g_hThread[1]);
}


///////////////////////////////////////////////////////////////


void Dlg_OnCommand (HWND hwnd, int id, HWND hwndCtl,
    UINT codeNotify) {

    HANDLE hThread;
    DWORD dw;

    switch (id) {
```

(continued)

Figure 10-1. *continued*

```
      case IDCANCEL:
         EndDialog(hwnd, id);
         break;

      case IDC_PRIORITYCLASS:
         if (codeNotify != CBN_SELCHANGE)
            break;

         // User is changing priority class.
         switch (ComboBox_GetCurSel(hwndCtl)) {
            case 0:
               dw = IDLE_PRIORITY_CLASS;
               break;

            case 1:
            default:
               dw = NORMAL_PRIORITY_CLASS;
               break;

            case 2:
               dw = HIGH_PRIORITY_CLASS;
               break;

            case 3:
               dw = REALTIME_PRIORITY_CLASS;
               break;
         }
         SetPriorityClass(GetCurrentProcess(), dw);
         break;

      case IDC_DSPYTHRDPRIORITY:
      case IDC_CNTRTHRDPRIORITY:
         if (codeNotify != CBN_SELCHANGE)
            break;

         switch (ComboBox_GetCurSel(hwndCtl)) {
            case 0:
               dw = (DWORD) THREAD_PRIORITY_IDLE;
               break;

            case 1:
               dw = (DWORD) THREAD_PRIORITY_LOWEST;
               break;
```

(continued)

Figure 10-1. *continued*

```
              case 2:
                 dw = (DWORD) THREAD_PRIORITY_BELOW_NORMAL;
                 break;

              case 3:
              default:
                 dw = (DWORD) THREAD_PRIORITY_NORMAL;
                 break;

              case 4:
                 dw = (DWORD) THREAD_PRIORITY_ABOVE_NORMAL;
                 break;

              case 5:
                 dw = (DWORD) THREAD_PRIORITY_HIGHEST;
                 break;

              case 6:
                 dw = (DWORD) THREAD_PRIORITY_TIME_CRITICAL;
                 break;
           }
           // User is changing the relative priority
           // of one of the threads.
           hThread = (id == IDC_CNTRTHRDPRIORITY) ?
                 g_hThread[0] : g_hThread[1];

           SetThreadPriority(hThread, dw);
           break;

        case IDC_PAUSE:
           // User is pausing or resuming both threads.
           if (Button_GetCheck(hwndCtl)) {

              SuspendThread(g_hThread[0]);
              SuspendThread(g_hThread[1]);

           } else {

              ResumeThread(g_hThread[0]);
              ResumeThread(g_hThread[1]);

           }
           break;
     }
  }
```

(continued)

Figure 10-1. *continued*

```
///////////////////////////////////////////////////////////////


BOOL CALLBACK Dlg_Proc (HWND hwnd, UINT uMsg,
   WPARAM wParam, LPARAM lParam) {

   switch (uMsg) {
      chHANDLE_DLGMSG(hwnd, WM_INITDIALOG, Dlg_OnInitDialog);
      chHANDLE_DLGMSG(hwnd, WM_DESTROY, Dlg_OnDestroy);
      chHANDLE_DLGMSG(hwnd, WM_COMMAND, Dlg_OnCommand);
   }
   return(FALSE);
}



///////////////////////////////////////////////////////////////


int WINAPI _tWinMain (HINSTANCE hinstExe,
   HINSTANCE hinstPrev, LPTSTR pszCmdLine, int nCmdShow) {

   chWARNIFUNICODEUNDERWIN95();
   DialogBox(hinstExe, MAKEINTRESOURCE(IDD_CRITSECS),
      NULL, Dlg_Proc);

   // Wait for both worker threads to terminate.
   WaitForMultipleObjects(2, g_hThread, TRUE, INFINITE);

   // Close our handles to the worker threads.
   CloseHandle(g_hThread[0]);
   CloseHandle(g_hThread[1]);

   // The worker threads can no longer be using the
   // critical section, so delete it.
   DeleteCriticalSection(&g_CriticalSection);

   return(0);
}


//////////////////////// End Of File ////////////////////////
```

(continued)

Figure 10-1. *continued*

```
CRITSECS.RC
//Microsoft Developer Studio generated resource script.
//
#include "Resource.h"

#define APSTUDIO_READONLY_SYMBOLS
/////////////////////////////////////////////////////////////////////
//
// Generated from the TEXTINCLUDE 2 resource.
//
#include "afxres.h"


/////////////////////////////////////////////////////////////////////
#undef APSTUDIO_READONLY_SYMBOLS


/////////////////////////////////////////////////////////////////////
// English (U.S.) resources

#if !defined(AFX_RESOURCE_DLL) || defined(AFX_TARG_ENU)
#ifdef _WIN32
LANGUAGE LANG_ENGLISH, SUBLANG_ENGLISH_US
#pragma code_page(1252)
#endif //_WIN32


/////////////////////////////////////////////////////////////////////
//
// Icon
//

// Icon with lowest ID value placed first to ensure application
// icon remains consistent on all systems.
IDI_CRITSECS             ICON    DISCARDABLE     "CritSecs.Ico"


/////////////////////////////////////////////////////////////////////
//
// Dialog
//

IDD_CRITSECS DIALOG DISCARDABLE  29, 28, 197, 208
STYLE WS_MINIMIZEBOX | WS_POPUP | WS_VISIBLE | WS_CAPTION|
   WS_SYSMENU
```

(continued)

Figure 10-1. *continued*

```
CAPTION "Critical Section Test Application"
FONT 8, "System"
BEGIN
    LTEXT           "&Process priority class:",
                    IDC_STATIC,4,4,74,8
    COMBOBOX        IDC_PRIORITYCLASS,88,4,64,48,
                    CBS_DROPDOWNLIST | WS_GROUP |
                    WS_TABSTOP
    CONTROL         "&Display thread priority:",
                    IDC_STATIC,"Static",
                    SS_LEFTNOWORDWRAP | WS_GROUP |
                    WS_TABSTOP,4,24,76,8
    COMBOBOX        IDC_DSPYTHRDPRIORITY,88,24,100,76,
                    CBS_DROPDOWNLIST | WS_GROUP |
                    WS_TABSTOP
    CONTROL         "&Counter thread priority:",
                    IDC_STATIC,"Static",
                    SS_LEFTNOWORDWRAP |
                    WS_GROUP | WS_TABSTOP,4,40,76,8
    COMBOBOX        IDC_CNTRTHRDPRIORITY,88,40,100,76,
                    CBS_DROPDOWNLIST | WS_GROUP |
                    WS_TABSTOP
    CONTROL         "&Synchronize",IDC_SYNCHRONIZE,
                    "Button",BS_AUTOCHECKBOX |
                    WS_TABSTOP,4,60,52,10
    CONTROL         "S&how counter thread",
                    IDC_SHOWCNTRTHRD,"Button",
                    BS_AUTOCHECKBOX | WS_TABSTOP,
                    4,72,77,10
    CONTROL         "P&ause",IDC_PAUSE,"Button",
                    BS_AUTOCHECKBOX | WS_TABSTOP,
                    4,84,32,10
    LISTBOX         IDC_DATABOX,88,60,100,144,
                    WS_VSCROLL | WS_GROUP |
                    WS_TABSTOP
END


#ifdef APSTUDIO_INVOKED
/////////////////////////////////////////////////////////////////
//
// TEXTINCLUDE
//
```

(continued)

Figure 10-1. *continued*

```
1 TEXTINCLUDE DISCARDABLE
BEGIN
    "Resource.h\0"
END

2 TEXTINCLUDE DISCARDABLE
BEGIN
    "#include ""afxres.h""\r\n"
    "\0"
END

3 TEXTINCLUDE DISCARDABLE
BEGIN
    "\r\n"
    "\0"
END


#endif    // APSTUDIO_INVOKED


#endif    // English (U.S.) resources
/////////////////////////////////////////////////////////////////////////



#ifndef APSTUDIO_INVOKED
/////////////////////////////////////////////////////////////////////////
//
// Generated from the TEXTINCLUDE 3 resource.
//


/////////////////////////////////////////////////////////////////////////
#endif    // not APSTUDIO_INVOKED
```

Synchronizing Threads with Kernel Objects

Critical sections are great for serializing access to data within a process because they are very fast. However, you might want to synchronize some applications with other special events occurring in the machine or with operations being performed in other processes. For example, you might want to create a child process to help accomplish some work, and as a result, the parent process might need to wait until the child process completes before continuing.

The following kernel objects can be used to synchronize threads:

- Processes
- Threads
- Files
- Console input
- File change notifications
- Mutexes
- Semaphores
- Events (auto-reset and manual-reset events)
- Waitable timers (Windows NT 4 or later only)

Each object can be in one of two states at any time: *signaled* or *nonsignaled*. Threads can be put to sleep until an object becomes signaled. If a thread in a parent process needs to wait for the child process to terminate, the parent's thread puts itself to sleep until the kernel object identifying the child process becomes signaled. You might recall from Chapter 3 that processes become signaled when they terminate. The same is true for thread objects. When a thread is created and running, its associated thread kernel object is nonsignaled. As soon as the thread terminates, its thread kernel object becomes signaled.

I like to think of the signaled state as a flag being raised. Threads sleep while the objects they are waiting for are nonsignaled (the flag is lowered). However, as soon as the object becomes signaled (the flag goes up), the sleeping thread sees the flag, wakes up, and resumes execution.

Some of the kernel objects listed above exist for no other purpose than to help with the synchronization of threads. For example, if a thread has a handle to a process object, the thread can call various Win32 functions to change the priority class of the process or to get the exit code of the process. In addition, a thread can use the handle of a process object to synchronize itself with the termination of the process.

Thread handles also serve the same two purposes. You can use a thread handle to manipulate a thread, and you can use a handle of a thread object to synchronize a thread with the termination of another thread.

Like process handles and thread handles, file handles can also be used for two purposes: you can read from and write to a file using its handle, and you can set a thread to synchronize itself with the completion of an asynchronous file I/O operation. Asynchronous file I/O and this type of thread synchronization are discussed in Chapter 15.

The last type of kernel object that serves two purposes is the console input object. This object is very similar to a file, and, in fact, you call the *CreateFile* function to create a console input object. A console-based application can use a handle of this object to read input from the application's input buffer, and a thread can use this handle to put itself to sleep until input is available for processing.

The other kernel objects—file change notifications, mutexes, semaphores, events, and waitable timers—exist for the sole purpose of thread synchronization. Likewise, there are Win32 functions that exist to create these objects, open these objects, synchronize threads with these objects, and close these objects. No other operations can be performed with these kernel objects. This chapter discusses how to use mutexes, semaphores, events, and waitable timers; file change notification objects are discussed in Chapter 14.

Threads use two main functions to put themselves to sleep while waiting for kernel objects to become signaled:

```
DWORD WaitForSingleObject(HANDLE hObject, DWORD dwTimeout);
```

and

```
DWORD WaitForMultipleObjects(DWORD cObjects, LPHANDLE lpHandles,
   BOOL bWaitAll, DWORD dwTimeout);
```

The *WaitForSingleObject* function tells the system that the thread is waiting for the kernel object identified by the *hObject* parameter to be signaled. The *dwTimeout* parameter tells the system how long the thread is willing to wait in milliseconds. If the specified kernel object does not become signaled in the specified time, the system should wake up the thread and allow it to continue executing.

WaitForSingleObject returns one of the following values:

Return Value	Defined As	Meaning
WAIT_OBJECT_0	0x00000000	The object reached the signaled state.
WAIT_TIMEOUT	0x00000102	The object did not reach the signaled state in *dwTimeout* milliseconds.

(continued)

continued

Return Value	Defined As	Meaning
WAIT_ABANDONED	0x00000080	The object was a mutex that reached the signaled state because it was abandoned. (See the "Mutexes" section later in this chapter.)
WAIT_FAILED	0xFFFFFFFF	An error occurred. Call *GetLastError* to get extended error information.

You can pass two special values as the *dwTimeout* parameter to *WaitForSingleObject*. Passing 0 tells the system that you don't want to wait at all and that the system should simply tell you if the object is signaled or nonsignaled. A return value of WAIT_OBJECT_0 indicates that the object is signaled, and a return value of WAIT_TIMEOUT indicates that the object is nonsignaled. Passing a value of INFINITE (defined as 0xFFFFFFFF) causes *WaitForSingleObject* to wait until the object reaches the signaled state. If the object never becomes signaled, the thread is never awakened and scheduled CPU time—which means that the thread is forever deadlocked.

The *WaitForMultipleObjects* function is similar to the *WaitForSingleObject* function except that it waits either for several objects to be signaled or for one object from a list of objects to be signaled. When calling this function, the *cObjects* parameter indicates the number of objects you want the function to check. This value cannot be larger than MAXIMUM_WAIT_OBJECTS, which is defined as 64. The *lpHandles* parameter is a pointer to an array of handles identifying these objects. An error occurs if the same object appears more than once in this list, even if the object is being identified by two different handle values.

The *bWaitAll* parameter indicates whether you want to wait for *one* of the objects in the list to become signaled or if you want *all* the objects in the list to become signaled. If *bWaitAll* is TRUE, *WaitForMultipleObjects* waits for all the objects to be signaled at the same time. If *bWaitAll* is FALSE, *WaitForMultipleObjects* waits until one of the objects becomes signaled. *WaitForMultipleObjects* scans the handle array from index 0 on up, and the first object that is signaled terminates the wait. The *dwTimeout* parameter is identical to the *dwTimeout* parameter for the *WaitForSingleObject* function. If multiple objects become signaled simultaneously, *WaitForMultipleObjects* returns the index of the first handle in the array identifying the object that became signaled.

WaitForMultipleObjects returns one of the following values:

Return Value	Defined As	Meaning
WAIT_OBJECT_0 to (WAIT_OBJECT_0 + cObjects − 1)	Start at 0x00000000	When waiting for all objects, this value indicates that the wait was completed successfully.
		When waiting for any object, this value indicates the index of the handle in the *lpHandles* array belonging to the object that satisfied the wait.
WAIT_TIMEOUT	0x00000102	The object or objects did not reach the signaled state in *dwTimeout* milliseconds.
WAIT_ABANDONED_0 to (WAIT_ABANDONED_0 + cObjects − 1)	Start at 0x00000080	When waiting for all objects, this value indicates that the wait was completed successfully and that at least one object was a mutex that became signaled because it was abandoned.
		When waiting for any object, this value indicates the index of the handle in the *lpHandles* array belonging to the mutex object that became signaled because it was abandoned.
WAIT_FAILED	0xFFFFFFFF	An error occurred. Call *GetLastError* to get extended error information.

The *WaitForSingleObject* and *WaitForMultipleObjects* functions have important side effects on certain kernel objects. For process and thread objects, there are no side effects. After process and thread objects become signaled, they stay signaled. Here's an example: if 10 threads are calling *WaitForSingleObject* and waiting for the same process object to become signaled, when the process terminates, the process object becomes signaled and all the waiting threads wake up to continue execution. The same is true for thread objects; once a thread object becomes signaled, it stays signaled.

For mutex, auto-reset event, and auto-reset waitable timer objects, the *WaitForSingleObject* and *WaitForMultipleObjects* functions change their states to nonsignaled. Once these objects become signaled and another thread is awakened, the object is immediately reset to its nonsignaled state. Because of this, only one thread waiting for a mutex, an auto-reset event, or an auto-reset waitable timer will awaken; other waiting threads will continue to sleep. These concepts will be made clearer as we go on and discuss each of these synchronization objects separately.

One more point regarding the *WaitForMultipleObjects* function: when *WaitForMultipleObjects* is called with *bWaitAll* passed as TRUE, none of the objects being waited for will be reset to their nonsignaled state until all the objects being waited for are signaled. In other words, the system periodically takes a snapshot of all the specified objects, and, if all of them are signaled, *WaitForMultipleObjects* resets any mutexes, auto-reset events, and auto-reset waitable timers back to their nonsignaled state. The system will not alter the state of any object unless all the specified objects are signaled simultaneously. The following discussion about *WaitForMultipleObjects* assumes that you understand the kernel synchronization objects. If you are new to thread synchronization, you might want to read the next section about mutexes and then return to these paragraphs.

Here is an example that demonstrates what I mean. Let's say that Thread 1 is waiting for two mutex objects: Mutex A and Mutex B. And let's say that Thread 2 is executing code and is just about to enter a wait for the Mutex A object that Thread 1 is also waiting for. If Mutex A now becomes signaled, Thread 1 has half of what it needs to stop waiting and continue execution—it still needs to wait for Mutex B. If Thread 2 now calls *WaitForSingleObject*, specifying Mutex A, the system will give ownership of Mutex A to Thread 2. Thread 1 must still wait for Mutex B to become available, but now it must also wait for Thread 2 to release Mutex A.

WaitForMultipleObjects does not take ownership of an object unless it can take ownership of all the specified objects. If *WaitForMultipleObjects* obtained ownership of the synchronization objects as they became available, a deadlock situation would likely occur. Here is what could happen: Let's say Thread 1 and Thread 2 are both suspended on a call to *WaitForMultipleObjects*, waiting for Mutex A and Mutex B to become signaled. Now a third thread releases Mutex A. The system detects this and gives ownership of Mutex A to Thread 1. The same third thread now releases Mutex B. The system detects this and gives Mutex B to Thread 2.

At this point, both Thread 1 and Thread 2 are still suspended, waiting for the other mutex object to become signaled.

Now you see the problem: Thread 1 has ownership of Mutex A but can't resume itself, so Mutex A can never be released. This means that Thread 2 will never gain ownership of Mutex A and is also stuck in its suspended state. To avoid this deadlock situation, *WaitForMultipleObjects* doesn't reset any objects to their nonsignaled state unless all of the specified objects are signaled simultaneously.

Mutexes

Mutexes are very much like critical sections except that they can be used to synchronize data access across multiple processes. To use a mutex, one process must first create the mutex with the *CreateMutex* function:

```
HANDLE CreateMutex(LPSECURITY_ATTRIBUTES lpsa, BOOL fInitialOwner,
    LPTSTR lpszMutexName);
```

The *lpsa* parameter points to a SECURITY_ATTRIBUTES structure. The *fInitialOwner* parameter indicates whether the thread creating the mutex should be the initial owner of the mutex. The value TRUE means that the thread will own the mutex and therefore the mutex will be in the nonsignaled state. Any thread that waits on the mutex will be suspended until the thread that created the mutex releases it. Passing FALSE for the *fInitialOwner* parameter of *CreateMutex* means that the mutex is not owned by any thread and is therefore created in the signaled state. The first thread to wait for the mutex will immediately gain ownership of the mutex and continue execution.

The *lpszMutexName* parameter is either NULL or an address of a zero-terminated string that identifies the mutex. When an application calls *CreateMutex*, the system allocates a mutex kernel object and assigns it the name indicated by *lpszMutexName*. This name is used to share a mutex between processes. (I'll discuss this later in the chapter.) The *CreateMutex* function returns a process-relative handle that identifies the new mutex object.

One of the big differences between mutexes and critical sections is that mutexes can be used to synchronize threads running in multiple processes. To do this, a thread in each process must have its own process-relative handle to a single mutex object. These handles can be obtained in several ways. The first and most common way is for one thread in each process to call *CreateMutex*, passing the identical string for the *lpszMutexName* parameter. The first thread to call *CreateMutex* will cause the system to create the mutex kernel object. As additional threads call

347

CreateMutex, the system determines that a mutex with the specified name already exists; as a result, it does not create a new mutex object but returns a process-relative handle identifying the existing mutex object.

A thread can determine whether *CreateMutex* actually created a new mutex object by calling *GetLastError* immediately after the call to *Create-Mutex*. If *GetLastError* reports ERROR_ALREADY_EXISTS, a new mutex object was not created. If you are expecting to share this mutex with other processes, you can ignore this last step.

Another method for obtaining the handle of a mutex involves a call to the *OpenMutex* function:

```
HANDLE OpenMutex(DWORD fdwAccess, BOOL fInherit, LPTSTR lpszName);
```

The *fdwAccess* parameter can be either SYNCHRONIZE or MUTEX-_ALL_ACCESS. The *fInherit* parameter indicates whether any child process created by this process should inherit this handle to this mutex object. The *lpszName* parameter is the zero-terminated string name of the mutex object.

When the call to *OpenMutex* is made, the system scans all existing mutex objects to see if any of them have the name indicated by *lpszName*. If the system finds a mutex object with the specified name, it creates a process-relative handle identifying the mutex and returns the handle to the calling thread. Any thread in the calling process can now use this handle in any function that accepts a mutex handle. If a mutex with the specified name cannot be found, NULL is returned.

Both methods described above require that the mutex be named. Two other methods don't require naming the mutex—one involves the use of the *DuplicateHandle* function, and the other involves parent-child handle inheritance. These methods are discussed in Chapter 2.

Using Mutexes Instead of Critical Sections

Let's rewrite the critical section example shown on pages 317 and 318 using mutexes, and you will see how similar the code is:

```
int    g_nIndex = 0;
const int MAX_TIMES = 1000;
DWORD g_dwTimes[MAX_TIMES];
HANDLE g_hMutex = NULL;

int WinMain (...) {
   HANDLE hThreads[2];
```

```
   // Create the mutex before the threads so that it
   // exists when the threads execute.
   g_hMutex = CreateMutex(NULL, FALSE, NULL);

   // Save the handles of the threads in an array.
   hThreads[0] = CreateThread(..., FirstThread, ...);
   hThreads[1] = CreateThread(..., SecondThread, ...);

   // Wait for both threads to terminate.
   WaitForMultipleObjects(2, hThreads, TRUE, INFINITE);

   // Close the thread handles.
   CloseHandle(hThreads[0]);
   CloseHandle(hThreads[1]);

   // Close the mutex.
   CloseHandle(g_hMutex);
}

DWORD WINAPI FirstThread (LPVOID lpvThreadParm) {
   BOOL fDone = FALSE;
   DWORD dw;

   while (!fDone) {
      // Wait forever for the mutex to become signaled.
      dw = WaitForSingleObject(g_hMutex, INFINITE);

      if (dw == WAIT_OBJECT_0) {
         // Mutex became signaled.
         if (g_nIndex >= MAX_TIMES) {
            fDone = TRUE;

         } else {
            g_dwTimes[g_nIndex] = GetTickCount();
            g_nIndex++;
         }

         // Release the mutex.
         ReleaseMutex(g_hMutex);
      } else {

         // The mutex was abandoned.
         break;   // Exit the while loop.
      }
   }
   return(0);
}
```

(continued)

```
DWORD WINAPI SecondThread (LPVOID lpvThreadParm) {
   BOOL fDone = FALSE;
   DWORD dw;

   while (!fDone) {
      // Wait forever for the mutex to become signaled.
      dw = WaitForSingleObject(g_hMutex, INFINITE);

      if (dw == WAIT_OBJECT_0) {
         // Mutex became signaled.
         if (g_nIndex >= MAX_TIMES) {
            fDone = TRUE;
         } else {
            g_nIndex++;
            g_dwTimes[g_nIndex - 1] = GetTickCount();
         }

         // Release the mutex.
         ReleaseMutex(g_hMutex);
      } else {
         // The mutex was abandoned.
         break;   // Exit the while loop.
      }
   }
   return(0);
}
```

Notice that I created the mutex before creating the threads. This is important—if I had done it the other way around, the threads might attempt to call *WaitForSingleObject,* passing the handle NULL because the mutex had not been created yet. You can write the code differently so that you create the threads first. That code looks like this:

```
:
:

// Create both threads, but do not allow them to begin executing.
hThreads[0] = CreateThread(..., FirstThread, NULL,
   CREATE_SUSPENDED, ...);
hThreads[1] = CreateThread(..., SecondThread, NULL,
   CREATE_SUSPENDED, ...);

// Create the mutex.
g_hMutex = CreateMutex(NULL, FALSE, NULL);

// Allow the threads to run.
ResumeThread(hThreads[0]);
ResumeThread(hThreads[1]);
:
:
```

Here I create both threads, but they are suspended. They won't be scheduled any CPU time until they are resumed. Then I create the mutex and save its handle in the global *g_hMutex* variable. Now that I know this handle is not NULL, I resume both of the suspended threads by calling *ResumeThread* twice. The order here is very important. In my own work, I've forgotten to create objects before referencing them more often than I care to remember.

Back in *WinMain* in the code on pages 348 and 349, I showed how the process's primary thread waits for the two threads to terminate; it does this by calling *WaitForMultipleObjects*. In this call, the value 2 indicates that the primary thread is waiting for two objects to be signaled, *hThreads* identifies the array of handles, and TRUE means that the thread wants to wait until all the objects are signaled simultaneously—which will tell us that both threads have terminated. The inclusion of the INFINITE identifier means that the primary thread will wait forever for both threads to terminate. When *WaitForMultipleObjects* returns, *WinMain* calls *CloseHandle* so that the mutex object is destroyed.

Both thread functions have been modified to use mutex objects instead of critical sections. The calls to *EnterCriticalSection* have been replaced by calls to *WaitForSingleObject*. *WaitForSingleObject* can return WAIT_OBJECT_0, WAIT_ABANDONED, or WAIT_TIMEOUT. WAIT-_TIMEOUT can never occur here because INFINITE was specified in the call. A return value of WAIT_OBJECT_0 means that the mutex was signaled and the thread can continue executing. When *WaitForSingle-Object* sees that the mutex has reached a signaled state, the thread immediately grabs ownership of the mutex, which places the mutex back into the nonsignaled state. The thread can then manipulate the data structure; when it no longer needs access to the structure, the thread calls the *ReleaseMutex* function:

```
BOOL ReleaseMutex(HANDLE hMutex);
```

ReleaseMutex is the function that changes the mutex from the non-signaled state to the signaled state just as the *LeaveCriticalSection* function does for critical sections. One important thing to remember is that this function has an effect only if the thread that is calling *ReleaseMutex* also has ownership of the mutex. Immediately after this function is called, any thread that is waiting for the mutex can grab hold of it and begin executing. Of course, when the thread grabs the mutex, the mutex again becomes nonsignaled. If no threads are waiting on the mutex, the mutex remains in the signaled state, indicating that no thread is accessing the protected data. If a thread comes along and waits on the mutex, it will immediately be able to grab the mutex, locking other threads out if they try to wait on the mutex.

Let me reiterate that when working with any kind of synchronization object, you always want to maintain ownership of that object for as short a time as possible. If other threads are waiting for the object, they are all sleeping and not doing their work.

Abandoned Mutexes

Mutex objects are different from all other synchronization kernel objects because mutex objects are owned by a thread. All other synchronization objects are either signaled or nonsignaled, period. Mutex objects, in addition to being signaled or nonsignaled, remember which thread owns them. A mutex is abandoned if a thread waits for a mutex object, grabs the object (putting it in the nonsignaled state), and then terminates. In this scenario, the mutex is nonsignaled and will never be signaled because no other thread can release the mutex by calling *ReleaseMutex*.

When the system sees that this has happened, it automatically sets the mutex back to the signaled state. Any threads that are currently waiting for the mutex with a call to *WaitForSingleObject* get awakened, and *WaitForSingleObject* returns WAIT_ABANDONED instead of WAIT_OB-JECT_0. In this way, a thread knows that the mutex has not been released gracefully. This is usually an indication that a bug exists in the source code. There is no way to know if the thread that previously owned the mutex finished what it was doing to the data before it terminated. (Remember that threads can be forcibly terminated by calling *ExitThread* or *TerminateThread*.)˙

In the code fragment on page 350, I check to see whether the mutex has been abandoned; if it has, I break out of the *while* loop, causing the thread to end. *WinMain* will eventually see that both threads have terminated, causing the mutex to be destroyed and the process to terminate. I could ignore the possibility that WAIT_ABANDONED can be returned from *WaitForSingleObject*, but I don't know what state the protected data might be in.

One last point about mutexes: mutexes have an ownership count associated with them. So if a thread calls *WaitForSingleObject* for a mutex object that the thread already owns, the call succeeds immediately every time because the system knows that this thread already owns the mutex. In addition, the reference count for the mutex is incremented each time. This means that the thread must call *ReleaseMutex* the same number of times before the mutex will be in the signaled state again. *EnterCriticalSection* and *LeaveCriticalSection* work for critical sections in the same way.

The Mutexes Sample Application

The Mutexes application (MUTEXES.EXE), listed in Figure 10-2, is simply the CritSecs program modified to use mutexes instead of critical sections. On the outside, the Mutexes program behaves identically to the CritSecs program. However, by using mutexes instead of critical sections, it would now be possible to put the *CounterThread* function in one process and the *DisplayThread* function in another process (although the sample does not demonstrate this). The source code and resource files for the application are in the MUTEXES directory on the companion disc.

Mutexes.ico

MUTEXES.C

```
/********************************************************************
Module name: Mutexes.C
Notices: Copyright (c) 1995-1997 Jeffrey Richter
********************************************************************/


#include "..\CmnHdr.H"                    /* See Appendix C. */
#include <windows.h>
#include <windowsx.h>
#include <tchar.h>
#include <stdio.h>                  // For sprintf
#include <process.h>               // For _beginthreadex
#include "Resource.H"



///////////////////////////////////////////////////////////////////


// Global variables
// g_fTerminate is set to TRUE when the dialog box is
// dismissed. It indicates to the worker threads that they
// need to terminate. It is volatile because it can change
// at any time.
volatile BOOL  g_fTerminate = FALSE;
```

Figure 10-2. *(continued)*

The Mutexes application.

Figure 10-2. *continued*

```
HWND    g_hwnd;
HANDLE  g_hThread[2];  // Counter[0] & Display[1] threads


// The data that needs protecting
TCHAR   g_szNumber[10] = __TEXT("0");

// The mutex used to protect the data
HANDLE g_hMutex;


///////////////////////////////////////////////////////////////////


// Add a string to a list box.
void AddToListBox (LPCTSTR szBuffer) {
   HWND hwndDataBox = GetDlgItem(g_hwnd, IDC_DATABOX);

   int x = ListBox_AddString(hwndDataBox, szBuffer);
   ListBox_SetCurSel(hwndDataBox, x);

   if (ListBox_GetCount(hwndDataBox) > 100)
      ListBox_DeleteString(hwndDataBox, 0);
}


///////////////////////////////////////////////////////////////////


// Thread to increment the protected counter data
DWORD WINAPI CounterThread (LPVOID lpThreadParameter) {
   unsigned int nNumber, nDigit;
   BOOL fSyncChecked;

   while (!g_fTerminate) {
      // Get the status of the Synchronize check box
      // and save it.
      fSyncChecked =
         IsDlgButtonChecked(g_hwnd, IDC_SYNCHRONIZE);

      if (fSyncChecked) {
         // If the user wants us synchronized, do it.
         WaitForSingleObject(g_hMutex, INFINITE);
      }
```

(continued)

Figure 10-2. *continued*

```
      // Convert the string number to an integer and add 1.
      _stscanf(g_szNumber, __TEXT("%d"), &nNumber);
      nNumber++;

      // Convert the new integer back to a string.
      nDigit = 0;
      while (nNumber != 0) {
         // Put a digit into the string.
         g_szNumber[nDigit++] = (TCHAR)
   (__TEXT('0') + (nNumber % 10));

         // A call to Sleep here tells the system that we want
         // to relinquish the remainder of our time slice to
         // another thread.  This call is needed for
         // single-CPU systems so that the results of the
         // synchronization or lack thereof are obvious.
         // Normally, your programs would NOT call Sleep here.
         Sleep(0);

         // Get ready to get the next digit.
         nNumber /= 10;
      }

      // All digits converted to characters.
      // Terminate the string.
      g_szNumber[nDigit] = 0;

      // Characters were generated in reverse order;
      // reverse the string.
      // Call _strrev if ANSI, Call _wcsrev if Unicode.
      _tcsrev(g_szNumber);

      if (fSyncChecked) {
         // If the user wants synchronization, do it.
         ReleaseMutex(g_hMutex);
      }

      // If the user wants to display something
      // after each iteration, do it.
      if (IsDlgButtonChecked(g_hwnd, IDC_SHOWCNTRTHRD))
         AddToListBox(__TEXT("Cntr: Increment"));
   }
   return(0);  // We get here when the window is dismissed.
}
```

(continued)

Figure 10-2. *continued*

```
/////////////////////////////////////////////////////////////////////


// Thread to add the current value of
// the counter (data) to the list box
DWORD WINAPI DisplayThread (LPVOID lpThreadParameter) {
   BOOL fSyncChecked;
   TCHAR szBuffer[50];

   while (!g_fTerminate) {

      // Determine whether the user wants the threads
      // to be synchronized.
      fSyncChecked =
         IsDlgButtonChecked(g_hwnd, IDC_SYNCHRONIZE);

      if (fSyncChecked)
         WaitForSingleObject(g_hMutex, INFINITE);

      // Construct a string with the string form of the number.
      _stprintf(szBuffer, __TEXT("Dspy: %s"), g_szNumber);

      if (fSyncChecked)
         ReleaseMutex(g_hMutex);

      // Add the string form of the number to the list box.
      AddToListBox(szBuffer);
   }
   return(0);  // We get here when the window is dismissed.
}


/////////////////////////////////////////////////////////////////////


BOOL Dlg_OnInitDialog (HWND hwnd, HWND hwndFocus,
   LPARAM lParam) {
   HWND hWndCtl;
   DWORD dwThreadID;

   // Associate an icon with the dialog box.
   chSETDLGICONS(hwnd, IDI_MUTEXES, IDI_MUTEXES);
```

(continued)

Figure 10-2. *continued*

```
// Save the handle of the dialog box in a global so that
// the threads can easily gain access to it.  This must be
// done before creating the threads.
g_hwnd = hwnd;

// Initialize the mutex object.  This must also be
// done before any threads try to use it. There
// should be error checking here.
g_hMutex = CreateMutex(NULL, FALSE, NULL);

// Create our counter thread and let it start running.
g_hThread[0] = chBEGINTHREADEX(NULL, 0,
   CounterThread, NULL, 0, &dwThreadID);

// Create our display thread and let it start running.
g_hThread[1] = chBEGINTHREADEX(NULL, 0,
   DisplayThread, NULL, 0, &dwThreadID);


// Fill the Process Priority Class combo box and select
// Normal.
hWndCtl = GetDlgItem(hwnd, IDC_PRIORITYCLASS);
ComboBox_AddString(hWndCtl, __TEXT("Idle"));
ComboBox_AddString(hWndCtl, __TEXT("Normal"));
ComboBox_AddString(hWndCtl, __TEXT("High"));
ComboBox_AddString(hWndCtl, __TEXT("Realtime"));
ComboBox_SetCurSel(hWndCtl, 1);  // Normal

// Fill the Display Thread Priority
// combo box and select Normal.
hWndCtl = GetDlgItem(hwnd, IDC_DSPYTHRDPRIORITY);
ComboBox_AddString(hWndCtl, __TEXT("Idle"));
ComboBox_AddString(hWndCtl, __TEXT("Lowest"));
ComboBox_AddString(hWndCtl, __TEXT("Below normal"));
ComboBox_AddString(hWndCtl, __TEXT("Normal"));
ComboBox_AddString(hWndCtl, __TEXT("Above normal"));
ComboBox_AddString(hWndCtl, __TEXT("Highest"));
ComboBox_AddString(hWndCtl, __TEXT("Timecritical"));
ComboBox_SetCurSel(hWndCtl, 3);  // Normal

// Fill the Counter Thread Priority
// combo box and select Normal.
```

(continued)

Figure 10-2. *continued*

```
   hWndCtl = GetDlgItem(hwnd, IDC_CNTRTHRDPRIORITY);
   ComboBox_AddString(hWndCtl, __TEXT("Idle"));
   ComboBox_AddString(hWndCtl, __TEXT("Lowest"));
   ComboBox_AddString(hWndCtl, __TEXT("Below normal"));
   ComboBox_AddString(hWndCtl, __TEXT("Normal"));
   ComboBox_AddString(hWndCtl, __TEXT("Above normal"));
   ComboBox_AddString(hWndCtl, __TEXT("Highest"));
   ComboBox_AddString(hWndCtl, __TEXT("Timecritical"));
   ComboBox_SetCurSel(hWndCtl, 3);   // Normal

   return(TRUE);
}


///////////////////////////////////////////////////////////////


void Dlg_OnDestroy (HWND hwnd) {
   // When the dialog box is destroyed, signal the worker
   // threads to terminate.
   g_fTerminate = TRUE;

   // Resume the worker threads in case they're paused.
   ResumeThread(g_hThread[0]);
   ResumeThread(g_hThread[1]);
}


///////////////////////////////////////////////////////////////


void Dlg_OnCommand (HWND hwnd, int id, HWND hwndCtl,
   UINT codeNotify) {

   HANDLE hThread;
   DWORD dw;

   switch (id) {
      case IDCANCEL:
         EndDialog(hwnd, id);
         break;

      case IDC_PRIORITYCLASS:
         if (codeNotify != CBN_SELCHANGE)
            break;
```

(continued)

Figure 10-2. *continued*

```
        // User is changing priority class.
        switch (ComboBox_GetCurSel(hwndCtl)) {
            case 0:
                dw = IDLE_PRIORITY_CLASS;
                break;

            case 1:
            default:
                dw = NORMAL_PRIORITY_CLASS;
                break;

            case 2:
                dw = HIGH_PRIORITY_CLASS;
                break;

            case 3:
                dw = REALTIME_PRIORITY_CLASS;
                break;
        }
        SetPriorityClass(GetCurrentProcess(), dw);
        break;

case IDC_DSPYTHRDPRIORITY:
case IDC_CNTRTHRDPRIORITY:
    if (codeNotify != CBN_SELCHANGE)
        break;

    switch (ComboBox_GetCurSel(hwndCtl)) {
        case 0:
            dw = (DWORD) THREAD_PRIORITY_IDLE;
            break;

        case 1:
            dw = (DWORD) THREAD_PRIORITY_LOWEST;
            break;

        case 2:
            dw = (DWORD) THREAD_PRIORITY_BELOW_NORMAL;
            break;

        case 3:
        default:
            dw = (DWORD) THREAD_PRIORITY_NORMAL;
            break;
```

(continued)

Figure 10-2. *continued*

```
            case 4:
                dw = (DWORD) THREAD_PRIORITY_ABOVE_NORMAL;
                break;

            case 5:
                dw = (DWORD) THREAD_PRIORITY_HIGHEST;
                break;

            case 6:
                dw = (DWORD) THREAD_PRIORITY_TIME_CRITICAL;
                break;
        }
        // User is changing the relative priority
        // of one of the threads.
        hThread = (id == IDC_CNTRTHRDPRIORITY) ?
            g_hThread[0] : g_hThread[1];

        SetThreadPriority(hThread, dw);
        break;

    case IDC_PAUSE:
        // User is pausing or resuming both threads.
        if (Button_GetCheck(hwndCtl)) {

            SuspendThread(g_hThread[0]);
            SuspendThread(g_hThread[1]);

        } else {

            ResumeThread(g_hThread[0]);
            ResumeThread(g_hThread[1]);

        }
        break;
    }
}


///////////////////////////////////////////////////////////////////


BOOL CALLBACK Dlg_Proc (HWND hwnd, UINT uMsg,
    WPARAM wParam, LPARAM lParam) {
```

(continued)

Figure 10-2. *continued*

```
    switch (uMsg) {
        chHANDLE_DLGMSG(hwnd, WM_INITDIALOG, Dlg_OnInitDialog);
        chHANDLE_DLGMSG(hwnd, WM_DESTROY, Dlg_OnDestroy);
        chHANDLE_DLGMSG(hwnd, WM_COMMAND, Dlg_OnCommand);
    }
    return(FALSE);
}


///////////////////////////////////////////////////////////////


int WINAPI _tWinMain (HINSTANCE hinstExe,
    HINSTANCE hinstPrev, LPTSTR pszCmdLine, int nCmdShow) {

    chWARNIFUNICODEUNDERWIN95();
    DialogBox(hinstExe, MAKEINTRESOURCE(IDD_MUTEXES),
        NULL, Dlg_Proc);

    // Wait for both worker threads to terminate.
    WaitForMultipleObjects(2, g_hThread, TRUE, INFINITE);

    // Close our handles to the worker threads.
    CloseHandle(g_hThread[0]);
    CloseHandle(g_hThread[1]);

    // The worker threads can no longer be using the
    // mutex, so destroy it.
    CloseHandle(g_hMutex);

    return(0);
}


///////////////////////// End Of File /////////////////////////
```

MUTEXES.RC
```
//Microsoft Developer Studio generated resource script.
//
#include "Resource.h"

#define APSTUDIO_READONLY_SYMBOLS
```

(continued)

Figure 10-2. *continued*

```
/////////////////////////////////////////////////////////////////
//
// Generated from the TEXTINCLUDE 2 resource.
//
#include "afxres.h"


/////////////////////////////////////////////////////////////////
#undef APSTUDIO_READONLY_SYMBOLS


/////////////////////////////////////////////////////////////////
// English (U.S.) resources

#if !defined(AFX_RESOURCE_DLL) || defined(AFX_TARG_ENU)
#ifdef _WIN32
LANGUAGE LANG_ENGLISH, SUBLANG_ENGLISH_US
#pragma code_page(1252)
#endif //_WIN32


#ifdef APSTUDIO_INVOKED
/////////////////////////////////////////////////////////////////
//
// TEXTINCLUDE
//

1 TEXTINCLUDE DISCARDABLE
BEGIN
    "Resource.h\0"
END

2 TEXTINCLUDE DISCARDABLE
BEGIN
    "#include ""afxres.h""\r\n"
    "\0"
END

3 TEXTINCLUDE DISCARDABLE
BEGIN
    "\r\n"
    "\0"
END

#endif    // APSTUDIO_INVOKED
```

(continued)

Figure 10-2. *continued*

```
//////////////////////////////////////////////////////////////////
//
// Dialog
//

IDD_MUTEXES DIALOG DISCARDABLE  29, 28, 197, 208
STYLE WS_MINIMIZEBOX | WS_POPUP | WS_VISIBLE | WS_CAPTION |
    WS_SYSMENU
CAPTION "Mutex Test Application"
FONT 8, "System"
BEGIN
    LTEXT           "&Process priority class:",IDC_STATIC,
                    4,4,74,8
    COMBOBOX        IDC_PRIORITYCLASS,88,4,64,48,
                    CBS_DROPDOWNLIST | WS_GROUP |
                    WS_TABSTOP
    CONTROL         "&Display thread priority:",IDC_STATIC,
                    "Static", SS_LEFTNOWORDWRAP | WS_GROUP |
                    WS_TABSTOP,4,24,76,8
    COMBOBOX        IDC_DSPYTHRDPRIORITY,88,24,100,76,
                    CBS_DROPDOWNLIST | WS_GROUP | WS_TABSTOP
    CONTROL         "&Counter thread priority:",IDC_STATIC,
                    "Static", SS_LEFTNOWORDWRAP | WS_GROUP |
                    WS_TABSTOP,4,40,76,8
    COMBOBOX        IDC_CNTRTHRDPRIORITY,88,40,100,76,
                    CBS_DROPDOWNLIST | WS_GROUP | WS_TABSTOP
    CONTROL         "&Synchronize",IDC_SYNCHRONIZE,"Button",
                    BS_AUTOCHECKBOX | WS_TABSTOP, 4,60,52,10
    CONTROL         "S&how counter thread",IDC_SHOWCNTRTHRD,
                    "Button", BS_AUTOCHECKBOX | WS_TABSTOP,
                    4,72,77,10
    CONTROL         "P&ause",IDC_PAUSE,"Button",
                    BS_AUTOCHECKBOX | WS_TABSTOP, 4,84,32,10
    LISTBOX         IDC_DATABOX,88,60,100,144,WS_VSCROLL |
                    WS_GROUP | WS_TABSTOP
END
```

(continued)

363

Figure 10-2. *continued*

```
////////////////////////////////////////////////////////////////
//
// Icon
//

// Icon with lowest ID value placed first to ensure application
// icon remains consistent on all systems.
IDI_MUTEXES              ICON    DISCARDABLE     "Mutexes.Ico"
#endif    // English (U.S.) resources
////////////////////////////////////////////////////////////////


#ifndef APSTUDIO_INVOKED
////////////////////////////////////////////////////////////////
//
// Generated from the TEXTINCLUDE 3 resource.
//


////////////////////////////////////////////////////////////////
#endif    // not APSTUDIO_INVOKED
```

Semaphores

Semaphore kernel objects are used for resource counting. They offer a thread the ability to query the number of resources available; if one or more resources are available, the count of available resources is decremented. Semaphores perform this test-and-set operation atomically; that is, when you request a resource from a semaphore, the operating system checks whether the resource is available and decrements the count of available resources without letting another thread interfere. Only after the resource count has been decremented does the system allow another thread to request a resource.

For example, let's say that a computer has three serial ports. No more than three threads can use the serial ports at any given time; each port can be assigned to one thread. This situation provides a perfect opportunity to use a semaphore. To monitor serial port usage, you can create a semaphore with a count of 3—one for each port. A semaphore is signaled when its resource count is greater than 0 and is nonsignaled when the count is equal to 0. (The count can never be less than 0.) Every time a thread calls *WaitForSingleObject* and passes the handle of a semaphore, the system checks whether the resource count for the semaphore is greater than 0. If it is, the system decrements the resource count and wakes the thread. If the resource count is 0 when the thread calls *WaitForSingleObject*, the system puts the thread to sleep until another thread releases the semaphore (increments the resource count).

Because several threads can affect a semaphore's resource count, a semaphore, unlike a critical section or a mutex, is not considered to be owned by a thread. This means that it's possible for one thread to wait for the semaphore object (decrement the object's resource count) and another thread to release the object (increment the object's resource count).

You create a semaphore by calling the *CreateSemaphore* function:

```
HANDLE CreateSemaphore(LPSECURITY_ATTRIBUTE lpsa,
    LONG cSemInitial, LONG cSemMax, LPTSTR lpszSemName);
```

This function creates a semaphore that has a maximum resource count of *cSemMax*. So in the previous example, you would pass the value 3 to represent the three serial ports. The *cSemInitial* parameter lets you specify the starting resource count for the semaphore. When the system starts, all three serial ports are available, so you would set this value to 3 as well. When the operating system initializes, you might want it to indicate that there are three serial ports but that none are available. To do this, you would pass 0 as the *cSemInitial* parameter.

The last parameter of *CreateSemaphore*, *lpszSemName*, assigns a string name to the semaphore. You can use this string name in other processes to get the handle of the semaphore by calling *CreateSemaphore* or *OpenSemaphore*:

```
HANDLE OpenSemaphore(DWORD fdwAccess, BOOL fInherit,
    LPTSTR lpszName);
```

This function's semantics are identical to those of the *OpenMutex* function, discussed previously.

To release a semaphore (increment its resource count), you call the *ReleaseSemaphore* function:

```
BOOL ReleaseSemaphore(HANDLE hSemaphore, LONG cRelease,
    LPLONG lplPrevious);
```

This function is similar to the *ReleaseMutex* function, but there are a few differences. First, any thread can call this function at any time because semaphore objects are not owned by a single thread. Second, the *Release-Semaphore* function can be used to increment the resource count of the semaphore by more than 1. The *cRelease* parameter indicates by how much the semaphore should be released. For example, let's say that we have an application that copies data from one serial port to another. The application has to acquire the semaphore twice by calling *WaitForSingle-Object* twice. However, it can release both resources with just a single call to *ReleaseSemaphore*. The following code fragment demonstrates:

```
// Get two serial ports.
WaitForSingleObject(g_hSemSerialPort, INFINITE);
WaitForSingleObject(g_hSemSerialPort, INFINITE);

    :
    :

// Use the serial ports to do the copy.

    :
    :

// Release the serial ports so that other applications
// can use them.
ReleaseSemaphore(g_hSemSerialPort, 2, NULL);
```

It would be nice if you could call *WaitForMultipleObjects* once instead of calling *WaitForSingleObject* twice. However, *WaitForMultipleObjects* does not allow the same handle to be used more than once in a single call. So although we must call *WaitForSingleObject* twice, it is convenient that we can call *ReleaseSemaphore* once at the end to increment the semaphore's count by 2.

ReleaseSemaphore's last parameter, *lplPrevious*, is a pointer to a long, which *ReleaseSemaphore* fills with the semaphore's resource count *before* adding *cRelease* back to it. If you are not interested in this value, you can simply pass NULL.

It would help if there were a Win32 function that determined the resource count of a semaphore without actually altering the semaphore's count. At first, I thought that calling *ReleaseSemaphore* and passing 0 for the second parameter might work by returning the actual count in the long pointed to by the *lplPrevious* parameter. But, unfortunately, this doesn't work; *ReleaseSemaphore* fills the long with 0. Next I tried passing a really big number as the second parameter, but *ReleaseSemaphore* still filled the long with 0. There is no way to get the count of a semaphore without altering it.

The Supermarket Sample Application

The SprMrkt (SPRMRKT.EXE) application, listed in Figure 10-4 beginning on page 380, demonstrates the use of mutexes and semaphores to control a supermarket simulation. The source code and resource files for the application are in the SPRMRKT directory on the companion disc. When you run SprMrkt, the following dialog box appears:

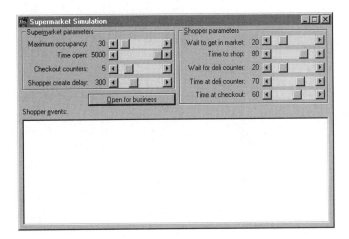

Using this dialog box, you can set up all the initial parameters before executing the simulation. When you have finished configuring the simulation parameters, click on the Open For Business button to create and start executing a thread that represents the supermarket. The function that identifies this thread is called *ThreadSuperMarket*.

The supermarket thread is responsible for the following events:

1. Opening the supermarket

2. Creating threads that represent individual shoppers

3. Closing the front doors when the store closes so that no more shoppers can enter

4. Waiting until all the shoppers in the store have checked out their groceries before ending the simulation

5. Notifying the GUI thread (or primary thread) that the supermarket simulation has ended so that the dialog box can re-enable able the simulation parameter controls and another simulation can be executed

As mentioned in number 2 above, each shopper is represented by his or her own thread. Every so often, the supermarket thread creates a new shopper thread by calling _beginthreadex:

```
hThread = (HANDLE) chBEGINTHREADEX (
    NULL,                      // Security attributes
    0,                         // Stack
    ThreadShopper,             // Thread function
    (LPVOID) ++nShopperNum,    // Shopper number as lpvParam
    0,                         // Flags
    &dwThreadId);              // Thread ID

CloseHandle(hThread);
```

The call to *CloseHandle* tells the system that the shopper thread isn't referenced directly from within the supermarket thread. After the supermarket thread creates a shopper thread, the shopper thread executes. When the shopper thread is finished shopping and exits the supermarket, the shopper thread terminates and its associated thread kernel object is destroyed with it.

I'm sure that by now you can guess what would happen if I had forgotten the call to *CloseHandle*: a resource leak would have occurred. Remember that the act of creating a thread causes the new thread object to have an initial usage count of 1. Then, because chBEGINTHREADEX[3] returns a handle to the thread object, the thread object's usage count is incremented to 2. When the shopper thread leaves the supermarket (terminates), the thread object's usage count decrements to 1. If *CloseHandle* is not called, the object's usage count never decrements to 0 and the system won't free the thread object from its internal memory until the whole process is terminated. Because shoppers are created frequently and because the user can run the simulation several times in a row without exiting and restarting the program, the number of unfreed thread objects could really add up. So, as you can see, the call to *CloseHandle* is really quite necessary.

After the supermarket has created a shopper, it waits a random amount of time before creating another. The maximum duration of this wait is specified by the Shopper Create Delay setting in the dialog box.

---

3. chBEGINTHREADEX is a macro that simply calls the C run-time's _beginthreadex function after performing some casting in order to make the compiler happy. The macro is defined in the *CmnHdr.h* header file supplied with this book and is discussed in Appendix B.

By having the supermarket running as its own thread and each shopper also executing as his or her own thread, you create the feeling that every shopper can move around the supermarket at his or her own pace and that the supermarket itself is operating at its own pace.

Shoppers perform the following actions:

1. Wait to get into the store

2. Perform a random amount of shopping

3. Go to the deli counter to order luncheon meats

4. Stand in line at the checkout counter to pay for items

5. Spend a random amount of time at the checkout counter

6. Leave the checkout counter

7. Leave the supermarket

After a shopper thread leaves the supermarket, it terminates.

As the simulation progresses, the Shopper Events list box notifies you of the various events that are occurring in the supermarket. By examining this information, you can see where potential bottlenecks occur and how a change to the configuration parameters might alter the scenario for the next run. This information might be used by a manager to determine the best number of open checkout registers or the best number of workers attending the deli counters. Figure 10-3 shows the results of a sample run using the parameter settings shown in the dialog box.

```
---> Opening the supermarket to shoppers.
0001: Waiting to get in store (11).
0002: Waiting to get in store (16).
0001: In supermarket, shopping for 46.
0002: In supermarket, shopping for 38.
0003: Waiting to get in store (17).
0003: In supermarket, shopping for 65.
0002: Not going to the deli counter.
0001: Waiting for service at deli counter (17).
0002: Waiting for an empty checkout counter.
0001: Being served at deli (49).
0002: Checking out (30).
0003: Waiting for service at deli counter (0).
```

Figure 10-3. *(continued)*

Simulation results using the dialog box settings.

369

Figure 10-3. *continued*

```
0003: Tired of waiting at deli.
0004: Waiting to get in store (7).
0002: Leaving checkout counter.
0001: Waiting for an empty checkout counter.
0005: Waiting to get in store (3).
0003: Waiting for an empty checkout counter.
0004: In supermarket, shopping for 9.
0006: Waiting to get in store (8).
0002: Left the supermarket.
0001: Checking out (0).
0005: In supermarket, shopping for 0.
0003: Checking out (22).
0006: In supermarket, shopping for 42.
0004: Not going to the deli counter.
0001: Leaving checkout counter.
0005: Not going to the deli counter.
0003: Leaving checkout counter.
0004: Waiting for an empty checkout counter.
0001: Left the supermarket.
0005: Waiting for an empty checkout counter.
0004: Checking out (36).
0003: Left the supermarket.
0006: Waiting for service at deli counter (13).
0007: Waiting to get in store (7).
0005: Checking out (3).
0006: Being served at deli (42).
0004: Leaving checkout counter.
0007: In supermarket, shopping for 41.
0008: Waiting to get in store (16).
0005: Leaving checkout counter.
0006: Waiting for an empty checkout counter.
0005: Left the supermarket.
0004: Left the supermarket.
0008: In supermarket, shopping for 24.
0007: Not going to the deli counter.
0006: Checking out (43).
0007: Waiting for an empty checkout counter.
0008: Not going to the deli counter.
0007: Checking out (8).
0009: Waiting to get in store (10).
0008: Waiting for an empty checkout counter.
0008: Checking out (27).
0006: Leaving checkout counter.
0009: In supermarket, shopping for 18.
0007: Leaving checkout counter.
```

(continued)

Figure 10-3. *continued*

```
0006: Left the supermarket.
0007: Left the supermarket.
0009: Not going to the deli counter.
0008: Leaving checkout counter.
0008: Left the supermarket.
0009: Waiting for an empty checkout counter.
0009: Checking out (46).
0010: Waiting to get in store (16).
0010: In supermarket, shopping for 79.
0009: Leaving checkout counter.
0009: Left the supermarket.
0011: Waiting to get in store (12).
0011: In supermarket, shopping for 31.
0010: Waiting for service at deli counter (5).
0011: Not going to the deli counter.
0010: Being served at deli (1).
0011: Waiting for an empty checkout counter.
0010: Waiting for an empty checkout counter.
0010: Checking out (22).
0011: Checking out (5).
0012: Waiting to get in store (1).
0011: Leaving checkout counter.
0010: Leaving checkout counter.
0012: In supermarket, shopping for 0.
0011: Left the supermarket.
0010: Left the supermarket.
0012: Not going to the deli counter.
0013: Waiting to get in store (5).
0012: Waiting for an empty checkout counter.
0012: Checking out (35).
0013: In supermarket, shopping for 55.
0014: Waiting to get in store (14).
0014: In supermarket, shopping for 38.
0012: Leaving checkout counter.
0013: Waiting for service at deli counter (14).
0013: Being served at deli (32).
0012: Left the supermarket.
0014: Waiting for service at deli counter (18).
0013: Waiting for an empty checkout counter.
0014: Tired of waiting at deli.
0014: Waiting for an empty checkout counter.
0015: Waiting to get in store (2).
0013: Checking out (35).
0014: Checking out (23).
0015: In supermarket, shopping for 58.
```

(continued)

Figure 10-3. *continued*

```
0013: Leaving checkout counter.
0013: Left the supermarket.
0014: Leaving checkout counter.
0015: Not going to the deli counter.
0014: Left the supermarket.
0015: Waiting for an empty checkout counter.
0016: Waiting to get in store (7).
0015: Checking out (9).
0016: In supermarket, shopping for 18.
0015: Leaving checkout counter.
0015: Left the supermarket.
0016: Waiting for service at deli counter (16).
0016: Being served at deli (36).
0017: Waiting to get in store (15).
0016: Waiting for an empty checkout counter.
0017: In supermarket, shopping for 27.
0016: Checking out (10).
0017: Not going to the deli counter.
0016: Leaving checkout counter.
0017: Waiting for an empty checkout counter.
0017: Checking out (29).
0016: Left the supermarket.
0017: Leaving checkout counter.
0017: Left the supermarket.
0018: Waiting to get in store (13).
0018: In supermarket, shopping for 75.
0019: Waiting to get in store (2).
0019: In supermarket, shopping for 11.
0019: Not going to the deli counter.
0018: Not going to the deli counter.
0020: Waiting to get in store (8).
0019: Waiting for an empty checkout counter.
0018: Waiting for an empty checkout counter.
0019: Checking out (4).
0020: In supermarket, shopping for 54.
0021: Waiting to get in store (3).
0018: Checking out (52).
0019: Leaving checkout counter.
0021: In supermarket, shopping for 65.
0019: Left the supermarket.
0020: Not going to the deli counter.
0020: Waiting for an empty checkout counter.
0018: Leaving checkout counter.
0021: Waiting for service at deli counter (3).
0020: Checking out (49).
```

(continued)

Figure 10-3. *continued*

```
0018: Left the supermarket.
0021: Being served at deli (35).
0022: Waiting to get in store (3).
0020: Leaving checkout counter.
0020: Left the supermarket.
0021: Waiting for an empty checkout counter.
0022: In supermarket, shopping for 58.
0023: Waiting to get in store (5).
0021: Checking out (34).
0023: In supermarket, shopping for 54.
0022: Not going to the deli counter.
0024: Waiting to get in store (9).
0021: Leaving checkout counter.
0023: Waiting for service at deli counter (7).
0022: Waiting for an empty checkout counter.
0024: In supermarket, shopping for 66.
0021: Left the supermarket.
0023: Being served at deli (2).
0022: Checking out (31).
0023: Waiting for an empty checkout counter.
0022: Leaving checkout counter.
0024: Not going to the deli counter.
0023: Checking out (56).
0025: Waiting to get in store (2).
0022: Left the supermarket.
0024: Waiting for an empty checkout counter.
0025: In supermarket, shopping for 73.
0024: Checking out (32).
0023: Leaving checkout counter.
0026: Waiting to get in store (9).
0023: Left the supermarket.
0025: Waiting for service at deli counter (16).
0024: Leaving checkout counter.
0026: In supermarket, shopping for 21.
0027: Waiting to get in store (9).
0025: Being served at deli (68).
0024: Left the supermarket.
0027: In supermarket, shopping for 45.
0028: Waiting to get in store (14).
0026: Waiting for service at deli counter (15).
0025: Waiting for an empty checkout counter.
0028: In supermarket, shopping for 67.
0026: Being served at deli (27).
0029: Waiting to get in store (17).
0027: Waiting for service at deli counter (19).
```

(continued)

Figure 10-3. *continued*

```
0025: Checking out (34).
0026: Waiting for an empty checkout counter.
0029: In supermarket, shopping for 4.
0028: Not going to the deli counter.
---> Waiting for shoppers to check out so store can close.
0027: Being served at deli (13).
0025: Leaving checkout counter.
0026: Checking out (50).
---> 0 shoppers NOT in store.
0028: Waiting for an empty checkout counter.
0029: Not going to the deli counter.
0027: Waiting for an empty checkout counter.
---> 1 shoppers NOT in store.
0025: Left the supermarket.
0028: Checking out (39).
0027: Checking out (11).
0029: Waiting for an empty checkout counter.
0026: Leaving checkout counter.
---> 2 shoppers NOT in store.
0027: Leaving checkout counter.
---> 3 shoppers NOT in store.
0029: Checking out (50).
0026: Left the supermarket.
0028: Leaving checkout counter.
0027: Left the supermarket.
---> 4 shoppers NOT in store.
0028: Left the supermarket.
0029: Leaving checkout counter.
---> 5 shoppers NOT in store.
0029: Left the supermarket.
---> 6 shoppers NOT in store.
---> 7 shoppers NOT in store.
---> 8 shoppers NOT in store.
---> 9 shoppers NOT in store.
---> 10 shoppers NOT in store.
---> 11 shoppers NOT in store.
---> 12 shoppers NOT in store.
---> 13 shoppers NOT in store.
---> 14 shoppers NOT in store.
---> 15 shoppers NOT in store.
---> 16 shoppers NOT in store.
---> 17 shoppers NOT in store.
---> 18 shoppers NOT in store.
---> 19 shoppers NOT in store.
---> 20 shoppers NOT in store.
```

(continued)

Figure 10-3. *continued*

```
---> 21 shoppers NOT in store.
---> 22 shoppers NOT in store.
---> 23 shoppers NOT in store.
---> 24 shoppers NOT in store.
---> 25 shoppers NOT in store.
---> 26 shoppers NOT in store.
---> 27 shoppers NOT in store.
---> 28 shoppers NOT in store.
---> 29 shoppers NOT in store.
---> Store closed--end of simulation.
```

Now let's imagine that this supermarket is open for business and inside several shoppers are going about their business. With so many things going on simultaneously, there must be some way to synchronize the actions of these executing threads. In this example, several forms of synchronization are being used.

When the supermarket thread starts executing, it immediately creates a semaphore object that is identified by the global *g_hSemEntrance* variable:

```
g_hSemEntrance = CreateSemaphore(
    NULL,                // Security attributes
    0,                   // Initial lock count
    g_nMaxOccupancy,     // Maximum people allowed in store
    NULL);               // Do not name the semaphore.
```

This object monitors the number of shoppers that are allowed into the supermarket at any one time. This maximum number of shoppers is identified by the Maximum Occupancy setting specified in the dialog box. For a brief moment after opening for business, the supermarket's doors are still closed, not allowing any shoppers into the store. This closed state is indicated by passing 0 as the initial lock count. When the store is ready to allow shoppers in, it calls

```
ReleaseSemaphore(g_hSemEntrance, g_nMaxOccupancy, NULL);
```

When a new shopper thread is created, the first thing it does is call

```
dwResult = WaitForSingleObject(g_hSemEntrance, nDuration);
```

This causes the shopper thread to suspend its execution if the supermarket is already filled with shoppers to maximum occupancy. If the supermarket is not filled with shoppers, *WaitForSingleObject* returns immediately, granting the shopper admittance to the store. The count of the semaphore is also decremented so that one fewer shopper is allowed into the store.

You'll notice that I specified a duration value in the call in the code fragment on the preceding page using the *nDuration* parameter. Shoppers will wait only so long to get into the supermarket before getting tired and going home. The maximum value of this duration can be set by using the Wait To Get In Market setting in the dialog box. If the shopper gets tired of waiting to enter the market, *WaitForSingleObject* returns WAIT_TIMEOUT. The shopper thread places the notification of this event in the Shopper Events list box and returns from the shopper thread, causing the thread to be terminated.

After the shopper has entered the store, some shopping must occur. The maximum duration of this shopping can be set by the Time To Shop setting in the dialog box. In the shopper thread, the action of shopping is performed simply by placing a call to the *Sleep* function and passing the value of the shopping duration.

After the shopper has picked up a few items (*Sleep* has returned), the shopper heads on over to the deli counter to buy roast beef (yummy—my favorite). Actually, as a friend pointed out to me, most people go to the market without stopping at the deli counter at all. So in the shopper thread, the shopper has only a one-in-three chance of going to the deli counter (which leaves more roast beef for me).

If, as luck would have it, the shopper does go to the deli counter, the shopper must be waited on. In the simulation, the deli counter is attended by only one worker. So the synchronization of shoppers with the deli counter is guarded by a mutex object. Only one shopper thread can own the mutex at any one time. If a shopper goes to the deli counter while another shopper is being waited on, the newly arriving shopper must wait until the first shopper completes his or her business at the counter. Completing his or her business means releasing the mutex so that another shopper can get waited on. A shopper thread spends time at the deli counter by calling *Sleep*, passing in a random duration whose maximum value is specified by the Time At Deli Counter setting in the dialog box.

It is also quite possible that the shopper currently being waited on is taking too long and a waiting shopper gets frustrated and leaves the deli counter. The maximum duration for waiting for service at the deli counter can be specified using the Wait For Deli Counter setting in the dialog box.

This part of the simulation has two problems. One, only one worker is attending the deli counter. You might want to add a simulation parameter in which the user controlling the simulation can specify the number of workers attending the deli counter. In this way, several shoppers could be served simultaneously. If you decide to do this, you could simply change the mutex object controlling the deli counter to a semaphore object in which the maximum count of the semaphore represents the number of people working at the deli counter. I chose not to do this because I wanted to show you another programming example using mutexes.

The second problem with this scheme is that shoppers are not necessarily waited on in the order in which they appear at the deli counter. In other words, let's say that Shopper 1 is currently being waited on when Shopper 2 appears, followed shortly by Shopper 3. When Shopper 1 leaves the counter, both Shopper 2 and Shopper 3 are still waiting to gain ownership of the mutex. The system makes no guarantee that it will give the mutex to Shopper 2 just because Shopper 2 was waiting for the mutex first. If you want to add this type of control for synchronizing threads, you'll have to add the logic yourself. The system and the Win32 API don't support any direct means of doing this automatically for you.

Regardless of how the shopper dealt with the deli counter, the next step is for the shopper to stand in line at the checkout counter. You can specify the number of checkout counters in the supermarket using the Checkout Counters setting in the dialog box.

Here is another place in which the simulation differs a little bit from reality. A standard pattern in all the supermarkets I've ever been in involves sauntering up to the checkout area and selecting a checkout line to stand in. This is usually a matter of examining what everyone else is buying to see which lines have the least number of items to be rung up before the cashier gets to your stuff. Then you see which lines contain people who have their checkbooks out—you know that these are the bad lines. And then, after you have used these factors to narrow down your decision, you take a quick glance to see which cashier looks friendliest and go with that line.

In the supermarket simulation, things are a little less detailed. Waiting for a checkout counter is more like raising your hand in class and hoping the teacher will call on you. When the teacher asks a question, all the students who think they know the answer raise their hands. But the teacher selects only one student (at random) to answer. In the supermarket simulation, there are a fixed number of checkout counters. These are guarded by a semaphore created by the supermarket thread, as shown at the top of the next page.

```
g_hSemCheckout = CreateSemaphore(
    NULL,                       // Security attributes
    g_nCheckoutRegisters,       // All registers are free.
    g_nCheckoutRegisters,       // The number of registers at the
                                // store
    NULL);                      // No name for the semaphore
```

When a shopper is ready to check out, the shopper thread waits for this semaphore. If a checkout counter is available, the shopper immediately starts checking out, and the semaphore is decremented. If all the checkout counters are in use, the shopper must wait. I designed the simulation so that a shopper cannot get tired of waiting for a checkout counter and leave the supermarket. Once a shopper thread begins waiting, it must continue waiting until it has checked out:

```
WaitForSingleObject(g_hSemCheckout, INFINITE);
```

After the shopper has gained access to a checkout counter, it takes some time for the cashier to ring up all his or her purchases. This time is determined by placing a call to *Sleep*, again passing it a random duration whose maximum value is specified by the Time At Checkout setting in the dialog box.

When all of the shopper's items have been totaled, the shopper leaves the checkout counter by releasing the *g_hSemCheckout* semaphore:

```
ReleaseSemaphore(g_hSemCheckout, 1, NULL);
```

This release allows another shopper waiting to check out to gain access to a checkout counter. The shopper who has checked out must exit the supermarket by releasing the *g_hSemCheckout* semaphore, as shown here:

```
ReleaseSemaphore(g_hSemEntrance, 1, NULL);
```

This release tells the semaphore controlling the admittance of shoppers into the market that one shopper has left and that another shopper can enter.

After the shopper has left the market, the shopper no longer has a reason for being and returns from the thread. Perhaps this is where the phrase "shop till you drop" comes from.

We have spent a good bit of time talking about the shopper threads. Let's return now to the supermarket thread. As mentioned at the beginning of this discussion, the supermarket thread is responsible for randomly creating shoppers. However, the supermarket also stays open for some amount of time and then closes. The amount of time that the supermarket stays open is set using the Time Open setting in the dialog box.

When the supermarket thread sees that the set amount of time has been reached, it stops creating shoppers. But the supermarket cannot close until all the existing shoppers have been served. The supermarket executes the following loop:

```
for (nMaxOccupancy = 0;
   nMaxOccupancy < g_nMaxOccupancy; nMaxOccupancy++) {

   WaitForSingleObject(g_hSemEntrance, INFINITE);
}
```

The loop simply calls *WaitForSingleObject* repeatedly until the supermarket has gained control of the entrance semaphore *g_nMaxOccupancy* times, which can happen only after every shopper has left the supermarket. You could have a problem here if a shopper thread was created just before the supermarket closed. In this case, both the supermarket and the shopper thread are waiting for the semaphore. The system makes no guarantee as to which thread will gain the semaphore when it becomes signaled. So it is possible that a waiting shopper can enter the supermarket even though the supermarket is closed.

It is also possible that the supermarket thread can gain all of the semaphore. In this case, any created shoppers that hadn't entered the store yet would just get tired of waiting and terminate themselves. In a real simulation, these areas would need to be cleaned up a bit.

It might be nice if the supermarket simply called *WaitForMultipleObjects* once instead of calling *WaitForSingleObject* repeatedly in a loop. But this can't be done, for two reasons. First, you can't pass a handle identifying a single object to *WaitForMultipleObjects* more than once. Second, *WaitForMultipleObjects* lets you wait for only MAXIMUM_WAIT_OBJECTS number of objects, which is currently defined as 64. Because we could set the maximum occupancy to be well over 64—maybe 500—calling *WaitForMultipleObjects* wouldn't work even if we could specify the handle to the semaphore more than once.

After the supermarket thread captures the *g_hSemEntrance* semaphore *g_nMaxOccupancy* number of times, it makes the following calls to be sure that all the synchronization objects are destroyed by the system:

```
CloseHandle(g_hSemCheckout);
CloseHandle(g_hMtxDeliCntr);
CloseHandle(g_hSemEntrance);
```

SprMrkt.ico

SPRMRKT.C

```
/***************************************************************
Module name: SprMrkt.C
Notices: Copyright (c) 1995-1997 Jeffrey Richter
***************************************************************/


#include "..\CmnHdr.H"                    /* See Appendix C. */
#include <windows.h>
#include <windowsx.h>
#include <tchar.h>
#include <stdio.h>
#include <stdlib.h>                // For random number stuff
#include <string.h>
#include <stdarg.h>
#include <process.h>              // For _beginthreadex
#include "Resource.H"


///////////////////////////////////////////////////////////////


// This is the correction to a bug in windowsx.h:
#undef FORWARD_WM_HSCROLL
#define FORWARD_WM_HSCROLL(hwnd, hwndCtl, code, pos, fn) \
   (void)(fn)((hwnd), WM_HSCROLL, \
      MAKEWPARAM((UINT)(code),(UINT)(pos)), \
      (LPARAM)(UINT)(hwndCtl))


///////////////////////////////////////////////////////////////


// Forward references to the supermarket
// and shopper thread functions.
DWORD WINAPI ThreadSuperMarket (LPVOID lpvParam);
DWORD WINAPI ThreadShopper (LPVOID lpvParam);


///////////////////////////////////////////////////////////////


// Global variables
HWND g_hwndLB = NULL;   // List box for shopper events
```

Figure 10-4. *(continued)*
The SprMrkt application.

Figure 10-4. *continued*

```
// User-settable simulation parameters.
int g_nMaxOccupancy;
int g_nTimeOpen;
int g_nCheckoutCounters;
int g_nMaxDelayBetweenShopperCreation;
int g_nMaxWaitToGetInMarket;
int g_nMaxTimeShopping;
int g_nMaxWaitForDeliCntr;
int g_nMaxTimeSpentAtDeli;
int g_nMaxTimeAtCheckout;

// Synchronization objects used to control the simulation
HANDLE g_hSemEntrance;
HANDLE g_hMtxDeliCntr;
HANDLE g_hSemCheckout;


///////////////////////////////////////////////////////////////


// This function constructs a string using the format string
// passed and the variable number of arguments and adds the
// string to the shopper events list box identified by the
// global g_hwndLB variable.
void AddStr (LPCTSTR szFmt, ...) {
   TCHAR szBuf[150];
   int nIndex;
   va_list va_params;

   // Make va_params point to the first argument after szFmt.
   va_start(va_params, szFmt);

   // Build the string to be displayed.
   _vstprintf(szBuf, szFmt, va_params);
   do {
      // Add the string to the end of the list box.
      nIndex = ListBox_AddString(g_hwndLB, szBuf);

      // If the list box is full, delete the first item in it.
      if (nIndex == LB_ERR)
         ListBox_DeleteString(g_hwndLB, 0);

   } while (nIndex == LB_ERR);
```

(continued)

Figure 10-4. *continued*

```
   // Select the newly added item.
   ListBox_SetCurSel(g_hwndLB, nIndex);

   // Indicate that we are done referencing
   // the variable arguments.
   va_end(va_params);
}


/////////////////////////////////////////////////////////////////////


// This function returns a random number
// between 0 and nMaxValue, inclusive.
int Random (int nMaxValue) {
   return(rand() / (RAND_MAX / (nMaxValue + 1)));
}


/////////////////////////////////////////////////////////////////////


BOOL Dlg_OnInitDialog (HWND hwnd, HWND hwndFocus,
   LPARAM lParam) {

   HWND hwndSB;

   // Associate an icon with the dialog box.
   chSETDLGICONS(hwnd, IDI_SPRMRKT, IDI_SPRMRKT);

   // Save the window handle to the shopper events list box
   // in a global variable so that the AddStr function has
   // access to it.
   g_hwndLB = GetDlgItem(hwnd, IDC_SHOPPEREVENTS);

   // Set the scroll bar range and default positions for all of
   // the simulation parameters.
   hwndSB = GetDlgItem(hwnd, IDC_MAXOCCUPANCY);
   ScrollBar_SetRange(hwndSB, 0, 500, TRUE);

   // Set the initial value of the scroll bar.
   FORWARD_WM_HSCROLL(hwnd, hwndSB, SB_THUMBTRACK,
      30, SendMessage);
```

(continued)

Figure 10-4. *continued*

```
hwndSB = GetDlgItem(hwnd, IDC_TIMEOPEN);
ScrollBar_SetRange(hwndSB, 0, 5000, TRUE);
FORWARD_WM_HSCROLL(hwnd, hwndSB, SB_THUMBTRACK,
   5000, SendMessage);

hwndSB = GetDlgItem(hwnd, IDC_NUMCOUNTERS);
ScrollBar_SetRange(hwndSB, 0, 30, TRUE);
FORWARD_WM_HSCROLL(hwnd, hwndSB, SB_THUMBTRACK,
   5, SendMessage);

hwndSB = GetDlgItem(hwnd, IDC_SHOPPERCREATIONDELAY);
ScrollBar_SetRange(hwndSB, 0, 1000, TRUE);
FORWARD_WM_HSCROLL(hwnd, hwndSB, SB_THUMBTRACK,
   300, SendMessage);

hwndSB = GetDlgItem(hwnd, IDC_DELAYTOGETIN);
ScrollBar_SetRange(hwndSB, 0, 100, TRUE);
FORWARD_WM_HSCROLL(hwnd, hwndSB, SB_THUMBTRACK,
   20, SendMessage);

hwndSB = GetDlgItem(hwnd, IDC_TIMETOSHOP);
ScrollBar_SetRange(hwndSB, 0, 100, TRUE);
FORWARD_WM_HSCROLL(hwnd, hwndSB, SB_THUMBTRACK,
   80, SendMessage);

hwndSB = GetDlgItem(hwnd, IDC_WAITDELICNTR);
ScrollBar_SetRange(hwndSB, 0, 100, TRUE);
FORWARD_WM_HSCROLL(hwnd, hwndSB, SB_THUMBTRACK,
   20, SendMessage);

hwndSB = GetDlgItem(hwnd, IDC_TIMEATDELICNTR);
ScrollBar_SetRange(hwndSB, 0, 100, TRUE);
FORWARD_WM_HSCROLL(hwnd, hwndSB, SB_THUMBTRACK,
   70, SendMessage);

hwndSB = GetDlgItem(hwnd, IDC_TIMEATCHECKOUT);
ScrollBar_SetRange(hwndSB, 0, 100, TRUE);
FORWARD_WM_HSCROLL(hwnd, hwndSB, SB_THUMBTRACK,
   60, SendMessage);

return(TRUE);
}
```

(continued)

Figure 10-4. *continued*

```
//////////////////////////////////////////////////////////////

void Dlg_OnHScroll(HWND hwnd, HWND hwndCtl,
   UINT code, int pos) {

   TCHAR szBuf[10];
   int nPosCrnt, nPosMin, nPosMax;

   // Get the current position and the legal range for the
   // scroll bar that the user is changing.
   nPosCrnt = ScrollBar_GetPos(hwndCtl);
   ScrollBar_GetRange(hwndCtl, &nPosMin, &nPosMax);

   switch (code) {
      case SB_LINELEFT:
         nPosCrnt--;
         break;

      case SB_LINERIGHT:
         nPosCrnt++;
         break;

      case SB_PAGELEFT:
         nPosCrnt -= (nPosMax - nPosMin + 1) / 10;
         break;

      case SB_PAGERIGHT:
         nPosCrnt += (nPosMax - nPosMin + 1) / 10;
         break;

      case SB_THUMBTRACK:
         nPosCrnt = pos;
         break;

      case SB_LEFT:
         nPosCrnt = nPosMin;
         break;

      case SB_RIGHT:
         nPosCrnt = nPosMax;
         break;
   }
```

(continued)

Figure 10-4. *continued*

```
    // Make sure that the new scroll bar position
    // is within the legal range.
    if (nPosCrnt < nPosMin)
      nPosCrnt = nPosMin;

    if (nPosCrnt > nPosMax)
      nPosCrnt = nPosMax;

    // Set the new scroll bar position.
    ScrollBar_SetPos(hwndCtl, nPosCrnt, TRUE);

    // Change the value displayed in the text box to
    // reflect the value in the scroll bar.
    _stprintf(szBuf, __TEXT("%d"), nPosCrnt);
    SetWindowText(GetPrevSibling(hwndCtl), szBuf);
}


///////////////////////////////////////////////////////////////


void Dlg_OnCommand (HWND hwnd, int id, HWND hwndCtl,
   UINT codeNotify) {

   DWORD dwThreadId;
   HANDLE hThread;

   switch (id) {
      case IDOK:
         // Load the scroll bar settings into the global
         // variables so that they can be used
         // by the simulation.
         g_nMaxOccupancy = ScrollBar_GetPos(
            GetDlgItem(hwnd, IDC_MAXOCCUPANCY));

         g_nTimeOpen = ScrollBar_GetPos(
            GetDlgItem(hwnd, IDC_TIMEOPEN));

         g_nCheckoutCounters = ScrollBar_GetPos(
            GetDlgItem(hwnd, IDC_NUMCOUNTERS));

         g_nMaxDelayBetweenShopperCreation = ScrollBar_GetPos(
            GetDlgItem(hwnd, IDC_SHOPPERCREATIONDELAY));
```

(continued)

Figure 10-4. *continued*

```
g_nMaxWaitToGetInMarket = ScrollBar_GetPos(
   GetDlgItem(hwnd, IDC_DELAYTOGETIN));

g_nMaxTimeShopping = ScrollBar_GetPos(
   GetDlgItem(hwnd, IDC_TIMETOSHOP));

g_nMaxWaitForDeliCntr = ScrollBar_GetPos(
   GetDlgItem(hwnd, IDC_WAITDELICNTR));

g_nMaxTimeSpentAtDeli = ScrollBar_GetPos(
   GetDlgItem(hwnd, IDC_TIMEATDELICNTR));

g_nMaxTimeAtCheckout = ScrollBar_GetPos(
   GetDlgItem(hwnd, IDC_TIMEATCHECKOUT));


// Clear out everything in the list box.
ListBox_ResetContent(
   GetDlgItem(hwnd, IDC_SHOPPEREVENTS));

// Disable the Open For Business button
// while simulation is in progress.

EnableWindow(hwndCtl, FALSE);

if (NULL == GetFocus()) {
   SetFocus(GetDlgItem(hwnd, IDC_MAXOCCUPANCY));
}


// The system overhead will cause the results
// of the simulation to be skewed. To help
// minimize this effect, we boost the priority class
// of this process.
SetPriorityClass(GetCurrentProcess(),
   HIGH_PRIORITY_CLASS);

// Create the thread representing the supermarket.
hThread = chBEGINTHREADEX(
   NULL,               // Security attributes
   0,                  // Stack
   ThreadSuperMarket,  // Thread function
   (LPVOID) hwnd,      // Thread function parameter
   0,                  // Flags
```

(continued)

Figure 10-4. *continued*

```
                &dwThreadId);        // Thread ID
            // Since we are not interested in manipulating the
            // thread object from this function, we can close
            // our handle to it.
            CloseHandle(hThread);
            break;

        case IDCANCEL:
            EndDialog(hwnd, id);
            break;
    }
}


///////////////////////////////////////////////////////////////


BOOL CALLBACK Dlg_Proc (HWND hwnd, UINT uMsg,
    WPARAM wParam, LPARAM lParam) {

    switch (uMsg) {
        chHANDLE_DLGMSG(hwnd, WM_INITDIALOG, Dlg_OnInitDialog);
        chHANDLE_DLGMSG(hwnd, WM_COMMAND,   Dlg_OnCommand);
        chHANDLE_DLGMSG(hwnd, WM_HSCROLL,   Dlg_OnHScroll);

        case WM_USER:
            // This message is sent by the SuperMarketThread
            // function to notify us that the simulation
            // has completed.

            // Return the priority class of the simulation
            // back to normal.
            SetPriorityClass(GetCurrentProcess(),
                NORMAL_PRIORITY_CLASS);

            // Enable the Open For Business button so that
            // the user can run the simulation again with
            // new parameters.
            EnableWindow(GetDlgItem(hwnd, IDOK), TRUE);
            break;
    }
    return(FALSE);
}
```

(continued)

Figure 10-4. *continued*

```
//////////////////////////////////////////////////////////////

int WINAPI _tWinMain (HINSTANCE hinstExe,
   HINSTANCE hinstPrev, LPTSTR pszCmdLine, int nCmdShow) {

   chWARNIFUNICODEUNDERWIN95();
   DialogBox(hinstExe, MAKEINTRESOURCE(IDD_SPRMRKT),
      NULL, Dlg_Proc);

   return(0);
}


//////////////////////////////////////////////////////////////


DWORD WINAPI ThreadSuperMarket (LPVOID lpvParam) {
   DWORD dwCloseTime;
   HANDLE hThread;
   DWORD dwThreadId;
   int nShopperNum = 0, nMaxOccupancy;

   g_hSemEntrance = CreateSemaphore(
      NULL,                 // Security attributes
      0,                    // Initial lock count
      g_nMaxOccupancy,      // Maximum people allowed in store
      NULL);                // Do not name the semaphore.

   g_hMtxDeliCntr = CreateMutex(
      NULL,                 // Security attributes
      FALSE,                // Initially no one is at the deli.
      NULL);                // Do not name the mutex.

   g_hSemCheckout = CreateSemaphore(
      NULL,                 // Security attributes
      g_nCheckoutCounters,  // All counters are free.
      g_nCheckoutCounters,  // The number of counters at the store
      NULL);                // No name for the semaphore


   // Open the store to the shoppers.
   AddStr(__TEXT("--> Opening the supermarket to shoppers."));
   ReleaseSemaphore(g_hSemEntrance, g_nMaxOccupancy, NULL);
```

(continued)

Figure 10-4. *continued*

```
// Get the time at which the store should
// stop creating shoppers.
dwCloseTime = GetTickCount() + g_nTimeOpen;

// Continue loop until the store closes.
while (GetTickCount() < dwCloseTime) {

   // Create the thread representing a shopper.
   hThread = chBEGINTHREADEX(
      NULL,                     // Security attributes
      0,                        // Stack
      ThreadShopper,            // Thread function
      (LPVOID) ++nShopperNum,   // Shopper number as lpvParam
      0,                        // Flags
      &dwThreadId);             // Thread ID

   // Since we are not interested in manipulating the
   // thread object from this function, we can close
   // our handle to it.
   CloseHandle(hThread);

   // Wait until another shopper comes to the supermarket.
   Sleep(Random(g_nMaxDelayBetweenShopperCreation));
}

// The supermarket wants to close;
// wait for all of the shoppers to leave.
AddStr(__TEXT("--> Waiting for shoppers to check out ")
   __TEXT("so store can close."));

nMaxOccupancy = 1;
for (; nMaxOccupancy <= g_nMaxOccupancy; nMaxOccupancy++) {
   WaitForSingleObject(g_hSemEntrance, INFINITE);
   AddStr(__TEXT("--> %d shoppers NOT in store."),
   nMaxOccupancy);
}

AddStr(__TEXT("--> Store closed--end of simulation."));

// Everybody has left the market--end of simulation.
CloseHandle(g_hSemCheckout);
CloseHandle(g_hMtxDeliCntr);
CloseHandle(g_hSemEntrance);

// Notify the GUI thread that the simulation has completed.
```

(continued)

Figure 10-4. *continued*

```
    // The window handle of the GUI thread's dialog box was
    // passed in the lpvParam parameter to this thread when
    // it was created.
    SendMessage((HWND) lpvParam, WM_USER, 0, 0);

    return(0);
}


///////////////////////////////////////////////////////////////////


DWORD WINAPI ThreadShopper (LPVOID lpvParam) {
    int nShopperNum = (int) lpvParam;
    DWORD dwResult;
    int nDuration;

    // Seed the random number generator for this thread
    // or every shopper thread will use the same seed and
    // generate the same set of random numbers.
    srand(GetTickCount() * nShopperNum);

    // Wait till the shopper can enter the supermarket.
    nDuration = Random(g_nMaxWaitToGetInMarket);
    AddStr(__TEXT("%04lu: Waiting to get in store (%lu)."),
        nShopperNum, nDuration);

    dwResult = WaitForSingleObject(g_hSemEntrance, nDuration);
    if (dwResult == WAIT_TIMEOUT) {
        // The shopper got tired of
        // waiting to be let in and left.
        AddStr(__TEXT("%04lu: Tired of waiting; went home."),
        nShopperNum);
        return(0);
    }


    // Shopper entered the supermarket.  Time to go shopping.
    nDuration = Random(g_nMaxTimeShopping);
    AddStr(__TEXT("%04lu: In supermarket, shopping for %lu."),
        nShopperNum, nDuration);
    Sleep(nDuration);
```

(continued)

Figure 10-4. *continued*

```
// Done with initial shopping. Shopper has a one-in-three
// chance of going to the deli counter.
if (Random(2) == 0) {

   // Shopper going to deli counter.
   nDuration = Random(g_nMaxWaitForDeliCntr);
   AddStr(
      __TEXT("%04lu: Waiting for service at ")
      __TEXT("Deli Counter (%lu)."),
      nShopperNum, nDuration);
   dwResult =
      WaitForSingleObject(g_hMtxDeliCntr, nDuration);

   if (dwResult == 0) {
      // Got attention at deli; order stuff.
      nDuration = Random(g_nMaxTimeSpentAtDeli);

      AddStr(__TEXT("%04lu: Being served at Deli (%lu)."),
         nShopperNum, nDuration);
      Sleep(nDuration);

      // Leave the deli counter.
      ReleaseMutex(g_hMtxDeliCntr);

   } else {
      // Tired of waiting at deli counter,
      // leave and continue shopping.
      AddStr(__TEXT("%04lu: Tired of waiting at Deli."),
         nShopperNum);
   }

} else {
   AddStr(__TEXT("%04lu: Not going to the Deli counter."),
      nShopperNum);
}


// Waiting for a checkout counter.
AddStr(
   __TEXT("%04lu: Waiting for an empty checkout counter."),
   nShopperNum);
WaitForSingleObject(g_hSemCheckout, INFINITE);
```

(continued)

Figure 10-4. *continued*

```
    // Checking out.
    nDuration = Random(g_nMaxTimeAtCheckout);
    AddStr(__TEXT("%04lu: Checking out (%lu)."),
        nShopperNum, nDuration);
    Sleep(nDuration);

    // Leaving the checkout counter.
    AddStr(__TEXT("%04lu: Leaving checkout counter."),
        nShopperNum);
    ReleaseSemaphore(g_hSemCheckout, 1, NULL);

    // Leaving the store.
    AddStr(__TEXT("%04lu: Left the supermarket."),
        nShopperNum);
    ReleaseSemaphore(g_hSemEntrance, 1, NULL);

    // Shopper shopped till he/she dropped.  Shopper dead.
    return(0);
}


////////////////////////// End Of File //////////////////////////
```

```
SPRMRKT.RC
//Microsoft Developer Studio generated resource script.
//
#include "Resource.h"

#define APSTUDIO_READONLY_SYMBOLS
/////////////////////////////////////////////////////////////////
//
// Generated from the TEXTINCLUDE 2 resource.
//
#include "afxres.h"


/////////////////////////////////////////////////////////////////
#undef APSTUDIO_READONLY_SYMBOLS


/////////////////////////////////////////////////////////////////
// English (U.S.) resources
```

(continued)

Figure 10-4. *continued*

```
#if !defined(AFX_RESOURCE_DLL) || defined(AFX_TARG_ENU)
#ifdef _WIN32
LANGUAGE LANG_ENGLISH, SUBLANG_ENGLISH_US
#pragma code_page(1252)
#endif //_WIN32

#ifdef APSTUDIO_INVOKED
/////////////////////////////////////////////////////////////////////
//
// TEXTINCLUDE
//

1 TEXTINCLUDE DISCARDABLE
BEGIN
    "Resource.h\0"
END

2 TEXTINCLUDE DISCARDABLE
BEGIN
    "#include ""afxres.h""\r\n"
    "\0"
END

3 TEXTINCLUDE DISCARDABLE
BEGIN
    "\r\n"
    "\0"
END

#endif    // APSTUDIO_INVOKED


/////////////////////////////////////////////////////////////////////
//
// Dialog
//

IDD_SPRMRKT DIALOG DISCARDABLE  4, 58, 360, 206
STYLE WS_MINIMIZEBOX | WS_POPUP | WS_VISIBLE | WS_CAPTION |
    WS_SYSMENU
CAPTION "Supermarket Simulation"
FONT 8, "MS Sans Serif"
```

(continued)

Figure 10-4. *continued*

```
BEGIN
    GROUPBOX        "Super&market parameters",IDC_STATIC,4,
                    0,176,64,WS_GROUP
    RTEXT           "Maximum occupancy:",IDC_STATIC,8,
                    12,72,8,NOT WS_GROUP
    RTEXT           "MO",IDC_STATIC,84,12,16,8,
                    SS_NOPREFIX | NOT WS_GROUP
    SCROLLBAR       IDC_MAXOCCUPANCY,104,12,72,10,WS_TABSTOP
    RTEXT           "Time open:",IDC_STATIC,8,24,72,8,
                    NOT WS_GROUP
    RTEXT           "TO",IDC_STATIC,84,24,16,8,
                    SS_NOPREFIX | NOT WS_GROUP
    SCROLLBAR       IDC_TIMEOPEN,104,24,72,10,WS_TABSTOP
    RTEXT           "Checkout counters:",IDC_STATIC,8,
                    38,72,8,NOT WS_GROUP
    RTEXT           "CC",IDC_STATIC,84,38,16,8,
                    SS_NOPREFIX | NOT WS_GROUP
    SCROLLBAR       IDC_NUMCOUNTERS,104,38,72,10,WS_TABSTOP
    RTEXT           "Shopper create delay:",IDC_STATIC,8,
                    52,72,8,NOT WS_GROUP
    RTEXT           "SC",IDC_STATIC,84,52,16,8,
                    SS_NOPREFIX | NOT WS_GROUP
    SCROLLBAR       IDC_SHOPPERCREATIONDELAY,104,52,
                    72,10,WS_TABSTOP
    GROUPBOX        "&Shopper parameters",IDC_STATIC,184,0,
                    172,80,WS_GROUP
    RTEXT           "Wait to get in market:",IDC_STATIC,188,
                    12,72,8,NOT
                    WS_GROUP
    RTEXT           "WTGI",IDC_STATIC,260,12,16,8,
                    SS_NOPREFIX | NOT WS_GROUP
    SCROLLBAR       IDC_DELAYTOGETIN,280,10,72,10,WS_TABSTOP
    RTEXT           "Time to shop:",IDC_STATIC,188,24,72,
                    8,NOT WS_GROUP
    RTEXT           "TTS",IDC_STATIC,260,24,16,8,
                    SS_NOPREFIX | NOT WS_GROUP
    SCROLLBAR       IDC_TIMETOSHOP,280,24,72,10,WS_TABSTOP
    RTEXT           "Wait for deli counter:",IDC_STATIC,188,
                    38,72,8,NOT
                    WS_GROUP
    RTEXT           "WFDC",IDC_STATIC,260,38,16,8,
                    SS_NOPREFIX | NOT WS_GROUP
    SCROLLBAR       IDC_WAITDELICNTR,280,38,72,10,WS_TABSTOP
```

(continued)

Figure 10-4. *continued*

```
      RTEXT              "Time at deli counter:",IDC_STATIC,188,
                         52,72,8,NOT WS_GROUP
      RTEXT              "TADC",IDC_STATIC,260,52,16,8,
                         SS_NOPREFIX | NOT WS_GROUP
      SCROLLBAR          IDC_TIMEATDELICNTR,280,52,72,10,WS_TABSTOP
      RTEXT              "Time at checkout:",IDC_STATIC,188,
                         66,72,8,NOT WS_GROUP
      RTEXT              "TAC",IDC_STATIC,260,66,16,8,
                         SS_NOPREFIX | NOT WS_GROUP
      SCROLLBAR          IDC_TIMEATCHECKOUT,280,66,72,10,WS_TABSTOP
      PUSHBUTTON         "&Open for business",IDOK,80,68,100,
                         12,WS_GROUP
      LTEXT              "Shopper &events:",IDC_STATIC,4,82,56,8
      LISTBOX            IDC_SHOPPEREVENTS,4,94,352,108,
                         LBS_NOINTEGRALHEIGHT |
                         WS_VSCROLL | WS_TABSTOP
END


/////////////////////////////////////////////////////////////////
//
// Icon
//

// Icon with lowest ID value placed first to ensure application
// icon remains consistent on all systems.
IDI_SPRMRKT            ICON    DISCARDABLE    "SprMrkt.Ico"
#endif    // English (U.S.) resources
/////////////////////////////////////////////////////////////////


#ifndef APSTUDIO_INVOKED
/////////////////////////////////////////////////////////////////
//
// Generated from the TEXTINCLUDE 3 resource.
//

/////////////////////////////////////////////////////////////////
#endif    // not APSTUDIO_INVOKED
```

Events

Event objects are the most primitive form of synchronization object and are quite different from mutexes and semaphores. Mutexes and semaphores are usually used to control access to data, but events are used to signal that some operation has completed. There are two different types of event objects: manual-reset events and auto-reset events. A manual-reset event is used to signal several threads simultaneously that an operation has completed, and an auto-reset event is used to signal a single thread that an operation has completed.

Events are most commonly used when one thread performs initialization work and then, when it completes, signals another thread to perform the remaining work. The initialization thread sets the event to the nonsignaled state and begins to perform the initialization. Then, after the initialization has completed, the thread sets the event to the signaled state. When the worker thread starts executing, it immediately suspends itself, waiting for the event to become signaled. When the initialization thread signals the event, the worker thread wakes up and performs the rest of the work necessary.

For example, a process might be running two threads. The first thread reads data from a file into a memory buffer. After the data has been read, the first thread signals the second thread that it can process the data. When the second thread finishes processing the data, it might need to signal the first thread again so that the first thread can read the next block of data from the file.

Let's start our discussion with how to create an event. The semantics for creating, opening, and closing events are identical to those for mutexes and semaphores. Events are created using the *CreateEvent* function:

```
HANDLE CreateEvent(LPSECURITY_ATTRIBUTES lpsa,
    BOOL fManualReset, BOOL fInitialState, LPTSTR lpszEventName);
```

The *fManualReset* parameter is a Boolean value that tells the system whether you want to create a manual-reset event (TRUE) or an auto-reset event (FALSE). The *fInitialState* parameter indicates whether the event should be initialized as signaled (TRUE) or nonsignaled (FALSE). After the system creates the event object, *CreateEvent* returns the process-relative handle to the event. Threads in other processes can gain access to the object by calling *CreateEvent* using the same value in the *lpszEventName* parameter; by using inheritance; by using the *DuplicateHandle* function; or by calling *OpenEvent* (shown on the facing page), specifying a name in the *lpszName* parameter that matches the name specified in the call to *CreateEvent*:

```
HANDLE OpenEvent(DWORD fdwAccess, BOOL fInherit, LPTSTR lpszName);
```

As always, events are closed by calling the very popular *CloseHandle* function.

Manual-Reset Events

Manual-reset events are not automatically reset to the nonsignaled state by the *WaitForSingleObject* and *WaitForMultipleObjects* functions. In the case of mutexes, when a thread calls *WaitForSingleObject* or *WaitForMultiple-Objects*, the functions wait for the mutex to be signaled and then automatically reset the mutex to nonsignaled. This is important because it guarantees that no more than one thread waiting on the mutex will be able to wake up and continue executing. If threads were responsible for manually resetting the mutex back to the nonsignaled state, it would be possible for two or more threads to have their waits satisfied before each one reset the mutex to nonsignaled.

For manual-reset events, the story is quite different. You might have several threads, all of them waiting for the same event to occur. When the event does occur, each waiting thread might be able to perform its own processing. Let's go back to our file reading and processing example. It might be that one thread is responsible for reading data from a file into a buffer. After the data has been read, we might want to start nine other threads. Each of these nine threads might process the data in a slightly different way. Let's say the file contains a word processing document. The first thread could count characters, the second thread could count words, the third thread could count pages, the fourth thread could perform a spell check, the fifth thread could print the document, and so on. The one extremely important characteristic that all these threads have in common is that none of them write to the data. All of them consider the data to be a read-only resource.

In this example, you most certainly would want to allow all the waiting threads to be satisfied when the event occurred. This is the reason for manual-reset events. When a manual-reset event is signaled, all threads waiting on the event are allowed to run. A thread sets an event object to the signaled state by calling

```
BOOL SetEvent(HANDLE hEvent);
```

This function takes the handle to an event object and simply sets it to the signaled state. *SetEvent* returns TRUE if the function is successful. After the manual-reset event has been signaled, it remains signaled until one thread explicitly (or manually) resets the event by calling

```
BOOL ResetEvent(HANDLE hEvent);
```

This function takes the handle to an event object and resets it to the non-signaled state. *ResetEvent* returns TRUE if the function is successful. See, I told you that events were the most primitive synchronization object.

For the file reading and processing example, the thread that reads the file data and puts it into the shared memory buffer would call *ResetEvent* just before reading the data into the buffer. It would then call *SetEvent* when the reading was completed.

I've left out one small issue: how does the file-read thread know when to read the next block of data? We know that it should read the next block of data when all the other threads have finished their work with the current block of data. But the other threads need a way to signal that they've finished. The best method is for each of the data processing threads to create their own event object. If all the handles for these event objects were stored in an array, the file-read thread could call *WaitForMultipleObjects*, indicating that it wanted to wait for all the event handles.

Because calling *SetEvent*, releasing waiting events, and immediately calling *ResetEvent* is quite common, Win32 offers another function that performs all three of these steps:

```
BOOL PulseEvent(HANDLE hEvent);
```

When *PulseEvent* returns, the event is left in the nonsignaled state. If the function is successful, TRUE is returned.

The Bucket of Balls Sample Application

A basic synchronization problem, commonly referred to as the classic multiple-readers/multiple-writers scenario, exists for many different applications. The problem involves an arbitrary number of threads that are attempting to access a global resource. Some of these threads (the writers) need to modify the contents of the global data, and some of the threads (the readers) need only to read the data. Synchronization is necessary because of the following rules:

1. When one thread is writing to the data, no other thread can write to the data.

2. When one thread is writing to the data, no other thread can read from the data.

3. When one thread is reading from the data, no other thread can write to the data.

4. When one thread is reading from the data, other threads can also read from the data.

Let's look at this problem in the context of a database application. Let's say we have five end users, all working on the same database: two employees are entering records into the database, and three employees are retrieving records from the database.

In this scenario, rule 1 is necessary because we certainly can't have both Employee 1 and Employee 2 updating record 3457 at the same time. If both employees attempt to modify the same record, Employee 1's changes and Employee 2's changes might be made to the database at the same time. We wouldn't want to have a situation in which a record in the database contained corrupted information.

Rule 2 prohibits an employee from accessing a record in the database if another employee is updating a record in the database. If this situation were not prevented, it would be possible for Employee 4 to read the contents of record 2543 while Employee 1 was altering that same record. When Employee 4's computer displayed record 2543, the record would contain some of the old information and some of the updated information—this is certainly unacceptable. Rule 3 is needed in order to solve the same problem. The difference in the wording of rules 2 and 3 prevents the situation regardless of who gains access to the database record first—an employee who is trying to write or an employee who is attempting to read.

The last rule, rule 4, exists for performance reasons. It makes sense that if no employees are attempting to modify records in the database, the content of the database is not changing and, therefore, any and all employees who are simply retrieving records from the database should be allowed to do so.

OK, there you have the gist of the problem. Now the question is, how do we solve it?

The Bucket (BUCKET.EXE) application, listed in Figure 10-5 beginning on page 410, demonstrates the solution by synchronizing the access of five threads to a small database. To accomplish this synchronization, Bucket uses three of the kernel synchronization objects discussed in this chapter: manual-reset events, semaphores, and mutexes. Although Bucket manages only five threads (two updating the database and three reading the database), the groundwork presented easily extends itself to a situation in which virtually any number of threads (readers and/or writers) can be synchronized. The source code and resource files for the application are in the BUCKET directory on the companion disc.

When you invoke Bucket, the following dialog box appears:

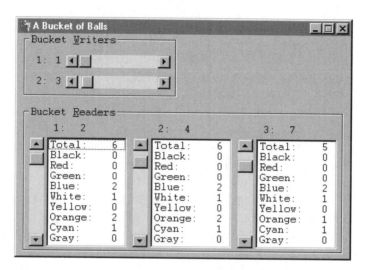

The database being managed is a bucket that can contain no more than 100 balls. Initially the bucket is empty. The Bucket Writers section in the upper portion of the dialog box represents the two threads that add, remove, or change the different colored balls in the bucket. To the right of the thread number is a time value specified in seconds. For Writer 1, this value is 1. This means that every second, Writer 1 attempts to gain access to the bucket and add another ball. The scroll bar at the right of the second's value allows you to change this delay time, which can range from 0 through 60 seconds. Writer 2 operates in the same way except that it starts out with an initial delay time of 3 seconds.

The bottom portion of the dialog box represents the three reader threads. These threads work similarly to the writer threads. After every specified number of seconds (0 through 60), each of the three reader threads erases the contents of its list box, counts the different colored balls in the bucket, and updates the list box to display the results.

The important thing to remember here is that all the threads are being synchronized. If a writer currently has permission to add, remove, or change a ball in the bucket, neither the other writer nor any of the readers will be granted access to the bucket. On the other hand, if a reader has access to the bucket and is counting the balls, any of the other readers requesting access to do the same will gain access, but none of the writers will be allowed to change any of the balls in the bucket until all the readers are finished.

Now that you see how the program operates, let's turn our attention to the source code listed in Figure 10-5.

Important

A point I've been trying to drive home throughout this chapter is that thread synchronization bugs are extremely difficult to locate and fix. As it turns out, I am far from immune to this problem myself (as several readers have so kindly pointed out to me). The Bucket sample that appears in the first edition of this book has bugs in it. I have (well, at least I'm pretty sure this time that I have) corrected the bugs in Bucket, and I have also improved the application's code and clarity significantly. If you used any code from my first edition's Bucket sample, you might want to examine this updated version and see whether you need to make any enhancements to your own code.

The SWMRG Compound Synchronization Object

When I started to fix Bucket for the second edition of the book, I realized that the code Bucket was using in the first edition for its thread synchronization was too complicated and error prone—a better method was definitely called for. Because the single-writer/multiple-reader scenario is a classic synchronization problem, I thought it best to create a generic, reusable object to solve it. This way, if any of you reading this need to solve this classic problem, you can just steal my code and incorporate it into your own application with few or no changes whatsoever. The result of my labor is something I like to call SWMRG (I pronounce it *swimerge*); it stands for single-writer/multiple-reader guard.

A SWMRG object is a data structure of my own creation. This SWMRG data structure and the functions that manipulate it can be found in the SWMRG.H and SWMRG.C files in the BUCKET directory on the companion disc. A SWMRG object is a compound synchronization object designed specifically for handling the classic single-writer/ multiple-reader synchronization problem. I call it a compound synchronization object because it uses three kernel objects: a mutex, a semaphore, and a manual-reset event. I discuss how it uses these later. For now, I'll simply discuss how an application uses a SWMRG object.

Let me start off by saying that you use a SWMRG object in exactly the same way you would use a CRITICAL_SECTION object. First you must create an instance of a SWMRG object in your application. As with CRITICAL_SECTION objects, you usually create a SWMRG object as a global variable so that all threads in the process have access to it:

```
#include "SWMRG.h"
SWMRG g_SWMRG;   // The global SWMRG object
```

Also, the data members in a SWMRG object should be considered opaque to the application—only the functions supplied in SWMRG.C reference the members in the structure; the application should never need to touch these data members. This is also how CRITICAL_SECTION objects are used.

Before any thread in the process can synchronize itself using the SWMRG object, the SWMRG object must be initialized (usually in the application's *WinMain* function). A SWMRG object is initialized by calling the *SWMRGInitialize* function:

```
BOOL  SWMRGInitialize (PSWMRG pSWMRG, LPCTSTR lpszName);
```

As you can see, the first parameter must be the address of a SWMRG object and the second parameter allows you to specify a name for the object. Although the *SWMRGInitialize* function is similar to the *InitializeCriticalSection* function, there is one really big difference: I have designed the SWMRG object so that it can be accessed by threads running in different processes. In order to do this, however, you must pass a string name as the *lpszName* parameter. This technique is similar to creating a mutex object and specifying a name for it. If you don't want to share the SWMRG object across processes, you should pass NULL for the *lpszName* parameter. I'll talk more about using the SWMRG object across processes a little later in this chapter.

When the process is ending and you are sure that no writer or reader threads will attempt to access the SWMRG object, the SWMRG object should be destroyed by calling the *SWMRGDelete* function:

```
void SWMRGDelete (PSWMRG pSWMRG);
```

Now, in between the calls to *SWMRGInitialize* and *SWMRGDelete*, any writer or reader thread can use the SWMRG object for synchronization. The interface is very simple. When a writer thread needs access to the shared data resource, it must first call a function that is similar to the *EnterCriticalSection* function:

```
DWORD SWMRGWaitToWrite (PSWMRG pSWMRG, DWORD dwTimeout);
```

The writer thread passes the address of the SWMRG object as the first parameter and a time-out value for the second parameter. This is another area in which SWMRG objects vary from critical sections: with a SWMRG object, you can specify a time-out value while waiting. *SWMRG-WaitToWrite* will return either WAIT_OBJECT_0 or WAIT_TIMEOUT.

If the writer thread was granted exclusive access to the shared data resource because *SWMRGWaitToWrite* returned WAIT_OBJECT_0, it must call *SWMRGDoneWriting* when it no longer needs access to the data. Calling *SWMRGDoneWriting* allows other writer or reader threads the opportunity to access the shared resource:

```
void SWMRGDoneWriting (PSWMRG pSWMRG);
```

This function is similar to the *LeaveCriticalSection* function.

So far we have discussed only the writer thread side of using a SWMRG object. Now let's discuss how a reader thread uses the SWMRG object. When a reader thread wants to access the shared data resource, it calls *SWMRGWaitToRead*:

```
DWORD SWMRGWaitToRead (PSWMRG pSWMRG, DWORD dwTimeout);
```

This function is similar to the *SWMRGWaitToWrite* function in that it takes the same parameters and has the same return values. The difference is in what it does internally, which we'll discuss shortly.

When a reader thread is done accessing the shared data, it must call *SWMRGDoneReading* so that a writer thread has the opportunity to access the shared data resource:

```
void SWMRGDoneReading (PSWMRG pSWMRG);
```

Of course, a writer thread will be granted access only if no reader threads are currently accessing the resource.

It's time now to discuss how the SWMRG object is actually implemented. We'll begin by examining the data members of the SWMRG structure:

```
typedef struct SingleWriterMultiReaderGuard {
    // This mutex guards access to the other objects
    // managed by this data structure and also indicates
    // when there are no writer threads writing.
    HANDLE hMutexNoWriter;

    // This manual-reset event is signaled when
    // there are no reader threads reading.
    HANDLE hEventNoReaders;
```

(continued)

```
// This semaphore is used simply as a counter that is
// accessible between multiple processes. It is NOT
// used for thread synchronization.
// The count is the number of reader threads reading.
HANDLE hSemNumReaders;

} SWMRG, *PSWMRG;
```

This data structure consists of three handles to kernel synchronization objects. The first handle, *hMutexNoWriter,* is used by the SWMRG functions to indicate whether a writer thread has access to the shared data resource. Remember that a writer thread having access to the resource locks out all other writer threads as well as all reader threads. So a mutex object seems an excellent choice because only one thread at a time can own a mutex object. When the mutex is signaled, we know that no writer thread is currently accessing the data.

The second handle, *hEventNoReaders,* indicates whether any reader threads are currently accessing the data. If no reader threads are accessing the data, this manual-reset event object is signaled.

The third handle, *hSemNumReaders,* indicates the number of reader threads that are currently accessing the shared resource. The SWMRG functions do not use this semaphore for synchronization purposes—they use it as a counter. The SWMRG object must maintain a counter that indicates the number of reader threads that are simultaneously accessing the data. This way, when the last reader thread calls *SWMRGDone-Reading,* the counter goes to 0 and the *hEventNoReaders* event can be signaled by calling the *SetEvent* function.

When I was developing SWMRG, I originally had a long variable declared in the SWMRG structure instead of this handle to a semaphore. I used this variable to count the number of reader threads accessing the resource. But then, as I continued to develop the SWMRG code, I got to the point where I wanted to make it work for threads in other processes. This meant that the counter variable needed to be accessible in each process's address space. So I thought about creating a memory-mapped file and mapping a view of this file into each process's address space when *SWMRGInitialize* is called. The thing I hated about this method was that a memory-mapped file can be no smaller than a page and all I needed was a 4-byte value. For a system with a page size of 4096 bytes, this meant a 102,400 percent overhead; on a system with a page size of 8192 (such as the DEC Alpha), the overhead would be 202,400 percent!

After racking my brain for a while, I realized that a semaphore kernel object maintains a counter, is accessible across processes, and uses much less than 4096 bytes of memory. So I create a semaphore and use this as my counter. Whenever I want to decrement the counter, I call *WaitForSingleObject*, passing the handle to the semaphore; and whenever I want to increment the counter, I call *ReleaseSemaphore*. The problem with using semaphores as counters is that you can't query the current value of the semaphore. The only thing you can do is check to see whether the semaphore has a count of 0 by calling *WaitForSingleObject* with a time-out value of 0. If *WaitForSingleObject* returns WAIT_TIME-OUT, the semaphore's count is 0; and if WAIT_OBJECT_0 is returned, the semaphore's count is greater than 0. This is all that we can know about the semaphore, and fortunately, this is all that the SWMRG object functions need to know. More on this later.

I've placed a lot of comments in the SWMRG.C file to explain each of the functions, but I'll also discuss them briefly here in the text.

The *SWMRGInitialize* function is used to initialize the SWMRG object. Basically, it creates the mutex, event, and semaphore objects. For threads in different processes to share the SWMRG object, each process must allocate its own instance of a SWMRG object. Then a thread in each process must pass the address of its SWMRG object as well as a name for the object when calling *SWMRGInitialize*. *SWMRGInitialize* uses this name when creating the mutex, event, and semaphore. For example, if you call *SWMRGInitialize*, passing "*Jeff*" for the *lpszName* parameter, the mutex object is created with the name *SWMRGMutexNoWriterJeff*, the event object is created with the name *SWMRGEventNoReadersJeff*, and the semaphore object is created with the name *SWMRGSemNumReadersJeff*. The static *ConstructObjName* function is just a small helper function that *SWMRGInitialize* calls in order to append the *lpszName* parameter to the kernel object name's prefix.

When a thread in another process calls *SWMRGInitialize* and passes the same name for the *lpszName* parameter, the calls to create the various kernel objects will see that kernel objects with the same names already exist and will return handles to the existing objects rather than create new objects. The threads in the different processes will be synchronized.

The *SWMRGDelete* function is by far the simplest of the functions. It calls *CloseHandle* three times, once for each kernel object.

When a writer thread is ready to modify the shared data resource, it must first request permission to do so by calling the *SWMRGWaitToWrite* function. This function calls the Win32 *WaitForMultipleObjects* function, telling it to wait for both the *hMutexNoWriter* mutex and the *hEventNoReaders* event. If *WaitForMultipleObjects* returns WAIT_OBJECT_0, the thread knows that no other writer threads and no reader threads are using the shared resource. If the function returns WAIT_TIMEOUT, the writer thread knows that it is not safe to modify the shared resource because another writer thread or at least one reader thread is currently accessing the data.

When a writer thread has completed modifying the shared resource, it must call the *SWMRGDoneWriting* function. This function releases the *hMutexNoWriter* semaphore so that any other writer or reader threads will see that no writer threads are accessing the data.

When a reader thread is ready to read the shared data resource, it must first request permission to do so by calling the *SWMRGWaitToRead* function. This function calls *WaitForSingleObject*, passing the *hMutexNoWriter* mutex handle. This is because a reader thread can always read the resource if no writer thread is currently accessing the resource. If the call to *WaitForSingleObject* times out while waiting for the mutex, *SWMRGWaitToRead* returns WAIT_TIMEOUT.

However, if the call to *WaitForSingleObject* successfully obtains ownership of the mutex, the semaphore that maintains the count of reader threads must be incremented. This is done simply by calling *ReleaseSemaphore*, passing it the *hSemNumReaders* handle and a value of 1 for the *cReleaseCount* parameter. The *ReleaseSemaphore* function returns the previous count of the semaphore in a DWORD whose address is passed as the last parameter. *SWMRGWaitToRead* examines this value, and, if no reader threads were accessing the shared resource prior to calling *ReleaseSemaphore*, *SWMRGWaitToRead* resets the *hEventNoReaders* manual-reset event. Resetting this event object indicates that some reader threads are accessing the shared data. If this reader thread is not the first reader thread to access the data, the *hEventNoReaders* event will already be in the nonsignaled state, so there is no reason to call *ResetEvent* again.

Just before *SWMRGWaitToRead* returns, it must call *ReleaseMutex*, passing the *hMutexNoWriter* handle. This call is necessary because when *SWMRGWaitToRead* successfully waits for this mutex, the mutex becomes nonsignaled as a side effect. This indicates, of course, that a writer thread is accessing the data. We must correct this side effect by calling *ReleaseMutex* so that the other threads know that a writer thread is not actually accessing the shared data.

The last function to discuss is *SWMRGDoneReading*. A reader thread must call this function when it has completed accessing the shared data. *SWMRGDoneReading* first calls *WaitForMultipleObjects*, passing the *hMutexNoWriter* handle, because the thread that is calling *SWMRGDoneReading* must have exclusive access to the *hEventNoReaders* and *hSemNumReaders* objects. This thread needs to alter the states of these objects, and other writer and reader threads must not be able to examine the states of these objects until the thread that has finished reading has completely updated them. Because the *SWMRGWaitToWrite*, *SWMRGDoneWriting*, *SWMRGWaitToRead*, and *SWMRGDoneReading* functions all must successfully wait on the *hMutexNoWriter* mutex before continuing, a reader thread calling *SWMRGDoneReading* can block these other threads until it has updated the event and semaphore objects.

I mentioned that *SWMRGDoneReading* calls *WaitForMultipleObjects* instead of *WaitForSingleObject*. The other handle that is passed to *WaitForMultipleObjects* is the *hSemNumReaders* handle. This has the effect of decrementing the number of readers. Remember that successfully waiting for a semaphore object means that the system automatically decrements the count of the semaphore by 1. Now that the semaphore has been decremented, *SWMRGDoneReading* must check to see whether the reader thread is the last reader thread.

Determining whether this thread is the last reader thread is not as straightforward as I would have hoped. It would be easy if Win32 offered a function that returned the current count associated with a semaphore, but Win32 does not offer such a function. So the only thing I can do is call *ReleaseSemaphore*, which returns the current count of the semaphore but also has the side effect of incrementing the semaphore. So, I must follow the call to *ReleaseSemaphore* with a call to *WaitForSingleObject*, passing the *hSemNumReaders* handle so that the count is decremented again. If *ReleaseSemaphore* sets the *lNumReaders* variables to zero, I know that this reader thread is the last one and I change the *hEventNoReaders* event to the signaled state by calling *SetEvent*.

Finally, just before *SWMRGDoneReading* returns, it must release the *hMutexNoWriter* mutex by calling *ReleaseMutex*. As with the *SWMRGWaitToRead* function, this is necessary so that any other writer and reader threads can now wake up and continue their business.

The Bucket Sample Source Code

When you invoke Bucket, the first thing it does is initialize a SWMRG synchronization object. Because the Bucket sample application is the only application that needs access to the mutex, event, and semaphore objects, NULL is passed to *SWMRGInitialize*'s *lpszName* parameter. After the SWMRG object has been initialized, Bucket calls *DialogBox* in order to display its user interface.

Displaying the dialog box causes the system to send a WM_INIT-DIALOG message. In the processing of the *Dlg_OnInitDialog* function, the scroll bars are initialized and the two writer and three reader threads are created. The handles to these five threads are saved in a global array because they'll be needed to cleanly terminate the process. All these threads work in exactly the same way. Each thread performs a small amount of initialization and then enters a *while* loop that terminates only when the global *g_lTerminate* variable is set to 1. (When the application starts, this variable is initialized to 0; we'll come back to this variable shortly.)

Inside the *while* loop, each thread first calls the Win32 *Sleep* function, passing it a value that is determined by the thread's associated scroll bar value:

```
Sleep(1000 * GetDlgItemInt(g_hwndDlg, nNumID, NULL, FALSE));
```

This call to *Sleep* simulates the writer or reader thread doing other work that does not require access to the shared data resource. When a writer thread awakens, it calls the *SWMRGWaitToWrite* function; when a reader thread awakens, it calls the *SWMRGWaitToRead* function. When a writer thread's call to *SWMRGWaitToWrite* returns, the writer thread knows that no other writer thread or reader thread has access to the data. The writer thread then calls the *Bucket_AlterContents* function to change the contents of the bucket.

When a reader thread's call to *SWMRGWaitToRead* returns, it knows that no writer threads are accessing the bucket, but other reader threads might be accessing it. The reader thread calls the *Bucket_DumpToLB* function, which examines the contents of the bucket (without altering the contents) and places the results in the thread's respective list box.

When a writer or reader thread has completed its access to the bucket, it calls *SWMRGDoneWriting* or *SWMRGDoneReading*, depending on the type of thread. This lets another writer or reader thread access the bucket. Then the *while* loop iterates back to the top.

Now we get to the point of discussing how the writer and reader threads know when to terminate. When the user closes the dialog box, the process's primary thread, which is responsible for managing the application's user interface, returns from the call to *DialogBox* in the program's *WinMain* function and executes the following line of code:

```
InterlockedIncrement((PLONG) &g_lTerminate);
```

This call increments the global *g_lTerminate* variable from 0 to 1. Eventually all the writer and reader threads will see that this variable has changed, indicating that they should terminate. The *InterlockedIncrement* function atomically changes the value of the long variable whose address is passed to it. This means that any threads attempting to examine the value of the *g_lTerminate* values will be momentarily suspended until the *InterlockedIncrement* function has completely updated the long variable's value. (The *InterlockedIncrement* function is discussed in more detail in the last section of this chapter.)

Because the *g_lTerminate* variable has been incremented, the writer and reader threads will eventually stop running. They might not stop for quite some time, however—if they are busy performing work, their *while* loops might not iterate for a while. To clean up nicely, the primary thread must wait for all the threads to terminate. It does this by calling *WaitForMultipleObjects*, passing the handles to the five threads. Remember that these handles were saved in a global array when the *Dlg_On-InitDialog* function was called. When all the threads have terminated, *WaitForMultipleObjects* returns and the primary thread calls *CloseHandle*, passing each of the writer and reader thread handles.

Finally, the primary thread calls *SWMRGDelete* so that the *hMutex-NoWriter*, *hEventNoReaders*, and *hSemNumReaders* objects have their usage counts decremented, thereby freeing these objects.

When I was testing Bucket's process and thread termination, I used the PERFMON.EXE application that ships with Windows NT to be sure that everything was working correctly. After starting BUCKET.EXE, I started PERFMON.EXE, selected the Add To Chart option from the Edit menu, and got the dialog box shown here:

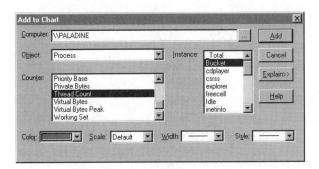

In this dialog box, I set the Object field to Process, the Instance field to Bucket, and the Counter field to Thread Count. Then I clicked on the Add button. This caused PerfMon to monitor the number of threads that were running in the Bucket process. The chart produced appears at the top of the next page.

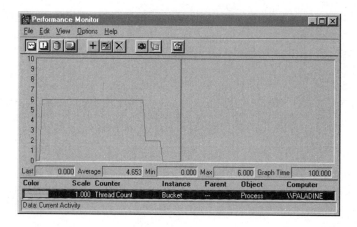

You can see from this chart that the Bucket application went from zero to six threads almost immediately. But then, around the time the vertical bar was under the toolbar button that looks like a camera, I closed the dialog box. Bucket's primary thread immediately incremented the *g_lTerminate* variable to 1, and it looks as if three threads saw this change right away and terminated. Then, after a little delay, the fourth thread iterated back to the top of its *while* loop, saw the change, and terminated. A little later, the fifth thread saw the changed variable and terminated. When the fifth thread terminated, the primary thread awakened immediately and also terminated. This is why the chart shows such a steep drop from two threads to zero threads.

The PERFMON.EXE application is an incredibly useful program that many developers ignore. This is an extremely minor example of what it can do. I am always finding new uses for PerfMon and encourage you to spend time experimenting with it to find out how it can give you additional perspectives on your own applications.

Bucket.ico

BUCKET.C
```
/************************************************************
Module name: Bucket.C
Notices: Copyright (c) 1995-1997 Jeffrey Richter
************************************************************/


#include "..\CmnHdr.H"                    /* See Appendix C. */
#include <windows.h>
```

Figure 10-5.
The Bucket application.

(continued)

Figure 10-5. *continued*

```c
#include <windowsx.h>
#include <tchar.h>
#include <stdio.h>                // For sprintf
#include <stdlib.h>               // For rand
#include <process.h>             // For _beginthreadex
#include "Resource.H"
#include "SWMRG.H"


///////////////////////////////////////////////////////////////////


// single-writer/multiple-reader guard synchronization object
SWMRG g_SWMRG;

// Array of thread handles needed for process termination
HANDLE g_hThreads[5];

// Flag indicating when the threads should terminate
// The flag is volatile because it is changed asynchronously.
long volatile g_lTerminate = 0;

// Window handle of dialog box.
HWND g_hwndDlg = NULL;


///////////////////////////////////////////////////////////////////
////// Data and routines for manipulating the bucket  ///////
///////////////////////////////////////////////////////////////////

// Enumerated list of valid ball colors
typedef enum {
   BC_FIRSTBALLCLR,
   // BC_NULL indicates an empty space in the bucket.
   BC_NULL = BC_FIRSTBALLCLR,
   BC_BLACK,
   BC_RED,
   BC_GREEN,
   BC_BLUE,
   BC_WHITE,
   BC_YELLOW,
   BC_ORANGE,
   BC_CYAN,
```

(continued)

Figure 10-5. *continued*

```
    BC_GRAY,
    BC_LASTBALLCLR = BC_GRAY
} BALLCOLOR;


// String list of valid ball colors
const TCHAR *szBallColors[] = {
    NULL,
    __TEXT("Black"),
    __TEXT("Red"),
    __TEXT("Green"),
    __TEXT("Blue"),
    __TEXT("White"),
    __TEXT("Yellow"),
    __TEXT("Orange"),
    __TEXT("Cyan"),
    __TEXT("Gray")
};


// Maximum number of balls in the bucket
#define MAX_BALLS    100


// Initially the bucket is empty.
// The bucket is volatile because its contents
// change asynchronously.
BALLCOLOR volatile g_Bucket[MAX_BALLS] = { BC_NULL };


///////////////////////////////////////////////////////////////


void Bucket_AlterContents (void) {

    // Add/remove a randomly colored ball to or from the bucket.
    g_Bucket[rand() % MAX_BALLS] = (BALLCOLOR) (rand() % 10);
}


///////////////////////////////////////////////////////////////


void Bucket_DumpToLB (HWND hwndLB) {
```

(continued)

412

Figure 10-5. *continued*

```
    int nBallNum;
    int nBallColor[BC_LASTBALLCLR - BC_FIRSTBALLCLR + 1] =
       { 0 };

    BALLCOLOR BallColor;
    TCHAR szBuf[50];

    // Calculate how many balls of each color are in the bucket.
    for (nBallNum = 0; nBallNum < MAX_BALLS; nBallNum++) {
       // Get the color of the nBallNum'th ball.
       BallColor = g_Bucket[nBallNum];

       // Increment the total for balls of this color.
       nBallColor[BallColor]++;
    }


    // Empty the list box.
    ListBox_ResetContent(hwndLB);

    // Build the contents of the list box.
    BallColor = BC_FIRSTBALLCLR;
    for (; BallColor <= BC_LASTBALLCLR; BallColor++) {

       if (szBallColors[BallColor] != NULL) {
          _stprintf(szBuf, __TEXT("%s: %*s%2d"),
             szBallColors[BallColor],
             7 - lstrlen(szBallColors[BallColor]), __TEXT(" "),
             nBallColor[BallColor]);
       } else {
          _stprintf(szBuf, __TEXT("Total:   %2d"),
             MAX_BALLS - nBallColor[BallColor]);
       }

       ListBox_AddString(hwndLB, szBuf);
    }
}


//////////////////////////////////////////////////////////////////


DWORD WINAPI Writer (LPVOID lpvParam) {
    int nWriterNum = (int) lpvParam, nNumID;
```

(continued)

Figure 10-5. *continued*

```
    switch (nWriterNum) {
       case 1:
          nNumID = IDC_WRITE1NUM;
          break;

       case 2:
          nNumID = IDC_WRITE2NUM;
          break;

       default:
          nNumID = 0;           // We should never get here.
          break;
    }


    // Continue looping until the process has been terminated.
    while (!g_lTerminate) {

       // Go to sleep for the user-defined amount of time.
       Sleep(1000 *
          GetDlgItemInt(g_hwndDlg, nNumID, NULL, FALSE));

       // Wait until safe to write: no writers and no readers.
       SWMRGWaitToWrite(&g_SWMRG, INFINITE);

       // Write to the shared data (the bucket).
       Bucket_AlterContents();

       // Inform the other writers/readers that we are done.
       SWMRGDoneWriting(&g_SWMRG);
    }

    return(0);
}


//////////////////////////////////////////////////////////////


DWORD WINAPI Reader (LPVOID lpvParam) {
   int nReaderNum = (int) lpvParam, nNumID = 0;
   HWND hwndLB = NULL;

   // Get the window handle of the reader's display list box.
```

(continued)

Figure 10-5. *continued*

```
    // Get the ID of the reader's number static control.
    switch (nReaderNum) {
        case 1:
            nNumID = IDC_READ1NUM;
            hwndLB  = GetDlgItem(g_hwndDlg, IDC_READ1LIST);
            break;

        case 2:
            nNumID = IDC_READ2NUM;
            hwndLB  = GetDlgItem(g_hwndDlg, IDC_READ2LIST);
            break;

        case 3:
            nNumID = IDC_READ3NUM;
            hwndLB  = GetDlgItem(g_hwndDlg, IDC_READ3LIST);
            break;

        default:
            nNumID = 0;          // We should never get here.
            hwndLB  = NULL;
            break;
    }


    // Continue looping until the process has been terminated.
    while (!g_lTerminate) {

        // Go to sleep for the user-defined amount of time.
        Sleep(1000 *
            GetDlgItemInt(g_hwndDlg, nNumID, NULL, FALSE));

        // Wait until safe to read: no writers
        SWMRGWaitToRead(&g_SWMRG, INFINITE);

        // Read from the shared data (the bucket).
        Bucket_DumpToLB(hwndLB);

        // Inform the other writers/readers that we are done.
        SWMRGDoneReading(&g_SWMRG);
    }
    return(0);
}
```

(continued)

Figure 10-5. *continued*

```
///////////////////////////////////////////////////////////


BOOL Dlg_OnInitDialog (HWND hwnd, HWND hwndFocus,
   LPARAM lParam) {

   DWORD dwThreadID;
   int x;

   // Associate an icon with the dialog box.
   chSETDLGICONS(hwnd, IDI_BUCKET, IDI_BUCKET);

   // Save the handle of the dialog box in a global so that
   // the threads can easily gain access to it. This must
   // be done before creating the threads.
   g_hwndDlg = hwnd;


   // Initialize the scroll bar values for the bucket writers.
   ScrollBar_SetRange(GetDlgItem(hwnd, IDC_WRITE1SCRL),
      0, 60, FALSE);
   ScrollBar_SetPos(GetDlgItem(hwnd, IDC_WRITE1SCRL), 1, TRUE);
   SetDlgItemInt(hwnd, IDC_WRITE1NUM, 1, FALSE);

   ScrollBar_SetRange(GetDlgItem(hwnd, IDC_WRITE2SCRL),
      0, 60, FALSE);
   ScrollBar_SetPos(GetDlgItem(hwnd, IDC_WRITE2SCRL), 3, TRUE);
   SetDlgItemInt(hwnd, IDC_WRITE2NUM, 3, FALSE);


   // Initialize the scroll bar values for the bucket readers.
   ScrollBar_SetRange(GetDlgItem(hwnd, IDC_READ1SCRL),
      0, 60, FALSE);
   ScrollBar_SetPos(GetDlgItem(hwnd, IDC_READ1SCRL), 2, TRUE);
   SetDlgItemInt(hwnd, IDC_READ1NUM, 2, FALSE);

   ScrollBar_SetRange(GetDlgItem(hwnd, IDC_READ2SCRL),
      0, 60, FALSE);
   ScrollBar_SetPos(GetDlgItem(hwnd, IDC_READ2SCRL), 4, TRUE);
   SetDlgItemInt(hwnd, IDC_READ2NUM, 4, FALSE);

   ScrollBar_SetRange(GetDlgItem(hwnd, IDC_READ3SCRL),
      0, 60, FALSE);
   ScrollBar_SetPos(GetDlgItem(hwnd, IDC_READ3SCRL), 7, TRUE);
```

(continued)

Figure 10-5. *continued*

```
    SetDlgItemInt(hwnd, IDC_READ3NUM, 7, FALSE);

    // Create the two writer and three reader threads.
    // NOTE: these threads MUST be created AFTER all other
    // synchronization objects.
    for (x = 0; x <= 1; x++) {
        g_hThreads[x] = chBEGINTHREADEX(NULL, 0, Writer,
            (LPVOID) (x + 1), 0, &dwThreadID);
    }

    for (x = 2; x <= 4; x++) {
        g_hThreads[x] = chBEGINTHREADEX(NULL, 0, Reader,
            (LPVOID) (x - 1), 0, &dwThreadID);
    }

    return(TRUE);
}


///////////////////////////////////////////////////////////


void Dlg_OnHScroll (HWND hwnd, HWND hwndCtl,
    UINT code, int pos) {

    int posCrnt, posMin, posMax;

    posCrnt = ScrollBar_GetPos(hwndCtl);
    ScrollBar_GetRange(hwndCtl, &posMin, &posMax);

    switch (code) {
        case SB_LINELEFT:
            posCrnt--;
            break;

        case SB_LINERIGHT:
            posCrnt++;
            break;

        case SB_PAGELEFT:
            posCrnt -= 10;
            break;

        case SB_PAGERIGHT:
```

(continued)

Figure 10-5. *continued*

```
            posCrnt += 10;
            break;

        case SB_THUMBTRACK:
            posCrnt = pos;
            break;

        case SB_LEFT:
            posCrnt = 0;
            break;

        case SB_RIGHT:
            posCrnt = posMax;
            break;
    }

    if (posCrnt < 0)
        posCrnt = 0;

    if (posCrnt > posMax)
        posCrnt = posMax;

    ScrollBar_SetPos(hwndCtl, posCrnt, TRUE);

    SetDlgItemInt(hwnd, GetDlgCtrlID(hwndCtl) - 1,
        posCrnt, FALSE);
}


///////////////////////////////////////////////////////////


void Dlg_OnVScroll (HWND hwnd, HWND hwndCtl,
    UINT code, int pos) {

    int posCrnt, posMin, posMax;

    posCrnt = ScrollBar_GetPos(hwndCtl);
    ScrollBar_GetRange(hwndCtl, &posMin, &posMax);

    switch (code) {
        case SB_LINEUP:
            posCrnt--;
            break;
```

(continued)

Figure 10-5. *continued*

```
        case SB_LINEDOWN:
            posCrnt++;
            break;

        case SB_PAGEUP:
            posCrnt -= 10;
            break;

        case SB_PAGEDOWN:
            posCrnt += 10;
            break;

        case SB_THUMBTRACK:
            posCrnt = pos;
            break;

        case SB_TOP:
            posCrnt = 0;
            break;

        case SB_BOTTOM:
            posCrnt = posMax;
            break;
    }

    if (posCrnt < 0)
        posCrnt = 0;

    if (posCrnt > posMax)
        posCrnt = posMax;

    ScrollBar_SetPos(hwndCtl, posCrnt, TRUE);

    SetDlgItemInt(hwnd, GetDlgCtrlID(hwndCtl) - 1,
        posCrnt, FALSE);
}


///////////////////////////////////////////////////////////////


void Dlg_OnCommand (HWND hwnd, int id,
    HWND hwndCtl, UINT codeNotify) {
```

(continued)

419

Figure 10-5. *continued*

```
    switch (id) {
        case IDCANCEL:
            EndDialog(hwnd, id);
            break;
    }
}


////////////////////////////////////////////////////////////


BOOL CALLBACK Dlg_Proc (HWND hwnd, UINT uMsg,
    WPARAM wParam, LPARAM lParam) {

    switch (uMsg) {
        chHANDLE_DLGMSG(hwnd, WM_INITDIALOG, Dlg_OnInitDialog);
        chHANDLE_DLGMSG(hwnd, WM_COMMAND, Dlg_OnCommand);
        chHANDLE_DLGMSG(hwnd, WM_HSCROLL, Dlg_OnHScroll);
        chHANDLE_DLGMSG(hwnd, WM_VSCROLL, Dlg_OnVScroll);
    }

    return(FALSE);
}


////////////////////////////////////////////////////////////


int WINAPI _tWinMain (HINSTANCE hinstExe,
    HINSTANCE hinstPrev, LPTSTR pszCmdLine, int nCmdShow) {

    int x;

    chWARNIFUNICODEUNDERWIN95();

    // Initialize the single-writer/multiple-reader
    // guard synchronization object. This must be done
    // before any thread attempts to use it.
    SWMRGInitialize(&g_SWMRG, NULL);


    // Display the process's user interface.
    DialogBox(hinstExe, MAKEINTRESOURCE(IDD_BUCKET),
        NULL, Dlg_Proc);
```

(continued)

Figure 10-5. *continued*

```
// When the user shuts down the process, clean up.
// 1. Inform the threads that the process is terminating.
InterlockedIncrement((PLONG) &g_lTerminate);

// 2. Wait for all of the threads to terminate. This
// might take a long time because some threads might be
// sleeping and therefore not checking the g_lTerminate
// variable.
WaitForMultipleObjects(chDIMOF(g_hThreads), g_hThreads,
   TRUE, INFINITE);

// 3. Close all of our handles to the threads.
for (x = 0; x < chDIMOF(g_hThreads); x++)
   CloseHandle(g_hThreads[x]);


// 4. Delete the Single Writer/Multiple Reader Guard
// synchronization object. This must be done when it
// is known that no threads will attempt to use it.
SWMRGDelete(&g_SWMRG);

return(0);
}


/////////////////////// End Of File ///////////////////////
```

SWMRG.C

```
/************************************************************
Module name: SWMRG.C
Notices: Copyright (c) 1995-1997 Jeffrey Richter
************************************************************/


#include "..\CmnHdr.H"                    /* See Appendix C. */
#include <windows.h>
#include <string.h>
#include <tchar.h>
#include "SWMRG.H"              // The header file


/////////////////////////////////////////////////////////////
```

(continued)

Figure 10-5. *continued*

```
static LPCTSTR ConstructObjName (
   LPCTSTR lpszPrefix, LPCTSTR lpszSuffix,
   LPTSTR lpszFullName, size_t cbFullName, PBOOL fOk) {
   *fOk = TRUE;      // Assume success.

   if (lpszSuffix == NULL)
      return(NULL);

   if ((_tcslen(lpszPrefix) + _tcslen(lpszSuffix)) >=
      cbFullName) {
      // If the strings will overflow the buffer,
      // indicate an error.
      *fOk = FALSE;
      return(NULL);
   }

   _tcscpy(lpszFullName, lpszPrefix);
   _tcscat(lpszFullName, lpszSuffix);
   return(lpszFullName);
}


///////////////////////////////////////////////////////////////


BOOL SWMRGInitialize(PSWMRG pSWMRG, LPCTSTR lpszName) {
   TCHAR szFullObjName[100];
   LPCTSTR lpszObjName;
   BOOL fOk;

   // Initialize all data members to NULL so that we can
   // accurately check whether an error has occurred.
   pSWMRG->hMutexNoWriter = NULL;
   pSWMRG->hEventNoReaders = NULL;
   pSWMRG->hSemNumReaders = NULL;

   // This mutex guards access to the other objects
   // managed by this data structure and also indicates
   // whether there are any writer threads writing.
   // Initially no thread owns the mutex.
   lpszObjName = ConstructObjName(
      __TEXT("SWMRGMutexNoWriter"), lpszName,
      szFullObjName, chDIMOF(szFullObjName), &fOk);
   if (fOk)
```

(continued)

Figure 10-5. *continued*

```
        pSWMRG->hMutexNoWriter =
            CreateMutex(NULL, FALSE, lpszObjName);

    // Create the manual-reset event that is signalled when
    // no reader threads are reading.
    // Initially no reader threads are reading.
    lpszObjName = ConstructObjName(
        __TEXT("SWMRGEventNoReaders"), lpszName,
        szFullObjName, chDIMOF(szFullObjName), &fOk);
    if (fOk)
        pSWMRG->hEventNoReaders =
            CreateEvent(NULL, TRUE, TRUE, lpszObjName);

    // Initialize the variable that indicates the number of
    // reader threads that are reading.
    // Initially no reader threads are reading.
    lpszObjName = ConstructObjName(
        __TEXT("SWMRGSemNumReaders"), lpszName,
        szFullObjName, chDIMOF(szFullObjName), &fOk);
    if (fOk)
        pSWMRG->hSemNumReaders =
            CreateSemaphore(NULL, 0, 0x7FFFFFFF, lpszObjName);


    if ((NULL == pSWMRG->hMutexNoWriter)    ||
        (NULL == pSWMRG->hEventNoReaders)   ||
        (NULL == pSWMRG->hSemNumReaders)) {
        // If a synchronization object could not be created,
        // destroy any created objects and return failure.
        SWMRGDelete(pSWMRG);
        fOk = FALSE;
    } else {
        fOk = TRUE;
    }

    // Return TRUE upon success, FALSE upon failure.
    return(fOk);
}


////////////////////////////////////////////////////////////////
```

(continued)

Figure 10-5. *continued*

```
void SWMRGDelete(PSWMRG pSWMRG) {

   // Destroy any synchronization objects that were
   // successfully created.
   if (NULL != pSWMRG->hMutexNoWriter)
      CloseHandle(pSWMRG->hMutexNoWriter);

   if (NULL != pSWMRG->hEventNoReaders)
      CloseHandle(pSWMRG->hEventNoReaders);

   if (NULL != pSWMRG->hSemNumReaders)
      CloseHandle(pSWMRG->hSemNumReaders);
}


///////////////////////////////////////////////////////////////


DWORD SWMRGWaitToWrite(PSWMRG pSWMRG, DWORD dwTimeout) {
   DWORD dw;
   HANDLE aHandles[2];

   // We can write if the following are true:
   // 1. The mutex guard is available and
   //    no other threads are writing.
   // 2. No threads are reading.
   aHandles[0] = pSWMRG->hMutexNoWriter;
   aHandles[1] = pSWMRG->hEventNoReaders;
   dw = WaitForMultipleObjects(2, aHandles, TRUE, dwTimeout);

   if (dw != WAIT_TIMEOUT) {
      // This thread can write to the shared data.

      // Because a writer thread is writing, the mutex
      // should not be released. This stops
      // other writers and readers.
   }

   return(dw);
}


///////////////////////////////////////////////////////////////
```

(continued)

Figure 10-5. *continued*

```
void SWMRGDoneWriting(PSWMRG pSWMRG) {
   // Presumably, a writer thread calling this function has
   // successfully called WaitToWrite. This means that we
   // do not have to wait on any synchronization objects
   // here because the writer already owns the mutex.

   // Allow other writer/reader threads to use
   // the SWMRG synchronization object.
   ReleaseMutex(pSWMRG->hMutexNoWriter);
}


///////////////////////////////////////////////////////////////


DWORD SWMRGWaitToRead(PSWMRG pSWMRG, DWORD dwTimeout) {
   DWORD dw;
   LONG lPreviousCount;

   // We can read if the mutex guard is available
   // and no threads are writing.
   dw = WaitForSingleObject(pSWMRG->hMutexNoWriter, dwTimeout);

   if (dw != WAIT_TIMEOUT) {
      // This thread can read from the shared data.

      // Increment the number of reader threads.
      ReleaseSemaphore(pSWMRG->hSemNumReaders, 1,
         &lPreviousCount);
      if (lPreviousCount == 0) {
         // If this is the first reader thread,
         // set our event to reflect this.
         ResetEvent(pSWMRG->hEventNoReaders);
      }

      // Allow other writer/reader threads to use
      // the SWMRG synchronization object.
      ReleaseMutex(pSWMRG->hMutexNoWriter);
   }

   return(dw);
}
```

(continued)

Figure 10-5. *continued*

```
/////////////////////////////////////////////////////////////

void SWMRGDoneReading (PSWMRG pSWMRG) {
   HANDLE aHandles[2];
   LONG lNumReaders;

   // We can stop reading if the mutex guard is available,
   // but when we stop reading we must also decrement the
   // number of reader threads.
   aHandles[0] = pSWMRG->hMutexNoWriter;
   aHandles[1] = pSWMRG->hSemNumReaders;
   WaitForMultipleObjects(2, aHandles, TRUE, INFINITE);

   // Get the remaining number of readers by releasing the
   // semaphore and then restoring the count by immediately
   // performing a wait.
   ReleaseSemaphore(pSWMRG->hSemNumReaders, 1,
      &lNumReaders);
   WaitForSingleObject(pSWMRG->hSemNumReaders, INFINITE);

   // If there are no remaining readers,
   // set the event to relect this.
   if (lNumReaders == 0) {
      // If there are no reader threads,
      // set our event to reflect this.
      SetEvent(pSWMRG->hEventNoReaders);
   }

   // Allow other writer/reader threads to use
   // the SWMRG synchronization object.
   ReleaseMutex(pSWMRG->hMutexNoWriter);
}


///////////////////////// End Of File /////////////////////////
```

SWMRG.H

```
/*************************************************************
Module name: SWMRG.H
Notices: Copyright (c) 1995-1997 Jeffrey Richter
*************************************************************/
```

(continued)

Figure 10-5. *continued*

```
// The single-writer/multiple-reader guard
// compound synchronization object
typedef struct SingleWriterMultiReaderGuard {
    // This mutex guards access to the other objects
    // managed by this data structure and also indicates
    // whether any writer threads are writing.
    HANDLE hMutexNoWriter;

    // This manual-reset event is signaled when
    // no reader threads are reading.
    HANDLE hEventNoReaders;

    // This semaphore is used simply as a counter that is
    // accessible between multiple processes. It is NOT
    // used for thread synchronization.
    // The count is the number of reader threads reading.
    HANDLE hSemNumReaders;

} SWMRG, *PSWMRG;


//////////////////////////////////////////////////////////////


// Initializes a SWMRG structure. This structure must be
// initialized before any writer or reader threads attempt
// to wait on it.
// The structure must be allocated by the application and
// the structure's address is passed as the first parameter.
// The lpszName parameter is the name of the object. Pass
// NULL if you do not want to share the object.
BOOL SWMRGInitialize (PSWMRG pSWMRG, LPCTSTR lpszName);


// Deletes the system resources associated with a SWMRG
// structure. The structure must be deleted only when
// no writer or reader threads in the calling process
// will wait on it.
void SWMRGDelete (PSWMRG pSWMRG);


// A writer thread calls this function to know when
// it can successfully write to the shared data.
DWORD SWMRGWaitToWrite (PSWMRG pSWMRG, DWORD dwTimeout);
```

(continued)

427

Figure 10-5. *continued*

```
// A writer thread calls this function to let other threads
// know that it no longer needs to write to the shared data.
void SWMRGDoneWriting (PSWMRG pSWMRG);


// A reader thread calls this function to know when
// it can successfully read the shared data.
DWORD SWMRGWaitToRead  (PSWMRG pSWMRG, DWORD dwTimeout);


// A reader thread calls this function to let other threads
// know when it no longer needs to read the shared data.
void SWMRGDoneReading (PSWMRG pSWMRG);


///////////////////////// End Of File /////////////////////////
```

```
BUCKET.RC
//Microsoft Developer Studio generated resource script.
//
#include "Resource.h"

#define APSTUDIO_READONLY_SYMBOLS
/////////////////////////////////////////////////////////////////
//
// Generated from the TEXTINCLUDE 2 resource.
//
#include "afxres.h"


/////////////////////////////////////////////////////////////////
#undef APSTUDIO_READONLY_SYMBOLS


/////////////////////////////////////////////////////////////////
// English (U.S.) resources

#if !defined(AFX_RESOURCE_DLL) || defined(AFX_TARG_ENU)
#ifdef _WIN32
LANGUAGE LANG_ENGLISH, SUBLANG_ENGLISH_US
#pragma code_page(1252)
#endif //_WIN32
```

(continued)

Figure 10-5. *continued*

```
/////////////////////////////////////////////////////////////
//
// Icon
//

// Icon with lowest ID value placed first to ensure application
// icon remains consistent on all systems.
IDI_BUCKET                   ICON    DISCARDABLE     "Bucket.Ico"


/////////////////////////////////////////////////////////////
//
// Dialog
//

IDD_BUCKET DIALOG DISCARDABLE  12, 48, 216, 171
STYLE WS_MINIMIZEBOX | WS_POPUP | WS_VISIBLE | WS_CAPTION |
    WS_SYSMENU
CAPTION "A Bucket of Balls"
FONT 8, "Courier"
BEGIN
    GROUPBOX        "Bucket &Writers",IDC_STATIC,4,0,100,48
    RTEXT           "1:",IDC_STATIC,8,16,12,8,SS_NOPREFIX
    RTEXT           "##",IDC_WRITE1NUM,20,16,9,8,SS_NOPREFIX
    SCROLLBAR       IDC_WRITE1SCRL,32,16,68,10
    RTEXT           "2:",IDC_STATIC,8,32,12,8,SS_NOPREFIX
    RTEXT           "##",IDC_WRITE2NUM,20,32,9,8,SS_NOPREFIX
    SCROLLBAR       IDC_WRITE2SCRL,32,32,68,10
    GROUPBOX        "Bucket &Readers",IDC_STATIC,4,56,208,112
    RTEXT           "1:",IDC_STATIC,20,68,12,8,SS_NOPREFIX
    RTEXT           "##",IDC_READ1NUM,36,68,9,8,SS_NOPREFIX
    SCROLLBAR       IDC_READ1SCRL,8,80,10,84,SBS_VERT
    LISTBOX         IDC_READ1LIST,20,80,52,84,
                    LBS_NOINTEGRALHEIGHT |
                    WS_TABSTOP
    RTEXT           "2:",IDC_STATIC,88,68,12,8,SS_NOPREFIX
    RTEXT           "##",IDC_READ2NUM,104,68,9,8,SS_NOPREFIX
    SCROLLBAR       IDC_READ2SCRL,76,80,10,84,SBS_VERT
    LISTBOX         IDC_READ2LIST,88,80,52,84,
                    LBS_NOINTEGRALHEIGHT |
                    WS_TABSTOP
    RTEXT           "3:",IDC_STATIC,156,68,12,8,SS_NOPREFIX
    RTEXT           "##",IDC_READ3NUM,172,68,9,8,SS_NOPREFIX
```

(continued)

Figure 10-5. *continued*

```
       SCROLLBAR        IDC_READ3SCRL,144,80,10,84,SBS_VERT
       LISTBOX          IDC_READ3LIST,156,80,52,84,
                        LBS_NOINTEGRALHEIGHT |
                        WS_TABSTOP
END


#ifdef APSTUDIO_INVOKED
/////////////////////////////////////////////////////////////////////////
//
// TEXTINCLUDE
//

1 TEXTINCLUDE DISCARDABLE
BEGIN
    "Resource.h\0"
END

2 TEXTINCLUDE DISCARDABLE
BEGIN
    "#include ""afxres.h""\r\n"
    "\0"
END

3 TEXTINCLUDE DISCARDABLE
BEGIN
    "\r\n"
    "\0"
END

#endif    // APSTUDIO_INVOKED

#endif    // English (U.S.) resources
/////////////////////////////////////////////////////////////////////////



#ifndef APSTUDIO_INVOKED
/////////////////////////////////////////////////////////////////////////
//
// Generated from the TEXTINCLUDE 3 resource.
//


/////////////////////////////////////////////////////////////////////////
#endif    // not APSTUDIO_INVOKED
```

Auto-Reset Events

Auto-reset events behave more like mutexes and semaphores than manual-reset events do. When a thread calls *SetEvent* to signal an event, the event stays signaled until another thread that is waiting for the event is awakened. Just before the waiting thread resumes, the system automatically resets the event to the nonsignaled state. Using an auto-reset event in this way has the effect of allowing only one thread waiting for the event to resume execution. Any other threads waiting for the event are left suspended, still waiting. You have no control over which of the suspended threads will resume execution—the operating system makes that decision. This statement is true not only of events but of all synchronization objects. If multiple waits are satisfied, the highest-priority thread will run.

You can manipulate an auto-reset event by using the same functions that manipulate a manual-reset event: *SetEvent, ResetEvent,* and *PulseEvent.* Usually, you don't use the *ResetEvent* function, however, because the system automatically resets an auto-reset event before *WaitForSingleObject* and *WaitForMultipleObjects* return.

The *PulseEvent* function performs the same operations for manual-reset events as it does for auto-reset events—that is, *PulseEvent* signals the event, releases a thread waiting for the event, and resets the event. However, there is one small difference between calling *PulseEvent* for an auto-reset event and calling it for a manual-reset event: pulsing an auto-reset event releases only a single thread that is waiting for the event, even if several threads are waiting. By contrast, pulsing a manual-reset event releases all the threads waiting for the event.

The Document Statistics Sample Application

The DocStats (DOCSTATS.EXE) application, listed in Figure 10-6 beginning on page 435, demonstrates the use of auto-reset events. The source code files and resource files for the application are in the DOCSTATS directory on the companion disc. When you run DocStats, the dialog box at the top of the next page appears.

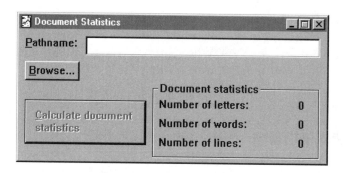

Before you can perform any statistical analysis, you must first enter a pathname or choose the Browse button to select a file. Note that DocStats can process only ANSI files; it will give incorrect results on Unicode or binary files.

DocStats analyzes the specified file and displays the number of characters, words, and lines in the file. What makes DocStats exciting is the way it accomplishes this heroic task.

When you choose the Calculate Document Statistics button, Doc-Stats creates three threads, one for each of the items (characters, words, and lines) to be counted. These threads are suspended until a global buffer contains data for them to process. Next DocStats opens the specified file and loads the first 1024 bytes of the file into the global data buffer. Now that the data is ready to be processed, DocStats notifies the three suspended threads that they can resume execution to process the global data.

While the three threads are processing the file data, the primary thread suspends itself so that it won't immediately loop around and read the next 1024 bytes from the data file. The primary thread waits until all three counting threads have completed processing the data before it reads the next chunk of data from the file. If the primary thread doesn't wait and reads the next chunk of data, that data overwrites the previous chunk of data in the global buffer while the three secondary threads are still processing it—a big no-no. When the primary thread has read the last chunk of the file's data, it closes the file, retrieves the results calculated by the three secondary threads, and displays the results.

The most interesting aspect of DocStats is how it synchronizes the execution of the primary thread with the three secondary threads. Initially, when the primary thread starts executing, it creates six auto-reset events—two for each secondary thread. One of these events notifies a single secondary thread that the primary thread has read the data from the file and that this data can now be processed. The handles to these events are stored in the *g_hEventsDataReady* array. When these events are created, they are initially set to nonsignaled, which indicates that the data buffer is not ready for processing.

The second of the two events indicates that the secondary thread has processed the file's data contained in the global buffer and that it's suspending itself, waiting for the primary thread to indicate that the next chunk of data has been read and is ready to be processed. The handles to these events are stored in the *g_hEventsProcIdle* array. When these events are created, they are initially set to signaled, which indicates that the secondary threads are idle.

Next the primary thread creates the three secondary threads. None of these threads are created in the suspended state—all are allowed to begin executing. The handles to these three threads are stored in the *hThreads* array. All three threads operate in the same way. After they begin executing, they immediately enter a loop that iterates with each chunk of file data read by the primary thread. However, before any of the secondary threads can start processing the global buffer, they must wait until the buffer has been initialized. So the first action in this loop is a call to *WaitForSingleObject*, passing the handle of an event contained in the *g_hEventsDataReady* array.

The primary thread then opens the file and waits for all three of the secondary threads to indicate that they are not processing the data in the global buffer. For the first iteration, all the event handles in the *g_hEventsProcIdle* array are signaled, so the primary thread won't need to wait at all. The primary thread reads the first 1024 bytes into the global buffer and, after reading the data, signals the three waiting threads that the data is ready by calling *SetEvent* three times, once for each event in the *g_hEventsDataReady* array.

When these events become signaled, the secondary threads wake up and begin processing the file's data. Because these are auto-reset events, the events are automatically set back to the nonsignaled state, indicating that the data is *not* ready for processing. The result is that the secondary threads have indicated that the data is not ready for processing—but they have already resumed execution and are no longer checking the events. The threads continue to run, thinking that the data is ready—and it is.

When I was first designing this application, I tried to get by with using only one event to signal that the data was ready. After all, there was only one block of data, and it seemed to me that one event should be able to indicate to all of the secondary threads that the block of data was ready. But I wasn't able to solve this problem using only a single event. When I tried using a single event, one of the secondary threads would see that the data was ready, and because an auto-reset event was used, the event would be reset to the nonsignaled state. This would happen before the other two secondary threads saw that the event had been signaled. As a result, the other two secondary threads would never get a chance to process the data. By using three different events to represent the "data-ready" event, each thread can look for its own event without affecting the other threads.

After each of the three secondary threads has scanned the whole buffer, each calls *SetEvent* on its respective event contained in the *g_h-EventsProcIdle* array. This call signals back to the primary thread that the secondary thread is finished accessing the buffer. Remember, the primary thread calls *WaitForMultipleObjects* at the top of its loop. This means that it will wait until all three secondary threads have completed processing the buffer and set their respective events to signaled before it reads the next chunk of the file's data.

When the primary thread's call to *WaitForMultipleObjects* returns, the three *g_hEventsProcIdle* events are automatically reset to their nonsignaled state, indicating that the secondary threads are not idle and are processing data. In reality, they are still waiting for the data-ready events to be signaled.

Let's consider what would happen if the *g_hEventsProcIdle* events were not automatically reset to nonsignaled. And imagine that we're running the program on a single-CPU system and that threads are allowed to execute for a full hour before being preempted.

In this case, the primary thread could read the file's data, set the three data-ready events to signaled, and loop back around to the top of its loop. This time, it would be waiting for the three *g_hEventsProcIdle* events to be signaled, and if they weren't automatically reset to non-signaled, the wait would end and the primary thread would read the next chunk of data into the buffer all before the secondary threads had a chance to process the contents of the previous chunk—a bug!

I'm sure you see the problem here. I know that having the CPU dedicated to a single thread for a full hour before preempting it is a bit excessive, but extreme thinking is a good practice when creating multithreaded applications. Writing and designing multithreaded applications isn't easy. A number of possible gotchas can occur. I've found it tremendously helpful to imagine that the computer system I'm using to implement my application actually preempts threads once an hour. It's always easier to consider the potential problem up front rather than let the system discover it for you.

As it turns out, it took me quite a few tries before I got DocStats to execute correctly. Even a machine that preempts threads every 20 milliseconds is enough for the application to fail.

Now back to DocStats. After the primary thread has finished reading the file's data, the secondary threads must return the results of their calculations. They do this by executing a return statement at the end of their thread functions, using the result as the function's return value. Once again, the primary thread calls *WaitForMultipleObjects*, suspending itself until all three secondary threads have terminated. The suspending is done by waiting for the thread handles contained in the *hThreads* array rather than waiting for any events.

After all three secondary threads have terminated, the primary thread calls *GetExitCodeThread* to get each thread's return value. The primary thread then calls *CloseHandle* for all six events and all three threads so that the system resources are freed. Finally, DocStats displays the results in the dialog box.

DocStats.ico

DOCSTATS.C

```
/*******************************************************************
Module name: DocStats.C
Notices: Copyright (c) 1995-1997 Jeffrey Richter
*******************************************************************/


#include "..\CmnHdr.H"                    /* See Appendix C. */
#include <windows.h>
#include <windowsx.h>
#include <tchar.h>
#include <stdio.h>                // For sprintf
#include <string.h>
#include <process.h>             // For _beginthreadex
#include "Resource.H"



///////////////////////////////////////////////////////////////////
```

Figure 10-6.
The DocStats application.

(continued)

Figure 10-6. *continued*

```
typedef enum {
    STAT_FIRST = 0,
    STAT_LETTERS = STAT_FIRST,
    STAT_WORDS,
    STAT_LINES,
    STAT_LAST = STAT_LINES
} STATTYPE;

HANDLE g_hEventsDataReady[STAT_LAST - STAT_FIRST + 1];
HANDLE g_hEventsProcIdle[STAT_LAST - STAT_FIRST + 1];

BYTE  g_bFileBuf[1024];
DWORD g_dwNumBytesInBuf;

// Forward reference
DWORD WINAPI StatThreadFunc(LPVOID lpvParam);


//////////////////////////////////////////////////////////////////


BOOL DocStats(LPCTSTR pszPathname, PDWORD pdwNumLetters,
  PDWORD pdwNumWords, PDWORD pdwNumLines) {

  HANDLE hThreads[STAT_LAST - STAT_FIRST + 1];
  HANDLE hFile;
  DWORD dwThreadID;
  STATTYPE StatType;

  *pdwNumLetters = 0;
  *pdwNumWords = 0;
  *pdwNumLines = 0;

  // Open the file for reading.
  hFile = CreateFile(pszPathname, GENERIC_READ, 0,
    NULL, OPEN_EXISTING, FILE_ATTRIBUTE_NORMAL, NULL);
  if (hFile == INVALID_HANDLE_VALUE) {
    // File open failed.
    chMB(__TEXT("File could not be opened."));
    return(FALSE);
  }

  for (StatType = STAT_FIRST; StatType < STAT_LAST + 1;
    StatType++) {
```

(continued)

Figure 10-6. *continued*

```
    // Signaled when not processing buffer.
    g_hEventsDataReady[StatType] =
        CreateEvent(NULL, FALSE, FALSE, NULL);
    g_hEventsProcIdle[StatType] =
        CreateEvent(NULL, FALSE, TRUE, NULL);

    // Create all the threads.  Threads MUST be
    // created AFTER the event objects.
    hThreads[StatType] = chBEGINTHREADEX(NULL, 0,
        StatThreadFunc, (PVOID) StatType, 0, &dwThreadID);
}


do {
    // Wait for the worker threads to be idle.
    WaitForMultipleObjects(STAT_LAST - STAT_FIRST + 1,
        g_hEventsProcIdle, TRUE, INFINITE);

    // Read part of the file into the global memory buffer.
    ReadFile(hFile, g_bFileBuf, chDIMOF(g_bFileBuf),
        &g_dwNumBytesInBuf, NULL);

    // Signal the works that the data is ready.
    for (StatType = STAT_FIRST; StatType < STAT_LAST + 1;
        StatType++) {
        SetEvent(g_hEventsDataReady[StatType]);
    }

} while (g_dwNumBytesInBuf != 0);


// All the statistics for the file have been accumulated;
// time to clean up.
CloseHandle(hFile);

// Wait for all of the threads to return.
WaitForMultipleObjects(STAT_LAST - STAT_FIRST + 1,
    hThreads, TRUE, INFINITE);

// Get the statistic from each thread.
GetExitCodeThread(hThreads[STAT_LETTERS], pdwNumLetters);
GetExitCodeThread(hThreads[STAT_WORDS], pdwNumWords);
GetExitCodeThread(hThreads[STAT_LINES], pdwNumLines);
```

(continued)

Figure 10-6. *continued*

```
    // Clean up the handles for all the threads
    for (StatType = STAT_FIRST; StatType < STAT_LAST + 1;
      StatType++) {
      CloseHandle(hThreads[StatType]);
      CloseHandle(g_hEventsDataReady[StatType]);
      CloseHandle(g_hEventsProcIdle[StatType]);
    }

    return(TRUE);
}


///////////////////////////////////////////////////////////////


DWORD WINAPI StatThreadFunc(LPVOID lpvParam) {
    STATTYPE StatType = (STATTYPE) lpvParam;
    DWORD dwNumBytesInBuf, dwByteIndex, dwNumStat = 0;
    BYTE bByte;
    BOOL fInWord = FALSE, fIsWordSep;

    do {
      // Wait for the data to be ready.
      WaitForSingleObject(g_hEventsDataReady[StatType],
        INFINITE);

      dwNumBytesInBuf = g_dwNumBytesInBuf;
      dwByteIndex = 0;
      for (; dwByteIndex < dwNumBytesInBuf; dwByteIndex++) {

        bByte = g_bFileBuf[dwByteIndex];
        // Note that this program works only on ANSI files
        // regardless of whether the source code is compiled
        // for ANSI or Unicode.
        switch (StatType) {
          case STAT_LETTERS:
            if (IsCharAlphaA(bByte))
              dwNumStat++;
            break;

          case STAT_WORDS:
            fIsWordSep = (strchr(" \t\n\r", bByte) != NULL);
            if (!fInWord && !fIsWordSep) {
```

(continued)

Figure 10-6. *continued*

```
                    dwNumStat++;
                    fInWord = TRUE;
                } else {
                    if (fInWord && fIsWordSep)
                        fInWord = FALSE;
                }
                break;

            case STAT_LINES:
                if ('\n' == bByte)
                    dwNumStat++;
                break;
            }
        }

        // Data processed; signal that we are done.
        SetEvent(g_hEventsProcIdle[StatType]);

    } while (dwNumBytesInBuf > 0);

    return(dwNumStat);
}


///////////////////////////////////////////////////////////////


BOOL Dlg_OnInitDialog (HWND hwnd, HWND hwndFocus,
    LPARAM lParam) {

    // Associate an icon with the dialog box.
    chSETDLGICONS(hwnd, IDI_DOCSTATS, IDI_DOCSTATS);

    // Initialize the dialog box by disabling all
    // the nonsetup controls.
    EnableWindow(GetDlgItem(hwnd, IDC_DODOCSTATS), FALSE);

    return(TRUE);
}


///////////////////////////////////////////////////////////////
```

(continued)

Figure 10-6. *continued*

```
void Dlg_OnCommand (HWND hwnd, int id, HWND hwndCtl,
   UINT codeNotify) {

   TCHAR szPathname[_MAX_PATH];
   OPENFILENAME ofn;
   DWORD dwNumLetters, dwNumWords, dwNumLines;

   switch (id) {
      case IDC_FILENAME:
         EnableWindow(GetDlgItem(hwnd, IDC_DODOCSTATS),
            Edit_GetTextLength(hwndCtl) > 0);
         break;

      case IDC_FILESELECT:
         chINITSTRUCT(ofn, TRUE);
         ofn.hwndOwner = hwnd;
         ofn.lpstrFile = szPathname;
         ofn.lpstrFile[0] = 0;
         ofn.nMaxFile = chDIMOF(szPathname);
         ofn.lpstrTitle = __TEXT("Select file for reversing");
         ofn.Flags = OFN_EXPLORER | OFN_FILEMUSTEXIST;
         GetOpenFileName(&ofn);
         SetDlgItemText(hwnd, IDC_FILENAME, ofn.lpstrFile);
         SetFocus(GetDlgItem(hwnd, IDC_DODOCSTATS));
         break;

      case IDC_DODOCSTATS:
         GetDlgItemText(hwnd, IDC_FILENAME, szPathname,
            chDIMOF(szPathname));
         if (DocStats(szPathname, &dwNumLetters, &dwNumWords,
            &dwNumLines) ) {
            SetDlgItemInt(hwnd, IDC_NUMLETTERS, dwNumLetters,
               FALSE);
            SetDlgItemInt(hwnd, IDC_NUMWORDS, dwNumWords,
               FALSE);
            SetDlgItemInt(hwnd, IDC_NUMLINES, dwNumLines,
               FALSE);
         }
         break;

      case IDCANCEL:
         EndDialog(hwnd, id);
         break;
   }
}
```

(continued)

Figure 10-6. *continued*

```
/////////////////////////////////////////////////////////////


BOOL CALLBACK Dlg_Proc (HWND hwnd, UINT uMsg,
   WPARAM wParam, LPARAM lParam) {

   switch (uMsg) {
      chHANDLE_DLGMSG(hwnd, WM_INITDIALOG, Dlg_OnInitDialog);
      chHANDLE_DLGMSG(hwnd, WM_COMMAND,  Dlg_OnCommand);
   }
   return(FALSE);
}



/////////////////////////////////////////////////////////////


int WINAPI _tWinMain (HINSTANCE hinstExe,
   HINSTANCE hinstPrev, LPTSTR pszCmdLine, int nCmdShow) {

   chWARNIFUNICODEUNDERWIN95();
   DialogBox(hinstExe, MAKEINTRESOURCE(IDD_DOCSTATS),
      NULL, Dlg_Proc);
   return(0);
}


/////////////////////// End Of File ///////////////////////
```

DOCSTATS.RC

```
//Microsoft Developer Studio generated resource script.
//
#include "Resource.h"

#define APSTUDIO_READONLY_SYMBOLS
/////////////////////////////////////////////////////////////
//
// Generated from the TEXTINCLUDE 2 resource.
//
#include "afxres.h"
```

(continued)

Figure 10-6. *continued*

```
///////////////////////////////////////////////////////////////
#undef APSTUDIO_READONLY_SYMBOLS

///////////////////////////////////////////////////////////////
// English (U.S.) resources

#if !defined(AFX_RESOURCE_DLL) || defined(AFX_TARG_ENU)
#ifdef _WIN32
LANGUAGE LANG_ENGLISH, SUBLANG_ENGLISH_US
#pragma code_page(1252)
#endif //_WIN32

///////////////////////////////////////////////////////////////
//
// Icon
//

// Icon with lowest ID value placed first to ensure application
// icon remains consistent on all systems.
IDI_DOCSTATS            ICON    DISCARDABLE     "DocStats.Ico"

#ifdef APSTUDIO_INVOKED
///////////////////////////////////////////////////////////////
//
// TEXTINCLUDE
//

1 TEXTINCLUDE DISCARDABLE
BEGIN
    "Resource.h\0"
END

2 TEXTINCLUDE DISCARDABLE
BEGIN
    "#include ""afxres.h""\r\n"
    "\0"
END

3 TEXTINCLUDE DISCARDABLE
BEGIN
    "\r\n"
    "\0"
END
```

(continued)

Figure 10-6. *continued*

```
#endif    // APSTUDIO_INVOKED


/////////////////////////////////////////////////////////////////
//
// Dialog
//

IDD_DOCSTATS DIALOG DISCARDABLE  15, 24, 200, 82
STYLE WS_MINIMIZEBOX | WS_POPUP | WS_VISIBLE | WS_CAPTION |
    WS_SYSMENU
CAPTION "Document Statistics"
FONT 8, "System"
BEGIN
    LTEXT            "&Pathname:",IDC_STATIC,4,4,35,8
    EDITTEXT         IDC_FILENAME,44,4,152,12,ES_AUTOHSCROLL
    PUSHBUTTON       "&Browse...",IDC_FILESELECT,4,20,36,12,
                     WS_GROUP
    DEFPUSHBUTTON    "&Calculate document statistics",
                     IDC_DODOCSTATS,4,44,80,28,BS_MULTILINE
    GROUPBOX         "Document statistics",IDC_STATIC,
                     88,32,108,48
    LTEXT            "Number of letters:",IDC_STATIC,92,42,58,8
    RTEXT            "0",IDC_NUMLETTERS,160,42,26,8
    LTEXT            "Number of words:",IDC_STATIC,92,54,57,8
    RTEXT            "0",IDC_NUMWORDS,160,54,26,8
    LTEXT            "Number of lines:",IDC_STATIC,92,66,55,8
    RTEXT            "0",IDC_NUMLINES,160,66,26,8
END


/////////////////////////////////////////////////////////////////
//
// DESIGNINFO
//
#ifdef APSTUDIO_INVOKED
GUIDELINES DESIGNINFO DISCARDABLE
BEGIN
    IDD_DOCSTATS, DIALOG
    BEGIN
        RIGHTMARGIN, 176
        BOTTOMMARGIN, 78
    END
END
```

(continued)

Figure 10-6. *continued*

```
#endif    // APSTUDIO_INVOKED

#endif    // English (U.S.) resources
/////////////////////////////////////////////////////////////////////////


#ifndef APSTUDIO_INVOKED
/////////////////////////////////////////////////////////////////////////
//
// Generated from the TEXTINCLUDE 3 resource.
//


/////////////////////////////////////////////////////////////////////////
#endif    // not APSTUDIO_INVOKED
```

Waitable Timers

Waitable timers are a new addition to Windows NT 4. Basically, waitable timers are kernel objects that signal themselves at a certain time and/or at regular intervals. Creating a waitable timer is simply a matter of calling *CreateWaitableTimer*:

```
HANDLE CreateWaitableTimer(LPSECURITY_ATTRIBUTES lpsa,
    BOOL bManualReset, LPCTSTR lpszTimerName);
```

The *lpsa* and *lpszTimerName* parameters indicate security attribute information and allow you to name the kernel object. If *bManualReset* is TRUE, when the timer is signaled all threads waiting on the timer wake up. If *bManualReset* is FALSE, only one waiting thread can wake up when the timer is signaled. (See the discussion of events earlier in this chapter for more on manual-reset versus auto-reset behavior.)

Windows 95 does not have any of the waitable timer functions presented in this section. If you write an application that calls these functions, you will not be able to load your application on Windows 95.

Of course, a process can obtain its own process relative handle to an existing waitable timer by calling *OpenWaitableTimer*:

```
HANDLE OpenWaitableTimer(DWORD dwDesiredAccess,
   BOOL bInheritHandle, LPCTSTR lpszTimerName);
```

Once a process has the handle to a waitable timer, the process can set the timer by calling

```
BOOL SetWaitableTimer(HANDLE hTimer,
   const LARGE_INTEGER *pDueTime, LONG lPeriod,
   PTIMERAPCROUTINE pfnCompletionRoutine,
   LPVOID lpArgToCompletionRoutine, BOOL fResume);
```

This function takes several parameters and can be quite confusing to use. Obviously, the *hTimer* parameter indicates the timer that you wish to set. The next two parameters, *pDueTime* and *lPeriod*, are used together. You use the *pDueTime* parameter to indicate when the timer should go off for the very first time, and you use the *lPeriod* parameter to indicate how frequently the timer should go off after that. The following code demonstrates how to set a timer to go off for the first time on January 1, 1999, at 1:00 P.M., and then to go off every 6 hours after that:

```
// Declare our local variables.
HANDLE hTimer;
SYSTEMTIME st;
FILETIME ftLocal, ftUTC;
LARGE_INTEGER liUTC;

// Create a timer that is automatically reset after a waiting
// thread sees that the timer is signaled (has gone off).
hTimer = CreateWaitableTimer(NULL, FALSE, NULL);

// The timer should first go off on January 1, 1999, at 1:00 P.M.
// (local time).
st.wYear         = 1999;
st.wMonth        = 1;  // January
st.wDayOfWeek    = 0;  // Ignored
st.wDay          = 1;  // The first of the month
st.wHour         = 13; // 1PM
st.wMinute       = 0;  // 0 minutes into the hour
st.wSecond       = 0;  // 0 seconds into the minute
st.wMilliseconds = 0;  // 0 milliseconds into the second

SystemTimeToFileTime(&st, &ftLocal);

// Convert local time to UTC time.
LocalFileTimeToFileTime(&ftLocal, &ftUTC);
```

(continued)

445

```
// Convert FILETIME to LARGE_INTEGER because of different alignment.
liUTC.LowPart  = ftUTC.dwLowDateTime;
liUTC.HighPart = ftUTC.dwHighDateTime;

// Set the timer.
SetWaitableTimer(hTimer, &liUTC, 6 * 60 * 60 * 1000,
   NULL, NULL, FALSE);
   .
   .
   .
```

The code above first initializes a SYSTEMTIME structure indicating when the timer should first go off (be signaled). I am setting this time in local time—the correct time for the logged-on user. *SetWaitableTimer*'s second parameter is prototyped as a const LARGE_INTEGER * and therefore cannot accept a SYSTEMTIME structure directly. However, a FILETIME structure and a LARGE_INTEGER structure have identical binary formats: both structures contain two 32-bit values. So, we can convert our SYSTEMTIME structure to a FILETIME structure. The next problem is that *SetWaitableTimer* expects the time always to be passed to it in Coordinated Universal Time (UTC) time. This conversion is easily made by calling *LocalFileTimeToFileTime*. Since FILETIME and LARGE_INTEGER structures have identical binary formats, you might be tempted to pass the address of the FILETIME structure directly to *SetWaitableTimer*:

```
// Set the timer.
SetWaitableTimer(hTimer, (PLARGE_INTEGER) &ftUTC,
   6 * 60 * 60 * 1000, NULL, NULL, FALSE);
```

In fact, this is what I originally did. However, this is a big mistake! Although it is true that FILETIME and LARGE_INTEGER structures have identical binary format, the alignment requirements of both structures are different. The address of all FILETIME structures must begin on an even 32-bit boundary, but the address of all LARGE_INTEGER structures must begin on an even 64-bit boundary. Calling *SetWaitableTimer* and passing it a FILETIME structure may or may not work correctly, depending on whether the FILETIME structure happens to be on an even 64-bit boundary. However, the compiler ensures that LARGE_INTEGER structures always begin on 64-bit boundaries, and so the proper thing to do (that is guaranteed to work all the time) is to copy the FILETIME's members into a LARGE_INTEGER's members and then pass the address of the LARGE_INTEGER to *SetWaitableTimer*.

Important

The *x*86 processors silently deal with unaligned data references. So, passing the address of a FILETIME to *SetWaitableTimer* would always work when your application is running on an *x*86 CPU. However, other processors, such as the Alpha, MIPS, and PowerPC, do not handle unaligned references as silently. In fact, most of these other processors raise an EXCEPTION_DATATYPE_MISALIGNMENT exception that causes your process to terminate. Alignment errors are the biggest cause of problems when porting code that works on *x*86 computers to other processors. Paying attention to alignment issues now can save months of porting effort later!

Now, to have the timer go off every 6 hours after January 1, 1999, at 1:00 P.M., we turn our attention to *SetWaitableTimer*'s *lPeriod* parameter. This parameter indicates, in milliseconds, how often the timer should go off after it initially goes off. For 6 hours, I pass 21,600,000 (6 hours * 60 minutes-per-hour * 60 seconds-per-minute * 1000 milliseconds-per-second).

I'll save the discussion of *SetWaitableTimer*'s last three parameters for the end of this section. For now, let's keep talking about the second and third parameters. Instead of setting an absolute time for when the timer should first go off, you also have the ability (by specifying a negative time) to give *SetWaitableTimer* a time relative to when you call the function (in nanoseconds). The following code demonstrates how to set a timer initially to go off 5 seconds after the call to *SetWaitableTimer*:

```
// Declare our local variables
HANDLE hTimer;
LARGE_INTEGER li;

// Create a timer that is automatically reset after a waiting
// thread sees that the timer is signaled (has gone off).
hTimer = CreateWaitableTimer(NULL, FALSE, NULL);

// Set the timer to go off 5 seconds after calling SetWaitableTimer.
const int nNanosecondsPerSecond = 10000000;
__int64 qwTimeFromNowInNanoseconds = 5 * nNanosecondsPerSecond;

// Negate the time so that SetWaitableTimer knows we
// want relative time instead of absolute time.
qwTimeFromNowInNanoseconds = -qwTimeFromNowInNanoseconds;
```

(continued)

```
// Copy the relative time from a quad-word (__int64) into a
// LARGE_INTEGER.
li.LowPart  = (DWORD) (qwTimeFromNowInNanoseconds & 0xFFFFFFFF);
li.HighPart = (LONG)  (qwTimeFromNowInNanoseconds >> 32);

// Passing a negative value for the second parameter tells the
// function to go off at a time relative to the time when we call
// the function.
SetWaitableTimer(hTimer, &li, 6 * 60 * 60 * 1000,
   NULL, NULL, FALSE);
   .
   .
   .
```

There may be an occasion when you do not want to use a periodic timer and simply want the timer to go off once. You can easily accomplish this by passing 0 for the *lPeriod* parameter. When you do this, the timer will become signaled at the specified absolute or relative time and will never become signaled again. At this time, you can either call *Close-Handle* to close the timer or you can call *SetWaitableTimer* again to reset the time, giving it new criteria to follow.

OK, so that you know how to set up a timer, let's now turn to *Set-WaitableTimer*'s next two parameters, *pfnCompletionRoutine* and *lpArg-ToCompletionRoutine*. Usually, you will pass NULL for both of these parameters, as I did in the two code fragments above. However, you do have the ability to have the system queue an asynchronous procedure call (APC) to the thread that calls *SetWaitableTimer* when the timer is signaled. Chapter 15 discusses APCs in detail, so I won't cover them here in this chapter.

If you want the timer to queue an APC, you must pass the address of a timer APC routine, which you must implement. The function must look like this:

```
VOID APIENTRY TimerAPCRoutine(LPVOID lpArgToCompletionRoutine,
   DWORD dwTimerLowValue, DWORD dwTimerHighValue) {

   // Do whatever you want here.
}
```

I've named the function *TimerAPCRoutine*, but you can name it anything you like. This function will be called using the same thread that called *SetWaitableTimer* when the timer goes off if and only if the calling thread is in an alertable state: in other words, the thread must be waiting in a call to *SleepEx, WaitForSingleObjectEx, WaitForMultipleObjectsEx, MsgWait-ForMultipleObjectsEx,* or *SignalObjectAndWait.* If the thread is not waiting in one of these functions, the system does not queue the timer APC routine and your thread misses the timer event. To illustrate, take a look at this code:

```
HANDLE hTimer = CreateWaitableTimer(NULL, FALSE, NULL);
SetWaitableTimer(hTimer, …, TimerAPCRoutine, …);
WaitForSingleObjectEx(hTimer, INFINITE, TRUE);
```

You should not write code like this because the call to *WaitForSingle-ObjectEx* is actually waiting on the timer twice. When the timer becomes signaled, the wait is successful and the thread wakes, which takes the thread out of the alertable state, and the APC routine will not be called. As I said earlier, you won't often have a reason to use an APC routine with waitable timers because you can always wait for the timer to be signaled and then do what you want. The only time you would want to use APC routines with timers is if your application is designed so that you *do* want to miss timer events if your thread is busy doing something else.

If your thread is in one of these functions when the timer goes off, the system makes your thread call the callback routine. The first parameter to the callback routine is the same value that you pass to *SetWaitableTimer*'s *lpArgToCompletionRoutine* parameter. This allows you to pass some data (usually a pointer to a structure that you define) to the *Timer-APCRoutine*. The remaining two parameters, *dwTimerLowValue* and *dwTimerHighValue,* indicate the time when the timer went off. The code here demonstrates how to take this information and show it to the user:

```
VOID APIENTRY TimerAPCRoutine(LPVOID lpArgToCompletionRoutine,
   DWORD dwTimerLowValue, DWORD dwTimerHighValue) {

   FILETIME ftUTC, ftLocal;
   SYSTEMTIME st;
   TCHAR szBuf[256];

   // Put the time in a FILETIME structure.
   ftUTC.dwLowDateTime  = dwTimerLowValue;
   ftUTC.dwHighDateTime = dwTimerHighValue;

   // Convert the UTC time to the user's local time.
   FileTimeToLocalFileTime(&ftUTC, &ftLocal);

   // Convert the FILETIME to the SYSTEMTIME structure
   // required by GetDateFormat and GetTimeFormat.
   FileTimeToSystemTime(&ftLocal, &st);
```

(continued)

```
    // Construct a string with the
    // date/time that the timer went off.
    GetDateFormat(LOCALE_USER_DEFAULT, DATE_LONGDATE,
       &st, NULL, szBuf, sizeof(szBuf) / sizeof(TCHAR));
    _tcscat(szBuf, __TEXT("  "));
    GetTimeFormat(LOCALE_USER_DEFAULT, 0,
       &st, NULL, _tcschr(szBuf, 0),
       sizeof(szBuf) / sizeof(TCHAR) - _tcslen(szBuf));

    // Show the time to the user.
    MessageBox(NULL, szBuf, "Timer went off at...", MB_OK);
}
```

SetWaitableTimer has just one more parameter to discuss, *fResume*. This parameter is useful for computers that support suspend and resume. Usually, you will pass FALSE for this argument, as I've done in the code fragments above. However, if you are, say, writing a Schedule+-like application in which you want to set timers that remind the user of scheduled meetings, you should pass TRUE for this argument. When the timer goes off, it will take the machine out of suspend mode (if it's in suspend mode) and wake up the threads that are waiting on the timer. A Schedule+-like application would now play a wave file and present a message box telling the user of the upcoming meeting.

Our discussion of waitable timers would not be complete unless we also talk about *CancelWaitableTimer*:

```
BOOL CancelWaitableTimer(HANDLE hTimer);
```

This function is very simple. It takes the handle of a timer and cancels it so that the timer will never go off unless there is a subsequent call to *SetWaitableTimer* to reset the timer. If you ever want to change the criteria for a timer, you do not have to call *CancelWaitableTimer* before calling *SetWaitableTimer*: as a convenience, each call to *SetWaitableTimer* cancels the criteria for the timer before setting the new criteria.

Any seasoned Windows developer will immediately want to make a comparison of waitable timers and User timers (set with the *SetTimer* function). The biggest difference is that waitable timers are implemented in the kernel. This means that waitable timers are lighter weight than User timers. It also means that waitable timers are secure objects.

User timers generate WM_TIMER messages that come back to the thread that called *SetTimer* (for callback timers) or that created the window (for window-based timers). So, only one thread is ever notified when a User timer goes off. Waitable timers, on the other hand, can be waited on by multiple threads, and several threads can wake up if the timer is a manual-reset timer.

If you are going to be performing user-interface-related events in response to a timer, it will probably be easier to structure your code using User timers. This is because using a waitable timer requires having your threads wait for messages as well as kernel objects.[4] Finally, with waitable timers, you're more likely to get notified when the time actually expires. As Chapter 11 explains, WM_TIMER messages are always the lowest-priority messages and are retrieved when no other messages are in a thread's queue. Waitable timers are not treated any differently than any other kernel object; if the timer goes off and your thread is waiting, your thread will wake up.

Thread Suspension

WaitForSingleObject and *WaitForMultipleObjects* are the functions that a thread most commonly calls to suspend itself until certain criteria are met. However, a thread can call a few other functions to suspend itself. The following sections discuss these functions briefly.

Sleep

The simplest of these functions is *Sleep*:

```
VOID Sleep(DWORD cMilliseconds);
```

This function causes the thread to suspend itself until *cMilliseconds* have elapsed. Note that *Sleep* allows a thread to voluntarily give up the remainder of its time slice. Even a call to *Sleep* passing a value of 0 causes the CPU to stop executing the current thread and assign itself to the next waiting thread. The CritSecs program discussed earlier in the chapter uses this technique.

Asynchronous File I/O

Asynchronous file I/O allows a thread to start a file-read or file-write operation without having to wait for the read or write operation to complete. For example, if an application needs to load a large file into memory, the application could tell the system to load the file into

---

4. If you want to restructure your code, the *MsgWaitForMultipleObjects* function exists for exactly this purpose.

memory. Then, as the system loads the file, the application can be busy performing other tasks—creating windows, initializing internal data structures, and so on. When the initialization is complete, the application can suspend itself, waiting for the system to notify it that the file has been read.

File objects are synchronizable kernel objects, which means that you can call *WaitForSingleObject*, passing the handle of a file. While the system is performing the asynchronous I/O, the file object is in the non-signaled state. As soon as the file operation is complete, the system changes the state of the file object to signaled so that the thread knows that the file operation has completed. At this point, the thread continues execution.

Asynchronous file I/O is discussed in more detail in Chapter 15.

WaitForInputIdle

A thread can also suspend itself by calling *WaitForInputIdle*:

```
DWORD WaitForInputIdle(HANDLE hProcess, DWORD dwTimeout);
```

This function waits until the process identified by *hProcess* has no input pending in the thread that created the application's first window. This function is useful for a parent process. The parent process spawns a child process to do some work. When the parent process's thread calls *Create-Process*, the parent's thread continues to execute while the child process is initializing. It might be that the parent's thread needs to get the handle of a window created by the child. The only way for the parent's thread to know when the child process has been fully initialized is for the parent's thread to wait until the child is no longer processing any input. So after the call to *CreateProcess*, the parent's thread would place a call to *WaitForInputIdle*.

You might also use *WaitForInputIdle* when you need to force keystrokes into an application. Let's say that you post the following messages to the main window of an application:

WM_KEYDOWN	with a virtual key of VK_MENU
WM_KEYDOWN	with a virtual key of VK_F
WM_KEYUP	with a virtual key of VK_F
WM_KEYUP	with a virtual key of VK_MENU
WM_KEYDOWN	with a virtual key of VK_O
WM_KEYUP	with a virtual key of VK_O

This sequence has the effect of sending Alt+F, O to an application, which, for most English-language applications, will select the application's File Open menu command. Selecting this command displays a dialog box; however, before the dialog box can appear, Windows must load the dialog box template from the file and cycle through all the controls in the template, calling *CreateWindow* for each one. This can take some time. So the application that posted the WM_KEY* messages can now call *WaitForInputIdle*, which causes the application to wait until the dialog box has been completely created and is ready for user input. The application can now force additional keys into the dialog box and its controls so that it can continue doing whatever it needs to do.

This particular problem was faced by many developers writing for 16-bit Windows. Applications wanted to post messages to a window but didn't know exactly when the window was created and ready. The *WaitForInputIdle* function solves this problem.

MsgWaitForMultipleObjects

A thread can call the *MsgWaitForMultipleObjects* function to cause the thread to wait for its own messages:

```
DWORD MsgWaitForMultipleObjects(DWORD dwCount, LPHANDLE lpHandles,
    BOOL bWaitAll, DWORD dwMilliseconds, DWORD dwWakeMask);
```

The *MsgWaitForMultipleObjects* function is similar to the *WaitForMultipleObjects* function, with the addition of the *dwWakeMask* parameter. This parameter can be used by an application to determine whether it should awaken to process certain types of messages. For example, if a thread wants to suspend itself until a keyboard or mouse message is in the queue, the application can make the following call:

```
MsgWaitForMultipleObjects(0, NULL, TRUE, INFINITE,
    QS_KEY | QS_MOUSE);
```

This statement says that we're not passing any handles of synchronization objects, as indicated by passing 0 and NULL for the *dwCount* and *lpHandles* parameters. We're telling the function to wait for all objects to be signaled. But because we're specifying only one object to wait on, the *fWaitAll* parameter could have easily been FALSE without altering the effect of this call. We are also telling the system that we want to wait however long it takes until either a keyboard message or a mouse message is available in the thread's input queue.

The legal domain of possible values that can be specified in the last parameter is the same as the values that can be passed to the *GetQueueStatus* function, which is discussed in Chapter 11. The *MsgWaitForMultipleObjects* function can be useful if your program is waiting for a particular object to become signaled and you want to allow the user to interrupt the wait. If your program is waiting for the object to become signaled and the user presses a key, the thread is awakened and the *MsgWaitForMultipleObjects* function returns. Normally, when the *WaitForMultipleObjects* function returns, it returns the index of the object that became signaled to satisfy the call (WAIT_OBJECT_0 to WAIT_OBJECT_0+*dwCount*−1). Adding the *dwWakeMask* parameter is like adding another handle to the call. If *MsgWaitForMultipleObjects* is satisfied because of the wake mask, the return value will be WAIT_OBJECT_0+*dwCount*. The FileChng application in Chapter 14 demonstrates how to use this function.

WaitForDebugEvent

The Win32-based operating systems offer excellent debugging support. When a debugger starts executing, it attaches itself to a debugee. The debugger simply sits idle waiting for the operating system to notify it of debug events related to the debugee. A debugger waits for these events by calling:

```
BOOL WaitForDebugEvent(LPDEBUG_EVENT lpde, DWORD dwTimeout);
```

When a debugger calls *WaitForDebugEvent*, the debugger's thread is suspended. The system will notify the debugger that a debug event has occurred by allowing the call to *WaitForDebugEvent* to return. The structure pointed to by the *lpde* parameter is filled by the system before it awakens the thread. This structure contains information regarding the debug event that has just occurred.

SignalObjectAndWait

Windows NT 4 adds a new function that signals a kernel object and waits on another kernel object in a single atomic operation:

```
BOOL SignalObjectAndWait(HANDLE hObjectToSignal,
    HANDLE hObjectToWaitOn, DWORD dwMilliseconds, BOOL bAlertable);
```

When you call this function, the *hObjectToSignal* parameter must identify a mutex, semaphore, or an event; any other type of object causes the function to return WAIT_FAILED, and *GetLastError* returns 6 (ERROR_INVALID_HANDLE). Internally, the function examines the type of object and performs the equivalent of *ReleaseMutex, Release-Semaphore* (with a count of 1), or *ResetEvent.*

Windows 95 does not have any implementation for the *SignalObject-AndWait* function. If you write an application that calls this function, you will not be able to load your application on Windows 95.

The *hObjectToWaitOn* parameter can identify any of the following kernel objects: mutex, semaphore, event, timer, process, thread, file change notification (discussed in Chapter 14), or console input. As usual, the *dwMilliseconds* parameter indicates how long the function should wait for this object to become signaled, and the *bAlertable* flag indicates whether the thread should be able to process any queued asynchronous procedure calls while the thread is waiting. (Alterable I/O and APCs are discussed in Chapter 15.)

The documentation for this function indicates that it returns a BOOL, but in reality, the function returns one of the following values: WAIT_OBJECT_0, WAIT_TIMEOUT, WAIT_FAILED, WAIT_ABAN-DONED, or WAIT_IO_COMPLETION.

This function is a welcome addition to the Win32 API for two reasons. First, because signaling one object and waiting on another is a fairly common task to perform, having a single function that does both operations saves some processing time. Each time you call a function that causes your thread to jump from user-mode to kernel-mode code, approximately 600 CPU instructions need to execute (on *x*86 platforms), so code such as

```
ReleaseMutex(hMutex);
WaitForSingleObject(hEvent, INFINITE);
```

causes about 1200 CPU instructions to execute. In high-performance server applications, *SignalObjectAndWait* saves a lot of processing time.

Second, without the *SignalObjectAndWait* function, there is no way for one thread to know when another thread is in a wait state. This knowledge is useful for functions such as *PulseEvent.* As mentioned earlier in this chapter, *PulseEvent* signals an event and immediately resets it. If no threads are currently waiting on the event, no events catch the pulse. I've seen people write code as shown at the top of the following page.

```
// Perform some work

   .
   .
   .

SetEvent(hEventWorkerThreadDone);
WaitForSingleObject(hEventMoreWorkToBeDone, INFINITE);
// Do more work

   .
   .
   .
```

This code fragment is executed by a worker thread that is performing some work and then calls *SetEvent* to indicate (to another thread) that the work is done. The other thread has code like this:

```
WaitForSingleObject(hEventWorkerThreadDone);
PulseEvent(hEventMoreWorkToBeDone);
```

The worker thread's code fragment is poorly designed because it does not work reliably. It is possible that after the worker thread calls *SetEvent*, the other thread may wake immediately and call *PulseEvent*. The problem is that the worker thread was preempted and hasn't yet had a chance to return from its call to *SetEvent*, let alone call *WaitForSingleObject*. The result is that the signaling of the *hEventMoreWorkToBeDone* event is missed entirely by the worker thread.

If you rewrite the worker thread's code to call *SignalObjectAndWait* as here,

```
// Perform some work

   .
   .
   .

SignalObjectAndWait(hEventWorkerThreadDone,
   hEventMoreWorkToBeDone, INFINITE, FALSE);
// Do more work

   .
   .
   .
```

the code will work reliably because the signaling and wait is performed atomically. When the nonworker thread wakes up, it can be 100% sure that the worker thread is waiting on the *hEventMoreWorkToBeDone* event and is therefore guaranteed to see the event be pulsed.

The Interlocked Family of Functions

The last five functions we'll discuss are *InterlockedIncrement, InterlockedDecrement, InterlockedExchange, InterlockedExchangeAdd,* and *InterlockedCompareExchange*:

```
LONG InterlockedIncrement(PLONG plValue);

LONG InterlockedDecrement(PLONG plValue);

LONG InterlockedExchange(PLONG plTarget, LONG lValue);

LONG InterlockedExchangeAdd(PLONG plAddend, LONG lIncrement);

PVOID InterlockedCompareExchange(PVOID *Destination, PVOID Exchange,
    PVOID Comperand);
```

The sole purpose of these functions is to change the value of a long variable. These functions absolutely guarantee that the thread changing the long variable has exclusive access to this variable—no other thread will be able to change this variable at the same time. This is true even if the two threads are being executed simultaneously by two different CPUs in the same machine.

It is important to note that all the threads should attempt to modify the shared long variable by calling these functions; no thread should ever attempt to modify the shared variable by using simple C statements:

```
// The long variable shared by many threads
LONG lValue;
.
.
.

// Incorrect way to increment the long
lValue++;
.
.
.

// Correct way to increment the long
InterlockedIncrement(&lValue);
```

Normally, the way to protect the long variable from being corrupted would be to use a form of synchronization, such as mutexes. But because the manipulation of a long variable is so common and useful, Microsoft added these five functions to the Win32 API.

The calls to *InterlockedIncrement* and *InterlockedDecrement* add 1 to and subtract 1 from the long variable whose address you pass as the *plValue* parameter to the functions. These functions *do not* return the new value of the long variable. Instead, they return a value that compares the new value of the long to 0. If the result of incrementing or decrementing the long variable causes the long variable to be 0, the functions return 0. If the value of the long becomes less than 0, the functions return a value that is less than 0. And you can probably guess that if the long variable becomes greater than 0, the functions return a value that is greater than 0. The return value is almost never the actual value of the long variable. I use both of these functions in the MULTINST.C and MODUSE.C source files, which are described in Chapter 12.

The third function, *InterlockedExchange*, is used to completely replace the current value of the long whose address is passed in the *plTarget* parameter with a long value that is passed in the *lValue* parameter. Again, this function protects the long variable from any other thread that is attempting to change the variable at the same time.

Another point about using these functions: no *Interlocked* function is available for one thread to read the value of a long while another thread is attempting to change the long because the function isn't necessary. If one thread calls *InterlockedIncrement* while another thread reads the contents of the long, the value read from the long will always be valid. The thread might get the value of the long before *InterlockedIncrement* changes the variable, or the thread might get the value after *Interlocked-Increment* changes the value. The thread has no idea which value it gets, but it is guaranteed to get a valid value and not a value that is partially incremented.

The last two functions are new for Windows NT 4. These new functions take advantage of CPU instructions that exist only on the Intel 486 or better processors. Microsoft added these interlocked functions to the Win32 API because Windows NT 4 now requires a 486 or better processor; 386 machines are no longer supported. This also means that these functions do not exist on Windows 95.

The *InterlockedExchangeAdd* function is similar to the *Interlocked-Increment* and *InterlockedDecrement* functions except that you can add or subtract the long by an arbitrary amount rather than always adding or subtracting 1. To subtract a value, just pass in a negative number for the second parameter:

```
LONG lVal = 5;
LONG lOrigVal = InterlockedExchangeAdd(&lVal, -2);
// lOrigVal contains 5, lVal contains 3
```

The *InterlockedCompareExchange* function performs an atomic test and set operation. The function compares the current value of the long (pointed to by the *Destination* parameter) with the value passed in the *Comperand* parameter. If the values are the same, the *Destination* parameter is changed to the value of the *Exchange* parameter. If the *Destination* parameter doesn't match the *Comperand* parameter, the *Destination* parameter is not changed.

The following code compares the current value of the *Destination* parameter with 5 and changes the value of the *Destination* parameter to 500 if they are the same:

```
LONG lVal = 5;
LONG lOrigVal = (LONG) InterlockedCompareExchange((PVOID) &lVal,
   (PVOID) 500, (PVOID) 5);
// lOrigVal contains 5, lVal contains 500
```

Here is another example:

```
LONG lVal = 5;
LONG lOrigVal = (LONG) InterlockedCompareExchange((PVOID) &lVal,
   (PVOID) 500, (PVOID) 10);
// lOrigVal contains 5, lVal contains 5
```

Notice the cast to PVOID in the calls to *InterlockedCompareExchange*. Unfortunately, these casts are necessary to avoid compiler warnings. For some unknown reason, Microsoft chose to prototype *InterlockedCompareExchange* as taking PVOIDs instead of the normal PLONGs. You'll also notice that the return value must also be cast to a LONG.

WINDOW MESSAGES AND ASYNCHRONOUS INPUT

Microsoft had some pretty big goals in mind when it started designing the Win32 environment: virtual memory management, preemptive multitasking, and security, to name just a few. The idea behind many of these goals was to create a robust environment in which one application could not adversely affect other applications. This is an area in which the 16-bit Windows environment is significantly lacking.

Unfortunately, to offer these improvements, Microsoft was forced to change many things that 16-bit Windows programmers had become accustomed to. For example, the Win32 system processes a user's keyboard and mouse input in a completely different manner than does the 16-bit Windows environment. For many applications, these changes to the environment will require that pieces of the application be redesigned rather than simply ported to Win32. These changes are the focus of this chapter.

Multitasking

I think multitasking is the single most important feature that separates 16-bit Windows from Win32. Although 16-bit Windows can run multiple applications simultaneously, it runs the applications non-preemptively; that is, one application must tell the operating system that it's finished processing before the scheduler can assign another application execution time, which creates problems for both users and application developers.

For users, it means that control of the system is lost for an arbitrary time period decided by the application (not the user). If an application takes a long time to execute a particular task, such as formatting a floppy disk, the user can't switch away from that task and work with a word processor while the formatting continues in the background. This situation is unfortunate because users want to make the most of their time.

Developers for 16-bit Windows recognize this limitation and try to implement their applications so that they execute tasks in spurts. For example, a formatting program might format a single track on a floppy disk and then return control to 16-bit Windows. Once 16-bit Windows has control, it can respond to other tasks for the user. When the user is idle, 16-bit Windows returns control to the format program so that another track can be formatted.

Well, this method of sharing time between tasks works, but it makes implementing a program significantly more difficult. One way the formatting program can accomplish its tasks is to set a timer for itself using the *SetTimer* function. The program is then notified with WM_TIMER messages when it's time to execute another part of the process. This type of implementation involves the following problems:

- 16-bit Windows offers a limited number of timers for application use. What should the program do if a timer is not available—not allow the user to format a disk until another application using a timer is terminated?

- The program must keep track of its progress. The formatting program must save, either in global variables or in a dynamically allocated block of memory, information such as the letter of the drive it is formatting, the track that has just been formatted, and so forth.

- The program code can't include a function that formats a disk; instead, it must include a function that formats a single track of a disk. This means that the functions in the program must be broken up in a way that is not natural for a programmer to implement. You don't usually design an algorithm thinking that the processor needs to be able to jump into the middle of it. You can imagine how difficult implementation would be if your algorithm required a series of nested loops to perform its operations and the processor needed to jump into the innermost loop.

- WM_TIMER messages occur at regular intervals. So if an application sets a timer to go off every second, WM_TIMER messages are received 60 times every minute. This is true whether a user is running the application on a 25-MHz 386 or a 90-MHz Pentium. If a user has a faster machine, the program should take advantage of that.

Another favorite method 16-bit Windows developers use to help their applications behave more courteously toward other applications involves the *PeekMessage* function. When an application calls *PeekMessage*, the application tells 16-bit Windows, "I have more work to process, but I'm willing to postpone doing it if another application needs to do something."

This method makes the code easier to implement because the implementer can design the algorithms assuming that the computer won't jump into the middle of a process. This method also doesn't require any timers and doesn't have any special system resource requirements. The method does have two problems, however: the implementer must sprinkle *PeekMessage* loops throughout the code, and the application must be written to handle all kinds of asynchronous events. For example, a spreadsheet might be recalculating cell values when another application attempts to initiate a DDE conversation with it. It is incredibly difficult to test your application to verify that it performs correctly in all possible scenarios.

As it turns out, even when developers use these methods to help their applications behave in a friendlier way, their programs still don't multitask smoothly. Sometimes a user might click on another application's window, and a full second or more might go by before 16-bit Windows changes to the active application. More important, though, if an application bug causes the application never to call *PeekMessage* or return control to 16-bit Windows, the entire 16-bit Windows system effectively hangs. At this point, the user can't switch to another application, can't save on disk any work that was in progress, and, more often than not, is forced to reboot the computer. These situations are unacceptable!

The Win32 environment solves these problems (and more that I haven't even mentioned) with preemptive multitasking. By adding a preemptive multitasking capability to Windows NT and Windows 95, Microsoft has done much more than allow multiple applications to run simultaneously. The environment is much more robust because a single application can't control all the system resources.

Preemptive Time Scheduling

In 16-bit Windows, there is only one thread of execution; that is, the microprocessor travels in a linear path from functions in one application to functions in another application, frequently dipping into the operating system's code. Whenever the user moves from executing one application, or task, to another, the operating system code performs a task switch. A task switch simply means that the operating system saves the state of the CPU's registers before deactivating the current task and restores the registers for the newly activated task. Notice that I said the operating system is responsible for performing the task switch. Because the system has only one thread of execution, if any code enters an infinite loop, the thread can never access the operating system code that performs the task switch, and the system hangs.

In addition, 16-bit Windows uses the concepts of modules and tasks. A module identifies an executable file that is loaded into memory. Every time an instance of the executable file is invoked, 16-bit Windows calls this instance a task. With few exceptions, resources (that is, memory blocks or windows) created (allocated) when the task is executing become owned by the particular task. Some resources, such as icons and cursors, are actually owned by the module, which allows these resources to be shared by all of the module's tasks.

Win32 still uses the term *module* to identify an executable file loaded into memory. However, Win32 takes the concept of a task and breaks it down into two new concepts—*processes* and *threads*.

As discussed in Chapter 3, a process refers to an instance of a running program. For example, if a single instance of Notepad and two instances of Calculator are running, three processes are running in the system. And, as discussed in Chapter 4, a thread describes a path of execution within a process. When an executable file is invoked, the operating system creates both a process and a thread. For example, when the user invokes a Win32 application, the system locates the program's EXE file, creates a process and a thread for the new instance, and tells the CPU to start executing the thread beginning with the C run-time startup code, which in turn calls your *WinMain* function. When the thread terminates (returns from *WinMain*), the system destroys the thread and the process.

Every process has at least one thread; the system schedules CPU time among threads of a process, not among processes themselves. After a thread begins executing, it can create additional threads within the process. These threads execute until they are destroyed or until they terminate on their own. The number of threads that can be created is limited only by system resources.

While a thread is executing, the system can steal the CPU away from the thread and give the CPU to another thread. But the CPU cannot be interrupted while it is executing a single instruction (a CPU instruction, not a line of source code). The operating system's ability to interrupt a thread at (almost) any time and assign the CPU to a waiting thread is called *preemptive multitasking*.

The life span of a process is directly tied to the threads it owns. Threads within a process have lives of their own, too. New threads are created, existing threads are paused and restarted, and other threads are terminated. When all the threads in a process terminate, the system terminates the process, frees any resources owned by the process, and removes the process from memory.

Most objects allocated by a thread are owned by the process that also owns the thread. For example, a block of memory allocated by a thread is owned by the process, not by the thread. All of the global and static variables in an application are also owned by the process. And all GDI objects (pens, brushes, bitmaps) are owned by the process. Most User objects (icons, cursors, window classes, menus, and accelerator tables) are owned by the process that owns the thread that created them or loaded them into memory. Only two User objects—windows and hooks—are owned by a thread instead of by a process.

You need to understand ownership so that you know what can be shared. If a process has seven threads operating within it and one thread makes a call to allocate a block of memory, the block of memory can then be accessed from any of the seven threads. This access can cause several problems if all the threads attempt to read and write from the same block simultaneously. Synchronizing several threads is discussed further in Chapter 10.

Ownership is also important because the Win32 system is much better than 16-bit Windows about cleaning up after a thread or a process terminates. If a thread terminates and neglects to destroy a window that it created, the system ensures that the window is destroyed, not sitting around somewhere soaking up precious memory and system resources. For example, if a thread creates or loads a cursor into memory and then the thread is terminated, the cursor is not destroyed. This is because the cursor is owned by the process and not by the thread. When the process terminates, the system ensures that the cursor is destroyed. In 16-bit Windows, a task has the equivalent of one and only one thread. As a result, the concept of ownership is less complicated.

Thread Queues and Message Processing

Much of the work performed by Win32 applications is initiated by window messages. In the 16-bit Windows environment, there is a single thread of execution. If your application sends a message to a window created by another task, your task stops running and the code to process the message starts running. After the message is processed, the system returns to your task's code so that it can continue executing. In a multithreaded environment, things are quite different.

In Win32, the code in a window procedure must be executed by the thread that created the window, which might not be the same thread that sent the message. In order to let other threads process messages, some sort of cooperation must occur in which the calling thread notifies the receiving thread that it needs it to perform an action. Then the calling thread suspends itself until the receiving thread has completed the request. In this section, we'll take a look at the various methods threads can use to send and post window messages.

Win32 Message Queue Architecture

As I have already said, one of the main goals of Win32 is to offer a robust environment for all the applications running. To meet this goal, each thread must run in an environment in which it believes that it is the only thread running. More specifically, each thread must have message queues that are totally unaffected by other threads. In addition, each thread must have a simulated environment that allows the thread to maintain its own notion of keyboard focus, window activation, mouse capture, and so on.

Whenever a thread is created, the system also creates a THREAD-INFO structure and associates this data structure with the thread. This THREADINFO structure contains a set of member variables that are used to make the thread think that it is running in its very own environment. The THREADINFO structure is an internal (undocumented) data structure that identifies the thread's posted-message queue, send-message queue, reply-message queue, virtualized input queue, and wake flags, as well as a number of variables that are used for the thread's local input state. Figure 11-1 illustrates how THREADINFO structures are associated with three threads.

The remainder of this chapter is dedicated to discussing the THREADINFO structure's data members.

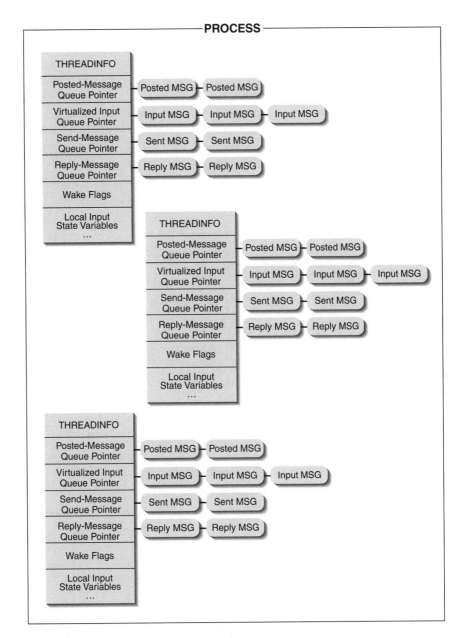

Figure 11-1.
Three threads with their respective THREADINFO structures.

Posting Messages to a Thread's Message Queue

In Win32, when a thread is first created, it is considered to be a worker thread; that is, the system tries to keep the thread lean and mean. But as soon as the thread makes its first call to a User or GDI function, it becomes a user-interface thread. User-interface threads have additional overhead associated with them, such as the THREADINFO structure. To say this another way, a thread does not have a THREADINFO structure associated with it until the thread makes its first User or GDI function call.

Once a thread has a THREADINFO structure associated with it, the thread also has its very own set of message queues. If a single process creates 10 threads and all these threads call *CreateWindow* (a User function), there will be 10 message queue sets. Messages are placed in a thread's posted-message queue by calling the *PostMessage* function:

```
BOOL PostMessage(HWND hWnd, UINT Msg, WPARAM wParam,
    LPARAM lParam);
```

When a thread calls this function, the system determines which thread created the window identified by the *hWnd* parameter and posts the specified message to the appropriate thread's posted-message queue.[1] *PostMessage* returns immediately after posting the message—the calling thread has no idea whether the posted message was processed by the specified window's window procedure. In fact, it is possible that the specified window will never receive the posted message. This could happen if the thread that created the specified window were somehow to terminate before processing all of the messages in its queue.

A message can also be placed in a thread's posted-message queue by calling *PostThreadMessage*:

```
BOOL PostThreadMessage(DWORD idThread, UINT Msg, WPARAM wParam,
    LPARAM lParam);
```

---

1. You can determine which thread created a window by calling *GetWindowThreadProcessId*:

```
DWORD GetWindowThreadProcessId(HWND hWnd, LPDWord lpdwProcessId);
```

This function returns the systemwide unique ID of the thread that created the window identified by the *hWnd* parameter. You can also get the systemwide unique ID of the process that owns this thread by passing the address of a DWORD for the *lpdwProcessId* parameter. Usually, we do not need the process ID and simply pass NULL for this parameter.

In 16-bit Windows, each task has its own message queue so that every application doesn't have to process the messages destined for other applications. By default, this message queue is large enough to hold up to eight messages. An application is able to increase or decrease the queue size by calling the *SetMessageQueue* function. This function exists in the Win32 API but is unnecessary because messages are stored in a linked list and there is no limit to the number of messages that can be placed in the list. In Win32, each thread's message queue is maintained as a doubly linked list. As messages are posted to the queue, MSG structures are linked onto the end of the linked list. When a message is pulled off the message queue, the system returns the first message in the linked list. The THREADINFO structure contains the pointer to the first message in the linked list rather than the actual message queue.

PostMessage's return value indicates whether there was enough room in the queue to post the specified message. For 16-bit Windows, *PostMessage* returns FALSE if the queue is full. For Win32, it is nearly impossible for *PostMessage* ever to return FALSE.

The desired thread is identified by the first parameter, *idThread*. When this message is placed in the queue, the *hWnd* member in the MSG structure will be set to NULL. This function is usually called when an application performs some special processing in its main message loop. The main message loop for the thread is written so that, after *GetMessage* or *PeekMessage* retrieves a message, the code checks for an *hWnd* of NULL and can examine the *msg* member of the MSG structure to perform the special processing. If the thread determines that this message is not destined for a window, *DispatchMessage* is not called, and the message loop iterates to retrieve the next message.

Like the *PostMessage* function, PostThreadMessage returns immediately after posting the message to the thread's queue. The calling thread has no idea when or if the message gets processed.

The *PostThreadMessage* function replaces the 16-bit Windows function *PostAppMessage*.

469

Sending Messages to a Window

Window messages can be sent directly to a window procedure by using the *SendMessage* function:

```
LRESULT SendMessage(HWND hWnd, UINT Msg, WPARAM wParam,
    LPARAM lParam);
```

The window procedure will process the message, and, only after the message has been processed, will return *SendMessage* to the caller. Because of its synchronous nature, *SendMessage* is used more frequently than either *PostMessage* or *PostThreadMessage* in Windows programming. The calling thread knows that the window message has been completely processed before the next line of code executes.

If the thread calling *SendMessage* is sending a message to a window created by the same thread, *SendMessage* is very simple: it just calls the specified window's window procedure as a subroutine. When the window procedure is finished processing the message, it returns a 32-bit value back to *SendMessage*. *SendMessage* returns this 32-bit value to the calling thread.

If a thread is sending a message to a window created by another thread, the internal workings of *SendMessage* are far more complicated.[2] Win32 requires that a window's message be processed by the thread that created the window. So if you call *SendMessage* to send a message to a window created by another process, and therefore to another thread, your thread cannot possibly process the window message because your thread is not running in the other process's address space and therefore does not have access to the window procedure's code and data. In fact, your thread is suspended while the other thread is processing the message. So in order to send a window message to a window created by another thread, the system must perform the actions I'll discuss next.

First, the sent message is appended to the receiving thread's send-message queue, which has the effect of setting the QS_SENDMESSAGE flag (discussed later) for that thread. Second, if the receiving thread is already executing code and isn't waiting for messages (on a call to *GetMessage*, *PeekMessage*, or *WaitMessage*), the sent message can't be processed—the system won't interrupt the thread to process the message immediately. When the receiving thread is waiting for messages, the system first checks to see whether the QS_SENDMESSAGE wake flag is set,

---

2. This is true even if the two threads are in the same process.

and if it is, the system scans the list of messages in the send-message queue to find the first sent message. It is possible that several sent messages could pile up in this queue. For example, several threads could each send a message to a single window at the same time. When this happens, the system simply appends these messages to the receiving thread's send-message queue.

When the receiving thread is waiting for messages, the system simply locates the first message in the send-message queue and calls the appropriate window procedure to process the message. If no more messages are in the send-message queue, the QS_SENDMESSAGE wake flag is turned off. While the receiving thread is processing the message, the thread that called *SendMessage* is sitting idle waiting for a message to appear in its reply-message queue. After the sent message is processed, the window procedure's return value is posted to the sending thread's reply-message queue. The sending thread will now wake up and retrieve the return value contained inside the reply message. This return value is the value that is returned from the call to *SendMessage*. At this point, the sending thread continues execution as normal.

While a thread is waiting for *SendMessage* to return, it basically sits idle. It is allowed to perform one task, however: if another thread in the system sends a message to a window created by a thread that is waiting for *SendMessage* to return, the system will process the sent message immediately. The system doesn't have to wait for the thread to call *GetMessage*, *PeekMessage*, or *WaitMessage* in this case.

Because the Win32 subsystem uses this method to handle the sending of interthread messages, it's possible that your thread could hang. For example, let's say that the thread processing the sent message has a bug and enters an infinite loop. What happens to the thread that called *SendMessage*? Will it ever be resumed? Does this mean that a bug in one application can cause another application to hang? The answer is yes!

Four functions allow you to write code defensively to protect yourself from this situation. The first function is *SendMessageTimeout*:

```
LRESULT SendMessageTimeout(HWND hwnd, UINT uMsg, WPARAM wParam,
    LPARAM lParam, UINT fuFlags, UINT uTimeout, LPDWORD lpdwResult);
```

The *SendMessageTimeout* function allows you to specify the maximum amount of time you are willing to wait for another thread to reply to your message. The first four parameters are the same parameters that you pass to *SendMessage*. For the *fuFlags* parameter, you can pass

SMTO_NORMAL, SMTO_ABORTIFHUNG, SMTO_BLOCK, or a combination of SMTO_ABORTIFHUNG and SMTO_BLOCK.

The SMTO_ABORTIFHUNG flag tells *SendMessageTimeout* to check whether the receiving thread is in a hung state[3] and, if so, to return immediately. The SMTO_BLOCK flag causes the calling thread not to process any other sent messages until *SendMessageTimeout* returns. The SMTO_NORMAL flag is defined as 0 in WINUSER.H; this is the flag to use if you don't specify either of the other two.

Earlier in this section I said that a thread can be interrupted while waiting for a sent message to return so that it can process another sent message. Using the SMTO_BLOCK flag stops the system from allowing this interruption. You should use this flag only if your thread could not process a sent message while waiting for its sent message to be processed. Using SMTO_BLOCK could create a deadlock situation until the timeout expires—for example, if you send a message to another thread and that thread needs to send a message to your thread. In this case, neither thread can continue processing and both threads effectively hang.

The *uTimeout* parameter specifies the number of milliseconds you are willing to wait for the reply message. If the function is successful, TRUE is returned and the result of the message is copied into the buffer whose address you specify in the *lpdwResult* parameter.

By the way, this function is prototyped incorrectly in the header file of WINUSER.H. The function should be prototyped simply as returning a BOOL since the LRESULT is actually returned via a parameter to the function. This actually raises some problems because *SendMessageTimeout* will return FALSE if you pass an invalid window handle or if it times out. The only way to know for sure why the function failed is by calling *GetLastError*. However, *GetLastError* will be 0 (ERROR_SUCCESS) if the function fails because of a timeout. If you pass an invalid handle, *GetLastError* will be 1400 (ERROR_INVALID_WINDOW_HANDLE).

If you call *SendMessageTimeout* to send a message to a window created by the calling thread, the system simply calls the window procedure and places the return value in *lpdwResult*. Because all processing must take place with one thread, the code following the call to *SendMessageTimeout* cannot start executing until after the message has been processed.

---

3. The operating system considers a thread to be hung if the thread stops processing messages for more than 5 seconds.

The second function that can help in sending interthread messages is

```
BOOL SendMessageCallback(HWND hwnd, UINT uMsg, WPARAM wParam,
    LPARAM lParam, SENDASYNCPROC lpResultCallBack, DWORD dwData);
```

Again, the first four parameters are the same as those used by the *Send-Message* function. When a thread calls *SendMessageCallback*, the function sends the message off to the receiving thread's send-message queue and immediately returns so that your thread can continue processing. When the receiving thread has finished processing the message, a message is posted to the sending thread's reply-message queue. Later, the system notifies your thread of the reply by calling a function that you write using the following prototype:

```
VOID CALLBACK ResultCallBack(HWND hwnd, UINT uMsg, DWORD dwData,
    LRESULT lResult);
```

You must pass the address to this function as the *lpResultCallBack* parameter of *SendMessageCallback*. When this function is called, it is passed the handle of the window that finished processing the message and the message value in the first two parameters. The third parameter, *dwData*, will always be the value that you passed in the *dwData* parameter to *SendMessageCallback*. The system simply takes whatever you specify here and passes it directly to your *ResultCallBack* function. The last parameter passed to your *ResultCallBack* function is the result from the window procedure that processed the message.

Because *SendMessageCallback* returns immediately when performing an interthread send, the callback function is not called as soon as the receiving thread finishes processing the message. Instead, the receiving thread posts a message to the sending thread's reply-message queue. The next time the sending thread calls *GetMessage*, *PeekMessage*, *WaitMessage*, or one of the *SendMessage** functions, the message is pulled from the reply-message queue and your *ResultCallBack* function is executed.

The *SendMessageCallback* function has another use. Win32 offers a method by which you can broadcast a message to all the existing overlapped windows in the system by calling *SendMessage* and passing HWND_BROADCAST (defined as −1) as the *hwnd* parameter. Use this method only to broadcast a message whose return value you aren't interested in, because the function can return only a single LRESULT. But by using the *SendMessageCallback* function, you can broadcast a message to every overlapped window and see the result of each. Your *ResultCallBack* function will be called with the result of every window processing the message.

If you call *SendMessageCallback* to send a message to a window created by the calling thread, the system immediately calls the window procedure, and then, after the message is processed, the system calls the *ResultCallBack* function. After the *ResultCallBack* function returns, execution begins at the line following the call to *SendMessageCallback*.

The third function that can help in sending interthread messages is

```
BOOL SendNotifyMessage(HWND hwnd, UINT Msg, WPARAM wParam,
    LPARAM lParam);
```

SendNotifyMessage places a message in the send-message queue of the receiving threads and returns to the calling thread immediately. This should sound familiar because it is exactly what the *PostMessage* function does. However, *SendNotifyMessage* differs from *PostMessage* in two ways.

First, if *SendNotifyMessage* sends a message to a window created by another thread, the sent message has higher priority than posted messages placed in the receiving thread's queue. In other words, messages that the *SendNotifyMessage* function places in a queue are always retrieved before messages that the *PostMessage* function posts to a queue.

Second, when you are sending a message to a window created by the calling thread, *SendNotifyMessage* works exactly like the *SendMessage* function: *SendNotifyMessage* doesn't return until the message has been processed.

As it turns out, most messages sent to a window are used for notification purposes; that is, the message is sent because the window needs to be aware that a state change has occurred so that it can perform some processing before you carry on with your work. For example, WM-_ACTIVATE, WM_DESTROY, WM_ENABLE, WM_SIZE, WM_SET-FOCUS, and WM_MOVE, just to name a few, are all notifications that are sent to a window by the system instead of being posted. However, these messages are notifications to the window; the system doesn't have to stop running so that the window procedure can process these messages. In contrast, when the system sends a WM_CREATE message to a window, the system must wait until the window has finished processing the message. If the return value is −1, the window is not created.

The fourth function that can help in sending interthread messages is

```
BOOL ReplyMessage(LRESULT lResult);
```

This function is different from the three functions we just discussed. Whereas the three *Send∗* functions are used by the thread sending a message to protect itself from hanging, *ReplyMessage* is called by the thread receiving the window message. When a thread calls *ReplyMessage*, it is telling the system that it has completed enough work to know the result of the message and that the result should be packaged up and posted to the sending thread's reply-message queue. This allows the sending thread to wake up, get the result, and continue executing.

The thread calling *ReplyMessage* specifies the result of processing the message in the *lResult* parameter. After *ReplyMessage* is called, the thread that sent the message resumes, and the thread processing the message continues to process the message. Neither thread is suspended, and both can continue executing normally. When the thread processing the message returns from its window procedure, any value that it returns is simply ignored.

The problem with *ReplyMessage* is that it has to be called from within the window procedure that is receiving the message and not by the thread that called one of the *Send∗* functions. So you are better off writing defensive code by replacing your calls to *SendMessage* with one of the three new *Send∗* functions instead of relying on the implementer of a window procedure to make calls to *ReplyMessage*.

You should also be aware that *ReplyMessage* does nothing if you call it while processing a message sent from the same thread. In fact, this is what *ReplyMessage*'s return value indicates. *ReplyMessage* returns TRUE if you call it while you are processing an interthread send and FALSE if you are processing an intrathread send.

At times, you may want to know if you are processing an interthread or an intrathread sent message. You can find this out by calling *InSendMessage*:

```
BOOL InSendMessage(VOID);
```

The name of this function does not accurately explain what it does. At first glance, you would think that this function returns TRUE if the thread is processing a sent message and FALSE if it's processing a posted message. This is not what the function does, however. The function returns TRUE if the thread is processing an interthread sent message and FALSE if it is processing an intrathread sent or posted message. The return values of *InSendMessage* and *ReplyMessage* are identical.

Waking a Thread

When a thread calls *GetMessage* or *WaitMessage* and there are no messages for the thread or windows created by the thread, the system can suspend the thread so that it is not scheduled any CPU time. However, when a message is posted or sent to the thread, the system sets a wake flag indicating that the thread should now be scheduled CPU time in order to process the message. Under normal circumstances, the user is not typing or moving the mouse and no messages are being sent to any of the windows. This means that most of the threads in the system are not being scheduled any CPU time.

When a thread is running, it can query the status of its queues by calling the *GetQueueStatus* function, shown here:

```
DWORD GetQueueStatus(UINT fuFlags);
```

The *fuFlags* parameter is a flag or a series of flags ORed together that allows you to test for specific wake bits. The following table shows the possible flag values and their meanings:

Flag	Message in the Queue
QS_KEY	WM_KEYUP, WM_KEYDOWN, WM_SYSKEYUP, or WM_SYSKEYDOWN
QS_MOUSE	Same as QS_MOUSEMOVE | QS_MOUSEBUTTON
QS_MOUSEMOVE	WM_MOUSEMOVE
QS_MOUSEBUTTON	WM_?BUTTON*[1]
QS_PAINT	WM_PAINT
QS_POSTMESSAGE	Posted message (other than from a hardware input event)
QS_SENDMESSAGE	Message sent by another thread (this includes reply messages, too)
QS_TIMER	WM_TIMER
QS_HOTKEY	WM_HOTKEY
QS_INPUT	Same as QS_MOUSE | QS_KEY
QS_ALLEVENTS	Same as QS_INPUT | QS_POSTMESSAGE | QS_TIMER | QS_PAINT | QS_HOTKEY[2]
QS_ALLINPUT	Same as QS_ALLEVENTS | QS_SENDMESSAGE

1. Where ? is L, M, or R, and * is DOWN, UP, or DBLCLK.

2. The QS_SENDMESSAGE flag is not ORed into the QS_ALLEVENTS flag because it's reserved for internal use by the system.

When you call the *GetQueueStatus* function, the *fuFlags* parameter tells *GetQueueStatus* the types of messages to check for in the queues. The fewer the number of QS_* identifiers you OR together, the faster the call executes. Then, when *GetQueueStatus* returns, the types of messages currently in the thread's queues can be found in the high-word of the return value. This returned set of flags will always be a subset of what you asked for. For example, if you make the call

```
BOOL fPaintMsgWaiting = HIWORD(GetQueueStatus(QS_TIMER)) & QS_PAINT;
```

the value of *fPaintMsgWaiting* will always be FALSE whether or not a WM_PAINT message is waiting in the queue, because QS_PAINT was not specified as a flag in the parameter passed to *GetQueueStatus*.

The low-word of *GetQueueStatus*'s return value indicates the types of messages that have been added to the queue and that haven't been processed since the last call to *GetQueueStatus*, *GetMessage*, or *PeekMessage*.

Not all the wake flags are treated equally by the system. For the QS_MOUSEMOVE flag, as long as an unprocessed WM_MOUSEMOVE message exists in the queue, the flag is turned on. When *GetMessage* or *PeekMessage* (with PM_REMOVE) pulls the last WM_MOUSEMOVE message from the queue, the flag is turned off until a new WM_MOUSE-MOVE message is placed in the input queue. The QS_KEY, QS_MOUSE-BUTTON, and QS_HOTKEY flags work in the same way for their respective messages.

The QS_PAINT flag is handled differently. If a window created by the thread has an invalid region, the QS_PAINT flag is turned on. When the area occupied by all windows created by this thread becomes validated (usually by a call to *ValidateRect*, *ValidateRegion*, or *BeginPaint*), the QS_PAINT flag is turned off. This flag is turned off only when all windows created by the thread are validated. Calling *GetMessage* or *Peek-Message* has no effect on this wake flag.

The QS_POSTMESSAGE flag is set whenever at least one message is in the thread's posted-message queue. This doesn't include hardware event messages that are in the thread's virtualized input queue. When all the messages in the thread's posted-message queue have been processed and the queue is empty, this flag is reset.

The QS_TIMER flag is set whenever a timer (created by the thread) goes off. After the WM_TIMER event is returned by *GetMessage* or *Peek-Message*, the QS_TIMER flag is reset until the timer goes off again.

The QS_SENDMESSAGE flag indicates that a message is in either the thread's send-message or reply-message queue. This flag is used by the system internally to identify and process messages being sent from one thread to another. It is not used for messages that a thread sends to itself. Although you can use the QS_SENDMESSAGE flag, it's very rare that you'd need to. I've never seen an application use this flag.

There is another queue status flag that is not documented—QS_QUIT. When a thread calls *PostQuitMessage*, the QS_QUIT flag is turned on. The system does not actually append a WM_QUIT message to the thread's message queue. The *GetQueueStatus* function does not return the state of this flag.

When a thread calls *GetMessage* or *PeekMessage*, the system must examine the state of the thread's queues and determine which message should be processed. Figure 11-2 and the following list illustrate the steps that the system performs when determining which message the thread should process next.

1. If the QS_SENDMESSAGE flag is turned on, the system sends the message to the proper window procedure. Both the *GetMessage* and *PeekMessage* functions handle this processing internally and do not return to the thread after the window procedure has processed the message; instead, these functions sit and wait for another message to process.

2. If messages are in the thread's posted-message queue, *GetMessage* and *PeekMessage* fill the MSG structure passed to these functions, and then the functions return. The thread's message loop usually calls *DispatchMessage* at this point to have the message processed by the appropriate window procedure.

3. If the QS_QUIT flag is turned on, *GetMessage* and *PeekMessage* return a WM_QUIT message and reset the QS_QUIT flag.

4. If messages are in the thread's virtualized input queue, *GetMessage* and *PeekMessage* return the hardware input message.

5. If the QS_PAINT flag is turned on, *GetMessage* and *PeekMessage* return a WM_PAINT message for the proper window.

6. If the QS_TIMER flag is turned on, *GetMessage* and *PeekMessage* return a WM_TIMER message.

Although you might find it hard to believe, there's a reason for this madness. The big assumption that Microsoft made when designing this algorithm was that applications should be user-driven and that the user

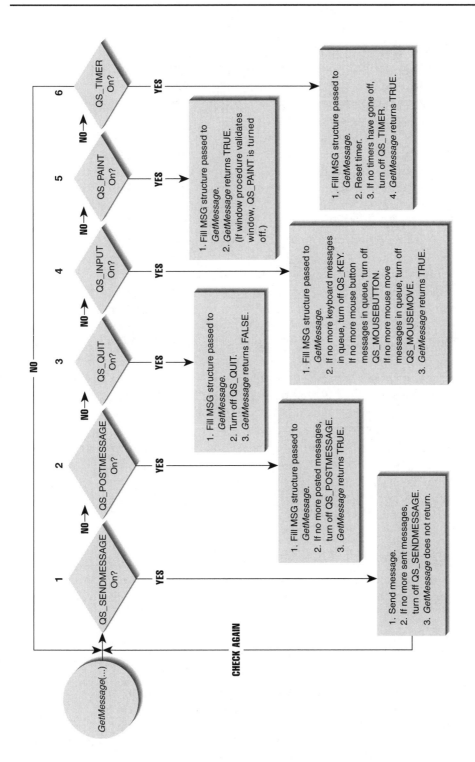

Figure 11-2.
How messages are retrieved for a thread.

drives the applications by creating hardware input events (keyboard and mouse operations). While using an application, the user might press a mouse button, which causes a sequence of events to occur. An application makes each of the individual events occur by posting messages to the thread's message queue.

So if you press the mouse button, the window that processes the WM_LBUTTONDOWN message might post three messages to different windows. Because it is the hardware event that sparks these three software events, the system processes the software events before retrieving the user's next hardware event. This explains why the posted-message queue is checked before the virtualized input queue.

An excellent example of this sequence of events is a call to the *TranslateMessage* function. This function checks whether a WM_KEY-DOWN or a WM_SYSKEYDOWN message was retrieved from the input queue. If one of these messages was retrieved, the system checks whether the virtual key information can be converted to a character equivalent. If the virtual key information can be converted, *TranslateMessage* calls *PostMessage* to place a WM_CHAR message or a WM_SYSCHAR message in the posted-message queue. The next time *GetMessage* is called, the system first checks the contents of the posted-message queue and, if a message exists there, pulls the message from the queue and returns it. The returned message will be the WM_CHAR message or the WM_SYSCHAR message. The next time *GetMessage* is called, the system checks the posted-message queue and finds it empty. The system then checks the input queue, where it finds the WM_(SYS)KEYUP message. *GetMessage* returns this message.

Because the system works this way, the following sequence of hardware events,

```
WM_KEYDOWN
WM_KEYUP
```

generates the following sequence of messages to your window procedure (assuming that the virtual key information can be converted to a character equivalent):

```
WM_KEYDOWN
WM_CHAR
WM_KEYUP
```

Now let's get back to discussing how the system decides what messages to return from *GetMessage* and *PeekMessage*. After the system checks the posted-message queue but before it checks the virtualized input queue, it checks the QS_QUIT flag. Remember that the QS_QUIT flag is set when the thread calls *PostQuitMessage*. Calling *PostQuitMessage* is similar (but not identical) to calling *PostMessage*, which places the message at the end of the message queue and causes the message to be processed before the input queue is checked. So why does *PostQuitMessage* set a flag instead of placing a WM_QUIT message in the message queue? There are two reasons.

First, in 16-bit Windows a queue can hold up to only eight messages. If the queue is full and the application attempts to post a WM_QUIT message to the queue, the WM_QUIT message gets lost and the application never terminates. Because the WM_QUIT message is handled as a special flag, the message never gets lost. Of course, in Win32 this reason is no longer valid because Win32 queues are linked lists that grow dynamically. The second reason for handling the QS_QUIT flag this way is to let the application finish processing all the other posted messages before the system terminates the application. So if you have the code fragment

```
case WM_CLOSE:
   PostQuitMessage(0);
   PostMessage(hwnd, WM_USER, 0, 0);
     .
     .
     .
```

the WM_USER message will be retrieved from the queue before a WM_QUIT message, even though the WM_USER message is posted to the queue after *PostQuitMessage* is called.

The last two messages are WM_PAINT and WM_TIMER. A WM_PAINT message has low priority because painting the screen is a slow process. If a WM_PAINT message were sent every time a window became invalid, the system would be too slow to use. By placing WM_PAINT messages after keyboard input, the system runs much faster. For example, you can select a menu item that invokes a dialog box, choose an item from the box, and press Enter all before the dialog box even appears on the screen. If you type fast enough, your keystroke messages will always be pulled from the queue before any WM_PAINT messages. When you press Enter to accept the dialog box options, the dialog box window is destroyed and the system resets the QS_PAINT flag.

The last message, WM_TIMER, has an even lower priority than a WM_PAINT message. To understand why, think about the Clock application that ships with the system. Clock updates its display every time it receives a WM_TIMER message. Imagine that WM_TIMER messages are returned before WM_PAINT messages and that Clock sets a timer of such short duration that it goes off continuously, never allowing a WM_PAINT message to be returned from *GetMessage*. In this case, Clock would never paint itself—it would just keep updating its internal time but would never get a WM_PAINT message.

Important

Remember that the *GetMessage* and *PeekMessage* functions check only the wake flags and message queues of the calling thread. This means that threads can never retrieve messages from a queue that is attached to another thread, including messages for threads that are part of the same process.

Sending Data with Messages

I have already explained that Win32 does not allow two applications to share a memory block by passing the handle of the memory block from one process to another. I have also said that you cannot share the block by passing the address to the data's location from one process to another. Both of these methods for sharing data work in 16-bit Windows but fail under Win32 for the same reason: each process has its own address space.

If you want to share memory between applications, I recommend using memory-mapped files, as explained in Chapter 8. However, let's look at a situation in which one process prepares a block of data for sharing with other applications. After the data is prepared, the creating process needs to signal the other applications that the data is ready. The creating process can accomplish this in several ways. One way is to use event objects as discussed in Chapter 10. Another way is to send a window message to a window in the other process. In this section, we'll examine how the system transfers data between processes using window messages.

Some window messages specify the address of a block of memory in their *lParam* parameter. For example, the WM_SETTEXT message uses the *lParam* parameter as a pointer to a zero-terminated string that identifies the new text for the window. Consider the following call:

```
SendMessage(FindWindow(NULL, "Calculator"), WM_SETTEXT,
    0, (LPARAM) "A Test Caption");
```

This call seems harmless enough—it determines the window handle of the Calculator application's window and attempts to change its caption to *A Test Caption*. But let's take a closer look at what happens here.

The string of the new title is contained in your process's address space. So the address of this string in your process space will be passed as the *lParam* parameter. When the window procedure for Calculator's window receives this message, it looks at the *lParam* parameter and attempts to manipulate what it thinks is a zero-terminated string in order to make it the new title.

But the address in *lParam* points to a string in your process's address space—not in Calculator's address space. This is a big problem because a memory access violation is sure to occur. But if you execute the line above, you'll see that it works successfully. How can this be?

The answer is that the system looks specifically for the WM_SETTEXT message and handles it differently from the way it handles most other messages. When you call *SendMessage*, the code in the function checks whether you are trying to send a WM_SETTEXT message. If you are, it packs the zero-terminated string from your address space into a block of memory that it is going to share with the other process. Then it sends the message to the thread in the other process. When the receiving thread is ready to process the WM_SETTEXT message, it determines the location, in its own address space, of the shared block of memory that contains a copy of the new window text. The *lParam* parameter is initialized to point to this address, and the WM_SETTEXT message is dispatched to the appropriate window procedure. Boy, doesn't this seem like a lot of work?

Fortunately, most messages don't require this type of processing, which takes place only when an application sends interprocess messages. Special processing like this has to be performed for any message whose *wParam* or *lParam* parameters represent a pointer to a data structure.

Let's look at another case that requires special handling by the system—the WM_GETTEXT message. Suppose your application contains the following code:

```
char szBuf[200];
SendMessage(FindWindow(NULL, "Calculator"), WM_GETTEXT,
   sizeof(szBuf), (LPARAM) szBuf);
```

The WM_GETTEXT message requests that Calculator's window procedure fill the buffer pointed to by *szBuf* with the title of its window. When you send this message to a window in another process, the system must actually send two messages. First the system sends a WM_GETTEXTLENGTH message to the window. The window procedure responds by returning the number of characters required to hold the window's title.

The system can use this count to allocate a block of memory that will end up being shared between the two processes.

Once the memory block has been allocated, the system can send the WM_GETTEXT message to fill the memory block. Then the system switches back to the process that called *SendMessage* in the first place, copies the data from the shared memory block into the buffer pointed to by *szBuf*, and returns from the call to *SendMessage*.

Well, all this is fine and good if you are sending messages that the system is aware of. But what if you create your own (WM_USER + x) message that you want to send from one process to a window in another? The system will not know that you want it to allocate a shared block of memory and to update pointers when sending. If you want to do this, you can use the new WM_COPYDATA message:

```
COPYDATASTRUCT cds;
SendMessage(hwndReceiver, WM_COPYDATA,
    (WPARAM) hwndSender, (LPARAM) &cds);
```

COPYDATASTRUCT is a structure defined in WINUSER.H, and it looks like this:

```
typedef struct tagCOPYDATASTRUCT {
    DWORD dwData;
    DWORD cbData;
    PVOID lpData;
} COPYDATASTRUCT;
```

When you're ready to send some data to a window in another process, you must first initialize the COPYDATASTRUCT structure. The *dwData* member is reserved for your own use. You can place any 32-bit value in it. For example, you might have occasion to send different types or categories of data to the other process. You can use this value to indicate the content of the data you are sending.

The *cbData* member specifies the number of bytes that you want to transfer to the other process, and the *lpData* member points to the first byte of the data. The address pointed to by *lpData* is, of course, in the sender's address space.

When *SendMessage* sees that you are sending a WM_COPYDATA message, it allocates a block of memory *cbData* bytes in size and copies the data from your address space to this block. It then sends the message to the destination window. When the receiving window procedure processes this message, the *lParam* parameter points to a COPYDATA-STRUCT that exists in the address space of the receiving process. The *lpData* member of this structure points to the copied block of memory, and the address has been changed to reflect where the memory exists in the receiving process's address space.

You should remember three important things about the WM-_COPYDATA message. First, always send this message; never post it. You can't post a WM_COPYDATA message because the system must free the copied memory after the receiving window procedure has processed the message. If you post the message, the system doesn't know when the WM_COPYDATA message is processed and therefore can't free the copied block of memory.

Second, it takes some time for the system to make a copy of the data in the other process's address space. This means that you shouldn't have another thread that modifies the contents of the memory block running in the sending application until the call to *SendMessage* returns.

Third, the WM_COPYDATA message works for sending data from a Win32 process to a 16-bit Windows application and vice versa. This is probably the best way to communicate across the 16-bit to 32-bit boundary.

The CopyData Sample Application

The CopyData application (COPYDATA.EXE), listed in Figure 11-3 beginning on page 487, demonstrates how to use the WM_COPYDATA message to send a block of data from one application to another. The source code and resource files for the application are in the COPYDATA directory on the companion disc. You'll need to have at least two copies of CopyData running to see it work. Each time you start a copy of CopyData, it presents a dialog box that looks like this:

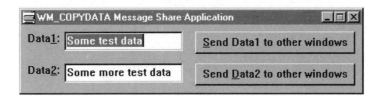

To see data copied from one application to another, first change the text in the Data1 and Data2 edit controls. Then click on one of the two Send Data* To Other Windows buttons, and the program sends the data to all the running instances of CopyData. Each instance updates the contents of its own edit box to reflect the new data.

The list on the next page describes how CopyData works. When a user clicks on one of the two buttons, CopyData performs the actions described.

1. Initializes the *dwData* member of COPYDATASTRUCT with 0 if the user clicked on the Send Data1 To Other Windows button or with 1 if the user clicked on the Send Data2 To Other Windows button.

2. Retrieves the length of the text string (in characters) from the appropriate edit box and adds 1 for a zero-terminating character. This value is converted from a number of characters to a number of bytes by multiplying by sizeof(TCHAR), and the result is then placed in the *cbData* member of COPYDATA-STRUCT.

3. Calls *HeapAlloc* to allocate a block of memory large enough to hold the length of the string in the edit box plus its zero-terminating character. The address of this block is stored in the *lpData* member of COPYDATASTRUCT.

4. Copies the text from the edit box into this memory block.

At this point, everything is ready to be sent to the other windows. To determine which windows to send the WM_COPYDATA message to, CopyData does the following:

1. Gets the handle of the first window that is a sibling to the instance of CopyData the user is running.

2. Gets the text of CopyData's title bar.

3. Cycles through all the sibling windows, comparing each window's title bar to CopyData's title bar. If the titles match, the WM_COPYDATA message is sent to the sibling window. Because I didn't do any special checks in this loop, the instance of CopyData that is calling *SendMessage* will send itself a WM-_COPYDATA message. This demonstrates that WM_COPY-DATA messages can be sent and received from the same thread.

4. After all the windows have been checked, CopyData calls *Heap-Free* to free the memory block that it was using to hold the edit box text.

And that's all there is to sending data from one application to another using messages.

CopyData.ico

COPYDATA.C

```
/*******************************************************************
Module name: CopyData.C
Notices: Copyright (c) 1995-1997 Jeffrey Richter
*******************************************************************/


#include "..\CmnHdr.H"                          /* See Appendix C. */
#include <windows.h>
#include <windowsx.h>
#include <tchar.h>
#include "Resource.H"


///////////////////////////////////////////////////////////////////


// Microsoft does not include message cracker macros for
// the WM_COPYDATA message in WINDOWSX.H.
// I have written them here....

/* BOOL Cls_OnCopyData(HWND hwnd, HWND hwndFrom,
      PCOPYDATASTRUCT cds) */

#define HANDLE_WM_COPYDATA(hwnd, wParam, lParam, fn) \
    ((fn)((hwnd), (HWND)(wParam), \
    (PCOPYDATASTRUCT)lParam), 0L)

#define FORWARD_WM_COPYDATA(hwnd, hwndFrom, cds, fn) \
    (BOOL)(UINT)(DWORD)(fn)((hwnd), WM_COPYDATA, \
    (WPARAM)(hwndFrom), (LPARAM)(cds))


///////////////////////////////////////////////////////////////////


BOOL Dlg_OnCopyData(HWND hwnd, HWND hwndFrom,
    PCOPYDATASTRUCT cds) {

    Edit_SetText(
      GetDlgItem(hwnd, cds->dwData ? IDC_DATA2 : IDC_DATA1),
      cds->lpData);
    return(TRUE);
}
```

Figure 11-3.   *(continued)*
The CopyData application.

Figure 11-3. *continued*

```
//////////////////////////////////////////////////////////////

BOOL Dlg_OnInitDialog (HWND hwnd, HWND hwndFocus,
   LPARAM lParam) {

   // Associate an icon with the dialog box.
   chSETDLGICONS(hwnd, IDI_COPYDATA, IDI_COPYDATA);

   // Initialize the edit control with some test data.
   Edit_SetText(GetDlgItem(hwnd, IDC_DATA1),
      __TEXT("Some test data"));
   Edit_SetText(GetDlgItem(hwnd, IDC_DATA2),
      __TEXT("Some more test data"));

   return(TRUE);
}


//////////////////////////////////////////////////////////////

void Dlg_OnCommand (HWND hwnd, int id, HWND hwndCtl,
   UINT codeNotify) {

   HWND hwndEdit, hwndSibling;
   COPYDATASTRUCT cds;
   TCHAR szCaption[100], szCaptionSibling[100];

   switch (id) {
      case IDC_COPYDATA1:
      case IDC_COPYDATA2:
         if (codeNotify != BN_CLICKED)
            break;

         hwndEdit = GetDlgItem(hwnd,
            (id == IDC_COPYDATA1) ? IDC_DATA1 : IDC_DATA2);

         // Prepare the contents of the COPYDATASTRUCT.
         // 0 = ID_DATA1, 1 = ID_DATA2
         cds.dwData = (DWORD) ((id == IDC_COPYDATA1) ? 0 : 1);
```

(continued)

Figure 11-3. *continued*

```
// Get the length of the data block
// that we are sending.
cds.cbData = (Edit_GetTextLength(hwndEdit) + 1) *
    sizeof(TCHAR);

// Allocate a block of memory to hold the string.
cds.lpData = HeapAlloc(GetProcessHeap(),
    HEAP_ZERO_MEMORY, cds.cbData);

// Put the edit control's string in the data block.
Edit_GetText(hwndEdit, cds.lpData, cds.cbData);

// Find the first overlapped window in the list.
hwndSibling = GetFirstSibling(hwnd);

// Get the caption of our window.
GetWindowText(hwnd, szCaption,
    chDIMOF(szCaption));

while (IsWindow(hwndSibling)) {
    // Get the caption of the potential
    // window to send the data to.
    GetWindowText(hwndSibling, szCaptionSibling,
        chDIMOF(szCaptionSibling));

    if (_tcscmp(szCaption, szCaptionSibling) == 0) {
        // If the window's caption is the same as ours,
        // send the data. This may mean that we are
        // sending the message to ourselves. This is OK;
        // it demonstrates that WM_COPYDATA can be
        // used to send data to ourselves.
        FORWARD_WM_COPYDATA(hwndSibling, hwnd,
            &cds, SendMessage);
    }

    // Get the handle of the next overlapped window.
    hwndSibling = GetNextSibling(hwndSibling);
}

// Free the data buffer.
HeapFree(GetProcessHeap(), 0, cds.lpData);
break;
```

(continued)

Figure 11-3. *continued*

```
      case IDCANCEL:
         EndDialog(hwnd, id);
         break;
   }
}


///////////////////////////////////////////////////////////////////


BOOL CALLBACK Dlg_Proc (HWND hwnd, UINT uMsg,
   WPARAM wParam, LPARAM lParam) {

   switch (uMsg) {
      chHANDLE_DLGMSG(hwnd, WM_INITDIALOG, Dlg_OnInitDialog);
      chHANDLE_DLGMSG(hwnd, WM_COMMAND, Dlg_OnCommand);
      chHANDLE_DLGMSG(hwnd, WM_COPYDATA, Dlg_OnCopyData);
   }
   return(FALSE);
}


///////////////////////////////////////////////////////////////////


int WINAPI _tWinMain (HINSTANCE hinstExe,
   HINSTANCE hinstPrev, LPTSTR pszCmdLine, int nCmdShow) {

   chWARNIFUNICODEUNDERWIN95();
   DialogBox(hinstExe, MAKEINTRESOURCE(IDD_COPYDATA),
      NULL, Dlg_Proc);

   return(0);
}


/////////////////////// End Of File ///////////////////////
```

COPYDATA.RC
```
//Microsoft Developer Studio generated resource script.
//
```

(continued)

Figure 11-3. *continued*

```
#include "Resource.h"

#define APSTUDIO_READONLY_SYMBOLS
/////////////////////////////////////////////////////////////
//
// Generated from the TEXTINCLUDE 2 resource.
//
#include "afxres.h"


/////////////////////////////////////////////////////////////
#undef APSTUDIO_READONLY_SYMBOLS


/////////////////////////////////////////////////////////////
// English (U.S.) resources

#if !defined(AFX_RESOURCE_DLL) || defined(AFX_TARG_ENU)
#ifdef _WIN32
LANGUAGE LANG_ENGLISH, SUBLANG_ENGLISH_US
#pragma code_page(1252)
#endif //_WIN32


/////////////////////////////////////////////////////////////
//
// Dialog
//

IDD_COPYDATA DIALOG DISCARDABLE  38, 36, 220, 42
STYLE WS_MINIMIZEBOX | WS_POPUP | WS_VISIBLE | WS_CAPTION
   | WS_SYSMENU
CAPTION "WM_COPYDATA Message Share Application"
FONT 8, "System"
BEGIN
    LTEXT           "Data&1:",IDC_STATIC,4,4,24,12
    EDITTEXT        IDC_DATA1,28,4,76,12
    PUSHBUTTON      "&Send Data1 to other windows",
                    IDC_COPYDATA1,112,4,104,14,WS_GROUP
    LTEXT           "Data&2:",IDC_STATIC,4,24,24,12
    EDITTEXT        IDC_DATA2,28,24,76,12
    PUSHBUTTON      "Send &Data2 to other windows",
                    IDC_COPYDATA2,112,24,104,14,WS_GROUP
END
```

(continued)

Figure 11-3. *continued*

```
//////////////////////////////////////////////////////////
//
// Icon
//

// Icon with lowest ID value placed first to ensure
// application icon remains consistent on all systems.
IDI_COPYDATA            ICON    DISCARDABLE    "CopyData.Ico"

#ifdef APSTUDIO_INVOKED
//////////////////////////////////////////////////////////
//
// TEXTINCLUDE
//

1 TEXTINCLUDE DISCARDABLE
BEGIN
    "Resource.h\0"
END

2 TEXTINCLUDE DISCARDABLE
BEGIN
    "#include ""afxres.h""\r\n"
    "\0"
END

3 TEXTINCLUDE DISCARDABLE
BEGIN
    "\r\n"
    "\0"
END

#endif    // APSTUDIO_INVOKED

#endif    // English (U.S.) resources
//////////////////////////////////////////////////////////


#ifndef APSTUDIO_INVOKED
//////////////////////////////////////////////////////////
//
// Generated from the TEXTINCLUDE 3 resource.
```

(continued)

Figure 11-3. *continued*

```
//



///////////////////////////////////////////////////////////////
#endif    // not APSTUDIO_INVOKED
```

Deserialized Input

Serialized input (used by 16-bit Windows) is when the system processes the user's input (keyboard and mouse events) in the order in which the input was entered by the user. The events are removed from the system queue as various applications request them. For example, let's say that the user types *ABC*, Alt+Tab, *XYZ* at the keyboard. This means that seven keyboard hardware events are added to the system queue.[4] The application with keyboard focus retrieves the *ABC* messages from the system queue and displays the characters in its client area. Let's say a bug in the program causes it to enter an infinite loop whenever it receives the letter *C*. At this point, the whole system is hung. Alt+Tab and *XYZ* will never be read from the system queue. In fact, if the user attempts to activate another application using the mouse, the mouse event will be appended to the system queue after the last keystroke event. And as you might expect, this mouse event will never be retrieved from the system queue either. The user has no recourse now but to reboot the computer.

Microsoft did try to improve this situation. Support was added to 16-bit Windows so that a user can press Ctrl+Alt+Del if an application is no longer responding to the system. When the system detects this input, it locates the currently active application and attempts to remove it from memory. My experience with this feature has been that 16-bit Windows usually cannot recover from the hung application gracefully and I still need to reboot.

The solution to this serialized input problem is *deserialized input*. With deserialized input, one hardware event isn't necessarily processed before another event. I know what you're thinking: "Does this mean that

---

4. Actually, more than seven events are appended to the system queue. For example, each keystroke generates a WM_KEYDOWN and a WM_KEYUP event. I'm calling it seven events just to simplify the discussion.

if you type *ABC* at the keyboard the thread will receive *CAB*?" No, of course not. However, it does mean that if you type *ABC*, Alt+Tab, *XYZ*, the thread that becomes active after Alt+Tab might process *XYZ* before the first thread finishes processing *ABC*.

In Win32, input is applied on a thread-level basis instead of on the systemwide basis employed by 16-bit Windows. A thread receives hardware events in the order in which the user enters them, which is how the system deserializes the hardware input.

How Input Is Deserialized

When the system starts running, the system creates itself a special thread called the *raw input thread* (RIT). When the user presses and releases a key, presses and releases a mouse button, or moves the mouse, the device driver for the hardware device appends a hardware event to the RIT's queue. This causes the RIT to wake up; examine the event at the head of its queue; translate the event into the appropriate WM_KEY*, WM-_?BUTTON*, or WM_MOUSEMOVE message; and post the message to the appropriate thread's virtualized input queue.

As shown in Figure 11-1 on page 467, each thread has its very own posted-message queue and virtualized input queue. Every time a thread creates a window, the system places all messages posted for this window in the creating thread's posted-message queue.

Assume the following scenario: a process creates two threads, Thread A and Thread B. Thread A then creates a window—Win A—and Thread B creates two windows—Win B and Win C. Figure 11-4 illustrates this scenario. If a thread in the system posts a message to Win A, this message is placed in Thread A's posted-message queue. Any messages posted for either Win B or Win C are placed in Thread B's posted-message queue.

When the RIT processes a hardware event, it must determine which virtualized input queue should receive the event. For a mouse event, the RIT first determines which window is under the mouse cursor and then places the mouse event (WM_?BUTTON* or WM_MOUSE-MOVE) in the virtualized input queue associated with the thread that created the window. For a keystroke event, the RIT determines which thread is the foreground thread—that is, the thread with which the user is currently working. The appropriate keyboard message is placed in the virtualized input queue associated with this foreground thread.

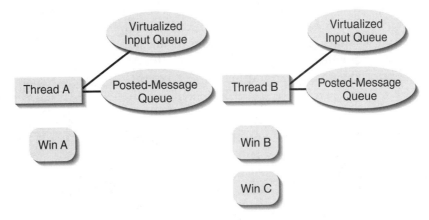

Figure 11-4.
Messages for Win A go in Thread A's queues; messages for Win B and Win C go in Thread B's queues.

For the system to switch threads, regardless of whether a thread is processing input, the RIT must examine each hardware input event before posting the event to a thread's virtualized input queue. For example, the RIT checks for the following key combinations and performs the corresponding action:

Key Combination	Windows 95	Windows NT
Alt+Tab	Activates another window connecting its thread to the RIT	Activates another window connecting its thread to the RIT
Alt+Esc	Activates another window connecting its thread to the RIT	Activates another window connecting its thread to the RIT
Ctrl+Esc	Pops open the Taskbar's Start menu	Pops open the Taskbar's Start menu
Ctrl+Alt+Del	Displays the system's Close Program dialog box	Displays the Windows NT Security dialog box

Sharing Thread Virtualized Input Queues

You can force two or more threads to share the same virtualized input queue and local input state variables (discussed later) by using the

AttachThreadInput function:

```
BOOL AttachThreadInput(DWORD idAttach, DWORD idAttachTo,
    BOOL fAttach);
```

This function tells the system to let two threads share the same virtualized input queue, as illustrated in Figure 11-5. The first parameter, *idAttach*, is the ID of the thread containing the virtualized input queue you no longer want. The second parameter, *idAttachTo*, is the ID of the thread containing the virtualized input queue you want the threads to share. The last parameter, *fAttach*, is TRUE if you want the sharing to occur or FALSE if you want to separate the two threads' virtualized input queues again. You can tell several threads to share the same virtualized input queue by making successive calls to the *AttachThreadInput* function.

Returning to the earlier example, let's say that Thread B calls *AttachThreadInput*, passing Thread B's ID as the first parameter, Thread A's ID as the second parameter, and TRUE as the last parameter:

```
AttachThreadInput(idThreadB, idThreadA, TRUE);
```

Now every hardware input event destined for either Win B or Win C will be appended to Thread A's virtualized input queue. Thread B's virtualized input queue will no longer receive input events unless the two queues are detached by calling *AttachThreadInput* a second time, passing FALSE as the *fAttach* parameter.

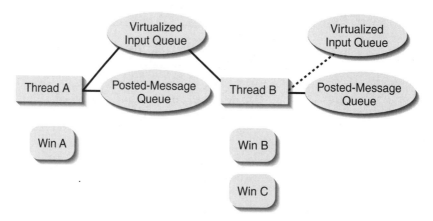

Figure 11-5.
Hardware messages for Win A, Win B, and Win C go in Thread A's virtualized input queue.

When you attach two threads to the same virtualized input queue, each thread still maintains its own message queue. Every time you attach another thread to the same virtualized input queue, you are making the system behave more and more like 16-bit Windows. After all, in 16-bit Windows all the tasks are attached to a single input queue—the system queue. In fact, when you run 16-bit Windows applications under Windows 95 or Windows NT, the system makes sure that all of the 16-bit Windows applications share a single input queue for backward compatibility because 16-bit Windows applications expect this behavior.

If you make all threads share a single queue, you severely curtail the robustness of the Win32 system. If one application receives a keystroke and hangs, another application can't receive any input. So think twice or three times before using the *AttachThreadInput* function.

Windows NT allows 16-bit Windows applications to run in separate address spaces. All the 16-bit applications in a single address space have their input queues attached to one another. However, if two 16-bit applications are running in different address spaces, the system does not attach their input queues. This makes Windows NT run 16-bit Windows applications more robustly than 16-bit Windows did. If a 16-bit Windows application hangs, all other 16-bit Windows applications in the same address space also hang. However, 16-bit Windows applications running in separate address spaces are not affected.

The system implicitly attaches the virtualized input queues of several threads if an application installs a journal record hook or a journal playback hook. When the hook is uninstalled, the system automatically restores all the threads so that they are using the same input queues they were using before the hook was installed.

When an application installs a journal record hook, it tells the system that it wants to be notified of all hardware events entered by the user. The application usually saves or records this information. In another session, the application installs a journal playback hook, which causes the system to ignore the user's input and to expect the application that installed the hook to play back the events it recorded earlier.

Playing back the recorded events simulates the user repeating his or her hardware input. The Recorder application that Microsoft ships with 16-bit Windows allows users to record events for later playback by installing journal record and journal playback hooks. You'll notice that

Recorder is not shipped with Windows 95 or Windows NT—this is because Recorder compromises the robustness of the system.

There is one other instance in which the system implicitly calls *AttachThreadInput* on your behalf. Let's say you have an application that creates two threads. The first thread creates a dialog box. After the dialog box has been created, the second thread calls *CreateWindow*, using the WS_CHILD style, and passes the handle of the dialog box to be the child's parent. The system calls *AttachThreadInput* with the child window's thread to tell the child's thread that it should use the same input queue that the dialog box thread is using. This action forces input to be synchronized among all the child windows in the dialog box. As you'll see later in this chapter, it's possible for windows created by different threads to look as if they all have the input focus simultaneously, which can confuse an end user. When you attach the input queues, only one window will appear to have the focus.

Local Input State

Back when programmers were developing applications for MS-DOS, it could always be presumed that the running application would be the only active application. As a result, applications frequently assumed that the whole display was theirs for the writing, the memory theirs for the allocating, the disk space theirs for the accessing, the keystrokes theirs for the taking, the CPU theirs for the computing—you get the idea.

Well, 16-bit Windows came around and programmers had to learn to cooperate with one another. Many programs, all running simultaneously, had to share the limited system resources. An application had to restrict its output to a small rectangular region on the display; allocate memory only when needed (as well as try to make it discardable); relinquish control of itself to other applications on certain keystrokes; and purposely put itself to sleep so that other applications could get a little CPU time. If an application was not as friendly as it should be, a user had no recourse but to terminate the piggish application or run it alone, which obviously defeated the idea of a multitasking environment.

Under Win32, much of this is still true. Developers still design their applications to use a small rectangular region on the display for output, allocate memory only when needed, and so on. The big difference is that Win32 makes applications behave courteously. The system forces limits on the amount of memory that an application can hog. It monitors the keyboard and allows the user to switch to another application whether the currently active application wants to allow this or not. It preempts a running application and gives time to another application regardless of how hungry for processing time the current application is.[5]

Who are the winners now that the system has so much control over the applications we write? Both the users and the developers. Because the system does all this no matter what we as programmers might do to stop it, we can relax a little and stop worrying about crowding out other applications. A big part of making this work is the concept of the *local input state.*

Each thread has its own input state, which is managed inside a thread's THREADINFO structure (discussed earlier). This input state consists of the thread's virtualized input queue as well as a set of variables. These variables keep track of the following input state management information:

Keyboard input and window focus information, such as

- Which window has keyboard focus

- Which window is active

- Which keys that are pressed on the keyboard are stored in the synchronous key state array

- The state of the caret

Mouse cursor management information, such as

- Which window has mouse capture

- The shape of the mouse cursor

- The visibility of the mouse cursor

Because each thread gets its very own set of input state variables, each thread has a different notion of focus window, mouse capture window, and so on. From a thread's perspective, either one of its windows has keyboard focus or no window in the system has keyboard focus, either one of its windows has mouse capture or no window has mouse capture, and so on. As you might expect, this separatism has several ramifications, which we'll discuss in this chapter.

---

5. You can set your process's priority class high; however, doing so might starve processes at a lower priority, making the lower-priority processes unresponsive. But even if you set a process's priority class high, the system still gives the user the ability to terminate the process.

Keyboard Input and Focus

Win32 and 16-bit Windows handle keyboard input in very different ways. When I was first getting started with Win32, I tried to understand how the system handles keyboard input by drawing on my knowledge of 16-bit Windows. As it turned out, my knowledge of how 16-bit Windows handles keyboard input made it *more* difficult to understand both how Win32 handles keyboard input and how it changes the input focus between windows.

In Win32, the raw input thread (RIT) directs the user's keyboard input to a thread's virtualized input queue—not to a window. The RIT places the keyboard events into the thread's virtualized input queue without referring to a particular window. When the thread calls *GetMessage*, the keyboard event is removed from the queue and assigned to the window (created by the thread) that currently has input focus. Figure 11-6 illustrates this process.

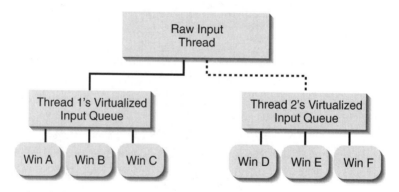

Figure 11-6.
The RIT directs the user's keyboard input to one thread's virtualized input queue at a time.

To instruct a different window to accept keyboard input, you need to specify to which thread's virtualized input queue the RIT should direct keyboard input *and* tell the thread's input state variables which window will have keyboard focus. Calling *SetFocus* alone does not accomplish both tasks. If Thread 1 is currently receiving input from the RIT, a call to *SetFocus*, passing the handle of Win A, Win B, or Win C, causes the focus to change. The window losing focus removes its focus rectangle or hides its caret, and the window gaining focus draws a focus rectangle or shows its caret.

However, let's say that Thread 1 is still receiving input from the RIT, and it calls *SetFocus*, passing the handle of Win E. In this case, the system prevents the call to *SetFocus* from doing anything because the window for which you are trying to set focus is not using the virtualized input queue that is currently "connected" to the RIT. After Thread 1 executes this call, there is no change in focus, and the appearance of the screen doesn't change.

In another situation, Thread 1 might be connected to the RIT and Thread 2 might call *SetFocus*, passing the handle of Win E. In this case, Thread 2's local input state variables are updated to reflect that Win E is the window to receive keyboard input the next time the RIT directs keystrokes to Thread 2. The call doesn't cause the RIT to direct input to Thread 2's virtualized input queue.

Because Win E now has focus for Thread 2, it receives a WM_SET-FOCUS message. If Win E is a pushbutton, it draws a focus rectangle for itself, so two windows with focus rectangles might appear on the screen. I found this very disconcerting at first—and now that I've seen it happen a few more times, I still find it disconcerting. You should be careful when you call *SetFocus* so that this situation doesn't occur.

By the way, if you give focus to a window that displays a caret when it receives a WM_SETFOCUS message, you can produce several windows on the screen that display carets simultaneously. This can be a bit bewildering to a user.

When focus is transferred from one window to another using conventional methods (such as clicking on a window with the mouse), the window losing focus receives a WM_KILLFOCUS message. If the window receiving focus belongs to a thread other than the thread associated with the window losing focus, the local input state variables of the thread that created the window losing focus are updated to reflect that no window has focus. Calling *GetFocus* at this time returns NULL, which makes the thread think that no window currently has the focus. This can be problematic when you're porting a 16-bit Windows application to Win32 because most 16-bit Windows applications never expect *GetFocus* to return NULL.

The *SetActiveWindow* function activates a top-level window in the system:

```
HWND SetActiveWindow(HWND hwnd);
```

In 16-bit Windows, an application typically calls this function to bring another application to the foreground. In Win32, this function behaves just like the *SetFocus* function; that is, if a thread calls *SetActiveWindow*, passing the handle of a window owned by a different thread, the system does nothing. But if the window was created by the same thread making the call, the system changes the active window.

The complement of *SetActiveWindow* is the *GetActiveWindow* function:

```
HWND GetActiveWindow(VOID);
```

This function works just like the *GetFocus* function except that it returns the handle of the active window indicated by the calling thread's local input state variables. So if the active window is owned by another thread, *GetActiveWindow* returns NULL.

These functions behave differently under Win32 than they do under 16-bit Windows for a reason: Microsoft is taking control away from applications and giving it back to the users. The assumption is that users find it confusing when windows pop up in the foreground under program control.

For example, a user might start a lengthy process in Application A and switch to Application B. When Application A is finished, it might activate its main window. You certainly wouldn't want Application A's main window to pop up on top of Application B's window while the user is still working with Application B. This could catch the user by surprise. Also, the user might not immediately notice that Application A's window had popped up on top of Application B's window, and the user might enter text into Application A by mistake. This could have disastrous effects.

However, sometimes an application really needs to bring a window to the foreground. The following functions not only change the window focus for a thread but also instruct the RIT to direct keystrokes to a different thread. One of these functions, the *SetForegroundWindow* function, is not in 16-bit Windows:

```
BOOL SetForegroundWindow(HWND hwnd);
```

This function brings the window identified by the *hwnd* parameter to the foreground. The system also activates the window and gives it the focus. This function sets the foreground window regardless of which thread created the window. The complementary function is *GetForeground-Window*:

```
HWND GetForegroundWindow(VOID);
```

This function returns the handle of the window that is currently in the foreground.

Other functions that can alter a window's z-order, activation status, and focus status include *BringWindowToTop* and *SetWindowPos*. The *BringWindowToTop* function, shown here, exists in both 16-bit Windows and Win32:

```
BOOL BringWindowToTop(HWND hwnd);
```

As long as the thread calling *BringWindowToTop* is in the foreground when you call this function, Win32 activates the window you specify regardless of which thread created the window. Win32 both redirects the RIT to the thread that created the window and sets the focus window for the thread's local input state variables. If the thread calling *BringWindowToTop* is not the foreground thread, the window order doesn't change.

The *SetWindowPos* function, shown here, brings a window to the foreground or the background by passing HWND_TOP or HWND_BOTTOM as the second parameter:

```
BOOL SetWindowPos(HWND hwnd, HWND hwndInsertAfter,
    int x, int y, int cx, int cy, UINT fuFlags);
```

Actually, *BringWindowToTop* is implemented internally as a call to *SetWindowPos* passing HWND_TOP as the second parameter.

Another aspect of keyboard management and the local input state is that of the synchronous key state array. Every thread's local input state variables include a synchronous key state array, but all threads share a single asynchronous key state array. These arrays reflect the state of all keys on a keyboard at any given time. The *GetAsyncKeyState* function determines whether the user is currently pressing a key on the keyboard:

```
SHORT GetAsyncKeyState(int nVirtKey);
```

The *nVirtKey* parameter identifies the virtual key code of the key to check. The high-bit of the result indicates whether the key is currently pressed (1) or not (0). I have often used this function during the processing of a single message to check whether the user has released the primary mouse button. I pass the virtual key value VK_LBUTTON and wait for the high-bit of the return value to be 0. This function has changed slightly for Win32. In Win32, *GetAsyncKeyState* always returns 0 (not pressed) if the thread calling the function did not create the window that currently has the input focus.

The *GetKeyState* function, which follows, differs from the *GetAsyncKeyState* function because it returns the keyboard state at the time the most recent keyboard message was removed from the thread's queue:

```
SHORT GetKeyState(int nVirtKey);
```

This function is not affected by which window has input focus and can be called at any time. For a more detailed discussion of these two key state arrays and these functions, refer to Chapter 8, "Keystroke Processing," in *Windows 95: A Developer's Guide* (Richter and Locke, 1995).

Mouse Cursor Management

Mouse cursor management is another component of the local input state. Because the mouse, like the keyboard, must be shared among all the different threads, Win32 must not allow a single thread to monopolize the mouse cursor by altering its shape or confining it to a small area of the screen. In this section, we'll take a look at how the mouse cursor is managed by the system.

One aspect of mouse cursor management is the cursor's hide/show capability. Let's say that a 16-bit Windows application calls *ShowCursor(FALSE)*, causing the mouse cursor to be hidden, and the application never calls *ShowCursor(TRUE)*. The user wouldn't be able to see the mouse when using a different application.

Win32 wouldn't allow this to happen. The system hides the cursor whenever the mouse is positioned over a window created by the thread that called *ShowCursor(FALSE)* and shows it whenever the cursor is positioned over a window not created by this thread.

Another aspect of mouse cursor management is the ability to clip the cursor to a rectangular region of the screen. In 16-bit Windows, it is possible for an application to clip the mouse cursor by calling the *Clip-Cursor* function:

```
BOOL ClipCursor(CONST RECT *lprc);
```

This function causes the mouse to be constrained within the screen coordinates specified in the rectangle pointed to by the *lprc* parameter. Again, we have the problem in which one application should not be able to limit the movement of the mouse cursor on the screen. But Win32 must also allow an application to clip a mouse cursor's motion to a specified rectangle. So the system allows the application to set the clipping rectangle and confines the mouse to that region of the screen. Then, if an asynchronous activation event occurs (when the user clicks on another application's window, when a call to *SetForegroundWindow* is made, or when Ctrl+Esc is pressed), the system stops clipping the cursor's movement, allowing the cursor to move freely across the entire screen.

Now we move to the issue of mouse capture. When a window "captures" the mouse (by calling *SetCapture*), it requests that all mouse messages be directed from the RIT to the thread's virtualized input queue and that all mouse messages from the virtualized input queue be directed to the window that set capture. This capturing of mouse messages continues until the application later calls *ReleaseCapture*.

Under 16-bit Windows, if an application calls *SetCapture* but never calls *ReleaseCapture*, mouse messages can never be directed to any other window in the system. Again, we have a situation that Win32 cannot allow, but solving this problem is a bit tricky. When an application calls *SetCapture*, the RIT is directed to place all mouse messages in the thread's virtualized input queue. *SetCapture* also sets the local input state variables for the thread that called *SetCapture*.

Usually an application calls *SetCapture* when the user presses a mouse button. However, there is no reason why a thread could not call *SetCapture* even if a mouse button is not down. If *SetCapture* is called when a mouse button is down, capture is performed systemwide, just as in 16-bit Windows. However, when the system detects that no mouse buttons are down, the RIT no longer directs mouse messages solely to the thread's virtualized input queue. Instead, the RIT directs mouse messages to the input queue associated with the window that is directly beneath the mouse cursor. This is normal behavior when the mouse is not captured.

However, the thread that originally called *SetCapture* still thinks that mouse capture is in effect. This means that whenever the mouse is positioned over any window created by the thread that has capture set, the mouse messages will be directed to the capture window for that thread. In other words, when the user releases all mouse buttons, mouse capture is no longer performed on a systemwide level—it is now performed on a thread-local level.

In addition, if the user attempts to activate a window created by another thread, the system automatically sends mouse button down and mouse button up messages to the thread that set capture. Then the system updates the thread's local input state variables to indicate that the thread no longer has mouse capture. It is clear from this implementation that Microsoft expects mouse clicking-and-dragging to be the most common reason for using mouse capture. If you are using mouse capture with techniques other than click-and-drag, you will definitely have to experiment to see how things may have changed from 16-bit Windows to Win32.

The final local input state variable pertaining to the mouse is its cursor shape. Whenever a thread calls *SetCursor* to change the shape of the mouse cursor, the local input state variables are updated to reflect the mouse cursor shape. In other words, the local input state variables always remember the most recent shape of the mouse cursor set by the thread.

Let's say that the user moves the mouse over your window, your window receives a WM_SETCURSOR message, and you call *SetCursor* to change the mouse cursor to an hourglass. After the call to *SetCursor*, you have code that enters into a lengthy process. (An infinite loop is a good example of a lengthy process.) Now the user moves the mouse cursor out of your window and over the window belonging to another application. In 16-bit Windows, the mouse cursor doesn't change, but in Windows 95 and Windows NT the mouse cursor can be changed by the other window procedure.

Local input state variables are not required in order for a thread to change the mouse cursor's shape when another thread executes a lengthy procedure. But now let's move the mouse cursor back into your window that is still executing its lengthy procedure. The system wants to send WM_SETCURSOR messages to the window, but the window is unable to retrieve them because it is still looping. So the system looks at the most recently set mouse cursor shape (contained in the thread's local input state variables) and automatically sets the mouse cursor back to this shape (the hourglass, in this example). This gives the user visual feedback that the process is still working and that the user must wait.

The Local Input State Laboratory Sample Application

The LISLab application (LISLAB.EXE), listed in Figure 11-7 beginning on page 514, is a laboratory that allows you to experiment with how local input states work. The source code and resource files for the application are in the LISLAB directory on the companion disc. Before invoking the application, you will want to run the Notepad application.

After Notepad is running, you can start LISLab and see the following dialog box appear:

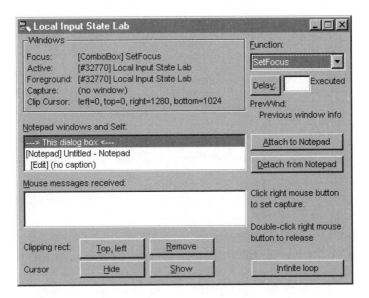

In the upper left corner is the Windows group box. The five entries in this box are updated once per second—that is, once every second the dialog box receives a WM_TIMER message, and in response, it calls the following functions: *GetFocus, GetActiveWindow, GetForegroundWindow, Get-Capture,* and *GetClipCursor.* The first four of these functions return window handles. From these window handles, I can determine the window's class and caption and display this information. Remember that these window handles are being retrieved from my own thread's local input state variables.

If I activate another application (for example, Notepad), the Focus and Active entries change to (No Window) and the Foreground entry changes to [Notepad] Untitled - Notepad. Notice that by activating Notepad you make LISLab think that no window has focus and that no window is active.

Next you can experiment with changing the window focus. First select SetFocus from the Function combo box at the upper right corner of the Local Input State Lab dialog box. Then enter the delay time (in seconds) that you want LISLab to wait before calling *SetFocus.* For this experiment, you'll probably want to specify a delay of 0 seconds. I'll explain shortly how the Delay field is used.

Next select a window that you want to pass in the call to *SetFocus*. You select a window using the Notepad Windows And Self list box on the left side of the Local Input State Lab dialog box. For this experiment, select [Notepad] Untitled–Notepad in the list box. Now you are ready to call *SetFocus*. Simply click on the Delay button and watch what happens to the Windows group box—nothing. The system does not perform a focus change.

If you really want *SetFocus* to change focus to Notepad, you can click on the Attach To Notepad button. Clicking on this button causes LISLab to call

```
AttachThreadInput(GetWindowThreadProcessId(g_hwndNotepad, NULL),
    GetCurrentThreadId(), TRUE);
```

This call tells LISLab's thread to use the same virtualized input queue as that of Notepad. In addition, LISLab's thread will also share the same local input state variables used by Notepad.

If after clicking on the Attach To Notepad button you click on Notepad's window, LISLab's dialog box looks like this:

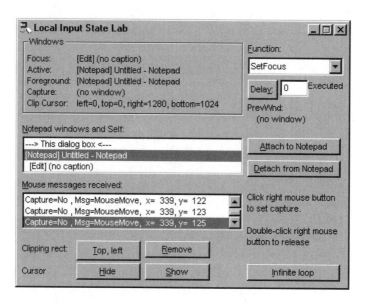

Notice that now, because the input queues are attached, LISLab can follow window focus changes made in Notepad. The above dialog box shows that the Edit control currently has the focus. If we display the File Open dialog box in Notepad, LISLab will continue to update its display and show us which Notepad window has focus, which window is active, and so on.

Now we can move back to LISLab, click on the Delay button, and have *SetFocus* attempt to give Notepad focus. This time the call to *SetFocus* succeeds because the input queues are attached.

You can continue to experiment by placing calls to *SetActiveWindow*, *SetForegroundWindow*, *BringWindowToTop*, and *SetWindowPos* by selecting the desired function from the Function combo box. Try calling these functions both when the input queues are attached and when they are detached, and notice the differences.

Now I'll explain why I include the delay option. The delay option causes LISLab to call the specified function after the number of seconds indicated. An example will help illustrate why you need it. First make sure that LISLab is detached from Notepad by clicking on the Detach From Notepad button. Then select ---> This Dialog Box <--- from the Notepad Windows And Self list box. Next select SetFocus from the Function combo box, and enter a delay of 10 seconds. Finally, click on the Delay button, and then quickly click on Notepad's window to make it active. You must make Notepad active before the 10 seconds elapse.

While LISLab is waiting for the 10 seconds to elapse, it displays the word Pending to the right of the seconds value. After the 10 seconds, Pending is replaced by Executed, and the result of calling the function is displayed. If you watch carefully, LISLab will give focus to the Function combo box and show that the combo box now has the focus. But Notepad will still be receiving your keystrokes. LISLab's thread thinks that the combo box has the focus, and Notepad's thread thinks that one of its windows has the focus. However, the RIT remains "connected" to Notepad's thread.

One final point about windows and the focus: both the *SetFocus* and *SetActiveWindow* functions return the handle to the window that originally had the focus or was active. The information for this window is displayed in the PrevWnd field in the LISLab dialog box. Also, just before LISLab calls *SetForegroundWindow*, it calls *GetForegroundWindow* to get the handle of the window that was originally in the foreground. This information is also displayed in the PrevWnd field.

It's time to move on to experiments involving the mouse cursor. Whenever you move the mouse over LISLab's dialog box (but not over any of its child windows), the mouse is displayed as a vertical arrow. As mouse messages are sent to the dialog box, they are also added to the Mouse Messages Received list box. In this way, you know when the dialog box is receiving mouse messages. If you move the mouse outside the dialog box or over one of its child windows, you'll see that messages are no longer added to the list box.

Now move the mouse to the right of the dialog box over the text Click Right Mouse Button To Set Capture, and click and hold the right mouse button. When you do this, LISLab calls *SetCapture* and passes the handle of LISLab's dialog box. Notice that LISLab reflects that it has capture by updating the Windows group box at the top.

Without releasing the right mouse button, move the mouse over LISLab's child windows and watch the mouse messages being added to the list box. Notice that if you move the mouse outside of LISLab's dialog box, LISLab continues to be notified of mouse messages. The mouse cursor retains its vertical arrow shape no matter where you move the mouse on the screen. This is exactly how mouse capture works in 16-bit Windows.

But now we're ready to see where the system behaves differently. Release the right mouse button and watch what happens. The capture window reflected at the top of LISLab continues to show that LISLab thinks it still has mouse capture. However, if you move the mouse outside of LISLab's dialog box, the cursor no longer remains a vertical arrow and mouse messages stop going to the Mouse Messages Received list box. If you move the mouse over any of LISLab's child windows, you'll see that capture is still in effect because all the windows are using the same set of local input state variables. This is very different from the way 16-bit Windows works.

When you're done experimenting with mouse capture, you can turn it off using one of two techniques:

■ Double-click the right mouse button anywhere in the Local Input State Lab dialog box to have LISLab place a call to *ReleaseCapture.*

■ Click on a window created by a thread other than LISLab's thread. When you do this, the system automatically sends mouse button up and mouse button down messages to LISLab's dialog box.

Regardless of which method you choose, watch how the Capture field in the Windows group box changes to reflect that no window has mouse capture.

There are only two more mouse-related experiments: one experiment involves clipping the mouse cursor's movement to a rectangle, and the other involves cursor visibility. When you click on the Top, Left button, LISLab executes the following code:

```
RECT rc;
  :
  :
SetRect(&rc, 0, 0,
   GetSystemMetrics(SM_CXSCREEN) / 2,
   GetSystemMetrics(SM_CYSCREEN) / 2);
```

This causes the mouse cursor to be confined to the top left quarter of the screen. If you use Alt+Tab to select another application's window, you'll notice that the clipping rectangle stays in effect. The system automatically stops clipping the mouse and allows it to traverse the entire screen when you perform any of the following operations:

Windows 95	Click on another application's title bar and move the window.
Windows NT	Click on another application's title bar. (You don't have to move the window.)
Windows NT	Invoke and dismiss the Task Manager.

You can also click on the Remove button in the Local Input State Lab dialog box (assuming that the button is in the clipping rectangle) to remove the clipping rectangle.

Clicking on the Hide or Show Cursor button causes LISLab to execute the following code:

```
ShowCursor(FALSE);
```

or

```
ShowCursor(TRUE);
```

When you hide the mouse cursor, it doesn't appear when you move the mouse over LISLab's dialog box. But the moment you move the mouse outside this dialog box, the cursor appears again. Use the Show button to counteract the effect of the Hide button. Note that the effects of hiding the cursor are cumulative; that is, if you click on the Hide button five times, you must click on the Show button five times to make the cursor visible.

The last experiment involves using the Infinite Loop button. When you click on this button, LISLab executes the following code:

```
SetCursor(LoadCursor(NULL, IDC_NO));
for (;;)
   ;
```

The first line changes the mouse cursor to a slashed circle, and the second line executes an infinite loop. After you click on the Infinite Loop button, LISLab stops responding to any input whatsoever. If you move the mouse over LISLab's dialog box, the cursor remains as the slashed circle. However, if you move the mouse outside the dialog box, the cursor changes to reflect the cursor of the window over which it is located. You can use the mouse to manipulate these other windows.

If you move the mouse back over LISLab's dialog box, the system sees that LISLab is not responding and automatically changes the cursor back to its most recent shape—the slashed circle. In 16-bit Windows, an application executing an infinite loop hangs not only the application but the whole system. As you can see, on a Win32-based operating system an infinite loop is just a minor inconvenience to the user.

Notice that if you move a window over the hung Local Input State Lab dialog box and then move it away, the system sends LISLab a WM_PAINT message. But the system also realizes that the thread is not responding. The system helps out here by repainting the window for the unresponsive application. Of course, the system cannot repaint the window correctly because it doesn't know what the application is supposed to be doing, so the system simply erases the window's background and redraws the frame.

Now the problem is that we have a window on the screen that isn't responding to anything we do. How do we get rid of it? In Windows 95, we must first press Ctrl+Alt+Del to display the Close Program window shown here:

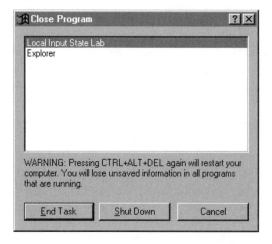

And in Windows NT, you can either right-click on the application's button on the Taskbar or you can display the Task Manager window shown here:

Then we simply select the application we want to terminate—Local Input State Lab, in this case—and click on the End Task button. The system will attempt to terminate LISLab in a nice way but will notice that the application isn't responding. This causes the system to display the following dialog box:

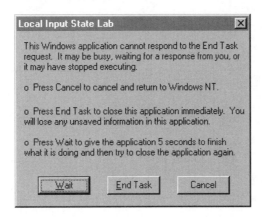

Choosing End Task causes the system to forcibly remove LISLab from the system. The Wait button (available only if you are running under Windows NT) delays the action; choose it if you think that an application will respond to input again within 5 seconds. We know that LISLab won't respond because its infinite loop will never end. The Cancel button tells the system that you changed your mind and no longer want to terminate the application. Choose End Task to remove LISLab from the system.

The whole point of these experiments is to demonstrate the system's robustness. It is almost impossible for one application to place the operating system in a state that would render the other applications unusable. Also, note that both Windows 95 and Windows NT automatically free all resources that were allocated by threads in the terminated process—there are no memory leaks!

LISLab.ico

```
LISLAB.C
/******************************************************************
Module name: LISLab.C
Notices: Copyright (c) 1995-1997 Jeffrey Richter
******************************************************************/


#include "..\CmnHdr.H"                    /* See Appendix C. */
#include <windows.h>
#include <windowsx.h>
#include <tchar.h>
#include <string.h>
#include <stdio.h>                 // For sprintf
#include "Resource.H"



///////////////////////////////////////////////////////////////////



#define TIMER_DELAY (1 * 1000) // 1 second * 1000 milliseconds

UINT   g_uTimerId = 1;
int    g_nEventId = 0;
DWORD  g_dwEventTime = 0;
HWND   g_hwndSubject = NULL;
HWND   g_hwndNotepad = NULL;
```

Figure 11-7.   *(continued)*

The LISLab application.

Figure 11-3. *continued*

```
////////////////////////////////////////////////////////////////


void CalcWndText (HWND hwnd, LPTSTR szBuf, int nLen) {
   TCHAR szClass[50], szCaption[50], szBufT[150];

   if (hwnd == (HWND) NULL) {
      _tcscpy(szBuf, __TEXT("(no window)"));
      return;
   }


   if (!IsWindow(hwnd)) {
      _tcscpy(szBuf, __TEXT("(invalid window)"));
      return;
   }


   GetClassName(hwnd, szClass, chDIMOF(szClass));
   GetWindowText(hwnd, szCaption, chDIMOF(szCaption));

   _stprintf(szBufT, __TEXT("[%s] %s"), (LPTSTR) szClass,
      (*szCaption == 0) ? (LPTSTR) __TEXT("(no caption)")
      : (LPTSTR) szCaption);
   _tcsncpy(szBuf, szBufT, nLen - 1);
   szBuf[nLen - 1] = 0; // Force zero-terminated string
}



////////////////////////////////////////////////////////////////


// To minimize stack use, one instance of WALKWINDOWTREEDATA
// is created as a local variable in WalkWindowTree() and a
// pointer to it is passed to WalkWindowTreeRecurse.

// Data used by WalkWindowTreeRecurse
typedef struct {
   HWND   hwndLB;        // Handle to the output list box
   HWND   hwndParent;    // Handle to the parent
   int    nLevel;        // Nesting depth
   int    nIndex;        // List box item index
   TCHAR  szBuf[100];    // Output buffer
   int    iBuf;          // Index into szBuf
```

(continued)

Figure 11-7. *continued*

```
} WALKWINDOWTREEDATA, *LPWALKWINDOWTREEDATA;


void WalkWindowTreeRecurse (LPWALKWINDOWTREEDATA pWWT) {

    const int nIndexAmount = 2;
    HWND hwndChild;

    pWWT->nLevel++;

    if (!IsWindow(pWWT->hwndParent))
        return;

    for (pWWT->iBuf = 0;
        pWWT->iBuf < pWWT->nLevel * nIndexAmount; pWWT->iBuf++)
        pWWT->szBuf[pWWT->iBuf] = __TEXT(' ');

    CalcWndText(pWWT->hwndParent, &pWWT->szBuf[pWWT->iBuf],
        chDIMOF(pWWT->szBuf) - pWWT->iBuf);
    pWWT->nIndex = ListBox_AddString(pWWT->hwndLB, pWWT->szBuf);
    ListBox_SetItemData(pWWT->hwndLB, pWWT->nIndex,
        pWWT->hwndParent);

    hwndChild = GetFirstChild(pWWT->hwndParent);
    while (hwndChild != NULL) {
        pWWT->hwndParent = hwndChild;
        WalkWindowTreeRecurse(pWWT);
        hwndChild = GetNextSibling(hwndChild);
    }

    pWWT->nLevel--;
}


//////////////////////////////////////////////////////////////


void WalkWindowTree (HWND hwndLB, HWND hwndParent) {

    WALKWINDOWTREEDATA WWT;

    WWT.hwndLB = hwndLB;
    WWT.hwndParent = hwndParent;
    WWT.nLevel = -1;
```

(continued)

Figure 11-7. *continued*

```
    WalkWindowTreeRecurse(&WWT);
}



/////////////////////////////////////////////////////////////////


BOOL Dlg_OnInitDialog (HWND hwnd, HWND hwndFocus,
    LPARAM lParam) {

    HWND hwndT;

    // Associate an icon with the dialog box.
    chSETDLGICONS(hwnd, IDI_LISLAB, IDI_LISLAB);

    // Associate the Up arrow cursor with the dialog box's
    // client area.
    SetClassLong(hwnd, GCL_HCURSOR,
        (LONG) LoadCursor(NULL, IDC_UPARROW));

    g_uTimerId = SetTimer(hwnd, g_uTimerId, TIMER_DELAY, NULL);

    hwndT = GetDlgItem(hwnd, IDC_WNDFUNC);
    ComboBox_AddString(hwndT, __TEXT("SetFocus"));
    ComboBox_AddString(hwndT, __TEXT("SetActiveWindow"));
    ComboBox_AddString(hwndT, __TEXT("SetForegroundWnd"));
    ComboBox_AddString(hwndT, __TEXT("BringWindowToTop"));
    ComboBox_AddString(hwndT, __TEXT("SetWindowPos-TOP"));
    ComboBox_AddString(hwndT, __TEXT("SetWindowPos-BTM"));
    ComboBox_SetCurSel(hwndT, 0);


    // Fill the windows list box with our window
    // and the windows of the Explorer.

    // First our own dialog box
    hwndT = GetDlgItem(hwnd, IDC_WNDS);
    ListBox_AddString(hwndT,
        __TEXT("--> This dialog box <--"));
    ListBox_SetItemData(hwndT, 0, hwnd);
    ListBox_SetCurSel(hwndT, 0);
```

(continued)

Figure 11-7. *continued*

```
    // Now the windows of Notepad
    g_hwndNotepad = FindWindow(__TEXT("Notepad"), NULL);
    WalkWindowTree(hwndT, g_hwndNotepad);

    return(TRUE);
}


//////////////////////////////////////////////////////////////


void Dlg_OnDestroy (HWND hwnd) {
    if (g_uTimerId != 0)
        KillTimer(hwnd, g_uTimerId);
}


//////////////////////////////////////////////////////////////


void Dlg_OnCommand (HWND hwnd, int id, HWND hwndCtl,
    UINT codeNotify) {

    HWND hwndT;
    RECT rc;

    switch (id) {

        case IDCANCEL:
            EndDialog(hwnd, 0);
            break;

        case IDC_FUNCSTART:
            g_dwEventTime = GetTickCount() + 1000 *
                GetDlgItemInt(hwnd, IDC_DELAY, NULL, FALSE);
            hwndT = GetDlgItem(hwnd, IDC_WNDS);
            g_hwndSubject = (HWND)
                ListBox_GetItemData(hwndT,
                    ListBox_GetCurSel(hwndT));
            g_nEventId =
                ComboBox_GetCurSel(GetDlgItem(hwnd, IDC_WNDFUNC));
            SetWindowText(GetDlgItem(hwnd, IDC_EVENTPENDING),
```

(continued)

Figure 11-7. *continued*

```
            __TEXT("Pending"));
        break;

    case IDC_THREADATTACH:
        AttachThreadInput(
            GetWindowThreadProcessId(g_hwndNotepad, NULL),
            GetCurrentThreadId(), TRUE);
        break;

    case IDC_THREADDETACH:
        AttachThreadInput(
            GetWindowThreadProcessId(g_hwndNotepad, NULL),
            GetCurrentThreadId(), FALSE);
        break;

    case IDC_SETCLIPRECT:
        SetRect(&rc, 0, 0,
            GetSystemMetrics(SM_CXSCREEN) / 2,
            GetSystemMetrics(SM_CYSCREEN) / 2);
        ClipCursor(&rc);
        break;

    case IDC_REMOVECLIPRECT:
        ClipCursor(NULL);
        break;

    case IDC_HIDECURSOR:
        ShowCursor(FALSE);
        break;

    case IDC_SHOWCURSOR:
        ShowCursor(TRUE);
        break;

    case IDC_INFINITELOOP:
        SetCursor(LoadCursor(NULL, IDC_NO));
        for (;;)
            ;
        break;
    }
}
```

(continued)

Figure 11-7. *continued*

```
//////////////////////////////////////////////////////////////


void AddStr (HWND hwndLB, LPCTSTR szBuf) {
   int nIndex;

   do {
      nIndex = ListBox_AddString(hwndLB, szBuf);
      if (nIndex == LB_ERR)
         ListBox_DeleteString(hwndLB, 0);
   } while (nIndex == LB_ERR);

   ListBox_SetCurSel(hwndLB, nIndex);
}


//////////////////////////////////////////////////////////////


int Dlg_OnRButtonDown (HWND hwnd, BOOL fDoubleClick,
   int x, int y, UINT keyFlags) {

   TCHAR szBuf[100];
   _stprintf(szBuf,
      __TEXT("Capture=%-3s, Msg=RButtonDown, ")
      __TEXT("DblClk=%-3s, x=%5d, y=%5d"),
      (GetCapture() == NULL) ? __TEXT("No") : __TEXT("Yes"),
      fDoubleClick ? __TEXT("Yes") : __TEXT("No"), x, y);

   AddStr(GetDlgItem(hwnd, IDC_MOUSEMSGS), szBuf);
   if (!fDoubleClick) {
      SetCapture(hwnd);
   } else {
      ReleaseCapture();
   }
   return(0);
}


//////////////////////////////////////////////////////////////


int Dlg_OnRButtonUp (HWND hwnd, int x, int y, UINT keyFlags) {
   TCHAR szBuf[100];
```

(continued)

Figure 11-7. *continued*

```
    _stprintf(szBuf,
       __TEXT("Capture=%-3s, Msg=RButtonUp,   x=%5d, y=%5d"),
       (GetCapture() == NULL)
          ? __TEXT("No") : __TEXT("Yes"), x, y);

    AddStr(GetDlgItem(hwnd, IDC_MOUSEMSGS), szBuf);
    return(0);
}


///////////////////////////////////////////////////////////////////


int Dlg_OnLButtonDown (HWND hwnd, BOOL fDoubleClick,
    int x, int y, UINT keyFlags) {

    TCHAR szBuf[100];
    _stprintf(szBuf,
       __TEXT("Capture=%-3s, Msg=LButtonDown, ")
       __TEXT("DblClk=%-3s, x=%5d, y=%5d"),
       (GetCapture() == NULL) ? __TEXT("No") : __TEXT("Yes"),
       fDoubleClick ? __TEXT("Yes") : __TEXT("No"), x, y);

    AddStr(GetDlgItem(hwnd, IDC_MOUSEMSGS), szBuf);
    return(0);
}


///////////////////////////////////////////////////////////////////


void Dlg_OnLButtonUp (HWND hwnd, int x, int y,
    UINT keyFlags) {
    TCHAR szBuf[100];

    _stprintf(szBuf,
       __TEXT("Capture=%-3s, Msg=LButtonUp,   x=%5d, y=%5d"),
       (GetCapture() == NULL)
          ? __TEXT("No") : __TEXT("Yes"), x, y);

    AddStr(GetDlgItem(hwnd, IDC_MOUSEMSGS), szBuf);
}
```

(continued)

Figure 11-7. *continued*

```
//////////////////////////////////////////////////////////////


void Dlg_OnMouseMove (HWND hwnd, int x, int y,
   UINT keyFlags) {

   TCHAR szBuf[100];

   _stprintf(szBuf,
      __TEXT("Capture=%-3s, Msg=MouseMove,  x=%5d, y=%5d"),
         (GetCapture() == NULL)
         ? __TEXT("No") : __TEXT("Yes"), x, y);

   AddStr(GetDlgItem(hwnd, IDC_MOUSEMSGS), szBuf);
}



//////////////////////////////////////////////////////////////


void Dlg_OnTimer (HWND hwnd, UINT id) {
   TCHAR szBuf[100];
   RECT rc;
   HWND hwndT;

   CalcWndText(GetFocus(), szBuf, chDIMOF(szBuf));
   SetWindowText(GetDlgItem(hwnd, IDC_WNDFOCUS), szBuf);

   CalcWndText(GetCapture(), szBuf, chDIMOF(szBuf));
   SetWindowText(GetDlgItem(hwnd, IDC_WNDCAPTURE), szBuf);

   CalcWndText(GetActiveWindow(), szBuf, chDIMOF(szBuf));
   SetWindowText(GetDlgItem(hwnd, IDC_WNDACTIVE), szBuf);

   CalcWndText(GetForegroundWindow(), szBuf,
      chDIMOF(szBuf));
   SetWindowText(GetDlgItem(hwnd, IDC_WNDFOREGROUND), szBuf);

   GetClipCursor(&rc);
   _stprintf(szBuf,
      __TEXT("left=%d, top=%d, right=%d, bottom=%d"),
        rc.left, rc.top, rc.right, rc.bottom);
   SetWindowText(GetDlgItem(hwnd, IDC_CLIPCURSOR), szBuf);
```

(continued)

Figure 11-7. *continued*

```
if ((g_dwEventTime == 0) ||
    (GetTickCount() < g_dwEventTime))
    return;

switch (g_nEventId) {
    case 0:  // SetFocus
        g_hwndSubject = SetFocus(g_hwndSubject);
        break;

    case 1:  // SetActiveWindow
        g_hwndSubject = SetActiveWindow(g_hwndSubject);
        break;

    case 2:  // SetForegroundWindow
        hwndT = GetForegroundWindow();
        SetForegroundWindow(g_hwndSubject);
        g_hwndSubject = hwndT;
        break;

    case 3:  // BringWindowToTop
        BringWindowToTop(g_hwndSubject);
        break;

    case 4:  // SetWindowPos w/HWND_TOP
        SetWindowPos(g_hwndSubject, HWND_TOP, 0, 0, 0, 0,
            SWP_NOMOVE | SWP_NOSIZE);
        g_hwndSubject = (HWND) 1;
        break;

    case 5:  // SetWindowPos w/ HWND_BOTTOM
        SetWindowPos(g_hwndSubject, HWND_BOTTOM, 0, 0, 0, 0,
            SWP_NOMOVE | SWP_NOSIZE);
        g_hwndSubject = (HWND) 1;
        break;
}

if (g_hwndSubject == (HWND) 1) {
    SetWindowText(GetDlgItem(hwnd, IDC_PREVWND),
        __TEXT("Can't tell."));
} else {
    CalcWndText(g_hwndSubject, szBuf, chDIMOF(szBuf));
    SetWindowText(GetDlgItem(hwnd, IDC_PREVWND), szBuf);
}
```

(continued)

Figure 11-7. *continued*

```
   g_hwndSubject = NULL; g_nEventId = 0; g_dwEventTime = 0;
   SetWindowText(GetDlgItem(hwnd, IDC_EVENTPENDING),
      __TEXT("Executed"));
}


///////////////////////////////////////////////////////////////


BOOL CALLBACK Dlg_Proc (HWND hwnd, UINT uMsg,
   WPARAM wParam, LPARAM lParam) {

   switch (uMsg) {
      chHANDLE_DLGMSG(hwnd, WM_INITDIALOG,
         Dlg_OnInitDialog);
      chHANDLE_DLGMSG(hwnd, WM_DESTROY,        Dlg_OnDestroy);
      chHANDLE_DLGMSG(hwnd, WM_COMMAND,        Dlg_OnCommand);

      chHANDLE_DLGMSG(hwnd, WM_MOUSEMOVE,      Dlg_OnMouseMove);

      chHANDLE_DLGMSG(hwnd, WM_LBUTTONDOWN,
         Dlg_OnLButtonDown);
      chHANDLE_DLGMSG(hwnd, WM_LBUTTONDBLCLK,
         Dlg_OnLButtonDown);
      chHANDLE_DLGMSG(hwnd, WM_LBUTTONUP,      Dlg_OnLButtonUp);

      chHANDLE_DLGMSG(hwnd, WM_RBUTTONDOWN,
         Dlg_OnRButtonDown);
      chHANDLE_DLGMSG(hwnd, WM_RBUTTONDBLCLK,
         Dlg_OnRButtonDown);
      chHANDLE_DLGMSG(hwnd, WM_RBUTTONUP,      Dlg_OnRButtonUp);

      chHANDLE_DLGMSG(hwnd, WM_TIMER,          Dlg_OnTimer);
   }
   return(FALSE);
}


///////////////////////////////////////////////////////////////


int WINAPI _tWinMain (HINSTANCE hinstExe,
   HINSTANCE hinstPrev, LPTSTR pszCmdLine, int nCmdShow) {
```

(continued)

Figure 11-7. *continued*

```
    chWARNIFUNICODEUNDERWIN95();
    DialogBox(hinstExe, MAKEINTRESOURCE(IDD_LISLAB),
        NULL, Dlg_Proc);

    return(0);
}



///////////////////////// End Of File //////////////////////////
```

LISLAB.RC
```
//Microsoft Developer Studio generated resource script.
//
#include "Resource.h"

#define APSTUDIO_READONLY_SYMBOLS
/////////////////////////////////////////////////////////////////
//
// Generated from the TEXTINCLUDE 2 resource.
//
#include "afxres.h"


/////////////////////////////////////////////////////////////////
#undef APSTUDIO_READONLY_SYMBOLS


/////////////////////////////////////////////////////////////////
// English (U.S.) resources

#if !defined(AFX_RESOURCE_DLL) || defined(AFX_TARG_ENU)
#ifdef _WIN32
LANGUAGE LANG_ENGLISH, SUBLANG_ENGLISH_US
#pragma code_page(1252)
#endif //_WIN32


/////////////////////////////////////////////////////////////////
//
// Icon
//

// Icon with lowest ID value placed first to ensure
// application icon remains consistent on all systems.
IDI_LISLAB              ICON    DISCARDABLE     "LISLab.Ico"
```

(continued)

Figure 11-7. *continued*

```
/////////////////////////////////////////////////////////
//
// Dialog
//


IDD_LISLAB DIALOG DISCARDABLE  12, 38, 286, 178
STYLE WS_MINIMIZEBOX | WS_VISIBLE | WS_CAPTION
   | WS_SYSMENU
CAPTION "Local Input State Lab"
FONT 8, "Arial"
BEGIN
    GROUPBOX          "Windows",IDC_STATIC,4,0,192,56
    LTEXT             "Focus:",IDC_STATIC,8,12,23,8
    LTEXT             "Focus window info",IDC_WNDFOCUS,
                      52,12,140,8
    LTEXT             "Active:",IDC_STATIC,8,20,24,8
    LTEXT             "Active window info",IDC_WNDACTIVE,
                      52,20,140,8
    LTEXT             "Foreground:",IDC_STATIC,8,28,40,8
    LTEXT             "Foreground window info",
                      IDC_WNDFOREGROUND,52,28,140,8
    LTEXT             "Capture:",IDC_STATIC,8,36,29,8
    LTEXT             "Capture window info",IDC_WNDCAPTURE,
                      52,36,140,8
    LTEXT             "Clip Cursor:",IDC_STATIC,8,44,39,8
    LTEXT             "Cursor clipping info",IDC_CLIPCURSOR,
                      52,44,140,8
    LTEXT             "&Function:",IDC_STATIC,200,4,32,8
    COMBOBOX          IDC_WNDFUNC,200,14,82,54,
                      CBS_DROPDOWNLIST | WS_VSCROLL
                      | WS_TABSTOP
    PUSHBUTTON        "Dela&y:",IDC_FUNCSTART,200,30,26,14
    EDITTEXT          IDC_DELAY,228,30,24,12,ES_AUTOHSCROLL
    LTEXT             "Executed",IDC_EVENTPENDING,
                      252,30,32,10
    LTEXT             "PrevWnd:",IDC_STATIC,200,46,34,8
    LTEXT             "Previous window info",IDC_PREVWND,
                      208,54,76,18
    LTEXT             "&Notepad windows and Self:",
                      IDC_STATIC,4,62,90,8
    LISTBOX           IDC_WNDS,4,72,192,32,WS_VSCROLL
                      | WS_TABSTOP
```

(continued)

Figure 11-7. *continued*

```
        PUSHBUTTON          "&Attach to Notepad",IDC_THREADATTACH,
                            200,72,80,12
        PUSHBUTTON          "&Detach from Notepad",
                            IDC_THREADDETACH,200,88,80,12
        LTEXT               "&Mouse messages received:",
                            IDC_STATIC,4,102,89,8
        LISTBOX             IDC_MOUSEMSGS,4,112,192,32,WS_VSCROLL
                            | WS_TABSTOP
        LTEXT               "Click right mouse button to set\
capture.\n\nDouble-click right mouse button to release\
capture.",
                            IDC_STATIC,200,110,80,40
        LTEXT               "Clipping rect:",IDC_STATIC,
                            4,148,44,8
        PUSHBUTTON          "&Top, left",IDC_SETCLIPRECT,
                            52,146,56,14
        PUSHBUTTON          "&Remove",IDC_REMOVECLIPRECT,
                            112,146,56,12
        PUSHBUTTON          "&Hide",IDC_HIDECURSOR,52,162,56,12
        PUSHBUTTON          "&Show",IDC_SHOWCURSOR,112,162,56,12
        PUSHBUTTON          "&Infinite loop",IDC_INFINITELOOP,200,
                            162,80,12,WS_GROUP | NOT WS_TABSTOP
        LTEXT               "Cursor visibility:",IDC_STATIC,
                            4,164,47,8
END


#ifdef APSTUDIO_INVOKED
/////////////////////////////////////////////////////////////
//
// TEXTINCLUDE
//

1 TEXTINCLUDE DISCARDABLE
BEGIN
    "Resource.h\0"
END

2 TEXTINCLUDE DISCARDABLE
BEGIN
    "#include ""afxres.h""\r\n"
    "\0"
END
```

(continued)

Figure 11-7. *continued*

```
3 TEXTINCLUDE DISCARDABLE
BEGIN
    "\r\n"
    "\0"
END

#endif    // APSTUDIO_INVOKED


/////////////////////////////////////////////////////////////
//
// DESIGNINFO
//

#ifdef APSTUDIO_INVOKED
GUIDELINES DESIGNINFO DISCARDABLE
BEGIN
    IDD_LISLAB, DIALOG
    BEGIN
        RIGHTMARGIN, 283
        BOTTOMMARGIN, 170
    END
END
#endif    // APSTUDIO_INVOKED

#endif    // English (U.S.) resources
/////////////////////////////////////////////////////////////



#ifndef APSTUDIO_INVOKED
/////////////////////////////////////////////////////////////
//
// Generated from the TEXTINCLUDE 3 resource.
//


/////////////////////////////////////////////////////////////
#endif    // not APSTUDIO_INVOKED
```

DYNAMIC-LINK LIBRARIES

Dynamic-link libraries (DLLs) have been the cornerstone of Windows since the very first version of the operating system. All the functions in the Win32 API are contained in DLLs. The three most important DLLs are KERNEL32.DLL, which consists of functions for managing memory, processes, and threads; USER32.DLL, which consists of functions for performing user-interface tasks such as window creation and message sending; and GDI32.DLL, which consists of functions for drawing graphical images and displaying text.

Windows also comes with several other DLLs that contain functions for performing more specialized tasks. For example, ADVAPI32.DLL contains functions for object security, registry manipulation, and event logging; COMDLG32.DLL contains the common dialogs (such as File Open and File Save); and LZ32.DLL supports file decompression.

In this chapter, we'll discuss how you can create Win32 DLLs for your own applications. In addition, some advanced techniques that require the use of DLLs are described at the end of the chapter; you'll find other advanced techniques in Chapter 18.

Creating a Dynamic-Link Library

It is often easier to create a dynamic-link library than it is to create an application. This is because a DLL usually consists of a set of autonomous functions that any application can use. There is usually no support code for processing message loops or creating windows within DLLs. A dynamic-link library is simply a set of source code modules, with each module containing a set of functions. These functions are written with the expectation that an application (EXE file) or another DLL will call them. After all the source code files have been compiled, they are then linked by the linker just as an application's EXE file would be. However, for a DLL you must specify the /DLL switch to the linker. This switch causes the linker to emit slightly different information into the resulting DLL file image so that the operating system loader recognizes the file image as a DLL rather than an application.

For an application (or another DLL) to call functions contained within a DLL, the DLL's file image must first be mapped into the calling process's address space. This can be accomplished using one of two methods: implicit load-time linking or explicit run-time linking. These methods will be discussed shortly.

Once a DLL's file image is mapped into the calling process's address space, the DLL's functions are available to all the threads running within the process. In fact, the DLL loses almost all of its identity as a DLL: to all the threads in the process, the DLL's code and data simply look like additional code and data that just happen to be in the process's address space. Whenever a thread calls any DLL function, the DLL function looks at the thread's stack to retrieve its passed parameters and also uses the thread's stack for any local variables that the DLL function might need. In addition, any objects created by code in the DLL's functions are owned by the calling thread or process—a DLL never owns anything in Win32.

For example, if *VirtualAlloc* is called by a function in a DLL, the region of address space is reserved from the address space of the calling thread's process. If the DLL is later unmapped from the process's address space, the address space region remains reserved because the system does not keep track of the fact that a function in the DLL reserved the region. The reserved region is owned by the process and will be freed only if a thread somehow calls the *VirtualFree* function or if the process terminates.

As you already know, the global and static variables of an EXE file are not shared between multiple running instances of the same EXE. Windows 95 ensures this by allocating storage for the EXE's global and static variables when the EXE is mapped into the process's address space; Windows NT ensures this by using the copy-on-write mechanism discussed in Chapter 5. Global and static variables in a DLL are handled in exactly the same way. When one process maps a DLL image file into its address space, the system creates instances of the global and static data variables as well. Later in this chapter, I'll talk about a technique that allows a DLL to share its global and static variables across multiple mappings of the DLL. However, this technique is not the default in Win32— you must perform some additional actions to get this behavior.

DLLs are managed quite differently in 16-bit Windows than in Win32. In 16-bit Windows, loading a DLL means that, in a sense, the DLL becomes part of the operating system. After the DLL is loaded, any and all applications currently running have immediate access to the DLL and the functions that the DLL contains. In the Win32 environment, a DLL *must* be mapped into the process's address space before an application can successfully call functions in the DLL.

The 16-bit Windows environment and the Win32 environment handle a DLL's global and static data quite differently as well. In 16-bit Windows, each DLL has its own data segment. This data segment houses all the static and global variables needed by the DLL as well as the DLL's own private local heap. When a DLL function allocates memory using *LocalAlloc,* the memory that satisfies this request is taken from the DLL's data segment. This segment, like all segments, is limited to 64 KB.

This design allows applications to share data among multiple processes because the DLL's local heap is available to the DLL regardless of which process called the function contained in the DLL. Here is an example of how a DLL can be used for sharing data between two applications:

```
HLOCAL g_hData = NULL;

void SetData (LPVOID lpvData, int nSize) {
    LPVOID lpv;
    g_hData = LocalAlloc(LMEM_MOVEABLE, nSize);
    lpv = LocalLock(g_hData);
    memcpy(lpv, lpvData, nSize);
    LocalUnlock(g_hData);
}

void GetData (LPVOID lpvData, int nSize) {
    LPVOID lpv = LocalLock(g_hData);
    memcpy(lpvData, lpv, nSize);
    LocalUnlock(g_hData);
}
```

When *SetData* is called, it allocates a block of memory out of the DLL's data segment, copies the data pointed to by the *lpvData* parameter into the block, and saves the handle to the block in a global variable, *g_hData.* A totally different application can now call *GetData. GetData* uses the global variable identifying the local memory handle, locks the block,

(continued)

16 ·· 32

(continued)

copies the data into the buffer identified by the *lpvData* parameter, and returns. This is an easy way to share data between two processes in 16-bit Windows.

Of course, this method doesn't work at all in Win32, for two reasons. First, DLLs in Win32 don't receive their own local heaps. Second, a Win32 DLL's global and static variables are not shared among multiple mappings of the DLL—the system creates an instance of the global *g_hData* variable for each process, and each instance will not have the same value when the DLL is mapped into the address spaces of mulitple processes.

Mapping a DLL into a Process's Address Space

As I mentioned earlier, in order for a thread to call a function in a DLL, the DLL's file image must be mapped into the address space of the calling thread's process. You can accomplish this in two ways: implicitly linking to functions in the DLL and explicitly loading the DLL.

Implicit Linking

Implicit linking is the most common method for mapping a DLL's file image into a process's address space. When you link an application, you must specify a set of LIB files to the linker. Each LIB file contains the list of functions that a DLL file is allowing an application (or another DLL) to call. When the linker sees that the application is calling a function that is referenced in a DLL's LIB file, the linker embeds information into the resultant EXE file image that indicates the name of the DLL containing the functions that the EXE requires. When the operating system loads an EXE file, the system examines the contents of the EXE file image to see which DLLs must be loaded for the application to run. The system then attempts to map the required DLL file images into the process's address space. When searching for the DLL, the system looks for the file image in the following locations:

1. The directory containing the EXE image file

2. The process's current directory

3. The Windows system directory

4. The Windows directory

5. The directories listed in the PATH environment variable

If the DLL file cannot be found, the operating system displays a message box that looks something like the one here and immediately terminates the entire process:

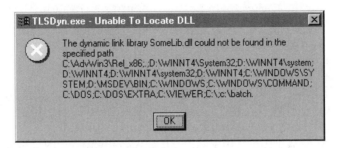

When using this method, any DLL file images mapped into the process's address space are not unmapped until the process is terminated.

Explicit Linking

A DLL's file image can be explicitly mapped into a process's address space when one of the process's threads calls either the *LoadLibrary* or the *LoadLibraryEx* function:

```
HINSTANCE LoadLibrary(LPCTSTR lpszLibFile);

HINSTANCE LoadLibraryEx(LPCTSTR lpszLibFile, HANDLE hFile,
    DWORD dwFlags);
```

Both of these functions locate a file image on the user's system (using the same search algorithm discussed in the previous section) and attempt to map the DLL's file image into the calling process's address space. The HINSTANCE value returned from both of these functions identifies the virtual memory address where the file image was mapped. If the DLL could not be mapped into the process's address space, the functions return NULL.

Under 16-bit Windows, *LoadLibrary* indicates that an error has occurred by returning a handle value less than 32. The value returned indicates the reason for the failure. In Win32, NULL is always returned if an error occurs. To determine the reason for the error, the thread must call *GetLastError.*

You'll notice that the *LoadLibraryEx* function has two additional parameters: *hFile* and *dwFlags*. The *hFile* parameter is reserved for future use and must be NULL for now.

For the *dwFlags* parameter, you must specify either 0 or a combination of the DONT_RESOLVE_DLL_REFERENCES, LOAD_LIBRARY_AS_DATAFILE, and LOAD_WITH_ALTERED_SEARCH_PATH flags. These flags are discussed briefly below.

DONT_RESOLVE_DLL_REFERENCES Specifying this flag tells the system to map the DLL into the calling process's address space. Normally, when a DLL is mapped into a process's address space, the system calls a special function in the DLL, usually named *DllMain* (discussed later in this chapter), that is used to initialize the DLL. Specifying the DONT_RESOLVE_DLL_REFERENCES flag causes the system simply to map the file image without calling the *DllMain* function.

In addition, a DLL might import functions contained in another DLL. When the system maps a DLL into a process's address space, the system also checks to see whether any additional DLLs are required by the DLL and automatically loads these as well. When the DONT_RESOLVE_DLL_REFERENCES flag is specified, the system does not automatically load any of these additional DLLs into the process's address space.

LOAD_LIBRARY_AS_DATAFILE This flag is very similar to the DONT_RESOLVE_DLL_REFERENCES flag; that is, the system simply maps the DLL into the process's address space as though it were a data file. The system spends no additional time preparing to execute any code in the file. For example, when a DLL is mapped into a process's address space, the system examines some information in the DLL to determine which page protection attributes should be assigned to different sections of the file. When you don't specify the LOAD_LIBRARY_AS_DATAFILE flag, the system sets the page protection attributes the same way it would if it were expecting to execute code in the file.

This flag is useful for several reasons. First, if you have a DLL that contains only resources and no functions, you might want to specify this flag. By doing so, the DLL's file image gets mapped into the process's address space and you can then use the HINSTANCE value returned from *LoadLibraryEx* in calls to functions that load resources. You might also use the LOAD_LIBRARY_AS_DATAFILE flag if you want to use resources that are contained inside an EXE file. Normally, loading an EXE file starts a new process, but you can also use the *LoadLibraryEx* function to map an EXE file's image into a process's address space. Again, once you have the mapped EXE's HINSTANCE value, you can access resources contained within it. Because an EXE file does not have the *DllMain* function, you'll have to specify the LOAD_LIBRARY_AS-_DATAFILE flag when calling *LoadLibraryEx* to load an EXE file.

LOAD_WITH_ALTERED_SEARCH_PATH Specifying this flag changes the search algorithm that *LoadLibraryEx* uses to locate the specified DLL file. Normally, *LoadLibraryEx* searches for files in the order shown at the bottom of page 532. However, if the LOAD_WITH_ALTERED-_SEARCH_PATH flag is specified, *LoadLibraryEx* searches for the file using the following algorithm:

1. The directory specified in the *lpszLibFile* parameter

2. The process's current directory

3. The Windows system directory

4. The Windows directory

5. The directories listed in the PATH environment variable

There is another force at work that can alter where the system locates DLLs. Inside the registry is a key called

```
HKEY_LOCAL_MACHINE\SYSTEM\CurrentControlSet\Control\
    Session Manager\KnownDLLs
```

The window at the top of the next page shows the contents of this key if you look it up using REGEDIT.EXE.

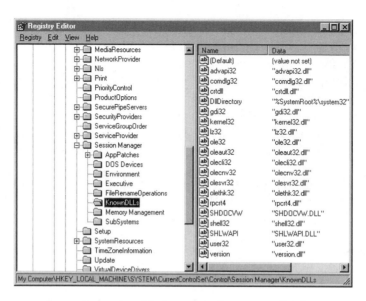

As you can see, this key contains a set of value names that are the names of certain DLLs. Each of these value names has value data that happens to be identical to the value name with a ".DLL" file extension. (This does not have to be the case, however, as I'll show you in an upcoming example.)

When *LoadLibrary* or *LoadLibraryEx* are called, these functions first check to see whether you are passing a DLL name that includes the ".DLL" extension. If you do not pass the extension, they search for the DLL using the search rules just mentioned.

If you do specify a ".DLL" extension, however, these functions remove the extension and then search the *KnownDLLs* registry key to see if it contains a value name that matches. If no matching name is found, the search rules previously mentioned are used. But if a matching value name is found in the *KnownDLLs* registry key, the system then looks up the associated value data and attempts to load a DLL using the value data instead. The system also begins searching for the DLL in the directory indicated by the *DllDirectory* value's data in the registry. By default, the *DllDirectory* value's data is "%SystemRoot%\System32" on Windows NT.

To illustrate, suppose we add the following value to the *KnownDLLs* registry key:

```
Value name: SomeLib
Value data: SomeOtherLib.DLL
```

When we call

```
LoadLibrary("SomeLib");
```

the system uses the normal search rules to locate the file. However, if we call

```
LoadLibrary("SomeLib.DLL");
```

the system sees that there is a matching value name (remember the system removes the ".DLL" extension when checking the registry value names). So the system attempts to load a library called "SomeOtherLib.DLL" instead of "SomeLib.DLL". And the system first looks for "SomeOther-Lib.DLL" in the "%SystemRoot%\System32" directory. If the file is found in this directory, it is loaded. If the file is not in this directory, *Load-Library(Ex)* fails and returns NULL, and a call to *GetLastError* returns 2 (ERROR_FILE_NOT_FOUND).

When explicitly loading a DLL, you may explicitly unmap the file image from the process's address space at any time by calling the *Free-Library* function:

```
BOOL FreeLibrary(HINSTANCE hinstDll);
```

When calling *FreeLibrary*, you must pass the HINSTANCE value that identifies the DLL you want to free. This value was returned by an earlier call to *LoadLibrary* or *LoadLibraryEx*.

In reality, the *LoadLibrary* and *LoadLibraryEx* functions increment a usage count associated with the specified library, and the *FreeLibrary* function decrements the library's usage count. For example, the first time you call *LoadLibrary* to load a DLL, the system maps the DLL's file image into the calling process's address space and associates a usage count of 1 with the DLL. If a thread in the same process later calls *LoadLibrary* to load the same DLL file image, the system does not map the DLL file image into the process's address space a second time. Instead, the system simply increments the usage count associated with the DLL. In order for the DLL file image to be unmapped from the process's address space, threads in the process must call *FreeLibrary* twice—the first call to *FreeLibrary* simply decrements the DLL's usage count to 1, and the second call to *FreeLibrary* decrements the DLL's usage count to 0. When the system sees that a DLL's usage count has reached 0, the system unmaps the DLL's file image from the process's address space. After the DLL's file image is unmapped, any thread that attempts to call a function in the DLL will raise an access violation because the code at the specified address is no longer mapped into the process's address space.

The system maintains a DLL's usage count on a per-process basis; that is, if a thread in Process A makes the call

```
HINSTANCE hinstDll = LoadLibrary("MyLib.DLL");
```

and then a thread in Process B makes the same call, MYLIB.DLL is mapped into both processes' address spaces—the DLL's usage count in Process A and the DLL's usage count in Process B are both 1. If a thread in Process B later calls

```
FreeLibrary(hinstDll);
```

the DLL's usage count with respect to Process B becomes 0, and the DLL is unmapped from Process B's address space. However, the mapping of the DLL in Process A's address space is unaffected, and the DLL's usage count with respect to Process A remains 1.

A thread can call the *GetModuleHandle* function

```
HINSTANCE GetModuleHandle(LPCTSTR lpszModuleName);
```

to determine whether a DLL is mapped into its process's address space. For example, the following code loads MYLIB.DLL only if it is not already mapped into the process's address space:

```
HINSTANCE hinstDll;
hinstDll = GetModuleHandle("MyLib");    // DLL extension assumed
if (hinstDll == NULL) {
   hinstDll = LoadLibrary("MyLib");     // DLL extension assumed
}
```

You can also determine the full pathname of a DLL (or an EXE) if all you have is the DLL's HINSTANCE value by using the *GetModuleFileName* function:

```
DWORD GetModuleFileName(HINSTANCE hinstModule,
   LPTSTR lpszPath, DWORD cchPath);
```

The first parameter is the DLL's (or EXE's) HINSTANCE. The second parameter, *lpszPath*, is the address of the buffer where the function will put the file image's full pathname. The third and last parameter, *cchPath*, specifies the size of the buffer in characters.

There is another Win32 function that you can use to decrement a DLL's usage count:

```
VOID FreeLibraryAndExitThread(HINSTANCE hinstDll,
   DWORD dwExitCode);
```

The 16-bit Windows API has a *GetModuleUsage* function:

```
int GetModuleUsage(HINSTANCE hinstDll);
```

When you pass this function the HINSTANCE value of a loaded DLL, the system returns the usage count of the DLL. The usage count tells you how many times *FreeLibrary* would have to be called in order to unload the DLL. Remember that in 16-bit Windows, DLLs become part of the operating system and are available to all running tasks. Because DLLs in Win32 become part of the calling process's address space rather than part of the operating system itself, *GetModuleUsage* is no longer supported in the Win32 API.

Personally, I think Microsoft should have kept *GetModuleUsage* in the Win32 API because it's useful to know the usage count of a DLL with respect to the calling process. The operating system keeps track of this information internally already—it would have been easy for Microsoft to modify *GetModuleUsage* so that it simply returned this information.

This function is implemented in KERNEL32.DLL as follows:

```
VOID FreeLibraryAndExitThread(HINSTANCE hinstDll,
    DWORD dwExitCode) {

    FreeLibrary(hinstDll);
    ExitThread(dwExitCode);
}
```

At first glance this doesn't look like such a big deal, and you might ask yourself why Microsoft went to the trouble of creating the *FreeLibraryAndExitThread* function. The reason has to do with the following scenario: Suppose you are writing a DLL that, when it is first mapped into a process's address space, creates a thread. When the thread is finished performing its work, the thread can unmap the DLL from the process's address space. For the thread to unmap the DLL, the thread must call *FreeLibrary* and then immediately call *ExitThread*.

But if the thread calls *FreeLibrary* and *ExitThread* individually, a very serious problem occurs. The problem, of course, is that the call to *FreeLibrary* unmaps the DLL from the process's address space immediately. By the time the call to *FreeLibrary* returns, the code that contains the call to *ExitThread* is no longer available and the thread will attempt to execute nothing. This will cause an access violation to be raised, and the entire process will be terminated!

However, if the thread calls *FreeLibraryAndExitThread*, this function calls *FreeLibrary*, causing the DLL to be immediately unmapped. The next instruction executed is in KERNEL32.DLL, not in the DLL that has just been unmapped. This means that the thread can continue executing and can call *ExitThread*. *ExitThread* will cause the thread to terminate and will not return.

Granted, you will probably not have much need for the *FreeLibrary-AndExitThread* function. I have needed it only once myself, and I was performing a very specialized task. Also, at the time I was writing my code for Windows NT 3.1, which did not offer this function. So I was very glad to see that Microsoft had added it to Windows NT 3.5 and Windows 95.

The DLL's Entry/Exit Function

A Win32 DLL can, optionally, have a single entry/exit function. The system calls this DLL entry/exit function at various times that I will discuss later. These calls are informational and are usually used by a DLL to perform any per-process or per-thread initialization and cleanup. If your DLL doesn't require these notifications, you do not have to implement this function in your DLL source code. For example, if you create a DLL that contains only resources, you do not need to implement this function. If you do have this entry/exit function, it must look like this:

```
BOOL WINAPI DllMain (HINSTANCE hinstDll, DWORD fdwReason,
  LPVOID fImpLoad) {

  switch (fdwReason) {
    case DLL_PROCESS_ATTACH:
      // The DLL is being mapped into
      // the process's address space.
      break;

    case DLL_THREAD_ATTACH:
      // A thread is being created.
      break;

    case DLL_THREAD_DETACH:
      // A thread is exiting cleanly.
      break;

    case DLL_PROCESS_DETACH:
      // The DLL is being unmapped from
      // the process's address space.
      break;
  }
  return(TRUE);     // Used only for DLL_PROCESS_ATTACH
}
```

540

When producing DLLs for 16-bit Windows, you always need to link a small assembly language module into your DLL. This module performs some low-level initialization and calls your *LibMain* function, passing parameters that the system has passed to the assembly language module in CPU registers. Fortunately, Microsoft includes the source code for this module on the SDK disks. The assembled OBJ file is also on the SDK disks, which is helpful to those of us who don't own a macro assembler.

As mentioned earlier, Win32 is designed as a portable API capable of running on different hardware platforms using different CPUs. To accomplish this, Microsoft needed to remove the necessity for any assembly language modules. To create a DLL, you need only to write your code and link it as if it were an application. Most of your DLLs should port directly to Win32 with very little modification. The two areas that will require modification are the *LibMain* and *Windows Exit Procedure (WEP)* functions.

In 16-bit Windows, the system calls the library's *LibMain* function whenever the library is loaded into the system and calls the library's *WEP* function whenever the library is being removed from the system. Conceptually, the *WEP* function was a nice addition to 16-bit Windows (it didn't exist prior to version 3.0), but there were many problems with the way that Windows made use of the function. In low-memory situations, the *WEP* function could actually be called before the *LibMain* function, and it might be called using the Kernel's very small stack. This meant that using local variables in the *WEP* function might cause the entire system to crash. You'll be happy to know that all these problems do not exist in Win32.

The *DllMain* function replaces the *LibMain* and *WEP* functions used in 16-bit Windows DLLs.

The operating system calls this entry/exit function at various times. Whenever the function is called, the *hinstDll* parameter contains the instance handle of the DLL. Like the *hinstExe* parameter to *WinMain*, this value identifies the virtual memory address of where the DLL's file image was mapped in the process's address space. Usually, you'll save this parameter in a global variable so that you can use it in calls that load resources, such as *DialogBox* and *LoadString*. The last parameter, *fImpLoad*, is nonzero if the DLL is implicitly loaded or zero if the DLL is explicitly loaded.

The *fdwReason* parameter indicates why the system is calling the function. This parameter can be one of four possible values: DLL-_PROCESS_ATTACH, DLL_PROCESS_DETACH, DLL_THREAD_AT-TACH, or DLL_THREAD_DETACH. These values and their meanings are discussed in the following sections.

DLL_PROCESS_ATTACH

When a DLL is first mapped into a process's address space, the system calls the DLL's *DllMain* function, passing it a value of DLL_PROCESS-_ATTACH for the *fdwReason* parameter. This happens only when the DLL's file image is first mapped. If a thread later calls *LoadLibrary* or *LoadLibraryEx* for a DLL that is already mapped into the process's address space, the operating system simply increments the DLL's usage count; it does *not* call the DLL's *DllMain* function again with a value of DLL_PROCESS_ATTACH.

When processing DLL_PROCESS_ATTACH, a DLL should perform any process-relative initialization required by functions contained within the DLL. For example, the DLL might contain functions that need to use their own heap (created in the process's address space). The DLL's *DllMain* function could create this heap by calling *HeapCreate* during its processing of the DLL_PROCESS_ATTACH notification. The handle to the created heap could be saved in a global variable that the DLL functions have access to.

When *DllMain* is processing a DLL_PROCESS_ATTACH notification, *DllMain*'s return value indicates whether the DLL's initialization was successful. If, for example, the call to *HeapCreate* was successful, you should return TRUE from *DllMain*. If the heap could not be created, return FALSE. For any of the other *fdwReason* values—DLL_PRO-CESS_DETACH, DLL_THREAD_ATTACH, and DLL_THREAD_DE-TACH—the system ignores the return value from *DllMain*.

Of course, there must be some thread in the system that is responsible for executing the code in the *DllMain* function. When a new process is created, the system allocates the process's address space and then maps the EXE file image and all of the required DLL file images into the process's address space. Then the system creates the process's primary thread and uses this thread to call each of the DLL's *DllMain* functions with a value of DLL_PROCESS_ATTACH. After all of the mapped DLLs have responded to this notification, the system causes the process's primary thread to begin executing the EXE's C run-time startup code, followed by the EXE's *WinMain* function. If any of the DLL's *DllMain* functions return FALSE, indicating unsuccessful initialization, the system terminates the entire process, removing all the file images from its address space and displaying a message box to the user stating that the process could not be started.

Now let's look at what happens when a DLL is loaded explicitly. When a thread in a process calls *LoadLibrary* or *LoadLibraryEx*, the system locates the specified DLL and maps the DLL into the process's address space. Then the system calls the DLL's *DllMain* function with a value of DLL_PROCESS_ATTACH, using the thread that placed the call to *LoadLibrary* or *LoadLibraryEx*. After the DLL's *DllMain* function has processed the notification, the system allows the call to *LoadLibrary* or *LoadLibraryEx* to return, and the thread continues processing as normal. If the *DllMain* function returned FALSE, indicating that the initialization was unsuccessful, the system automatically unmaps the DLL's file image from the process's address space and NULL is returned from the call to *LoadLibrary* or *LoadLibraryEx*.

In 16-bit Windows, a DLL's *LibMain* function is called only once, when the DLL is loaded. If other applications are loaded and require the same DLL, 16-bit Windows doesn't call the DLL's *LibMain* function again. In contrast, a Win32 DLL's *DllMain* function is called with a value of DLL-_PROCESS_ATTACH every time the DLL is mapped into another process's address space. If 10 applications require LIBXYZ.DLL, LIBXYZ's *DllMain* is called 10 times with a value of DLL_PROCESS_ATTACH.

DLL_PROCESS_DETACH

When a DLL is unmapped from a process's address space, the system calls the DLL's *DllMain* function, passing it an *fdwReason* value of DLL-_PROCESS_DETACH. A DLL should perform any process-relative cleanup when processing this value. For example, a DLL might call *HeapDestroy* to destroy a heap that it created during the DLL_PROCESS_ATTACH notification.

Important

If a DLL's *DllMain* function is called with an *fdwReason* value of DLL-_PROCESS_ATTACH and *DllMain* returns FALSE, indicating unsuccessful initialization, the system will still call the DLL's *DllMain* function with a value of DLL_PROCESS_DETACH. For this reason, you must make sure that you don't try to clean up anything that wasn't successfully initialized.

For example, examine the following *DllMain* function to see whether you can determine where a possible memory access violation might occur:

```
BOOL WINAPI DllMain(HINSTANCE hinstDll, DWORD fdwReason,
   LPVOID fImpLoad) {

   static PVOID pvData = NULL;
   BOOL fOk = TRUE;   // Assume success.

   switch (fdwReason) {
      case DLL_PROCESS_ATTACH:
         pvData = HeapAlloc(GetProcessHeap(), 0, 1000);
         if (pvData == NULL)
            fOk = FALSE;
         break;

      case DLL_PROCESS_DETACH:
         HeapFree(GetProcessHeap(), 0, pvData);
         break;
   }

   return(fOk);   // Used only for DLL_PROCESS_ATTACH
}
```

The code looks harmless enough. When the DLL is attached to the process's address space, a small memory block is allocated. If the block could not be allocated, *DllMain* returns FALSE, indicating that the DLL was unable to initialize properly. When the DLL is unmapped from the process's address space, the allocated memory block is freed. Here's the problem: In the fragment above, note that if a library's *DllMain* returns FALSE when processing its DLL_PROCESS_ATTACH notification, the system calls *DllMain* again with a value of DLL_PROCESS_DETACH.

(continued)

This means that *HeapFree* will be called to free a memory block, even though that memory block was never allocated successfully. To correct the problem, you must rewrite the DLL_PROCESS_DETACH case as follows:

```
case DLL_PROCESS_DETACH:
   if (pvData != NULL)
      HeapFree(GetProcessHeap(), 0, pvData);
   break;
```

If the DLL is being unmapped because the process is terminating, the thread that calls *ExitProcess* is responsible for executing the *DllMain* function's code. Under normal circumstances, this is the application's primary thread. When your *WinMain* function returns to the C run-time library's startup code, the startup code explicitly calls the *ExitProcess* function to terminate the process.

If the DLL is being unmapped because a thread in the process called *FreeLibrary*, the *DllMain* function code is executed by the thread that called *FreeLibrary*. The call to *FreeLibrary* will not return until after the *DllMain* function has finished executing.

If a process terminates because some thread in the system calls *Terminate-Process*, the system does *not* call the DLL's *DllMain* function with a value of DLL_PROCESS_DETACH. This means that any DLLs mapped into the process's address space will not have the chance to perform any cleanup before the process terminates. This could result in the loss of data. You should use the *TerminateProcess* function only as a last resort!

Figure 12-1 on the following page shows the steps that are performed when a thread calls *LoadLibrary*.

Figure 12-2 on page 547 shows the steps that are performed when a thread calls *FreeLibrary*.

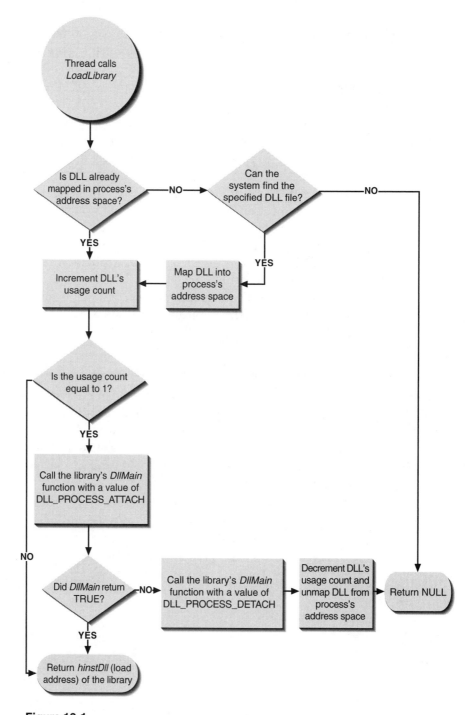

Figure 12-1.
The steps performed by the system when a thread calls LoadLibrary.

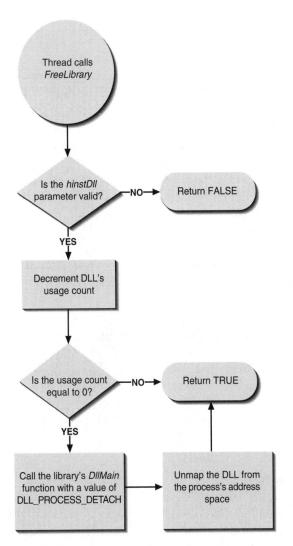

Figure 12-2.
The steps performed by the system when a thread calls FreeLibrary.

DLL_THREAD_ATTACH

When a thread is created in a process, the system examines all of the DLL file images currently mapped into the process's address space and calls each of these DLL's *DllMain* functions with a value of DLL_THREAD-_ATTACH. This notification tells all the DLLs to perform any per-thread initialization. For example, the DLL version of the C run-time library allocates a block of data so that a multithreaded application can safely use functions contained in the C run-time library.

The newly created thread is responsible for executing the code in all of the DLL's *DllMain* functions. Only after all the DLLs have had a chance to process this notification will the system allow the new thread to begin executing its thread function.

If a process already has several threads running in it when a new DLL is mapped into its address space, the system does *not* call the DLL's *DllMain* function with a value of DLL_THREAD_ATTACH for any of the already existing threads. The system calls the DLL's *DllMain* with a value of DLL_THREAD_ATTACH only if the DLL is mapped into the process's address space at the time that a new thread is created.

Also note that the system does not call any *DllMain* functions with a value of DLL_THREAD_ATTACH for the process's primary thread. Any DLLs that are mapped into the process's address space when the process is first invoked receive the DLL_PROCESS_ATTACH notification but do not receive the DLL_THREAD_ATTACH notification.

DLL_THREAD_DETACH

When a thread terminates by calling *ExitThread*,[1] the system examines all the DLL file images currently mapped into the process's address space and calls each DLL's *DllMain* function with a value of DLL_THREAD-_DETACH. This notification tells all the DLLs to perform any per-thread cleanup. For example, the DLL version of the C run-time library frees the data block that it uses to manage multithreaded applications.

---

1. If you allow your thread function to return instead of calling *ExitThread*, the system calls the *ExitThread* function automatically.

Important

If a thread terminates because a thread in the system calls *Terminate-Thread*, the system does *not* call all of the DLL's *DllMain* functions with a value of DLL_THREAD_DETACH. This means that any DLLs mapped into the process's address space will not have the chance to perform any cleanup before the thread terminates. This may result in the loss of data. Like *TerminateProcess*, use the *TerminateThread* function only as a last resort!

If any threads are still running when the DLL is detached, *DllMain* is not called with DLL_THREAD_DETACH for any of the threads. You might want to check for this in your DLL_PROCESS_DETACH processing so that you can perform any necessary cleanup.

Because of the rules stated above, it is possible for the following situation to occur: A thread in a process calls *LoadLibrary* to load a DLL, causing the system to call the DLL's *DllMain* function with a value of DLL_PROCESS_ATTACH. Next the thread that loaded the DLL exits, causing the DLL's *DllMain* function to be called again, this time with a value of DLL_THREAD_DETACH. Notice that the DLL is being notified that the thread is detaching but that it never received a DLL_THREAD_ATTACH notifying the library that the thread had attached. For this reason, you must be extremely careful when performing any thread-relative cleanup. Fortunately, most programs are written so that the thread that calls *LoadLibrary* is the same thread that calls *FreeLibrary*.

How the System Serializes Calls to *DllMain*

The system serializes calls to a DLL's *DllMain* function. To understand what this means, consider the following scenario. A process has two threads, Thread A and Thread B. The process also has a DLL, SOME-DLL.DLL, mapped into its address space. Both threads are about to call the *CreateThread* function in order to create two more threads: Thread C and Thread D.

When Thread A calls *CreateThread* to create Thread C, the system calls SOMEDLL's *DllMain* function with a value of DLL_THREAD_AT-TACH. While Thread C is executing the code in the *DllMain* function, Thread B calls *CreateThread* in order to create Thread D. The system needs to call the *DllMain* function again with a value of DLL_THREAD-_ATTACH, this time having Thread D execute the code. However, calls to *DllMain* are serialized by the system, and the system will suspend

Thread D until Thread C has completely processed the code in *DllMain* and returned.

After Thread C has finished processing the *DllMain* function, it can begin executing its thread function. Now the system wakes up Thread D and allows it to process the code in *DllMain*. When it returns, Thread D will begin processing its thread function.

Normally, you don't even think about this *DllMain* serialization. The reason I'm making a big deal out of it is that I worked with someone who had a bug in his code caused by *DllMain* serialization. His code looked something like this:

```
BOOL WINAPI DllMain (HINSTANCE hinstDll, DWORD fdwReason,
    LPVOID fImpLoad) {

    HANDLE hThread;
    DWORD dwThreadId;

    switch (fdwReason) {
    case DLL_PROCESS_ATTACH:
        // The DLL is being mapped into the
        // process's address space.

        // Create a thread to do some stuff.
        hThread = CreateThread(NULL, 0, SomeFunction, NULL,
            0, &dwThreadId);

        // Suspend our thread until the new thread terminates.
        WaitForSingleObject(hThread, INFINITE);

        // We no longer need access to the new thread.
        CloseHandle(hThread);
        break;

    case DLL_THREAD_ATTACH:
        // A thread is being created.
        break;

    case DLL_THREAD_DETACH:
        // A thread is exiting cleanly.
        break;

    case DLL_PROCESS_DETACH:
        // The DLL is being unmapped from the
        // process's address space.
        break;
    }
    return(TRUE);
}
```

It took us several hours to discover the problem with this code. Can you see it? When *DllMain* receives a DLL_PROCESS_ATTACH notification, a new thread is created. The system needs to call this *DllMain* function again with a value of DLL_THREAD_ATTACH. However, the new thread is suspended because the thread that caused the DLL_PROCESS_ATTACH notification to be sent to *DllMain* has not finished processing yet. The problem is the call to *WaitForSingleObject*. This function suspends the currently executing thread until the new thread terminates. However, the new thread will never get a chance to run, let alone terminate, because it is suspended waiting for the current thread to exit the *DllMain* function. What we have here is a deadlock situation—both threads are suspended forever!

When I first started thinking about ways to solve this problem, I discovered the *DisableThreadLibraryCalls* function:

```
BOOL DisableThreadLibraryCalls(HINSTANCE hinstDll);
```

This function was introduced with Windows NT 3.5 and exists in Windows 95 as well.

When you call *DisableThreadLibraryCalls*, you are telling the system that you do not want DLL_THREAD_ATTACH and DLL_THREAD_-DETACH notifications sent to the specified DLL's *DllMain* function. It seemed reasonable to me that, if we told the system not to send DLL notifications to the DLL, the deadlock situation would not occur. However, when I tested my solution, which follows, I soon discovered that the problem was not solved.

```
BOOL WINAPI DllMain (HINSTANCE hinstDll, DWORD fdwReason,
   LPVOID fImpLoad) {

   HANDLE hThread;
   DWORD dwThreadId;

   switch (fdwReason) {
   case DLL_PROCESS_ATTACH:
      // The DLL is being mapped into the process's address space.

      // Prevent the system from calling DllMain
      // when threads are created or destroyed.
      DisableThreadLibraryCalls(hinstDll);

      // Create a thread to do some stuff.
      hThread = CreateThread(NULL, 0, SomeFunction, NULL,
         0, &dwThreadId);
```

(continued)

```
    // Suspend our thread until the new thread terminates.
    WaitForSingleObject(hThread, INFINITE);

    // We no longer need access to the new thread.
    CloseHandle(hThread);
    break;

case DLL_THREAD_ATTACH:
    // A thread is being created.
    break;

case DLL_THREAD_DETACH:
    // A thread is exiting cleanly.
    break;

case DLL_PROCESS_DETACH:
    // The DLL is being unmapped from the process's address
    // space.
    break;
}
return(TRUE);
}
```

Upon further research I discovered why. When a process is created, the system also creates a mutex object. Each process has its own mutex object—the mutex object is not shared by multiple processes. The purpose of this mutex object is to synchronize all of a process's threads when the threads call the *DllMain* functions of the DLLs mapped into the process's address space.

When the *CreateThread* function is called, the system first creates the thread kernel object and the thread's stack. Then the system internally calls the *WaitForSingleObject* function, passing the handle of the process's mutex object. Once the new thread has ownership of the mutex, the system makes the new thread call each of the DLL's *DllMain* functions with a value of DLL_THREAD_ATTACH. Only after all of the DLL's *DllMain* functions have been called does the system call *ReleaseMutex* to relinquish ownership of the process's mutex object. Because the system works this way, adding the call to *DisableThreadLibraryCalls* does not prevent the threads from deadlocking. The only way I could think of to prevent the threads from being suspended was to redesign this part of the source code so that *WaitForSingleObject* is not called inside any DLL's *DllMain* function.

DllMain and the C Run-Time Library

In the discussion of the *DllMain* function on the previous page, I have been assuming that you are using Microsoft's Visual C++ compiler to build your dynamic-link library. When you write a DLL, it is likely that you will need some startup assistance from the C run-time library. For example, say that you are building a DLL that contains a global variable and that this global variable is an instance of a C++ class. Before the DLL can safely use the global variable, the variable must have its constructor called—this is a job for the C run-time library's DLL startup code.

When you link your DLL, the linker embeds the address of the DLL's entry/exit function in the resulting DLL file image. You specify the address of this function using the linker's /ENTRY switch. By default, when you use Microsoft's linker and specify the /DLL switch, the linker assumes that the entry function is called *_DllMainCRTStartup*. This function is contained inside the C run-time's library file and is statically linked in your DLL file's image when you link your DLL. The function is statically linked even if you use the DLL version of the C run-time library.)

When your DLL file image is mapped into a process's address space, the system actually calls this *_DllMainCRTStartup* function instead of your *DllMain* function. The *_DllMainCRTStartup* function initializes the C run-time library and ensures that any global or static C++ objects are constructed when *_DllMainCRTStartup* receives the DLL_PROCESS-_ATTACH notification. After any C run-time initialization has been performed, the *_DllMainCRTStartup* function calls your *DllMain* function.

When the DLL receives a DLL_PROCESS_DETACH notification, the system again calls the *_DllMainCRTStartup* function. This time, the function calls your *DllMain* function, and when *DllMain* returns, *_DllMainCRTStartup* calls any destructors for any global or static C++ objects in the DLL. The *_DllMainCRTStartup* function is also responsible for doing any additional C run-time–related initialization and cleanup when DLL_THREAD_ATTACH and DLL_THREAD_DETACH notifications are sent to the DLL.

I mentioned earlier in this chapter that you do not have to implement a *DllMain* function in your DLL's source code. If you don't have your own *DllMain* function, the C run-time library has its own implementation of a *DllMain* function that looks like this:

```
BOOL WINAPI DllMain(HINSTANCE hinstDll, DWORD fdwReason,
  LPVOID fImpLoad) {

  return(TRUE);
}
```

When the linker links your DLL, it will link the C run-time's implementation of the *DllMain* function if the linker cannot find a *DllMain* function in your DLL's OBJ files.

Exporting Functions and Variables from a DLL

When you create a DLL, you are creating a set of functions that you want an EXE or other DLLs to be able to call. When a DLL function is made available to an EXE or another DLL file, the function is said to be *exported*. Win32 makes it possible to export global data variables as well as functions. In this section, we look at the steps you need to perform in order to export a DLL's functions and global variables.

The following code (taken from a DLL's source file) demonstrates how to export a function called *Add* and a global integer variable called *g_nUsageCount* from a DLL:

```
__declspec(dllexport) int Add (int nLeft, int nRight) {
   return(nLeft + nRight);
}

__declspec(dllexport) int g_nUsageCount = 0;
```

For the most part, nothing in this code should be new to you except for the *__declspec(dllexport)*. Microsoft's C/C++ compiler recognizes this as a new keyword. When the compiler compiles the *Add* function and the *g_nUsageCount* variable, the compiler embeds some additional information in the resulting OBJ file. This information is intended to be parsed and processed by the linker when all of the OBJ files for the DLL are linked.

When the DLL is linked, the linker detects this embedded information about the exported function and variable. The linker then automatically produces a LIB file that contains the list of symbols exported by the DLL. This LIB file will, of course, be required to link any EXE that calls the exported functions in the DLL. In addition to creating the LIB file, the linker embeds a table of exported symbols in the resulting DLL file. Each entry in this table consists of the exported function's or variable's name and the address at which the function or variable is located within the DLL's file image. The linker ensures that the list is sorted alphabetically by symbol name.

You can run the DumpBin utility that comes with Visual C++ to see what the export table looks like. The following sample output shows a fragment of the Windows 95 KERNEL32.DLL's export table:

```
DUMPBIN -EXPORTS KERNEL32.DLL

Microsoft (R) COFF Binary File Dumper Version 4.0
Copyright (C) Microsoft Corp 1992-96. All rights reserved.


Dump of file kernel32.dll

File Type: DLL

        Section contains the following Exports for KERNEL32.dll

              0 characteristics
       2EAC6946 time date stamp Mon Oct 24 19:11:18 1994
            0.0 version
              1 base
            320 # functions
            320 # names

        ordinal hint    name

              1    0    AddAtomA  (000334b2)
              2    1    AddAtomW  (000108a9)
              3    2    AddConsoleAliasA  (0001094b)
              4    3    AddConsoleAliasW  (0001094b)
              5    4    AllocConsole  (0001707e)
              6    5    AllocLSCallback  (0002250a)
              7    6    AllocMappedBuffer  (00031b4f)
              8    7    AllocSLCallback  (0002253d)
              9    8    BackupRead  (00010930)
              A    9    BackupSeek  (0001091e)
              B    A    BackupWrite  (00010930)
              C    B    Beep  (000108c4)
              D    C    BeginUpdateResourceA  (000108c4)
              E    D    BeginUpdateResourceW  (000108c4)
              F    E    BuildCommDCBA  (00033f45)
             10    F    BuildCommDCBAndTimeoutsA  (00033f70)
             11   10    BuildCommDCBAndTimeoutsW  (000108df)
             12   11    BuildCommDCBW  (000108c4)
             13   12    CallNamedPipeA  (00033dae)
             14   13    CallNamedPipeW  (00010930)
                           .
                           .
                           .
            316  315    lstrcmpiA  (00032c80)
            317  316    lstrcmpiW  (000108c4)
            318  317    lstrcpy  (00032cba)
            319  318    lstrcpyA  (00032cba)
```

(continued)

```
31A  319   lstrcpyW   (000108c4)
31B  31A   lstrcpyn   (00032cf4)
31C  31B   lstrcpynA  (00032cf4)
31D  31C   lstrcpynW  (000108df)
31E  31D   lstrlen    (00032d6b)
31F  31E   lstrlenA   (00032d6b)
320  31F   lstrlenW   (000108a9)
```

Summary

```
 4000 .data
 6000 .edata
12000 .rsrc
41000 .text
 3000 LOCKCODE
 3000 LOCKDATA
 2000 _FREQASM
 2000 _INIT
```

As you can see, the symbols are in alphabetical order, and the numbers in parentheses identify the symbol's address in the DLL file image. The hint column simply indicates the entry number in the list; the first entry is 0. The value in the ordinal column is always 1 greater than the value in the hint column.

Important

Many developers are used to exporting DLL functions by assigning functions an ordinal value. This is especially true if you are coming from a 16-bit Windows background. However, Microsoft does not publish ordinal values for the Win32 system DLLs. When your EXE or DLL links to any Win32 function, Microsoft wants you to link using the symbol's name. If you decide to link by ordinal, you run the risk that your application will not run on other Win32 platforms.

In fact, this has happened to me. I published a sample application that used ordinal numbers in the *Microsoft Systems Journal*. My application ran fine on Windows NT 3.1, but when Windows NT 3.5 came out, my application did not run correctly. To fix the problem, I had to replace the ordinal numbers with function names. Now the application runs on both Windows NT 3.1 and later versions.

I asked Microsoft why it is getting away from ordinals and got this response: "We [Microsoft] feel that the PE format provides the benefit of ordinals (fast lookup) with the flexibility of import by name. We can

(continued)

Important

(continued)

add APIs at any time. Ordinals are very hard to manage in a large project with multiple implementations."

You can use ordinals for any DLLs that you create and have your EXE files link to these DLLs by ordinal. Microsoft guarantees that this method will continue to work even in future versions of the operating system. However, I personally am avoiding the use of ordinals in my own work and will link by name only from now on.

Importing Functions and Variables from a DLL

When you want your EXE to call functions or access variables contained within a DLL, you must tell the compiler that the functions or variables you want to access are contained inside a DLL. For example, the following code fragment shows how to import the *Add* function and the *g_n-UsageCount* variable exported by the DLL discussed on page 554:

```
__declspec(dllimport) int Add (int nLeft, int nRight);

__declspec(dllimport) int g_nUsageCount;
```

Like *__declspec(dllexport)*, *__declspec(dllimport)* is a keyword recognized by Microsoft's C/C++ compiler. This keyword informs the compiler that the *Add* function and the *g_nUsageCount* variable are contained in a DLL that the EXE will have access to when it loads. This causes the compiler to generate special code for these imported symbols.

The compiler also embeds special information in the resulting OBJ file. This information is used in linking the EXE file. It tells the linker which functions it needs to look for in the various LIB files in order to successfully link the EXE file image. When the linker is attempting to link the EXE, it looks for the imported functions and variables. As the linker discovers which LIB file contains the imported symbols, the linker adds entries to an import table. Each entry contains the name of the DLL file that contains the symbol, and also contains the name of the symbol itself. When the linker finally writes the EXE file image to the hard drive, the image contains this import table.

You can run the DumpBin utility that comes with Visual C++ to see what the import table looks like. The sample output on the following pages shows the Windows 95 CALC.EXE's import table.

DUMPBIN -IMPORTS CALC.EXE

Microsoft (R) COFF Binary File Dumper Version 4.0
Copyright (C) Microsoft Corp 1992-96. All rights reserved.

Dump of file calc.exe

File Type: EXECUTABLE IMAGE

        Section contains the following Imports

            SHELL32.dll
            2EAC769C time date stamp Mon Oct 24 20:08:12 1994
                7E982F73   32   ShellAboutA

            KERNEL32.dll
            2EAC6964 time date stamp Mon Oct 24 19:11:48 1994
                BFFA1F51   184   GlobalUnlock
                BFF936B8   16C   GlobalAlloc
                BFFA1EA7   17D   GlobalReAlloc
                BFFA1EC9   17E   GlobalSize
                BFF936EB   16E   GlobalCompact
                BFFA1F73   175   GlobalFree
                BFFA1F0D   17A   GlobalLock
                BFFA2D6B   321   lstrlenA
                BFFA2D31   312   lstrcatA
                BFFA35DE   2F4   WriteProfileStringA
                BFFA3186   115   GetModuleHandleA
                BFFA3248   13F   GetStartupInfoA
                BFF9F4FC   F8   GetEnvironmentStrings
                BFF9F4EE   C8   GetCommandLineA
                BFF96741   29E   Sleep
                BFFA2C46   315   lstrcmpA
                BFFA3581   13A   GetProfileStringA
                BFF8C136   2B8   UnhandledExceptionFilter
                BFFA3167   113   GetModuleFileNameA
                BFFAAB12   BE   GetACP
                BFFAAB18   11F   GetOEMCP
                BFFAAB1E   C1   GetCPInfo
                BFF8E3D4   141   GetStdHandle
                BFF8E4DF   104   GetFileType
                BFF94904   2C4   VirtualFree
                BFF9476E   2C3   VirtualAlloc
                BFFA21EE   21F   RaiseException
                BFFAAC19   1FB   MultiByteToWideChar
                BFFAB259   2DD   WideCharToMultiByte
                BFFA1E78   12D   GetProcAddress

```
BFF9FCFD   10B   GetLastError
BFF936B8   1D8   LocalAlloc
BFFA1FFC   1DF   LocalReAlloc
BFFA2CBA   31B   lstrcpyA
BFFA354F   136   GetProfileIntA
BFF8A63D   15B   GetTickCount
BFF937D4   1DC   LocalFree
BFF8A150   161   GetVersion
BFF9F25B    7B   ExitProcess
BFF8BE06   23B   RtlUnwind
```

USER32.dll
2EAC7672 time date stamp Mon Oct 24 20:07:30 1994

```
BFF610F6   223   WinHelpA
BFF62386    D6   GetDC
BFF6446D   122   GetWindowRect
BFF62D77    45   CreateDialogParamA
BFF616A8    30   CheckRadioButton
BFF64950   165   LoadStringA
BFF63B36   192   RegisterClassA
BFF642DF   112   GetSysColorBrush
BFF64DB4   157   LoadCursorA
BFF64D9E   15B   LoadIconA
BFF61639   1C5   SetDlgItemTextA
BFF64416    DB   GetDlgItem
BFF62042    B6   FillRect
BFF64798   1DA   SetRect
BFF62B9E    2E   CheckMenuItem
BFF61A54   110   GetSubMenu
BFF62302    F1   GetMenu
BFF6147E   1EB   SetWindowPos
BFF616C9   16B   MapDialogRect
BFF6203C   138   InvalidateRect
BFF6236E   1C8   SetFocus
BFF64597   14A   IsIconic
BFF642BE   111   GetSysColor
BFF623E4    7F   DestroyMenu
BFF61B41   208   TrackPopupMenuEx
BFF61251   161   LoadMenuA
BFF61E22   19F   ReleaseCapture
BFF62376   1B6   SetCapture
BFF64450    DA   GetDlgCtrlID
BFF62BA6    A4   EnableMenuItem
BFF6470D   144   IsClipboardFormatAvailable
BFF61F5C   1A0   ReleaseDC
BFF64527   1A7   ScreenToClient
```

(continued)

BFF623B8	80	DestroyWindow
BFF623A8	18D	PostQuitMessage
BFF64F9B	77	DefWindowProcA
BFF623EC	172	MessageBeep
BFF61720	123	GetWindowTextA
BFF619F7	98	DrawFrameControl
BFF644AD	CC	GetClientRect
BFF62EF9	1F4	ShowCursor
BFF62B62	1BE	SetCursor
BFF61798	A9	EndPaint
BFF619FD	95	DrawEdge
BFF61747	9	BeginPaint
BFF62B50	36	CloseClipboard
BFF63F9B	29	CharUpperA
BFF61165	CE	GetClipboardData
BFF62F01	184	OpenClipboard
BFF61510	1EC	SetWindowTextA
BFF61F70	A6	EnableWindow
BFF61689	2D	CheckDlgButton
BFF61F64	1F7	ShowWindow
BFF623D4	217	UpdateWindow
BFF611A1	4F	CreateWindowExA
BFF64BD0	1AD	SendMessageA
BFF61255	153	LoadAcceleratorsA
BFF64AD7	FD	GetMessageA
BFF64B96	146	IsDialogMessageA
BFF64B3C	20A	TranslateAcceleratorA
BFF64B03	20D	TranslateMessage
BFF63DDB	85	DispatchMessageA
BFF63902	173	MessageBoxA

```
GDI32.dll
2EAC7672 time date stamp Mon Oct 24 20:07:30 1994
```

BFF344AD	C2	GetStockObject
BFF3133F	94	GetDeviceCaps
BFF310E1	D3	GetTextMetricsA
BFF34C28	135	SetTextColor
BFF34C2F	114	SetBkColor
BFF3219E	145	TextOutA
BFF31B26	CF	GetTextExtentPointA
BFF324A9	115	SetBkMode
BFF3214F	10E	SelectObject
BFF32461	46	DeleteObject

Summary

```
1000 .bss
2000 .data
1000 .idata
```

```
1000 .rdata
2000 .reloc
2000 .rsrc
A000 .text
```

When an EXE file is invoked, the operating system loader examines the EXE's import table and attempts to locate and map any required DLLs into the process's address space. The loader then obtains the addresses of the symbols referenced by the EXE file and saves these addresses in a table. Naturally, this can take some processing time—but it is done only when the process is first invoked. Whenever the application references one of these symbols, the code generated by the compiler pulls the symbol's address from the table and completes the link. The number to the left of the imported symbol is called a *hint* and is used by the loader to speed up the process of resolving the symbol's address. The number to the left of the hint is the address of the function if the executable file has been bound.[2]

When you want to import a symbol, you do not have to use the __*declspec(dllimport)* keyword. Instead, you can simply use the standard C *extern* keyword. However, the compiler is able to produce slightly more efficient code if it knows ahead of time that the symbol you are referencing is going to be imported from a DLL's LIB file. So I highly recommend that you use the __*declspec(dllimport)* keyword for imported function and data symbols.

A thread can obtain the address of a DLL's exported function or variable by calling the *GetProcAddress* function:

```
FARPROC GetProcAddress(HINSTANCE hinstDll, LPCSTR lpszProc);
```

The *hinstDll* parameter specifies the handle to the DLL. The return value from *LoadLibrary* or *LoadLibraryEx* identifies this handle value. The *lpszProc* parameter can take one of two forms. First, it can be the address to a zero-terminated string containing the name of the function whose address we want:

```
lpfn = GetProcAddress(hinstDll, "SomeFuncInDll");
```

Notice that the *lpszProc* parameter is prototyped as an LPCSTR, as opposed to an LPCTSTR. This means that the *GetProcAddress* function will accept only ANSI strings—you cannot pass a Unicode string to this function. This is because the function and variable symbols are always stored as ANSI strings in the DLL's export table.

---

2. A DLL is bound using the BIND utility; this utility does not ship with Visual C++ but is included in the Win32 SDK.

The second form the *lpszProc* parameter can take indicates the ordinal number of the function whose address we want:

```
lpfn = GetProcAddress(hinstDll, MAKEINTRESOURCE(2));
```

This usage assumes that we know that the *SomeFuncInDll* function was assigned the ordinal value of 2 by the creator of the DLL. Again, let me reiterate that Microsoft is strongly discouraging the use of ordinals, so you will not see this second usage of *GetProcAddress* very often.

Either method provides the address to the *SomeFuncInDll* function contained inside the DLL. If the function cannot be found, *GetProcAddress* returns NULL. Each method has its own subtle disadvantages. The first method works more slowly than the second because the system must perform string comparisons and searches on the function name string passed in. In the second method, if you pass an ordinal number that hasn't been assigned to any of the exported functions, *GetProcAddress* might return a non-NULL value. (This is true for 16-bit Windows as well.) This return value will trick your application into thinking that you have a valid address when in fact you don't. Attempting to call this address will almost certainly cause the thread to raise an access violation. Early in my Windows programming career, I didn't fully understand this behavior and was burned by it several times—so watch out. (This behavior is yet another reason to avoid ordinals in favor of symbol names.)

A DLL's Header File

Usually, when you create a DLL you also create a header file. This header file has the prototypes for all the functions and variables that the DLL is exporting. When you compile your EXE's source code files, you will include this header file. Often you will want to include this header file when you compile the DLL's source code files as well. To create a single header file that you can include for both the EXE's and the DLL's source code files, you should create the header file as follows:

```
// MYLIBAPI is defined as __declspec(dllexport) in the
// implementation file (MyLib.c). Thus, when this header
// file is included by MyLib.c, functions will be
// exported instead of imported.


#ifndef MYLIBAPI
#define MYLIBAPI __declspec(dllimport)
#endif
```

```
//////////////////////////////////////////////////

MYLIBAPI int Add (int nLeft, int nRight);
MYLIBAPI int g_nUsageCount;
```

Then, at the top of your DLL's source code files, include the above header file as follows:

```
// We must define MYLIBAPI as __declspec(dllexport)
// before including MyLib.h. MyLib.h will see that we
// have already defined MYLIBAPI and will not
// (re)define it as __declspec(dllimport).

#define MYLIBAPI __declspec(dllexport)
#include "MyLib.h"


//////////////////////////////////////////////////


int Add (int nLeft, int nRight) {
   return(nLeft + nRight);
}


MYLIBAPI int g_nUsageCount;
   :
   :
```

When you compile the library's source code file, you have explicitly set MYLIBAPI to _declspec(dllexport)_ so that the compiler knows to export the functions. Because the compiler knows from the header that the functions are exported, you don't have to repeat the _declspec(dllexport)_ in front of the function bodies or variables. Notice that there is no _declspec(dllexport)_ before the _Add_ function's body.

For source code that imports the symbols from the DLL, you just need to include the header file. Since MYLIBAPI will not be defined, the header file will define it as _declspec(dllimport)_ so that the compiler knows which symbols are contained in a DLL. If you examine the Windows header files, such as WINUSER.H, you'll see that Microsoft uses the same technique that I've just explained here.

Creating DLLs for Use with Non–Visual C++ Tools

If you are using Visual C++ to build a DLL, and if you are using Visual C++ to build an EXE that will link with the DLL, everything that I've just said is completely true and you can safely skip this entire section. However, if you are building a DLL with Visual C++ that is to be linked with an EXE built using any arbitrary vendor's tools, you must perform some additional work.

The problem is that most exported functions are C (as opposed to C++) and use the *stdcall* calling convention. When C functions are exported using *stdcall*, the Visual C++ compiler mangles the function names by prepending a leading underscore and by adding a suffix of an @ sign followed by a number that indicates the count of bytes that are passed to the function as parameters. For example, the function

```
__declspec(dllexport) LONG __stdcall MyFunc(int a, int b);
```

is exported by Visual C++ as *_MyFunc@8* in the DLL's export table. If you now build an EXE using another vendor's tools, it will attempt to link to a function named *_MyFunc*—a function that does not exist in the Visual C++–built DLL—and the link will fail.

To build a DLL with Visual C++ that is to be linked with other compiler vendor's tools, you must tell Visual C++ to export the function names without mangling. You can do this in two ways.

The first way is to create a DEF file for your Visual C++ project and include in the DEF file an EXPORTS section like this:

```
EXPORTS
   MyFunc
```

When the Visual C++ linker interprets this DEF file, it sees that both *_MyFunc@8* and *MyFunc* are being exported. Because these two function names match (except for the mangling), the linker decides to export the function using the DEF file name of *MyFunc* and does not export a function with the name of *_MyFunc@8* at all.

Now, you might think that if you build an EXE with Visual C++ and attempt to link to the DLL containing the unmangled name, the Visual C++ linker would fail because it would try to link to a function called *_MyFunc@8*. Well, you'll be pleased to know that the Visual C++ linker does the right thing and links the EXE to the function named *MyFunc*.

If you want to avoid using a DEF file, you can use the second way of exporting an unmangled version of the function. Inside one of the DLL's source code modules, add a line like this:

```
#pragma comment(linker, "/export:MyFunc=_MyFunc@8")
```

This line causes the compiler to emit a linker directive instructing the linker that a function called *MyFunc* is to be exported with the same entry point as a function called *_MyFunc@8*. This second technique is a bit less convenient to use than the first because you must mangle the function name yourself to construct the line. Also, when you use this second technique, the DLL will actually be exporting two symbols identifying a single function: *MyFunc* and *_MyFunc@8*, whereas the first technique exported only the *MyFunc* symbol. The second technique really doesn't buy you very much—it just enables you to avoid using a DEF file.

By the way, exporting and importing C++ functions using different compiler vendor tools is almost impossible because Win32 compiler vendors do not agree on the algorithm for mangling function names. For this reason, you should avoid creating DLLs that export C++ classes unless you're guaranteed that the consumers of your DLL are using the same compiler tools as you are.

Sharing Data Across Mappings of an EXE or a DLL

As you know by now, the system creates instances of any global or static variables contained in an EXE or a DLL file image for multiple mappings of the file image. In other words, if an EXE has a global variable and you invoke two or more instances of the application, each process gets its very own copy of the global variable—the multiple instances of the EXE do not share a single copy of the global variable. Normally, this is exactly what we want. However, on some occasions it is useful and convenient for multiple mappings of an EXE to share a single instance of a variable.

For example, Win32 offers no easy way to determine whether the user is running multiple instances of an application. But if you could get all the instances to share a single global variable, this global variable could reflect the number of instances running. When the user invoked an instance of the application, the new instance's thread could simply check the value of the global variable (which had been updated by another instance), and if the count were greater than 1, the second instance could notify the user that only one instance of the application is allowed to run and the second instance would terminate.

This section discusses a technique that allows you to share variables among all instances of an EXE or a DLL. But before we get heavily into the details, you'll need a little background information.

The Sections of an EXE or a DLL

Every EXE or DLL file image is composed of a collection of sections. By convention, each standard section name begins with a period. For example, when you compile your program, the compiler places all the code in a section called .text. The compiler also places all the uninitialized data in a .bss section and all the initialized data in a .data section.

Each section has a combination of the following attributes associated with it:

Attribute	Meaning
READ	The bytes in the section can be read from.
WRITE	The bytes in the section can be written to.
EXECUTE	The bytes in the section can be executed.
SHARED	The bytes in the section are shared across multiple instances.

By running the DumpBin utility, you can see the list of sections in an executable or a DLL. The following listing shows the result of running the DumpBin utility on the MODULE.DLL file included with this book's companion CD:

```
Microsoft (R) COFF Binary File Dumper Version 4.0
Copyright (C) Microsoft Corp 1992-1996. All rights reserved.


Dump of file module.dll

File Type: DLL

    Summary

        1000 .data
        1000 .idata
        1000 .rdata
        1000 .reloc
        1000 .text
        1000 Shared
```

In addition to the summary list of sections above, you can get a more detailed list of each section by specifying the -HEADERS switch to DumpBin.

The following table shows the names of some of the more common sections and lists what each section contains:

Section Name	Contains
.text	Application's or DLL's code
.bss	Uninitialized data
.rdata	Read-only run-time data
.rsrc	Resources
.edata	Exported names table
.data	Initialized data
.xdata	Exception handling table
.idata	Imported names table
.CRT	Read-only C run-time data
.reloc	Fixup table information
.debug	Debugging information
.tls	Thread-local storage

Notice how the MODULE.DLL has an additional section—called Shared. I created this section myself. You can easily create sections when compiling an application or a DLL by using the following directive when you compile:

```
#pragma data_seg("segname")
```

So, for example, the MODULE.C file (on page 570) contains these lines:

```
#pragma data_seg("Shared")
LONG g_lModuleUsage = 0;
#pragma data_seg()
```

When the compiler compiles this code, it creates a new section—Shared—and places all the *initialized* data variables that it sees after the pragma in this new section. In the example above, the variable is placed in the Shared section. Following the variable, the *#pragma dataseg()* line tells the compiler to stop putting initialized variables in the Shared section and to start putting them back in the default data section. It is extremely important to remember that the compiler will store only initialized variables in the new section. The compiler always places uninitialized variables in the .bss section. For example, if I had removed the initialization from the previous code fragment as follows, the compiler would have ended up putting this variable in a .bss section and not in the Shared section:

```
#pragma data_seg("Shared")
LONG g_lModuleUsage;
#pragma data_seg()
```

Probably the most common reason to put variables in their own section is to share them among multiple mappings of an application or a DLL. By default, each mapping of an application or a DLL gets its very own set of variables. However, you can group into their own section any variables that you want to share among all mappings of an application or a DLL. When you group variables, the system doesn't create new instances of the variables for every mapping of the application or DLL.

Just telling the compiler to place certain variables in their own section is not enough to share those variables. You must also tell the linker that the variables in a particular section are to be shared. You can do this by using the /SECTION switch on the linker's command line:

```
/SECTION:name, attributes
```

Following the colon, place the name of the section for which you want to alter attributes.

For MODULE.DLL, we want to change the attributes of the Shared section. You must specify the attributes of the section following the comma. Use an *R* for READ, a *W* for WRITE, an *E* for EXECUTE, and an *S* for SHARED. So to make the Shared section readable, writable, and shared, the switch must look like this:

```
/SECTION:Shared,RWS
```

If you want to change the attributes of more than one section, you must specify the /SECTION switch multiple times—once for each section for which you want to change attributes.

You can also embed linker switches inside your source code:

```
#pragma comment(linker, "/SECTION:.Shared,RWS")
```

This line tells the compiler to embed the above string inside a special section named ".drectve". When the linker combines all the OBJ modules together, the linker examines each OBJ module's ".drectve" section and pretends that all the strings were passed to the linker as command-line arguments. I use this technique all the time because it is so convenient—if you move a source code file into a new project, you don't have to remember to set linker switches in Visual C++'s Build Settings dialog box. My common header file discussed in Appendix C uses this *pragma*.

Although it is possible to create shared sections, Microsoft discourages the use of shared sections for two reasons. First, sharing memory in this way violates B-level security policy. Second, sharing variables means that an error in one application can affect the operation of another application because there is no way to protect a block of data from being randomly written to by an application.

Imagine that you have written two applications, each requiring the user to enter a password. However, you decide to add a feature to your applications that makes things a little easier on the user: if the user is already running one of the applications when the second is started, the second application examines the contents of shared memory to get the password. This way, the user doesn't need to enter the password a second time if one of the programs is already being used.

This sounds innocent enough. After all, no other applications but your own load the DLL and know where to find the password contained within the shared section. However, hackers lurk about, and if they want to get your password, all they need to do is write a small program of their own to load your company's DLL and monitor the shared memory blocks. When the user enters a password, the hacker's program can learn the user's password.

An industrious program such as the hacker's might also try to guess repeatedly at passwords and write them to the shared memory. Once the program guesses the correct password, it can send all kinds of commands to one of the two applications.

Perhaps this problem could be solved if there were a way to grant access to only certain applications for loading a particular DLL. But currently this is not the case—any program can call *LoadLibrary* to explicitly load a DLL.

The ModUse Sample Application

Earlier in this chapter, I said that Win32 does not support the *GetModuleUsage* function offered by 16-bit Windows. However, by using shared memory, you can implement the *GetModuleUsage* function yourself. The MODUSE.EXE and MODULE.DLL files demonstrate how to do this.

Figure 12-3 shows MODULE.DLL, which we'll look at first. The source code and resource files for the library are in the MODUSE directory on the companion disc.

MODULE.C

```
/***************************************************************
Module name: Module.C
Notices: Copyright (c) 1995-1997 Jeffrey Richter
***************************************************************/


#include "..\CmnHdr.H"                        /* See Appendix C. */
#include <windows.h>

#define MODULEAPI __declspec(dllexport)
#include "Module.H"


///////////////////////////////////////////////////////////////


// Instruct the compiler to put the g_lModuleUsage data
// variable in its own data section, called Shared. We
// then instruct the linker that we want the data in this
// section to be shared by all instances of this application.
#pragma data_seg("Shared")
LONG g_lModuleUsage = 0;
#pragma data_seg()

// Instruct the linker to make the Shared section
// readable, writable, and shared.
#pragma comment(linker, "/section:Shared,rws")


///////////////////////////////////////////////////////////////


// 'g_uMsgModCountChange' could be shared, but I chose not to.
UINT g_uMsgModCntChange = 0;


///////////////////////////////////////////////////////////////
```

Figure 12-3.
The Module dynamic-link library.

(continued)

Figure 12-3. *continued*

```
BOOL WINAPI DllMain (HINSTANCE hinstDll, DWORD fdwReason,
   LPVOID lpvReserved) {

   switch (fdwReason) {

   case DLL_PROCESS_ATTACH:
      // DLL is attaching to the address
      // space of the current process.

      // Increment this module's usage count when it is
      // attached to a process.
      InterlockedIncrement((PLONG) &g_lModuleUsage);

      // Reserve a systemwide window message for ourselves.
      // This message is used to notify all of the top-level
      // windows that this module's usage count has changed.
      g_uMsgModCntChange =
         RegisterWindowMessage(__TEXT("MsgModUsgCntChange"));

      // Notify all of the top-level windows that this
      // module's usage count has changed.
      PostMessage(HWND_BROADCAST, g_uMsgModCntChange, 0, 0);
      break;

   case DLL_THREAD_ATTACH:
      // A new thread is being created in the current process.
      break;

   case DLL_THREAD_DETACH:
      // A thread is exiting cleanly.
      break;

   case DLL_PROCESS_DETACH:
      // The calling process is detaching
      // the DLL from its address space.

      // Decrement this module's usage count when it
      // gets detached from a process.
      InterlockedDecrement((PLONG) &g_lModuleUsage);

      // Notify all of the top-level windows that this
      // module's usage count has changed.
      PostMessage(HWND_BROADCAST, g_uMsgModCntChange, 0, 0);
```

(continued)

Figure 12-3. *continued*

```
      break;
   }

   return(TRUE);
}


////////////////////////////////////////////////////////////////


MODULEAPI LONG GetModuleUsage (void) {
   return(g_lModuleUsage);
}


//////////////////////// End Of File ////////////////////////
```

MODULE.H
```
/*********************************************************
Module name: Module.H
Notices: Copyright (c) 1995-1997 Jeffrey Richter
*********************************************************/


#if !defined(MODULEAPI)
#define MODULEAPI __declspec(dllimport)
#endif


// Function to return the module's usage count.
MODULEAPI LONG GetModuleUsage (void);


//////////////////////// End Of File ////////////////////////
```

The most important thing to note in MODULE.C is that I have created a global variable, *g_lModuleUsage*, in its very own section and have specified that this section be shared by specifying the /SECTION switch to the linker. I have also initialized *g_lModuleUsage* to be 0. Now whenever MODULE.DLL is mapped into a process's address space, *DllMain* is called with a value of DLL_PROCESS_ATTACH. The DLL processes this call by calling

```
InterlockedIncrement(&g_lModuleUsage);
```

This call increments the *g_lModuleUsage* variable. You might wonder why I increment this long by calling *InterlockedIncrement* instead of just using

```
g_lModuleUsage++;
```

I admit that the difference between the two statements is subtle, and that most of the time you wouldn't even notice a difference and everything would work just fine. However, if I use only the C postfix increment operator, there is a potential problem. If two processes call *LoadLibrary* to load MODULE.DLL into memory at the same time, the value of *g_lModuleUsage* can become corrupted. By using *InterlockedIncrement*, the system guarantees that no more than one CPU can access the 4 bytes of memory at any one time.

The next step in maintaining MODULE.DLL's usage count is to decrement the usage count whenever *DllMain* is called with a value of DLL_PROCESS_DETACH. When this happens, *g_lUsageCount* is decremented by making a call to *InterlockedDecrement*. Refer to Chapter 10 for more information on the *InterlockedIncrement* and *InterlockedDecrement* functions.

The only other function in this DLL is *GetModuleUsage*:

```
LONG GetModuleUsage(void);
```

This function accepts no parameters and simply returns the value in the *g_lUsageCount* variable. An application can now call this function to determine the number of processes that have mapped MODULE.DLL into their own address spaces.

To make this demonstration a little more exciting, I also created the ModUse (MODUSE.EXE) sample application, listed in Figure 12-4. This is a very simple program that displays a dialog box. After the dialog box is displayed, its dialog box procedure simply sits around and waits for the registered window message[3] "MsgModCntChange". This message is registered by MODULE.DLL when its *DllMain* function is called with a value of DLL_PROCESS_ATTACH. This same message is registered by MODUSE.EXE first when its *WinMain* function is called. The value for the message is saved in the global *g_uMsgModCntChange* variable.

Whenever the DLL is attached or detached from a process, it calls

```
PostMessage(HWND_BROADCAST, g_uMsgCntChange, 0, 0);
```

This causes the value of the registered window message to be broadcast to all the overlapped windows in the system. The only windows that will

---

3. For more information about using registered window messages, see the *RegisterWindowMessage* function in the *Microsoft Win32 Programmer's Reference*.

recognize this systemwide window message are the dialog boxes created by any active instances of the ModUse application. MODUSE.C's dialog box procedure contains an explicit check for this registered window message:

```
if (uMsg == g_uMsgModCntChange) {
    SetDlgItemInt(hDlg, IDC_MODCNT, GetModuleUsage(), FALSE);
}
```

When this message is received, the DLL's *GetModuleUsage* function is called to get the current module usage. This value is then placed in a static window control that is a child of the dialog box.

When you run the ModUse program, the MODULE.DLL file is implicitly mapped into the process's address space. The attachment of this DLL to the process causes the registered message to be posted to all the overlapped windows in the system. The windows will ignore this message except for the dialog box displayed by ModUse. When the dialog box receives the message, it calls the *GetModuleUsage* function in the DLL to obtain MODULE.DLL's usage count, which is 1. This value is then placed in the dialog box:

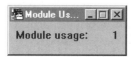

If you run a second instance of ModUse, the same sequence of events will occur. This time, MODULE.DLL's usage count is 2, and two dialog boxes that can process the registered window message are displayed. Both dialog box procedures call *GetModuleUsage*, see that the count is 2, and then update their static controls appropriately:

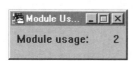 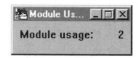

This technique for sharing data in a section across multiple file mappings is not limited to DLLs alone—applications (EXEs) can also use it. For an application, the data is shared among all running instances of the application.

ModUse.ico

MODUSE.C

```c
/************************************************************
Module name: ModUse.C
Notices: Copyright (c) 1995-1997 Jeffrey Richter
************************************************************/


#include "..\CmnHdr.H"                    /* See Appendix C. */
#include <windows.h>
#include <windowsx.h>
#include <tchar.h>
#include "Resource.H"
#include "..\Module\Module.H"


///////////////////////////////////////////////////////////


UINT g_uMsgModCntChange = 0;


///////////////////////////////////////////////////////////


BOOL Dlg_OnInitDialog (HWND hwnd, HWND hwndFocus,
   LPARAM lParam) {

   // Associate an icon with the dialog box.
   chSETDLGICONS(hwnd, IDI_MODUSE, IDI_MODUSE);

   // Force the static control to be initialized correctly.
   PostMessage(hwnd, g_uMsgModCntChange, 0, 0);
   return(TRUE);
}


///////////////////////////////////////////////////////////


void Dlg_OnCommand (HWND hwnd, int id, HWND hwndCtl,
   UINT codeNotify) {

   switch (id) {
      case IDCANCEL:
         EndDialog(hwnd, id);
```

Figure 12-4.
The ModUse application.

(continued)

575

Figure 12-4. *continued*

```
            break;
    }
}


//////////////////////////////////////////////////////////////


BOOL CALLBACK Dlg_Proc (HWND hwnd, UINT uMsg,
   WPARAM wParam, LPARAM lParam) {

   if (uMsg == g_uMsgModCntChange) {
      SetDlgItemInt(hwnd, IDC_USAGECOUNT,
         GetModuleUsage(), FALSE);
   }

   switch (uMsg) {
      chHANDLE_DLGMSG(hwnd, WM_INITDIALOG, Dlg_OnInitDialog);
      chHANDLE_DLGMSG(hwnd, WM_COMMAND, Dlg_OnCommand);
   }
   return(FALSE);
}


//////////////////////////////////////////////////////////////


int WINAPI _tWinMain (HINSTANCE hinstExe,
   HINSTANCE hinstPrev, LPTSTR pszCmdLine, int nCmdShow) {

   chWARNIFUNICODEUNDERWIN95();

   // Get the numeric value of the systemwide window message
   // used by the module to notify all top-level windows when
   // the module's usage count has changed.
   g_uMsgModCntChange =
      RegisterWindowMessage(__TEXT("MsgModUsgCntChange"));

   DialogBox(hinstExe, MAKEINTRESOURCE(IDD_MODUSE),
      NULL, Dlg_Proc);

   return(0);
}


/////////////////////////// End Of File ///////////////////////////
```

(continued)

Figure 12-4. *continued*

MODUSE.RC

```
//Microsoft Developer Studio generated resource script.
//
#include "Resource.h"

#define APSTUDIO_READONLY_SYMBOLS
/////////////////////////////////////////////////////////////
//
// Generated from the TEXTINCLUDE 2 resource.
//
#include "afxres.h"

/////////////////////////////////////////////////////////////
#undef APSTUDIO_READONLY_SYMBOLS

/////////////////////////////////////////////////////////////
// English (U.S.) resources

#if !defined(AFX_RESOURCE_DLL) || defined(AFX_TARG_ENU)
#ifdef _WIN32
LANGUAGE LANG_ENGLISH, SUBLANG_ENGLISH_US
#pragma code_page(1252)
#endif //_WIN32

#ifdef APSTUDIO_INVOKED
/////////////////////////////////////////////////////////////
//
// TEXTINCLUDE
//

1 TEXTINCLUDE DISCARDABLE
BEGIN
    "Resource.h\0"
END

2 TEXTINCLUDE DISCARDABLE
BEGIN
    "#include ""afxres.h""\r\n"
    "\0"
END

3 TEXTINCLUDE DISCARDABLE
BEGIN
    "\r\n"
```

(continued)

Figure 12-4. *continued*

```
    "\0"
END

#endif    // APSTUDIO_INVOKED


/////////////////////////////////////////////////////////////
//
// Dialog
//

IDD_MODUSE DIALOG DISCARDABLE  0, 0, 76, 20
STYLE WS_MINIMIZEBOX | WS_POPUP | WS_VISIBLE | WS_CAPTION
   | WS_SYSMENU
CAPTION "Module Usage"
FONT 8, "System"
BEGIN
    LTEXT           "Module usage:",IDC_STATIC,
                    4,4,49,8,SS_NOPREFIX
    RTEXT           "#",IDC_USAGECOUNT,56,4,
                    16,12,SS_NOPREFIX
END


/////////////////////////////////////////////////////////////
//
// Icon
//

// Icon with lowest ID value placed first to ensure
// application icon remains consistent on all systems.
IDI_MODUSE              ICON    DISCARDABLE     "ModUse.Ico"
#endif    // English (U.S.) resources
/////////////////////////////////////////////////////////////


#ifndef APSTUDIO_INVOKED
/////////////////////////////////////////////////////////////
//
// Generated from the TEXTINCLUDE 3 resource.
//


/////////////////////////////////////////////////////////////
#endif    // not APSTUDIO_INVOKED
```

The MultInst Sample Application

In 16-bit Windows, many programmers used the value of *hinstPrev*, which 16-bit Windows passed to *WinMain* to determine whether an instance of an application was already running. Applications that allowed only one instance of themselves to run at a time would check the value of *hinstExePrev*, and, if its value wasn't NULL, they would terminate. Under Win32, the value of *hinstExePrev* passed to *WinMain* is always NULL. Because of this, an application cannot easily determine whether another instance of itself is running.

One way for an application to know how many instances of itself are running is to use the shared data section technique just discussed. The MultInst (MULTINST.EXE) sample application, listed in Figure 12-5, demonstrates how to allow only one instance of an application to run. The source code and resource files for the application are in the MULT-INST directory on the companion disc.

MultInst.ico

MULTINST.C
```
/***************************************************************
Module name: MultInst.C
Notices: Copyright (c) 1995-1997 Jeffrey Richter
***************************************************************/


#include "..\CmnHdr.H"                    /* See Appendix C. */
#include <windows.h>
#include <tchar.h>
#include "Resource.H"


///////////////////////////////////////////////////////////////


// We instruct the compiler to put the g_lUsageCount data
// variable in its own data section called Shared. We
// then instruct the linker that we want the data in this
// section to be shared by all instances of this application.
#pragma data_seg("Shared")
LONG g_lUsageCount = -1;
#pragma data_seg()

// Instruct the linker to make the Shared section
// readable, writable, and shared.
#pragma comment(linker, "/section:Shared,rws")
```

Figure 12-5. *(continued)*
The MultInst application.

Figure 12-5. *continued*

```
///////////////////////////////////////////////////////////

int WINAPI _tWinMain (HINSTANCE hinstExe,
   HINSTANCE hinstPrev, LPTSTR pszCmdLine, int nCmdShow) {

   // An instance is running; increment the counter.
   BOOL fFirstInstance =
      (InterlockedIncrement(&g_lUsageCount) == 0);

   chWARNIFUNICODEUNDERWIN95();

   // If more than one instance is running, tell
   // the user and terminate the program.
   if (!fFirstInstance) {
      MessageBox(NULL,
         __TEXT("Application is already running - ")
         __TEXT("Terminating this instance."),
         __TEXT("Multiple Instance"),
            MB_OK | MB_ICONINFORMATION);
   } else {

      // We are the only instance running;
      // wait for the user to terminate us.
      MessageBox(NULL,
         __TEXT("Running first instance of application.\n")
         __TEXT("Select OK to terminate."),
         __TEXT("Multiple Instance"),
         MB_OK | MB_ICONINFORMATION);
   }

   // We are no longer running; decrement the usage counter.
   InterlockedDecrement(&g_lUsageCount);

   return(0);
}


////////////////////// End Of File //////////////////////////
```

(continued)

Figure 12-5. *continued*

MULTINST.RC

```
//Microsoft Developer Studio generated resource script.
//
#include "Resource.h"

#define APSTUDIO_READONLY_SYMBOLS
/////////////////////////////////////////////////////////////
//
// Generated from the TEXTINCLUDE 2 resource.
//
#include "afxres.h"


/////////////////////////////////////////////////////////////
#undef APSTUDIO_READONLY_SYMBOLS


/////////////////////////////////////////////////////////////
// English (U.S.) resources

#if !defined(AFX_RESOURCE_DLL) || defined(AFX_TARG_ENU)
#ifdef _WIN32
LANGUAGE LANG_ENGLISH, SUBLANG_ENGLISH_US
#pragma code_page(1252)
#endif //_WIN32


#ifdef APSTUDIO_INVOKED
/////////////////////////////////////////////////////////////
//
// TEXTINCLUDE
//

1 TEXTINCLUDE DISCARDABLE
BEGIN
    "Resource.h\0"
END

2 TEXTINCLUDE DISCARDABLE
BEGIN
    "#include ""afxres.h""\r\n"
    "\0"
END
```

(continued)

Figure 12-5. *continued*

```
3 TEXTINCLUDE DISCARDABLE
BEGIN
    "\r\n"
    "\0"
END

#endif    // APSTUDIO_INVOKED


/////////////////////////////////////////////////////////////////
//
// Icon
//

// Icon with lowest ID value placed first to ensure
// application icon remains consistent on all systems.
IDI_MULTINST           ICON    DISCARDABLE    "MultInst.Ico"
#endif    // English (U.S.) resources
/////////////////////////////////////////////////////////////////



#ifndef APSTUDIO_INVOKED
/////////////////////////////////////////////////////////////////
//
// Generated from the TEXTINCLUDE 3 resource.
//


/////////////////////////////////////////////////////////////////
#endif    // not APSTUDIO_INVOKED
```

THREAD-LOCAL STORAGE

Sometimes it's convenient to associate data with an instance of an object. For example, window extra bytes associate data with a specific window by using the *SetWindowWord* and *SetWindowLong* functions. Thread-local storage (TLS) allows you to associate data with a specific thread of execution. For example, you might want to associate the creation time of a thread with a thread. Then, when the thread terminates, you can determine the lifetime of the thread.

The C run-time library uses TLS. Because the library was designed years before multithreaded applications, most functions in the library are intended for use with single-threaded applications. The *strtok* function is an excellent example. The first time an application calls *strtok*, the function passes the address to a string and saves the address of the string in its own static variable. When you make future calls to *strtok*, passing NULL, the function refers to the saved string address.

In a multithreaded environment, it's possible that one thread can call *strtok*, and then, before it can make another call, another thread can also call *strtok*. In this case, the second thread causes *strtok* to overwrite its static variable with a new address, which happens unbeknownst to the first thread. And the first thread's future calls to *strtok* use the second thread's string, which can lead to all kinds of difficult-to-find-and-fix bugs.

To fix this problem, the C run-time library uses TLS, which means each thread is assigned its own string pointer that is reserved for use by the *strtok* function. Other C run-time functions that require the same treatment include *asctime* and *gmtime*.

Thread-local storage can be a lifesaver if your application relies heavily on global or static variables. Fortunately, software developers tend to minimize the use of such variables and rely much more on automatic (stack-based) variables and data passing via function parameters.

This is good because stack-based variables are always associated with a particular thread.

It is both fortunate and unfortunate that the standard C run-time library has existed for so many years. It has been implemented and reimplemented by various compiler vendors; no C compiler would be worth buying if it didn't include the standard C library. Programmers have used it for years and will continue to do so, which means that the prototype and behavior of functions such as *strtok* must remain exactly as the standard C library describes them. If the C run-time library were to be redesigned today, it would be designed for environments that support multithreaded applications, and extreme measures would be taken to avoid the use of global and static variables.

In my own software projects, I avoid global variables as much as possible. If your application uses global and static variables, I strongly suggest that you examine each variable and investigate the possibilities for changing it to a stack-based variable. This effort can save you an enormous amount of time if you decide to add additional threads to your application, and even single-threaded applications can benefit.

Although the two TLS techniques discussed in this chapter can be used in both applications and DLLs, you will more frequently find them useful when creating DLLs because DLLs often don't know the structure of the application to which they are linked. If you're writing an application (rather than a DLL), you typically know how many threads will be created and how those threads will be used. The application developer can then create makeshift methods or, better yet, use stack-based methods (local variables) for associating data with each created thread.

A DLL implementer typically doesn't know how the application to which it is linked creates and uses threads. Thread-local storage was created with the intent of helping the DLL developer. However, the information discussed in this chapter can be used just as easily by an application developer.

Dynamic Thread-Local Storage

An application takes advantage of dynamic thread-local storage by calling a set of four functions. Although these functions can be used by an application or a DLL, they are most often used by DLLs.

Figure 13-1 shows the internal data structures that Microsoft Windows 95 and Microsoft Windows NT use for managing TLS.

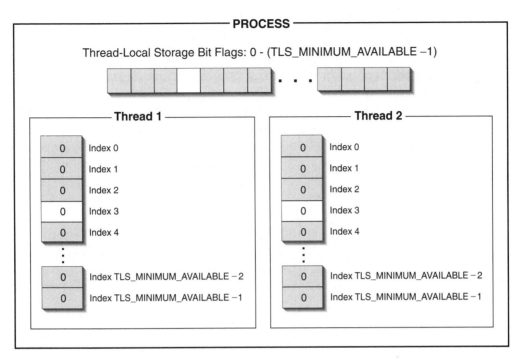

Figure 13-1.
Internal data structures that manage thread-local storage.

The figure shows a single set of in-use flags for each process running in the system. Each flag is either FREE or INUSE, indicating whether the TLS slot is in use. Microsoft guarantees that at least TLS-_MINIMUM_AVAILABLE bit flags will be available on all Win32 platforms. By the way, TLS_MINIMUM_AVAILABLE is defined as 64 in WINNT.H. On some platforms, the system might expand this flag array to accommodate the needs of the application or the DLL.

To use dynamic TLS, a call must first be made to *TlsAlloc*:

```
DWORD TlsAlloc(VOID);
```

This function instructs the system to scan the bit flags in the process and locate a FREE flag. The system then changes the flag from FREE to INUSE, and *TlsAlloc* returns the index of the flag in the bit array. A DLL (or an application) usually saves the index in a global variable.[1]

---

1. This is one of those times when a global variable is actually the better choice because the value is used on a per-process basis rather than a per-thread basis.

If *TlsAlloc* cannot find a FREE flag in the list, it returns TLS_OUT-_OF_INDEXES (defined as 0xFFFFFFFF in WINBASE.H). The first time *TlsAlloc* is called, the system recognizes that the first flag is FREE and changes the flag to INUSE, and *TlsAlloc* returns 0. That's 99% of what *TlsAlloc* does. I'll get to the other 1% later.

When a thread is created, an array of TLS_MINIMUM_AVAIL-ABLE 32-bit values (LPVOIDs) is allocated, initialized to 0, and associated with the thread by the system. As Figure 13-1 shows, each thread gets its own array, and each LPVOID in the array can store any 32-bit value.

Before you can store information in a thread's LPVOID array, you must know which index in the array is available for use—this is what the earlier call to *TlsAlloc* is for. Conceptually, *TlsAlloc* is reserving an index for you. If *TlsAlloc* returns index 3, it is effectively saying that index 3 is reserved for you in every thread currently executing in the process as well as in any threads that might be created in the future.

To place a value in a thread's array, you call the *TlsSetValue* function:

```
BOOL TlsSetValue(DWORD dwTlsIndex, LPVOID lpvTlsValue);
```

This function puts an LPVOID value or any other 32-bit value, identified by the *lpvTlsValue* parameter, into the thread's array at the index identified by the *dwTlsIndex* parameter. The value of *lpvTlsValue* is associated with the thread making the call to *TlsSetValue*. If the call is successful, TRUE is returned.

A thread changes its own array when it calls *TlsSetValue*. But a thread cannot set a thread-local storage value for another thread. Personally, I wish there were another *Tls* function that allowed one thread to store data in another thread's array, but no such function exists. Currently, the only way to pass data from one thread to another is to pass a single 32-bit value to *CreateThread* or *_beginthreadex*. *CreateThread* or *_beginthreadex* then passes this value to the thread function as its only parameter.

When calling *TlsSetValue*, be extremely careful that you always pass an index returned from an earlier call to *TlsAlloc*. Microsoft designed these functions to be as fast as possible and, in so doing, gave up error checking. If you pass an index that was never allocated by a call to *Tls-Alloc*, the system stores the 32-bit value in the thread's array anyway—no error check is performed.

To retrieve a value from a thread's array, you call *TlsGetValue*:

```
LPVOID TlsGetValue(DWORD dwTlsIndex);
```

This function returns the value that was associated with the TLS slot at index *dwTlsIndex*. Like *TlsSetValue*, *TlsGetValue* looks only at the array that belongs to the calling thread. And again like *TlsSetValue*, *TlsGetValue* performs no test to check the validity of the passed index.

When you come to a point in your process where you no longer need to reserve a TLS slot among all threads, you should call *TlsFree*:

```
BOOL TlsFree(DWORD dwTlsIndex);
```

This function simply tells the system that this slot no longer needs to be reserved. The INUSE flag managed by the process's bit flags array is set to FREE again and might be allocated in the future if a thread later calls *TlsAlloc*. *TlsFree* returns TRUE if the function is successful. Attempting to free a slot that was not allocated results in an error.

Using Dynamic Thread-Local Storage

Usually, if a DLL uses TLS, it calls *TlsAlloc* when its *DllMain* function is called with DLL_PROCESS_ATTACH, and it calls *TlsFree* when *DllMain* is called with DLL_PROCESS_DETACH. The calls to *TlsSetValue* and *Tls-GetValue* are most likely made during calls to functions contained within the DLL.

One method for adding TLS to an application is to add it when you need it. For example, you might have a function in a DLL that works similarly to *strtok*. The first time your function is called, the thread passes a pointer to a 40-byte structure. You need to save this structure so that future calls can reference it. So you might code your function like this:

```
DWORD g_dwTlsIndex;    // Assume that this is initialized
                       // with the result of a call to TlsAlloc.
 .
 .
 .
void MyFunction (LPSOMESTRUCT lpSomeStruct) {
   if (lpSomeStruct != NULL) {
      // The caller is priming this function.

      // See if we already allocated space to save the data.
      if (TlsGetValue(g_dwTlsIndex) == NULL) {
         // Space was never allocated. This is the first
         // time this function has ever been called by this thread.
         TlsSetValue(g_dwTlsIndex,
            HeapAlloc(GetProcessHeap(), 0,
               sizeof(*lpSomeStruct)));
      }
```

(continued)

587

```
        // Memory already exists for the data; save the newly
        // passed values.
        memcpy(TlsGetValue(g_dwTlsIndex), lpSomeStruct,
            sizeof(*lpSomeStruct));

    } else {

        // The caller already primed the function. Now it
        // wants to do something with the saved data.

        // Get the address of the saved data.
        lpSomeStruct = (LPSOMESTRUCT) TlsGetValue(g_dwTlsIndex);

        // The saved data is pointed to by lpSomeStruct; use it.
        :
        :

    }
```

If the application's thread never calls *MyFunction*, a memory block is never allocated for the thread.

It might seem that 64 (at least) TLS locations are more than you will ever need. However, keep in mind that an application can dynamically link to several DLLs. One DLL can allocate 10 TLS indexes, a second DLL can allocate 5 indexes, and so on. So it is always best to reduce the number of TLS indexes you need. The best way to do this is to use the same method that *MyFunction* uses above. Sure, I can save all 40 bytes across 10 TLS indexes, but doing so is not only wasteful, it makes working with the data difficult. Instead, allocate a memory block for the data and simply save the pointer in a single TLS index just as *MyFunction* does.

When I discussed the *TlsAlloc* function earlier, I described only 99% of what it did. To help you understand the remaining 1%, look at this code fragment:

```
DWORD dwTlsIndex;
LPVOID lpvSomeValue;

:
:

dwTlsIndex = TlsAlloc();
TlsSetValue(dwTlsIndex, (LPVOID) 12345);
TlsFree(dwTlsIndex);

// Assume that the dwTlsIndex value returned from
// this call to TlsAlloc is identical to the index
// returned by the earlier call to TlsAlloc.
dwTlsIndex = TlsAlloc();

lpvSomeValue = TlsGetValue(dwTlsIndex);
```

What do you think *lpvSomeValue* contains after this code executes? 12345? The answer is 0. *TlsAlloc*, before returning, cycles through every thread existing in the process and places a 0 in each thread's array at the newly allocated index. This is very fortunate.

It's possible that an application will call *LoadLibrary* to load a DLL. And the DLL might call *TlsAlloc* to allocate an index. Then the thread might call *FreeLibrary* to remove the DLL. The DLL should free its index with a call to *TlsFree*, but who knows which values the DLL code placed in any of the thread's arrays? Next a thread calls *LoadLibrary* to load a different DLL into memory. This DLL also calls *TlsAlloc* when it starts and gets the same index used by the previous DLL. If *TlsAlloc* didn't set the returned index for all threads in the process, a thread might see an old value and the code might not execute correctly.

For example, this new DLL might want to check whether memory for a thread has ever been allocated by calling *TlsGetValue*, as in the last code fragment shown on the facing page. If *TlsAlloc* doesn't clear out the array entry for every thread, the old data from the first DLL is still available. If a thread calls *MyFunction*, *MyFunction* thinks that a memory block has already been allocated and calls *memcpy* to copy the new data into what *MyFunction* thinks is a memory block. This could have disastrous results. Fortunately, *TlsAlloc* initializes the array elements so that the disaster can never happen.

The Dynamic Thread-Local Storage Sample Application

The TLSDyn (TLSDYN.EXE) application, listed in Figure 13-2 beginning on page 592, demonstrates how to take advantage of dynamic TLS. The program implicitly links to a dynamic-link library called SOMELIB-.DLL, listed in Figure 13-3 beginning on page 597. This DLL allocates a single TLS index when it receives its DLL_PROCESS_ATTACH notification and frees this TLS index when it receives a DLL_PROCESS_DE-TACH notification. The source code and resource files for TLSDyn and SOMELIB.DLL are in the TLSDYN directory on the companion disc.

SOMELIB.DLL contains a function called *LoadResString*. When this function is called, it first checks whether the calling thread previously called *LoadResString*. *LoadResString* determines this by calling *TlsGetValue* and checking whether the return value is NULL. A NULL value indicates a first-time call to *LoadResString*. In this case, *LoadResString* allocates a block of memory from the process's heap and stores the address of the block in the calling thread's TLS slot.

Whether or not this is the first time this thread is calling *Load-ResString*, we have an address to a block of memory in the heap allocated for this thread. *LoadResString* now calls *LoadString* to load a string from the DLL's string table into this block of memory. This string is now associated with the calling thread.

Finally, *LoadResString* increments an internal counter (stored in the static variable *nStringId*) and returns the address of the loaded string resource. Every time a thread calls *LoadResString*, a different string is retrieved from the DLL's string table.

Now let's look at how the TLSDyn application works. When you invoke it, the following message box appears:

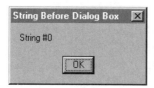

When *WinMain* begins executing, it makes a call to the *LoadResString* function, which in turn loads String #0 from the DLL's string table and associates the string with the process's primary thread. The primary thread then makes a call to *MessageBox* to show you that it was successful.

After you click on the OK button, the primary thread creates a dialog box and five threads. Each of these threads makes its own initial call to *LoadResString* so that each will have its own associated string. Then each thread iterates through a loop four times. With each iteration, each thread creates a string containing the thread number and its associated string. The string is then added to the list box. After all five threads have completed their loops, the following dialog box appears:

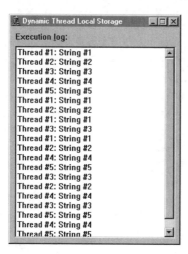

The order of the strings might be different on your machine. Simply note that the *LoadResString* function assigns every thread its own string. Also note that if no thread in the program ever makes a call to *LoadResString*, memory isn't allocated from the heap for this thread. We could allocate the memory in the *DllMain* function whenever the program received either a DLL_PROCESS_ATTACH or a DLL_PROCESS-_DETACH notification, but that would mean allocating memory from the heap for all threads created by the process, even if they never called *LoadResString*. The method used by SOMELIB.DLL is more efficient.

After the program runs, you can terminate it, which causes another message box to appear:

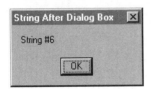

This message box appears as a result of *WinMain* making another call to *LoadResString*. *LoadResString* associates a new string with the primary thread, overwriting the original string, String #0.

Notice how the *DllMain* function in SOMELIB.C cleans up after itself when it receives either a DLL_THREAD_DETACH or a DLL_PRO-CESS_DETACH. In both cases, the DLL checks whether memory from the heap was allocated for the thread and, if so, frees that memory block. Although the memory would be freed automatically when TLSDyn terminated, it's best to clean up yourself. Always check that memory is in fact allocated before attempting to free it (just as *DllMain* does). Also, notice how *TLSFree* is called when *DllMain* is notified that the library is being detached from the process.

Now suppose that an application is already running when one of its threads calls *LoadLibrary* to attach to SOMELIB.DLL. SOMELIB's *DllMain* allocates a TLS index that is guaranteed to be unique for all existing threads and all new threads for this process. Let's say that some threads call *LoadResString*, which results in memory allocation, and a thread calls *FreeLibrary* to detach SOMELIB.DLL. *DllMain* receives a DLL_PROCESS_DETACH message and frees any memory block associated with the calling thread. But what about other threads in the process that might have called *LoadResString*? The memory allocated by these threads will never be freed—we have a pretty bad memory leak here.

Unfortunately, this problem has no good solutions. Your DLL needs to track its allocations in an array, and when it receives a DLL_PROCESS_DETACH notification, it needs to traverse through all the pointers in the array and call *HeapFree* for each one.

TLSDyn.ico

TLSDYN.C

```
/***************************************************************
Module name: TLSDyn.C
Notices: Copyright (c) 1995-1997 Jeffrey Richter
***************************************************************/


#include "..\CmnHdr.H"                      /* See Appendix C. */
#include <windows.h>
#include <windowsx.h>
#include <tchar.h>
#include <stdio.h>         // For sprintf
#include <process.h>       // For _beginthreadex
#include "..\SomeLib\SomeLib.H"
#include "Resource.H"



///////////////////////////////////////////////////////////////


HWND g_hwndLog = NULL;



///////////////////////////////////////////////////////////////


DWORD WINAPI ThreadFunc (LPVOID lpvThreadParm) {
   int nThreadNum = (int) lpvThreadParm;
   int nNumCycles = 4;
   TCHAR szBuf[100];
   LPCTSTR szString = LoadResString();

   while (nNumCycles--) {
      _stprintf(szBuf, __TEXT("Thread #%d: %s"),
         nThreadNum, szString);

      ListBox_AddString(g_hwndLog, szBuf);
```

Figure 13-2.
The TLSDyn application.

(continued)

Figure 13-2. *continued*

```
      Sleep(nThreadNum * 50);
   }
   return(0);
}


//////////////////////////////////////////////////////////////


BOOL Dlg_OnInitDialog (HWND hwnd, HWND hwndFocus,
   LPARAM lParam) {

   int nThreadNum;

   // Associate an icon with the dialog box.
   chSETDLGICONS(hwnd, IDI_TLSDYN, IDI_TLSDYN);

   g_hwndLog = GetDlgItem(hwnd, IDC_LOG);


   for (nThreadNum = 1; nThreadNum <= 5; nThreadNum++) {
      HANDLE hThread;
      DWORD dwIDThread;

      hThread = chBEGINTHREADEX(NULL, 0, ThreadFunc,
         (LPVOID) nThreadNum, 0, &dwIDThread);

      CloseHandle(hThread);
   }

   return(TRUE);
}


//////////////////////////////////////////////////////////////


void Dlg_OnCommand (HWND hwnd, int id, HWND hwndCtl,
   UINT codeNotify) {

   switch (id) {
      case IDCANCEL:
         EndDialog(hwnd, id);
         break;
```

(continued)

Figure 13-2. *continued*

```
   }
}


/////////////////////////////////////////////////////////////////


BOOL CALLBACK Dlg_Proc (HWND hwnd, UINT uMsg,
   WPARAM wParam, LPARAM lParam) {

   switch (uMsg) {
      chHANDLE_DLGMSG(hwnd, WM_INITDIALOG, Dlg_OnInitDialog);
      chHANDLE_DLGMSG(hwnd, WM_COMMAND, Dlg_OnCommand);
   }
   return(FALSE);
}


/////////////////////////////////////////////////////////////////


int WINAPI _tWinMain (HINSTANCE hinstExe,
   HINSTANCE hinstPrev, LPTSTR pszCmdLine, int nCmdShow) {

   chWARNIFUNICODEUNDERWIN95();

   MessageBox(NULL, LoadResString(),
      __TEXT("String Before Dialog Box"), MB_OK);

   DialogBox(hinstExe, MAKEINTRESOURCE(IDD_TLSDYN),
      NULL, Dlg_Proc);

   MessageBox(NULL, LoadResString(),
      __TEXT("String After Dialog Box"), MB_OK);

   return(0);
}


//////////////////////// End Of File ////////////////////////
```

(continued)

Figure 13-2. *continued*

TLSDYN.RC

```
//Microsoft Developer Studio generated resource script.
//
#include "Resource.h"

#define APSTUDIO_READONLY_SYMBOLS
/////////////////////////////////////////////////////////////////
//
// Generated from the TEXTINCLUDE 2 resource.
//
#include "afxres.h"


/////////////////////////////////////////////////////////////////
#undef APSTUDIO_READONLY_SYMBOLS

/////////////////////////////////////////////////////////////////
// English (U.S.) resources

#if !defined(AFX_RESOURCE_DLL) || defined(AFX_TARG_ENU)
#ifdef _WIN32
LANGUAGE LANG_ENGLISH, SUBLANG_ENGLISH_US
#pragma code_page(1252)
#endif //_WIN32

#ifdef APSTUDIO_INVOKED
/////////////////////////////////////////////////////////////////
//
// TEXTINCLUDE
//

1 TEXTINCLUDE DISCARDABLE
BEGIN
    "Resource.h\0"
END

2 TEXTINCLUDE DISCARDABLE
BEGIN
    "#include ""afxres.h""\r\n"
    "\0"
END

3 TEXTINCLUDE DISCARDABLE
BEGIN
    "\r\n"
```

(continued)

Figure 13-2. *continued*

```
    "\0"
END

#endif    // APSTUDIO_INVOKED


/////////////////////////////////////////////////////////////
//
// Icon
//

// Icon with lowest ID value placed first to ensure
// application icon remains consistent on all systems.
IDI_TLSDYN              ICON   DISCARDABLE    "TLSDyn.Ico"


/////////////////////////////////////////////////////////////
//
// Dialog
//

IDD_TLSDYN DIALOG DISCARDABLE  25, 21, 147, 180
STYLE WS_MINIMIZEBOX | WS_VISIBLE | WS_CAPTION | WS_SYSMENU
CAPTION "Dynamic Thread Local Storage"
FONT 8, "System"
BEGIN
    LTEXT           "Execution &log:",IDC_STATIC,4,4,47,8
    LISTBOX         IDC_LOG,4,16,140,160,NOT LBS_NOTIFY |
                    LBS_NOINTEGRALHEIGHT | WS_VSCROLL
END

#endif    // English (U.S.) resources
/////////////////////////////////////////////////////////////



#ifndef APSTUDIO_INVOKED
/////////////////////////////////////////////////////////////
//
// Generated from the TEXTINCLUDE 3 resource.
//



/////////////////////////////////////////////////////////////
#endif    // not APSTUDIO_INVOKED
```

SOMELIB.C

```
/*************************************************************
Module name: SomeLib.C
Notices: Copyright (c) 1995-1997 Jeffrey Richter
*************************************************************/


#include "..\CmnHdr.H"                    /* See Appendix C. */
#include <windows.h>
#include "Resource.h"

#define _SOMELIBLIB_
#include "SomeLib.H"


///////////////////////////////////////////////////////////


// Out thread local storage slot
DWORD g_dwTlsIndex = TLS_OUT_OF_INDEXES;

// Per mapping instance data for this DLL
HINSTANCE g_hinstDll = NULL;

// This mutex is required to guard access to the static
// nStringId variable inside the LoadResString function.
HANDLE g_hMutex = NULL;


///////////////////////////////////////////////////////////


BOOL WINAPI DllMain (HINSTANCE hinstDll, DWORD fdwReason,
    LPVOID lpvReserved) {

    LPTSTR lpszStr;

    switch (fdwReason) {

        case DLL_PROCESS_ATTACH:
            // DLL is attaching to the address space
            // of the current process.
            g_hinstDll = hinstDll;
```

Figure 13-3.
The SomeLib.DLL file.

(continued)

597

Figure 13-3. *continued*

```
        // Allocate a thread-local storage index.
        g_dwTlsIndex = TlsAlloc();

        if (g_dwTlsIndex == TLS_OUT_OF_INDEXES) {
            // The TLS index couldn't be allocated--have the
            // DLL return that initialization was
            // NOT successful.
            return(FALSE);
        }

        g_hMutex = CreateMutex(NULL, FALSE, NULL);
        if (g_hMutex == NULL) {
            // The mutex couldn't be created--have the
            // DLL return that initialization was
            // NOT successful.
            return(FALSE);
        }

        break;

    case DLL_THREAD_ATTACH:
        // A new thread is being created in the process.
        break;

    case DLL_THREAD_DETACH:
        // A thread is exiting cleanly.

        // Ensure that the TLS index was
        // allocated successfully.
        if (g_dwTlsIndex != TLS_OUT_OF_INDEXES) {

            // Get the pointer to the allocated memory.
            lpszStr = TlsGetValue(g_dwTlsIndex);

            // Test whether memory was ever allocated
            // for this thread.
            if (lpszStr != NULL) {
                HeapFree(GetProcessHeap(), 0, lpszStr);
            }
        }
        break;

    case DLL_PROCESS_DETACH:
        // The calling process is detaching the DLL
        // from its address space.
```

(continued)

Figure 13-3. *continued*

```
                // Ensure that the TLS index was
                // allocated successfully.
                if (g_dwTlsIndex != TLS_OUT_OF_INDEXES) {

                    // Get the pointer to the allocated memory.
                    lpszStr = TlsGetValue(g_dwTlsIndex);

                    // Test whether memory was ever allocated
                    // for this thread.
                    if (lpszStr != NULL) {
                        HeapFree(GetProcessHeap(), 0, lpszStr);
                    }

                    // Free the TLS index.
                    TlsFree(g_dwTlsIndex);
                }

                // Ensure that the mutex was created successfully.
                if (g_hMutex != NULL) {
                    CloseHandle(g_hMutex);
                }
                break;
        }
        return(TRUE);
}


//////////////////////////////////////////////////////////////////


#define RESSTR_SIZE      (1000 * sizeof(TCHAR))

SOMELIBAPI LPCTSTR LoadResString (void) {
    static int nStringId = 0;

    LPTSTR lpszStr = TlsGetValue(g_dwTlsIndex);

    if (lpszStr == NULL) {
        lpszStr = HeapAlloc(GetProcessHeap(), 0, RESSTR_SIZE);
        TlsSetValue(g_dwTlsIndex, lpszStr);
    }

    WaitForSingleObject(g_hMutex, INFINITE);
    LoadString(g_hinstDll, IDS_STRINGFIRST + nStringId,
        lpszStr, RESSTR_SIZE);
```

(continued)

Figure 13-3. *continued*

```
    nStringId = (nStringId + 1) % IDS_STRINGNUM;
    ReleaseMutex(g_hMutex);

    return(lpszStr);
}


//////////////////////// End Of File ////////////////////////
```

SOMELIB.H

```
/**************************************************************
Module name: SomeLib.H
Notices: Copyright (c) 1995-1997 Jeffrey Richter
**************************************************************/


#if !defined(_SOMELIBLIB_)
#define SOMELIBAPI __declspec(dllimport)
#else
#define SOMELIBAPI __declspec(dllexport)
#endif


// IDs for use by the string table resource
#define IDS_STRINGLAST    (IDS_STRINGFIRST + 9)
#define IDS_STRINGNUM     (IDS_STRINGLAST - \
                           IDS_STRINGFIRST + 1)


// Function to return the address of a string in memory
SOMELIBAPI LPCTSTR LoadResString (void);


//////////////////////// End Of File ////////////////////////
```

(continued)

Figure 13-3. *continued*

```
SOMELIB.RC
//Microsoft Visual C++ generated resource script.
//
#include "Resource.h"

#define APSTUDIO_READONLY_SYMBOLS
/////////////////////////////////////////////////////////////
//
// Generated from the TEXTINCLUDE 2 resource.
//
#include "afxres.h"


/////////////////////////////////////////////////////////////
#undef APSTUDIO_READONLY_SYMBOLS


#ifdef APSTUDIO_INVOKED
/////////////////////////////////////////////////////////////
//
// TEXTINCLUDE
//

1 TEXTINCLUDE DISCARDABLE
BEGIN
    "Resource.h\0"
END

2 TEXTINCLUDE DISCARDABLE
BEGIN
    "#include ""afxres.h""\r\n"
    "\0"
END

3 TEXTINCLUDE DISCARDABLE
BEGIN
    "\r\n"
    "\0"
END

/////////////////////////////////////////////////////////////
#endif    // APSTUDIO_INVOKED
```

(continued)

Figure 13-3. *continued*

```
//////////////////////////////////////////////////////////////
//
// String Table
//

STRINGTABLE DISCARDABLE
BEGIN
    1008                    "String #8"
    1009                    "String #9"
END


STRINGTABLE DISCARDABLE
BEGIN
    IDS_STRINGFIRST         "String #0"
    1001                    "String #1"
    1002                    "String #2"
    1003                    "String #3"
    1004                    "String #4"
    1005                    "String #5"
    1006                    "String #6"
    1007                    "String #7"
END



#ifndef APSTUDIO_INVOKED
//////////////////////////////////////////////////////////////
//
// Generated from the TEXTINCLUDE 3 resource.
//



//////////////////////////////////////////////////////////////
#endif    // not APSTUDIO_INVOKED
```

Static Thread-Local Storage

Static thread-local storage uses the same concept as dynamic TLS—it associates data with a thread. However, static TLS is much easier to use in your code because you don't need to call any functions to take advantage of it.

Let's say that you want to associate a start time with every thread created by your application. All you need to do is declare the start-time variable as follows:

```
__declspec(thread) DWORD gt_dwStartTime = 0;
```

The *__declspec(thread)* prefix in the line above is a new modifier that Microsoft added to the Visual C++ compiler. It tells the compiler that the corresponding variable should be placed in its own section inside the EXE or DLL file. The variable following *__declspec(thread)* must be declared as either a global variable or a static variable inside (or outside) a function. You can't declare a local variable to be of type *__declspec-(thread)*. This shouldn't be a problem because local variables are always associated with a specific thread anyway. I use the *gt_* prefix for global TLS variables and *st_* for static TLS variables.

When the compiler compiles your program, it puts all the TLS variables into their own section named, unsurprisingly enough, .tls. The linker combines all the .tls sections together from all the object modules to produce one big .tls section in the resulting EXE or DLL file.

To make static TLS work, the operating system needs to get involved. When your application is loaded into memory, the system looks for the .tls section in your EXE file and dynamically allocates a block of memory large enough to hold all the static TLS variables. Every time the code in your application refers to one of these variables, the reference resolves to a memory location contained in the allocated block of memory. As a result, the compiler must generate additional code in order to reference the static TLS variables, which makes your application both larger in size and slower to execute. On an *x86* CPU, three additional machine instructions are generated for every reference to a static TLS variable.

If another thread is created in your process, the system traps it and automatically allocates another block of memory to contain the new thread's static TLS variables. The new thread has access only to its own static TLS variables and isn't able to access the TLS variables belonging to any other thread.

That's basically how static TLS works. Now let's add DLLs to the story. It's likely that your application will use static TLS variables and that you will link to a DLL that also wants to use static TLS variables. When the system loads your application, it first determines the size of your application's .tls section and adds the value to the size of any .tls sections contained in any DLLs to which your application links. When threads are created in your process, the system automatically allocates a block of memory large enough to hold all the TLS variables required by your application and all the implicitly linked DLLs. This is pretty cool.

But let's look at what happens when your application calls *Load-Library* to link to a DLL that also contains static TLS variables. The system needs to look at all the threads that already exist in the process and enlarge their TLS memory blocks to accommodate the additional memory requirements of the new DLL. Also, if *FreeLibrary* is called to free a DLL containing static TLS variables, the memory block associated with each thread in the process should be compacted.

Alas, this is too much for the operating system to manage. The system allows libraries containing static TLS variables to be explicitly loaded at run time; however, the TLS data isn't properly initialized, and any attempt to access it may result in an access violation. This is the only disadvantage of using static TLS; this problem doesn't occur when using dynamic TLS. Libraries that use dynamic TLS can be loaded at run time and freed at run time with no problems at all.

The Static Thread-Local Storage Sample Application

The TLSStat (TLSSTAT.EXE) application, listed in Figure 13-4 beginning on page 607, demonstrates the use of static TLS. The source code and resource files for the application are in the TLSSTAT directory on the companion disc. When you first invoke TLSStat, the following dialog box appears:

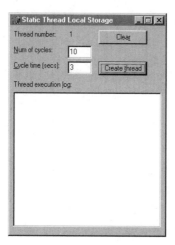

This dialog box allows you to dynamically create new threads and monitor their execution.

The following line is included near the top of TLSSTAT.C:

```
__declspec(thread) DWORD gt_dwStartTime = 0;
```

This line declares a static TLS variable called *gt_dwStartTime*. The system creates a new instance of this variable every time a new thread is created in the process. Whenever any thread refers to *gt_dwStartTime*, that thread is always referring to its own copy of this variable.

Clicking on the Create Thread button dynamically creates a new thread by allocating a data structure from the heap and filling the members of the structure with information that needs to be passed to the newly created thread. This information includes the thread number, the number of cycles that the thread should execute, and the duration of each cycle. The pointer to this data structure is then passed to _beginthreadex, which passes the pointer to the thread function. The thread function is responsible for freeing this memory block when it no longer needs it.[2]

When each new thread begins, it records the system time in the *gt_dwStartTime* variable and starts executing a loop. As each iteration of the loop begins, the thread displays the total amount of time that the thread has been in existence in the Thread Execution Log list box.

You should notice that in this example I could have done away with the *gt_dwStartTime* variable by creating a local (stack-based) variable called *dwStartTime* and placing it inside *ThreadFunc*. In fact, this would have been a better way to write the application because it would have avoided the additional size and speed overhead incurred when using static TLS. However, if I had done this, the demonstration program would no longer have demonstrated static TLS.

The real point I'm trying to make is that an application "understands" the nature of the program, whereas a DLL most likely doesn't. This is why TLS was really designed for DLLs, although it can be used in applications.

Before creating a thread, you can set the number of iterations in the loop and the duration of each iteration by adjusting the contents of the Num Of Cycles and Cycle Time (Secs) edit boxes. Because a new thread can take several seconds to execute, you can create additional threads before the first thread finishes executing by adjusting the Num

---

2. While I was writing this section of code, I thought it would be useful to have a new Win32 function that offered some way for one thread to alter the thread-local storage variables used by another thread. If this function existed, I probably could have avoided using the heap altogether by assigning values to the new thread.

Of Cycles and Cycle Time (Secs) edit boxes and clicking on the Create Thread button again. The following screen shot was taken while three threads were executing simultaneously:

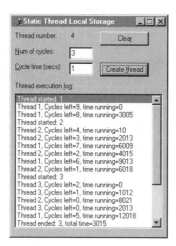

The three threads were created using the following settings:

Thread Number	Num Of Cycles	Cycle Time (Secs)
1	10	3
2	5	2
3	3	1

Every time a new thread is created, the Thread Number value is incremented. You can reset the application by clicking on the Clear button, which causes the Thread Number value to reset to 1 and the contents of the list box to be cleared.

One last thing to note. When you terminate TLSStat, it displays the following message box:

This box displays the total amount of time that the application (or primary thread) has been executing by referencing its own *gt_dwStartTime* TLS variable.

TLSStat.ico

TLSSTAT.C

```
/*******************************************************************
Module name: TLSStat.C
Notices: Copyright (c) 1995-1997 Jeffrey Richter
*******************************************************************/


#include "..\CmnHdr.H"                    /* See Appendix C. */
#include <windows.h>
#include <windowsx.h>
#include <tchar.h>
#include <stdlib.h>              // For rand
#include <stdio.h>               // For sprintf
#include <process.h>            // For _beginthreadex
#include "Resource.H"



///////////////////////////////////////////////////////////////////


// Structure used to pass data from one thread to another
typedef struct {
    int nThreadNum;         // The number used for recordkeeping
    int nNumCycles;         // Number of iterations in the loop
    DWORD dwCycleTime;      // Time spent in each loop iteration
} THREADDATA, *LPTHREADDATA;


// Global handle to list box window used for
// logging execution
HWND g_hwndLogLB = NULL;


// Our global static TLS variable
// to hold each thread's start time
// The system will automatically allocate one of these
// for every thread created in this process.
__declspec(thread) DWORD gt_dwStartTime = 0;


///////////////////////////////////////////////////////////////////


DWORD WINAPI ThreadFunc (LPVOID lpvThreadParm) {
    // The parameter passed to us is a pointer to a THREADDATA
    // structure.  Let's save it in a local variable.
```

Figure 13-4.   *(continued)*
The TLSStat application.

Figure 13-4. *continued*

```
LPTHREADDATA lpThreadData = (LPTHREADDATA) lpvThreadParm;

TCHAR szBuf[100];

// Store the thread's start time in its very
// own static TLS variable.
gt_dwStartTime = GetTickCount();

// Write a log entry stating that we're starting.
_stprintf(szBuf, __TEXT("Thread started: %d"),
   lpThreadData->nThreadNum);
ListBox_AddString(g_hwndLogLB, szBuf);
ListBox_SetCurSel(g_hwndLogLB, 0);

// Start doing some work....
while (lpThreadData->nNumCycles--) {
   // Write to the log how many cycles this thread
   // has left before it dies and how long this thread
   // has been running.
   _stprintf(szBuf,
      __TEXT("Thread %d, Cycles left=%d, time running=%d"),
      lpThreadData->nThreadNum, lpThreadData->nNumCycles,
      GetTickCount() - gt_dwStartTime);

   ListBox_AddString(g_hwndLogLB, szBuf);

   // Sleep for a while and let other threads run.
   Sleep(lpThreadData->dwCycleTime);
}

// This thread is done executing; write a log entry
// that says so and displays the total execution time
// of the thread.
_stprintf(szBuf, __TEXT("Thread ended: %d, total time=%d"),
   lpThreadData->nThreadNum,
   GetTickCount() - gt_dwStartTime);
ListBox_AddString(g_hwndLogLB, szBuf);

// The thread is responsible for deleting the THREADDATA
// structure that was allocated by the primary thread.
HeapFree(GetProcessHeap(), 0, lpvThreadParm);

return(0);
}
```

(continued)

Figure 13-4. *continued*

```
//////////////////////////////////////////////////////////

BOOL Dlg_OnInitDialog (HWND hwnd, HWND hwndFocus,
   LPARAM lParam) {

   // Associate an icon with the dialog box.
   chSETDLGICONS(hwnd, IDI_TLSSTAT, IDI_TLSSTAT);

   // Default the thread number to 1.
   SetDlgItemInt(hwnd, IDC_THREADNUM, 1, FALSE);

   // Default the number of cycles to 10.
   SetDlgItemInt(hwnd, IDC_NUMCYCLES, 10, FALSE);

   // Default the maximum cycle time to 3 seconds.
   SetDlgItemInt(hwnd, IDC_CYCLETIME, 3, FALSE);

   // Save the handle of the dialog box in a global
   // variable so that it can be accessed easily from
   // the thread function.
   g_hwndLogLB = GetDlgItem(hwnd, IDC_LOG);

   // Let's start with the Create Thread
   // button having focus.
   SetFocus(GetDlgItem(hwnd, IDOK));

   // I set focus, so the Dialog Manager shouldn't.
   return(FALSE);
}


//////////////////////////////////////////////////////////

void Dlg_OnCommand (HWND hwnd, int id, HWND hwndCtl,
   UINT codeNotify) {

   DWORD        dwIDThread;
   HANDLE       hThread;
   LPTHREADDATA lpThreadData;

   switch (id) {
```

(continued)

Figure 13-4. *continued*

```
case IDC_CLEAR:
   // Reset the application.
   SetDlgItemInt(hwnd, IDC_THREADNUM, 1, FALSE);
   ListBox_ResetContent(g_hwndLogLB);
   break;

case IDOK:
   // Allocate a block of memory that can be used to
   // give data from this thread to the new thread we
   // are about to create.
   lpThreadData = (LPTHREADDATA)
      HeapAlloc(GetProcessHeap(), 0,
         sizeof(THREADDATA));

   if (lpThreadData == NULL) {
      // Memory could not be allocated; display message
      // box and break.
      chMB(__TEXT("Error creating ThreadData"));
      break;
   }

   // Fill the memory block with the data from
   // the dialog box.
   lpThreadData->nThreadNum =
      GetDlgItemInt(hwnd, IDC_THREADNUM, NULL, FALSE);
   lpThreadData->nNumCycles =
      GetDlgItemInt(hwnd, IDC_NUMCYCLES, NULL, FALSE);

   // Multiply the cycle time by 1000
   // to convert to seconds.
   lpThreadData->dwCycleTime = (DWORD)
      (1000 * GetDlgItemInt(hwnd,
      IDC_CYCLETIME, NULL, FALSE));


   // Increment the thread number for the next thread.
   SetDlgItemInt(hwnd, IDC_THREADNUM,
      lpThreadData->nThreadNum + 1, FALSE);

   // Create the new thread and pass it the address of
   // our allocated memory block containing the
   // attributes that the thread should use.  The
   // thread is responsible for freeing the memory
   // block when it no longer needs it.
```

(continued)

Figure 13-4. *continued*

```
        hThread = chBEGINTHREADEX(NULL, 0, ThreadFunc,
            (LPVOID) lpThreadData, 0, &dwIDThread);

        if (hThread != NULL) {
            // If the thread was created successfully, close
            // the handle because this thread never needs
            // to refer to the new thread again.
            CloseHandle(hThread);

        } else {

            // The thread could not be created;
            // display message box and break.
            chMB(__TEXT("Error creating the new thread"));
            HeapFree(GetProcessHeap(), 0,
                (LPVOID) lpThreadData);
        }
        break;

    case IDCANCEL:
        EndDialog(hwnd, id);
        break;
    }
}


//////////////////////////////////////////////////////////////


BOOL CALLBACK Dlg_Proc (HWND hwnd, UINT uMsg,
    WPARAM wParam, LPARAM lParam) {

    switch (uMsg) {
        chHANDLE_DLGMSG(hwnd, WM_INITDIALOG, Dlg_OnInitDialog);
        chHANDLE_DLGMSG(hwnd, WM_COMMAND, Dlg_OnCommand);
    }
    return(FALSE);
}


//////////////////////////////////////////////////////////////
```

(continued)

Figure 13-4. *continued*

```
int WINAPI _tWinMain (HINSTANCE hinstExe,
   HINSTANCE hinstPrev, LPTSTR pszCmdLine, int nCmdShow) {

   TCHAR szBuf[100];

   chWARNIFUNICODEUNDERWIN95();

   // The primary thread also gets its own TLS copy
   // of the gt_dwStartTime variable.  Let's initialize it to
   // the time when the application started executing.
   gt_dwStartTime = GetTickCount();

   DialogBox(hinstExe, MAKEINTRESOURCE(IDD_TLSSTAT),
      NULL, Dlg_Proc);

   // The user has terminated the dialog box; let's show
   // how long the whole application has been running.
   _stprintf(szBuf,
      __TEXT("Total time running application=%d."),
      GetTickCount() - gt_dwStartTime);
   chMB(szBuf);

   return(0);
}


//////////////////////// End Of File ////////////////////////
```

TLSSTAT.RC

```
//Microsoft Developer Studio generated resource script.
//
#include "Resource.h"

#define APSTUDIO_READONLY_SYMBOLS
/////////////////////////////////////////////////////////////
//
// Generated from the TEXTINCLUDE 2 resource.
//
#include "afxres.h"


/////////////////////////////////////////////////////////////
#undef APSTUDIO_READONLY_SYMBOLS
```

(continued)

Figure 13-4. *continued*

```
/////////////////////////////////////////////////////////
// English (U.S.) resources

#if !defined(AFX_RESOURCE_DLL) || defined(AFX_TARG_ENU)
#ifdef _WIN32
LANGUAGE LANG_ENGLISH, SUBLANG_ENGLISH_US
#pragma code_page(1252)
#endif //_WIN32

#ifdef APSTUDIO_INVOKED
/////////////////////////////////////////////////////////
//
// TEXTINCLUDE
//

1 TEXTINCLUDE DISCARDABLE
BEGIN
    "Resource.h\0"
END

2 TEXTINCLUDE DISCARDABLE
BEGIN
    "#include ""afxres.h""\r\n"
    "\0"
END

3 TEXTINCLUDE DISCARDABLE
BEGIN
    "\r\n"
    "\0"
END

#endif    // APSTUDIO_INVOKED


/////////////////////////////////////////////////////////
//
// Dialog
//

IDD_TLSSTAT DIALOG DISCARDABLE  18, 18, 180, 215
STYLE WS_MINIMIZEBOX | WS_VISIBLE | WS_CAPTION | WS_SYSMENU
CAPTION "Static Thread Local Storage"
FONT 8, "Helv"
```

(continued)

Figure 13-4. *continued*

```
BEGIN
    LTEXT           "Thread number:",IDC_STATIC,4,4,52,8
    RTEXT           "1",IDC_THREADNUM,60,4,13,8
    PUSHBUTTON      "Clea&r",IDC_CLEAR,104,4,56,14
    LTEXT           "&Num of cycles:",IDC_STATIC,4,20,50,8
    EDITTEXT        IDC_NUMCYCLES,68,20,28,13
    LTEXT           "&Cycle time (secs):",IDC_STATIC,
                    4,36,59,8
    EDITTEXT        IDC_CYCLETIME,68,36,28,13
    DEFPUSHBUTTON   "Create &thread",IDOK,104,36,56,14,
                    WS_GROUP
    LTEXT           "Thread execution &log:",IDC_STATIC,
                    4,56,72,8
    LISTBOX         IDC_LOG,4,68,172,144,NOT LBS_NOTIFY |
                    WS_VSCROLL | WS_GROUP | WS_TABSTOP
END


/////////////////////////////////////////////////////////////
//
// Icon
//


// Icon with lowest ID value placed first to ensure
// application icon remains consistent on all systems.
IDI_TLSSTAT             ICON    DISCARDABLE     "TLSStat.Ico"
#endif    // English (U.S.) resources
/////////////////////////////////////////////////////////////



#ifndef APSTUDIO_INVOKED
/////////////////////////////////////////////////////////////
//
// Generated from the TEXTINCLUDE 3 resource.
//


/////////////////////////////////////////////////////////////
#endif    // not APSTUDIO_INVOKED
```

FILE SYSTEMS

One important aspect of any operating system is the way in which it manages files. In good old MS-DOS, managing files is about all the operating system did, especially when 16-bit Windows was running on top of it. 16-bit Windows pretty much took care of everything except the manipulation of files on hard disks and floppy disks, which it left up to MS-DOS. (As time went on, though, 16-bit Windows took on more of even this responsibility by adding direct 32-bit access support and going right to the disk controller to manipulate the system's paging file.)

Now both Microsoft Windows 95 and Microsoft Windows NT have greatly enhanced 32-bit file support for managing the user's files and drives. In fact, both of these operating systems sport an installable file system that is capable of supporting multiple file systems—all of them simultaneously.

The main file system of Windows 95 is the File Allocation Table (FAT) file system. Windows NT also supports the FAT file system. The FAT file system supports file and directory names up to 255 characters long. These names are stored on the disk using Unicode. Using Unicode to store filenames means among other things that files will retain their names when they are copied to systems that use different languages. The FAT file system also associates three time stamps with each file: when the file was created, when the file was last accessed, and when the file was last modified.

In addition to the FAT file system, Windows NT supports the NT file system (NTFS). The NTFS file system offers all of the features of the FAT file system plus some additional ones. The most important feature of NTFS is a file system recovery scheme that allows for quick restoration of disk-based data after a system failure. Other features of NTFS allow you to manipulate extremely large storage media. Several security features, such as execute-only files (which make it far more difficult for a virus to attach itself to an application), have been added. For POSIX compatibility, NTFS supports file system features such as hard links, case-sensitive filenames, and the ability to retain information regarding when a file was last opened.

NTFS was designed to be extended. Features that will be supported include transaction-based operations to support fault tolerant applications, user-controlled version numbers for files, multiple data streams per file, flexible options for file naming and file attributes, and support for the popular file servers. For security-minded installations, NTFS will certainly become the standard, and it should eventually replace the FAT file system standard.

The CD-ROM File System (CDFS) is used specifically for a CD-ROM drive, once considered a high-ticket peripheral for a personal computer. Today a CD-ROM drive is becoming more a necessity than a luxury. More and more software is available on CD-ROM—even Windows 95 and Windows NT are available on CD-ROM. In the future, more software programs will use CD-ROMs as their distribution medium because CD-ROMs offer several advantages:

- CD-ROMs are less expensive to mass-produce when compared to the sheer number of floppy disks involved in so much of software distribution. This should lower the cost of retail software products.

- Because the average end user doesn't have CD-ROM duplication equipment, it's much harder for end users to pirate copies of software distributed on CD-ROM. People who want to use the software will have to buy it. This should also help lower the cost of retail software products.

- CD-ROMs are more reliable than floppies because CD-ROMs aren't magnetic and therefore, unlike floppies, aren't subject to magnetic disturbances.

- Data can be accessed directly from a CD-ROM without having to be installed on your hard drive. This can save enormous amounts of precious hard disk space.

- Applications are much easier to install from a CD-ROM because you don't have to baby-sit the computer, switching floppies on demand.

Microsoft's having built CD-ROM support directly into Windows 95 and Windows NT will certainly help to promote the use and wide acceptance of CD-ROMs in the marketplace.

The best aspect of all these file systems is that they provide simultaneous operating system support. If you are using Windows NT, you can easily have one partition on your hard disk formatted for FAT and another formatted for NTFS. Then you can easily copy files from either of these partitions to a floppy disk formatted for the FAT file system.

Win32's Filename Conventions

So that Win32 can support several different file systems, all the file systems must observe some ground rules. The most important rule is that each file system must organize files into a hierarchical directory tree just as the FAT file system does. Directory names and filenames in the pathname must be separated by the backslash (\) character. In addition to the rules for constructing pathnames, there are rules for constructing directory names and filenames.

- All pathnames must be zero-terminated.

- Directory names and filenames must not contain the backslash separator character (\), a character whose ASCII value is in the range 0 through 31, or any character explicitly disallowed by any of the file systems.

- Directory names and filenames can be created in mixed case, but users must anticipate that searches for directories and files will always be performed by means of case-insensitive comparisons. If a file called ReadMe.Txt already exists and you try to name another file README.TXT, the naming of the second file will fail.

- When used to specify a directory name, the period (.) identifies the current directory. For example, the pathname .\README-.TXT indicates that the file is in the current directory.

- When used to specify a directory name, two periods (..) identify the parent directory of the current directory. For example, the pathname ..\README.TXT indicates that the file is in the current directory's parent directory.

- When used as part of a directory name or filename, a period (.) separates individual components of the name. For example, in the file README.TXT, the period separates the file's name (in the smaller sense) from the file's extension.

- Directory names and filenames must not contain some special characters; these include the less than sign (<), the greater than sign (>), the colon (:), the double quotation marks ("), and the pipe (|).

All file systems supported by Win32 must follow these ground rules. The differences among the file systems have to do with how each file system interprets the ground rules and with the additional features or information a file system adds that distinguishes it from others. For example, the NTFS file system allows directories and files to be secured, whereas the FAT file system does not.

System and Volume Operations

Let's look at the file system at the highest level first and work our way down to the nitty-gritty stuff. At the highest level, your application might need to know what logical drives exist in the user's environment. The most primitive call you can make to determine this is

```
DWORD GetLogicalDrives(void);
```

This function simply returns a 32-bit value in which each bit represents whether a logical drive exists. For example, if the system has a drive A, bit 0 will be set, and if the system has a drive Z, bit 25 will be set.

You can determine whether a particular drive letter was assigned to a logical drive on the system by executing this function:

```
BOOL DoesDriveExist (TCHAR cDriveLetter) {
   cDriveLetter = (TCHAR) CharUpper(cDriveLetter);
   return(GetLogicalDrives() & (1 << (cDriveLetter - __TEXT('A'))));
}
```

The result from *GetLogicalDrives* can also be used to count the number of logical drives in the system:

```
UINT GetNumDrivesInSys (void) {
   DWORD dw = GetLogicalDrives();
   UINT uDrivesInSys = 0;
```

```
// Repeat until there are no more drives.
while (dw != 0) {

    if (dw & 1) {
        // If low-bit is set, drive exists.
        uDrivesInSys++;
    }

    // Shift all the drive information down 1 bit.
    dw >>= 1;
}

// Return number of logical drives.
return(uDrivesInSys);
}
```

The *GetLogicalDrives* function is very fast but doesn't return a lot of useful information.

The *GetLogicalDriveStrings* function doesn't require all the bit manipulations and returns more complete information:

```
DWORD GetLogicalDriveStrings(DWORD cchBuffer, LPTSTR lpszBuffer);
```

This function fills the buffer pointed to by *lpszBuffer* with the root directory information associated with every logical drive on the system. The *cchBuffer* parameter tells the function the maximum size of the buffer. The function returns the number of characters required to hold all the data. When calling this function, you should always compare the return value with the value passed in the *cchBuffer* parameter. If the return value is smaller, the buffer was large enough to hold all the data. If the return value is larger, there was more data than could fit into the buffer.

The best way to use this function is to call it once, passing in 0 as the *cchBuffer* parameter. Then use the return value to dynamically allocate a block of memory of the size returned by the call to *GetLogicalDriveStrings*. Then call the function again, this time passing in the address of the newly allocated buffer:

```
DWORD dw = GetLogicalDriveStrings(0, NULL);
LPTSTR lpDriveStrings = HeapAlloc(GetProcessHeap(), 0, dw *
    sizeof(TCHAR));
GetLogicalDriveStrings(dw, lpDriveStrings);
```

The contents of the returned buffer have the same format as an environment string buffer, that is, items separated by a zero character with an extra, terminating zero character at the end. For example, on my machine the buffer comes back looking like this:

```
A:\<null>
B:\<null>
C:\<null>
D:\<null>
E:\<null>
F:\<null>
G:\<null>
<null>
```

Now that you have the root directories for every logical drive on the system, you might want to determine exactly what type of drive each is located on. You can use *GetDriveType*:

```
UINT GetDriveType(LPTSTR lpszRootPathName);
```

The *GetDriveType* function returns the type of drive identified by the *lpszRootPathName* parameter. Here are the possible return values:

Identifier	Meaning
DRIVE_UNKNOWN	Drive type can't be determined.
DRIVE_NO_ROOT_DIR	Root directory doesn't exist.
DRIVE_REMOVABLE	Disk can be removed from the drive. This value is returned for floppy drives.
DRIVE_FIXED	Disk can't be removed from the drive. This value is returned for hard drives.
DRIVE_REMOTE	Drive is a remote drive. This value is returned for network drives.
DRIVE_CDROM	Drive is a CD-ROM drive.
DRIVE_RAMDISK	Drive is a RAM disk.

Getting Volume-Specific Information

When developing a Win32 application, you should always keep in mind that the user might be using any combination of file systems (FAT, NTFS, and CDFS) and that new file systems may emerge in the future. Any new file systems will need to follow the ground rules, and with a little extra work you can write an application so that it runs correctly regardless of which file system or systems the user has. If your application needs some specific information about a particular file system, it can call *Get-VolumeInformation*:

```
BOOL GetVolumeInformation(LPTSTR lpRootPathName,
    LPTSTR lpVolumeNameBuffer, DWORD nVolumeNameSize,
    LPDWORD lpVolumeSerialNumber, LPDWORD lpMaximumComponentLength,
    LPDWORD lpFileSystemFlags, LPTSTR lpFileSystemNameBuffer,
    DWORD nFileSystemNameSize);
```

The *GetVolumeInformation* function returns file system–specific information associated with the directory path specified in the *lpRootPathName* parameter. Most of the remaining parameters are pointers to buffers or DWORDs that the function will fill.

GetVolumeInformation returns the volume label of the disk in *lpVolumeNameBuffer*. The *nVolumeNameSize* parameter indicates the maximum size of the buffer in characters. The DWORD pointed to by the *lpVolumeSerialNumber* parameter gets filled with the serial number of the volume. If you are not interested in this information, NULL can be passed as the *lpVolumeSerialNumber* parameter.

The serial number is most useful when another disk has been inserted in the drive. Starting with MS-DOS 4.0, the FORMAT command puts serial number information on a disk. This way, even if two disks have the same volume label, each has its own unique serial number. If the user removes one disk and inserts the other, the volume labels could be the same but the serial numbers would be different. An application can check to determine whether the user has swapped disks.

The DWORD pointed to by the *lpMaximumComponentLength* parameter gets filled with the maximum number of characters supported for directory names and filenames. For the FAT, NTFS, and CDFS file systems, the value is 255. Many applications hard-code lengths in their source code for pathname and filename buffers. This is a big no-no! For many applications, everything might seem OK at first, as the application manipulates files and paths with short filenames; but when the application manipulates files with long filenames, you'll get stack overwrites, invalid memory accesses, and other assorted problems.

When you are developing an application, create some lo-o-ong filenames and some hu-u-uge pathnames, and bury some of your application's data files deep down in the bowels of the directory hierarchy to see how your application performs. It's much better for you to catch file system problems during development rather than after you ship.

Another easy-to-forget consideration is Unicode. If you are using Unicode in your application, your buffers need to be twice as big. Only the FAT and the NTFS file systems store filenames as Unicode strings, and the system knows whether your application manipulates Unicode filenames. When you request paths and filenames, the system will perform any and all conversions for you, but you must ensure that your buffers will be big enough to hold the results of these conversions.

The DWORD pointed to by the *lpFileSystemFlags* parameter is filled with flags about the file system. Here are the possible values:

Flag Identifier	Meaning
FS_CASE_IS_PRESERVED	The case of a filename is preserved when the name is put on disk.
FS_CASE_SENSITIVE	The file system supports case-sensitive filename lookup.
FS_UNICODE_STORED_ON_DISK	The file system supports Unicode in filenames as they appear on disk.
FS_PERSISTENT_ACLS	The file system preserves and enforces access control lists (NTFS only).
FS_FILE_COMPRESSION	The file system supports file-based compression. NTFS supports the ability to compress individual files; FAT can compress only full volumes at a time. So for an NTFS volume, this flag will be on, and for FAT, it will be off.
FS_VOL_IS_COMPRESSED	The file system supports volume-based compression. NTFS supports the ability to compress individual files; FAT can compress only full volumes at a time. So for an NTFS volume, this flag will be off, and for FAT, it will be on.

The *lpFileSystemNameBuffer* parameter points to a buffer that *GetVolumeInformation* will fill with the name of the file system (FAT, NTFS, or CDFS). The last parameter, *nFileSystemNameSize*, is the maximum size of the *lpFileSystemNameBuffer* buffer in characters.

If you're calling *GetVolumeInformation* to detect whether a disk is in a drive, you will probably want to call

```
SetErrorMode(SEM_FAILCRITICALERRORS);
```

first so that the system does not display a message box if a disk is not in the drive.

Most of the information returned by *GetVolumeInformation* is determined when the user's disk is formatted, and it can't be changed unless the user's disk is reformatted. The one piece of information that you can change without reformatting is the disk's volume label. You can change it by calling

```
BOOL SetVolumeLabel(LPTSTR lpRootPathName, LPTSTR lpVolumeName);
```

The first parameter of *SetVolumeLabel* is the root directory of the file system whose volume label you want to change. If you specify NULL here, the system changes the volume label for the process's current disk. The *lpVolumeName* parameter indicates the new name you want the volume to have. Specifying NULL here causes *SetVolumeLabel* to remove any volume label from the disk.

Another function you can call to get disk volume information is the *GetDiskFreeSpace* function:

```
BOOL GetDiskFreeSpace(LPTSTR lpszRootPathName,
   LPDWORD lpSectorsPerCluster, LPDWORD lpBytesPerSector,
   LPDWORD lpFreeClusters, LPDWORD lpClusters);
```

The *GetDiskFreeSpace* function returns space availability statistics about the volume identified by the *lpszRootPathName* parameter. All the bytes available on floppy disks and hard drives are packaged together into sectors, usually with 512 bytes per sector. Sectors are then grouped together to form clusters. In the FAT file system, the number of sectors per cluster can vary dramatically, as this table indicates:

Disk Type	Sectors per Cluster
360-KB floppy disk	2
1.2-MB floppy disk	4
200-MB hard disk	8
400-MB hard disk	32

When parts of a disk are allocated to a file, the minimum amount of memory that can be allocated to a file is a single cluster. For example, a 10-byte file would occupy 2 sectors, or 1 KB (2 × 512 bytes), on a 360-KB floppy; but the same file would occupy 8 sectors, or 4 KB (8 × 512 bytes), on a 200-MB hard disk.

Let's say that we have two 1-KB files on a floppy disk and try to copy both files to a 200-MB hard drive that has only 4 KB of free space. The first file will be copied successfully, but there will be insufficient disk space on the hard drive for the second file. We've tried to copy 2 KB of data into a 4-KB space and failed. On very large media, this cluster overhead can become a serious problem.

While I was writing the first edition of this book, I upgraded my 250-MB hard drive to a 1-GB hard drive. I also decided to partition the new drive into two 512-MB partitions. Each partition used 32 sectors per cluster. This meant that a 1-byte file required a minimum of 16 KB. After I'd finished installing about 200 MB of file data, the amount of wasted space was about 100 MB. That 100 MB of wasted space was almost half my original hard drive's total capacity. I was impressed by the extent of the clustering overhead. I quickly repartitioned my new hard drive into several partitions, each about 250 MB because clusters for a 250-MB drive contain only 8 sectors each.

Microsoft has a new FAT32 file system that is similar to FAT but that alleviates this clustering problem. Unfortunately, FAT32, although wasting far less disk space, breaks some MS-DOS and 16-bit Windows applications because the on-disk file structures had to be changed. Microsoft expects that most users will prefer the additional disk space and will upgrade any applications that are broken. Applications that use the Win32 API for manipulating disk volumes will not be affected by this new on-disk structure.

As of this writing, Windows NT does not support the FAT32 file system. For this reason, you should not use FAT32 file systems for disk volumes that you intend to access with both Windows 95 and Windows NT.

From the values returned by the *GetDiskFreeSpace* function, you can calculate the total disk space, the amount of free disk space, and the amount of used disk space:

```
DWORD dwSectorsPerCluster, dwBytesPerSector;
DWORD dwFreeClusters, dwClusters;
DWORD dwTotalDiskSpace, dwFreeDiskSpace, dwUsedDiskSpace;

GetDiskFreeSpace("C:\\", &dwSectorsPerCluster,
    &dwBytesPerSector, &dwFreeClusters, &dwClusters);

dwTotalDiskSpace =
    dwSectorsPerCluster * dwBytesPerSector * dwClusters;

dwFreeDiskSpace =
    dwSectorsPerCluster * dwBytesPerSector * dwFreeClusters;

dwUsedDiskSpace =
    dwSectorsPerCluster * dwBytesPerSector *
      (dwClusters - dwFreeClusters);
    .
    .
    .
```

Windows NT 4 introduces the new *GetDiskFreeSpaceEx* function:

```
BOOL GetDiskFreeSpaceEx(LPCTSTR lpDirectoryName,
    PULARGE_INTEGER lpFreeBytesAvailableToCaller,
    PULARGE_INTEGER lpTotalNumberOfBytes,
    PULARGE_INTEGER lpTotalNumberOfFreeBytes);
```

This function will also be available on future versions of Windows 95. It is similar to the *GetDiskFreeSpace* function except that it multiplies the bytes per cluster by the number of clusters for you. The value returned in the unsigned large integer pointed to by the *lpFreeBytesAvailableToCaller* parameter indicates the number of bytes associated with the calling thread that are available to the user. This is useful when working on a system that supports disk quotas for users.

The Disk Information Viewer Sample Application

The DiskInfo (DISKINFO.EXE) application, listed in Figure 14-1 beginning on page 628, demonstrates the use of most of the functions we've just surveyed. The source code and resource files for the application are in the DISKINFO directory on the companion disc. When you execute DiskInfo, the Disk Volume Information Viewer dialog box appears. On the next two pages, this dialog box shows the results when I select various logical drives on my computer.

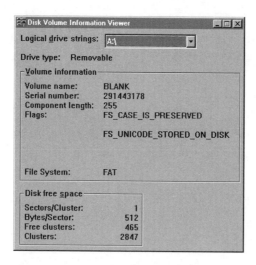

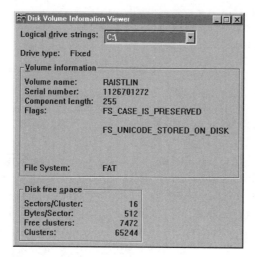

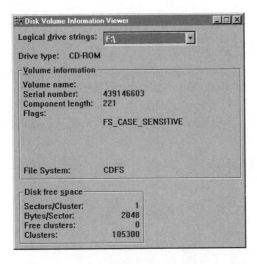

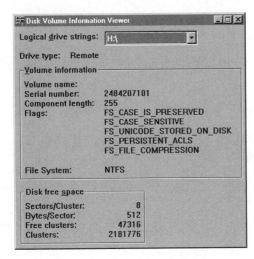

The combo box at the top of the dialog box shows all the logical drives connected to the system. This information is obtained by a call to *GetLogicalDriveStrings*. When you select a logical drive, the remaining fields in the dialog box change to show information about the newly selected drive. The Drive Type field is updated by a call to *GetDriveType*, the fields in the Volume Information group box are updated by a call to *GetVolumeInformation*, and the fields in the Disk Free Space group box are updated by a call to *GetDiskFreeSpace*.

DiskInfo.ico

DISKINFO.C

```
/********************************************************
Module name: DiskInfo.C
Notices: Copyright (c) 1995-1997 Jeffrey Richter
********************************************************/


#include "..\CmnHdr.H"                    /* See Appendix C. */
#include <windows.h>
#include <windowsx.h>

#include <tchar.h>
#include <stdio.h>                // For sprintf
#include <string.h>               // For strchr
#include "Resource.H"



///////////////////////////////////////////////////////////////


void Dlg_FillDriveInfo (HWND hwnd, LPTSTR lpszRootPathName) {
    // Variables for processing the drive type information.
    int nDriveType;
    LPCTSTR p;

    // Variables for processing the volume information
    TCHAR szBuf[200];
    TCHAR lpVolumeNameBuffer[200];
    DWORD dwVolumeSerialNumber, dwMaximumComponentLength;
    DWORD dwFileSystemFlags;
    TCHAR lpFileSystemNameBuffer[50];

    // Variables for processing the disk space information
    DWORD dwSectorsPerCluster, dwBytesPerSector;
```

Figure 14-1.
The DiskInfo application.

(continued)

Figure 14-1. *continued*

```
DWORD dwFreeClusters, dwClusters;
// Get the drive type information.
nDriveType = GetDriveType(lpszRootPathName);
switch (nDriveType) {
  case DRIVE_UNKNOWN:
    p = __TEXT("Cannot be determined.");
    break;

  case DRIVE_NO_ROOT_DIR:
    p = __TEXT("Path does not exist.");
    break;

  case DRIVE_REMOVABLE:
    p = __TEXT("Removable");
    break;

  case DRIVE_FIXED:
    p = __TEXT("Fixed");
    break;

  case DRIVE_REMOTE:
    p = __TEXT("Remote");
    break;

  case DRIVE_CDROM:
    p = __TEXT("CD-ROM");
    break;

  case DRIVE_RAMDISK:
    p = __TEXT("RAM disk");
    break;

  default:
    p = __TEXT("Unknown");
    break;
}

SetWindowText(GetDlgItem(hwnd, IDC_DRIVETYPE), p);

// Get the volume information.
if (GetVolumeInformation(lpszRootPathName,
  lpVolumeNameBuffer,
  chDIMOF(lpVolumeNameBuffer), &dwVolumeSerialNumber,
```

(continued)

Figure 14-1. *continued*

```
        &dwMaximumComponentLength, &dwFileSystemFlags,
        lpFileSystemNameBuffer,
        chDIMOF(lpFileSystemNameBuffer))) {

        _stprintf(szBuf, __TEXT("%s\n%u\n%u\n"),
            lpVolumeNameBuffer, dwVolumeSerialNumber,
            dwMaximumComponentLength);

        if (dwFileSystemFlags & FS_CASE_IS_PRESERVED)
            _tcscat(szBuf, __TEXT("FS_CASE_IS_PRESERVED"));
        _tcscat(szBuf, __TEXT("\n"));

        if (dwFileSystemFlags & FS_CASE_SENSITIVE)
            _tcscat(szBuf, __TEXT("FS_CASE_SENSITIVE"));
        _tcscat(szBuf, __TEXT("\n"));

        if (dwFileSystemFlags & FS_UNICODE_STORED_ON_DISK)
            _tcscat(szBuf, __TEXT("FS_UNICODE_STORED_ON_DISK"));
        _tcscat(szBuf, __TEXT("\n"));

        if (dwFileSystemFlags & FS_PERSISTENT_ACLS)
            _tcscat(szBuf, __TEXT("FS_PERSISTENT_ACLS"));
        _tcscat(szBuf, __TEXT("\n"));

        if (dwFileSystemFlags & FS_FILE_COMPRESSION)
            _tcscat(szBuf, __TEXT("FS_FILE_COMPRESSION"));
        _tcscat(szBuf, __TEXT("\n"));

        if (dwFileSystemFlags & FS_VOL_IS_COMPRESSED)
            _tcscat(szBuf, __TEXT("FS_VOL_IS_COMPRESSED"));
        _tcscat(szBuf, __TEXT("\n"));

        _tcscat(szBuf, lpFileSystemNameBuffer);
    } else {
        _tcscpy(szBuf, __TEXT("NO VOLUME INFO"));
    }
    SetWindowText(GetDlgItem(hwnd, IDC_VOLINFO), szBuf);


    // Get the disk space information.
    if (GetDiskFreeSpace(lpszRootPathName,
        &dwSectorsPerCluster, &dwBytesPerSector,
        &dwFreeClusters, &dwClusters)) {
```

(continued)

Figure 14-1. *continued*

```
      _stprintf(szBuf, __TEXT("%u\n%u\n%u\n%u"),
         dwSectorsPerCluster, dwBytesPerSector,
         dwFreeClusters, dwClusters);
   } else {
      _tcscpy(szBuf, __TEXT("NO\nDISK\nSPACE\nINFO"));
   }
   SetWindowText(GetDlgItem(hwnd, IDC_DISKINFO), szBuf);
}


///////////////////////////////////////////////////////////////


BOOL Dlg_OnInitDialog (HWND hwnd, HWND hwndFocus,
   LPARAM lParam) {

   DWORD   dwNumBytesForDriveStrings;
   HANDLE  hHeap;
   LPTSTR  pszAllDrives, pszDrive;
   TCHAR   szLogDrive[100];
   HWND    hwndCtl = GetDlgItem(hwnd, IDC_LOGDRIVES);
   int     nNumDrives = 0, nDriveNum;

   // Associate an icon with the dialog box.
   chSETDLGICONS(hwnd, IDI_DISKINFO, IDI_DISKINFO);

   // Get the number of bytes needed to hold all
   // the logical drive strings.
   dwNumBytesForDriveStrings =
      GetLogicalDriveStrings(0, NULL) * sizeof(TCHAR);

   // The GetLogicalDriveStrings function is
   // supported on this platform.

   // Allocate memory from the heap for the drive
   // string names.
   hHeap = GetProcessHeap();
   pszAllDrives = (LPTSTR) HeapAlloc(hHeap,
      HEAP_ZERO_MEMORY, dwNumBytesForDriveStrings);

   // Get the drive string names in our buffer.
   GetLogicalDriveStrings(
      dwNumBytesForDriveStrings / sizeof(TCHAR),
      pszAllDrives);
```

(continued)

631

Figure 14-1. *continued*

```
      // Parse the memory block, and fill the combo box.
      pszDrive = pszAllDrives;
      while (pszDrive[0] != 0) {
         ComboBox_AddString(hwndCtl, pszDrive);
         nNumDrives++;
         pszDrive = _tcschr(pszDrive, 0) + 1; // Go to next string.
      }

      HeapFree(hHeap, 0, pszAllDrives);

      // Initialize the volume information for the first fixed
      // drive so that we don't try to read volume
      // information from a drive that doesn't contain a
      // diskette.
      for (nDriveNum = 0; nDriveNum < nNumDrives; nDriveNum++) {
         ComboBox_GetLBText(hwndCtl, nDriveNum, szLogDrive);
         if (GetDriveType(szLogDrive) == DRIVE_FIXED)
            break;
      }

      if (nDriveNum == nNumDrives) {
         // There are no fixed drives--just use the
         // first drive.
         ComboBox_GetLBText(hwndCtl, nDriveNum = 0, szLogDrive);
      }

      // Select the first fixed drive, or select the first
      // drive if no fixed drives exist.
      ComboBox_SetCurSel(hwndCtl, nDriveNum);

      Dlg_FillDriveInfo(hwnd, szLogDrive);

      return(TRUE);
   }


   ///////////////////////////////////////////////////////////////


   void Dlg_OnCommand (HWND hwnd, int id, HWND hwndCtl,
      UINT codeNotify) {

      TCHAR szLogDrive[100];

      switch (id) {
```

(continued)

Figure 14-1. *continued*

```
        case IDC_LOGDRIVES:
            if (codeNotify != CBN_SELCHANGE)
                break;

            ComboBox_GetText(hwndCtl, szLogDrive,
                chDIMOF(szLogDrive));
            Dlg_FillDriveInfo(hwnd, szLogDrive);
            break;

        case IDCANCEL:
            EndDialog(hwnd, id);
            break;
    }
}


///////////////////////////////////////////////////////////


BOOL CALLBACK Dlg_Proc (HWND hwnd, UINT uMsg,
    WPARAM wParam, LPARAM lParam) {

    switch (uMsg) {
        chHANDLE_DLGMSG(hwnd, WM_INITDIALOG, Dlg_OnInitDialog);
        chHANDLE_DLGMSG(hwnd, WM_COMMAND, Dlg_OnCommand);
    }
    return(FALSE);
}


///////////////////////////////////////////////////////////


int WINAPI _tWinMain (HINSTANCE hinstExe,
    HINSTANCE hinstPrev, LPTSTR pszCmdLine, int nCmdShow) {

    chWARNIFUNICODEUNDERWIN95();
    DialogBox(hinstExe, MAKEINTRESOURCE(IDD_DISKINFO),
        NULL, Dlg_Proc);

    return(0);
}


/////////////////////// End Of File ///////////////////////
```

(continued)

Figure 14-1. *continued*

```
DISKINFO.RC
//Microsoft Developer Studio generated resource script.
//
#include "Resource.h"

#define APSTUDIO_READONLY_SYMBOLS
/////////////////////////////////////////////////////////
//
// Generated from the TEXTINCLUDE 2 resource.
//
#include "afxres.h"


/////////////////////////////////////////////////////////
#undef APSTUDIO_READONLY_SYMBOLS


/////////////////////////////////////////////////////////
// English (U.S.) resources

#if !defined(AFX_RESOURCE_DLL) || defined(AFX_TARG_ENU)
#ifdef _WIN32
LANGUAGE LANG_ENGLISH, SUBLANG_ENGLISH_US
#pragma code_page(1252)
#endif //_WIN32


#ifdef APSTUDIO_INVOKED
/////////////////////////////////////////////////////////
//
// TEXTINCLUDE
//

1 TEXTINCLUDE DISCARDABLE
BEGIN
    "Resource.h\0"
END

2 TEXTINCLUDE DISCARDABLE
BEGIN
    "#include ""afxres.h""\r\n"
    "\0"
END

3 TEXTINCLUDE DISCARDABLE
BEGIN
    "\r\n"
```

(continued)

Figure 14-1. *continued*

```
    "\0"
END


#endif    // APSTUDIO_INVOKED


//////////////////////////////////////////////////////
//
// Dialog
//

IDD_DISKINFO DIALOG DISCARDABLE  15, 24, 198, 185
STYLE DS_NOIDLEMSG | WS_MINIMIZEBOX | WS_POPUP |
    WS_VISIBLE | WS_CAPTION | WS_SYSMENU
CAPTION "Disk Volume Information Viewer"
FONT 8, "System"
BEGIN
    LTEXT              "Logical &drive strings:",
                       IDC_STATIC,4,4,70,8
    COMBOBOX           IDC_LOGDRIVES,78,4,80,76,
                       CBS_DROPDOWNLIST | WS_GROUP |
                       WS_TABSTOP
    LTEXT              "Drive type:",IDC_STATIC,4,20,37,8
    LTEXT              "Text",IDC_DRIVETYPE,48,20,96,8
    GROUPBOX           "&Volume information",IDC_STATIC,
                       4,32,192,96,WS_GROUP | WS_TABSTOP
    LTEXT              "Volume name:\nSerial number:\
\nComponent length:\nFlags:\n\n\n\n\n\nFile System:",
                       IDC_STATIC,8,44,64,80
    LTEXT              "Label\n12345678\n10\n\
FS_CASE_IS_PRESERVED\nFS_CASE_SENSITIVE\n\
FS_UNICODE_STORED_ON_DISK\nFS_PERSISTENT_ACLS\
\nFS_FILE_COMPRESSION\nFS_VOL_IS_COMPRESSED\nNTFS",
                       IDC_VOLINFO,77,44,116,80,
                       SS_NOPREFIX
    GROUPBOX           "Disk free &space",IDC_STATIC,
                       4,134,108,48,WS_GROUP | WS_TABSTOP
    LTEXT              "Sectors/Cluster:\nBytes/Sector:\
\nFree clusters:\nClusters:",
                       IDC_STATIC,8,146,52,32
    RTEXT              "8\n512\n300\n400",IDC_DISKINFO,
                       64,146,44,32,SS_NOPREFIX
END
```

(continued)

Figure 14-1. *continued*

```
/////////////////////////////////////////////////////////
//
// Icon
//

// Icon with lowest ID value placed first to ensure
// application icon remains consistent on all systems.
IDI_DISKINFO        ICON    DISCARDABLE    "DiskInfo.Ico"


/////////////////////////////////////////////////////////
//
// DESIGNINFO
//

#ifdef APSTUDIO_INVOKED
GUIDELINES DESIGNINFO DISCARDABLE
BEGIN
    IDD_DISKINFO, DIALOG
    BEGIN
        BOTTOMMARGIN, 176
    END
END
#endif    // APSTUDIO_INVOKED

#endif    // English (U.S.) resources
/////////////////////////////////////////////////////////



#ifndef APSTUDIO_INVOKED
/////////////////////////////////////////////////////////
//
// Generated from the TEXTINCLUDE 3 resource.
//


/////////////////////////////////////////////////////////
#endif    // not APSTUDIO_INVOKED
```

Directory Operations

Every process has a directory associated with it called the current directory. By default, file operations are performed inside the process's current directory. When a process is first created, it inherits the current directory used by its parent process.

Getting the Current Directory

A process determines its current directory by calling

```
DWORD GetCurrentDirectory(DWORD cchCurDir, LPTSTR lpszCurDir);
```

The *GetCurrentDirectory* function fills the buffer pointed to by *lpszCurDir* with the process's current path. The *cchCurDir* parameter indicates the maximum size of the buffer in characters. If the function fails, 0 is returned; otherwise, the function returns the number of characters copied to the buffer, not including the terminating zero. If the buffer isn't large enough to hold the current path, the return value indicates the number of characters required to hold the path. To ensure that *GetCurrentDirectory* succeeds, you need to write code similar to this:

```
TCHAR szCurDir[MAX_PATH];

DWORD dwResult = GetCurrentDirectory(
   sizeof(szCurDir) / sizeof(TCHAR), szCurDir);

if (dwResult == 0) {
   // Total function failure
} else {
   if (dwResult < (sizeof(szCurDir) / sizeof(TCHAR))) {
      // Buffer was big enough for the full path
   } else {
      // Buffer was too small
   }
}
```

Notice the use of MAX_PATH in this routine. The MAX_PATH value is defined in WINDEF.H as 260. For MS-DOS development, some C compilers define a macro called _MAX_PATH as only 80. The big difference in this value is attributable to the long filenames now supported by Windows 95 and Windows NT. It's difficult to stress enough the significance of long filename support. I've seen too many programs that create buffers for filenames along these lines:

```
char szFileName[13];    // "Filename" + '.' + "ext" + zero byte
```

These buffers will be far too small to hold long filenames. It's likely that a function in the application will overwrite a buffer because the application will make the assumption that filenames will never be longer than 13 characters.

One way to handle the longer filenames is to make your buffers much larger. Using MAX_PATH as we've just seen is an example of this approach. Unfortunately, the Win32 header files don't define a macro called MAX_FILE, but you could define MAX_FILE as 260 as well.

This approach would work for today's long filenames, but a new file system in the future might allow filenames as long as 512 characters. So the best way to allocate buffers for file system components is dynamically, by first calling *GetVolumeInformation* and checking the value returned in the buffer pointed to by the *lpMaximumComponentLength* parameter.

Changing the Current Directory

A process can change its current directory by calling

```
BOOL SetCurrentDirectory(LPTSTR lpszCurDir);
```

Changing the current directory alters the current directory of only the process making the call; the change of directory doesn't affect any other running processes. However, if the process making the call spawns a new process after changing its current directory, the new process will inherit the current directory of the parent, which will now be the directory that was specified in the last call to *SetCurrentDirectory*.

Getting the System Directory

In addition to getting its own current directory, an application can determine the system directory by calling

```
UINT GetSystemDirectory(LPTSTR lpszSysPath, UINT cchSysPath);
```

The *GetSystemDirectory* function fills the buffer pointed to by *lpszSysPath* with the system directory name. Usually, this directory will be something like this:

```
C:\WINDOWS\SYSTEM    (Windows 95)
C:\WINNT\SYSTEM32    (Windows NT)
```

The return values for *GetSystemDirectory* should be interpreted just as they were for the *GetCurrentDirectory* function. Applications typically don't use the system directory for anything. In fact, on shared versions of Windows, the system directory is protected so that files can't be created in the directory; nor can files already in the system directory be modified. A benefit of this protection is that viruses won't be able to attach themselves to any of the files contained in the system directory.

Getting the Windows Directory

If a process wants to create or write to a file that is to be shared by multiple processes, the process can use the Windows directory. The path of the Windows directory can be obtained by calling

```
UINT GetWindowsDirectory(LPTSTR lpszWinPath, UINT cchWinPath);
```

The *GetWindowsDirectory* function fills the buffer pointed to by *lpszWinPath* with the Windows directory. Usually, this directory will be something like this:

```
C:\WINDOWS    (Windows 95)
C:\WINNT      (Windows NT)
```

When running a shared version of Windows, the system creates a Windows directory private to each user. This is the only directory guaranteed to be private for an individual user. If a user wants to keep certain files hidden from all other users, the files must be created either in the Windows directory or in a subdirectory of the Windows directory.

Creating and Removing Directories

Finally, there are three additional functions for manipulating directories:

```
BOOL CreateDirectory(LPTSTR lpszPath, LPSECURITY_ATTRIBUTES lpsa);

BOOL CreateDirectoryEx(LPCTSTR lpTemplateDirectory,
    LPCTSTR lpNewDirectory,
    LPSECURITY_ATTRIBUTES lpSecurityAttributes);

BOOL RemoveDirectory(LPTSTR lpszDir);
```

As their names imply, these functions allow a process to create and remove directories. When creating a directory, a process can specify a SECURITY_ATTRIBUTES structure to assign special privileges to the directory. For example, an application could create the directory so that another user couldn't go into or remove the directory. Security is available when creating the directory on an NTFS partition only. Because the *CreateDirectory* and *CreateDirectoryEx* functions do not return handles, the *bInheritHandle* member in the SECURITY_ATTRIBUTES structure is ignored.

639

The *CreateDirectoryEx* function allows you to take the attributes associated with an existing directory and have the new directory use them. An example of an attribute is whether all files in the directory should be compressed.

All three of these functions return TRUE when they're successful and FALSE when they fail. *RemoveDirectory* will fail if the directory contains files or other subdirectories or if the process doesn't have delete access for removing the directory.

Copying, Deleting, Moving, and Renaming Files

Both 16-bit Windows and MS-DOS have always lacked a function for copying files from one place to another. Applications have typically implemented this important functionality by opening a source file for reading and creating a destination file for writing. Then, using a buffer, the application would read part of the source file into memory and write the buffer back out to the destination file. After the source file had been read and written, the application would close both files. And the time stamp of the destination file would reflect the time of the copy—not the time of the source file's last update. This problem would usually have to be fixed by the addition of a few more function calls.

Copying a File

With Win32, we finally have an operating system call available to us for copying files:

```
BOOL CopyFile(LPTSTR lpszExistingFile, LPTSTR lpszNewFile,
    BOOL fFailIfExists);
```

CopyFile is a simple function that copies the file identified by the *lpszExistingFile* parameter to a new file whose pathname is specified by the *lpszNewFile* parameter. The last parameter, *fFailIfExists*, specifies whether you want the function to fail if a file already exists that matches the name pointed to by the *lpszNewFile* parameter. If a file with the same name does exist and *fFailIfExists* is TRUE, the function fails; otherwise, the function destroys the existing file and creates the new file. *CopyFile* returns TRUE if it is successful. Only closed files or files that are open with read-access only can be copied. The function fails if any process has the existing file open with write-access.

Windows NT 4 has a new *CopyFileEx* function:

```
BOOL CopyFileEx(LPCWSTR lpExistingFileName, LPCWSTR lpNewFileName,
    LPPROGRESS_ROUTINE lpProgressRoutine, LPVOID lpData,
    LPBOOL pbCancel, DWORD dwCopyFlags);
```

This function exists so that you can give the user feedback as the copy operation progresses. The first two parameters are identical to *Copy-File*'s first two parameters. The third parameter, *lpProgressRoutine*, can be either NULL, if you don't want to give the user feedback, or the address of a callback function, which is called periodically as the file is copied. (I'll talk about this function shortly.) The *lpData* parameter is just a 32-bit value that is passed to the callback function. The *pbCancel* is a pointer to a BOOL that is filled in by *CopyFileEx*. When the callback function is called, it can tell *CopyFileEx* to stop copying the file. If the copy is stopped prematurely, *bCancel* will be TRUE when *CopyFileEx* terminates. If the file is copied in its entirety, *bCancel* will be FALSE. The *dwCopyFlags* can be any combination of the following flags:

Flag	Description
COPY_FILE_FAIL_IF_EXISTS	Causes *CopyFileEx* to not copy the file if the file specified by the *lpNewFileName* already exists.
COPY_FILE_RESTARTABLE	Causes *CopyFileEx* to keep progress information about the copy in the target file. If the copy is canceled, a subsequent call to *CopyFileEx* can just copy the remainder of the file without having to start over from the beginning.

If you specify the address of a callback function, the callback function must look like this:

```
DWORD WINAPI CopyProgressRoutine(
    LARGE_INTEGER TotalFileSize, LARGE_INTEGER TotalBytesTransferred,
    LARGE_INTEGER StreamSize,    LARGE_INTEGER StreamBytesTransferred,
    DWORD dwStreamNumber, DWORD dwCallbackReason,
    HANDLE hSourceFile, HANDLE hDestinationFile, LPVOID lpData) {
    :
    :
}
```

The first two parameters indicate the total size of the file and the number of bytes copied so far. A progress dialog box will use these two parameters to show the user what percentage of the copy has completed. A file can consist of multiple streams. To date, the fact that a file can consist of multiple streams has not been documented very well in the Win32 API, but it will be becoming more prominent with future versions of NTFS and Windows NT. Most files that exist today consist of a single stream. *CopyProgressRoutine*'s next three parameters indicate which stream is currently being copied (*dwStreamNumber*), the size of that stream (*StreamSize*), and how many bytes of that stream have been copied (*StreamBytesTransferred*). The first stream in a file is numbered 1.

The *dwCallbackReason* parameter indicates why the system is calling the callback function. The following table shows the possible reasons:

Reason	Description
CALLBACK_STREAM_SWITCH	Indicates that a stream is just starting to be copied
CALLBACK_CHUNK_FINISHED	Indicates that more data in the current stream has been copied

The last three parameters contain the handle of the source file, the handle of the destination file, and the user-defined 32-bit value that was passed to the *CopyFileEx* function.

The *CopyProgressRoutine* must return one of the following values:

Return Value	Description
PROGRESS_CONTINUE	The copy operation should continue.
PROGRESS_CANCEL	The copy operation should stop, and the destination file should be deleted.
PROGRESS_STOP	The copy operation should stop, but the destination file should not be deleted. This allows the copy to continue at a later time. Return this value only if *CopyFileEx* was called using the COPY_FILE_RESTARTABLE flag.
PROGRESS_QUIET	The copy operation should continue, but the *CopyProgressRoutine* should no longer be called.

Deleting a File

Deleting a file by means of the *DeleteFile* function is even easier than copying a file:

```
BOOL DeleteFile(LPTSTR lpszFileName);
```

This function deletes the file identified by the *lpszFileName* parameter and returns TRUE if successful. The function fails if the specified file doesn't exist or if the file is open. If any process has the file open, the file can't be deleted.

Under Windows 95, the *DeleteFile* function will actually delete an open file, whereas Windows NT guards against this possibility. Deleting an open file, of course, means that the file may lose data. It is up to you to ensure that files are closed prior to deleting them with *DeleteFile*.

Moving a File

Two functions allow you to move a file from one directory to another directory:

```
BOOL MoveFile(LPTSTR lpszExisting, LPTSTR lpszNew);

BOOL MoveFileEx(LPTSTR lpszExisting, LPTSTR lpszNew,
    DWORD fdwFlags);
```

Both functions move the existing file, which is identified by the *lpszExisting* parameter, to the new location identified by the *lpszNew* parameter. The *lpszNew* parameter must include the name of the file. For example, the following instruction won't move the CLOCK.EXE file from the WINNT directory on drive C to the root directory of drive C:

```
MoveFile("C:\\WINNT\\CLOCK.EXE", "C:\\");
```

This instruction will:

```
MoveFile("C:\\WINNT\\CLOCK.EXE", "C:\\CLOCK.EXE");
```

Moving a file is not always the same as copying the file to another location and then deleting the original file. If you are moving a file from one directory to another directory on the same drive, *MoveFile* and *MoveFileEx* don't move any of the data in the file. Both functions simply remove the file's entry in the first directory and add a new entry to the second directory the file is supposedly copied to. Simply adjusting the directory entries "copies" a file significantly faster because no data is moved around. Less disk space is needed during the move too. When a file is moved from one drive to another, the system must create a duplicate file before it deletes the original. At the moment after the copy and before the deletion of the original, there are two whole copies of the file in existence. If the file is huge, this can take up a serious amount of disk space.

If the system had to copy and delete a file it was moving from one directory to another on the same drive, the function might fail because of insufficient disk space. If the file were 1 MB long and only 512 KB of disk space were available, the system wouldn't be able to copy the file before deleting the original. But because only directory entries are altered, no additional disk space is required and the move is much more likely to succeed.

If the move does succeed, both *MoveFile* and *MoveFileEx* return TRUE. The move can fail if insufficient disk space is available for interdrive moves or if a filename matching the name specified in *lpszNew* already exists.

You wouldn't be able to guess it from their names, but both *MoveFile* and *MoveFileEx* can also be used to change the name of a subdirectory. For example, to change the name of the subdirectory UTILITY to TOOLS, use this statement:

```
MoveFile("C:\\UTILITY", "C:\\TOOLS");
```

It would certainly be useful if *MoveFile* and *MoveFileEx* could move an entire subdirectory tree elsewhere in the drive's directory hierarchy, but these functions are not capable of this sweeping kind of operation. To move a subdirectory tree to another location on the same drive, you would have to use the *FindFirstFile*, *FindFirstFileEx*, *FindNextFile*, and *FindClose* functions discussed later in this chapter to walk down the directory hierarchy three different times. The first time you'd need to call *CreateDirectory* to create a similar directory structure in the new location. The second time you'd need to call *MoveFile* to move each individual file in the directory structure. The last time you'd need to call *RemoveDirectory* to remove the old directory hierarchy.

The Differences Between *MoveFile* and *MoveFileEx*

By offering one more parameter, *fdwFlags*, *MoveFileEx* gives you more control over moving a file or renaming a subdirectory than the *MoveFile* function does.

Under Windows 95, the *MoveFileEx* function has no useful implementation and simply returns FALSE; calling *GetLastError* returns ERROR-_CALL_NOT_IMPLEMENTED.

MoveFileEx comes into its own when moving a file fails because a filename matching the name specified in *lpszNew* already exists. To destroy the existing file and give the moved file the same name anyway, you can specify the MOVEFILE_REPLACE_EXISTING flag when you call *MoveFileEx*. This flag has no effect when you're renaming a subdirectory.

By default, *MoveFileEx* will not move a file from one drive to another drive. If you want to allow this behavior, you must specify the MOVE-FILE_COPY_ALLOWED flag. On Windows NT, the *MoveFile* function calls the *MoveFileEx* function internally, specifying the MOVEFILE-_COPY_ALLOWED flag, so you don't have to worry about this if you use the *MoveFile* function instead of the *MoveFileEx* function. Like the MOVE-FILE_REPLACE_EXISTING flag, this flag has no effect when you're renaming a subdirectory.

The MOVEFILE_DELAY_UNTIL_REBOOT flag provokes some interesting behavior. If this flag is specified, the system doesn't move the file or rename the directory at the time the call is placed. Instead, it keeps a list in the registry of all the files that have been moved with this flag specified. Then the next time the operating system is booted, the system examines the registry and moves or renames all the files in the list. The files are moved or renamed just after the drives are checked and before any paging files are created.

The MOVEFILE_DELAY_UNTIL_REBOOT flag is customarily used by installation programs. Let's say that you recently received a new device driver for your video card. When you try to install the new driver, the system can't delete or overwrite the old video driver because the file is still in use by the system. In this case, the Setup program will copy the new driver into another directory, leaving the original driver file. Setup will then issue a call to *MoveFileEx*, specifying the current path of the new file in the *lpszExisting* parameter and the location where the file should be in the *lpszNew* parameter. Setup will also pass the MOVEFILE_DE-LAY_UNTIL_REBOOT flag to *MoveFileEx*. The system will add the new path to its list in the registry and simply return to Setup. When the system is rebooted, it will replace the old video driver with the new driver before the system is fully started. Once the system is up, the new device driver will be used instead of the old one.

The last flag, MOVEFILE_WRITE_THROUGH, is ignored on all platforms except Windows NT 4. This flag ensures that *MoveFileEx* does not return until the file has been moved. This flag is most useful when *MoveFileEx* is copying a file to another disk and then deleting the original file. This flag is ignored if you also specify the MOVEFILE_DELAY_UNTIL_REBOOT flag.

One other way in which *MoveFileEx* differs from *MoveFile* is that it provides a novel way of deleting a file. You can delete a file with *MoveFileEx* by passing NULL as the *lpszNew* parameter. In a sense, you are telling the system you want to move the existing file (*lpszExisting*) to nowhere, which has the effect of deleting the file.

Renaming a File

There is no *RenameFile* function. To rename a file, you must call *MoveFile* or *MoveFileEx*. All you do is move the file from its directory to the same directory. To rename CLOCK.EXE to WATCH.EXE, for example, you'd use this statement:

```
MoveFile("C:\\WINNT\\CLOCK.EXE", "C:\\WINNT\\WATCH.EXE");
```

Because we're not moving the file from one drive to another drive or from one directory to another directory, the system simply removes WINNT's directory entry for CLOCK.EXE and adds a new directory entry for WATCH.EXE—the file is effectively renamed.

The Setup program could have copied the new video device driver file to the system directory, giving it a different name. Then the Setup program would issue a call to *MoveFileEx*, still specifying the MOVEFILE_DELAY_UNTIL_REBOOT flag. This time, since the file would already be in the correct directory, rebooting the system would have the effect of renaming the file instead of copying it.

I'd like to see Microsoft enhance these file functions by adding wildcard support. Wouldn't it be nice to be able to issue a command like

```
DeleteFile("*.BAK");
```

and have the system delete all of the BAK files in the current directory? Currently, if you want to do a mass deletion, you must first create a list of all the BAK files in the current directory and then call *DeleteFile* for each file. To create a list of the BAK files, you would use *FindFirstFile*, *FindFirstFileEx*, *FindNextFile*, and *FindClose*—functions discussed in detail later in this chapter.

Searching for Files

Almost all applications use files. Because an application can create many files and because applications are often designed to read files created by other applications (for example, Microsoft Excel can read Lotus 1-2-3 files), file searching has become a common task—so common, in fact, that Microsoft has created a set of common dialog boxes that help users search their drives for particular files. For some applications, though, the File Open and File Save As dialog boxes aren't enough. Some applications might need to search for files or allow access to files using methods not accommodated by the standard file dialog boxes.

One common operation is to convert a simple filename or a file with a relative path to its full pathname. In 16-bit Windows, a call to *Open-File* using the OF_PARSE flag accomplishes the conversion. In Win32, the call is to

```
DWORD GetFullPathName(LPCTSTR lpszFile, DWORD cchPath,
    LPTSTR lpszPath, LPTSTR *ppszFilePart);
```

The *GetFullPathName* function accepts a filename (and optional path information) in the *lpszFile* parameter. The function then uses the current drive and current directory information associated with the process, calculates the full pathname for the file, and fills the buffer pointed to by *lpszPath*. The *cchPath* parameter indicates the maximum size of the buffer for the drive and path in characters. In the *ppszFilePart* parameter, you must pass the address of an LPTSTR variable. *GetFullPathName* will fill the variable with the address within *lpszPath* at which the filename resides. Applications can use this information when they construct their caption text.

For example, if I am using Wordpad and open a file called HIMOM-.TXT, Wordpad's caption becomes

```
HIMOM.TXT - Wordpad
```

This last parameter, *ppszFilePart*, is simply a convenience. You could get the address of the filename by calling

```
szFilePart = strrchr(szPath, '\\') + 1;
```

GetFullPathName doesn't really search for a file on the system. It just converts a filename to its full pathname. In fact, *GetFullPathName* doesn't examine anything on the disk.

If you want to scan the user's disks for a file, you can use

```
DWORD SearchPath(LPCTSTR lpszPath, LPCTSTR lpszFile,
    LPCSTR lpszExtension, DWORD cchReturnBuffer,
    LPTSTR lpszReturnBuffer, LPTSTR *plpszFilePart);
```

The *SearchPath* function looks for a file in a list of directories you specify. You pass the list of paths to be scanned in the *lpszPath* parameter. If this parameter is NULL, the file is searched for in the paths in the following order:

1. The directory from which the application was loaded

2. The current directory

3. The Windows system directory

4. The Windows directory

5. The directories listed in the PATH environment variable

You specify the file you want to search for in the *lpszFile* parameter. If the *lpszFile* parameter includes an extension, you should pass in NULL for the *lpszExtension* parameter; otherwise, you can pass an extension in the *lpszExtension* parameter that must begin with a period. The extension is appended to the filename only if the filename doesn't have an extension already. The last three parameters have the same meanings as the last three parameters of the *GetFullPathName* function.

Another method of looking for files allows you to find a file by traversing the user's entire hard disk, looking at every directory and file in existence if you want. You tell the system what directory to start in and the filename to search for by calling *FindFirstFile*:

```
HANDLE FindFirstFile(LPTSTR lpszSearchFile,
    LPWIN32_FIND_DATA lpffd);
```

The *FindFirstFile* function tells the system you want to search for a file. The first parameter, *lpszSearchFile*, points to a zero-terminated string containing a filename. The filename can include wildcard characters (* and ?), and you can preface the filename with a starting path. The *lpffd* parameter is the address to a WIN32_FIND_DATA structure:

```
typedef struct _WIN32_FIND_DATA {
    DWORD dwFileAttributes;
    FILETIME ftCreationTime;
    FILETIME ftLastAccessTime;
    FILETIME ftLastWriteTime;
```

```
    DWORD nFileSizeHigh;
    DWORD nFileSizeLow;
    DWORD dwReserved0;
    DWORD dwReserved1;
    CHAR cFileName[ MAX_PATH ];
    CHAR cAlternateFileName[ 14 ];
} WIN32_FIND_DATA, *PWI32_FIND_DATA, *LPWIN32_FIND_DATA;
```

If *FindFirstFile* succeeds in locating a file matching the filespec in the specified directory, it fills in the members of the WIN32_FIND_DATA structure and returns a handle. If *FindFirstFile* fails to find a file that matches the filespec, it returns INVALID_HANDLE_VALUE, and the structure isn't changed.

Important

The *FindFirstFile* function returns INVALID_HANDLE_VALUE rather than NULL when it fails.

The WIN32_FIND_DATA structure contains information about the matching file—its attributes, its time stamps, and its size. At the end of the structure are two names for the file. The *cFileName* member is the real name of the file. This is the member you should use most often. The *cAlternateFileName* is a synthesized name for the file.

Let's say you are using a program designed for 16-bit Windows. When you select the application's File Open dialog box, you see a list of the files in the current directory. If the current directory is on an NTFS file system and the names of the files in that directory average 50 characters, what gets displayed?

Under OS/2, a program that wasn't designed to recognize HPFS filenames couldn't see HPFS files at all. For Win32, Microsoft decided (correctly) that such files should be made accessible to the user. Well, since the 16-bit Windows application isn't prepared to work with long filenames, the system must convert the long filenames to fit an 8.3 system. This converted, or alternate, filename is what you'll find in the *cAlternateFileName* member of the WIN32_FIND_DATA structure.

For short filenames, the contents of the *cFileName* and *cAlternateFileName* members will be identical; for long filenames, the *cFileName* member will contain the real name, and the *cAlternateFileName* member will contain the synthesized name. For example, the filename "Hello Mom and Dad" can have the truncated, or alternate, name "HELLOM~1."

There is a *GetShortPathName* function:

```
DWORD GetShortPathName (LPCTSTR lpszLongPath, LPTSTR lpszShortPath,
    DWORD cchBuffer);
```

You pass the address to a buffer containing a file's long name in the *lpszLongPath* parameter, and the function fills the buffer pointed to by the *lpszShortPath* parameter with the file's corresponding short name. You must pass the size, in characters, of the *lpszShortPath* buffer in the *cchBuffer* parameter. The function returns the number of characters copied to the *lpszShortPath* buffer.

If *FindFirstFile* has successfully found a matching file, you can call *FindNextFile* to search for the next file matching the file specification originally passed to *FindFirstFile*:

```
BOOL FindNextFile(HANDLE hFindFile, LPWIN32_FIND_DATA lpffd);
```

The *hFindFile* parameter is the handle that was returned by the earlier call to *FindFirstFile*, and the *lpffd* parameter is, again, the address to a WIN32_FIND_DATA structure—not necessarily the same structure you used in the earlier call to *FindFirstFile*, although it can be if you'd like.

If *FindNextFile* is successful, it returns TRUE and fills the WIN32-_FIND_DATA structure. If the function can't find a match, it returns FALSE.

The Windows 95 implementation of *FindFirstFile* and *FindNextFile* has a bug. Windows 95 interprets the ? wildcard character to mean "any character" rather than "zero or one character." So if you pass a search string of FIL??.??? to *FindFirstFile*, FILEA.TXT will be found but FILE.TXT will not be found. On Windows NT, both these files would be found.

When you have finished finding files, you must close the handle returned by *FindFirstFile* by calling *FindClose*:

```
BOOL FindClose(HANDLE hFindFile);
```

This is one of the very few times in Win32 that you don't call *CloseHandle* to close a handle. You must call *FindClose* instead so that some additional bookkeeping information maintained by the system will also be freed.

650

The *FindFirstFile* and *FindNextFile* functions just cycle through all the files (and subdirectories) within a single directory you've specified. If you want to walk up and down the entire directory hierarchy, you will need to write a recursive function.

Windows NT 4 includes a new *FindFirstFileEx* function:

```
HANDLE FindFirstFileEx(LPCTSTR lpFileName,
    FINDEX_INFO_LEVELS fInfoLevelId, LPVOID lpFindFileData,
    FINDEX_SEARCH_OPS fSearchOp, LPVOID lpSearchFilter,
    DWORD dwAdditionalFlags);
```

If you can demand your users to run Windows NT 4, this function can save you a lot of effort and increase your application execution time. The first parameter, *lpFileName*, contains the starting directory and specification using wildcards of the file/directory names you wish to find. The *fInfoLevelId* parameter indicates the type of information you want returned for each matching entry. For Windows NT 4, you must pass *FindExInfoStandard*. The *lpFindFileData* parameter is a pointer to a structure that receives the information for a matching entry. Each *fInfoLevelId* will have a corresponding data structure. For an *fInfoLevelId* of *FindExInfoStandard*, *lpFindFileData* must point to a WIN32_FIND_DATA structure.

The *fSearchOp* and *lpSearchFilter* parameters are what makes *FindFirstFileEx* more powerful than *FindFirstFile*. These parameters apply additional filters to the search. For *fSearchOp*, you can pass only one of the following flags:

Flag	Description
FindExSearchNameMatch	This flag performs a normal search against the specification in the *lpFileName* parameter.
FindExSearchLimitToDirectories	A match is made only if the "file" is a directory. (Some file systems do not support this flag and return matches against files and directories.)
FindExSearchLimitToDevices	Only device names are returned.

Each *fSearchOp* can have an associated data structure that contains additional search criteria used for filtering. Currently none of the documented search operations have additional criteria, so you must always pass NULL for the *lpSearchFilter* parameter. However, you can easily imagine a search operation that causes *FindFirstFileEx* to return files modified within a certain date range or files containing a text string. If either of these two search operations existed, the *lpSeachFilter* would point to a structure containing the date range or the ANSI/Unicode text string.

FindFirstFileEx's last parameter, *dwAdditionalFlags*, allows you to specify even more flags when calling the function. Currently, only one flag is defined: FIND_FIRST_EX_CASE_SENSITIVE. By default, all Win32 functions perform case-insensitive comparisons for file and directory names. However, this flag allows you to override this behavior and allow case-sensitive matches. It was necessary to add this flag for Windows NT because of the POSIX subsystem. POSIX applications have the ability to create case-sensitive names like ReadMe.txt, README.TXT, and readme.txt. If a user ran a Win32 application, the Win32 application would be able to open only one of these files—the other two files would not be accessible to a Win32 application. The FIND_FIRST_EX_CASE-_SENSITIVE flag allows a Win32 application to access these other files.

Like *FindFirstFile*, *FindFirstFileEx* returns a handle that can be used in subsequent calls to *FindNextFile* and *FindClose*.

Important

This is one of the very few times in Win32 that you don't call *CloseHandle* to close a handle. You must call *FindClose* instead so that some additional bookkeeping information maintained by the system will also be freed.

The Directory Walker Sample Application

The DirWalk (DIRWALK.EXE) application, listed in Figure 14-2 beginning on page 656, demonstrates the use of the *FindFirstFile*, *FindNextFile*, *FindClose*, *GetCurrentDirectory*, and *SetCurrentDirectory* functions to walk the entire directory tree of a disk volume. The source code and resource files for the application are in the DIRWALK directory on the companion disc. When the user executes DIRWALK.EXE, it starts at the root directory of the current drive, walks the whole tree, and displays a dialog box containing a list box that shows the entire drive's directory tree. This is how the Directory Walker dialog box appears when DirWalk is run on my machine:

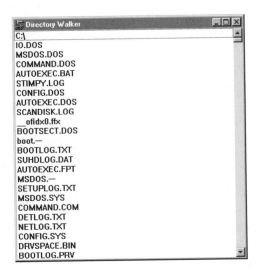

When the dialog box receives its WM_INITDIALOG message, it performs some simple initialization and calls the *DirWalk* function located in DIRWALK.C:

```
void DirWalk (HWND hwndTreeLB, LPCTSTR pszRootPath);
```

The *hwndTreeLB* parameter is the handle of the list box window that the function should fill, and the *pszRootPath* is the starting directory. The call to *DirWalk* passes "\\" in the *pszRootPath* parameter so that the directory walk starts at the root of the current drive. It would certainly be possible to specify a different directory here so that the tree would be walked from the specified directory downward.

When the *DirWalk* function is called, it performs some initialization before calling the *DirWalkRecurse* function. This recursive function will be called by itself over and over as different levels of the drive's directory tree are walked. Before the directory tree can be walked, *DirWalk* performs some initialization by saving the current directory in a temporary variable and then setting the current directory to the path specified in the *pszRootPath* parameter.

Then the thread is ready to start walking by calling *DirWalkRecurse*. This function first adds the current directory to the list box. Then it calls *FindFirstFile* to get the name of the first file in the current directory. If a file is found, its name is displayed and *FindNextFile* is called in order to get the next file in the directory.

After all of the files have been displayed, *DirWalkRecurse* tests the *fRecurse* member of the DIRWALKDATA structure to see if it should recurse into subdirectories. In the DirWalk sample application, this member will always be TRUE. I added the *fRecurse* member because these functions are used in the FILECHNG.EXE application, presented later in this chapter.

When *DirWalkRecurse* needs to go into a subdirectory, it calls *FindFirstChildDir*. This little function, which appears in DIRWALK.C, is a simple wrapper around the *FindFirstFile* function. *FindFirstChildDir* filters out all the filenames in a directory and returns only subdirectory names. The helper function *FindNextChildDir* is just a wrapper around the *FindNextFile* function that also filters out filenames.

As each subdirectory is found, *DirWalkRecurse* moves into the new subdirectory and calls itself so that the new subtree can be walked. After the subtree is walked, *DirWalkRecurse* calls

```
SetCurrentDirectory(__TEXT(".."));
```

so that the current directory is restored to what it was before making the recursive call to *DirWalkRecurse*.

Before any tree walking can start, the *DirWalk* function creates a local DIRWALKDATA structure, called *DW*, on the stack. This structure contains information used by *DirWalkRecurse*.

When I first wrote this program, I had all the members inside the DIRWALKDATA structure as local variables declared inside *DirWalkRecurse*. Then each time *DirWalkRecurse* called itself, another set of these variables was created on the stack. As I soon discovered, this can eat up quite a bit of stack space if a directory tree goes down pretty deep, so I looked for a more efficient method of storing these variables.

The next method I tried was to create the DIRWALKDATA members as static variables. That way, I thought, there would be only one set of them and they wouldn't be allocated on the stack at all. This sounded pretty good to me except that it meant that the *DirWalk* and *DirWalkRecurse* functions were no longer multithread safe. If two threads wanted to walk the tree simultaneously, they would be sharing the same static local variables—with undesirable effects. This realization led me to modify the program again.

I made all the variables static thread-local storage variables by putting *__declspec(thread)* in front of each one. This, I thought, would force a new set of the static variables for every thread created in the process. The

only thing I didn't like about this approach was that a set of these variables would be created for every thread, even for those threads that never called *DirWalk* or *DirWalkRecurse*.

This problem could be fixed by using dynamic thread-local storage. This way, I reasoned, I'd be allocating only a TLS index, which isn't a memory allocation anyway. Then when *DirWalk* was called, it would call *HeapAlloc* to allocate a DIRWALKDATA structure and store the address of this structure using *TlsSetValue*. This dynamic approach solved the problem of allocating additional memory for threads that never called *DirWalk*, and as a bonus, the memory containing the data structure would be around only while the *DirWalk* function was being called. Just before *DirWalk* returned, it would free the buffer.

After I got to this point, the best solution finally hit me: create a data structure on the stack for the thread, and provide just the pointer to the structure with each recursive call. This solution is what you see in the sample program's code. This method creates the variables on the stack, memory is allocated for them only when it is needed, and only a 4-byte pointer is passed on the stack with each recursive call. This seems to me to be the best compromise among all the possibilities.

In spite of all this effort, it turns out that *DirWalk* and *DirWalkRecurse* are still not multithread safe. Can you guess why? Because of the calls to *SetCurrentDirectory*. You should think of the current directory as being stored in a global variable for a process. If you change the current directory in one thread, you are changing it for all threads in the process. To make *DirWalk* and *DirWalkRecurse* multithread safe, you would have to get rid of the calls to *SetCurrentDirectory*. You could get rid of the calls to *SetCurrentDirectory* by managing the walked path in a string variable and by calling *FindFirstDir* using a full path instead of using paths relative to the current directory. Because I also wanted to demonstrate the use of the *GetCurrentDirectory* and *SetCurrentDirectory* functions, I leave this last modification of the program as an exercise for you.

DirWalk.ico

DIRWALK.C

```
/*****************************************************************
Module name: DirWalk.C
Written by: Jim Harkins and Jeffrey Richter
Notices: Copyright (c) 1995-1997 Jeffrey Richter
*****************************************************************/


#include "..\CmnHdr.H"                      /* See Appendix C. */
#include <windows.h>
#include <windowsx.h>

#include <tchar.h>
#include <stdlib.h>
#include <stdio.h>                  // For sprintf
#include <string.h>
#include "Resource.H"


///////////////////////////////////////////////////////////////


static BOOL IsChildDir (WIN32_FIND_DATA *lpFindData) {

   return(
      ((lpFindData->dwFileAttributes &
         FILE_ATTRIBUTE_DIRECTORY) != 0) &&
      (lstrcmp(lpFindData->cFileName, __TEXT("."))  != 0) &&
      (lstrcmp(lpFindData->cFileName, __TEXT("..")) != 0));
}


///////////////////////////////////////////////////////////////


static BOOL FindNextChildDir (HANDLE hFindFile,
   WIN32_FIND_DATA *lpFindData) {

   BOOL fFound = FALSE;

   do {
      fFound = FindNextFile(hFindFile, lpFindData);
   } while (fFound && !IsChildDir(lpFindData));

   return(fFound);
}
```

Figure 14-2. *(continued)*
The DirWalk application.

Figure 14-2. *continued*

```
/////////////////////////////////////////////////////////////////


static HANDLE FindFirstChildDir (LPTSTR szPath,
    WIN32_FIND_DATA *lpFindData) {

    BOOL fFound;
    HANDLE hFindFile = FindFirstFile(szPath, lpFindData);

    if (hFindFile != INVALID_HANDLE_VALUE) {
        fFound = IsChildDir(lpFindData);

        if (!fFound)
            fFound = FindNextChildDir(hFindFile, lpFindData);

        if (!fFound) {
            FindClose(hFindFile);
            hFindFile = INVALID_HANDLE_VALUE;
        }
    }
    return(hFindFile);
}


/////////////////////////////////////////////////////////////////


// To minimize stack use, one instance of the DIRWALKDATA
// structure is created as a local variable in DirWalk,
// and a pointer to it is passed to DirWalkRecurse.

// Data used by DirWalkRecurse
typedef struct {
    HWND    hwndTreeLB;     // Handle to the output list box
    int     nDepth;         // Nesting depth
    BOOL    fRecurse;       // Set to TRUE to list subdirectories.
    TCHAR   szBuf[1000];    // Output formatting buffer
    int     nIndent;        // Indentation character count
    BOOL    fOk;            // Loop control flag
    BOOL    fIsDir;         // Loop control flag
    WIN32_FIND_DATA FindData; // File information
} DIRWALKDATA, *LPDIRWALKDATA;


/////////////////////////////////////////////////////////////////
```

(continued)

Figure 14-2. *continued*

```
// Walk the directory structure and fill a list box with
// filenames. If pDW->fRecurse is set, list any child
// directories by recursively calling DirWalkRecurse.
static void DirWalkRecurse (LPDIRWALKDATA pDW) {
   HANDLE hFind;

   pDW->nDepth++;

   pDW->nIndent = 3 * pDW->nDepth;
   _stprintf(pDW->szBuf, __TEXT("%*s"), pDW->nIndent,
      __TEXT(""));

   GetCurrentDirectory(chDIMOF(pDW->szBuf) - pDW->nIndent,
      &pDW->szBuf[pDW->nIndent]);
   ListBox_AddString(pDW->hwndTreeLB, pDW->szBuf);

   hFind = FindFirstFile(__TEXT("*.*"), &pDW->FindData);
   pDW->fOk = (hFind != INVALID_HANDLE_VALUE);

   while (pDW->fOk) {
      pDW->fIsDir = pDW->FindData.dwFileAttributes &
         FILE_ATTRIBUTE_DIRECTORY;
      if (!pDW->fIsDir ||
         (!pDW->fRecurse && IsChildDir(&pDW->FindData))) {

         _stprintf(pDW->szBuf,
            pDW->fIsDir ? __TEXT("%*s[%s]") : __TEXT("%*s%s"),
            pDW->nIndent, __TEXT(""),
            pDW->FindData.cFileName);

         ListBox_AddString(pDW->hwndTreeLB, pDW->szBuf);
      }
      pDW->fOk = FindNextFile(hFind, &pDW->FindData);
   }
   if (hFind != INVALID_HANDLE_VALUE)
      FindClose(hFind);

   if (pDW->fRecurse) {
      // Get the first child directory.
      hFind = FindFirstChildDir(
         __TEXT("*.*"), &pDW->FindData);
      pDW->fOk = (hFind != INVALID_HANDLE_VALUE);
      while (pDW->fOk) {
         // Change into the child directory.
         if (SetCurrentDirectory(pDW->FindData.cFileName)) {
```

(continued)

Figure 14-2. *continued*

```
            // Perform the recursive walk into the child
            // directory.  Remember that some members of pDW
            // will be overwritten by this call.
            DirWalkRecurse(pDW);

            // Change back to the child's parent directory.
            SetCurrentDirectory(__TEXT(".."));
        }

        pDW->fOk = FindNextChildDir(hFind, &pDW->FindData);
    }

    if (hFind != INVALID_HANDLE_VALUE)
        FindClose(hFind);
    }
    pDW->nDepth--;
}


///////////////////////////////////////////////////////////////


// Walk the directory structure and fill a list box with
// filenames. This function sets up a call to
// DirWalkRecurse, which does the real work.

void DirWalk (
    HWND hwndTreeLB,         // List box to fill
    LPCTSTR pszRootPath,     // Starting point of the tree walk
    BOOL fRecurse) {         // Expand subdirectories.

    TCHAR szCurrDir[_MAX_DIR];
    DIRWALKDATA DW;

    // Clear out the list box.
    ListBox_ResetContent(hwndTreeLB);

    // Save the current directory so that it can
    // be restored later.
    GetCurrentDirectory(chDIMOF(szCurrDir), szCurrDir);

    // Set the current directory to where we want
    // to start walking.
    SetCurrentDirectory(pszRootPath);
```

(continued)

Figure 14-2. *continued*

```
      // nDepth is used to control indenting. The value -1 will
      // cause the first level to display flush left.
      DW.nDepth = -1;

      DW.hwndTreeLB = hwndTreeLB;
      DW.fRecurse = fRecurse;

      // Call the recursive function to walk the subdirectories.
      DirWalkRecurse(&DW);

      // Restore the current directory to what it was
      // before the function was called.
      SetCurrentDirectory(szCurrDir);
   }


   ///////////////////////////////////////////////////////////////


   BOOL Dlg_OnInitDialog (HWND hwnd, HWND hwndFocus,
      LPARAM lParam) {

      RECT rc;

      // Associate an icon with the dialog box.
      chSETDLGICONS(hwnd, IDI_DIRWALK, IDI_DIRWALK);

      DirWalk(GetDlgItem(hwnd, IDC_TREE), __TEXT("\\"), TRUE);

      GetClientRect(hwnd, &rc);
      SetWindowPos(GetDlgItem(hwnd, IDC_TREE), NULL,
         0, 0, rc.right, rc.bottom, SWP_NOZORDER);

      return(TRUE);
   }


   ///////////////////////////////////////////////////////////////


   void Dlg_OnSize (HWND hwnd, UINT state, int cx, int cy) {
      SetWindowPos(GetDlgItem(hwnd, IDC_TREE), NULL, 0, 0,
         cx, cy, SWP_NOZORDER);
   }
```

(continued)

Figure 14-2. *continued*

```
///////////////////////////////////////////////////////////


void Dlg_OnCommand (HWND hwnd, int id, HWND hwndCtl,
   UINT codeNotify) {

   switch (id) {
      case IDCANCEL:
         EndDialog(hwnd, id);
         break;

      case IDOK:
         // Call the recursive routine to walk the tree.
         DirWalk(GetDlgItem(hwnd, IDC_TREE), __TEXT("\\"),
            TRUE);
         break;
   }
}


///////////////////////////////////////////////////////////


BOOL CALLBACK Dlg_Proc (HWND hwnd, UINT uMsg,
   WPARAM wParam, LPARAM lParam) {

   switch (uMsg) {
      chHANDLE_DLGMSG(hwnd, WM_INITDIALOG,  Dlg_OnInitDialog);
      chHANDLE_DLGMSG(hwnd, WM_SIZE,        Dlg_OnSize);
      chHANDLE_DLGMSG(hwnd, WM_COMMAND,     Dlg_OnCommand);
   }
   return(FALSE);
}


///////////////////////////////////////////////////////////


int WINAPI _tWinMain (HINSTANCE hinstExe,
   HINSTANCE hinstPrev, LPTSTR pszCmdLine, int nCmdShow) {

   chWARNIFUNICODEUNDERWIN95();
   DialogBox(hinstExe, MAKEINTRESOURCE(IDD_DIRWALK),
      NULL, Dlg_Proc);
```

(continued)

Figure 14-2. *continued*

```
    return(0);
}



///////////////////////// End Of File /////////////////////////
```

DIRWALK.RC

```
//Microsoft Developer Studio generated resource script.
//
#include "Resource.h"

#define APSTUDIO_READONLY_SYMBOLS
/////////////////////////////////////////////////////////////////
//
// Generated from the TEXTINCLUDE 2 resource.
//
#include "afxres.h"


/////////////////////////////////////////////////////////////////
#undef APSTUDIO_READONLY_SYMBOLS


/////////////////////////////////////////////////////////////////
// English (U.S.) resources

#if !defined(AFX_RESOURCE_DLL) || defined(AFX_TARG_ENU)
#ifdef _WIN32
LANGUAGE LANG_ENGLISH, SUBLANG_ENGLISH_US
#pragma code_page(1252)
#endif //_WIN32


/////////////////////////////////////////////////////////////////
//
// Icon
//


// Icon with lowest ID value placed first to ensure
// application icon remains consistent on all systems.
IDI_DIRWALK             ICON    DISCARDABLE     "DirWalk.Ico"


/////////////////////////////////////////////////////////////////
//
// Dialog
//
```

(continued)

Figure 14-2. *continued*

```
IDD_DIRWALK DIALOG DISCARDABLE  10, 18, 250, 250
STYLE WS_MINIMIZEBOX | WS_MAXIMIZEBOX | WS_POPUP |
      WS_VISIBLE | WS_CAPTION | WS_SYSMENU | WS_THICKFRAME
CAPTION "Directory Walker"
FONT 8, "System"
BEGIN
    LISTBOX             IDC_TREE,0,0,0,0,NOT LBS_NOTIFY |
                        LBS_NOINTEGRALHEIGHT | NOT WS_BORDER |
                        WS_VSCROLL | WS_HSCROLL | WS_GROUP |
                        WS_TABSTOP
END


#ifdef APSTUDIO_INVOKED
/////////////////////////////////////////////////////////////
//
// TEXTINCLUDE
//

1 TEXTINCLUDE DISCARDABLE
BEGIN
    "Resource.h\0"
END

2 TEXTINCLUDE DISCARDABLE
BEGIN
    "#include ""afxres.h""\r\n"
    "\0"
END

3 TEXTINCLUDE DISCARDABLE
BEGIN
    "\r\n"
    "\0"
END

#endif    // APSTUDIO_INVOKED

#endif    // English (U.S.) resources
/////////////////////////////////////////////////////////////



#ifndef APSTUDIO_INVOKED
```

(continued)

Figure 14-2. *continued*

```
//////////////////////////////////////////////////////////////
//
// Generated from the TEXTINCLUDE 3 resource.
//


//////////////////////////////////////////////////////////////
#endif    // not APSTUDIO_INVOKED
```

File System Change Notifications

Many applications would like to be notified when something in the file system has been altered. Although you probably have not noticed it, the Explorer-like Open common dialog box updates its window automatically to reflect any changes made to the file system. To see this in action, perform the following experiment. Select the File Open menu option in any application that displays the File Open common dialog box. Now, from the command prompt, copy a file from a floppy disk to the directory that is currently viewed in the dialog box. After the file is copied, the dialog box will automatically update its contents to show that the new file is now present in the viewed directory.

This has been a feature long wished for in 16-bit Windows—and actually, 16-bit Windows does have a function, *FileCDR*, that an application can call in order to be notified of changes in the file system. There are two problems with *FileCDR*, though: it's an undocumented function, and it allows only one application at a time to get file system notifications. If another application calls the *FileCDR* function, the first application will stop getting notifications.

So many people requested that applications be notified dynamically of file system changes that Microsoft built direct support for this capability into Windows 95 and Windows NT. Here is how it works. First your application must tell the system that it is interested in being notified of file system changes by calling *FindFirstChangeNotification*:

```
HANDLE FindFirstChangeNotification(LPTSTR lpszPath,
    BOOL fWatchSubTree, DWORD fdwFilter);
```

The *lpszPath* parameter specifies the root of the directory tree that you want to monitor. You can specify the root directory of a drive or any subdirectory. If you specify a subdirectory, you won't be notified of events occurring in directories above the specified subdirectory. If you want to monitor directory trees on different drives, you must make multiple calls to *FindFirstChangeNotification*—one for each drive that you want to monitor.

The second parameter, *fWatchSubTree*, tells the system whether you want to watch events that occur in directories beneath the *lpszPath* directory. If you pass FALSE, you will be notified only of events that occur in the single directory you've specified.

In the *fdwFilter* parameter, you tell the system what type of file changes you're interested in. You can combine the *fdwFilter* flags by ORing them. Here's the list of valid flags and their meanings:

Flag	Meaning
FILE_NOTIFY_CHANGE_FILE_NAME	A file has been created, renamed, or deleted.
FILE_NOTIFY_CHANGE_DIR_NAME	A directory has been created, renamed, or deleted.
FILE_NOTIFY_CHANGE_ATTRIBUTES	A file's attribute has changed.
FILE_NOTIFY_CHANGE_SIZE	A file's size has changed.
FILE_NOTIFY_CHANGE_CREATION	A file's creation time has changed.
FILE_NOTIFY_CHANGE_LAST_WRITE	A file's last write time has changed.
FILE_NOTIFY_CHANGE_LAST_ACCESS	A file's last access time has changed.
FILE_NOTIFY_CHANGE_SECURITY	A security descriptor for a directory or file has been changed.

Note that the system frequently buffers file changes. A file's size doesn't change, for example, until buffered information is flushed to the disk. You will be notified of the change in the file size only when the system flushes the data to disk, not when an application actually changes the data.

If *FindFirstChangeNotification* is successful, it returns a handle your thread can use with the various synchronization functions such as *WaitForSingleObject* and *WaitForMultipleObjects*. If you pass an invalid parameter, such as a nonexistent path, INVALID_HANDLE_VALUE is returned.

Important

Like the *FindFirstFile* function, the *FindFirstChangeNotification* function returns INVALID_HANDLE_VALUE rather than NULL when it fails.

Personally, I think it would have made more sense to name the *FindFirstChangeNotification* function something like *CreateFileChangeNotification* because the function doesn't really find a file change at all; it simply creates a file change notification object and returns its handle.

Once you have the notification object's handle, you can use it when you make calls to the *WaitForSingleObject* and *WaitForMultipleObjects* functions. Whenever a change occurs in the file system that meets the criteria you specified in the call to *FindFirstChangeNotification*, the object will become signaled. You can think of a file change notification object as a manual-reset event with some additional logic built into it—when a change occurs in the file system, the event is signaled. When your call to *WaitForSingleObject* or *WaitForMultipleObjects* returns, you know that you need to walk the drive's directory tree (starting from *lpszPath*) so that you can refresh the directory and file information in your application.

The system accumulates many file changes and notifies you of them all at once. For example, if the user entered the command

```
deltree .     (Windows 95)
rmdir . /s    (Windows NT)
```

on the command line to erase all the files in the current directory and all its subdirectories, the command shell's thread might delete several files before the system signaled the file change notification object, allowing your thread to resume execution. The handle won't be signaled separately for every single file change. This greatly improves performance.

When the file change notification object is signaled, your thread wakes up and you can perform whatever operations you want. When you have finished, you must call *FindNextChangeNotification*:

```
BOOL FindNextChangeNotification(HANDLE hChange);
```

The *FindNextChangeNotification* function resets the file change notification object to its nonsignaled state, similar to calling *ResetEvent*. However, this is where file change notification objects differ from manual-reset events. While your thread was walking the drive's directory tree, the command shell's thread might have preempted your thread and been able to continue deleting more files and directories. The call to *FindNextChangeNotification* checks to see whether this has happened, and if more file

666

change events have occurred since the object became signaled, the object is not reset to the nonsignaled state and remains signaled.

That way, if your thread waits for the object again, the wait will be satisfied immediately and you will again walk the drive's directory tree. You should always wait for a file change notification object after every call to *FindNextChangeNotification*. Without this wait, your thread might miss a file change event.

As usual, when you no longer want file change notifications, you must close the object. You close the file change notification object by calling

```
BOOL FindCloseChangeNotification(HANDLE hChange);
```

Important

This is one of the very few times in Win32 that you don't call *CloseHandle* to close a handle. You must call *FindCloseChangeNotification* instead so that the system deletes any record of file changes that have been made since the file change notification object was last signaled.

As mentioned above, the problem with *FindFirstChangeNotification* is that you are notified only when a change occurs. To discover the exact nature of the change, you must walk the directory or directory tree. Because this is not convenient, Windows NT 4 adds a new *ReadDirectory-ChangesW* function:

```
BOOL ReadDirectoryChangesW(HANDLE hDirectory,
    LPVOID lpBuffer, DWORD nBufferLength,
    BOOL bWatchSubtree, DWORD dwNotifyFilter,
    LPDWORD lpBytesReturned, LPOVERLAPPED lpOverlapped,
    LPOVERLAPPED_COMPLETION_ROUTINE lpCompletionRoutine);
```

As the *W* at the end of the function name implies, this function exists only in a Unicode version, which means that it can return strings only in Unicode characters. The first parameter to this function is a handle to a directory that you can obtain by calling *CreateFile* (Chapter 15 discusses the *CreateFile* function in more detail) as follows:

```
HANDLE hdir = CreateFile(
    "C:\\Program Files",            // Directory path
    FILE_LIST_DIRECTORY,           // Access
                                   // (ReadDirectoryChangesW
                                   // requires
                                   // FILE_LIST_DIRECTORY)
```

(continued)

667

```
              FILE_SHARE_READ | FILE_SHARE_DELETE,   // Sharing mode
              NULL,                                   // Security descriptor
              OPEN_EXISTING,                          // Creation disposition
              FILE_FLAG_BACKUP_SEMANTICS,             // Attributes
                                                      // BACKUP_SEMANTICS required
                                                      // for dir
              NULL);                                  // Ignored when opening a
                                                      // file/dir
```

When you're done using the directory handle, you close it simply by calling

```
CloseHandle(hdir);
```

The *lpBuffer* and *nBufferLength* arguments indicate the address to a block of memory and the length of that memory block (in bytes). The block of memory contains an array of FIND_NOTIFY_INFORMATION structures:

```
typedef struct _FILE_NOTIFY_INFORMATION {
    DWORD NextEntryOffset;
    DWORD Action;
    DWORD FileNameLength;
    WCHAR FileName[1];
} FILE_NOTIFY_INFORMATION;
```

When changes to a directory occur, *ReadDirectoryChangesW* fills in this block of memory with the exact nature of the changes. Because each of these structures has a variable length, the *NextEntryOffset* member contains the number of bytes in the entry. By adding this number to the beginning of the entry, you can get to the next entry. When the *NextEntryOffset* member contains 0 (zero), you have reached the end of the list. The action member indicates why this entry is present in the list. The following table shows the possible reasons:

Action	Description
FILE_ACTION_ADDED	The file was added to the directory.
FILE_ACTION_REMOVED	The file was removed from the directory.
FILE_ACTION_MODIFIED	The file was modified. This can be a change in the time stamp or attributes.
FILE_ACTION_RENAMED_OLD_NAME	The file was renamed and this is the old name.
FILE_ACTION_RENAMED_NEW_NAME	The file was renamed and this is the new name.

The *FileNameLength* member indicates the name of the changed file. This length is in bytes, so you will have to divide the number by sizeof(WCHAR) (which evaluates to 2) to get the actual number of characters. Also, this count does not include a terminating zero character. The *FileName* member is the first character of the filename. The filename is not zero-terminated and is always in Unicode.

ReadDirectoryChangesW's *bWatchSubtree* parameter indicates whether you want the function to monitor subdirectories as well as the specified directory. The *dwNotifyFilter* parameter indicates the types of changes that you're interested in. You can pass any combination of the FILE_NO-TIFY_* flags (shown on page 665) that can also be passed to the *FindFirstChangeNotification* function.

If you open the handle to the directory as I have in the above call to *CreateFile*, *ReadDirectoryChangesW* will perform its work synchronously, which means that the function will not return until it has filled the buffer with the directory's changes. For synchronous calls to *ReadDirectoryChangesW*, the *lpBytesReturned* parameter is the address of a DWORD that will be filled in with the number of bytes written to the buffer pointed to by the *lpBuffer* parameter.

ReadDirectoryChangesW can also do its work asynchronously, however, so that when you call it, the function returns immediately and the system watches for directory changes on your behalf. When the system detects directory changes, you'll want to be notified of the changes. These notifications can happen in one of three different ways, which I'll describe shortly. First, to have *ReadDirectoryChangesW* work asynchronously, you must open the directory using the FILE_FLAG_OVERLAP-PED flag as shown here:

```
HANDLE hdir = CreateFile(
   "C:\\Program Files",                       // Directory path
   FILE_LIST_DIRECTORY,                       // Access
                                              // (ReadDirectoryChangesW
                                              // requires
                                              // FILE_LIST_DIRECTORY)
   FILE_SHARE_READ | FILE_SHARE_DELETE,       // Sharing mode
   NULL,                                      // Security descriptor
   OPEN_EXISTING,                             // Creation disposition
   FILE_FLAG_BACKUP_SEMANTICS |               // Attributes
      FILE_FLAG_OVERLAPPED,                   // BACKUP_SEMANTICS required
                                              // for dir OVERLAPPED
                                              // required for async
   NULL);                                     // Ignored when opening a
                                              // file/dir
```

Now when you call *ReadDirectoryChangesW*, it will return immediately.

You can be notified of directory changes using any of three different methods:

■ You can allocate an OVERLAPPED structure and initialize the *hEvent* member to the handle of an event kernel object. Then pass the address of this structure in *ReadDirectoryChangesW*'s *lpOverlapped* parameter. Somewhere else in your code, you can then call *WaitForSingleObject* or one of the other wait functions to wait on the event. When directory changes occur, the system will automatically signal the event.

■ You can pass in the address of an overlapped completion routine for *ReadDirectoryChangesW*'s *lpCompletionRoutine* parameter. When directory changes occur, the system will automatically queue an APC to the thread that called *ReadDirectoryChangesW*. The completion routine will be called when your thread enters an alertable state by calling *WaitForSingleObjectEx*, *WaitForMultipleObjectsEx*, *SleepEx*, and so on.

■ You can associate the directory handle with an I/O completion port and then have a thread wait on the completion port using *GetQueuedCompletionStatus*.

All of these methods are discussed in far more detail in Chapter 15.

The File Change Sample Application

The FileChng (FILECHNG.EXE) application, listed in Figure 14-3 beginning on page 673, uses the three change notification functions to monitor changes made to a drive's directory tree. The source code and resource files for the application are in the FILECHNG directory on the companion disc. When the user executes FileChng, the File Change Notifications dialog box appears:

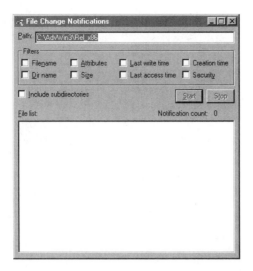

Before the program starts monitoring file changes, you must tell it what you are interested in monitoring by setting some or all the parameters in the Filters group box. When you click on the Start button, the program retrieves all of the parameters from the dialog box controls and calls *FindFirstChangeNotification* so that the system will start to notify the program of any file system changes. The program also resets the Notification Count value to 0 and performs an initial directory tree walk starting at the path you've specified, filling the list box with a list of the directories and files in the tree.

The program then sits idle waiting for the system to signal the file change notification object. When a change occurs in the file system that matches your filter criteria, the system signals the notification object, causing FileChng's thread to wake up, increment the Notification Count value, and rewalk the directory tree. After each walk, the thread calls *FindNextChangeNotification* and waits for the object again. You can stop monitoring changes to the file system by clicking on the Stop button or by changing some of the notification criteria values.

The program code is pretty self-explanatory, but I do want to draw your attention to the *WinMain* function, which I've structured differently than the other sample programs in this book. I wanted to write the File-Chng program so that it had only a single thread of execution. To do this, I needed a method whereby my thread could suspend itself until either a window message entered the thread's queues or the file change notification object became signaled. I racked my brain for a while and then remembered the *MsgWaitForMultipleObjects* function.

This function was just what the doctor ordered. It's just like *WaitForMultipleObjects* except that it also checks for window messages. Using *MsgWaitForMultipleObjects* meant that I couldn't create a modal dialog box for this program, though, because modal dialog boxes call *GetMessage* for their message processing and there would be no way for me to wait for the file change notification object. Since I had to get more involved with the message loop for the program, I had to use *CreateDialog* instead of *DialogBox* to create a modeless dialog box. Then I had to code the message loop myself.

Here's a little more detail on what the program does. First it calls *CreateDialog* to create a modeless dialog box that will be the user interface for the program. Next the thread starts executing the message loop, which repeatedly checks the *fQuit* variable to find out when it should terminate. The *fQuit* variable is initialized to FALSE when the program starts and is set to TRUE when a WM_QUIT message is pulled from the thread's queue.

Once in the message loop, the thread checks whether the handle to the file change notification object is valid and stores the result in the *fWait4FileChanges* variable. The handle won't be valid if the user hasn't clicked on the Start button yet. Then the program makes this call:

```
dwResult = MsgWaitForMultipleObjects(
   (fWait4FileChanges) ? 1 : 0,
   &s_hChange, FALSE, INFINITE, QS_ALLEVENTS);
```

If there is a valid handle to a file change notification object, the call to *MsgWaitForMultipleObjects* tells the system to wait either for this object to become signaled or for a message to enter one of the thread's message queues. If the handle is invalid, the thread will just wait until a message is available.

When the system awakens the thread, the thread checks to see what the reason is. If it has been awakened because of a file change, the Notification Count value is incremented, the directory tree is rewalked, and *FindNextChangeNotification* is called. The thread then loops around to the top of the message loop and makes another call to *MsgWaitForMultipleObjects*.

If the thread has been awakened because of a window message, the message must now be retrieved from the queue by a call to *PeekMessage* specifying the PM_REMOVE flag. Next *IsDialogMessage* is called, passing the retrieved message. This call allows the user to navigate through the controls in the modeless dialog box using the keyboard. If the message isn't a navigational keyboard message, the thread checks to see whether it is a WM_QUIT message. If it is, the *fQuit* variable is set to TRUE, causing the message loop to terminate before it begins its next iteration.

If the message isn't a navigational keyboard message and is also not a WM_QUIT message, *TranslateMessage* is called, followed by *DispatchMessage*, just as they would be called in any normal message loop.

You'll notice that I call *PeekMessage* in a loop here—I do this to give the user interface a higher priority than the processing for file change notifications.

FileChng.ico

FILECHNG.C

```
/************************************************************
Module name: FileChng.C
Written by: Jim Harkins and Jeffrey Richter
Notices: Copyright (c) 1995-1997 Jeffrey Richter
************************************************************/


#include "..\CmnHdr.H"               /* See Appendix C. */
#include <windows.h>
#include <windowsx.h>
#include <tchar.h>
#include <stdio.h>
#include <stdlib.h>
#include <string.h>
#include "Resource.H"


///////////////////////////////////////////////////////////
// The following functions are taken directly from DirWalk.C.


static BOOL IsChildDir (WIN32_FIND_DATA *lpFindData) {

   return(
      ((lpFindData->dwFileAttributes &
         FILE_ATTRIBUTE_DIRECTORY) != 0) &&
      (lstrcmp(lpFindData->cFileName, __TEXT(".")) != 0) &&
      (lstrcmp(lpFindData->cFileName, __TEXT("..")) != 0));
}


///////////////////////////////////////////////////////////
```

Figure 14-3. *(continued)*
The FileChng application.

Figure 14-3. *continued*

```
static BOOL FindNextChildDir (HANDLE hFindFile,
   WIN32_FIND_DATA *lpFindData) {

   BOOL fFound = FALSE;

   do {
      fFound = FindNextFile(hFindFile, lpFindData);
   } while (fFound && !IsChildDir(lpFindData));

   return(fFound);
}


///////////////////////////////////////////////////////////////


static HANDLE FindFirstChildDir (LPTSTR szPath,
   WIN32_FIND_DATA *lpFindData) {

   BOOL fFound;
   HANDLE hFindFile = FindFirstFile(szPath, lpFindData);

   if (hFindFile != INVALID_HANDLE_VALUE) {
      fFound = IsChildDir(lpFindData);

      if (!fFound)
         fFound = FindNextChildDir(hFindFile, lpFindData);

      if (!fFound) {
         FindClose(hFindFile);
         hFindFile = INVALID_HANDLE_VALUE;
      }
   }
   return(hFindFile);
}


///////////////////////////////////////////////////////////////


// To minimize stack use, one instance of the DIRWALKDATA
// structure is created as a local variable in DirWalk,
// and a pointer to it is passed to DirWalkRecurse.
```

(continued)

Figure 14-3. *continued*

```
// Data used by DirWalkRecurse
typedef struct {
    HWND    hwndTreeLB;     // Handle to the output list box
    int     nDepth;         // Nesting depth
    BOOL    fRecurse;       // Set to TRUE to list subdirectories.
    TCHAR   szBuf[1000];    // Output formatting buffer
    int     nIndent;        // Indentation character count
    BOOL    fOk;            // Loop control flag
    BOOL    fIsDir;         // Loop control flag
    WIN32_FIND_DATA FindData; // File information
} DIRWALKDATA, *LPDIRWALKDATA;


///////////////////////////////////////////////////////////////


// Walk the directory structure and fill a list box with
// filenames. If pDW->fRecurse is set, list any child
// directories by recursively calling DirWalkRecurse.
void DirWalkRecurse (LPDIRWALKDATA pDW) {
    HANDLE hFind;

    pDW->nDepth++;

    pDW->nIndent = 3 * pDW->nDepth;
    _stprintf(pDW->szBuf, __TEXT("%*s"), pDW->nIndent,
        __TEXT(""));

    GetCurrentDirectory(chDIMOF(pDW->szBuf) - pDW->nIndent,
        &pDW->szBuf[pDW->nIndent]);
    ListBox_AddString(pDW->hwndTreeLB, pDW->szBuf);

    hFind = FindFirstFile(__TEXT("*.*"), &pDW->FindData);
    pDW->fOk = (hFind != INVALID_HANDLE_VALUE);

    while (pDW->fOk) {
        pDW->fIsDir = pDW->FindData.dwFileAttributes &
            FILE_ATTRIBUTE_DIRECTORY;
        if (!pDW->fIsDir ||
            (!pDW->fRecurse && IsChildDir(&pDW->FindData))) {

            _stprintf(pDW->szBuf,
                pDW->fIsDir ? __TEXT("%*s[%s]") : __TEXT("%*s%s"),
```

(continued)

Figure 14-3. *continued*

```
            pDW->nIndent, __TEXT(""),
            pDW->FindData.cFileName);

        ListBox_AddString(pDW->hwndTreeLB, pDW->szBuf);
      }
      pDW->fOk = FindNextFile(hFind, &pDW->FindData);
   }
   if (hFind != INVALID_HANDLE_VALUE)
      FindClose(hFind);

   if (pDW->fRecurse) {
      // Get the first child directory.
      hFind = FindFirstChildDir(
         __TEXT("*.*"), &pDW->FindData);
      pDW->fOk = (hFind != INVALID_HANDLE_VALUE);
      while (pDW->fOk) {
         // Change into the child directory.
         if (SetCurrentDirectory(pDW->FindData.cFileName)) {

            // Perform the recursive walk into the child
            // directory.  Remember that some members of pDW
            // will be overwritten by this call.
            DirWalkRecurse(pDW);

            // Change back to the child's parent directory.
            SetCurrentDirectory(__TEXT(".."));
         }

         pDW->fOk = FindNextChildDir(hFind, &pDW->FindData);
      }

      if (hFind != INVALID_HANDLE_VALUE)
         FindClose(hFind);
   }
   pDW->nDepth--;
}


//////////////////////////////////////////////////////////////


// Walk the directory structure and fill a list box with
// filenames. This function sets up a call to
// DirWalkRecurse, which does the real work.
```

(continued)

Figure 14-3. *continued*

```
void DirWalk (
    HWND hwndTreeLB,        // List box to fill
    LPCTSTR pszRootPath,    // Starting point of the tree walk
    BOOL fRecurse) {        // Expand subdirectories.

    TCHAR szCurrDir[_MAX_DIR];
    DIRWALKDATA DW;

    // Clear out the list box.
    ListBox_ResetContent(hwndTreeLB);

    // Save the current directory so that it can
    // be restored later.
    GetCurrentDirectory(chDIMOF(szCurrDir), szCurrDir);

    // Set the current directory to where we want
    // to start walking.
    SetCurrentDirectory(pszRootPath);

    // nDepth is used to control indenting. The value -1 will
    // cause the first level to display flush left.
    DW.nDepth = -1;

    DW.hwndTreeLB = hwndTreeLB;
    DW.fRecurse = fRecurse;

    // Call the recursive function to walk the subdirectories.
    DirWalkRecurse(&DW);

    // Restore the current directory to what it was
    // before the function was called.
    SetCurrentDirectory(szCurrDir);
}


////////////////////////////////////////////////////////////////


HANDLE g_hChange = INVALID_HANDLE_VALUE;
int    g_nCount = 0;


////////////////////////////////////////////////////////////////
```

(continued)

677

Figure 14-3. *continued*

```
void Dlg_ErrorBox (LPCTSTR pszSource) {
   TCHAR szBuf[100];   // Output formatting buffer.

   _stprintf(szBuf, __TEXT("%s reported error %lu"),
      pszSource, GetLastError());

   chMB(szBuf);
}


///////////////////////////////////////////////////////////////////


DWORD Dlg_GetFilter (HWND hwnd) {
   DWORD fdwFilter = 0;

   if (IsDlgButtonChecked(hwnd, IDC_FILENAME))
      fdwFilter |= FILE_NOTIFY_CHANGE_FILE_NAME;

   if (IsDlgButtonChecked(hwnd, IDC_DIRNAME))
      fdwFilter |= FILE_NOTIFY_CHANGE_DIR_NAME;

   if (IsDlgButtonChecked(hwnd, IDC_ATTRIBS))
      fdwFilter |= FILE_NOTIFY_CHANGE_ATTRIBUTES;

   if (IsDlgButtonChecked(hwnd, IDC_SIZEFLTR))
      fdwFilter |= FILE_NOTIFY_CHANGE_SIZE;

   if (IsDlgButtonChecked(hwnd, IDC_LASTWRITE))
      fdwFilter |= FILE_NOTIFY_CHANGE_LAST_WRITE;

   if (IsDlgButtonChecked(hwnd, IDC_LASTACCESS))
      fdwFilter |= FILE_NOTIFY_CHANGE_LAST_ACCESS;

   if (IsDlgButtonChecked(hwnd, IDC_CREATION))
      fdwFilter |= FILE_NOTIFY_CHANGE_CREATION;

   if (IsDlgButtonChecked(hwnd, IDC_SECURITY))
      fdwFilter |= FILE_NOTIFY_CHANGE_SECURITY;

   return(fdwFilter);
}


///////////////////////////////////////////////////////////////////
```

(continued)

Figure 14-3. *continued*

```
// Validate the dialog box controls and configure a
// valid call to FindFirstChangeNotification:
// At least one filter flag must be set, and
// the path must be valid.
BOOL Dlg_Validate (HWND hwnd) {
   BOOL  fValid = FALSE;
   TCHAR szPath[_MAX_DIR];

   // Test to see whether at least one flag is set.
   if (0 != Dlg_GetFilter(hwnd)) {

      // Verify that the path exists.
      GetDlgItemText(hwnd, IDC_PATH, szPath,
         chDIMOF(szPath));
      fValid = SetCurrentDirectory(szPath);
   }
   return(fValid);
}


///////////////////////////////////////////////////////////////


// Stop close change notification.
void Dlg_CloseChange (HWND hwnd) {
   BOOL fDisableFocus =
      (GetFocus() == GetDlgItem(hwnd, IDC_STOP));

   EnableWindow(GetDlgItem(hwnd, IDC_STOP), FALSE);

   if (Dlg_Validate(hwnd)) {
      EnableWindow(GetDlgItem(hwnd, IDC_START), TRUE);
      if (fDisableFocus) {
         SetFocus(GetDlgItem(hwnd, IDC_START));
      }
   } else {
      fDisableFocus = fDisableFocus ||
         (GetFocus() == GetDlgItem(hwnd, IDC_START));

      EnableWindow(GetDlgItem(hwnd, IDC_START), FALSE);
      if (fDisableFocus) {
         SetFocus(GetDlgItem(hwnd, IDC_INCSUBDIRS));
      }
   }
```

(continued)

Figure 14-3. *continued*

```
    if (INVALID_HANDLE_VALUE != g_hChange) {
        if (!FindCloseChangeNotification(g_hChange)) {
            Dlg_ErrorBox(__TEXT("FindCloseChangeNotification"));
        }
        g_hChange = INVALID_HANDLE_VALUE;
    }
}


///////////////////////////////////////////////////////////////


// Start close change notification.
void Dlg_OpenChange (HWND hwnd) {
    TCHAR szPath[_MAX_DIR];
    BOOL fDisableFocus =
        (GetFocus() == GetDlgItem(hwnd, IDC_START));

    Dlg_CloseChange(hwnd);

    g_nCount = 0;
    SetDlgItemInt(hwnd, IDC_NCOUNT, g_nCount, FALSE);

    GetDlgItemText(hwnd, IDC_PATH, szPath, chDIMOF(szPath));

    g_hChange = FindFirstChangeNotification(szPath,
        IsDlgButtonChecked(hwnd, IDC_INCSUBDIRS),
        Dlg_GetFilter(hwnd));

    if (INVALID_HANDLE_VALUE == g_hChange) {
        Dlg_ErrorBox(__TEXT("FindFirstChangeNotification"));
        g_hChange = INVALID_HANDLE_VALUE;
    } else {
        EnableWindow(GetDlgItem(hwnd, IDC_START), FALSE);
        EnableWindow(GetDlgItem(hwnd, IDC_STOP), TRUE);

        if (fDisableFocus) {
            SetFocus(GetDlgItem(hwnd, IDC_STOP));
        }
        DirWalk(GetDlgItem(hwnd, IDC_TREE), szPath,
            IsDlgButtonChecked(hwnd, IDC_INCSUBDIRS));
    }
}
```

(continued)

Figure 14-3. *continued*

```
////////////////////////////////////////////////////////////////

BOOL Dlg_OnInitDialog (HWND hwnd, HWND hwndFocus,
    LPARAM lParam) {
    TCHAR szPath[_MAX_DIR];

    // Associate an icon with the dialog box.
    chSETDLGICONS(hwnd, IDI_FILECHNG, IDI_FILECHNG);

    // Path defaults to the current path
    GetCurrentDirectory(chDIMOF(szPath), szPath);
    SetDlgItemText(hwnd, IDC_PATH, szPath);

    Dlg_CloseChange(hwnd);

    return(TRUE);
}


////////////////////////////////////////////////////////////////

void Dlg_OnCommand (HWND hwnd, int id, HWND hwndCtl,
    UINT codeNotify) {

    switch (id) {
        case IDC_PATH:
            // If change notification is started and
            // the user updates the path,
            // stop notifications.
            if (EN_CHANGE == codeNotify) {
                Dlg_CloseChange(hwnd);
            }
            break;

        case IDC_INCSUBDIRS:
        case IDC_FILENAME:
        case IDC_DIRNAME:
        case IDC_ATTRIBS:
        case IDC_SIZEFLTR:
        case IDC_LASTWRITE:
        case IDC_LASTACCESS:
```

(continued)

Figure 14-3. *continued*

```
      case IDC_CREATION:
      case IDC_SECURITY:
      case IDC_STOP:
         Dlg_CloseChange(hwnd);
         break;

      case IDC_START:
         Dlg_OpenChange(hwnd);
         break;

      case IDCANCEL:
         Dlg_CloseChange(hwnd);
         PostQuitMessage(0);
         break;

   }
}


///////////////////////////////////////////////////////////////


BOOL CALLBACK Dlg_Proc (HWND hwnd, UINT uMsg, WPARAM wParam,
   LPARAM lParam) {

   switch (uMsg) {
      chHANDLE_DLGMSG(hwnd, WM_INITDIALOG, Dlg_OnInitDialog);
      chHANDLE_DLGMSG(hwnd, WM_COMMAND, Dlg_OnCommand);
   }
   return(FALSE);
}


///////////////////////////////////////////////////////////////


int WINAPI _tWinMain (HINSTANCE hinstExe,
   HINSTANCE hinstPrev, LPTSTR pszCmdLine, int nCmdShow) {

   HWND  hwnd;
   MSG   msg;
   DWORD dwResult;
   BOOL  fQuit = FALSE, fWait4FileChanges;
   TCHAR szPath[_MAX_DIR];
```

(continued)

Figure 14-3. *continued*

```
chWARNIFUNICODEUNDERWIN95();

// Create a modeless dialog box instead of a modal
// dialog box because we need to have more control over
// the message loop processing.
hwnd = CreateDialog(hinstExe,
    MAKEINTRESOURCE(IDD_FILECHNG), NULL, Dlg_Proc);

// Continue to loop until a WM_QUIT
// message comes out of the queue.
while (!fQuit) {

    // Do we have a valid file change notification handle?
    fWait4FileChanges = (INVALID_HANDLE_VALUE != g_hChange);

    // If we do, wait until a file change occurs OR until
    // a message shows up in our queue.
    dwResult = MsgWaitForMultipleObjects(
        (fWait4FileChanges) ? 1 : 0,
        &g_hChange, FALSE, INFINITE, QS_ALLEVENTS);


    if (fWait4FileChanges && (WAIT_OBJECT_0 == dwResult)) {
        // We awoke because of a file change notification.
        // Let's update the list box.

        // Increment the counter indicating the number
        // of notifications we have received.
        SetDlgItemInt(hwnd, IDC_NCOUNT, ++g_nCount, FALSE);

        // Get the root path and fill the list box with the
        // list of files in the path and the root
        // directory's subdirectories if the Include
        // Subdirectories check box is checked.
        GetDlgItemText(hwnd, IDC_PATH, szPath,
            chDIMOF(szPath));
        DirWalk(GetDlgItem(hwnd, IDC_TREE), szPath,
            IsDlgButtonChecked(hwnd, IDC_INCSUBDIRS));

        // Tell the system that we processed the
        // notification.
        FindNextChangeNotification(g_hChange);
    } else {
```

(continued)

Figure 14-3. *continued*

```
        // We awoke because there is at least one message in
        // the queue. Let's dispatch all the queued messages.
        while (PeekMessage(&msg, NULL, 0, 0, PM_REMOVE)) {

            // Call IsDialogMessage so that the keyboard can
            // be used to control focus in the dialog box.
            if (!IsDialogMessage(hwnd, &msg)) {
                if (msg.message == WM_QUIT) {
                    // If we have a WM_QUIT message,
                    // set the flag so that the
                    // loop terminates.
                    fQuit = TRUE;
                } else {
                    // Not a WM_QUIT message. Translate it
                    // and dispatch it.
                    TranslateMessage(&msg);
                    DispatchMessage(&msg);
                }
            }  // if (!IsDialogMessage())
        }  // while messages are still in the queue
    }  // if file change notification OR message
}  // while (!fQuit)

// The application is terminating. Destroy the modeless
// dialog box.
DestroyWindow(hwnd);

return(0);
}


//////////////////////// End Of File ////////////////////////
```

FILECHNG.RC
```
//Microsoft Developer Studio generated resource script.
//
#include "Resource.h"

#define APSTUDIO_READONLY_SYMBOLS
/////////////////////////////////////////////////////////////
//
// Generated from the TEXTINCLUDE 2 resource.
//
```

(continued)

Figure 14-3. *continued*

```
#include "afxres.h"

/////////////////////////////////////////////////////////
#undef APSTUDIO_READONLY_SYMBOLS

/////////////////////////////////////////////////////////
// English (U.S.) resources

#if !defined(AFX_RESOURCE_DLL) || defined(AFX_TARG_ENU)
#ifdef _WIN32
LANGUAGE LANG_ENGLISH, SUBLANG_ENGLISH_US
#pragma code_page(1252)
#endif //_WIN32


/////////////////////////////////////////////////////////
//
// Icon
//

// Icon with lowest ID value placed first to ensure
// application icon remains consistent on all systems.
IDI_FILECHNG            ICON    DISCARDABLE    "FileChng.Ico"


/////////////////////////////////////////////////////////
//
// Dialog
//

IDD_FILECHNG DIALOG DISCARDABLE  6, 18, 256, 237
STYLE WS_MINIMIZEBOX | WS_VISIBLE | WS_CAPTION | WS_SYSMENU
CAPTION "File Change Notifications"
FONT 8, "Helv"
BEGIN
    LTEXT           "&Path:",IDC_STATIC,4,4,19,8
    EDITTEXT        IDC_PATH,24,4,228,12,ES_AUTOHSCROLL
    GROUPBOX        "Filters",IDC_STATIC,4,20,248,40
    CONTROL         "File&name",IDC_FILENAME,"Button",
                    BS_AUTOCHECKBOX | WS_TABSTOP,8,32,42,10
    CONTROL         "&Dir name",IDC_DIRNAME,"Button",
                    BS_AUTOCHECKBOX | WS_TABSTOP,8,44,40,10
    CONTROL         "&Attributes",IDC_ATTRIBS,"Button",
                    BS_AUTOCHECKBOX | WS_TABSTOP,64,32,42,10
    CONTROL         "Si&ze",IDC_SIZEFLTR,"Button",
                    BS_AUTOCHECKBOX | WS_TABSTOP,64,44,25,10
```

(continued)

Figure 14-3. *continued*

```
    CONTROL         "&Last write time",IDC_LASTWRITE,
                    "Button",BS_AUTOCHECKBOX | WS_TABSTOP,
                    120,32,58,10
    CONTROL         "Last access time",IDC_LASTACCESS,
                    "Button",BS_AUTOCHECKBOX | WS_TABSTOP,
                    120,44,69,10
    CONTROL         "Creation time",IDC_CREATION,"Button",
                    BS_AUTOCHECKBOX | WS_TABSTOP,192,32,
                    57,10
    CONTROL         "Securit&y",IDC_SECURITY,"Button",
                    BS_AUTOCHECKBOX | WS_TABSTOP,192,44,
                    38,10
    CONTROL         "&Include subdirectories",
                    IDC_INCSUBDIRS,"Button",
                    BS_AUTOCHECKBOX | WS_TABSTOP,
                    4,64,83,10
    DEFPUSHBUTTON   "&Start",IDC_START,184,64,32,14
    PUSHBUTTON      "S&top",IDC_STOP,220,64,32,14
    LTEXT           "&File list:",IDC_STATIC,4,84,27,8
    LISTBOX         IDC_TREE,4,96,248,136,NOT LBS_NOTIFY |
                    LBS_NOINTEGRALHEIGHT | WS_VSCROLL |
                    WS_HSCROLL | WS_TABSTOP
    LTEXT           "Notification count:",IDC_STATIC,
                    164,84,62,9,SS_NOPREFIX
    LTEXT           "0",IDC_NCOUNT,228,84,24,8,SS_NOPREFIX
END


#ifdef APSTUDIO_INVOKED
/////////////////////////////////////////////////////////
//
// TEXTINCLUDE
//

1 TEXTINCLUDE DISCARDABLE
BEGIN
    "Resource.h\0"
END

2 TEXTINCLUDE DISCARDABLE
BEGIN
    "#include ""afxres.h""\r\n"
    "\0"
END
```

(continued)

Figure 14-3. *continued*

```
3 TEXTINCLUDE DISCARDABLE
BEGIN
    "\r\n"
    "\0"
END

#endif    // APSTUDIO_INVOKED

#endif    // English (U.S.) resources
/////////////////////////////////////////////////////////////


#ifndef APSTUDIO_INVOKED
/////////////////////////////////////////////////////////////
//
// Generated from the TEXTINCLUDE 3 resource.
//


/////////////////////////////////////////////////////////////
#endif    // not APSTUDIO_INVOKED
```

Manipulating File Attributes

A set of attributes is associated with every file. Many of the file attributes are initialized when the file is created, some are altered when a file is accessed, and some can be altered specifically under program control. Often you might not have any interest in altering the values but just want to see what the current attributes are for a file. Most file attributes have to do with flag settings, file size, and file time stamps.

Executable File Type

Occasionally you come across a situation in which you have an executable file and you need to determine what type of file it is. To do this, you can call the *GetBinaryType* function:

```
BOOL GetBinaryType (LPCTSTR lpApplicationName,
    LPDWORD lpBinaryType);
```

All you do is pass the pathname of a file on the disk, and the function returns, in the DWORD pointed to by the *lpBinaryType* parameter, the type of executable that is in the file. The following types of executable files are possible:

Executable Type	Description
SCS_32BIT_BINARY	A Win32-based application
SCS_DOS_BINARY	An MS-DOS–based application
SCS_OS216_BINARY	A 16-bit OS/2-based application
SCS_PIF_BINARY	A PIF file that executes an MS-DOS–based application
SCS_POSIX_BINARY	A POSIX-based application
SCS_WOW_BINARY	A 16-bit Windows-based application

Under Windows 95, the *GetBinaryType* function has no useful implementation and simply returns FALSE; calling *GetLastError* returns ERROR-_CALL_NOT_IMPLEMENTED.

File Attributes

A file's attributes are initially set when the file is created with the *CreateFile* function. When *CreateFile* is called, the *fdwAttrsAndFlags* parameter specifies the attributes the file should have when it is created. To see what these attributes are later, an application can call:

```
DWORD GetFileAttributes(LPTSTR lpszFileName);
```

The *GetFileAttributes* function retrieves the attributes associated with the file identified by the *lpszFileName* parameter. When the function returns, you can AND the return value with any of the following file attribute identifiers:

FILE_ATTRIBUTE_ARCHIVE
FILE_ATTRIBUTE_COMPRESSED,
FILE_ATTRIBUTE_DIRECTORY
FILE_ATTRIBUTE_HIDDEN
FILE_ATTRIBUTE_NORMAL
FILE_ATTRIBUTE_OFFLINE

FILE_ATTRIBUTE_READONLY

FILE_ATTRIBUTE_SYSTEM

FILE_ATTRIBUTE_TEMPORARY

(These file attribute identifiers will be discussed in more detail in Chapter 15.)

In addition to *GetFileAttributes*, Windows NT 4 offers a new *GetFileAttributesEx* function:

```
BOOL GetFileAttributesEx(LPCTSTR lpFileName,
    GET_FILEEX_INFO_LEVELS fInfoLevelId, LPVOID lpFileInformation);
```

This function returns much more information than does *GetFileAttributes*. It is designed to make getting file attributes faster. Rather than calling *GetFileAttributes*, *GetFileTimes* (discussed shortly), and *GetFileSize* (also discussed shortly), *GetFileAttributesEx* allows you to get the same information with just a single function call.

Obviously, *lpFileName* identifies the pathname of the file whose attributes you want to query. The *fInfoLevelId* parameter indicates what file attribute information you're interested in. Currently, just one information level is available: *GetFileExInfoStandard*. When you request an information level of *GetFileExInfoStandard*, the *lpFileInformation* parameter has to be a pointer to a WIN32_FILE_ATTRIBUTE_DATA structure:

```
typedef struct _WIN32_FILE_ATTRIBUTE_DATA {
    DWORD       dwFileAttributes;
    FILETIME    ftCreationTime;
    FILETIME    ftLastAccessTime;
    FILETIME    ftLastWriteTime;
    DWORD       nFileSizeHigh;
    DWORD       nFileSizeLow;
} WIN32_FILE_ATTRIBUTE_DATA, *LPWIN32_FILE_ATTRIBUTE_DATA;
```

Although it's not frequently done, you can alter any of these file attributes by calling *SetFileAttributes*:

```
BOOL SetFileAttributes(LPTSTR lpFileName, DWORD dwFileAttributes);
```

SetFileAttributes returns TRUE if it successfully alters the file's attributes. The following code turns off the archive flag for CALC.EXE:

```
DWORD dwFileAttributes = GetFileAttributes("CALC.EXE");
dwFileAttributes &= ~FILE_ATTRIBUTE_ARCHIVE;
SetFileAttributes("CALC.EXE", dwFileAttributes);
```

There are some limitations when using *SetFileAttributes*. For example, you cannot change a file into a directory (or vice versa) by using the FILE_ATTRIBUTE_DIRECTORY flag. Nor can you compress a file simply by specifying the FILE_ATTRIBUTE_COMPRESSED flag. To compress a file, you must call the *DeviceIoControl* function using the FSCTL_SET_COMPRESSION operation.

You can also use the COMPACT.EXE utility that ships with Windows NT to compress files and directories.

File Size

You might also want to query a file's size by calling *GetFileSize*:

```
DWORD GetFileSize(HANDLE hFile, LPDWORD lpdwFileSizeHigh);
```

You'll immediately notice that the *GetFileSize* function requires that the file be open and that the handle to the file be passed as the *hFile* parameter. You get this handle by calling the *CreateFile* function, which is discussed in Chapter 15. *GetFileSize* returns the low 32-bit value representing the file's size directly. If you are interested in the high 32-bit part of the file's size, you need to pass an address to a DWORD that *GetFileSize* will fill with this information. A file's size can be altered only by writing to the file or by calling *SetEndOfFile*.

GetFileSize returns the full size of the file, which is what you want 99 percent of the time. On rare occasions, you might want to know the compressed size of a file. You can get this information by calling *GetCompressedFileSize*:

```
DWORD GetCompressedFileSize(LPCTSTR lpFileName,
    LPDWORD lpFileSizeHigh);
```

Unlike *GetFileSize*, this function does not require a handle to the file; you simply pass in the pathname of the file instead. However, the *lpFileSizeHigh* and return value have the same meaning as they have for the *GetFileSize* function.

File Time Stamps

In MS-DOS, and more specifically in FAT file systems prior to Windows 95 and Windows NT 3.5, a file has only one time stamp associated with it—the stamp indicating the last time the file was written to. But in recent FAT file systems, as well as in NTFS, a file can have three time stamps associated with it: the date and time the file was created, the date and time the file was last accessed, and the date and time the file was last written to (or modified). To retrieve the time stamp information for a file, call

```
BOOL GetFileTime(HANDLE hFile, LPFILETIME lpftCreation,
    LPFILETIME lpftLastAccess, LPFILETIME lpftLastWrite);
```

As with *GetFileSize*, the file must be opened before the call to *Get-FileTime* is made so that we can pass its file handle as the *hFile* parameter. The next three parameters are all pointers to FILETIME structures:

```
typedef struct _FILETIME {
    DWORD dwLowDateTime;
    DWORD dwHighDateTime;
} FILETIME, *PFILETIME, *LPFILETIME;
```

If you aren't interested in when the file was created, you can pass in NULL as the *lpftCreation* parameter. The same is true for either of the other two time stamp parameters.

The 64-bit value composed of the *dwLowDateTime* and *dwHighDate-Time* members in the FILETIME structure represents the number of 100-nanosecond intervals since January 1, 1601. I'll grant you that this isn't very useful, but the date does, after all, mark the start of a new quadricentury. Still not too impressed? I guess Microsoft didn't think you'd be too impressed either, so it wrote some additional functions to help you realize the usefulness of file times.

Perhaps all you need to do is check to see which of two files is older. That's easy:

```
LONG CompareFileTime(LPFILETIME lpft1, LPFILETIME lpft2);
```

CompareFileTime returns one of these long values:

Result of *CompareFileTime*	Meaning
−1	*lpft1* is less than (older than) *lpft2*
0	*lpft1* is same (age) as *lpft2*
+1	*lpft1* is greater than (younger than) *lpft2*

Using *CompareFileTime*, you can also check to see whether a file was written to the last time it was accessed:

```
lResult = CompareFileTime(&ftLastAccess, &ftLastWrite);
if (lResult == 0) {
    // Last access was a write
} else {
    // Last access was not a write
}
```

You might want to show the user one of the file's time stamps. In this case, you will need to convert FILETIME structures to SYSTEM-TIME structures, or vice versa, using

```
BOOL FileTimeToSystemTime(LPFILETIME lpft, LPSYSTEMTIME lpst);
```

and

```
BOOL SystemTimeToFileTime(LPSYSTEMTIME lpst, LPFILETIME lpft);
```

These functions convert the time stamp easily between the FILETIME and SYSTEMTIME structures.

A SYSTEMTIME structure looks like this:

```
typedef struct _SYSTEMTIME {
    WORD wYear;
    WORD wMonth;
    WORD wDayOfWeek;
    WORD wDay;
    WORD wHour;
    WORD wMinute;
    WORD wSecond;
    WORD wMilliseconds;
} SYSTEMTIME;
typedef SYSTEMTIME *PSYSTEMTIME, *LPSYSTEMTIME;
```

With this information, it's easy to construct a string that will be meaningful to an end user. Note that when you convert from SYSTEMTIME to FILETIME, the *wDayOfWeek* member in the SYSTEMTIME structure is ignored.

You can convert a file's time to local time and back again by using these functions:

```
BOOL FileTimeToLocalFileTime(LPFILETIME lpft,
    LPFILETIME lpftLocal);
```

and

```
BOOL LocalFileTimeToFileTime(LPFILETIME lpftLocal,
    LPFILETIME lpft);
```

Both these functions take two pointers to FILETIME structures. When you use these functions, be careful not to pass the same address as both parameters—the functions won't work correctly.

And if you're an MS-DOS and FAT diehard who doesn't want to port the existing file time stamp code in your applications over to the new way of doing things just yet, you can use these two functions to convert a FILETIME structure to the time format used by MS-DOS and vice versa:

```
BOOL FileTimeToDosDateTime(LPFILETIME lpft,
    LPWORD lpwDOSDate, LPWORD lpwDOSTime);
```

```
BOOL DosDateTimeToFileTime(WORD wDOSDate, WORD wDOSTime,
    LPFILETIME lpft);
```

The *FileTimeToDosDateTime* function takes the address of the FILE-TIME structure containing the file's time and converts it to two WORD values that MS-DOS uses—one WORD for the date and the other WORD for the time.

Important

Under Windows 95, the *FileTimeToDosDateTime* and *DosDateTimeToFile-Time* functions allow dates up to 12/31/2099. Under Windows NT, these functions allow dates up to 12/31/2107.

After you have manipulated and converted the time values all you want, you can change the time associated with a file by calling *GetFile-Time*'s complementary function:

```
BOOL SetFileTime(HANDLE hFile, LPFILETIME lpftCreation,
    LPFILETIME lpftLastAccess, LPFILETIME lpftLastWrite);
```

If you don't want to change one or more time stamps of the file, you can pass in NULL for the desired parameters.

The other way to get the attribute information associated with a file is to call the *GetFileInformationByHandle* function:

```
BOOL GetFileInformationByHandle(HANDLE hFile,
    LPBY_HANDLE_FILE_INFORMATION lpFileInformation);
```

This function requires the handle of an open file identified by the *hFile* parameter and the address of a BY_HANDLE_FILE_INFORMATION structure, which the function fills with information about the file:

```
typedef struct _BY_HANDLE_FILE_INFORMATION {
    DWORD dwFileAttributes;
    FILETIME ftCreationTime;
    FILETIME ftLastAccessTime;
    FILETIME ftLastWriteTime;
    DWORD dwVolumeSerialNumber;
    DWORD nFileSizeHigh;
    DWORD nFileSizeLow;
    DWORD nNumberOfLinks;
    DWORD nFileIndexHigh;
    DWORD nFileIndexLow;
} BY_HANDLE_FILE_INFORMATION,
    *PBY_HANDLE_FILE_INFORMATION, *LPBY_HANDLE_FILE_INFORMATION;
```

The *GetFileInformationByHandle* function gathers all of the attribute information available for the file. In addition to the file attributes contained in the *dwFileAttributes* member and the three time stamps that are contained in the *ftCreationTime*, *ftLastAccessTime*, and *ftLastWriteTime* members, the function gets the serial number of the disk volume on which the file resides in the *dwVolumeSerialNumber* member, and the file's size in the *nFileSizeHigh* and *nFileSizeLow* members. It finds the number of links (used by the POSIX subsystem in Windows NT) in the *nNumber-OfLinks* member.

The system assigns every file, each time it's opened, a unique ID contained in the *nFileIndexHigh* and *nFileIndexLow* members. The ID might not be constant across openings of the file and will almost definitely be different if the file is opened during a different session. However, if one application opens a file and another application opens the same file, the ID will be the same. An application can use the ID in conjunction with the volume's serial number to determine whether two (or more) different file handles reference the same file.

Creating Temporary Files

Many applications need to create temporary files while they operate. Win32 offers two functions that make it easy to create temporary files:

```
DWORD GetTempPath(DWORD nBufferLength, LPTSTR lpBuffer);
```

```
UINT GetTempFileName(LPCTSTR lpPathName, LPCTSTR lpPrefixString,
    UINT uUnique, LPTSTR lpTempFileName);
```

GetTempPath fills the *lpBuffer* pointed to by *lpBuffer* with the full path where the operating system stores temporary files. The temporary path is determined as follows:

1. If a TMP environment variable is defined, it identifies the path.

2. If TMP is not defined, the TEMP environment variable identifies the path.

3. If both TMP and TEMP are not defined, the current directory is used.

The *GetTempFileName* function constructs a filename that is guaranteed not to conflict with an existing file. The *lpPathName* parameter must identify the directory where the temporary file should be created. You will usually call *GetTempPath* first and pass the returned buffer for this parameter. The *lpPrefixString* parameter identifies a three-character prefix that the temporary file name will start with. This prefix is used so that an application can identify the temporary files that it creates.

The *uUnique* parameter should almost always be 0 (zero). When this parameter is zero, *GetTempFileName* uses the system time to create a unique suffix for the filename. If a temporary file with this name exists, the system uses an algorithm until it arrives at a unique filename. When a unique name has been found, *GetTempFileName* creates the file and returns the file's name in the buffer pointed to by *GetTempFileName*'s *lpTempFileName* parameter.

If *uUnique* is not zero, *GetTempFileName* simply constructs a filename using the specified three-character prefix and the unique number (converted to hex) and returns the filename in the buffer pointed to by *GetTempFileName*'s *lpTempFileName* parameter. When you pass a nonzero value for *uUnique*, *GetTempFileName* does not attempt to ensure that the filename is unique, nor does it attempt to create the file. To work with this temporary file, you will have to open it calling *CreateFile* (discussed in Chapter 15).

DEVICE I/O

One of the strengths of both Microsoft Windows NT and Microsoft Windows 95 is the sheer number of devices that they support. In this context, I define a device to be anything that allows communication. The following table lists some devices and their most common usage:

Device	Most Common Usage
File	Persistent storage of arbitrary data
Directory	Attributes and file compression
Logical disk drive	Formatting
Physical disk drive	Partition table access
Serial port	Data transmission over a phone line
Parallel port	Data transmission to a printer
Mailslot	One-to-many transmission of data, usually over a network to a Windows machine
Named pipe	One-to-one transmission of data, usually over a network to a Windows machine
Anonymous pipe	One-to-one transmission of data on a single machine (never over the network)
Socket	Datagram or stream transmission of data, usually over a network to any machine supporting sockets (the machine need not be running Windows)
Console	A text window screen buffer

In this chapter, we discuss the Win32 device architecture. As you'll see, Win32 tries to hide device differences from the software developer as much as possible. That is, once you open a device, the Win32 functions that allow you to read and write data to the device are the same no matter what device you are communicating with. The bulk of this chapter explains the different mechanisms available for reading and writing data to devices.

Although only a few Win32 functions are available for reading and writing data regardless of the device, devices are certainly different from one another. For example, it makes sense to set a baud rate for serial communications, but a baud rate has no meaning when using a named pipe to communicate over a network (or the local machine). Because these different devices have many subtle differences, I will not attempt to address all the nuances of all these devices. However, I will spend some additional time addressing files since files are so common.

Opening and Closing Devices

To perform any type of I/O, you must first open the desired device and get a handle to it. How you get the handle to a device depends on the specific device. The table on the facing page lists various devices and the functions you should call to open them.

All of these functions return a 32-bit handle that identifies the device. You can pass the handle to various functions to communicate with the device. For example, you call *SetCommConfig* to set the baud rate of a serial port:

```
BOOL SetCommConfig(HANDLE hCommDev, LPCOMMCONFIG lpCC,
    DWORD dwSize);
```

And you use *SetMailslotInfo* to set the time-out value when waiting to read data:

```
BOOL SetMailslotInfo(HANDLE hMailslot, DWORD lReadTimeout);
```

As you can see, these functions require a handle to a device for their first argument.

When you are finished manipulating a device, you must close it. On most devices, you do this by calling the very popular *CloseHandle*:

```
BOOL CloseHandle(HANDLE hObject);
```

However, if the device is a socket, you must call *closesocket* instead:

```
int closesocket(SOCKET s);
```

Also, if you have a handle to a device, you can find out what type of device it is by calling *GetFileType*:

```
DWORD GetFileType(HANDLE hFile);
```

Device	Function Used to Open the Device
File	*CreateFile* (*pszName* is pathname or UNC pathname)
Directory[1]	*CreateFile* (*pszName* is dirname or UNC dirname using **FILE_FLAG_BACKUP_SEMANTICS**)
Logical drive[2]	*CreateFile* (*pszName* is "\\.\x:")
Physical drive[3]	*CreateFile* (*pszName* is "\\.\PHYSICALDRIVE*x*")
Serial port	*CreateFile* (*pszName* is "COM?")
Parallel port	*CreateFile* (*pszName* is "LPT?")
Mailslot server	*CreateMailslot* (*pszName* is "\\.\mailslot*mailslotname*")
Mailslot client	*CreateFile* (*pszName* is "*servername*\mailslot*mailslotname*")
Named pipe server	*CreateNamedPipe* (*pszName* is "\\.\pipe*pipename*")
Named pipe client	*CreateFile* (*pszName* is "*servername*\pipe*pipename*")
Anonymous pipe client and server	*CreatePipe*
Socket	*socket, accept, AcceptEx*
Console	*CreateConsoleScreenBuffer, GetStdHandle*

1. Windows NT allows you to open a directory if you specify the FILE_FLAG_BACKUP_SEMANTICS flag in the call to *CreateFile*. This allows you to change the directory's attributes (normal, hidden, and so on) and its time stamp. Windows 95 does not allow you to open a directory.

2. Windows NT allows you to open a logical drive if you specify a string in the form of "\\.\x:" where *x* is a drive letter. For example, to open drive A, you specify "\\.\A:". Opening a drive allows you to format the drive or determine the media size of the drive. Windows 95 does not allow you to open a logical drive.

3. Windows NT allows you to open a physical drive if you specify a string in the form of "\\.\PHYSICALDRIVE*x*" where *x* is a physical drive number. For example, to read or write to physical sectors on the user's first physical hard disk, you specify "\\.\PHYSICALDRIVE0". Opening a physical drive allows you to access the hard drive's partition tables directly. Opening the physical drive is potentially dangerous; an incorrect write to the drive could make the disk's contents inaccessible by the operating system's file system. Windows 95 does not allow you to open a physical drive.

All you do is pass to this function the handle to a device and the function returns one of the values indicated in the following table:

Flag	Description
FILE_TYPE_UNKNOWN	The type of the specified file is unknown.
FILE_TYPE_DISK	The specified file is a disk file.
FILE_TYPE_CHAR	The specified file is a character file, typically an LPT device or a console.
FILE_TYPE_PIPE	The specified file is either a named or an anonymous pipe.

A Detailed Look at *CreateFile*

As you can see from the table on the preceding page, most devices are opened using the *CreateFile* function:

```
HANDLE CreateFile(LPCTSTR pszName, DWORD dwDesiredAccess,
    DWORD dwShareMode, LPSECURITY_ATTRIBUTES pSecurityAttributes,
    DWORD dwCreationDistribution, DWORD dwFlagsAndAttrs,
    HANDLE hTemplateFile);
```

Don't let the name of this function fool you. Of course this function creates and opens disk files, but it opens lots of other devices as well.

In 16-bit Windows, files are created and opened by means of the *OpenFile*, *_lcreat*, and *_lopen* functions. For backward compatibility, these functions were carried over into Win32, but they're considered obsolete, and you should avoid using them. For Win32 applications, files should be created or opened by means of the much more powerful *CreateFile* function.

When you call this function, the *pszName* parameter identifies the type of device as well as a specific instance of the device. The table on page 699 shows the various device syntaxes that *CreateFile* recognizes.

If you are opening a file, you can pass a pathname that is up to _MAX_PATH (defined as 260) characters long. However, on Windows NT you can transcend this limit by calling *CreateFileW* (the Unicode version of the function) and precede the pathname with "\\?\". If you prefix these characters to your path, *CreateFileW* will remove this prefix and allow you to pass a path that is almost 32,000 Unicode characters long. Remember, however, that you must use fully qualified paths when using this prefix; the system does not process relative directories such as "." and "..".

The *dwDesiredAccess* parameter specifies how you want to transmit data to and from the device. You can pass four possible values here, as shown in the following table:

Value	Meaning
0	You do not intend to read or write data to the device. Pass 0 when you just want to change the device's configuration settings—for example, if you want to change only a file's time stamp.
GENERIC_READ	Allows read-only access from the device.
GENERIC_WRITE	Allows write-only access to the device. Note that GENERIC_WRITE does not imply GENERIC_READ. This value is used to send data to a printer and by backup software.
GENERIC_READ | GENERIC_WRITE	Allows both read and write access to the device. This value is the most common since it allows the free exchange of data.

The *dwShareMode* parameter specifies device-sharing privileges. In Windows 95 and Windows NT more so than in 16-bit Windows, it is likely that a single device can and will be accessed by several computers at the same time (in a networking environment) or by several processes at the same time (in a multithreaded environment). The potential for device sharing means that you must think about whether you should and how you will restrict other computers or processes from accessing the device's data. The table on the next page shows the possible values that can be passed for the *dwShareMode* parameter and their meanings.

Value	Meaning
0	You want exclusive access to the device. If the device is already opened, *CreateFile* fails. If you open the device and *CreateFile* is called in the future to open the device, the second call to *CreateFile* fails.
FILE_SHARE_READ	You want the device to be read-only. If the device is already opened for writing, *CreateFile* fails. If you open the device and *CreateFile* is called in the future to open the device for writing, the second call to *CreateFile* fails.
FILE_SHARE_WRITE	You want the device to be write-only. If the device is already opened for reading, *CreateFile* fails. If you open the device and *CreateFile* is called in the future to open the device for reading, the second call to *CreateFile* fails.
FILE_SHARE_READ | FILE_SHARE_WRITE	You want the device to be readable and writable. If the device is already opened for exclusive access, *CreateFile* fails. If you open the device and *CreateFile* is called in the future to open the device for reading or writing, the second call to *CreateFile* succeeds.

The fourth parameter of *CreateFile* is *pSecurityAttributes*. As always, this parameter points to a SECURITY_ATTRIBUTES structure that allows you to specify security information with the device's associated kernel object and whether the returned handle should be inheritable (allowing child processes to access the device). The parameter can be NULL if you want default security for the object and the handle to be noninheritable.

The *dwCreationDistribution* parameter is most meaningful when *CreateFile* is being called to open a file as opposed to another type of device. The following table indicates the possible values that you can pass for this parameter:

When you are calling *CreateFile* to open a device other than a file, you should pass OPEN_EXISTING for the *dwCreationDistribution* parameter.

CreateFile's *dwFlagsAndAttrs* parameter has two purposes: it allows you to set flags that fine-tune the communication with the device, and if the device is a file, you also get to set the file's attributes. We'll take a look at the flags first and then discuss the file attributes.

Identifier	Meaning
CREATE_NEW	Tells *CreateFile* to create a new file and to fail if a file with the same name already exists.
CREATE_ALWAYS	Tells *CreateFile* to create a file regardless of whether a file with the same name already exists. If the file already exists, *CreateFile* overwrites the existing file.
OPEN_EXISTING	Tells *CreateFile* to open an existing file and to fail if the file doesn't already exist.
OPEN_ALWAYS	Tells *CreateFile* to open a file if it exists and to create the file if it doesn't exist.
TRUNCATE_EXISTING	Tells *CreateFile* to open an existing file, truncate its size to 0 bytes, and fail if the file doesn't already exist. The GENERIC_WRITE flag must be used with this flag.

Most of these flags are signals that tell the system how you intend to access the device. The system can then optimize its caching algorithms to help your application work more efficiently.

The FILE_FLAG_NO_BUFFERING flag affects I/O to and from the file systems. To improve performance, the system caches data to and from disk drives. Normally, you would not specify this flag, and the cache manager will keep recently accessed portions of the file system in memory. This way, if you read a couple of bytes from a file and then read a few more bytes, the file's data is most likely loaded in memory and the disk needs to be accessed only once instead of twice. This greatly improves performance. However, it does mean that portions of the file's data are in memory twice: the cache manager has a buffer, and you have called some function (such as *ReadFile*) that has copied some of the data from the cache manager's buffer into your own buffer.

In addition, when the cache manager is buffering data, it may also read-ahead so that the next bytes you're likely to read are already in memory. Again, speed is improved by reading more bytes than necessary from the file. However, memory is potentially wasted if you never attempt to read further in the file. (See the FILE_FLAG_SEQUENTIAL-_SCAN and FILE_FLAG_RANDOM_ACCESS flags below for more about read-ahead.)

By specifying the FILE_FLAG_NO_BUFFERING flag, you tell the cache manager that you do not want it to buffer any data—you take on this responsibility yourself! Depending on what you're doing, this flag may improve your application's speed and memory usage. Because the file system's device driver is writing the file's data directly into the buffers that you supply, you must follow certain rules:

- You must always access the file using offsets that are exact multiples of the disk volume's sector size.[1]

- You must always read/write a number of bytes that is an exact multiple of the sector size.

- You must make sure that the buffer in your process's address space begins on an address that is evenly divisible by the sector size.

The next two flags, FILE_FLAG_SEQUENTIAL_SCAN and FILE_FLAG_RANDOM_ACCESS, are useful only if you allow the system to buffer the file data for you. If you specify the FILE_FLAG_NO_BUFFERING flag, both these flags are ignored.

If you specify the FILE_FLAG_SEQUENTIAL_SCAN flag, the system thinks that you are accessing the file sequentially. When you read some data from the file, the system will actually read more of the file's data than what you requested. This reduces the number of hits to the hard disk and improves the speed of your application. If you perform any direct seeks on the file, the system has spent a little extra time and memory caching data that you are not accessing. This is perfectly OK, but if you do it often, you'd be better off specifying the FILE_FLAG_RANDOM_ACCESS flag. This flag tells the system not to preread file data.

The last cache-related flag is FILE_FLAG_WRITE_THROUGH. This flag disables intermediate caching of file-write operations to reduce the potential for data loss. When you specify this flag, the system writes all file modifications directly to the disk. However, the system still maintains an internal cache of the file's data, and file-read operations use the cached data (if available) instead of reading data directly from the disk. When this flag is used to open a file on a network server, the Win32 file-write functions do not return to the calling thread until the data is written to the server's disk drive.

---

1. Use the *GetDiskFreeSpace* function to determine the disk volume's sector size.

That's it for the buffer-related flags. The remaining *CreateFile dw-FlagsAndAttrs* flags don't fall into any one category.

Use the FILE_FLAG_DELETE_ON_CLOSE flag to have the system delete the file after the file is closed. This flag is most frequently used with the FILE_ATTRIBUTE_TEMPORARY attribute. When these two flags are used together, your application can create a temporary file, write to it, read from it, and close it. When the file is closed, the system automatically deletes the file—what a convenience! If your process closes its handle to the file and the same file is opened by somebody else, the system won't immediately close the file. The system will wait until all open handles to the file are closed before deleting it.

Use the FILE_FLAG_BACKUP_SEMANTICS flag in backup and restore software. Before opening or creating any files, the system normally performs security checks to be sure that the process trying to open or create a file has the requisite access privileges. However, backup and restore software is special in that it can override certain file security checks. When you specify the FILE_FLAG_BACKUP_SEMANTICS flag, the system checks to be sure that a process has the access rights and, if it does, allows the file to be opened for backup or restore purposes only. You can also use the FILE_FLAG_BACKUP_SEMANTICS flag to open a handle to a directory.

Windows 95 does not support the FILE_FLAG_BACKUP_SEMANTICS flag.

Use the FILE_FLAG_POSIX_SEMANTICS flag to tell the system to use POSIX rules for accessing a file. File systems used by POSIX allow case-sensitive filenames. This means that the files named JEFFREY.DOC, Jeffrey.Doc, and jeffrey.doc are all different files. MS-DOS, 16-bit Windows, and Win32 were designed to expect that filenames would be case-insensitive. Use the FILE_FLAG_POSIX_SEMANTICS flag with extreme caution. If you use this flag when you create a file, that file might not be accessible to MS-DOS, 16-bit Windows, and Win32 applications.

The last flag, FILE_FLAG_OVERLAPPED, tells the system that you want to access a device asynchronously. You'll notice that the default way of opening a device is for synchronous I/O (not specifying FILE_FLAG-_OVERLAPPED). Synchronous I/O is what most MS-DOS and 16-bit Windows developers are used to. When you read data from a file, your program is suspended, waiting for the information to be read. Once the information has been read, your program regains control and continues executing.

Because device I/O is slow when compared with most other operations, you might want to consider communicating with some devices asynchronously. Basically, you call a function telling the operating system to read or write data; but instead of waiting for the I/O to complete, your call returns immediately, and the operating system finishes the I/O on your behalf using its own threads. When the operating system has finished performing your requested I/O, you can be notified. Asynchronous I/O can be a very convenient means of designing an application, especially a server application. Win32 offers several different methods of asynchronous I/O, all of which are discussed later in this chapter.

Windows 95 does not support asynchronous I/O when using files. However, some asynchronous I/O is available for other devices, such as serial ports.

Now it's time to examine the file attribute flags. These flags are completely ignored unless you are creating a brand new file and you pass NULL for *CreateFile*'s *hTemplateFile* parameter. Most of the attributes should already be familiar to you.

Identifier	Meaning
FILE_ATTRIBUTE_ARCHIVE	The file is an archive file. Applications use this flag to mark files for backup or removal. When *CreateFile* creates a new file, this flag is automatically set.
FILE_ATTRIBUTE_HIDDEN	The file is hidden. It won't be included in an ordinary directory listing.
FILE_ATTRIBUTE_NORMAL	The file has no other attributes set. This attribute is valid only if it's used alone.
FILE_ATTRIBUTE_READONLY	The file is read-only. Applications can read the file but can't write to it or delete it.
FILE_ATTRIBUTE_SYSTEM	The file is part of the operating system or is used exclusively by the operating system.

(continued)

Identifier	Meaning
FILE_ATTRIBUTE_COMPRESSED	The file or directory is compressed. For a file, this means that all the data in the file is compressed. For a directory, this means that compression is the default for newly created files and subdirectories.
FILE_ATTRIBUTE_OFFLINE	The file exists, but its data has been moved to offline storage. This flag is useful for hierarchical storage systems.
FILE_ATTRIBUTE_TEMPORARY	The file's data is going to be used only for a short time. The file system tries to keep the file's data in RAM rather than on disk to keep the access time to a minimum.

Use FILE_ATTRIBUTE_TEMPORARY if you are creating a temporary file. When *CreateFile* creates a file with the temporary attribute, it tries to keep the file's data in memory instead of on the disk. This makes accessing the file's contents much faster. If you keep writing to the file and the system can no longer keep the data in RAM, the operating system will be forced to start writing the data to the hard disk. You can improve the system's performance by combining the FILE_ATTRIBUTE_TEMPORARY flag with the FILE_FLAG_DELETE_ON_CLOSE flag (discussed earlier). Normally, the system flushes a file's cached data when the file is closed. However, if the system sees that the file is to be deleted when it is closed, the system doesn't need to flush the file's cached data.

CreateFile's last parameter, *hTemplateFile*, identifies the handle of an open file or is NULL. If *hTemplateFile* identifies a file handle, *CreateFile* ignores the attribute flags in the *dwFlagsAndAttrs* parameter completely and uses the attributes associated with the file identified by *hTemplateFile*. The file identified by *hTemplateFile* must have been opened with the GENERIC_READ flag for this to work. If *CreateFile* is opening an existing file (as opposed to creating a new file), the *hTemplateFile* parameter is ignored.

Under Windows 95, the *hTemplateFile* parameter must always be NULL or *CreateFile* will always fail; calling *GetLastError* returns ERROR_NOT-_SUPPORTED.

If *CreateFile* succeeds in creating or opening a file or device, the handle of the file/device is returned. If *CreateFile* fails, INVALID_HAN-DLE_VALUE is returned.

Important

Most Win32 functions that return a handle return NULL if the function fails. However, *CreateFile* returns INVALID_HANDLE_VALUE (defined as 0xFFFFFFFF) instead. I have often seen code like this:

```
HANDLE hFile = CreateFile(...);
if (hFile == NULL) {
   // We'll never get in here
} else {
   // File may or may not be created OK
}
   .
   .
   .
```

This code is incorrect. Here's the correct way to check for an invalid file handle:

```
HANDLE hFile = CreateFile(...);
if (hFile == INVALID_HANDLE_VALUE) {
   // File not created
} else {
   // File created OK
}
   .
   .
   .
```

Working with File Devices

Because working with files is so common, I want to spend some time addressing issues that apply specifically to file devices. This section shows how to position a file's pointer, change a file's size, and unlock and lock regions within a file.

Positioning a File Pointer

When *CreateFile* returns a handle to a file, the system associates a file pointer with the handle. This file pointer indicates the 64-bit offset within the file where the next synchronous read or write should be performed. Initially, this file pointer is set to 0; so if you call *ReadFile* immediately after a call to *CreateFile*, you will start reading from offset 0 in the file. If you read 100 bytes of the file into memory, the system updates the pointer associated with the file handle so that the next call to *ReadFile* starts reading at the 101st byte in the file. Remember that a file pointer is associated with a file handle and not with file operations or the file kernel object itself. For example, look at this code:

```
HFILE hFile = CreateFile(…);
ReadFile(hFile, lpBuffer, 100, &dwBytesRead, NULL);
WriteFile(hFile, lpBuffer, 100, &dwBytesWritten, NULL);
```

In this code fragment, the first 100 bytes from the file are read into the buffer, and these same 100 bytes are written to the file. The bytes are written from offset 100 in the file to offset 199. If there is another file operation after the call to *WriteFile*, it will start at offset 200 in the file.

It is also possible to open the same file two or more times. Every time the file is opened, a new file handle is returned. Because a file pointer is associated with each file handle, file manipulations using one file handle don't affect the pointer associated with other file handles, even if all handles refer to the same file. Look at this code:

```
HFILE hFile1 = CreateFile("MYFILE.DAT", …);
HFILE hFile2 = CreateFile("MYFILE.DAT", …);
ReadFile(hFile1 lpBuffer, 100, &dwBytesRead, NULL);
WriteFile(hFile2, lpBuffer, 100, &dwBytesWritten, NULL);
```

In this code, the first 100 bytes from MYFILE.DAT are read into a buffer. After this read, the pointer associated with *hFile1* points to the 101st byte in the file. Now the code writes 100 bytes back to the same file. In this case, the pointer associated with *hFile2* is still initialized to 0, causing the first 100 bytes in MYFILE.DAT to be overwritten with the same data that was originally read from the file. The net result is that there is no change to the contents of the file. But after the calls to *ReadFile* and *WriteFile* have been completed, both handles' file pointers point to the 101st byte in the file.

If you need to access a file randomly, you will need to alter the file pointer associated with the file's handle. You do this by calling *SetFilePointer*, as shown on the next page.

```
DWORD SetFilePointer(HANDLE hFile, LONG lDistanceToMove,
   PLONG lpDistanceToMoveHigh, DWORD dwMoveMethod);
```

The *hFile* parameter identifies the file handle the pointer is associated with. The *lDistanceToMove* parameter tells the system by how many bytes you want to move the pointer. The number you specify is added to the current value of the file's pointer, so a negative number has the effect of stepping backward in the file. For most files, being able to move the pointer forward or backward by a 32-bit value is good enough. But for really big files, you might need a 64-bit value.

These giant files are exactly what the *lpDistanceToMoveHigh* parameter is for. If you are moving the pointer within plus or minus 2 GB of its current position, pass NULL in the *lpDistanceToMoveHigh* parameter. If you want to move the pointer somewhere within 18 billion GB of its current position, you need to pass the high 32-bit part of this value in the *lpDistanceToMoveHigh* parameter. Actually, you can't pass the high 32-bit part of the value directly; you must store the value in a variable and pass the address of this variable as the parameter.

The reason for this indirection is that *SetFilePointer* returns the previous location of the file pointer. If all you are interested in is the low 32 bits of this pointer, the function returns that value directly. If you are also interested in the high 32 bits of the pointer, the *SetFilePointer* function fills the variable pointed to by *lpDistanceToMoveHigh* before it returns.

The last parameter, *dwMoveMethod*, tells *SetFilePointer* how to interpret the two parameters *lDistanceToMove* and *lpDistanceToMoveHigh*. Here are the three possible values you can pass via *dwMoveMethod* to specify the starting point for the move:

Identifier	Meaning
FILE_BEGIN	The file's pointer becomes the unsigned value specified by the two *DistanceToMove* parameters.
FILE_CURRENT	The file's pointer is added to the signed value specified by the two *DistanceToMove* parameters.
FILE_END	The file's pointer becomes the number of bytes in the file added to the signed value specified by the two *DistanceToMove* parameters. The *DistanceToMove* parameters should identify a negative number in this case.

710

If *SetFilePointer* fails to alter the file's pointer, it returns 0xFFFFFFFF and the contents of the *lpDistanceToMoveHigh* buffer will contain NULL. Because it is possible for a large file to be positioned successfully to location 0xFFFFFFFF, it is better to verify that *SetFilePointer* is successful by calling *GetLastError* and checking to see whether it returns NO_ERROR.

Setting the End of a File

Usually, the system takes care of setting the end of a file when the file is closed. However, you might sometimes want to force a file to be smaller or larger. On those occasions, call

```
BOOL SetEndOfFile(HANDLE hFile);
```

This *SetEndOfFile* function changes the length of a file so that the value indicated by the file pointer becomes the length of the file. For example, if you wanted to force a file to be 1024 bytes long, you'd use *SetEndOfFile* this way:

```
HFILE hFile = CreateFile(…);
SetFilePointer(hFile, 1024, NULL, FILE_BEGIN);
SetEndOfFile(hFile);
CloseHandle(hFile);
```

If you use the Explorer to examine the directory containing this file, you'll see that the file is exactly 1024 bytes long.

Locking and Unlocking Regions of a File

The FILE_SHARE_READ and FILE_SHARE_WRITE flags let you tell the system whether and how a file can be opened by others. But think of a company that has a large customer database that contains a million records. Such a database is probably opened by almost everyone in the company. If everybody is performing searches only, that's fine—the file can always be opened with just the FILE_SHARE_READ flag specified. But what if a group in the company needs to enter additional names and addresses in the customer database? These employees will need to open the database for writing. And somehow, write access will need to be coordinated so that when one employee is appending a record to the database, another employee won't be able to append a record at the same time. If both employees were able to write to the database simultaneously, the integrity of the database would be compromised. File locking is a solution to this problem.

File locking is similar to using the FILE_SHARE_* flags, but the FILE_SHARE_* flags affect an entire file, whereas file locking affects small sections of a file. For example, if a customer moves to a new address, you'll need to update the customer's record. Before you write out the new information, you'll want to be sure that no one else can access the customer's data record while you're updating it. You'll want to lock that part of the database by calling

```
BOOL LockFile(HANDLE hFile, DWORD dwFileOffsetLow,
    DWORD dwFileOffsetHigh, DWORD cbLockLow, DWORD cbLockHigh);
```

The first parameter, *hFile*, identifies the handle to the file you want to lock a subsection of. The next two parameters, *dwFileOffsetLow* and *dwFileOffsetHigh*, specify the 64-bit offset into the file where you want to begin the file lock. The last two parameters, *cbLockLow* and *cbLockHigh*, specify the number of bytes you want to lock. If you were going to update the 100th customer record in the database, you would use *LockFile* this way:

```
LockFile(hFile, sizeof(CUSTOMER_RECORD) * (100 - 1), 0,
    sizeof(CUSTOMER_RECORD), 0);
```

If *LockFile* is successful, TRUE is returned. While a region of a file is locked, all other processes that try to read from or write to the locked region will fail. This is why it's crucial to check the number of bytes read or written when *ReadFile* and *WriteFile* return—in case some other process has already locked regions of the file. You must design your program to handle such a case gracefully, perhaps by allowing the user to close other applications and try to read or write the data again.

It's perfectly legal to lock a region that falls beyond the current end of the file. You'd want to do that when you were adding customer records to the end of the file. You'd lock the region of the file just beyond the end of the file and write the new customer record to this region.

Note that you can't lock a region that includes an already locked region. The second call to *LockFile* here, for example, will fail:

```
LockFile(hFile, sizeof(CUSTOMER_RECORD) * (100 - 1), 0,
    sizeof(CUSTOMER_RECORD), 0);
```

```
LockFile(hFile, sizeof(CUSTOMER_RECORD) * (100 - 2), 0,
    2 * sizeof(CUSTOMER_RECORD), 0);
```

In the first call to *LockFile*, we locked the 100th customer record. In the second call, we're trying to lock the 99th through 100th customer records. Because the 100th record has already been locked, this second call fails.

Naturally, when you have finished with a locked region of a file, you'll need to unlock it:

```
BOOL UnlockFile(HANDLE hFile, DWORD dwFileOffsetLow,
    DWORD dwFileOffsetHigh, DWORD cbUnlockLow, DWORD cbUnlockHigh);
```

The *UnlockFile* parameters correspond to the *LockFile* parameters, and the return value is the same. When you unlock a region, you must unlock it in the same way that it was locked. For example, the following calls won't work together correctly:

```
LockFile(hFile, sizeof(CUSTOMER_RECORD) * (100 - 1), 0,
    sizeof(CUSTOMER_RECORD), 0);

LockFile(hFile, sizeof(CUSTOMER_RECORD) * (100 - 2), 0,
    sizeof(CUSTOMER_RECORD), 0);

UnlockFile(hFile, sizeof(CUSTOMER_RECORD) * (100 - 2), 0,
    2 * sizeof(CUSTOMER_RECORD), 0);
```

The first two calls to *LockFile* lock the 100th and 99th records of the database, respectively. Then the call to *UnlockFile* tries to unlock both records with one call. This call to *UnlockFile* will fail. If two separate calls are made to *LockFile*, two separate and similar calls must be made to *UnlockFile*.

Important

Remember to unlock all locked regions of a file before you close the file or terminate the process.

You can call two other functions to lock and unlock a region of a file:

```
BOOL LockFileEx(HANDLE hFile, DWORD dwFlags, DWORD dwReserved,
    DWORD nNumberOfBytesToLockLow, DWORD nNumberOfBytesToLockHigh,
    LPOVERLAPPED lpOverlapped);

BOOL UnlockFileEx(HANDLE hFile, DWORD dwReserved,
    DWORD nNumberOfBytesToUnlockLow,
    DWORD nNumberOfBytesToUnlockHigh,
    LPOVERLAPPED lpOverlapped);
```

The *LockFileEx* and *UnlockFileEx* functions offer a superset of the *LockFile* and *UnlockFile* file capabilities.

Under Windows 95, the *LockFileEx* and *UnlockFileEx* functions have no useful implementations and simply return FALSE; calling *GetLastError* returns ERROR_CALL_NOT_IMPLEMENTED.

LockFileEx adds two capabilities to *LockFile*. You can use *LockFileEx* to lock a region of a file so that no other process can write to the locked region, as with *LockFile*; but with *LockFileEx*, you can allow other processes to continue reading from the locked region. By default, the *LockFileEx* function requests such a shared lock; you can request an exclusive lock by ORing with the LOCKFILE_EXCLUSIVE_LOCK flag in the *dwFlags* parameter. (*LockFile* is implemented internally as calling *LockFileEx* passing the LOCKFILE_EXCLUSIVE_LOCK flag.)

The other capability *LockFileEx* adds to *LockFile* is that you can tell *LockFileEx* to wait until a lock is granted if a thread in your process asks to lock a region of a file that is already locked by another process. In such a case, the *LockFile* function would return immediately, indicating that the call had failed. If your thread couldn't continue processing unless it could lock the region of the file, you would have to call *LockFile* repeatedly until it was able to lock the region and return TRUE. To simplify your program, you can call *LockFileEx*, which by default won't return until it has been able to lock the region of the file you've asked it to. If you want the function to return immediately, regardless of whether it can lock the region, OR the LOCKFILE_FAIL_IMMEDIATELY flag into the *dwFlags* parameter.

Most of the other *LockFileEx* parameters—*hFile, nNumberOfBytesToLockLow,* and *nNumberOfBytesToLockHigh*—are self-explanatory. The *dwReserved* parameter is reserved for Microsoft's future use, so it should always be 0. The last parameter, *lpOverlapped,* must point to an OVERLAPPED structure:

```
typedef struct _OVERLAPPED {
    DWORD   Internal;
    DWORD   InternalHigh;
    DWORD   Offset;
    DWORD   OffsetHigh;
    HANDLE  hEvent;
} OVERLAPPED;
typedef OVERLAPPED *LPOVERLAPPED;
```

The only members of the OVERLAPPED structure that *LockFileEx* uses are the *Offset* and *OffsetHigh* members; *LockFileEx* ignores all the other members. Before calling *LockFileEx*, you must initialize the *Offset* and *OffsetHigh* members so that they indicate the starting byte of the region of the file you want to lock.

When you're ready to unlock the locked region of the file, you can call either *UnlockFile* or *UnlockFileEx*. The *UnlockFileEx* function will someday offer enhancements over *UnlockFile*. It currently offers no capabilities in addition to those offered by *UnlockFile*.

Performing Synchronous I/O

This section discusses the Win32 functions that allow you to perform synchronous I/O on devices. Keep in mind that a device can be a file, mailslot, pipe, socket, and so on. No matter what the device, the I/O is performed using the same functions.

Without a doubt, the easiest and most commonly used functions for reading from and writing to devices are the following two functions:

```
BOOL ReadFile(HANDLE hFile, LPVOID lpBuffer,
    DWORD nNumberOfBytesToRead, LPDWORD lpNumberOfBytesRead,
    LPOVERLAPPED lpOverlapped);

BOOL WriteFile(HANDLE hFile, CONST VOID *lpBuffer,
    DWORD nNumberOfBytesToWrite, LPDWORD lpNumberOfBytesWritten,
    LPOVERLAPPED lpOverlapped);
```

Even though these functions have the word "File" in their names, they can be used for any type of device. The *hFile* parameter identifies the handle of the device you want to access. When this device is opened, you must not specify the FILE_FLAG_OVERLAPPED flag or the system will think that you want to perform I/O with this device asynchronously. The *lpBuffer* parameter points to the buffer to which the device's data should be read or to the buffer containing the data that should be written out to the device. The *nNumberOfBytesToRead* and *nNumberOfBytesToWrite* parameters tell *ReadFile* and *WriteFile* how many bytes to read from the device and how many bytes to write to the device, respectively.

The *lpNumberOfBytesRead* and *lpNumberOfBytesWritten* parameters indicate the address of a DWORD that the functions will fill with the number of bytes successfully transmitted to/from the device. The last parameter, *lpOverlapped*, should be NULL when performing synchronous I/O. We'll examine this parameter in more detail when we discuss asynchronous I/O shortly.

Both *ReadFile* and *WriteFile* return TRUE if successful. By the way, *ReadFile* can be called only for devices that were opened with the GENERIC_READ flag. Likewise, *WriteFile* can be called only if the device was opened with the GENERIC_WRITE flag.

Flushing Data to the Device

You'll remember from our look at the *CreateFile* function that there were quite a few flags you could pass to alter the way in which the system cached file data. Some other devices, such as serial ports, mailslots, and pipes, also cache data. If you want to force the system to write cached data to the device, you can call *FlushFileBuffers*:

```
BOOL FlushFileBuffers(HANDLE hFile);
```

The *FlushFileBuffers* function forces all the buffered data that is associated with a device identified by the *hFile* parameter to be written. The device must have been opened with the GENERIC_WRITE flag. If the function is successful, TRUE is returned.

Performing Asynchronous I/O

Compared to most other operations carried out by a computer, device I/O is one of the slowest. The CPU performs arithmetic operations and even paints the screen much faster than it reads data from or writes data to a file or across a network. By taking advantage of Win32's multi-threaded architecture, you can perform asynchronous device I/O; that is, you can tell the system to read from or write to the device while the rest of the code in your application continues to execute in parallel.

Suppose you were developing a simple database application. When the user opened a database, you'd have to have your application read the contents of the database into memory as well as into an index file. After the user selected the OK button in the File Open dialog box, your application would display an hourglass cursor while the database file was opened and read. After reading the database records into memory, the application would have to open the index file and read the index as well. While all this work went on, the hourglass cursor would be displayed, and the user wouldn't be able to start manipulating the records in the database until all the files had been read.

By taking advantage of asynchronous file I/O, you can cut down this file opening time substantially. If the user will run the database application on a machine with several CPUs, one CPU could be assigned responsibility for opening and reading the database records and another CPU could be assigned responsibility for opening and reading the index file. Since each of these tasks would be assigned to its very own CPU, the two tasks could execute at the same time. This would reduce the time it would take to open the database, and the user would be able to start manipulating records much sooner.

Of course, the file containing the index for the database would probably be much smaller than the file containing the records themselves. The index file would probably be loaded into memory before the database records were loaded. The application couldn't allow the user access until both files had been completely read into memory, though. So that the application would know when both files had been completely read, you'd have to use some form of thread synchronization.

To access a device asynchronously, you must first open the device by calling *CreateFile*, specifying the FILE_FLAG_OVERLAPPED flag in the *dwFlagsAndAttrs* parameter. This flag notifies the system that you intend to access the device asynchronously.

Win32 allows four different techniques to perform asynchronous I/O, and this chapter covers all of them. The techniques have a common theory of operation. When performing asynchronous I/O, you must first issue an I/O request to the operating system. The operating system queues the various I/O requests and handles them internally. While the system is handling the I/O requests, your thread is allowed to return and continue processing—this is what makes the I/O asynchronous in the first place.

At some point, the operating system will finish processing your I/O request and will now have to notify you that data has been sent, that data has been received, or that an error occurred. The way that you issue I/O requests is almost identical for the four techniques. What really distinguishes one technique from another is the way that you are notified of the result.

The following table quickly summarizes the four different techniques. The techniques are shown in order of complexity, from easiest to understand and implement (device handle signaling) to hardest to understand and implement (I/O completion ports).

Technique	Summary
Signaling a device kernel object	Not useful if you're going to perform multiple simultaneous I/O requests against a single device. Allows one thread to issue an I/O request and another thread to process it.
Signaling an event kernel object	Allows multiple simultaneous I/O requests against a single device. Allows one thread to issue an I/O request and another thread to process it.
Alertable I/O	Allows multiple simultaneous I/O requests against a single device. The thread that issued an I/O request must also process it.
I/O completion ports	Allows multiple simultaneous I/O requests against a single device. Allows one thread to issue an I/O request and another thread to process it. This technique is highly scalable, with the most flexibility.

Signaling a Device Kernel Object

The simplest technique for performing asynchronous device I/O is to use device handle signaling. To issue the I/O request, you again use the *ReadFile* and *WriteFile* functions:

```
BOOL ReadFile(HANDLE hFile, LPVOID lpBuffer,
    DWORD nNumberOfBytesToRead, LPDWORD lpNumberOfBytesRead,
    LPOVERLAPPED lpOverlapped);

BOOL WriteFile(HANDLE hFile, CONST VOID *lpBuffer,
    DWORD nNumberOfBytesToWrite, LPDWORD lpNumberOfBytesWritten,
    LPOVERLAPPED lpOverlapped);
```

We have already discussed these functions in the "Performing Synchronous I/O" section earlier in the chapter, but to perform asynchronous I/O, you must pass the address to an initialized OVERLAPPED structure as the *lpOverlapped* parameter. Win32 uses the word *overlapped* in this context to indicate that the time spent performing the I/O request overlaps the time your thread spends doing other things. Here's the form of an OVERLAPPED structure:

```
typedef struct _OVERLAPPED {
    DWORD    Internal;
    DWORD    InternalHigh;
    DWORD    Offset;
    DWORD    OffsetHigh;
    HANDLE   hEvent;
} OVERLAPPED;
typedef OVERLAPPED *LPOVERLAPPED;
```

When you call either *ReadFile* or *WriteFile*, you must allocate an OVERLAPPED structure and initialize the *Offset*, *OffsetHigh*, and *hEvent* members of the structure. The *Offset* and *OffsetHigh* members are used only when the device is a file; they must be set to 0 for other devices.

Important

The *Offset* and *OffsetHigh* members are *not* ignored for non–file devices— you must initialize these members to 0 or the I/O request may fail and *GetLastError* will return ERROR_INVALID_PARAMETER.

When accessing a file, the *Offset* and *OffsetHigh* members indicate the 64-bit offset within the file where you want the I/O operation to begin. For example, if you want to read 100 bytes from the file starting at byte position 345, write the following code:

```
// Open file for asynchronous file I/O.
HANDLE hFile = CreateFile(…, FILE_FLAG_OVERLAPPED, …);

// Create a buffer to hold the data.
BYTE bBuffer[100];

// DWORD used for the number of bytes read
DWORD dwNumBytesRead;

// Initialize an OVERLAPPED structure to tell
// the system where to start reading the data.
OVERLAPPED Overlapped;
Overlapped.Offset = 345;
Overlapped.OffsetHigh = 0;

Overlapped.hEvent = NULL;    // Explained later

// Start reading the data asynchronously.
ReadFile(hFile, bBuffer, sizeof(bBuffer),
    &dwNumBytesRead, &Overlapped);

// Code below ReadFile executes while the system
// reads the file's data into the buffer.
  :
  :
```

As you perform asynchronous file I/O, you need to keep in mind several things. In synchronous file I/O, each file handle has a file pointer associated with it. When another request to read from or write to the file is made, the system knows to start accessing the file at the location identified by the file pointer. After the operation is complete, the system updates the file pointer automatically so that the next operation can pick up where the last operation left off.

Things work quite differently in asynchronous file I/O. Imagine what would happen if you didn't have to use an OVERLAPPED structure. If your code placed a call to *ReadFile* immediately followed by another call to *ReadFile* (for the same file handle), the system wouldn't know where to start reading the file for the second call to *ReadFile*. You probably wouldn't want to start reading the file at the same location used by the first call to *ReadFile*. You might want to start the second read at the byte in the file following the last byte read by the first call to *ReadFile*. To avoid confusion, Microsoft designed *ReadFile* and *WriteFile* so that for every asynchronous I/O operation the starting byte in the file must be specified in the OVERLAPPED structure.

When you call *ReadFile* or *WriteFile* to queue an I/O request, the system checks to see whether the data you're requesting just happens to be in the system's cache already. If the data is already in the cache, the system copies the data to your buffer and then your call to *ReadFile* or *WriteFile* returns. At this point, either your buffer contains the requested data or the buffer's data has been sent. You are now free to use the buffer in any way that you desire. You are also told how many bytes were transferred by examining the DWORD value stored in the *lpNumberOfBytesRead* or *lpNumberOfBytesWritten* parameter. If the I/O request is performed synchronously and is successful, *ReadFile* and *WriteFile* both return TRUE.

If the I/O request is performed asynchronously, then *ReadFile* and *WriteFile* both return FALSE, which indicates that the I/O request did not complete. An I/O request may not complete for a variety of reasons; to find out why a particular request did not complete, you must call *GetLastError*. If *GetLastError* returns ERROR_IO_PENDING, the I/O request was successfully queued and will complete later.

An I/O request might also fail because the system maintains a fixed list (in nonpaged pool) of outstanding I/O requests. If this list is full when you issue another request, *ReadFile* and *WriteFile* return FALSE, and *GetLastError* returns either ERROR_INVALID_USER_BUFFER or ERROR_NOT_ENOUGH_MEMORY. Also, when you issue an I/O request, the system must page lock your data buffer.[2] This data buffer is part of your process's working set, and each process has a maximum working-set

---

2. See the *VirtualLock* and *VirtualUnlock* functions in Chapter 7 for more information about page locking.

size. If you do not have enough room in your process's working set, issuing the I/O request will fail and *GetLastError* returns ERROR_NOT_ENOUGH_QUOTA. You can increase your process's working-set size by calling *SetProcessWorkingSetSize*:

```
BOOL SetProcessWorkingSetSize(HANDLE hProcess,
  DWORD dwMinimumWorkingSetSize, DWORD dwMaximumWorkingSetSize);
```

Let me summarize: when you attempt to issue a new I/O request and the function fails, with *GetLastError* returning either ERROR_INVALID_USER_BUFFER, ERROR_NOT_ENOUGH_MEMORY, or ERROR_NOT_ENOUGH_QUOTA, you must make your thread wait until a previously issued I/O request completes and then attempt to reissue the new I/O request.

Important

While an I/O request is being processed, the data buffer and the OVERLAPPED structure must not be destroyed! The system will be moving data into or out of this buffer shortly, and it will refer to the overlapped structure later as well. You can safely destroy these memory blocks only after the I/O request has completed.

Once the asynchronous file operation has begun, your thread can continue initializing or do any other processing it sees fit to do. Eventually, you will need to synchronize your thread with the completion of the I/O operation. In other words, you'll hit a point in your thread's code at which the thread can't continue to execute unless the data from the device is fully loaded into the buffer.

Win32 considers a device handle to be a synchronization object—that is, it can be in either a signaled or a nonsignaled state. When you call *ReadFile* or *WriteFile*, one of the first things these functions do is reset the device handle to its nonsignaled state. Then, when all the data has been read from or written to the device, the system sets the device handle to the signaled state. By calling the *WaitForSingleObject* or *WaitForMultipleObjects* function, your thread can determine when the asynchronous device operation has completed—that is, when the device handle has been set to the signaled state. An extension of the code we've been looking at appears on the next page.

```
// Open file for asynchronous file I/O.
HANDLE hFile = CreateFile(…, FILE_FLAG_OVERLAPPED, …);

// Create a buffer to hold the data.
BYTE bBuffer[100];

// DWORD used for the number of bytes read
DWORD dwNumBytesRead;

// Initialize an OVERLAPPED structure to tell
// the system where to start reading the data.
OVERLAPPED Overlapped;
Overlapped.Offset = 345;
Overlapped.OffsetHigh = 0;

Overlapped.hEvent = NULL;    // Explained later

// Start reading the data asynchronously.
ReadFile(hFile, bBuffer, sizeof(bBuffer),
    &dwNumBytesRead, &Overlapped);

// Code below ReadFile executes while the system
// reads the file's data into the buffer.
:
:

// The thread can't continue until we know that all
// the requested data has been read into our buffer.
WaitForSingleObject(hFile, INFINITE);

// Initialization complete and file data read;
// the thread can continue.
:
:
```

Something important is missing from this code. We should be checking to be sure that the file operation has completed successfully before we allow the thread to continue running. We can get the result of an asynchronous device operation by calling

```
BOOL GetOverlappedResult(HANDLE hFile, LPOVERLAPPED lpOverlapped,
    LPDWORD lpcbTransfer, BOOL fWait);
```

When we call the *GetOverlappedResult* function, the *hFile* and *lpOverlapped* parameters must indicate the same file handle and OVERLAPPED structure that were used in the call to *ReadFile* or *WriteFile*. The *lpcbTransfer* parameter points to a DWORD that will be filled with the number of bytes that were successfully transferred to or from the buffer during the write or read operation. If you aren't interested in this information, you must still pass a valid address here to avoid an access violation.

The last parameter, *fWait*, is a Boolean value that tells *GetOverlappedResult* whether it should wait until the overlapped file operation is complete before returning. If *fWait* is FALSE, *GetOverlappedResult* doesn't wait and returns immediately to the application. An application can call *GetOverlappedResult*, passing TRUE for the *fWait* parameter to suspend the thread while an operation continues execution, instead of calling *WaitForSingleObject* as in the code we just looked at.

GetOverlappedResult returns TRUE if the function is successful. If you pass FALSE for the *fWait* parameter and the I/O operation has not yet been completed, *GetOverlappedResult* will also return FALSE. You can determine whether the call failed or whether the I/O operation is still proceeding by following the call to *GetOverlappedResult* with a call to *GetLastError*. If *GetLastError* returns ERROR_IO_INCOMPLETE, the call was good but the I/O operation is still in progress.

> Under Windows 95, the *GetOverlappedResult* function works only on serial devices.

Note that you can't reuse the OVERLAPPED structure in your application until the I/O request has been completed. The example shown here is totally incorrect:

```
void Func1 (void) {

    // Open file for asynchronous file I/O.
    HANDLE hFile = CreateFile(…, FILE_FLAG_OVERLAPPED, …);

    // Create a buffer to hold the data.
    BYTE bBuffer[100];

    Func2(hFile, bBuffer, sizeof(bBuffer));
        ⋮
        ⋮

}

void Func2 (HANDLE hFile, LPVOID bBuffer, DWORD dwBufSize) {

    DWORD dwNumBytesRead;
```

(continued)

723

```
    // Initialize an OVERLAPPED structure to tell
    // the system where to start reading the data.
    OVERLAPPED Overlapped;
    memset(&Overlapped, 0, sizeof(Overlapped));

    // Start reading the data asynchronously.
    ReadFile(hFile, bBuffer,
        dwBufSize, &dwNumBytesRead, &Overlapped);
}
```

This code fragment is incorrect because the locally defined OVER-
LAPPED structure in *Func2* will go out of scope when *Func2* returns. The
system remembers the address of the OVERLAPPED structure when you
call *ReadFile* or *WriteFile*. When the I/O request is complete, the system
needs to reference the *Internal*, *InternalHigh*, and *hEvent* members of the
structure. If the structure goes out of scope, the system will manipulate
whatever garbage happens to be on the stack—and this could introduce
difficult-to-find bugs into your application!

The *Internal* and *InternalHigh* members of the OVERLAPPED
structure, which the system must update when the I/O request is complete, were reserved for internal use during very early betas of Windows
NT. As time went on, it became clear to Microsoft that the information
contained in these members would be useful to all of us. Microsoft left
the names of the members *Internal* and *InternalHigh* so that any code already relying on these names wouldn't have to be changed. If the I/O
request is completed because of an error, the *Internal* member contains a
system-dependent status. The *InternalHigh* member is updated with the
number of bytes that have been transferred. This is the same value that is
put into the buffer pointed to by the *lpcbTransfer* parameter of *GetOverlappedResult*.

Signaling an Event Kernel Object

The technique shown in the previous section is very simple and straightforward, but it turns out not to be all that useful because it does not
handle multiple I/O requests well. For example, suppose you were trying to carry out multiple asynchronous operations on a single file at the
same time. Say that you wanted to read a sequence of bytes from the beginning of the file and simultaneously write another sequence of bytes to
the end of the file. In this situation, you can't synchronize your thread by
waiting for the file handle to become signaled.

The handle becomes signaled as soon as either of the file operations completes, so if you call *WaitForSingleObject*, passing it the file handle, you will be unsure whether it returned because the read operation completed or because the write operation completed. Clearly, there needs to be a better way to perform multiple, simultaneous asynchronous I/O requests so that we don't run into this predicament—fortunately, there is.

The last member of the OVERLAPPED structure, *hEvent*, identifies an event kernel object you must create by calling *CreateEvent*. (For more information on events, see Chapter 10.) When the system completes an asynchronous I/O request, it checks to see whether the *hEvent* member of the OVERLAPPED structure is NULL. If *hEvent* is not NULL, the system signals the event by calling *SetEvent*, passing *hEvent* as the event handle. The system also sets the file handle to the signaled state just as it did before. However, if you are using events to determine when a file operation has completed, you shouldn't wait for the file handle object to become signaled—wait for the event instead.

If you want to perform multiple asynchronous device I/O requests simultaneously, you should create an event for each request, initialize the *hEvent* member in each request's OVERLAPPED structure, and then call *ReadFile* or *WriteFile*. When you reach the point in your code at which you need to synchronize with the completion of the I/O request, simply call *WaitForMultipleObjects*, passing in the event handles associated with each outstanding I/O request's OVERLAPPED structures. With this scheme, you can easily and reliably perform multiple asynchronous device I/O operations simultaneously, using the same device handle.

You can also use the *GetOverlappedResult* function to synchronize your application with its impending device I/O. If you pass in TRUE as the *fWait* parameter for *GetOverlappedResult*, the function internally calls *WaitForSingleObject* and passes the *hEvent* member of the OVERLAPPED structure.

The potential problem here is that if you are using an auto-reset event instead of a manual-reset event to signal the end of an I/O request, you might permanently suspend your thread. If you use an auto-reset event and call *WaitForSingleObject* from your own code to wait for the I/O request to be completed, the event will be reset automatically to the nonsignaled state when *WaitForSingleObject* returns. If you then call *GetOverlappedResult* to determine the number of bytes that were successfully transferred and pass TRUE for *fWait*, you will cause *GetOverlappedResult* to make its own call to *WaitForSingleObject*. When *GetOverlappedResult* does this, the call to *WaitForSingleObject* will never return because the I/O request already completed will have caused the event to become signaled. The event won't be signaled again. *GetOverlappedResult* will never return to your thread's code, and the thread will be hung!

Alertable I/O

Whenever a thread is created, the system also creates a queue and associates it with the thread. This queue is called the Asynchronous Procedure Call (APC) queue. The thread's APC queue works similarly to the message queue that was discussed in Chapter 11. However, the APC queue is implemented by the low-level guts of the kernel, whereas the message queue is implemented at a much higher level: the user-interface components of the system. Because the APC queue is implemented by the kernel, it is more efficient and operations involving it execute much quicker.

It is possible to make I/O requests and have the results of these requests queued to the calling thread's APC queue. To have completed I/O requests queued to your thread's APC queue, you call the *ReadFileEx* and *WriteFileEx* functions:

```
BOOL ReadFileEx(HANDLE hFile, LPVOID lpBuffer,
    DWORD nNumberOfBytesToRead, LPOVERLAPPED lpOverlapped,
    LPOVERLAPPED_COMPLETION_ROUTINE lpCompletionRoutine);

BOOL WriteFileEx(HANDLE hFile, CONST VOID *lpBuffer,
    DWORD nNumberOfBytesToWrite, LPOVERLAPPED lpOverlapped,
    LPOVERLAPPED_COMPLETION_ROUTINE lpCompletionRoutine);
```

Under Windows 95, the *ReadFileEx* and *WriteFileEx* functions have no useful implementation and simply return FALSE; calling *GetLastError* returns ERROR_CALL_NOT_IMPLEMENTED.

ReadFileEx and *WriteFileEx* issue I/O requests to the operating system, and the functions return immediately. Eventually, the system will process your I/O request and will need to notify you somehow that your request has been processed. We have already looked at two methods of getting these notifications: device handle signaling and event handle signaling. When an I/O request that was issued via a call to *ReadFileEx* or *WriteFileEx* completes, the system signals the device handle and appends an entry to the thread's APC queue.[3] Note that the system always appends the entry to the queue associated with the thread that issued the I/O request by calling *ReadFileEx* or *WriteFileEx*.

The *ReadFileEx* and *WriteFileEx* functions have the same parameters as the *ReadFile* and *WriteFile* functions, with two exceptions. First, the *Ex* functions do not get passed a pointer to a DWORD that gets filled with the number of bytes transferred; this information can be retrieved only by the callback function. Second, the *Ex* functions require that you pass the address of a callback function, called a *completion routine*. This routine must have the following prototype:

```
VOID WINAPI FileIOCompletionRoutine(DWORD fdwError,
    DWORD cbTransferred, LPOVERLAPPED lpo);
```

I'll get back to this completion routine function shortly. First let's look at how the system handles the asynchronous I/O requests. For example, the following code queues three different asynchronous file operations:

```
hFile = CreateFile(…);

// Perform first ReadFileEx.
ReadFileEx(hFile, …);

// Perform first WriteFileEx.
WriteFileEx(hFile, …);

// Perform second ReadFileEx.
ReadFileEx(hFile, …);

SomeFunc();
```

If the call to *SomeFunc* takes some time to execute, the system will complete the three file operations before *SomeFunc* returns. While the thread is executing the *SomeFunc* function, the system is appending completed I/O entries to the thread's APC queue. The list might look something like this:

```
1st WriteFileEx completed
2nd ReadFileEx completed
1st ReadFileEx completed
```

---

3. The *hEvent* member in the OVERLAPPED structure is ignored when using this technique. You may use the *hEvent* member for your own purposes if you like.

The APC queue is maintained internally by the system. You'll also notice from the list that the system can execute your queued I/O requests in any order and that I/O requests that you issue last may be completed first and vice versa. Each entry in your thread's APC queue contains information about the complete I/O request: error code, number of bytes transferred, address of the OVERLAPPED structure passed to *ReadFileEx* or *WriteFileEx*, and the address of the callback routine.

As I/O requests complete, they are simply queued to your thread's APC queue—the callback routine is not immediately called because your thread may be busy doing something else and cannot be interrupted. To process entries in your thread's APC queue, the thread must put itself in an *alertable* state. This simply means that your thread has reached a position in its execution where it can handle being interrupted. Five Win32 functions can place a thread into an alertable state:

```
DWORD SleepEx(DWORD dwTimeout, BOOL fAlertable);

DWORD WaitForSingleObjectEx(HANDLE hObject, DWORD dwTimeout,
    BOOL fAlertable);

DWORD WaitForMultipleObjectsEx(DWORD cObjects,
    LPHANDLE lphObjects, BOOL fWaitAll, DWORD dwTimeout,
    BOOL fAlertable);

BOOL SignalObjectAndWait(HANDLE hObjectToSignal,
    HANDLE hObjectToWaitOn, DWORD dwMilliseconds,
    BOOL bAlertable);

DWORD MsgWaitForMultipleObjectsEx(DWORD nCount, LPHANDLE pHandles,
    DWORD dwMilliseconds, DWORD dwWakeMask, DWORD dwFlags);
```

The last argument to the first four functions is a Boolean value indicating whether the calling thread should place itself into an alertable state. For *MsgWaitForMultipleObjectsEx*, you must use the MWMO_ALERTABLE flag to have the thread enter an alertable state. If you're familiar with the *Sleep*, *WaitForSingleObject*, and *WaitForMultipleObjects* functions, you should know that, internally, these non-*Ex* functions call their *Ex* counterparts, always passing FALSE for the *fAlertable* parameter.

When you call one of the five functions above and place your thread in an alertable state, the system first checks your thread's APC queue. If at least one entry is in the queue, the system does not put your thread to sleep; instead, the system pulls the entry from the APC queue and your thread calls the callback routine, passing it the completed I/O request's error code, number of bytes transferred, and address of the OVERLAPPED structure. When the callback routine returns to the system, the system checks for more entries in the APC queue. If more entries exist, they are processed. However, if no more entries exist, your call to the alertable function returns. Something to keep in mind is that if any entries are in your thread's APC queue when you call any of these functions, your thread never sleeps!

The only time these functions suspend your thread is if no entries are in your thread's APC queue at the time when you call the function. Now while your thread is suspended, it will wake up if the kernel object(s) that you're waiting on become signaled or if an APC entry appears in your thread's queue. As soon as an APC entry appears, since your thread is in an alertable state, the system wakes your thread and empties the queue (by calling the callback routines); and then the functions immediately return to the caller—your thread does not go back to sleep waiting for kernel objects to become signaled.

The return value from these five functions indicates why they have returned. If the return value is WAIT_IO_COMPLETION, you know that the thread is continuing to execute because at least one entry was processed from the thread's APC queue. If the return value is anything else, it indicates that the thread woke up either because the sleep period expired, the specified kernel object(s) became signaled, or a mutex was abandoned. (See Chapter 10 for a more detailed discussion of these return values.)

Windows 95 and Windows NT 4, introduce a new function that allows you to manually queue an entry to a thread's APC queue:

```
DWORD QueueUserAPC(PAPCFUNC pfnAPC, HANDLE hThread, DWORD dwData);
```

The first parameter is a pointer to an APC function that must have the following prototype:

```
VOID WINAPI APCFunc(DWORD dwParam);
```

The second parameter is the handle of the thread for which you want to queue the entry. Note that this can be any thread in the system. If *hThread* identifies a thread in a different process's address space, then *pfnAPC* must specify the memory address of a function that is in the address space of the target thread. The last parameter to *QueueUserAPC*, *dwData*, is a 32-bit value that simply gets passed to the callback function.

Even though *QueueUserAPC* is prototyped as returning a DWORD, it actually returns a BOOL indicating success or failure. You can use

QueueUserAPC as a means of performing interthread communication even across process boundaries. It's just unfortunate that you can pass only a 32-bit value.

QueueUserAPC is undocumented for Windows 95, but it does exist and is exported from Kernel32.DLL. Feel free to call this function, because it is now completely documented and supported for both Windows 95 and Windows NT 4.

These alertable functions in their extended form are most useful in a client/server situation. You might have a server application that guards a database of information. You might also have a client application that periodically needs to request data from the server application. The server and client applications would communicate with each other using named pipes.

The server application would start by calling *ReadFileEx* and then pass to the server the handle to a named pipe instead of the handle to a file. When a client application sent information to the server through the named pipe, the asynchronous call would read the client's request and call the *FileIOCompletionRoutine* function. The *FileIOCompletionRoutine* function would interpret the client's request and locate the requested information in the database. The server would do this by initiating its own call to *ReadFileEx*. When the database information had been read, another *FileIOCompletionRoutine* call would be executed and the retrieved data would be transferred back through the named pipe to the client application.

One of the main drawbacks of using alertable I/O requests is that the thread that issues the I/O request must be the same thread to process the result. In some server applications, this is not the best architecture. For example, imagine a thread that issues an I/O request and then stays busy doing something else. If the I/O request completes, it might be nice to have another thread handle the incoming data. But the data will just sit in a buffer until the issuing thread finishes its current processing so that it can place itself in an alertable state. To overcome this limitation of alertable I/O, Microsoft added I/O completion ports (discussed later in this chapter) to the Win32 API.

The Alertable I/O Application

The AlertIO (ALERTIO.EXE) application, listed in Figure 15-1 beginning on page 733, demonstrates the use of alertable device I/O. The source code and resource files for the application are in the ALERTIO directory on the companion disc. The program simply copies a file the user specifies to a new file called ALERTIO.CPY. When the user executes AlertIO, the Alertable I/O File Copy dialog box appears:

The user clicks on the Browse button to select the file that is to be copied. After the user selects a file to be copied, the Pathname and File Size fields are updated. When the user clicks on the Copy button, the program calls the *FileCopy* function, which in turn calls *PrepareDstFile*. *PrepareDstFile* is responsible for opening the source file and for creating the destination file. You'll notice that both calls to *CreateFile* specify the FILE_FLAG_NO_BUFFERING flag so that the system's cache does not waste memory keeping its own copy of the source and destination file's data.

Important

If both files are opened successfully, the destination file size is immediately set to the appropriate size by calling *SetFilePointer* and *SetEndOfFile*. Adjusting the destination file's size now is extremely important because NTFS maintains a high-water marker that indicates the highest point at which the file was written. If you read past this marker, the system knows to return zeroes. If you write past the marker, the file's data from the old high-water mark to the write offset is filled with zeroes, your data is then written to the file, and the file's high-water marker is updated. This behavior satisfies C2 security requirements pertaining to not presenting prior data. When you write to the end of a file on an NTFS partition causing the high-water marker to move, NTFS must perform the I/O request synchronously. If AlertIO did not set the size of the destination file, none of the overlapped I/O requests would be performed asynchronously.

Now we're ready to create a set of I/O requests. We do this by initializing MAX_PENDING_IO_REQS IOREQ structures. Each of these structures contains an OVERLAPPED structure used when calling *Read-FileEx* and *WriteFileEx*. The OVERLAPPED structure's *Offset* and *Offset-High* members are initialized to point to the starting byte offset inside the source file where the I/O request should begin reading. The *hEvent* member is initialized to NULL; however, you can put whatever value you want in this member because the system ignores the contents of the *hEvent* member when performing I/O requests using *ReadFileEx* and *WriteFileEx*.

Each I/O request requires a memory buffer in addition to an OVERLAPPED structure. I chose to implement this by placing a *pbData* member inside my IOREQ structure. This *pbData* member is initialized to a block of memory that is allocated using *VirtualAlloc*. Using *Virtual-Alloc* ensures that the block begins on an even allocation-granularity boundary, which satisfies the requirement of the FILE_FLAG_NO_BUF-FERING flag: the buffer must begin on an address that is evenly divisible by the volume's sector size.

After each IOREQ structure is initialized, *ReadFileEx* is called to is-sue the request and a counter of the outstanding read requests is incre-mented. When the request completes, an APC entry is placed in AlertIO's thread queue. After all I/O requests are issued, a loop is entered that continues until there are no more outstanding I/O requests issued on any file. Inside this loop, *SleepEx* is called, passing a time-out value of IN-FINITE, and places the thread into an alertable state. The only time *SleepEx* returns is when one or more queued APC entries are processed.

As each read I/O request completes, the APC entries are queued to the thread's queue. When the thread is in an alertable state (*SleepEx* is called), the entries are removed from the APC queue and *ReadComple-tionRoutine* is called. This function casts the *pOverlapped* parameter to a PIOREQ pointer. Here is a very common trick: append your own data members to the end of an OVERLAPPED structure, and pass this address to *ReadFile(Ex)* or *WriteFile(Ex)*. Then when the pointer to the OVER-LAPPED structure is passed back to you, you can cast it to your own structure to gain access to your own data members.

Now *ReadCompletionRoutine* decrements the number of outstanding read I/O requests. Note that because the AlertIO program uses a single thread, no thread synchronization issues are involved when manipulat-ing these variables. Then *ReadCompletionFunction* rounds up the number-of-bytes-transferred to an even multiple of the host system's page size, which again is required because we used the FILE_FLAG_NO_BUF-FERING flag when calling *CreateFile*. After this, *WriteFileEx* is called to issue another I/O request to write the data to the destination file, and the number of outstanding write requests is incremented.

When this write I/O request completes, another APC entry is placed in the thread's queue. When the thread is in an alertable state, the entry is removed from the queue and *WriteCompletionFunction* is called. This function parallels the code in the *ReadCompletionFunction* function: the number of outstanding write requests is decremented, and if we have not tried to read beyond the end of the file, a call to *ReadFileEx* is issued to queue another I/O request against the source file.

The main loop terminates when *SleepEx* returns and there are no outstanding I/O requests. At this point, the I/O request buffers are freed and *CopyCleanup* is called. *CopyCleanup* closes the source and destination files. Then it reopens the destination file without specifying the FILE_FLAG_NO_BUFFERING flag. Because we are not using this flag, file operations do not have to be performed on sector boundaries. This allows us to shrink the size of the destination file to the same size as the source file.

AlertIO.ico

```
ALERTIO.C
/***********************************************************
Module name: AlertIO.C
Notices: Copyright (c) 1997 Jeffrey Richter
***********************************************************/


#include "..\CmnHdr.H"                    /* See Appendix C. */
#include <windows.h>
#include <windowsx.h>
#include <tchar.h>
#include <stdio.h>
#include <stdlib.h>
#include "Resource.H"



///////////////////////////////////////////////////////////////////
```

Figure 15-1.
The AlertIO application.

(continued)

Figure 15-1. *continued*

```
static BOOL PrepareDstFile(LPCTSTR pszFileSrc,
   LPCTSTR pszFileDst, PHANDLE phFileSrc, PHANDLE phFileDst,
   PULARGE_INTEGER pulFileSize, DWORD dwPageSize) {

   ULARGE_INTEGER ulFileSizeDst;
   DWORD dwError;
   BOOL fOk = FALSE;

   __try {
      // Open the existing source file for input.
      *phFileSrc = CreateFile(pszFileSrc, GENERIC_READ,
         FILE_SHARE_READ, NULL, OPEN_EXISTING,
         FILE_FLAG_NO_BUFFERING | FILE_FLAG_OVERLAPPED, NULL);

      if (*phFileSrc == INVALID_HANDLE_VALUE)
         __leave;

      // Create the new destination file for output.
      *phFileDst = CreateFile(pszFileDst, GENERIC_WRITE,
         0, NULL, CREATE_ALWAYS,
         FILE_FLAG_NO_BUFFERING | FILE_FLAG_OVERLAPPED,
         *phFileSrc);

      if (*phFileDst == INVALID_HANDLE_VALUE)
         __leave;

      // Get the size of the original file.
      pulFileSize->LowPart = GetFileSize(*phFileSrc,
         &pulFileSize->HighPart);

      // Round up the source file size
      // to an even multiple of pages.
      ulFileSizeDst.QuadPart = (pulFileSize->QuadPart +
         dwPageSize - 1) & ~(dwPageSize - 1);

      // Force the destination file to the size needed.
      dwError = SetFilePointer(*phFileDst,
         ulFileSizeDst.LowPart,
         (PLONG) ulFileSizeDst.HighPart, FILE_BEGIN);
      if ((dwError == 0xffffffff) &&
         (GetLastError() != NO_ERROR))
         __leave;

      if (!SetEndOfFile(*phFileDst))
         __leave;
```

(continued)

Figure 15-1. *continued*

```
      fOk = TRUE; // We did everything successfully.
   }
   __finally {

      // If anything failed, clean up entirely.
      if (!fOk) {
         if (*phFileSrc != INVALID_HANDLE_VALUE) {
            CloseHandle(*phFileSrc);
            *phFileSrc = INVALID_HANDLE_VALUE;
         }
         if (*phFileSrc != INVALID_HANDLE_VALUE) {
            CloseHandle(*phFileDst);
            *phFileDst = INVALID_HANDLE_VALUE;
         }
      }
   }
   return(fOk);
}


///////////////////////////////////////////////////////////////


static void CopyCleanup(LPCTSTR pszFileDst, HANDLE hFileSrc,
   HANDLE hFileDst, PULARGE_INTEGER pulFileSize) {

   // Close the source and destination files.
   CloseHandle(hFileDst);
   CloseHandle(hFileSrc);

   // We need another handle to the destination file that is
   // opened without FILE_FLAG_NO_BUFFERING. This allows us
   // to set the end-of-file marker to a position that is not
   // sector-aligned.
   hFileDst = CreateFile(pszFileDst, GENERIC_WRITE,
      FILE_SHARE_READ | FILE_SHARE_WRITE, NULL,
      OPEN_EXISTING, 0, NULL);

   if (hFileDst != INVALID_HANDLE_VALUE) {

      // Set the destination file's size to the size of the
      // source file, in case the size of the source file was
      // not a multiple of the page size.
      SetFilePointer(hFileDst, pulFileSize->LowPart,
         (PLONG) pulFileSize->HighPart, FILE_BEGIN);
```

(continued)

Figure 15-1. *continued*

```
        SetEndOfFile(hFileDst);
        CloseHandle(hFileDst);
    }
}


////////////////////////////////////////////////////////////////


typedef struct {
    // The page size used on the host machine
    DWORD dwPageSize;

    // Handles of the source and destination files
    HANDLE hFileSrc, hFileDst;

    // Size of source file
    ULARGE_INTEGER ulFileSize;

    // Offset in source file where next read begins
    ULARGE_INTEGER ulNextReadOffset;

    // The number of pending read and write I/O requests
    int nReadsInProgress;
    int nWritesInProgress;
} COPYSTATE, *PCOPYSTATE;


COPYSTATE g_cs;


// Each IO requires an OVERLAPPED structure and a buffer.
typedef struct {
    OVERLAPPED Overlapped;
    PBYTE      pbData;
} IOREQ, *PIOREQ;

#define MAX_PENDING_IO_REQS    4
#define BUFFSIZE               (64 * 1024)


////////////////////////////////////////////////////////////////
```

(continued)

Figure 15-1. *continued*

```
VOID WINAPI WriteCompletionRoutine(DWORD dwErrorCode,
   DWORD dwNumberOfBytesTransferred,
   LPOVERLAPPED pOverlapped);


/////////////////////////////////////////////////////////////


VOID WINAPI ReadCompletionRoutine(DWORD dwErrorCode,
   DWORD dwNumberOfBytesTransferred,
   LPOVERLAPPED pOverlapped) {

   PIOREQ pIOReq = (PIOREQ) pOverlapped;
   chASSERT(dwErrorCode == NO_ERROR);
   g_cs.nReadsInProgress--;

   // Round up the number of bytes to write
   // to a sector boundary.
   dwNumberOfBytesTransferred =
      (dwNumberOfBytesTransferred + g_cs.dwPageSize - 1) &
      ~(g_cs.dwPageSize - 1);

   chVERIFY(WriteFileEx(g_cs.hFileDst, pIOReq->pbData,
      dwNumberOfBytesTransferred, pOverlapped,
      WriteCompletionRoutine));

   g_cs.nWritesInProgress++;
}


/////////////////////////////////////////////////////////////


VOID WINAPI WriteCompletionRoutine(DWORD dwErrorCode,
   DWORD dwNumberOfBytesTransferred,
   LPOVERLAPPED pOverlapped) {

   PIOREQ pIOReq = (PIOREQ) pOverlapped;
   chASSERT(dwErrorCode == NO_ERROR);
   g_cs.nWritesInProgress--;

   if (g_cs.ulNextReadOffset.QuadPart <
      g_cs.ulFileSize.QuadPart) {
      // We haven't read past the end of the file yet.
```

(continued)

Figure 15-1. *continued*

```
        // Read the next chunk of data.
        pOverlapped->Offset     = g_cs.ulNextReadOffset.LowPart;
        pOverlapped->OffsetHigh = g_cs.ulNextReadOffset.HighPart;
        chVERIFY(ReadFileEx(g_cs.hFileSrc, pIOReq->pbData,
            BUFFSIZE, pOverlapped, ReadCompletionRoutine));

        g_cs.nReadsInProgress++;
        // Offset in source file where next read begins.
        g_cs.ulNextReadOffset.QuadPart += BUFFSIZE;
    }
}


///////////////////////////////////////////////////////////////////


BOOL FileCopy (LPCTSTR pszFileSrc, LPCTSTR pszFileDst) {

    // Maintain info about each IO request.
    IOREQ IOReq[MAX_PENDING_IO_REQS] = { 0 };

    SYSTEM_INFO si;
    int nIOReq;
    BOOL fOk;

    // Initialize the global COPYSTATE variable.
    GetSystemInfo(&si);
    g_cs.dwPageSize = si.dwPageSize;
    g_cs.ulNextReadOffset.QuadPart = 0;
    g_cs.nReadsInProgress = 0;
    g_cs.nWritesInProgress = 0;

    // Open the existing source file for input.
    fOk = PrepareDstFile(pszFileSrc, pszFileDst,
        &g_cs.hFileSrc, &g_cs.hFileDst,
        &g_cs.ulFileSize, g_cs.dwPageSize);
    if (!fOk)
        return(fOk);

    // Start the copy engine by posting a number of read
    // IO requests against the source file.
    for (nIOReq = 0; nIOReq < MAX_PENDING_IO_REQS; nIOReq++) {
        IOReq[nIOReq].Overlapped.Internal = 0;
        IOReq[nIOReq].Overlapped.InternalHigh = 0;
```

(continued)

Figure 15-1. *continued*

```
    IOReq[nIOReq].Overlapped.Offset =
       g_cs.ulNextReadOffset.LowPart;
    IOReq[nIOReq].Overlapped.OffsetHigh =
       g_cs.ulNextReadOffset.HighPart;
    IOReq[nIOReq].Overlapped.hEvent = NULL;
    IOReq[nIOReq].pbData = VirtualAlloc(NULL,
       BUFFSIZE, MEM_RESERVE | MEM_COMMIT, PAGE_READWRITE);

    if (g_cs.ulNextReadOffset.QuadPart <
       g_cs.ulFileSize.QuadPart) {
       chVERIFY(ReadFileEx(g_cs.hFileSrc,
          IOReq[nIOReq].pbData, BUFFSIZE,
          &IOReq[nIOReq].Overlapped,
          ReadCompletionRoutine));
       g_cs.nReadsInProgress++;
       g_cs.ulNextReadOffset.QuadPart += BUFFSIZE;
    }
}

// Loop until an error has occurred or until the
// destination file has been written.
while ((g_cs.nReadsInProgress > 0) ||
       (g_cs.nWritesInProgress > 0)) {
   SleepEx(INFINITE, TRUE);
}

// Free the memory buffers used for the copy.
for (nIOReq = 0; nIOReq < MAX_PENDING_IO_REQS; nIOReq++) {
   VirtualFree(IOReq[nIOReq].pbData, 0, MEM_RELEASE);
}

// Close the source and destination files; force the
// destination file to be the same size as the source.
CopyCleanup(pszFileDst, g_cs.hFileSrc,
   g_cs.hFileDst, &g_cs.ulFileSize);

return(TRUE);
}


///////////////////////////////////////////////////////////////
```

(continued)

Figure 15-1. *continued*

```
BOOL Dlg_OnInitDialog (HWND hwnd, HWND hwndFocus,
   LPARAM lParam) {

   // Associate an icon with the dialog box.
   chSETDLGICONS(hwnd, IDI_ALERTIO, IDI_ALERTIO);

   // Disable the "Copy" button because no file
   // has been selected yet.
   EnableWindow(GetDlgItem(hwnd, IDOK), FALSE);

   return(TRUE);
}


/////////////////////////////////////////////////////////////////


void Dlg_OnCommand (HWND hwnd, int id,
   HWND hwndCtl, UINT codeNotify) {

   TCHAR szPathname[_MAX_DIR];
   BOOL fOk;
   OPENFILENAME ofn;

   switch (id) {
      case IDOK:
         // Copy the source file to the destination file.
         Static_GetText(GetDlgItem(hwnd, IDC_SRCFILE),
            szPathname, sizeof(szPathname));
         SetCursor(LoadCursor(NULL, IDC_WAIT));
         FileCopy(szPathname, __TEXT("AlertIO.CPY"));
         break;

      case IDC_BROWSE:
         chINITSTRUCT(ofn, TRUE);
         ofn.hwndOwner = hwnd;
         ofn.lpstrFilter = __TEXT("*.*\0");
         _tcscpy(szPathname, __TEXT("*.*"));
         ofn.lpstrFile = szPathname;
         ofn.nMaxFile = sizeof(szPathname);
         ofn.Flags = OFN_FILEMUSTEXIST;
         fOk = GetOpenFileName(&ofn);
```

(continued)

Figure 15-1. *continued*

```
            if (fOk) {
               HANDLE hFile;
               Static_SetText(GetDlgItem(hwnd, IDC_SRCFILE),
                  szPathname);
               hFile = CreateFile(szPathname, GENERIC_READ,
                  0, NULL, OPEN_EXISTING, 0, NULL);

               SetDlgItemInt(hwnd, IDC_SRCFILESIZE,
                  GetFileSize(hFile, NULL), FALSE);
               CloseHandle(hFile);
            }

            // Enable the "Copy" button if the user selected
            // a valid pathname.
            GetWindowText(GetDlgItem(hwnd, IDC_SRCFILE),
               szPathname, sizeof(szPathname));
            EnableWindow(GetDlgItem(hwnd, IDOK),
               szPathname[0] != __TEXT('('));

            if (fOk) {
               // If the user pressed the OK button in the file
               // dialog box, change focus to the "Copy" button.
               FORWARD_WM_NEXTDLGCTL(hwnd,
                  GetDlgItem(hwnd, IDOK), TRUE, SendMessage);
            }
            break;

         case IDCANCEL:
            EndDialog(hwnd, id);
            break;
      }
   }


   //////////////////////////////////////////////////////////////


   BOOL CALLBACK Dlg_Proc (HWND hwnd, UINT uMsg,
      WPARAM wParam, LPARAM lParam) {

      switch (uMsg) {
         chHANDLE_DLGMSG(hwnd, WM_INITDIALOG, Dlg_OnInitDialog);
         chHANDLE_DLGMSG(hwnd, WM_COMMAND, Dlg_OnCommand);
      }
```

(continued)

741

Figure 15-1. *continued*

```
    return(FALSE);
}


/////////////////////////////////////////////////////////////


int WINAPI _tWinMain (HINSTANCE hinstExe,
   HINSTANCE hinstPrev, LPTSTR pszCmdLine, int nCmdShow) {

   chWARNIFUNICODEUNDERWIN95();
   DialogBox(hinstExe, MAKEINTRESOURCE(IDD_ALERTIO),
      NULL, Dlg_Proc);

   return(0);
}


/////////////////////// End Of File ///////////////////////
```

ALERTIO.RC

```
//Microsoft Developer Studio generated resource script.
//
#include "Resource.h"

#define APSTUDIO_READONLY_SYMBOLS
/////////////////////////////////////////////////////////////
//
// Generated from the TEXTINCLUDE 2 resource.
//
#include "afxres.h"


/////////////////////////////////////////////////////////////
#undef APSTUDIO_READONLY_SYMBOLS


/////////////////////////////////////////////////////////////
// English (U.S.) resources

#if !defined(AFX_RESOURCE_DLL) || defined(AFX_TARG_ENU)
#ifdef _WIN32
LANGUAGE LANG_ENGLISH, SUBLANG_ENGLISH_US
```

(continued)

Figure 15-1. *continued*

```
#pragma code_page(1252)
#endif //_WIN32


/////////////////////////////////////////////////////////////
//
// Icon
//

// Icon with lowest ID value placed first to ensure
// application icon remains consistent on all systems.
IDI_ALERTIO              ICON    DISCARDABLE     "AlertIO.Ico"


/////////////////////////////////////////////////////////////
//
// Dialog
//


IDD_ALERTIO DIALOG DISCARDABLE  15, 24, 214, 37
STYLE WS_MINIMIZEBOX | WS_POPUP | WS_VISIBLE | WS_CAPTION |
    WS_SYSMENU
CAPTION "Alertable I/O File Copy"
FONT 8, "System"
BEGIN
    LTEXT           "&Pathname:",IDC_STATIC,4,6,35,8
    EDITTEXT        IDC_SRCFILE,44,4,168,12,ES_AUTOHSCROLL
    PUSHBUTTON      "&Browse...",IDC_BROWSE,4,20,36,12,
                    WS_GROUP
    DEFPUSHBUTTON   "&Copy",IDOK,52,20,36,12
    LTEXT           "File size:",IDC_STATIC,144,20,31,8
    LTEXT           "0",IDC_SRCFILESIZE,180,20,34,8
END



#ifdef APSTUDIO_INVOKED
/////////////////////////////////////////////////////////////
//
// TEXTINCLUDE
//

1 TEXTINCLUDE DISCARDABLE
BEGIN
    "Resource.h\0"
END
```

(continued)

Figure 15-1. *continued*

```
2 TEXTINCLUDE DISCARDABLE
BEGIN
    "#include ""afxres.h""\r\n"
    "\0"
END

3 TEXTINCLUDE DISCARDABLE
BEGIN
    "\r\n"
    "\0"
END


#endif    // APSTUDIO_INVOKED



/////////////////////////////////////////////////////////////////
//
// DESIGNINFO
//

#ifdef APSTUDIO_INVOKED
GUIDELINES DESIGNINFO DISCARDABLE
BEGIN
    IDD_ALERTIO, DIALOG
    BEGIN
        RIGHTMARGIN, 190
        BOTTOMMARGIN, 33
    END
END
#endif    // APSTUDIO_INVOKED

#endif    // English (U.S.) resources
/////////////////////////////////////////////////////////////////



#ifndef APSTUDIO_INVOKED
/////////////////////////////////////////////////////////////////
//
// Generated from the TEXTINCLUDE 3 resource.
//


/////////////////////////////////////////////////////////////////
#endif    // not APSTUDIO_INVOKED
```

I/O Completion Ports

Windows NT is designed to be a secure, robust operating system running applications that service literally thousands of users. This capability to remain secure and robust while servicing many users is true of Windows NT Workstation and is even more true of Windows NT Server.

> Under Windows 95, I/O completion port functions have no useful implementation.

You can generally architect a service application in two ways:

- In the *serial model,* a single thread waits for a client to make a request (usually over the network). When the request comes in, the thread wakes and handles the client's request.

- In the *concurrent model,* a single thread waits for a client request and then creates a new thread to handle the request. While the new thread is handling the client's request, the original thread loops back around and waits for another client request. When the thread handling the client's request is completely processed, the thread dies.

The problem with the serial model is that it does not handle multiple, simultaneous requests well. If two clients make requests at the same time, only one can be processed at a time; the second request must wait for the first request to finish processing. A service that is designed using the serial approach cannot take advantage of SMP machines. Obviously, the serial model is good only for the simplest of server applications, in which few client requests are made and requests can be handled very quickly. A Ping server is a good example of a serial server.

Because of the limitations in the serial model, the concurrent model is extremely popular. In the concurrent model, a thread is created to handle each client request. The advantage is that the thread that waits for incoming requests has very little work to do. Most of the time, this thread is sleeping. When a client request comes in, the thread wakes, creates a new thread to handle the request, and then waits for another client request. This means that incoming client requests are handled expediently. Also, because each client request gets its own thread, the server application scales well and can easily take advantage of SMP machines.

745

So by upgrading the hardware (adding another CPU), the performance of the server application improves when you use the concurrent model.

As server applications using the concurrent model were implemented on Windows NT, the Windows NT team noticed that the performance of these applications was not as high as they would like it to be. In particular, handling many simultaneous client requests meant that many threads were running in the system concurrently. Because all of these threads were runnable (not suspended and waiting for something to happen), Microsoft realized that the Windows NT kernel spent too much time context switching between the running threads, and the threads were not getting as much CPU time to do their work.

To make Windows NT an awesome server environment, Microsoft needed to address this problem. The result is a new kernel object called the *I/O completion port,* which was first introduced in Windows NT 3.5. The theory behind the I/O completion port is that the number of threads running concurrently must have an upper bound; that is, 500 simultaneous client requests cannot allow 500 runnable threads to exist. But what is the proper number of concurrent, runnable threads? Well, if you think about this question for a moment, you'll come to the realization that if a machine has two CPUs, it really doesn't make sense to have more than two runnable threads—one for each processor. As soon as you have more runnable threads than CPUs available, the system has to spend time performing thread context switches, which wastes precious CPU cycles.

Another deficiency of the concurrent model is that a new thread is created for each client request. Creating a thread is cheap when compared to creating a new process with its own 4-GB virtual address space, but creating threads is far from free. The server application's performance can be further improved if a pool of threads is created when the application initializes and if these threads then hang around for the duration of the application. I/O completion ports were designed to work with a pool of threads.

An I/O completion port is probably the most complex kernel object offered by Win32. To create an I/O completion port, you call *CreateIoCompletionPort*:

```
HANDLE CreateIoCompletionPort(HANDLE hFileHandle,
    HANDLE hExistingCompletionPort, DWORD dwCompletionKey,
    DWORD dwNumberOfConcurrentThreads);
```

This function does two different things: it creates an I/O completion port, and it also associates a device with an I/O completion port. This function is overly complex, however, and in my opinion, Microsoft should have split it into two separate functions. When I work with I/O completion ports, I separate these two capabilities by creating two very tiny functions that abstract the call to *CreateIoCompletionPort*. The first function I write is called *CreateNewCompletionPort*, and I implement it as follows:

```
HANDLE CreateNewCompletionPort(DWORD dwNumberOfConcurrentThreads) {
   return(CreateIoCompletionPort(INVALID_HANDLE_VALUE,
      NULL, 0, dwNumberOfConcurrentThreads));
}
```

This function takes a single argument, *dwNumberOfConcurrentThreads*, and then calls the Win32 *CreateIoCompletionPort* function, passing in hard-coded values for the first three parameters and *dwNumberOfConcurrentThreads* for the last parameter. You see, the first three parameters to *CreateIoCompletionPort* are used only when you are associating a device with a completion port. (I'll talk about this shortly.) To create just a completion port, I pass INVALID_HANDLE_VALUE, NULL, and 0, respectively.

The *dwNumberOfConcurrentThreads* parameter tells the I/O completion port the maximum number of threads that should be runnable at the same time. If you pass 0 for the *dwNumberOfConcurrentThreads* parameter, the completion port defaults to allowing as many concurrent threads as there are CPUs on the host machine. This is usually exactly what you want so that extra context switching is avoided. You may want to increase this value if the processing of a client request requires a lengthy computation that rarely blocks. You might experiment with the *dwNumberOfConcurrentThreads* parameter by trying different values and comparing your application's performance.

You'll notice that *CreateIoCompletionPort* is about the only Win32 function that creates a kernel object but that does not have an LP-SECURITY_ATTRIBUTES parameter. This is because completion ports are intended to be used within a single process only. The reason for this will be made clearer when I explain how to use completion ports.

When you create an I/O completion port, the kernel actually creates five different data structures, as shown in Figure 15-2. You will want to refer to this figure as you continue reading this section.

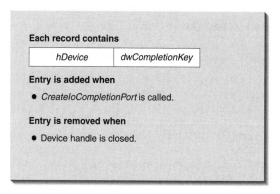

Device List

Each record contains

hDevice	dwCompletionKey

Entry is added when

- *CreateIoCompletionPort* is called.

Entry is removed when

- Device handle is closed.

I/O Completion Queue (FIFO)

Each record contains

dwBytesTransferred	dwCompletionKey	pOverlapped	dwError

Entry is added when

- I/O request completes.
- *PostQueuedCompletionStatus* is called.

Entry is removed when

- Completion port removes an entry from the Waiting Thread Queue.

Figure 15-2.   *(continued)*

The internal workings of an I/O completion port.

Figure 15-2. *continued*

Waiting Thread Queue (LIFO)

Each record contains

> *dwThreadId*

Entry is added when

- Thread calls *GetQueuedCompletionStatus.*

Entry is removed when

- I/O completion queue is not empty and the number of running threads is less than the maximum number of concurrent threads (entry is removed from I/O Completion Queue, *dwThreadId* moves to Released Thread List, and *GetQueuedCompletionStatus* returns).

Released Thread List

Each record contains

> *dwThreadId*

Entry is added when

- Completion port wakes a thread in the Waiting Thread Queue.
- Paused thread wakes up.

Entry is removed when

- Thread again calls *GetQueuedCompletionStatus* (*dwThreadId* moves back to the Waiting Thread Queue).
- Thread calls a function that suspends itself (*dwThreadId* moves to Paused Thread List).

Paused Thread List

Each record contains

> *dwThreadId*

Entry is added when

- Released thread calls a function that suspends itself.

Entry is removed when

- Suspended thread wakes up (*dwThreadId* moves back to Released Thread List).

The first data structure is a device list. For a completion port to be useful, you must associate a device or multiple devices with the port. You do this by also calling *CreateIoCompletionPort*. Again, I have created my own function, *AssociateDeviceWithCompletionPort*, which abstracts the call to *CreateIoCompletionPort*:

```
BOOL AssociateDeviceWithCompletionPort(
    HANDLE hCompPort, HANDLE hDevice, DWORD dwCompKey) {
    HANDLE h = CreateIoCompletionPort(hDevice,
      hCompPort, dwCompKey, 0);
    return(h == hCompPort);
}
```

AssociateDeviceWithCompletionPort appends an entry to an existing completion port's device list. You pass the function the handle of an existing completion port (returned by a previous call to *CreateNewCompletionPort*), the handle of the device (this can be a file, a socket, a mailslot, a pipe, and so on), and a completion key (a 32-bit value that has meaning to you; the operating system doesn't care what you pass here). Each time you associate a device with the port, the system appends this information to the completion port's device list.

Important

Even though I recommend that you mentally separate the two different reasons for calling *CreateIoCompletionPort*, there is one advantage to having the function be so complex: you can create an I/O completion port and associate a device with it at the same time. For example, the code below opens a file and creates a new completion port associating the file with it. All I/O requests to the file will complete with a completion key of COMPKEY_FILE, and the port will allow as many as two threads to execute concurrently.

```
#define COMPKEY_FILE    1
HANDLE hfile = CreateFile(…);
HANDLE hCompPort = CreateIoCompletionPort(NULL, hfile,
    COMPKEY_FILE, 2);
```

Windows NT 3.5 requires that a device always be associated with a completion port at the time when the completion port is created. In other words, Windows NT 3.5 does not allow you to pass INVALID-_HANDLE_VALUE as the second parameter to *CreateIoCompletionPort*. In Windows NT 3.51, Microsoft modified the function so that you can now pass INVALID_HANDLE_VALUE to create a completion port without associating a device with it.

The second data structure is an I/O completion queue. When an asynchronous I/O request for a device completes, the system checks to see whether the device is associated with a completion port, and if so, the system appends the completed I/O request entry to the end of the completion port's I/O completion queue. Each entry in this queue indicates the number of bytes transferred, the 32-bit completion key value that was set when the device was associated with the port, the pointer to the I/O request's OVERLAPPED structure, and an error code. We'll discuss how entries are removed from this queue shortly.

Important

It is possible to issue an I/O request to a device and not have an I/O completion entry queued to the I/O completion port. This is not usually necessary, but it can come in handy occasionally. For example, there are times when you send data over a socket and you don't care whether the data actually makes it or not.

To issue an I/O request without having a completion entry queued, you must load the OVERLAPPED structure's *hEvent* member with a valid event handle and bitwise-OR this value with 1, like this:

```
Overlapped.hEvent = CreateEvent(NULL, TRUE, FALSE, NULL);
Overlapped.hEvent |= 1;
ReadFile(…, &Overlapped);
```

Now you can issue your I/O request passing the address of this OVERLAPPED structure to the desired Win32 function (like *ReadFile* above).

It would be nice if you didn't have to create an event just to stop the queuing of the I/O completion. I would like to be able to do the following, but this doesn't work:

```
Overlapped.hEvent = 1;
ReadFile(…, &Overlapped);
```

Also, don't forget to reset the low-order bit before closing this event handle:

```
CloseHandle(Overlapped.hEvent & ~1);
```

When your server application initializes, it should create the I/O completion port by calling something like *CreateNewCompletionPort*. The application should then create a pool of threads to handle client requests. The question now is how many threads should be in the pool?

This is a tough question to answer, and I will address it in more detail later. For right now, a standard rule of thumb is to take the number of CPUs on the host machine and multiply it by 2. So on a dual-processor machine, you should create a pool of four threads.

All of these threads in the pool should execute a single thread function. Typically, this thread function performs some sort of initialization and then enters a loop that should terminate when the server process is stopping. Inside the loop, the thread puts itself to sleep waiting for device I/O requests to complete to the completion port. This is done by calling *GetQueuedCompletionStatus*:

```
BOOL GetQueuedCompletionStatus(HANDLE hCompletionPort,
    LPDWORD lpdwNumberOfBytesTransferred, LPDWORD lpdwCompletionKey,
    LPOVERLAPPED *lpOverlapped, DWORD dwMilliseconds);
```

The first parameter, *hCompletionPort*, indicates which completion port the thread is interested in monitoring. Many server applications will use a single I/O completion port and have all I/O request notifications complete to this one port. Basically, the job of *GetQueuedCompletionStatus* is to put the calling thread to sleep until an entry appears in the specified completion port's I/O completion queue or until the specified time-out occurs (as specified in the *dwMilliseconds* parameter).

The third data structure associated with an I/O completion port is the waiting thread queue. As each thread in the thread pool calls *GetQueuedCompletionStatus*, the ID of the calling thread is placed in this waiting thread queue. This way, the I/O completion port kernel object always knows which threads are currently waiting to handle completed I/O requests. When an entry appears in the port's I/O completion queue, the completion port wakes one of the threads in the waiting thread queue. This thread will get the pieces of information that make up a completed I/O entry: the number of bytes transferred, the completion key, and the address of the OVERLAPPED structure. This information is returned to the thread via the *lpdwNumberOfBytesTransferred*, *lpdwCompletionKey*, and *lpOverlapped* parameters passed to *GetQueuedCompletionStatus*.

GetQueuedCompletionStatus may return for various reasons. Obviously, if you call the function improperly (that is, pass an invalid completion port handle), the function returns FALSE and *GetLastError* returns an error (such as ERROR_INVALID_HANDLE). If the function times out while waiting for an I/O completion entry, FALSE is returned and *GetLastError* returns WAIT_TIMEOUT.

When an entry is removed from the I/O completion queue, the variables pointed to by the *lpdwNumberOfBytesTransferred*, *lpdwCompletion-Key*, and *lpOverlapped* parameters are set to reflect the entry's information. If the removed entry represents a successfully completed I/O request, *GetQueuedCompletionStatus* returns TRUE. However, if the entry removed from the I/O completion queue represents a failed I/O request, *GetQueuedCompletionStatus* returns FALSE and a call to *GetLastError* returns the reason for the I/O request failure.

You can tell whether *GetQueuedCompletionStatus* returns a failed I/O completion entry or failed because of a time-out or another reason by checking the value of the *lpOverlapped* variable, as shown in the following code fragment:

```
DWORD dwNumberOfBytesTransferred, dwCompletionKey;
LPOVERLAPPED lpOverlapped;
   .
   .
   .
// hIOCompPort is initialized somewhere else in the program.
BOOL fOk = GetQueuedCompletionStatus(hIOCompPort,
   &dwNumberOfBytesTransferred,
   &dwCompletionKey, &lpOverlapped, 1000);
DWORD dwError = GetLastError();
if (fOk) {

   // Process a successfully completed I/O request.
      .
      .
      .

} else {

   if (lpOverlapped != NULL) {

      // Process a failed completed I/O request.
      // dwError contains the reason for failure.
         .
         .
         .

   } else {

      if (dwError == WAIT_TIMEOUT) {
         // Time-out while waiting for completed I/O entry
            .
            .
            .

      } else {
```

(continued)

753

```
        // Bad call to GetQueuedCompletionStatus
        // dwError contains the reason for the bad call.
        .
        .
        .

    }
  }
}
```

As you would expect, entries are removed from the I/O completion queue in a first-in-first-out (FIFO) fashion. However, as you might not expect, threads that call *GetQueuedCompletionStatus* are awakened in a last-in-first-out (LIFO) fashion. The reason for this is again to improve performance. For example, let's say that four threads are waiting in the waiting thread queue. If a single completed I/O entry appears, the last thread to call *GetQueuedCompletionStatus* wakes up to process the entry. When this thread is finished processing the entry, it again calls *Get-QueuedCompletionStatus* to enter the waiting thread queue. Now if another I/O completion entry appears, the same thread that processed the first entry will be awakened to process the new entry.

As long as I/O requests complete so slowly that a single thread can handle them, the system will just keep waking the one thread and the other three threads will continue to sleep. By using this LIFO algorithm, threads that don't get scheduled can have their memory resources (like stack space) swapped out to the disk and flushed from a processor's cache. This means that it's not bad to have many threads waiting on a completion port. If you do have several threads waiting but few I/O requests completing, the extra threads have most of their resources swapped out of the system anyway.

Now it's time to discuss why I/O completion ports are so useful. First, when you create the I/O completion port, you specify the number of threads that can run concurrently. As I said, you usually set this value to the number of CPUs on the host machine.[4] As completed I/O entries are queued, the I/O completion port wants to wake up waiting threads. However, the completion port will wake up only as many threads as you have specified. So if four I/O requests complete and four threads are waiting in a call to *GetQueuedCompletionStatus*, the I/O completion port will allow only two threads to wake up; the other two threads continue to sleep. As each thread processes a completed I/O entry, it again calls *GetQueuedCompletionStatus*. The system sees that more entries are queued and wakes the same threads to go and process the remaining entries.

---

4. You can determine the number of CPUs on the host machine by calling *GetSystemInfo* (discussed in Chapter 6).

If you're thinking about this carefully, you should be noticing that something just doesn't make a lot of sense: if the completion port only ever allows the specified number of threads to wake up concurrently, why have more threads waiting in the thread pool? For example, if we're running on a machine with two CPUs, we create the I/O completion port telling it to allow no more than two threads to process entries concurrently, but we create four (twice the number of CPUs) in the thread pool. It seems as though we are creating two additional threads that will never be awakened to process anything.

I/O completion ports are very smart. When a completion port wakes a thread, the completion port places the thread's ID in the fourth data structure associated with the completion port, a released thread list. (See Figure 15-2.) This allows the completion port to remember which threads it awakened and allows the completion port to monitor the execution of these threads. If a released thread calls any function that places the thread in a wait state, the completion port detects this and updates its internal data structures by moving the thread's ID from the released thread list to the paused thread list (the fifth and final data structure that is part of an I/O completion port).

The goal of the completion port is to keep as many entries in the released thread list as specified by the concurrent number of threads value used when creating the completion port. If a released thread enters a wait state for any reason, the released thread list shrinks and the completion port releases another waiting thread. If a paused thread wakes, it leaves the paused thread list and reenters the released thread list. This means that it is now possible for the released thread list to have more entries in it than are allowed by the maximum concurrency value.

Let's tie all of this together now. Say that we are again running on a machine with two CPUs. We create a completion port that allows no more than two threads to wake concurrently, and we create four threads that are waiting for completed I/O requests. If three completed I/O requests get queued to the port, only two threads are awakened to process the requests. This reduces the number of runnable threads and saves context switching time. Now if one of the running threads calls *Sleep, WaitForSingleObject, WaitForMultipleObjects, SignalObjectAndWait*, or any function that would cause the thread not to be runnable, the I/O completion detects this and wakes a third thread immediately.

Eventually, the first thread will become runnable again. When this happens, the number of runnable threads will be higher than the number of CPUs in the system. However, the completion port again is aware of this and will not allow any additional threads to wake up until the number of threads drops below the number of CPUs. It is presumed that the number of runnable threads will stay above the maximum for only a short time and will die down quickly as the threads loop around and again call *GetQueuedCompletionStatus*. This explains why the thread pool should contain more threads than the concurrent thread count set in the completion port.

Now is a good time to discuss how many threads should be in the thread pool. First, when the server application initializes, you want to create a minimum set of threads so that you don't have to create and destroy threads on a regular basis. Remember that creating and destroying threads wastes CPU time, so it's best to minimize this as much as possible. Second, you want to set a maximum number of threads, too, because creating too many threads wastes system resources. Even if most of these resources can be swapped out of RAM, it's best to minimize system resource usage and not waste even paging file space if you can help it.

You will probably want to experiment with different numbers of threads. Microsoft's Internet Information Service (IIS) uses a fairly complex algorithm to manage its thread pool. The maximum number of threads that IIS will create in the pool is dynamic. When IIS initializes, it allows at most 10 threads per CPU to be created. However, depending on what clients request, this maximum may grow. IIS sets a high maximum of two times the number of megabytes of RAM in the machine.[5]

When a client's request causes code in an ISAPI DLL to execute, IIS increases the maximum count of threads in the pool. When the ISAPI function returns, IIS decrements the count. This is because IIS has no idea what the ISAPI DLL function is going to do. If the function enters an infinite loop, IIS has lost one of its threads. This is why IIS increments the maximum number of threads that can be in the pool.

So far, we have just talked about incrementing a counter that indicates the maximum number of threads that can be in the pool. New threads are not added to the pool as soon as the counter changes. If a client request comes in and all the threads currently in the pool are busy, a new thread is created (assuming that there are fewer threads than the current maximum). IIS knows the number of busy threads by keeping a counter. This counter is decremented just before *GetQueuedCompletion-Status* is called and is incremented just after *GetQueuedCompletionStatus* returns.[6]

---

5. I asked Microsoft's IIS team how they arrived at this formula for a maximum and was told that it just felt right. You should arrive at an algorithm that "feels right" for your application.

6. You'll want to use *InterlockedIncrement* and *InterlockedDecrement* functions to accomplish this.

I have now explained how the maximum thread pool count is maintained and how threads are added to the pool. But what if the thread pool is high and few requests come into the server application? If this happens, we want to start killing off threads that are in the pool. IIS does this by having each thread in the pool call *GetQueuedCompletionStatus* with a time-out value of 24 hours. If a thread in the pool sleeps for 24 hours straight, then the thread wakes up and exits, removing itself from the pool.

A very important thing to keep in mind is that you should always have at least one thread in the pool that can accept incoming client requests. If all the threads in the pool are busy, a client request might be denied. It is always better to accept the request and process it with extra context switching rather than to deny the request completely.

Simulating Completed I/O Requests

In Windows NT 3.51, Microsoft added a new function related to I/O completion ports, *PostQueuedCompletionStatus*:

```
BOOL PostQueuedCompletionStatus(HANDLE hCompletionPort,
    DWORD dwNumberOfBytesTransferred, DWORD dwCompletionKey,
    LPOVERLAPPED lpOverlapped);
```

This function allows you to manually append a completed I/O request to a completion port's I/O completion queue. The *hCompletionPort* parameter identifies the completion port that you wish to queue the entry for. The remaining three parameters, *dwNumberOfBytesTransferred*, *dwCompletionKey*, and *lpOverlapped*, indicate the values that should be returned by a thread's call to *GetQueuedCompletionStatus*. When a thread pulls a simulated entry from the I/O completion queue, *GetQueuedCompletionStatus* returns TRUE, indicating a successfully executed I/O request.

The *PostQueuedCompletionStatus* function is incredibly useful; it gives you a way to communicate with all the threads in your pool. For example, if the user wants to terminate a service application, you want to have all the threads exit cleanly. But if the threads are waiting on the completion port and no I/O requests are coming in, the threads can't wake up. By calling *PostQueuedCompletionStatus* once for each thread in the pool, each thread can wake up, examine the values returned from *GetQueuedCompletionStatus*, see that the application is terminating, and clean up and exit appropriately.

You must be careful when using a technique like this. My example above works because the threads in the pool are dying and not calling

GetQueuedCompletionStatus again. However, if you want to notify the threads of something and have them loop back around to call *GetQueued-CompletionStatus* again, you may have a problem. This is because the threads wake up in a LIFO order. So you will have to employ some additional thread synchronization in your application to ensure that each worker thread gets the opportunity to see its simulated I/O entry. Without this additional thread synchronization, it is possible that one thread might see the same notification several times.

The I/O Completion Port Application

The IOCmpPrt (IOCMPPRT.EXE) application, listed in Figure 15-3 beginning on page 758, demonstrates the use of I/O completion ports. The source code and resource files for the application are in the IOCMP-PRT directory on the companion disc. The program simply copies a file the user specifies to a new file called IOCMPPRT.CPY. When the user executes IOCmpPrt, the I/O Completion Port File Copy dialog box appears:

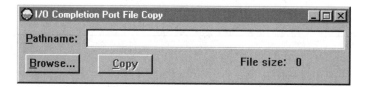

The user clicks on the Browse button to select the file to be copied. After you've selected a file to be copied, the Pathname and File Size fields are updated. When the user clicks on the Copy button, the program calls the *FileCopy* function, which in turn calls *PrepareDstFile*. *PrepareDstFile* was discussed in the AlertIO application section early in the chapter, so I won't go into it here.

After opening the source file and creating the destination file, the I/O completion port kernel object is created by calling *CreateNewCompletionPort*. *CreateNewCompletionPort* is my function that internally calls the Win32 *CreateIoCompletionPort* function to create the completion port. Once the completion port is created, you can associate devices with it. You do this by calling *AssociateDeviceWithCompletionPort*, which is also a function of my own that internally calls *CreateIoCompletionPort*. Once the device is associated with the port, all completed I/O request notifications get appended to the completion port's queue. Each device is also assigned its own completion key: as I/O requests against the source file complete, the completion key will be COMPKEY_READ, and as I/O requests against the destination file complete, the completion key will be COMPKEY_WRITE.

Now we're ready to initialize a set of I/O requests (OVERLAPPED structures) and their memory buffers. To issue the initial read requests, I perform a little trick: I call *PostQueuedCompletionStatus* to simulate completed write I/O requests into the completion port's queue. When the main loop runs, it thinks that some write I/O requests have completed. In processing these completed I/O requests, the program checks to see whether we've attempted to read beyond the end of the file; if we haven't, *ReadFile* is called to issue a read I/O request.

The main loop terminates when there are no outstanding I/O requests. As long as I/O requests are outstanding, the interior of the loop calls *GetQueuedCompletionStatus*. This call puts the thread to sleep until an I/O request completes to the completion port. When *GetQueuedCompletionStatus* returns, the returned completion key, *dwCompKey*, is checked. If *dwCompKey* is COMPKEY_READ, an I/O request against the source file is completed. We then call *WriteFile* to issue a write I/O request against the destination file. If *dwCompKey* is COMPKEY_WRITE, an I/O request against the destination file is completed. If we haven't read beyond the end of the source file, we then call *ReadFile* to continue reading the source file.

When there are no more outstanding I/O requests, the loop terminates. We then destroy the I/O completion port kernel object by calling *CloseHandle*; we free the memory buffers and then call *CopyCleanup*, which closes the files and adjusts the size of the destination file.

IOCmpPrt.ico

IOCMPPRT.C

```
/*****************************************************************
Module name: IOCmpPrt.C
Notices: Copyright (c) 1997 Jeffrey Richter
*****************************************************************/


#include "..\CmnHdr.H"                     /* See Appendix C. */
#include <windows.h>
#include <windowsx.h>
#include <tchar.h>
#include <stdio.h>
#include <stdlib.h>
#include "Resource.H"
```

Figure 15-3.   *(continued)*

The IOCmpPrt application.

Figure 15-3. *continued*

```
//////////////////////////////////////////////////////////////

HANDLE CreateNewCompletionPort(DWORD cSimultaneousClients) {
   return(CreateIoCompletionPort(INVALID_HANDLE_VALUE,
      NULL, 0, cSimultaneousClients));
}


BOOL AssociateDeviceWithCompletionPort(
   HANDLE hCompPort, HANDLE hDevice, DWORD dwCompKey) {
   HANDLE h = CreateIoCompletionPort(hDevice,
      hCompPort, dwCompKey, 0);
   return(h == hCompPort);
}



//////////////////////////////////////////////////////////////


static BOOL PrepareDstFile(LPCTSTR pszFileSrc,
   LPCTSTR pszFileDst,
   PHANDLE phFileSrc, PHANDLE phFileDst,
   PULARGE_INTEGER pulFileSize, DWORD dwPageSize) {

   ULARGE_INTEGER ulFileSizeDst;
   DWORD dwError;
   BOOL fOk = FALSE;

   __try {
      // Open the existing source file for input.
      *phFileSrc = CreateFile(pszFileSrc, GENERIC_READ,
         FILE_SHARE_READ, NULL, OPEN_EXISTING,
         FILE_FLAG_NO_BUFFERING | FILE_FLAG_OVERLAPPED,
         NULL);

      if (*phFileSrc == INVALID_HANDLE_VALUE)
         __leave;

      // Create the new destination file for output.
      *phFileDst = CreateFile(pszFileDst, GENERIC_WRITE,
         0, NULL, CREATE_ALWAYS,
         FILE_FLAG_NO_BUFFERING | FILE_FLAG_OVERLAPPED,
         *phFileSrc);
```

(continued)

Figure 15-3. *continued*

```
      if (*phFileDst == INVALID_HANDLE_VALUE)
         __leave;

      // Get the size of the original file.
      pulFileSize->LowPart = GetFileSize(*phFileSrc,
         &pulFileSize->HighPart);

      // Round up the source file size
      // to an even multiple of pages.
      ulFileSizeDst.QuadPart = (pulFileSize->QuadPart +
         dwPageSize - 1) & ~(dwPageSize - 1);

      // Force the destination file to the size needed.
      dwError = SetFilePointer(*phFileDst,
         ulFileSizeDst.LowPart,
         (PLONG) ulFileSizeDst.HighPart, FILE_BEGIN);
      if ((dwError == 0xffffffff) &&
         (GetLastError() != NO_ERROR))
         __leave;

      if (!SetEndOfFile(*phFileDst))
         __leave;

      fOk = TRUE; // We did everything successfully.
   }
   __finally {

      // If anything failed, clean up entirely.
      if (!fOk) {
         if (*phFileSrc != INVALID_HANDLE_VALUE) {
            CloseHandle(*phFileSrc);
            *phFileSrc = INVALID_HANDLE_VALUE;
         }
         if (*phFileSrc != INVALID_HANDLE_VALUE) {
            CloseHandle(*phFileDst);
            *phFileDst = INVALID_HANDLE_VALUE;
         }
      }
   }
   return(fOk);
}


///////////////////////////////////////////////////////////////
```

(continued)

Figure 15-3. *continued*

```
static void CopyCleanup(LPCTSTR pszFileDst, HANDLE hFileSrc,
   HANDLE hFileDst, PULARGE_INTEGER pulFileSize) {

   // Close the source and destination files.
   CloseHandle(hFileDst);
   CloseHandle(hFileSrc);

   // We need another handle to the destination file that is
   // opened without FILE_FLAG_NO_BUFFERING. This allows us
   // to set the end-of-file marker to a position that is
   // not sector-aligned.
   hFileDst = CreateFile(pszFileDst, GENERIC_WRITE,
      FILE_SHARE_READ | FILE_SHARE_WRITE, NULL,
      OPEN_EXISTING, 0, NULL);

   if (hFileDst != INVALID_HANDLE_VALUE) {

      // Set the destination file's size to the size of the
      // source file, in case the size of the source file was
      // not a multiple of the page size.
      SetFilePointer(hFileDst, pulFileSize->LowPart,
         (PLONG) pulFileSize->HighPart, FILE_BEGIN);
      SetEndOfFile(hFileDst);
      CloseHandle(hFileDst);
   }
}


/////////////////////////////////////////////////////////////////


typedef struct {
   // The page size used on the host machine
   DWORD dwPageSize;

   // Handles of the source and destination files
   HANDLE hFileSrc, hFileDst;

   // Size of source file
   ULARGE_INTEGER ulFileSize;

   // Offset in source file where next read begins
   ULARGE_INTEGER ulNextReadOffset;
```

(continued)

Figure 15-3. *continued*

```
    // The number of pending read and write I/O requests
    int nReadsInProgress;
    int nWritesInProgress;
} COPYSTATE, *PCOPYSTATE;


// Each IO requires an OVERLAPPED structure and a buffer.
typedef struct {
    OVERLAPPED Overlapped;
    PBYTE      pbData;
} IOREQ, *PIOREQ;

#define MAX_PENDING_IO_REQS    4
#define BUFFSIZE               (64 * 1024)

// The keys indicating the type of completed IO
#define COMPKEY_READ  1
#define COMPKEY_WRITE 2


//////////////////////////////////////////////////////////////


BOOL FileCopy (LPCTSTR pszFileSrc, LPCTSTR pszFileDst) {

    // We need a local copy state variable.
    COPYSTATE cs;

    // Maintain info about each IO request.
    IOREQ IOReq[MAX_PENDING_IO_REQS] = { 0 };

    SYSTEM_INFO si;
    int nIOReq;
    BOOL fOk, fDone = FALSE;

    // I/O Completion Port where read and writes complete to
    HANDLE hIOCompPort = NULL;

    DWORD dwNumBytesXfer, dwCompKey;
    LPOVERLAPPED pOverlapped;

    // Initialize the global COPYSTATE variable.
    GetSystemInfo(&si);
    cs.dwPageSize = si.dwPageSize;
    cs.ulNextReadOffset.QuadPart = 0;
```

(continued)

Figure 15-3. *continued*

```
    cs.nReadsInProgress = 0;
    cs.nWritesInProgress = 0;

    // Open the existing source file for input.
    fOk = PrepareDstFile(pszFileSrc, pszFileDst,
        &cs.hFileSrc, &cs.hFileDst,
        &cs.ulFileSize, cs.dwPageSize);
    if (!fOk)
        return(fOk);

    // Create a new completion port kernel object.
    hIOCompPort = CreateNewCompletionPort(0);
    chASSERT(hIOCompPort != NULL);

    // Associate completed IOs to/from the source file with
    // IO Completion Port. All completed IOs have a
    // completion key of COMPKEY_READ.
    chVERIFY(AssociateDeviceWithCompletionPort(hIOCompPort,
        cs.hFileSrc, COMPKEY_READ));

    // Associate completed IOs to/from the destination file
    // with IO Completion Port. All completed IOs have a
    // completion key of COMPKEY_WRITE.
    chVERIFY(AssociateDeviceWithCompletionPort(hIOCompPort,
        cs.hFileDst, COMPKEY_WRITE));

    // Start the copy engine by posting a number of read
    // IO requests against the source file.
    for (nIOReq = 0; nIOReq < MAX_PENDING_IO_REQS;
        nIOReq++) {
        IOReq[nIOReq].Overlapped.Internal = 0;
        IOReq[nIOReq].Overlapped.InternalHigh = 0;
        IOReq[nIOReq].Overlapped.Offset = 0;
        IOReq[nIOReq].Overlapped.OffsetHigh = 0;
        IOReq[nIOReq].Overlapped.hEvent = NULL;
        IOReq[nIOReq].pbData = VirtualAlloc(NULL,
            BUFFSIZE, MEM_RESERVE | MEM_COMMIT,
            PAGE_READWRITE);

        cs.nWritesInProgress++;
        PostQueuedCompletionStatus(hIOCompPort, 0,
            COMPKEY_WRITE, &IOReq[nIOReq].Overlapped);
    }
```

(continued)

Figure 15-3. *continued*

```
// Loop until an error has occurred or until the
// destination file has been written.
while ((cs.nReadsInProgress > 0) ||
       (cs.nWritesInProgress > 0)) {
   PIOREQ pIOReq;
   fOk = GetQueuedCompletionStatus(hIOCompPort,
      &dwNumBytesXfer, &dwCompKey, &pOverlapped,
      INFINITE);
   chASSERT(fOk || (GetLastError() == NO_ERROR));
   pIOReq = (PIOREQ) pOverlapped;

   switch (dwCompKey) {
      case COMPKEY_READ:
         cs.nReadsInProgress--;
         // Round up the number of bytes to write
         // to a sector boundary.
         dwNumBytesXfer =
            (dwNumBytesXfer + cs.dwPageSize - 1) &
            ~(cs.dwPageSize - 1);
         fOk = WriteFile(cs.hFileDst, pIOReq->pbData,
            dwNumBytesXfer, &dwNumBytesXfer,
            pOverlapped);
         // The write either completed or is pending.
         chASSERT(fOk || (!fOk &&
            (GetLastError() == ERROR_IO_PENDING)));
         cs.nWritesInProgress++;
         break;

      case COMPKEY_WRITE:
         cs.nWritesInProgress--;
         if (cs.ulNextReadOffset.QuadPart >=
             cs.ulFileSize.QuadPart)
            break;

         // We haven't read past the end of the file yet.
         // Read the next chunk of data.
         pOverlapped->Offset    =
            cs.ulNextReadOffset.LowPart;
         pOverlapped->OffsetHigh =
            cs.ulNextReadOffset.HighPart;
         fOk = ReadFile(cs.hFileSrc, pIOReq->pbData,
            BUFFSIZE, &dwNumBytesXfer, pOverlapped);
         // The read either completed or is pending.
         chASSERT(fOk || (!fOk &&
```

(continued)

Figure 15-3. *continued*

```
                (GetLastError() == ERROR_IO_PENDING)));
            cs.nReadsInProgress++;
            // Offset in source file where next read begins
            cs.ulNextReadOffset.QuadPart += BUFFSIZE;
            break;
        }
    }

    // Destroy the I/O completion port.
    CloseHandle(hIOCompPort);

    // Free the memory buffers used for the copy.
    for (nIOReq = 0; nIOReq < MAX_PENDING_IO_REQS;
        nIOReq++) {
        VirtualFree(IOReq[nIOReq].pbData, 0, MEM_RELEASE);
    }

    // Close the source and destination files; force the
    // destination file to be the same size as the source.
    CopyCleanup(pszFileDst, cs.hFileSrc, cs.hFileDst,
        &cs.ulFileSize);

    return(TRUE);
}


/////////////////////////////////////////////////////////////////


BOOL Dlg_OnInitDialog (HWND hwnd, HWND hwndFocus,
    LPARAM lParam) {

    // Associate an icon with the dialog box.
    chSETDLGICONS(hwnd, IDI_IOCMPPRT, IDI_IOCMPPRT);

    // Disable the "Copy" button because no file
    // has been selected yet.
    EnableWindow(GetDlgItem(hwnd, IDOK), FALSE);

    return(TRUE);
}


/////////////////////////////////////////////////////////////////
```

(continued)

Figure 15-3. *continued*

```
void Dlg_OnCommand (HWND hwnd, int id,
    HWND hwndCtl, UINT codeNotify) {

    TCHAR szPathname[_MAX_DIR];
    BOOL fOk;
    OPENFILENAME ofn;

    switch (id) {
        case IDOK:
            // Copy the source file to the destination file.
            Static_GetText(GetDlgItem(hwnd, IDC_SRCFILE),
                szPathname, sizeof(szPathname));
            SetCursor(LoadCursor(NULL, IDC_WAIT));
            FileCopy(szPathname, __TEXT("IOCmpPrt.CPY"));
            break;

        case IDC_BROWSE:
            chINITSTRUCT(ofn, TRUE);
            ofn.hwndOwner = hwnd;
            ofn.lpstrFilter = __TEXT("*.*\0");
            _tcscpy(szPathname, __TEXT("*.*"));
            ofn.lpstrFile = szPathname;
            ofn.nMaxFile = sizeof(szPathname);
            ofn.Flags = OFN_FILEMUSTEXIST;
            fOk = GetOpenFileName(&ofn);

            if (fOk) {
                HANDLE hFile;
                Static_SetText(GetDlgItem(hwnd, IDC_SRCFILE),
                    szPathname);
                hFile = CreateFile(szPathname, GENERIC_READ,
                    0, NULL, OPEN_EXISTING, 0, NULL);

                SetDlgItemInt(hwnd, IDC_SRCFILESIZE,
                    GetFileSize(hFile, NULL), FALSE);
                CloseHandle(hFile);
            }

            // Enable the "Copy" button if the user selected
            // a valid pathname.
            GetWindowText(GetDlgItem(hwnd, IDC_SRCFILE),
                szPathname, sizeof(szPathname));
            EnableWindow(GetDlgItem(hwnd, IDOK),
                szPathname[0] != __TEXT('('));
```

(continued)

Figure 15-3. *continued*

```
            if (fOk) {
                // If the user pressed the OK button in the file
                // dialog box, change focus to the "Copy" button.
                FORWARD_WM_NEXTDLGCTL(hwnd,
                    GetDlgItem(hwnd, IDOK), TRUE, SendMessage);
            }
            break;

        case IDCANCEL:
            EndDialog(hwnd, id);
            break;
    }
}


///////////////////////////////////////////////////////////////


BOOL CALLBACK Dlg_Proc (HWND hwnd, UINT uMsg,
    WPARAM wParam, LPARAM lParam) {

    switch (uMsg) {
        chHANDLE_DLGMSG(hwnd, WM_INITDIALOG, Dlg_OnInitDialog);
        chHANDLE_DLGMSG(hwnd, WM_COMMAND, Dlg_OnCommand);
    }

    return(FALSE);
}


///////////////////////////////////////////////////////////////


int WINAPI _tWinMain (HINSTANCE hinstExe,
    HINSTANCE hinstPrev, LPTSTR pszCmdLine, int nCmdShow) {

    chWARNIFUNICODEUNDERWIN95();
    DialogBox(hinstExe, MAKEINTRESOURCE(IDD_IOCMPPRT),
        NULL, Dlg_Proc);

    return(0);
}


////////////////////////// End Of File //////////////////////////
```

(continued)

Figure 15-3. *continued*

IOCMPPRT.RC

```
//Microsoft Developer Studio generated resource script.
//
#include "Resource.h"

#define APSTUDIO_READONLY_SYMBOLS
/////////////////////////////////////////////////////////////
//
// Generated from the TEXTINCLUDE 2 resource.
//
#include "afxres.h"


/////////////////////////////////////////////////////////////
#undef APSTUDIO_READONLY_SYMBOLS


/////////////////////////////////////////////////////////////
// English (U.S.) resources

#if !defined(AFX_RESOURCE_DLL) || defined(AFX_TARG_ENU)
#ifdef _WIN32
LANGUAGE LANG_ENGLISH, SUBLANG_ENGLISH_US
#pragma code_page(1252)
#endif //_WIN32


/////////////////////////////////////////////////////////////
//
// Icon
//


// Icon with lowest ID value placed first to ensure
// application icon remains consistent on all systems.
IDI_IOCMPPRT            ICON    DISCARDABLE     "IOCmpPrt.Ico"


/////////////////////////////////////////////////////////////
//
// Dialog
//


IDD_IOCMPPRT DIALOG DISCARDABLE  15, 24, 214, 37
STYLE WS_MINIMIZEBOX | WS_POPUP | WS_VISIBLE | WS_CAPTION |
    WS_SYSMENU
CAPTION "I/O Completion Port File Copy"
FONT 8, "System"
```

(continued)

Figure 15-3. *continued*

```
BEGIN
    LTEXT            "&Pathname:",-1,4,6,35,8
    EDITTEXT         IDC_SRCFILE,44,4,168,12,ES_AUTOHSCROLL
    PUSHBUTTON       "&Browse...",IDC_BROWSE,4,20,36,12,
                     WS_GROUP
    DEFPUSHBUTTON    "&Copy",IDOK,52,20,36,12
    LTEXT            "File size:",-1,144,20,31,8
    LTEXT            "0",IDC_SRCFILESIZE,180,20,34,8
END


#ifdef APSTUDIO_INVOKED
/////////////////////////////////////////////////////////////
//
// TEXTINCLUDE
//

1 TEXTINCLUDE DISCARDABLE
BEGIN
    "Resource.h\0"
END

2 TEXTINCLUDE DISCARDABLE
BEGIN
    "#include ""afxres.h""\r\n"
    "\0"
END

3 TEXTINCLUDE DISCARDABLE
BEGIN
    "\r\n"
    "\0"
END

#endif     // APSTUDIO_INVOKED


/////////////////////////////////////////////////////////////
//
// DESIGNINFO
//

#ifdef APSTUDIO_INVOKED
GUIDELINES DESIGNINFO DISCARDABLE
```

(continued)

Figure 15-3. *continued*

```
BEGIN
    IDD_IOCMPPRT, DIALOG
    BEGIN
        RIGHTMARGIN, 190
        BOTTOMMARGIN, 33
    END
END
#endif    // APSTUDIO_INVOKED


#endif    // English (U.S.) resources
/////////////////////////////////////////////////////////////



#ifndef APSTUDIO_INVOKED
/////////////////////////////////////////////////////////////
//
// Generated from the TEXTINCLUDE 3 resource.
//


/////////////////////////////////////////////////////////////
#endif    // not APSTUDIO_INVOKED
```

Determining Whether an
I/O Request Has Completed

The Win32 SDK that includes the new functions for Windows NT 4 defines a macro called *HasOverlappedIoCompleted*:

```
#define HasOverlappedIoCompleted(lpOverlapped) \
    ((lpOverlapped)->Internal != STATUS_PENDING)
```

This is a macro and therefore can be used with versions of Windows NT prior to 4. This macro allows an application to very quickly check whether a specific I/O request has completed. All you have to do is pass the address of the OVERLAPPED structure associated with the request into this macro. If the request is still pending, FALSE is returned; if the I/O request completed, TRUE is returned.

Once you know that the I/O request has completed, you can get the details of the operation by calling *GetOverlappedResult* or *GetQueued-CompletionStatus*, or by placing the thread in an alertable state so that the I/O completion callback routine gets a chance to execute.

Canceling Outstanding I/O Requests

In Windows NT 4, a new function was added that allows a thread to cancel all its outstanding I/O requests to a specific device:

```
BOOL CancelIO(HANDLE hFile);
```

Note that this function cancels only requests that were made by the calling thread; you cannot cancel requests made by other threads. If the function fails, FALSE is returned.

If the thread that issued the I/O request did so using *ReadFileEx* or *WriteFileEx*, *CancelIO* causes an entry to be placed in the thread's APC queue. When the thread is in an alertable state, the callback function is called with an error code of ERROR_OPERATION_ABORTED.

If completed I/O requests for the device get queued to an I/O completion port, an entry will get queued and *GetQueuedCompletionStatus* will return; a subsequent call to *GetLastError* returns ERROR_OPERA-TION_ABORTED.

You should also be aware that calling *CloseHandle* on a device that has outstanding I/O requests against it causes the I/O requests to be canceled.

STRUCTURED EXCEPTION HANDLING

Close your eyes for a moment and imagine writing your application as though your code could never fail. That's right—there's always enough memory, no one ever passes you an invalid pointer, and files you count on always exist. Wouldn't it be a pleasure to write your code if you could make these assumptions? Your code would be so much easier to write, to read, and to understand. No more fussing with *if* statements here and *goto*s there—in each function, you'd just write your code top to bottom.

If this kind of straightforward programming environment seems like a dream to you, you'll love structured exception handling (SEH). The virtue of SEH is that as you write your code, you can focus on getting your task done. If something goes wrong at run time, the system catches it and notifies you of the problem.

With SEH, you can't totally ignore the possibility of an error in your code, but SEH does allow you to separate the main job from the error handling chores. This division makes it easy to concentrate on the problem at hand and focus on the possible errors later.

One of Microsoft's main motivations for adding structured exception handling to Win32 was to ease the development of Windows 95 and Windows NT and make the operating systems more robust. The developers of the Windows NT operating system and its various subsystems used SEH to make the system more robust. And we can use SEH to make our own applications more robust.

The burden of making SEH work falls more on the compiler than on the operating system. Your compiler must generate special code when exception blocks are entered into and exited from. The compiler must produce tables of support data structures to handle SEH and also must supply callback functions that the operating system can call so that exception blocks can be traversed. The compiler is also responsible for preparing stack frames and other internal information that is used and referenced by the operating system. Adding SEH support to a compiler is not an easy task, and you shouldn't be surprised if your favorite compiler vendor delays shipment of its Win32-capable compiler because of SEH implementation problems.

Nor should it surprise you that different compiler vendors implement SEH in different ways. Fortunately, we can ignore compiler implementation details and just use the compiler's SEH capabilities.

Differences among compiler implementations of SEH could make it difficult to discuss in specific ways with specific code examples how you can take advantage of SEH. However, most compiler vendors follow Microsoft's suggested syntax. The syntax and keywords I use in my examples may differ from those of another company's compiler, but the main SEH concepts are the same. I'll use the Microsoft Visual C++ compiler's syntax throughout this chapter.

Important

Don't confuse structured exception handling with C++ exception handling. C++ exception handling is a different form of exception handling, one that makes use of the C++ keywords *catch* and *throw*. Microsoft has added C++ exception handling in Visual C++ version 2.0. Microsoft's implementation of C++ exception handling is accomplished by taking advantage of the structured exception handling capabilities already present in the compiler and Windows operating systems.

Structured exception handling really consists of two main capabilities: termination handling and exception handling. We'll turn our attention to termination handlers first.

Termination Handlers

A termination handler guarantees that a block of code (the termination handler) will be called and executed regardless of how another section of code (the guarded body) is exited. The syntax (using the Microsoft Visual C++ compiler) for a termination handler is as follows:

```
__try {
  // Guarded body
  .
  .
  .
}
__finally {
  // Termination handler
  .
  .
  .
}
```

The *__try* and *__finally* keywords delineate the two sections of the termination handler. In the code fragment above, the operating system and the compiler work together to guarantee that the *__finally* block code in the termination handler will be executed no matter how the guarded body is exited. Regardless of whether you put a *return*, a *goto*, or even a call to *longjump* in the guarded body, the termination handler will be called. Here's the flow of code execution:

```
// 1. Code before the try block executes

__try {
  // 2. Code inside the try block executes
}
__finally {
  // 3. Code inside the finally block executes
}

// 4. Code after the finally block executes
```

Understanding Termination Handlers by Example

Because the compiler and the operating system are intimately involved with the execution of your code when you use SEH, I believe that the best way to demonstrate how SEH works is by examining source code samples and discussing the order in which the statements execute in each example.

Therefore, the next few sections show different source code fragments, and the text associated with each fragment explains how the compiler and operating system alter the execution order of your code.

Funcenstein1

To appreciate the ramifications of using termination handlers, let's examine a more concrete coding example on the next page.

```
DWORD Funcenstein1 (void) {
   DWORD dwTemp;

   // 1. Do any processing here.
      .
      .
      .
   __try {
      // 2. Request permission to access
      //    protected data, and then use it.
      WaitForSingleObject(g_hSem, INFINITE);

      g_dwProtectedData = 5;
      dwTemp = g_dwProtectedData;
   }
   __finally {
      // 3. Allow others to use protected data.
      ReleaseSemaphore(g_hSem, 1, NULL);
   }

   // 4. Continue processing.
   return(dwTemp);
}
```

In *Funcenstein1*, using the *try-finally* blocks really isn't doing very much for you. The code will wait for a semaphore, alter the contents of the protected data, save the new value in the local variable *dwTemp*, release the semaphore, and return the new value to the caller.

Funcenstein2

Now let's modify the function a little and see what happens:

```
DWORD Funcenstein2 (void) {
   DWORD dwTemp;

   // 1. Do any processing here.
      .
      .
      .
   __try {
      // 2. Request permission to access
      //    protected data, and then use it.
      WaitForSingleObject(g_hSem, INFINITE);

      g_dwProtectedData = 5;
      dwTemp = g_dwProtectedData;

      // Return the new value.
```

```
    return(dwTemp);
}
__finally {
    // 3. Allow others to use protected data.
    ReleaseSemaphore(g_hSem, 1, NULL);
}

// Continue processing--this code
// will never execute in this version.
dwTemp = 9;
return(dwTemp);
}
```

In *Funcenstein2*, a *return* statement has been added to the end of the *try* block. This *return* statement tells the compiler that you want to exit the function and return the contents of the *dwTemp* variable, which now contains the value 5. However, if this *return* statement had been executed, the semaphore would not have been released by the thread—and no other thread would ever be able to gain control of the semaphore. As you can imagine, this kind of sequence can become a really big problem because threads waiting for the semaphore might never be able to resume execution.

However, by using the termination handler, you have avoided the premature execution of the *return* statement. When the *return* statement tries to exit the *try* block, the compiler makes sure that the code in the *finally* block executes first. The code inside the *finally* block is guaranteed to execute before the *return* statement in the *try* block is allowed to exit. In *Funcenstein2*, putting the call to *ReleaseSemaphore* into a termination handler block ensures that the semaphore will always be released—there is no chance for a thread to accidentally retain ownership of the semaphore, which would mean that all other threads waiting for the semaphore would never be scheduled CPU time.

After the code in the *finally* block executes, the function does, in fact, return. Any code appearing below the *finally* block doesn't execute because the function returns in the *try* block. Therefore, this function returns the value 5, not the value 9.

You might be asking yourself how the compiler guarantees that the *finally* block executes before the *try* block can be exited. When the compiler examines your source code, it sees that you have coded a *return* statement inside a *try* block. Having seen this, the compiler generates code to save the return value (5 in our example) in a temporary variable created by the compiler. The compiler then generates code to execute the instructions contained inside the *finally* block; this is called a *local unwind.* More specifically, a local unwind occurs when the system executes the contents of a *finally* block because of the premature exit of code in a *try* block. After the instructions inside the *finally* block execute, the value in the compiler's temporary variable is retrieved and returned from the function.

As you can see, the compiler must generate additional code and the system must perform additional work to pull this whole thing off. On different CPUs, the steps necessary to make termination handling work vary. The MIPS, Alpha, and PowerPC processors, for example, must execute several hundred or even several thousand instructions to capture the *try* block's premature return and call the *finally* block. You should avoid writing code that causes premature exits from the *try* block of a termination handler because the performance of your application could be adversely impacted. Later in this chapter, I'll discuss the __leave keyword, which can help you avoid writing code that forces local unwinds.

Exception handling is designed to capture exceptions (in our example, the premature *return*)—the exceptions to the rule that you expect to happen infrequently. If a situation is the norm, it's much more efficient to check for the situation explicitly rather than to rely on the SEH capabilities of the operating system and your compiler to trap common occurrences.

Note that when the flow of control naturally leaves the *try* block and enters the *finally* block (as shown in *Funcenstein1*), the overhead of entering the *finally* block is minimal. On the *x86* CPUs using the Microsoft compiler, a single machine instruction is executed as execution leaves the *try* block to enter the *finally* block—I doubt that you will even notice this overhead in your application. When the compiler has to generate additional code and the system has to perform additional work, as in *Funcenstein2*, the overhead is much more noticeable.

Funcenstein3

Now let's modify the function again and take a look at what happens:

```
DWORD Funcenstein3 (void) {
    DWORD dwTemp;

    // 1. Do any processing here.
    :

    __try {
```

```
    // 2. Request permission to access
    //    protected data, and then use it.
    WaitForSingleObject(g_hSem, INFINITE);

    g_dwProtectedData = 5;
    dwTemp = g_dwProtectedData;

    // Try to jump over the finally block.
    goto ReturnValue;
  }

  __finally {
    // 3. Allow others to use protected data.
    ReleaseSemaphore(g_hSem, 1, NULL);
  }

  dwTemp = 9;
  // 4. Continue processing.
  ReturnValue:
  return(dwTemp);
}
```

In *Funcenstein3*, when the compiler sees the *goto* statement in the *try* block, it generates a local unwind to execute the contents of the *finally* block first. However, this time, after the code in the *finally* block executes, the code after the ReturnValue label is executed because no return occurs in either the *try* or the *finally* block. This code causes the function to return a 5. Again, because you have interrupted the natural flow of control from the *try* block into the *finally* block, you may incur a high performance penalty depending on the CPU your application is running on.

Funcfurter1

Now let's look at another scenario in which termination handling really proves its value. Look at this function:

```
DWORD Funcfurter1 (void) {
  DWORD dwTemp;

  // 1. Do any processing here.
    .
    .
    .
  __try {
    // 2. Request permission to access
    //    protected data, and then use it.
    WaitForSingleObject(g_hSem, INFINITE);
```

(continued)

```
      dwTemp = Funcinator(g_dwProtectedData);
   }
   __finally {
      // 3. Allow others to use protected data.
      ReleaseSemaphore(g_hSem, 1, NULL);
   }

   // 4. Continue processing.
   return(dwTemp);
}
```

Now imagine that the *Funcinator* function called in the *try* block contains a bug that causes an invalid memory access. In a 16-bit Windows application, this would present the user with the ever-popular Application Error dialog box. When the user dismissed the error dialog box, the application would be terminated. If the code were running in a Win32 application with no *try-finally* block, and the application were terminated because *Funcinator* generated an invalid memory access, the semaphore would still be owned and would never be released—any threads in other processes that were waiting for this semaphore would never be scheduled CPU time. But placing the call to *ReleaseSemaphore* in a *finally* block guarantees that the semaphore gets released even if some other function causes a memory access violation.

If termination handlers are powerful enough to capture an application terminating because of an invalid memory access, we should have no trouble believing that they will also capture *setjump/longjump* combinations and, of course, simple statements such as *break* and *continue*.

Pop Quiz Time: *FuncaDoodleDoo*

Now for a test. Can you determine what the following function returns?

```
DWORD FuncaDoodleDoo (void) {
   DWORD dwTemp = 0;

   while (dwTemp < 10) {

      __try {
         if (dwTemp == 2)
            continue;

         if (dwTemp == 3)
            break;
      }
```

```
    __finally {
        dwTemp++;
    }

    dwTemp++;
}

dwTemp += 10;
return(dwTemp);
}
```

Let's analyze what the function does step by step. First *dwTemp* is set to 0. The code in the *try* block executes, but neither of the *if* statements evaluates to TRUE. Execution moves naturally to the code in the *finally* block, which increments *dwTemp* to 1. Then the instruction after the *finally* block increments *dwTemp* again, making it 2.

When the loop iterates, *dwTemp* is 2 and the *continue* statement in the *try* block will execute. Without a termination handler to force execution of the *finally* block before exit from the *try* block, execution would immediately jump back up to the *while* test, *dwTemp* would not be changed, and we would have started an infinite loop. With a termination handler, the system notes that the *continue* statement causes the flow of control to exit the *try* block prematurely and moves execution to the *finally* block. In the *finally* block, *dwTemp* is incremented to 3. However, the code after the *finally* block doesn't execute because the flow of control moves back to *continue* and thus to the top of the loop.

Now we are processing the loop's third iteration. This time, the first *if* statement evaluates to FALSE, but the second *if* statement evaluates to TRUE. The system again catches our attempt to break out of the *try* block and executes the code in the *finally* block first. Now *dwTemp* is incremented to 4. Because a *break* statement was executed, control resumes after the loop. Thus, the code after the *finally* block and still inside the loop doesn't execute. The code below the loop adds 10 to *dwTemp* for a grand total of 14—the result of calling this function. It should go without saying that you should never actually write code like *FuncaDoodleDoo*. I placed the *continue* and *break* statements in the middle of the code only to demonstrate the operation of the termination handler.

Although a termination handler will catch most situations in which the *try* block would otherwise be exited prematurely, it can't cause the code in a *finally* block to be executed if the thread or process is terminated. A call to *ExitThread* or *ExitProcess* will immediately terminate the

thread or process without executing any of the code in a *finally* block. Also, if your thread or process should die because some application called *TerminateThread* or *TerminateProcess,* the code in a *finally* block again won't execute. Some C run-time functions, such as *abort,* which in turn call *ExitProcess,* again preclude the execution of *finally* blocks. You can't do anything to prevent another application from terminating one of your threads or processes, but you can prevent your own premature calls to *ExitThread* and *ExitProcess.*

Funcenstein4

Let's take a look at one more termination handling scenario.

```
DWORD Funcenstein4 (void) {
    DWORD dwTemp;
    // 1. Do any processing here.
    :
    :

    __try {
        // 2. Request permission to access
        //    protected data, and then use it.
        WaitForSingleObject(g_hSem, INFINITE);

        g_dwProtectedData = 5;
        dwTemp = g_dwProtectedData;

        // Return the new value.
        return(dwTemp);
    }
    __finally {
        // 3. Allow others to use protected data.
        ReleaseSemaphore(g_hSem, 1, NULL);
        return(103);
    }

    // Continue processing--this code will never execute.
    dwTemp = 9;
    return(dwTemp);
}
```

In *Funcenstein4,* the *try* block will execute and try to return the value of *dwTemp* (5) back to *Funcenstein4*'s caller. As noted in the discussion of *Funcenstein2,* trying to return prematurely from a *try* block causes the generation of code that puts the return value into a temporary variable created by the compiler. Then the code inside the *finally* block is executed. Notice that in this variation on *Funcenstein2* I have added a *return*

statement to the *finally* block. Will *Funcenstein4* return 5 to the caller, or 103? The answer is that 103 will be returned because the *return* statement in the *finally* block causes the value 103 to be stored in the same temporary variable in which the value 5 has been stored, overwriting the 5. When the *finally* block completes execution, the value now in the temporary variable (103) is returned from *Funcenstein4* to its caller.

We've seen termination handlers do an effective job of rescuing execution from a premature exit of the *try* block, and we've also seen termination handlers produce an unwanted result because they prevented a premature exit of the *try* block. A good rule of thumb is to avoid any statements that would cause a premature exit of the *try* block part of a termination handler. In fact, it is always best to remove all *returns, continues, breaks, gotos,* and so on from inside both the *try* and the *finally* blocks of a termination handler and to put these statements outside the handler. Such a practice will cause the compiler to generate both a smaller amount of code because it won't have to catch premature exits from the *try* block and faster code because it will have fewer instructions to execute in order to perform the local unwind. In addition, your code will be much easier to read and maintain.

Funcarama1

We have pretty much covered the basic syntax and semantics of termination handlers. Now let's look at how a termination handler could be used to simplify a more complicated programming problem. Let's look at a function that doesn't take advantage of termination handlers at all.

```
BOOL Funcarama1 (void) {
   HANDLE hFile = INVALID_HANDLE_VALUE;
   LPVOID lpBuf = NULL;
   DWORD dwNumBytesRead;
   BOOL fOk;

   hFile = CreateFile("SOMEDATA.DAT", GENERIC_READ,
      FILE_SHARE_READ, NULL, OPEN_EXISTING,
      0, NULL);
   if (hFile == INVALID_HANDLE_VALUE) {
      return(FALSE);
   }

   lpBuf = VirtualAlloc(NULL, 1024, MEM_COMMIT,
      PAGE_READWRITE);
   if (lpBuf == NULL) {
      CloseHandle(hFile);
```

(continued)

```
      return(FALSE);
   }

   fOk = ReadFile(hFile, lpBuf, 1024,
      &dwNumBytesRead, NULL);
   if (!fOk || (dwNumBytesRead == 0)) {
      VirtualFree(lpBuf, MEM_RELEASE | MEM_DECOMMIT);
      CloseHandle(hFile);
      return(FALSE);
   }

   // Do some calculation on the data.
      .
      .
      .
   // Clean up all the resources.
   VirtualFree(lpBuf, MEM_RELEASE | MEM_DECOMMIT);
   CloseHandle(hFile);
   return(TRUE);
}
```

All the error checking in *Funcarama1* makes the function difficult to read, which also makes the function difficult to understand, maintain, and modify.

Funcarama2

Of course, it's possible to rewrite *Funcarama1* so that it is a little cleaner and easier to understand:

```
BOOL Funcarama2 (void) {
   HANDLE hFile = INVALID_HANDLE_VALUE;
   LPVOID lpBuf = NULL;
   DWORD dwNumBytesRead;
   BOOL fOk, fSuccess = FALSE;

   hFile = CreateFile("SOMEDATA.DAT", GENERIC_READ,
      FILE_SHARE_READ, NULL, OPEN_EXISTING,
      0, NULL);

   if (hFile != INVALID_HANDLE_VALUE) {

      lpBuf = VirtualAlloc(NULL, 1024, MEM_COMMIT,
         PAGE_READWRITE);

      if (lpBuf != NULL) {

         fOk = ReadFile(hFile, lpBuf, 1024,
            &dwNumBytesRead, NULL);
```

```
        if (fOk && (dwNumBytesRead != 0)) {
            // Do some calculation on the data.
                :
                :
            fSuccess = TRUE;
        }

    }

    VirtualFree(lpBuf, MEM_RELEASE | MEM_DECOMMIT);

  }

  CloseHandle(hFile);
  return(fSuccess);
}
```

Funcarama 2 is easier to understand, but it is still difficult to modify and maintain. Also, the indentation level gets to be pretty extreme as more conditional statements are added; with such a rewrite, you soon end up writing code on the far right of your screen and wrapping statements after every five characters!

Funcarama3

Let's rewrite the first version, *Funcarama1*, to take advantage of an SEH termination handler:

```
DWORD Funcarama3 (void) {
   HANDLE hFile = INVALID_HANDLE_VALUE;
   LPVOID lpBuf = NULL;

   __try {
      DWORD dwNumBytesRead;
      BOOL fOk;

      hFile = CreateFile("SOMEDATA.DAT", GENERIC_READ,
         FILE_SHARE_READ, NULL, OPEN_EXISTING,
         0, NULL);
      if (hFile == INVALID_HANDLE_VALUE) {
         return(FALSE);
      }

      lpBuf = VirtualAlloc(NULL, 1024, MEM_COMMIT,
         PAGE_READWRITE);
      if (lpBuf == NULL) {
         return(FALSE);
      }
```

(continued)

```
        fOk = ReadFile(hFile, lpBuf, 1024,
            &dwNumBytesRead, NULL);
        if (!fOk || (dwNumBytesRead != 1024)) {
            return(FALSE);
        }

        // Do some calculation on the data.
        .
        .
        .

    }

    __finally {
        // Clean up all the resources.
        if (lpBuf != NULL)
            VirtualFree(lpBuf, MEM_RELEASE | MEM_DECOMMIT);
        if (hFile != INVALID_HANDLE_VALUE)
            CloseHandle(hFile);
    }
    // Continue processing.
    return(TRUE);
}
```

The real virtue of the *Funcarama3* version is that all of the function's cleanup code is localized in one place and one place only: the *finally* block. If we ever need to add some additional code to this function, we can simply add a single cleanup line in the *finally* block—we won't have to go back to every possible location of failure and add our cleanup line to each failure location.

Funcarama4: The Final Frontier

The real problem with the *Funcarama3* version is the overhead. As mentioned after the discussion of *Funcenstein4*, you really should avoid putting *return* statements into *try* blocks as much as possible.

To help make such avoidance easier, Microsoft added another keyword, __*leave*, to its C++ compiler. Here is the *Funcarama4* version, which takes advantage of the __*leave* keyword:

```
DWORD Funcarama4 (void) {
    HANDLE hFile = INVALID_HANDLE_VALUE;
    LPVOID lpBuf = NULL;

    // Assume that the function will not execute successfully.
    BOOL fFunctionOk = FALSE;
```

```
__try {
   DWORD dwNumBytesRead;
   BOOL fOk;

   hFile = CreateFile("SOMEDATA.DAT", GENERIC_READ,
      FILE_SHARE_READ, NULL, OPEN_EXISTING,
      0, NULL);
   if (hFile == INVALID_HANDLE_VALUE) {
      __leave;
   }

   lpBuf = VirtualAlloc(NULL, 1024, MEM_COMMIT,
      PAGE_READWRITE);

   if (lpBuf == NULL) {
      __leave;
   }

   fOk = ReadFile(hFile, lpBuf, 1024,
      &dwNumBytesRead, NULL);
   if (!fOk || (dwNumBytesRead == 0)) {
      __leave;
   }

   // Do some calculation on the data.
      :
      :

   // Indicate that the entire function executed successfully.
   fFunctionOk = TRUE;
}
__finally {
   // Clean up all the resources.
   if (lpBuf != NULL)
      VirtualFree(lpBuf, MEM_RELEASE | MEM_DECOMMIT);
   if (hFile != INVALID_HANDLE_VALUE)
      CloseHandle(hFile);
}
// Continue processing.
return(fFunctionOk);
}
```

The use of the _leave keyword in the *try* block causes a jump to the end of the *try* block. You can think of it as jumping to the *try* block's closing brace. Because the flow of control will exit *naturally* from the *try* block and enter the *finally* block, no overhead is incurred. However, it was necessary to introduce a new Boolean variable, *fFunctionOk*, to indicate the success or failure of the function—a relatively small price to pay.

When designing your functions to take advantage of termination handlers in this way, remember to initialize all of your resource handles to invalid values before entering your *try* block. Then, in the *finally* block, you can check to see which resources have been allocated successfully so that you'll know which ones to free. Another popular method for tracking which resources will need to be freed is to set a flag when a resource allocation is successful. Then the code in the *finally* block can examine the state of the flag to determine whether the resource needs freeing.

Notes About the *finally* Block

So far we have explicitly identified two scenarios that force the *finally* block to be executed:

- Normal flow of control from the *try* block into the *finally* block

- Local unwind: premature exit from the *try* block (*goto*, *longjump, continue, break, return*, and so on) forcing control to the *finally* block

A third scenario, a *global unwind,* occurred without explicit identification as such in the *Funcfurter1* function we saw earlier on pages 779 and 780. Inside the *try* block of this function was a call to the *Funcinator* function. If the *Funcinator* function caused a memory access violation, a global unwind caused *Funcfurter1*'s *finally* block to execute. We'll look at global unwinding in greater detail when we get to the "Exception Filters and Exception Handlers" section of this chapter.

Code in a *finally* block always starts executing as a result of one of these three situations. To determine which of the three possibilities caused the *finally* block to execute, you can call the intrinsic function[1] *AbnormalTermination:*

```
BOOL AbnormalTermination(VOID);
```

---

1. An intrinsic function is a special function recognized by the compiler. The compiler generates the code for the function inline rather than generating code to call the function. For example, *memcpy* is an intrinsic function (if the /Oi compiler switch is specified). When the compiler sees a call to *memcpy*, it puts the *memcpy* code directly into the function that called *memcpy* instead of generating a call to the *memcpy* function. This usually has the effect of making your code run faster at the expense of code size.

The intrinsic *AbnormalTermination* function is different from the intrinsic *memcpy* function in that it exists only in an intrinsic form. No C run-time library contains the *Abnormal-Termination* function.

This intrinsic function can be called only from inside a *finally* block and returns a Boolean value indicating whether the *try* block associated with the *finally* block was exited prematurely. In other words, if the flow of control leaves the *try* block and naturally enters the *finally* block, *AbnormalTermination* will return FALSE. If the flow of control exits the *try* block abnormally—usually because a local unwind has been caused by a *goto*, *return*, *break*, or *continue* statement or because a global unwind has been caused by a memory access violation—a call to *AbnormalTermination* will return TRUE. If *AbnormalTermination* returns TRUE, it is not possible to distinguish whether a local unwind or a global unwind caused the *finally* block to execute. It is impossible to determine whether a *finally* block is executing because of a global or a local unwind.

Funcfurter2

Here is *Funcfurter2*, which demonstrates use of the *AbnormalTermination* intrinsic function:

```
DWORD Funcfurter2 (void) {
   DWORD dwTemp;

   // 1. Do any processing here.
   :
   :

   __try {
      // 2. Request permission to access
      //    protected data, and then use it.
      WaitForSingleObject(g_hSem, INFINITE);

      dwTemp = Funcinator(g_dwProtectedData);
   }
   __finally {
      // 3. Allow others to use protected data.
      ReleaseSemaphore(g_hSem, 1, NULL);

      if (!AbnormalTermination()) {
         // No errors occurred in the try block, and
         // control flowed naturally from try into finally.
         :
         :

      } else {
```

(continued)

789

```
        // Something caused an exception, and
        // because there is no code in the try block
        // that would cause a premature exit, we must
        // be executing in the finally block
        // because of a global unwind.

        // If there were a goto in the try block,
        // we wouldn't know how we got here.
        .
        .
        .
    }
}

// 4. Continue processing.
return(dwTemp);
}
```

Now that you know how to write termination handlers, you'll see that they can be even more useful and important when we look at exception filters and exception handlers later in the chapter. Before we move on, let's review the reasons for using termination handlers:

- They simplify error processing because all cleanup is in one location and is guaranteed to execute.

- They improve program readability.

- They make code easier to maintain.

- They have minimal speed and size overhead if used correctly.

The SEH Termination Sample Application

The SEHTerm (SEHTERM.EXE) application, listed in Figure 16-1 beginning on page 794, demonstrates the use of termination handlers by simulating the execution of a function that counts the number of words in a file. The source code and resource files for the application are in the SEHTERM directory on the companion disc. Here are the steps that the program's *Dlg_CountWordsInFile* function performs:

1. Opens the file.

2. Gets the size of the file.

3. Allocates a memory block using the result of step 2.

4. Reads the contents of the file into the allocated memory block.

5. Calculates the number of words in the file in the memory block.

After the calculation, the function cleans up everything it has done and returns the number of words counted. It performs these tasks in the following order:

6. Frees the memory block.

7. Closes the file.

8. Returns the number of words in the file. If an error occurred, returns −1.

During the initialization for this function, any of steps 1 through 4 could fail. If this happens, the function needs to clean up any allocations it's already made before returning −1 to the caller. Termination handlers ensure that everything is cleaned up properly.

When you first invoke SEHTerm, this dialog box appears:

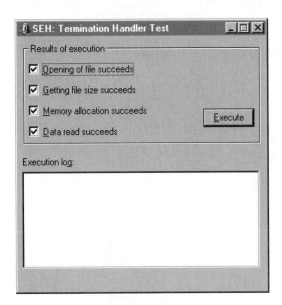

In the Results Of Execution group box at the top of the dialog box, you get to specify which of the four initialization operations will succeed and which will fail. Remember, this program only simulates the work to be done; it doesn't actually open a file, read the file's contents, or count the number of words in the file. In a sense, you get to play operating system here—you can tell the simulation which operations you want to succeed and which operations you want to fail.

After you have set the four check boxes the way you want them, click on the Execute button. The simulation will now try to perform steps 1 through 4 in the list of steps that the *Dlg_CountWordsInFile* function performs. All four steps are performed from within a single *try* block. If any of the steps fails, a __*leave* statement in the *try* block is executed and processing moves immediately into the *finally* block, skipping the remainder of the code in the *try* block.

The code in the *finally* block examines the state of the initialization by checking the *hFile* and *lpvFileData* variables, and then it executes the appropriate cleanup routines. The Execution Log list box at the bottom of the SEH Termination Handler Test dialog box shows the result of each step of *Dlg_CountWordsInFile*'s execution.

In our first experiment, we'll allow all four operations to succeed. To simulate this success, we must be sure that all four check boxes are checked before we click on the Execute button. After the code executes, we can see the results in the Execution Log:

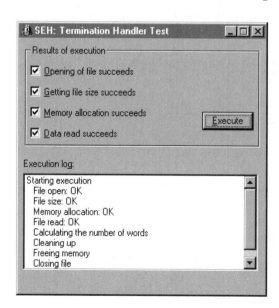

The Execution Log tells us that everything was successfully initialized, the number of words was calculated, and everything was cleaned up OK.

Now let's pretend that the memory allocation failed when the *Dlg-_CountWordsInFile* function attempted it. Here is the result:

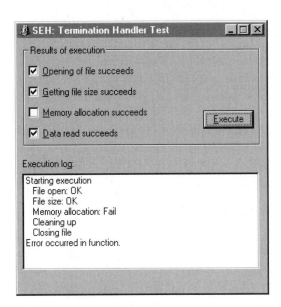

The function opened the file, obtained its size, and tried to allocate a block of memory. When we forced this allocation to fail, execution jumped over the remainder of the *try* block code to an immediate execution of the *finally* block code. The code in the *finally* block can see that the file was opened successfully by checking the *hFile* variable. It calls *CloseHandle* to close the file.

The *finally* block code also checks the *lpvFileData* variable to see whether the memory allocation was successful. Since *lpvFileData* is NULL, the code doesn't try to free the memory block. That's why *Freeing memory* doesn't appear in the Execution Log this time.

The function will also return –1, indicating that an error has occurred. This causes the line *Error occurred in function* to appear in the Execution Log.

Let's do just one more experiment. You can try others on your own machine. On the next page is another simulation.

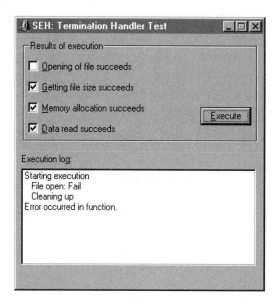

In this experiment, we force the opening of the file to fail and everything else to succeed. However, the code in the *try* block stops executing as soon as it can't open the file. In this case, the remainder of the initialization doesn't execute and the code in the *finally* block starts executing. The cleanup code sees that the file was never opened and that the memory block was never allocated and therefore does nothing.

You can experiment yourself by checking and unchecking the various options and clicking on the Execute button. Notice how the Execution Log changes with each test. As you experiment, it's a good idea to have the SEHTerm source code (in Figure 16-1) beside you to help you understand how termination handlers work.

SEHTerm.ico

SEHTERM.C

```
/*******************************************************************
Module name: SEHTerm.C
Notices: Copyright (c) 1995-1997 Jeffrey Richter
*******************************************************************/


#include "..\CmnHdr.H"              /* See Appendix C. */
#include <windows.h>
#include <windowsx.h>
```

Figure 16-1.
The SEHTerm application.

(continued)

Figure 16-1. *continued*

```
#include <tchar.h>
#include <stdio.h>
#include "Resource.H"


///////////////////////////////////////////////////////////////


// The SIMULATION define should always be defined.
// It exists so that you can easily separate the simulation
// aspects of this program from the actual code that you would
// use to perform the various operations.
#define SIMULATION


///////////////////////////////////////////////////////////////


BOOL Dlg_OnInitDialog (HWND hwnd, HWND hwndFocus,
   LPARAM lParam) {

   // Associate an icon with the dialog box.
   chSETDLGICONS(hwnd, IDI_SEHTERM, IDI_SEHTERM);

   Button_SetCheck(GetDlgItem(hwnd, IDC_OPENSUCCEEDS), TRUE);
   Button_SetCheck(GetDlgItem(hwnd, IDC_SIZESUCCEEDS), TRUE);
   Button_SetCheck(GetDlgItem(hwnd, IDC_MEMSUCCEEDS), TRUE);
   Button_SetCheck(GetDlgItem(hwnd, IDC_READSUCCEEDS), TRUE);
   return(TRUE);
}


///////////////////////////////////////////////////////////////


LONG Dlg_CountWordsInFile (HWND hwndLog,
   BOOL fOpenSucceeds, BOOL fFileSizeSucceeds,
   BOOL fMemSucceeds, BOOL fReadSucceeds) {

   HANDLE hFile = INVALID_HANDLE_VALUE;
   DWORD  dwFileSize = 0;
   LPVOID lpvFileData = NULL;
   BOOL   fFileReadOk = FALSE;
```

(continued)

Figure 16-1. *continued*

```
LONG    lNumWords = -1;
DWORD   dwLastError;

__try {
   // Clear the Execution Log list box.
   ListBox_ResetContent(hwndLog);
   ListBox_AddString(hwndLog,
      __TEXT("Starting execution"));

   // Open the file.
#ifdef SIMULATION
   hFile = (fOpenSucceeds ?
      (HANDLE) !INVALID_HANDLE_VALUE :
      INVALID_HANDLE_VALUE);
#else
   hFile = CreateFile(…);
#endif
   if (hFile == INVALID_HANDLE_VALUE) {
      // The file could not be opened.
      ListBox_AddString(hwndLog,
         __TEXT("   File open: Fail"));
      __leave;
   } else {
      ListBox_AddString(hwndLog,
         __TEXT("   File open: OK"));
   }

   // Determine the size of the file.
#ifdef SIMULATION
   dwLastError = fFileSizeSucceeds ? NO_ERROR : !NO_ERROR;
#else
   dwFileSize = GetFileSize(hFile);
   dwLastError = GetLastError();
#endif

   if (dwLastError != NO_ERROR) {
      // The file size could not be obtained.
      ListBox_AddString(hwndLog,
         __TEXT("   File size: Fail"));
      __leave;
   } else {
      ListBox_AddString(hwndLog,
         __TEXT("   File size: OK"));
   }
```

(continued)

Figure 16-1. *continued*

```
      // Allocate a block of memory to store the entire file.
#ifdef SIMULATION
      lpvFileData = fMemSucceeds ? !NULL : NULL;
#else
      lpvFileData = HeapAlloc(GetProcessHeap(), 0, dwFileSize);
#endif
      if (lpvFileData == NULL) {
         // Allocation failed.
         ListBox_AddString(hwndLog,
            __TEXT("   Memory allocation: Fail"));
         __leave;
      } else {
         ListBox_AddString(hwndLog,
            __TEXT("   Memory allocation: OK"));
      }


      // Read the file into the buffer.
#ifdef SIMULATION
      fReadSucceeds = fReadSucceeds;
#else
      fReadSucceeds =ReadFile(hFile, lpvFileData, dwFileSize,
         NULL, NULL);
#endif
      if (!fReadSucceeds) {
         // The file's data could not be loaded into memory.
         ListBox_AddString(hwndLog,
            __TEXT("   File read: Fail"));
         __leave;
      } else {
         ListBox_AddString(hwndLog,
            __TEXT("   File read: OK"));
         fFileReadOk = TRUE;
      }


      // Calculate the number of words in the file.
      // The algorithm to calculate the number of words in the
      // file would go here. For simulation purposes, I'll
      // just set lNumWords to 37.
      ListBox_AddString(hwndLog,
         __TEXT("   Calculating the number of words"));
      lNumWords = 37;
```

(continued)

797

Figure 16-1. *continued*

```
    } // try

    __finally {
        // Display a notification that we are cleaning up.
        ListBox_AddString(hwndLog, __TEXT("   Cleaning up"));

        // Guarantee that the memory is freed.
        if (lpvFileData != NULL) {
            ListBox_AddString(hwndLog,
                __TEXT("   Freeing memory"));
#ifndef SIMULATION
            HeapFree(GetProcessHeap(), 0, lpvFileData);
#endif
        }

        // Guarantee that the file is closed.
        if (hFile != INVALID_HANDLE_VALUE) {
            ListBox_AddString(hwndLog,
                __TEXT("   Closing file"));
#ifndef SIMULATION
            CloseHandle(hFile);
#endif
        }

    } // finally

    return(lNumWords);
}


//////////////////////////////////////////////////////////////


void Dlg_OnCommand (HWND hwnd, int id, HWND hwndCtl,
    UINT codeNotify) {

    TCHAR szBuf[100];
    LONG  lNumWords;

    switch (id) {
        case IDOK:
            lNumWords = Dlg_CountWordsInFile(
                GetDlgItem(hwnd, IDC_LOG),
                Button_GetCheck(GetDlgItem(hwnd,
```

(continued)

Figure 16-1. *continued*

```
            IDC_OPENSUCCEEDS)),
        Button_GetCheck(GetDlgItem(hwnd,
            IDC_SIZESUCCEEDS)),
        Button_GetCheck(GetDlgItem(hwnd, IDC_MEMSUCCEEDS)),
        Button_GetCheck(GetDlgItem(hwnd, IDC_READSUCCEEDS))
        );

    if (lNumWords == -1) {
        ListBox_AddString(GetDlgItem(hwnd, IDC_LOG),
            __TEXT("Error occurred in function."));
    } else {
        _stprintf(szBuf,
            __TEXT("Result: Words in file = %d"),
            lNumWords);
        ListBox_AddString(GetDlgItem(hwnd,
            IDC_LOG), szBuf);
    }

    break;

    case IDCANCEL:
        EndDialog(hwnd, id);
        break;
    }
}


///////////////////////////////////////////////////////////////


BOOL CALLBACK DlgProc (HWND hwnd, UINT uMsg,
    WPARAM wParam, LPARAM lParam) {

    switch (uMsg) {
        chHANDLE_DLGMSG(hwnd, WM_INITDIALOG, Dlg_OnInitDialog);
        chHANDLE_DLGMSG(hwnd, WM_COMMAND, Dlg_OnCommand);
    }
    return(FALSE);
}


///////////////////////////////////////////////////////////////
```

(continued)

Figure 16-1. *continued*

```
int WINAPI _tWinMain (HINSTANCE hinstExe,
   HINSTANCE hinstPrev, LPTSTR pszCmdLine, int nCmdShow) {

   chWARNIFUNICODEUNDERWIN95();
   DialogBox(hinstExe, MAKEINTRESOURCE(IDD_SEHTERM),
      NULL, DlgProc);

   return(0);
}


/////////////////////// End Of File ///////////////////////////
```

SEHTERM.RC
```
//Microsoft Developer Studio generated resource script.
//
#include "Resource.h"

#define APSTUDIO_READONLY_SYMBOLS
/////////////////////////////////////////////////////////////////
//
// Generated from the TEXTINCLUDE 2 resource.
//
#include "afxres.h"


/////////////////////////////////////////////////////////////////
#undef APSTUDIO_READONLY_SYMBOLS

/////////////////////////////////////////////////////////////////
// English (U.S.) resources

#if !defined(AFX_RESOURCE_DLL) || defined(AFX_TARG_ENU)
#ifdef _WIN32
LANGUAGE LANG_ENGLISH, SUBLANG_ENGLISH_US
#pragma code_page(1252)
#endif //_WIN32

#ifdef APSTUDIO_INVOKED
/////////////////////////////////////////////////////////////////
//
// TEXTINCLUDE
//
```

(continued)

Figure 16-1. *continued*

```
1 TEXTINCLUDE DISCARDABLE
BEGIN
    "Resource.h\0"
END

2 TEXTINCLUDE DISCARDABLE
BEGIN
    "#include ""afxres.h""\r\n"
    "\0"
END

3 TEXTINCLUDE DISCARDABLE
BEGIN
    "\r\n"
    "\0"
END

#endif    // APSTUDIO_INVOKED


/////////////////////////////////////////////////////////////
//
// Dialog
//

IDD_SEHTERM DIALOG DISCARDABLE  18, 18, 214, 196
STYLE WS_MINIMIZEBOX | WS_VISIBLE | WS_CAPTION | WS_SYSMENU
CAPTION "SEH: Termination Handler Test"
FONT 8, "Helv"
BEGIN
    GROUPBOX        "Results of execution",IDC_STATIC,
                    5,5,204,78,WS_GROUP
    CONTROL         "&Opening of file succeeds",
                    IDC_OPENSUCCEEDS,"Button",
                    BS_AUTOCHECKBOX | WS_GROUP | WS_TABSTOP,
                    10,20,92,10
    CONTROL         "&Getting file size succeeds",
                    IDC_SIZESUCCEEDS,"Button",
                    BS_AUTOCHECKBOX | WS_GROUP | WS_TABSTOP,
                    10,36,95,10
    CONTROL         "&Memory allocation succeeds",
                    IDC_MEMSUCCEEDS,"Button",
                    BS_AUTOCHECKBOX | WS_GROUP | WS_TABSTOP,
                    10,52,103,10
```

(continued)

Figure 16-1. *continued*

```
        CONTROL         "&Data read succeeds",IDC_READSUCCEEDS,
                        "Button",BS_AUTOCHECKBOX | WS_GROUP |
                        WS_TABSTOP,10,68,77,10
        PUSHBUTTON      "&Execute",IDOK,160,56,44,14,WS_GROUP
        LTEXT           "Execution lo&g:",IDC_STATIC,4,92,48,8
        LISTBOX         IDC_LOG,4,104,204,88,NOT LBS_NOTIFY |
                        WS_VSCROLL | WS_GROUP | WS_TABSTOP
END


/////////////////////////////////////////////////////////////
//
// Icon
//

// Icon with lowest ID value placed first to ensure
// application icon remains consistent on all systems.
IDI_SEHTERM             ICON    DISCARDABLE     "SEHTerm.Ico"
#endif    // English (U.S.) resources
/////////////////////////////////////////////////////////////



#ifndef APSTUDIO_INVOKED
/////////////////////////////////////////////////////////////
//
// Generated from the TEXTINCLUDE 3 resource.
//



/////////////////////////////////////////////////////////////
#endif    // not APSTUDIO_INVOKED
```

Exception Filters and Exception Handlers

An exception is an event you don't expect. In a well-written application, you don't expect attempts to access an invalid memory address or divide a value by 0. Nevertheless, such errors do occur. The CPU is responsible for catching invalid memory accesses and divides by 0, and it will raise an exception in response to these errors. When the CPU raises an exception, it's known as a *hardware exception*. We'll see later that the operating system and your applications can raise their own exceptions, known as *software exceptions*.

When a hardware or software exception is raised, the operating system offers your application the opportunity to see what type of exception was raised and allows the application to handle the exception itself. Here is the syntax for an exception handler:

```
__try {
   // Guarded body
   .
   .
   .
}
__except (exception filter) {
   // Exception handler
   .
   .
   .
}
```

Notice the __*except* keyword. Whenever you create a *try* block, it must be followed by either a *finally* block or an *except* block. A *try* block can't have both a *finally* block and an *except* block, and a *try* block can't have multiple *finally* or *except* blocks. However, it is possible to nest *try-finally* blocks inside *try-except* blocks and vice versa.

Understanding Exception Filters and Exception Handlers by Example

Unlike termination handlers, exception filters and exception handlers are executed directly by the operating system—the compiler has little to do with evaluating exception filters or executing exception handlers. The next six sections demonstrate the normal execution of *try-except* blocks, explain how and why the operating system evaluates exception filters, and show the circumstances under which the operating system executes the code inside an exception handler.

Funcmeister1

Here's a more concrete coding example of a *try-except* block:

```
DWORD Funcmeister1 (void) {
   DWORD dwTemp;

   // 1. Do any processing here.
   .
   .
   .
```

(continued)

```
__try {
   // 2. Perform some operation.
   dwTemp = 0;
}
__except (EXCEPTION_EXECUTE_HANDLER) {
   // Handle an exception; this never executes.
      .
      .
      .
}

// 3. Continue processing.
return(dwTemp);
}
```

In the *Funcmeister1 try* block, we simply move a 0 into the *dwTemp* variable. This operation will never cause an exception to be raised, so the code inside the *except* block will never execute. Note this difference from *try-finally* behavior. After *dwTemp* is set to 0, the next instruction to execute is the *return* statement.

Although *return, goto, continue,* and *break* statements are strongly discouraged in the *try* block of a termination handler, no speed or code-size penalty is associated with using these statements inside the *try* block of an exception handler. Such a statement in the *try* block associated with an *except* block won't incur the overhead of a local unwind.

Funcmeister2

Let's modify the function and see what happens:

```
DWORD Funcmeister2 (void) {
   DWORD dwTemp = 0;

   // 1. Do any processing here.
      .
      .
      .
   __try {
      // 2. Perform some operation(s).
      dwTemp = 5 / dwTemp;      // Generates an exception
      dwTemp += 10;             // Never executes
   }
   __except ( /* 3. Evaluate filter. */ EXCEPTION_EXECUTE_HANDLER) {
      // 4. Handle an exception.

      MessageBeep(0);
         .
         .
         .
```

```
        }

        // 5. Continue processing.
        return(dwTemp);
}
```

In *Funcmeister2*, an instruction inside the *try* block calls for the attempt to divide 5 by 0. The CPU will catch this event and raise a hardware exception. When this exception is raised, the system will locate the beginning of the *except* block and evaluate the exception filter expression, an expression that must evaluate to one of the following three identifiers as defined in the Win32 EXCPT.H file:

Identifier	Defined As
EXCEPTION_EXECUTE_HANDLER	1
EXCEPTION_CONTINUE_SEARCH	0
EXCEPTION_CONTINUE_EXECUTION	−1

EXCEPTION_EXECUTE_HANDLER

In *Funcmeister2*, the exception filter expression evaluates to EXCEPTION_EXECUTE_HANDLER. This value basically says to the system, "I recognize the exception; that is, I had a feeling that this exception might occur sometime, and I've written some code to deal with it that I'd like to execute now." Execution immediately jumps to the code inside the *except* block (the exception handler code). After the code in the *except* block has executed, the system considers the exception to be handled and allows your application to continue executing.

This is pretty different from 16-bit Windows applications, where a divide by 0 causes a System Error box to appear that allows the user one option only: to close the application right then and there. In Win32 applications, you can trap the error, handle it in your own way, and allow your application to continue running without the user ever knowing that the error happened.

But where in the code does execution resume? With a little bit of thought, it's easy to imagine several possibilities.

The first possibility would be for execution to resume after the CPU instruction that generates the exception. In *Funcmeister2*, execution would resume with the instruction that adds 10 to *dwTemp*. This may seem like a reasonable thing to do, but in reality, most programs are written so that they cannot continue executing successfully if one of the earlier instructions fails to execute.

In *Funcmeister2*, the code can continue to execute normally; however, *Funcmeister2* is not the normal situation. Most likely, your code will be structured so that the CPU instructions following the instruction that generates the exception will expect a valid return value. For example, you might have a function that allocates memory, in which case a whole series of instructions will be executed to manipulate that memory. If the memory cannot be allocated, all the lines will fail, making the program generate exceptions repeatedly.

Here is another example of why execution cannot continue after the failed CPU instruction. Let's replace the C statement that generated the exception in *Funcmeister2* with the following line:

```
malloc(5 / dwTemp);
```

For the line above, the compiler generates CPU instructions to perform the division, pushes the result on the stack, and calls the *malloc* function. If the division fails, the code can't continue executing properly. The system has to push something on the stack; if it doesn't, the stack gets corrupted.

Fortunately, Microsoft has not made it possible for us to have the system resume execution on the instruction following the instruction that generates the exception. This decision saves us from potential problems like these.

The second possibility would be for execution to resume with the instruction that generated the exception. This is an interesting possibility. What if inside the *except* block you had this statement:

```
dwTemp = 2;
```

With this assignment in the *except* block, you could resume execution with the instruction that generated the exception. This time, you would be dividing 5 by 2, and execution would continue just fine without raising another exception. You can alter something and have the system retry the instruction that generated the exception. However, you should be aware that this technique can result in some subtle behaviors. We'll discuss this technique in the following section.

The third and last possibility would be for execution to pick up with the first instruction following the *except* block. This is actually what happens when the exception filter expression evaluates to EXCEPTION_EX-

ECUTE_HANDLER. After the code inside the *except* block finishes executing, control resumes at the first instruction after the *except* block.

EXCEPTION_CONTINUE_EXECUTION

Let's take a closer look at the exception filter to see how it evaluates to one of the three exception identifiers defined in EXCPT.H. In *Funcmeister2*, the EXCEPTION_EXECUTE_HANDLER identifier is hard-coded directly into the filter for simplicity's sake, but you can make the filter call a function that will determine which of the three identifiers should be returned. Let's look at another code example:

```
char g_szBuffer[100];

void FunclinRoosevelt1 (void) {
   int x = 0;
   char *lpBuffer = NULL;

   __try {
      *lpBuffer = 'J';
      x = 5 / x;
   }
   __except (OilFilter1(&lpBuffer)) {
      MessageBox(NULL, "An exception occurred", NULL, MB_OK);
   }
   MessageBox(NULL, "Function completed", NULL, MB_OK);
}

LONG OilFilter1 (char **lplpBuffer) {
   if (*lplpBuffer == NULL) {
      *lplpBuffer = g_szBuffer;
      return(EXCEPTION_CONTINUE_EXECUTION);
   }
   return(EXCEPTION_EXECUTE_HANDLER);
}
```

We first run into a problem when we try to put a *'J'* into the buffer pointed to by *lpBuffer*. Unfortunately, we didn't initialize *lpBuffer* to point to our global buffer *g_szBuffer*, and *lpBuffer* points to NULL instead. The CPU will generate an exception and evaluate the exception filter in the *except* block associated with the *try* block in which the exception occurred. In the *except* block, the *OilFilter1* function is passed the address of the *lpBuffer* variable.

When *OilFilter1* gets control, it checks to see whether *lplpBuffer* is NULL and, if it is, sets it to point to the global buffer *g_szBuffer*. The filter then returns EXCEPTION_CONTINUE_EXECUTION. When the system sees that the filter evaluated to EXCEPTION_CONTINUE_EXECUTION, it jumps back to the instruction that generated the exception and tries to execute it again. This time, the instruction will succeed, and '*J*' will be put into the first byte of the *g_szBuffer* buffer.

As the code continues to execute, we run up against the divide by 0 problem in the *try* block. Again the system evaluates the exception filter. This time, *OilFilter1* sees that **lplpBuffer* is not NULL and returns EXCEPTION_EXECUTE_HANDLER, which tells the system to execute the *except* block code. This causes a message box to appear displaying the text *An exception occurred*.

As you can see, you can do an awful lot of work inside an exception filter. Of course, the filter must return one of the three exception identifiers, but the filter can also perform any other tasks you want it to.

Use EXCEPTION_CONTINUE_EXECUTION with Caution

As it turns out, trying to correct the situation shown in the function just discussed and having the system continue execution might or might not work—it depends on the target CPU for your application, on how your compiler generates instructions for C statements, and on your compiler options.

A compiler might generate two machine instructions to perform the statement

```
*lpBuffer = 'J';
```

The first instruction would load the contents of *lpBuffer* into a register, and the second instruction would try to copy a '*J*' into the address to which the register points. It is this second instruction that would generate the exception. The exception filter would catch the exception, correct the value in *lpBuffer*, and tell the system to reexecute the second instruction. The problem is that the contents of the register wouldn't be changed to reflect the new value loaded into *lpBuffer*, and reexecuting the instruction would therefore generate another exception. We'd have an infinite loop!

Continuing execution might be fine if the compiler optimizes the code but might fail if the compiler doesn't optimize the code. This can be an incredibly difficult bug to fix, and you will have to examine the assembly language generated for your source code to determine what has gone wrong in your application. The moral of this story is to be very, very careful when returning EXCEPTION_CONTINUE_EXECUTION from an exception filter.

EXCEPTION_CONTINUE_SEARCH

The examples have been pretty tame so far. Let's shake things up a bit by adding a function call:

```
void FunclinRoosevelt2 (void) {
   char *lpBuffer = NULL;

   __try {
      FuncSinatra2(lpBuffer);
   }
   __except (OilFilter2(&lpBuffer)) {
      MessageBox(NULL, …);
   }
}

void FuncSinatra2 (char *sz) {
   *sz = 0;
}

LONG OilFilter2 (char **lplpBuffer) {
   if (*lplpBuffer == NULL) {
      *lplpBuffer = g_szBuffer;
      return(EXCEPTION_CONTINUE_EXECUTION);
   }
   return(EXCEPTION_EXECUTE_HANDLER);
}
```

When *FunclinRoosevelt2* executes, it calls *FuncSinatra2*, passing it NULL. When *FuncSinatra2* executes, an exception is generated. Just as before, the system evaluates the exception filter associated with the most recently executing *try* block. In this example, the *try* block inside *FunclinRoosevelt2* is the most recently executing *try* block, so the system calls the *OilFilter2* function to evaluate the exception filter—even though the exception was generated inside the *FuncSinatra2* function.

Now let's stir things up a little more by adding another *try-except* block.

```
void FunclinRoosevelt3 (void) {

   char *lpBuffer = NULL;

   __try {
      FuncSinatra3(lpBuffer);
   }
   __except (OilFilter3(&lpBuffer)) {
      MessageBox(NULL, …);
```

(continued)

```
      }
   }

void FuncSinatra3 (char *sz) {
   __try {
      *sz = 0;
   }
   __except (EXCEPTION_CONTINUE_SEARCH) {
      // This never executes.
         .
         .
         .
   }
}

LONG OilFilter3 (char **lplpBuffer) {
   if (*lplpBuffer == NULL) {
      *lplpBuffer = g_szBuffer;
      return(EXCEPTION_CONTINUE_EXECUTION);
   }
   return(EXCEPTION_EXECUTE_HANDLER);
}
```

Now, when *FuncSinatra3* tries to fill address NULL with 0, an exception is still generated but *FuncSinatra3*'s exception filter will get executed. *FuncSinatra3*'s exception filter is very simple and evaluates to EXCEPTION_CONTINUE_SEARCH. This identifier tells the system to walk up to the previous *try* block that's matched with an *except* block and call this previous *try* block's exception filter.

Because *FuncSinatra3*'s filter evaluates to EXCEPTION_CONTINUE_SEARCH, the system will walk up to the previous *try* block (in *FunclinRoosevelt3*) and evaluate its exception filter, *OilFilter3*. *OilFilter3* will see that *lpBuffer* is NULL, will set *lpBuffer* to point to the global buffer, and will then tell the system to resume execution on the instruction that generated the exception. This will allow the code inside *FuncSinatra3*'s *try* block to execute, but unfortunately, *FuncSinatra3*'s local *sz* variable will not have been changed, and resuming execution on the failed instruction will simply cause another exception to be generated. What we have here is another infinite loop!

You'll notice I said that the system walks up to the most recently executing *try* block that's matched with an *except* block and evaluates its filters. This means that any *try* blocks that are matched with *finally* blocks instead of *except* blocks are skipped by the system while it walks up the chain. The reason for this should be pretty obvious: *finally* blocks don't have exception filters and therefore give the system nothing to evaluate.

If *FuncSinatra3* in the last example contained a *finally* block instead of its *except* block, the system would have started evaluating exception filters beginning with *FunclinRoosevelt3*'s *OilFilter3*.

Figure 16-2 on the next page shows a flowchart describing the actions taken by the system when an exception is generated.

Global Unwinds

Exception handling involves a global unwind. When an exception filter evaluates to EXCEPTION_EXECUTE_HANDLER, the system must perform a global unwind. The global unwind causes all of the outstanding *try-finally* blocks that started executing below the *try-except* block that is handling the exception to resume execution. These two functions are an example:

```
void FuncOStimpy1 (void) {

    // 1. Do any processing here.
    :
    :

    __try {
        // 2. Call another function.
        FuncORen1();

        // Code here never executes.
    }

    __except ( /* 6. Evaluate filter. */ EXCEPTION_EXECUTE_HANDLER) {
        // 8. After the unwind, the exception handler executes.
        MessageBox(NULL, …);
    }

    // 9. Exception handled--continue execution.
    :
    :

}
void FuncORen1 (void) {
    DWORD dwTemp = 0;

    // 3. Do any processing here.
    :
    :
```

(continued on page 813)

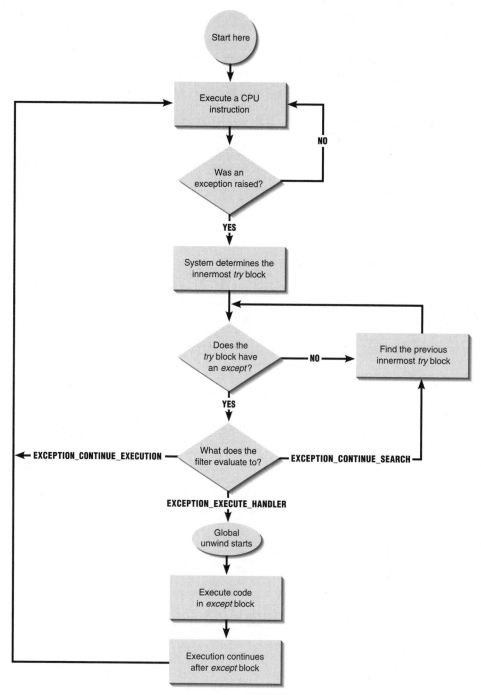

Figure 16-2.
How the system processes an exception.

```
__try {
    // 4. Request permission to access protected data.
    WaitForSingleObject(g_hSem, INFINITE);

    // 5. Modify the data.
    //    An exception is generated here.
    g_dwProtectedData = 5 / dwTemp;
}
__finally {
    // 7. Global unwind occurs because filter evaluated
    //    to EXCEPTION_EXECUTE_HANDLER.

    // Allow others to use protected data.
    ReleaseSemaphore(g_hSem, 1, NULL);
}

// Continue processing--never executes.
    .
    .
    .
}
```

FuncOStimpy1 and *FuncORen1* together illustrate the most confusing aspects of structured exception handling. The numbers at the beginnings of the comments show the order of execution, but let's hold hands and go through it together.

FuncOStimpy1 begins execution by entering its *try* block and calling *FuncORen1*. *FuncORen1* starts by entering its own *try* block and waits to obtain a semaphore. Once it has the semaphore, *FuncORen1* tries to alter the global data variable, *g_dwProtectedData*. However, the division by 0 causes an exception to be generated. The system grabs control now and searches for a *try* block matched with an *except* block. Since the *try* block in *FuncORen1* is matched by a *finally* block, the system searches upward for another *try* block. This time, it finds the *try* block in *FuncOStimpy1*, and it sees that *FuncOStimpy1*'s *try* block is matched by an *except* block.

The system now evaluates the exception filter that's associated with *FuncOStimpy1*'s *except* block and waits for the return value. When the system sees that the return value is EXCEPTION_EXECUTE_HANDLER, the system begins a global unwind in *FuncORen1*'s *finally* block. Note that the unwind takes place *before* the system begins execution of the code in *FuncOStimpy1*'s *except* block. For a global unwind, the system starts back at the bottom of all outstanding *try* blocks and searches this time for *try* blocks matched by *finally* blocks. The *finally* block that the system finds here is the one contained inside *FuncORen1*.

When the system executes the code in *FuncORen1*'s *finally* block, you can really see the power of structured exception handling. Because *FuncORen1*'s *finally* block is executed, the semaphore is released, allowing other threads to resume execution. If the call to *ReleaseSemaphore* were not contained inside the *finally* block, the semaphore would never be released.

After the code contained in the *finally* block has executed, the system continues to walk upward looking for outstanding *finally* blocks that need to be executed. In this example, there are none. The system stops walking upward when it reaches the *try-except* block that decided to handle the exception. At this point, the global unwind is complete, and the system can execute the code contained inside the *except* block.

Figure 16-3 shows a flowchart that describes how the system performs a global unwind.

That's how structured exception handling works. SEH can be difficult to understand because the system really gets involved with the execution of your code. No longer does the code flow from top to bottom; the system gets involved and makes sections of code execute according to its notions of order. This order of execution is complex but predictable, and by following the flowcharts in Figure 16-2 and Figure 16-3, you should be able to use SEH with confidence.

Halting Global Unwinds

It's possible to stop the system from completing a global unwind by putting a *return* statement inside a *finally* block. Let's look at the code here:

```
void FuncMonkey (void) {
   __try {
      FuncFish();
   }
   __except (EXCEPTION_EXECUTE_HANDLER) {
      MessageBeep(0);
   }
   MessageBox(…);
}

void FuncFish (void) {
   FuncPheasant();
   MessageBox(…);
}
```

(continued on page 816)

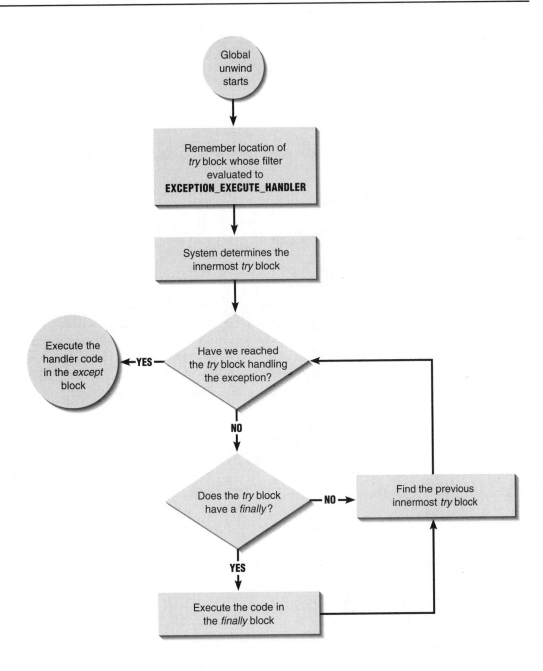

Figure 16-3.
How the system performs a global unwind.

```
void FuncPheasant (void) {

   __try {
      strcpy(NULL, NULL);
   }

   __finally {
      return;
   }
}
```

When the *strcpy* function is called in *FuncPheasant*'s *try* block, a memory access violation exception will be generated. When this happens, the system will start scanning to see whether any exception filters exist that can handle the exception. The system will find that the exception filter in *FuncMonkey* wants to handle the exception, and the system will start a global unwind.

The global unwind starts by executing the code inside *FuncPheasant*'s *finally* block. However, this block of code contains a *return* statement. The *return* statement causes the system to stop unwinding, and *FuncPheasant* will actually end up returning to *FuncFish*. *FuncFish* will continue executing and will display a message box on the screen. *FuncFish* will then return to *FuncMonkey*. The code in *FuncMonkey* continues executing by calling *MessageBox*.

Notice that the code inside *FuncMonkey*'s exception block never executes the call to *MessageBeep*. The *return* statement in *FuncPheasant*'s *finally* block causes the system to stop unwinding altogether, and execution continues as though nothing ever happened.

Microsoft has designed SEH to work this way on purpose. You might occasionally want to stop unwinding and allow execution to continue, and this method allows you to do this. Usually, though, this isn't the sort of thing you want to do. As a rule, be careful to avoid putting *return* statements inside *finally* blocks.

More About Exception Filters

Often an exception filter must analyze the situation before it can determine what value to return. For example, your handler might know what to do if a divide by 0 exception occurs, but it might not know how to handle a memory access exception. The exception filter has the responsibility for examining the situation and returning the appropriate value.

This code demonstrates a method for identifying the kind of exception that has occurred:

```
__try {
    x = 0;
    y = 4 / x;
}

__except ((GetExceptionCode() == EXCEPTION_INT_DIVIDE_BY_ZERO) ?
    EXCEPTION_EXECUTE_HANDLER : EXCEPTION_CONTINUE_SEARCH) {
    // Handle divide by zero exception.
}
```

The *GetExceptionCode* intrinsic function returns a value identifying the kind of exception that has occurred:

```
DWORD GetExceptionCode(VOID);
```

The following list of all predefined exceptions and their meanings is adapted from the Win32 documentation. The exception identifiers can be found in the Win32 WINBASE.H header file.

EXCEPTION_ACCESS_VIOLATION The thread tried to read from or write to a virtual address for which it doesn't have the appropriate access.

EXCEPTION_ARRAY_BOUNDS_EXCEEDED The thread tried to access an array element that is out of bounds, and the underlying hardware supports bounds checking.

EXCEPTION_BREAKPOINT A breakpoint was encountered.

EXCEPTION_DATATYPE_MISALIGNMENT The thread tried to read or write data that is misaligned on hardware that doesn't provide alignment. For example, 16-bit values must be aligned on 2-byte boundaries, 32-bit values on 4-byte boundaries, and so on.

EXCEPTION_FLT_DENORMAL_OPERAND One of the operands in a floating-point operation is denormal. A denormal value is one that is too small to represent a standard floating-point value.

EXCEPTION_FLT_DIVIDE_BY_ZERO The thread tried to divide a floating-point value by a floating-point divisor of 0.

EXCEPTION_FLT_INEXACT_RESULT The result of a floating-point operation can't be represented exactly as a decimal fraction.

EXCEPTION_FLT_INVALID_OPERATION Represents any floating-point exception not included in this list.

EXCEPTION_FLT_OVERFLOW The exponent of a floating-point operation is greater than the magnitude allowed by the corresponding type.

EXCEPTION_FLT_STACK_CHECK The stack overflowed or underflowed as the result of a floating-point operation.

EXCEPTION_FLT_UNDERFLOW The exponent of a floating-point operation is less than the magnitude allowed by the type.

EXCEPTION_GUARD_PAGE A thread attempted to access a page of memory that has the PAGE_GUARD protection attribute. The page is made accessible, and an EXCEPTION_GUARD_PAGE exception is raised.

EXCEPTION_ILLEGAL_INSTRUCTION A thread executed an invalid instruction. This exception is defined by the specific CPU architecture; executing an invalid instruction may cause a trap error on different CPUs.

EXCEPTION_IN_PAGE_ERROR A page fault couldn't be satisfied because the file system or a device driver returned a read error.

EXCEPTION_INT_DIVIDE_BY_ZERO The thread tried to divide an integer value by an integer divisor of 0.

EXCEPTION_INT_OVERFLOW The result of an integer operation caused a carry out of the most significant bit of the result.

EXCEPTION_INVALID_DISPOSITION An exception handler returned a value other than EXCEPTION_EXECUTE_HANDLER, EXCEPTION_CONTINUE_SEARCH, or EXCEPTION_CONTINUE-_EXECUTION.

EXCEPTION_NONCONTINUABLE_EXCEPTION The thread tried to continue execution after a noncontinuable exception occurred.

EXCEPTION_PRIV_INSTRUCTION The thread tried to execute an instruction whose operation is not allowed in the current machine mode.

EXCEPTION_SINGLE_STEP A trace trap or other single-instruction mechanism signaled that one instruction has been executed.

EXCEPTION_STACK_OVERFLOW The user stack is exhausted and cannot be expanded.

The *GetExceptionCode* intrinsic function can be called only in an exception filter (between the parentheses following __*except*) or inside an exception handler. The following code is legal:

```
__try {
   y = 0;
   x = 4 / y;
}

__except (
   ((GetExceptionCode() == EXCEPTION_ACCESS_VIOLATION) ||
    (GetExceptionCode() == EXCEPTION_INT_DIVIDE_BY_ZERO)) ?
   EXCEPTION_EXECUTE_HANDLER : EXCEPTION_CONTINUE_SEARCH) {

   switch (GetExceptionCode()) {
      case EXCEPTION_ACCESS_VIOLATION:
         // Handle the access violation.
         :
         :
         break;

      case EXCEPTION_INT_DIVIDE_BY_ZERO:
         // Handle the integer divide by 0.
         :
         :
         break;
   }
}
```

However, you cannot call *GetExceptionCode* from inside an exception filter function. To help you catch such errors, the compiler will produce a compilation error if you try to compile the following code:

```
__try {
   y = 0;
   x = 4 / y;
}

__except (CoffeeFilter()) {

   // Handle the exception.
   :
```

(continued)

```
}

LONG CoffeeFilter (void) {
   // Compilation error: illegal call to GetExceptionCode.
   return((GetExceptionCode() == EXCEPTION_ACCESS_VIOLATION) ?
      EXCEPTION_EXECUTE_HANDLER : EXCEPTION_CONTINUE_SEARCH);
}
```

You can get this effect by rewriting the code this way:

```
__try {
   y = 0;
   x = 4 / y;
}

__except (CoffeeFilter(GetExceptionCode())) {

   // Handle the exception.
   .
   .
   .
}

LONG CoffeeFilter (DWORD dwExceptionCode) {
   return((dwExceptionCode == EXCEPTION_ACCESS_VIOLATION) ?
      EXCEPTION_EXECUTE_HANDLER : EXCEPTION_CONTINUE_SEARCH);
}
```

Exception codes follow the rules for error codes in Win32 as defined inside the WINERROR.H file. Each DWORD is divided as shown in this table:

Bits:	31–30	29–28	27–16	15–0
Contents:	Severity	Flags	Facility code	Exception code
Meaning:	0 = Success	Bit 29	Microsoft-defined	Microsoft/Programmer-defined
	1 = Informational	0 = Microsoft		
	2 = Warning	1 = Customer		
	3 = Error	Bit 28 is reserved (must be 0)		

Currently, Microsoft defines the following facility codes:

Facility Code	Value
FACILITY_NULL	0
FACILITY_RPC	1
FACILITY_DISPATCH	2
FACILITY_STORAGE	3
FACILITY_ITF	4
FACILITY_WIN32	7
FACILITY_WINDOWS	8
FACILITY_CONTROL	10

The following table shows the meaning of all the system-defined exception codes:

Exception Code	Code	Severity
EXCEPTION_ACCESS_VIOLATION	0xC0000005	Error
EXCEPTION_ARRAY_BOUNDS_EXCEEDED	0xC000008C	Error
EXCEPTION_BREAKPOINT	0x80000003	Warning
EXCEPTION_DATATYPE_MISALIGNMENT	0x80000002	Warning
EXCEPTION_FLT_DENORMAL_OPERAND	0xC000008D	Error
EXCEPTION_FLT_DIVIDE_BY_ZERO	0xC000008E	Error
EXCEPTION_FLT_INEXACT_RESULT	0xC000008F	Error
EXCEPTION_FLT_INVALID_OPERATION	0xC0000030	Error
EXCEPTION_FLT_OVERFLOW	0xC0000091	Error
EXCEPTION_FLT_STACK_CHECK	0xC0000032	Error
EXCEPTION_FLT_UNDERFLOW	0xC0000033	Error
EXCEPTION_GUARD_PAGE	0x80000001	Warning
EXCEPTION_ILLEGAL_INSTRUCTION	0xC000001D	Error
EXCEPTION_IN_PAGE_ERROR	0xC0000006	Error
EXCEPTION_INT_DIVIDE_BY_ZERO	0xC0000094	Error
EXCEPTION_INT_OVERFLOW	0xC0000035	Error
EXCEPTION_INVALID_DISPOSITION	0xC0000026	Error
EXCEPTION_NONCONTINUABLE_EXCEPTION	0xC0000025	Error
EXCEPTION_PRIV_INSTRUCTION	0xC0000096	Error
EXCEPTION_SINGLE_STEP	0x80000004	Warning
EXCEPTION_STACK_OVERFLOW	0xC00000FD	Error

GetExceptionInformation

When an exception occurs, the operating system pushes the following three structures on the stack of the thread that raised the exception: the EXCEPTION_RECORD structure, the CONTEXT structure, and the EXCEPTION_POINTERS structure.

The EXCEPTION_RECORD structure contains CPU-independent information about the raised exception, and the CONTEXT structure contains CPU-dependent information about the raised exception. The EXCEPTION_POINTERS structure has only two data members that are pointers to the pushed EXCEPTION_RECORD and CONTEXT data structures:

```
typedef struct _EXCEPTION_POINTERS {
    PEXCEPTION_RECORD ExceptionRecord;
    PCONTEXT ContextRecord;
} EXCEPTION_POINTERS;
```

To retrieve this information and use it in your own application, you will need to call the *GetExceptionInformation* function:

```
LPEXCEPTION_POINTERS GetExceptionInformation(VOID);
```

This intrinsic function returns a pointer to an EXCEPTION_POINTERS structure.

The most important thing to remember about the *GetExceptionInformation* function is that it can be called only in an exception filter—never inside an exception handler and never inside an exception filter function because the CONTEXT, EXCEPTION_RECORD, and EXCEPTION_POINTERS data structures are valid only during the exception filter processing. Once control has been transferred to the exception handler, the data on the stack is destroyed, which is why the function can be called only during evaluation of the exception filter.

If you have a need to access the exception information from inside your exception handler block, you must save the EXCEPTION_RECORD data structure and/or CONTEXT data structure pointed to by the EXCEPTION_POINTERS structure in one or more variables that you create. The following code demonstrates how to save both the EXCEPTION_RECORD and CONTEXT data structures:

```
void FuncSkunk (void) {
    // Declare variables that we can use to save the exception
    // record and the context if an exception should occur.
    EXCEPTION_RECORD SavedExceptRec;
```

```
CONTEXT SavedContext;
  .
  .
  .
__try {
  .
  .
}

__except (
   SavedExceptRec =
     *(GetExceptionInformation())->ExceptionRecord,
   SavedContext =
     *(GetExceptionInformation())->ContextRecord,
   EXCEPTION_EXECUTE_HANDLER) {

   // We can use the SavedExceptRec and SavedContext
   // variables inside the handler code block.
   switch (SavedExceptRec.ExceptionCode) {
     .
     .
   }
  }
  .
  .
}
```

Notice the use of the C language's comma (,) operator in the exception filter. Many programmers aren't used to seeing this operator. It tells the compiler to execute the comma-separated expressions from left to right. When all of the expressions have been evaluated, the result of the last (or rightmost) expression is returned.

In *FuncSkunk*, the left expression will execute, which causes the **EXCEPTION_RECORD** structure on the stack to be stored in the *SavedExceptRec* local variable. The result of this expression is the value of *SavedExceptRec*. However, this result is discarded and the next expression to the right is evaluated. This second expression causes the **CONTEXT** structure on the stack to be stored in the *SavedContext* local variable. The result of the second expression is *SavedContext*, and again, this expression is discarded as the third expression is evaluated. This is a very simple expression that evaluates to EXCEPTION_EXECUTE_HAN-DLER. The result of this rightmost expression is the result of the entire comma-separated expression.

Because the exception filter evaluated to EXCEPTION_EXECUTE-_HANDLER, the code inside the *except* block executes. At this point, the

SavedExceptRec and *SavedContext* variables have been initialized and can be used inside the *except* block. Keep in mind it is important that the *SavedExceptRec* and *SavedContext* variables be declared outside the *try* block.

As you've probably guessed, the *ExceptionRecord* member of the EXCEPTION_POINTERS structure points to an EXCEPTION_RECORD structure:

```
typedef struct _EXCEPTION_RECORD {
    DWORD ExceptionCode;
    DWORD ExceptionFlags;
    struct _EXCEPTION_RECORD *ExceptionRecord;
    PVOID ExceptionAddress;
    DWORD NumberParameters;
    DWORD ExceptionInformation[EXCEPTION_MAXIMUM_PARAMETERS];
} EXCEPTION_RECORD;
```

The EXCEPTION_RECORD structure contains detailed, CPU-independent information about the exception that has most recently occurred:

- *ExceptionCode* contains the code of the exception. This is the same information that is returned from the *GetExceptionCode* intrinsic function.

- *ExceptionFlags* contains flags about the exception. Currently the only two values are 0 (which indicates a continuable exception) and EXCEPTION_NONCONTINUABLE (which indicates a noncontinuable exception). Any attempt to continue execution after a noncontinuable exception causes an EXCEPTION-_NONCONTINUABLE_EXCEPTION exception to be raised.

- *ExceptionRecord* points to an EXCEPTION_RECORD structure for another unhandled exception. While handling one exception, it is possible to raise another exception. For example, the code in your exception filter could attempt to divide a number by 0. Exception records can be chained to provide additional information when nested exceptions occur. A nested exception occurs if an exception is generated during the processing of an exception filter. If there are no unhandled exceptions, this member will contain NULL.

- *ExceptionAddress* specifies the address of the instruction in your code at which the exception occurred.

- *NumberParameters* specifies the number of parameters associated with the exception. This is the number of defined elements in the *ExceptionInformation* array.

- *ExceptionInformation* specifies an array of additional 32-bit arguments that describe the exception. For most exception codes, the array elements are undefined.

The last two members of the EXCEPTION_RECORD structure, *NumberParameters* and *ExceptionInformation*, offer the exception filter some additional information about the exception. Currently only one type of exception involves additional information: EXCEPTION_ACCESS_VIOLATION. All other possible exceptions will have the *NumberParameters* member set to 0. When you look at the additional information about a generated exception, you can examine the *NumberParameters* member to see how many DWORDs of information are available.

For an EXCEPTION_ACCESS_VIOLATION exception, *ExceptionInformation[0]* contains a read-write flag that indicates the type of operation that caused the access violation. If this value is 0, the thread tried to read the inaccessible data. If this value is 1, the thread tried to write to an inaccessible address. *ExceptionInformation[1]* specifies the virtual address of the inaccessible data.

By using these members, you can produce exception filters that offer you a significant amount of information about your application. For example, you might write an exception filter like this one:

```
__try {
   :
   :
}
__except (ExpFltr(GetExceptionInformation()->ExceptionRecord)) {
   :
   :
}

LONG ExpFltr (LPEXCEPTION_RECORD lpER) {
    char szBuf[300], *p;
    DWORD dwExceptionCode = lpER->ExceptionCode;

    sprintf(szBuf, "Code = %x, Address = %x",
        dwExceptionCode, lpER->ExceptionAddress);
```

(continued)

825

```
    // Find the end of the string.
    p = strchr(szBuf, 0);

    // I used a switch statement in case Microsoft adds
    // information for other exception codes in the future.
    switch (dwExceptionCode) {
       case EXCEPTION_ACCESS_VIOLATION:
          sprintf(p, "Attempt to %s data at address %x",
             lpER->ExceptionInformation[0] ? "write" : "read",
             lpER->ExceptionInformation[1]);
          break;

       default:
          break;
    }

    MessageBox(NULL, szBuf, "Exception",
       MB_OK | MB_ICONEXCLAMATION);

    return(EXCEPTION_CONTINUE_SEARCH);
}
```

The *ContextRecord* member of the EXCEPTION_POINTERS structure points to a CONTEXT structure. This structure is platform-dependent; that is, the contents of this structure will differ from one CPU platform to another. Here is the CONTEXT structure for an *x*86 CPU:

```
typedef struct _CONTEXT {

    // Flags describing contents of CONTEXT record
    DWORD ContextFlags;

    // Debug registers
    DWORD    Dr0;
    DWORD    Dr1;
    DWORD    Dr2;
    DWORD    Dr3;
    DWORD    Dr6;
    DWORD    Dr7;

    // Floating-point registers
    FLOATING_SAVE_AREA FloatSave;

    // Segment registers
    DWORD    SegGs;
    DWORD    SegFs;
```

```
DWORD    SegEs;
DWORD    SegDs;

// Integer registers
DWORD    Edi;
DWORD    Esi;
DWORD    Ebx;
DWORD    Edx;
DWORD    Ecx;
DWORD    Eax;

// Control registers
DWORD    Ebp;
DWORD    Eip;
DWORD    SegCs;
DWORD    EFlags;
DWORD    Esp;
DWORD    SegSs;

} CONTEXT;
```

Basically, this structure contains one member for each of the registers available on the CPU. When an exception is raised, you can find out even more information by examining the members of this structure. Unfortunately, realizing the benefit of such a possibility requires you to write platform-dependent code that recognizes the machine it's running on and uses the appropriate CONTEXT structure. The best way to handle this is to put *#ifdefs* into your code. The CONTEXT structures for the *x*86, MIPS, Alpha, and PowerPC CPUs are in the WINNT.H header file.

The SEH Exceptions Sample Application

The SEHExcpt (SEHEXCPT.EXE) sample application, listed in Figure 16-4 beginning on page 831, demonstrates the use of exception filters and handlers. The source code and resource files for the application are in the SEHEXCPT directory on the companion disc. When you invoke SEHExcpt, the dialog box on the top of the next page appears.

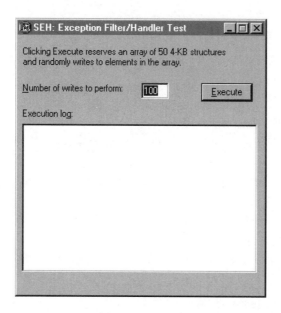

When you click on the Execute button, the program calls *Virtual-Alloc* to reserve a region of memory in the process's address space big enough to contain an array of 50 elements, each 4 KB in size. Notice that I said the region is reserved—not committed.

After reserving the region, the program tries to write to randomly selected elements in the array. You get to specify the number of accesses the program will try by entering a number in the Number Of Writes To Perform field.

For the first randomly selected element, an access violation exception will occur because memory has only been reserved, not committed. At this point, the exception filter, identified by the *ExpFilter* function in SEHEXCPT.C, gets called by the operating system.

This filter is responsible for calling *VirtualAlloc* again, but this time it passes MEM_COMMIT to *VirtualAlloc* in order to actually commit memory to the reserved region. But before the filter can do this, it must determine that the exception that it is filtering occurred because of an invalid memory access in the reserved region.

It's important that the program not accidentally absorb exceptions. When you implement an exception filter, be sure to perform whatever tests are necessary to ensure that you are actually handling the exception for which you designed the filter. If any other exception occurs that the filter can't handle, the filter must return EXCEPTION_CONTINUE-_SEARCH.

The *ExpFilter* function determines whether the occurring exception comes from an invalid array access by performing the following tests:

1. Is the exception code EXCEPTION_ACCESS_VIOLATION?

2. Had memory for the array been reserved when the exception occurred? An exception might have occurred before memory for the array was even reserved.

3. Is the address of the invalid memory access within the memory region reserved for the array?

If any of the three tests fails, the filter was not written to handle the occurring exception and the filter returns EXCEPTION_CONTINUE-_SEARCH. If all three tests succeed, the filter assumes that the invalid access was in the array and calls *CommitMemory*. *CommitMemory* determines whether the invalid memory access was an attempt to read from or to write to the array and creates a string to be displayed in the Execution Log list box. For this sample program, the memory access will always be an attempt to write to the memory. Finally, *CommitMemory* calls *VirtualAlloc* to commit memory to the region of the array memory occupied by the individual array element that was accessed.

When *CommitMemory* returns to the exception filter, the filter returns EXCEPTION_CONTINUE_EXECUTION. This value causes the machine instruction that raised the exception to execute again. This time, the memory access will succeed because memory will have been committed.

Earlier in this chapter, I said that you must be careful when returning EXCEPTION_CONTINUE_EXECUTION from a filter. I said that you could run into a problem if your compiler generates multiple machine instructions for a single C/C++ statement. In the case I've just discussed, there would *never* be a problem. This example is guaranteed to work on any CPU platform using any programming language or compiler because we are not trying to change any variables that the compiler might decide to load into registers.

OK, turn the page and let's look at a sample run of the program.

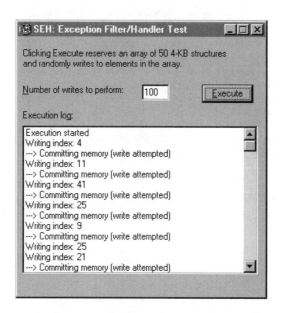

The log shows the results of performing 100 randomly selected write accesses to the array. At first the array had no memory committed to it, causing the exception filter to be invoked for array indexes 4, 11, 41, 25, and 9. But then index 25 was written to again. This time, no access violation occurred, and the exception filter didn't get called.

Now let's scroll to the bottom of the Execution Log:

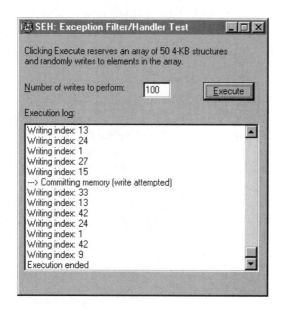

At the end of the 100 accesses, very few exceptions occur because most of the array indexes have already been selected and memory for these indexes has been committed.

You'll notice that I put a *try-finally* block inside the *ExpFilter* function. I did this to demonstrate that it's perfectly legal and useful to use structured exception handling inside an exception filter. It's also possible to put *try-finally* or *try-except* blocks inside *finally* blocks or *except* blocks, and it's even possible to nest *try-finally* and *try-except* blocks inside one another. Nesting of exception handlers inside an exception filter will be demonstrated in the SEHSoft sample application, coming up a little later.

As with the SEHTerm program we looked at earlier, you can experiment with SEHExcpt yourself by changing the number of array accesses and seeing how this change affects the number of times that the exception filter is called.

SEHExcpt.ico

SEHEXCPT.C

```
/***************************************************************
Module name: SEHExcpt.C
Notices: Copyright (c) 1995-1997 Jeffrey Richter
***************************************************************/


#include "..\CmnHdr.H"                    /* See Appendix C. */
#include <windows.h>
#include <windowsx.h>
#include <tchar.h>
#include <stdio.h>                  // For sprintf
#include <stdlib.h>                 // For rand
#include "Resource.H"



///////////////////////////////////////////////////////////////


#define NUMELEMENTS       (50)

// Declare each array element to be 4 KB.
typedef struct {
    BYTE bReserved[4 * 1024];
} ELEMENT, *LPELEMENT;
```

Figure 16-4.   *(continued)*
The SEHExcpt application.

Figure 16-4. *continued*

```
////////////////////////////////////////////////////////////////

void CommitMemory (HWND hwndLog, LPEXCEPTION_POINTERS lpEP,
   LPBYTE lpbAttemptedAddr) {

   BOOL fAttemptedWrite;
   TCHAR szBuf[100];

   // Find out whether a memory access was tried.
   fAttemptedWrite = (BOOL)
      lpEP->ExceptionRecord->ExceptionInformation[0];

   // Add an entry to the Execution Log list box.
   _stprintf(szBuf,
      __TEXT("--> Committing memory (%s attempted)"),
      fAttemptedWrite ? __TEXT("write") : __TEXT("read"));
   ListBox_AddString(hwndLog, szBuf);

   // The attempted memory access did occur while the program
   // was accessing an element in our array. Let's try to
   // commit memory to an individual element of the reserved
   // array's address space.
   VirtualAlloc(lpbAttemptedAddr, sizeof(ELEMENT),
      MEM_COMMIT, PAGE_READWRITE);
}


////////////////////////////////////////////////////////////////

int ExpFilter (LPEXCEPTION_POINTERS lpEP, LPBYTE lpbArray,
   LONG lNumBytesInArray, HWND hwndLog) {

   LPBYTE lpbAttemptedAddr = NULL;

   // Get the exception code explaining
   // why the filter is executing.
   DWORD dwExceptionCode = lpEP->ExceptionRecord->ExceptionCode;

   // Assume that this filter will NOT handle the exception
   // and will let the system continue scanning
   // for other filters.
   int nFilterResult = EXCEPTION_CONTINUE_SEARCH;
```

(continued)

Figure 16-4. *continued*

```
__try {
   // We must first determine whether the exception is
   // occurring because of a memory access to our array of
   // elements. This filter and handler do not process
   // any other types of exceptions.

   if (dwExceptionCode != EXCEPTION_ACCESS_VIOLATION) {
      // If the exception is not a memory access violation,
      // the exception doesn't come from an array element
      // access. The system should continue its search for
      // another exception filter.
      nFilterResult = EXCEPTION_CONTINUE_SEARCH;
      __leave;
   }

   if (lpbArray == NULL) {
      // The exception occurred either before the program
      // tried to reserve the address space or the
      // array's address space was unsuccessfully reserved.
      nFilterResult = EXCEPTION_CONTINUE_SEARCH;
      __leave;
   }

   // Get the address of the attempted memory access.
   lpbAttemptedAddr = (LPBYTE)
      lpEP->ExceptionRecord->ExceptionInformation[1];

   if ((lpbAttemptedAddr < lpbArray) ||
      ((lpbArray + lNumBytesInArray) < lpbAttemptedAddr)) {

      // Address attempted is BELOW the beginning of the
      // array's reserved space or is ABOVE the end of the
      // array's reserved space. We'll let some other
      // filter handle this exception.
      nFilterResult = EXCEPTION_CONTINUE_SEARCH;
      __leave;
   }

   // This filter will handle the exception.

   CommitMemory(hwndLog, lpEP, lpbAttemptedAddr);

   // Memory is committed now. Let's restart the
   // instruction that caused the exception in the first
```

(continued)

Figure 16-4. *continued*

```
      // place. This time, the instruction will succeed
      // and not cause another exception.
      nFilterResult = EXCEPTION_CONTINUE_EXECUTION;
   }

   __finally {
   }

   // Now that memory is committed, we can continue execution
   // at the instruction that generated the exception in
   // the first place.
   return(nFilterResult);
}


//////////////////////////////////////////////////////////////


void Dlg_ReserveArrayAndAccessIt (HWND hwndLog,
   int nNumAccesses) {

   LPELEMENT lpArray = NULL;
   ELEMENT Element;
   TCHAR szBuf[100];
   int nElementNum;
   const LONG lNumBytesInArray = sizeof(ELEMENT) *
      NUMELEMENTS;

   // Clear the Execution Log list box.
   ListBox_ResetContent(hwndLog);
   ListBox_AddString(hwndLog, __TEXT("Execution started"));

   __try {
      // Reserve an address space large enough to
      // hold NUMELEMENTS number of ELEMENTs.
      lpArray = VirtualAlloc(NULL, lNumBytesInArray,
         MEM_RESERVE, PAGE_NOACCESS);

      while (nNumAccesses--) {
         // Get the index of a random element to access.
         nElementNum = rand() % NUMELEMENTS;

         // Try a write access.
         _stprintf(szBuf,
```

(continued)

Figure 16-4. *continued*

```
            __TEXT("Writing index: %d"), nElementNum);
        ListBox_AddString(hwndLog, szBuf);

        // The exception will occur on this line.
        lpArray[nElementNum] = Element;

    } // while

    // We have finished the execution.
    ListBox_AddString(hwndLog, __TEXT("Execution ended"));

    // Decommit and free the array of ELEMENTs.
    VirtualFree(lpArray, 0, MEM_RELEASE);
    } // __try

    __except (
        ExpFilter(GetExceptionInformation(), (LPBYTE) lpArray,
            lNumBytesInArray, hwndLog)) {

        // Because the filter never returns
        // EXCEPTION_EXECUTE_HANDLER, there is nothing
        // to do in the except block.

    } // __except
}


///////////////////////////////////////////////////////////////


BOOL Dlg_OnInitDialog (HWND hwnd, HWND hwndFocus,
    LPARAM lParam) {

    // Associate an icon with the dialog box.
    chSETDLGICONS(hwnd, IDI_SEHEXCPT, IDI_SEHEXCPT);

    // Default the number of accesses to 100.
    SetDlgItemInt(hwnd, IDC_NUMACCESSES, 100, FALSE);
    return(TRUE);
}


///////////////////////////////////////////////////////////////
```

(continued)

Figure 16-4. *continued*

```
void Dlg_OnCommand (HWND hwnd, int id,
   HWND hwndCtl, UINT codeNotify) {

   int  nNumAccesses;
   BOOL fTranslated;

   switch (id) {
      case IDOK:
         nNumAccesses = GetDlgItemInt(hwnd, IDC_NUMACCESSES,
            &fTranslated, FALSE);

         if (fTranslated) {
            Dlg_ReserveArrayAndAccessIt(
               GetDlgItem(hwnd, IDC_LOG), nNumAccesses);
         } else {
            chMB(__TEXT("Invalid number of accesses."));
         }
         break;

      case IDCANCEL:
         EndDialog(hwnd, id);
         break;
   }
}


///////////////////////////////////////////////////////////////


BOOL CALLBACK Dlg_Proc (HWND hwnd, UINT uMsg,
   WPARAM wParam, LPARAM lParam) {

   switch (uMsg) {
      chHANDLE_DLGMSG(hwnd, WM_INITDIALOG, Dlg_OnInitDialog);
      chHANDLE_DLGMSG(hwnd, WM_COMMAND, Dlg_OnCommand);
   }
   return(FALSE);
}


///////////////////////////////////////////////////////////////


int WINAPI _tWinMain (HINSTANCE hinstExe,
   HINSTANCE hinstPrev, LPTSTR pszCmdLine, int nCmdShow) {
```

(continued)

Figure 16-4. *continued*

```
    chWARNIFUNICODEUNDERWIN95();
    DialogBox(hinstExe, MAKEINTRESOURCE(IDD_SEHEXCPT),
        NULL, Dlg_Proc);

    return(0);
}



///////////////////////// End Of File /////////////////////////
```

SEHEXCPT.RC

```
//Microsoft Developer Studio generated resource script.
//
#include "Resource.h"

#define APSTUDIO_READONLY_SYMBOLS
/////////////////////////////////////////////////////////////
//
// Generated from the TEXTINCLUDE 2 resource.
//
#include "afxres.h"


/////////////////////////////////////////////////////////////
#undef APSTUDIO_READONLY_SYMBOLS


/////////////////////////////////////////////////////////////
// English (U.S.) resources

#if !defined(AFX_RESOURCE_DLL) || defined(AFX_TARG_ENU)
#ifdef _WIN32
LANGUAGE LANG_ENGLISH, SUBLANG_ENGLISH_US
#pragma code_page(1252)
#endif //_WIN32

#ifdef APSTUDIO_INVOKED
/////////////////////////////////////////////////////////////
//
// TEXTINCLUDE
//

1 TEXTINCLUDE DISCARDABLE
BEGIN
```

(continued)

Figure 16-4. *continued*

```
    "Resource.h\0"
END

2 TEXTINCLUDE DISCARDABLE
BEGIN
    "#include ""afxres.h""\r\n"
    "\0"
END

3 TEXTINCLUDE DISCARDABLE
BEGIN
    "\r\n"
    "\0"
END

#endif     // APSTUDIO_INVOKED


/////////////////////////////////////////////////////////////////
//
// Dialog
//

IDD_SEHEXCPT DIALOG DISCARDABLE  18, 18, 214, 200
STYLE WS_MINIMIZEBOX | WS_VISIBLE | WS_CAPTION | WS_SYSMENU
CAPTION "SEH: Exception Filter/Handler Test"
FONT 8, "Helv"
BEGIN
    LTEXT           "Clicking Execute reserves an array of\
50 4-KB structures and randomly writes to elements in the\
array.",
                    IDC_STATIC,4,8,188,24
    LTEXT           "&Number of writes to perform:",
                    IDC_STATIC,4,36,93,8
    EDITTEXT        IDC_NUMACCESSES,108,36,24,12
    PUSHBUTTON      "&Execute",IDD_SEHEXCPT,160,36,44,14,
                    WS_GROUP
    LTEXT           "Execution lo&g:",IDC_STATIC,4,56,48,8
    LISTBOX         IDC_LOG,4,68,204,128,NOT LBS_NOTIFY |
                    WS_VSCROLL | WS_GROUP | WS_TABSTOP
END
```

(continued)

Figure 16-4. *continued*

```
/////////////////////////////////////////////////////////
//
// Icon
//

// Icon with lowest ID value placed first to ensure
// application icon remains consistent on all systems.
IDI_SEHEXCPT            ICON   DISCARDABLE      "SEHExcpt.Ico"
#endif    // English (U.S.) resources
/////////////////////////////////////////////////////////


#ifndef APSTUDIO_INVOKED
/////////////////////////////////////////////////////////
//
// Generated from the TEXTINCLUDE 3 resource.
//


/////////////////////////////////////////////////////////
#endif    // not APSTUDIO_INVOKED
```

The SEH Sum Sample Application

The SEHSum (SEHSUM.EXE) sample application, listed in Figure 16-5 beginning on page 842, demonstrates how to use exception filters and exception handlers to recover gracefully from a stack overflow. The source code and resource files for the application are in the SEHSUM directory on the companion disc. You might want to review the section "A Thread's Stack" in Chapter 7 in order to fully understand how this application works.

The SEHSum application sums all of the numbers from 0 through x, where x is a number entered by the user. Of course, the simplest way to do this would be to create a function called *Sum* that simply performs the following calculation:

```
Sum = (x * (x + 1)) / 2;
```

For this sample, I have written the *Sum* function to be recursive.

When the program starts, it displays the dialog box shown here:

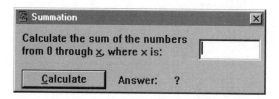

In this dialog box, you can enter a number in the edit control and then click on the Calculate button. This causes the program to create a new thread whose sole responsibility is to total all of the numbers between 0 and *x*. While the new thread is running, the program's primary thread tells the system not to schedule it any CPU time by calling *WaitForSingleObject*. When the new thread terminates, the system reschedules CPU time to the primary thread. The primary thread retrieves the sum by getting the new thread's exit code through a call to *GetExitCodeThread*. Finally—and this is extremely important—the primary thread closes its handle to the new thread so that the system can completely destroy the thread object and so that our application does not have a resource leak.

Now the primary thread examines the summation thread's exit code. If the exit code is UINT_MAX, it indicates that an error occurred—the summation thread overflowed the stack while totaling the numbers—and the primary thread will display a message box to this effect. If the exit code is not UINT_MAX, the summation thread completed successfully and the exit code is the summation. In this case, the primary thread will simply put the summation answer in the dialog box.

Now let's turn to the summation thread. The thread function for this thread is called *SumThreadFunc*. When this thread is created by the primary thread, it is passed the number of integers that it should total as its only parameter, *p*. The function then initializes the *uSum* variable to UINT_MAX, which means that the function is assuming that it will not complete successfully. Next *SumThreadFunc* sets up SEH so that it can catch any exception that might be raised while the thread executes. The recursive *Sum* function is then called to calculate the sum.

If the sum is calculated successfully, *SumThreadFunc* simply returns the value of the *uSum* variable; this is the thread's exit code. However, if an exception is raised while the *Sum* function is executing, the system will immediately evaluate the SEH filter expression. In other words, the system will call the *FilterFunc* function and pass it the code that identifies the raised exception. For a stack overflow exception, this code is EXCEP-

TION_STACK_OVERFLOW. If you want to see the program gracefully handle a stack overflow exception, tell the program to sum the first 44,000 numbers.

My *FilterFunc* function is very simple. It begins by assuming that it is not prepared to handle the type of exception that has been raised. When a filter does not know how to handle an exception, it should return EXCEPTION_CONTINUE_SEARCH. Then the filter should check to see whether the raised exception is EXCEPTION_STACK_OVERFLOW. If this is true, the filter should return EXCEPTION_EXECUTE_HAN-DLER. This indicates to the system that the filter was expecting this exception and that the code contained in the *except* block should execute. For this sample application, EXCEPTION_EXECUTE_HANDLER indicates that an error occurred while the thread was executing the *Sum* function and that the thread should simply exit returning UINT_MAX (the value in *uSumNum*) because I'm pretending that the *Sum* function was never called.

The last thing that I want to discuss is why I execute the *Sum* function in its own thread instead of just setting up an SEH block in the primary thread and calling the *Sum* function from within the *try* block. I created this additional thread for three reasons.

First, each time a thread is created, it gets its very own 1-MB stack region. If I called the *Sum* function from within the primary thread, some of the stack space would already be in use and the *Sum* function would not be able to use its full 1 MB of stack space. Granted, my sample is a very simple program and is probably not using all that much stack, but other programs will probably be more complicated. I can easily imagine a situation in which *Sum* might successfully total the integers from 0 through 1000; then, when *Sum* is called again later, the stack might be deeper, causing a stack overflow to occur when *Sum* is trying only to total the integers from 0 through 750. So to make the *Sum* function behave more consistently, I ensure that it has a full stack that has not been used by any other code.

The second reason for using a separate thread is that a thread is notified only once of a stack overflow exception. If I called the *Sum* function in the primary thread and a stack overflow occurred, the exception could be trapped and handled gracefully. However, at this point, all of the stack's reserved address space is committed with physical storage, and there are no more pages with the guard protection flag turned on. If the user performs another sum, the *Sum* function could overflow the stack and a stack overflow exception would not be raised. Instead, an access violation exception would be raised, and it would be too late to handle this situation gracefully.

The final reason for using a separate stack is so that the physical storage for the stack can be freed. Take this scenario as an example: The user asks the *Sum* function to calculate the sum of the integers from 0 through 30,000. This will require quite a bit of physical storage to be committed to the stack region. Then the user might do several summations in which the highest number is only 5000. In this case, a large amount of storage is committed to the stack region but is no longer being used. This physical storage is allocated from the paging file. It's better to free this storage and give it back to the system and other processes. By having the *SumThreadFunc* thread terminate, the system automatically reclaims the physical storage that was committed to the stack's region.

SEHSum.ico

```
SEHSUM.C
/****************************************************************
Module name: SEHSum.C
Notices: Copyright (c) 1995-1997 Jeffrey Richter
****************************************************************/


#include "..\CmnHdr.H"                    /* See Appendix C. */
#include <windows.h>
#include <windowsx.h>
#include <limits.h>
#include <process.h>              // For _beginthreadex
#include <tchar.h>
#include "Resource.H"



///////////////////////////////////////////////////////////////


// An example of calling Sum for uNum = 0 through 9
// uNum: 0 1 2 3  4  5  6  7  8  9 …
// Sum:  0 1 3 6 10 15 21 28 36 45 …
UINT Sum (UINT uNum) {

   if (uNum == 0)
      return(0);
```

Figure 16-5.
The SEHSum application.

(continued)

Figure 16-5. *continued*

```
    // Call Sum recursively.
    return(uNum + Sum(uNum - 1));
}


////////////////////////////////////////////////////////////


long FilterFunc (DWORD dwExceptionCode) {

    // Assume that we do not know how to handle the exception;
    // tell the system to continue to search for an SEH
    // handler.
    long lRet = EXCEPTION_CONTINUE_SEARCH;

    if (dwExceptionCode == STATUS_STACK_OVERFLOW) {
        // If the exception raised is a stack overflow,
        // we do know how to handle it.
        lRet = EXCEPTION_EXECUTE_HANDLER;
    }

    return(lRet);
}


////////////////////////////////////////////////////////////


// The separate thread that is responsible for calculating the
// sum. I use a separate thread for the following reasons:
// 1. A separate thread gets its own 1 MB of stack space.
// 2. A thread can be notified of a stack overflow only once.
// 3. The stack's storage is freed when the thread exits.
DWORD WINAPI SumThreadFunc (PVOID p) {

    // The parameter, p, is really a UINT containing
    // the number of integers to sum.
    UINT uSumNum = (UINT) p;

    // uSum contains the summation of the numbers
    // from 0 through uSumNum. If the sum cannot be calculated,
    // a sum of UINT_MAX is returned.
    UINT uSum = UINT_MAX;
```

(continued)

Figure 16-5. *continued*

```
    __try {
        // To catch the stack overflow exception, we must
        // execute the Sum function while inside an SEH block.
        uSum = Sum(uSumNum);
    }
    __except (FilterFunc(GetExceptionCode())) {
        // If we get in here, it's because we have trapped
        // a stack overflow. We can now do whatever is
        // necessary to gracefully continue execution.
        // This sample application has nothing to do, so
        // no code is placed in this exception handler block.
    }

    // The thread's exit code is the sum of the first uSumNum
    // numbers, or UINT_MAX if a stack overflow occurred.
    return(uSum);
}


///////////////////////////////////////////////////////////


BOOL Dlg_OnInitDialog (HWND hwnd, HWND hwndFocus,
    LPARAM lParam) {

    // Associate an icon with the dialog box.
    chSETDLGICONS(hwnd, IDI_SEHSUM, IDI_SEHSUM);

    return(TRUE);
}


///////////////////////////////////////////////////////////


void Dlg_OnCommand (HWND hwnd, int id,
    HWND hwndCtl, UINT codeNotify) {

    UINT uSumNum, uSum;
    BOOL fTranslated;
    DWORD dwThreadId;
    HANDLE hThread;
```

(continued)

844

Figure 16-5. *continued*

```
switch (id) {
   case IDC_CALC:
      // Get the number of integers the user wants to sum.
      uSumNum = GetDlgItemInt(hwnd, IDC_SUMNUM,
         &fTranslated, FALSE);

      // Create a thread (with its own stack) that is
      // responsible for performing the summation.
      hThread = chBEGINTHREADEX(NULL, 0, SumThreadFunc,
         (PVOID) uSumNum, 0, &dwThreadId);

      // The thread's exit code is the resulting summation.

      // We must first wait for the thread to terminate.
      WaitForSingleObject(hThread, INFINITE);

      // Now we can get the thread's exit code.
      GetExitCodeThread(hThread, (PDWORD) &uSum);

      // Finally, we close the handle to the thread so
      // that the system can destroy the thread object.
      CloseHandle(hThread);

      // Update the dialog box to show the result.
      if (uSum == UINT_MAX) {
         // If the thread's exit code is UINT_MAX, a stack
         // overflow occurred.  Update the dialog box
         // and display a message box.
         SetDlgItemText(hwnd, IDC_ANSWER, __TEXT("Error"));
         chMB(__TEXT("The number is too big, ")
            __TEXT("please enter a smaller number"));
      } else {
         // The sum was calculated successfully;
         // update the dialog box.
         SetDlgItemInt(hwnd, IDC_ANSWER, uSum, FALSE);
      }

      break;

   case IDCANCEL:
      EndDialog(hwnd, id);
      break;
   }
}
```

(continued)

Figure 16-5. *continued*

```
//////////////////////////////////////////////////////////////


BOOL CALLBACK Dlg_Proc (HWND hwnd, UINT uMsg,
   WPARAM wParam, LPARAM lParam) {

   switch (uMsg) {
      chHANDLE_DLGMSG(hwnd, WM_INITDIALOG, Dlg_OnInitDialog);
      chHANDLE_DLGMSG(hwnd, WM_COMMAND, Dlg_OnCommand);
   }

   return(FALSE);
}



//////////////////////////////////////////////////////////////


int WINAPI _tWinMain (HINSTANCE hinstExe,
   HINSTANCE hinstPrev, LPTSTR pszCmdLine, int nCmdShow) {

   chWARNIFUNICODEUNDERWIN95();
   DialogBox(hinstExe, MAKEINTRESOURCE(IDD_SUMMATION),
      NULL, Dlg_Proc);

   return(0);
}


/////////////////////////// End Of File ///////////////////////////
```

SEHSUM.RC
```
//Microsoft Developer Studio generated resource script.
//
#include "Resource.h"

#define APSTUDIO_READONLY_SYMBOLS
//////////////////////////////////////////////////////////////
//
// Generated from the TEXTINCLUDE 2 resource.
//
```

(continued)

Figure 16-5. *continued*

```
#define APSTUDIO_HIDDEN_SYMBOLS
#include "windows.h"
#undef APSTUDIO_HIDDEN_SYMBOLS

/////////////////////////////////////////////////////////////////
#undef APSTUDIO_READONLY_SYMBOLS

/////////////////////////////////////////////////////////////////
// English (U.S.) resources

#if !defined(AFX_RESOURCE_DLL) || defined(AFX_TARG_ENU)
#ifdef _WIN32
LANGUAGE LANG_ENGLISH, SUBLANG_ENGLISH_US
#pragma code_page(1252)
#endif //_WIN32


/////////////////////////////////////////////////////////////////
//
// Icon
//

// Icon with lowest ID value placed first to ensure
// application icon remains consistent on all systems.
IDI_SEHSUM              ICON    DISCARDABLE     "SEHSum.ICO"


/////////////////////////////////////////////////////////////////
//
// Dialog
//

IDD_SUMMATION DIALOG DISCARDABLE  18, 18, 162, 41
STYLE WS_POPUP | WS_CAPTION | WS_SYSMENU
CAPTION "Summation"
FONT 8, "System"
BEGIN
    LTEXT           "Calculate the sum of the numbers\
  from 0 through &x, where x is: ",
                    IDC_STATIC,4,4,112,20
    EDITTEXT        IDC_SUMNUM,120,8,40,13,ES_AUTOHSCROLL
    DEFPUSHBUTTON   "&Calculate",IDC_CALC,4,28,56,12
    LTEXT           "Answer:",IDC_STATIC,68,30,30,8
    LTEXT           "?",IDC_ANSWER,104,30,56,8
END
```

(continued)

Figure 16-5. *continued*

```
#ifdef APSTUDIO_INVOKED
/////////////////////////////////////////////////////////////
//
// TEXTINCLUDE
//

1 TEXTINCLUDE DISCARDABLE
BEGIN
    "Resource.h\0"
END

2 TEXTINCLUDE DISCARDABLE
BEGIN
    "#define APSTUDIO_HIDDEN_SYMBOLS\r\n"
    "#include ""windows.h""\r\n"
    "#undef APSTUDIO_HIDDEN_SYMBOLS\r\n"
    "\0"
END

3 TEXTINCLUDE DISCARDABLE
BEGIN
    "\r\n"
    "\0"
END

#endif    // APSTUDIO_INVOKED

#endif    // English (U.S.) resources
/////////////////////////////////////////////////////////////



#ifndef APSTUDIO_INVOKED
/////////////////////////////////////////////////////////////
//
// Generated from the TEXTINCLUDE 3 resource.
//


/////////////////////////////////////////////////////////////
#endif    // not APSTUDIO_INVOKED
```

Software Exceptions

So far we have been looking at handling hardware exceptions in which the CPU catches an event and raises an exception. Often it's useful to raise software exceptions in which the operating system or your application raises its own exceptions. The *HeapAlloc* function provides a good occasion for software exception use. When you call the *HeapAlloc* function, you can specify the HEAP_GENERATE_EXCEPTIONS flag. Then, if *HeapAlloc* is unable to satisfy the memory request, *HeapAlloc* generates a STATUS_NO_MEMORY software exception.

If you want to take advantage of this exception, you can code your *try* block as though the memory allocation will always succeed; if the allocation fails, you can either handle the exception by using an *except* block or have your function clean up by matching the *try* block with a *finally* block.

Your application doesn't need to know whether it is processing a hardware exception or a software exception, and you implement your *try-finally* and *try-except* blocks identically. However, you can have portions of your code raise software exceptions themselves, just as *HeapAlloc* does. To raise a software exception in your code, call the *RaiseException* function:

```
VOID RaiseException(DWORD dwExceptionCode, DWORD dwExceptionFlags,
    DWORD cArguments, LPDWORD lpArguments);
```

The first parameter, *dwExceptionCode*, must be a value that identifies the raised exception. The *HeapAlloc* function passes STATUS_NO_MEMORY for this parameter. If you raise your own exception identifiers, you should follow the same format as the standard Win32 error codes as defined in the WINERROR.H file. Recall that each DWORD is divided as shown in the table on the top of the next page.

Bits:	31–30	29–28	27–16	15–0
Contents:	Severity	Flags	Facility code	Exception code
Meaning:	0 = Success	Bit 29	Microsoft-defined	Microsoft/Programmer-defined
	1 = Informational	0 = Microsoft		
	2 = Warning	1 = Customer		
	3 = Error	Bit 28 is reserved (must be 0)		

If you create your own exception code, fill out all four fields of the DWORD: bits 31 and 30 should contain the severity; bit 29 should be 1 (0 is reserved for Microsoft-created exceptions, such as *HeapAlloc*'s STATUS-_NO_MEMORY); bit 28 should be 0; bits 27 through 16 should be one of Microsoft's predefined facility codes; and bits 15 through 0 should be an arbitrary value that you choose to identify the section of your application that raised the exception.

RaiseException's second parameter, *dwExceptionFlags*, must be either 0 or EXCEPTION_NONCONTINUABLE. Specifying the EXCEPTION-_NONCONTINUABLE flag tells the system that the type of exception you are raising can't be continued. The EXCEPTION_NONCONTINU-ABLE flag is used internally in the operating system to signal fatal (non-recoverable) errors.

When *HeapAlloc* raises the STATUS_NO_MEMORY exception, it uses the EXCEPTION_NONCONTINUABLE flag to tell the system that this exception cannot be continued and that it is illegal for an exception filter to evaluate to EXCEPTION_CONTINUE_EXECUTION. If this type of exception is raised and an exception filter does evaluate to EX-CEPTION_CONTINUE_EXECUTION, the system raises a new exception: EXCEPTION_NONCONTINUABLE_EXCEPTION.

That's right—it is possible for an exception to be raised while the application is trying to process another exception. This of course makes sense. While we're at it, let's note that it's also possible for an invalid memory access to occur inside a *finally* block, an exception filter, or an exception handler. When this happens, the system stacks exceptions. Remember the *GetExceptionInformation* function? This function returns the address of an EXCEPTION_POINTERS structure. The *ExceptionRec-ord* member of the EXCEPTION_POINTERS structure points to an

EXCEPTION_RECORD structure that contains another *ExceptionRecord* member. This member is a pointer to another EXCEPTION_RECORD, which contains information about the previously raised exception.

Usually the system is processing only one exception at a time, and the *ExceptionRecord* member is NULL. However, if during the processing of one exception another exception is raised, the first EXCEPTION-_RECORD structure contains information about the most recently raised exception and the *ExceptionRecord* member of this first EXCEP-TION_RECORD structure points to the EXCEPTION_RECORD structure for the previously raised exception. If additional exceptions have not been processed completely, you can continue to walk this linked list of EXCEPTION_RECORD structures to determine how to handle the exception.

RaiseException's third and fourth parameters, *cArguments* and *lpAr-guments*, are used to pass additional information about the generated exception. If you don't need additional arguments, you can pass NULL to *lpArguments*, in which case *RaiseException* ignores the *cArguments* parameter. If you do want to pass additional arguments, the *cArguments* parameter must indicate the number of elements in the DWORD array pointed to by the *lpArguments* parameter. This parameter cannot exceed EXCEP-TION_MAXIMUM_PARAMETERS, which is defined in WINNT.H as 15.

During the processing of this exception, you can have an exception filter refer to the *NumberParameters* and *ExceptionInformation* members of the EXCEPTION_RECORD structure to examine the information in the *cArguments* and *lpArguments* parameters.

You might want to generate your own software exceptions in your application for any of several reasons. For example, you might want to send informational messages to the system's event log. Whenever a function in your application sensed some sort of problem, you could call *RaiseException* and have some exception handler further up the call tree look for certain exceptions and either add them to the event log or pop up a message box. You might also want to create software exceptions to signal internal fatal errors in your application. This would be much easier than trying to return error values all the way up the call tree.

The SEH Software Exceptions Sample Application

The SEHSoft (SEHSOFT.EXE) application, listed in Figure 16-6 beginning on page 855, demonstrates how to create and use your own software exceptions. The source code and resource files for the application are in the SEHSOFT directory on the companion disc. The program is based on the earlier SEHExcpt sample program. When you invoke SEHSoft, this dialog box appears:

This box is similar to SEHExcpt's dialog box, but this program will try to read from as well as write to the array of elements.

In the *Dlg_ReserveArrayAndAccessIt* function, the access loop gets the index of a random element to access; it has been modified to then select another random number. This second number is used to determine whether the program should try to write the element to the array or read the element from the array.

You might be asking yourself what it means to read an element from the array if the array has never been initialized. You'd be quite correct to ask this. I have enhanced the program to automatically zero the contents of an array element when memory is committed because the program has tried to read an array element. I did this by raising a software exception.

Inside the *ExpFilter* function, instead of just calling *CommitMemory* as I did in SEHEXCPT.C, I put the call to *CommitMemory* into a *try* block. The filter expression for the *except* block associated with this *try* block checks whether the call to *CommitMemory* has generated an exception and whether that exception code is SE_ZERO_ELEM.

SE_ZERO_ELEM is a *#define* that identifies a software exception code I have created near the top of SEHSOFT.C:

```
// Useful macro for creating our own software exception codes
#define MAKESOFTWAREEXCEPTION(Severity, Facility, Exception) \
   ((DWORD) ( \
   /* Severity code */      (Severity       ) |   \
   /* MS(0) or Cust(1) */   (1         << 29) |   \
   /* Reserved(0) */        (0         << 28) |   \
   /* Facility code */      (Facility  << 16) |   \
   /* Exception code */     (Exception <<  0)))

// Our very own software exception. This exception is raised
// when an element of the array needs to be initialized
// to all zeros.
#define SE_ZERO_ELEM\
   MAKESOFTWAREEXCEPTION(ERROR_SEVERITY_ERROR,\
   FACILITY_NULL, 1)
```

The exception filter expression looks like this:

```
__except ((GetExceptionCode() == SE_ZERO_ELEM) ?
   (SavedExceptRec =
      *((GetExceptionInformation())->ExceptionRecord),
   EXCEPTION_EXECUTE_HANDLER) :
   EXCEPTION_CONTINUE_SEARCH) {
   .
   .
   .
}
```

The exception handler is prepared to handle only SE_ZERO_EL-EM exceptions. If *GetExceptionCode* returns any other exception, EXCEPTION_CONTINUE_SEARCH is returned. If the exception code is SE_ZERO_ELEM, EXCEPTION_EXECUTE_HANDLER should be returned so that the code inside the *except* block will be executed. But the code inside the *except* block will need access to the exception information, so a call to *GetExceptionInformation* is made before the return. EXCEPTION_EXECUTE_HANDLER and the information inside the EXCEPTION_RECORD structure are stored in the local *SavedExceptRec* variable.

Now that the code inside the *except* block is executing, it gets the address of the array element that needs to be zeroed by looking into the *SavedExceptRec* structure and calls *memset* to zero this one array element.

The only thing that I've left out is how the exception is generated. The code appears at the bottom of the *CommitMemory* function:

```
if (!fAttemptedWrite) {
    // The program is trying to read an array element
    // that has never been created. We'll raise our very own
    // software exception so that this array element will be
    // zeroed before it is accessed.
    RaiseException(SE_ZERO_ELEM, 0, 1, (LPDWORD) &lpAttemptedAddr);
}
```

If the attempted access is a read, the program calls *RaiseException*, passing it a SE_ZERO_ELEM software exception code and a 0 flag. We can also pass, using the third and fourth arguments, a maximum of EXCEPTION_MAXIMUM_PARAMETERS (15) parameters to the exception filter. In this example, I want to pass just one parameter to the filter: the address to the array element that needs to be zeroed. To do this, I send 1 as the third argument to *RaiseException* and the address to that parameter as the fourth argument.

Here is an example of what SEHSoft looks like when it's executed:

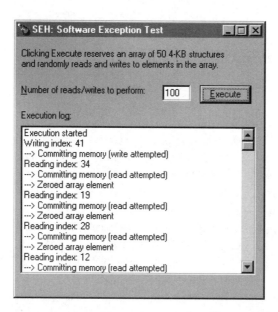

Every time the software exception is raised, the exception handler adds an entry to the Execution Log showing that it zeroed the array element.

SEHSoft.ico

SEHSOFT.C

```
/*************************************************************
Module name: SEHSoft.C
Notices: Copyright (c) 1995-1997 Jeffrey Richter
*************************************************************/


#include "..\CmnHdr.H"                      /* See Appendix C. */
#include <windows.h>
#include <windowsx.h>
#include <tchar.h>
#include <stdio.h>                 // For sprintf
#include <stdlib.h>                // For rand
#include "Resource.H"


///////////////////////////////////////////////////////////////


#define NUMELEMENTS      (50)


// Declare each array element to be 4 KB.
typedef struct {
   BYTE bReserved[4 * 1024];
} ELEMENT, *LPELEMENT;


// Useful macro for creating our own software exception codes
#define MAKESOFTWAREEXCEPTION(Severity, Facility, Exception) \
   ((DWORD) ( \
   /* Severity code */      (Severity            |    \
   /* MS(0) or Cust(1) */   (1          << 29) |      \
   /* Reserved(0) */        (0          << 28) |      \
   /* Facility code */      (Facility  << 16) |       \
   /* Exception code */     (Exception <<  0)))


// Our very own software exception. This exception is raised
// when an element of the array needs to be initialized
// to all zeros.
#define SE_ZERO_ELEM \
   MAKESOFTWAREEXCEPTION(ERROR_SEVERITY_ERROR,\
   FACILITY_NULL, 1)


///////////////////////////////////////////////////////////////
```

Figure 16-6.
The SEHSoft application.

(continued)

Figure 16-6. *continued*

```
void CommitMemory(HWND hwndLog, LPEXCEPTION_POINTERS lpEP,
   LPBYTE lpbAttemptedAddr) {

   BOOL fAttemptedWrite;
   TCHAR szBuf[100];

   // Find out whether a memory read or write was tried.
   fAttemptedWrite = (BOOL)
      lpEP->ExceptionRecord->ExceptionInformation[0];

   // Add an entry to the Execution Log list box.
   _stprintf(szBuf,
      __TEXT("--> Committing memory (%s attempted)"),
      fAttemptedWrite ? __TEXT("write") : __TEXT("read"));
   ListBox_AddString(hwndLog, szBuf);

   // The attempted memory access did occur while the
   // program was accessing an element in our array.
   // Let's try to commit memory to an individual element
   // of the reserved array's address space.
   VirtualAlloc(lpbAttemptedAddr, sizeof(ELEMENT),
      MEM_COMMIT, PAGE_READWRITE);

   if (!fAttemptedWrite) {
      // The program is trying to read an array element
      // that has never been created. We'll raise our very
      // own software exception so that this array element
      // will be zeroed before it is accessed.
      RaiseException(SE_ZERO_ELEM, 0, 1,
         (LPDWORD) &lpbAttemptedAddr);
   }
}


///////////////////////////////////////////////////////////////


int ExpFilter (LPEXCEPTION_POINTERS lpEP, LPBYTE lpbArray,
   LONG lNumBytesInArray, HWND hwndLog) {

   LPBYTE lpbAttemptedAddr = NULL;

   // Get the exception code explaining
   // why the filter is executing.
   DWORD dwExceptionCode = lpEP->ExceptionRecord->ExceptionCode;
```

(continued)

Figure 16-6. *continued*

```
// Assume that this filter will NOT handle the exception
// and will let the system continue scanning
// for other filters.
int nFilterResult = EXCEPTION_CONTINUE_SEARCH;

__try {
    // Declare an EXCEPTION_RECORD structure that is local
    // to this __try frame. This variable is used in the
    // __except block below.
    EXCEPTION_RECORD SavedExceptRec;

    // We must first determine whether the exception is
    // occurring because of a memory access to our array of
    // elements. This filter and handler do not process
    // any other types of exceptions.

    if (dwExceptionCode != EXCEPTION_ACCESS_VIOLATION) {
        // If the exception is not a memory access violation,
        // the exception did not occur because of an array
        // element access. The system should continue its
        // search for another exception filter.
        nFilterResult = EXCEPTION_CONTINUE_SEARCH;
        __leave;
    }

    if (lpbArray == NULL) {
        // The exception occurred before the program
        // tried to reserve the address space, or else the
        // array's address space was unsuccessfully reserved.
        nFilterResult = EXCEPTION_CONTINUE_SEARCH;
        __leave;
    }

    // Get the address of the attempted memory access.
    lpbAttemptedAddr = (LPBYTE)
        lpEP->ExceptionRecord->ExceptionInformation[1];

    if ((lpbAttemptedAddr < lpbArray) ||
        ((lpbArray + lNumBytesInArray) < lpbAttemptedAddr)) {
        // Address attempted is BELOW the beginning of the
        // array's reserved space or is ABOVE the end of the
        // array's reserved space. We'll let some other
        // filter handle this exception.
```

(continued)

Figure 16-6. *continued*

```
        nFilterResult = EXCEPTION_CONTINUE_SEARCH;
        __leave;
    }


    // *** The exception is to be handled by this filter.

    __try {
        // Call the function that commits memory to the
        // accessed array element. This function will raise
        // a software exception if read access was attempted.
        // In this case, we want to zero the contents of the
        // array element before the read continues.
        CommitMemory(hwndLog, lpEP, lpbAttemptedAddr);
    }

    // We want to handle the exception only if it is our
    // very own software exception telling us to zero the
    // contents of the array element. If this is the case, we
    // need to save the additional information given to us
    // with the SE_ZERO_ELEM exception code so that the
    // handler knows which array element to zero.
    __except ((GetExceptionCode() == SE_ZERO_ELEM) ?
        (SavedExceptRec =
        *((GetExceptionInformation())->ExceptionRecord),
        EXCEPTION_EXECUTE_HANDLER) :
        EXCEPTION_CONTINUE_SEARCH) {

        // Get the address of the array element to zero.
        LPELEMENT lpArrayElementToZero = (LPELEMENT)
            SavedExceptRec.ExceptionInformation[0];

        // Zero the array element before reading from it.
        chINITSTRUCT(*lpArrayElementToZero, FALSE);

        ListBox_AddString(hwndLog,
            __TEXT("--> Zeroed array element"));
    }

    // Memory is committed now; let's restart the
    // instruction that caused the exception in the first
    // place. This time, it will succeed and not cause
    // another exception.
    nFilterResult = EXCEPTION_CONTINUE_EXECUTION;
}
```

(continued)

Figure 16-6. *continued*

```
    __finally {
    }

    // Now that memory is committed, we can continue execution
    // on the instruction that generated the exception in
    // the first place.
    return(nFilterResult);
}



///////////////////////////////////////////////////////////////


void Dlg_ReserveArrayAndAccessIt (HWND hwndLog,
    int nNumAccesses) {

    LPELEMENT lpArray = NULL;
    ELEMENT Element;
    TCHAR szBuf[100];
    int nElementNum = 0;
    const LONG lNumBytesInArray = sizeof(ELEMENT) *
        NUMELEMENTS;

    // Clear the Execution Log list box.
    ListBox_ResetContent(hwndLog);
    ListBox_AddString(hwndLog, __TEXT("Execution started"));

    __try {
        // Reserve an address space large enough to
        // hold NUMELEMENTS number of ELEMENTs.
        lpArray = VirtualAlloc(NULL, lNumBytesInArray,
            MEM_RESERVE, PAGE_NOACCESS);

        while (nNumAccesses--) {
            // Get the index of a random element to access.
            nElementNum = rand() % NUMELEMENTS;

            // Give us a 50 percent chance of reading and a
            // 50 percent chance of writing.
            if ((rand() % 2) == 0) {
                // Attempt a read access.
                _stprintf(szBuf, __TEXT("Reading index: %d"),
                    nElementNum);
                ListBox_AddString(hwndLog, szBuf);
```

(continued)

Figure 16-6. *continued*

```
                // The exception will occur on this line.
                Element = lpArray[nElementNum];

        } else {

                // Attempt a write access.
                _stprintf(szBuf, __TEXT("Writing index: %d"),
                    nElementNum);
                ListBox_AddString(hwndLog, szBuf);

                // The exception will occur on this line.
                lpArray[nElementNum] = Element;
        }

    }   // while

    // We have finished the execution.
    ListBox_AddString(hwndLog, __TEXT("Execution ended"));

    // Decommit and free the array of ELEMENTs.
    VirtualFree(lpArray, 0, MEM_RELEASE);
}   // __try

__except (
    ExpFilter(GetExceptionInformation(), (LPBYTE) lpArray,
        lNumBytesInArray, hwndLog)) {

    // Because the filter never returns
    // EXCEPTION_EXECUTE_HANDLER, there is
    // nothing to do here.

}   // __except
}


//////////////////////////////////////////////////////////////


BOOL Dlg_OnInitDialog (HWND hwnd, HWND hwndFocus,
    LPARAM lParam) {

    // Associate an icon with the dialog box.
    chSETDLGICONS(hwnd, IDI_SEHSOFT, IDI_SEHSOFT);
```

(continued)

Figure 16-6. *continued*

```
    // Default the number of accesses to 100.
    SetDlgItemInt(hwnd, IDC_NUMACCESSES, 100, FALSE);
    return(TRUE);
}


//////////////////////////////////////////////////////////////


void Dlg_OnCommand (HWND hwnd, int id,
    HWND hwndCtl, UINT codeNotify) {

    int   nNumAccesses;
    BOOL  fTranslated;

    switch (id) {
        case IDOK:
            nNumAccesses = GetDlgItemInt(hwnd, IDC_NUMACCESSES,
                &fTranslated, FALSE);

            if (fTranslated) {
                Dlg_ReserveArrayAndAccessIt(
                    GetDlgItem(hwnd, IDC_LOG), nNumAccesses);
            } else {
                chMB(__TEXT("Invalid number of accesses."));
            }
            break;

        case IDCANCEL:
            EndDialog(hwnd, id);
            break;
    }
}


//////////////////////////////////////////////////////////////


BOOL CALLBACK Dlg_Proc (HWND hwnd, UINT uMsg,
    WPARAM wParam, LPARAM lParam) {

    switch (uMsg) {
        chHANDLE_DLGMSG(hwnd, WM_INITDIALOG, Dlg_OnInitDialog);
```

(continued)

Figure 16-6. *continued*

```
        chHANDLE_DLGMSG(hwnd, WM_COMMAND, Dlg_OnCommand);
   }
   return(FALSE);
}


//////////////////////////////////////////////////////////////


int WINAPI _tWinMain (HINSTANCE hinstExe,
   HINSTANCE hinstPrev, LPTSTR pszCmdLine, int nCmdShow) {

   chWARNIFUNICODEUNDERWIN95();
   DialogBox(hinstExe, MAKEINTRESOURCE(IDD_SEHSOFT),
      NULL, Dlg_Proc);

   return(0);
}


////////////////////////// End Of File //////////////////////////
```

SEHSOFT.RC

```
//Microsoft Developer Studio generated resource script.
//
#include "Resource.h"

#define APSTUDIO_READONLY_SYMBOLS
//////////////////////////////////////////////////////////////
//
// Generated from the TEXTINCLUDE 2 resource.
//
#include "afxres.h"


//////////////////////////////////////////////////////////////
#undef APSTUDIO_READONLY_SYMBOLS


//////////////////////////////////////////////////////////////
// English (U.S.) resources

#if !defined(AFX_RESOURCE_DLL) || defined(AFX_TARG_ENU)
#ifdef _WIN32
```

(continued)

Figure 16-6. *continued*

```
LANGUAGE LANG_ENGLISH, SUBLANG_ENGLISH_US
#pragma code_page(1252)
#endif //_WIN32


#ifdef APSTUDIO_INVOKED
/////////////////////////////////////////////////////////////////
//
// TEXTINCLUDE
//

1 TEXTINCLUDE DISCARDABLE
BEGIN
    "Resource.h\0"
END

2 TEXTINCLUDE DISCARDABLE
BEGIN
    "#include ""afxres.h""\r\n"
    "\0"
END

3 TEXTINCLUDE DISCARDABLE
BEGIN
    "\r\n"
    "\0"
END


#endif    // APSTUDIO_INVOKED



/////////////////////////////////////////////////////////////////
//
// Dialog
//

IDD_SEHSOFT DIALOG DISCARDABLE  18, 18, 214, 200
STYLE WS_MINIMIZEBOX | WS_VISIBLE | WS_CAPTION | WS_SYSMENU
CAPTION "SEH: Software Exception Test"
FONT 8, "Helv"
BEGIN
    LTEXT           "Clicking Execute reserves an array of\
 50 4-KB structures and randomly reads and writes to\
 elements in the array.",
```

(continued)

Figure 16-6. *continued*

```
                         IDC_STATIC,4,8,188,24
        LTEXT            "&Number of reads/writes to perform:",
                         IDC_STATIC,4,36,114,8
        EDITTEXT         IDC_NUMACCESSES,128,36,24,12
        PUSHBUTTON       "&Execute",IDOK,160,36,44,14,WS_GROUP
        LTEXT            "Execution lo&g:",IDC_STATIC,4,56,48,8
        LISTBOX          IDC_LOG,4,68,204,128,NOT LBS_NOTIFY |
                         WS_VSCROLL | WS_GROUP | WS_TABSTOP
END


/////////////////////////////////////////////////////////////
//
// Icon
//

// Icon with lowest ID value placed first to ensure
// application icon remains consistent on all systems.
IDI_SEHSOFT             ICON    DISCARDABLE    "SEHSoft.Ico"
#endif    // English (U.S.) resources
/////////////////////////////////////////////////////////////


#ifndef APSTUDIO_INVOKED
/////////////////////////////////////////////////////////////
//
// Generated from the TEXTINCLUDE 3 resource.
//


/////////////////////////////////////////////////////////////
#endif    // not APSTUDIO_INVOKED
```

Unhandled Exceptions

All through this chapter, I've been pointing out that when an exception is raised, the system tries to locate an exception filter that is willing to handle the exception. This is true, but it's not the first thing the system does when an exception occurs. When an exception is raised, the system first checks to see whether the process is attached to a debugger. If the process isn't attached to a debugger, the system then scans for exception filters.

If the process is being debugged, the system sends a debugging event to the debugger and fills out this EXCEPTION_DEBUG_INFO structure:

```
typedef struct _EXCEPTION_DEBUG_INFO {
    EXCEPTION_RECORD ExceptionRecord;
    DWORD dwFirstChance;
} EXCEPTION_DEBUG_INFO;
```

The EXCEPTION_DEBUG_INFO structure tells the debugger that an exception has occurred. The *ExceptionRecord* member contains the same information you would get by calling the *GetExceptionInformation* function. The debugger can use this information to determine how it wants to handle the exception. The *dwFirstChance* member will be set to nonzero. Typically, a debugger will be written to process breakpoint and single-step exceptions and can thus stop these exceptions from percolating up through your thread.

If a debugger is monitoring the process and handles the exception, the process is allowed to continue processing. The debugger can also decide to freeze the threads in the process and allow you to inspect the reason for the generated exception.

If the debugger doesn't handle the exception, the system scans your thread in search of an exception filter that returns either EXCEPTION_EXECUTE_HANDLER or EXCEPTION_CONTINUE_EXECUTION. As soon as an exception filter returns one of these identifiers, execution continues in the manner described for each identifier earlier in this chapter.

If the system reaches the top of the thread without locating an exception filter to handle the exception, the system notifies the debugger again. This time, the *dwFirstChance* member in the EXCEPTION_DEBUG_INFO structure will be 0. The debugger can tell from this value that an unhandled exception occurred in one of the process's threads; the debugger will display a message box notifying you of this unhandled exception and will allow you to start debugging the process.

Unhandled Exceptions Without a Debugger Attached

But now let's look at what happens if every exception filter returns EXCEPTION_CONTINUE_SEARCH when your process is not being debugged. In this case, the system traverses all the way to the top of the thread without finding an exception filter willing to handle the exception. When this happens, the system uses the SEH frame that was initialized in the system's *StartOfThread* function (see page 77 in Chapter 4) to call a built-in exception filter function called *UnhandledExceptionFilter*:

```
LONG UnhandledExceptionFilter(
   LPEXCEPTION_POINTERS lpexpExceptionInfo);
```

The first thing that this function does is check whether the process is being debugged; if it is being debugged, *UnhandledExceptionFilter* returns EXCEPTION_CONTINUE_SEARCH, which causes the debugger to be notified of the exception.

If the process is not being debugged, the function displays a message box notifying the user that an exception occurred in the process. This message box looks similar to the following on Windows 95:

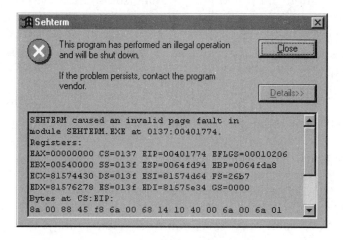

On Windows NT, it looks like this:

In the Windows NT message box, the first paragraph of text indicates which exception occurred and the address of the instruction in the process's address space that generated the exception. It just so happens that a memory access violation caused this message box to appear, so the system can report the invalid memory address that was accessed and specify that the attempted access was for reading. The *UnhandledExceptionFilter* function gets this additional information by referencing the

ExceptionInformation member of the EXCEPTION_RECORD structure generated for this exception.

Following the description of the exception, the message box indicates the user's two choices. The first choice is to click on the OK button, which causes *UnhandledExceptionFilter* to return EXCEPTION_EXE-CUTE_HANDLER. This causes the system to execute a built-in exception handler that terminates the process by calling:

```
ExitProcess(GetExceptionCode());
```

The second choice, clicking on the Cancel button, is a developer's dream come true. When you click on the Cancel button, *UnhandledExceptionFilter* attempts to load a debugger and attach the debugger to the process. With the debugger attached to the process, you can examine the state of variables, set breakpoints, restart the process, and do anything else you would normally do when you debug a process.

The real boon is that you can handle the failure of your application when it occurs. Under most other operating systems, you must invoke your application through the debugger to debug it. If an exception occurs in a process on one of these other operating systems, you have to terminate the process, start a debugger, and invoke the application again using the debugger. The problem is that you would have to try to reproduce the bug before you could fix it. And who knows what the values of the different variables were when the problem originally occurred? It's much harder to resolve a bug this way. The ability to dynamically attach a debugger to a process as it's running is one of Win32's best features.

UnhandledExceptionFilter invokes the debugger by looking into the Registry. Specifically, the key contains the command line that *UnhandledExceptionFilter* executes:

```
HKEY_LOCAL_MACHINE\SOFTWARE\Microsoft\
    Windows NT\CurrentVersion\AeDebug\Debugger
```

When you install Visual C++ 4.*x*, the value of this key is set to:

```
F:\MSDEV\BIN\MSDEV.EXE -p %ld -e %ld
```

This line tells the system which program to run (MSDEV.EXE) and where to find it (in F:\MSDEV\BIN on my machine). *UnhandledExceptionFilter* also passes two parameters on the command line to MSDEV.EXE. The first parameter is the ID of the process that is to be debugged. The second parameter identifies an inheritable manual-reset event that was created in the nonsignaled state by the *UnhandledExceptionFilter* function.

MSDEV recognizes the *-p* and *-e* switches as identifying the process ID and the event handle.

After the process ID and event handle are parsed into the string, *UnhandledExceptionFilter* executes the debugger by calling *CreateProcess* and waits for the manual-reset event to become signaled. The debugger can then attach itself to the process by calling *DebugActiveProcess* and passing it the ID of the process to be debugged:

```
BOOL DebugActiveProcess(DWORD idProcess);
```

When the debugger attaches to the process, the system sends debug events back to the debugger so that the debugger is aware of the process's state. For example, the system sends information about active threads in the process and about dynamic-link libraries mapped into the process's address space.

While the system is bringing the debugger up to date, all the threads in the debuggee are suspended, still waiting for the manual-reset event to become signaled. When the debugger is ready to let you debug the process, it calls the *SetEvent* function, passing the handle of the manual-reset event. The debugger can use the event's handle value directly because the event was created so that it could be inherited by any child processes of the debuggee. And because the *UnhandledException-Filter* function is in the process called *CreateProcess* to invoke the debugger, the debugger is a child of the process.

When the debuggee sees that the manual-reset event has become signaled, it wakes up and *UnhandledExceptionFilter* returns EXCEPTION_CONTINUE_SEARCH. Returning EXCEPTION_CONTINUE-_SEARCH causes the unhandled exception to be filtered up again. This time, the process is being debugged, and the debugger will be notified of the exception.

Turning Off the Exception Message Box

There might be times when you don't want the exception message box to be displayed if an exception occurs. For example, you might not want the message box to appear in the shipping version of your product. If it did appear, it could easily lead an end user to accidentally start debugging your application. An end user needs only to click on the Cancel button in the message box to enter unfamiliar, scary territory—the debugger. You can use a variety of methods to prevent this message box from appearing.

To prevent *UnhandledExceptionFilter* from displaying the exception message box, you can call the *SetErrorMode* function,

```
UINT SetErrorMode(UINT fuErrorMode);
```

passing it the SEM_NOGPFAULTERRORBOX identifier. Then when *UnhandledExceptionFilter* is called to handle the exception, it simply terminates your application. The user is given no warning; the application just goes away.

Another method you can use to disable the message box is to place a *try-except* block around the entire contents of your *WinMain* function. Make sure that the exception filter always evaluates to EXCEPTION-_EXECUTE_HANDLER so that the exception is handled, preventing the system from calling the *UnhandledExceptionFilter* function. In *Win-Main*'s exception handler, you can display a dialog box with some diagnostic information. The user can copy the information and report it to your customer service lines to help you track the sources of problems in your application. You should create the dialog box so that the user can only terminate the application and not invoke the debugger.

The problem with this method is that it catches only exceptions that occur in your process's primary thread. If any other threads are running, and an unhandled exception occurs in one of these threads, the system calls the built-in *UnhandledExceptionFilter* function. To fix this, you would need to include *try-except* blocks before all the thread functions in your code and in the *WinMain* function.

Because it is so easy to forget this when writing new code, Microsoft added another Win32 function, *SetUnhandledExceptionFilter*, to help you:

```
LPTOP_LEVEL_EXCEPTION_FILTER SetUnhandledExceptionFilter(
   LPTOP_LEVEL_EXCEPTION_FILTER lpTopLevelExceptionFilter);
```

After your process calls this function, an unhandled exception occurring in any of your process's threads causes your own exception filter to be called. You need to pass the address of this filter as the only parameter to *SetUnhandledExceptionFilter*. The prototype of this function looks like this:

```
LONG UnhandledExceptionFilter(
   LPEXCEPTION_POINTERS lpexpExceptionInfo);
```

You'll notice that this function is identical in form to the *Unhandled-ExceptionFilter* function. You can perform any processing you desire in your exception filter as long as you return one of the three EXCEP-TION_* identifiers. The following table shows what happens when each identifier is returned:

Identifier	What Happens
EXCEPTION_EXECUTE_HANDLER	The process simply terminates because the system doesn't perform any action in its exception handler block.
EXCEPTION_CONTINUE_EXECUTION	Execution continues at the instruction that raised the exception. You can modify the exception information referenced by the LPEXCEPTION_POINTERS parameter.
EXCEPTION_CONTINUE_SEARCH	The normal Win32 *UnhandledExceptionFilter* function is called.

To make the *UnhandledExceptionFilter* function the default filter again, you can simply call *SetUnhandledExceptionFilter* and pass it NULL. Also, whenever you set a new unhandled exception filter, *SetUnhandledExceptionFilter* returns the address of the previously installed exception filter. This address will be NULL if *UnhandledExceptionFilter* was the currently installed filter.

The last method for turning off *UnhandledExceptionFilter*'s message box is really designed for the software developer and not for the end user. Another subkey in the registry affects the *UnhandledExceptionFilter* function:

```
HKEY_LOCAL_MACHINE\SOFTWARE\Microsoft\
   Windows NT\CurrentVersion\AeDebug\Auto
```

This Auto subkey can be set to either 0 or 1. If the Auto subkey is set to 1, *UnhandledExceptionFilter* does not display a message box showing the user the exception and immediately invokes the debugger. If the Auto subkey is set to 0, *UnhandledExceptionFilter* displays the exception message box first and operates as described in the previous section.

Calling *UnhandledExceptionFilter* Yourself

The *UnhandledExceptionFilter* function is a Win32 function that you can call directly from within your own code. Here is an example of how you can use it:

```
void Funcadelic (void) {
   __try {
      .
      .
      .
   }
   __except (ExpFltr(GetExceptionInformation())) {
      .
      .
      .
   }
}

LONG ExpFltr (LPEXCEPTION_POINTERS lpEP) {
   DWORD dwExceptionCode = lpEP->ExceptionRecord.ExceptionCode;

   if (dwExceptionCode == EXCEPTION_ACCESS_VIOLATION) {
      // Do some work here….
      return(EXCEPTION_CONTINUE_EXECUTION);
   }

   return(UnhandledExceptionFilter(lpEP));
}
```

In the *Funcadelic* function, an exception in the *try* block causes the *ExpFltr* function to be called. The *ExpFilter* function is passed the return value from *GetExceptionInformation*. Inside the exception filter, the exception code is determined and compared with EXCEPTION_ACCESS-_VIOLATION. If an access violation has occurred, the exception filter corrects the situation and returns EXCEPTION_CONTINUE_EXECU-TION from the filter. The return value causes the system to continue execution at the instruction that originally caused the exception in the first place.

If any other exception has occurred, *ExpFltr* calls *UnhandledEx-ceptionFilter*, passing it the address of the EXCEPTION_POINTERS structure. *UnhandledExceptionFilter* then displays a message box that allows you to terminate the process or to begin debugging the process. The return value from *UnhandledExceptionFilter* is returned from *ExpFltr*.

Windows NT–Specific: Unhandled Kernel-Mode Exceptions

So far in this chapter we have looked at what happens when a user-mode thread generates an exception—but a kernel-mode thread might also generate an exception. Exceptions in kernel mode are handled exactly the same as exceptions in user mode. If a low-level virtual memory function generates an exception, the system checks whether any kernel-mode exception filters are prepared to handle the exception. If the system cannot find an exception filter to handle the exception, the exception is unhandled. In the case of a kernel-mode exception, the unhandled exception is in the operating system and not in an application. Such an exception would be a serious bug in the operating system!

It isn't safe for the system to continue running if an unhandled exception occurs in kernel mode, so Windows NT doesn't call the *UnhandledExceptionFilter* function in such a case; instead, Windows NT switches the video mode back to text mode, displays some debugging information on the screen, and halts the system. You should jot down the debugging information and send it to Microsoft so that it can be used to correct the code in future versions of the operating system. You'll need to reboot your machine before you can do anything else; any unsaved work is lost.

UNICODE

With Microsoft Windows becoming more and more popular around the world, it is increasingly important that we, as developers, target the various international markets. Previously, it was common for U.S. versions of software to ship as much as six months prior to the shipping of international versions. But increasing international support in the operating system is making it easier to produce applications for international markets and therefore reducing the time lag between distribution of the U.S. and international versions of our software.

Windows has always offered support to help developers localize their applications. An application can get country-specific information from various functions and can examine Control Panel settings to determine the user's preferences. Windows even supports different fonts for our applications.

Character Sets

The real problem with localization has always been manipulating different character sets. For years, most of us have been coding text strings as a series of single-byte characters with a zero at the end. This is second nature to us. When we call *strlen*, it returns the number of characters in a zero-terminated array of single-byte characters.

The problem is that some languages and writing systems (kanji being the classic example) have so many symbols in their character sets that a single byte, which offers no more than 256 different symbols at best, is just not enough. So double-byte character sets (DBCSs) were created to support these languages and writing systems.

Single-Byte and Double-Byte Character Sets

In a double-byte character set, each character in a string consists of either 1 or 2 bytes. For Japanese kanji, if the first character is between 0x81 and 0x9F or between 0xE0 and 0xFC, you must look at the next byte to determine the full character in the string. Working with double-byte character sets is a programmer's nightmare because some characters are 1 byte wide and some are 2 bytes wide.

Simply placing a call to *strlen* doesn't really tell you how many characters are in the string—it tells you the number of bytes before you hit a terminating zero. The ANSI C run-time library has no functions that allow you to manipulate double-byte character sets. However, the Visual C++ run-time library does include a number of functions, such as _mbslen, that allow you to manipulate multibyte (that is, both single-byte and double-byte) character strings.

To help manipulate DBCS strings, Win32 offers a set of helper functions:

Function	Description
LPTSTR CharNext(LPCTSTR lpszCurrentChar);	Returns the address of the next character in a string
LPTSTR CharPrev(LPCTSTR lpszStart, LPCTSTR lpszCurrentChar);	Returns the address of the previous character in a string
BOOL IsDBCSLeadByte(BYTE bTestChar);	Returns TRUE if the byte is the first byte of a DBCS character

The two functions *CharNext* and *CharPrev* allow you to traverse forward or backward through a DBCS string one character at a time. The third function, *IsDBCSLeadByte*, returns TRUE if the byte passed to it is the first byte of a 2-byte character.

Although these functions make manipulating DBCS strings a little easier, a better approach is definitely needed. Enter Unicode.

When Microsoft was porting the *AnsiNext* and *AnsiPrev* functions to the Win32 API, someone realized that the functions are really used by DBCS strings instead of ANSI strings and that the functions should undergo name-change surgery. So the *AnsiNext* and *AnsiPrev* functions have been renamed and added to the Win32 API as *CharNext* and *CharPrev*: the Win32 header files define the following macros so that 16-bit Windows code ports easily to Win32:

```
#define AnsiNext CharNextA
#define AnsiPrev CharPrevA
```

Unicode: The Wide-Byte Character Set

Unicode is a standard founded by Apple and Xerox in 1988. In 1991, a consortium was created to develop and promote Unicode. The consortium consists of Adobe, Aldus, Apple, Borland, Digital, Go, IBM, Lotus, Metaphor, Microsoft, NeXT, Novell, the Research Libraries Group, Sun, Taligent, Unisys, WordPerfect, and Xerox. This group of companies is responsible for maintaining the Unicode standard. The full description of Unicode can be found in *The Unicode Standard: Worldwide Character Encoding,* published by Addison-Wesley.

Unicode offers a simple and consistent way of representing strings. All characters in a Unicode string are 16-bit values (2 bytes). There are no special bytes that indicate whether the next byte is part of the same character or is a new character. This means that you can traverse the characters in a string by simply incrementing or decrementing a pointer. Calls to functions such as *CharNext, CharPrev,* and *IsDBCSLeadByte* are no longer necessary.

Because Unicode represents each character with a 16-bit value, more than 65,000 characters are available, making it possible to encode all the characters that make up written languages throughout the world. This is a far cry from the 256 characters available with a single-byte character set.

Currently, Unicode code points[1] are defined for the Arabic, Chinese bopomofo, Cyrillic (Russian), Greek, Hebrew, Japanese kana, Korean hangul, and Latin (English) alphabets, as well as for others. A large number of punctuation marks, mathematical symbols, technical symbols, arrows, dingbats, diacritics, and other characters are also included

---

1. A code point is the position of a symbol in a character set.

in the character sets. When you add all these alphabets and symbols together, they total about 34,000 different code points, which leaves about half of the 65,000 total code points available for future expansion.

These 65,536 characters are divided into regions. The following table shows some of the regions and the characters that are assigned to them:

16-Bit Code	Characters
0000–007F	ASCII
0080–00FF	Latin1 characters
0100–017F	European Latin
0180–01FF	Extended Latin
0250–02AF	Standard phonetic
02B0–02FF	Modified letters
0300–036F	Generic diacritical marks
0370–03FF	Greek
0400–04FF	Cyrillic
0530–058F	Armenian
0590–05FF	Hebrew
0600–06FF	Arabic
0900–097F	Devanagari

Approximately 29,000 code points are currently unassigned, but they are reserved for future use. And approximately 6000 code points are reserved for your own personal use.

Why You Should Use Unicode

When developing an application, you should definitely consider taking advantage of Unicode. Even if you're not planning to localize your application today, developing with Unicode in mind will certainly simplify conversion in the future. In addition, Unicode does the following:

- Enables easy data exchange between languages

- Allows you to distribute a single binary EXE or DLL file that supports all languages

- Improves the efficiency of your application (discussed in more detail later in the chapter)

How to Write Unicode Source Code

Microsoft designed the Win32 API for Unicode so that it would have as little impact on your code as possible. In fact, it is possible to write a single source code file so that it can be compiled with or without using Unicode—you need only define two macros to make the change and then recompile.

Windows NT and Unicode

Microsoft Windows NT is the first operating system to be built from the ground up using Unicode. All the core functions for creating windows, displaying text, performing string manipulations, and so forth expect Unicode strings. If you call any Win32 function and pass it an ANSI string, the system first converts the string to Unicode and then passes the Unicode string to the operating system. If you are expecting ANSI strings back from a function, the system converts the Unicode string to an ANSI string before returning to your application. All these conversions occur invisibly to you. Of course, a slight time overhead is involved for the system to carry out all these string conversions.

For example, if you call *CreateWindowEx* and pass non-Unicode strings for the class name and window caption text, *CreateWindowEx* must allocate blocks of memory (in your process's default heap), convert the non-Unicode strings to Unicode strings and store the result in the allocated memory blocks, and make a function call to the Unicode version of *CreateWindowEx*.

For functions that fill buffers with strings, the system must convert from Unicode to non-Unicode equivalents before your application can process the string. Because the system must perform all these conversions, your application requires more memory and runs slower. You can make your application perform more efficiently by developing your application using Unicode from the start.

Windows 95 and Unicode

Microsoft Windows 95 is not a completely new operating system. It has a 16-bit Windows heritage that was not designed to handle Unicode. Adding Unicode support would have been too large a task and was dropped from the product's feature list. For this reason, Windows 95, like its predecessors, does almost everything internally using ANSI strings.

It is still possible to write a Win32 application that processes Unicode characters and strings, but it is much harder to call the Win32 functions. For example, if you want to call *CreateWindowEx* and pass it ANSI strings, the call is very fast; no buffers need to be allocated from your process's default heap, and no string conversions need to be done. However, if you want to call *CreateWindowEx* and pass it Unicode strings, you must explicitly allocate buffers and call Win32 functions to perform the conversion from Unicode to ANSI. You can then call *CreateWindowEx*, passing the ANSI strings. When *CreateWindowEx* returns, you can free the temporary buffers. This is far less convenient than using Unicode on Windows NT. I will describe how you can perform these conversions under Windows 95 later in this chapter.

Although it is true that most implementations of Unicode functions do nothing in Windows 95, a few Unicode functions do have useful implementations. These functions are *ExtTextOutW*, *GetCharWidthW*, *GetTextExtentExPointW*, *GetTextExtentPointW*, *MessageBoxExW*, *MessageBoxW*, and *TextOutW*.

Unicode Support in the C Run-Time Library

To take advantage of Unicode character strings, some new data types have been defined. The standard C header file, STRING.H, has been modified to define a data type named *wchar_t*, which is the data type of a Unicode character:

```
typedef unsigned short wchar_t;
```

For example, if you want to create a buffer to hold a Unicode string of up to 99 characters and a terminating zero character, you can use the following statement:

```
wchar_t szBuffer[100];
```

This statement creates an array of 100 16-bit values. Of course, the standard C run-time string functions, such as *strcpy*, *strchr*, and *strcat*, operate on ANSI strings only; they don't process Unicode strings correctly. So a complementary set of functions was created. Figure 17-1 shows the standard C ANSI string functions followed by their equivalent Unicode functions.

```
char * strcat(char *, const char *);
wchar_t * wcscat(wchar_t *, const wchar_t *);

char * strchr(const char *, int);
wchar_t * wcschr(const wchar_t *, wchar_t);

int strcmp(const char *, const char *);
int wcscmp(const wchar_t *, const wchar_t *);

int _stricmp(const char *, const char *);
int _wcsicmp(const wchar_t *, const wchar_t *);

int strcoll(const char *, const char *);
int wcscoll(const wchar_t *, const wchar_t *);

int _stricoll(const char *, const char *);
int _wcsicoll(const wchar_t *, const wchar_t *);

char * strcpy(char *, const char *);
wchar_t * wcscpy(wchar_t *, const wchar_t *);

size_t strcspn(const char *, const char *);
size_t wcscspn(const wchar_t *, const wchar_t *);

char * _strdup(const char *);
wchar_t * _wcsdup(const wchar_t *);

size_t strlen(const char *);
size_t wcslen(const wchar_t *);

char * _strlwr(char *);
wchar_t * _wcslwr(wchar_t *);

char * strncat(char *, const char *, size_t);
wchar_t * wcsncat(wchar_t *, const wchar_t *, size_t);

int strncmp(const char *, const char *, size_t);
int wcsncmp(const wchar_t *, const wchar_t *, size_t);

int _strnicmp(const char *, const char *, size_t);
int _wcsnicmp(const wchar_t *, const wchar_t *, size_t);

char * strncpy(char *, const char *, size_t);
wchar_t * wcsncpy(wchar_t *, const wchar_t *, size_t);
```

Figure 17-1. *(continued)*

Standard C ANSI string functions and their Unicode equivalents.

Figure 17-1. *continued*

```
char * _strnset(char *, int, size_t);
wchar_t * _wcsnset(wchar_t *, wchar_t, size_t);

char * strpbrk(const char *, const char *);
wchar_t * wcspbrk(const wchar_t *, const wchar_t *);

char * strrchr(const char *, int);
wchar_t * wcsrchr(const wchar_t *, wchar_t);

char * _strrev(char *);
wchar_t * _wcsrev(wchar_t *);

char * _strset(char *, int);
wchar_t * _wcsset(wchar_t *, wchar_t);

size_t strspn(const char *, const char *);
size_t wcsspn(const wchar_t *, const wchar_t *);

char * strstr(const char *, const char *);
wchar_t * wcsstr(const wchar_t *, const wchar_t *);

char * strtok(char *, const char *);
wchar_t * wcstok(wchar_t *, const wchar_t *);

char * _strupr(char *);
wchar_t * _wcsupr(wchar_t *);

size_t strxfrm (char *, const char *, size_t);
size_t wcsxfrm(wchar_t *, const wchar_t *, size_t);
```

Notice that all the Unicode functions begin with *wcs*, which stands for *wide character set*. To call the Unicode function, you simply replace the *str* prefix of any ANSI string function with the *wcs* prefix.

Code that includes explicit calls to either the *str* functions or the *wcs* functions cannot be compiled easily for both ANSI and Unicode. Earlier in this chapter, I said it's possible to make a single source code file that can be compiled for both. To set up the dual capability, you include the TCHAR.H file instead of including STRING.H.

TCHAR.H exists for the sole purpose of helping you create ANSI/Unicode generic source code files. It consists of a set of macros that you should use in your source code instead of making direct calls to either the *str* or the *wcs* functions. If you define _UNICODE when you compile your source code, the macros reference the *wcs* set of functions. If you

don't define _UNICODE, the macros reference the *str* set of functions.
Figure 17-2 lists the macros in TCHAR.H and what they reference, depending on whether _UNICODE is defined.

TCHAR.H Macro	_UNICODE Defined	_UNICODE Not Defined
_tprintf	wprintf	printf
_ftprintf	fwprintf	fprintf
_stprintf	swprintf	sprintf
_sntprintf	_snwprintf	_snprintf
_vtprintf	vwprintf	vprintf
_vftprintf	vfwprintf	vfprintf
_vstprintf	vswprintf	vsprintf
_vvsntprintf	_vsnwprintf	_vsnprintf
_tscanf	wscanf	scanf
_ftscanf	fwscanf	fscanf
_stscanf	swscanf	sscanf
_fgettc	fgetwc	fgetc
_fgettchar	fgetwchar	fgetchar
_fgetts	fgetws	fgets
_fputtc	fputwc	fputc
_fputtchar	fputwchar	fputchar
_fputts	fputws	fputs
_gettc	getwc	getc
_getts	getws	gets
_puttc	putwc	putc
_putts	putws	puts
_ungettc	ungetwc	ungetc
_tcstod	wcstod	strtod
_tcstol	wcstol	strtol
_tcstoul	wcstoul	strtoul
_tcscat	wcscat	strcat
_tcschr	wcschr	strchr
_tcscmp	wcscmp	strcmp
_tcscpy	wcscpy	strcpy

Figure 17-2.   *(continued)*

Macros in TCHAR.H and their references.

Figure 17-2. *continued*

TCHAR.H Macro	_UNICODE Defined	_UNICODE Not Defined
_tcscspn	wcspn	strcspn
_tcslen	wcslen	strlen
_tcsncat	wcsncat	strncat
_tcsncmp	wcsncmp	strncmp
_tcsncpy	wcsncpy	strncpy
_tcspbrk	wcspbrk	strpbrk
_tcsrchr	wcsrchr	strrchr
_tcsspn	wcsspn	strspn
_tcsstr	wcsstr	strstr
_tcstok	wcstok	strtok
_tcsdup	_wcsdup	strdup
_tcsicmp	_wcsicmp	stricmp
_tcsnicmp	_wcsnicmp	_strnicmp
_tcsnset	_wcsnset	_strnset
_tcsrev	_wcsrev	_strrev
_tcsset	_wcsset	_strset
_tcslwr	_wcslwr	_strlwr
_tcsupr	_wcsupr	_strupr
_tcsxfrm	wcsxfrm	strxfrm
_tcscoll	wcscoll	strcoll
_tcsicoll	_wcsicoll	_stricoll
_istalpha	iswalpha	isalpha
_istupper	iswupper	isupper
_istlower	iswlower	islower
_istdigit	iswdigit	isdigit
_istxdigit	iswxdigit	isxdigit
_istspace	iswspace	isspace
_istpunct	iswpunct	ispunct
_istalnum	iswalnum	isalnum
_istprint	iswprint	isprint
_istgraph	iswgraph	isgraph
_istcntrl	iswcntrl	iscntrl
_istascii	iswascii	isascii
_totupper	towupper	toupper
_totlower	towlower	tolower

By using the identifiers listed in the left column, you can write your source code so that it can be compiled using either Unicode or ANSI. This isn't quite the whole story, however. TCHAR.H includes some additional macros.

To define an array of string characters that is ANSI/Unicode generic, use the following TCHAR data type. If _UNICODE is defined, TCHAR is declared as follows:

```
typedef wchar_t TCHAR;
```

If _UNICODE is not defined, TCHAR is declared as

```
typedef char TCHAR;
```

Using this data type, you can allocate a string of characters as follows:

```
TCHAR szString[100];
```

You can also create pointers to strings:

```
TCHAR *szError = "Error";
```

However, there is a problem with the previous line. By default, Microsoft's C++ compiler compiles all strings as though they were ANSI strings, not Unicode strings. As a result, the compiler will compile this line correctly if _UNICODE is not defined but will generate an error if _UNICODE is defined. To generate a Unicode string instead of an ANSI string, you would have to rewrite the line as follows:

```
TCHAR *szError = L"Error";
```

An uppercase *L* before a literal string informs the compiler that the string should be compiled as a Unicode string. When the compiler places the string in the program's data section, it intersperses zero bytes between every character. The problem with this change is that now the program will compile successfully only if _UNICODE is defined. We need another macro that selectively adds the uppercase *L* before a literal string. This is the job of the _TEXT macro, also defined in TCHAR.H. If _UNICODE is defined, _TEXT is defined as

```
#define _TEXT(x)    L ## x
```

If _UNICODE is not defined, _TEXT is defined as

```
#define _TEXT(x)    x
```

Using this macro, we can rewrite the line above so that it compiles correctly whether or not the _UNICODE macro is defined, as shown here:

```
TCHAR *szError = _TEXT("Error");
```

The _TEXT macro can also be used for literal characters. For example, to check whether the first character of a string is an uppercase *J*, execute the following:

```
if (szError[0] == _TEXT('J')) {
    // First character is a 'J'
    :
    :
} else {
    // First character is not a 'J'
    :
    :
}
```

Unicode Data Types Defined by Win32

The Win32 header files define the data types listed here:

Data Type	Description
WCHAR	Unicode character
LPWSTR	Pointer to a Unicode string
LPCWSTR	Pointer to a constant Unicode string

These data types always refer to Unicode characters and strings. The Win32 header files also define the ANSI/Unicode generic data types LPTSTR and LPCTSTR. These data types point to either an ANSI string or a Unicode string, depending on whether the UNICODE macro is defined when you compile the module.

Notice that this time the UNICODE macro is not preceded by an underscore. The _UNICODE macro is used for the C run-time header files, and the UNICODE macro is used for the Win32 header files. You usually need to define both macros when compiling a source code module.

Unicode and ANSI Functions in Win32

Earlier I implied that there are two functions called *CreateWindowEx*: a *CreateWindowEx* that accepts Unicode strings and a second *CreateWindowEx* that accepts ANSI strings. This is true, but the two functions are actually prototyped as follows:

```
HWND WINAPI CreateWindowExW(DWORD dwExStyle, LPCWSTR lpClassName,
    LPCWSTR lpWindowName, DWORD dwStyle, int X, int Y,
    int nWidth, int nHeight, HWND hWndParent, HMENU hMenu,
    HINSTANCE hInstance, LPVOID lpParam);

HWND WINAPI CreateWindowExA(DWORD dwExStyle, LPCSTR lpClassName,
    LPCSTR lpWindowName, DWORD dwStyle, int X, int Y,
    int nWidth, int nHeight, HWND hWndParent, HMENU hMenu,
    HINSTANCE hInstance, LPVOID lpParam);
```

CreateWindowExW is the version that accepts Unicode strings. The uppercase *W* at the end of the function name stands for *wide*. Unicode characters are 16 bits each, so they are frequently referred to as wide characters. *CreateWindowExA* has an uppercase *A* at the end, which indicates that it accepts ANSI character strings.

But we usually just include a call to *CreateWindowEx* in our code and don't directly call either *CreateWindowExW* or *CreateWindowExA*. In WINUSER.H, *CreateWindowEx* is actually a macro defined as

```
#ifdef UNICODE
#define CreateWindowEx   CreateWindowExW
#else
#define CreateWindowEx   CreateWindowExA
#endif // !UNICODE
```

Whether UNICODE is defined when you compile your source code module determines which version of *CreateWindowEx* is called. When you port a 16-bit Windows application to Win32, you probably won't define UNICODE when you compile. Any calls you make to *CreateWindowEx* evaluate to calls to *CreateWindowExA*—the ANSI version of *CreateWindowEx*. Because 16-bit Windows offers only an ANSI version of *CreateWindowEx*, your porting will go much easier.

Under Windows NT, Microsoft's source code for *CreateWindowExA* is simply a thunking, or translation, layer that allocates memory to convert ANSI strings to Unicode strings; the code then calls *CreateWindowExW*, passing the converted strings. When *CreateWindowExW* returns, *CreateWindowExA* frees its memory buffers and returns the window handle to you.

If you're creating dynamic-link libraries that other software developers will use, consider using this technique: supply two entry points in the DLL—an ANSI version and a Unicode version. In the ANSI version, simply allocate memory, perform the necessary string conversions, and call the Unicode version of the function. (This process is demonstrated later in this chapter.)

Under Windows 95, Microsoft's source code for *CreateWindowExA* is the function that does the work. Windows 95 offers all the entry points to all the Win32 functions that accept a Unicode parameter, but these functions do not translate Unicode strings to ANSI strings—they just return failure. A call to *GetLastError* returns ERROR_CALL_NOT-_IMPLEMENTED. Only ANSI versions of these functions work properly. If your compiled code makes calls to any of the wide-character Win32 functions, your application will not run under Windows 95.

Certain functions in the Win32 API, such as *WinExec* and *OpenFile*, exist solely for backward compatibility with 16-bit Windows programs and should be avoided. You should replace any calls to *WinExec* and *OpenFile* with calls to the *CreateProcess* and *CreateFile* functions. Internally, the old functions call the new functions anyway.

The big problem with the old functions is that they don't accept Unicode strings. When you call these functions, you must pass ANSI strings. All the new and nonobsolete functions, on the other hand, do have both ANSI and Unicode versions on Windows NT.

Making Your Application ANSI- and Unicode-Aware

It's a good idea to start converting your application to make it Unicode-aware even if you don't plan to use Unicode right away. Here are the basic steps you should follow:

- Start thinking of text strings as arrays of characters, not as arrays of *char*s or arrays of bytes.

- Use generic data types (such as TCHAR and LPTSTR) for text characters and strings.

- Use explicit data types (such as BYTE and LPBYTE) for bytes, byte pointers, and data buffers.

- Use the _TEXT macro for literal characters and strings.

- Perform global replaces. (For example, replace LPSTR with LPTSTR.)

- Modify string arithmetic problems. (For example, convert *sizeof(szBuffer)* to *(sizeof(szBuffer) / sizeof(TCHAR))*.) This is the most difficult step to remember—I have forgotten to do this more times than I care to remember.

When I was developing the sample programs for the first edition of this book, I originally wrote them so that they compiled natively as ANSI only. Then, when I began to write this chapter, I knew that I wanted to encourage the use of Unicode and was going to create sample programs to demonstrate how easy it is to create programs that can be compiled in both Unicode and ANSI. I decided that the best course of action was to convert all the sample programs in the book so that they could be compiled in both Unicode and ANSI.

I converted all the programs in about four hours, which isn't bad, considering that I didn't have any prior conversion experience.

String Functions in Win32

The Win32 API also offers a set of functions for manipulating Unicode strings, as described here:

Function	Description
lstrcat	Concatenates one string onto the end of another
lstrcmp	Performs case-sensitive comparison of two strings
lstrcmpi	Performs case-insensitive comparison of two strings
lstrcpy	Copies one string to another location in memory
lstrlen	Returns the length of a string in characters

These functions are implemented as macros that call either the Unicode version of the function or the ANSI version of the function, depending on whether UNICODE is defined when the source module is compiled. For example, if UNICODE is not defined, *lstrcat* will expand to *lstrcatA*, and if UNICODE is defined, *lstrcat* will expand to *lstrcatW*.

Two Win32 string functions, *lstrcmp* and *lstrcmpi*, behave differently from their equivalent C run-time functions. The C run-time functions *strcmp*, *strcmpi*, *wcscmp*, and *wcscmpi* simply compare the values of the code points in the strings; that is, the functions ignore the meaning of the actual characters and simply check the numeric value of each character in the first string with the numeric value of the character in the second string. The Win32 functions *lstrcmp* and *lstrcmpi*, on the other hand, are implemented as calls to the Win32 function *CompareString*:

```
int CompareString(LCID lcid, DWORD fdwStyle,
    LPCWSTR lpString1, int cch1, LPCTSTR lpString2, int cch2);
```

This function compares two Unicode strings. The first parameter to *CompareString* specifies a locale ID (LCID), a 32-bit value that identifies a particular language. *CompareString* uses this LCID to compare the two strings by checking the meaning of the characters as they apply to a particular language. This action is much more meaningful than the simple number comparison performed by the C run-time functions.

When any of the *lstrcmp* family of functions calls *CompareString*, the function passes the result of calling the Win32 *GetThreadLocale* function as the first parameter:

```
LCID GetThreadLocale(VOID);
```

Every time a thread is created, it is assigned a locale. This function returns the current locale setting for the thread.

The second parameter of *CompareString* identifies flags that modify the method used by the function to compare the two strings. The following table shows the possible flags:

Flag	Meaning
NORM_IGNORECASE	Ignore case differences
NORM_IGNOREKANATYPE	Do not differentiate between hiragana and katakana characters
NORM_IGNORENONSPACE	Ignore nonspacing characters
NORM_IGNORESYMBOLS	Ignore symbols
NORM_IGNOREWIDTH	Do not differentiate between a single-byte character and the same character as a double-byte character
SORT_STRINGSORT	Treat punctuation the same as symbols

When *lstrcmp* calls *CompareString*, it passes 0 for the *fdwStyle* parameter. But when *lstrcmpi* calls *CompareString*, it passes NORM_IGNORECASE. The remaining four parameters of *CompareString* specify the two strings and their respective lengths. If you pass –1 for the *cch1* parameter, the function assumes that the *lpString1* string is zero-terminated and calculates the length of the string. This also is true for the *cch2* parameter with respect to the *lpString2* string.

Other C run-time functions don't offer good support for manipulating Unicode strings. For example, the *tolower* and *toupper* functions don't properly convert characters with accent marks. To compensate for these deficiencies in the C run-time library, you'll need to call the Win32 functions described on the following page to convert the case of a Unicode string. These functions also work correctly for ANSI strings.

The first two functions,

```
LPTSTR CharLower(LPTSTR lpszString);
```

and

```
LPTSTR CharUpper(LPTSTR lpszString);
```

convert either a single character or an entire zero-terminated string. To convert an entire string, simply pass the address of the string. To convert a single character, you must pass the individual character as follows:

```
TCHAR cLowerCaseChar = CharLower((LPTSTR) szString[0]);
```

Casting the single character to an LPTSTR causes the high 16 bits of the pointer to be set to 0 and the low 16 bits to contain the character. When the function sees that the high 16 bits are 0, the function knows that you want to convert a single character rather than a whole string. The value returned will be a 32-bit value with the converted character in the low 16 bits.

The next two functions are similar to the previous two except that they convert the characters contained inside a buffer (which does not need to be zero-terminated):

```
DWORD CharLowerBuff(LPTSTR lpszString, DWORD cchString);
```

```
DWORD CharUpperBuff(LPTSTR lpszString, DWORD cchString);
```

Other C run-time functions, such as *isalpha, islower,* and *isupper,* return a value that indicates whether a given character is alphabetic, lowercase, or uppercase. The Win32 API offers functions that return this information as well, but the Win32 functions also consider the language indicated by the user in the Control Panel:

```
BOOL IsCharAlpha(TCHAR ch);
```

```
BOOL IsCharAlphaNumeric(TCHAR ch);
```

```
BOOL IsCharLower(TCHAR ch);
```

```
BOOL IsCharUpper(TCHAR ch);
```

The *printf* family of functions is the last group of C run-time functions we'll discuss. If you compile your source module with _UNICODE defined, the *printf* family of functions expects that all the character and string parameters represent Unicode characters and strings. However, if you compile without defining _UNICODE, the *printf* family expects that all the characters and strings passed to it are ANSI.

The Win32 function *wsprintf* is an enhanced version of the C run-time's *sprintf* function. It offers some additional field types that allow you to state explicitly whether a character or string is ANSI or Unicode. Using these extended field types, you can mix ANSI and Unicode characters and strings in a single call to *wsprintf.*

Resources

When the resource compiler compiles all your resources, the output file is a binary representation of the resources. String values in your resources (string tables, dialog box templates, menus, and so on) are always written as Unicode strings. Under both Windows 95 and Windows NT, the system performs internal conversions if your application doesn't define the UNICODE macro. For example, if UNICODE is not defined when you compile your source module, a call to *LoadString* will actually call the *LoadStringA* function. *LoadStringA* will then read the string from your resources and convert the string to ANSI. The ANSI representation of the string will be returned from the function to your application.

Text Files

To date, there have been very few Unicode text files. None of the text files that ship with any Microsoft operating system or product have been in Unicode. However, I expect that this trend may change in the future (albeit a long way into the future). Certainly, the Windows NT Notepad application allows you to open both Unicode and ANSI files as well as to create them.

For many applications that open text files and process them, such as compilers, it would be convenient if, after opening a file, the application could determine whether the text file contained ANSI characters or Unicode characters. Windows NT 3.5 introduced the *IsTextUnicode* function, which can help make this distinction:

```
DWORD IsTextUnicode(CONST LPVOID lpvBuffer, int cb, LPINT lpResult);
```

The problem with text files is that there are no hard and fast rules as to their content. This makes it extremely difficult to determine whether the file contains ANSI or Unicode characters. *IsTextUnicode* uses a series of statistical and deterministic methods in order to guess at the content of the buffer. Because this is not an exact science, it is possible that *IsTextUnicode* will return an incorrect result.

The first parameter, *lpvBuffer*, identifies the address of a buffer that you want to test. The data is a void pointer because you don't know whether you have an array of ANSI characters or an array of Unicode characters.

The second parameter, *cb*, specifies the number of bytes that *lpvBuffer* points to. Again, because you don't know what's in the buffer, *cb* is a count of bytes rather than a count of characters. Note that you do not have to specify the entire length of the buffer. Of course, the more bytes *IsTextUnicode* can test, the more accurate a response you're likely to get.

The third parameter, *lpResult*, is the address of an integer that you must initialize before calling *IsTextUnicode*. You initialize this integer to indicate which tests you want *IsTextUnicode* to perform. (See the *Microsoft Win32 Programmer's Reference* for details.) You can also pass NULL for this parameter, in which case *IsTextUnicode* will perform every test it can.

If *IsTextUnicode* thinks that the buffer contains Unicode text, TRUE is returned; otherwise, FALSE is returned. If specific tests were requested in the integer pointed to by the *lpResult* parameter, the function sets the bits in the integer before returning to reflect the results of each test.

Under Windows 95, the *IsTextUnicode* function has no useful implementation and simply returns FALSE; calling *GetLastError* returns ERROR_CALL_NOT_IMPLEMENTED.

The FileRev sample application presented in Chapter 8 demonstrates the use of the *IsTextUnicode* function.

Translating Strings Between Unicode and ANSI

The Win32 function *MultiByteToWideChar* converts multibyte-character strings to wide-character strings:

```
int MultiByteToWideChar(UINT uCodePage, DWORD dwFlags,
    LPCSTR lpMultiByteStr, int cchMultiByte,
    LPWSTR lpWideCharStr, int cchWideChar);
```

The *uCodePage* parameter identifies a code page number that is associated with the multibyte string. The *dwFlags* parameter allows you to specify additional control that affects characters with diacritical marks such as accents. Usually the flags aren't used, and 0 is passed in the *dwFlags* parameter. The *lpMultiByteStr* parameter specifies the string to be converted, and the *cchMultiByte* parameter indicates the length (in bytes) of the string. The function determines the length of the source string if you pass −1 for the *cchMultiByte* parameter.

The Unicode version of the string resulting from the conversion is written to the buffer located in memory at the address specified by the *lpWideCharStr* parameter. You must specify the maximum size of this buffer (in characters) in the *cchWideChar* parameter. If you call *MultiByte-ToWideChar*, passing 0 for the *cchWideChar* parameter, the function doesn't perform the conversion and instead returns the size of the buffer required for the conversion to succeed. Typically, you will convert a multibyte character string to its Unicode equivalent by performing the following steps:

1. Call *MultiByteToWideChar*, passing NULL for the *lpWideCharStr* parameter and 0 for the *cchWideChar* parameter.

2. Allocate a block of memory large enough to hold the converted Unicode string. This size is returned by the previous call to *MultiByteToWideChar*.

3. Call *MultiByteToWideChar* again, this time passing the address of the buffer as the *lpWideCharStr* parameter and passing the size returned by the first call to *MultiByteToWideChar* as the *cchWideChar* parameter.

4. Use the converted string.

5. Free the memory block occupying the Unicode string.

The Win32 function *WideCharToMultiByte* converts a wide-character string to its multibyte string equivalent, as shown here:

```
int WideCharToMultiByte(UINT uCodePage, DWORD dwFlags,
   LPCWSTR lpWideCharStr, int cchWideChar,
   LPSTR lpMultiByteStr, int cchMultiByte,
   LPCSTR lpDefaultChar, LPBOOL lpfUsedDefaultChar);
```

This function is very similar to the *MultiByteToWideChar* function. Again, the *uCodePage* parameter identifies the code page to be associated with the newly converted string. The *dwFlags* parameter allows you to specify additional control over the conversion. The flags affect characters with diacritical marks and characters that the system is unable to convert.

Most often, you won't need this degree of control over the conversion, and you'll pass 0 for the *dwFlags* parameter.

The *lpWideCharStr* parameter specifies the address in memory of the string to be converted, and the *cchWideChar* parameter indicates the length (in characters) of this string. The function determines the length of the source string if you pass –1 for the *cchWideChar* parameter.

The multibyte version of the string resulting from the conversion is written to the buffer indicated by the *lpMultiByteStr* parameter. You must specify the maximum size of this buffer (in bytes) in the *cchMultiByte* parameter. Passing 0 as the *cchMultiByte* parameter of the *WideChar-ToMultiByte* function causes the function to return the size required by the destination buffer. You'll typically convert a wide-byte character string to a multibyte character string using a sequence of events similar to those discussed when converting a multibyte string to a wide-byte string.

You'll notice that the *WideCharToMultiByte* function accepts two parameters more than the *MultiByteToWideChar* function: *lpDefaultChar* and *lpfUsedDefaultChar*. These parameters are used by the *WideCharTo-MultiByte* function only if it comes across a wide character that doesn't have a representation in the code page identified by the *uCodePage* parameter. If the wide character cannot be converted, the function uses the character pointed to by the *lpDefaultChar* parameter. If this parameter is NULL, which is most common, the function uses a system default character. This default character is usually a question mark. This is dangerous for filenames because the question mark is a wildcard character.

The *lpfUsedDefaultChar* parameter points to a Boolean variable that the function sets to TRUE if at least one character in the wide-character string could not be converted to its multibyte equivalent. The function sets the variable to FALSE if all the characters convert successfully. You can test this variable after the function returns to check whether the wide-character string was converted successfully. Again, you usually pass NULL for this parameter.

For a more complete description of how to use these functions, please refer to the *Microsoft Win32 Programmer's Reference.*

You could use these two functions to easily create both Unicode and ANSI versions of functions. For example, you might have a dynamic-link library that contains a function that reverses all the characters in a string. You could write the Unicode version of the function as shown at the top of the next page.

```
BOOL StringReverseW (LPWSTR lpWideCharStr) {

   // Get a pointer to the last character in the string.
   LPWSTR lpEndOfStr = lpWideCharStr + wcslen(lpWideCharStr) - 1;
   wchar_t cCharT;
   // Repeat until we reach the center character in the string.
   while (lpWideCharStr < lpEndOfStr) {
      // Save a character in a temporary variable.
      cCharT = *lpWideCharStr;

      // Put the last character in the first character.
      *lpWideCharStr = *lpEndOfStr;

      // Put the temporary character in the last character.
      *lpEndOfStr = cCharT;

      // Move in one character from the left.
      lpWideCharStr++;

      // Move in one character from the right.
      lpEndOfStr--;
   }

   // The string is reversed; return success.
   return(TRUE);
}
```

And you could write the ANSI version of the function so that it doesn't perform the actual work of reversing the string at all. Instead, you could write the ANSI version so that it converts the ANSI string to Unicode, passes the Unicode string to the *StringReverseW* function, and then converts the reversed string back to ANSI. The function would look like this:

```
BOOL StringReverseA (LPSTR lpMultiByteStr) {
   LPWSTR lpWideCharStr;
   int nLenOfWideCharStr;
   BOOL fOk = FALSE;

   // Calculate the number of characters needed to hold
   // the wide-character version of the string.
   nLenOfWideCharStr = MultiByteToWideChar(CP_ACP, 0,
      lpMultiByteStr, -1, NULL, 0);

   // Allocate memory from the process's default heap to
   // accommodate the size of the wide-character string.
   // Don't forget that MultiByteToWideChar returns the
```

```
// number of characters, not the number of bytes, so
// you must multiply by the size of a wide character.
lpWideCharStr = HeapAlloc(GetProcessHeap(), 0,
    nLenOfWideCharStr * sizeof(WCHAR));

if (lpWideCharStr == NULL)
    return(fOk);

// Convert the multibyte string to a wide-character string.
MultiByteToWideChar(CP_ACP, 0, lpMultiByteStr, -1,
    lpWideCharStr, nLenOfWideCharStr);

// Call the wide-character version of this
// function to do the actual work.
fOk = StringReverseW(lpWideCharStr);

if (fOk) {
    // Convert the wide-character string back
    // to a multibyte string.
    WideCharToMultiByte(CP_ACP, 0, lpWideCharStr, -1,
        lpMultiByteStr, strlen(lpMultiByteStr), NULL, NULL);
}

// Free the memory containing the wide-character string.
HeapFree(GetProcessHeap(), 0, lpWideCharStr);

return(fOk);
}
```

Finally, in the header file that you distribute with the dynamic-link library, you would prototype the two functions as follows:

```
BOOL StringReverseW (LPWSTR lpWideCharStr);
BOOL StringReverseA (LPSTR lpMultiByteStr);

#ifdef UNICODE
#define StringReverse   StringReverseW
#else
#define StringReverse   StringReverseA
#endif // !UNICODE
```

Windows NT: Window Classes and Procedures

When you register a new window class, you must tell the system the address of the window procedure responsible for processing messages for this class. For certain messages (such as WM_SETTEXT), the *lParam* parameter for the message is a pointer to a string. The system needs to know whether the window procedure requires that the string be in ANSI or Unicode before dispatching the message so that the message will be processed correctly.

You tell the system whether a window procedure expects ANSI strings or Unicode strings depending on which function you use to register the window class. If you construct the WNDCLASS structure and call *RegisterClassA*, the system thinks that the window procedure expects all strings and characters to be ANSI. Registering the window class with *RegisterClassW* causes the system to dispatch only Unicode strings and characters to the window procedure. Of course, the macro *RegisterClass* expands to either *RegisterClassA* or *RegisterClassW*, depending on whether UNICODE is defined when you compile the source module.

If you have a handle to a window, you can determine what type of characters and strings the window procedure expects by calling

```
BOOL IsWindowUnicode(HWND hwnd);
```

If the window procedure for the specified window expects Unicode, the function returns TRUE; otherwise, FALSE is returned.

If you create an ANSI string and send a WM_SETTEXT message to a window whose window procedure expects Unicode strings, the system will automatically convert the string for you before sending the message. It is very rare that you'll ever need to call the *IsWindowUnicode* function.

The system will also perform automatic translations if you subclass a window procedure. Let's say that the window procedure for an edit control expects its characters and strings to be in Unicode. Then somewhere in your program you create an edit control and subclass the window's procedure by calling

```
LONG SetWindowLongA(HWND hwnd, int nIndex, LONG lNewLong);
```

or

```
LONG SetWindowLongW(HWND hwnd, int nIndex, LONG lNewLong);
```

and passing GWL_WNDPROC as the *nIndex* parameter and the address to your subclass procedure as the *lNewLong* parameter. But what happens if your subclass procedure expects ANSI characters and strings? This could potentially create a big problem. The system determines how to convert the strings and characters depending on which of the two functions above you use to perform the subclassing. If you call *SetWindow-LongA*, you're telling the system that the new window procedure (your subclass procedure) is to receive ANSI characters and strings. In fact, if you were to call *IsWindowUnicode* after calling *SetWindowLongA*, you would see that it would return FALSE, indicating that the subclassed edit window procedure no longer expects Unicode characters and strings.

But now we have a new problem: how do we ensure that the original window procedure gets the correct type of characters and strings? The system needs to have two pieces of information to correctly convert the characters and strings. The first is the form that the characters and strings are currently in. We inform the system by calling either *Call-WindowProcA* or *CallWindowProcW*:

```
LRESULT CallWindowProcA(WNDPROC wndprcPrev, HWND hwnd,
    UINT uMsg, WPARAM wParam, LPARAM lParam);

LRESULT CallWindowProcW(WNDPROC wndprcPrev, HWND hwnd,
    UINT uMsg, WPARAM wParam, LPARAM lParam);
```

If the subclass procedure has ANSI strings that it wants to pass to the original window procedure, the subclass procedure must call *Call-WindowProcA*. If the subclass procedure has Unicode strings that it wants to pass to the original window procedure, the subclass procedure must call *CallWindowProcW*.

The second piece of information that the system needs is the type of characters and strings that the original window procedure expects. The system gets this information from the address of the original window procedure. When you call the *SetWindowLongA* or the *SetWindow-LongW* function, the system checks to see whether you are subclassing a Unicode window procedure with an ANSI subclass procedure or vice versa. If you're not changing the type of strings expected, *SetWindowLong* simply returns the address of the original window procedure. If you're changing the type of characters and strings that the window procedure expects, *SetWindowLong* doesn't return the actual address of the original window procedure; instead, it returns a handle to an internal Win32 subsystem data structure.

This structure contains the address of the original window procedure and a value that indicates whether that procedure expects Unicode or ANSI strings. When you call *CallWindowProc*, the system checks whether you are passing a handle of one of the internal data structures or the address of a window procedure. If you're passing the address of a window procedure, the original window procedure is called and no character and string conversions need to be performed.

If, on the other hand, you're passing the handle of an internal data structure, the system converts the characters and strings to the appropriate type (Unicode or ANSI) and then calls the original window procedure.

CHAPTER EIGHTEEN

BREAKING THROUGH PROCESS BOUNDARY WALLS

In the Win32 environment, each process gets its own 4-GB address space that can be accessed using 32-bit addresses ranging from 0x00000000 through 0xFFFFFFFF. When you use pointers to reference memory, the value of the pointer refers to a memory address in your own process's address space. It is not possible for your process to create a pointer that references memory belonging to another process. So if your process has a bug that overwrites memory at a random address, the bug can't affect the memory used by another process.

One of the biggest problems with the 16-bit Windows operating system is that all processes run in the same address space. If one process writes to memory, it is possible that the memory belongs to another process or, even worse, to the operating system itself. With the individual address spaces used by Win32, it is very difficult for one process to affect another process.

Win32 processes running under Windows 95 share the 2-GB address space from 0x80000000 through 0xFFFFFFFF. Only memory-mapped files and system components are mapped into this region. For more information, see chapters 5 and 8.

Win32's separate address spaces are a great advantage for both developers and users. For developers, the Win32 environment is more likely to catch wild memory reads and writes. For users, the operating system is more robust because one application cannot bring down another process or the operating system. However, many 16-bit Windows-based programs take advantage of the fact that all programs share a single address space. These programs are now much more difficult for developers to port to Win32.

Here are some examples of situations that require breaking through process boundary walls to access another process's address space:

- Subclassing a window created by another process

- Debugging aids (for example, determining which DLLs another process is using)

- Hooking other processes

In this chapter, I'll show you three mechanisms by which a Win32 process can break through the process boundary walls. All three are based on the concept of injecting a DLL into another process's address space.

Why Process Boundary Walls Need to Be Broken: An Example

Say that you want to subclass an instance of a window created by another process. You may recall that subclassing allows you to alter the behavior of a window. In 16-bit Windows, you simply call *SetWindowLong* to change the window procedure address in the window's memory block to point to a new (your own) *WndProc*. The entry for the *SetWindowLong* function in the Win32 documentation states that an application cannot subclass a window created by another process. This statement is not exactly true. The problem with subclassing another process's window really has to do with process address space boundaries. When you call *SetWindowLong* in both 16-bit Windows and Win32 to subclass a window,

```
SetWindowLong(hwnd, GWL_WNDPROC, MySubclassProc);
```

you are telling the system that all messages sent or posted to the window specified by *hwnd* should now be directed to *MySubclassProc* instead of the window's normal window procedure. In other words, whenever the system needs to dispatch a message to the specified window's *WndProc*, the system looks up its address and then makes a direct call to the *WndProc*. In this example, the system will see that the address of the *MySubclassProc* function is associated with the window and make a direct call to *MySubclassProc* instead.

The problem with subclassing a window created by another process in Win32 is that the subclass procedure is in another address space.

Figure 18-1 shows a simplified view of how a window procedure receives messages. Process A is running and has created a window. The USER-32.DLL file is mapped into the address space of Process A. This mapping of USER32.DLL is responsible for receiving and dispatching all sent and posted messages destined for any window created by any thread running in Process A. When this mapping of USER32.DLL detects a message, it first determines the address of the window's *WndProc* and then calls it, passing the window handle, the message, and the *wParam* and *lParam* values. After the *WndProc* processes the message, USER32 loops back around and waits for another window message to be processed.

Now let's suppose that your process is Process B and you want to subclass a window created by a thread in Process A. Your code in Process B must first determine the handle to the window you want to subclass. This can be done easily in a variety of ways. The example shown in Figure 18-1 simply calls *FindWindow* to obtain the desired window. Next the thread in Process B calls *SetWindowLong* in an attempt to change the address of the window's *WndProc*. Notice that I wrote "attempt." In Win32, this call does nothing and simply returns NULL. The code in *SetWindowLong* checks to see whether one process is attempting to change

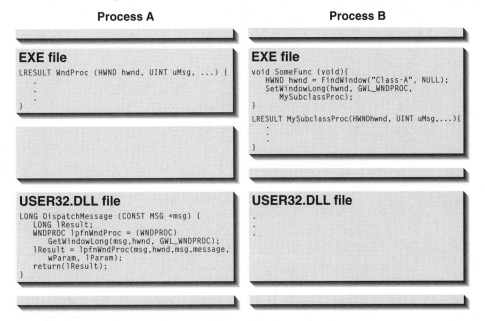

Figure 18-1.
A thread in Process B attempts to subclass a window created by a thread in Process A.

the *WndProc* address for a window created by another process and simply ignores the call.

What if Win32's *SetWindowLong* function could change the window's *WndProc*? The system would associate the address of *MySubclassProc* with the specified window. Then when this window was sent a message, the USER32 code in Process A would retrieve the message, get the address of *MySubclassProc*, and attempt to call this address. But then there would be a big problem. *MySubclassProc* would be in Process B's address space, but Process A would be the active process. Obviously, if USER32 were to call this address, USER32 would be calling an address in Process A's address space, most likely resulting in a memory access violation.

To avoid this problem, you would like the system to know that *MySubclassProc* is in Process B's address space and then have the system perform a context switch before calling the subclass procedure. This additional functionality was not implemented for several reasons:

- Subclassing windows created by threads in other processes is done fairly infrequently. Most applications subclass windows that they create, and the memory architecture of Win32 does not hinder this.

- Switching active processes is very expensive in terms of CPU time.

- A thread in Process B would have to execute the code in *MySubclassProc*. Which thread should the system try to use? An existing thread or a new thread?

- How could USER32 tell whether the address associated with the window was for a procedure in another process or in the same process?

Because there are no great solutions to these problems, Microsoft decided not to allow *SetWindowLong* to change the window procedure of a window created by another process.

But it is possible to subclass a window created by another process; you just have to go about it in a different way. The problem isn't really a question of subclassing but more a question of process address space boundaries. If you could somehow get the code for your subclass procedure into Process A's address space, you could easily call *SetWindowLong* and pass Process A's address to *MySubclassProc*. I call this technique injecting a DLL into a process's address space. I know three ways to do this. Let's discuss each of these in turn, going from easiest to most difficult.

Injecting a DLL Using the Registry

If you have been using Windows 95 or Windows NT for any period of time, you should be familiar with the registry. If you're not, get familiar with it! The configuration for the entire system is maintained in the registry, and you can alter the behavior of the system by tweaking various settings. The entry I'm going to discuss is in the following key:

```
HKEY_LOCAL_MACHINE\Software\Microsoft\Windows
    NT\CurrentVersion\Windows\AppInit_DLLs.
```

Windows 95 ignores this registry key. Therefore, this technique cannot be used to inject a DLL under Windows 95.

The window below shows what the entries in this key look like when viewed from the Windows NT Registry Editor. The value for this key might contain a single DLL pathname or a set of DLL pathnames (separated by spaces). In the window, I have set the value to a single DLL pathname, C:\MYLIB.DLL.

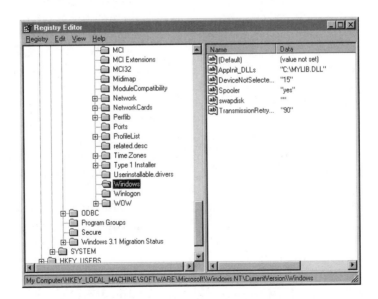

When you restart your machine and Windows NT initializes, the Win32 subsystem saves the value of this key. Then, whenever the USER-32.DLL library is mapped into a process, USER32 retrieves the saved value of this key from the Win32 subsystem and calls *LoadLibrary* for each DLL specified in the string. As each library is loaded, the library's associated *DllMain* is called with an *fdwReason* value of DLL_PROCESS_AT-TACH so that each library can initialize itself. USER32 does not check whether each library has been successfully loaded or initialized.

Of all the methods for injecting a DLL, this is by far the easiest. All you need to do is add a value to an already existing registry key. But this technique also has some disadvantages.

First, because the Win32 subsystem reads the value of this key during initialization, you must restart your computer after changing this value. Even logging off and logging back on won't work—you must restart. Of course, the opposite is also true; if you remove a DLL from this key's value, the system won't stop mapping the library until the computer is restarted.

Second, your DLL is mapped only into processes that also map USER32.DLL. Whereas all GUI-based applications will map USER32, most CUI-based applications will not. So if you need to inject your DLL into a compiler or linker, this method will not work at all.

Third, your DLL is mapped into every GUI-based application. Most likely, you need only to inject your library into one or a few processes. The more processes your DLL is mapped into, the greater the chance of crashing the "container" processes. After all, your code is now being executed by threads running in these processes. If your code causes an infinite loop or accesses memory incorrectly, you are affecting the behavior and robustness of the processes in which your code is running. Therefore, it is best to inject your library into as few processes as possible.

Finally, your DLL is mapped into every GUI-based application for its entire lifetime. This is similar to the previous problem. Since it is better to be mapped into just the processes you need, it follows that it is best for the DLL to be mapped into those processes for the minimum amount of time. Suppose that when the user invokes your application, you want to subclass WordPad's main window. Your DLL doesn't have to be mapped into WordPad's address space until the user invokes your application. If the user later decides to terminate your application, you'll want to unsubclass WordPad's main window. In this case, your DLL no longer needs to be injected into WordPad's address space. It's best to keep your DLL injected only when necessary.

Injecting a DLL Using Windows Hooks

It is possible to inject a DLL into a process's address space using hooks. To get hooks to work in Win32 as they do in 16-bit Windows, Microsoft was forced to devise a mechanism that allows a DLL to be injected into the address space of another process. Let's look at an example.

Process A (a Spy++-like utility) installs a WH_GETMESSAGE hook to see messages processed by windows in the system. The hook is installed by calling *SetWindowsHookEx* as follows:

```
HHOOK hHook = SetWindowsHookEx(WH_GETMESSAGE, GetMsgProc,
    hinstDll, NULL);
```

The first parameter, WH_GETMESSAGE, indicates the type of hook to install. The second parameter, *GetMsgProc*, identifies the address (in your address space) of the function that the system should call whenever a window is about to process a message. The third parameter, *hinstDll*, identifies the DLL that contains the *GetMsgProc* function. In Win32, a DLL's *hinstDll* value identifies the 32-bit virtual memory address where the DLL is mapped into the process's address space. Finally, the last parameter, NULL, identifies the thread to hook. It is possible for one thread to call *SetWindowsHookEx* and to pass the ID of another thread in the system. By passing a value of NULL for this parameter, we are telling the system that we want to hook all threads in the system.

Now let's take a look at what happens:

1. A thread in Process B is about to dispatch a message to a window.

2. The system checks to see whether a WH_GETMESSAGE hook is installed on this thread.

3. The system checks to see whether the DLL containing the *GetMsgProc* function is mapped into Process B's address space.

4. If the DLL has not been mapped, the system forces the DLL to be mapped into Process B's address space and increments a lock count on the DLL's mapping in Process B.

5. The system looks at the DLL's *hinstDll* as it applies to Process B and checks to see whether the DLL's *hinstDll* is at the same location as it applies to Process A. If the *hinstDll*s are the same, the memory address of the *GetMsgProc* function is also the same in the two process address spaces. In this case, the system can simply call the *GetMsgProc* function in Process A's address space.

6. If the *hinstDll*s are different, the system must determine the virtual memory address of the *GetMsgProc* function in Process B's address space. This address is determined with the following formula:

```
GetMsgProc B = hinstDll B + (GetMsgProc A - hinstDll A)
```

By subtracting *hinstDll A* from *GetMsgProc A*, you get the offset in bytes for the *GetMsgProc* function. Adding this offset to *hinstDll B* gives the location of the *GetMsgProc* function as it applies to the DLL's mapping in Process B's address space.

7. The system increments a lock count on the DLL's mapping in Process B.

8. The system calls the *GetMsgProc* function in Process B's address space.

9. When *GetMsgProc* returns, the system decrements a lock count on the DLL's mapping in Process B.

That's it. This is how hooks had to be implemented in the Win32 environment. You should note that when the system injects or maps the DLL containing the hook filter function, the whole DLL is mapped—not just the hook filter function. This means that any and all functions contained in the DLL now exist and can be called from threads running in Process B's context.

So, to subclass a window created by a thread in another process, you can first set a WH_GETMESSAGE hook on the thread that created the window, and then, when the *GetMsgProc* function is called, call *SetWindowLong* to subclass the window. Of course, the subclass procedure must be in the same DLL as the *GetMsgProc* function.

Unlike the Registry method of injecting a DLL, this method allows you to unmap the DLL when it is no longer needed in the other process's address space by simply calling the following:

```
BOOL UnhookWindowsHookEx(HHOOK hhook);
```

When a thread calls the *UnhookWindowsHookEx* function, the system cycles through its internal list of processes into which it had to inject the DLL and decrements the DLL's lock count. When this lock count reaches 0, the DLL is automatically unmapped from the process's address space. You'll recall that just before the system calls the *GetMsgProc* function, the system increments the DLL's lock count. (See step 7 above.) This prevents a memory access violation. Without incrementing this lock count, another thread running in the system could call *Unhook-WindowsHookEx* while Process B's thread attempts to execute the code in the *GetMsgProc* function.

All this means that you can't subclass the window and immediately unhook the hook. The hook must stay in effect for the lifetime of the subclass.

The Desktop Item Position Saver Utility

Most of the time, I use my computer for business-related tasks, and I find that a screen resolution of 1152 x 864 works best for me. However, I have recently started playing games on my computer, and most games are designed for a 640 x 480 resolution display. So when I feel like playing a game, I go to the Control Panel's Display applet and change the display's resolution to 640 x 480. When I'm done playing the game, I go back to the Display applet and raise the resolution to 1152 x 864 again.

This ability to change the display resolution on the fly is awesome and a very welcome feature on Windows 95 and Wndows NT 4. However, I do despise one thing about changing the display resolution: the desktop icons don't remember where they were. I have several icons on my desktop to access applications immediately and to get to files that I use frequently. I have these icons layed out on my desktop just so. When I change the display resolution, the desktop window changes size and my icons are rearranged in a way that makes it impossible for me to find anything. Then, when I change the display resolution back, all my icons are rearranged again, in some new order. To fix this, I have to manually reposition all the desktop icons back to how I like them—how annoying!

I hated manually rearranging these icons so much that I created the Desktop Item Position Saver utility, DIPS. DIPS consists of a small executable and a small dynamic-link library. When you run the executable, the following message box appears:

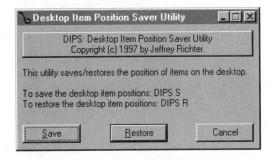

This message box shows how to use the utility. When you pass an *S* as the command-line argument to DIPS, it creates the following registry subkey:

```
HKEY_CURRENT_USER\Software\Richter\Desktop Item Position Saver
```

and adds a value for each item on your desktop window. Each item has a position value saved with it. You would run DIPS S just before changing the screen resolution to play a game. Then when you're done playing the game, change the screen resolution back to normal and run DIPS R. This causes DIPS to open the registry subkey, and for each item on your desktop that matches an item saved in the registry, the item's position is set back to where it was when you ran DIPS S.

At first, you might think that DIPS would be fairly easy and almost trivial to implement. After all, you just need to get the window handle of the desktop's ListView control, send it messages to enumerate the items, get their positions, and then save this information in the registry. However, if you try this, you'll see that it is not quite this simple. The problem is that most common control window messages, such as LVM_GETITEM and LVM_GETITEMPOSITION, do not work across process boundaries.

Here is why these messages don't work across process boundaries: the LVM_GETITEM message requires that you pass in the address of an LV_ITEM data structure for the message's LPARAM parameter. Because this memory address is meaningful only to the process that is sending the message, the process receiving the message cannot safely use it.[1] So to make DIPS work as advertised, it is necessary to inject code into EXPLORER.EXE that sends LVM_GETITEM and LVM_GETITEMPO-SITION messages successfully to the desktop's ListView control.

The DIPS application consists of two parts: a DIPS.EXE file built using the DIPS.C source file and the DIPSLIB.DLL file built using the

---

1. Unlike the new common controls, you can send window messages across process boundaries to interact with the built-in controls (such as button, edit, static, combo box, list box, and so on). For example, you can send a list box control created by a thread in another process an LB_GETTEXT message where the LPARAM parameter points to a string buffer in the sending process. The reason this works is because Microsoft checks specifically to see if a LB_GETTEXT message is being sent, and if so, the operating system internally creates memory-mapped files and copies the string data across process boundaries.

Why did Microsoft decide to do this for the built-in controls and not for the new common controls? The answer is portability. In 16-bit Windows, where all applications run in a single address space, one application could send an LB_GETTEXT message to a window created by another application. To port these 16-bit applications to Win32 easily, Microsoft went to the extra effort of making sure that this still works. However, the new common controls do not exist in 16-bit Windows and therefore there was no porting issue involved, so Microsoft chose not to do the additional work for the common controls.

DIPSLIB.C source file. Both source files also include the DIPSLIB.H file. All of these files are shown in Figure 18-2 beginning on page 911.

When you run DIPS.EXE, it first gets the window handle of the desktop's ListView control:

```
// The Desktop ListView window is the
// grandchild of the ProgMan window.
hwndLV = GetFirstChild(
    GetFirstChild(FindWindow(__TEXT("ProgMan"), NULL)));
```

This code first looks for a window whose class is ProgMan. Even though no Program Manager application is running, the new shell creates a window of this class for backward compatibility with applications that were designed for older versions of Windows. This ProgMan window has a single child window whose class is SHELLDLL_DefView and this child window also has a single child window whose class is SysListView32. This SysListView32 window is the desktop's ListView control window.[2]

Once I have the ListView's window handle, I can determine the ID of the thread that created the window by calling *GetWindowThreadProcessId*. I pass this ID to the *SetDIPSHook* function (implemented inside DIPSLIB.C). *SetDIPSHook* installs a WH_GETMESSAGE hook on this thread and calls

```
PostThreadMessage(dwThreadId, WM_NULL, 0, 0);
```

to force Explorer's thread to wake up. Because I have installed a WH_GETMESSAGE hook on this thread, the operating system automatically injects my DIPSLIB.DLL file into Explorer's address space and calls my *GetMsgProc* function. This function first checks to see whether it is being called for the first time, and if so, creates a hidden window with a caption of "Richter DIPS." Keep in mind that it is Explorer's thread that is creating this hidden window. While this window is being created, the DIPS.EXE thread returns from *SetDIPSHook* and then calls

```
GetMessage(&msg, NULL, 0, 0);
```

This call puts the thread to sleep until a message shows up in the queue. Even though DIPS.EXE does not create any windows of its own, it still has a message queue, and messages can be placed in this queue only by calling *PostThreadMessage*. If you look at the code in DIPSLIB.C's *GetMsgProc* function, you'll see that immediately after the call to *CreateDialog*, there is a call to *PostThreadMessage* that will cause the DIPS.EXE

---

2. By the way, I obtained all this information using Visual C++'s Spy++ tool.

thread to wake back up. The thread ID was saved in a shared variable inside the *SetDIPSHook* function.

Notice that I am using the thread's message queue for thread synchronization. There is absolutely nothing wrong with doing this, and sometimes it's much easier to synchronize threads in this way rather than using the various kernel objects: mutexes, semaphores, events, and so on. Win32 is a very rich API; take advantage of it.

When the thread in the DIPS executable wakes up, it knows that the server dialog box has been created and calls *FindWindow* to get the window handle. We now can use window messages to communicate between the client (the DIPS applications) and the server (the hidden dialog box). Because the dialog box was created by a thread running inside the context of the Explorer process, we do have a few limitations on what we can do to the Explorer.

To tell our dialog box to save/restore the desktop icon positions, all we do is send a message:

```
// Tell the DIPS window which ListView window to manipulate
// and whether the items should be saved or restored.
SendMessage(hwndDIPS, WM_APP, (WPARAM) hwndLV, fSave);
```

I have coded the dialog box's dialog box procedure to look for the WM_APP message. When it receives this message, the WPARAM parameter indicates the handle of the ListView control that is to be manipulated, and the LPARAM parameter is a Boolean value indicating whether the current item positions should be saved to the registry or whether the items should be repositioned based on the saved information read from the registry.

Because I use *SendMessage* instead of *PostMessage* here, the function will not return until the operation is complete. If you wanted to, you could add messages to the dialog's dialog box procedure to give the program more control over the Explorer process. When I'm finished communicating with the dialog box and wish to terminate the server (so to speak), I send a WM_CLOSE message that tells the dialog box to destroy itself.

Finally, just before the DIPS application terminates, it calls *SetDIPS-Hook* again but passes 0 as the thread ID. The 0 is a sentinel value that tells the function to unhook the WH_GETMESSAGE hook. When the hook is uninstalled, the operating system automatically unloads the DIPSLIB.DLL file from Explorer's address space, which means that the dialog box's dialog box procedure is no longer inside Explorer's address space. It is important that the dialog box be destroyed first, before uninstalling the hook, or the next message received by the dialog box would cause Explorer's thread to raise an access violation. If this happens, Explorer is terminated by the operating system—you must be very careful when using DLL injection!

DIPS.ico

```
DIPS.C
/******************************************************************
Module name: DIPS.c
Notices: Copyright (c) 1996-1997 Jeffrey Richter
******************************************************************/


#include "..\CmnHdr.H"                    /* See Appendix C. */
#include <Windows.H>
#include <WindowsX.H>
#include <tchar.h>
#include "Resource.h"
#include "..\DIPSLib\DIPSLib.h"



///////////////////////////////////////////////////////////////////


BOOL Dlg_OnInitDialog (HWND hwnd, HWND hwndFocus,
   LPARAM lParam) {

   // Associate an icon with the dialog box.
   chSETDLGICONS(hwnd, IDI_DIPS, IDI_DIPS);

   return(TRUE);
}



///////////////////////////////////////////////////////////////////


void Dlg_OnCommand (HWND hwnd, int id,
   HWND hwndCtl, UINT codeNotify) {

   switch (id) {
      case IDC_SAVE:
      case IDC_RESTORE:
      case IDCANCEL:
```

Figure 18-2.
The DIPS utility.

(continued)

Figure 18-2. *continued*

```
        EndDialog(hwnd, id);
        break;
    }
}


//////////////////////////////////////////////////////////////


BOOL CALLBACK Dlg_Proc (HWND hwnd, UINT uMsg,
    WPARAM wParam, LPARAM lParam) {

    switch (uMsg) {
        chHANDLE_DLGMSG(hwnd, WM_INITDIALOG, Dlg_OnInitDialog);
        chHANDLE_DLGMSG(hwnd, WM_COMMAND, Dlg_OnCommand);
    }

    return(FALSE);
}


//////////////////////////////////////////////////////////////


int WINAPI _tWinMain (HINSTANCE hinstExe,
    HINSTANCE hinstPrev, LPTSTR pszCmdLine, int nCmdShow) {

    HWND hwndDIPS;
    HWND hwndLV;
    MSG msg;
    TCHAR cWhatToDo;

    chWARNIFUNICODEUNDERWIN95();

    // Convert command-line character to uppercase.
    CharUpperBuff(pszCmdLine, 1);
    cWhatToDo = pszCmdLine[0];

    if ((cWhatToDo != __TEXT('S')) &&
        (cWhatToDo != __TEXT('R'))) {

        // An invalid command-line argument; prompt the user.
        cWhatToDo = 0;
    }
```

(continued)

Figure 18-2. *continued*

```
if (cWhatToDo == 0) {
   // No command-line argument was used to tell us what to
   // do; show usage dialog box and prompt the user.
   switch (DialogBox(hinstExe, MAKEINTRESOURCE(IDD_DIPS),
      NULL, Dlg_Proc)) {
      case IDC_SAVE:
         cWhatToDo = __TEXT('S');
         break;

      case IDC_RESTORE:
         cWhatToDo = __TEXT('R');
         break;
   }
}

if (cWhatToDo == 0) {
   // The user doesn't want to do anything.
   return(0);
}

// The Desktop ListView window is the
// grandchild of the ProgMan window.
hwndLV = GetFirstChild(
   GetFirstChild(FindWindow(__TEXT("ProgMan"), NULL)));
chASSERT(IsWindow(hwndLV));

// Set hook that injects our DLL into the Explorer's
// address space. After setting the hook, the DIPS hidden
// modeless dialog box is created. We send messages to
// this window to tell it what we want it to do.
chVERIFY(SetDIPSHook(
   GetWindowThreadProcessId(hwndLV, NULL)));

// Wait for the DIPS server window to be created.
GetMessage(&msg, NULL, 0, 0);

// Find the handle of the hidden dialog box window.
hwndDIPS = FindWindow(NULL, __TEXT("Richter DIPS"));

// Make sure that the window was created.
chASSERT(IsWindow(hwndDIPS));

// Tell the DIPS window which ListView window to manipulate
// and whether the items should be saved or restored.
```

(continued)

Figure 18-2. *continued*

```
        SendMessage(hwndDIPS, WM_APP, (WPARAM) hwndLV,
           (cWhatToDo == __TEXT('S')));

        // Tell the DIPS window to destroy itself. Use SendMessage
        // instead of PostMessage so that we know the window is
        // destroyed before the hook is removed.
        SendMessage(hwndDIPS, WM_CLOSE, 0, 0);

        // Make sure that the window was destroyed.
        chASSERT(!IsWindow(hwndDIPS));

        // Unhook the DLL removing the DIPS dialog box procedure
        // from the Explorer's address space.
        SetDIPSHook(0);

        return(0);
    }


/////////////////////////// End of File ///////////////////////////
```

DIPSLIB.C
```
/****************************************************************
Module name: DIPSLib.c
Notices: Copyright (c) 1996-1977 Jeffrey Richter
****************************************************************/


#include "..\CmnHdr.H"                           /* See Appendix C. */
#include <Windows.H>
#include <WindowsX.H>
#include <CommCtrl.H>

#define DIPSLIBAPI __declspec(dllexport)
#include "DIPSLib.H"
#include "Resource.H"



///////////////////////////////////////////////////////////////////
```

(continued)

Figure 18-2. *continued*

```
#ifdef _DEBUG
// This function forces the debugger to be invoked.
void ForceDebugBreak() {
   __try { DebugBreak(); }
   __except(UnhandledExceptionFilter(
      GetExceptionInformation())) {
   }
}
#else
#define ForceDebugBreak()
#endif


///////////////////////////////////////////////////////////


// Forward references
LRESULT WINAPI GetMsgProc (int nCode, WPARAM wParam,
   LPARAM lParam);
BOOL WINAPI DIPS_DlgProc(HWND hwnd, UINT uMsg,
   WPARAM wParam, LPARAM lParam);


///////////////////////////////////////////////////////////


// Instruct the compiler to put the g_hhook data variable in
// its own data section called Shared. We then instruct the
// linker that we want to share the data in this section
// with all instances of this application.
#pragma data_seg("Shared")
HHOOK g_hhook = NULL;
DWORD g_dwThreadIdDIPS = 0;
#pragma data_seg()

// Instruct the linker to make the Shared section
// readable, writable, and shared.
#pragma comment(linker, "/section:Shared,rws")


///////////////////////////////////////////////////////////


// Nonshared variables
HINSTANCE g_hinstDll = NULL;
```

(continued)

Figure 18-2. *continued*

```
/////////////////////////////////////////////////////////////////

BOOL WINAPI DllMain (HINSTANCE hinstDll, DWORD fdwReason,
   LPVOID fImpLoad) {

   switch (fdwReason) {

      case DLL_PROCESS_ATTACH:
         // DLL is attaching to the address space
         // of the current process.
         g_hinstDll = hinstDll;
         break;

      case DLL_THREAD_ATTACH:
         // A new thread is being created
         // in the current process.
         break;

      case DLL_THREAD_DETACH:
         // A thread is exiting cleanly.
         break;

      case DLL_PROCESS_DETACH:
         // The calling process is detaching the
         // DLL from its address space.
         break;
   }
   return(TRUE);
}


/////////////////////////////////////////////////////////////////


BOOL WINAPI SetDIPSHook(DWORD dwThreadId) {
   BOOL fOk = FALSE;

   if (dwThreadId != 0) {
      // Make sure that the hook is not already installed.
      chASSERT(g_hhook == NULL);

      // Install the hook on the specified thread.
```

(continued)

Figure 18-2. *continued*

```
        g_hhook = SetWindowsHookEx(WH_GETMESSAGE, GetMsgProc,
           g_hinstDll, dwThreadId);

        if (fOk = (g_hhook != NULL)) {
           // Save our thread ID in a shared variable so that
           // our GetMsgProc function can post a message back
           // to our thread when the server window has been
           // created.
           g_dwThreadIdDIPS = GetCurrentThreadId();

           // The hook was installed successfully; force a
           // benign message to the thread's queue so that
           // the hook function gets called.
           fOk = PostThreadMessage(dwThreadId, WM_NULL, 0, 0);
        }
     } else {

        // Make sure that a hook has been installed.
        chASSERT(g_hhook != NULL);
        fOk = UnhookWindowsHookEx(g_hhook);
        g_hhook = NULL;
     }

     return(fOk);
}


///////////////////////////////////////////////////////////


LRESULT WINAPI GetMsgProc (int nCode,
   WPARAM wParam, LPARAM lParam) {

   static BOOL fFirstTime = TRUE;

   if (fFirstTime) {
      // The DLL just got injected.
      fFirstTime = FALSE;

      // Uncomment the line below to invoke the debugger
      // on the process that just got the injected DLL.
      // ForceDebugBreak();

      // Create the DTIS Server window to
```

(continued)

917

Figure 18-2. *continued*

```
      // handle the client request.
      CreateDialog(g_hinstDll, MAKEINTRESOURCE(IDD_DIPS),
         NULL, DIPS_DlgProc);

      // Tell the DIPS application that the server is
      // up and ready to handle requests.
      PostThreadMessage(g_dwThreadIdDIPS, WM_NULL, 0, 0);
   }

   return(CallNextHookEx(g_hhook, nCode, wParam, lParam));
}


///////////////////////////////////////////////////////////////


void DIPS_OnClose(HWND hwnd) {
   DestroyWindow(hwnd);
}


///////////////////////////////////////////////////////////////


static const TCHAR g_szRegSubKey[] =
   __TEXT("Software\\Richter\\Desktop Item Position Saver");


///////////////////////////////////////////////////////////////


void SaveListViewItemPositions(HWND hwndLV) {
   int nItem, nMaxItems = ListView_GetItemCount(hwndLV);
   HKEY hkey;
   DWORD dwDisposition;

   // When saving new positions, delete the old position
   // information that is currently in the registry.
   LONG l = RegDeleteKey(HKEY_CURRENT_USER, g_szRegSubKey);

   // Create the registry key to hold the info
   l = RegCreateKeyEx(HKEY_CURRENT_USER, g_szRegSubKey,
      0, NULL, REG_OPTION_NON_VOLATILE, KEY_SET_VALUE,
      NULL, &hkey, &dwDisposition);
```

(continued)

Figure 18-2. *continued*

```
   chASSERT(1 == ERROR_SUCCESS);

   for (nItem = 0; nItem < nMaxItems; nItem++) {
      TCHAR szName[_MAX_PATH];
      POINT pt;

      // Get the name and position of a listview item.
      ListView_GetItemText(hwndLV, nItem, 0, szName,
         chDIMOF(szName));
      ListView_GetItemPosition(hwndLV, nItem, &pt);

      // Save the name and position in the registry.
      1 = RegSetValueEx(hkey, szName, 0,
         REG_BINARY, (PBYTE) &pt, sizeof(pt));
      chASSERT(1 == ERROR_SUCCESS);
   }
   RegCloseKey(hkey);
}


///////////////////////////////////////////////////////////////


void RestoreListViewItemPositions(HWND hwndLV) {
   HKEY hkey;
   LONG l = RegOpenKeyEx(HKEY_CURRENT_USER, g_szRegSubKey,
      0, KEY_QUERY_VALUE, &hkey);
   if (l == ERROR_SUCCESS) {
      int nIndex;

      // If the listview has AutoArrange on,
      // temporarily turn it off.
      DWORD dwStyle = GetWindowStyle(hwndLV);
      if (dwStyle & LVS_AUTOARRANGE)
         SetWindowLong(hwndLV, GWL_STYLE,
            dwStyle & ~LVS_AUTOARRANGE);

      for (nIndex = 0; TRUE; nIndex++) {
         TCHAR szName[_MAX_PATH];
         POINT pt;
         LV_FINDINFO lvfi;
         int cbValueName = chDIMOF(szName);
         int cbData = sizeof(pt), nItem;
         DWORD dwType;
```

(continued)

Figure 18-2. *continued*

```
            // Read a value name and position from the registry.
            l = RegEnumValue(hkey, nIndex, szName, &cbValueName,
                NULL, &dwType, (PBYTE) &pt, &cbData);

            if (l == ERROR_NO_MORE_ITEMS)
                break;

            if ((dwType == REG_BINARY) &&
                (cbData == sizeof(pt))) {
                // The value is something that we recognize; try
                // to find an item in the listview control that
                // matches the name.
                lvfi.flags = LVFI_STRING;
                lvfi.psz = szName;
                nItem = ListView_FindItem(hwndLV, -1, &lvfi);
                if (nItem != -1) {
                    // We found a match; change the
                    // item's position.
                    ListView_SetItemPosition(hwndLV, nItem,
                        pt.x, pt.y);
                }
            }
        }
        // Turn AutoArrange back on if it was originally on.
        SetWindowLong(hwndLV, GWL_STYLE, dwStyle);
        RegCloseKey(hkey);
    }
}


///////////////////////////////////////////////////////////////


BOOL WINAPI DIPS_DlgProc(HWND hwnd, UINT uMsg,
    WPARAM wParam, LPARAM lParam) {

    switch (uMsg) {
        chHANDLE_DLGMSG(hwnd, WM_CLOSE, DIPS_OnClose);

        case WM_APP:
            // Uncomment the line below to invoke the debugger
            // on the process that just got the injected DLL.
            // ForceDebugBreak();
```

(continued)

Figure 18-2. *continued*

```
            if (lParam)
                SaveListViewItemPositions((HWND) wParam);
            else
                RestoreListViewItemPositions((HWND) wParam);
            break;
    }
    return(FALSE);
}



////////////////////// End of File //////////////////////
```

DIPSLIB.H
```
/**************************************************************
Module name: DIPSLib.h
Notices: Copyright (c) 1996-1997 Jeffrey Richter
**************************************************************/


#if !defined(DIPSLIBAPI)
#define DIPSLIBAPI __declspec(dllimport)
#endif


///////////////////////////////////////////////////////////


// External function prototypes
DIPSLIBAPI BOOL WINAPI SetDIPSHook(DWORD dwThreadId);


////////////////////// End of File //////////////////////
```

DIPSLIB.RC
```
//Microsoft Developer Studio generated resource script.
//
#include "resource.h"

#define APSTUDIO_READONLY_SYMBOLS
```

(continued)

Figure 18-2. *continued*

```
//////////////////////////////////////////////////////////
//
// Generated from the TEXTINCLUDE 2 resource.
//
#include "afxres.h"


//////////////////////////////////////////////////////////
#undef APSTUDIO_READONLY_SYMBOLS


//////////////////////////////////////////////////////////
// English (U.S.) resources

#if !defined(AFX_RESOURCE_DLL) || defined(AFX_TARG_ENU)
#ifdef _WIN32
LANGUAGE LANG_ENGLISH, SUBLANG_ENGLISH_US
#pragma code_page(1252)
#endif //_WIN32


//////////////////////////////////////////////////////////
//
// Dialog
//

IDD_DIPS DIALOG DISCARDABLE  0, 0, 132, 13
STYLE WS_CAPTION
CAPTION "Richter DIPS"
FONT 8, "MS Sans Serif"
BEGIN
END



#ifdef APSTUDIO_INVOKED
//////////////////////////////////////////////////////////
//
// TEXTINCLUDE
//

1 TEXTINCLUDE DISCARDABLE
BEGIN
    "resource.h\0"
END

2 TEXTINCLUDE DISCARDABLE
BEGIN
```

(continued)

Figure 18-2. *continued*

```
    "#include ""afxres.h""\r\n"
    "\0"
END

3 TEXTINCLUDE DISCARDABLE
BEGIN
    "\r\n"
    "\0"
END

#endif    // APSTUDIO_INVOKED

#endif    // English (U.S.) resources
/////////////////////////////////////////////////////////////


#ifndef APSTUDIO_INVOKED
/////////////////////////////////////////////////////////////
//
// Generated from the TEXTINCLUDE 3 resource.
//


/////////////////////////////////////////////////////////////
#endif    // not APSTUDIO_INVOKED
```

Injecting a DLL Using Remote Threads

This method of injecting a DLL was the most difficult to develop, but it offers the greatest amount of flexibility. It uses many of the features in Win32: processes, threads, thread synchronization, structured exception handling, virtual memory management, and Unicode. (If you're unclear about any of these features, please refer to their respective chapters in this book.) To inject DLLs using this method, you need to create and execute threads in the target process's address space and access the physical storage committed to a thread's stack. But first you must understand how the system creates threads and how a thread uses its stack. You might want to refresh your memory on these details by referring to the section "The *CreateThread* Function" in Chapter 4 and the section "A Thread's Stack" in Chapter 7.

How a DLL Is Loaded

As we all know, the function *LoadLibrary* causes the system to load the specified library into the calling thread's process's address space:

```
HINSTANCE LoadLibrary(LPCTSTR lpszLibFile);
```

If you look up *LoadLibrary* in the WINBASE.H header file, you find the following:

```
HINSTANCE WINAPI LoadLibraryA(LPCSTR lpLibFileName);
HINSTANCE WINAPI LoadLibraryW(LPCWSTR lpLibFileName);
#ifdef UNICODE
#define LoadLibrary   LoadLibraryW
#else
#define LoadLibrary   LoadLibraryA
#endif // !UNICODE
```

There are actually two *LoadLibrary* functions: *LoadLibraryA* and *LoadLibraryW*. The only difference between them is the type of parameter that you pass to the function. If you have the library's filename stored as an ANSI string, you must call *LoadLibraryA* (the *A* stands for ANSI); if the filename is stored as a Unicode string, you must call *LoadLibraryW* (the *W* stands for wide characters). No single *LoadLibrary* function exists—only *LoadLibraryA* and *LoadLibraryW*. For most applications, the LoadLibrary macro expands to *LoadLibraryA*.

Win32 Functions That Affect Other Processes

By this point in the book, you should have a pretty good understanding of threads and their stacks. But before I dive into further discussions about injecting a DLL into another process's address space, I want to briefly discuss the Win32 functions that allow one process to alter another. Very few functions allow such alterations because they usually compromise the robustness of an application. Many of the functions that do allow a process to alter another process were created by Microsoft for use by debuggers. Most Win32-based applications should have very little or no need to call any of these functions. The following two tables show all of the Win32 functions that accept handles to processes and threads as parameters.

Win32 Process Function	Description
CreateProcess	Creates another process
FlushInstructionCache	Flushes another process's instruction cache
VirtualProtectEx	Changes access protection on another process's committed pages
VirtualQueryEx	Provides information about a range of pages in another process
VirtualAllocEx	New Windows NT 4 function that reserves address space and/or commits storage in another process
VirtualFreeEx	New Windows NT 4 function that decommits storage and/or releases address space in another process
GetProcessAffinityMask	Indicates the processors on which a process is allowed to run
GetProcessTimes	Obtains another process's timing information
GetProcessWorkingSetSize	Gets the minimum and maximum working set sizes for a specified process
SetProcessWorkingSetSize	Sets the minimum and maximum working set sizes for a specified process
TerminateProcess	Terminates another process
GetExitCodeProcess	Gets another process's exit code
CreateRemoteThread	Creates a thread in another process
ReadProcessMemory	Reads memory from another process's address space
WriteProcessMemory	Writes memory to another process's address space
GetPriorityClass	Gets another process's priority class
SetPriorityClass	Sets another process's priority class
WaitForInputIdle	Waits until another process has no input pending in its thread's input queue

Win32 Thread Function	Description
SetThreadAffinityMask	Sets the processors on which a thread is allowed to run
GetThreadPriority	Gets another thread's scheduling priority
SetThreadPriority	Sets another thread's scheduling priority

(continued)

Win32 Thread Function	Description
GetThreadTimes	Gets another thread's timing information
TerminateThread	Terminates another thread
GetExitCodeThread	Gets another thread's exit code
GetThreadSelectorEntry	Gets another thread's descriptor table entry (for *x86* systems only)
GetThreadContext	Gets a thread's CPU registers
SetThreadContext	Changes a thread's CPU registers
ResumeThread	Increments another thread's suspend count
SuspendThread	Decrements another thread's suspend count

Of all these functions, we need to use only nine to inject a DLL into another process's address space. Let's take a brief look at these nine functions.

CreateRemoteThread

CreateRemoteThread allows one process to create a thread that runs in the context of another process.

```
HANDLE CreateRemoteThread (HANDLE hProcess, LPSECURITY_ATTRIBUTES
    lpsa, DWORD cbStack, LPTHREAD_START_ROUTINE lpStartAddr,
    LPVOID lpvThreadParm, DWORD fdwCreate, LPDWORD lpIDThread);
```

CreateRemoteThread is identical to *CreateThread* except that it has one additional parameter, *hProcess*. The *hProcess* parameter identifies the process that is to own the newly created thread. The *lpStartAddr* parameter identifies the memory address of the thread function. This memory address is, of course, relative to the remote process—the thread function's code cannot be in your own process's address space.

In Windows NT, the more commonly used *CreateThread* function is implemented by calling *CreateRemoteThread*. *CreateThread* is implemented as follows:

```
HANDLE CreateThread (LPSECURITY_ATTRIBUTES lpsa, DWORD cbStack,
    LPTHREAD_START_ROUTINE lpStartAddr, LPVOID lpvThreadParm,
    DWORD fdwCreate, LPDWORD lpIDThread) {

    return(CreateRemoteThread(GetCurrentProcess(), lpsa, cbStack,
        lpStartAddr, lpvThreadParm, fdwCreate, lpIDThread));
}
```

Under Windows 95, the *CreateRemoteThread* function has no useful implementation and simply returns FALSE; calling *GetLastError* returns ERROR_CALL_NOT_IMPLEMENTED. (The *CreateThread* function contains the complete implementation of the code that creates a thread in the calling process.) Because *CreateRemoteThread* is not implemented, this technique cannot be used to inject a DLL under Windows 95.

GetThreadContext and *SetThreadContext*

The Win32 API contains just one data structure, called CONTEXT, that is CPU-specific. The code fragment below shows the CONTEXT structure for an *x*86 CPU. A CONTEXT structure is divided into five sections. CONTEXT_CONTROL contains the control registers of the CPU such as the instruction pointer, stack pointer, flags, and function return address. (Unlike the *x*86 processor, which pushes a function's return address on the stack when making a call, both MIPS and Alpha CPUs place a function's return address in a register when making a call.) CONTEXT_INTEGER identifies the CPU's integer registers; CONTEXT_FLOATING_POINT identifies the CPU's floating-point registers; CONTEXT_SEGMENTS identifies the CPU's segment registers (*x*86 only); and CONTEXT_DEBUG_REGISTERS identifies the CPU's debug registers (*x*86 only).

```
typedef struct _CONTEXT {

    //
    // The flags values within this flag control the contents of
    // a CONTEXT record.
    //
    // If the context record is used as an input parameter, then
    // for each portion of the context record controlled by a flag
    // whose value is set, it is assumed that that portion of the
    // context record contains valid context. If the context record
    // is being used to modify a thread's context, then only that
    // portion of the thread's context will be modified.
    //
    // If the context record is used as an IN OUT parameter to
    // capture the context of a thread, then only those portions
    // of the thread's context corresponding to set flags will be
    // returned.
    // The context record is never used as an OUT only parameter.
    //
```

(continued)

```
DWORD ContextFlags;

//
// This section is specified/returned if CONTEXT_DEBUG_REGISTERS
// is set in ContextFlags. Note that CONTEXT_DEBUG_REGISTERS is
// NOT included in CONTEXT_FULL.
//

DWORD    Dr0;
DWORD    Dr1;
DWORD    Dr2;
DWORD    Dr3;
DWORD    Dr6;
DWORD    Dr7;

//
// This section is specified/returned if the
// ContextFlags word contains the flag CONTEXT_FLOATING_POINT.
//

FLOATING_SAVE_AREA FloatSave;

//
// This section is specified/returned if the
// ContextFlags word contains the flag CONTEXT_SEGMENTS.
//

DWORD    SegGs;
DWORD    SegFs;
DWORD    SegEs;
DWORD    SegDs;

//
// This section is specified/returned if the
// ContextFlags word contains the flag CONTEXT_INTEGER.
//

DWORD    Edi;
DWORD    Esi;
DWORD    Ebx;
DWORD    Edx;
DWORD    Ecx;
DWORD    Eax;

//
// This section is specified/returned if the
// ContextFlags word contains the flag CONTEXT_CONTROL.
//
```

```
DWORD    Ebp;
DWORD    Eip;
DWORD    SegCs;              // MUST BE SANITIZED
DWORD    EFlags;            // MUST BE SANITIZED
DWORD    Esp;
DWORD    SegSs;

} CONTEXT;
```

One member of a CONTEXT structure that does not correspond to any CPU registers is *ContextFlags*. This member exists in all CONTEXT structure definitions regardless of the CPU architecture. The *ContextFlags* member indicates to the *GetThreadContext* function which registers you are interested in retrieving. For example, if you wanted to get the control registers for a thread, you would write something like this:

```
// Create a CONTEXT structure.
CONTEXT Context;

// Tell the system that we are interested in only the
// control registers.
Context.ContextFlags = CONTEXT_CONTROL;

// Tell the system to get the registers associated with a thread.
GetThreadContext(hThread, &Context);

// The control register members in the CONTEXT structure
// reflect the thread's control registers. The other members
// are undefined.
```

Notice that you must first initialize the *ContextFlags* member in the CONTEXT structure prior to calling *GetThreadContext*. If you want to get a thread's control and integer registers, you should initialize *ContextFlags* as follows:

```
// Tell the system that we are interested
// in the control and integer registers.
Context.ContextFlags = CONTEXT_CONTROL | CONTEXT_INTEGER;
```

There is also an identifier that you can use to get all of the thread's important registers (that is, the ones Microsoft deems to be most commonly used):

```
// Tell the system we are interested
// in the important registers.
Context.ContextFlags = CONTEXT_FULL;
```

CONTEXT_FULL is defined in WINNT.H as shown in the following table:

CPU Type	Definition of CONTEXT_FULL
*x*86	CONTEXT_CONTROL | CONTEXT_INTEGER | CONTEXT_SEGMENTS
MIPS	CONTEXT_CONTROL | CONTEXT_FLOATING_POINT | CONTEXT_INTEGER | CONTEXT_EXTENDED_INTEGER
Alpha	CONTEXT_CONTROL | CONTEXT_FLOATING_POINT | CONTEXT_INTEGER
PowerPC	CONTEXT_CONTROL | CONTEXT_FLOATING_POINT | CONTEXT_INTEGER

When *GetThreadContext* returns, you can easily examine any of the thread's register values, but remember this means writing code that is CPU-dependent. The following table lists the instruction pointer and stack pointer members of a CONTEXT structure according to the CPU type:

CPU Type	Instruction Pointer	Stack Pointer
*x*86	CONTEXT.Eip	CONTEXT.Esp
MIPS	CONTEXT.Fir	CONTEXT.IntSp
Alpha	CONTEXT.Fir	CONTEXT.IntSp
PowerPC	CONTEXT.Iar	CONTEXT.Gpr1

Important

On the PowerPC, the stack pointer register, Gpr1, is part of the integer registers, not the control registers. So for the PowerPC, you must set the *ContextFlags* member of the CONTEXT structure to CONTEXT_INTEGER instead of CONTEXT_CONTROL.

It's also possible to modify any of the members in the CONTEXT structure. Of course, changing any member in the CONTEXT structure does not change the registers associated with the thread. After you do change some of the members in the CONTEXT structure, you could call *SetThreadContext* to set the register values of the specified thread to reflect the values of CONTEXT's members.

```
BOOL SetThreadContext(HANDLE hThread, CONST CONTEXT *lpContext);
```

Before calling *SetThreadContext,* you must initialize the *ContextFlags* member of CONTEXT again, as shown here:

```
CONTEXT Context;

// Stop the thread from running.
SuspendThread(hThread);

// Get the thread's context registers.
Context.ContextFlags = CONTEXT_CONTROL;
GetThreadContext(hThread, &Context);

// Make the instruction pointer point to the address of your choice.
// Here I've arbitrarily set the address instruction pointer to
// 0x00010000.
#if defined(_ALPHA_)
Context.Fir = 0x00010000;
#elif defined(_MIPS_)
Context.Fir = 0x00010000;
#elif defined(_X86_)
Context.Eip = 0x00010000;
#elif defined(_PPC_)
Context.Iar = 0x00010000;
#else
#error Module contains CPU-specific code; modify and recompile.
#endif


// Set the thread's registers to reflect the changed values.
// It's not really necessary to reset the ControlFlags member
// because it was set earlier.
Context.ControlFlags = CONTEXT_CONTROL;
SetThreadContext(hThread, &Context);

// Resuming the thread will cause it to begin execution
// at address 0x00010000.
ResumeThread(hThread);
```

VirtualQueryEx and *VirtualProtectEx*

The *VirtualQueryEx* function returns information about a process's address space:

```
DWORD VirtualQueryEx(HANDLE hProcess, LPCVOID lpvAddress,
    PMEMORY_BASIC_INFORMATION pmbiBuffer, DWORD cbLength);
```

This function is very similar to the *VirtualQuery* function discussed in Chapter 7 except that *VirtualQueryEx* has one additional parameter, *hProcess*. This parameter allows you to select a process whose address space you wish to query.

The *VirtualProtectEx* function allows a thread in one process to alter the protection attributes on pages of physical storage that are used by another process:

```
BOOL VirtualProtectEx(HANDLE hProcess, LPVOID lpvAddress,
    DWORD cbSize, DWORD fdwNewProtect, LPDWORD pfdwOldProtect);
```

This function is very similar to the *VirtualProtect* function discussed in Chapter 7. Again, the only difference is that the *VirtualProtectEx* function has one additional parameter, *hProcess*.

VirtualAllocEx and VirtualFreeEx

The *VirtualAllocEx* and *VirtualFreeEx* functions were added in Windows NT 4. Like the previous two *Ex* functions, these functions allow one process to reserve address space and/or commit storage in another process using *VirtualAllocEx*:

```
LPVOID VirtualAllocEx(HANDLE hProcess, LPVOID lpAddress,
    DWORD dwSize, DWORD flAllocationType, DWORD flProtect);
```

or to decommit storage and/or release address space using *VirtualFreeEx*:

```
BOOL VirtualFreeEx(HANDLE hProcess, LPVOID lpAddress,
    DWORD dwSize, DWORD dwFreeType);
```

Both these functions are similar to their non-*Ex* versions, which are discussed in Chapter 7. The difference is that these two functions require a handle to a process as their first argument. This handle indicates the process where the operation is to be performed.

ReadProcessMemory and WriteProcessMemory

The *ReadProcessMemory* and *WriteProcessMemory* functions allow a thread to copy data from its process's address space to another process's address space and vice versa.

```
BOOL ReadProcessMemory (HANDLE hProcess, LPVOID lpBaseAddress,
    LPVOID lpBuffer, DWORD cbRead, LPDWORD lpNumberOfBytesRead);
```

```
BOOL WriteProcessMemory (HANDLE hProcess, LPVOID lpBaseAddress,
    LPVOID lpBuffer, DWORD cbWrite, LPDWORD lpNumberOfBytesWritten);
```

The remote process is identified by the *hProcess* parameter. The *lp-BaseAddress* parameter is the base address of memory in the remote process, *lpBuffer* is the base address of memory in the local process, *cbRead* and *cbWrite* are the requested number of bytes to transfer, and *lpNumberOfBytesRead* and *lpNumberOfBytesWritten* are filled on return with the number of bytes actually transferred.

Creating a Function to Inject a DLL into Any Process's Address Space

Now I'm ready (finally) to discuss the third method of injecting a DLL into another process. Up to this point, one problem has remained unsolved: a call to the *LoadLibrary* function causes the system to map the specified DLL into the address space of the process that owns the calling thread, when what you need to do is to force a thread in another process to call *LoadLibrary* for you.

Solving this problem was certainly a learning experience for me. My code went through a series of major revisions before I got to the final result, which you see in Figure 18-5 later in this chapter. I will not show the results of all the attempts, but I will try to explain how I was led to the final result, a function I named *InjectLib*.

Version 0: Why the Obvious Method Just Doesn't Work

On the surface, the simple solution to this problem seems to be the following:

```
HANDLE hProcessRemote;
DWORD dwThreadId;
HINSTANCE hinstKrnl = GetModuleHandle(__TEXT("Kernel32"));

CreateRemoteThread(hProcessRemote, NULL, 0,
   (LPTHREAD_START_ROUTINE)
      GetProcAddress(hinstKrnl, "LoadLibraryA"),
      "C:\\MYLIB.DLL", 0, &dwThreadId);
```

This call to *CreateRemoteThread* doesn't work the way you'd think, but let's first reexamine what I am trying to do here. I am trying to create a thread in the remote process. This thread should begin execution by calling *LoadLibraryA*. Fortunately, *LoadLibraryA* takes a single 32-bit parameter that is an address to an ANSI string identifying the DLL to be loaded. When *LoadLibraryA* is called to map a DLL into a process's address space, the DLL is mapped into the process that owns the thread that is calling *LoadLibraryA*. After *LoadLibraryA* loads the DLL, it should return to the *StartOfThread* function, and the thread then exits. Of course, MYLIB.DLL would forever be mapped into the remote process's address space because its lock count would never be decremented, but let's just take this problem one step at a time.

Can you see why the call above doesn't work? It's because the string "C:\\MYLIB.DLL" is in the calling process's address space. You are passing this string's address (in the local address space) to the remote thread. When *LoadLibraryA* is called by the remote thread, *LoadLibraryA* is going to think that the address identifies a string in its own address space and will try to process whatever is at that address. Most likely this will cause an access violation in the remote thread; the unhandled exception message box will be presented to the user, and the remote process will be terminated. That's right, the remote process will be terminated—not your process. You will have successfully crashed another process while yours continues to execute just fine!

What you really need to do now is somehow copy the string identifying the DLL into the address space of the remote process. So where do you copy this string to? This question will be answered as I progress.

You may be wondering why I bothered to get the address of *Load-LibraryA* by calling *GetProcAddress* instead of calling *CreateRemoteThread* like this:

```
CreateRemoteThread(hProcessRemote, NULL, 0, LoadLibraryA,
    "C:\\MYLIB.DLL", 0, &dwThreadId);
```

The reason is quite subtle. When you compile and link a Win32-based program, the resulting binary contains a jump table. This table consists of a series of thunks to imported functions. So when your code calls a function such as *LoadLibraryA*, the linker generates a call to a thunk in your EXE's or your DLL's jump table. The jump table in turn makes a jump to the actual function. The linker does this to reduce the load time of your EXE or DLL and to save on memory.

If you used a direct reference to *LoadLibraryA* in the call to *CreateRemoteThread*, this would resolve to the address of the *LoadLibraryA* thunk in your jump table. Passing the address of the thunk as the starting address of the remote thread would cause the remote thread to begin executing who-knows-what. Again, the result most likely would be an access violation. To force a direct call to the *LoadLibraryA* function, bypassing the jump table, you need to get the exact location of *Load-LibraryA* by calling *GetProcAddress*.

The call to *CreateRemoteThread* assumes that KERNEL32.DLL is mapped to the same memory location in both the local and the remote processes' address spaces. Every application requires KERNEL32.DLL, and in my experience the system maps KERNEL32.DLL to the same address in every process. I can't think of a situation in which this isn't true. In fact, if you compile, link, and run the program

```
void __cdecl main (void) {
}
```

and then run PVIEW.EXE, you'll see that even this teeny-tiny program requires that NTDLL.DLL and KERNEL32.DLL be mapped into the process's address space.

Version 1: Hand-Coded Machine Language

The very first version of the *InjectLib* function that I actually implemented went like this. First I created a thread in the remote process by calling *CreateRemoteThread*:

```
hThread = CreateRemoteThread(hProcess, NULL, 1024, 0x00000000,
   NULL, CREATE_SUSPENDED, &dwThreadId);
```

This is a pretty bizarre way to create a thread, because the address of the thread function is 0x00000000. This is sure to guarantee an access violation as soon as the thread starts running. However, note that I also specified the CREATE_SUSPENDED flag. This means that the thread will have an initial suspend count of 1 and will therefore not be scheduled any CPU time.

Next I had to locate the new thread's stack. I did this by calling *GetThreadContext* and examining the address contained in the stack pointer register.

From this address, I used *WriteProcessMemory* to copy the name of the DLL to the remote thread's stack. I then created a buffer in my own process's address space in which I placed hand-coded Intel *x*86 machine language to do the following:

```
mov     eax, <address of DLL pathname on stack>
push    eax             ; Push address of DLL's pathname
                        ; on the stack.
call    LoadLibraryA    ; Call LoadLibraryA function.
push    eax             ; Save the DLL's hinstDll
                        ; (returned in EAX) on the stack.
push    eax             ; Save the DLL's hinstDll again.
call    FreeLibrary     ; The DLL's hinstDll is on the stack
                        ; for this call.
call    ExitThread      ; Force the thread to terminate.
                        ; (DLL's hinstDll is the exit code.)
```

935

That's right, I looked up the machine language instructions for each of the assembly-language instructions above and filled this buffer with these instructions. Then I again called *WriteProcessMemory* to write this code to the remote thread's stack. I wrote this code just below the DLL's pathname.

Next I changed the remote thread's context structure so that the stack pointer pointed to the memory below the hand-coded machine language, and I changed the instruction pointer so that it pointed to the first byte of the hand-coded machine language. (See Figure 18-3.) I then called *SetThreadContext* to put the new values in the remote thread's registers.

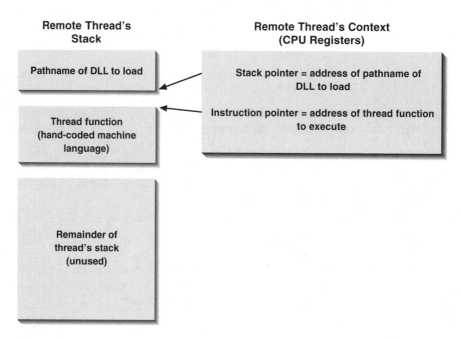

Figure 18-3.
The CPU registers of a remote thread pointing to the contents of another remote thread's stack.

Now I was all ready to go. All I had to do was call *ResumeThread*, and the remote thread would start executing my hand-coded machine language instructions, load the DLL, free the DLL, and exit the thread.

There are a number of points to discuss about this method. First, I needed to call *ExitThread* myself because I changed the instruction pointer. Remember that a thread's instruction pointer is initialized to point to the *StartOfThread* function. (See page 77 in Chapter 4 for a discussion of the *StartOfThread* function.) A side effect of my changing the instruction pointer was that the *StartOfThread* function would never execute. Normally, *StartOfThread* calls the thread function, but because I changed the instruction pointer register, *StartOfThread* did not call my thread function. Therefore, I couldn't put an Intel *x*86 RET instruction at the end of my code—the CPU would not know where to return. So, to make the remote thread terminate cleanly, I had to call *ExitThread* explicitly.

Second, if the library does not initialize properly, *LoadLibraryA* returns NULL to me. At this point, my code would push NULL on the stack and call *FreeLibrary*. This is probably not the best thing it could do. It would be better to compare the EAX register with zero and call *FreeLibrary* only if EAX is nonzero. I didn't put this check in the code because I didn't want to figure out what the hand-coded machine language for these additional instructions would be. Instead, I thought that the *FreeLibrary* function would figure out that I was passing an invalid *hinstDll* value and would just return FALSE, indicating that the call was bad.

Third, skipping the execution of the *StartOfThread* function means that a default structured exception handling (SEH) frame is not set up properly for this thread. This is a problem only if the thread's code causes an exception to be raised. At first, you might not think that this problem is very serious. After all, what could possibly go wrong with a call to *LoadLibraryA*, a call to *FreeLibrary*, and a call to *ExitThread*? Well, as you may remember from Chapter 12, this thread is also responsible for executing the library's *DllMain* function with an *fdwReason* value of DLL_PROCESS_ATTACH and an *fdwReason* value of DLL_PROCESS_DETACH. If any of this code raises an unhandled exception, the system terminates the process on the spot without a message box or any notification to the end user whatsoever. Again, I could have written additional hand-coded machine language instructions to create an SEH frame, but this would have been *very* difficult. The implementation of SEH varies dramatically among given CPU architectures and is extremely complicated.

Finally, as you can see, the biggest problem with this whole approach is the hand-coded assembly language. As it is, I have already copped out on adding features or correcting potential problems because I didn't feel like figuring out the additional instructions. But I needed to redo all this work for each CPU platform. I did, in fact, go ahead and do this for the MIPS platform and was starting to do it for the

Alpha when a friend suggested that there might be a way to write this code so that it was CPU-independent.

I have to admit that my friend and I were both skeptical at first, but we started tossing ideas around, and then we started typing up some of our ideas in Notepad. When it actually started to seem like there might be a way to do it, I started modifying my code (after making a backup of the original, of course). Several hours later (around 2:00 A.M.), we had something working on the Intel and MIPS platforms—which takes us to version 2.

Version 2: *AllocProcessMemory* and *CreateRemoteThread*

Eventually I wound up with a method that works something like this:

1. Allocate memory space in the remote process's address space.

2. Copy the code of a function from your process's address space to the remote process's address space. I will discuss this in detail later in this chapter.

3. Copy an INJLIBINFO data structure containing the DLL's pathname and other important data to the remote process's address space.

4. Call *CreateRemoteThread*, passing the remote address of the copied function as the *lpStartAddr* parameter and the remote address of the INJLIBINFO structure as the *lpvThreadParm* parameter.

5. Wait for the remote thread to exit.

6. Free the memory allocated in step 1.

Now let's look into each of these steps in more detail. Let's begin with how to allocate and free memory in another process's address space.

When I first started to look for a way to allocate memory in a remote process, I looked feverishly for the two Win32 functions *Virtual-AllocEx* and *VirtualFreeEx*. I knew that the Win32 API has a *VirtualQueryEx* function that allows a thread in one process to examine the state of memory owned by another process and a *VirtualProtectEx* function that allows a thread in one process to change the page protection of memory owned by another process. Given these two functions, I was sure that I would find *VirtualAllocEx* and *VirtualFreeEx* functions as well. But I was wrong! It seemed awfully strange to me that *VirtualAllocEx* and *Virtual-*

FreeEx functions didn't exist at that time. There just had to be another way to allocate memory in another process's address space! Then I remembered that when I create a thread, the system allocates memory for the thread's stack—eureka! If I create a remote thread, the stack is allocated in the remote process's address space.

Important

In Windows NT 4, Microsoft added the *VirtualAllocEx* and *VirtualFreeEx* functions to the Win32 API, making DLL injection much simpler. However, for those of you that want to use this technique on Windows NT 3.51 or earlier, I'll explain what I had to do to simulate *VirtualAllocEx* and *VirtualFreeEx*. If you can require Windows NT 4 or later, delete my *Alloc-ProcessMemory* and *FreeProcessMemory* functions (described below) and replace calls to these functions with calls to *VirtualAllocEx* and *VirtualFreeEx*, respectively.

After I came to this realization, the implementation of functions to allocate and free memory in a remote process's address space was pretty straightforward. The result is shown in the PROCMEM.C file. (See Figure 18-4 beginning on page 943.) This file contains two functions, *Alloc-ProcessMemory* and *FreeProcessMemory*.

Let's look at *AllocProcessMemory* first:

```
PVOID AllocProcessMemory (HANDLE hProcess, DWORD dwNumBytes);
```

As its name implies, this function allocates memory in another process's address space. The *hProcess* parameter identifies the process in whose address space memory should be allocated, and the *dwNumBytes* parameter indicates the number of bytes to allocate. The function returns the address where the memory was allocated in the remote process; if the memory could not be allocated, the function returns NULL.

Here is how the function works. First I call *CreateRemoteThread* as follows:

```
HINSTANCE hinstKrnl = GetModuleHandle(__TEXT("Kernel32"));
    :
    :
hThread = CreateRemoteThread(hProcess, NULL,
    dwNumBytes + sizeof(HANDLE),
    (LPTHREAD_START_ROUTINE)GetProcAddress(hinstKrnl, "ExitThread"),
    0, CREATE_SUSPENDED, &dwThreadId);
```

You know that creating a thread causes the system to allocate a stack for the thread. So for the third parameter to *CreateRemoteThread*, I pass the number of bytes to commit for the thread's stack. This value is the number of bytes passed to *AllocProcessMemory* plus the size of a HANDLE. For reasons you'll see later, I need a place to save the thread handle; I chose to save it at the beginning of the allocated memory block.

I tell the system that the thread should start executing at the address where the *ExitThread* function resides. As soon as the thread starts executing, it immediately invokes *ExitThread*, passing it a parameter value of 0. This, of course, causes the thread to terminate immediately and the system to free the thread's stack. But I need the thread's stack to hang around for awhile, so I pass the CREATE_SUSPENDED flag to *CreateRemoteThread*. This flag tells the system not to let the thread execute—the CPU registers and the stack for the thread are initialized, but the thread is not scheduled any CPU time. After the system creates the remote thread, the thread's ID is placed in the *dwThreadId* variable and the handle to the thread is returned.

But why do I need to call *ExitThread* at all? It would be nice to create the remote thread as follows:

```
hThread = CreateRemoteThread(hProcess, NULL,
   dwNumBytes + sizeof(HANDLE),
   0x00000000, 0, CREATE_SUSPENDED, &dwThreadId);
```

This specifies that the remote thread should start executing at address 0x00000000, which would certainly cause a memory access violation if the thread resumed execution. However, I don't ever need to resume the thread. When the time comes to free the memory block, I could just make the following call:

```
TerminateThread(hThread, 0);
```

TerminateThread forces the system to terminate the thread. Unfortunately, *TerminateThread* does not cause the thread's stack to be freed. (See the discussion of the *TerminateThread* function on page 87 in Chapter 4.) *ExitThread*, however, does free a thread's stack. So to ensure that the memory allocated in the remote process is freed, the remote thread calls *ExitThread* when it is resumed.

Now, after creating the remote thread, I need to determine where in the remote process's address space the stack is located. This is done as shown here:

```
CONTEXT Context;
:
:

Context.ContextFlags = CONTEXT_CONTROL | CONTEXT_INTEGER;
GetThreadContext(hThread, &Context);

// Address of top of stack is in stack pointer register
```

GetThreadContext retrieves the CPU registers for the specified thread—in this case, the remote thread. The CONTEXT structure contains a stack pointer register that is initialized by the system when the thread is created and that contains the 32-bit memory address at the top of the stack. Actually, this address is 4 bytes above the top of the stack. When a function pushes something onto the stack, the CPU first decrements the stack pointer by 4 bytes and then puts the new data on the stack. You have to subtract 4 bytes (or the size of a 32-bit value) from the stack pointer address to get the address of the last 32-bit value on the stack.

The stack pointer's register name varies among CPUs, so I created a macro, STACKPTR, that abstracts the stack pointer's register name based on the CPU type. This is the only CPU-dependent portion of my code:

```
#if defined(_X86_)
#define STACKPTR(Context)   ((Context).Esp)
#endif

#if defined(_MIPS_)
#define STACKPTR(Context)   ((Context).IntSp)
#endif

#if defined(_ALPHA_)
#define STACKPTR(Context)   ((Context).IntSp)
#endif

if defined(_PPC_)
#define STACKPTR(Context)   ((Context).Gpr1)
#endif

#if !defined(STACKPTR)
#error Module contains CPU specific code; modify and recompile.
#endif
```

Notice that at the end I check to see if STACKPTR is defined. If it is not, I force the compilation to halt by taking advantage of the preprocessor's *#error* directive. If, in the future, this code is compiled for another CPU architecture, it will have to be modified to abstract the new architecture's stack pointer register.

After I have the address of the top of the stack, I call *VirtualQueryEx*:

```
MEMORY_BASIC_INFORMATION mbi;
LPVOID pvMem;
:
:

VirtualQueryEx(hProcess, (PDWORD) STACKPTR(Context) - 1,
    &mbi, sizeof(mbi));
pvMem = (PVOID) mbi.BaseAddress;
```

As mentioned earlier, this function looks into the address space of another process and fills a **MEMORY_BASIC_INFORMATION** structure with data describing the nature of the memory. I am interested in the *BaseAddress* member of this structure. This member gives the memory address at the bottom of the stack's committed memory—this is the address of my allocated memory block.

At this point, I have the remote memory address to return to the caller. However, if I want to free the allocated memory later by calling *ResumeThread*, I must save the handle of the remote thread somewhere. I could have forced the caller to pass *AllocProcessMemory* the address of a HANDLE variable that I could fill before returning, but I didn't like this method for two reasons. One, the caller would need to know too much of my internal implementation of this function. Two, the caller would be responsible for maintaining this handle and passing the correct handle back to me when calling *FreeProcessMemory*.

Instead, I decided to save the thread's handle at the bottom of the newly allocated memory block in the remote process's address space. To do this, I write the thread's handle there by calling *WriteProcessMemory*.

```
fOk = WriteProcessMemory(hProcess, pvMem, &hThread,
    sizeof(hThread), &dwNumBytesXferred);
```

Next, I increment the pointer to the block by the size of a thread handle and return this address to the caller:

```
pvMem = (PVOID) ((PHANDLE) pvMem + 1);
return(pvMem);
```

Freeing the memory is much simpler. When the local thread wants to free the remote memory, it calls *FreeProcessMemory*:

```
BOOL FreeProcessMemory (HANDLE hProcess, PVOID pvMem);
```

and passes the remote process's handle and the memory address that was returned by the previous call to *AllocProcessMemory*. The first thing that *FreeProcessMemory* must do is get the handle to the remote thread.

AllocProcessMemory stored this handle in the first 4 bytes of the allocated memory. To get it back, you must subtract the size of a thread handle from the memory address and call *ReadProcessMemory*:

```
pvMem = (PVOID) ((PHANDLE) pvMem - 1);
fOk = ReadProcessMemory(hProcess, pvMem, &hThread,
    sizeof(hThread), &dwNumBytesXferred);
```

Now all you have to do is allow the thread to begin executing. This is done by calling *ResumeThread*.

```
ResumeThread(hThread);
CloseHandle(hThread);
```

When the thread starts executing, it will immediately call *Exit-Thread*; the thread will stop running and the system will destroy the thread's stack. Also, the local thread must call *CloseHandle* so that you don't accidentally accumulate another thread handle in your process whenever a call to *AllocProcessMemory* is made.

The ProcMem Utility Functions

The *AllocProcessMemory* and *FreeProcessMemory* functions allocate and free memory in another process's address space. The code for these functions is contained in PROCMEM.C, listed in Figure 18-4. Any code that uses the functions should, of course, include the PROCMEM.H header file, also listed in Figure 18-4. These source code files are in the TINJLIB directory on the companion disc. If you are targeting Windows NT 4 or later, you can completely ignore the PROCMEM.C and PROCMEM.H files and simply call the *VirtualAllocEx* and *VirtualFreeEx* functions instead.

```
PROCMEM.C
/*******************************************************************
Module name: ProcMem.C
Notices: Copyright (c) 1995-1997 Jeffrey Richter
*******************************************************************/


include "..\CmnHdr.H"                    /* See Appendix C. */
#include <windows.h>
#include "ProcMem.H"
```

Figure 18-4.   *(continued)*
The ProcMem utility functions.

Figure 18-4. *continued*

```
//////////////////////////////////////////////////////////////


#if defined(_X86_)
#define STACKPTR(Context)   ((Context).Esp)
#endif

#if defined(_MIPS_)
#define STACKPTR(Context)   ((Context).IntSp)
#endif

#if defined(_ALPHA_)
#define STACKPTR(Context)   ((Context).IntSp)
#endif

#if defined(_PPC_)
#define STACKPTR(Context)   ((Context).Gpr1)
#endif

#if !defined(STACKPTR)
#error Module contains CPU-specific code; modify and recompile.
#endif


//////////////////////////////////////////////////////////////


PVOID AllocProcessMemory (HANDLE hProcess, DWORD dwNumBytes) {
   CONTEXT Context;
   DWORD dwThreadId, dwNumBytesXferred, dwError;
   HANDLE hThread;
   HINSTANCE hinstKrnl = GetModuleHandle(__TEXT("Kernel32"));
   PVOID pvMem = NULL;
   MEMORY_BASIC_INFORMATION mbi;
   BOOL fOk = FALSE;     // Assume failure.

   __try {
      hThread = CreateRemoteThread(
         hProcess,
         NULL,              // Default security
         dwNumBytes + sizeof(HANDLE),
                            // Amount of memory to allocate in
                            // the remote process plus 4 bytes
                            // for a thread handle
```

(continued)

Figure 18-4. *continued*

```
        (LPTHREAD_START_ROUTINE)
          GetProcAddress(hinstKrnl, "ExitThread"),
                          // Address of function where thread
                          // should begin execution. We pass the
                          // address of ExitThread so that the
                          // stack will be destroyed.
          0,              // Parameter passed to thread function.
                          // This will be passed to ExitThread.
          CREATE_SUSPENDED, // Flags. We must create the thread
                          // suspended so that the thread
                          // doesn't terminate before we use
                          // the allocated memory.
          &dwThreadId);   // ID of the new thread

      if (hThread == NULL) {
         dwError = GetLastError();  // For debugging
         __leave;
      }

      Context.ContextFlags = CONTEXT_CONTROL | CONTEXT_INTEGER;
      if (!GetThreadContext(hThread, &Context))
         __leave;

      // Determine the bottom address of the committed memory.
      if (sizeof(mbi) != VirtualQueryEx(hProcess,
         (PDWORD) STACKPTR(Context) - 1, &mbi, sizeof(mbi)))
         __leave;

      // Store the remote thread's handle in the bottommost
      // bytes of the allocated memory.
      pvMem = (PVOID) mbi.BaseAddress;

      fOk = WriteProcessMemory(hProcess, pvMem, &hThread,
         sizeof(hThread), &dwNumBytesXferred);

      if (!fOk)
         __leave;

      // Point past the thread's handle.
      pvMem = (PVOID) ((PHANDLE) pvMem + 1);
   }
   __finally {
      if (!fOk) {
         if (hThread) {
```

(continued)

Figure 18-4. *continued*

```
            ResumeThread(hThread);
            CloseHandle(hThread);
         }
         pvMem = NULL;
      }
   }

   return(pvMem);
}


//////////////////////////////////////////////////////////////////


BOOL FreeProcessMemory (HANDLE hProcess, PVOID pvMem) {
   BOOL fOk;
   HANDLE hThread;
   DWORD dwNumBytesXferred;


   // Get the handle of the remote thread from the block of
   // memory.
   pvMem = (PVOID) ((PHANDLE) pvMem - 1);

   fOk = ReadProcessMemory(hProcess, pvMem, &hThread,
      sizeof(hThread), &dwNumBytesXferred);
   if (fOk) {
      if (ResumeThread(hThread) == 0xffffffff) {
         // Resume failed, probably because the application
         // overwrote the memory containing the handle.
         fOk = FALSE;
      }
      CloseHandle(hThread);
   }

   return(fOk);
}


//////////////////////// End Of File ////////////////////////
```

(continued)

Figure 18-4. *continued*

```
PROCMEM.H
/****************************************************************
Module name: ProcMem.H
Notices: Written 1995 Jeffrey Richter
****************************************************************/


PVOID AllocProcessMemory (HANDLE hProcess, DWORD dwNumBytes);
BOOL  FreeProcessMemory (HANDLE hProcess, PVOID pvMem);


//////////////////////////// End Of File ////////////////////////////
```

The *InjectLib* Function

The *InjectLib* function, listed in Figure 18-5 beginning on page 953, shows how I injected a DLL into another process's address space. The source code files are in the TINJLIB directory on the companion disc. First I'll discuss how I determine the amount of memory I need to allocate in the remote process's address space. After I allocate the memory, I "squirt" the *ThreadFunc* function and INJLIBINFO structure into this memory block and start the function executing.

When *ThreadFunc* runs in the remote process, it calls *LoadLibrary* to inject the function. The secret to creating a CPU-independent version of *ThreadFunc* is to write the function using a high-level language (C in this case) and let the compiler generate the machine-language code for the whole function. You can then copy the function from your address space to the remote process's address space and let the function execute. Regardless of the CPU type, the compiler will generate the proper machine language for this function.

When I was designing the *ThreadFunc* function, I had to keep in mind that in the local process's address space the function is located at one memory address, but that when the function is copied to the remote process's address space, it almost definitely is not copied to the same address. This means that I had to design the function to contain no references to anything outside of itself! This is very difficult.

More specifically, the function could not contain any references to global or static variables because the references would be to exact memory locations, and the data variables would not exist in the remote process's address space. *ThreadFunc* also couldn't contain any direct references or calls to other functions. The compiler and linker optimize these calls to call thunks in the jump table, which would not be in the remote process.

The function also could not use more than a page's worth of local variables. Whenever the compiler sees that the amount of memory required by a single function's local variables is more than a page, the compiler generates a hidden call to the C run-time library's stack checking function. This call to the stack checking function is a direct reference to another function that would cause the remote thread to raise an exception when it was allowed to execute.

Even with all these prohibitions, you can still access the stack. So I put a pointer on the stack that points to an INJLIBINFO data structure containing all the information needed by *ThreadFunc*. The data structure contains three members:

```
typedef HINSTANCE (WINAPI *PROCLOADLIBRARY)(LPBYTE);
typedef BOOL (WINAPI *PROCFREELIBRARY)(HINSTANCE);

typedef struct {
    PROCLOADLIBRARY fnLoadLibrary;
    PROCFREELIBRARY fnFreeLibrary;
    BYTE pbLibFile[MAX_PATH * sizeof(WCHAR)];
} INJLIBINFO, *PINJLIBINFO;
```

The first member, *fnLoadLibrary*, holds the absolute address of either the *LoadLibraryA* or the *LoadLibraryW* function, depending on whether the *pbLibFile* member contains an ANSI or a Unicode string. The second member, *fnFreeLibrary*, contains the absolute address of the *FreeLibrary* function. The last member, *pbLibFile*, contains either the ANSI or the Unicode version of the pathname for the DLL to be loaded.

When the remote thread executes *ThreadFunc*, *ThreadFunc* is passed the address to this data structure; the address was copied into the memory allocated by the earlier call to *AllocProcessMemory*. *ThreadFunc* simply calls one of the *LoadLibrary* functions:

```
HINSTANCE hinstDll;
hinstDll = pInjLibInfo->fnLoadLibrary(pInjLibInfo->pbLibFile);
```

Remember, this call will not return until the library's *DllMain* function has processed its DLL_PROCESS_ATTACH notification. When the call does return, the HINSTANCE of the DLL is saved in the local variable, *hinstDll*. Then, after the library has loaded and successfully initialized, *ThreadFunc* calls *FreeLibrary*:

```
if (hinstDll != NULL) {
    pInjLibInfo->fnFreeLibrary(hinstDll);
}
```

The call to *FreeLibrary* will not return until the library's *DllMain* function has finished processing its DLL_PROCESS_DETACH notification.

Finally, *ThreadFunc* returns the HINSTANCE of the loaded DLL. (NULL is returned if the DLL failed to load successfully.) This return value becomes the exit code for this thread. As long as another thread in the system has a handle to this remote thread, the remote thread's thread kernel object remains in the system, and *GetExitCodeThread* can be called to retrieve the thread's exit code. This way, the thread running in the local process can determine whether the DLL loaded successfully.

You should notice two advantages of *ThreadFunc* over version 1's thread function. As mentioned earlier, the biggest advantage is that there is no hand-coded machine language. The second is that the remote *ThreadFunc* function is called by the *StartOfThread* function. This means that *ThreadFunc* can simply return when it is finished, rather than having to call *ExitThread*, and that the default structured exception handling frame is set up and ready to capture unhandled exceptions.

InjectLib, *InjectLibA*, *InjectLibW*, and *InjectLibWorA*

Now let's look at the function responsible for injecting the *ThreadFunc* function into the remote process's address space. Because I wanted to supply a complete library function, I created this function to have full ANSI and Unicode entry points. This means that there are two functions—one for ANSI (*InjectLibA*) and one for Unicode (*InjectLibW*)—as well as a macro, *InjectLib*, that expands to one of these two functions depending on whether UNICODE is defined during compilation.

```
BOOL InjectLibA (HANDLE hProcess, LPCSTR lpszLibFile);
BOOL InjectLibW (HANDLE hProcess, LPCWSTR lpszLibFile);

#ifdef UNICODE
#define InjectLib InjectLibW
#else
#define InjectLib InjectLibA
#endif // !UNICODE
```

The two function prototypes and the macro are defined in the INJLIB.H file. (See Figure 18-5.)

Both *InjectLibA* and *InjectLibW* are one-line stub functions that simply call the real workhorse function, *InjectLibWorA*. *InjectLibWorA* is a static function that cannot be called from any code outside the INJLIB.C file. (See Figure 18-5.) When the stub functions call *InjectLibWorA*, they pass the information at the top of the next page.

- The handle of the process in which the library is to be injected.

- The address to the DLL's pathname. This may be either an ANSI string or a Unicode string.

- A Boolean value that indicates what type of string *lpszLibFile* is. TRUE indicates Unicode and FALSE indicates ANSI.

The value returned by *InjectLibWorA* indicates whether the DLL was successfully loaded in the remote process. *InjectLibA* and *InjectLibW* simply return *InjectLibWorA*'s return value back to their callers.

```
BOOL InjectLibA (HANDLE hProcess, LPCSTR lpszLibFile) {
    return(InjectLibWorA(hProcess, (LPBYTE) lpszLibFile, FALSE));
}

BOOL InjectLibW (HANDLE hProcess, LPCWSTR lpszLibFile) {
    return(InjectLibWorA(hProcess, (LPBYTE) lpszLibFile, TRUE));
}
```

So how does *InjectLibWorA* actually inject a DLL into another process's address space? The first step is to create and initialize an INJLIB-INFO data structure:

```
HINSTANCE hinstKrnl = GetModuleHandle(__TEXT("Kernel32"));

INJLIBINFO InjLibInfo;
 :
 :
InjLibInfo.fnLoadLibrary = (PROCLOADLIBRARY)
    GetProcAddress(hinstKrnl,
      (fUnicode ? "LoadLibraryW" : "LoadLibraryA"));
InjLibInfo.fnFreeLibrary = (PROCFREELIBRARY)
    GetProcAddress(hinstKrnl, "FreeLibrary");
InjLibInfo.pbLibFile[0] = 0;  // Initialized later
 :
 :
if (fUnicode)
    wcscpy((LPWSTR) InjLibInfo.pbLibFile, (LPCWSTR) pbLibFile);
else
    strcpy((LPSTR) InjLibInfo.pbLibFile, (LPCSTR) pbLibFile);
```

This structure is eventually copied into the memory allocated within the remote process. The structure is initialized by obtaining the absolute address of the *LoadLibraryA* or *LoadLibraryW* function as well as the *FreeLibrary* function. Then the DLL's pathname is copied from the *pbLibFile* parameter to the *pbLibFile* member of the INJLIBINFO structure.

The code assumes that both the local process and the remote process have KERNEL32.DLL mapped into their respective address spaces and that KERNEL32.DLL is mapped to the same address in both processes. As mentioned earlier, this is actually a very safe bet—I have never seen a situation where this failed to be the case.

Now I need to determine the size of the memory block to allocate in the remote process's address space. This memory block is going to hold a copy of *ThreadFunc* and a copy of INJLIBINFO. The size of *ThreadFunc* is determined by taking its address in memory and subtracting the memory address of the function after it, *AfterThreadFunc*:

```
const int cbCodeSize = ((LPBYTE) (DWORD)
   AfterThreadFunc - (LPBYTE) (DWORD) ThreadFunc);
```

This assumes that the compiler and linker will place the *After-ThreadFunc* function immediately after the *ThreadFunc* function in the resulting object code. For the Intel, MIPS, Alpha, and PowerPC compilers that ship with Visual C++, this is true. However, I've been told than an Alpha compiler (for operating systems other than Windows NT) compiles functions and places them backward in the resulting object file. It's possible that other compilers for Windows NT might come up with a different result when subtracting *ThreadFunc* from *AfterThreadFunc*, which would break this code.

Even if a Windows NT–based compiler did reverse the functions, this problem would be easy to correct. You would simply need to add a function before *ThreadFunc* and call the new function *BeforeThreadFunc*. Then you could compare the address of *BeforeThreadFunc* with the address of *AfterThreadFunc* and subtract the memory address of *ThreadFunc* from the larger function. Of course, it's always possible that some future compiler will reorganize functions in a way I haven't anticipated, although I think this is unlikely.

So now you have the size of the *ThreadFunc* function, but you also need enough memory in the remote process to hold an INJLIBINFO structure:

```
const DWORD cbMemSize = cbCodeSize + sizeof(InjLibInfo) + 3;
```

You'll notice that I added *3* to the memory size above. This is because all structures must start on an even 32-bit boundary. The same is true for code. For example, if the *ThreadFunc* function required 65 bytes, and I put the INJLIBINFO structure immediately after the code, the structure would start at byte 65. As soon as the *ThreadFunc* function attempted to access the structure, the CPU would raise a datatype misalignment exception. For *x*86 architectures, this is not a problem because they automatically correct for misaligned data; but on RISC architectures, this is a really big problem. It wouldn't help to put the INJLIBINFO structure before *ThreadFunc*'s code. In calculating the size of the required memory block, I just assumed that in a worst case situation I'd need to leave at most a 3-byte gap after the code and before the structure.

The memory space is now allocated in the remote process using my *AllocProcessMemory* function.

```
pdwCodeRemote = (PDWORD) AllocProcessMemory(hProcess, cbMemSize);
```

When the system commits stack space for a new thread, the system gives the memory pages of that space the protection of PAGE_READ-WRITE. This means that any attempt to read or write to the memory is OK, but if an attempt is made to execute code on these pages, the CPU raises an exception. This causes a small problem because I'm purposely putting code on the stack so that it can be executed. This problem is solved with a simple call to *VirtualProtectEx*:

```
fOk = VirtualProtectEx(hProcess, pdwCodeRemote, cbMemSize,
    PAGE_EXECUTE_READWRITE, &dwOldProtect);
```

This is the kind of problem that can go unnoticed for a long time. In fact, I figured it out only while writing this text—long after I had finished writing and testing the code on *x*86, MIPS, and Alpha platforms. How'd I manage that? While I was working on the code I must have tested it occasionally, and I should have seen immediately that the remote thread was raising exceptions, right? Well, Win32 supports these different page protections, but the CPU might not. In fact, the *x*86, MIPS, Alpha, and PowerPC CPUs all ignore the execute page protection. With these CPUs, if a page is readable, it's executable. I decided to add this call to *VirtualProtectEx* anyway for aesthetic reasons and because this code is more likely to work on future CPU architectures.

Now it's time to copy the *ThreadFunc* function and the INJLIBINFO structure over to the memory that was allocated in the remote process's address space:

```
fOk = WriteProcessMemory(hProcess, pdwCodeRemote,
    (LPVOID) (DWORD) ThreadFunc, cbCodeSize, &dwNumBytesXferred);

// Force the structure to begin on an even 32-bit boundary.
PINJLIBINFO pInjLibInfoRemote = (PINJLIBINFO)
    (pdwCodeRemote + ((cbCodeSize + 4) & ~3));
```

```
fOk = WriteProcessMemory(hProcess, pInjLibInfoRemote,
    &InjLibInfo, sizeof(InjLibInfo), &dwNumBytesXferred);
```

At this point, everything is initialized in the remote process. The next step is to create a remote thread that will execute the *ThreadFunc* function using the data in the INJLIBINFO structure. Because this thread will execute asynchronously with your local thread, you must put the local thread to sleep until you know that the remote thread has finished loading the DLL and exited:

```
HANDLE hThread = CreateRemoteThread(hProcess, NULL, 0,
    (LPTHREAD_START_ROUTINE) (DWORD) pdwCodeRemote,
    pInjLibInfoRemote, 0, &dwThreadId);

WaitForSingleObject(hThread, INFINITE);
```

After the remote thread has finished executing, you want to get the remote thread's exit code. This exit code is the HINSTANCE of the remotely loaded DLL. If the HINSTANCE is NULL, you know that the DLL did not initialize successfully. *InjectLibWorA* returns FALSE if the HINSTANCE value is NULL; otherwise it returns TRUE. After you have the remote thread's exit code, you no longer need to maintain your handle to the remote thread and you can free the memory allocated in the remote process's address space:

```
GetExitCodeThread(hThread, (PDWORD) &hinstDllRemote);
CloseHandle(hThread);
FreeProcessMemory(hProcess, pdwCodeRemote);

return(hinstDllRemote != NULL);
```

INJLIB.C

```
/***************************************************************
Module name: InjLib.C
Notices: Copyright (c) 1995-1997 Jeffrey Richter
***************************************************************/


#include "..\CmnHdr.H"                    /* See Appendix C. */
#include <windows.h>
#include "ProcMem.H"
#include "InjLib.H"


///////////////////////////////////////////////////////////////
```

Figure 18-5.   *(continued)*
Implementation of the InjectLib *function.*

Figure 18-5. *continued*

```
typedef HINSTANCE (WINAPI *PROCLOADLIBRARY)(LPBYTE);
typedef BOOL (WINAPI *PROCFREELIBRARY)(HINSTANCE);

typedef struct {
   PROCLOADLIBRARY fnLoadLibrary;
   PROCFREELIBRARY fnFreeLibrary;
   BYTE pbLibFile[MAX_PATH * sizeof(WCHAR)];
} INJLIBINFO, *PINJLIBINFO;



///////////////////////////////////////////////////////////////////



// Calls to the stack checking routine must be disabled.
#pragma check_stack (off)

static DWORD WINAPI ThreadFunc (PINJLIBINFO pInjLibInfo) {
   // There must be less than a page worth of local
   // variables used in this function.
   HINSTANCE hinstDll;


   // Call LoadLibrary(A/W) to load the DLL.
   hinstDll = pInjLibInfo->
      fnLoadLibrary(pInjLibInfo->pbLibFile);

   // Calling LoadLibrary causes the system to map the DLL
   // into the remote process's address space and call
   // the DLL's DllMain with an fdwReason value of
   // DLL_PROCESS_ATTACH. The DLL can do whatever it wants
   // during this processing. When DllMain returns, the system
   // returns the HINSTANCE of the DLL back from our call to
   // LoadLibrary.  At this point, we call FreeLibrary,
   // passing the library's HINSTANCE in order to free it.

   // If the DLL could not be loaded or if the library's
   // DllMain (DLL_PROCESS_ATTACH) returns FALSE, hinstDll
   // will come back as NULL.

   // If the library initialized successfully, free it.
   if (hinstDll != NULL) {
      // Calling FreeLibrary causes the system to call the
      // DLL's DllMain with a reason of DLL_PROCESS_DETACH.
      // The DLL can perform whatever cleanup is necessary.
```

(continued)

Figure 18-5. *continued*

```
        pInjLibInfo->fnFreeLibrary(hinstDll);
    }

    // The thread's exit code is the handle of the DLL.
    return((DWORD) hinstDll);
}


///////////////////////////////////////////////////////////////


// This function marks the memory address after ThreadFunc.
// ThreadFuncCodeSizeInBytes =
//    (PBYTE) AfterThreadFunc - (PBYTE) ThreadFunc.
static void AfterThreadFunc (void) {
}
#pragma check_stack


///////////////////////////////////////////////////////////////


static BOOL InjectLibWorA (HANDLE hProcess,
    const BYTE * const pbLibFile, BOOL fUnicode) {

    // Kernel32.DLL's HINSTANCE is used to get the
    // address of LoadLibraryA or LoadLibraryW and
    // FreeLibrary.
    HINSTANCE hinstKrnl = GetModuleHandle(__TEXT("Kernel32"));

    INJLIBINFO InjLibInfo;

    // The address to which code will be copied in the
    // remote process
    PDWORD pdwCodeRemote = NULL;

    // Calculate the number of bytes in the ThreadFunc
    // function.
    const int cbCodeSize = ((LPBYTE)(DWORD)
        AfterThreadFunc - (LPBYTE)(DWORD) ThreadFunc);

    // The address to which INJLIBINFO will be copied in
    // the remote process
    PINJLIBINFO pInjLibInfoRemote = NULL;
```

(continued)

Figure 18-5. *continued*

```
// The number of bytes written to the remote process
DWORD dwNumBytesXferred = 0;

// The handle and ID of the thread executing the
// remote copy of ThreadFunc
DWORD dwThreadId = 0;
const DWORD cbMemSize =
   cbCodeSize + sizeof(InjLibInfo) + 3;
HANDLE hThread = NULL;
HINSTANCE hinstDllRemote = NULL;


BOOL fOk = FALSE;
DWORD dwOldProtect;


// Initialize the INJLIBINFO structure here, and
// then copy it to memory in the remote process.
InjLibInfo.fnLoadLibrary = (PROCLOADLIBRARY)
   GetProcAddress(hinstKrnl,
      (fUnicode ? "LoadLibraryW" : "LoadLibraryA"));
InjLibInfo.fnFreeLibrary = (PROCFREELIBRARY)
   GetProcAddress(hinstKrnl, "FreeLibrary");
InjLibInfo.pbLibFile[0] = 0;   // Initialized later

__try {
   // Finish initializing the INJLIBINFO structure
   // by copying the desired DLL's pathname.
   if (fUnicode)
      wcscpy((LPWSTR) InjLibInfo.pbLibFile,
         (LPCWSTR) pbLibFile);
   else
      strcpy((LPSTR) InjLibInfo.pbLibFile,
         (LPCSTR) pbLibFile);

   // Allocate enough memory in the remote process's
   // address space to hold our ThreadFunc function
   // and an INJLIBINFO structure.
   pdwCodeRemote = (PDWORD)
      AllocProcessMemory(hProcess, cbMemSize);

   if (pdwCodeRemote == NULL)
      __leave;

   // Change the page protection of the allocated memory
   // to executable, read, and write.
```

(continued)

Figure 18-5. *continued*

```
      fOk = VirtualProtectEx(hProcess, pdwCodeRemote,
         cbMemSize, PAGE_EXECUTE_READWRITE, &dwOldProtect);
      if (!fOk)
         __leave;

      // Write a copy of ThreadFunc to the remote process.
      fOk = WriteProcessMemory(hProcess, pdwCodeRemote,
         (LPVOID)(DWORD) ThreadFunc, cbCodeSize,
         &dwNumBytesXferred);
      if (!fOk)
         __leave;



      // Write a copy of INJLIBINFO to the remote process.
      // (The structure MUST start on an even 32-bit boundary.)
      pInjLibInfoRemote = (PINJLIBINFO)
         ((PBYTE) pdwCodeRemote + ((cbCodeSize + 4) & ~3));

      // Put InjLibInfo in the remote thread's memory block.
      fOk = WriteProcessMemory(hProcess, pInjLibInfoRemote,
         &InjLibInfo, sizeof(InjLibInfo), &dwNumBytesXferred);
      if (!fOk)
         __leave;


      hThread = CreateRemoteThread(hProcess, NULL, 0,
         (LPTHREAD_START_ROUTINE)(DWORD) pdwCodeRemote,
         pInjLibInfoRemote, 0, &dwThreadId);
      if (hThread == NULL)
         __leave;

      WaitForSingleObject(hThread, INFINITE);
   } // __try
   __finally {
      if (hThread != NULL) {
         GetExitCodeThread(hThread, (PDWORD) &hinstDllRemote);
         CloseHandle(hThread);
      }

      // Let the remote thread start executing the remote
      // ThreadFunc function using our modified stack, which
      // now contains an initialized INJLIBINFO structure.
      FreeProcessMemory(hProcess, pdwCodeRemote);
   } //__finally
```

(continued)

Figure 18-5. *continued*

```
   // Return TRUE if the DLL loaded successfully.
   return(hinstDllRemote != NULL);
}


///////////////////////////////////////////////////////////////////


BOOL WINAPI InjectLibA (HANDLE hProcess, LPCSTR lpszLibFile) {

   return(InjectLibWorA(hProcess, (LPBYTE) lpszLibFile,
     FALSE));
}


///////////////////////////////////////////////////////////////////


BOOL WINAPI InjectLibW (HANDLE hProcess, LPCWSTR lpszLibFile) {

   return(InjectLibWorA(hProcess, (LPBYTE) lpszLibFile, TRUE));
}


/////////////////////// End Of File ///////////////////////
```

INJLIB.H
```
/****************************************************************
Module name: InjLib.H
Notices: Copyright (c) 1995-1997 Jeffrey Richter
****************************************************************/


BOOL WINAPI InjectLibA (HANDLE hProcess, LPCSTR lpszLibFile);
BOOL WINAPI InjectLibW (HANDLE hProcess, LPCWSTR lpszLibFile);


#ifdef UNICODE
#define InjectLib InjectLibW
#else
#define InjectLib InjectLibA
#endif // !UNICODE


/////////////////////// End Of File ///////////////////////
```

Testing the *InjectLib* Function

Having written the *InjectLib* function, I needed to devise a way to test it. I describe how I did so in this section. Testing *InjectLib* involves two parts. First, I wrote an application, which I call TInjLib, to call the *InjectLib* function. Second, I wrote a DLL to be injected into a remote process. This DLL retrieves information that is specific to the application that contains the injected DLL. If I get back information that seems correct based on the process that I inject into, I know that the *InjectLib* function is working successfully.

The Inject Library Test Sample Application

The TINJLIB.EXE application, listed in Figure 18-6 beginning on the following page, shows how to call *InjectLib*. The source code and resource files for the application are in the TINJLIB directory on the companion disc. The program simply accepts a process ID of a running process. You can obtain a process's ID by using the PVIEW.EXE or PSTAT.EXE tool that ships with Visual C++ or the Task Manager that ships with Windows NT 4. With the ID, the program attempts to open a handle to this running process by calling *OpenProcess*, requesting the appropriate access rights:

```
hProcess = OpenProcess(
    PROCESS_CREATE_THREAD |       // For CreateRemoteThread
    PROCESS_QUERY_INFORMATION |   // For VirtualQueryEx
    PROCESS_VM_OPERATION |        // For VirtualProtectEx,
                                  // VirtualAllocEx, and
                                  // VirtualFreeEx
    PROCESS_VM_READ |             // For ReadProcessMemory
    PROCESS_VM_WRITE,             // For WriteProcessMemory
    FALSE, dwProcessId);
```

If *OpenProcess* returns NULL, TInjLib cannot open a handle to the process. This will happen in a highly secure system or if you attempt to open a handle to a secure process. The Win32 subsystem and some other processes (such as WinLogon, ClipSrv, and EventLog) are secure so that an application cannot obtain a handle to any of them when requesting the above access flags.

If *OpenProcess* is successful, TInjLib creates a buffer with the full pathname of the DLL that you want to inject and calls *InjectLib*. When *InjectLib* returns, the program displays a message box indicating whether the DLL successfully loaded in the remote process; it then closes the handle to the process. That's all there is to it.

You may notice when examining the code that I make a special check to see whether the process ID passed is 0. If so, I set the process ID to TINJLIB.EXE's own process ID by calling *GetCurrentProcessId*. This way, when TInjLib calls *InjectLib*, TInjLib is injecting the DLL into its own address space. I do this to make debugging easier. As you can imagine, when bugs popped up it was sometimes difficult to determine whether the bugs were in the local process or in the remote process. Originally, I started debugging my code with two debuggers, one watching TInjLib and the other watching the remote process. This turned out to be terribly inconvenient. And then it dawned on me that TInjLib can also inject a DLL into itself—that is, into the same address space as the caller. This made it much easier to debug my code.

TInjLib.ico

```
TINJLIB.C
/*************************************************************
Module name: TInjLib.C
Notices: Copyright (c) 1995-1997 Jeffrey Richter
*************************************************************/
#include "..\CmnHdr.H"                    /* See Appendix C. */
#include <windows.h>
#include <windowsx.h>
#include <stdio.h>
#include <tchar.h>
#include "InjLib.H"
#include "Resource.h"


///////////////////////////////////////////////////////////////


BOOL Dlg_OnInitDialog (HWND hwnd, HWND hwndFocus,

    LPARAM lParam) {

    // Associate an icon with the dialog box.
    chSETDLGICONS(hwnd, IDI_TINJLIB, IDI_TINJLIB);

    return(TRUE);
}


///////////////////////////////////////////////////////////////
```

Figure 18-6.
The TInjLib application.

(continued)

Figure 18-6 *continued*

```
void Dlg_OnCommand (HWND hwnd, int id,
   HWND hwndCtl, UINT codeNotify) {

   BOOL fTranslated;
   DWORD dwProcessId;
   HANDLE hProcess;

   switch (id) {
      case IDC_INJECT:
         dwProcessId = GetDlgItemInt(hwnd, IDC_PROCESSID,
            &fTranslated, FALSE);
         if (dwProcessId == 0) {
            // A process ID of 0 causes everything to take
            // place in the local process; this makes things
            // easier for debugging.
            dwProcessId = GetCurrentProcessId();
         }

         // Get a handle for the target process.
         hProcess = OpenProcess(
            PROCESS_CREATE_THREAD |      // For CreateRemoteThread
            PROCESS_QUERY_INFORMATION |  // For VirtualQueryEx
            PROCESS_VM_OPERATION |       // For VirtualProtectEx
            PROCESS_VM_READ |            // For ReadProcessMemory
            PROCESS_VM_WRITE,            // For WriteProcessMemory
            FALSE, dwProcessId);

         if (hProcess == NULL) {

            chMB((GetLastError() == ERROR_ACCESS_DENIED) ?
               __TEXT("Insufficient access to process")
                  : __TEXT("Invalid process Id"));
         } else {

            TCHAR szLibFile[MAX_PATH];
            GetModuleFileName(NULL,
               szLibFile, sizeof(szLibFile));
            _tcscpy(_tcsrchr(szLibFile,
               __TEXT('\\')) + 1, __TEXT("ImgWalk.DLL"));
            chMB(InjectLib(hProcess, szLibFile) ?
```

(continued)

Figure 18-6 *continued*

```
                __TEXT("Remote DLL Loaded") :
                __TEXT("Remote DLL failed load"));
            CloseHandle(hProcess);
         }
         break;

      case IDCANCEL:
         EndDialog(hwnd, id);
         break;
   }
}


///////////////////////////////////////////////////////////////


BOOL CALLBACK Dlg_Proc (HWND hwnd, UINT uMsg,
   WPARAM wParam, LPARAM lParam) {

   switch (uMsg) {
      chHANDLE_DLGMSG(hwnd, WM_INITDIALOG, Dlg_OnInitDialog);
      chHANDLE_DLGMSG(hwnd, WM_COMMAND, Dlg_OnCommand);
   }

   return(FALSE);
}


///////////////////////////////////////////////////////////////


int WINAPI _tWinMain (HINSTANCE hinstExe,
   HINSTANCE hinstPrev, LPTSTR pszCmdLine, int nCmdShow) {

   chWARNIFUNICODEUNDERWIN95();
   DialogBox(hinstExe, MAKEINTRESOURCE(IDD_TINJLIB),
      NULL, Dlg_Proc);

   return(0);
}


///////////////////////// End Of File /////////////////////////
```

(continued)

Figure 18-6 *continued*

```
TINJLIB.RC
//Microsoft Developer Studio generated resource script.
//
#include "resource.h"

#define APSTUDIO_READONLY_SYMBOLS
/////////////////////////////////////////////////////////////////
//
// Generated from the TEXTINCLUDE 2 resource.
//
#include "afxres.h"


/////////////////////////////////////////////////////////////////
#undef APSTUDIO_READONLY_SYMBOLS


/////////////////////////////////////////////////////////////////
// English (U.S.) resources

#if !defined(AFX_RESOURCE_DLL) || defined(AFX_TARG_ENU)
#ifdef _WIN32
LANGUAGE LANG_ENGLISH, SUBLANG_ENGLISH_US
#pragma code_page(1252)
#endif //_WIN32


/////////////////////////////////////////////////////////////////
//
// Icon
//

// Icon with lowest ID value placed first to ensure
// application icon remains consistent on all systems.
IDI_TINJLIB             ICON    DISCARDABLE     "TInjLib.ico"

#ifdef APSTUDIO_INVOKED
/////////////////////////////////////////////////////////////////
//
// TEXTINCLUDE
//

1 TEXTINCLUDE DISCARDABLE
BEGIN
    "resource.h\0"
END
```

(continued)

Figure 18-6 *continued*

```
2 TEXTINCLUDE DISCARDABLE
BEGIN
    "#include ""afxres.h""\r\n"
    "\0"
END

3 TEXTINCLUDE DISCARDABLE
BEGIN
    "\r\n"
    "\0"
END

#endif    // APSTUDIO_INVOKED


/////////////////////////////////////////////////////////////
//
// Dialog
//

IDD_TINJLIB DIALOG DISCARDABLE  15, 24, 158, 24
STYLE DS_3DLOOK | DS_CENTER | WS_MINIMIZEBOX | WS_VISIBLE |
    WS_CAPTION | WS_SYSMENU
CAPTION "Inject Library Tester"
FONT 8, "System"
BEGIN
    LTEXT           "&Process Id (decimal):",-1,4,6,69,8
    EDITTEXT        IDC_PROCESSID,78,4,36,12,ES_AUTOHSCROLL
    DEFPUSHBUTTON   "&Inject",IDC_INJECT,120,4,36,12,
                    WS_GROUP
END


/////////////////////////////////////////////////////////////
//
// DESIGNINFO
//

#ifdef APSTUDIO_INVOKED
GUIDELINES DESIGNINFO DISCARDABLE
BEGIN
    IDD_TINJLIB, DIALOG
    BEGIN
        RIGHTMARGIN, 134
        BOTTOMMARGIN, 20
```

(continued)

Figure 18-6 *continued*

```
      END
  END
  #endif    // APSTUDIO_INVOKED

  #endif    // English (U.S.) resources
  /////////////////////////////////////////////////////////////


  #ifndef APSTUDIO_INVOKED
  /////////////////////////////////////////////////////////////
  //
  // Generated from the TEXTINCLUDE 3 resource.
  //


  /////////////////////////////////////////////////////////////
  #endif    // not APSTUDIO_INVOKED
```

The Image Walk Dynamic-Link Library

IMGWALK.DLL, listed in Figure 18-7 beginning on page 967, is a DLL that, once injected into a process's address space, can report on all the DLLs that the process is using. The source code and resource files for the DLL are in the IMGWALK directory on the companion disc. For example, if I first run Notepad and then run TInjLib, passing it Notepad's process ID, TInjLib injects the IMGWALK.DLL into Notepad's address space. Once there, ImgWalk determines which file images (EXEs and DLLs) are being used by Notepad and displays the message box on the next page, which shows the results.

At first glance, it seems that there is practically no way to accomplish what ImgWalk does without using undocumented functions. A process's image information can be obtained by debugging the desired process. However, there are problems associated with creating a debugger—the biggest being that a debugger attached to a debuggee can never detach itself without terminating the debuggee. This is clearly visible in the way that terminating a debugger also terminates its debuggee. The *InjectLib* function does not have this problem—it attaches the DLL to a process, and then *InjectLib* detaches the DLL from that process.

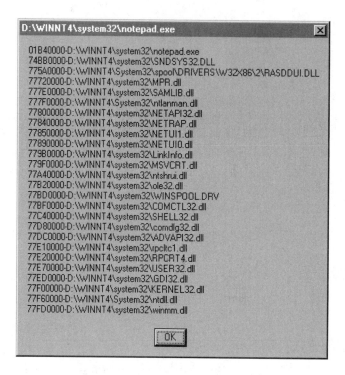

ImgWalk walks through a process's address space looking for mapped file images by repeatedly calling *VirtualQuery* to fill a MEMORY-_BASIC_INFORMATION structure. With each iteration of the loop, ImgWalk checks to see whether there's a file pathname to concatenate with a string. This string appears in the message box.

```
while (VirtualQuery(lp, &mbi, sizeof(mbi)) == sizeof(mbi)) {
   if (mbi.State == MEM_FREE)
      mbi.AllocationBase = mbi.BaseAddress;

   if ((mbi.AllocationBase == hinstDll) ||
      (mbi.AllocationBase != mbi.BaseAddress) ||
      (mbi.AllocationBase == NULL)) {
      // Do not add the module name to the list
      // if any of the following is true:
      // 1. If this region contains this DLL
      // 2. If this block is NOT the beginning of a region
      // 3. If the address is NULL
      nLen = 0;
   } else {
      nLen = GetModuleFileName((HINSTANCE) mbi.AllocationBase,
         szModName, ARRAY_SIZE(szModName));
   }
```

```
if (nLen > 0) {
   _stprintf(_tcschr(szBuf, 0), __TEXT("\n%08X-%s"),
      mbi.AllocationBase, szModName);
}

lp += mbi.RegionSize;
}
```

First I check to see whether the region's base address matches the base address of the injected DLL. If we have a match, I set *nLen* to 0 so that I do not show the injected library in the message box. If we don't have a match, I attempt to get the filename for the module loaded at the region's base address. If the *nLen* variable is greater than 0, the system recognizes that the address identifies a loaded module and the system fills the *szModName* buffer with the full pathname of the module. I then concatenate the module's HINSTANCE (base address) and its pathname with the *szBuf* string that will eventually be displayed in the message box. When the loop is finished, the DLL presents a message box with the final string as its contents.

```
IMGWALK.C
/**************************************************************
Module name: ImgWalk.C
Notices: Copyright (c) 1995-1997 Jeffrey Richter
**************************************************************/


#include "..\CmnHdr.H"                     /* See Appendix C. */
#include <windows.h>
#include <stdio.h>
#include <tchar.h>



///////////////////////////////////////////////////////////////



BOOL WINAPI DllMain (HINSTANCE hinstDll, DWORD fdwReason,
   LPVOID lpvReserved) {

   TCHAR szBuf[MAX_PATH * 30], szModName[MAX_PATH];

   if (fdwReason == DLL_PROCESS_ATTACH) {
      LPBYTE lp = NULL;
```

Figure 18-7.
Source code for IMGWALK.DLL.

(continued)

Figure 18-7. *continued*

```
        MEMORY_BASIC_INFORMATION mbi;
        int nLen;
        szBuf[0] = 0;
        szBuf[1] = 0;

        while (VirtualQuery(lp, &mbi, sizeof(mbi))
            == sizeof(mbi)) {
            if (mbi.State == MEM_FREE)
                mbi.AllocationBase = mbi.BaseAddress;

            if ((mbi.AllocationBase == hinstDll) ||
                (mbi.AllocationBase != mbi.BaseAddress) ||
                (mbi.AllocationBase == NULL)) {
                // Do not add the module name to the list
                // if any of the following is true:
                // 1. If this region contains this DLL
                // 2. If this block is NOT the beginning of
                //    a region
                // 3. If the address is NULL
                nLen = 0;
            } else {
                nLen = GetModuleFileName(
                    (HINSTANCE) mbi.AllocationBase,
                    szModName, chDIMOF(szModName));
            }

            if (nLen > 0) {
                _stprintf(_tcschr(szBuf, 0), __TEXT("\n%08X-%s"),
                    mbi.AllocationBase, szModName);
            }

            lp += mbi.RegionSize;
        }

        chMB(&szBuf[1]);
    }
    return(TRUE);
}


/////////////////////////// End Of File ///////////////////////////
```

A Summary

The following table summarizes the pros and cons of the three library injection methods discussed in this chapter.

Features	AppInit_DLLs	Hooks	Remote Threads
Method works under Windows 95?	No	Yes	No
Method works under Windows NT?	Yes	Yes	Yes
Requires restarting the computer?	Yes	No	No
Requires the target process map USER32.DLL?	Yes	Yes	No
Requires the target process map KERNEL32.DLL?	Yes	Yes	Yes
Can the injected library be unloaded from the target process?	No	Yes	Yes
Is the library injected into every process that maps USER32.DLL?	Yes	No	No
Is the source code CPU platform independent?	Yes	Yes	99% Yes

FIBERS

Microsoft Windows NT 3.51 service pack 3 introduced new functionality, called fibers, into the operating system. The fiber functions were added to the Win32 API to help companies quickly port their existing UNIX server applications to Windows NT. These UNIX server applications are single-threaded (using the Win32 definition) but are designed in a way that enables them to serve multiple clients. In other words, the developers of these applications have created their own threading architecture library and use it to simulate pure threads. This threading package creates multiple stacks, saves certain CPU registers, and switches among them to service the client requests.

Obviously, to get the best performance, these UNIX applications should be redesigned, removing the simulated threading library and replacing it with the pure threads offered by Windows. However, because this redesign can take several months (or longer) to complete, companies are first porting their existing UNIX code to Win32 so they can ship something to the Windows market while a Win32-redesigned version of their application is in the works.

When porting the UNIX code to Win32, however, problems can arise. In particular, the way in which Windows manages a thread stack is much more sophisticated than simply allocating memory. Windows stacks start out with relatively little physical storage and grow as necessary. The details of this process are described in the "A Thread's Stack" section beginning on page 224 in Chapter 7. Porting is also complicated by the Win32 structured exception handling mechanism, which is described in Chapter 16.

To help these companies port their code more quickly and correctly to Win32, Microsoft added fibers to the operating system. So as you can see, fibers are a very useful addition to the Win32 API; but you should avoid them in favor of more properly designed applications that use Windows native threads. Having put in that disclaimer, I'll now explain the concept of a fiber, the functions that manipulate fibers, and how to take advantage of fibers.

The first thing to keep in mind is that threads are implemented by the Windows kernel. The operating system has intimate knowledge of threads and schedules them according to the algorithm defined by Microsoft. A fiber is implemented in user-mode code; the kernel does not have knowledge of fibers, and they are scheduled according to the algorithm *you* define. Because you are defining the fiber-scheduling algorithm, fibers are nonpreemptively scheduled as far as the kernel is concerned.

The next thing to be aware of is that a single thread may contain one or more fibers. As far as the kernel is concerned, a thread is being preemptively scheduled and is executing code. However, the thread will be executing one fiber's code at a time—you decide which fiber is executing. (These concepts will become clearer as we go on.)

The first step you must perform when using fibers is to turn your existing thread into a fiber. You do this by calling *ConvertThreadToFiber*:

```
LPVOID ConvertThreadToFiber(LPVOID lpParameter);
```

This function allocates memory for the fiber's execution context (about 200 bytes in size). This execution context consists of the following elements:

- A user-defined 32-bit value that is initialized to the value passed to *ConvertThreadToFiber*'s *lpParameter* argument.
- The head of a structured exception handling chain.
- The top and bottom memory addresses of the fiber's stack. When converting a thread to a fiber, this is also the thread's stack.
- Various CPU registers, including a stack pointer, an instruction pointer, and others.

After the fiber execution context has been allocated and initialized, the address of the execution context is associated with the thread—the thread has been converted to a fiber, and the fiber is now running on this thread. *ConvertThreadToFiber* actually returns the memory address of the fiber's execution context. You will need to use this address later, but you should never read from or write to the execution context data yourself—the fiber functions will manipulate the contents of the structure for you when necessary. Now if your fiber (thread) returns or calls *ExitThread*, the fiber and the thread both die.

There is no reason to convert a thread to a fiber unless you plan to create additional fibers to run on the same thread. To create another fiber, the thread (currently running fiber) calls *CreateFiber*:

```
LPVOID CreateFiber(DWORD dwStackSize,
   LPFIBER_START_ROUTINE lpStartAddress, LPVOID lpParameter);
```

CreateFiber first attempts to create a new stack whose size is indicated by the *dwStackSize* parameter. Usually 0 is passed, which, by default, creates a stack that can grow to 1 MB in size but initially has 2 pages of storage committed to it. If you specify a nonzero size, a stack is reserved and committed using the specified size.

After the stack is created, *CreateFiber* allocates a new fiber execution context structure and initializes it: the user-defined value is set to the value passed to *CreateFiber*'s *lpParameter*, the top and bottom memory addresses of the new stack are saved, and the memory address of the fiber function (passed as the *lpStartAddress* argument) is saved.

The *lpStartAddress* argument must specify the address of a fiber routine that you must implement and that must have the following prototype:

```
VOID WINAPI FiberFunc(PVOID lpParameter);
```

When the fiber is scheduled for the first time, this function executes and is passed the *lpParameter* value that was originally passed to *CreateFiber*. You can do whatever you like in this fiber function. However, you'll notice that the function is prototyped as returning VOID. This is not because the return value has no meaning; it is because this function should never return at all! If a fiber function does return, the thread and all the fibers created on it are destroyed immediately.

Like *ConvertThreadToFiber*, *CreateFiber* returns the memory address of the fiber's execution context. However, unlike *ConvertThreadToFiber*, this new fiber is not executing, because the currently running fiber is still executing. Only one fiber at a time can be executing on a single thread. To make the new fiber execute, *SwitchToFiber* must be called:

```
VOID SwitchToFiber(LPVOID lpFiber);
```

SwitchToFiber takes a single parameter, *lpFiber*, which is the memory address of a fiber's execution context as returned by a previous call to *ConvertThreadToFiber* or *CreateFiber*. This memory address tells the function which fiber to schedule now. Internally, *SwitchToFiber* performs the following steps:

1. Some of the current CPU registers, including the instruction pointer register and the stack pointer register, are saved in the currently running fiber's execution context.

2. The registers previously saved in the soon-to-be-running fiber's execution context are loaded into the CPU registers. These registers include the stack pointer register so that this fiber's stack will be used when the thread continues execution.

3. The fiber's execution context is associated with the thread—the thread is now running the specified fiber.

4. The thread's instruction pointer is set to the saved instruction pointer. The thread (fiber) will continue execution where this fiber was last executing.

SwitchToFiber is the only way for a fiber to get any CPU time. Because your code must explicitly call *SwitchToFiber* at the appropriate times, you are in complete control of the fiber scheduling. Keep in mind that fiber scheduling has nothing to do with thread scheduling. The thread that the fibers are running on is always preemptable by the operating system. It's just that when the thread is scheduled, the currently selected fiber runs—no other fiber will run unless *SwitchToFiber* is explicitly called.

When you want to destroy a fiber, call *DeleteFiber*:

```
VOID DeleteFiber(LPVOID lpFiber);
```

This function deletes the fiber indicated by the *lpFiber* parameter, which is, of course, the address of a fiber's execution context. This function frees the memory used by the fiber's stack and then destroys the fiber's execution context. But note: if you pass the address of the fiber that is currently associated with the thread, this function calls *ExitThread* internally, which causes the thread and all the fibers created on the thread to die.

DeleteFiber is usually called by one fiber to delete another fiber. The deleted fiber's stack is destroyed, and the fiber's execution context is freed. Notice the difference here between fibers and threads: threads usually kill themselves by calling *ExitThread*. In fact, it is considered bad form for one thread to terminate another thread using *TerminateThread*. And, if you do call *TerminateThread*, the system does not destroy the terminated thread's stack. We can use this ability for a fiber to cleanly delete another fiber to our advantage. I'll discuss how when I explain the sample application later in this appendix.

Two additional fiber functions are provided simply for your convenience. A thread can be executing a single fiber at a time, and the operating system always knows which fiber is currently associated with the thread. If you want to get the address of the currently running fiber's execution context, you can call *GetCurrentFiber*:

```
PVOID GetCurrentFiber(VOID)
```

The other convenience function is *GetFiberData*:

```
PVOID GetFiberData(VOID)
```

As I've mentioned, each fiber's execution context contains a 32-bit user-defined value. This value is initialized with the value that is passed as the *lpParameter* argument either to *ConvertThreadToFiber* or to *CreateFiber*. This value is also passed as an argument to a fiber function. *GetFiberData* simply looks in the currently executing fiber's execution context and returns the saved 32-bit value.

Both *GetCurrentFiber* and *GetFiberData* are very fast functions and are usually implemented as intrinsic functions, which means that the compiler generates the code for these functions inline.

The Counter Sample Application

The Counter (COUNTER.EXE) application in Figure A-1 beginning on page 979 demonstrates how to use fibers to easily implement background processing. When you run the application, the dialog box below appears. (I highly recommend that you run the application to really understand what's happening here and to see the behavior as you read the remainder of this discussion.)

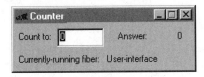

You can think of this application as a superminiature spreadsheet consisting of two cells. The first cell is a writable cell implemented as an edit control (after the "Count to" text), and the second cell is a read-only cell implemented as a static control (after the "Answer" text). As you change the number in the edit control, the Answer cell automatically recalculates. For this simple application, the recalculation is a counter that starts at 0 and increments slowly until the value in the Answer cell becomes the same value as the entered number. For demonstration purposes, the static control at the bottom of the dialog box updates to indicate which fiber is currently executing. This fiber can be either the User-interface fiber or the Recalculation fiber.

To test the application, type a 5 into the edit control: the currently running fiber field will change to "Recalculation," and the number in the Answer field will slowly increment from 0 to 5. When the counting is finished, the currently running fiber field will change back to User-interface and the thread will go to sleep. Now, in the edit control, type a 0 after the 5 (making 50) and watch the counting start over from 0 and go to 50. But this time, while the Answer is incrementing, move the window on the screen. When you do this, you'll notice that the recalculation fiber is preempted and that the user-interface fiber is rescheduled so that the application's user interface stays responsive to the user. When you stop moving the window, the recalculation fiber is rescheduled and the Answer field continues counting from where it left off.

One last thing to test: while the recalculation fiber is counting, change the number in the edit control. Again, notice that the user interface is responsive to your input; but also notice that when you stop typing, the recalculation fiber starts counting from the very beginning. This is exactly the kind of behavior that is desired by a full-blown spreadsheet application.

Keep in mind that no critical sections or other thread synchronization objects are used in this application—everything is done using a single thread consisting of two fibers. Now, we'll discuss how this application is implemented.

When the process's primary thread starts by executing *WinMain* (at the end of the listing), *ConvertThreadToFiber* is called to turn the thread into a fiber and to allow us to create another fiber later. Then a modeless dialog box is created, which is the application's main window. Next a state variable is initialized to indicate the background processing state (BPS). This state variable is the *bps* member contained inside the global *g_FiberInfo* variable. Three states are possible, as described in the following table:

State	Description
BPS_DONE	The recalculation ran to completion and the user has not changed anything that would require a recalculation.
BPS_STARTOVER	The user has changed something that requires a recalculation to start from the beginning.
BPS_CONTINUE	The recalculation was started but has not finished. Also, the user has not changed anything that would require the recalculation to start over from the beginning.

The background processing state variable is examined in the thread's message loop, which is more complicated than a normal message loop. Here is what the message loop does: First, if a window message exists (the user interface is active), process the message. Keeping the user interface responsive is always a higher priority than recalculating values.

If the user interface has nothing to do, check to see whether any recalculations need to be performed (the background processing state is BPS_STARTOVER or BPS_CONTINUE). If there are no recalculations to do (BPS_DONE), suspend the thread by calling *WaitMessage*; only a user-interface event can cause a recalculation to be required.

Now if the user-interface fiber has nothing to do and the user has just changed the value in the edit control, we need to start the recalculation over from the beginning (BPS_STARTOVER). The first thing to realize here is that we may already have a recalculation fiber running. If this is the case, we need to delete the fiber and create a new fiber that will start its counting from the very beginning. The user-interface fiber calls *DeleteFiber* to destroy the existing recalculation fiber. This is where fibers (as opposed to threads) come in very handy. Deleting the recalculation fiber is perfectly OK: the fiber's stack and execution context are completely and cleanly destroyed. If we were using threads instead of fibers, it would not be possible to have the user-interface thread destroy the recalculation thread cleanly—we would have to use some form of interthread communication and wait for the recalculation thread to die on its own. Once we know that no recalculation fiber exists, we can create a new recalculation fiber and set the background processing state to BPS_CONTINUE.

When the user interface is idle and the recalculation fiber has something to do, we schedule it time by calling *SwitchToFiber*. *SwitchToFiber* will not return until the recalculation fiber calls *SwitchToFiber*, again passing the address of the user-interface fiber's execution context.

The *Counter_FiberFunc* function contains the code executed by the recalculation fiber. This fiber function is passed the address of the global *g_FiberInfo* structure so that it knows the handle of the dialog box window, the address of the user-interface fiber's execution context, and the current background processing state. It's true that the address of this structure does not need to be passed since it is in a global variable, but I wanted to demonstrate how to pass arguments to fiber functions. Besides, passing the address places fewer dependencies on the code, which is always a good practice.

The fiber function first updates the status control in the dialog box to indicate that the recalculation fiber is now executing. Then the function gets the number inside the edit control and enters a loop that starts counting from 0 to the number. Each time the number is about to be incremented, *GetQueueStatus* is called to see whether any messages have shown up in the thread's message queue (all fibers running on a single thread share the thread's message queue). When a message does show up, the user-interface fiber has something to do; and because we want it to take priority over the recalculations, *SwitchToFiber* is called immediately so that the user-interface fiber can process the message. After the message(s) have been processed, the user-interface fiber will reschedule the recalculation fiber (as described earlier), and the background processing will continue.

When there are no messages to be processed, the recalculation fiber updates the Answer field in the dialog box and then sleeps for 200 milliseconds. In production code, you should remove the call to Sleep; I have it here to exaggerate the time required to perform the recalculation.

When the recalculation fiber has finished calculating the answer, the background processing state variable is set to BPS_DONE and the user-interface fiber is rescheduled by calling *SwitchToFiber*. At this point, if the user-interface fiber has nothing to do, it will call *WaitMessage*, suspending the thread so that no CPU time is wasted.

Counter.ico

COUNTER.C

```
/*****************************************************************
Module name: Counter.c
Notices: Copyright (c) 1996-1997 Jeffrey Richter
*****************************************************************/


#include "..\CmnHdr.h"
#include <Windows.h>
#include <WindowsX.h>
#include <tchar.h>
#include "Resource.h"


///////////////////////////////////////////////////////////////


// The possible state of the background processing
typedef enum {
    BPS_STARTOVER,  // Start the background processing from
                    // the beginning.
    BPS_CONTINUE,   // Continue the background processing.
    BPS_DONE        // There is no background processing to do.
} BKGNDPROCSTATE;


typedef struct {
    // User-interface fiber execution context
    PVOID pFiberUI;

    // Handle of main UI window
    HWND  hwnd;

    // State of background processing
    BKGNDPROCSTATE bps;
} FIBERINFO, *PFIBERINFO;


// A global that contains application state information. This
// global is accessed directly by the UI fiber and indirectly
// by the background processing fiber.
FIBERINFO g_FiberInfo;
```

Figure A-1. *(continued)*

The Counter application.

Figure A-1. *continued*

```
//////////////////////////////////////////////////////////////


void WINAPI Counter_FiberFunc (LPVOID pvParam) {
   PFIBERINFO pFiberInfo = (PFIBERINFO) pvParam;
   BOOL fTranslated;
   int x, nCount;

   // Update the window showing which fiber is executing.
   SetDlgItemText(pFiberInfo->hwnd,
      IDC_FIBER, __TEXT("Recalculation"));

   // Get the current count in the EDIT control.
   nCount = GetDlgItemInt(
      pFiberInfo->hwnd, IDC_COUNT, &fTranslated, FALSE);

   // Count from 0 to nCount, updating the STATIC control.
   for (x = 0; x <= nCount; x++) {

      // UI events have higher priority than counting.
      // If there are any UI events, handle them ASAP.
      if (HIWORD(GetQueueStatus(QS_ALLEVENTS)) != 0) {

         // The UI fiber has something to do; temporarily
         // pause counting and handle the UI events.
         SwitchToFiber(pFiberInfo->pFiberUI);

         // The UI has no more events; continue counting.
         SetDlgItemText(pFiberInfo->hwnd,
            IDC_FIBER, __TEXT("Recalculation"));
      }

      // Update the STATIC control with the most recent count.
      SetDlgItemInt(pFiberInfo->hwnd, IDC_ANSWER, x, FALSE);

      // Sleep for a while to exaggerate the effect; remove
      // the call to Sleep in production code.
      Sleep(200);
   }


   // Indicate that counting is complete.
   pFiberInfo->bps = BPS_DONE;
```

(continued)

Figure A-1. *continued*

```
    // Reschedule the UI thread. When the UI thread is running
    // and has no events to process, the thread is put to sleep.
    // NOTE: If we just allow the fiber function to return,
    // the thread and the UI fiber die -- we don't want this!
    SwitchToFiber(pFiberInfo->pFiberUI);
}


//////////////////////////////////////////////////////////////////


BOOL Counter_OnInitDialog(HWND hwnd,
    HWND hwndFocus, LPARAM lParam) {

    // Associate an icon with the dialog box.
    chSETDLGICONS(hwnd, IDI_COUNTER, IDI_COUNTER);

#ifdef _DEBUG
    // In debug versions, move the window to the top left so
    // that the rest of the screen is available to the debugger.
    SetWindowPos(hwnd, NULL, 0, 0, 0, 0,
        SWP_NOZORDER | SWP_NOSIZE);
#endif

    SetDlgItemInt(hwnd, IDC_COUNT, 0, FALSE);
    return(TRUE);
}


//////////////////////////////////////////////////////////////////


void Counter_OnCommand(HWND hwnd,
    int id, HWND hwndCtl, UINT codeNotify) {

    switch (id) {
        case IDCANCEL:
            // If the Escape key is hit, destroy the modeless
            // dialog box, terminating the application.
            DestroyWindow(hwnd);
            break;

        case IDC_COUNT:
            if (codeNotify == EN_CHANGE) {
```

(continued)

Figure A-1. *continued*

```
                   // When the user changes the count, start the
                   // background processing over from the beginning.
                   g_FiberInfo.bps = BPS_STARTOVER;
               }
               break;
        }
}


///////////////////////////////////////////////////////////////////


BOOL WINAPI Counter_DlgProc (HWND hwnd, UINT uMsg,
   WPARAM wParam, LPARAM lParam) {

   switch (uMsg) {
      HANDLE_MSG(hwnd, WM_INITDIALOG, Counter_OnInitDialog);
      HANDLE_MSG(hwnd, WM_COMMAND, Counter_OnCommand);
   }
   return(FALSE);
}


///////////////////////////////////////////////////////////////////


int WINAPI _tWinMain (HINSTANCE hinstExe,
   HINSTANCE hinstPrev, LPTSTR pszCmdLine, int nCmdShow) {

   // Counter fiber execution context
   PVOID pFiberCounter = NULL;

   chWARNIFUNICODEUNDERWIN95();

   // Convert this thread to a fiber.
   g_FiberInfo.pFiberUI = ConvertThreadToFiber(NULL);

   // Create the application's UI window.
   g_FiberInfo.hwnd = CreateDialog(hinstExe,
      MAKEINTRESOURCE(IDD_COUNTER), NULL, Counter_DlgProc);

   // Update the window showing which fiber is executing.
   SetDlgItemText(g_FiberInfo.hwnd,
      IDC_FIBER, __TEXT("User-interface"));
```

(continued)

Figure A-1. *continued*

```
// Initially, there is no background processing to be done.
g_FiberInfo.bps = BPS_DONE;

// While the UI window still exists...
while (IsWindow(g_FiberInfo.hwnd)) {

    // UI messages are higher priority
    // than background processing.
    MSG msg;
    if (PeekMessage(&msg, NULL, 0, 0, PM_REMOVE)) {

        // If a message exists in the queue, process it.
        if (!IsDialogMessage(g_FiberInfo.hwnd, &msg)) {
            TranslateMessage(&msg);
            DispatchMessage(&msg);
        }

    } else {

        // If no UI messages exist, check the
        // state of the background processing.
        switch (g_FiberInfo.bps) {
            case BPS_DONE:
                // No messages exist and there is no background
                // processing to do; wait for a UI event.
                WaitMessage();
                break;

            case BPS_STARTOVER:
                // The user has changed the count; start the
                // background processing over from
                // the beginning.

                if (pFiberCounter != NULL) {
                    // If a recalculation fiber already exists,
                    // delete it so that background processing
                    // will start over from the beginning.
                    DeleteFiber(pFiberCounter);
                    pFiberCounter = NULL;
                }

                // Create a new recalc fiber that
                // starts over from the beginning.
                pFiberCounter = CreateFiber(
```

(continued)

Figure A-1. *continued*

```
                0, Counter_FiberFunc, &g_FiberInfo);

        // Indicate that we have started the background
        // processing and that it should continue.
        g_FiberInfo.bps = BPS_CONTINUE;

        // Fall through to BPS_CONTINUE case...

    case BPS_CONTINUE:
        // Allow the background processing to execute...
        SwitchToFiber(pFiberCounter);

        // The background processing has been paused
        // (because a UI message showed up) or has been
        // stopped (because the counting has completed).

        // Update the window showing which fiber
        // is executing.
        SetDlgItemText(g_FiberInfo.hwnd,
            IDC_FIBER, __TEXT("User-interface"));

        if (g_FiberInfo.bps == BPS_DONE) {
            // If the background processing ran to
            // completion, delete the background fiber
            // so that background processing will start
            // over from the beginning next time.
            DeleteFiber(pFiberCounter);
            pFiberCounter = NULL;
        }
        break;
    }  // switch on background processing state

  }  // No UI messages exist
}  // while the window still exists

return(0);  // End the application.
}


/////////////////////// End Of File //////////////////////////
```

(continued)

Figure A-1. *continued*

COUNTER.RC

```
//Microsoft Developer Studio generated resource script.
//
#include "resource.h"

#define APSTUDIO_READONLY_SYMBOLS
/////////////////////////////////////////////////////////////
//
// Generated from the TEXTINCLUDE 2 resource.
//
#include "afxres.h"


/////////////////////////////////////////////////////////////
#undef APSTUDIO_READONLY_SYMBOLS


/////////////////////////////////////////////////////////////
// English (U.S.) resources

#if !defined(AFX_RESOURCE_DLL) || defined(AFX_TARG_ENU)
#ifdef _WIN32
LANGUAGE LANG_ENGLISH, SUBLANG_ENGLISH_US
#pragma code_page(1252)
#endif //_WIN32


/////////////////////////////////////////////////////////////
//
// Dialog
//

IDD_COUNTER DIALOG DISCARDABLE  0, 0, 156, 37
STYLE DS_3DLOOK | DS_CENTER | WS_MINIMIZEBOX | WS_VISIBLE |
    WS_CAPTION | WS_SYSMENU
CAPTION "Counter"
FONT 8, "MS Sans Serif"
BEGIN
    LTEXT           "Count to:",IDC_STATIC,4,6,34,8
    EDITTEXT        IDC_COUNT,38,4,40,14,ES_AUTOHSCROLL |
                    ES_NUMBER
    LTEXT           "Answer:",IDC_STATIC,90,6,25,8
    RTEXT           "0",IDC_ANSWER,122,6,23,8
    LTEXT           "Currently-running fiber:",IDC_STATIC,
                    4,24,75,8
```

(continued)

Figure A-1. *continued*

```
    LTEXT              "Fiber",IDC_FIBER,80,24,72,8
END


/////////////////////////////////////////////////////////////
//
// DESIGNINFO
//

#ifdef APSTUDIO_INVOKED
GUIDELINES DESIGNINFO DISCARDABLE
BEGIN
    IDD_COUNTER, DIALOG
    BEGIN
        LEFTMARGIN, 7
        RIGHTMARGIN, 149
        TOPMARGIN, 7
        BOTTOMMARGIN, 30
    END
END
#endif    // APSTUDIO_INVOKED


#ifdef APSTUDIO_INVOKED
/////////////////////////////////////////////////////////////
//
// TEXTINCLUDE
//

1 TEXTINCLUDE DISCARDABLE
BEGIN
    "resource.h\0"
END

2 TEXTINCLUDE DISCARDABLE
BEGIN
    "#include ""afxres.h""\r\n"
    "\0"
END

3 TEXTINCLUDE DISCARDABLE
```

(continued)

Figure A-1. *continued*

```
BEGIN
    "\r\n"
    "\0"
END

#endif    // APSTUDIO_INVOKED


/////////////////////////////////////////////////////////////
//
// Icon
//

// Icon with lowest ID value placed first to ensure
// application icon remains consistent on all systems.
IDI_COUNTER           ICON    DISCARDABLE    "Counter.ico"
#endif    // English (U.S.) resources
/////////////////////////////////////////////////////////////



#ifndef APSTUDIO_INVOKED
/////////////////////////////////////////////////////////////
//
// Generated from the TEXTINCLUDE 3 resource.
//


/////////////////////////////////////////////////////////////
#endif    // not APSTUDIO_INVOKED
```

A P P E N D I X   B

MESSAGE CRACKERS

When Windows was introduced, there were only two programming languages that could be used for developing Windows-based applications: C and assembly language. And the only C compiler that could produce executable files for Windows was Microsoft's; no other compiler on the market supported the development of applications for Windows. Well, things have changed significantly over the past few years. Now you can develop Windows-based applications using Ada, assembly language, C, C++, COBOL, FORTRAN, Java, LISP, Modula-2, Pascal, REXX, and Smalltalk/V. And let's not forget Basic.

But even with all these languages that support Windows coming out of the woodwork, C is still the language used most often, with C++ slowly gaining popularity. When it came time to choose a language for presenting the sample code in this book, I narrowed down the choices to these four:

1. Straight C

2. C with message crackers

3. Straight C++

4. C++ using the Microsoft Foundation Classes

It was a tough decision.

Because I wanted the book to appeal to the broadest possible audience, I decided to rule out option 4. Since several companies produce C++ class libraries for Windows development, I didn't want to require one particular class library. Also, some class libraries do more for you than just put a wrapper around the Windows APIs, and I didn't want to introduce extraneous code or procedures into the code samples. I will say, however, that I personally love the Microsoft Foundation Classes and use them when I develop large applications of my own.

Option 3 didn't seem to offer much either. Even without a class library, developing Windows-based applications in C++ can be easier than using straight C, but because the programs in this book are relatively small, using C++ wouldn't have offered many advantages. Another big reason for not choosing option 3 or 4 is that most people are still doing development for Windows in C and haven't yet switched to C++.

Option 1 would have been a good choice because there would have been almost no learning curve for people trying to understand my programs, but I chose to go with option 2. When I go to conferences, I frequently ask people if they are using message crackers, and I usually get a "no" response. When I probe further, I discover that they don't even know what message crackers are or what they do. By using C with message crackers to present the sample code in this book, I get to introduce these little-known but useful macros to many people who might not know about them.

Message crackers are contained in the WINDOWSX.H file supplied with Visual C++. You usually include this file immediately after the WINDOWS.H file. The WINDOWSX.H file is nothing more than a bunch of *#define* statements that create a set of macros for you to use. Microsoft designed the macros to provide the following advantages:

- They reduce the amount of casting necessary in an application and make the casting that is required error free. One of the big problems with programming for Windows in C has been the amount of casting required. You hardly ever see a call to a Win32 API function that doesn't require some sort of cast. Casts should be avoided because they prevent the compiler from catching potential errors in your code. A cast tells the compiler, "I know I'm passing the wrong type here, but that's OK; I know what I'm doing." When you do so much casting, it's easy to make a mistake. The compiler should be doing as much work to help us as it possibly can. If you use these macros, you'll have much less casting to perform.

- They make your code more readable.

- They simplify porting between the 16-bit Windows API and the Win32 API.

- They're easy to understand—they're just macros, after all.

- They're easy to incorporate into existing code. You can leave old code alone and immediately start using the macros in new code. You don't have to retrofit an entire application.

■ They can be used in C and C++ code, although they're not necessary if you're using a class library.

■ If you need a feature that the macros don't support, you can easily write your own macros by following the model used in the header file.

■ If you use the macros, you don't need to reference or remember obscure Windows constructs. For example, many functions in Windows expect a long parameter where the value in the long's high-word means one thing and the value in its low-word means something else. Before calling these functions, you must construct a long value out of the two individual values. This is usually done by using the MAKELONG macro from WINDEF.H. But I can't tell you how many times I've accidentally reversed the two values, causing an incorrect value to be passed to a function. The macros in WINDOWSX.H come to the rescue.

The macros contained in WINDOWSX.H are actually divided into three groups: message crackers, child control macros, and API macros.

Message Crackers

Message crackers make it easier to write window procedures. Typically, window procedures are implemented as one huge *switch* statement. In my travels, I have seen window procedure *switch* statements that contained well over 500 lines of code. We all know that implementing window procedures this way is a bad practice, but we do it anyway. I have been known to do it myself on occasion. Message crackers force you to break up your *switch* statements into smaller functions—one function per window message. This makes your code much more manageable.

Another problem with window procedures is that every message has *wParam* and *lParam* parameters, and depending on the message, these parameters have different meanings. In some cases, such as for a WM_COMMAND message, *wParam* contains two different values. The high-word of the *wParam* parameter is the notification code, and the low-word is the ID of the control. Or is it the other way around? I always forget. Even worse, in 16-bit Windows, the *lParam* parameter for a WM-_COMMAND message contains the window handle and the notification code. If you use message crackers, you don't have to remember or look up any of this. These macros are called message crackers because they crack apart the parameters for any given message. If you want to process the WM_COMMAND message, you simply write a function that looks like this:

```
void Cls_OnCommand(HWND hwnd, int id, HWND hwndCtl,
   UINT codeNotify) {

   switch (id) {

      case ID_SOMELISTBOX:
         if (codeNotify != LBN_SELCHANGE)
            break;

         // Do LBN_SELCHANGE processing.
         break;

      case ID_SOMEBUTTON:
         break;

         :
         :

   }
}
```

Look how easy it is! The crackers look at the message's *wParam* and *lParam* parameters, break the parameters apart, and call your function. There is a WINDOWSX.H file for Win32 and a WINDOWSX.H file for 16-bit Windows. The WM_COMMAND cracker for 16-bit Windows cracks *wParam* and *lParam* differently from the Win32 version. No matter how the parameters are cracked, you still write just the one function. You instantly have code that will compile and work correctly for both 16-bit Windows and Win32!

To use message crackers, you need to make some changes to your window procedure's *switch* statement. Take a look at the window procedure here:

```
LRESULT WndProc (HWND hwnd, UINT uMsg,
   WPARAM wParam, LPARAM lParam) {

   switch (uMsg) {
      HANDLE_MSG(hwnd, WM_COMMAND, Cls_OnCommand);
      HANDLE_MSG(hwnd, WM_PAINT, Cls_OnPaint);
      HANDLE_MSG(hwnd, WM_DESTROY, Cls_OnDestroy);
      default:
         return(DefWindowProc(hwnd, uMsg, wParam, lParam));
   }
}
```

The HANDLE_MSG macro is defined as follows in both the 16-bit Windows and the Win32 version of WINDOWSX.H:

```
#define HANDLE_MSG(hwnd, message, fn)    \
    case (message): \
        return HANDLE_##message((hwnd), (wParam), (lParam), (fn));
```

For a WM_COMMAND message, the preprocessor expands this line to read as follows:

```
case (WM_COMMAND):
    return HANDLE_WM_COMMAND((hwnd), (wParam), (lParam),
        (Cls_OnCommand));
```

The HANDLE_WM_* macros are also defined in WINDOWSX.H. These macros are actually message crackers. They crack the contents of the *wParam* and *lParam* parameters, perform all the necessary casting, and call the appropriate message function, such as the *Cls_OnCommand* function shown earlier. The macro for the 16-bit Windows version of HANDLE_WM_COMMAND is

```
#define HANDLE_WM_COMMAND(hwnd, wParam, lParam, fn) \
    ((fn)((hwnd), (int)(wParam), (HWND)LOWORD(lParam),
    (UINT) HIWORD(lParam)), 0L)
```

The macro for the Win32 version is

```
#define HANDLE_WM_COMMAND(hwnd, wParam, lParam, fn) \
    ( (fn) ((hwnd), (int) (LOWORD(wParam)), (HWND)(lParam),
    (UINT) HIWORD(wParam)), 0L)
```

When the preprocessor expands either of these macros, the result is a call to the *Cls_OnCommand* function with the contents of the *wParam* and *lParam* parameters broken down into their respective parts and cast appropriately.

When you are going to use message cracker macros to process a message, you should open the WINDOWSX.H file and search for the message you want to process. For example, if you search for WM-_COMMAND, you see the part of the file that contains these lines:

```
/* void Cls_OnCommand(HWND hwnd, int id, HWND hwndCtl,
        UINT codeNotify); */
#define HANDLE_WM_COMMAND(hwnd, wParam, lParam, fn) \
    ((fn)((hwnd), (int)(LOWORD(wParam)), (HWND)(lParam),
    (UINT)HIWORD(wParam)), 0L)
#define FORWARD_WM_COMMAND(hwnd, id, hwndCtl, codeNotify, fn) \
    (void)(fn)((hwnd), WM_COMMAND,
    MAKEWPARAM((UINT)(id),(UINT)(codeNotify)),
    (LPARAM)(HWND)(hwndCtl))
```

The first line is a comment that shows you the prototype of the function you have to write. This prototype is the same whether you are looking at the 16-bit Windows version or the Win32 version of the WINDOWSX.H file. The next line is the HANDLE_WM_* macro, which we have already discussed. The last line is a message forwarder. Let's say that during your processing of the WM_COMMAND message you want to call the default window procedure to have it do some work for you. This function would look like this:

```
void Cls_OnCommand (HWND hwnd, int id, HWND hwndCtl,
    UINT codeNotify) {

    // Do some normal processing.

    // Do default processing.
    FORWARD_WM_COMMAND(hwnd, id, hwndCtl, codeNotify,
        DefWindowProc);
}
```

The FORWARD_WM_* macro takes the cracked message parameters and reconstructs them to their *wParam* and *lParam* equivalents. The macro then calls a function that you supply. In the example above, the macro calls the *DefWindowProc* function, but you could just as easily have used *SendMessage* or *PostMessage*. In fact, if you want to send (or post) a message to any window in the system, you can use a FORWARD-_WM_* macro to help combine the individual parameters. Like the HANDLE_WM_* macros, the FORWARD_WM_* macros are defined differently depending on whether you are compiling for 16-bit Windows or for Win32.

Child Control Macros

The child control macros make it easier to send messages to child controls. They are very similar to the FORWARD_WM_* macros. Each of the macros starts with the type of control you are sending the message to, followed by an underscore and the name of the message. For example, to send an LB_GETCOUNT message to a list box, you would use the following macro from WINDOWSX.H:

```
#define ListBox_GetCount(hwndCtl)
    ((int)(DWORD)SendMessage((hwndCtl), LB_GETCOUNT, 0, 0L))
```

Let me point out a couple of things about this macro. First, it takes only one parameter, *hwndCtl*, which is the window handle of the list box. Because the LB_GETCOUNT message ignores the *wParam* and *lParam* parameters, you don't need to bother with them at all. The macro will pass zeros in, as you can see on the preceding page.

Second, when *SendMessage* returns, the result is cast to an *int* to remove the necessity for you to supply your own cast. Normally you would write code like this:

```
int n = (int) SendMessage(hwndCtl, LB_GETCOUNT, 0, 0);
```

When this line is compiled for 16-bit Windows, the compiler warns you that you might lose significant digits. The reason for this is that you are attempting to put a DWORD value (returned from *SendMessage*) into an integer. It's much simpler to write

```
int n = ListBox_GetCount(hwndCtl);
```

Also, I'm sure you'll agree that the line above is a little easier to read than the *SendMessage* line.

The one thing I don't like about the child control macros is that they all take the handle of the control window. Most of the time, the controls you need to send messages to are children of a dialog box. So you end up having to call *GetDlgItem* all the time, producing code like this:

```
int n = ListBox_GetCount(GetDlgItem(hDlg, ID_LISTBOX));
```

This code doesn't run any slower than it would if you had used *SendDlgItemMessage*, but your application does contain some extra code because of the additional call to *GetDlgItem*. If you need to send several messages to the same control, you may want to call *GetDlgItem* once, save the child window's handle, and then call all the macros you need, as shown in the following code:

```
HWND hwndCtl = GetDlgItem(hDlg, ID_LISTBOX);
int n = ListBox_GetCount(hwndCtl);
ListBox_AddString(hwndCtl, "Another string");
    :
    :
```

If you design your code in this way, your application runs faster because it doesn't repeatedly call *GetDlgItem*. *GetDlgItem* can be a slow function if your dialog box has many controls and the control you are looking for is toward the end of the z-order.

API Macros

The API macros exist to make some common operations a little simpler. For example, one common operation is to create a new font, select the font into a device context, and save the handle of the original font. This code looks something like this:

```
HFONT hfontOrig = (HFONT) SelectObject(hdc, (HGDIOBJ) hfontNew);
```

This statement requires two casts in order to get a warning-free compilation. One of the macros in WINDOWSX.H was designed for exactly this purpose:

```
#define SelectFont(hdc, hfont) \
   ((HFONT) SelectObject( (hdc), (HGDIOBJ) (HFONT) (hfont)))
```

If you use this macro, the line of code in your program becomes

```
HFONT hfontOrig = SelectFont(hdc, hfontNew);
```

This code is easier to read and is far less subject to error.

Several more API macros are defined in WINDOWSX.H to help with commonly performed Windows tasks. I urge you to examine them and to use them.

THE BUILD ENVIRONMENT

To build the sample applications in this book, you must be concerned with compiler and linker switch settings. I have tried to isolate these details from the sample applications by putting almost all of these settings in a single header file, called CMNHDR.H, that is included in all of the sample application source code files. Unfortunately, there are some settings I wasn't able to put in this header file; I was therefore forced to make some changes to each sample application's project make file. This appendix discusses why I chose the compiler and linker switches that I did and how I went about setting them for the sample applications.

The CMNHDR.H Header File

All the sample programs in this book include the CMNHDR.H header file before including any other header file. I wrote the CMNHDR.H header file, listed in Figure C-1 beginning on page 1004, to make life a little easier for myself. The file contains macros, linker directives, and other code that I wanted to be common across all the applications. Sometimes when I want to try out different things, all I need to do is modify the CMNHDR.H file and rebuild all the sample applications. The CMNHDR.H file is in the root directory on the companion disc.

The remainder of this appendix discusses each section contained within the CMNHDR.H header file. I explain the rationale for each section and also describe how and why you might want to make changes before rebuilding all the sample applications.

Warning Level 4

When I develop software, I always do my best to ensure that the code compiles both error and warning free. I also like to compile at the highest warning level possible. This way, the compiler is doing the most work for me and is examining even the most minute details of my code. For the Microsoft C/C++ compilers, this means that I built all the sample applications on the companion disc using warning level 4.

Unfortunately, Microsoft's Operating Systems group doesn't share my sentiments about compiling using warning level 4, and as a result, when I set the sample applications to compile at warning level 4, many lines in the Microsoft Windows header files cause the compiler to generate warnings. Fortunately, these warnings do not represent problems in the code—most are generated by unconventional uses of the C language. These uses rely on compiler extensions that almost all vendors of PC-compatible compilers implement.

The first part of the CMNHDR.H header file explicitly tells the compiler to ignore some common warnings using the #*pragma warning* directive.

Windows Version

Because some of my sample applications call new functions that exist only in Microsoft Windows NT 4, this section defines the _WIN32_WINNT symbol as follows:

```
#define _WIN32_WINNT 0x0400
```

The reason I must do this is because the new Windows NT 4 functions are prototyped in the windows header files like this:

```
#if (_WIN32_WINNT >= 0x0400)
WINBASEAPI
BOOL
WINAPI
TryEnterCriticalSection(
   LPCRITICAL_SECTION lpCriticalSection
   );
#endif /* _WIN32_WINNT >= 0x0400 */
```

Unless you specifically define _WIN32_WINNT as I have (before including WINDOWS.H), the prototypes for the new Win32 functions will not be declared and the compiler will generate errors if you attempt to call these functions. Microsoft protected these functions with the _WIN32_WINNT symbol to help ensure that applications you develop can run on multiple versions of Windows NT (and Windows 95).

The STRICT Macro

All my sample applications are compiled taking advantage of the strict type-checking support available in the Windows header files. This support makes sure that I assign HWNDs to HWNDs and HDCs to HDCs and so forth. With STRICT defined, the compiler will issue a warning if, for example, I attempt to assign an HWND to an HDC.

To turn on strict type-checking, the compiler must have the STRICT macro defined prior to including the Windows header files.

CPU Portability Macros

To support the targeting of multiple CPU architectures, this section defines a few symbols to indicate where certain CPU-specific files are kept.

Unicode

I have written all the sample applications so that they can be compiled as either ANSI or Unicode. When compiling the applications for the x86 CPU architecture, ANSI is the default so that the applications will execute on Windows 95. However, Unicode is used when building the applications for any other CPU architecture so that the applications use less memory and execute faster.

If you want to create Unicode versions for the x86 architecture, all you need to do is uncomment the single line that defines UNICODE and rebuild. By defining the UNICODE macro in CMNHDR.H, it is easy for me to control how I want the sample applications to build. For more information on Unicode, see Chapter 17.

The chDIMOF Macro

The chDIMOF macro is a useful macro that I tend to use in many programs I write. It simply returns the number of elements in an array. It does this by using the *sizeof* operator to first calculate the size of the entire array in bytes. It then divides this number by the number of bytes required for a single entry in the array.

The chBEGINTHREADEX Macro

All the multithreaded samples in this book use the *_beginthreadex* function, supplied in Microsoft's C run-time library, instead of Win32's *CreateThread* function. This is because the *_beginthreadex* function prepares the new thread so that it can use the C run-time library functions and also ensures that the per-thread C run-time library information is destroyed when the thread returns. (See Chapter 4 for more details.)

Unfortunately, the _beginthreadex function is prototyped as follows:

```
unsigned long __cdecl _beginthreadex(void *lpsa, unsigned cbStack,
    unsigned (__stdcall *) (void *lpStartAddr), void *lpvThreadParm,
    unsigned fdwCreate, unsigned *lpIDThread);
```

Although the parameter values for _beginthreadex are identical to the parameter values for the Win32 CreateThread function, the data types of the parameters do not match. Here is the prototype for the CreateThread function:

```
HANDLE CreateThread (LPSECURITY_ATTRIBUTES lpsa, DWORD cbStack,
    LPTHREAD_START_ROUTINE lpStartAddr, LPVOID lpvThreadParm,
    DWORD fdwCreate, LPDWORD lpIDThread);
```

Microsoft did not use the Win32 data types when creating the _beginthreadex function's prototype because Microsoft's C run-time group does not want to have any dependencies on the Operating System group. I commend this decision; however, this makes using the _beginthreadex function more difficult in your code, especially if you define the STRICT macro when you compile.

There are really two problems with the way Microsoft prototyped the _beginthreadex function. First, some of the data types used for the function do not match the primitive types used by the CreateThread function. For example, the Win32 data type DWORD is defined as follows:

```
typedef unsigned long DWORD;
```

This data type is used for CreateThread's cbStack parameter as well as for its fdwCreate parameter. The problem is that _beginthreadex prototypes these two parameters as unsigned, which really means unsigned int. The compiler considers an unsigned int to be different from an unsigned long and generates a warning. Because the _beginthreadex function is not a part of the standard C run-time library and exists only as an alternative to calling the Win32 CreateThread function, I believe that Microsoft should have prototyped _beginthreadex this way so that warnings are not generated:

```
unsigned long __cdecl _beginthreadex(void *lpsa,
    unsigned long cbStack,
    unsigned (__stdcall *) (void *lpStartAddr), void *lpvThreadParm,
    unsigned long fdwCreate, unsigned long *lpIDThread);
```

The second problem is just a small variation of the first. The _beginthreadex function returns an unsigned long representing the handle of the newly created thread. An application will typically want to store this return value in a data variable of type HANDLE as follows:

```
HANDLE hThread = _beginthreadex(…);
```

The line of code above causes the compiler to generate another warning if you define STRICT when you compile your code. To avoid the compiler warning, you must rewrite the line above introducing a cast as follows:

```
HANDLE hThread = (HANDLE) _beginthreadex(…);
```

Again, this is very inconvenient. To make my life a little easier, I define a chBEGINTHREADEX macro in CMNHDR.H to perform all of this casting for me.

The chASSERT and chVERIFY Macros

To help find potential problems while developing the applications, I frequently sprinkled chASSERT macros throughout the code. This macro tests whether the expression identified by *x* is TRUE and, if not, displays a message box indicating the file, line, and the expression that failed. In release builds of the applications, this macro expands to nothing. The chVERIFY macro is almost identical to the chASSERT macro except that the expression is evaluated in release builds as well as debug builds.

The chHANDLE_DLGMSG Macro

When using message crackers with dialog boxes, you should not use the HANDLE_MSG macro from Microsoft's WINDOWSX.H header file. The reason to avoid this macro is that it doesn't return TRUE or FALSE to indicate whether a message was handled by the dialog box procedure.

As much as I hate to admit it, the previous two editions of this book made the mistake of using the HANDLE_MSG macro. I was very lucky that the applications in the previous editions worked correctly. I have corrected all of the applications in this edition to use the chHANDLE-_DLGMSG macro.

The chMB Macro

The chMB macro simply puts up a message box. The caption is the full pathname of the executable file for the calling process.

The chINITSTRUCT Macro

The chINITSTRUCT macro is by far my favorite of all the macros in CMNHDR.H. I love this macro! In Win32 programming, we frequently have to allocate a data structure, zero it, and initialize the first member of the structure to the size of the structure. I have seen many programmers either forget to do one or both of these things. The result is that their calls to Win32 functions fail for no apparent reason, or worse, coincidentally work—sometimes!

If you religiously use the chINITSTRUCT macro, you will be ensured that the structure's members are always set to zero. You must explicitly state whether or not you want the first member to be initialized to the size of the structure. If you pass TRUE as the second parameter, the size will be automatically initialized—this way, you will never forget!

The chSETDLGICONS Macro

Because most of the applications use a dialog box as their main window, the dialog box's icon must be changed manually so that it is displayed correctly on the TaskBar, in the task switch window, and in the application's caption itself. The chSETDLGICONS macro is always called when dialog boxes receive a WM_INITDIALOG message so that the icons are set correctly.

The chWARNIFUNICODEUNDERWIN95 Macro

Windows 95 does not support Unicode as completely as does Windows NT. In fact, applications that call Unicode functions will not run on Windows 95! Unfortunately, Windows 95 does not give any notification if an application compiled for Unicode is invoked. For the applications in this book, this means that the applications start and terminate with no indication that they ever attempted to execute. This drove me absolutely nuts! So, I created this chWARNIFUNICODEUNDERWIN95 macro so that I would know when I attempted to run a Unicode-compiled application under Windows 95.

The Pragma Message Helper Macro

While working on code, I often like to get something working immediately and then make it bulletproof later. When I need to remind myself that some code needs additional attention, I used to place a line like this in the code:

```
#pragma message("Fix this later")
```

Whenever the compiler compiled this line, it would output a string reminding me that I had some more work to do. Sadly, the message displayed by the compiler is not as helpful as it could be. What would be really cool is if the compiler output the name of the source code file and the line number that the pragma appeared on. This way, not only would I know that I have some work to do, but I could also locate the surrounding code immediately.

To get this behavior, you have to trick the pragma comment directive using a series of macros. The end result is that you can use the chMSG macro like this:

```
#pragma chMSG(Fix this later)
```

When the line above is compiled, the compiler produces a line that looks like this:

```
C:\Document\AdvWin\Code\Sysinfo.06\..\CmnHdr.H(296):Fix this later
```

Now, using Visual C++, I can double-click on this line in the output window and the environment will automatically open the appropriate file and position the caret directly on the pragma line.

As a convenience, the chMSG macro does not require quotes to be used around the text string.

Linker Directives

One of my goals when creating the sample applications in the book was to avoid putting a lot of dependencies in the applications' project make files. For example, I could have used Visual C++'s Project Settings dialog box to add the STRICT, UNICODE, and _UNICODE macros to the project's settings, but that would have created a dependency on the project's make file. If you ever wanted to create the project's make file from scratch, you might forget to select certain options and some of the programs might not work properly.

In fact, this is what happened to me while I was developing some of the sample applications. Some of the sample DLLs require that certain linker switches be set in order for them to function correctly. Whenever I would create a new project make file for these DLLs, I always forgot to set one of the linker switches, the DLL functioned improperly, and I would have to start debugging the application and the DLL to find out why. As soon as I realized that the code was fine but that I had forgotten to set a linker switch, I would kick myself.

I knew that this was going to continue to be a problem for me as well as for readers of this book, so I set out on a mission to remove specific project settings from all the make files for the samples. Starting with Visual C++ 4.0, you can easily set linker switches inside your source code file using a pragma comment directive. For example, the code:

```
// Instruct the linker to make the Shared section
// readable, writable, and shared.
#pragma comment(linker, "/section:Shared,rws")
```

causes the compiler to embed a linker switch inside this source file's associated OBJ module. When the linker links the module, it looks for any embedded linker switches and pretends that the switches were specified on the command line. This is very convenient.

CMNHDR.H

```
/****************************************************************
Module name: CmnHdr.h
Written by: Jeffrey Richter
Notices: Copyright (c) 1995-1997 Jeffrey Richter
Purpose: Common header file containing handy macros and
         definitions used throughout all the applications
         in the book.
****************************************************************/


/* Disable ridiculous warnings so that the code */
/* compiles cleanly using warning level 4.      */

/* nonstandard extension 'single line comment' was used */
#pragma warning(disable: 4001)

// nonstandard extension used : nameless struct/union
#pragma warning(disable: 4201)

// nonstandard extension used : bit field types other than int
#pragma warning(disable: 4214)

// Note: Creating precompiled header
#pragma warning(disable: 4699)

// unreferenced inline function has been removed
#pragma warning(disable: 4514)

// unreferenced formal parameter
#pragma warning(disable: 4100)

// indirection to slightly different base types
#pragma warning(disable: 4057
```

Figure C-1.
The CMNHDR.H header file.

(continued)

Figure C-1. *continued*

```
// named type definition in parentheses
#pragma warning(disable: 4115)

// nonstandard extension used : benign typedef redefinition
#pragma warning(disable: 4209)


/////////////// Windows Version Build Option ////////////////


#define _WIN32_WINNT 0x0400


/////////////////// STRICT Build Option ////////////////////


// Force all EXEs/DLLs to use STRICT type checking.
#define STRICT


/////////////////// CPU Portability Macros //////////////////


// If no CPU platform was specified, default to the
// current platform.
#if !defined(_PPC_) && !defined(_ALPHA_) && !defined(_MIPS_)\
   && !defined(_X86_)
   #if defined(_M_IX86)
      #define _X86_
   #endif
   #if defined(_M_MRX000)
      #define _MIPS_
   #endif
   #if defined(_M_ALPHA)
      #define _ALPHA_
   #endif
   #if defined(_M_PPC)
      #define _PPC_
   #endif
#endif
```

(continued)

Figure C-1. *continued*

```
//////////////////// Unicode Build Option ////////////////////


// If we are not compiling for an x86 CPU, we always
// compile using Unicode.
#ifndef _X86_
#define UNICODE
#endif


// To compile using Unicode on the x86 CPU, uncomment the
// line below.
//#define UNICODE

// When using Unicode Win32 functions, use Unicode
// C-Runtime functions, too.
#ifdef UNICODE
#define _UNICODE
#endif


//////////////////////// chDIMOF Macro ////////////////////////


// This macro evaluates to the number of elements in an array.
#define chDIMOF(Array) (sizeof(Array) / sizeof(Array[0]))


//////////////////// chBEGINTHREADEX Macro ////////////////////


// Create a chBEGINTHREADEX macro that calls the C run-time's
// _beginthreadex function. The C run-time library doesn't
// want to have any reliance on Win32 data types such as
// HANDLE. This means that a Win32 programmer needs to cast
// the return value to a HANDLE. This is terribly inconvenient,
// so I have created this macro to perform the casting.
typedef unsigned (__stdcall *PTHREAD_START) (void *);
#define chBEGINTHREADEX(lpsa, cbStack, lpStartAddr, \
    lpvThreadParm, fdwCreate, lpIDThread)           \
      ((HANDLE)_beginthreadex(                      \
        (void *) (lpsa),                            \
        (unsigned) (cbStack),                       \
```

(continued)

Figure C-1. *continued*

```
            (PTHREAD_START) (lpStartAddr),              \
            (void *) (lpvThreadParm),                   \
            (unsigned) (fdwCreate),                     \
            (unsigned *) (lpIDThread)))



/////////////////// Assert/Verify Macros ///////////////////


#define chFAIL(szMSG) {                                 \
    MessageBox(GetActiveWindow(), szMSG,               \
        __TEXT("Assertion Failed"), MB_OK | MB_ICONERROR); \
    DebugBreak();                                       \
  }

// Put up an assertion failure message box.
#define chASSERTFAIL(file,line,expr) {                  \
    TCHAR sz[128];                                      \
    wsprintf(sz, __TEXT("File %hs, line %d : %hs"),     \
        file, line, expr);                              \
    chFAIL(sz);                                         \
  }

// Put up a message box if an assertion fails in a debug build.
#ifdef _DEBUG
#define chASSERT(x) if (!(x))\
   chASSERTFAIL(__FILE__, __LINE__, #x)
#else
#define chASSERT(x)
#endif

// Assert in debug builds, but don't remove the code in
// retail builds.
#ifdef _DEBUG
#define chVERIFY(x) chASSERT(x)
#else
#define chVERIFY(x) (x)
#endif
```

(continued)

Figure C-1. *continued*

```
///////////////////// chHANDLE_DLGMSG Macro /////////////////////


// The normal HANDLE_MSG macro in WINDOWSX.H does not work
// properly for dialog boxes because DlgProcs return a BOOL
// instead of an LRESULT (like WndProcs). This chHANDLE_DLGMSG
// macro corrects the problem:
#define chHANDLE_DLGMSG(hwnd, message, fn)                     \
   case (message): return (SetDlgMsgResult(hwnd, uMsg,        \
      HANDLE_##message((hwnd), (wParam), (lParam), (fn))))


///////////////////// Quick MessageBox Macro /////////////////////


#define chMB(s) {                                              \
     TCHAR szTMP[128];                                         \
     GetModuleFileName(NULL, szTMP, chDIMOF(szTMP));           \
     MessageBox(GetActiveWindow(), s, szTMP, MB_OK);           \
   }


///////////////////// Zero Variable Macro /////////////////////


// Zero out a structure. If fInitSize is TRUE, initialize
// the first int to the size of the structure. Many structures
// like WNDCLASSEX and STARTUPINFO require that their first
// member be set to the size of the structure itself.
#define chINITSTRUCT(structure, fInitSize)                     \
   (ZeroMemory(&(structure), sizeof(structure)),              \
   fInitSize ? (*(int*) &(structure) = sizeof(structure)) : 0)


/////////////// Dialog Box Icon Setting Macro///////////////

// The call to SetClassLong is for Windows NT 3.51 or less.
// The WM_SETICON messages are for Windows NT 4.0 and
// Windows 95.

#define chSETDLGICONS(hwnd, idiLarge, idiSmall)                \
   {                                                           \
     OSVERSIONINFO VerInfo;                                    \
```

(continued)

Figure C-1. *continued*

```
        chINITSTRUCT(VerInfo, TRUE);                               \
        GetVersionEx(&VerInfo);                                    \
        if ((VerInfo.dwPlatformId == VER_PLATFORM_WIN32_NT) && \
            (VerInfo.dwMajorVersion <= 3 &&                        \
              VerInfo.dwMinorVersion <= 51)) {                     \
          SetClassLong(hwnd, GCL_HICON, (LONG)                     \
            LoadIcon(GetWindowInstance(hwnd),                      \
              MAKEINTRESOURCE(idiLarge)));                         \
        } else {                                                   \
          SendMessage(hwnd, WM_SETICON, TRUE,  (LPARAM)            \
            LoadIcon(GetWindowInstance(hwnd),                      \
              MAKEINTRESOURCE(idiLarge)));                         \
          SendMessage(hwnd, WM_SETICON, FALSE, (LPARAM)            \
            LoadIcon(GetWindowInstance(hwnd),                      \
              MAKEINTRESOURCE(idiSmall)));                         \
        }                                                          \
    }


///////////////// UNICODE Check Macro /////////////////////////


#ifdef UNICODE

#define chWARNIFUNICODEUNDERWIN95()                               \
   if (GetWindowsDirectoryW(NULL, 0) <= 0)                        \
      MessageBoxA(NULL,                                           \
         "This operating system doesn't support Unicode.",   \
         NULL, MB_OK)

#else

#define chWARNIFUNICODEUNDERWIN95()

#endif


/////////////// Pragma message helper macro //////////////

/*
When the compiler sees a line like this:
#pragma chMSG(Fix this later)
it outputs a line like this:
```

(continued)

1009

Figure C-1. *continued*

```
C:\Document\AdvWin\Code\Sysinfo.06\..\CmnHdr.H(296):
    Fix this later

You can easily jump directly to this line and examine
the surrounding code.
*/
#define chSTR(x)        #x
#define chSTR2(x)    chSTR(x)
#define chMSG(desc)                                              \
    message(__FILE__ "(" chSTR2(__LINE__) "):" #desc)


////////////// End of File //////////////////////////////////////
```

Project Settings I Couldn't Set in the Source Files

The only project setting that you might have to change is in the Output Directories group box. When you create a Visual C++ project, the integrated environment chooses a subdirectory for the resultant binary files. If you are building an executable that requires a DLL or a DLL that has an associated executable, you will have to change the Output Directories information so that the final EXE or DLL files are in the same subdirectory.

INDEX

Italic page-number references indicate a figure, a listing, a table, or a footnote.

About the author...

Jeffrey Richter is a Win32 trainer and has given programming seminars to thousands of software developers. His clients include such companies as Allen-Bradley, AT&T, Caterpillar, Digital, GE Medical Systems, Hewlett Packard, IBM, Intel, Intuit, Microsoft, Pitney Bowes, and Sybase. (For training information, please see www.solsem.com.)

Jeff also speaks regularly at industry conferences, including Software Development and COMDEX, and is a technical advisor for Boston University's WinDev conference. In 1995, Jeff authored *Windows 95: A Developer's Guide* (M & T Books), which covers Win32 user-interface programming. Jeff is also a contributing editor to *Microsoft Systems Journal*, for which he authors the Win32 Q & A column and has written several feature articles.

Jeff now lives in Bellevue, Washington, where he is a frequent consultant to Microsoft. His code appears in Visual C++ and other applications produced by Microsoft's Personal Operating Systems group. He likes to eat teriyaki chicken bowls from Costco and top them off with Ben and Jerry's ice cream while watching *The Simpsons*. He has a passion for classic rock and jazz fusion bands.

You can reach Jeff at this e-mail address: *v-jeffrr@microsoft.com*.

The manuscript for this book was prepared and submitted to Microsoft Press in electronic form. Text files were prepared using Microsoft Word for Windows 95. Pages were composed by Microsoft Press using Adobe PageMaker 6.01, with text in New Baskerville and display type in Helvetica Bold. Composed pages were delivered to the printer as electronic prepress files.

Art Direction
Gregory Erickson

Cover Graphic Designer
Robin Hjellen

Cover Illustrator
Glenn Mitsui

Interior Graphic Designer
Kim Eggleston

Interior Graphic Artist
Travis Beaven

Principal Typographers
Peggy Herman
Jeffrey Brendecke

Indexer
Richard Shrout

Other *UNUSUAL Seminars*

FROM David Solomon Expert Seminars

David Solomon Expert Seminars offer the following leading-edge Win32®, Windows® 95, Windows NT®, Visual C++®, and MFC seminars to corporate clients. Each seminar has been **developed personally by the instructor who gives it.** Seminars are one day in duration (except where noted) and can be combined to form a multi-day event. Hands-on labs can be added to most of our seminars (add $1/2$ day of lab time per one seminar day).

On-Site Seminars—These seminars are available for delivery onsite at companies worldwide (minimum of 15 students per class).

Public Seminars—We occasionally run public seminars. Contact us to see if one is scheduled in your area.

Hands-on Labs—Hands-on labs are available as an optional add-on for most of our seminars. This gives students an opportunity to put into practice what they have learned while having access to the instructor for personalized assistance.

Scheduling—To schedule a seminar, we must receive a purchase order four weeks prior to the seminar date. A two-week notice is required to cancel a seminar without incurring a cancellation fee.

For More Information:

World Wide Web:	http://www.solsem.com/
Email:	seminars@solsem.com
Telephone:	800-492-4898, outside USA: +1-860-355-9029
Facsimile:	860-355-9050

Jamie Hanrahan

- ▶ Windows NT Internal Architecture
- ▶ Windows NT Kernel-Mode Device Driver Programming
- ▶ Windows NT Kernel-Mode Device Driver Programming Advanced Driver Topics

Ken Miller

- ▶ Taking advantage of VB's New Features
- ▶ Developing Visual Basic®/SQL Server™ Applications
- ▶ Programming the Windows NT/Win32 API with VB

Matt Pietrek

- ▶ Windows 95 Internals
- ▶ Advanced Win32 Programming & Debugging for Windows NT & 95

Jeff Prosise

- ▶ Programming Windows NT & Windows 95 with Visual C++ & MFC

David Solomon

- ▶ Windows NT Internal Architecture
- ▶ Windows NT & Win32 for VMS Programmers
- ▶ Windows NT for VMS System Managers

Ken Spencer
- ▶ Windows NT for System/Network Managers
- ▶ Taking Advantage of VB's New Features
- ▶ Developing Visual Basic/SQL Server Applications
- ▶ Programming the Windows NT/Win32 API with VB

New!

Brian Catlin
- ▶ Writing Windows NT Display/Video Drivers

You've read the book— Now hear the man! *On Site!*

Have Jeff Richter come on site to your company to deliver one of his high-powered Win32® programming seminars!

Register Today!

Return this
ADVANCED WINDOWS, *Third Edition*
registration card for a
Microsoft Press® catalog

U.S. and Canada addresses only. Fill in information below and mail postage-free. Please mail only the bottom half of this page.

1-57231-548-2A   **ADVANCED WINDOWS®, Third Edition**   *Owner Registration Card*

_____
NAME

_____
INSTITUTION OR COMPANY NAME

_____
ADDRESS

_____
CITY   STATE   ZIP

Microsoft®*Press*
Quality Computer Books

**For a free catalog of
Microsoft Press® products, call
1-800-MSPRESS**

BUSINESS REPLY MAIL

FIRST-CLASS MAIL   PERMIT NO. 53   BOTHELL, WA

POSTAGE WILL BE PAID BY ADDRESSEE

MICROSOFT PRESS REGISTRATION
ADVANCED WINDOWS,* Third Edition*
PO BOX 3019
BOTHELL WA 98041-9946

BREWERY
REDCHURCH
PARADISE PALE ALE

BREWERY
REDCHURCH
BRICK LANE LAGER

BREWERY
REDCHURCH
BETHNAL PALE ALE

BREWERY
REDCHURCH
SHOREDITCH BLONDE

BREWERY
REDCHURCH
BETHNAL PALE ALE

BREWERY
REDCHURCH
HOXTON STOUT

BREWERY
REDCHURCH
GREAT EASTERN IPA

BREWERY
REDCHURCH
PARADISE PALE ALE

BREWERY
REDCHURCH
BRICK LANE LAGER

BREWERY
REDCHURCH
GREAT EASTERN IPA

BREWERY
REDCHURCH
SHOREDITCH BLONDE

BREWERY
REDCHURCH
OLD FORD EXPORT STOU

16

Gabriel Lluelles Rabadà (Barcelona 1932–2012) was a Catalan industrial designer. He completed his studies in industrial mechanics and industrial electro-mechanics at the Industrial School of Barcelona. Between 1947 and 1962 he worked at Pimax Industria as a craftsman, eventually becoming the head of technical services and finally taking over as technical director. From 1962 to 1970 he was the director of the department of development and construction at Braun Spain. In 1971, after a period of activity as an independent designer he joined Taurus as a design overseer and director of a new line of products. He worked there until his retirement in 1998. Throughout those years, Lluelles actively collaborated with ADI-FAD, BCD and ADP to promote industrial design. His designs have been awarded on multiple occasions and his work has been exhibited in numerous design exhibitions. Among his more creations are the vocal Neopreno and the Olicromàtic M12-2 juicer designed together with Dieter Rams.

Gabriel Lluelles

Leopoldo Milà i Sagnier (Barcelona, 1921–2006) was a Catalan industrial designer, founder of the Pulmex and DAE companies. In 1958 he became the technical director of the motorcycle company Montesa, where he created and designed the highly successful Impala model, winner of the Golden Delta Award (ADI-FAD) in 1962. Based on a simple 2 stroke monocylinder engine and a very stable frame, it is characterized by a rounded tank, a unique engine sound and a guitar shaped seat. The clean and simple design of the Impala quickly became an icon of the motorcycling industry. To demonstrate the quality and reliability of the motorcycle, three Impala prototypes successfully crossed Africa from all the way from Cape Town to Tunis in a historic endeavour baptised the "Impala operation". Milà went on to create the award winning Montesa Cota 247. He continues being a reference in the Spanish motorbike industry.

Leopoldo Milá

23
Museu del Disseny de Barcelona

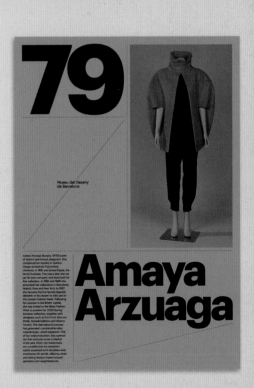

79
Museu del Disseny de Barcelona

Amaya Arzuaga (Burgos, 1970) is one of Spain's best known designers. She completed her studies in Fashion Design at bloc4:uk Polytechnic University. In 1992 and joined Elypse, the family business. Two years later she set up her own company and launched her first collection. In 1995 and 1996 she presented her collections in Barcelona, Madrid, Paris and New York. In 1997 she became the first female Spanish designer to be chosen to take part in the London Fashion Week. Following her success in the British capital, she was invited to the Milan Fashion Week to present her 2003 Spring Summer collection, together with designers such as Tom Ford, Marcial Prada, Dolce&Gabbana and Alberto Favetti. This international success has generated considerable sales outside Spain, which represent 70% of her total production. She opened her first exclusive store in Madrid in 1998 and 2000. Her restraints are a predilection for minimalism, subtly accented with shoulders and developing 3D profils, offering urban and daring designs typed around geometry and weightlessness.

Amaya Arzuaga

ASTRONAUT OF INNER SPACES: SUNDRIDGE PARK, SOHO, LONDON … MARS

MARLBOROUGH

CENTURY

CATTLE & SON

PORTLAND

St JAMES

BERWICK

CHARITY

Quintessentializes
Photosynthesised
College of Justice
E Pluribus Unum
Bank of England
Gamesomeness

NE
SO
GATE

EVERY
BODY
DANCE
NOW

Airport Terminal Specialists   Tim Mein Architects

MEIN

Auckland New Zealand

+64 9 354 3723   An independent airport terminal design consultancy, specialising in the planning and design of airport terminals

LHR London Heathrow T3	SYD Sydney International Airport	SYD Sydney Domestic T3	YYC Calgary International Airport
CXI Cassidy International Airport	YQR Regina International Airport	DBO Dubbo Airport	PER Perth International Airport
VAV Lopepau'u Airport	FUN Funafuti International Airport	IUE Niue International Airport	TRG Tauranga Airport

↳CHAPEAU
SPECIMEN
CHAPEAU&
SPEC1MEN
⊛CHAPEAU
SPECIMEN
CHAPEAU*
SPE€IMEN
√CHAPEAU
SPECIMEN

Exposició
**Extraordinàries!
Col·leccions d'arts
decoratives i arts
d'autor (segles III-XX)**

2

−1B01   23 4

Exposició
**Extraordinàries!
Col·leccions d'arts
decoratives i arts
d'autor (segles III-XX)**

Diese Woche:

21.8.23.8.25.8.27.8.

Manuel Aires Mateus
Manuel Graça Dias
Maria Helena Barreiros
Pedro Campos Costa
Ricardo Agarez
Ricardo Carvalho

/ UAL
00-185 Lisboa

na.pt

Habitar
pensar
nvestigar
fazer

Peter Dawson

Foreword by
Tobias Frere-Jones

The Essential Type Directory

A Sourcebook of Over 1,800 Typefaces and Their Histories

BLACK DOG
& LEVENTHAL
PUBLISHERS
NEW YORK

Contents

Script 560

Foundry Profiles

Designer Profiles

Foreword
by Tobias Frere-Jones

Looking back on the recent history of type design, it's tempting to see a story of technology, liberating makers, and users alike. In the last few decades, the tools for making digital type became available to anyone with a computer and enough patience. Designing a typeface—let alone preparing it for the marketplace—was a lengthy and daunting task. Throughout most of the 20th century, this had been an industrial-scale undertaking (literally). It was thrilling to watch the old ways being usurped and swept away. As it turned out, that was really the smaller part of the story.

The quieter and more profound change has been in education. Those slow, onerous ways of making type were also the venue for training young designers. No school taught these very particular skills, so the young and eager would learn on the job, as they had for centuries. Techniques were closely guarded from competitors, with most designers ("punch-cutters" for many years) declining to publish any detailed guide to their craft. It was a black art, and deliberately so.

But in the digital age, access to tools begat the demand for skills. And now typeface design is a regular feature of design programs around the world, with a few schools in Europe and the United States even offering degrees or certificates in this very specialized discipline. The spread of type education has brought digital type to its more mature state. And now there are more trained type designers than at any point in history. This discipline has never been so thoroughly populated.

But the question is often posed: why do we need more typefaces? Depending on how you hear it, the question may imply not only a redundancy but an ongoing dilution: the more we make the less it means. But the opposite is true. That diversity—even in fine shades—is a source of strength. If we all used the same type, that choice would become meaningless and we'd lose a chance for expression.

We can (and should) discuss the associations the type will accrue through use: the typeface that was used for this ad campaign, this political candidate, that movie poster. But it glosses over an important point: these choices, any choices, have the chance to mean more because other designers used something else. That constant refresh of inventory is the foundation of power. As long as the flavor is distinct and the execution is sound, typefaces will support one another regardless of style. Not in spite of their differences but because of them.

Gathering typefaces from the last centuries as well as the present day, this book hopes to consider that expanding world.

Opposite. Specimen examples of sans serif design Mallory. It was the first typeface released under Frere-Jones Type (see p. 80), the independent type design studio of Tobias Frere-Jones. A humanist design combining British and US typographic traditions to provide a distinctive and unique sans serif font family.

FREQUENTS HERZEGOVINA

World Leagues Grand Prix

Every December Sunday

€207 ₺214 ₦981 ₹835 ₽160

MEN'S NATIONAL TEAM

5408 SAN FRANCISCO BLVD

QUILTING WORKSHOPS!

Unjustifiable Alternatives

Gjøvik to Logroño quickest

RYE WHISKEY TASTINGS

Introduction

I had my first forays into working with type in my youth, when I spent my later school studies honing my skills to become a commercial illustrator. My ambition was to illustrate graphic novels. Designing posters and graphic ephemera, I used type mainly in the form of hand drawings with a liberal dash of Letraset dry-transfer lettering. At such a tender age, I was not fully aware of the existence of typeface designers or typefaces as a commercial craft and industry.

I was formally introduced to typography and typefaces during my first year of studying for a degree in Graphic Design at Kingston University, Surrey, UK, when my lecturer, the designer Eugenie Dodd, asked me to complete a typographic project. It was a momentous moment as I realized that a whole world of typefaces and their infinite possibilities lay before me. I changed tack in my studies and never looked back. Gone was my ambition of becoming a comic-book illustrator as my attentions turned to becoming a typographic graphic designer.

More than twenty-five years later, I am writing the introduction to *The Essential Type Directory*, having enjoyed a career that has been more like a vocation. I love my role and, more importantly, I am still learning. Over the years, I have used numerous typefaces on a wide variety of projects and have always admired the creative ingenuity, dedication, craftsmanship, and attention to detail of the unsung heroes of the world of type design. These highly skilled members of the creative community past and present number in their thousands. Many are revered as icons in the typographic world thanks to their creative genius and unassuming daily passion. What are invariably their labors of love enable those who work with type to have their creations read in print or online across the world.

The Essential Type Directory aims to pay tribute to these heroes of type by presenting a selection of the many typefaces that are available for a designer. The book is a visual celebration of the craft, innovation, and beauty of these letterforms. It is a comparative guide across a range of type styles and their subcategories, providing the historical background to their creation as well as insight into the evolution of the international industry and community that revolves around typefaces. There are now more than 250,000 individual fonts that make up typeface families, and they comprise the good, the bad, and the excellent. This collection presents a portfolio of diverse creations with the aim of being an essential and informative sourcebook for the graphic designer and design studio. Given there are so many types available, not all can be included here and inevitably there are typefaces that have been omitted but which are popular with practitioners. (Other factors are the extent, permissions, and contributions offered). This collection comprises more than 1,800 typefaces with all manners of style, geographical location, and historical periods, as well as aesthetic appeal and practicality. *The Essential Type Directory* also profiles some of the world's most innovative type design studios and their work, as well as significant type designers who have created landmark typefaces and contributed to the development of type design and graphic design.

The Essential Type Directory is a typographic time capsule. It is by no means complete but it provides a snapshot of what has come before, shows where typeface design is now and signals the directions it is heading. Type design evolves, not simply according to fashion, designers' interests, and aesthetic urges, but most importantly in keeping with the technological advances in how people read information in print and on screen. In recent years, there have been a wealth of highly crafted typefaces with extensive families that bridge the gap between print and online legibility, working across all media at all sizes. A number of these typefaces are commissions specifically created for brands and organizations, large and small, to communicate their position and messages, but as is often the case, the typefaces created become the visual essence of the brands.

Designing new and ever-more refined and advanced types is a perpetual benefit to all, from the largest studios to the independent designer.

Above. A typesetter in the late 1940s assembles letters of lead type into a block at the Wick printing works of Partridge & Love, Bristol. This traditional method of printing with blocks of individual type remained in use by some printers for small jobs until the 1970s. It was labor-intensive but provided high-quality impressions.

Above right. Editors and typesetters working in the composing room of the *Washington Times-Herald* newspaper in 1954.

Right. Phototypesetting systems became prevalent by the 1970s (shown here in Germany c. 1980s). As a result of their introduction, the use of metal type for commercial mass-market printing declined and eventually ceased. Phototypesetting systems projected letterforms onto photographic material for use in offset lithographic printing.

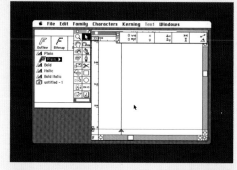

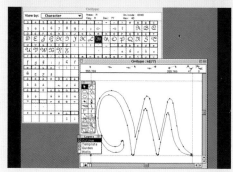

Top. When the Apple Macintosh computer was released in 1984, it triggered a seismic change in the ways that users could work with type and how type could be designed. Early type-design software such as Font Studio and Fontographer led the way.

Above. Today, the same design principles, attention to detail, and lengthy processes still apply to the creation of any new typefaces. Shown above are on-screen refinements being undertaken at Fontsmith and, right, the numerous workings for Fedra Serif by Typotheque.

The encouragement of businesses, cultural organizations, and media empires to engage with type, and the desires of type foundries to create beautifully crafted, aesthetically pleasing and technically competent typefaces will ensure that the craft of these individuals across the world continues. Just as their predecessors have influenced today's designers, so contemporary creations become cultural, creative, and historical reference points in their turn.

— Peter Dawson

About the Book

To compile the final edit of the 1,800-plus typefaces included in this book took six months of research, examination, addition, deletion, and refinement, with a further eight months for building the book and evolving the content. Many foundries from around the globe were invited to participate; sadly, several could not contribute due to commercial, logistical, or timing reasons.

Once all the classic and key historical types and subsequent variations and revivals were included, the foundries who kindly contributed their libraries were added. This has resulted in a diverse range of contemporary and highly crafted submissions.

The final collection is of typefaces that work as a resource and reference point to help graphic designers in selecting typefaces for their projects, as well as acting as an encyclopedia of type development and history.

Each typeface is presented with uppercase and lowercase alphabetical letterforms along with numerals, key punctuation marks, and symbols. All typeface examples are presented at 20-point size on 22-point leading, thereby creating a direct comparison across the entire book for letter spacing, x-height, and cap height. In addition, readers can see the line length occupied by each typeface. However, because of the structure of the book and page size it is not possible on some occasions to present the whole of the uppercase alphabet. Those typefaces that appear only in uppercase will have no lowercase option and some of the typefaces possess alternate characters, so discrete differences in their letter designs or certain of the characters are shown.

A short descriptive text accompanies each entry, explaining its origin and / or significant design features. Each entry also contains a section that provides information on the foundry, the name of the designer/s, the designer's nationality, and the type's date of origination. Earlier dates invariably refer to metal production, whether punches or hot metal. Later dates refer to phototypesetting and digital production. The team of writers who assisted in this extensive challenge was confronted by many cases of conflicting information regarding origination credits and dates of typefaces that in some instances are centuries old and come from all over the world. The hope is that their diligence has achieved clarity and historical accuracy. Typefaces of particular value, visual interest, or innovative contemporary designs are presented as half-, single- or double-page spread features. This allows for additional information and images showcasing how they were created or their usage. At the end of the book there are several indexes to help readers locate typeface entries: an A to Z index of typefaces, an index of typefaces by designer, and an index by foundry.

Glossary

Anti-aliasing
The addition of intermediate pixels (especially on curves) on screen, where bitmapped type possesses stepped pixels to create smooth transitions by blurring the edges.

Antiqua
A classification or grouping of serif types with calligraphic Old Style letterforms. Used as a German and Scandinavian common name for serif types.

Aperture
The opening of a part-closed counter, such as "C" and "S," or the upper half of a lowercase double-storey "a."

Apex
The point where two strokes meet at the top of a letter, such as on an uppercase "A" or "M."

Arc
Any part of a curve of a letter, leading into a stem.

Arm
The horizontal stroke in a character that does not connect to a stem at one side such as on an "E," or on both sides such as a "T."

Ascender
The vertical stroke or feature of a lowercase letter that rises above the font's x-height, as in "b," "d," "f," and "k."

Axis (stress)
A key feature of most typefaces, an invisible line that runs through the character, from top to bottom, through its thinnest points, creating direction in its form. This assists in classification, with Old Style typefaces having a slanted axis and transitional types having invariably a vertical stress.

Back slant
A reverse italic / oblique with a left tilt or lean.

Ball terminal
A circular rounded shape found at the end of a stroke instead of a serif or a sharp cut-off. To be found on lowercase double-storey serif letters such as "a," "c," and "f."

Baseline
Invisible line on which all lower- and uppercase letters sit.

Beak
A decorative pronounced stroke, similar to a serif, found at the end of the arm of a letter, such as capital "S."

Bitmap
Character or form defined by pixels set within a grid. What was a part of PostScript fonts containing information for the typeface to display correctly on-screen on older computer systems that had no rasterizing capability. Also referred to as "screen fonts."

Blackletter
A classification or grouping of heavy calligraphic script types, also known as Gothic Script and Old English script, employing broad-nibbed uniform vertical strokes connected by angular lines. Created from the Middle Ages onward and used commonly for manuscript books and documents throughout Europe at the time.

Body
The full height of a typeface including ascenders, descenders, and clearance space. The height of the body is equal to the point size.

Bold
A heavier drawn variation of a regular weight of a typeface.

Bowl
The enclosed rounded / oval form found on letterforms such as "b," "o," and "p."

Bracket
The curved or wedge-shaped element found between the serif and the stem that joins them together.

Calligraphy
The craft of writing elegant letterforms by hand using a writing tool.

Cap height
The height of a capital or uppercase letter from its baseline to the letterform's highest point.

Capital
A large set of initial letters. Also referred to as "uppercase" and "caps."

Character
Any individual letter, number, punctuation mark, symbol, or sign within a typeface.

Color (typographic)
The tonal value of a block of text when it is set on a page. Referred to in shades of gray to black.

Condensed
Typeface appearance designed with a narrower character width over Roman types.

Constructivist
Russian 20th-century art and architectural movement, influenced by Cubism and Futurism, and which was an influence at the Bauhaus schools in Germany.

Contrast
The difference between thick and thin strokes of a character design. Can also be referred to in terms of size, color, and weight of differing types.

Counter
The enclosed or partially enclosed negative space within a letter, such as in "b" and the lower part of "e."

Cross stroke
The horizontal strokes across the stem found in lowercase letterforms, such as "t" and "f."

Crossbar
The horizontal strokes found in letterforms, such as "A" and "H." Also known as a "bar."

Crotch
Inside angle where two strokes join, such as in a "V."

Cursive
Type reminiscent of handwritten letterforms. Also known as "script" or "longhand" with characters joined up.

Descender
The part of a lowercase letter that sits below the baseline, such as on a "g" or "p."

Didone
A serif family that possesses very high stroke contrast with unbracketed hairline serifs. Also referred to as "modern."

Dingbat
A non-alphabetical character consisting of a symbol, shape, or other pictorial element.

Display
Typefaces designed for title or headline applications rather than for reading texts. Commonly used in advertising or banner applications, often decorative and used for larger settings rather than the setting of extended lengths of text.

Double-storey
Lowercase "a" and "g" that possess two counters over each other. Single-storey types have just the one.

Drop shadow
Creation of an offset replication of a letterform positioned behind a character to provide a 3D effect or shadow design.

Ear
Decorative flourish found on a lowercase double-storey "g" on the upper right of the top bowl.

Egyptian
Serif type with low stroke contrast and large, heavy, squared serifs.

English roundhand
Calligraphic connecting handwritten script originating from England in the mid 17th century. Features include a low stroke contrast as drawn with metal pointed nibs.

Expanded (extended)
A type design whereby the letterforms are created as if stretched across the horizontal axis to make wider character widths than in a regular design.

Expert
A reference for a font that possesses an extended character set such as non-aligning numerals and other alternative characters.

Eye
Specifically the counter within a lowercase "e."

Family
A collection of fonts of varying weights and styles sharing a common design approach and construction.

Fat Face
Heavily emboldened serif display typefaces. The earliest recorded designs were in England during the early 19th century, where they were used for posters and lottery bills.

Figures
Alternative name for numbers and numerals.

Finial
A tapered or curved end to a stroke.

Fleuron
Decorative typographic ornament such as a flower or botanical symbol that is placed at the beginning or ends of paragraphs.

Font / fount
A collection of all the letterforms, punctuation marks, numerals, and font metrics attributed to a single typeface design and weight such as Roman. A typeface family is made up of several fonts, each of its own style and weight.

Foot
The element of a stem that sits on the baseline.

Foundry
The historical name of a place used for casting hot-metal type. It is employed today to describe type studios.

Fraktur
A form of decorative blackletter type, commonly found in Germany from the 16th century and widely used there until the mid 20th century.

Glyph
A single character (number or letter), punctuation mark, or symbol within a typeface.

Grotesque
From the German "grotesk"; a type classification of sans serif typefaces.

Hot metal
A process that involved the injection of molten metal into a cast formed of differing glyphs to create type blocks (slugs) to be used for printing, when inked up and pressed into the paper. Developed in the late 19th century, it fell out of fashion for mass-market printing with the appearance of phototypesetting in the late 1950s. It became obsolete with the advent of digital processes in the 1980s. Also known as "mechanical typesetting."

Humanist
A classification of serif and sans serif typefaces based on calligraphic minuscule letterforms dating to the 7th and 9th centuries and the proportions of the Roman capital.

Ink trap
A feature within a typeface's design where counters and corners of letterforms are removed to counter the build-up of ink when printed, negating dark spots, especially if material is of a low quality such as newsprint.

Italic
A slanted, script version of a Roman typeface; a bespoke design incorporating distinctive and individual letterforms that appear handwritten. More often found in serif designs. See "oblique."

Italienne
Decorative display type inspired by the large wood type of the American Wild West identified by large, heavy banded serifs and extreme contrast in stroke weight.

Junction
Intersection at which the end of one stroke meets a point in another stroke in a letter.

Kerning
The spacing and plus / minus adjustment between individual pairs of letters to improve readability and appearance.

Leading
The term dates to the use of metal type when compositors inserted thin strips of lead between lines to increase line spacing. Traditionally, it refers to the adjustment and addition of vertical distance between lines of horizontal type, expressed in points, fractions of points, or millimetres. Today, the term is widely used to describe line spacing.

Leg
The downward sloping stroke on a "k" and "R."

Legibility
The ability of one letter to be easily distinguished and recognizable from another.

Letter spacing
The adjustment of space between letters in typesetting, either uniformly or optically, to achieve optimum positioning.

Ligature
Two characters joined to form one letterform such as "fi," "ff," or "fl."

Light
A thinner drawn variation of a regular weight of a typeface.

Line spacing
The vertical distance between lines of horizontal type, expressed in points, fractions of points, or millimetres. Measured from the baseline of one line to the baseline of the next.

Lining figures
Numeral characters of common size and cap height resting on the baseline.

Lithographic (litho) printing
Printing onto paper from inked etched metal plates. The most common form of printing worldwide today. It is used for the printing of books, catalogues, and posters due to its high quality.

Loop
The lower portion of a double-storey lowercase 'g' that sits below the baseline.

Lowercase
Small letters of the Latin alphabet derived from handwritten minuscules. The name derives from the use of metal type, when the letterforms were kept in tray. The lower part of the tray contained the lowercase letter whereas the capitals were in the upper trays and were hence named "uppercase."

Metrics
Numerical values and units of measure contained within a digital font file to ensure accurate spacing and positioning of type.

Minuscule
The small or lowercase letters of the alphabet based on cursive letterforms from the 7th to 9th century.

Modern
A serif family that possesses very high stroke contrast often with unbracketed hairline serifs. Also referred to as "didone."

Monoline
A typeface where the letterform's stroke weight possesses a constant width.

Monospaced
A typeface where each of its character occupies the same amount of space, irrespective of its width. Commonly seen in typefaces based on manual typewriters.

Neo-grotesque
A type classification of sans serif typefaces. These types are simpler in appearance than earlier grotesque counterparts with more consistent stroke contrast and increased legibility.

Non-aligning figures
Numeral characters of varying height and position on the baseline. Also referred to as "Old Style" numerals.

Oblique
Slanted (mechanically sheared) Roman letter forms; not to be confused with "Italic," which has a more cursive construction. More often seen with sans serif than serif types. See "Italic."

OCR
Abbreviation of "optical character recognition." A typeface that can be scanned and read by a machine as well as read by people. Invariably used when large amounts of data require processing.

Old Style
A classification for serif types that appear with low stroke contrast, an angled stress to the left, bracketed serifs, and angled head serifs. Originally created between the late 15th and mid 18th centuries.

OpenType
Cross-platform font format by Microsoft and Adobe, which was developed in the late 1990s and became widespread in the industry after 2000. Not only does the typeface allow for cross-platform compatibility working on both PCs and Macs but it also allows for very large character sets to be created and contained within a single file. As OpenType fonts support Unicode, one font can contain more than 65,000 glyphs, making it possible to work with multiple languages within one file.

Phototypesetting (photocomposition)
Typesetting process whereby typefaces were created on glass negatives and were exposed to photosensitive paper by shining light through them to create hard-copy versions. Became obsolete with the introduction of the personal computer and desktop-publishing software.

Pica
An Anglo-American standard typographic unit of measure possessing a width of 12 points.

Pixel
Smallest unit of a digital image and a display screen.

Point
A standard typographic unit of measure equal roughly to $1/72$nd of an inch (0.351 mm) with 72.27 points to the inch.

Point size
A unit of measure of type based on roughly $1/72$ in. In the Anglo-American point system, one point typically equals 0.01383 in. (0.351 mm). In desktop publishing the figure is usually rounded off to exactly $1/72$ in., which matches with screen display resolutions of 72 pixels to the inch.

PostScript
Adobe's page-description programing language that allows for vector-based elements to be accurately rendered. Now replaced by OpenType.

Proportional spacing
A typeface whose characters possess spacing based on their individual character widths rather than a uniform, identical spacing, thus creating better readability within running text.

Punch (punchcutter)
A steel die faced with an individual letter hand-carved in relief. This die was then punched into a softer metal with other letter punches to create text blocks / page layouts and the resultant printing blocks to reproduce them.

Readability
The ability of being able to read and absorb lengthy typeset text when composed with ease.

Regular
A classification term for a standard weight of typeface.

Roman
Regular, upright style of letter. Also used as a term for a typeface of book / normal weight as opposed to a bolder weight.

Running text
Continuous typeset reading text, as commonly seen in textbooks.

Sans serif
A typeface classification of a group of typefaces with no serif features in its construction. First became popular in the early 19th century.

Semibold
An intermediary weight between Roman / Medium and Bold.

Serif
The small stroke that appears at the beginning or end of a serif letter stroke. There are a number of differing shapes that include bracketed, slab, hairline, banded, and wedge.

Slab serif
A typestyle where the serifs are squared in construction and equal, or close to, the optical weight of the strokes.

Slope
Oblique simulated Roman letterforms, more often used with sans serif.

Small caps (capitals)
Capital letterforms but with a height roughly that of lowercase letters.

Spacing
See "Letter spacing."

Spine
The central curved stroke in both lower- and uppercase "s."

Stem
The main vertical stroke in a letter.

Stress
See "Axis."

Stroke
The line that creates the letterform / character.

Style
Typographic term that describes the varieties of a single typeface, such as Roman, Bold, and Italic.

Swash
An elegant addition, usually to uppercase italics or script types, which is a decorative extension to the letterform.

Tabular figures
Numerals that share a fixed width so that when they are employed in columns for accounting purposes they can be aligned to be easily read.

Tail
Decorative stroke on uppercase letter "Q" that sits below the baseline.

Thicks and thins
Terminology to describe the widths of the stroke.

Titling
A display style of typeface designed for large settings, capitals, and numerals only.

Tittle
The dot of a lowercase "i" and "j."

Tracking
Spacing applied to characters in a line of text as a whole, adjusting the inter-letter spacing as a consistent unit rather than kerning that focuses on just a pair of letters.

Transitional
A group of typefaces emerging in the 18th century which are the bridge between their predecessors' Old Style types with elements of the soon-to-emerge modern-style serifs. Possessing a higher contrast stroke weight and a more vertical stress to their construction. Many contemporary serif designs can be categorized as transitional.

Typeface
The harmonious design of a font as a collection of all the character elements (letters, numerals, and punctuation marks) that share the same design principles and / or construction elements.

Unicase
Typeface where both uppercase and lowercase share the same height so that they can be mixed together.

Unicode
The international computer industry standard for the handling and presentation of text.

Uppercase
The capital letters in a typeface.

Vector
Mathematical formula that creates and defines a curved or straight line that is at the heart of every digital font. The vector outlines allow for the typeface to be scaled at any size without loss of quality and the information is translated into a bitmap representation for screen use as pixels.

Weight
Definition for the lightness or heaviness of a typeface's design.

x-height
The height of lowercase letters from the baseline exemplified by the letter "x," ignoring both ascenders and descenders. Typefaces with a large x-height appear much bigger than typefaces with a smaller x-height even if they share the same point size when set.

The Essential Type Directory

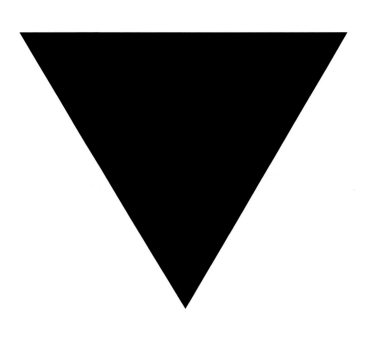

S TALENTS *of* RIDICUL

ut pleaded excuse for

much the rather

N NEW YORK C

y that nasty weee

ndeterminatel

ID THE SPANI

and smiled at her apprehension

Serif

Opposite. Detail of specimen of Emigre foundry's MrsEavesXL. Designed by Zuzana Licko in 2009; this variant is built upon the success of the original Mrs Eaves design but with more consideration to designs where space is at a premium.

The earliest serif forms date to Roman times, when Latin letterforms were carved into stone. Research indicates that these inscriptions were first painted or marked on to the stone for stone carvers to follow as a guide, hence the introduction of a serif flare at the end of a line to close the stroke. This provided a tidy and clean closure, as well as neatening the end of the lines once carved.

In the 1400s, all type had to be carved before it was set and printed, and type cutters adopted existing Roman forms in their designs. Soon the Blackletter (see p. 562) forms of the day were replaced by the handwriting-influenced designs of these early Roman forms. The earliest serif forms, described as Venetian or humanist (see p. 71), had a more calligraphic feel. The stress of the drawn letter reflected a handwritten approach with the stroke contrast being less markedly different.

In the 1500s, these types gave way to what is referred to as Old Style (see p. 110). This was a period of great invention and innovation as designers and printers created their own designs. These Old Style letterforms built further on the handwritten aspect of their construction. The axis of their curved strokes inclined to the left, the serifs were almost always bracketed and the head serifs were angled. These types had a more upright composure and, as letter-cutting and printing techniques improved, more refinement was introduced into the stroke weights. Printers worked closely with type designers experimenting with letterforms, ink mixtures, and paper manufacture.

By the mid to late 1700s, the fashion for an increased contrast between the thick and thin strokes and a vertical stress, or close to vertical, in the construction of the letters with flat bracketed serifs resulted in the evolution of transitional typefaces (see p. 150). This was the period where type forms evolved from Old Style to the Modern / Didone (see p. 93) typeface designs. One of the lead innovators of the time was English type designer and printer John Baskerville. His tireless efforts researching and developing all aspects of producing the printed word had a huge impact on type design and his principles still apply. As such, many contemporary serif typefaces fall into this category.

By the 1800s, technological developments in type design and printing resulted in the creation of Modern / Didone or neoclassical typefaces. Notable exponents of these styles include Italy's Giambattista Bodoni and France's Firmin Didot.

Because printing was at a relatively sophisticated point by then, these types possessed very high contrast in their stroke weights with hairline thins and heavyweight thicks. Their serifs were often unbracketed, allowing for sharp junctures between horizontal and vertical strokes and the serifs.

At the start of the 20th century, type design and manufacture began to expand industrially as a global *tour de force*. Slab serif designs (also referred to as square serif or Egyptian) had emerged. These types were primarily born out of increased newspaper usage and the need to create bold headlines with impact. The rise in consumerism resulted in their use for product advertising too, notably including Clarendon (see p. 38), Rockwell (see p. 58), and later ITC Lubalin Graph (see p. 55). Their forms have minimal stroke contrast, so as to be more impactful on the page, and invariably come with unbracketed serifs. Slab serifs can be further broken down from the accepted subcategories of serif to Clarendon-style slab serifs (see p. 35), geometric-style slab serifs (see p. 419), and humanist slab serifs (see p. 521).

Amalia

ABCDEFGHIJKLMNOPQRSTUVWXYZ
abcdefghijklmnopqrstuvwxyz
1234567890 !@#?:;"*&

Foundry: Typotheque
Designer: Nikola Djurek
Designer Nationality: Croatian
Date: 2006

While taking inspiration from Dutch classical typography in general, Amalia has a moderate contrast that is similar to modern faces such as Didot and Bodoni. *Typographica* review chose Amalia as one of its "Favorite Typefaces of 2006." The font was remastered in 2018.

Barbedor

ABCDEFGHIJKLMNOPQRSTUVWXYZ
abcdefghijklmnopqrstuvwxyz
1234567890 !@#?:;"*&

Foundry: Hell
Designer: Hans Eduard Meier
Designer Nationality: Swiss
Date: 1987

Created for the Hell Digiset machine (but sketched out on paper), Barbedor is influenced by 15th-century humanist book scripts. Its characters appear as if they have been formed by broad-tipped pens, and its handwritten nature is further emphasized by its subtle serif elements.

Bernhard Modern

ABCDEFGHIJKLMNOPQRSTUVWXYZ
abcdefghijklmnopqrstuvwxyz
1234567890 !@#?:;"*&

Foundry: American Type Founders
Designer: Lucian Bernhard
Designer Nationality: German
Date: 1937

Originally named "Booklet," Bernhard Modern has a low x-height, reminiscent of the engravers' Old Style faces that were popular in the 1930s. The difference in line weight gives it a handwritten flavor, which is emphasized by its rounded line terminals and gently tapered serifs.

Brioni

ABCDEFGHIJKLMNOPQRSTUVWXYZ
abcdefghijklmnopqrstuvwxyz
1234567890 !@#?:;"*&

Foundry: Typotheque
Designer: Nikola Djurek
Designer Nationality: Croatian
Date: 2008

Nikola Djurek received the Icograda Excellence Award for Brioni (along with Plan Grotesque and Marlene) in 2010. Three years later, a Greek version by Peter Biľak and a Cyrillic version Alexander Tarbeev was added. It is a sophisticated serif designed for use in books and magazines.

Byngve

ABCDEFGHIJKLMNOPQRSTUVWXYZ
abcdefghijklmnopqrstuvwxyz
1234567890 !@#?:;"'*&

Foundry: Linotype
Designer: Bo Berndal
Designer Nationality: Swedish
Date: 2004

This unpronounceable font is an amalgamation of the designer's two Christian names, "Bo" and "Yngve." Byngve takes its inspiration from elegant 15th-century Italian calligraphic letterforms. Swedish typographer Bo Berndal drew the laid-back serif entirely by hand before digitizing it.

Calligraphic 810

ABCDEFGHIJKLMNOPQRSTUVWXYZ
abcdefghijklmnopqrstuvwxyz
1234567890 !@#?:;"'*&

Foundry: Stempel / Bitstream
Designer: Gudrun Zapf von Hesse
Designer Nationality: German
Date: 1952 / c. 1980s

Calligraphic 810 is Bitstream's cut of Gudrun Zapf von Hesse's serif Diotima originally made for Stempel in 1952 and available in roman and italic. Linotype released a new four-weight cut in 2008 as Diotima Classic, which includes additional light and heavy weight.

Cataneo

ABCDEFGHIJKLMNOPQRSTUVWXYZ
abcdefghijklmnopqrstuvwxyz
1234567890 !@#?:;"'*&

Foundry: Bitstream
Designer: Richard Lipton / Jacqueline Sakwa
Designer Nationality: American
Date: 1993

This elegant cursive serif was inspired by the 16th-century Italian master calligrapher Bernardino Cataneo, who is best known for his single manuscript copy book of twenty pages. It has three weights—Light, Regular, and Bold—as well as complementary swash characters and extensions.

Corvallis

ABCDEFGHIJKLMNOPQRSTUVWXYZ
abcdefghijklmnopqrstuvwxyz
1234567890 !@#?:;"'*&

Foundry: ITC
Designer: Philip Bouwsma
Designer Nationality: American
Date: 1994

This beautifully crafted serif came as a result of Philip Bouwsma's lifetime appreciation of the classics and the craft of calligraphy. Like many of his typefaces, Corvallis is clearly influenced by the broad-pen calligraphy of historic scripts. It is available in regular and oblique.

De Worde

ABCDEFGHIJKLMNOPQRSTUVWXYZ
abcdefghijklmnopqrstuvwxyz
1234567890 !@#?:;"&*

This expertly crafted seven-weight font was inspired by the early italic used extensively by the 16th-century printer and publisher Wynkyn de Worde, who is known as the Father of Fleet Street. It was released to coincide with the 60th anniversary of the Wynkyn de Worde Society.

Foundry: Jeremy Tankard Typography
Designer: Jeremy Tankard
Designer Nationality: British
Date: 2016

Diotima

ABCDEFGHIJKLMNOPQRSTUVWXYZ
abcdefghijklmnopqrstuvwxyz
1234567890 !@#?:;"*&

A delicate, rounded serif, Diotima is named after a slim and beautiful Greek priestess in one of Plato's texts. This typeface, originally released as a hot-metal typeface with a single weight, is complemented perfectly by Gudrun Zapf von Hesse's headline type Smaragd, and Ariadne Initials.

Foundry: Stempel
Designer: Gudrun Zapf von Hesse
Designer Nationality: German
Date: 1951

Ellington

ABCDEFGHIJKLMNOPQRSTUVWXYZ
abcdefghijklmnopqrstuvwxyz
1234567890 !@#?:;"*&

This calligraphy-influenced font was named for the jazz musician Duke Ellington and was designed by lettering artist and stone carver Michael Harvey. Its condensed letterforms were developed with utility in mind, to be both legible and distinctive in body text and display contexts.

Foundry: Monotype
Designer: Michael Harvey
Designer Nationality: British
Date: 1990

Empirica

ABCDEFGHIJKLMNOPQRSTUVWXYZ
abcdefghijklmnopqrstuvwxyz
1234567890 !@#?:;"*&

Empirica is a combination of the grand style of Ancient Rome and the French tradition, and its close spacing and delicate serifs make it a perfect headline font. It comprises six weights plus italics, and there are alternate short descenders for tighter line spacing at the largest headline settings.

Foundry: Frere-Jones Type
Designer: Tobias Frere-Jones / Nina Stössinger
Designer Nationality: American / Swiss
Date: 2018

Exlibris

ABCDEFGHIJKLMNOPQRSTUVWXYZ
abcdefghijklmnopqrstuvwxyz
1234567890 !@#?:;"*&

Foundry: ITC
Designer: Bo Berndal
Designer Nationality: Swedish
Date: 1993

Bo Berndal's remarkable seventy-year-long career spanned book design, illustration, calligraphy, advertising, and teaching, and he created more than 200 typefaces over the course of his life. This graceful yet robust serif, available in three weights, was his first design for ITC.

Footlight

ABCDEFGHIJKLMNOPQRSTUVWXYZ
abcdefghijklmnopqrstuvwxyz
1234567890 !@#?:;"*&

Foundry: Monotype
Designer: Ong Chong Wah
Designer Nationality: Malaysian
Date: 1986

Malaysian designer Ong Chong Wah first created Footlight as an italic, before expanding his design to include the roman. This approach is reflected in the distinctive, calligraphic appearance of the font, which was made widely available by Microsoft within many of its products.

FS Olivia

ABCDEFGHIJKLMNOPQRSTUVWXYZ
abcdefghijklmnopqrstuvwxyz
1234567890 !@#?:;"*&

Foundry: Fontsmith
Designer: Eleni Beveratou
Designer Nationality: Greek
Date: 2012

Eleni Beveratou's design for FS Olivia was inspired in part by the work of Dutch type designer Sjoerd Hendrik de Roos, and was created to capture a sense of the movement of pen on paper. It is an expressive, textural serif, and the Pro edition also includes Cyrillic and Greek character sets.

Gilgamesh

ABCDEFGHIJKLMNOPQRSTUVWXYZ
abcdefghijklmnopqrstuvwxyz
1234567890 !@#?:;"*&

Foundry: Letraset
Designer: Michael Gills
Designer Nationality: British
Date: 1994

Michael Gills's exploration of calligraphic type styles during his time at Letraset resulted in a range of new designs, among them Gilgamesh. This Old Style typeface features narrower letterforms and counterbalanced serifs, making it a useful and legible choice for body text.

GT Sectra

ABCDEFGHIJKLMNOPQRSTUVWXYZ
abcdefghijklmnopqrstuvwxyz
1234567890 !@#?:;"*&

Foundry: Grilli Type
Designer: Marc Kappeler /
Dominik Huber / Noël Leu
Designer Nationality: Swiss
Date: 2011 / 2014

GT Sectra was originally created for use in the reportage magazine *Reportagen*. The typeface combines "the calligraphic influence of the broad nib pen with the sharpness of the scalpel knife." *Reportagen* was designed by Zurich-based studio Moiré and the journal required a typeface that was flexible and extensive in weights following expenditure on its start-up.

At first, *Reportagen* used Times Bold for headlines and a typewriter typeface for texts, but once more funding was achieved a typeface was commissioned to work with the many hierarchies and sizes being employed in the magazine, whose impact was nearly all typographic. This sole use of text throughout was also at the core of the magazine's visual identity, from the cover through to the articles it contained.

Swiss foundry Grilli Type (see p. 238) published the design by Marc Kappeler and Dominik Huber of Moiré. The typeface's edgy appearance and distinctive, cut calligraphic forms, led to its name Sectra, derived from the Latin for "to cut," *secare*.

Sectra has undergone many iterations since its inception in 2011. Moiré joined forces with Noël Leu from Grilli Type to refine the concept behind it, and every issue of *Reportagen* saw improvements to the typeface. Initially, the letterforms possessed a softer and more traditional feel, but gradually curves were replaced by cuts, resulting in simpler shapes. The result is a design with a high legibility factor and strong, angular lines. The family contains fifteen weights divided into three subfamilies.

Below. GT Sectra was created for use in the current affairs magazine *Reportagen*, designed in conjunction with Zurich-based studio Moiré.

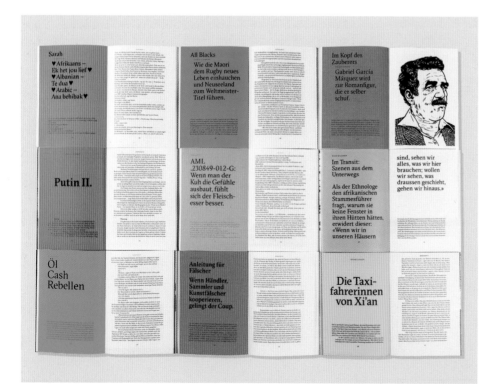

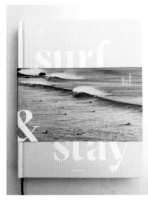

Above. Travel guide *Surf & Stay* highlights the best spots on the coastlines of Spain and Portugal to camp and surf. Written by Veerle Helsen and designed by Elke Treunen of Antwerp-based design studio MAFF.

Left. Designed by London studio Land of Plenty, GT Sectra is employed on the cover of *The Association of Photographers Annual* and used at both headline and text sizes.

Hiroshige

ABCDEFGHIJKLMNOPQRSTUVWXYZ
abcdefghijklmnopqrstuvwxyz
1234567890 !@#?:;"*&

Hiroshige was originally commissioned to appear in a book of woodcuts by renowned 19th-century Japanese artist Andō Hiroshige. The calligraphic details within the font's letterforms are very reminiscent of brushstrokes and could be seen as a nod to its namesake.

Foundry: AlphaOmega Typography
Designer: Cynthia Hollandsworth Batty
Designer Nationality: American
Date: 1986

ITC Anima

ABCDEFGHIJKLMNOPQRSTUVWXYZ
abcdefghijklmnopqrstuvwxyz
1234567890 !@#?:;"*&

For ITC Anima, Serbian designer Olivera Stojadinovic set out to create a font that captured a sense of movement and vivacity within its forms. She hand-drew Anima before making digital amendments, and its angled serifs and calligraphic feel reflect the spontaneity of the sketching process.

Foundry: ITC
Designer: Olivera Stojadinovic
Designer Nationality: Serbian
Date: 2006

ITC Cerigo

ABCDEFGHIJKLMNOPQRSTUVWXYZ
abcdefghijklmnopqrstuvwxyz
1234567890 !@#?:;"*&

This distinctive serif was created by French type designer Jean-Renaud Cuaz, who wanted to develop a new interpretation of Renaissance calligraphic lettering styles that stood apart from existing revivals, such as Chancery by Hermann Zapf (see p. 574). It is available in three weights.

Foundry: ITC
Designer: Jean-Renaud Cuaz
Designer Nationality: French
Date: 1993

ITC Kallos

ABCDEFGHIJKLMNOPQRSTUVWXYZ
abcdefghijklmnopqrstuvwxyz
1234567890 !@#?:;"*&

Phill Grimshaw was taught by typographer Tony Forster at Bolton College of Art, Greater Manchester, England before studying at London's Royal College of Art. ITC Kallos is an elegant, calligraphic text typeface and one of more than forty fonts he designed in his career.

Foundry: ITC
Designer: Phill Grimshaw
Designer Nationality: British
Date: 1996

ITC New Veljovic

ABCDEFGHIJKLMNOPQRSTUVWXYZ
abcdefghijklmnopqrstuvwxyz
1234567890 !@#?:;"'*&

Foundry: ITC
Designer: Jovica Veljović
Designer Nationality: Serbian
Date: 2014

This revised version of Serbian designer Jovica Veljović's eponymous first typeface was published by ITC thirty years after the original, with the addition of several weights, styles, and character sets. Veljović's amendments enhance the typeface's suitability for a broad range of applications.

ITC Syndor

ABCDEFGHIJKLMNOPQRSTUVWXYZ
abcdefghijklmnopqrstuvwxyz
1234567890 !@#?:;"*&

Foundry: ITC
Designer: Hans Eduard Meier
Designer Nationality: Swiss
Date: 1992

Swiss type designer Hans Eduard Meier held a fascination with the evolution of written letterforms; his book on the subject, *Die Schriftenwicklung* (*The Development of Script and Type*, 1959), remains in print to this day. This elegant humanist serif design of his was published by ITC in 1992.

Mariposa

ABCDEFGHIJKLMNOPQRSTUVWXYZ
abcdefghijklmnopqrstuvwxyz
1234567890 !@#?:;"'*&

Foundry: Agfa Compugraphic
Designer: Philip Bouwsma
Designer Nationality: American
Date: 1994

US graphic designer Philip Bouwsma has a background in calligraphy and an interest in historical scripts. This is evident in this distinctive serif that features subtle curves and small, square serifs. Mariposa comes in Book and Bold, with italics, and can be paired with Mariposa Sans.

Nocturno

ABCDEFGHIJKLMNOPQRSTUVWXYZ
abcdefghijklmnopqrstuvwxyz
1234567890 !@#?:;"'*&

Foundry: Typotheque
Designer: Nikola Djurek
Designer Nationality: Croatian
Date: 2013

Nocturno comes in four weights, with italics, from the Dutch foundry Typotheque (see p. 90), which describes it as an "unapologetically calligraphic typeface with slightly oblique stress and sculpted, concave, almost flare serifs." It is easy on the eyes as a text face due to its large x-height.

Oxalis

ABCDEFGHIJKLMNOPQRSTUVWXYZ
abcdefghijklmnopqrstuvwxyz
1234567890 !@#?:;"*&

Oxalis is a quirky, calligraphic font with minimal serifs. It was created by French type designer Franck Jalleau, a teacher at the École Estienne, Paris and designer of typefaces for French passports. Oxalis was made for the Creative Alliance and is also available from Monotype in four weights.

Foundry: Creative Alliance
Designer: Franck Jalleau
Designer Nationality: French
Date: 1996

Runa Serif

ABCDEFGHIJKLMNOPQRSTUVWXYZ
abcdefghijklmnopqrstuvwxyz
1234567890 !@#?:;"*&

For Runa Serif, Swedish calligrapher Lennart Hansson was influenced by the forms of ancient Viking runes, which were used to write various Germanic languages. His design won the Nordic Typeface Competition in Copenhagen in 1993 and the Runa Serif family was published three years later.

Foundry: Monotype
Designer: Lennart Hansson
Designer Nationality: Swedish
Date: 1996

Semper

ABCDEFGHIJKLMNOPQRSTUVWXYZ
abcdefghijklmnopqrstuvwxyz
1234567890 !@#?:;"*&

Semper is named after the Latin for "always." It is a transitional serif inspired by the expressive forms of calligraphic lettering. Franko Luin's design balances the angular strokes and stresses of calligraphic forms with the moderate contrast and symmetrical serifs of the transitional style.

Foundry: Omnibus
Designer: Franko Luin
Designer Nationality: Swedish
Date: 1993

Thema

ABCDEFGHIJKLMNOPQRSTUVWXYZ
abcdefghijklmnopqrstuvwxyz
1234567890 !@#?:;"*&

Thema is a versatile, calligraphic serif face designed for both continuous text and striking headlines. The distinct contrast between strokes, alongside the sharp serifs and open counters, make it highly legible at small sizes, as well as being very effective in larger formats.

Foundry: Typotheque
Designer: Nikola Djurek
Designer Nationality: Croatian
Date: 2012

Algebra

ABCDEFGHIJKLMNOPQRSTUVWXYZ
abcdefghijklmnopqrstuvwxyz
1234567890 !@#?:;"*&

Foundry: Commercial Type
Designer: Susana Carvalho / Kai Bernau
Designer Nationality: Portuguese / German
Date: 2016

Algebra was informed by Granger, the headline face designed by Susana Carvalho and Kai Bernau for the US edition of *Esquire* magazine in 2011.

Algebra was conceived for flexible editorial use, and has loose spacing and little contrast, so it sits comfortably in long runs of text.

Algebra Display

ABCDEFGHIJKLMNOPQRSTUVWXYZ
abcdefghijklmnopqrstuvwxyz
1234567890 !@#?:;"*&

Foundry: Commercial Type
Designer: Susana Carvalho / Kai Bernau
Designer Nationality: Portuguese / German
Date: 2017

Algebra Display is the beefier sibling of Algebra, which is designed to inject authority into headlines and initials. While the broad strokes and serifs feature a considerable addition of muscle, the thin strokes are made even slimmer, to help maintain the font's dynamic balance.

Amariya

ABCDEFGHIJKLMNOPQRSTUVWXYZ
abcdefghijklmnopqrstuvwxyz
1234567890 !@#?:;"*&

Foundry: Monotype
Designer: Nadine Chahine
Designer Nationality: Lebanese
Date: 2017

Created primarily for on-screen use, this refined nine-weight font family supports the Arabic, Persian, and Urdu languages. It shares many qualities with traditional Middle Eastern text faces, but has been optimized for on-screen reading by its lower level of stroke contrast.

Ascender Serif

ABCDEFGHIJKLMNOPQRSTUVWXYZ
abcdefghijklmnopqrstuvwxyz
1234567890 !@#?:;"*&

Foundry: Ascender
Designer: Steve Matteson
Designer Nationality: American
Date: 2005

Created for on-screen legibility, this serif is metrically compatible with Times New Roman, offering a width-compatible font for developers to use across different platforms. The Ascender foundry worked closely with type developers for the Xbox 360, Android phone, and Windows core fonts.

Bonobo

ABCDEFGHIJKLMNOPQRSTUVWXYZ
abcdefghijklmnopqrstuvwxyz
1234567890 !@#?:;"*&

Foundry: Typodermic
Designer: Ray Larabie
Designer Nationality: Canadian
Date: 2006

Bonobo is a relaxed slab serif with distinctive curls on letters "a," "c," and "s." This playful typeface was created by Canadian Ray Larabie, a video games art director turned typeface designer. Larabie is based in Nagoya, Japan where he has set up his own foundry, Typodermic.

Bookman Old Style

ABCDEFGHIJKLMNOPQRSTUVWXYZ
abcdefghijklmnopqrstuvwxyz
1234567890 !@#?:;"*&

Foundry: Monotype
Designer: Alexander Phemister / Ong Chong Wah
Designer Nationality: British / Malaysian
Date: 1858 / 1990

This typeface has its origins in Alexander Phemister's Old Style Antique created *c.* 1858 for the Scottish foundry Miller & Richard. Many versions were made of the typeface, which became known as Bookman. This version is based on models for Lanston Monotype and American Type Founders.

Century Expanded

ABCDEFGHIJKLMNOPQRSTUVWXYZ
abcdefghijklmnopqrstuvwxyz
1234567890 !@#?:;"*&

Foundry: American Type Founders
Designer: Linn Boyd Benton / Morris Fuller Benton
Designer Nationality: American
Date: 1900

Century Expanded is a very legible text font. It is a version of Century Broadface, which is a version of Linn Boyd Benton's font Century, commissioned by *Century Magazine* in 1894. This expanded version was designed with his son, Morris Fuller, and references the Bruce Type foundry's #16 Roman.

CG Clarendon

ABCDEFGHIJKLMNOPQRSTUVWXYZ
abcdefghijklmnopqrstuvwxyz
1234567890 !@#?:;"*&

Foundry: Fann Street
Designer: Robert Besley
Designer Nationality: British
Date: 1845

Clarendon is a sturdy serif with a large x-height, short ascenders and descenders and strong bracketed serifs. It has inspired numerous copies and revivals. The slab serif became immediately popular, although many designers consider the later 20th-century versions to be superior.

Claridge

ABCDEFGHIJKLMNOPQRSTUVWXYZ
abcdefghijklmnopqrstuvwxyz
1234567890 !@#?:;"*&

Foundry: Cofino
Designer: Adrian Williams
Designer Nationality: British
Date: 1979

The lowercase "g" of this distinguished slab serif has a distinctive central join to its loop. Its designer Adrian Williams collaborated with Dr Rosemary Sassoon in 1985 to create typefaces for children; the partnership has produced some of the most notable educational typefaces for British schools.

Clarion

ABCDEFGHIJKLMNOPQRSTUVWXYZ
abcdefghijklmnopqrstuvwxyz
1234567890 !@#?:;"*&

Foundry: Monotype
Designer: Robin Nicholas
Designer Nationality: British
Date: 1985

Clarion is derived from Robin Nicholas's font Nimrod (1980) and made use of much of the research he completed for it, but with very distinctive detailing. He designed this sturdy serif with a large x-height specifically to be compatible with the emerging newspaper technology of the 1980s.

Congress

ABCDEFGHIJKLMNOPQRSTUVWXYZ
abcdefghijklmnopqrstuvwxyz
1234567890 !@#?:;"*&

Foundry: Elsner+Flake
Designer: Adrian Williams
Designer Nationality: British
Date: 1980

Congress is designed to look good when used in different European languages and was shown for the first time to an appreciative audience at the ATypI Congress held by the Association Typographique Internationale in Kiel, Germany in 1980. Adrian Williams added a sans version in 1985.

Cosmiqua

ABCDEFGHIJKLMNOPQRSTUVWXYZ
abcdefghijklmnopqrstuvwxyz
1234567890 !@#?:;"*&

Foundry: Linotype
Designer: Akira Kobayashi
Designer Nationality: Japanese
Date: 2007

This 1950s-inspired serif sits somewhere between formal italic types and casual handwriting scripts. Its name is an amalgamation of the French word cosmique (cosmic) and the German word Antiqua (the term for "serif"). Cosmiqua's distinctive serifs and terminals give it an informal, almost kitsch feel.

Clarendon LT

ABCDEFGHIJKLMNOPQRSTUVWXYZ
abcdefghijklmnopqrstuvwxyz
1234567890 !@#?:;"*&

Foundry: Fann Street Foundry / Linotype
Designer: Robert Besley / Hermann Eidenbenz
Designer Nationality: British / Swiss
Date: 1845 / 1953

Clarendon LT is a revival of the English slab serif typeface Clarendon created in 1953 by Hermann Eidenbenz of the Haas Type Foundry (Haas'sche Schriftgiesserei), a Swiss manufacturer of types that went on to produce Helvetica. Its distinctive bracketed square serifs, known as slab serifs, make for a more refined, Egyptian-style design. When employed with lighter serif typefaces, its heavier appearance helps to bring definition, and significantly aids access and navigation in expansive texts such as dictionaries.

This particular version of the typeface was refined from early slab serif designs that emerged from England in the early decades of the 19th century. The first Clarendon was created by Robert Besley of the Fann Street Foundry in London in 1845 and it was named after the Clarendon Press in Oxford. The origins of the design were from wooden display types, and Clarendon is often used for titles and display work. However, the Clarendon LT Light variant is perfectly adaptable for text applications.

Clarendon has influenced many slab serif designs and its popularity has resulted in the name being employed as a generic term for fonts of this style. Its characterful appearance and timeless design still make it a strong candidate for use in contemporary designs.

Below. A selection of prints from the calendar series "Cats Let Nothing Darken Their Roar," created by multi-discipline Spanish designer, Noa Bembibre. Clarendon is employed to convey a selection of abstract and emotive phrases.

I FELT BRIEFLY THAT YOU LIKED ARGUING SYNTAX

SENDING A POETIC, TENDER MOMENT BACK TO EARTH

LITTLE INFINITY

Right. *Inimigo Público* (Public Enemy) is a series of political protest posters, designed by the Brazilian husband and wife team of graphic designer and illustrator Johnny Brito and visual artist and photographer Maria Clara Feitosa, who collaborate as Vertentes Coletivo. The posters focus on four political figures from the 2018 elections and feature controversial comments they had made. The background is typeset in Fit by David Jonathan Ross, an ultra squared-off display type with keyline counters and apertures.

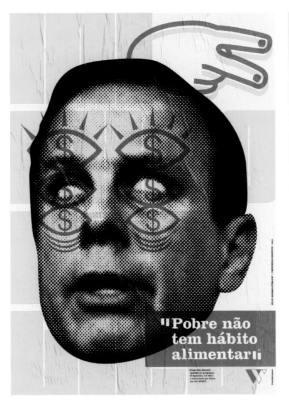

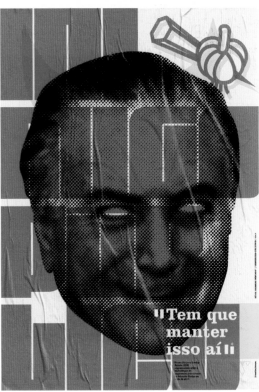

Delima

ABCDEFGHIJKLMNOPQRSTUVWXYZ
abcdefghijklmnopqrstuvwxyz
1234567890 !@#?:;"*&

Foundry: Monotype
Designer: Ong Chong Wah
Designer Nationality: Malaysian
Date: 1993

Delima has similarities to the slab serif Clarendon, and combines open counters and generous lowercase x-heights. Its serifs are short but sturdy, thus allowing closer letter spacing, which makes it extremely space efficient and therefore perfect for use as a text font.

Devin

ABCDEFGHIJKLMNOPQRSTUVWXYZ
abcdefghijklmnopqrstuvwxyz
1234567890 !@#?:;"*&

Foundry: Omnibus
Designer: Franko Luin
Designer Nationality: Swedish
Date: 1994

Despite being created primarily as a display typeface, Devin still remains surprisingly legible at smaller point sizes. The typeface is loosely influenced by Egyptian fonts. It is named after a ruined castle in Bratislava, Slovakia by its ex-Ericsson designer Franko Luin.

Digi Antiqua

ABCDEFGHIJKLMNOPQRSTUVWXYZ
abcdefghijklmnopqrstuvwxyz
1234567890 !@#?:;"*&

Foundry: Hell
Designer: Hell Design Studio
Designer Nationality: German
Date: 1968

The Hell Design Studio created Digi Antiqua primarily for use with its Digiset typesetting machines. Its letterforms were influenced by the slab serif fonts produced in England in the early 19th century. Its clear and elegant forms make it extremely legible at small point sizes.

Egizio

ABCDEFGHIJKLMNOPQRSTUVWXYZ
abcdefghijklmnopqrstuvwxyz
1234567890 !@#?:;"*&

Foundry: Nebiolo
Designer: Aldo Novarese
Designer Nationality: Italian
Date: 1955–58

Influential typeface designer Aldo Novarese created the heavily Clarendon-influenced Egizio. It comes with an italic, and was initially designed for the Italian foundry Nebiolo. Subsequent cuts have appeared courtesy of the German type foundries URW and Elsner+Flake.

Egyptian 505

ABCDEFGHIJKLMNOPQRSTUVWXYZ
abcdefghijklmnopqrstuvwxyz
1234567890 !@#?:;"*&

Foundry: Bitstream
Designer: André Gürtler
Designer Nationality: Swiss
Date: 1966 / c. 1980s

This is Bitstream's version of a typeface by Swiss designer André Gürtler. He worked on the font with his lettering class at the Allgemeine Gewerbeschule in Basle, which was held in classroom number 505. It won first prize in Visual Graphics Corporation's typeface design competition in 1966.

Egyptian 710

ABCDEFGHIJKLMNOPQRSTUVWXYZ
abcdefghijklmnopqrstuvwxyz
1234567890 !@#?:;"*&

Foundry: Figgins Foundry / Bitstream
Designer: Figgins Foundry
Designer Nationality: British
Date: 1860 / 1987

This is Bitstream's version of Antique No. 3. "Antique" was an early name for Egyptian types. The London-based Figgins Foundry cast a number of these types in the mid 19th century, which helped to define the contemporary styles of British printing. Bitstream digitized its font based on the original design.

Egyptienne F

ABCDEFGHIJKLMNOPQRSTUVWXYZ
abcdefghijklmnopqrstuvwxyz
1234567890 !@#?:;"*&

Foundry: Deberny & Peignot
Designer: Adrian Frutiger
Designer Nationality: Swiss
Date: 1956

Egyptienne F is the first attempt at a slab serif font by Adrian Frutiger (see p. 290). Later, he produced the Serifa typeface in 1966 and the recut Glypha in 1980. Egyptienne F is a sturdy Clarendon-style Egyptian with a medium x-height and excellent legibility at small sizes.

Else NPL

ABCDEFGHIJKLMNOPQRSTUVWXYZ
abcdefghijklmnopqrstuvwxyz
1234567890 !@#?:;"*&

Foundry: Norton Photosetting
Designer: Robert Norton
Designer Nationality: British
Date: 1982

This lively interpretation of the Century tradition was designed by Robert Norton, a shrewd businessman keen to engage with developing type technologies. He went on to join Microsoft in the 1990s, and was instrumental in the development of the company's TrueType font library.

Excelsior

ABCDEFGHIJKLMNOPQRSTUVWXYZ
abcdefghijklmnopqrstuvwxyz
1234567890 !@#?:;"*&

Foundry: Linotype
Designer: Chauncey H. Griffith
Designer Nationality: American
Date: 1931

Designer Chauncey H. Griffith consulted an optometrists' legibility survey before beginning work on Excelsior, which is an Ionic slab serif created with newspapers in mind. It is one of five designs by Griffith for Linotype's Legibility Group of typefaces and remains highly regarded within editorial design.

FS Clerkenwell

ABCDEFGHIJKLMNOPQRSTUVWXYZ
abcdefghijklmnopqrstuvwxyz
1234567890 !@#?:;"*&

Foundry: Fontsmith
Designer: Phil Garnham / Jason Smith
Designer Nationality: British
Date: 2003

The asymmetric details and upwardly angled leading serifs of this characterful font were the result of extensive experimentation by Phil Garnham and Jason Smith. Their resulting design is a distinctive, contemporary interpretation of the slab serif style, available in four weights.

ITC Bookman

ABCDEFGHIJKLMNOPQRSTUVWXYZ
abcdefghijklmnopqrstuvwxyz
1234567890 !@#?:;"*&

Foundry: ITC
Designer: Ed Benguiat
Designer Nationality: American
Date: 1975

Ed Benguiat (see p. 514) designed ITC Bookman based on several 19th-century antique or slab serif typefaces that themselves referenced Old Style serifs such as Caslon. Its bold texture and set of decorative swashes made the typeface popular within advertising after its release.

ITC Century

ABCDEFGHIJKLMNOPQRSTUVWXYZ
abcdefghijklmnopqrstuvwxyz
1234567890 !@#?:;"*&

Foundry: ITC
Designer: Linn Boyd Benton / Morris Fuller Benton / Tony Stan
Designer Nationality: American
Date: 1894 / 1980

This ITC typeface is based on a late 19th-century design for *Century Magazine* by Linn Boyd Benton, whose son Morris Fuller Benton further extended the font family for American Type Founders over the following decades. Tony Stan's revival of the original Century features narrower letter spacing.

ITC Charter

ABCDEFGHIJKLMNOPQRSTUVWXYZ
abcdefghijklmnopqrstuvwxyz
1234567890 !@#?:;"*&

Foundry: ITC
Designer: Matthew Carter
Designer Nationality: British
Date: 1987

Matthew Carter (see p. 616) designed Charter for ITC in 1987, with the intention of creating a typeface that would perform well in both high-resolution digital contexts and in lower-quality print conditions. ITC Charter's square skeleton ensures it reproduces well even at small point sizes.

ITC Cheltenham

ABCDEFGHIJKLMNOPQRSTUVWXYZ
abcdefghijklmnopqrstuvwxyz
1234567890 !@#?:;"*&

Foundry: ITC
Designer: Bertram Goodhue / Tony Stan
Designer Nationality: American
Date: 1896 / 1975

ITC stalwart Tony Stan was enlisted in the mid 1970s to fine-tune the proportions of the original Cheltenham, designed in 1896 by architect Bertram Goodhue. A subsequent condensed version for headlines, designed by Matthew Carter (see p. 616), was commissioned in 2003 by *The New York Times*.

ITC Cushing

ABCDEFGHIJKLMNOPQRSTUVWXYZ
abcdefghijklmnopqrstuvwxyz
1234567890 !@#?:;"*&

Foundry: ITC
Designer: J. Stearns Cushing / Vincent Pacella
Designer Nationality: American
Date: 1897 / 1992

Cushing was based on a design by New England printer and typographer J. Stearns Cushing from 1897, which was licensed and released by several other foundries more than a century after its appearance. Vincent Pacella's update adjusts the design of the uppercase letterforms.

ITC Pacella

ABCDEFGHIJKLMNOPQRSTUVWXYZ
abcdefghijklmnopqrstuvwxyz
1234567890 !@#?:;"*&

Foundry: ITC
Designer: Vincent Pacella
Designer Nationality: American
Date: 1987

This sturdy typeface by US designer Vincent Pacella was influenced by the highly legible forms of Century Schoolbook and Corona, among others. Characterful details such as the open bowls of the uppercase P and R ensure that it displays a distinct personality all of its own.

Margaret Calvert

Typographer and graphic designer Margaret Calvert is renowned for her work, alongside design partner Jock Kinneir, creating the typographical and pictorial architecture and typefaces for British airports, road, and rail networks in the 1960s.

She was born in South Africa and moved to the UK, where she studied at the Chelsea College of Art. There Kinneir, a graphic designer, was her tutor and mentor. In 1957, he asked for her assistance with the design of the wayfinding signage at the UK's second largest airport, Gatwick. Their first-ever foray into a project of this magnitude resulted in a solution of employing a black on yellow scheme as a highly effective way to aid passenger navigation. Calvert went on to work further with Kinneir and in 1966, they formed Kinneir Calvert Associates. Soon, the firm was appointed by the government's Anderson Committee to design the system for the UK's road and motorway network.

A key factor of this daunting challenge was designing a new typeface, one to be employed across the nation that could be easily read at high speeds, provide concise information, and in varying light conditions. After much testing, Calvert created and drew a mixed-case sans-serif design using Akzidenz-Grotesk as a starting point, which gave rise to a new typeface, Transport. In addition to this hugely successful typeface and graphical structure for the signage, Calvert developed an easy-to-understand pictogram system for warnings and instructions, taking their cue from pre-existing European road signs. The structures for these signs were formed of triangular frames for warnings, circles for instructions, and squares for information.

Calvert and Kinneir then designed the Rail Alphabet typeface used on the British railway system in the early 1960s. Its first outing was in National Health Service hospitals. It was then adopted by the British Rail network and later by all British Airports Authority airports as well as the Danish railway corporation, DSB. It was employed until the early 1990s, when the privatization of the networks meant an amalgam of identities and differing typefaces were introduced. In 2009, a digital version of Rail Alphabet was created from Calvert's original drawings and letterforms. Called New Rail Alphabet, it was created by A2-Type's Henrik Kubel and Scott Williams, who worked closely with Calvert on the project.

Calvert has also designed a number of commercial fonts for Monotype, including the slab serif design Calvert (see p. 51) in 1980. She served as a lecturer and head of graphic design at London's Royal College of Art between 1961 and 2001. In 2004, she was granted an honorary degree by the University of the Arts London and in 2016 was awarded the Order of the British Empire for services to typography and road safety.

Date: 1936–
Nationality: British
Notable typefaces:
Calvert (see p. 51)

Below left. The plethora of differing styles, sizes, and formats of the UK's road signs prior to Calvert and Kinneir's redesign. Here newly made road signs are being stored at the RAC sign factory in London, 1936.

Below middle / right. Margaret Calvert, Jock Kinneir.

Opposite. Examples of the redesigned warning and road signs employing the Transport sans serif and the new graphical structure. Motorway signs are always in blue with all white lettering, with non-primary routes in black lettering on white backgrounds as shown in the London Design Museum show *This is Design*. A green background on signs signifies the routes are primary with destinations in white and road numbers in yellow.

ITC Stone Informal

ABCDEFGHIJKLMNOPQRSTUVWXYZ
abcdefghijklmnopqrstuvwxyz
1234567890 !@#?:;"*&

Foundry: ITC
Designer: Sumner Stone / Bob Ishi
Designer Nationality: American
Date: 1988

US type designer Sumner Stone studied sociology and mathematics before moving into typeface design, a field in which he has since had a distinguished career. This rounded serif style, part of the extensive Stone superfamily, was designed with a colleague of his at Adobe, Bob Ishi.

ITC Stone Serif

ABCDEFGHIJKLMNOPQRSTUVWXYZ
abcdefghijklmnopqrstuvwxyz
1234567890!@#?:;"*&

Foundry: ITC
Designer: Sumner Stone
Designer Nationality: American
Date: 1987

This stately predecessor to ITC Stone Informal was designed to complement the other members of the Stone family, offering a versatile toolkit to serve a range of typesetting needs. Type designer John Renner added more than 300 phonetic characters to the typeface in 1992.

Kleukens-Egyptienne FSL

ABCDEFGHIJKLMNOPQRSTUVWXYZ
abcdefghijklmnopqrstuvwxyz
1234567890 !@#?:;"+&

Foundry: Forgotten Shapes
Designer: Friedrich Wilhelm Kleukens / Reymund Schröder
Designer Nationality: German
Date: 1929 / 2018

Kleukens-Egyptienne FSL is Reymund Schröder's digitization of German designer Friedrich Wilhelm Kleukens's design of 1929. Schröder worked from a low-resolution scan of the trial proof, alongside three initial sketches, to reproduce the strength and details of Kleukens's original concept.

Marlene

ABCDEFGHIJKLMNOPQRSTUVWXYZ
abcdefghijklmnopqrstuvwxyz
1234567890 !@#?:;"*&

Foundry: Typotheque
Designer: Nikola Djurek
Designer Nationality: Croatian
Date: 2008

Marlene is a high-contrast Egyptian face designed by Nikola Djurek. It has long vertical serifs with square edges, a sharp italic, and a large x-height. It comes in four weights, ranging from Light to Bold. The family also contains three display faces: Marlene Grand, Stencil, and Display.

Melior

ABCDEFGHIJKLMNOPQRSTUVWXYZ
abcdefghijklmnopqrstuvwxyz
1234567890 !@#?:;”*&

Foundry: Stempel
Designer: Hermann Zapf
Designer Nationality: German
Date: 1952

Melior is a fairly heavy and square roman serif by Hermann Zapf (see p. 574). It has short ascenders and descenders, and an italic that is the roman at an angle, although the "a" switches from two-storey to single in the italic. Zapf was inspired by the squared-off circle shape of a superellipse.

(see p. 574)

Monotype Century Schoolbook

ABCDEFGHIJKLMNOPQRSTUVWXYZ
abcdefghijklmnopqrstuvwxyz
1234567890 !@#?:;”*&

Foundry: Monotype
Designer: Morris Fuller Benton / Monotype Studio
Designer Nationality: American
Date: 1894 / 1915

Linn Boyd Benton designed Century for *Century Magazine* in 1894. Schoolbook, which has prominent slab serifs and open spacing, was an adaption by his son, Morris Fuller, intended for school textbooks and young readers in 1915. Legibility, clarity, and easy reading were the key aims.

Monotype Clarendon

ABCDEFGHIJKLMNOPQRSTUVWXYZ
abcdefghijklmnopqrstuvwxyz
1234567890 !@#?:;”*&

Foundry: Monotype
Designer: Robert Besley / Monotype Studio
Designer Nationality: British
Date: 1845 / *c.* 1960s

Clarendon was initially released by London's Fann Street Foundry as an evolution of the Egyptian style. It introduced varied stroke widths but kept the large, square serifs. Clarendon is a robust, friendly face best used for headlines and display, rather than body text.

Monotype Ionic

ABCDEFGHIJKLMNOPQRSTUVWXYZ
abcdefghijklmnopqrstuvwxyz
1234567890 !@#?:;”*&

Foundry: Monotype
Designer: Vincent Figgins
Designer Nationality: British
Date: 1821

Ionic was designed by London based typefounder Vincent Figgins in the early 19th century. Its large x-height, short ascenders and descenders, and prominent serifs, makes it highly readable at small sizes. Its legibility has made it a popular choice for newspapers for well over a century.

Monotype New Clarendon

ABCDEFGHIJKLMNOPQRSTUVWXYZ
abcdefghijklmnopqrstuvwxyz
1234567890 !@#?:;"*&

Foundry: Monotype
Designer: Robert Besley / Monotype Studio
Designer Nationality: British
Date: 1845 / 1960

New Clarendon has slightly more contrast and thinner serifs than the standard Clarendon, and also has a much shorter "t" and no top serif on the "q."

Monotype released this update in 1960 following Clarendon's popularity during the 1950s. It is available in regular and bold versions.

New Century Schoolbook

ABCDEFGHIJKLMNOPQRSTUVWXYZ
abcdefghijklmnopqrstuvwxyz
1234567890 !@#?:;"*&

Foundry: Linotype
Designer: Morris Fuller Benton / Matthew Carter
Designer Nationality: American / British
Date: 1915 / 1980

New Century Schoolbook is an update of Morris Fuller Benton's typeface Century Schoolbook, made in 1980 by Matthew Carter (see p. 616) for Linotype.

It is an extremely legible text face, with a large x-height, a vertical axis, and strong, bracketed serifs. It is available in roman and bold with italics.

News 701

ABCDEFGHIJKLMNOPQRSTUVWXYZ
abcdefghijklmnopqrstuvwxyz
1234567890 !@#?:;"*&

Foundry: Bitstream
Designer: Chauncey H. Griffith
Designer Nationality: American
Date: 1925

News 701 is Bitstream's version of Chauncey H. Griffith's Ionic No. 5 of 1925, which was the first release from Linotype's Legibility Group, a series of easily read faces designed to be used by newspapers with Linotype's hot-metal typesetting system. News 701 comes in regular, italic, and bold.

News 702

ABCDEFGHIJKLMNOPQRSTUVWXYZ
abcdefghijklmnopqrstuvwxyz
1234567890 !@#?:;"*&

Foundry: Bitstream
Designer: Chauncey H. Griffith
Designer Nationality: American
Date: 1931

News 702 is Bitstream's version of Chauncey H. Griffith's Excelsior, the second release from Linotype's Legibility Group in 1931, created for newspapers printing with rubber-roller presses. News 702 is a newspaper text face with horizontal serifs and a fairly even color.

Nimrod

ABCDEFGHIJKLMNOPQRSTUVWXYZ
abcdefghijklmnopqrstuvwxyz
1234567890 !@#?:;"*&

Foundry: Monotype
Designer: Robin Nicholas
Designer Nationality: British
Date: 1980

Monotype produced the Nimrod superfamily of eighteen fonts in response to the needs of the modern newspaper industry. It is an evolution of traditional Ionic newspaper faces with less fine detail, making it easier to read when small and less prone to degradation when cast in metal.

Scherzo

ABCDEFGHIJKLMNOPQRSTUVWXYZ
abcdefghijklmnopqrstuvwxyz
1234567890 !@#?:;"*&

Foundry: Monotype
Designer: Albert Boton
Designer Nationality: French
Date: 1996

Scherzo is a Clarendon serif designed for both body text and headlines. The minimal stroke contrast, elongated serifs, and abrupt brackets provide muscle in the demi and bold weights, while also ensuring the face has character and clarity in the regular weight.

Superclarendon

ABCDEFGHIJKLMNOPQRSTUVWXY
abcdefghijklmnopqrstuvwxyz
1234567890 !@#?:;"*&

Foundry: Typodermic
Designer: Ray Larabie
Designer Nationality: Canadian
Date: 2007

Superclarendon is a salute to Robert Besley's Clarendon font family from the mid 1800s, and is both a revival and expansion of Besley's design. Alongside the original features, details from other popular 19th-century faces were added to enhance its character and complexion.

Ysobel

ABCDEFGHIJKLMNOPQRSTUVWXYZ
abcdefghijklmnopqrstuvwxyz
1234567890 !@#?:;"*&

Foundry: Monotype
Designer: Robin Nicholas /
Delve Withrington / Alice Savoie
Designer Nationality: British /
American / French
Date: 2009

Ysobel is a clarendon serif designed for the diverse needs of editorial design. In all four weights, including a redrawn Display version, Ysobel fuses the approachability of open, gentle forms with the precision of incised serifs and robust strokes for optimal legibility.

Belwe Mono

ABCDEFGHIJKLMNOPQRSTUVWXYZ
abcdefghijklmnopqrstuvwxyz
1234567890 !?:;"*&

Foundry: Letraset
Designer: Georg Belwe / Alan Meeks
Designer Nationality: German / British
Date: 1926 / 1976

With unusual detailing and proportions, Belwe is an Art Nouveau-inspired slab serif with blackletter influences. Its many quirky characters, angled serifs, and calligraphic flourishes made it a popular choice when released by Schelter & Giesecke. After its first revival by Letraset, it was reissued many times.

Beton

ABCDEFGHIJKLMNOPQRSTUVWXYZ
abcdefghijklmnopqrstuvwxyz
1234567890 !@#?:;"*&

Foundry: Bauersche Giesserei
Designer: Heinrich Jost
Designer Nationality: German
Date: 1931–36

Beton's name references the French term *Béton* (raw concrete). A geometric slab serif, it shares many similarities with Memphis, its competitor when it was released in the 1930s. What distinguishes this monoline typeface is its double-storey "a." It was updated later by URW and Linotype.

Courier 10 Pitch

ABCDEFGHIJKLMNOPQRSTUVWXYZ
abcdefghijklmnopqrstuvwxyz
1234567890 !@#?:;"*&

Foundry: Bitstream
Designer: Howard Kettler
Designer Nationality: American
Date: 1955

Bitstream's version of the instantly recognizable monospaced slab serif displays all the characteristics of the original typewriter font designed by Howard Kettler for IBM. The typeface was made freely available and soon became the industry standard typeface for all machines.

Courier LT Round

ABCDEFGHIJKLMNOPQRSTUVWXYZ
abcdefghijklmnopqrstuvwxyz
1234567890 !@#?:;"*&

Foundry: Linotype
Designer: Howard Kettler
Designer Nationality: American
Date: 1955

Linotype's version of this well-known IBM typewriter font has Regular and Bold weights, with obliques and rounded terminals. Its sister version, Courier, has flat terminals, an optional oblique, a Medium weight, and Central European and Cyrillic companions.

Calvert

ABCDEFGHIJKLMNOPQRSTUVWXYZ
abcdefghijklmnopqrstuvwxyz
1234567890 !@#?:;"*&

Foundry: Monotype
Designer: Margaret Calvert
Designer Nationality: British
Date: 1980

Calvert takes its name from Margaret Calvert (see p. 44), who is renowned for having worked with Jock Kinneir to design most of the British road and traffic-warning signs of the 1950s and 1960s. This typeface is based on a commission for the Tyne and Wear Metro system in north-east England during the 1980s.

Calvert is a timeless slab serif, and its contemporary appearance and unique design come from the fact many of the characters have only half serifs, such as the "A," "M," and "X." This design choice results in a typeface with a constructed aesthetic that still retains a humanist quality to the characters. The typeface possesses a beautiful consistency in its letterforms, making for a very clear presentation in display applications.

Margaret Calvert is known for her typeface designs on British transportation signage. Her notable creations include Transport, which was created between 1957 and 1963 and is used on road signs throughout Britain, and Rail Alphabet, which was devised in 1964 and is employed on the nation's railway system.

Below. Cartlidge Levene's wayfinding system employing Margaret Calvert's eponymously titled slab serif typeface in the Royal College of Arts Dyson Building in London. The signage features a specially created reduced stencil version of Calvert, titled Calvert Brody, which was created by three generations of RCA type design luminaries: Margaret Calvert, Neville Brody, and Henrik Kubel of A2-Type.

Courier New

ABCDEFGHIJKLMNOPQRSTUVWXYZ
abcdefghijklmnopqrstuvwxyz
1234567890 !@#?:;"*&

Foundry: Monotype
Designer: Howard Kettler / Adrian Frutiger
Designer Nationality: American / Swiss
Date: 1955 / 2008

Howard Kettler and the Monotype Studio designed Courier in 1955 as a commission for IBM. The highly recognizable monospaced slab serif is the original typewriter typeface, spawning many variants from other foundries big and small. This was possible because IBM decided not to seek any form of copyright or trademark over the design.

Courier's monospacing reflects the charm of old typewritten letters where all the characters were evenly spaced out when struck, therefore creating unsightly gaps when set. By incorporating this mechanical restraint within its design, Courier has a certain rawness when used as text. However, in lists or tables it can be used as an advantage in aligning content. Despite the awkwardness of the typeface's setting and the distinctive appearance of emulating typewriter's letterforms, it has remained incredibly

popular. Its functional and basic appearance have meant it has been widely used in everything from official-looking documents, through to designs emulating telegrams and letters, and on advertising.

Renowned Swiss type designer Adrian Frutiger (see p. 290) redrew this later version, Courier New, for Monotype. The font family includes Courier New, Courier New Bold, Courier New Italic, and Courier New Bold Italic. Primarily used on IBM's popular model range of Selectric electric typewriters in the early 1960s, the family was later used as a system font appearing on Windows 3.1 and has remained the default font for monospaced typesetting and plain text usage on PCs.

Below left. Graphic identity, infographics and UI design for an exhibition about language in the Estonian National Museum by Margus Tamm.

Below right. Acoustic by Noize MC. Contributed by Mikhail Rul on 26 February 2016. Artwork published in 2015.

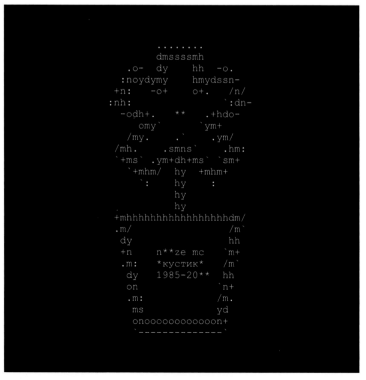

Cumberland

ABCDEFGHIJKLMNOPQRSTUVWXYZ
abcdefghijklmnopqrstuvwxyz
1234567890 !@#?:;"'*&

Foundry: Monotype
Designer: Monotype Studio
Designer Nationality: British
Date: 1999

This monospaced typewriter-style typeface is very much in the same genre as the ubiquitous Courier. Cumberland was designed and digitized in-house at the Monotype Studio in Redhill, Surrey, England to offer as an alternative to. It supports up to fifty languages.

Egyptian Slate

ABCDEFGHIJKLMNOPQRSTUVWXYZ
abcdefghijklmnopqrstuvwxyz
1234567890 !@#?:;"'*&

Foundry: Monotype
Designer: Rod McDonald
Designer Nationality: Canadian
Date: 2008

Rod McDonald developed Egyptian Slate from the Slate sans serif typeface he created in 2006. It is a poised slab serif available in six weights from Light to Black with complementary italics. Following on from Slate, the typeface was later reissued as Gibson in 2011.

Gelo

ABCDEFGHIJKLMNOPQRSTUVWXYZ
abcdefghijklmnopqrstuvwxyz
1234567890 !@#?:;"'*&

Foundry: Dalton Maag
Designer: Tom Foley / Sebastian Losch
Designer Nationality: Irish / German
Date: 2017

Gelo is an expressive font family that merges the structural authority of a slab serif with the approachable strokes of brush lettering. While the font's shape is principally geometric, the serifs and joints hint toward a more organic construction. It was designed for both print and digital use.

Geometric Slabserif 703

ABCDEFGHIJKLMNOPQRSTUVWXYZ
abcdefghijklmnopqrstuvwxyz
1234567890 !@#?:;"'*&

Foundry: Bitstream
Designer: Rudolf Wolf
Designer Nationality: German
Date: 1929 / 1990

This Bitstream typeface is a digitization of Rudolf Wolf's Memphis of 1929, which added slab serifs to the geometric forms popularized within Modernist type designs such as Futura. Bitstream's revival of this popular font adds a range of condensed weights to the original family.

Geometric Slabserif 712

ABCDEFGHIJKLMNOPQRSTUVWXYZ
abcdefghijklmnopqrstuvwxyz
1234567890 !@#?:;"*&

This is a Bitstream digitization of an earlier slab serif. Its monolinear design is based on Monotype's popular Rockwell typeface of 1934, which was itself based on a US slab serif design from 1910, Litho Antique. Rockwell is more suited for display type than lengthy body text.

Foundry: Bitstream
Designer: William Schraubstadter / Frank Hinman Pierpont / Manvel Shmavonyan / Isay Slutsker
Designer Nationality: American / American / Armenian / Russian
Date: 1910 / 1934 / 1999

HoTom

ABCDEFGHIJKLMNOPQRSTUVWXYZ
abcdefghijklmnopqrstuvwxyz
1234567890 !@#?:;"*&

The uncluttered design of this orderly slab serif is particularly well-suited to long passages of body text. HoTom was submitted to Linotype for its International Digital Type Design Contest in 1994 and later released as part of the foundry's TakeType Library that features competition winners.

Foundry: Linotype
Designer: Thomas Hofmann
Designer Nationality: German
Date: 1994

ITC American Typewriter

ABCDEFGHIJKLMNOPQRSTUVWXYZ
abcdefghijklmnopqrstuvwxyz
1234567890 !@#?:;"*&

Foundry: ITC
Designer: Joel Kaden / Tony Stan
Designer Nationality: American
Date: 1974

International Typeface Corporation (ITC) launched the ITC American Typewriter typeface as part of the celebrations in 1974 to commemorate the 100th anniversary of the invention of the office typewriter. ITC adopted the charm of this genre of letterforms as an homage to the forerunners of today's digital machines, yet reworked them to be a far more usable and aesthetically pleasing experience. The foundry chose to break away from the monospaced setting of existing designs and create a proportionally spaced font. This change allows the design to be used for a wider range of applications, just as a conventional text typeface would. The accompanying improvement in readability means it also works far better in roles such as text setting.

ITC Lubalin Graph

ABCDEFGHIJKLMNOPQRSTUVWXYZ
abcdefghijklmnopqrstuvwxyz
1234567890 !@#?:;"*&

ITC Lubalin Graph is a giant among the extensive range of geometric slab serif, or Egyptian types. Lubalin Graph's striking rectangular slab serifs and powerful circular forms create a practical yet friendly design. It is ideal for display and titling work or short extents of text, and the larger the typeface when used, the more striking any design becomes.

Designer Herb Lubalin (see p. 62) based the design of Lubalin Graph around that of his ITC Avant Garde Gothic san serif. The two faces share the basic geometric character shapes, tight letter spacing, and generous x-height. When paired together, they make for an ideal marriage between sans and serif.

To create the design, Lubalin collaborated with Ed Benguiat (see p. 514). It was then drawn up to fit the requirements of typographic reproduction by Tony DiSpigna and Joe Sundwall in 1974. Condensed weights, including small caps and Old Style figures, were added to the family by Helga Jörgenson and Sigrid Engelmann in 1992.

Foundry: ITC
Designer: Herb Lubalin / Ed Benguiat / Tony DiSpigna / Joe Sundwall
Designer Nationality: American
Date: 1974

Below. Vinyl single cover design employing ITC Lubalin Graph Extra Light for Aretha Franklin and George Benson released in 1981.

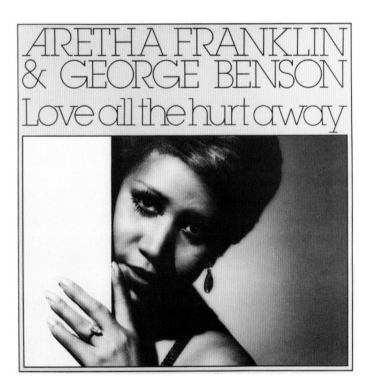

Lexia Mono

ABCDEFGHIJKLMNOPQRSTUVWXYZ
abcdefghijklmnopqrstuvwxyz
1234567890 !@#?:;"*&

Foundry: Dalton Maag
Designer: Ron Carpenter /
Elí Castellanos / Spike Spondike
Designer Nationality: British /
Mexican / American
Date: 2018

Lexia Mono is a monospaced slab serif designed intentionally for complex, text-heavy compositions. Its clean rhythm helps make it easy to read. Unlike most monospaced fonts, Lexia Mono is available in several weights, each with a true italic, and has an elevated x-height for readability in small sizes.

Memphis

ABCDEFGHIJKLMNOPQRSTUVWXYZ
abcdefghijklmnopqrstuvwxyz
1234567890 !@#?:;"*&

Foundry: Stempel
Designer: Rudolf Wolf
Designer Nationality: German
Date: 1929

Rudolf Wolf designed the Memphis slab serif for Stempel at the end of the 1920s. Its timeless look helped it remain popular throughout the 20th century and it is considered one of the first Egyptian revivals. Initially, Memphis was available in four weights: Light, Medium, Bold, and Extra Bold.

Memphis Soft Rounded

ABCDEFGHIJKLMNOPQRSTUVWXYZ
abcdefghijklmnopqrstuvwxyz
1234567890 !@#?:;"*&

Foundry: Linotype
Designer: Rudolf Wolf /
Linotype Design Studio
Designer Nationality: German
Date: 1929 / Unknown

Memphis Soft Rounded is an adaption of Rudolf Wolf's Memphis slab serif of 1929 done in-house by Linotype. It takes the original and replaces all of the right angles with soft curves. The result is a far friendlier typeface that comes in three weights: Medium, Bold, and Extra Bold.

Monotype Courier 12

ABCDEFGHIJKLMNOPQRSTUVWXYZ
abcdefghijklmnopqrstuvwxyz
1234567890 !@#?:;"*&

Foundry: Monotype
Designer: Howard Kettler
Designer Nationality: American
Date: 1955

Courier 12 is a version of the monospaced typewriter font Courier, which was created by US designer Howard Kettler for IBM in 1955. Courier 12 comes in one weight, which is lighter, finer, and more widely spaced than the regular weight of the standard Courier.

November Slab

ABCDEFGHIJKLMNOPQRSTUVWXYZ
abcdefghijklmnopqrstuvwxyz
1234567890 !@#?:;"*&

Foundry: Typotheque
Designer: Peter Biľak
Designer Nationality: Slovakian
Date: 2018

A functional, robust slab serif, Biľak's November Slab is a large type family available in three widths—regular, condensed, and compressed—and nine weights—hairline to black, all with italics for Latin, Cyrillic, and Greek. The original sans serif November was released in 2016.

Peggs

ABCDEFGHIJKLMNOPQRSTUVWXYZ
abcdefghijklmnopqrstuvwxyz
1234567890 !@#?:;"*&

Foundry: Colophon
Designer: The Entente
Designer Nationality: British
Date: 2009

Based on monospaced typewriter fonts and the quirks that appear from using unsophisticated printing techniques and materials, Peggs was first created in a singular bold weight for the identity of Brighton fashion shop Peggs & Son. It was later redrawn, re-spaced, and extended.

Prestige 12 Pitch

ABCDEFGHIJKLMNOPQRSTUVWXYZ
abcdefghijklmnopqrstuvwxyz
1234567890 !@#?:;"*&

Foundry: Bitstream
Designer: Clayton Smith
Designer Nationality: American
Date: 1953 / c. 1980s

Prestige 12 Pitch is Bitstream's digitization of Clayton Smith's Prestige Elite Typewriter design of 1953. Smith designed typewriter fonts at IBM, Lexington and developed this monospaced slab serif to improve both the character and legibility of typewriter text.

Rockwell Nova

ABCDEFGHIJKLMNOPQRSTUVWXYZ
abcdefghijklmnopqrstuvwxyz
1234567890 !@#?:;"*&

Foundry: Monotype
Designer: Monotype Studio
Date: Unknown

Rockwell Nova builds upon the original Rockwell font family. It retains all the quintessential qualities of the design while adding depth and diversity. The expanded font family includes thirteen variations, ranging from Condensed to Extra Bold, and suits both display and text uses.

Rockwell

ABCDEFGHIJKLMNOPQRSTUVWXYZ
abcdefghijklmnopqrstuvwxyz
1234567890 !@#?:;"*&

Foundry: Monotype
Designer: Frank Hinman Pierpont
Designer Nationality: American
Date: 1934

Slab serifs, or Egyptian, types were derived from early wood-carved typefaces and were used for large display types. Because of the difficulty in carving wood and the inability to create intricate and subtle shapes, these types adopted slab serifs for ease of creation. Rockwell's ancestry is no different; it is based on the Litho Antique font cast in 1910 by William A. Schraubstadter for the Inland Type Foundry. It, and similar typefaces, became popular over the next twenty years in the United States and Europe. Consequently, in 1931, the American Type Founders foundry asked Morris Fuller Benton to create a reissue with added characters and refinements, called Rockwell Antique.

However, Rockwell's evolution was still not over. In 1934, the esteemed type designer Frank Hinman Pierpont, in partnership with Monotype, created the Rockwell typeface family that exists today. This final design incorporated many refinements in spacing, letter weights and glyphs.

Rockwell is highly versatile, can be used in both display and text applications and is available in nine variations including italics, differing weights, and condensed versions. As with most slab serifs, its consistency and boldness allow it to be used in signage, wayfinding applications, and branding.

Below. Rockwell employed on the walls of the Achievement First Endeavor Middle School in Brooklyn, New York. Created by renowned Pentagram partner Paula Scher with Andrew Freeman and Drea Zlanabitnig.

Rockwell WGL

ABCDEFGHIJKLMNOPQRSTUVWXYZ
abcdefghijklmnopqrstuvwxyz
1234567890 !@#?:;"'*&

Foundry: Monotype
Designer: Monotype Studio
Date: 1934 / c. 1980s

Rockwell WGL is an update of the original Rockwell font family, designed for enhanced compatibility with Microsoft's Windows operating system. Unlike other Rockwell font families, Rockwell WGL includes the Windows Glyph List character set. It supports more than seventy-nine languages.

Serifa

ABCDEFGHIJKLMNOPQRSTUVWXYZ
abcdefghijklmnopqrstuvwxyz
1234567890 !@#?:;"*&

Foundry: Bauer
Designer: Adrian Frutiger
Designer Nationality: Swiss
Date: 1968

Serif is a traditional slab serif designed by Adrian Frutiger (see p. 290) and adapted from Univers, the sans serif face that he created in the 1950s. By lowering the x-height, Frutiger was able to balance the addition of block serifs with the original frame and geometry of Univers.

Square Slabserif 711

ABCDEFGHIJKLMNOPQRSTUVWXYZ
abcdefghijklmnopqrstuvwxyz
1234567890 !@#?:;"*&

Foundry: Bitstream
Designer: Georg Trump
Designer Nationality: German
Date: c. 1900–10 / 1990

Square Slabserif 711 is a revival of the slab serif types of the early 20th century. It was republished by Bitstream for the digital devices that emerged in the 1990s, because its geometric frame balances right angles and opposing curves, ensuring readability on screen and in print.

Stymie

ABCDEFGHIJKLMNOPQRSTUVWXYZ
abcdefghijklmnopqrstuvwxyz
1234567890 !@#?:;"*&

Foundry: ATF / Bitstream
Designer: Morris Fuller Benton / Sol Hess / Gerry Powell
Designer Nationality: American
Date: 1931 / c. 1980s

Stymie is Bitstream's digitization of an early 20th-century slab serif of the same name by Morris Fuller Benton. American Type Founders (ATF) commissioned it as a reworking of popular slab serifs of the time. Weights were added later by Sol Hess at Lanston Monotype and Gerry Powell at ATF

Tesla Slab

ABCDEFGHIJKLMNOPQRSTUVWXYZ
abcdefghijklmnopqrstuvwxyz
1234567890 !@#?:,"*&

Foundry: Typotheque
Designer: Nikola Djurek
Designer Nationality: Croatian
Date: 2015

Tesla Slab is an expressive slab serif with smooth curves, which boasts true italics and six different weights, from Hairline to Bold. Unlike many slabs, the strong strokes of Nikola Djurek's design features a slight variation in their width in order to convey both eloquence and industry.

Tribunal

ABCDEFGHIJKLMNOPQRSTUVWXYZ
abcdefghijklmnopqrstuvwxyz
1234567890 !@#?:,"*&

Foundry: Typotheque
Designer: Aljaž Vindiš
Designer Nationality: Slovenian
Date: 2011

Tribunal was conceived as a custom typeface for a cross-platform Slovenian student magazine, *Tribuna*, and was always intended for both printed and digital environments. The type family won the Brumen Award for typeface design at the 5th Slovene Biennale of Visual Communication in 2011.

Trilogy Egyptian

ABCDEFGHIJKLMNOPQRSTUVWXYZ
abcdefghijklmnopqrstuvwxyz
1234567890 !@#?:,"*&

Foundry: Jeremy Tankard Typography
Designer: Jeremy Tankard
Designer Nationality: British
Date: 2009

Trilogy Egyptian is a bold, headline slab serif inspired by the visual richness of 19th-century printed ephemera. Unlike the geometric forms of most early 20th-century slabs, the typeface combines a modern shape with the decorative details of late Victorian type design.

Typewriter

ABCDEFGHIJKLMNOPQRSTUVWXYZ
abcdefghijklmnopqrstuvwxyz
1234567890 !@#?: ;"*&

Foundry: Monotype
Designer: Monotype Studio
Date: Unknown

The Typewriter font family is a fixed-pitch, slab serif typeface, designed to imitate the letterforms produced on a typewriter. The characters are monospaced and mix symmetrical, flat serifs with bulbous terminals, alongside artificial ink traps and dark spots.

Albertus

ABCDEFGHIJKLMNOPQRSTUVWXYZ
abcdefghijklmnopqrstuvwxyz
1234567890 !@#?:;"✷&

Foundry: Monotype
Designer: Berthold Wolpe
Designer Nationality: German
Date: 1932

Albertus was designed by German type designer and typographer Berthold Wolpe to satisfy a commission by renowned British typographer Stanley Morrison for Monotype in 1932. The typeface was inspired by raised letterform inscriptions carved out of bronze, and the first release was in an all-capital, titling weight in 1935. A Roman upper- and lowercase design followed in 1938 and a Light weight in 1940. Albertus's bold simple strokes with subtle, minimal glyphic serifs make it an elegant and highly legible typeface used for display and titling applications. In 1941, Wolpe joined book publisher Faber & Faber in London, where he remained until his retirement in 1975. He became one of the great book-cover designers of the time, publishing more than 1,500 covers and dust jackets.

Right: Page designs from the exhibition catalogue to accompany the exhibition *David Bowie Is* at the V&A Museum, London. Albertus was used as the headline face in the book and the exhibition. Design by Barnbrook studio.

Albertus Nova

ABCDEFGHIJKLMNOPQRSTUVWXYZ
abcdefghijklmnopqrstuvwxyz
1234567890 !@#?:;"✷&

Foundry: Monotype
Designer: Berthold Wolpe / Toshi Omagari
Designer Nationality: German / Japanese
Date: 1932 / 2017

Berthold Wolpe's distinctive Albertus design is famous for its use on signage in the City of London. Toshi Omagari's Albertus Nova revives and extends it, revisiting some of the compromises made for metal typesetting. It comprises five weights, Greek and Cyrillic characters, and alternative caps.

Americana

ABCDEFGHIJKLMNOPQRSTUVWXYZ
abcdefghijklmnopqrstuvwxyz
1234567890 !@#?:;"*&

Foundry: American Type Founders
Designer: Richard Isbell
Designer Nationality: American
Date: 1965

Americana was named in honour of the United States Bicentennial in 1976 and is the last face cut by American Type Founders. The stylized design features generous letterforms, large counters, short ascenders and descenders, flared serifs, and a large x-height. It is best suited for short text.

Herb Lubalin

Herb Lubalin was a giant in the field of US graphic and type designers of the 1960s and 1970s. His groundbreaking and cutting-edge designs as designer/art director for the design and creative journal *Avant Garde* and the International Typeface Corporation's (ITC) magazine *U&lc*, along with his typeface ITC Avant Garde Gothic influenced design in the United States and internationally.

Born in New York in 1918, it wasn't until art school at the Cooper Union that his drawing pastime was directed into a passion for typography. From 1939, he was a freelance designer and typographer and then art director at a number of New York advertising agencies for more than two decades. It was during this period that his reputation was established as a master of "expressive typography" — conceptual ideas embedded within typographical arrangements as imagery. In 1964, he set up his own studio, Herb Lubalin, and quickly established a reputation for excellence. Three years later, he joined with Ernie Smith and Tom Carnase to found Lubalin, Smith, Carnase.

At this time, Lubalin had a working relationship with Ralph Ginzburg. An author, editor, publisher, and photojournalist, Ginzburg had gained notoriety for publishing books and journals on erotica and in 1963 was convicted for violating obscenity laws. He worked with Lubalin on a number of revolutionary magazines: *Eros* (1962), *Fact* (1964–67) and *Avant Garde* (1968–71). The latter had the greatest impact on Lubalin's output and legacy.

In 1970, Lubalin formed ITC with partners Aaron Burns and Edward Rondthaler. A new foundry, and one of the first created, which had no history or materials emanating from the period of type design from the hot-metal era. One of its first official releases was ITC Avant Garde Gothic, based around the masthead Lubalin had created for *Avant Garde* magazine, an entire typeface was developed from its geometric sans serif design that made full use of the advantages of phototypesetting. In addition to a set of standard characters, it possessed special characters and ligatures that were constructed around 45° angles allowing the designer to experiment with the letters when setting. Although coming under some criticism at the time for its grid-based approach and consistency, it has proved to be a highly legible and one of the most successful and popular sans serif display typeface designs of all time.

In 1973, ITC launched its quarterly journal, *U&lc* with Lubalin as editor and art director. His experimentation and ideas were given free rein and he worked on the journal until his death in 1981. *U&lc* was not only an international success it was a must-have journal with a circulation of more than 170,000 readers. These are impressive numbers for a journal on creative typography and reflect the immeasurable impact had Lubalin had on the field of design and typography.

Date: 1918–1981
Nationality: American
Notable typefaces:
ITC Avant Garde Gothic (see p.202)
ITC Lubalin Graph (see p.55)

Below. Lubalin's famous Mother & Child logotype and the *Avant Garde* journal masthead designed by Lubalin and drawn by colleague Tom Carnase under Lubalin's direction .

Opposite top. Specimen booklet for ITC Serif Gothic typeface, designed by Lubalin and fellow partner at Lubalin Associates Tony di Spigna.

Opposite middle. Herb Lubalin Inc. logo (left); Herb Lubalin; and a selection of the numerous logos created and collaborated with by Lubalin over his career.

Opposite bottom. Striking logotypes (from left) for Families (1980), proposed New York City logo NY,NY (1966), masthead for *Fact* magazine (1967).

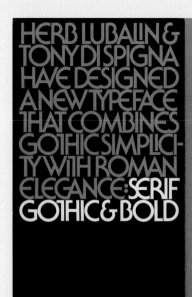

HERB LUBALIN & TONY DI SPIGNA HAVE DESIGNED A NEW TYPEFACE THAT COMBINES GOTHIC SIMPLICITY WITH ROMAN ELEGANCE: SERIF GOTHIC & BOLD

ITC SERIF GOTHIC & BOLD
ALTERNATE CHARACTERS

ITC Serif Gothic with bold is also available for headline use on our photo display typesetting machines.
Several alternate characters have been designed but unless specifically requested normal font characters will always be used.

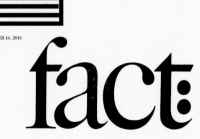

FLAT FILE
Nº1 — FEB 16, 2016

*Herb Lubalin Study Center
of Design & Typography*

Amerigo BT

ABCDEFGHIJKLMNOPQRSTUVWXYZ
abcdefghijklmnopqrstuvwxyz
1234567890 !@#?:;"*&

Foundry: Bitstream
Designer: Gerard Unger
Designer Nationality: Dutch
Date: 1987

Amerigo BT is the result of a commission to create a font similar to Optima. Gerard Unger's design is narrower and sharper than Optima, with wider ending terminals, and a greater contrast between thick and thin. The font is available in three weights with matching true italics.

Baker Signet

ABCDEFGHIJKLMNOPQRSTUVWXYZ
abcdefghijklmnopqrstuvwxyz
1234567890 !@#?:;"*&

Foundry: VGC
Designer: Arthur Baker
Designer Nationality: American
Date: 1965

Calligrapher Arthur Baker created this serif with its delicate strokes and triangular serifs. The lowercase "y" and capital "Q" have spirited descenders that demonstrate the typeface's close connection to handwriting. Coca-Cola adopted Baker Signet Bold for the word "Coke" in its product branding.

Canela Deck

ABCDEFGHIJKLMNOPQRSTUVWXYZ
abcdefghijklmnopqrstuvwxyz
1234567890 !@#?:;"*&

Foundry: Commercial Type
Designer: Miguel Reyes
Designer Nationality: Mexican
Date: 2018

Canela Deck is a glyphic serif, with sturdy strokes and wedged feet, crafted for use in the middle sizes of editorial layouts. Its graceful and imposing characters are suited to texts of between 20 and 40 points in size, such as headlines on web pages or a printed pull-quote.

Canela Text

ABCDEFGHIJKLMNOPQRSTUVWXYZ
abcdefghijklmnopqrstuvwxyz
1234567890 !@#?:;"*&

Foundry: Commercial Type
Designer: Miguel Reyes
Designer Nationality: Mexican
Date: 2018

Canela Text is optimized for small sizes and designed to preserve the character and precision of Canela Deck, while adding the many features required for text use. This includes the addition of a full range of weights, alongside small caps, fractions, and tabular figures.

Cantoria

ABCDEFGHIJKLMNOPQRSTUVWXYZ
abcdefghijklmnopqrstuvwxyz
1234567890 !@#?:;"*&

Foundry: Monotype
Designer: Ron Carpenter
Designer Nationality: British
Date: 1986

With its open counters and large capitals, Cantoria is a low-key but charming serif based on marks typical of stone-cut letters. It was inspired by Thomas Maitland Cleland's typeface Della Robbia of 1902, which was in turn inspired by 15th-century Florentine inscriptional capitals.

Charlotte Serif

ABCDEFGHIJKLMNOPQRSTUVWXYZ
abcdefghijklmnopqrstuvwxyz
1234567890 !@#?:;"*&

Foundry: ITC
Designer: Michael Gills
Designer Nationality: British
Date: 1992

Charlotte Serif is a modern roman typeface influenced by the 18th-century French type designer Pierre-Simon Fournier. It is a formal serif with strong vertical stress and unbracketed serifs. Described as having an authoritative tone, it is suitable for use in most text applications.

Flareserif 821

ABCDEFGHIJKLMNOPQRSTUVWXYZ
abcdefghijklmnopqrstuvwxyz
1234567890 !@#?:;"*&

Foundry: Bitstream
Designer: Berthold Wolpe / Matthew Carter
Designer Nationality: German / British
Date: 1938 / 1998

This version of Berthold Wolpe's perennially popular Albertus was one of several similar digitizations released in the late 20th century. Wolpe's work was a key source of inspiration for Bitstream founder Matthew Carter (see p. 616), who revived several of his fonts over the course of his career.

Foundry Wilson

ABCDEFGHIJKLMNOPQRSTUVWXYZ
abcdefghijklmnopqrstuvwxyz
1234567890 !@#?:;"*&

Foundry: The Foundry
Designer: David Quay / Freda Sack
Designer Nationality: British
Date: 1993

Scotsman Alexander Wilson was a fascinating figure—an astronomer, surgeon, and meteorologist, he also established a successful foundry in St Andrews in 1742. This respectful revival of one of his designs includes a set of ornamental printers' flowers reproduced from the original source.

FS Benjamin

ABCDEFGHIJKLMNOPQRSTUVWXYZ
abcdefghijklmnopqrstuvwxyz
1234567890 !@#?:;"*&

Foundry: Fontsmith
Designer: Stuart de Rozario / Jason Smith
Designer Nationality: British
Date: 2018

FS Benjamin is designed by Stuart de Rozario, senior type designer at leading London foundry Fontsmith (see p. 272), with creative direction from company founder and creative director Jason Smith. The typeface is de Rozario's tribute to the capital city he calls home, and it was inspired by London's sounds and contrasts.

The font's name references Big Ben, the nickname given to the Great Bell in the clock at the Houses of Parliament. This may refer to Sir Benjamin Hall, who oversaw the bell's installation, or a contemporary English heavyweight boxer called Benjamin "Big Ben" Caunt.

FS Benjamin is a highly versatile design with an elegant flared serif. Despite Benjamin's elegant and delicate nature, the design features brutal chiseled angles on closer inspection, reflecting the traditional roots of the craft. However, this is no retrospective design and it aims to work in a contemporary setting. The classic proportions of the design's x-height to cap height and ascender to descender ratio help make it accessible and highly legible across a wide variety of media. It comes in six weights with matching italics.

Below. For the launch of FS Benjamin, Fontsmith worked with London design studio DixonBaxi and released *Sounds of London*. In collaboration with Zelig Sound, they produced a unique track that remixed field recordings taken from across the capital by the studio staff, into a soundtrack of London, which was then pressed into a limited-edition vinyl release.

Light
Light Italic
Book
Book Italic
Regular
Regular Italic
Medium
Medium Italic
SemiBold
SemiBold Italic
Bold
Bold Italic

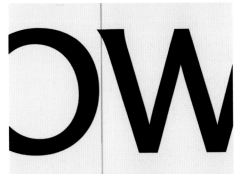

Friz Quadrata

ABCDEFGHIJKLMNOPQRSTUVWXYZ
abcdefghijklmnopqrstuvwxyz
1234567890 !@#?:;"*&

Foundry: VGC
Designer: Ernst Friz
Designer Nationality: Swiss
Date: 1965

Ernst Friz designed this distinctive, display-friendly serif for a competition held by phototypesetting foundry Visual Graphics Corporation (VGC). ITC reissued it in 1974 with the addition of a bold cut by Victor Caruso; Thierry Puyfoulhoux contributed italics two decades later.

FS Maja

ABCDEFGHIJKLMNOPQRSTUVWXYZ
abcdefghijklmnopqrstuvwxyz
1234567890 !@#?:;"*&

Foundry: Fontsmith
Designer: Jason Smith
Designer Nationality: British
Date: 2013

FS Maja was developed by Fontsmith (see p. 272) for a commission from Channel 4, which briefed the foundry to create a new typeface for its Freeview channel, E4. FS Maja is rounded and approachable, and designed to work well in physical and screen-based contexts, as well as at a variety of scales.

Icone

ABCDEFGHIJKLMNOPQRSTUVWXYZ
abcdefghijklmnopqrstuvwxyz
1234567890 !@#?:;"*&

Foundry: Linotype
Designer: Adrian Frutiger
Designer Nationality: Swiss
Date: 1980

The inscriptional style of this expansive font family features swollen, flared serifs, inspired by carved stone type found in northern France and Ireland. It was designed by Adrian Frutiger (see p. 290) to explore the intersection of classical type styles with developing digital type technology.

ITC Barcelona

ABCDEFGHIJKLMNOPQRSTUVWXYZ
abcdefghijklmnopqrstuvwxyz
1234567890 !@#?:;"*&

Foundry: ITC
Designer: Ed Benguiat
Designer Nationality: American
Date: 1981

Type designer and jazz musician Ed Benguiat (see p. 514) has designed more than 600 typefaces over the course of his career; he is widely renowned for his work both at Photo-Lettering and ITC. His design for ITC Barcelona features wedged brackets and distinctive curled curve terminals.

ITC Novarese

ABCDEFGHIJKLMNOPQRSTUVWXYZ
abcdefghijklmnopqrstuvwxyz
1234567890 !@#?:;"*&

Foundry: ITC
Designer: Aldo Novarese
Designer Nationality: Italian
Date: 1978

Aldo Novarese developed this typeface after his departure from the Nebiolo foundry in Turin and it can be seen as a consolidation of ideas expressed within many of his published typefaces. He took elements from what he considered to be his most successful typefaces to create this new design.

Masqualero

ABCDEFGHIJKLMNOPQRSTUVWXYZ
abcdefghijklmnopqrstuvwxyz
1234567890 !@#?:;"*&

Foundry: Monotype
Designer: Jim Ford
Designer Nationality: American
Date: 2017

Masqualero was designed by Jim Ford at Monotype and named after a song by jazz legend Miles Davis. It is a sophisticated, high-contrast contemporary serif that comes in six weights with italics. There are also two attractive, decorative display versions in uppercase: Stencil and Groove.

Memento

ABCDEFGHIJKLMNOPQRSTUVWXYZ
abcdefghijklmnopqrstuvwxyz
1234567890 !@#?:;"*&

Foundry: Omnibus
Designer: Franko Luin
Designer Nationality: Swedish
Date: 1993

Memento has little, triangular serifs reminiscent of Dutch typefaces of the 17th century. This is a versatile serif with a large x-height, which makes it legible at small sizes, and a distinctive "g" with an open lower loop. It is available in four different weights with italics.

Memo

ABCDEFGHIJKLMNOPQRSTUVWXYZ
abcdefghijklmnopqrstuvwxyz
1234567890 !@#?:;"*&

Foundry: Monotype
Designer: Albert Boton
Designer Nationality: French
Date: 1998

Memo was designed by French typographer Albert Boton, who trained under, and later worked with, leading Swiss designer Adrian Frutiger (see p. 290). The typeface has very minimal, triangular serifs and is a very slight variation on Agora, which Boton created for Berthold in 1990.

Meridien

ABCDEFGHIJKLMNOPQRSTUVWXYZ
abcdefghijklmnopqrstuvwxyz
1234567890 !@#?:;"*&

Foundry: Deberny & Peignot
Designer: Adrian Frutiger
Designer Nationality: Swiss
Date: 1957

A classical roman text face, Meridien was the fourth font created by Adrian Frutiger (see p. 290) and it established his name. Meridien was hard to obtain outside of France, leading to Monotype commissioning Frutiger to create the very similar Apollo, released in 1964.

Odense

ABCDEFGHIJKLMNOPQRSTUVWXYZ
abcdefghijklmnopqrstuvwxyz
1234567890 !@#?:;"*&

Foundry: Omnibus
Designer: Franko Luin
Designer Nationality: Swedish
Date: 1994

Named after a Danish town, Odense is like Optima but with tiny flared serifs. The family contains seventeen fonts: Roman to Extra Bold with italics; two weights of small caps; compressed, condensed and condensed bold with italics; and a display version, Odense Neon.

Pompei

ABCDEFGHIJKLMNOPQRSTUVWXYZ
abcdefghijklmnopqrstuvwxyz
1234567890 !@#?:;"*&

Foundry: Monotype
Designer: Albert Boton
Designer Nationality: French
Date: 1996

Albert Boton's Pompei is a glyphic serif with a muscular body that has been designed for great readability at small sizes. The font family features four weights, which range from Regular to Bold, with accompanying italics for both the Light and Regular weights.

Pompei New

ABCDEFGHIJKLMNOPQRSTUVWXYZ
abcdefghijklmnopqrstuvwxyz
1234567890 !@#?:;"*&

Foundry: Monotype
Designer: Albert Boton
Designer Nationality: French
Date: 2004

Pompei New is an update and expansion of Albert Boton's original font family of 1996. Alongside the initial styles, Pompei New includes the addition of a small caps design and an Old version, which includes extended ascenders and shrunken lowercase characters.

Versailles

ABCDEFGHIJKLMNOPQRSTUVWXYZ
abcdefghijklmnopqrstuvwxyz
1234567890 !@#?:;"*&

Foundry: Linotype
Designer: Adrian Frutiger
Designer Nationality: Swiss
Date: 1984

Versailles is inspired by the liberated letterforms of 19th-century French lithography, as well as the characters found on the memorial to French architect Charles Garnier in Paris. The shapes are modern in style, but the triangular serifs are reminiscent of earlier forms carved by hand.

Weiss

ABCDEFGHIJKLMNOPQRSTUVWXYZ
abcdefghijklmnopqrstuvwxyz
1234567890 !@#?:;"*&

Foundry: Bauer
Designer: Emil Rudolf Weiss
Designer Nationality: German
Date: 1928

Weiss was inspired by typefaces from the Italian Renaissance. It is one of the earliest contemporary serif types with italics based on the chancery style of writing. Originally known as Weiss Antiqua, it has sharp apex points and tall ascenders and its uppercase characters have a low-slung midsection.

Wolpe Pegasus

ABCDEFGHIJKLMNOPQRSTUVWXYZ
abcdefghijklmnopqrstuvwxyz
1234567890 !@#?:;"*&

Foundry: Monotype
Designer: Berthold Wolpe / Toshi Omagari
Designer Nationality: German / Japanese
Date: 1937 / 2017

Wolpe Pegasus is an update and digitization of Berthold Wolpe's serif Pegasus created in 1937. True to Wolpe's original design, Monotype's font maintains the initial quirks, which include varying stroke thicknesses, the occasional oversized serif and atypical loops and links.

Xenois Serif

ABCDEFGHIJKLMNOPQRSTUVWXYZ
abcdefghijklmnopqrstuvwxyz
1234567890 !@#?:;"*&

Foundry: Linotype
Designer: Erik Faulhaber
Designer Nationality: German
Date: 2013

Xenois Serif is a glyphic serif designed as part of a larger font family whose typefaces all interrelate well. It is notable for its expansive counters and apertures, reminiscent of those found in a sans serif, and its omission of serifs on several of the lowercase characters.

Alda

ABCDEFGHIJKLMNOPQRSTUVWXYZ
abcdefghijklmnopqrstuvwxyz
1234567890 !@#?:;"*&

Foundry: Emigre
Designer: Berton Hasebe
Designer Nationality: American
Date: 2008

Berton Hasebe conceived Alda during his master's at the Royal Academy of Art in The Hague. His idea was to generate different weights according to characteristics of physical objects, with the boldest weight echoing the tension of bent steel, and the lightest being as slight as a rubber band.

Breughel

ABCDEFGHIJKLMNOPQRSTUVWXYZ
abcdefghijklmnopqrstuvwxyz
1234567890 !@#?:;"*&

Foundry: Linotype
Designer: Adrian Frutiger
Designer Nationality: Swiss
Date: 1981

Breughel is inspired by 16th-century fonts and is one of the more experimental designs by Adrian Frutiger (see p. 290). It appears to slant to the right, due to the right sides of the stems being vertical and at 90° to the baseline, and the left sides curving into the serifs.

Cardea

ABCDEFGHIJKLMNOPQRSTUVWXYZ
abcdefghijklmnopqrstuvwxyz
1234567890 !@#?:;"*&

Foundry: Emigre
Designer: David Cabianca
Designer Nationality: Canadian
Date: 2004

David Cabianca created Cardea as part of his master's in Type Design at the University of Reading, Berkshire, England. With its high contrast and crisp edges, it has a strong, sculptural feel. Designed as a text face, it has three weights with accompanying italics and small caps.

Demos

ABCDEFGHIJKLMNOPQRSTUVWXYZ
abcdefghijklmnopqrstuvwxyz
1234567890 !@#?:;"*&

Foundry: Linotype
Designer: Gerard Unger
Designer Nationality: Dutch
Date: 1975

Gerard Unger's Demos was one of the first commercially available digital typefaces created for Hell's Digiset composing machines. It has a smooth appearance with an unusually tall x-height and relatively little difference between its thick vertical and thin horizontals.

Demos Next

ABCDEFGHIJKLMNOPQRSTUVWXYZ
abcdefghijklmnopqrstuvwxyz
1234567890 !@#?:;"*&

Demos Next is the latest incarnation of Gerard Unger's original Demos font from 1975. It follows on from 2001's Demos Neue, which was the typeface of the German federal government for more than ten years. Demos Next has been extended to several weights and adjusted for multiple languages.

Foundry: Linotype
Designer: Gerard Unger / Linda Hintz / Dan Reynolds
Designer Nationality: Dutch / German / American
Date: 1975 / 2015

Enigma

ABCDEFGHIJKLMNOPQRSTUVWXYZ
abcdefghijklmnopqrstuvwxyz
1234567890 !@#?:;"*&

For Enigma, Jeremy Tankard drew upon his research into innovations in 16th-century Dutch type design, the blending of Roman and Gothic styles, and the work of William A. Dwiggins. Since its initial release, Enigma now includes more weights and optical versions —Enigma Text, Enigma Display, and Enigma Fine.

Foundry: Jeremy Tankard Typography
Designer: Jeremy Tankard
Designer Nationality: British
Date: 1999

Fairplex Wide

ABCDEFGHIJKLMNOPQRSTUVWXYZ
abcdefghijklmnopqrstuvwxyz
1234567890 !@#?:;"*&

Fairplex Wide is a low-contrast serif that is reminiscent of a sans serif. Its intermediate weights were created by interpolating the Book and Black, with the exception of several characters, such as "n," which needed specially designed features to yield a pleasing weight balance and avoid serifs colliding.

Foundry: Emigre
Designer: Zuzana Licko
Designer Nationality: Slovakian
Date: 2002

FF Meta Serif

ABCDEFGHIJKLMNOPQRSTUVWXYZ
abcdefghijklmnopqrstuvwxyz
1234567890 !@#?:;"*&

This serif counterpart to FF Meta was designed by Erik Spiekermann (see p. 304) along with Christian Schwartz and Kris Sowersby, who developed its form over three years. It is versatile and warm, with subtle idiosyncrasies that sit comfortably alongside the sans serif original.

Foundry: FontFont
Designer: Erik Spiekermann / Christian Schwartz / Kris Sowersby / Ralph du Carrois / Botio Nikoltchev
Designer Nationality: German / American / New Zealander / German / Bulgarian
Date: 2007

Fedra Serif

ABCDEFGHIJKLMNOPQRSTUVWXYZ
abcdefghijklmnopqrstuvwxyz
1234567890 !@#?:;"'*&

Foundry: Typotheque
Designer: Peter Biľak
Designer Nationality: Slovakian
Date: 2003

Fedra Serif is a contemporary serif typeface designed in 2003 by Peter Biľak, the founder and type designer of Typotheque (see p. 90). It is a truly global and comprehensive typeface with each style supporting more than ninety languages. Biľak based his design on humanistic roots and the "rhythm" of handwriting married with the "rational drawing" of "a coarse computer-screen grid."

The typeface comes in two versions with varying stem heights. Version A has short ascenders and descenders, and low contrast; it can be used at very small sizes and for low-quality print applications, such as newspapers. Version A also matches the proportions of the sister sans serif typeface Fedra Sans for partnering serif and sans serif. Version B has longer stems and more contrast. Both versions

have the same character widths and kerning pairs, so are interchangeable without texts reflowing. In 2005, the OpenType Pro version was released with a wealth of features. The Fedra Serif Pro OpenType font supports all European languages, with Latin-based (Western, Central and Eastern European, Baltic, and Turkish), Cyrillic-based, and Greek-based versions. Arabic and Hebrew versions are available separately.

The detailing on some of the characters include a diamond-shaped point above the letter "i"; open counters for "P," "b," "9," and "6"; and curved terminating and sharp, angled connections for joining the strokes. Each weight has a collection of symbols, arrows, pictograms, and alternative characters, and a set of characters for science and mathematics.

Below. The elegant Fedra Serif, here shown in its Display cut at various sizes and mixed cases, includes details such as diamond-shaped points above the letter "i" and alternate characters such as the extended leg to the capital R, and custom ligatures for the T and U.

HEADLINE
maximum impact
LIGATURES

FF Scala

ABCDEFGHIJKLMNOPQRSTUVWXYZ
abcdefghijklmnopqrstuvwxyz
1234567890 !@#?:;"*&

Foundry: FontFont
Designer: Martin Majoor
Designer Nationality: Dutch
Date: 1990

This humanist serif takes its name from La Scala opera house in Milan and was commissioned by the Bredenburg Music Center of Utrecht. FF Scala Sans is its companion sans serif, along with FF Scala Jewels, which has a Dutch Baroque influence and decorative capitals.

Freight Text Pro

ABCDEFGHIJKLMNOPQRSTUVWXYZ
abcdefghijklmnopqrstuvwxyz
1234567890 !@#?:;"*&

Foundry: GarageFonts
Designer: Joshua Darden
Designer Nationality: American
Date: 2009

Freight was first published by David Carson's GarageFonts foundry in 2005; an extensive set of variant styles and weights have since been added. Freight Text Pro offers clarity and legibility thanks to its generous x-height, and it includes an expressive italic counterpart.

Frutiger Serif

ABCDEFGHIJKLMNOPQRSTUVWXYZ
abcdefghijklmnopqrstuvwxyz
1234567890 !@#?:;"*&

Foundry: Linotype
Designer: Adrian Frutiger / Akira Kobayashi
Designer Nationality: Swiss / Japanese
Date: 1957 / 2008

This serif counterpart to the eponymous sans from Adrian Frutiger (see p. 290) was developed from another of his designs, Meridien, first published by Deberny & Peignot in 1957. Frutiger Serif features a slightly narrower width than Meridien and contains an expanded range of sizes and weights.

Givens Antiqua

ABCDEFGHIJKLMNOPQRSTUVWXYZ
abcdefghijklmnopqrstuvwxyz
1234567890 !@#?:;"*&

Foundry: Monotype
Designer: George Ryan
Designer Nationality: American
Date: 2007

George Ryan began his career at Mergenthaler Linotype, and spent more than a decade at Bitstream before joining Monotype in 2003. He developed Givens Antiqua from sketches inspired by hand-drawn magazine typography; the font was named for Monotype co-founder Robert M. Givens.

Greta Text

ABCDEFGHIJKLMNOPQRSTUVWXYZ
abcdefghijklmnopqrstuvwxyz
1234567890 !@#?:;"*&

Foundry: Typotheque
Designer: Peter Biľak
Designer Nationality: Slovakian
Date: 2007

Greta Text was designed with the practicalities and limitations of newspaper use and web offset printing in mind. It is available in several grades of each weight for fine control of its visual texture, and its character set is tailored to the demands of a range of journalistic contexts.

ITC Resavska

ABCDEFGHIJKLMNOPQRSTUVWXYZ
abcdefghijklmnopqrstuvwxyz
1234567890 !@#?:;"*&

Foundry: ITC
Designer: Olivera Stojadinovic
Designer Nationality: Serbian
Date: 2004

This is Olivera Stojadinovic's serif counterpart to ITC Resavska Sans, which she designed for editorial use. She added geometric serifs to the original design to create four weights in serif and sans serif subfamilies. She went on to co-found the Serbia-based foundry Typolis in 2017.

Kingfisher

ABCDEFGHIJKLMNOPQRSTUVWXYZ
abcdefghijklmnopqrstuvwxyz
1234567890 !@#?:;"*&

Foundry: Jeremy Tankard Typography
Designer: Jeremy Tankard
Designer Nationality: British
Date: 2005

Jeremy Tankard intended Kingfisher to be ideal for continuous reading, especially for books. He found inspiration in the subtleties of letterpress typefaces such as Bembo and Ehrhardt, paying attention to their printed image. He added a slight irregularity to the letters to make the type appear less rigid.

Marathon

ABCDEFGHIJKLMNOPQRSTUVWXYZ
abcdefghijklmnopqrstuvwxyz
1234567890 !@#?:;"*&

Foundry: Monotype
Designer: Rudolf Koch / Ute Harder
Designer Nationality: German
Date: 1930 / 2003

Marathon is a digitization of one of the last fonts by Rudolf Koch, who is best known for his Kabel sans serif. Marathon was his serif text face, for which he cut the punches himself. Ute Harder based her digitization on a 48-point metal alphabet of Marathon, improving the spacing and adding characters.

Amasis

ABCDEFGHIJKLMNOPQRSTUVWXYZ
abcdefghijklmnopqrstuvwxyz
1234567890 !@#?:;"*&

Foundry: Monotype
Designer: Ron Carpenter
Designer Nationality: British
Date: 1992

Ron Carpenter created Amasis during his twenty-five-year-long stint at Monotype. The slab serif is unusual in that it takes a humanist rather than geometric approach. It was designed to work well at small sizes, and had the advantage of being suited for use with low-resolution printers and faxes.

Aptifer Slab

ABCDEFGHIJKLMNOPQRSTUVWXYZ
abcdefghijklmnopqrstuvwxyz
1234567890 !@#?:;"*&

Foundry: Linotype
Designer: Mårten Thavenius
Designer Nationality: Swedish
Date: 2006

This wedge slab serif channels two very different influences: the robust American Gothic and the more open humanist traditions. It shares many similarities, including stroke contrast and vertical stress, with its sister typeface, Aptifer Sans, which Swedish designer Mårten Thavenius also created.

Bariol Serif

ABCDEFGHIJKLMNOPQRSTUVWXYZ
abcdefghijklmnopqrstuvwxyz
1234567890 !@#?:;"*&

Foundry: Atipo
Designer: Raúl García del Pomar / Ismael González
Designer Nationality: Spanish
Date: 2015

Bariol Serif is a modern, functional serif designed as a sister typeface to the popular rounded sans serif Bariol. This accessible typeface is free for Regular and italic versions, or whatever a potential user can afford for the full set, and has proved popular as a low-budget option.

Brighton

ABCDEFGHIJKLMNOPQRSTUVWXYZ
abcdefghijklmnopqrstuvwxyz
1234567890 !@#?:;"*&

Foundry: ITC
Designer: Alan Bright
Designer Nationality: British
Date: 1979

Brighton was conceived as a text face but became more popular as a display face. Its rounded shapes and curved corners are often likened to Art Nouveau letters. It is perhaps most recognizable as the font used since 1984 in the logo of US supermarket chain Whole Foods Market.

Archer

ABCDEFGHIJKLMNOPQRSTUVWXYZ
abcdefghijklmnopqrstuvwxyz
1234567890 !@#?:;"'*&

Foundry: Hoefler & Co.
Designer: Tobias Frere-Jones / Jonathan Hoefler
Designer Nationality: American
Date: 2001

US foundry Hoefler & Co (then called Hoefler & Frere-Jones) designed this elegant slab serif in 2001 for *Martha Stewart Living* magazine. It possesses a humanist and gentle character yet retains the geometry of a slab serif that meets the challenges of editorial demands. From information graphics to reading text through to headlines and tables, Archer is a typeface family that is incredibly flexible and legible but also personable and inviting to read.

The rationale behind the design was that slab serifs generally fall into two camps. One is the Antique style, which comes from the 19th-century tradition that produced the Modern and Scotch styles with a more old-fashioned feel. The other is the geometric style, which is a Bauhaus type with a more rationalized discipline to the design. Archer combines the two approaches to get the best of both.

The typeface has fifty-five styles, including italics. Such a large range means not only that it is perfect for print applications but also that it can be employed on screen, ideally for headline sizes and larger. Details such as ball terminals on a number of the lowercase characters add to its unique character and friendliness. Such details are also seen on the typeface's uppercase, thus reinforcing its accessibility and legibility.

Below. The redesign of the identity and the packaging for Weingut Zähringer by Schmidt / Thurner / von Keisenberg features Archer with a vertical umlaut over the a in Zähringer.

PMN Caecilia

ABCDEFGHIJKLMNOPQRSTUVWXYZ
abcdefghijklmnopqrstuvwxyz
1234567890 !@#?:;"'*&

Foundry: Linotype
Designer: Peter Matthias Noordzij
Designer Nationality: Dutch
Date: 1990

The first-ever Neo-humanist slab serif, PMN Caecilia is Peter Matthias Noordzij's debut typeface. Replicating the writing style of a broad nib pen, it has subtle variations in stroke thickness and a large x-height, providing excellent legibility. It is used as the default font on Kindle e-readers.

Candida

ABCDEFGHIJKLMNOPQRSTUVWXYZ
abcdefghijklmnopqrstuvwxyz
1234567890 !@#?:;" *&

Foundry: Ludwig & Mayer / Bitstream
Designer: Jakob Erbar
Designer Nationality: German
Date: 1935–45 / c. 1980s

Candida was released after the designer's death in 1935, with subsequent weights drawn by other people. It was reworked in 1945, with a digitized version subsequently released by Bitstream. Described as a modest serif, it retains its legibility when used in text at small sizes.

Charlie

ABCDEFGHIJKLMNOPQRSTUVWXYZ
abcdefghijklmnopqrstuvwxyz
1234567890 !@#?:;"'*&

Foundry: Typotheque
Designer: Ross Milne
Designer Nationality: Canadian
Date: 2010

This affable serif was originally Ross Milne's thesis project when he was studying for his master's on the Type and Media course at the Royal Academy of Art, The Hague. A versatile slab serif, Charlie has narrow proportions, high x-height, and some unique finishing details.

Compatil Letter

ABCDEFGHIJKLMNOPQRSTUVWXYZ
abcdefghijklmnopqrstuvwxyz
1234567890 !@#?:;"'*&

Foundry: Linotype
Designer: Olaf Leu
Designer Nationality: German
Date: 2001

Compatil Letter is a robust serif that is described as being "informative yet poetic." It forms part of German font designer Olaf Leu's Compatil system. Compatil Letter is comprised of four weights and can easily be combined with the other typefaces in the Compatil family.

DIN Next Slab

ABCDEFGHIJKLMNOPQRSTUVWXYZ
abcdefghijklmnopqrstuvwxyz
1234567890 !@#?:;"*&

Foundry: Linotype
Designer: Akira Kobayashi / Tom Grace / Sandra Winter
Designer Nationality: Japanese / American / German
Date: 1931 / 2014

This is a new slab serif version of the typeface introduced by the Deutsches Institut für Normung (German Institute for Standardization) in the 1930s.

DIN Next Slab is available in seven weights from Ultra Light to Black. Its sister typefaces are DIN Next and DIN Next Rounded.

Diverda Serif

ABCDEFGHIJKLMNOPQRSTUVWXYZ
abcdefghijklmnopqrstuvwxyz
1234567890 !@#?:;"*&

Foundry: Linotype
Designer: Daniel Lanz
Designer Nationality: Swiss
Date: 2004

Diverda is a contemporary and very legible ornament-free serif with small x-heights and proportions that stay true to those of the Roman

alphabet. Swiss designer Daniel Lanz was inspired by pen on paper, and Diverda's downstrokes are heavier than its upstrokes.

Elante

ABCDEFGHIJKLMNOPQRSTUVWXYZ
abcdefghijklmnopqrstuvwxyz
1234567890 !@#?:;"*&

Foundry: Compugraphic
Designer: William A. Dwiggins
Designer Nationality: American
Date: 1935

Elante is Compugraphic's cold-type revival of Electra, a modern roman typeface designed by William A. Dwiggins in 1935 with long-form reading

in mind. This version, which has since been digitized, incorporates the set of shorter descenders included in Dwiggins's metal type original.

Exchange

ABCDEFGHIJKLMNOPQRSTUVWXYZ
abcdefghijklmnopqrstuvwxyz
1234567890 !@#?:;"*&

Foundry: Frere-Jones Type
Designer: Tobias Frere-Jones
Designer Nationality: American
Date: 2017

Exchange was originally designed as a newspaper text font, as is evident in its condensed proportions and wide range of historical references, from the

Depression-era United States to 19th-century Britain. Its additional MicroPlus styles make it ideal for use across all forms of digital media.

Frere-Jones Type

Tobias Frere-Jones is a superstar in the typographic world. He is one of the United States's leading and most prolific typeface designers and has designed more than 500 typefaces for retail, personal work, and private commissions. He also has numerous awards to his name for his contributions to design, typography, and type education.

After graduating with a Bachelor of Fine Arts degree from the Rhode Island School of Design he started his career at Font Bureau in Boston, where he went on to be senior designer. There he designed some of the foundry's best-known types, including Interstate and Garage Gothic. He went on to become a partner at New York foundry Hoefler & Frere-Jones, where he collaborated on many projects, creating some of his most recognizable designs such as Gotham (see p. 198), Surveyor, and Whitney.

In 2015, he founded his own type studio, Frere-Jones Type. In a short time, the new foundry's offerings received recognition. The first release was Mallory, a humanist sans serif, which includes twenty-six fonts—sixteen standard styles and ten MicroPlus styles that address the challenges of small print text and screen text simultaneously.

Working closely with Frere-Jones in the creation of typefaces are senior type designer Nina Stössinger and type designer Fred Shallcrass. Nina, originally from Switzerland, studied multimedia design in Germany, where she discovered her passion for type, and went on to an MA in Type and Media at Royal Academy of Art in The Hague. She also teaches type design at Yale School of Art, and currently serves on the Board of Directors of the Type Directors Club.

Fred, who gained editorial, brand, and lettering experience in New Zealand, moved to New York in 2015 and joined Frere-Jones soon after. He is also a teaching assistant at Type@Cooper Extended program.

Founded: 2015
Country: USA
Website: frerejones.com
Notable typefaces:
Conductor (see p. 458)

Below, clockwise from left. With British and American traits, sans serif Mallory is available in twenty-six fonts; inspired by Ancient Rome, headline face Empirica offers a full palette and is ideal for editorial and branding projects; display typeface Conductor is inspired by the letterforms on Bulgarian lottery tickets.

Opposite. Slab serif Exchange was originally designed as a newspaper text face.

DER GROßE DUDEN (1957)
FREQUENTS HERZEGOVINA
World Leagues Grand Prix
Every December Sunday
€207 ₺214 ₦981 ₹835 ₱160
MEN'S NATIONAL TEAM
5408 SAN FRANCISCO BLVD
QUILTING WORKSHOPS!
Unjustifiable Alternatives
Gjøvik to Logroño quickest
RYE WHISKEY TASTINGS
New Small Lizard Research

Quintessentializes
Photosynthesised
College of Justice
E Pluribus Unum
Bank of England
Gamesomeness

Overcompensating
Acts of Parliament
Goodbye to Berlin
Radiotherapeutic
Metamorphosed
Antimonarchist

Queensboro Plaza
Concept Album
Understated
Lineament

Track Connections
Revolving Mass
Photosphere
Quicksilver

PROBLEM SOLVING

CONSERVATION OF MATTER

BINARY NOTATION

PICKLED MUSTARD GREENS

ELECTRIC HEATER

APPROACH WHILE DRIVING

HOMEMADE WINE

CORRUGATED CARDBOARD

KEYNOTE SPEECH

FF Unit Slab

ABCDEFGHIJKLMNOPQRSTUVWXYZ
abcdefghijklmnopqrstuvwxyz
1234567890 !@#?:;"*&

Foundry: FontFont
Designer: Erik Spiekermann /
Christian Schwartz /
Kris Sowersby
Designer Nationality: German /
American / New Zealander
Date: 2009

This counterpart to the existing sans serif typeface FF Unit was developed from the early sketches for Meta Serif by New Zealand typeface designer Kris Sowersby. The precise, humanist slab serif design is suitable for both body text and headline use, and it also pairs well with typefaces from the Meta family.

FS Rufus

ABCDEFGHIJKLMNOPQRSTUVWXYZ
abcdefghijklmnopqrstuvwxyz
1234567890 !@#?:;"*&

Foundry: Fontsmith
Designer: Emanuela Conidi /
Mitja Miklavčič / Jason Smith
Designer Nationality: Italian /
Slovenian / British
Date: 2009

The extended letterforms of FS Rufus feature exaggerated ink traps—a detail traditionally incorporated into metal type that was designed for use at small point sizes. With more than eighty discretionary ligatures included, Rufus offers plenty of scope for creative typesetting.

FS Silas Slab

ABCDEFGHIJKLMNOPQRSTUVWXYZ
abcdefghijklmnopqrstuvwxyz
1234567890 !@#?:;"*&

Foundry: Fontsmith
Designer: Phil Garnham /
Jason Smith
Designer Nationality: British
Date: 2015

Fontsmith (see p. 272) created this angular serif as a counterpart to FS Silas Sans, and its design is more blunt and square than in the foundry's other explorations of the slab style. Its forms display an effective balance of expressiveness and clarity, and it is equally suitable for both print and digital use.

Generis Slab

ABCDEFGHIJKLMNOPQRSTUVWXYZ
abcdefghijklmnopqrstuvwxyz
1234567890 !@#?:;"*&

Foundry: Linotype
Designer: Erik Faulhaber
Designer Nationality: German
Date: 2006

German font designer Erik Faulhaber designed the comprehensive Generis type system to offer a versatile, complementary palette of typefaces that could be easily and harmoniously combined. The economical proportions of Generis Slab work well alongside its Serif, Sans, and Simple siblings.

Glypha

ABCDEFGHIJKLMNOPQRSTUVWXYZ
abcdefghijklmnopqrstuvwxyz
1234567890 !@#?:;"*&

Foundry: Stempel
Designer: Adrian Frutiger
Designer Nationality: Swiss
Date: 1977

Adrian Frutiger (see p. 290) designed this balanced serif. It is one of two such slab styles that he developed from the skeleton of Univers; its predecessor, Serifa, displays slightly more extended letterforms. True to its heritage, Glypha works well alongside Univers and other Neo-grotesques.

HFJ Sentinel

ABCDEFGHIJKLMNOPQRSTUVWXYZ
abcdefghijklmnopqrstuvwxyz
1234567890 !@#?:;"*&

Foundry: Hoefler & Frere-Jones
Designer: Tobias Frere-Jones / Jonathan Hoefler
Designer Nationality: American
Date: 2009

Sentinel was designed to address some of the shortcomings of earlier slab serif fonts, which frequently featured inconsistent character sets, missing italics and a limited range of weights. Sentinel Screensmart, a version design specially for screen use, is also available.

Humanist Slabserif 712

ABCDEFGHIJKLMNOPQRSTUVWXYZ
abcdefghijklmnopqrstuvwxyz
1234567890 !@#?:;"*&

Foundry: Bitstream
Designer: Adrian Frutiger
Designer Nationality: Swiss
Date: 1956

This Bitstream digitization is based on Egyptienne F, which was designed by Adrian Frutiger (see p. 290) for Deberny & Peignot in 1956; it was the first font to be created specifically for phototypesetting. Its bracketed serifs set it apart from Frutiger's later explorations of the slab style.

ITC Napoleone Slab

ABCDEFGHIJKLMNOPQRSTUVWXYZ
abcdefghijklmnopqrstuvwxyz
1234567890 !@#?:;"*&

Foundry: ITC
Designer: Silvio Napoleone
Designer Nationality: American
Date: 2002

This contemporary slab serif is the work of award-winning type and graphic designer Silvio Napoleone, co-founder of the Canadian consultancy Nubrand. Its chiseled, calligraphy-inspired forms make it a distinctive and legible choice for print and screen-based applications.

ITC Officina Serif

ABCDEFGHIJKLMNOPQRSTUVWXYZ
abcdefghijklmnopqrstuvwxyz
1234567890 !@#?:;"*&

Foundry: ITC
Designer: Erik Spiekermann
Designer Nationality: German
Date: 1990–98

This highly functional and very legible typeface was conceived for use in office correspondence and business documentation, and has proved suitable for many different applications. It is also available in sans serif and display versions (plus dingbats), each with five weights and matching italics.

ITC Tactile

ABCDEFGHIJKLMNOPQRSTUVWXYZ
abcdefghijklmnopqrstuvwxyz
1234567890 !@#?:;"*&

Foundry: ITC
Designer: Joseph Stitzlein
Designer Nationality: American
Date: 2002

This typeface, which won the Type Directors Club Award, features an intriguing blend of contradictory details, including both straight slab and bracketed serifs, and calligraphic diagonal line endings. It is available in a range of weights, each with its own distinctive tone of voice.

ITC Tyke

ABCDEFGHIJKLMNOPQRSTUVWXYZ
abcdefghijklmnopqrstuvwxyz
1234567890 !@#?:;"*&

Foundry: ITC
Designer: Tomi Haaparanta
Designer Nationality: Finnish
Date: 2005

The soft and friendly letterforms of ITC Tyke were developed by Finnish type designer Tomi Haaparanta to communicate in a similar tone to Cooper Black, but this contemporary typeface is available in a much broader range of weights, plus italics. It was published by ITC in 2005.

Jeunesse Slab

ABCDEFGHIJKLMNOPQRSTUVWXYZ
abcdefghijklmnopqrstuvwxyz
1234567890 !@#?:;"*&

Foundry: Monotype
Designer: Johannes Birkenbach
Designer Nationality: German
Date: 1993

Jeunesse Slab was created by German typographer Johannes Birkenbach, who had worked at Stempel, Linotype, and then Monotype. He designed it to complement Jeunesse and Jeunesse Sans; all were conceived as a full family in 1993. It is a slab serif available in one weight with italics.

Joanna

ABCDEFGHIJKLMNOPQRSTUVWXYZ
abcdefghijklmnopqrstuvwxyz
1234567890 !@#?:;"*&

Eric Gill designed Joanna following the release of Gill Sans, and named it after his daughter. He first used the typeface for the text in his book *An Essay* *on Typography* (1931). Joanna pairs very well with Gill Sans and is economical due to its narrow width and almost vertical italics.

Foundry: Monotype
Designer: Eric Gill
Designer Nationality: British
Date: 1930–31

Joanna Nova

ABCDEFGHIJKLMNOPQRSTUVWXYZ
abcdefghijklmnopqrstuvwxyz
1234567890 !@#?:;"*&

Monotype released this extensive update of Joanna, along with Gill Sans Nova and Joanna Sans, as part of the Eric Gill Series collection of seventy-seven fonts across the families. Ben Jones revisited Eric Gill's original drawings to reinstate some lost features while also improving usability.

Foundry: Monotype
Designer: Eric Gill / Ben Jones
Designer Nationality: British
Date: 1930–31 / 2015

Karloff Neutral

ABCDEFGHIJKLMNOPQRSTUVWXYZ
abcdefghijklmnopqrstuvwxyz
1234567890 !@#?:;"*&

Designed by a team lead by Peter Biľak, the Karloff family explores extremes. Neutral was an attempt to find a middle ground between high-contrast didone serifs and reverse-contrast Italian typefaces; the result is a slab serif that shares some of the humanistic features of a grotesque.

Foundry: Typotheque
Designer: Peter Biľak / Pieter van Rosmalen / Nikola Djurek
Designer Nationality: Slovakian / Dutch / Croatian
Date: 2012

LinoLetter

ABCDEFGHIJKLMNOPQRSTUVWXYZ
abcdefghijklmnopqrstuvwxyz
1234567890 !@#?:;"*&

LinoLetter is a slab serif that is ideal for newspaper work and mass-produced printing thanks to its heavy forms, low contrast, and legibility at small sizes. It was the result of a collaboration, began during the 1980s, between the Linotype foundry and the Basel School of Design, Switzerland.

Foundry: Linotype
Designer: André Gürtler / Reinhard Haus
Designer Nationality: Swiss / German
Date: 1992

Lumin

ABCDEFGHIJKLMNOPQRSTUVWXYZ
abcdefghijklmnopqrstuvwxyz
1234567890 !@#?:;"*&

Foundry: Typotheque
Designer: Nikola Djurek
Designer Nationality: Croatian
Date: 2013

Lumin is a dark slab serif by Croatian Nikola Djurek and forms part of a family that contains sans serif, condensed, and display faces. It has a big x-height, large counters, and horizontal terminals on unbracketed serifs. Lumin was designed with editorial usage in mind and comes in four weights.

Madawaska

ABCDEFGHIJKLMNOPQRSTUVWXYZ
abcdefghijklmnopqrstuvwxyz
1234567890 !@#?:;"*&

Foundry: Typodermic
Designer: Ray Larabie
Designer Nationality: Canadian
Date: 2008

Madawaska is a clean slab serif named after a county in New Brunswick, Canada. It is available in eight weights—Ultra Light to Heavy—each with italics and small caps. Canadian Ray Larabie, the proprietor of Typodermic, also designed two digitally distressed versions, Madawaska Jeans and River.

Malaga

ABCDEFGHIJKLMNOPQRSTUVWXYZ
abcdefghijklmnopqrstuvwxyz
1234567890 !@#?:;"*&

Foundry: Emigre
Designer: Xavier Dupré
Designer Nationality: French
Date: 2007

Malaga is a characterful sans serif inspired by everything from blackletter script to Latin fonts, and from the first Venetian Antiquas of the 15th century to brushstroke types. It has a number of unorthodox details but is still legible when used for extended text as well as display.

Mantika News

ABCDEFGHIJKLMNOPQRSTUVWXYZ
abcdefghijklmnopqrstuvwxyz
1234567890 !@#?:;"*&

Foundry: Linotype
Designer: Jürgen Weltin
Designer Nationality: German
Date: 2016

The newest of the Mantika family, News is a robust, contemporary serif in four weights, with Light and ExtraBold display versions that have shorter ascenders and a lower x-height. The Mantika family has shared character widths, making them ideal to use in tandem.

Marconi

ABCDEFGHIJKLMNOPQRSTUVWXYZ
abcdefghijklmnopqrstuvwxyz
1234567890 !@#?:;"*&

Foundry: Hell
Designer: Hermann Zapf
Designer Nationality: German
Date: 1976

Hermann Zapf (see p. 574) designed Marconi for the Digiset early digital typesetting system produced by Hell. It has a large x-height, very open lowercase letters and less height difference between upper and lowercases, all of which were suggested by the results of readability tests.

Museo Slab

ABCDEFGHIJKLMNOPQRSTUVWXYZ
abcdefghijklmnopqrstuvwxyz
1234567890 !@#?:;"*&

Foundry: exljbris
Designer: Jos Buivenga
Designer Nationality: Dutch
Date: 2009

Dutch designer Jos Buivenga of foundry exljbris added a slab serif to the family in 2009, a year after the successful release of Museo, his first commercial typeface. The standard Museo has square serifs, which are more prominent in the slab version that comes in six weights.

Neue Aachen

ABCDEFGHIJKLMNOPQRSTUVWXYZ
abcdefghijklmnopqrstuvwxyz
1234567890 !@#?:;"*&

Foundry: Monotype
Designer: Alan Meeks /
Colin Brignall / Jim Wasco
Designer Nationality: British /
British / American
Date: 1969 / 2012

Colin Brignall and Alan Meeks designed Aachen or Letraset in 1969. Jim Wasco gave the heavy, tightly spaced headline font an extensive update in 2012. Wasco designed nine weights with italics, a vast increase on the original Aachen, which came in just regular and bold.

Pica 10 Pitch

ABCDEFGHIJKLMNOPQRSTUVWXYZ
abcdefghijklmnopqrstuvwxyz
1234567890 !@#?:;"*&

Foundry: Bitstream
Designer: Bitstream
Designer Nationality: American
Date: 1953 / 1990

Pica 10 Pitch is named after the measuring system used for typewriter faces. Bitstream's revival is a digitization of the Pica typeface designed for the IBM Standard and Selectric typewriters. Pica 10 Pitch is fixed width, monospaced, and features capitals but no bold or italics.

Prima Serif

ABCDEFGHIJKLMNOPQRSTUVWXYZ
abcdefghijklmnopqrstuvwxyz
1234567890 !@#?:;"*&

Foundry: Bitstream
Designer: Jim Lyles
Designer Nationality: American
Date: 1998

Prima Serif was released in the middle of the dot-com boom when there was a period of rapid growth in internet usage. It was designed to provide outstanding quality at low screen resolutions, making it an ideal font for prolonged periods of web browsing or on-screen reading.

Proteus

ABCDEFGHIJKLMNOPQRSTUVWXYZ
abcdefghijklmnopqrstuvwxyz
1234567890 !@#?:;"*&

Foundry: ITC
Designer: Freda Sack
Designer Nationality: British
Date: 1983

British designer Freda Sack created the Proteus squared slab serif in the style of 16th-century poster and handbill typography. Similar to letterforms of this period, its design is expressive and robust, a formula that resonates in each of its four weights: Light, Book, Medium, and Bold.

Quitador

ABCDEFGHIJKLMNOPQRSTUVWXYZ
abcdefghijklmnopqrstuvwxyz
1234567890 !@#?:;"*&

Foundry: Linotype
Designer: Arne Freytag
Designer Nationality: German
Date: 2014

German designer Arne Freytag created the Quitador slab serif for multiple platforms, from mobile devices to magazine headlines. The font's shape is based on the superellipse, providing the letterforms with an open character that works at both small and large sizes.

Schadow

ABCDEFGHIJKLMNOPQRSTUVWXYZ
abcdefghijklmnopqrstuvwxyz
1234567890 !@#?:;"*&

Foundry: Bitstream
Designer: Georg Trump
Designer Nationality: German
Date: 1938–52

German font designer Georg Trump's Schadow was originally released by the Weber type foundry to rival Ludwig & Mayer's Candida typeface. Bitstream chose to digitize Schadow because its geometric letterforms suit the small sizes typically required for screen displays.

Siseriff

ABCDEFGHIJKLMNOPQRSTUVWXYZ
abcdefghijklmnopqrstuvwxyz
1234567890 !@#?:;"*&

Foundry: Linotype
Designer: Bo Berndal
Designer Nationality: Swedish
Date: 2002

Swedish designer Bo Berndal created the Siseriff slab serif to accommodate the various hierarchies of editorial design. Comprised of nine styles, the font family includes weights from Light to Black, and unlike the majority of slab serif families, features true italics instead of standard obliques.

Soho

ABCDEFGHIJKLMNOPQRSTUVWXYZ
abcdefghijklmnopqrstuvwxyz
1234567890 !@#?:;"*&

Foundry: Monotype
Designer: Seb Lester
Designer Nationality: British
Date: 2007

The product of three years of work, Soho is a slab serif family comprised of forty fonts and 32,668 characters. With a catalogue of weights that range from Condensed Extra Light to Ultra Extended, Soho is a typeface designed for the multiple platforms of 21st-century typography.

Vectipede

ABCDEFGHIJKLMNOPQRSTUVWXYZ
abcdefghijklmnopqrstuvwxyz
1234567890 !@#?:;"*&

Foundry: Typodermic
Designer: Ray Larabie / Chikako Larabie
Designer Nationality: Canadian / Japanese
Date: 2010

Vectipede is a technical slab serif with seven weights, ranging from Ultralight to Black, for maximum versatility. The letterforms have a squared character, smooth curves, and short serifs. Unlike most slab serifs, Vectipede combines curled terminals with keen edges.

Venus Egyptienne

ABCDEFGHIJKLMNOPQRSTUVWXYZ
abcdefghijklmnopqrstuvwxyz
1234567890 !@#?:;"*&

Foundry: Linotype
Designer: Bauersche Giesserei / Linotype Design Studio
Designer Nationality: German
Date: Unknown

Venus Egyptienne is Linotype's revival of the Bauersche Giesserei's font family, initially designed as a highly legible slab serif for German map production. Contrary to many slab serif designs, Venus Egyptienne has a narrow width, curved brackets, and no bold weight.

Typotheque

Based in a former school building in The Hague, Netherlands, Typotheque is a foundry that offers an expansive range of high-quality retail typefaces while also providing custom solutions for a range of applications and languages. It was established by founder Peter Biľak, who is committed to continuing the traditions of independent type foundries by creating typefaces that will stand the test of time but also reflect and serve today's needs. This is a concept they describe as "contemporaneity."

Typotheque focuses on extended language support for its typefaces, with its range of fonts covering most Latin-based languages as well as those based on Greek, Cyrillic, Arabic, Armenian, and Devanagari scripts. This comprehensive consideration for languages is visible in most of their releases, such as Fedra Sans (see p. 261), which is also available in Bengali, Tamil, and Inuktitut. In 2009, Typotheque was the first commercial type foundry to license its entire type library for use on the web.

Typotheque is also a publisher and a design studio managed by Peter along with his Slovak partner, Johanna, and Croatian designer Nikola Djurek. As a design studio, Typotheque has created an impressive body of cultural and commercial work over the years, using its own typefaces. This ranges from postage stamps to posters, and ceramic tiles to exhibition architecture and design.

Founded: 1999
Country: Netherlands
Website: typotheque.com
Notable typefaces:
Fedra Sans (see p. 261)
Fedra Serif (see p. 73)
Julien (see p. 429)

Below left. "Threesome" for the Karloff typeface family showing its three personalities: Positive, Neutral, and Negative.

Below middle. Specimen for Greta Sans and its extensive type system and language variants.

Below right. Experimental display typeface Calcula.

Right. The History typeface system conceived and designed by Peter Biľak (with assistance from Eike Dingler, Ján Filípek, Ondrej Jób, Ashfaq Niazi, and Ilya Ruderman) is a typeface that is based on the skeleton of Roman inscriptional capitals. The end design for History consists of twenty-one independent typefaces that share widths and other metric information so that they can be combined to reflect the evolution of typography. With the potential to create thousands of different designs with the twenty-one layers, the designer is provided with a huge opportunity for experimentation and play.

HISTORY

TRASH BAG OF RANDOM COINCIDENCES TORN OPEN IN A WIND

SURELY, WATT WITH HIS STEAM ENGINE, FARADAY WITH HIS ELECTRIC MOTOR, AND EDISON WITH HIS INCANDESCENT LIGHT BULB DID NOT HAVE IT AS THEIR GOAL TO CONTRIBUTE TO A FUEL SHORTAGE SOME DAY THAT WOULD PLACE THEIR COUNTRIES AT THE MERCY OF ARAB OIL.

RELAY RACE

JIGSAW PUZZLE

LIVING WHOLE, IF ONE ORGAN BE REMOVED, IT IS NOTHING BUT A LIFELESS MASS

ACTION AND REACTION

DIRTY POLITICS CLEANED UP FOR THE CONSUMPTION OF CHILDREN AND OTHER INNOCENTS

SUM TOTAL OF THE THINGS THAT COULD HAVE BEEN AVOIDED

GREAT DUST HEAP

PROPAGANDA OF THE VICTORS

ARGUMENT WITHOUT END

THAT LITTLE SEWER WHERE MAN LOVES TO WALLOW

COLLECTION OF CRIMES, FOLLIES, AND MISFORTUNES AMONG WHICH WE HAVE NOW AND THEN MET WITH A FEW VIRTUES, AND SOME HAPPY TIMES

GALLERY OF PICTURES IN WHICH THERE ARE FEW ORIGINALS AND MANY COPIES

SUDDEN STAGETRICK

STORY OF EVENTS, WITH PRAISE OR BLAME

ONE DAMNED THING AFTER ANOTHER

PATTERN-BOOK OF POSSESSED IDEOLOGIES

DISTILLATION OF RUMOR

TRANSFORMATION OF EVENTS INTO FOOTNOTES

GOSSIP WHO TEASE THE DEAD

EXCITABLE AND UNRELIABLE OLD LADY

DISCIPLINE CLOSEST TO LIFE

COLLECTION OF EPITAPHS

NIGHTMARE FROM WHICH I AM TRYING TO AWAKE

SOUND OF SILKEN SLIPPERS GOING DOWN-STAIRS AND WOOD-EN SHOES COMING UP

LESSON

VAST EARLY WARNING SYSTEM

AN AGGREGATION OF TRUTHS, HALF-TRUTHS, SEMI-TRUTHS, FABLES, MYTHS, RUMORS, PREJUDICES, PERSONAL NARRATIVES, GOSSIP, AND OFFICIAL PREVARICATIONS. IT IS A CANVAS UPON WHICH THOUSANDS OF ARTISTS THROUGHOUT THE AGES HAVE SPLASHED THEIR CONCEPTIONS AND INTERPRETATIONS OF A DAY AND AN ERA. SOME MOTIFS ARE GROTESQUE AND SOME ARE MAGNIFICENT.

HISTORY is the longest project that Typotheque has undertaken. Its beginnings trace to mid 1990s when Peter Biľak experimented with decorative layering systems inspired by 19th century Tuscan types. HISTORY goes a step forward and based on a skeleton of Roman inscriptional capitals creates 21 layers, 21 independent typefaces which share widths and other metric information, so they can be recombined. Potentially thousands of different unique styles can be created by superimposition of layers, ranging from conventional rennaisance, transitional, baroque, script like, commercial accidental, to digital types. Since they can share different all elements, the most interesting is when various seemingly incompatible elements are combiner. Just try putting on pixel letters the Didot-like serifs, or put 19th century slab serifs on top of a rennaisance construction. Happy accidents are not only amazing but suprisingly fresh and usable. Realising that controlling 21 different layers can be a daunting task, Typotheque delivers history not only as a set of OpenType fonts, but provides an application entitled History Remixer. This web based application uses single text input, and familiar Photoshop-like interface, where users select which layers should be on, layer order, colour and luminosity, and application generates an open PDF files.

Designed by Peter Biľak
Published by Typotheque, 2008

Vista Slab

ABCDEFGHIJKLMNOPQRSTUVWXYZ
abcdefghijklmnopqrstuvwxyz
1234567890 !@#?:;"*&

Foundry: Emigre
Designer: Xavier Dupré
Designer Nationality: French
Date: 2008

Vista Slab, by French typographer and type designer Xavier Dupré, was published in 2008 along with Vista Sans Narrow as an extension to the Vista Sans typeface he created three years earlier. The addition of the new versions extended the family to 108 fonts.

Dupré's intention for the design of the Vista family was to combine the simpler forms of a sans serif typeface with the "humanist appeal of calligraphic forms." When enlarged, the typeface provides insight into the many refined details it possesses, such as bulging edges on a selection of the stroke endings, ink traps in some of the characters and squared-up notches on inside cusps. Overall, it is a slab serif that provides a warmth and character to any texts set using it.

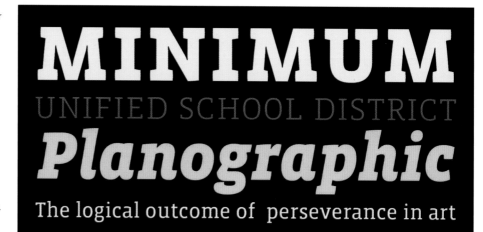

Xenois Slab

ABCDEFGHIJKLMNOPQRSTUVWXYZ
abcdefghijklmnopqrstuvwxyz
1234567890 !@#?:;"*&

Foundry: Linotype
Designer: Erik Faulhaber
Designer Nationality: German
Date: 2013

Xenois Slab is a further component of the extensive Xenois font family. The characters provide the font with a unique disposition while retaining the proportions and stroke weights of other Xenois fonts, allowing each style to harmonize across platforms and projects.

Zico

ABCDEFGHIJKLMNOPQRSTUVWXYZ
abcdefghijklmnopqrstuvwxyz
1234567890 !@#?:;"*&

Foundry: Typotheque
Designer: Marko Hrastovec
Designer Nationality: Croatian
Date: 2016

Marko Hrastovec's Zico is a humanist slab serif, influenced by the muscular letterforms found on sports jerseys. Throughout its seven weights, from Thin to Black, the characters propose a sporting aesthetic, seen primarily in their dynamic joints and robust strokes.

Archive

ABCDEFGHIJKLMNOPQRSTUVWXYZ
abcdefghijklmnopqrstuvwxyz
1234567890 !@#?:;"*&

Foundry: Colophon
Designer: The Entente
Designer Nationality: British
Date: 2013

Archive was initially created for a publication by Brighton-based photographic publisher Photoworks, and has small indents on the top and bottom of each serif that align parallel to the baseline and cap height. It is available in four weights plus italics, and a monospaced version.

Basilia

ABCDEFGHIJKLMNOPQRSTUVWXYZ
abcdefghijklmnopqrstuvwxyz
1234567890 !@#?:;"*&

Foundry: Haas
Designer: André Gürtler
Designer Nationality: Swiss
Date: 1978

Basilia has a classical look, expressed by the strong contrast between its robust verticals and fine horizontal strokes and serifs. Its round forms and softer strokes differentiate it from traditional Modern faces, with straight horizontal serifs set at right angles to the strokes.

Boberia

ABCDEFGHIJKLMNOPQRSTUVWXYZ
abcdefghijklmnopqrstuvwxyz
1234567890 !@#?:;"*&

Foundry: Linotype
Designer: Bo Berndal
Designer Nationality: Swedish
Date: 1994

Bo Berndal's expressive serif won the Linotype International Digital Type Design Contest in 1994. It is inspired by early 20th-century neoclassicism, and its narrow letterforms, large x-height and high stroke contrast give it a sophisticated feel, reminiscent of Art Deco designs.

Bodoni Classico

ABCDEFGHIJKLMNOPQRSTUVWXYZ
abcdefghijklmnopqrstuvwxyz
1234567890 !@#?:;"*&

Foundry: Omnibus
Designer: Giambattista Bodoni / Franko Luin
Designer Nationality: Italian / Swedish
Date: 1767 / 1995

This is one of the numerous variations on Giambattista Bodoni's hugely influential design of 1767, which was dominant until the end of the 19th century. Franko Luin's take is notable for displaying less stroke contrast than Bodoni's original design, making it ideal for use at smaller point sizes.

Bauer Bodoni

ABCDEFGHIJKLMNOPQRSTUVWXYZ
abcdefghijklmnopqrstuvwxyz
1234567890 !@#?:;"*&

Foundry: Bauer
Designer: Giambattista Bodoni / Heinrich Jost
Designer Nationality: Italian / German
Date: 1798 / 1926

Bauer Bodoni was designed for the Bauer Type Foundry in 1926 by Heinrich Jost, the German typographer and type designer, and is a revival of the famous Didone cut in 1798 by Italian typographer and printer Giambattista Bodoni. Bodoni's design was heavily influenced by the first of the modern faces cut by the Frenchman Firmin Didot, his contemporary and rival, in the early 1780s in Paris.

Bodoni and Didot were the key instigators in the development of serif typefaces from the transitional to the modern, along with Frenchman Pierre-Simon Fournier. However, it is the former pair who are most recognized, and the term "didone" is a combination of both of their surnames.

Bodoni pushed at the boundaries of what was achievable to be cut and printed. His typeface design was revolutionary; discarding brackets, with serifs just defined by a thin stroke and creating a huge contrast between the thick and thin strokes that defined each character. The technical precision and elegance of the typeface made for a classic.

The Bauer version of Bodoni is most often seen employed in graphic design for fashion, and in display and headline applications. This version retains the high contrast of Bodoni's original design and more of its features than many other published versions from different foundries, which have sometimes aimed to improve legibility by reducing the extreme tolerances of the overall design.

Below. f32 is an American trend-watching company. Blok Design, based in Canada, worked with the organization to create both its name (f32 comes from photography terminology, a setting that provides the most depth of field), and its visual identity across print, including stationery, trend reports, and a new website. The san-serif employed is Montserrat, a geometric sans serif by Argentinian designer Julieta Ulanovsky.

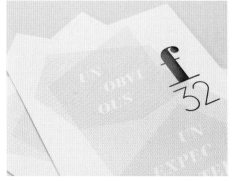

Bodoni LT

ABCDEFGHIJKLMNOPQRSTUVWXYZ
abcdefghijklmnopqrstuvwxyz
1234567890 !@#?:;"*&

Foundry: ATC
Designer: Giambattista Bodoni / Morris Fuller Benton
Designer Nationality: Italian / American
Date: 1767 / 1911

Giambattista Bodoni was a prolific type designer, and many interpretations of his 18th-century typeface have been created. Although some of the finer details of the original are missing from this cut, the high contrast and vertical stress typical of this style of serif are very much present.

Brenner

ABCDEFGHIJKLMNOPQRSTUVWXYZ
abcdefghijklmnopqrstuvwxyz
1234567890 !@#?:;"*&

Foundry: Typotheque
Designer: Nikola Djurek
Designer Nationality: Croatian
Date: 2018

Although inspired by the high-contrast fonts of Giambattista Bodoni and Firmin Didot, Brenner has the feel of handwritten pointed-pen writing. The typeface forms part of a superfamily with a Serif, Sans, Display, Mono, Script, Condensed, and Slab. It is best used at 14 point and above.

Bressay

ABCDEFGHIJKLMNOPQRSTUVWXYZ
abcdefghijklmnopqrstuvwxyz
1234567890 !@#?:;"*&

Foundry: Dalton Maag
Designer: Stuart Brown
Designer Nationality: British
Date: 2015

A revision of 19th-century Scotch Roman letterforms, Bressay is a versatile serif designed for use at all sizes. Slight modifications to classical features, such as the ball terminals, ensure character and readability across both print and digital platforms.

Chiswick Deck

ABCDEFGHIJKLMNOPQRSTUVWXYZ
abcdefghijklmnopqrstuvwxyz
1234567890 !@#?:;"*&

Foundry: Commercial Type
Designer: Paul Barnes
Designer Nationality: British
Date: 2017

Informed by a collection of 18th- and 19th-century types, Chiswick Deck is a lively modern serif. While the strokes are high in contrast and largely formal, the serifs and tails, especially those in the wonderfully rich italics, are treated with the more expressive forms of hand-lettering.

Didot

ABCDEFGHIJKLMNOPQRSTUVWXYZ
abcdefghijklmnopqrstuvwxyz
1234567890 !@#?:,"*&

Swiss type designer Adrian Frutiger (see p. 290) drew on the type designs and letterforms of Parisian designer Firmin Didot when he created Didot for Linotype in 1991. Frutiger's sensitive revival typeface captures the spirit and innovation of the Enlightenment, yet is also representative of Firmin Didot's later designs drawn up in the first decade of the 19th century.

Firmin Didot was working at a time when advances in type design, printing techniques, and paper technology led to huge improvements in letter-cutting. This contributed to increased innovation and the creation of ever-more sophisticated types. Didot's Modern approach (so-called because of its position after Old Style and Transitional) type design reflected the progression of these types, as did those of French designer Pierre-Simon Fournier and Italian designer Giambattista Bodoni in developing increasingly refined type designs.

A key design feature in the construction of Didot is the greater contrast between the thick and thin strokes making up the characters. In the 18th and 19th centuries, this feature pushed the boundaries of printing reproduction, but its style captured the pioneering zeitgeist of the time. The lack of curved serifs and the use of horizontal strokes is also part of the aesthetic for this typeface. Its elegance and refinement have made it a go-to typeface for fashion and classical-art applications.

Foundry: Linotype
Designer: Firmin Didot / Adrian Frutiger
Designer Nationality: French / Swiss
Date: c.1810 / 1991

Below left. Identity and branding for American Friends Musée d'Orsay using Linotype Didot with the sans serif Cantarell. Design: Trüf Creative, USA.

Below. Detail from an advert for The JFK Presidential Library and Museum. Design: The Martin Agency, USA.

Chiswick Text

ABCDEFGHIJKLMNOPQRSTUVWXYZ
abcdefghijklmnopqrstuvwxyz
1234567890 !@#?:;"*&

Foundry: Commercial Type
Designer: Paul Barnes
Designer Nationality: British
Date: 2017

Chiswick Text is a serif designed in the modern style and intended for texts that require smaller sizes. Like Chiswick Deck, its characters are informed by British lettering at the dawn of the Industrial Revolution and combine formal precision with lively, calligraphic flourishes.

Electra

ABCDEFGHIJKLMNOPQRSTUVWXYZ
abcdefghijklmnopqrstuvwxyz
1234567890 !@#?:;"*&

Foundry: Linotype
Designer: William A. Dwiggins
Designer Nationality: American
Date: 1935

William A. Dwiggins, the polymath and graphic-design pioneer, created Electra as a celebration of the new machine age within typography. Its crisp forms proved popular among US book designers following its release, and it has since been the subject of several digital revivals.

Estrella

ABCDEFGHIJKLMNOPQRSTUVWXYZ
abcdefghijklmnopqrstuvwxyz
1234567890 !@#?:;"*&

Foundry: Neutura
Designer: Alexander McCracken
Designer Nationality: American
Date: 2009

Created by San Francisco-based type designer Alexander McCracken for his foundry Neutura (see p. 472), this dignified, high-contrast Didone font supports more than thirty Latin-based languages. Alongside Regular and Hairline Regular weights, a decorative cut, Estrella Neuvo, is also available.

Fournier

ABCDEFGHIJKLMNOPQRSTUVWXYZ
abcdefghijklmnopqrstuvwxyz
1234567890 !@#?:;"*&

Foundry: Monotype
Designer: Pierre-Simon Fournier / Stanley Morison
Designer Nationality: French / British
Date: c. 1700s / 1924

Fournier MT was created under the direction of British typographer Stanley Morison. It is based on the designs of 18th-century French typefounder Pierre-Simon Fournier, whose work has been the subject of several revivals and influenced the development of modern-style serifs such as Bodoni.

Filosofia

ABCDEFGHIJKLMNOPQRSTUVWXYZ
abcdefghijklmnopqrstuvwxyz
1234567890 !@#?:;"*&

Foundry: Emigre
Designer: Zuzana Licko
Designer Nationality: Slovakian
Date: 1996

The Filosofia typeface family was designed by type designer Zuzana Licko, the founder of the type foundry Emigre (see p. 106). It is her interpretation of a Bodoni font design. Licko's creation incorporates slightly bulging round serif endings, which reflect the appearance of original Bodoni fonts printed in letterpress. She has also reduced the contrast between the thick and thin strokes of the characters to allow her design to be used in small text sizes for text either in print or on a computer.

Filosofia is a family of seven fonts, featuring a regular, bold, italic, and small caps, for use in a variety of text applications. The Grand character set has been further refined and is more delicate, with increased contrast in the stroke weights, and is intended for use at larger sizes. An additional style included in the Grand family package is a Unicase version that sets the characters at a single height irrespective of upper or lowercase.

Below. Specimen examples created by the Emigre foundry presenting Filosofia in both titling and text applications.

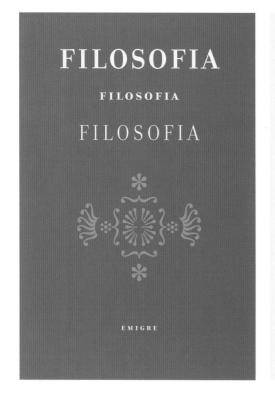

Right. Specimen example showing the unicase version (manifest destiny) where both lower and uppercase characters are set at the same height.

Below. Designed by Vignelli Associates in 1996, this poster was created to promote the Filosofia typeface. It describes Licko's underlying approach to the process of the design of their Bodoni tribute.

moccasin
UNIFIED SCHOOL DISTRICT
manifest destiny
The logical outcome of perseverance in art

My Favorite Typeface

Before the age of personal computers, when I used to spec typefaces out of photo typesetters' style books, my favorite typeface was Bodoni. I was attracted to its clean lines and geometric shapes, and the variety of headline style choices. However, for practical reasons, I often decided against using Bodoni for long texts, as the extreme contrast made it difficult to read at small sizes.

Since then, there have been many digital font revivals and reworkings of Bodoni's typefaces, some of which

have brought to light the numerous variations in Bodoni's type designs not evident in the earlier photo types. For example, the recent ITC Bodoni was released in three variants, each optimized for a range of sizes, and each with very distinct features, reflecting the variety of Bodoni's work.

In fact, Bodoni spent his entire life building a large collection of over 400 fonts. He started with Fournier's types as a model, and over time developed a personal style that tended toward simplicity, austerity and a greater contrast between the vertical stems and hairlines than previously seen, resulting in what we know today as the modern face.

In the preface of his "Manuale Tipografico" Bodoni stated: "It is proper here to offer the four different heads under which it seems to me are derived the beauties of type, and the first to these is regularity – conformity without ambiguity, variety without dissonance, and equality and symmetry without confusion."

This apparent development toward the geometry of Modern Face may explain the prevalence of excessively geometric Bodoni revivals which may have gone a step further in this progression than Bodoni intended.

Bodoni's many fonts also included small increments in sizes, sometimes down to half point sizes. As was common practice at the time, each size varied in design to accommodate the effects of the printing process. The characters comprising small text sizes were slightly widened to accommodate ample counters which resisted the tendency to clog up, as well as reduced contrast to ensure that the hairlines would not break up. The display sizes, in turn, were slightly narrower with more contrast, yielding graceful and delicate features which the letterpress process could only maintain at the larger sizes.

This practice disappeared with the introduction of photo type since it became most efficient to simply scale a single design to the various sizes as needed. Since then, technical advancements, including improvements in the printing process itself, have made it less necessary to have size specific design variations. However, it does remain a necessity for the optimum legibility of certain designs, such as Bodoni, which were designed for different manufacturing and printing processes

than those used today. In fact, the extreme contrast problem of many Bodoni revivals may be the result of choosing a display size for the model, which subsequently cause the hairlines to erode when reduced to small text sizes.

Although the computer is capable of addressing multiple size masters more readily than photo type did, (Adobe's Multiple Master format can accommodate this), optical scaling remains to be added as a standard feature to the popular font formats, and probably never will, since most contemporary typefaces which are designed for today's technology do not so critically demand such technical wizardry.

Because Bodoni created so many variations, many different Bodoni revivals and interpretations are possible. However, determining which most truly reflect Bodoni's work can be eternally debated. Filosofia is my interpretation of a Bodoni. It shows my personal preference for a geometric Bodoni, while incorporating such features as the slightly bulging round serif endings which often appeared in printed samples of Bodoni's work and reflect Bodoni's origins in letterpress technology. The Filosofia Regular family is designed for text applications. It is somewhat rugged with reduced contrast to withstand the reduction to text sizes. The Filosofia Grand family is intended for display applications and is therefore more delicate and refined.

An additional variant, included in the Grand package, is a Unicase version which uses a single height for characters that are otherwise separated into upper and lower case. This is similar to Bradbury Thompson's Alphabet Twenty Six, except that Thompson's goal was to create a text alphabet free of such redundancies as the two different forms which represent the character "a" or "A," whereas Filosofia Unicase does have stylistic variants to provide flexibility for headline use.

Zuzana Licko

'It's their Bodoni'

Industrial 736

ABCDEFGHIJKLMNOPQRSTUVWXYZ
abcdefghijklmnopqrstuvwxyz
1234567890 !@#?:;"*&

Foundry: Bitstream
Designer: Alessandro Butti
Designer Nationality: Italian
Date: 1908

Industrial 736 is a Bitstream digitization of the Torino font family, a neoclassical design for the Nebiolo foundry in Turin in 1908. Some attribute the design to the Italian type designer Alessandro Butti, who was director of the Nebiolo foundry from 1936 to 1952, when he was succeeded by Aldo Novarese.

Iridium

ABCDEFGHIJKLMNOPQRSTUVWXYZ
abcdefghijklmnopqrstuvwxyz
1234567890 !@#?:;"*&

Foundry: Stempel
Designer: Adrian Frutiger
Designer Nationality: Swiss
Date: 1972

This warm and delicate interpretation of the neoclassical style was commissioned by Stempel as one of the foundry's first fonts for phototypesetting. Adrian Frutiger (see p. 290) paid especially close attention to the harmony between its letterforms, and cut the final films himself, by hand.

ITC Bodoni Seventytwo

ABCDEFGHIJKLMNOPQRSTUVWXYZ
abcdefghijklmnopqrstuvwxyz
1234567890 !@#?:;"*&

Foundry: ITC
Designer: Giambattista Bodoni / Janice Fishman / Holly Goldsmith / Jim Parkinson / Sumner Stone
Designer Nationality: Italian / American / American / American / American
Date: 1790 / 1994

Bodoni Seventytwo is the display cut of ITC's Bodoni revival, and was developed by a four-strong team of type designers who traveled to Parma, Italy to research Giambattista Bodoni's original steel punches first-hand. Its design is carefully tailored for headline use.

ITC Bodoni Six

ABCDEFGHIJKLMNOPQRSTUVWXYZ
abcdefghijklmnopqrstuvwxyz
1234567890 !@#?:;"*&

Foundry: ITC
Designer: Giambattista Bodoni / Janice Fishman / Holly Goldsmith / Jim Parkinson / Sumner Stone
Designer Nationality: Italian / American / American / American / American
Date: 1790 / 1994

ITC's interpretation of Bodoni was cut in three different optical styles, of which this version was specifically developed for small type. With lower contrast than its display counterpart, ITC Bodoni Seventytwo, it remains legible within contexts such as captions and footnotes.

ITC Bodoni Twelve

ABCDEFGHIJKLMNOPQRSTUVWXYZ
abcdefghijklmnopqrstuvwxyz
1234567890 !@#?:;"'*&

Designed for text use, ITC Bodoni Twelve is an archetypal modern design reflecting the fine details of Giambattista Bodoni's original. This meticulous ITC revival includes a set of delicate typographic ornaments derived from examples found in Bodoni's *Manuale tipografico* (*Manual of Typography*, 1818).

Foundry: ITC
Designer: Giambattista Bodoni / Janice Fishman / Holly Goldsmith / Jim Parkinson / Sumner Stone
Designer Nationality: Italian / American / American / American / American
Date: 1790 / 1994

ITC Fenice

ABCDEFGHIJKLMNOPQRSTUVWXYZ
abcdefghijklmnopqrstuvwxyz
1234567890 !@#?:;"*&

Aldo Novarese is well known for his work at the Italian foundry Nebiolo, but he also designed typefaces for several other companies over the course of his career. This neoclassical serif builds on the high-contrast forms of Bodoni, but with contemporary details added throughout.

Foundry: ITC
Designer: Aldo Novarese
Designer Nationality: Italian
Date: 1980

ITC Jamille

ABCDEFGHIJKLMNOPQRSTUVWXYZ
abcdefghijklmnopqrstuvwxyz
1234567890 !@#?:;"*&

Jamille was US designer Mark Jamra's first typeface, begun during his postgraduate studies, and ITC acquired it for publication in 1988. The Pro version, sold through Jamra's own TypeCulture foundry, includes an expanded character set, and an attractive alphabet of swash caps.

Foundry: ITC
Designer: Mark Jamra
Designer Nationality: American
Date: 1988

ITC Modern No 216

ABCDEFGHIJKLMNOPQRSTUVWXYZ
abcdefghijklmnopqrstuvwxyz
1234567890 !@#?:;"*&

This Didone typeface displays a warmth that is characteristic of many of the designs by Ed Benguiat (see p. 514), with balanced, shapely curves evident within many of its letterforms. Offering eight different styles, the ITC Modern No 216 family performs at its best in display contexts.

Foundry: ITC
Designer: Ed Benguiat
Designer Nationality: American
Date: 1982

ITC Týfa

ABCDEFGHIJKLMNOPQRSTUVWXYZ
abcdefghijklmnopqrstuvwxyz
1234567890 !@#?:;"*&

Foundry: Grafotechna / ITC
Designer: Josef Týfa /
František Štorm
Designer Nationality: Czech
Date: 1959 / 1998

A fine example of mid 20th-century Czech type design, this distinctive serif was designed by Josef Týfa in 1959 and released by Grafotechna. It was digitized for ITC by František Štorm, working in collaboration with Týfa, nearly forty years later. Its delicate set of true italics has a distinctive character.

ITC Zapf Book

ABCDEFGHIJKLMNOPQRSTUVWXYZ
abcdefghijklmnopqrstuvwxyz
1234567890 !@#?:;"*&

Foundry: ITC
Designer: Hermann Zapf
Designer Nationality: German
Date: 1976

Zapf Book was created by Hermann Zapf, the illustrious German type designer and calligrapher (see p. 290), and was his first typeface for ITC. It is a blend of elements and characteristics from the existing typefaces Walbaum and Melior, and with the contrasting strokes of a modern typeface such as Bodoni.

Though it was designed as a text face, Zapf suggested the addition of swashes for display purposes, but these were never designed and realized. Highly distinctive in appearance, Zapf Book has been crafted in keeping with Zapf's ethos that an alphabet should not just work as a collection of single letters but also have a sense of unity in itself. Zapf designed his fonts using pen and paper, and was a master of calligraphy.

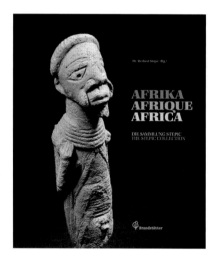

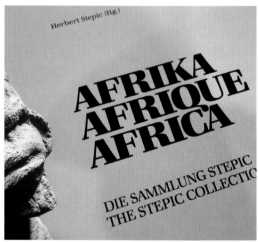

Karloff Positive

ABCDEFGHIJKLMNOPQRSTUVWXYZ
abcdefghijklmnopqrstuvwxyz
1234567890 !@#?:;"*&

Foundry: Typotheque
Designer: Peter Biľak / Pieter van Rosmalen / Nikola Djurek
Designer Nationality: Slovakian / Dutch / Croatian
Date: 2012

Inspired by the high-contrast of Didot and Bodoni, Karloff Positive is the beauty in this experimental family, while the reverse-contrast Karloff Negative is the beast, and Karloff Neutral is a mixture of both. The name is a nod to Boris Karloff, the actor famed for playing the monster in *Frankenstein* (1931).

Linotype Didot eText

ABCDEFGHIJKLMNOPQRSTUVWXYZ
abcdefghijklmnopqrstuvwxyz
1234567890 !@#?:,"*&

Foundry: Linotype
Designer: Adrian Frutiger
Designer Nationality: Swiss
Date: 2013

This modification of Didot by Adrian Frutiger (see p. 290) was specifically created for use in text-heavy digital contexts, such as e-readers, tablets, mobile devices, and websites. eText fonts are made with higher x-heights, wider spacing and modulated stroke weights to improve on-screen legibility.

Linotype Gianotten

ABCDEFGHIJKLMNOPQRSTUVWXYZ
abcdefghijklmnopqrstuvwxyz
1234567890 !@#?:,"*&

Foundry: Linotype
Designer: Giambattista Bodoni / Antonio Pace
Designer Nationality: Italian
Date: 1790 / 1999

Linotype Gianotten took Italian designer Antonio Pace more than five years to develop and it is his attempt to adapt Bodoni's modern text faces for the digital age. Hairlines are thicker and serifs shorter to aid readability. It was named after the Dutch typographer Henk W. J. Gianotten.

Madison Antiqua

ABCDEFGHIJKLMNOPQRSTUVWXYZ
abcdefghijklmnopqrstuvwxyz
1234567890 !@#?:,"*&

Foundry: Stempel
Designer: Heinrich Wilhelm Hoffmeister
Designer Nationality: German
Date: 1965

Madison Antiqua is based on Amts-Antiqua, designed by Heinrich Wilhelm Hoffmeister between 1909 and 1919. Stempel rereleased six of the original eight weights of Hoffmeister's design in 1965 as Madison Antiqua. It shares its name with the Manhattan Avenue famed for advertising agencies.

Menhart

ABCDEFGHIJKLMNOPQRSTUVWXYZ
abcdefghijklmnopqrstuvwxyz
1234567890 !@#?:,"*&

Foundry: Monotype
Designer: Oldrich Menhart
Designer Nationality: Czech
Date: 1934

Named after its creator Oldrich Menhart, the Czech type designer, calligrapher, and book designer, this is a roman with small serifs and an almost cursive feel to the lowercase alphabet. The Czech alphabet has fifteen accented letters and Menhart included these diacritics as an integral part of his design

Modern 880

ABCDEFGHIJKLMNOPQRSTUVWXYZ
abcdefghijklmnopqrstuvwxyz
1234567890 !@#?:;"*&

Foundry: Bitstream
Designer: Walter Tracy
Designer Nationality: British
Date: 1969

Modern 880 is Bitstream's version of Linotype Modern, a typeface designed by Walter Tracy, who worked at Linotype for more than thirty years from 1948. Modern 880, which comes in roman, italic, and bold, is a highly legible book type. Roman has square dots on the "i" and "j."

Modern No. 20

ABCDEFGHIJKLMNOPQRSTUVWXYZ
abcdefghijklmnopqrstuvwxyz
1234567890 !@#?:;"*&

Foundry: Stephenson, Blake & Co. / Bitstream
Date: 1905 / c. 1980s

Modern No. 20 is an attractive didone serif face released by British foundry Stephenson, Blake & Co. at the start of the 20th century, but like all of the many numbered modern faces it was inspired by the earlier forms of Bodoni and Didot. Modern No. 20 comes in roman and italic.

Monotype Bodoni

ABCDEFGHIJKLMNOPQRSTUVWXYZ
abcdefghijklmnopqrstuvwxyz
1234567890 !@#?:;"*&

Foundry: Monotype
Designer: Giambattista Bodoni
Designer Nationality: Italian
Date: 1790

Monotype Bodoni comes in five weights with italics and has a condensed bold too. Designed by Giambattista Bodoni and one of the first modern faces, it is high-contrast with vertical stress and has flat, unbracketed serifs. Monotype's cut is heavier than that of other foundries.

Monotype Modern

ABCDEFGHIJKLMNOPQRSTUVWXYZ
abcdefghijklmnopqrstuvwxyz
1234567890 !@#?:;"*&

Foundry: Monotype
Designer: Monotype Studio
Date: 1896

The first typeface produced by Monotype—then known as the Lanston Monotype Machine Company—was the condensed cut of Modern, an upright, high-contrast serif face with thin hairlines. It is available in four versions: bold, condensed, extended, and wide, all with italics.

Nara

ABCDEFGHIJKLMNOPQRSTUVWXYZ
abcdefghijklmnopqrstuvwxyz
1234567890 !@#?:;"*&

Foundry: Typotheque
Designer: Andrej Krátky /
Nikola Djurek / Peter Biľak
Designer Nationality: Czech /
Croatian / Slovakian
Date: 2009

Nara is a distinctive hybrid serif designed by Andrej Krátky between 1989 and 2009, and finished with help from Nikola Djurek and Peter Biľak. It comes in five weights, with two types of italic—both regular and an upright cursive. Originally called Adriq, it was renamed Nara after the Japanese city in Honshu.

New Caledonia

ABCDEFGHIJKLMNOPQRSTUVWXYZ
abcdefghijklmnopqrstuvwxyz
1234567890 !@#?:;"*&

Foundry: Linotype
Designer: William A. Dwiggins /
Alex Kaczun
Designer Nationality: American
Date: 1939 / 2007

Caledonia is a serif face designed for Mergenthaler Linotype in 1939 by William A. Dwiggins—the US designer credited with coining the term "graphic design." It is a popular choice for book text. New Caledonia is a digital update made by Alex Kaczun at Linotype in the late 1980s.

Otama

ABCDEFGHIJKLMNOPQRSTUVWXYZ
abcdefghijklmnopqrstuvwxyz
1234567890 !@#?:;"*&

Foundry: Tim Donaldson Design
Designer: Tim Donaldson
Designer Nationality: New
Zealander
Date: 2012

It took New Zealander Tim Donaldson more than two years to design this high-contrast didone serif. Otama features more than 8,000 different characters in the twenty-eight fonts that make up the superfamily, which contains regular, display, and text versions, in six weights, all with italics.

Parma

ABCDEFGHIJKLMNOPQRSTUVWXYZ
abcdefghijklmnopqrstuvwxyz
1234567890 !@#?:;"*&

Foundry: Monotype
Designer: Monotype Studio
Date: 2008

Named after the Italian city where Giambattista Bodoni worked, Parma is a high-contrast didone available in regular, italic, display and bold, with support for the Latin, Greek, and Cyrillic alphabets. It was designed by the Monotype Studio using research conducted at the Museo Bodoniano, Parma.

Emigre

Founded in 1984, Emigre can rightly be described as a pioneer and an innovator in the world of type, its launch coinciding with the arrival of the Macintosh computer in the design industry. The impact of these two events on design can never be underestimated. Founded in Berkeley, California by the Dutch designer Rudy VanderLans and his wife, Slovak designer Zuzana Licko, the foundry gained worldwide acclaim through its quarterly magazine, *Emigre*. An often-controversial journal, it challenged the conventions of legibility and explored readability through adventurous and experimental layouts that used its own digital typefaces, which were some of the very first to be created. *Emigre* magazine drew both acclaim and criticism worldwide because it altered the understanding of what could be achieved using a PC to design typefaces and create layouts.

As one of the first foundries distributing digital fonts, Emigre created systems that have been adopted by many smaller foundries across the world and still used today. Having won numerous awards for its own work and huge contribution to type design, Emigre has also collaborated with many esteemed type designers around the world using the Emigre platform to distribute their designs. Key contributors include Barry Deck, Miles Newlyn, Jonathan Barnbrook, P. Scott Makela, Jeffery Keedy, and Xavier Dupré.

In 2011, five digital typefaces from the *Emigre* Type Library were honoured when they were acquired by the Museum of Modern Art in New York for its permanent design and architecture collection. The final issue of *Emigre* magazine, No. 69, was published in 2005 and sold out, as has most of the back catalogue. This was a fitting tribute to the creativity and invention of the Emigre foundry and its influential library of design, which continues to have an impact today.

Founded: 1984
Country: USA
Website: emigre.com
Notable typefaces:
Mrs Eaves (see p. 171)
Base 900 (see p. 190)
Filosofia (see p. 98)

Below and opposite. As a ground-breaking showcase of not only their design abilities but also their innovative typeface creations, the *Emigre* magazines are still highly coveted publications today and reflect the digital revolution in graphic design through the years. From left, front covers of Issue Nos. 11, 14, 68, and 70.

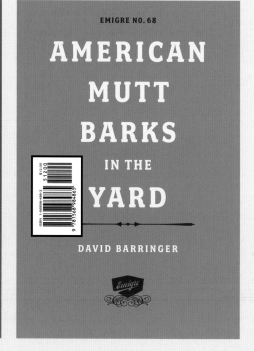

EMIGRE

No.70

The Look Back Issue

SELECTIONS FROM EMIGRE MAGAZINE #1 ~ #69

1984 ~ 2009

CELEBRATING 25 YEARS

In Graphic Design

Parmigiano Text

ABCDEFGHIJKLMNOPQRSTUVWXYZ
abcdefghijklmnopqrstuvwxyz
1234567890 !@#?:;"*&

Foundry: Typotheque
Designer: Riccardo Olocco /
Jonathan Pierini
Designer Nationality: Italian
Date: 2014

Parmigiano Text is part of the Parmigiano superfamily by Italians Riccardo Olocco and Jonathan Pierini. It is the family's Bodoni-inspired text face in six weights with italics. The Cyrillic was designed by Ilya Ruderman and Irina Smirnova, a Greek version by Irene Vlachou followed in 2015.

Pax

ABCDEFGHIJKLMNOPQRSTUVWXYZ
abcdefghijklmnopqrstuvwxyz
1234567890 !@#?:;"*&

Foundry: Omnibus
Designer: Franko Luin
Designer Nationality: Swedish
Date: 1995

Pax, which takes its name from the Latin for "peace," is a narrow didone designed by Franko Luin. A versatile family, Pax comes in roman, semibold, and bold, with italics; a condensed version comes in regular and bold, with italics. There are small-cap versions for roman and condensed.

Pax 2

ABCDEFGHIJKLMNOPQRSTUVWXYZ
abcdefghijklmnopqrstuvwxyz
1234567890 !@#?:;"*&

Foundry: Omnibus
Designer: Franko Luin
Designer Nationality: Swedish
Date: 1995

Released by Franko Luin the same year as the first Pax (1995), Pax 2 is almost identical, but since the original was somewhat narrow, Luin decided to create a second version that was a little broader and darker. Less versatile than its forebear, Pax 2 has no condensed versions.

Scotch Roman

ABCDEFGHIJKLMNOPQRSTUVWXYZ
abcdefghijklmnopqrstuvwxyz
1234567890 !@#?:;"*&

Foundry: A. D. Farmer
Designer: William Miller /
A. D. Farmer Foundry
Designer Nationality: Scottish /
American
Date: 1813 / 1904

Scotch Roman is modeled on Pica No. 2, a typeface designed in Edinburgh by William Miller in the 19th century and believed to be the first example of the style with a marked contrast in stroke weight. The font's name was applied to a recasting of Miller's type by the A. D. Farmer Foundry of New York.

Tiemann

ABCDEFGHIJKLMNOPQRSTUVWXYZ
abcdefghijklmnopqrstuvwxyz
1234567890 !@#?:,"*&

Foundry: Kingspor
Designer: Walter Tiemann
Designer Nationality: German
Date: 1923

The Tiemann font family, designed early in the 20th century, is a serif that both respects and challenges the modern style. While the significant stroke contrasts and flat serifs remain conventional, the shapes and proportions take their cue from neoclassical letterforms.

VentiQuattro

ABCDEFGHIJKLMNOPQRSTUVWXYZ
abcdefghijklmnopqrstuvwxyz
1234567890 !@#?:,"*&

Foundry: Playtype
Designer: Jonas Hecksher
Designer Nationality: Danish
Date: 2009

This elegant didone-style serif was designed by Jonas Hecksher, award-winning partner and creative director at the Danish design agency e-Types. VentiQuattro means "twenty-four" in Italian. It comprises four weights from Regular to Bold, plus an italic.

Walbaum

ABCDEFGHIJKLMNOPQRSTUVWXYZ
abcdefghijklmnopqrstuvwxyz
1234567890 !@#?:,"*&

Foundry: Monotype
Designer: Justic Erich Walbaum / Charles Nix / Carl Crossgrove / Juan Villanueva
Designer Nationality: German / American / American / Peruvian
Date: c. 1800s / 2018

A restoration of a typeface designed by Justus Erich Walbaum in the 19th century, Monotype's Walbaum is a 21st-century take on the modern serif. Designed for multiplatform use, Walbaum consists of thirty-two weights, and unlike earlier modern serifs, includes a wealth of ornaments.

WTC Our Bodoni

ABCDEFGHIJKLMNOPQRSTUVWXYZ
abcdefghijklmnopqrstuvwxyz
1234567890 !@#?:,"*&

Foundry: Monotype
Designer: Giambattista Bodoni / Tom Carnase / Massimo Vignelli
Designer Nationality: Italian / American / American
Date: 1767 /1989

WTC Our Bodoni was commissioned by the World Typeface Center, New York and is a redesign of the 18th-century modern serif cut by Giambattista Bodoni. Designed by Tom Carnase and Massimo Vignelli, this face takes the original forms of Bodoni and applies the ratios of the Helvetica font.

Adobe Caslon

ABCDEFGHIJKLMNOPQRSTUVWXYZ
abcdefghijklmnopqrstuvwxyz
1234567890 !@#?:;"*&

Foundry: Adobe
Designer: William Caslon / Carol Twombly
Designer Nationality: British / American
Date: *c.* 1720s / 1990

This revival by esteemed US type designer Carol Twombly for Adobe as part of its Adobe Originals program was developed from her studies of specimen pages printed by English typefounder William Caslon in the mid-1700s. It is considered by many to be the best text typeface ever to come out of the Adobe design studio and it retains an elegance no matter what the application.

A gunsmith and engraver by trade, William Caslon created his first typefaces in 1722, basing them on Old Style designs from the Netherlands. His typefaces proved to be a success at home and internationally, and were employed widely because of their simplicity, practicality, and legibility. His work contributed greatly to the development of English type design and toward creating an English national typographic style.

After Caslon's death in 1766, the usage of his typefaces declined until the mid to late 1800s, when they gained favor thanks to the Arts and Crafts movement in Britain. They remain a popular choice for printers and typesetters even to this day. The success of Caslon's types means there have been many revivals and the number of types referred to as "Caslon" is extensive. In addition, there is much variation between foundries and technological developments have also impacted on the way type is produced.

As a standard over three centuries, Caslon can rightly be said to be one of the most significant typefaces of all time. It has been used as text on the American Declaration of Independence, in classic works of literature by writers including George Bernard Shaw, and in *The New Yorker* magazine.

Right. Detail from *The First Six Books of the Elements of Euclid* annotated with Caslon Roman and Italic.

THE FIRST SIX BOOKS OF

THE ELEMENTS OF EUCLID

IN WHICH COLOURED DIAGRAMS AND SYMBOLS

ARE USED INSTEAD OF LETTERS FOR THE

GREATER EASE OF LEARNERS

BY OLIVER BYRNE

SURVEYOR OF HER MAJESTY'S SETTLEMENTS IN THE FALKLAND ISLANDS
AND AUTHOR OF NUMEROUS MATHEMATICAL WORKS

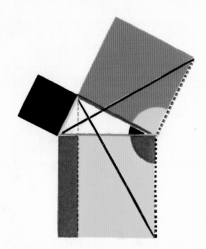

LONDON
WILLIAM PICKERING
1847

Administer

ABCDEFGHIJKLMNOPQRSTUVWXYZ
abcdefghijklmnopqrstuvwxyz
1234567890 !@#?:;"*&

Foundry: Typsettra
Designer: Les Usherwood /
Steve Jackaman
Designer Nationality: British
Date: *c.* 1980s / 2000

British-born designer Les Usherwood moved to Canada in 1957, where he co-founded the Typsettra foundry. His Administer now forms part of the Red Rooster Collection. Steve Jackaman digitized the new version of this elegant Old Style serif, which remains true to Usherwood's original drawings.

Adobe Garamond Pro

ABCDEFGHIJKLMNOPQRSTUVWXYZ
abcdefghijklmnopqrstuvwxyz
1234567890 !@#?:;"*&

Foundry: Adobe
Designer: Claude Garamond /
Robert Slimbach
Designer Nationality: French /
American
Date: 1480–1561 / 1989

This is considered an Old Style face due to the oblique nature of the slimmest parts of the letterforms. It is based on Claude Garamond's 16th-century design cut by Garamond's assistant Robert Granjon and is regarded as a more faithful interpretation than earlier versions.

Agmena

ABCDEFGHIJKLMNOPQRSTUVWXYZ
abcdefghijklmnopqrstuvwxyz
1234567890 !@#?:;"*&

Foundry: Linotype
Designer: Jovica Veljović
Designer Nationality: Serbian
Date: 2012

Created by Serbian designer Jovica Veljović, Agmena shares many traits with the group of Renaissance Antiqua fonts. Its generous x-height, large counters and open forms all help its legibility at small sizes, making it an ideal book font. It was a Type Directors Club Typeface Design Winner in 2013.

Alcuin

ABCDEFGHIJKLMNOPQRSTUVWXYZ
abcdefghijklmnopqrstuvwxyz
1234567890 !@#?:;"*&

Foundry: Linotype
Designer: Gudrun Zapf
von Hesse
Designer Nationality: German
Date: 1991

Gudrun Zapf von Hesse's expressive design retains the flow of handwritten letters, and Alcuin is based on the Carolingian minuscule calligraphic script that was introduced so the Latin alphabet could be recognized from region to region. It is named after an advisor to Emperor Charlemagne.

Aldine 401

ABCDEFGHIJKLMNOPQRSTUVWXYZ
abcdefghijklmnopqrstuvwxyz
1234567890 !@#?:;"*&

Foundry: Bitstream
Designer: Francesco Griffo
Designer Nationality: Italian
Date: *c.* 1495

This digitized Old Style serif was released by Bitstream and later updated by Paratype. It is based on Bembo, which itself was based on a design from *c.* 1495 cut by the Italian punchcutter Francesco Griffo for Aldus Manutius, the Venetian scholar, printer, and founder of the Aldine Press.

Aldine 721

ABCDEFGHIJKLMNOPQRSTUVWXYZ
abcdefghijklmnopqrstuvwxyz
1234567890 !@#?:;"*&

Foundry: Bitstream
Designer: Frank Hinman Pierpont
Designer Nationality: American
Date: 2000

One of many digitized versions of typefaces originally designed by Frank Hinman Pierpont (the engineer-turned-type-designer who became President of Monotype in 1899), this classic Old Style font is based on Plantin, itself based on a 16th-century design by Robert Granjon.

Aldus

ABCDEFGHIJKLMNOPQRSTUVWXYZ
abcdefghijklmnopqrstuvwxyz
1234567890 !@#?:;"*&

Foundry: Stempel
Designer: Hermann Zapf
Designer Nationality: German
Date: 1954

Initially called Palatino Light but later named Aldus, this was originally created as a text weight by Hermann Zapf (see p. 574) for his Palatino family. It was released in its own right with italic, small caps, and Old Style figures, and its narrow forms and light weight made it a popular choice for book typography.

Aldus Nova

ABCDEFGHIJKLMNOPQRSTUVWXYZ
abcdefghijklmnopqrstuvwxyz
1234567890 !@#?:;"*&

Foundry: Linotype
Designer: Hermann Zapf / Akira Kobayashi
Designer Nationality: German / Japanese
Date: 1954 / 2005

Hermann Zapf (see p. 574) collaborated with Akira Kobayashi to rework his designs for Palatino to form a new typeface family, Palatino Nova. It includes this updated version of his Aldus typeface from 1954, plus two titling weights based on Zapf's metal typeface Michelangelo and all caps Sistina.

Alisal

ABCDEFGHIJKLMNOPQRSTUVWXYZ
abcdefghijklmnopqrstuvwxyz
1234567890 !@#?:;"*&

Foundry: Monotype
Designer: Matthew Carter
Designer Nationality: British
Date: 1995

This handsome calligraphic font was a labor of love for Matthew Carter (see p. 616), who worked on the design for many years. Influenced by 15th- and 16th-century Italian Old Style fonts, Alisal is heavier and has distinctive serifs with no bracketing, which appear to cross the main vertical.

Arrus BT

ABCDEFGHIJKLMNOPQRSTUVWXYZ
abcdefghijklmnopqrstuvwxyz
1234567890 !@#?:;"*&

Foundry: Bitstream
Designer: Richard Lipton
Designer Nationality: American
Date: 1991

Arrus BT is influenced by classic Roman inscriptions and displays vertical strokes that gently expand. It is based on calligraphic alphabets that US designer Richard Lipton drew by hand using a brush rather than a pen. Lipton also created its distinctive sister typeface, Arrus Black.

Aurelia

ABCDEFGHIJKLMNOPQRSTUVWXYZ
abcdefghijklmnopqrstuvwxyz
1234567890 !@#?:;"*&

Foundry: Hell
Designer: Hermann Zapf
Designer Nationality: German
Date: 1963

Named after the Roman emperor Aurelianus, this typeface is based on Nicolas Jenson's classic Old Style typeface Jenson, created in 1470. Hermann Zapf (see p. 574) added his own personal flourishes, and updated it for use with the typesetting machines introduced in the 1960s by Rudolf Hell.

Bara

ABCDEFGHIJKLMNOPQRSTUVWXYZ
abcdefghijklmnopqrstuvwxyz
1234567890 !@#?:;"*&

Foundry: Typotheque
Designer: Nikola Djurek
Designer Nationality: Croatian
Date: 2016

Bara is a loose interpretation of a 16th-century typeface Schefferletter (or Enschedé English-bodied Roman No. 6). It is a slim, refined family, which has many of the idiosyncrasies found in the original metal type, such as the abruptly ended strokes of the letters "c" and "e."

Bembo

ABCDEFGHIJKLMNOPQRSTUVWXYZ
abcdefghijklmnopqrstuvwxyz
1234567890 !@#?:;"★&

Foundry: Monotype
Designer: Francesco Griffo /
Stanley Morison
Designer Nationality: Italian /
British
Date: 1496 / 1929

Bembo's origins date to the 15th century, when legendary Italian Renaissance printer Aldus Manutius of the Aldine Press in Venice, published a short book *De Aetna* (1496) on the travels of scholar and poet Pietro Bembo and his ascent of Mount Etna. Manutius employed a new roman typeface for the dialogue, which was created by punchcutter Francesco Griffo. The type's design adopted less of a heavy calligraphic, hand-drawn approach in favor of the more elegant appearance seen in serif types today. This resulted in many type designers of the time moving away from the established approach toward the evolution of serif roman designs.

In 1929, Monotype consultant Stanley Morison oversaw the recreation of the typeface as part of Monotype's restoration of historic typeface designs and titled it "Bembo." The 15th-century design had a number of characters refined and redrawn to meet the technical requirements of contemporary machine typesetting. Bembo comes in thirty-one weights, with small caps, Old Style figures, and expert characters. It is ideal for book typography but also functions as an all-rounder. Bembo has also had great influence on well-known typefaces such as Garamond, Times Roman and, in recent times, Robert Slimbach's Minion.

Section 25-Always now friend ly fires dirty disco c.p. loose tal k costs lives inside out melt clos e hit babies in the bardo be bra ve new horizon produced by martin hannett engineer joh n caffrey recorded at brittania row disegnatori : grafica indu stria e typografica berthold a factory records product fact 45

16.5 mm (60p)   10   20

Above. Vinyl album cover *Always Now* from English post-punk and electronic band Section 25. Released in 1981, the cover was designed by renowned UK graphic designer Peter Saville and Grafica Industria, his studio at the time.

Bembo Book

ABCDEFGHIJKLMNOPQRSTUVWXYZ
abcdefghijklmnopqrstuvwxyz
1234567890 !@#?:;"★&

Foundry: Monotype
Designer: Francesco Griffo /
Stanley Morison / Robin Nicholas
Designer Nationality: Italian /
British
Date: 1496 / 1929 / 2005

Stanley Morison's version (1929) of the typeface inspired by Francesco Griffo's 15th-century design was followed by a number of revisions by Monotype.

Robin Nicholas's Bembo Book is widely considered to be the most faithful interpretation of this classic and much-copied Old Style serif.

Bembo Infant

ABCDEFGHIJKLMNOPQRSTUVWXYZ
abcdefghijklmnopqrstuvwxyz
1234567890 !@#?:;"★&

Foundry: Monotype
Designer: Francesco Griffo /
Monotype Studio
Designer Nationality: Italian /
British
Date: 1495–1501 / 1929

One of many versions of Francesco Griffo's Bembo, this friendly serif has different forms for the letters "a," "g," and "y," the first two of which are both single storey. The traditional "Infant" or "Schoolbook" versions of typefaces were designed to help children with their reading.

Berling

ABCDEFGHIJKLMNOPQRSTUVWXYZ
abcdefghijklmnopqrstuvwxyz
1234567890 !@#?:;"*&

Foundry: Berlingska Stilgjuteriet
Designer: Karl-Erik Forsberg
Designer Nationality: Swedish
Date: 1951

This elegant serif with its sharp, beak-like serifs was designed for the Berlingska Stilgjuteriet foundry in Lund in 1951. It was followed by several more weights in 1958. A full-scale redesign was commissioned in 2004 by the Swedish publisher Verbum, under the title "Berling Nova."

Bertham

ABCDEFGHIJKLMNOPQRSTUVWXYZ
abcdefghijklmnopqrstuvwxyz
1234567890 !@#?:;"*&

Foundry: Continental
Designer: Frederic W. Goudy /
Steve Matheson
Designer Nationality: American
Date: 1936 / 2009

Frederic W. Goudy named this refined serif in memory of his wife Bertha, who had died the year before. It was commissioned by *American Printer* magazine and inspired by a design used by Lienhart Holle for Ptolemy's *Geographica* (*Geography*) in 1482. It was revived by Ascender as Bertham Pro.

Binny Old Style

ABCDEFGHIJKLMNOPQRSTUVWX
abcdefghijklmnopqrstuvwxyz
1234567890 !@#?:;"*&

Foundry: MacKellar, Smiths & Jordan
Designer: Alexander Kay
Designer Nationality: Scottish
Date: c. 1863 / 1908

Adapted by Alexander Kay, this sophisticated serif was itself an adaptation from Old Style No. 77, a typeface from the Philadelphia-based foundry MacKellar, Smiths & Jordan, dating from c. 1863. While influenced by Caslon, Binny Old Style is a more modern take on the classic typeface.

Buccardi

ABCDEFGHIJKLMNOPQRSTUVWXYZ
abcdefghijklmnopqrstuvwxyz
1234567890 !@#?:;"*&

Foundry: Agfa Compugraphic
Designer: Bo Berndal
Designer Nationality: Swedish
Date: 2003

This jaunty serif is designed by the calligrapher, author, and lecturer Bo Berndal, one of Sweden's most prolific type designers. Buccardi features a distinctive, almost top-heavy lowercase "a." It is available in both Pro and Standard versions in regular and bold, and with matching italics.

Calisto

ABCDEFGHIJKLMNOPQRSTUVWXYZ
abcdefghijklmnopqrstuvwxyz
1234567890 !@#?:;"*&

Foundry: Monotype
Designer: Ron Carpenter
Designer Nationality: British
Date: 1986

A graceful Old Style serif, with classical proportions and minimal stroke contrast, Calisto is reminiscent of typefaces such as Palatino and Belwe. Highly legible, its terminals are cut on an angle to the baseline and concavely indented. It was created by British typographer Ron Carpenter.

Cardamon

ABCDEFGHIJKLMNOPQRSTUVWXYZ
abcdefghijklmnopqrstuvwxyz
1234567890 !@#?:;"*&

Foundry: Linotype
Designer: Brigitte Schuster
Designer Nationality: Swiss
Date: 2015

Swiss designer Brigitte Schuster's first typeface was conceived while she was still a student at the Royal Academy of Art in The Hague. This legible, well-crafted serif was inspired by 16th-century punchcutters. It has angular forms, slightly inclined characters, and tapering stems.

Carmina BT

ABCDEFGHIJKLMNOPQRSTUVWXYZ
abcdefghijklmnopqrstuvwxyz
1234567890 !@#?:;"*&

Foundry: Bitstream
Designer: Gudrun Zapf
von Hesse
Designer Nationality: German
Date: 1987

Also known as Calligraphic 811, Carmina forms part of a calligraphic series commissioned by Bitstream from German designer Gudrun Zapf von Hesse.

The adaptable serif font displays the designer's love of calligraphy and is suitable for use in everything from books to signage.

Carré Noir

ABCDEFGHIJKLMNOPQRSTUVWXYZ
abcdefghijklmnopqrstuvwxyz
1234567890 !@#?:;"*&

Foundry: Monotype
Designer: Albert Boton
Designer Nationality: French
Date: 1996

French font designer Albert Boton became head of the type department at the Paris-based agency Carré Noir in 1981; fifteen years later he created this

sophisticated serif typeface with the same name, which is available in four weights, from Light to Bold, plus an italic and small caps.

Cartier Book

ABCDEFGHIJKLMNOPQRSTUVWXYZ
abcdefghijklmnopqrstuvwxyz
1234567890 !@#?:;"*&

Foundry: Linotype
Designer: Carl Dair /
Rod McDonald
Designer Nationality: Canadian
Date: 1967 / 1997

Carl Dair's CG Cartier was not suitable as a text font. Rod McDonald redrew the original typeface thirty years later, when it became Cartier Book.

He referenced the original drawings and removed inconsistencies, creating a functional but elegant face with three weights, an italic, and small caps.

Caslon 540

ABCDEFGHIJKLMNOPQRSTUVWXYZ
abcdefghijklmnopqrstuvwxyz
1234567890 !@#?:;"*&

Foundry: American Type
Founders
Designer: William Caslon /
American Type Founders
Designer Nationality: British /
American
Date: 1725 / 1902

This is the second version of Caslon to be released by American Type Founders. Caslon 540 has shortened descenders, which allow for tighter line

spacing. It features Old Style figures, small caps, and an italic, which was distributed by Letraset with a matching set of swashes.

Caslon Classico

ABCDEFGHIJKLMNOPQRSTUVWXYZ
abcdefghijklmnopqrstuvwxyz
1234567890 !@#?:;"'*&

Foundry: Omnibus
Designer: William Caslon /
Franko Luin
Designer Nationality: British /
Swedish
Date: 1725 / 1993

This five-weight version of Caslon, which is one of many cuts, was based closely on the 18th-century original by William Caslon. He was known as the first great English punchcutter, and typeface as "the script of kings." It was the type chosen for the United States Declaration of Independence in 1776.

Caslon Old Face

ABCDEFGHIJKLMNOPQRSTUVWXYZ
abcdefghijklmnopqrstuvwxyz
1234567890 !@#?:;"'*&

Foundry: Bitstream
Designer: William Caslon /
George Ostrochulski
Designer Nationality: British /
German
Date: 1725 / c. 1950s

The Bitstream version of Caslon Old Face is based largely on the hot-metal revival of the original Caslon fonts by English type founder William Caslon, and was created in digital form by George Ostrochulski at Mergenthaler Linotype. As with other revivals, it is a faithful recreation of the original.

Caxton

ABCDEFGHIJKLMNOPQRSTUVWXYZ
abcdefghijklmnopqrstuvwxyz
1234567890 !@#?:;"'*&

Foundry: ITC
Designer: Leslie Usherwood
Designer Nationality: American
Date: 1981

Fully justified (meaning that all the lines fit to the same margin), with concave-shaped serifs and diamond-shaped dots on the letters "i" and "j," Caxton is named after the font created in 1478 by printer William Caxton, which has been revised a number of times over the years.

Centaur

ABCDEFGHIJKLMNOPQRSTUVWXYZ
abcdefghijklmnopqrstuvwxyz
1234567890 !@#?:;"'*&

Foundry: Monotype
Designer: Bruce Rogers
Designer Nationality: American
Date: 1914 / 1929

An elegant and very slender humanist Old Style serif loosely based on Nicolas Jenson's 15th-century designs, this revival by Bruce Rogers first appeared as titling capitals in 1914 for the Metropolitan Museum of Art. The completed family, including lowercase and italics, was released in 1929.

Cochin

ABCDEFGHIJKLMNOPQRSTUVWXYZ
abcdefghijklmnopqrstuvwxyz
1234567890 !@#?:;"*&

Foundry: G. Peignot et Fils
Designer: Charles Malin
Designer Nationality: French
Date: 1914

This serif is named after the 18th-century French engraver Charles-Nicolas Cochin and is based on his copperplate engravings. The typeface was made for the Paris foundry G. Peignot et Fils (later Deberny & Peignot). It has particularly wide letterforms and was popular at the start of the 20th century.

Columbus

ABCDEFGHIJKLMNOPQRSTUVWXYZ
abcdefghijklmnopqrstuvwxyz
1234567890 !@#?:;"*&

Foundry: Monotype
Designer: David Saunders / Patricia Saunders
Designer Nationality: British
Date: 1992

Columbus was created to celebrate the 400th anniversary of Christopher Columbus crossing the Atlantic Ocean and the 1992 Summer Olympic Games in Barcelona. It is an interpretation of a typeface used by printer Jorge Coci in Spain c. 1513, which still retains traces of the Antique letterforms.

Della Robbia

ABCDEFGHIJKLMNOPQRSTUVWXYZ
abcdefghijklmnopqrstuvwxyz
1234567890 !@#?:;"*&

Foundry: American Type Founders
Designer: Thomas Maitland Cleland
Designer Nationality: American
Date: 1902

Inspired by a trip to Rome, US type designer Thomas Maitland Cleland created this serif in 1902 and named it after the Florentine sculptor Luca della Robbia. Its lowercase has long ascenders and short descenders. It was cast as Westminster Oldstyle by British foundry Stephenson, Blake & Co. in 1907.

Dutch 766

ABCDEFGHIJKLMNOPQRSTUVWXYZ
abcdefghijklmnopqrstuvwxyz
1234567890 !@#?:;"*&

Foundry: Bitstream
Designer: Gerard Meynell / John Henry Mason / F. Ernest Jackson / Edward Johnston
Designer Nationality: British
Date: 1913 / c. 1980s

This is Bitstream's digital version of Imprint Antiqua, a restrained large x-height serif that was heavily inspired by Caslon. Imprint Antiqua was created as the text face for *The Imprint,* a short-lived periodical published in London in 1913 about typography, lettering, and fine printing.

Elysium

ABCDEFGHIJKLMNOPQRSTUVWXYZ
abcdefghijklmnopqrstuvwxyz
1234567890 !@#?:;"*&

Foundry: Letraset
Designer: Michael Gills
Designer Nationality: British
Date: 1992

Designed during Michael Gills's time at Letraset, Elysium has distinctive, crisp letterforms and calligraphic details that were influenced by the work of Czech type designer Oldrich Menhart. It was designed for body text, to accompany Gills's earlier headline typeface, Prague (1991).

Engravers Oldstyle 205

ABCDEFGHIJKLMNOPQRSTUVWXYZ
abcdefghijklmnopqrstuvwxyz
1234567890 !@#?:;"*&

Foundry: Bitstream
Designer: Georges Peignot /
Sol Hess / Matthew Carter
Designer Nationality: French /
American / British
Date: 1912 / 1921 / 1977

This generously proportioned font is a revival of Cochin, designed by Georges Peignot in 1912. Building upon Sol Hess's work on Cochin Bold (1921), it adds further weights and corresponding italics to the original roman, whose design was based on 18th-century copper engravings.

Fairfield

ABCDEFGHIJKLMNOPQRSTUVWXYZ
abcdefghijklmnopqrstuvwxyz
1234567890 !@#?:;"*&

Foundry: Linotype
Designer: Rudolph Ruzicka
Designer Nationality: Czech
Date: 1939

Linotype recruited Rudolph Ruzicka on the recommendation of William A. Dwiggins. Ruzicka's economical approach to type design prioritized the reader's experience. His original designs for Fairfield Light and Medium were later developed by Alex Kaczun into an extensive digital font family.

Figural

ABCDEFGHIJKLMNOPQRSTUVWXYZ
abcdefghijklmnopqrstuvwxyz
1234567890 !@#?:;"*&

Foundry: ITC
Designer: Oldrich Menhart /
Michael Gills
Designer Nationality: Czech /
British
Date: 1940 / 1992

Figural was first published by Czech foundry Grafotechna in 1940; like much of Oldrich Menhart's work, it was designed to convey a sense of the spirit of Czech culture. This revival by Michael Gills preserves the character of the original, while smoothing some of its sharper edges.

Fleischman BT

ABCDEFGHIJKLMNOPQRSTUVWXYZ
abcdefghijklmnopqrstuvwxyz
1234567890 !@#?:;"*&

Foundry: Bitstream
Designer: Johann Fleischmann / Charles Gibbons
Designer Nationality: German / American
Date: 1739 / 2002

Charles Gibbons based this design on the work of German punchcutter Johann Fleischmann, whose 8-point roman (1739) inspired several revivals. This Old Style serif was well-received upon its release, offers an extensive character set, and supports a range of Latin-based languages.

FS Brabo

ABCDEFGHIJKLMNOPQRSTUVWXYZ
abcdefghijklmnopqrstuvwxyz
1234567890 !@#?:;"*&

Foundry: Fontsmith
Designer: Fernando Mello
Designer Nationality: Brazilian
Date: 2015

Fernando Mello's design for FS Brabo draws inspiration from classic book serifs such as Garamond and Bembo, reinterpreting their key characteristics to create a rounded and highly readable font. Its selection of OpenType swashes and ligatures offer versatility and flair.

Garamond Classico

ABCDEFGHIJKLMNOPQRSTUVWXYZ
abcdefghijklmnopqrstuvwxyz
1234567890 !@#?:;"*&

Foundry: Omnibus
Designer: Franko Luin
Designer Nationality: Swedish
Date: 1993

This Garamond revival builds upon the work of Jean Jannon, whose designs were for many years mistaken for Claude Garamond's originals. Of his choice to create yet another interpretation of this popular font, Franko Luin remarked "if so many others have done it, why not me too?"

Gloucester

ABCDEFGHIJKLMNOPQRSTUVWXYZ
abcdefghijklmnopqrstuvwxyz
1234567890 !@#?:;"*&

Foundry: Monotype
Designer: Bertram G. Goodhue / Monotype Studio
Designer Nationality: American
Date: 1896 / 1911

Originally known as Gloucester Old Style, this typeface was developed by Monotype from a font drawn by renowned US architect Bertram G. Goodhue for the Cheltenham Press. Goodhue's design proved popular, and numerous digitizations of his design have since been released.

Goudy

ABCDEFGHIJKLMNOPQRSTUVWXYZ
abcdefghijklmnopqrstuvwxyz
1234567890 !@#?:;"*&

Foundry: Monotype
Designer: Frederic W. Goudy /
Morris Fuller Benton
Designer Nationality: American
Date: 1915 / 1916 / 1927

Monotype's digitization of this enduringly popular font, created by the prolific US type designer Frederic W. Goudy, incorporates five styles and an elegant set of fleurons. Its bold and extrabold cuts were first created by Morris Fuller Benton in 1916 and 1927 respectively.

Goudy Catalogue

ABCDEFGHIJKLMNOPQRSTUVWXYZ
abcdefghijklmnopqrstuvwxyz
1234567890 !@#?:;"*&

Foundry: American Type Founders
Designer: Morris Fuller Benton
Designer Nationality: American
Date: 1919

Sporting a slightly heavier weight than the original Goudy Old Style, this Catalogue cut was designed in 1919 by Morris Fuller Benton, who led the design department at American Type Founders for nearly forty years. An italic counterpart to Goudy Catalogue, also by Benton, was published in 1921.

Goudy Old Style

ABCDEFGHIJKLMNOPQRSTUVWXYZ
abcdefghijklmnopqrstuvwxyz
1234567890 !@#?:;"*&

Foundry: American Type Founders
Designer: Frederic W. Goudy
Designer Nationality: American
Date: 1915

While this Old Style serif might appear visually similar to many Renaissance-era Italian typefaces, it was an original design by Frederic W. Goudy rather than a revival. Extensively expanded since its first release, the font is accompanied by a range of alternate cuts and weights.

Griffo Classico

ABCDEFGHIJKLMNOPQRSTUVWXYZ
abcdefghijklmnopqrstuvwxyz
1234567890 !@#?:;"*&

Foundry: Omnibus
Designer: Francesco Griffo /
Franko Luin
Designer Nationality: Italian /
Swedish
Date: 1496 / 1993

Franko Luin designed several accomplished revivals over the course of his career; this example builds upon the work of Francesco Griffo, a punchcutter for the influential printer and scholar Aldus Manutius. Its design was developed from Griffo's 1496 roman cut for Piero Bembo's book *De Aetna*.

Guardi

ABCDEFGHIJKLMNOPQRSTUVWXYZ
abcdefghijklmnopqrstuvwxyz
1234567890 !@#?:;"*&

Foundry: Linotype
Designer: Reinhard Haus
Designer Nationality: German
Date: 1986

Reinhard Haus's elegant design for Guardi was influenced by Venetian typefaces from the 15th century. It incorporates subtle calligraphic characteristics throughout, with a dynamic diagonal emphasis evident in both its letterforms and in the angle of its serifs.

Haarlemmer

ABCDEFGHIJKLMNOPQRSTUVWXYZ
abcdefghijklmnopqrstuvwxyz
1234567890 !@#?:;"*&

Foundry: Monotype
Designer: Jan van Krimpen / Frank E. Blokland
Designer Nationality: Dutch
Date: c. 1930s / 1998

Jan van Krimpen created the first drawings for Haarlemmer in the 1930s, but its production was thwarted by the outbreak of World War II. Freed from the limitations of metal typecasting, this revival presents a comprehensive realization of Van Krimpen's ambitions for the original.

Hadriano

ABCDEFGHIJKLMNOPQRSTUVWXYZ
abcdefghijklmnopqrstuvwxyz
1234567890 !@#?:;"*&

Foundry: Monotype
Designer: Frederic W. Goudy
Designer Nationality: American
Date: 1918

First released in uppercase only, Hadriano was developed from rubbings taken by Frederic W. Goudy of carved type on display in the Louvre. His later lowercase letterforms were not included in its earliest Monotype release; they would finally be incorporated within a much later digitization.

Hollander

ABCDEFGHIJKLMNOPQRSTUVWXYZ
abcdefghijklmnopqrstuvwxyz
1234567890 !@#?:;"*&

Foundry: Hell
Designer: Gerhard Unger
Designer Nationality: German
Date: 1983

Gerhard Unger designed Hollander during his time at Rudolf Hell's eponymous foundry, which pioneered digital-typesetting technology and went on to merge with Linotype in 1990. The generous curves and large x-height of its letterforms retain legibility within a wide range of contexts.

Commercial Type

Collaborating designers Paul Barnes and Christian Schwartz have worked together across the Atlantic since 2004 and formalized their arrangement as Commercial Type three years later. A joint venture, the foundry is based in New York and London and publishes retail fonts developed by Barnes and Schwartz as well as creations from their design team and third-party collaborators. Contributors from an international Who's Who in type design include Erik van Blokland, Susana Carvalho, Kai Bernau, Sandrine Nugue, and Ilya Ruderman.

As well as designing their own typefaces Commercial Type takes on numerous commissions, and one of Barnes and Schwartz's first and most ambitious projects—and one of the most ambitious undertaken by any foundry in recent years—was the creation of a new typeface family for the British newspaper the *Guardian* in 2005. As part of the redesign of the newspaper, headed up by its creative director Mark Porter, the title underwent a change in size from a broadsheet to the smaller

Berliner format. Porter needed a new typeface suite to get the most out of the new format. The result was the award-winning Guardian Egyptian, a contemporary slab serif with accompanying sans serif consisting of more than 130 styles. As a result of their work, the redesign team was awarded the coveted Black Pencil by D&AD and in 2006, *Wallpaper** magazine named Barnes and Schwartz two of the forty most influential designers under the age of forty. Other notable commissions include typefaces for the Empire State Building and *The Wall Street Journal*.

Founded: 2007
Countries: Britain / America
Website: commercialtype.com
Notable typefaces:
Portrait (see p. 143)
Druk (see p. 463)

Below. Britain's largest heritage organization, the National Trust, with over 3 million members, asked Commercial Type to produce their new corporate typeface. The new design was to replace its existing mixed usage of Helvetica, Bembo and Albertus. Paul Barnes' final design takes its cues from 19th-century British vernacular types yet incorporates the necessities that a contemporary corporate typeface is required to possess.

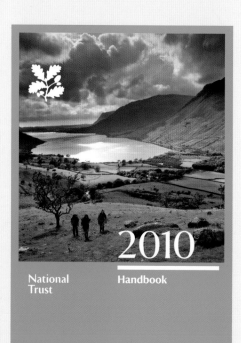

Antony

Torpoint, Cornwall PL11 2QA

Map ① E8

'**Because Antony is still a family experience of visiting is unique. coming back again and again.**' Helen Munzer, York

Faced in silver-grey Pentewan stone by colonnaded wings of mellow bric classically beautiful house is a beguil of the formal and informal. Still the Carew Pole family, it contains fine c of paintings, furniture and textiles. T bordering the Lynher estuary, lands

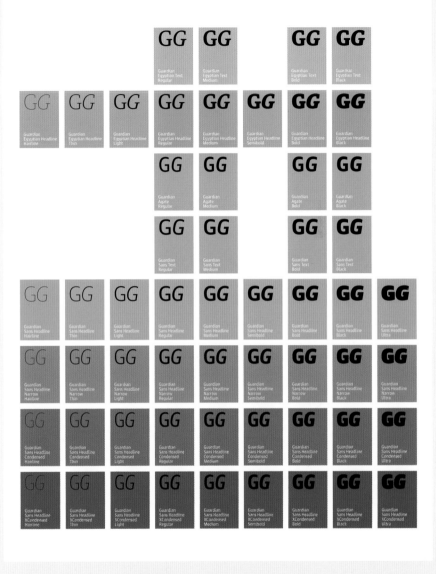

Above. The multi-award-winning typeface for the UK's *Guardian* newspaper was commissioned by Mark Porter for the *Guardian* and designed by Paul Barnes and Christian Schwartz with Berton Hasebe and Vincent Chan. The complete family took from 2009 through to 2012 to design and comprises a slab serif Egyptian (Guardian Egyptian), with accompanying italics used for headlines, and an accompanying version for text usage as well. There is also a sans serif variant for headline text and an agate version. The full family is employed across all print and online media and apps, from titling and texts through to infographics and tables.

Horley Old Style

ABCDEFGHIJKLMNOPQRSTUVWXYZ
abcdefghijklmnopqrstuvwxyz
1234567890 !@#?:;"'*&

Foundry: Monotype
Designer: Frank Hinman Pierpont
Designer Nationality: American
Date: 1925

This cheerful, well-crafted serif was developed by Monotype in response to the popularity of similar typefaces designed by Frederic W. Goudy—in particular, Kennerley and Goudy Old Style. A version suitable for phototypesetting systems was designed by Robert Norton in 1977.

Imprint

ABCDEFGHIJKLMNOPQRSTUVWXYZ
abcdefghijklmnopqrstuvwxyz
1234567890 !@#?:;"'*&

Foundry: Monotype
Designer: Frank Hinman Pierpont / Fritz Stelzer
Designer Nationality: American
Date: 1912

This Caslon-influenced design was commissioned by publisher Gerard Meynell for his short-lived print trade journal *The Imprint*, which counted type designers Edward Johnston and Stanley Morison among its contributors. It has since proved a popular choice for book typesetting.

Iowan Old Style BT

ABCDEFGHIJKLMNOPQRSTUVWXYZ
abcdefghijklmnopqrstuvwxyz
1234567890 !@#?:;"'*&

Foundry: Bitstream
Designer: John Downer
Designer Nationality: American
Date: 1991

Designer and sign-painter John Downer first created this hard-working font for ITC, but after plans to publish it were shelved, Bitstream stepped in. Its tall x-height, comprehensive character set, and compact form make Iowan Old Style BT a versatile choice for book designers.

ITC Berkeley Old Style

ABCDEFGHIJKLMNOPQRSTUVWXYZ
abcdefghijklmnopqrstuvwxyz
1234567890 !@#?:;"'*&

Foundry: ITC
Designer: Frederic W. Goudy / Tony Stan
Designer Nationality: American
Date: 1938 / 1983

This legible design is based on Frederic W. Goudy's University of California Old Style typeface (1938), which was created for exclusive use by the University of California Press. Tony Stan's revival of the font for ITC made it available to designers worldwide for the first time.

ITC Caslon No 224

ABCDEFGHIJKLMNOPQRSTUVWXYZ
abcdefghijklmnopqrstuvwxyz
1234567890 !@#?:;"*&

Foundry: ITC
Designer: Ed Benguiat
Designer Nationality: American
Date: 1982

Another design by Ed Benguiat (see p. 514), this revival of William Caslon's eponymous 18th-century font was developed with the methodologies and demands of contemporary graphic design in mind. Designed for body text, it was preceded by a version optimized for display use, ITC Caslon 223.

ITC Galliard

ABCDEFGHIJKLMNOPQRSTUVWXYZ
abcdefghijklmnopqrstuvwxyz
1234567890 !@#?:;"*&

Foundry: Linotype / ITC
Designer: Matthew Carter
Designer Nationality: British
Date: 1978 /1982

This interpretation of Robert Granjon's 16th-century design by Matthew Carter (see p. 616) was not intended as a direct revival; instead he wanted to capture the spirit of Granjon's designs in a contemporary typeface. ITC's reissue of the Linotype original is in the Museum of Modern Art collection.

ITC Galliard eText

ABCDEFGHIJKLMNOPQRSTUVWXYZ
abcdefghijklmnopqrstuvwxyz
1234567890 !@#?:;"*&

Foundry: ITC
Designer: Matthew Carter / Carl Crossgrove
Designer Nationality: British / American
Date: 2013

Type designer Carl Crossgrove developed this version of Galliard in 2013 for screen-based use. It is part of Monotype's eText offering, optimized to appear legible and true to its original forms on a range of screens, and at many different pixel resolutions.

ITC Garamond

ABCDEFGHIJKLMNOPQRSTUVWXYZ
abcdefghijklmnopqrstuvwxyz
1234567890 !@#?:;"*&

Foundry: ITC
Designer: Tony Stan
Designer Nationality: American
Date: 1975

This revival of Jean Jannon's 16th-century Garalde was originally developed by Tony Stan for ITC as a display typeface in two weights; its popularity and regular misuse as a text face prompted the development of a more extensive family, which now includes sixteen different styles.

ITC Giovanni

ABCDEFGHIJKLMNOPQRSTUVWXYZ
abcdefghijklmnopqrstuvwxyz
1234567890 !@#?:;"*&

Foundry: ITC
Designer: Robert Slimbach
Designer Nationality: American
Date: 1986

Designed by Robert Slimbach shortly before he joined Adobe in 1987, ITC Giovanni is a contemporary reinterpretation of classic Old Style serifs such as Garamond and Bembo. The result is a clean and legible typeface, with a generous x-height and an open visual texture.

ITC Golden Cockerel

ABCDEFGHIJKLMNOPQRSTUVWXYZ
abcdefghijklmnopqrstuvwxyz
1234567890 !@#?:;"*&

Foundry: ITC
Designer: Eric Gill / Richard Dawson / David Farey
Designer Nationality: British
Date: 1929 / 1996

This ITC typeface is a revival of a design by British type designer and sculptor Eric Gill in 1929 for the Golden Cockerel Press, a publisher renowned for finely crafted editions of classic works featuring wood-engraved illustrations. Gill's original design displays the influence of his work as a stone-carver.

ITC Legacy Serif

ABCDEFGHIJKLMNOPQRSTUVWXYZ
abcdefghijklmnopqrstuvwxyz
1234567890 !@#?:;"*&

Foundry: ITC
Designer: Ronald Arnholm
Designer Nationality: American
Date: 1993

Nicolas Jenson's type was designed for a 1470 edition of Eusebius's *De praeparatione evangelica* (*Preparation for the Gospel*), and Ronald Arnholm began this revival for his master's thesis at Yale; he refined its design over several decades, improving its fidelity to Jenson's original.

ITC Legacy Square Serif

ABCDEFGHIJKLMNOPQRSTUVWXYZ
abcdefghijklmnopqrstuvwxyz
1234567890 !@#?:;"*&

Foundry: ITC
Designer: Ronald Arnholm
Designer Nationality: American
Date: 2009

Ron Arnholm built on the success of his Legacy typeface following its release, designing numerous variant styles to develop an extensive superfamily. This square cut, traced from specimens of the serif and sans letterforms, was a Type Directors Club Typeface Design Winner in 2010.

ITC Mendoza Roman

ABCDEFGHIJKLMNOPQRSTUVWXYZ
abcdefghijklmnopqrstuvwxyz
1234567890 !@#?:;"*&

Foundry: ITC
Designer: José Mendoza y Almeida
Designer Nationality: French
Date: 1991

This Old Style serif, created by renowned French illustrator and type designer José Mendoza y Almeida, features low-contrast letterforms with subtly cupped serifs. The regularity of its forms makes it a useful choice for body text at small point sizes, and in suboptimal printing conditions.

ITC New Esprit

ABCDEFGHIJKLMNOPQRSTUVWXYZ
abcdefghijklmnopqrstuvwxyz
1234567890 !@#?:;"*&

Foundry: ITC
Designer: Jovica Veljović
Designer Nationality: Serbian
Date: 2010

Jovica Veljović won the coveted ATypI Prix Charles Peignot award in 1985, the same year he designed the first letterforms of this typeface for ITC. Revisiting his work several years later, he expanded the original design to encompass separate cuts for display and body text use.

ITC New Winchester

ABCDEFGHIJKLMNOPQRSTUVWXYZ
abcdefghijklmnopqrstuvwxyz
1234567890 !@#?:;"*&

Foundry: ITC
Designer: Jim Speice
Designer Nationality: American
Date: 1999

William A. Dwiggins' design for Winchester, through which he tested several ideas that he hoped would improve the legibility of serif faces, was never properly published. Jim Speice's revival of the font, more than five decades later, finally made its distinctive forms available digitally.

ITC Souvenir

ABCDEFGHIJKLMNOPQRSTUVWXYZ
abcdefghijklmnopqrstuvwxyz
1234567890 !@#?:;"*&

Foundry: ITC
Designer: Morris Fuller Benton / Ed Benguiat
Designer Nationality: American
Date: 1914 / 1972

This revival of Morris Fuller Benton's 1914 design went on to wildly outstrip its predecessor in popularity. One of ITC's first releases, the typeface is indelibly associated with 1970s graphic design, though its ubiquity prompted something of a backlash in subsequent decades.

ITC Souvenir Monospaced

ABCDEFGHIJKLMNOPQRSTUVWXYZ
abcdefghijklmnopqrstuvwxyz
1234567890 !@#?:;"*&

Foundry: ITC
Designer: Ed Benguiat /
Ned Bunnel
Designer Nationality: American
Date: 1972 / 1983

This monospaced cut of Souvenir was designed by Ned Bunnel, who was also responsible for the monospaced cut of ITC AvantGarde. First developed to accommodate the limitations of typewriters and early digital displays, such styles now offer a distinctive character of their own.

ITC Usherwood

ABCDEFGHIJKLMNOPQRSTUVWXYZ
abcdefghijklmnopqrstuvwxyz
1234567890 !@#?:;"*&

Foundry: ITC
Designer: Leslie Usherwood
Designer Nationality: Canadian
Date: 1983

Designed for ITC by Leslie Usherwood and the team at his Canadian foundry Typsettra, this approachable serif features asymmetrical styles throughout, and is well-suited for the setting of body text. ITC Usherwood is available in four weights, with corresponding italics.

ITC Veljovic

ABCDEFGHIJKLMNOPQRSTUVWXYZ
abcdefghijklmnopqrstuvwxyz
1234567890 !@#?:;"*&

Foundry: ITC
Designer: Jovica Veljović
Designer Nationality: Serbian
Date: 1984

Before ITC commissioned Jovica Veljović to design this, his eponymous first typeface, his calligraphic work appeared on the pages of the foundry's type journal, *U&lc*. His design for ITC Veljovic was influenced by the work of Hermann Zapf (see p. 574) and Henri Friedlaender.

ITC Weidemann

ABCDEFGHIJKLMNOPQRSTUVWXYZ
abcdefghijklmnopqrstuvwxyz
1234567890 !@#?:;"*&

Foundry: ITC
Designer: Kurt Weidemann
Designer Nationality: German
Date: 1983

Originally called Biblica, this typeface was commissioned for a new German edition of the Bible; its condensed letterforms reflect the need to set large volumes of text economically and legibly. Kurt Weidemann took inspiration from early Venetian faces for the design of the font.

Jenson Classico

ABCDEFGHIJKLMNOPQRSTUVWXYZ
abcdefghijklmnopqrstuvwxyz
1234567890 ! @#?:;"*&

Foundry: Linotype
Designer: Nicolas Jenson / Franko Luin
Designer Nationality: French / Swedish
Date: 1470 / 1993

In 1458, the French King Charles VII sent Nicolas Jenson to Mainz to learn about movable type. The type Jenson later used as a printer working in Venice from 1470 to 1480 has been called the original roman; it survived in books, providing a source for this digitization by Franko Luin.

King's Caslon

ABCDEFGHIJKLMNOPQRSTUVWXYZ
abcdefghijklmnopqrstuvwxyz
1234567890 !@#?:;"*&

Foundry: Dalton Maag
Designer: Marc Weymann / Ron Carpenter
Designer Nationality: British
Date: 2007

King's Caslon is a reinterpretation of William Caslon's 16th-century letterforms, designed with two optical sizes. The Text style is more transitional in character, with symmetrical serifs and moderate contrast, while the Display version combines strong contrast with softer details.

Kuenstler 480

ABCDEFGHIJKLMNOPQRSTUVWXYZ
abcdefghijklmnopqrstuvwxyz
1234567890 !@#?:;"*&

Foundry: Bitstream
Designer: Georg Trump
Designer Nationality: American
Date: 1954

Kuenstler 480 is a Bitstream version of Trump Mediaeval (1954). It has features of both an Old Style serif and a Venetian, as well as a sloping roman italic and angular serifs. In 2010, ParaType released a Cyrillic version of Kuenstler 480 by Vladimir Yefimov and Isabella Chaeva.

Latin 725

ABCDEFGHIJKLMNOPQRSTUVWXYZ
abcdefghijklmnopqrstuvwxyz
1234567890 !@#?:;"*&

Foundry: Bitstream
Designer: Adrian Frutiger
Designer Nationality: Swiss
Date: 1955

Latin 725 is Bitstream's version of the sharp-serifed Latin typeface Méridien by Adrian Frutiger (see p. 290), which was released by Deberny & Peignot in 1957. It was later re-envisioned as Frutiger Serif by Frutiger and Akira Kobayashi for Linotype. Latin 725 is ideal for setting large amounts of text.

Lava

ABCDEFGHIJKLMNOPQRSTUVWXYZ
abcdefghijklmnopqrstuvwxyz
1234567890 !@#?:;"*&

Foundry: Typotheque
Designer: Peter Biľak
Designer Nationality: Slovakian
Date: 2013

Peter Biľak created Lava for his magazine *Works That Work* (2013–18). The first issue was designed by Carvalho Bernau and used Lava alone. A highly legible face designed for both digital and print, Lava is available in four weights and has a Cyrillic alphabet designed by Ilya Ruderman.

Linotype Syntax Serif

ABCDEFGHIJKLMNOPQRSTUVWXYZ
abcdefghijklmnopqrstuvwxyz
1234567890 !@#?:;"*&

Foundry: Linotype
Designer: Hans Eduard Meier
Designer Nationality: Swiss
Date: 2000

Syntax Serif was released as part of the Syntax Next family forty-five years after Swiss designer Hans Eduard Meier originally began drawing Syntax, its sans serif partner. A highly legible face, described by Linotype as a "workhorse," Syntax Serif has a double-storey "g" and is ideal for long text.

Mantika Book

ABCDEFGHIJKLMNOPQRSTUVWXYZ
abcdefghijklmnopqrstuvwxyz
1234567890 !@#?:;"*&

Foundry: Linotype
Designer: Jürgen Weltin
Designer Nationality: German
Date: 2014

Mantika Book is the Antiqua serif of the Mantika superfamily, which also has a sans and an informal sans, by German designer Jürgen Weltin of Type Matters. Mantika Book comes in two weights—regular and bold—each of which has an italic that is relatively upright.

Matt Antique

ABCDEFGHIJKLMNOPQRSTUVWXYZ
abcdefghijklmnopqrstuvwxyz
1234567890 !@#?:;"*&

Foundry: Bitstream
Designer: John Matt
Designer Nationality: American
Date: 1979

Although drawn in the 1960s by US designer and Pratt Institute graduate John Matt, this elegant calligraphic serif was not released by Compugraphic until 1979. It was first known as Garth Graphic, after the company's founder William W. Garth Jr, and Bitsteam's version comes in roman, italic, and bold.

Mengelt Basel Antiqua

ABCDEFGHIJKLMNOPQRSTUVWXYZ
abcdefghijklmnopqrstuvwxyz
1234567890 !@#?:;"*&

Foundry: Linotype
Designer: Christian Mengelt
Designer Nationality: Swiss
Date: 2014

Drawing inspiration from book fonts used in 16th-century Switzerland, Christian Mengelt designed Basel Antiqua for a reprint of *De humani corporis fabrica* (*On the fabric of the human body*, 1543). Rather than an exact revival, Mengelt adapted the face used on the original book.

Minion

ABCDEFGHIJKLMNOPQRSTUVWXYZ
abcdefghijklmnopqrstuvwxyz
1234567890 !@#?:;"*&

Foundry: Adobe
Designer: Robert Slimbach
Designer Nationality: American
Date: 1990

Robert Slimbach, a type designer at Adobe since 1987, was inspired by late Renaissance typefaces to create Minion, a classic text face. A huge family of more than sixty fonts, it was updated as Minion Pro in 2000 and is a popular choice thanks to its inclusion in all of the Adobe applications.

Minister

ABCDEFGHIJKLMNOPQRSTUVWXYZ
abcdefghijklmnopqrstuvwxyz
1234567890 !@#?:;"*&

Foundry: Linotype
Designer: Carl Albert Fahrenwaldt / Alex Kaczun
Designer Nationality: German / American
Date: 1929 / 1987

Designed by Carl Albert Fahrenwaldt for East Geman foundry Schriftguss, Minister was digitized by Alex Kaczun for Linotype in 1987. Minister comes in four weights and has a calligraphic feel, with concave serifs and ovoid tittles. Adobe, Elsner+Flake and Scangraphic also have versions.

Miramar

ABCDEFGHIJKLMNOPQRSTUVWXYZ
abcdefghijklmnopqrstuvwxyz
1234567890 !@#?:;"*&

Foundry: Omnibus
Designer: Franko Luin
Designer Nationality: Swedish
Date: 1993

Franko Luin named Miramar after a castle north of his birthplace, Trieste. It is an elegant, Old Style text face with fine serifs. It comes in roman and bold, each with italics, and a single weight of small caps. Luin admits that he would use it only "for very special tasks."

Monotype Garamond

ABCDEFGHIJKLMNOPQRSTUVWXYZ
abcdefghijklmnopqrstuvwxyz
1234567890 !@#?:;"'*&

Foundry: Monotype
Designer: Claude Garamond /
Jean Jannon / Stanley Morison
Designer Nationality: French /
British
Date: c. 1540s / 1621 / 1922

Monotype Garamond is considered to be one of the more elegant cuts of the Garamond design. It was cut in 1922 from designs drawn up by Monotype consultant and type designer Stanley Morison from the original Garamond designs held in the archives of the French Imprimerie Nationale, the printing department of the French government. Many of these designs were created in 1621 by French designer Jean Jannon, who based his designs on the work of French type cutter Claude Garamond, whose types were published some eighty years before Jannon's interpretations.

It was Jannon's work that was adopted by the French leadership of the day and which became the house style for the Royal Printing Office. However, in the early 19th century, the designs were attributed by the French National Printing Office to Garamond rather than Jannon. This oversight was corrected in 1926 following research by US writer and type academic Beatrice Warde, one of the few women typographers in the world in the mid 20th century.

Garamond's legibility and classic good looks have meant it has been widely used for the printing of reading texts in books. It remains popular to this day and in recent times "Garamond" has become an umbrella term for types influenced by the work of Garamond and Jannon. Most foundries offer a version that draws on the principles of the original designs, yet all of them possess refinements and adjustments to distinguish them from one other.

Right. Website for the *Pittori di Cinema* book, published by Lazy Dog press, Milan, focussing on the work of cinema artists. The sans serif used is Tungsten, released by Hoefler & Frere-Jones (now known as Hoefler & Co.) in 2009.

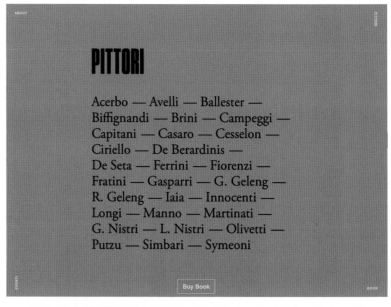

"MONOTYPE" SERIES No. 156
GARAMOND
Unit Arrangement 37 (6 point to 12D)

156—6 (6D) 6 Set   Line ·1186

THE invention of Printing from movable types was one of the chief events affecting the history of European civilization. The task of duplicating texts without variance was impossible before Gutenberg equipped the scholar with the accuracy of type. Prejudiced connoisseurs in the fifteenth century deplored the new mass-production *The invention of Printing from movable types was one of the chief events* THE INVENTION OF PRINTING FROM MOVABLE TYPES

156—8 (8D) 8 Set   Line ·125

DIE Erfindung des Buchdrucks mit beweglichen Lettern war eines der wichtigsten Ereignisse in der Geschichte der Zivilisation, denn die originalgetreue *Die Erfindung des Buchdrucks mit beweglichen Lettern war* DIE ERFINDUNG DES BUCHDRUCKS MIT

156—9 (8D) 8¾ Set   Line ·1268

L'INVENTION de l'Imprimerie au moyen de caractères mobiles fut l'un des principaux événements de l'histoire de la civilisation européenne, car *L'invention de l'Imprimerie au moyen de caractères* L'INVENTION DE L'IMPRIMERIE AU M

156—10 (9D) 9¼ Set   Line ·1276

THE invention of Printing from movable types was one of the chief events affecting *The invention of Printing from movable types was* THE INVENTION OF PRINTING FRO

156—11 (10D) 10¼ Set   Line ·13

DIE Erfindung des Buchdrucks mit beweglichen Lettern war eines der wich- *Die Erfindung des Buchdrucks mit beweglichen* DIE ERFINDUNG DES BUCHDRU

156—12 (12D) 11¼ Set   Line ·1338

L'INVENTION de l'Imprimerie au moyen de caractères mobiles fut l'un *L'invention de l'Imprimerie au moyen de* L'INVENTION DE L'IMPRIME

156—12D 12¼ Set (cast on 13 point E.) Line ·1368

THE invention of Printing from movable types was one of the *The invention of Printing from movable* THE INVENTION OF PRINT

156—14 (14D) 12¾ Set   ·2″ × ·2″   Line ·1486
Unit Arrangement 99

The invention of Printing from movable types was one of the *The invention of Printing from mova* THE INVENTION OF PRIN

156—14 12¾ Set Unit Arrangement 114   Line ·1395

His family has farmed the land for two hundred years, and although the estate, since the bad time, HAS PASSED FROM HIS POSSESSION HE

156—14 Display Matrices   Line ·1395

Fashions change, and each succeeding generation has its own tastes. That is to say, of the most infinite OF NATURE'S ASPECTS SOME MAY GIVE

156—16 14 Set Unit Arrangement 114   Line ·1599

There are few more striking indications of the changes in manners and customs that time has BROUGHT ABOUT THAN THESE OLD

156—18 16 Set Unit Arrangement 114   Line ·181

By that time the great green slope that rises away from the farmhouse garden IS TOUCHED WITH AN AUTUMN

156—18 Display Matrices   Line ·181

His family has farmed the land for two HUNDRED YEARS AND SINCE A

156—24 21¼ Set Unit Arrangement 114   Line ·2364

There are so many changes in ALL OUR MANNERS OR

156—24 Display Matrices   Line ·2364

Having arrived, we can now EXPLAIN IN A MANNER

156—30 Display Matrices   Line ·2918

This family has farmed the LANDS FOR OVER A

ABCDEFGHIJKLMNOPQRSTUVWXYZÆŒ&   *ABCDEFGHIJKLMNOPQRSTUVWXYZÆŒ&*
abcdefghijklmnopqrstuvwxyzæœ   ABCDEFGHIJKLMNOPQRSTUVWXYZÆŒ   *abcdefghijklmnopqrstuvwxyzæœ*
ÀÁÂÄÈÉÊËÌÍÎÏÒÓÔÖÙÚÛÜÑÇ   Q U   Qu   *Qu*   *AAAÄÈÉÊËÌÍÎÏÒÓÔÖÙÚÛÜÑÇ*
àáâäèéêëìíîïòóôöùúûüñç   ÀÁÂÄÈÉÊËÌÍÎÏÒÓÔÖÙÚÛÜÑÇ   *àáâäèéêëìíîïòóôöùúûüñç*
1234567890   .,:;-!?°-.().·[]*†‡§¶...£.-$ ﬀﬁﬂﬃﬄ   ij ß ÿ ß   ,.;:'"!?   *ﬀﬁﬂﬃﬄ*   *1234567890*
Alternative Figures: F214 1234567890 and F341 *1234567890*   Alternative *h*(75H) *s*(669S)   Qu Qu qu QU *QU*
A B C D E F G H J K M P T U Ex Na Ne Ni No Nu Qu Qu Ra Re Ri Ro Ru
as ÆÆ e et fr q gg gj gy is k ky ll m nt ſa ſb ſe ſh ſi ſk ſo ſa ſſ ſt ſu ſſa ſſe ſſi ſſl ſſo ſſu ſb ſt ta tt us v zy

5-41   B

LONDON : THE MONOTYPE CORPORATION LTD   PARIS : SOCIÉTÉ ANONYME MONOTYPE   BERLIN : SETZMASCHINEN-FABRIK MONOTYPE G.M.B.H.
(Printed in Great Britain)   *(Imprimé en Grande-Bretagne)*   *(Gedruckt in Großbritannien)*

Monotype Goudy

ABCDEFGHIJKLMNOPQRSTUVWXYZ
abcdefghijklmnopqrstuvwxyz
1234567890 !@#?:;''"*&

Foundry: Monotype
Designer: Frederic W. Goudy
Designer Nationality: American
Date: 1915

The acclaimed Goudy typeface was made by the master of US type design, Frederic W. Goudy, who designed more than one hundred typefaces over fifty years. The typeface is valued for its legibility and readability in print, its flexibility, and its range of weights, which means it is equally at home on a billboard as on the printed page.

When the American Type Foundry released the typeface in roman form only as Goudy Old Style in 1915, it was an immediate success. Its use became widespread because of its legibility as a text face compared to its contemporaries, thanks to its rounder curves and a softer design. Such features were partly due to the Renaissance types from which it drew its inspiration. However, it was also because of Goudy's clever hand in adding many personal and distinct touches to the character designs. He created an italic and a revision, Goudy Modern, in 1918, and a Heavyface in 1925. Other variants have also been drawn up by other designers, including Morris Fuller Benton who created Goudy Bold (1916–19), Goudy Extra Bold (1927), and the shaded version, Goudy Handtooled (1922). Today, the Goudy family is wide and extensive with a number of foundries offering versions.

Early in the 21st Century, THE TYRELL CORPORATION advanced Robot evolution into the NEXUS phase — a being virtually identical to a human — known as a *Replicant.*

The NEXUS 6 *Replicants* were superior in strength and agility, and at least equal in intelligence, to the genetic engineers

Left. Goudy employed in the opening titles for director Ridley Scott's 1982 science-fiction classic *Bladerunner*.

Monotype Century Old Style

ABCDEFGHIJKLMNOPQRSTUVWXYZ
abcdefghijklmnopqrstuvwxyz
1234567890 !@#?:;"*&

Foundry: Monotype
Designer: Morris Fuller Benton
Designer Nationality: American
Date: 1906

Century Old Style is an evolution of Century Expanded (1900), which Morris Fuller Benton cut as an extension of his father Linn Boyd Benton's Century (1894). He kept similar weights and proportions to Expanded but replaced the modern characteristics with more restrained Old Style features.

Monotype Goudy Catalogue

ABCDEFGHIJKLMNOPQRSTUVWXYZ
abcdefghijklmnopqrstuvwxyz
1234567890 !@#?:;"*&

Foundry: Monotype
Designer: Frederic W. Goudy / Morris Fuller Benton
Designer Nationality: American
Date: 1915 / 1919

Goudy Catalogue is Morris Fuller Benton's adaption of Goudy Old Style (1915); it comes in one weight with an italic and is heavier than the original Goudy. As the name implies, it is a good choice for book text. The typeface has short descenders and once had a display version called Goudy Handtooled.

Monotype Goudy Modern

ABCDEFGHIJKLMNOPQRSTUVWXYZ
abcdefghijklmnopqrstuvwxyz
1234567890 !@#?:;"*&

Foundry: Monotype
Designer: Frederic W. Goudy
Designer Nationality: American
Date: 1918

The result of prolific designer Frederic W. Goudy filling in the white spaces he had left in Goudy Open (1918), an earlier decorative face, Goudy Modern has sturdy, flat serifs. Monotype has held a version since 1928 which is available digitally in regular and bold with italics.

Monotype Italian Old Style

ABCDEFGHIJKLMNOPQRSTUVWXYZ
abcdefghijklmnopqrstuvwxyz
1234567890 !@#?:;"*&

Foundry: Monotype
Designer: Frederic W. Goudy
Designer Nationality: American
Date: 1924

Frederic W. Goudy designed this for Lanston Monotype, which wanted a competitor to Morris Fuller Benton's Cloister Old Style (1913). Italian Old Style was inspired by the forms of 15th-century Italian typefaces. It is available in regular and bold with italics, and is ideal as a book face.

Monotype Old Style

ABCDEFGHIJKLMNOPQRSTUVWXYZ
abcdefghijklmnopqrstuvwxyz
1234567890 !@#?:;"'*&

Foundry: Monotype
Designer: Alexander Phemister
Designer Nationality: Scottish
Date: 1860 / 1901

Monotype Old Style is a Lanston Monotype recut of a typeface first produced by the Scottish foundry Miller & Richard in 1860 as an update of Caslon Old Style. It is a mixture of Old Style and modern serifs, with vertical stress and sharp, straight serifs, and is ideal for text use.

Nevia BT

ABCDEFGHIJKLMNOPQRSTUVWXYZ
abcdefghijklmnopqrstuvwxyz
1234567890 !@#?:;"*&

Foundry: Bitstream
Designer: Hal Taylor
Designer Nationality: American
Date: 2002

Nevia is a characterful serif with many nuances and distinctive letters. The terminal of the "a" joins with the lower loop, the "M" has two different top serifs, and the crossbars of the "B," "P," and "R" do not meet their stems. The typeface is available in regular and bold with italics.

Orion

ABCDEFGHIJKLMNOPQRSTUVWXYZ
abcdefghijklmnopqrstuvwxyz
1234567890 !@#?:;"*&

Foundry: Monotype
Designer: Hermann Zapf
Designer Nationality: German
Date: 1974

Legendary typographer Hermann Zapf (see p. 574) started Orion in 1963. It was finally released in 1974 for the Linofilm photocomposing machine and was intended to be a neutral, legible text face for newspapers and books. Orion is available in roman and italic, which has a distinctive "et" ampersand.

Palatino

ABCDEFGHIJKLMNOPQRSTUVWXYZ
abcdefghijklmnopqrstuvwxyz
1234567890 !@#?:;"*&

Foundry: Stempel
Designer: Hermann Zapf
Designer Nationality: German
Date: 1950

Palatino is an Old Style serif by Hermann Zapf (see p. 574). It is named after the 16th-century Italian calligrapher Giovanni Battista Palatino, and inspired by the Renaissance typefaces of other Italian typographers such as Aldus Manutius. The German foundry Stempel released Palatino in 1950.

Palatino Linotype

ABCDEFGHIJKLMNOPQRSTUVWXYZ
abcdefghijklmnopqrstuvwxyz
1234567890 !@#?:;"*&

Foundry: Linotype
Designer: Hermann Zapf
Designer Nationality: German
Date: 1950 / 1999

Palatino was an instant hit when it was released, garnering much acclaim for Hermann Zapf (see p. 290). This led to many new versions—and copies—such as Linotype's, which became even more prominent when it was included in Windows 2000 and bundled with all Microsoft software.

Palatino Nova

ABCDEFGHIJKLMNOPQRSTUVWXYZ
abcdefghijklmnopqrstuvwxyz
1234567890 !@#?:;"*&

Foundry: Linotype
Designer: Hermann Zapf / Akira Kobayashi
Designer Nationality: German / Japanese
Date: 2005

Many foundries released sanctioned digitizations of Palatino, including Bitstream and URW, while Monotype put out the almost identical Book Antiqua. In 2005, Hermann Zapf (see p. 574) worked with Akira Kobayashi on a redesign called Palatino Nova to provide a definitive digitized version.

Pastonchi

ABCDEFGHIJKLMNOPQRSTUVWXYZ
abcdefghijklmnopqrstuvwxyz
1234567890 !@#?:;"*&

Foundry: Monotype
Designer: Francesco Pastonchi / Eduardo Cotti / Robin Nicholas
Designer Nationality: Italian / Italian / British
Date: 1927 / 1998

When poet Francesco Pastonchi was commissioned to produce a new edition of classic Italian books he failed to find a type he felt suitable, so he set about designing his own, with help from Eduardo Cotti at the Royal School of Typography in Turin. Pastonchi was digitized by Robin Nicholas in 1998.

Pescadero

ABCDEFGHIJKLMNOPQRSTUVWXYZ
abcdefghijklmnopqrstuvwxyz
1234567890 !@#?:;"*&

Foundry: Ascender
Designer: Steve Matteson
Designer Nationality: American
Date: 2006

Taking its name from the historic farming and ranching valley on California's coastline, Pescadero is an Old Style serif that references the calligraphic style of inscriptional letterforms. The characters strike a balance between swelling curves and stringent strokes.

Plantin

ABCDEFGHIJKLMNOPQRSTUVWXYZ
abcdefghijklmnopqrstuvwxyz
1234567890 !@#?:;"*&

Foundry: Monotype
Designer Frank Hinman
Pierpont / Fritz Stelzer
Designer Nationality: American /
German
Date: 1913

Though it possesses his name, the hugely influential 16th-century French printer and publisher Christophe Plantin did not design the Plantin typeface. Rather, it is an homage to the types he collected and employed as founder of the Plantin Press in Antwerp, Belgium.

Plantin was first cut in 1913 by German draughtsman Fritz Stelzer under the guidance of Frank Hinman Pierpont, a US engineer and works manager at Monotype in Surrey, England. Pierpoint instigated the creation of Plantin after a visit to the Plantin-Moretus Museum in Antwerp. He took away copies of a vast wealth of material, including unused types by 16th-century French type designer and printer Robert Granjon. Many believe that these, together with samples of Granjon's work printed by the Plantin Press, were the foundations of Plantin.

In the 21st century, Plantin has seen a resurgence in its use, especially in editorial and publishing arenas; it is highly legible and has a distinctive design, while its thicker characters allow it to hold more ink on press, aiding the printing process. Plantin has also influenced a number of designs, including another Monotype creation, Times New Roman. The Plantin family includes Light, Regular, Semi Bold, and Bold weights with a suite of small caps, ligatures, and Old Style figures for the text weights.

Below and opposite. The joint overall winner in the 2014 International Society of Typographic Designers International Typographic Awards was *Eros und Thanatos*. Written by Mark Gisbourne and published by Lubok Verlag in Germany, this stunning book is wholly set in Plantin, and was art directed and designed by Maria Magdalena Meyer with Maria Ondrej of studio MMKoehn in Leipzig. Its classic, understated style belies a highly crafted and elegant design solution with Plantin at the core of its success. Plantin's flexibility and suitability as a titling and text face is used to maximum effect from cover to cover.

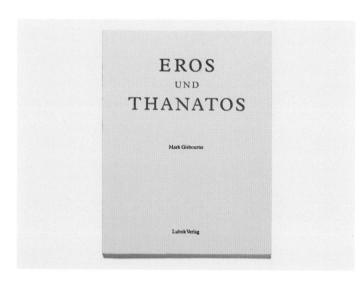

ns in Geis Bild mit Justine Ottos *Lonestar I*, könn

r ein Mädchen ähnlichen Alters dar, zeigt aber zu

kultureller Differenzen.[87] Weniger skizzenhaft un

n von unten, wie sie stolz ihre perspektivisch ver

chten falschen Fingernägeln präsentiert. Während

hsene imaginiert, konzentriert sie sich ganz dar

nte sagen, dass zwischen Sargents kleinem Mädch

Jahrhundert der Kinderpsychologie steht. Ihr Se

ken Eindruck proto-adoleszenter sexueller Selb

ch ist das Mädchen noch ein Mädchen, nicht älte

MPORARY PAINTING

hardly surprising given that Thomas Rusche, wh
ch Baroque paintings, is deeply concerned with
ion that link both his Baroque and contemporary
roque Age and the contemporary practice of paint
ne.[4] The idea of a monad-like parallelism, or 'var
modernist ideas of linear cause and effect (argu
used recently as a powerful analogous argumen
extension the plurality of different approaches tha
lso a fundamental corollary that profoundly conn
amely Eros (desire, the 'life drive') and Thanatos
which we must all succumb in our different ways.
d through 'deistic' principles, and in the Moder
l' or libidinal structures of explanation.[6] However, n
ning emotive power or experiences that these impu
que and contemporary parallels are no less signific
understanding of the motives and meaning behind t
rks.

ual aesthetic medium, has always been deeply conn
the isolation of the studio, long hours of solitude
form of personal expression, and the dissatisfa
s of a painter's life. Similarly, to a passionate colle
esire to possess the un-possessable, to grasp the
ors no less a sense of personal and unresolved frus
uously seeking out, a yearning for the complete inn
the creative aesthetics of 'Eros' and 'Thanatos',
ut inescapable. But desire and the death of desire
merely different aspects of human identity forged i
e civilising processes of life, as binary necessities t
reciprocity is the shadow that exists because ther
n simultaneously at a sense of discovery, and at res
que personal and ever deepening relationship to pai
through his extensive acquisitions over recent year
t a very small part of Thomas Rusche's contemp
reflect upon the aforementioned affinities. A featur
hirty years is the return to genre categories that we
ries of landscape and still life, and many sub-genr
first born of seventeenth century painting, and by
nting practitioners.[8] It not only reflects a Nietzsch
ng as a practice has the continuous ability to
painting, it has returned and facilitates an enorm
mporary world.[10] With the abandonment of so-ca
minism, the end game often argued by minimal
to the historical past and the great traditions of pas

BAROCKE UND ZEITGENÖSSISCHE MALEREI

VOR dem bisher Gesagten erstaunt es nicht, dass Thomas Rusche, der auch über eine umfangreiche Sammlung niederländischer Barockmalerei verfügt, sich intensiv mit den Konzepten und unterschiedlichen Verfahren der Überlieferung beschäftigt, die seine barocken und zeitgenössischen Kunstwerke miteinander verbinden.[3] Bemerkenswerterweise war das Verhältnis zwischen den barocken und zeitgenössischen Praktiken nie relevanter als zum gegenwärtigen Zeitpunkt.[4] Die Vorstellung von parallelen Monaden oder von „variablen Inflexionslinien" (Deleuze) wurde – im Gegensatz zu den vormals üblichen Ideen der Moderne von Ursache und Wirkung (die verschiedene Modi des stilistischen Determinismus begründeten) – in letzter Zeit oft als überzeugendes Argument verwendet, um mittels der Analogie die häufig so titulierte Postmoderne und, im weiteren Sinn, auch die Vielfalt der unterschiedlichen Zugänge zeitgenössischer Malpraktiken zu erklären.[5] Es gibt zudem eine grundlegende logische Konsequenz, die 17., 20. und 21. Jahrhundert tiefgreifend miteinander verbindet: die Prinzipien von Eros (Begehren, Lebenstrieb) und Thanatos (Todestrieb). Sie sind die menschlichen variablen „Inflexionslinien", nach denen wir uns alle auf unsere jeweils eigene Art und Weise ausrichten müssen. Im Zeitalter des Barock waren diese beiden Impulse üblicherweise Teil von „deistischen" Prinzipien, an deren Stelle in der Moderne weitgehend vielfältige „psychologische" oder libidinöse Erklärungsmuster getreten sind.[6] Aber nichts vermag jene emotive Macht und die Erfahrungen abzumildern, mit denen diese Impulse noch immer unsere zeitgenössischen menschlichen Leben konfrontieren. Diese Parallelen zwischen dem Barock und der Gegenwart sind aber auch hilfreich, um die Beweggründe und Bedeutungen, die der SØR Rusche Sammlung mit ihren weit über zweitausend Arbeiten zugrunde liegen, zu verstehen.

Die Praxis der Malerei war schon immer mehr als jede andere visuelle ästhetische Sprache tief mit Eros und Thanatos, dem Lebens- und Todestrieb verbunden: Die Isolation im Atelier, lange Stunden der Einsamkeit und Innenschau, das ehrgeizige Verlangen, eine vollkommene Form des persönlichen Ausdrucks zu finden und die Unzufriedenheit, wenn diese nicht gelingt, bestimmen die gespannte Unruhe im Leben eines Malers. Ähnlich spürt ein leidenschaftlicher Sammler wie Thomas Rusche das unstillbare Drängen und Begehren, Unbesitzbares besitzen und das Greifbare im nicht greifbaren Inhalt eines Gemäldes erfassen zu wollen, und er erlebt nicht weniger das Gefühl persönlicher, nicht zu besänftigender Enttäuschung. Das Sammeln ist naturgemäß ein Akt kontinuierlichen Aufspürens, ein Verlangen nach einem erfüllten Innenleben persönlicher ästhetischer Vertiefung. In diesem Zusammenhang sind die schöpferischen Ästhetiken von Eros und Thanatos, als Ausdruck sowohl des Lebens im Tod als auch des Todes im Leben, unausweichlich. Begehren und Tod des Begehrens sind jedoch nicht als schlichtweg entgegengesetzte Kräfte zu verstehen, sondern lediglich als verschiedene Aspekte der menschlichen Identität – parallel ausgebildet wohnen sie uns ein. Als duale Grundbedingungen der Malerei und der conditio humana sind sie Teil und ermöglichen sie die zivilisierenden Prozesse des Lebens. Sie bedingen einander wie der Schatten und das Licht.[7] Die in dieser Edition reproduzierten Werke zielen gleichzeitig auf den Sinn für Entdeckung sowie auf Vermittlung und Assimilation ab. Sie reflektieren Thomas Rusches einzigartige persönliche und sich stets vertiefende Beziehung zur Malerei, die er mit seinen umfassenden Erwerbungen der letzten Jahre bewiesen hat.

Die fünfzig ausgewählten Arbeiten sind nur ein kleiner Teil von Thomas Rusches Sammlung zeitgenössischer Kunst. Sie wurden ausgesucht, weil sich an ihnen die genannten Affinitäten gut verdeutlichen lassen. Ein Merkmal postmoderner oder zeitgenössischer Malerei der letzten dreißig Jahre ist die Rückkehr zu Genrekategorien, die auch im Barock verwendet wurden. Die Genres der Landschafts- und Stillebenmalerei, aber auch Subgenres wie Vanitas-Darstellungen oder das Memento-mori-Motiv wurden zuerst von der Malerei des 17. Jahrhunderts hervorgebracht und kehrten nun zurück, und viele zeitgenössische Maler beschäftigen sich mit ihnen.[8] Darin zeigt sich nicht nur eine nietzscheanische Geisteshaltung, sondern auch, dass die Praxis der Malerei sich beständig selbst wieder zu beleben vermag.[9] Weit entfernt vom „Betrauern" oder dem Tod der Malerei, ist sie lebendig und zeigt heute eine enorme Vielfalt an Ausdrucksformen und Anwendungsweisen.[10] Mit dem Ungültigwerden der sogenannten „großen Erzählungen", der starren Ideen des historischen Determinismus und der oft von den Minimalisten behaupteten Endphase hat sich die Malerei ein neues Leben geschaffen, das sie nicht nur mit der Vergangenheit und den großen Traditionen der Malerei verbindet, sondern zudem ihre Praxis bereichert und weiterführt.

3

Zeitgenössische Kunst der SØR Rusche Sammlung wurde gemeinsam mit Rusches Werken barocker Meister gezeigt: Gera Landscapes: *Landschaft entdecken*; Anhaltische Gemäldegalerie Dessau *Still Lifes: Stilleben – Niederländische Kunst des 17. Jahrhunderts im Dialog mit zeitgenössischen Positionen der Sammlung SØR Rusche*; Schloss Corvey *Genre: Von Liebeslust und Lebenslast – das inszenierte Alltag*; Museum Abtei Liesborn *Portraits: Menschenbilder 1629–2009*; Anhaltische Gemäldegalerie Dessau *Portraits: Blickkontakte – Niederländische Portraits des 17. Jahrhunderts im Dialog mit Kunst der Gegenwart, Sammlung SØR Rusche*. In den letzten drei Jahren wurden mehr als 1200 Gemälde der SØR Rusche Sammlung an über zwanzig Museen verliehen.

4

„Was ist barock?", 3. Kapitel in Deleuze, Gilles: *Die Falte. Leibniz und der Barock*. Frankfurt am Main: Suhrkamp 2000. S. 49–67. Der Text widmet sich teilweise den verwandten ästhetischen Aspekten barocker und zeitgenössischer Malerei und Architektur. (Originalausgabe: Deleuze, Gilles: Le Pli. Leibniz et le Baroque. Paris: Les Editions de Minuit 1988).

5

Lyotard, Jean-François: Beantwortung der Frage: Was ist postmodern? In: *Wege aus der Postmoderne. Schlüsseltexte der Postmoderne-Diskussion*. Hrsg. von Wolfgang Welsch. Weinheim: VCH Acta Humanaria 1988. S. 193–203. „Ein Werk ist nur modern, wenn es zuvor postmodern war. So gesehen, bedeutet der Postmodernismus nicht das Ende des Modernismus, sondern dessen permanente Geburt." S. 201. (Originalausgabe: Lyotard, Jean-François: La Condition postmoderne: Rapport sur le savoir. Paris: Les Editions de Minuit 1979).

6

Es gibt viele moderne psychologische Theorien von Eros und Thanatos, aber sie alle hielten sich an den Definitionen, die Freud in seinen berühmten Aufsätzen „Die Widerstände gegen die Psychoanalyse" (1925) und „Jenseits des Lustprinzips" (1920) formulierte. Ursprünglich nutzte Freud nicht den Begriff „Eros" (er bevorzugte „Lebenstrieb"), stellte ihn jedoch mit „Libido" (libidinöse oder sexuelle Energie) gleich, jedoch nicht als als Geschlechtlichkeit im genitalen Sinn verstanden zu wissen, sondern als lebensschaffende Kraft im schöpferischen Sinn. Thanatos (der Todesinstinkt oder Todestrieb), ein Begriff, der in der Psychoanalyse zuerst von Freuds Anhänger Wilhelm Stekel geprägt wurde, taucht bei Freud als ungelöste, in sich gegensätzliche Neigung, die den Menschen denaturiert und ihn oft zu Wiederholungen und Nachstellungen traumatischer Ereignisse zwingt, deren Funktion es ist sicherzustellen, dass der Organismus seinem eigenen Weg des Todes folgen solle. In einem nicht-freudschen Sprachrahmen gebracht und die theistisch-philosophische Beschreibung nutzend, bei dies der menschliche Hang, über die Sterblichkeit und den letztendlichen Ausgang des menschlichen Lebens, den Tod, zu meditieren. In gewissem Sinne entwickelte Freud diese Idee (wie auch die Idee des Es) vom Werk des deutschen Philosophen des Pessimismus, Arthur Schopenhauer (1788–1860), und dessen Vorstellung vom „Willen zum Leben" und anderen menschlichen Neigungen zur „Verneinung d[ie]ses Willens". Siehe dazu: Schopenhauer, Arthur: Die Welt als Wille und Vorstellung (1918).

7

„Das Gemälde ändert seinen Status, die Dinge tauchen vor dem Hintergrund auf, die Farben entspringen dem gemeinsamen Grund [,fond'], der ihre dunkle Natur bezeugt, die Figuren definieren sich eher durch die Deckung als durch ihren Umriß. Das aber geschieht nicht im Gegensatz zum Licht, sondern im Gegenteil aufgrund der neuen Herrschaft des Lichts. Leibniz sagt in der *Confessio philosophi*: ‚Es gleitet nur ein Spalt in die Mitte der Finsternis.'" Deleuze, G.: Die Falte. S. 57.

8

Allgemeine Publikationen jüngeren Datums dazu sind: Buttner, Nils: *Landscape Painting. A History*. New York: Abbeville Press 2006; Meijer, Fred G.: *Dutch and Flemish Still-life Paintings*. Zwolle: Waanders 2005; Sander, Jochen: *Die Magie der Dinge. Stillebenmalerei 1500–1800*. Ostfildern: Hatje Cantz 2008.

9

Friedrich Nietzsches Theorie der ewigen Wiederkunft erschien zuerst in seinem Buch *Die fröhliche Wissenschaft* (1882) und wurde ausgiebig von Martin Heidegger analysiert. Siehe „Die ewige Wiederkunft des Gleichen" in: Heidegger, Martin: Nietzsche II. 7. Auflage. Stuttgart: Klett-Cotta 2008. S. 254–261.

10

Bois, Yve-Alain: Painting. The Task of Mourning. In: Ders.: *Painting as Model*. Cambridge, Mass.: The MIT Press (1990) 1993. S. 229–244. Der Bois' Aufsatz beigefügte Aphorismus stammt von Sherry Levine: „[Meine Gemälde] behandeln auf gewisse Art den Tod, den unbehaglichen Tod des Modernismus."

Pilgrim

ABCDEFGHIJKLMNOPQRSTUVWXYZ
abcdefghijklmnopqrstuvwxyz
1234567890 !@#?:;"*&

Foundry: Linotype
Designer: Eric Gill / Walter Tracy / Linotype Design Studio
Designer Nationality: British
Date: 1934 / 1953 / 2005

Pilgrim is an Old Style serif informed by Eric Gill's design for a book published for the Limited Editions Club in New York in 1934. Much like Gill's original face, Pilgrim combines the traditional shapes and contrasts of an Old Style serif with the incised strokes typical of monumental Roman lettering.

Plantin Headline

ABCDEFGHIJKLMNOPQRSTUVWXYZ
abcdefghijklmnopqrstuvwxyz
1234567890 !@#?:;"*&

Foundry: Monotype
Designer: Monotype Studio
Date: 1913

Plantin Headline is one of several designs based on the 16th-century specimens held in the Plantin-Moretus Museum in Antwerp. Intended for use at larger sizes, Plantin Headline maintains the shape of Old Style letterforms while adding contrast to the strokes and serifs.

Plantin Infant

ABCDEFGHIJKLMNOPQRSTUVWXYZ
abcdefghijklmnopqrstuvwxyz
1234567890 !@#?:;"*&

Foundry: Monotype
Designer: Monotype Studio
Date: 1913

Plantin Infant is an Old Style text face based on the 16th-century specimens held in the Plantin-Moretus Museum in Antwerp. Like other traditional serifs designed in the French tradition, it combines pronounced strokes with a lowered x-height, for legibility at small sizes.

Poliphilus

ABCDEFGHIJKLMNOPQRSTUVWXYZ
abcdefghijklmnopqrstuvwxyz
1234567890 !@#::;"*&

Foundry: Monotype
Designer: Francesco Griffo / Monotype Studio
Designer Nationality: Italian
Date: 2001

Poliphilus is an exact replica of a text face cut by Francesco Griffo and used in *Hypnerotomachia Poliphili* (*The Dream of Poliphilus*), a romantic tale published by Aldus Manutius in 1499. Monotype's design even replicates the ink spreads caused by its original printing on handmade paper.

Portrait

ABCDEFGHIJKLMNOPQRSTUVWXYZ
abcdefghijklmnopqrstuvwxyz
1234567890 !@#?:;"'*&

Foundry: Commercial Type
Designer: Berton Hasebe
Designer Nationality: American
Date: 2013

The distinctive Portrait typeface by New York-based type designer Berton Hasebe was inspired by the forms of French Renaissance types produced by designers such as Claude Garamond and Robert Granjon. It encompasses his love of types from the period and is a marriage of classical proportions but with an edge.

Portrait has a striking clean and aggressively sharp tone, employing pointed Latin serifs across the design. It started out as a display typeface and possesses nuanced details that are clearly visible when scaled up. However, it comes in four families—Portrait, Portrait Text, Portrait Condensed, and Portrait Inline—and thirty-five styles, so it can be employed in every scenario. Its hard, chiseled serifs and minimal yet confident appearance make it ideal for contemporary publications; it has been used in influential art, design, and fashion magazines such as Document Journal and Wallpaper*.

Hasebe was born in Hawaii and studied design and typography in Los Angeles and the Netherlands. When he was completing his master's on the Type and Media course at the Royal Academy of Art in The Hague, he designed the Alda typeface, which was released by Emigre in 2008. Hasebe went on to become an in-house type designer at Commercial Type (see p. 124) from 2008 to 2013, after which he left to form his own studio. Through Commercial Type he has also released Platform (2010) and Druk (2014).

Below. Example setting for Portrait—from left, regular, medium, and bold. Possessing many traits of type with classical proportions, Hasebe's design contemporizes these serif types of old with minimal, triangular sharp chiseled serifs for lighter and roman weights and with heavier woodcut type forms with the bold weights. Portrait's main inspiration comes from a design attributed to French punchcutter Maitre Constantin (c. 1530) for the printer Robert I. Estienne in Paris.

Cabin boys
BOUNCE
Macédoine

PORTRAIT REGULAR 100 PT

Dandelion
YAWNER
Porquerías

PORTRAIT MEDIUM 100 PT

Ultimates
X-RATED
Tabulator

PORTRAIT BOLD 100 PT

Łódź & Kęty
OBESITIES
Fired Games

PORTRAIT REGULAR ITALIC 100 PT

Tuscan Sun
EQUINOX
N'est-ce pas

PORTRAIT MEDIUM ITALIC 100 PT [SWASH: Q]

Affiliations
MÖGÖTT
Littérateur

PORTRAIT BOLD ITALIC 100 PT [LIGATURE: ffl]

Portrait Condensed

ABCDEFGHIJKLMNOPQRSTUVWXYZ
abcdefghijklmnopqrstuvwxyz
1234567890 !@#?:;"*&

Foundry: Commercial Type
Designer: Berton Hasabe
Designer Nationality: American
Date: 2013

Portrait Condensed is a narrow, Old Style serif, inspired by the Vendôme Condensed font family, designed by François Ganeau in 1952. Like Ganeau's design, Portrait Condensed takes its cues, such as the sharp, triangular serifs, from the type designs of the French Renaissance.

Portrait Text

ABCDEFGHIJKLMNOPQRSTUVWXYZ
abcdefghijklmnopqrstuvwxyz
1234567890 !@#?:;"*&

Foundry: Commercial Type
Designer: Berton Hasabe
Designer Nationality: American
Date: 2013

Portrait Text is a streamlined Old Style serif that first appeared in style-led magazines such as the *Document Journal* and *Wallpaper**. The characters are trim and articulate, and are reminiscent of the faces used by 16th-century French printer and scholar Robert I Estienne.

Raleigh

ABCDEFGHIJKLMNOPQRSTUVWXYZ
abcdefghijklmnopqrstuvwxyz
1234567890 !@#?:;"*&

Foundry: Linotype
Designer: Carl Dair / David Anderson / Adrian Williams / Robert Norton
Designer Nationality: Canadian / Canadian / British / British
Date: 1967 / 1978

An Old Style serif, Raleigh is based on the Cartier typeface designed by Carl Dair in 1967 for the Canadian Centennial and the Expo held in Montreal. It was renamed after Dair's death that year. The Raleigh font family includes Robert Norton's text version and Adrian Williams's three display weights.

Renner Antiqua

ABCDEFGHIJKLMNOPQRSTUVWXYZ
abcdefghijklmnopqrstuvwxyz
1234567890 !@#?:;"*&

Foundry: Linotype
Designer: Paul Renner / Patrick Strietzel
Designer Nationality: German
Date: 1939 / 2008

Renner Antiqua was initially designed by Paul Renner in 1939 and later updated by Patrick Strietzel in 2008. Strietzel's design was produced in both text and display sizes and maintains the distinctive features of the original, such as bowed serifs and heightened stroke contrasts.

Revival 555

ABCDEFGHIJKLMNOPQRSTUVWXYZ
abcdefghijklmnopqrstuvwxyz
1234567890 !@#?:;"*&

Foundry: Bitstream
Designer: Frank Hinman Pierpont
Designer Nationality: American
Date: 1951

A romantic revival of Old Style letterforms, supervised by Frank Hinman Pierpont and later published by Bitstream, Revival 555 is a font family in the style of 15th- and 18th-century faces. The design features low x-heights, long ascenders, and minimal stroke contrasts.

Rotation

ABCDEFGHIJKLMNOPQRSTUVWXYZ
abcdefghijklmnopqrstuvwxyz
1234567890 !@#?:;"*&

Foundry: Linotype
Designer: Arthur Ritzel
Designer Nationality: German
Date: 1971

Rotation is a serif font family designed for use on the rotation printing press; it was intended for newspapers and for setting at small point sizes. Unlike Ionic style font families, which dominated newsprint after the end of World War II, Rotation utilizes the more traditional qualities of Old Style letterforms.

Rustika

ABCDEFGHIJKLMNOPQRSTUVWXYZ
abcdefghijklmnopqrstuvwxyz
1234567890 !@#?:;"*&

Foundry: Linotype
Designer: Franko Luin
Designer Nationality: Swedish
Date: 1995

The Rustika font family is a traditional Old Style serif with a rough edge. It takes its name from the Esperanto spelling of "rustic" and was designed to emulate the process of shaping characters by chisel. The resulting jagged letterforms give Rustika a historical feel.

Simoncini Garamond

ABCDEFGHIJKLMNOPQRSTUVWXYZ
abcdefghijklmnopqrstuvwxyz
1234567890 !@#?:;"*&

Foundry: Ludwig & Mayer
Designer: Francesco Simoncini / Wilhelm Bilz
Designer Nationality: Italian / German
Date: 1961

This was created by Italian font designer Francesco Simoncini and the art director of German type foundry Ludwig & Mayer, Wilhelm Bilz. It is based on the Jean Jannon model, and is lighter and more delicate than other Garamonds. Variations are Garamond Simoncini and Italian Garamond.

Stempel Garamond

ABCDEFGHIJKLMNOPQRSTUVWXYZ
abcdefghijklmnopqrstuvwxyz
1234567890 !@#?:;"'*&

Foundry: Stempel
Designer: Claude Garamond / David Stempel
Designer Nationality: French / German
Date: 1592 / 1925

Based on the Egenolff-Berner specimen, produced in 1592, Stempel Garamond is a restoration of the original Garamond types. One of the most popular renditions of the style, Stempel Garamond distinguishes itself through its keen curves and sharp terminals.

Stempel Schneidler

ABCDEFGHIJKLMNOPQRSTUVWXYZ
abcdefghijklmnopqrstuvwxyz
1234567890 !@#¿:;"'*&

Foundry: Linotype
Designer: F. H. Ernst Schneidler / Linotype Design Studio
Designer Nationality: German
Date: 1936 / 1982

First designed by Friedrich Hermann Ernst Schneidler in 1936, and titled Schneidler Old Style, this font family is a humanist serif inspired by the Renaissance typefaces of Venice. The Stempel foundry in Frankfurt later reworked the design, before being acquired by Linotype.

Thesaurus

ABCDEFGHIJKLMNOPQRSTUVWXYZ
abcdefghijklmnopqrstuvwxyz
1234567890 !@#?:;"'*&

Foundry: Typotheque
Designer: Fermín Guerrero
Designer Nationality: Uruguayan
Date: 2017

Thesaurus is an Old Style serif but with a modern feel. It was inspired by the metal types that Robert Estienne took from Paris to Geneva in the 16th century. Unlike the original letterforms, Thesaurus features an extended x-height, a narrower width, and multiple weights.

Thorndale

ABCDEFGHIJKLMNOPQRSTUVWXYZ
abcdefghijklmnopqrstuvwxyz
1234567890 !@#?:;"'*&

Foundry: Monotype
Designer: Monotype Studio
Date: 1999

Thorndale is a traditional Old Style serif, manufactured for the digital age. Thorndale was designed primarily for web browsers, but its asymmetrical serifs, low-contrast strokes, and classical characters ensure optimal legibility across multiple digital platforms.

Tribute

ABCDEFGHIJKLMNOPQRSTUVWXYZ
abcdefghijklmnopqrstuvwxyz
1234567890 !@#?:;"*&

Foundry: Emigre
Designer: Frank Heine
Designer Nationality: American
Date: 2003

Inspired by a photocopied type specimen from 1565 featuring letters cut by the French punchcutter François Guyot, and echoing his idiosyncratic approach, Tribute is a contemporary interpretation that features a roman and an italic and an accompanying set of ornaments.

Truesdell

ABCDEFGHIJKLMNOPQRSTUVWXYZ
abcdefghijklmnopqrstuvwxyz
1234567890 !@#?:;"*&

Foundry: Monotype
Designer: Frederic Goudy / Steve Matteson
Designer Nationality: American
Date: 1930 / 1994

Originally drawn by Frederic W. Goudy in 1930, Truesdell was subsequently lost in the fire that destroyed Goudy's studio in 1939. Almost sixty years later, using the only surviving examples of the initial design, Steve Matteson revived the Old Style serif for digital use.

Trump Mediaeval

ABCDEFGHIJKLMNOPQRSTUVWXYZ
abcdefghijklmnopqrstuvwxyz
1234567890 !@#?:;"*&

Foundry: Weber
Designer: Georg Trump
Designer Nationality: German
Date: 1954

Trump Mediaeval is a reworking of the traditional Old Style font family. It was designed for use with mid 20th-century technology, such as fax machines, so the letterforms utilize angled strokes and joints alongside sliced serifs and brackets to remain legible in low-resolution outputs.

Trump Mediaeval Office

ABCDEFGHIJKLMNOPQRSTUVWXYZ
abcdefghijklmnopqrstuvwxyz
1234567890 !@#?:;"*&

Foundry: Linotype
Designer: Georg Trump / Akira Kobayashi
Designer Nationality: German / Japanese
Date: 1954 / 2006

Trump Mediaeval Office is Linotype's revival of Trump Mediaeval for use in the 21st-century office. Reworking Georg Trump's original, Akira Kobayashi adds a variety of features to adapt the face to updated technology, such as the synchronization of character shapes across weights.

Van Dijck

ABCDEFGHIJKLMNOPQRSTUVWXYZ
abcdefghijklmnopqrstuvwxyz
1234567890 !@#?:;"★*&

Foundry: Monotype
Designer: Christoffel van Dijck /
Jan van Krimpen
Designer Nationality: Dutch
Date: *c.* 1600s / 1935

Van Dijck is Jan van Krimpen's revision of an Old Style serif attributed to 17th-century typefounder Christoffel van Dijck. Despite persisting doubts over the initial specimen's true author, the font family exhibits all the characteristics of Dutch type design in the 1600s.

Vendetta

ABCDEFGHIJKLMNOPQRSTUVWXYZ
abcdefghijklmnopqrstuvwxyz
1234567890 !@ #?:;"*&

Foundry: Emigre
Designer: John Downer
Designer Nationality: American
Date: 1999

Vendetta is a homage to the roman types of 15th-century punchcutters, who were themselves influenced by the work of Nicholas Jenson, and displays a very distinctive blend of old and new. The typeface comes in four weights from Light to Volume, and two matching italics.

Vendome

ABCDEFGHIJKLMNOPQRSTUVWXYZ
abcdefghijklmnopqrstuvwxyz
1234567890 !@#?:;"*&

Foundry: Olive
Designer: François Ganeau
Designer Nationality: French
Date: 1952

Vendome is an Old Style serif and the single result of French artist and sculptor François Ganeau's foray into the field of type design. The characters are calligraphic in their strokes and irregular in shape, with decorative features found in both the upper- and lowercase families.

Venetian 301

ABCDEFGHIJKLMNOPQRSTUVWXYZ
abcdefghijklmnopqrstuvwxyz
1234567890 !@#?:;"*&

Foundry: Bitstream
Designer: Bruce Rogers / Dmitry
Kirsanov
Designer Nationality: American /
Russian
Date: 1914 / 2006

Venetian 301 is Bitstream's digital version of Bruce Rogers's font family, Centaur (1914). Dmitry Kirsanov's design maintains the distinguishing features of the initial design, such as the arching strokes and gradual brackets, but favors smooth curves over the original angular shapes.

Whitenights

ABCDEFGHIJKLMNOPQRSTUVWXYZ
abcdefghijklmnopqrstuvwxyz
1234567890 !@#?:;""*&

Foundry: Linotype
Designer: Lars Bergquist
Designer Nationality: Swedish
Date: 2002

Whitenights is a versatile serif with variants that include Titling for headlines, Math for mathematical glyphs and a series of supplementary ligatures in all weights. Its characters are moderate in contrast and maintain a standard x-height for legibility in continuous text.

Wile

ABCDEFGHIJKLMNOPQRSTUVWXYZ
abcdefghijklmnopqrstuvwxyz
1234567890 !@#?:;"*&

Foundry: Monotype
Designer: Cynthia Hollandsworth Batty
Designer Nationality: American
Date: 1998

Wile is an Old Style serif, designed as a gift to the Agfa Compugraphic executive Don Wile upon his retirement. Its characters exhibit the influence of inscriptional letterforms, as seen in the wedged serifs, and are designed to work in both text and display sizes.

Wilke

ABCDEFGHIJKLMNOPQRSTUVWXYZ
abcdefghijklmnopqrstuvwxyz
1234567890 !@#?:;"*&

Foundry: Linotype
Designer: Martin Wilke
Designer Nationality: German
Date: 1988

Wilke is an energetic serif font family influenced by the styles of Irish handwriting found in the *Book of Kells*, a 9th-century illuminated manuscript. The strokes are somewhat typical of an Old Style face, but the serifs and terminals, especially in the numerals, express the idiosyncrasy of penmanship.

William Text

ABCDEFGHIJKLMNOPQRSTUVWXYZ
abcdefghijklmnopqrstuvwxyz
1234567890 !@#?:;"*&

Foundry: Typotheque
Designer: Maria Doreuli
Designer Nationality: Russian
Date: 2016

William Text is an elegant serif inspired by the legacy of English typefounder William Caslon. As with Caslon's 16th-century designs, William Text has a large x-height and is intended primarily for book text. The standard characters are accompanied by 200 refined ornaments.

Apollo

ABCDEFGHIJKLMNOPQRSTUVWXYZ
abcdefghijklmnopqrstuvwxyz
1234567890 !@#?:;''*&

Foundry: Monotype
Designer: Adrian Frutiger
Designer Nationality: Swiss
Date: 1964

Apollo is one of the lesser known fonts by Adrian Frutiger (see p. 290). He designed it to print accurately on smooth paper stocks. One of the first fonts created for Monotype's new phototypesetting machine, the robust design has a small x-height, open counters, bracketed serifs, and a primarily oblique axis.

(see p. 290)

Austin News Deck

ABCDEFGHIJKLMNOPQRSTUVWXYZ
abcdefghijklmnopqrstuvwxyz
1234567890 !@#?:;"*&

Foundry: Commercial Type
Designer: Paul Barnes
Designer Nationality: British
Date: 2016

Austin News Deck is a flexible transitional serif. It was conceived to work as an intermediate between the delicacy of the original Austin, designed by British graphic designer and typographer Paul Barnes for *Harper's Bazaar* fashion magazine in 2014, and the full body of Austin Text.

Austin News Headline

ABCDEFGHIJKLMNOPQRSTUVWXYZ
abcdefghijklmnopqrstuvwxyz
1234567890 !@#?:;"*&

Foundry: Commercial Type
Designer: Paul Barnes
Designer Nationality: British
Date: 2016

Making its debut in Jon Hill's redesign of the *Daily Telegraph* in 2015, Austin News Headline is a transitional serif suited to the demands of news media. It is an update of Austin, its increased x-height and shorter ascenders and descenders improving both readability and spatial economy.

Austin News Headline Condensed

ABCDEFGHIJKLMNOPQRSTUVWXYZ
abcdefghijklmnopqrstuvwxyz
1234567890 !@#?:;"*&

Foundry: Commercial Type
Designer: Paul Barnes
Designer Nationality: British
Date: 2016

Like its Austin News siblings, Austin News Headline Condensed was designed to meet the spatial requirements of 21st-century news media. Building on the economic forms of Austin News Headline, this font is a true condensed serif and includes a family of eight distinct weights.

Austin Text

ABCDEFGHIJKLMNOPQRSTUVWXYZ
abcdefghijklmnopqrstuvwxyz
1234567890 !@#?:;"*&

Designed specifically for use at smaller sizes, Austin Text is a robust transitional serif informed by the original types of 18th-century English punchcutter Richard Austin. The letterforms are each proportionally balanced to suit easy reading in long runs of dense text.

Foundry: Commercial Type
Designer: Paul Barnes
Designer Nationality: British
Date: 2014

Baskerville Classico

ABCDEFGHIJKLMNOPQRSTUVWXYZ
abcdefghijklmnopqrstuvwxyz
1234567890 !@#?:;"*&

John Baskerville was a highly influential 18th-century writer, stonecutter, and printer, known internationally for his innovative ideas and fastidious approach to his craft. One of numerous versions of Baskerville's classic serif, this cut was created by the Swedish type designer Franko Luin.

Foundry: Omnibus
Designer: John Baskerville / Franko Luin
Designer Nationality: British / Swedish
Date: 1724 / 1995

Baskerville LT

ABCDEFGHIJKLMNOPQRSTUVWXYZ
abcdefghijklmnopqrstuvwxyz
1234567890 !@#?:;"*&

George W. Jones, the master printer and typeface designer, was hired by the British branch of Mergenthaler to develop a series of typefaces for its hot-metal typesetting machines. He created this faithful revival of Baskerville's dignified serif in partnership with Linotype draughtsman Harry Smith.

Foundry: Mergenthaler Linotype
Designer: John Baskerville / George W. Jones
Designer Nationality: British
Date: 1724 / 1923

Baskerville No 2

ABCDEFGHIJKLMNOPQRSTUVWXYZ
abcdefghijklmnopqrstuvwxyz
1234567890 !@#?:;"*&

Bitstream's version of Baskerville was digitized following Monotype's version of 1924, which was created from proofs of John Baskerville's Great Primer (16 point) rather than the metal. There are many versions of Baskerville, which was the first transitional (between old-face and modern) type.

Foundry: Monotype / Bitstream
Designer: John Baskerville
Designer Nationality: British
Date: 1724 / 1924 / 1980

Jeremy Tankard Typography

British type designer Jeremy Tankard started his career after his studies at London's Central St Martins and then the Royal College of Art. He worked in corporate graphic design, advising and creating typography for many well-known international brands. Tankard established his own studio in 1998 to concentrate on his designs and since then has gone on to create an enviable portfolio of award-winning typefaces and a worldwide reputation for the outstanding quality and innovative designs of his types. They include the highly lauded Bliss (see p. 255), Enigma, Shire Types (see p. 483), and Hawkland (see p. 162).

Tankard has produced typographic solutions for commercial clients and design / advertising studios for several decades (such as Corbel for Microsoft and Blue Island for Adobe), and the typefaces he has created are highly flexible and adaptable to changes in technology and usage. The studio offers a diverse range of styles for nearly every application, providing both excellence and functionality, whether for a pre-established font or a bespoke commission typeface or logotype.

Founded: 1998
Country: UK
Website: typography.net
Notable typefaces:
Bliss (see p. 255)
Hawkland (see p. 162)
Shire Types (see p. 483)

Below left. De Worde typeface specimen designed by Alistair Hall at We Made This.

Below. Fenland specimen page.

Opposite. Promotional fold-out poster highlighting a selection of varying typefaces on offer.

Fenland a 14 font typeface

JEREMY TANKARD
– REDISTURBED REGULAR –

HAS
– TRILOGY EGYPTIAN HEAVY WIDE –

A FRESH NEW
– BLISS HEAVY –

SITE
– TRILOGY FATFACE REGULAR –

THAT'S QUITE WONDERFULLY EASY TO USE
– KINGFISHER ITALIC –

AND REPLETE WITH MANY
– ALCHEMY –

MARVELLOUS
– DE WORDE EXTRA BOLD –

TYPEFACES
– CAPLINE REGULAR –

Bell

ABCDEFGHIJKLMNOPQRSTUVWXYZ
abcdefghijklmnopqrstuvwxyz
1234567890 !@#?:;"*&

Richard Austin cut Bell in 1788 for John Bell, who used it in his newspaper *The Oracle*, and Monotype typographer Stanley Morison considered it to be the first English modern face. In 1931, Monotype cut a new version for hot metal based on original designs, with updates added over the years.

Foundry: British Letter / Monotype
Designer: Richard Austin / Monotype Studio
Designer Nationality: British
Date: 1788 / 1931

Berling Nova

ABCDEFGHIJKLMNOPQRSTUVWXYZ
abcdefghijklmnopqrstuvwxyz
1234567890 !@#?:;"*&

This redesign of Swedish designer Karl-Erik Forsberg's classic was created using much of his original source material from Linotype and is available in two weights. It has an increased x-height and bigger, more curved serifs, as well as the addition of small caps and Old Style figures.

Foundry: Verbum
Designer: Karl-Erik Forsberg / Örjan Nordling
Designer Nationality: Swedish
Date: 1951 / 2004

Berndal

ABCDEFGHIJKLMNOPQRSTUVWXYZ
abcdefghijklmnopqrstuvwxyz
1234567890 !@#?:;"*&

A refined serif from Sweden's master typographer, Berndal has large x-heights, open counters and short ascenders. Legible at small sizes, its letterforms are relatively wide, but consistent in width. There is a contrast in the thickness of the strokes, and a subtle calligraphic influence.

Foundry: Linotype
Designer: Bo Berndal
Designer Nationality: Swedish
Date: 2003

Birka

ABCDEFGHIJKLMNOPQRSTUVWXYZ
abcdefghijklmnopqrstuvwxyz
1234567890 !@#?:;"*&

Birka is named after the ancient Viking town near Stockholm. It is the first typeface that Franko Luin designed from scratch and he said it taught him everything he knows about type design. Inspired by the classic forms of Garamond, this polished serif has been described as "unmistakably Swedish."

Foundry: Omnibus
Designer: Franko Luin
Designer Nationality: Swedish
Date: 1992

Bohemia

ABCDEFGHIJKLMNOPQRSTUVWXYZ
abcdefghijklmnopqrstuvwxyz
1234567890 !@#?:,"'*&

Foundry: Linotype
Designer: Eduardo Manso
Designer Nationality: Spanish
Date: 2004

Bohemia was influenced by the refined design of transitional typefaces, such as Baskerville, but its more curvy letterforms give it a distinctive appearance. In 2003, it won first prize in the text category of Linotype's International Digital Type Design Contest.

Bruce Old Style

ABCDEFGHIJKLMNOPQRSTUVWXYZ
abcdefghijklmnopqrstuvwxyz
1234567890 !@#?:,"*&

Foundry: Monotype / Bitstream
Designer: Sol Hess
Designer Nationality: American
Date: 1909 / c. 1980s

This was originally Bruce Foundry's Old Style No. 20 (1869), which was based on Miller & Richard's Old Style (1858). Sol Hess recut the typeface at Lanston Monotype in 1909, and this was digitized by Bitstream. It is used as the complementary typeface in the Sears mail-order catalogue.

Bulmer

ABCDEFGHIJKLMNOPQRSTUVWXYZ
abcdefghijklmnopqrstuvwxyz
1234567890 !@#?:,"*&

Foundry: ATF / Monotype
Designer: Morris Fuller Benton / Robin Nicholas
Designer Nationality: American / British
Date: 1792 / 1995

A late transitional face heavily influenced by Baskerville, Bulmer has a greater contrast, along with sharper serifs and a distinctive curved-tailed uppercase "R." It was revived in the early 20th century by Morris Fuller Benton at American Type Founders, and then by Robin Nicholas at Monotype.

Burgess

ABCDEFGHIJKLMNOPQRSTUVWXYZ
abcdefghijklmnopqrstuvwxyz
1234567890 !@#?:,""*&

Foundry: Colophon
Designer: The Entente
Designer Nationality: British
Date: 2014

This subjective reinterpretation of mid-century cuts by Photostat (an early projection photocopier) of Times New Roman Bold and Bold Italic is named after William Starling Burgess. Some historians credit him, rather than Lardent and Morison, with the original design of Times New Roman in 1904.

Byington

ABCDEFGHIJKLMNOPQRSTUVWXYZ
abcdefghijklmnopqrstuvwxyz
1234567890 !@#?:;"*&

Foundry: Typodermic
Designer: Ray Larabie
Designer Nationality: Canadian
Date: 2005

Byington was inspired by the carvings on Trajan's Column in Rome and shares their classical lines, but its serifs are bolder and its curves more defined, making it ideal for low-resolution applications. Its lowercase letterforms are influenced by Sabon and Garamond, but retain the uppercase's elegant lines.

Carniola

ABCDEFGHIJKLMNOPQRSTUVWXYZ
abcdefghijklmnopqrstuvwxyz
1234567890 !@#?:;" *&

Foundry: Omnibus
Designer: Franko Luin
Designer Nationality: Swedish
Date: 1993

Swedish designer Franko Luin has described Carniola as "a pastiche of different type designs from the beginning of the 20th century, mostly American." In a reference to Luin's Slovene origins, the typeface takes its name from a historical region that comprised parts of present-day Slovenia.

CG Adroit

ABCDEFGHIJKLMNOPQRSTUVWXYZ
abcdefghijklmnopqrstuvwxyz
1234567890 !@#?:;" *&

Foundry: TypeSpectra
Designer: Phil Martin
Designer Nationality: American
Date: 1981

With its a distinctive lowercase "g," diagonal stress and strong contrast between thick and thin strokes, Adroit is available in six weights, from Light to Extra Bold. Its designer Phil Martin spent many years designing cartoons, before setting up the foundry TypeSpectra in Dallas, Texas in 1974.

Charter BT

ABCDEFGHIJKLMNOPQRSTUVWXYZ
abcdefghijklmnopqrstuvwxyz
1234567890 !@#?:;"*&

Foundry: Bitstream
Designer: Matthew Carter
Designer Nationality: British
Date: 1987

Charter is an economical serif with squared-off serifs and moderate curves and diagonals. It was created to deal with the limitations of low-resolution printers in the late 1980s. A new version, Charter Pro, was released in 2004 and was later added to Apple's OSX operating system.

Compatil Exquisit

ABCDEFGHIJKLMNOPQRSTUVWXYZ
abcdefghijklmnopqrstuvwxyz
1234567890 !@#?:;"'*&

Foundry: Linotype
Designer: Olaf Leu
Designer Nationality: German
Date: 2001

Compatil Exquisit is a refined serif forming part of the Compatil type system, created specifically for use in annual reports. This system comprises four compatible typefaces each with four weights, making it possible to set any combination of different styles effortlessly.

Compatil Text

ABCDEFGHIJKLMNOPQRSTUVWXYZ
abcdefghijklmnopqrstuvwxyz
1234567890 !@#?:;"'*&

Foundry: Linotype
Designer: Olaf Leu
Designer Nationality: German
Date: 2001

An authoritative serif, Compatil Text is designed for setting large blocks of text. It comes in four styles and supports ninety-three different languages. As it has identical letter spacing within individual heights, it can easily be combined with any of the other typefaces in the Compatil type superfamily.

Corona

ABCDEFGHIJKLMNOPQRSTUVWXYZ
abcdefghijklmnopqrstuvwxyz
1234567890 !@#?:;"'*&

Foundry: Mergenthaler Linotype
Designer: Chauncey H. Griffith
Designer Nationality: American
Date: 1941

With its narrow widths and large x-height giving a strong, modern feel, Corona forms part of Chauncey H. Griffith's Legibility Group, which contained typefaces especially suited to printing on newsprint. He commenced work on the series of typefaces in 1922, with Ionic No. 5 being the first face.

Dante

ABCDEFGHIJKLMNOPQRSTUVWXYZ
abcdefghijklmnopqrstuvwxyz
1234567890 !@#?:;"'*&

Foundry: Monotype
Designer: Giovanni Mardersteig / Charles Malin
Designer Nationality: German / French
Date: c. 1950s / 1991

Dante is one of Giovanni Mardersteig's most frequently used typefaces. It is a classic book face designed with an italic to work harmoniously with the roman. The face is named after the first book in which it was used, a biography of Dante, published by Mardersteig's private press Officina Bodoni in 1955.

Dante eText

ABCDEFGHIJKLMNOPQRSTUVWXYZ
abcdefghijklmnopqrstuvwxyz
1234567890 !@#?:;”★&

Foundry: Monotype
Designer: Giovanni Mardersteig / Ron Carpenter
Designer Nationality: German / British
Date: c. 1950s / 1993

One of a number of digitized versions of the original serif by German publisher and typographer Giovanni Mardersteig, this version was revised by Ron Carpenter for Monotype. It comprises three weights with titling capitals and was designed to be especially effective for screen use.

Diotima Classic

ABCDEFGHIJKLMNOPQRSTUVWXYZ
abcdefghijklmnopqrstuvwxyz
1234567890 !@#?:;”*&

Foundry: Linotype
Designer: Gudrun Zapf von Hesse / Akira Kobayashi
Designer Nationality: German / Japanese
Date: 1948 / 2008

Diotima Classic is a four-weight cut of the original single-weight design created in 1948. It includes a heavy weight added by Gudrun Zapf von Hesse, as well as a light, regular, and italic. With more robust serifs and thicker hairlines, the regular weight is ideal for text sizes.

Dutch 801

ABCDEFGHIJKLMNOPQRSTUVWXYZ
abcdefghijklmnopqrstuvwxyz
1234567890 !@#?:;”*&

Foundry: Bitstream
Designer: Stanley Morison / Victor Lardent
Designer Nationality: British
Date: 1931 / c. 1980s

Bitstream's Dutch 801 is one of many variants of Times New Roman, the typeface created by Stanley Morison for *The Times* newspaper. It was in use for forty years from 1931, though the newspaper had exclusive rights for just one year before it was released for general use.

Dutch 809

ABCDEFGHIJKLMNOPQRSTUVWXYZ
abcdefghijklmnopqrstuvwxyz
1234567890 !@#?:;”*&

Foundry: Bitstream
Designer: Günter Gerhard Lange
Designer Nationality: German
Date: 1969 / 1990

Dutch 809 is Bitstream's version of Concorde, the face created by Berthold art director Günter Gerhard Lange in 1969 as opposed to the typeface of the same name created by Adrian Frutiger (see p. 290). It is a highly legible typeface that is particularly well-suited for use in large areas of text.

Dutch 811

ABCDEFGHIJKLMNOPQRSTUVWXYZ
abcdefghijklmnopqrstuvwxyz
1234567890 !@#?:;"*&

Foundry: Bitstream
Designer: Matthew Carter
Designer Nationality: British
Date: 1970 / c. 1980s

This confident serif is Bitstream's version of the Olympian typeface created in 1970 by Matthew Carter (see p. 616). It was one of the next generation of newspaper fonts, combining old-face, transitional, and modern forms, and was later customized by Carter & Cone Type for *The Philadelphia Inquirer*.

Dutch 823

ABCDEFGHIJKLMNOPQRSTUVWXYZ
abcdefghijklmnopqrstuvwxyz
1234567890 !@#?:;"*&

Foundry: Bitstream
Designer: Francesco Simoncini
Designer Nationality: Italian
Date: 1958 / c. 1980s

Bitstream's version of Francesco Simoncini's Aster typeface, which he designed in 1958 for his Bologna-based Simoncini foundry and line-caster manufacturer. This typeface has delicate detailed serifs and was originally intended to be employed in books and newspapers.

Emona

ABCDEFGHIJKLMNOPQRSTUVWXYZ
abcdefghijklmnopqrstuvwxyz
1234567890 !@#?:;"*&

Foundry: Omnibus
Designer: Franko Luin
Designer Nationality: Swedish
Date: 1992

Franko Luin was born to Slovenian parents in Trieste in 1941 and immigrated to Sweden in 1961. He created more than fifty fonts during his career, working on original designs and digital revivals. Emona is a Luin original built on a superelliptical skeleton. Its letterforms share some similarities with Bodoni.

Esperanto

ABCDEFGHIJKLMNOPQRSTUVWXYZ
abcdefghijklmnopqrstuvwxyz
1234567890 !@#?:;"*&

Foundry: Omnibus
Designer: Franko Luin
Designer Nationality: Swedish
Date: 1992

Esperanto's design was inspired by the letterforms found in Renaissance manuscripts. It was named after an auxiliary language developed in the late 1800s to foster global peace and understanding; ironically, the Esperanto character set is not compatible with its namesake language.

Foundry Form Serif

ABCDEFGHIJKLMNOPQRSTUVWXYZ
abcdefghijklmnopqrstuvwxyz
1234567890 !@#?:;"*&

Designed concurrently with Foundry Form Sans, this open, legible typeface with a pronounced horizontal emphasis upholds the reputation of The Foundry (see p. 284) for well-formed fonts. Offering a comprehensive character set, it also includes a genuine italic, small caps, and Old Style figures.

Foundry: The Foundry
Designer: Freda Sack / David Quay
Designer Nationality: British
Date: 1999

FS Sally

ABCDEFGHIJKLMNOPQRSTUVWXYZ
abcdefghijklmnopqrstuvwxyz
1234567890 !@#?:;"*&

Fontsmith (see p. 272) expanded the versatile and elegant FS Sally family in 2016 to include support for Cyrillic and Greek alphabets, reflecting an increasing global demand for multilingual fonts. Available in five weights with corresponding italics, it boasts an exhaustive character set.

Foundry: Fontsmith
Designer: Phil Garnham / Jason Smith
Designer Nationality: British
Date: 2009

Garth Graphic

ABCDEFGHIJKLMNOPQRSTUVWXYZ
abcdefghijklmnopqrstuvwxyz
1234567890 !@#?:;"*&

Garth Graphic was developed from a single surviving proof of Matt Antique, a serif created during the 1960s by John Matt for use with the American Type Founders phototypesetter. This revival of Matt's design was named for Compugraphic founder William W. Garth Jr.

Foundry: Compugraphic
Designer: John Matt / Constance Blanchard / Renee LeWinter
Designer Nationality: American
Date: c. 1960s / 1979

Gazette

ABCDEFGHIJKLMNOPQRSTUVWXYZ
abcdefghijklmnopqrstuvwxyz
1234567890 !@#?:;"*&

As its name implies, Gazette was created for newspaper text, with compact proportions designed to retain legibility. The font was originally published by Intertype in 1954 as Imperial; details of its reissue as Gazette are the subject of debate within the typographic community.

Foundry: Intertype / Linotype
Designer: Edwin W. Shaar
Designer Nationality: American
Date: 1954 / 1977

Granjon

ABCDEFGHIJKLMNOPQRSTUVWXYZ
abcdefghijklmnopqrstuvwxyz
1234567890 !@#?:;"*&

Foundry: Linotype
Designer: George W. Jones
Designer Nationality: British
Date: 1928

Based on a cut of Garamond from 1592, this interpretation of the French Renaissance style was well-received following its release. To avoid confusion with other Garamond revivals it was named for Robert Granjon, whose italic designs were often paired with Garamond's original romans.

GT Alpina

ABCDEFGHIJKLMNOPQRSTUVWXYZ
abcdefghijklmnopqrstuvwxyz
1234567890 !@#?:;"*&

Foundry: Grilli Type
Designer: Reto Moser
Designer Nationality: Swiss
Date: 2019

GT Alpina is a large workhorse serif family designed by Swiss designer Reto Moser of Grilli Type (see p. 238) and Studio RM. It is a typeface that pushes the boundaries but never sacrifices function for form: its letters are robust and finely crafted, yet show a healthy disregard for convention.

Hawkhurst

ABCDEFGHIJKLMNOPQRSTUVWXYZ
abcdefghijklmnopqrstuvwxyz
1234567890 !@#?:;"*&

Foundry: Linotype
Designer: Richard Yeend
Designer Nationality: British
Date: 2002

Alongside his successful career in the editorial field as a designer, art director, and cartoonist, Richard Yeend was also an accomplished type designer, creating numerous fonts for both Monotype and Linotype. Hawkhurst, released in 2002, is expressive and transitional in style.

Imperial

ABCDEFGHIJKLMNOPQRSTUVWXYZ
abcdefghijklmnopqrstuvwxyz
1234567890 !@#?:;"*&

Foundry: Intertype
Designer: Edwin W. Shaar
Designer Nationality: American
Date: 1954

US type designer Edwin W. Shaar designed this compact, newspaper-friendly font for Intertype; it was created to compete with Linotype's legibility group of typefaces, which were also designed for editorial use. Imperial has been used within *The New York Times* since 1967.

Hawkland

ABCDEFGHIJKLMNOPQRSTUVWXYZ
abcdefghijklmnopqrstuvwxyz
1234567890 !@#?:;"*&

Foundry: Jeremy Tankard Typography
Designer: Jeremy Tankard
Designer Nationality: British
Date: 2018

Hawkland is the result of British type designer Jeremy Tankard's aim to create a transitional typeface with an unbracketed serif. Tankard was inspired by type styles from the late 18th century, and Hawkland owes more to type models drawn along mechanical lines using a ruler and compass than the calligraphic structure that lies at the heart of Old Style typefaces. At the end of the 17th century, French type engraver Philippe Grandjean cut a new type for the Imprimerie Royale printing works. Compared to Old Style, it had a vertical axis in the rounded letters and the serifs were sharper and flatter. Termed *roman du roi*, it is the forerunner of modern letters. This approach underlined Hawkland's development, and its serifs are much sharper and unbracketed compared to existing transitional types and owe more to those of a modern design.

The development work for Hawkland began in 2012 after Tankard completed his Fenland sans serif typeface and initially explored ideas for a serif based on Fenland. However, because of other commitments, the design of Hawkland was a stop-start process until 2017, when Tankard recommenced work on it toward completion.

The Hawkland family comes in six weights in roman and italic styles. It is suitable within a variety of contexts from editorial design to packaging and brand styling. Tankard also developed Hawkland Fine for larger display use. Hawkland Fine comes in a greater range of weights, and its thinner weights in particular evoke an engraved appearance.

Below. Jeremy Tankard's sketchbook below provides insight into the thought processes and experimentation— even at the initial stages—in establishing the design principles behind a new typeface.

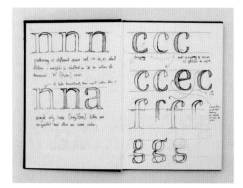

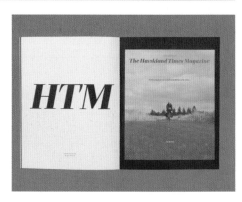

Isolde

ABCDEFGHIJKLMNOPQRSTUVWXYZ
abcdefghijklmnopqrstuvwxyz
1234567890 !@#?:;"*&

The wide letterforms, exaggerated serifs and heavily slanted italics of this Caslon-influenced typeface are well-suited for headline and display use. Designer Franko Luin named the font after the story of Tristan and Isolde, and created its specimen in the form of a fairy tale.

Foundry: Omnibus
Designer: Franko Luin
Designer Nationality: Swedish
Date: 1993

ITC Leawood

ABCDEFGHIJKLMNOPQRSTUVWXYZ
abcdefghijklmnopqrstuvwxyz
1234567890 !@#?:;"*&

Leslie Usherwood's designs for this characterful serif were completed by the team at Typsettra, his Toronto-based phototypesetting company, following his death in 1983. Its confident strokes, distinct serifs, and generous x-height aid legibility when close character spacing is required.

Foundry: ITC
Designer: Leslie Usherwood
Designer Nationality: Canadian
Date: 1985

ITC Slimbach

ABCDEFGHIJKLMNOPQRSTUVWXYZ
abcdefghijklmnopqrstuvwxyz
1234567890 !@#?:;"*&

Robert Slimbach designed this serif typeface for ITC on a freelance basis during the mid 1980s. It displays the influence of his training in calligraphy. Slimbach joined Adobe during the year of its release, and went on to be instrumental in the development of the company's digital typefaces.

Foundry: ITC
Designer: Robert Slimbach
Designer Nationality: American
Date: 1987

ITC Zapf International

ABCDEFGHIJKLMNOPQRSTUVWXYZ
abcdefghijklmnopqrstuvwxyz
1234567890 !@#?:;"*&

Zapf International is named after its designer, the leading German typographer Hermann Zapf (see p. 574). He designed the typeface for ITC in 1976 after a ten-year type design hiatus. Various flourishes indicate his calligraphic background, such as the long tail of the "Q" and the open bowl of the "g."

Foundry: ITC
Designer: Hermann Zapf
Designer Nationality: German
Date: 1976

ITC New Baskerville

ABCDEFGHIJKLMNOPQRSTUVWXYZ
abcdefghijklmnopqrstuvwxyz
1234567890 !@#?:;"*&

Foundry: ITC
Designer: John Baskerville /
John Quaranda
Designer Nationality: British /
American
Date: 1762 / 1982

This revival of one of the world's most widely used typefaces was created in 1978 by US type designer John Quaranda and arguably remains one of the most popular of all the Baskerville designs. The original Baskerville was created in the 18th century by English printer, stonecutter, writer, and type designer John Baskerville. This classic was then punchcut by his assistant, John Handy.

When John Baskerville designed this typeface, his ambition was to improve on the letterforms created by his contemporary, the English typefounder William Caslon. Baskerville brought in a more refined, elegant cut to the serifs, increased contrast and introduced thinner stroke weights. He also employed a more consistent design across the characters, which helped to increase legibility and recognition.

John Baskerville was also known as a perfectionist and his experimentation as a printer in all aspects of the printing process caused long delays to his own work. He invested his energies in all aspects of the printing process; from how the paper was made, the ink mixtures, the construction of the printing presses and the type itself. Consequently, although he set up his printing company in 1750, he did not produce his first book until 1757. However, his contribution to the creation of type foundries and printing in England is immeasurable. Although his endeavours were not so well-received at home, his work was greatly admired by his contemporaries in Europe and North America.

In its earliest incarnation, Baskerville was released in roman and italic. ITC New Baskerville comes in four weights with matching italics.

Right/opposite. Thirty-six-page promotional booklet for specifying ITC foundry's ITC New Baskerville, printed 1982.

abcdefghijklmnopqrstuv
ABCDEFGHIJKLMNOP
30

abcdefghijklmnopqr
ABCDEFGHIJKLNP
36

abcdefghijklmn
ABCDEFGHIK
48

abcdefghijkn
ABCDEFGH
60

abcdehikn
ABCDEHI
72

abcdeh
ABCDI
1" on Caps

Above display sizes, 30 pt to 1" are based on cap heights and are not necessarily in direct relation to text heights.

abcdefghijklmnopqrstuvwxyz
ABCDEFGHIJKLMNOPQRSTUVWXYZ
1234567890&1234567890$$¢f£%@
ÇŁØÆŒßçłøäëâèéfi˘ˇ˜˚
(.:,.!?·-—""''/#*)[†‡§»«1234567890]aeilmorst

COMPLETE ITC DISPLAY ALPHABET

26
good
reasons
to use
ITC
New
Baskerville™
Roman

6

7

Jante Antiqua

ABCDEFGHIJKLMNOPQRSTUVWXYZ
abcdefghijklmnopqrstuvwxyz
1234567890 !@#?:;"*&

Foundry: ITC
Designer: Poul Søgren
Designer Nationality: Danish
Date: 1992

Danish type and graphic designer Poul Søgren studied in Copenhagen before going to Paris to study under French type designer José Mendoza y Almeida at the Imprimerie Nationale. Søgren designed Jante Antiqua with newspaper usage in mind, and its ample x-height makes it ideal for body text.

Kalix

ABCDEFGHIJKLMNOPQRSTUVWXYZ
abcdefghijklmnopqrstuvwxyz
1234567890 !@#?:;"*&

Foundry: Linotype
Designer: Franko Luin
Designer Nationality: Swedish
Date: 1994

Designer Franko Luin named Kalix after a town in northern Sweden. He suggested that it be used "mainly for books and magazines." The typeface is a transitional serif, with many reference points. It comes in three weights—Roman, Semi Bold, and Bold—with italics and small caps.

Kis

ABCDEFGHIJKLMNOPQRSTUVWXYZ
abcdefghijklmnopqrstuvwxyz
1234567890 !@#?:;"*&

Foundry: Bitstream
Designer: Miklós Tótfalusi Kis
Designer Nationality: Hungarian
Date: 1685 / 1985

Kis is Bitstream's digital revival of Miklós Tótfalusi Kis's Old Style serif Janson. Kis was a Hungarian printer working in Amsterdam during the late 17th century and was revealed as the originator of the font, rather than the Dutch punchcutter Anton Janson, thanks to the work of type scholars in 1954.

Kis Classico

ABCDEFGHIJKLMNOPQRSTUVWXYZ
abcdefghijklmnopqrstuvwxyz
1234567890 !@#?:;"*&

Foundry: Omnibus
Designer: Franko Luin
Designer Nationality: Swedish
Date: 1993

Kis Classico is the work of Swedish type designer Franko Luin at his own studio, Omnibus, and comes in five weights. The typeface is named after a Hungarian monk called Miklós Kis, who traveled to Amsterdam toward the end of the 17th century to discover the art of printing.

Lapidary 333

ABCDEFGHIJKLMNOPQRSTUVWXYZ
abcdefghijklmnopqrstuvwxyz
1234567890 !@#?:;"*&

Foundry: Bitstream
Designer: Eric Gill
Designer Nationality: British
Date: 1929–32 / c. 1980s

Lapidary 333 is Bitstream's release of Eric Gill's Perpetua and comes in five styles. In 1925, Monotype's Stanley Morison commissioned Gill to make a roman for use in books; it was released commercially in 1932. Its small, angled serifs were inspired by Gill's background in stone carving.

Laurentian

ABCDEFGHIJKLMNOPQRSTUVWXYZ
abcdefghijklmnopqrstuvwxyz
1234567890 !@#?:;"*&

Foundry: Monotype
Designer: Rod McDonald
Designer Nationality: Canadian
Date: 2001

Canadian designer Rod McDonald created Laurentian as a commission for *Maclean's* magazine, which wanted a new masthead and a neutral, custom type family. Usage in tight columns meant the face needed to be slightly narrow, while economical printing meant contrast had to be modest.

Lector FSL

ABCDEFGHIJKLMNOPQRSTUVWXYZ
abcdefghijklmnopqrstuvwxyz
1234567890 !@#?:;"*&

Foundry: Forgotten Shapes
Designer: Gert Wunderlich / Reymund Schröder
Designer Nationality: German
Date: 1963 / 2018

Lector FSL is a revision and extension of Lector, a font initially designed by Gert Wunderlich for the Typoart foundry in the 1960s. The typeface is a collaboration between Wunderlich and his former student Reymund Schröder, and retains the character of a sharp, transitional serif.

Levato

ABCDEFGHIJKLMNOPQRSTUVWXYZ
abcdefghijklmnopqrstuvwxyz
1234567890 !@#?:;"*&

Foundry: Monotype
Designer: Felix Bonge
Designer Nationality: German
Date: 2011

Levato is German designer Felix Bonge's debut font and grew out of his studies at Hamburg University of Applied Sciences, taking inspiration from Renaissance Antiqua typefaces. It comes in five weights with a cursive italic, many ligatures, and swatch options for some letters.

Life

ABCDEFGHIJKLMNOPQRSTUVWXYZ
abcdefghijklmnopqrstuvwxyz
1234567890 !@#?:;"*&

Life's co-designer Francesco Simoncini grew up with type as his father Vincenzo ran a repair shop for typesetting machines. After World War II, they worked on matrices for Linotype and Intertype systems. Life is a newsprint font mainly inspired by Times, which mixes elements of many serif forms.

Foundry: Ludwig & Mayer
Designer: Wilhelm Bilz / Francesco Simoncini
Designer Nationality: German / Italian
Date: 1965

Linotype Centennial

ABCDEFGHIJKLMNOPQRSTUVWXYZ
abcdefghijklmnopqrstuvwxyz
1234567890 !@#?:;"*&

Adrian Frutiger (see p. 290) created Centennial to honour Linotype's 100th anniversary. It was inspired by Linn Boyd Benton and Morris Fuller Benton's Century, released by American Type Founders in the late 19th century. Frutiger deviated considerably from Century, enhancing it for a modern audience.

Foundry: Linotype
Designer: Adrian Frutiger
Designer Nationality: Swiss
Date: 1986

Linotype Really

ABCDEFGHIJKLMNOPQRSTUVWXYZ
abcdefghijklmnopqrstuvwxyz
1234567890 !@#?:;"*&

Really, by American designer Gary Munch, is available in six weights with italics and small caps. It functions well as a clean, legible text face, blending details from Caslon, Baskerville, and Bodoni. Munch later updated it as Really No. 2 with more weights and language support.

Foundry: Linotype
Designer: Gary Munch
Designer Nationality: American
Date: 1999

Marion

ABCDEFGHIJKLMNOPQRSTUVWXYZ
abcdefghijklmnopqrstuvwxyz
1234567890 !@#?:;"*&

Ray Larabie is a Canadian font designer who lives in Nagoya, Japan. He describes his Marion typeface family as an "unambiguous transitional serif typeface with an 18th-century flair." It comes in regular and bold with italics, ligatures, and the occasional flamboyant swash option.

Foundry: Typodermic
Designer: Ray Larabie
Designer Nationality: Canadian
Date: 2006

Maxime

ABCDEFGHIJKLMNOPQRSTUVWXYZ
abcdefghijklmnopqrstuvwxyz
1234567890 !@#?:;"*&

Foundry: Monotype
Designer: Éric de Berranger
Designer Nationality: French
Date: 1999

French designer Éric de Berranger has created fonts for Monotype, ITC, Agfa, Linotype, T-26, and 2Rebels. His Maxime design is a highly legible serif available in regular and bold with italics. The family also contains Maxime Ornaments, which consists of twenty-six custom typographic ornaments.

Mentor

ABCDEFGHIJKLMNOPQRSTUVWXYZ
abcdefghijklmnopqrstuvwxyz
1234567890 !@#?:;"*&

Foundry: Monotype
Designer: Michael Harvey /Andy Benedek
Designer Nationality: British
Date: 2004

According to Michael Harvey, three designers influenced the development of his Mentor serif: Eric Gill, Hermann Zapf (see p. 574), and Harvey's former boss, Reynolds Stone. Harvey and Andy Benedek designed type for Monotype before starting their own foundry, Fine Fonts, in 2000.

Monotype Baskerville

ABCDEFGHIJKLMNOPQRSTUVWXYZ
abcdefghijklmnopqrstuvwxyz
1234567890 !@#?:;"*&

Foundry: Monotype
Designer: John Baskerville / Monotype Studio
Designer Nationality: British
Date: 1754 / 1923

The Monotype Baskerville font family is a transitional serif created by the Monotype Studio in 1923, based on the original by John Baskerville in the mid 18th century. It is a popular choice for text in books and magazines, having a higher contrast and sharper serifs than Caslon.

Monotype Janson

ABCDEFGHIJKLMNOPQRSTUVWXYZ
abcdefghijklmnopqrstuvwxyz
1234567890 !@#?:;"*&

Foundry: Monotype
Designer: Miklós Tótfalusi Kis / Robin Nicholas / Patricia Saunders
Designer Nationality: Hungarian / British / British
Date: 1685 / c. 1930s

Monotype's cut of Miklós Tótfalusi Kis's Old Style serif Janson comes in regular and bold, with italics. Its legibility and even color make it perfect for text use in publications. An earlier Monotype version created in the 1930s was slightly less condensed and named Ehrhardt, after the foundry in Leipzig.

Monotype Sabon

ABCDEFGHIJKLMNOPQRSTUVWXYZ
abcdefghijklmnopqrstuvwxyz
1234567890 !@#?:;"'*&

Foundry: Monotype
Designer: Jan Tschichold
Designer Nationality: German
Date: 1967

German graphic designer, type designer, and typographer Jan Tschichold was an advocate of modernist design and inspired by the principles of the Bauhaus. Sabon came about from a joint commission in the early 1960s by three German foundries—Monotype, Linotype, and Stempel—to create a unifying design that would provide consistency in printing across the metal type technology of the day, either through mechanical composition or set by hand.

Released in 1967, the design of Sabon is loosely based on a 14-point Garamond Roman sample sheet printed in 1592 by Konrad Berner, a German printer based in Frankfurt. Berner married the widow of Jaques Sabon, a French typefounder, who brought some Garamond matrices to Frankfurt. The story is the inspiration behind Sabon's name as well as its appearance.

Although inspired by Old Style principles to letterforms, there is a reduced level of calligraphic construction and the characters are more balanced with rounded forms, resulting in a design with a moderate contrast in its stroke weights. This aids printing and reading in poor conditions. Another innovative feature, one of many in the design, was that the differing weights of roman, italic, and bold would occupy the same width, thus reducing the time required to do calculations for working out text extents. In addition, the typeface was fractionally narrower, meaning more characters could be set on line, reducing paper and ink costs.

Sabon is a truly classic typeface that is flexible, legible, and resilient with an elegant presentation, and it works as well for editorial tasks as for display settings.

Left. To achieve differentiation for their record releases, which are set entirely with Sabon (bold, italic, and regular), Sacred Bones Records use a template system, employing varying color and illustration styles. The independent record label is based in Brooklyn, New York.

Mrs Eaves

ABCDEFGHIJKLMNOPQRSTUVWXYZ
abcdefghijklmnopqrstuvwxyz
1234567890 !@#?:;"*&

Foundry: Emigre
Designer: Zuzana Licko
Designer Nationality: Slovakian
Date: 1996

Mrs Eaves is a revival of Baskerville by Zuzana Licko, the co-founder of the type foundry Emigre (see p. 106). In the best traditions of transitional serif typeface design, it appears traditional and elegant but offers a contemporary take on the past.

The softer appearance and yet heavier weight of Mrs Eaves when compared to other transitional designs is intentional. It reflects Licko's desire to give the impression it has been formed using lead type so that texts set on paper appear as if printed with letterpress. This distinguishes it from types with the crispness typical of modern reproduction.

Mrs Eaves is named after Sarah Eaves, who was housekeeper and then mistress to the 18th-century English printer and type designer John Baskerville. The pair married after her estranged husband died. Mrs Eaves's character and charm are further enhanced by its notable ligatures. There are 213 ligatures in all, which range from the standard to the ornate, with a number of elegant swash designs featured. As well as the standard ligatures, Mrs Eaves also contains the 18th-century variations of "ct" and "st."

In 2009, several variations were launched. Mrs Eaves XL features a larger x-height that makes it more suitable for body text. Mr Eaves and Mr Eaves XL are sans serif humanist variants that echo the designs of Gill Sans and Johnston.

Below. This ever-popular design is not only one of Emigre's most popular typefaces but is also one of the best-selling serif types from the last two decades, thanks to its elegant aesthetic and its flexibility, being ideal for both titling and text usages.

FABLE LIII. **The Trumpeter.**
— [SET IN MRS EAVES XL NARROW] —

A Trumpeter in a certain army happened to be taken prisoner.
HE WAS ORDERED *immediately* TO EXECUTION
but pleaded **excuse** for
HIMSELF,
that it was *unjust*
a person should suffer *death*, who, far from an intention
of mischief, *did not even wear* an offensive weapon.
So much the rather,
replied one of the enemy
SHALT THOU DIE;
since without any design of *fighting thyself*,
THOU EXCITEST OTHERS TO THE
bloody business:
for he that is the *abettor* of a
BAD ACTION
IS AT LEAST EQUALLY WITH HIM THAT
commit it.

FABLE LII. **The Mock-bird.**
— [SET IN MRS EAVES XL] —

There is a certain bird
in the West-Indies,
WHICH HAS THE *faculty* OF
MIMICKING THE NOTES
of *every* other songster,
without being able himself to add *any* original strains to the concert.
As one of these Mock-birds was displaying
HIS TALENTS *of* RIDICULE
among the branches of a *venerable wood*:
'Tis very well,
SAID A LITTLE WARBLER,
speaking in the name of all the rest,
we grant you that our music
is *not* without its faults:
but why will you not favour us
with a strain of
YOUR OWN?

Monticello

ABCDEFGHIJKLMNOPQRSTUVWXYZ
abcdefghijklmnopqrstuvwxyz
1234567890 !@#?:;"*&

Foundry: Linotype
Designer: Chauncey H. Griffith / Matthew Carter
Designer Nationality: American / British
Date: 1946 / 2002

Chauncey H. Griffith based Monticello on James Ronaldsons' Roman No. 1 (c. 1796) and American Type Founders' Oxford (1892). He created it as a historically apt face for Princeton University Press' publication of *The Papers of Thomas Jefferson.* Matthew Carter (see p. 616) refined the family for Linotype in 2002.

New Aster

ABCDEFGHIJKLMNOPQRSTUVWXYZ
abcdefghijklmnopqrstuvwxyz
1234567890 !@#?:;"*&

Foundry: Linotype
Designer: Francesco Simoncini / Linotype Design Studio
Designer Nationality: Italian
Date: 1958

Aster was first designed in 1958 by Italian designer Francesco Simoncini for newspaper and book text; thus it has a large x-height, fine serifs, and short ascenders and descenders. New Aster, available in four weights with italics, was the result of improvements made by Linotype.

News Plantin

ABCDEFGHIJKLMNOPQRSTUVWXYZ
abcdefghijklmnopqrstuvwxyz
1234567890 !@#?:;"*&

Foundry: Monotype
Designer: Frank Hinman Pierpont
Designer Nationality: American
Date: 1979

Designed by Monotype for use by the British newspaper *The Observer,* News Plantin is slightly more condensed, and therefore efficient, than the standard Plantin typeface. Plantin was named after an Antwerp printer, and created by Frank Hinman Pierpont based on fonts from the 16th century.

Nicolas Cochin

ABCDEFGHIJKLMNOPQRSTUVWXYZ
abcdefghijklmnopqrstuvwxyz
1234567890 !@#?:;"*&

Foundry: Deberny & Peignot
Designer: Charles Malin / Georges Peignot
Designer Nationality: French
Date: 1912

Named after the 18th-century French artist, writer, and critic Charles-Nicolas Cochin, whose engraved lettering provided inspiration to Georges Peignot, this typeface cut by Charles Malin for Deberny & Peignot in 1912 is a distinct serif with wide capitals and very tall, slender ascenders.

Octavian

ABCDEFGHIJKLMNOPQRSTUVWXYZ
abcdefghijklmnopqrstuvwxyz
1234567890 !@#?:;"'*&

Foundry: Monotype
Designer: Will Carter / David Kindersley
Designer Nationality: British
Date: 1961

Will Carter and David Kindersley designed Octavian for Monotype in 1961. They were inspired by the letterforms of classical inscriptions cut in stone; however, they reduced the width of letters and added weight to make it more economical in print. The typeface is available in one weight with an italic.

Old Style 7

ABCDEFGHIJKLMNOPQRSTUVWXYZ
abcdefghijklmnopqrstuvwxyz
1234567890 !@#?:;"'*&

Foundry: Miller & Richard
Designer: Alexander Phemister
Designer Nationality: Scottish
Date: 1860

Alexander Phemister cut Old Style 7 at the Scottish foundry Miller & Richard. It was one of the first of the much-imitated "modernized old face" types, which updated the forms of Caslon for the needs of the mid-19th-century printing industry, removing details considered to be old-fashioned.

Olympian

ABCDEFGHIJKLMNOPQRSTUVWXYZ
abcdefghijklmnopqrstuvwxyz
1234567890 !@#?:;"'*&

Foundry: Linotype
Designer: Matthew Carter
Designer Nationality: British
Date: 1970

British typographer Matthew Carter (see p. 616) designed Olympian for economical newspaper text use in 1970. It has a large x-height and is suited to being set in narrow columns. Available in roman and bold with italics, Olympian is believed to be the first copyrighted typeface in the United States.

Omnibus

ABCDEFGHIJKLMNOPQRSTUVWXYZ
abcdefghijklmnopqrstuvwxyz
1234567890 !@#?:;"'*&

Foundry: Omnibus
Designer: Franko Luin
Designer Nationality: Swedish
Date: 1993

Franko Luin was inspired by Baskerville when designing Omnibus, which shares its name with his type foundry, but decided to aim for a darker color. A legible serif text face, it is available in roman, semibold, and bold, all with italics, plus a single weight of small capitals.

Oranda

ABCDEFGHIJKLMNOPQRSTUVWXYZ
abcdefghijklmnopqrstuvwxyz
1234567890 !@#?:;"*&

Foundry: Bitstream
Designer: Gerard Unger
Designer Nationality: Dutch
Date: 1992

Dutch printer manufacturer Océ commissioned Dutch typographer Gerard Unger to design Oranda as a custom project in 1986. The typeface is named after the Japanese word for "Holland." Unger said he "had a look at typewriter fonts and came up with a subtler and more modern variant."

Paperback

ABCDEFGHIJKLMNOPQRSTUVWXYZ
abcdefghijklmnopqrstuvwxyz
1234567890 !@#?:;"*&

Foundry: House Industries
Designer: John Downer
Designer Nationality: American
Date: 2005

Paperback is a transitional font family intended for both headline and text purposes. Unlike most serif designs, which develop characters for use at a single scale, Paperback has features that are designed to shift with its size, enabling the letterforms to adapt to their context.

Parkinson Electra

ABCDEFGHIJKLMNOPQRSTUVWXYZ
abcdefghijklmnopqrstuvwxyz
1234567890 !@#?:;"*&

Foundry: Linotype
Designer: William A. Dwiggins / Jim Parkinson
Designer Nationality: American
Date: c. 1930s / 2010

In 2010, Jim Parkinson undertook a remodeling and digitization of the 1930s serif text face Electra to bring it into the modern age. Parkinson, who reworked Electra before for the *San Francisco Chronicle* in the 1990s, looked to William A. Dwiggins's original drafts for inspiration.

Perrywood

ABCDEFGHIJKLMNOPQRSTUVWXYZ
abcdefghijklmnopqrstuvwxyz
1234567890 !@#?:;"*&

Foundry: Monotype
Designer: Johannes Birkenbach
Designer Nationality: German
Date: 1993

German designer Johannes Birkenbach, who worked at Monotype in the UK from 1988 to 1993, took inspiration from Bembo and Plantin when designing Perrywood, a legible text face with an even color. A family of thirty fonts, Perrywood includes three versions in five weights with italics.

Perpetua

ABCDEFGHIJKLMNOPQRSTUVWXYZ
abcdefghijklmnopqrstuvwxyz
1234567890 !@#?:;"*&

Foundry: Monotype
Designer: Eric Gill
Designer Nationality: British
Date: 1929–32

This serif classic by English sculptor and type designer Eric Gill is as popular today as it was upon release. Monotype's Stanley Morison commissioned Gill in 1925, but the design process was a struggle and not without setbacks. Not only did Morison have to contend with his management's dislike for his new ideas and proposals, he also had to deal with Gill's dislike for the mechanical arts. Yet Gill had recently become involved in making books, and fonts were an essential part of that process, so he agreed to take on the project. He based Perpetua on old engravings, and using his sculpting skills patterned it after epigraphic, rather than calligraphic, letters.

However, despite progressing with the serif design, Gill was reassigned to a more pressing matter, the design of Gill Sans, which put Perpetua

on hold. Perpetua was first set in a limited edition of a new edition of *The Passion of Perpetua and Felicity* (c. 203) in 1929. When finally ready for release in 1930, further issues gathered apace. Perpetua was to be released with an accompanying italic called Felicity, a sloped roman, rather than a cursive italic. Despite Morison favoring the sloped approach, the Monotype management disliked the italic intensely, and with no italic, there was no release. So Gill returned to the drawing board and the completed family was finally launched in 1932. Perpetua is the culmination of a lengthy, drawn-out process, but it is a timeless design that has become Gill's most popular and enduring typeface.

Below. Designed by John Overton, then production manager at Penguin Books, these original Penguin Classic covers employ Eric Gill's Perpetua for titling. The series was redesigned after seven titles by Jan Tschichold in 1947.

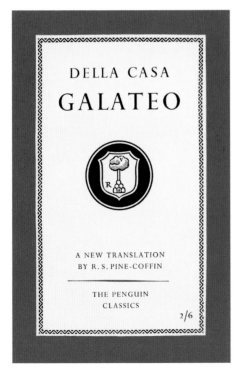

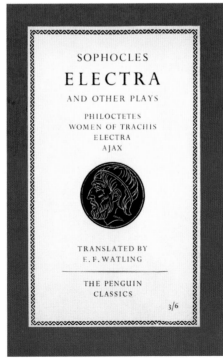

Photina

ABCDEFGHIJKLMNOPQRSTUVWXYZ
abcdefghijklmnopqrstuvwxyz
1234567890 !@#?:;"*&

Foundry: Monotype
Designer: José Mendoza y Almeida
Designer Nationality: French
Date: 1971

Photina was only the third serif produced by Monotype specifically for phototypesetting systems. Its sharp serifs and robust frame indicate the new forms made possible by phototypesetting technology. The face's high typographic quality made it popular for magazine and book text.

Rabenau

ABCDEFGHIJKLMNOPQRSTUVWXYZ
abcdefghijklmnopqrstuvwxyz
1234567890 !@#?:;"*&

Foundry: Linotype
Designer: Alex Bertram / Andreas Frohloff
Designer Nationality: German
Date: 2011

Rabenau is the result of more than a decade of research and experimentation by its co-creators, the German type designers Alex Bertram and Andreas Frohloff. The typeface mixes high-contrast strokes with smoothly curved serifs in each of its sixteen weights.

Really No. 2

ABCDEFGHIJKLMNOPQRSTUVWXYZ
abcdefghijklmnopqrstuvwxyz
1234567890 !@#?:;"*&

Foundry: Linotype
Designer: Gary Munch
Designer Nationality: American
Date: 1999 / 2008

Really No. 2 is an update of the Really serif Gary Munch designed for Linotype in 1999. It offers an expanded seven weights alongside extended language capabilities. Much like the initial design, Really No. 2 balances impact in the bold weights with clarity in the lighter versions.

Res Publica

ABCDEFGHIJKLMNOPQRSTUVWXYZ
abcdefghijklmnopqrstuvwxyz
1234567890 !@#?:;"*&

Foundry: Linotype
Designer: Franko Luin
Designer Nationality: Swedish
Date: 1992

Res Publica is a serif designed in the transitional style. Its name means "public matters" in Latin, from which is also derived the word "republic." The font's title is an indication of its purpose: to provide clarity in text-heavy documents, such as official reports, magazines, and school books.

Romana

ABCDEFGHIJKLMNOPQRSTUVWXYZ
abcdefghijklmnopqrstuvwxyz
1234567890 !@#?:,"*&

Romana is Bitstream's digitization of a popular 19th-century transitional serif face of the same name. The narrow and nimble frame of the lighter weights makes Romana legible at smaller sizes, while its compact design in the heavier styles increases its impact at display sizes.

Foundry: Bitstream
Designer: Theophile Beaudoire / Gustav F. Schroeder
Designer Nationality: French / German
Date: 1892 / c. 1990s

Sabon eText

ABCDEFGHIJKLMNOPQRSTUVWXYZ
abcdefghijklmnopqrstuvwxyz
1234567890 !@#?:,"*&

Designed specifically for the screens of e-readers, mobile phones and computers, Sabon eText is a conversion of Jan Tschichold's original design of 1967. Sabon eText contains several adjustments, to counters, line thickness, and x-height, to optimize the face for smaller sizes.

Foundry: Linotype
Designer: Jan Tschichold / Linotype Design Studio
Designer Nationality: German
Date: 1967 / 2013

Sabon Next

ABCDEFGHIJKLMNOPQRSTUVWXYZ
abcdefghijklmnopqrstuvwxyz
1234567890 !@#?:,"*&

Sabon Next is Jean François Porchez's revival of Jan Tschichold's Sabon, itself based on a Claude Garamond typeface. Working from both Tschichold's design and Garamond's original specimens, Porchez designed four extra weights and a series of alternate characters and ornaments.

Foundry: Linotype
Designer: Jan Tschichold / Jean François Porchez
Designer Nationality: German / French
Date: 1967 / 2002

Selune

ABCDEFGHIJKLMNOPQRSTUVWXYZ
abcdefghijklmnopqrstuvwxyz
1234567890 !@#?:,"*&

Selune is a transitional serif by French designer Jean Lochu of Studio Hollenstein in Paris. Lochu, whose early passion for calligraphy reveals itself in the refined strokes and bowls, designed the font in four weights, from Pale to Sombre, alongside a set of typographic accessories.

Foundry: Monotype
Designer: Jean Lochu
Designer Nationality: French
Date: 1999

Spectrum MT

ABCDEFGHIJKLMNOPQRSTUVWXYZ
abcdefghijklmnopqrstuvwxyz
1234567890 !@#?:;"*&

Foundry: Enschedé Foundry / Monotype
Designer: Jan Van Krimpen / Monotype Studio
Designer Nationality: Dutch / British
Date: 1952–1955

Dutch typographer, book designer, and type designer Jan van Krimpen created his Spectrum typeface in the early 1950s for a Bible project for the Spectrum publishing house in Utrech while he was employed by the Koninklijke Joh. Enschedé type foundry and printer in Haarlem. However, the book project was canceled.

Fortunately, Van Krimpen had a relationship with Monotype in England, which released many of his designs outside the Netherlands. The company was so enamored by the design's refinement, elegance, and balance, it acquired the typeface, completing it for release in 1955. The process of getting it published was a fractious one, with many letters passing between Van Krimpen and Monotype's Stanley Morison over disagreements in the design process. Spectrum's enlarged x-height and calligraphic nature make for a precise and incisive tone. It possesses some similar forms to Eric Gill's Perpetua: both share distinctive Old Style figures and numerals, and each is very legible across all ranges of size.

Van Krimpen was also a leading book designer with an international reputation, designing titles in the Netherlands and for the Limited Editions Club of New York. Spectrum's crisp and precise nature made it ideal as a book typeface although it was rarely used in contemporary publishing.

Swift

ABCDEFGHIJKLMNOPQRSTUVWXYZ
abcdefghijklmnopqrstuvwxyz
1234567890 !@#?:;"*&

Foundry: Linotype
Designer: Gerard Unger
Designer Nationality: Dutch
Date: 1984–89

Dutch typeface designer and professor of typography Gerard Unger developed Swift between 1984 and 1989. His design brief was to create a modern digital type for newspapers that could maintain legibility and consistency on ever higher speed printing presses yet on low-quality paper.

Swift's appearance with its sturdy stems, low-contrast strokes, enlarged serifs, tall x-height, and open counters, all contribute toward increasing legibility for what has become a contemporary classic. Ever popular among graphic designers, its versatility has meant its usage has stretched far beyond that of the newspaper industry: it is often seen employed in corporate identities, editorial, and publishing applications.

Right. *Typografische Monatsblätter* (*Swiss Typographic Monthly Magazine*) No. 4 created in 1987 by Swiss type designer and lecturer Max Caflisch.

Tempera Biblio

ABCDEFGHIJKLMNOPQRSTUVWXYZ
abcdefghijklmnopqrstuvwxyz
1234567890 !@#?:;"*G

Foundry: Typotheque
Designer: Nikola Djurek
Designer Nationality: Croatian
Date: 2006

Tempera Biblio is a transitional book face designed for continuous text. The font family features calligraphic features and low contrast, and comprises three weights, each maintaining a standard width, which allows the text to facilitate a variety of styles without altering its length.

Times Eighteen

ABCDEFGHIJKLMNOPQRSTUVWXYZ
abcdefghijklmnopqrstuvwxyz
1234567890 !@#?:;"*&

Foundry: Linotype
Designer: Stanley Morison / Victor Lardent / Walter Tracy
Designer Nationality: British
Date: 1931 / 1972

Times Eighteen is a transitional serif, designed specifically for headline type. Unlike the Times New Roman variation, this design is ideally suited to sizes of 18 point and above and features slightly condensed letterforms and finer hairline strokes for a bolder character.

Times Europa

ABCDEFGHIJKLMNOPQRSTUVWXYZ
abcdefghijklmnopqrstuvwxyz
1234567890 !@#?:;"*&

Foundry: Linotype
Designer: Stanley Morison / Victor Lardent / Walter Tracy
Designer Nationality: British
Date: 1931 /1972

Walter Tracy's Times Europa is a sweeping update of Stanley Morison's Times New Roman (1931). The muscular forms and wide counters of Tracy's design preserve legibility while adapting to the faster printing presses and lower-quality paper of the 1970s newspaper industry.

Times Europa Office

ABCDEFGHIJKLMNOPQRSTUVWXYZ
abcdefghijklmnopqrstuvwxyz
1234567890 !@#?:;"*&

Foundry: Linotype
Designer: Stanley Morison / Victor Lardent / Walter Tracy / Akira Kobayashi
Designer Nationality: British / Japanese
Date: 1931 /1972 / 2006

Times Europa Office is a revision of Times Europa to optimize Walter Tracy's design for office use. Akira Kobayashi, Linotype's type director, removed several irregularities, which were initially included to smooth the text in print, and redrew them to suit the clarity of digital displays.

Times New Roman

ABCDEFGHIJKLMNOPQRSTUVWXYZ
abcdefghijklmnopqrstuvwxyz
1234567890 !@#?:;"'*&

Foundry: Monotype
Designer: Stanley Morison / Victor Lardent
Designer Nationality: British
Date: 1931

Times New Roman was created in 1931 by Monotype typographic consultant Stanley Morison and *The Times* newspaper lettering artist Victor Lardent. Their historic font was first used by the British newspaper on 3 October 1932, and was made available to purchase in 1933.

By 1929, Morison was typographic advisor not only to Monotype but also to *The Times*. In 1931, he criticized the newspaper for the poor quality of its printing, and so the publication commissioned him to create a typeface to replace the existing outdated 19th-century face. The new typeface needed to be clearer, larger, and heavier on the page without taking up more space.

Morison and Lardent's design starting point was another of Monotype's existing serifs, Plantin, but Perpetua and Baskerville were also considered. For more than two years, Morison as art director and Lardent as designer labored to achieve their goal. The new typeface was incredibly successful and was used for forty years.

Although the newspaper no longer uses this particular version of Times New Roman, with many updates and revisions having been created over the years due to changes in production techniques, digital technologies, and format changes, the typeface's popularity has endured. It is still widely used in book and general printing while also being Monotype's biggest selling metal type of all time.

Today, Times New Roman is available on all computer operating systems as standard. However, it is still available to purchase with a wider range of styles and optical sizes offered for differing and more precise print applications.

Right. Monotype's Stanley Morison and Victor Lardent present their brand new Times New Roman typeface in the 3rd October, 1932 edition of *The Times*.

fact:

JANUARY–FEBRUARY 1964   VOLUME ONE, ISSUE ONE – $1.25

Bertrand Russell considers *Time* magazine to be "scurrilous and utterly shameless in its willingness to distort." **Ralph Ingersoll:** "In ethics, integrity, and responsibility, *Time* is a monumental failure." **Irwin Shaw:** *Time* is "nastier than any other magazine of the day." **Sloan Wilson:** "Any enemy of *Time* is a friend of mine." **Igor Stravinsky:** "Every music column I have read in *Time* has been distorted and inaccurate." **Tallulah Bankhead:** "Dirt is too clean a word for *Time*." **Mary McCarthy:** "*Time*'s falsifications are numerous." **Dwight Macdonald:** "The degree of credence one gives to *Time* is inverse to one's degree of knowledge of the situation being reported on." **David Merrick:** "There is not a single word of truth in *Time*." **P. G. Wodehouse:** "*Time* is about the most inaccurate magazine in existence." **Rockwell Kent:** *Time* "is inclined to value smartness above truth." **Eugene Burdick:** *Time* employs "dishonest tactics." **Conrad Aiken:** "*Time* slants its news." **Howard Fast:** *Time* provides "distortions and inaccuracies by the bushel." **James Gould Cozzens:** "My knowledge of inaccuracies in *Time* is first-hand." **Walter Winchell:** "*Time*'s inaccuracies are a staple of my column." **John Osborne:** "*Time* is a vicious, dehumanizing institution." **Eric Bentley:** "More pervasive than *Time*'s outright errors is its misuse of truth." **Vincent Price:** "Fortunately, most people read *Time* for laughs and not for facts." **H. Allen Smith:** "*Time*'s inaccuracies are as numerous as the sands of the Sahara." **Taylor Caldwell:** "I could write a whole book about *Time* inaccuracies." **Sen. John McClellan:** "*Time* is prejudiced and unfair."

fact:

VOLUME ONE, ISSUE FIVE $1.25

1,189 Psychiatrists Say Goldwater Is Psychologically Unfit To Be President!

fact:

VOLUME ONE, ISSUE FOUR $1.25

"Bobby Kennedy is the most vicious, evil ___ ___ ___ ___ in American politics today," says lawyer Melvin Belli.

fact:

VOLUME ONE, ISSUE THREE $1.25

American Cars Are Death Traps
This issue reveals which car makes are the most dangerous of all

Times Ten

ABCDEFGHIJKLMNOPQRSTUVWXYZ
abcdefghijklmnopqrstuvwxyz
1234567890 !@#?:;"*&

Foundry: Linotype
Designer: Stanley Morison
Designer Nationality: British
Date: 1931

Times Ten is a transitional serif and a member of the Times font family, which Stanley Morison designed explicitly for typography of twelve point and below. To retain character and legibility at such sizes, Times Ten features a wider build and additional muscle in the strokes.

Transitional 511

ABCDEFGHIJKLMNOPQRSTUVWXYZ
abcdefghijklmnopqrstuvwxyz
1234567890 !@#?:;"*&

Foundry: Bitstream
Designer: William A. Dwiggins
Designer Nationality: American
Date: 1938 / c. 1980s

Transitional 511 is Bitstream's digitization of William A. Dwiggins's transitional serif Caledonia from the 1930s. While most of the details were faithfully translated, such as the contrast of the joints and the calligraphic cross strokes, Transitional 511 has distinctly shorter descenders.

Transitional 521

ABCDEFGHIJKLMNOPQRSTUVWXYZ
abcdefghijklmnopqrstuvwxyz
1234567890 !@#?:;"*&

Foundry: Bitstream
Designer: William A. Dwiggins
Designer Nationality: American
Date: 1935 / c. 1980s

Transitional 521 is Bitstream's digitized version of William A. Dwiggins's 1930s serif, Electra, which became a standard book face. Taking its cue from Dwiggins's original metal design, Transitional 521 has distinctly sharp characters, as seen in the right-angled brackets and keen terminals.

Transitional 551

ABCDEFGHIJKLMNOPQRSTUVWXYZ
abcdefghijklmnopqrstuvwxyz
1234567890 !@#?:;"*&

Foundry: Bitstream
Designer: Rudolf Ruzicka
Designer Nationality: Czech
Date: 1939 / c. 1980s

Transitional 551 is Bitstream's digital translation of the Fairfield serif by Czech-born US illustrator and designer Rudolf Ruzicka. The significance of this font, designed for book text, lies in its unique design, with each letterform, from stem to serif, designed separately to provide the utmost legibility.

Vega

ABCDEFGHIJKLMNOPQRSTUVWXYZ
abcdefghijklmnopqrstuvwxyz
1234567890 !@#?:;"*&

Foundry: Omnibus
Designer: Franko Luin
Designer Nationality: Swedish
Date: 1994

Vega takes its name from several sources, which vary from a constellation, to a mathematician, to a research ship. Vega finds its shape in typefaces from the 16th and 17th centuries but includes its own unique details, seen in the blunt serifs of the "s." It is ideal not only for print but also for web usage.

Winthorpe

ABCDEFGHIJKLMNOPQRSTUVWXYZ
abcdefghijklmnopqrstuvwxyz
1234567890 !@#?:;"*&

Foundry: Typodermic
Designer: Ray Larabie
Designer Nationality: Canadian
Date: 2007

Ray Larabie's Winthorpe is a transitional serif designed to cover the breadth of styles required in 21st-century typesetting. The Winthorpe font family includes small caps, Old Style and lining numerals, ordinals, fractions, inferiors, and superiors, in each of its three weights.

Zapf Calligraphic 801

ABCDEFGHIJKLMNOPQRSTUVWXYZ
abcdefghijklmnopqrstuvwxyz
1234567890 !@#?:;"*&

Foundry: Bitstream
Designer: Hermann Zapf
Designer Nationality: German
Date: 1950 / c. 1980s

Zapf Calligraphic 801 is Bistream's digitization of the Palatino family from the 1950s by Hermann Zapf (see p. 574). As with the original design, produced for the Stempel foundry in Germany, Bitstream's version preserves the calligraphic styling of the letterforms which defines the lowercase of the font.

Zapf Elliptical 711

ABCDEFGHIJKLMNOPQRSTUVWXYZ
abcdefghijklmnopqrstuvwxyz
1234567890 !@#?:;"*&

Foundry: Bitstream
Designer: Hermann Zapf
Designer Nationality: German
Date: 1952 / c. 1980s

This font is Bitstream's version of Melior, a modern font family initially designed in 1952 for newsprint by Hermann Zapf (see p. 574). Zapf Elliptical 711 takes both its name and character from the superellipse, a squared circle that was central to Zapf's original design.

EFGHIJK
LMNOP
QRSTUV
WXYZ

Now see the movie:

Helvetica

Sans Serif

Opposite. Detail from the film poster for *Helvetica*, directed by US filmmaker Gary Hustwit, to celebrate the global popularity of Max Meidinger and Eduard Hoffmann's typeface on its 50th anniversary.

Sans serif forms have been found in Greek inscriptions as early as the 5th century BC, but more readily available sans serif types emerged toward the end of the 18th century, which is far later than for their serif equivalents. Sans serif forms are not constructed with serifs and, compared to serif forms, the stroke thickness has far less variation. Initially, printers adopted sans serifs for use in newspaper advertisements, theater programs, posters, and tickets because of their simplicity, legibility, utilitarian appearance, and immediacy.

William Caslon IV printed one of the first sans serif specimens in England in *c.* 1816, "Two Lines English Egyptian." It was subsequently digitized as Caslon Egyptian, although that design has monoline stroke widths and circular forms for its rounded letters. This became a reference point for many ensuing designs.

The development of sans serif types took off in the early 20th century. Many classic sans serif types were created after World War I (1914–18) through to the 1960s. After the horrors of the war, people anticipated a modern technological age of peace and innovation. Art and cultural movements such as the Bauhaus led to the creation of early geometric types such as Jakob Erbar's Erbar (*c.* 1920s) and Paul Renner's Futura (1928). These types reflected a purist and mechanical consideration to their construction with a simplicity formed around geometric shapes, producing circular, squared-up and triangular forms, in contrast to earlier types

influenced by handwritten rhythms. Such types were popular throughout the 1920s and 1930s. In the 1970s, designs such as ITC Avant Garde Gothic by Tom Carnase and Herb Lubalin (see p. 62) re-energized interest in these purist types. More recent designs for geometric typefaces, such as Avenir (1988) by Adrian Frutiger (see p. 290) and Gotham (2000) by Tobias Frere-Jones (see p. 80) maintained their international design appeal.

The term "grotesque." (also "grotesk" and "Gothic") is used to describe sans serifs with subtle variations of construction. It is a general term, although nuances do exist between grotesk and Gothic, the latter being a US approach to the design of grotesque fonts which is less geometric and more based on oval shapes. Invariably, Gothic has an increased contrast in stroke weight, regular proportions, uniform widths, and a lowercase of double-storey construction with relatively closed apertures. More modern grotesque designs are referred to as Neo-grotesque and for the purpose of comparison on the page they have been grouped together here. They usually have a greater range in weights within their families and possess slightly more geometric qualities to their designs. They also provide better legibility than their earlier counterparts. These designs aim to offer readability as well as legibility and can be used for far greater lengths of texts than their predecessors in print and online and digital media. This classification came to the fore in the 1950s thanks to a movement known

as the International Typographic Style (aka Swiss Style). However, the starting point was the Akzidenz Grotesk design dating to the end of the 19th century, which inspired the titan sans serifs Helvetica and Univers, both of which are employed across the globe in a vast array of applications.

Humanist sans serifs take their inspiration from more classical Roman letterforms. They adopt stroke contrast and construction forms from traditional serif types. Their italic variants are true italic designs based on a calligraphic approach rather than slanted variants. Humanist types are regarded as being the most legible and readable among the sans serif for lengthy texts, given their association with serif influences. They are ideal for headline and text purposes. Such flexibility gives them an edge when used by designers and means they are increasingly popular and are being created for screen applications.

Square sans serifs adopt many of the traits of grotesque and geometric designs but with the rounded ovals forming letter shapes being squared off to create a far more rectangular appearance. Sans serif designs over the last twenty years have drawn on a melting pot of influences and historical references. The result of this wealth of resources is that the distinctions between newer sans serifs are blurring. Sans serif types are ever increasing as many new and established foundries strive for perfection and innovation in creating designs that evoke modernity and simplicity.

Aperçu

ABCDEFGHIJKLMNOPQRSTUVWXYZ
abcdefghijklmnopqrstuvwxyz
1234567890 !@#?:;"*&

Foundry: Colophon
Designer: Anthony Sheret / Edd Harrington
Designer Nationality: British
Date: 2010

From the award-winning independent type foundry Colophon (see p. 210), which is based in London and Los Angeles, comes Aperçu, a contemporary geometric sans serif whose forms are drawn from classic typefaces such as Johnston (see p. 278), Gill Sans (see p. 276), and Franklin Gothic (see p. 235). Its elegant, rounded forms possess much charm and upon closer examination reveal quirks and details that make it stand out from similar designs. Its cleanliness and readability make it ideal for print and online use.

Developing Aperçu was one of Colophon's earliest projects, and it was trialled and tested on a number of live commissions during the creative process, the final design being published in August 2010. An extensive and highly flexible family, it has been expanded over the years to accommodate differing languages (with an Arabic version released in 2018) and enhanced OpenType features. Its four core weights consist of Light, Regular, Medium, and Bold with matching italics.

Since its release, Aperçu has been employed by cultural institutions such as New York's Museum of Modern Art, the Jewish Museum in London, and the Walker Art Center, Minneapolis. It has also been used in journals such as *Zeit Magazin* and by a host of commercial organizations.

Right. Aperçu specimen book (second edition), which includes overviews of both language support extensions and new cuts in Black, Black Italic, and Mono Bold. Design by Colophon.

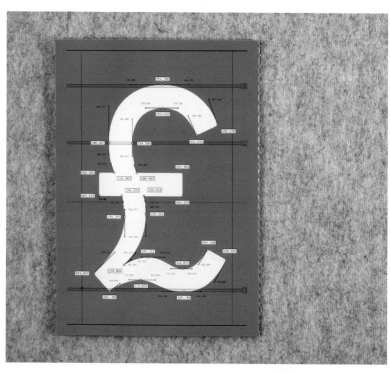

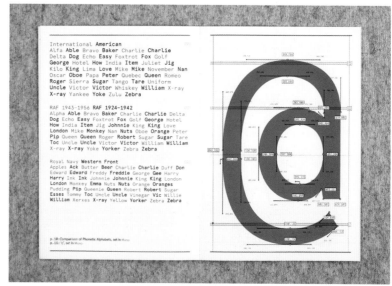

Black

ÀÁÂÃÄÅÆÇÐÈÉÊËÌÍÎÏŁÑ
ÒÓÔÕÖØŒÞŠÙÚÛÜÝŸŽ
№ ¼ ½ ¾ ⅓ ⅔ ⅛ ⅜ ⅝ ⅞
@& +©® £€¶# − [({!?})]

Black Italic

ÀÁÂÃÄÅÆÇÐÈÉÊËÌÍÎÏŁÑ
ÒÓÔÕÖØŒÞŠÙÚÛÜÝŸŽ
№ ¼ ½ ¾ ⅓ ⅔ ⅛ ⅜ ⅝ ⅞
@& +©® £€¶# − [({!?})]

Black & *Black Italic*

←→↑↓↖↙↘ ←→↑↓↖↗↘

p. 28 : 'E!' Waterfall, set in Black
p. 29 : Additional Characters, set in Black and *Black Italic*

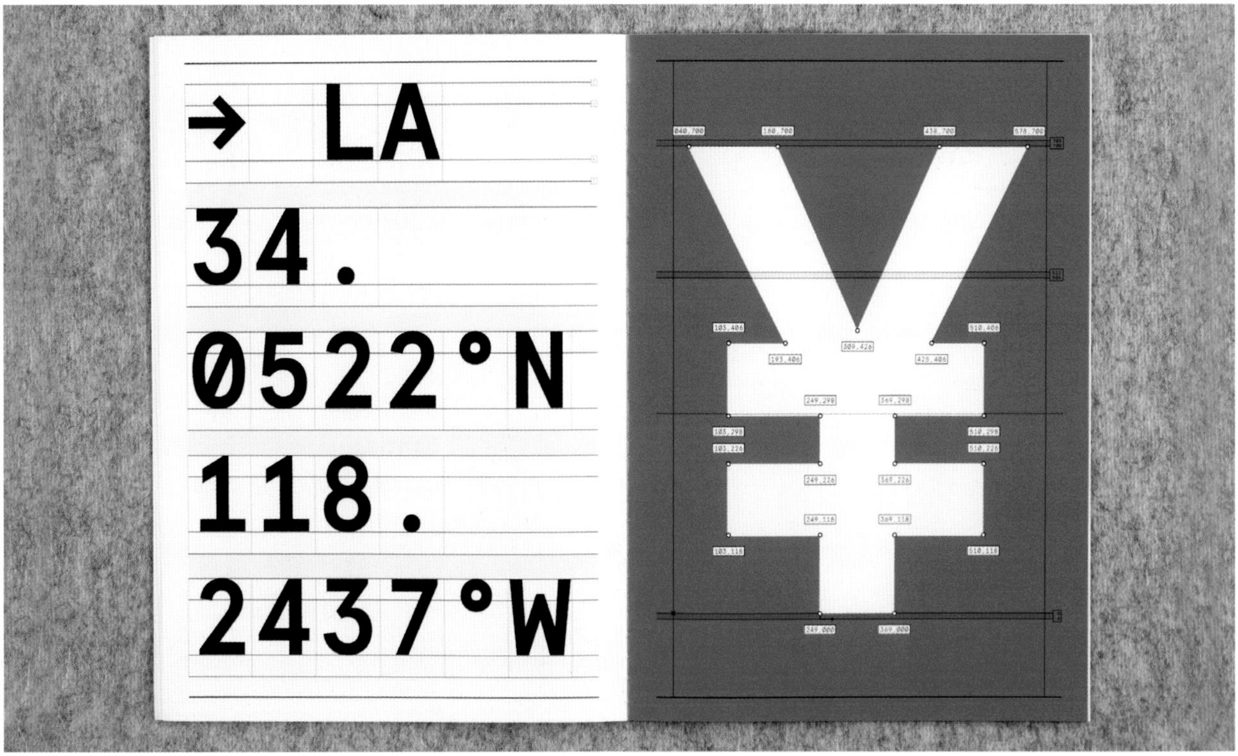

→ LA
34.
0522°N
118.
2437°W

Aperture

ABCDEFGHIJKLMNOPQRSTUVWXYZ
abcdefghijklmnopqrstuvwxyz
1234567890 !@#?:;"*&

Foundry: Neutura
Designer: Alexander McCracken
Designer Nationality: American
Date: 2009

Aperture was created by graphic designer and type designer Alexander McCracken, founder of Neutura (see p. 472) in San Francisco. Its geometric forms are based around an increased x-height, a strong use of vertical construction in its letterforms, low contrast in its stroke weights, and particular details such as unbracketed serifs on certain characters (see lowercase 'i' and 'r.') Its vertical extended appearance is offset by the use of shallow sloping diagonals for the continuation of the stroke in many of the characters, creating a consistency and modernity yet retaining legibility. Aperture is available as Extra Light, Regular, and Heavy.

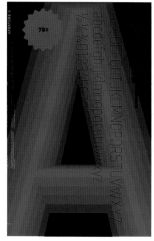

Avenir Next

ABCDEFGHIJKLMNOPQRSTUVWXYZ
abcdefghijklmnopqrstuvwxyz
1234567890 !@#?:;"*&

Foundry: Linotype
Designer: Adrian Frutiger /
Akira Kobayashi / Akaki Razmadze
Designer Nationality: Swiss /
Japanese / Georgian
Date: 2004

Adrian Frutiger (see p. 290) and the in-house team at Linotype designed Avenir Next as an expanded version of the original from 1988. It features six weights with a roman and italic and two widths, Normal and Condensed. Small caps, text figures and ligatures were also added.

Avenir Next Rounded

ABCDEFGHIJKLMNOPQRSTUVWXYZ
abcdefghijklmnopqrstuvwxyz
1234567890 !@#?:;"*&

Foundry: Linotype
Designer: Adrian Frutiger /
Akira Kobayashi / Sandra Winter
Designer Nationality: Swiss /
Japanese / German
Date: 2012

This version of Avenir Next featuring rounded terminals was created by the in-house team at Linotype in consultation with Adrian Frutiger (see p. 290). Comprising of four weights along with complementary italics, it is a playful and welcoming version of the popular sans serif.

Avenir

ABCDEFGHIJKLMNOPQRSTUVWXYZ
abcdefghijklmnopqrstuvwxyz
1234567890 !@#?:;"*&

Foundry: Linotype
Designer: Adrian Frutiger
Designer Nationality: Swiss
Date: 1988

The elegant geometric sans serif created by Swiss type designer Adrian Frutiger (see p. 290) takes its inspiration from the structured geometric typefaces of the early 20th century yet is endowed with a humanist touch, creating a warmer, more approachable typeface that is more akin in tone to his typeface Frutiger. Avenir reflects the aesthetic approaches of the later 20th century rather than the hardened perfection of its ancestors and inspiration, the typefaces Futura and Erbar.

"Avenir" means "future" in French and it has become a most appropriate title. Linotype released this refined and pure typeface in 1988, and it has become a timeless classic. The family includes three weights with matching italics. As with Univers, Frutiger employed a double-digit naming system to convey weight and width for each of the styles.

Avenir has many subtle details such as thicker vertical strokes and shortened ascenders, which all contribute towards its heightened legibility.

In 2004, Frutiger created a revised version with Linotype type director Akira Kobayashi, titled Avenir Next (see p. 188). It contains true italics, condensed styles, and small caps.

Below. The famous letters standing on Amsterdam's Museumplein, *I am amsterdam*, were hugely popular wth residents and tourists alike. Introduced in 2014 as part of a marketing campaign for the city, the logotype is set in Avenir. Sadly their popularity was so great, and the crowds so large, that they were removed by the council at the end of 2018 but are now on tour, being sited in other areas across the Dutch city.

Base 900

ABCDEFGHIJKLMNOPQRSTUVWXYZ
abcdefghijklmnopqrstuvwxyz
1234567890 !@#?:;"*&

Foundry: Emigre
Designer: Zuzana Licko
Designer Nationality: Slovakian
Date: 2010

Developed from a bitmap typeface, Base 900 from Emigre (see p. 106) is a typeface born from technological restraint. Refined from a simple bitmap form to a full, high-resolution typeface, Base 900 reflects its origins in early computer type in appearance and modular geometry, both enhanced to create an elegant and distinguished design.

Base 900 takes its origins from an earlier design by Zuzana Licko, Base 9, created in 1994, which was formed from a simple grid construction. Licko's aim with the Base 9 design was to create a comprehensive family of screen and printer fonts, similar to Verdana by British type designer Matthew Carter (see p. 616). These forms were primarily worked in a reverse manner to how modern fonts are designed, in that the screen-based appearance took dominance over the printer version. The design and adjustment of a grid-based letterform is far harder to adjust than the vector line-based forms of the printer fonts, so it was tackled first. In addition, a bitmap form is quite crude in its makeup and can be very limiting when designing letters, so it is necessary to get the screen version correct first.

It was from this simple Base 9 design that Base 900 was developed. It takes on a number of the quirks of Base 9, such as the triangular spur element that appears on many of the letterforms and the narrowed "m" that follows the grid construction over regular forms, which all originated in the Lo-Res 9 Bold bitmap. These features were incorporated and adapted as stylistic elements, giving the family its own highly distinctive geometric appearance.

IJANTING
SOJOURN
1,395,456,780
1,395,456,780
AWARD
AWARD **AWARD**
5037
5037

13

Base 900 : TYPE SPECIMEN

Boutique

ABCDEFGHIJKLMNOPQRSTUVWXYZ
abcdefghijklmnopqrstuvwxyz
1234567890 !@#?:;”*&

Foundry: Milieu Grotesque
Designer: Timo Gaessner
Designer Nationality: German
Date: 2012

Boutique is a sans serif with several geometric gestures. It was initiated as an experiment in 2008, and developed for the rebranding of German fashion label A. D. Deertz in 2009. The font family, finally released in 2012, features distinctly linear characters and a high stroke contrast.

Castledown

ABCDEFGHIJKLMNOPQRSTUVWXYZ
abcdefghijklmnopqrstuvwxyz
1234567890 !@#?:;“*&

Foundry: Colophon
Designer: The Entente
Designer Nationality: British
Date: 2014

Colophon (see p. 210) initiated Castledown in 2012 as a bespoke typeface for Castledown Primary School in Hastings, UK. It is a geometric sans serif with both Regular and Fun versions. Both styles include proportional weights, alongside variants such as Dotted and Cursive.

Century Gothic

ABCDEFGHIJKLMNOPQRSTUVWXYZ
abcdefghijklmnopqrstuvwxyz
1234567890 !@#?:;”*&

Foundry: Monotype
Designer: Monotype Studio
Date: 1991

Heavily influenced by geometric fonts Futura and Avant Garde, Century Gothic is a version of Futura created to match the proportions of Avant Garde. It also has its roots in Sol Hess's typeface Twentieth Century, but lacks the slanted characters and visual flair of the classic by Herb Lubalin (see p. 62).

Chalet

ABCDEFGHIJKLMNOPQRSTUVWXYZ
abcdefghijklmnopqrstuvwxyz
1234567890 !@#?:;”*&

Foundry: House Industries
Designer: Ken Barber /
Paul van der Laan
Designer Nationality: American /
Dutch
Date: 1993

Credited to the fictional 1940s designer René Albert Chalet, this functional sans serif has three variations: Chalet 1960, Chalet 1970, and Chalet 1980. Each has three weights: Paris (Light), London (Regular), and New York (Bold). Chalet also comes with more than one hundred useful silhouette images.

Chapeau

ABCDEFGHIJKLMNOPQRSTUVWXYZ
abcdefghijklmnopqrstuvwxyz
1234567890 !@#?:;"*&

Chapeau's geometric design is inspired by IBM's proportionally aligned typeface Doric, which Timo Gaessner encountered in a letter written by Johnny Cash on an IBM typewriter. Since its first release in 2010, Chapeau has been updated to include six weights and two monospaced styles.

Foundry: Milieu Grotesque
Designer: Timo Gaessner
Designer Nationality: German
Date: 2016

DIN Neuzeit Grotesk

ABCDEFGHIJKLMNOPQRSTUVWXYZ
abcdefghijklmnopqrstuvwxyz
1234567890 !@#?:;"*&

Neuzeit Grotesk was once the standard typeface used by the print industry. In 1970 the *Deutsches Institut für Normung* (German Institute for Industrial Standards) chose a version for use in signage and traffic directional systems across Germany, and the abbreviation "DIN" was then added to its name.

Foundry: Stempel
Designer: Wilhelm Pischner
Designer Nationality: German
Date: 1928

Drescher Grotesk BT

ABCDEFGHIJKLMNOPQRSTUVWXYZ
abcdefghijklmnopqrstuvwxyz
1234567890 !@#?:;"*&

This geometric design is Nicolai Gogoll's award-winning revival of Arno Drescher's Super Grotesk created in 1930, which became known as the "East German Futura" because Futura was unavailable. It is available in six weights, plus a special weight for use at small point sizes.

Foundry: Bitstream
Designer: Arno Drescher / Nicolai Gogoll
Designer Nationality: German
Date: 1930 / 2001

Erbar

ABCDEFGHIJKLMNOPQRSTUVWXYZ
abcdefghijklmnopqrstuvwxyz
1234567890 !@#?:;"*&

Erbar is a revival of Erbar Grotesk, one of the first geometric sans serifs that predates Futura. Erbar has eleven extra styles, including two weights with a smaller x-height, longer ascenders and two condensed weights. There are a number of different digitized versions, including CJ Type's Dunbar.

Foundry: Ludwig & Mayer
Designer: Jakob Erbar
Designer Nationality: German
Date: c. 1920s / 1995

Erbar AT

ABCDEFGHIJKLMNOPQRSTUVWXYZ
abcdefghijklmnopqrstuvwxyz
1234567890 !@#?:;"*&

Jakob Erbar's groundbreaking typeface was one of the first geometric sans serifs and predates both Rudolf Koch's Kabel and Paul Renner's Futura by five years. The original Erbar has Light Condensed and Bold Condensed weights, whereas this version has Light Condensed and Medium Condensed.

Foundry: Ludwig & Mayer
Designer: Jakob Erbar
Designer Nationality: German
Date: c. 1920s / 1995

FS Alvar

ABCDEFGHIJKLMNOPQRSTUVWXYZ
abcdefghijklmnopqrstuvwxyz
1234567890 !@#?:;"*&

A departure from the type styles for which Fontsmith (see p. 272) has traditionally been known, this Modernist-inspired sans serif was developed from sketches made by Phil Garnham during his undergraduate studies. Available in three weights, its stencilled letterforms are built on a modular grid.

Foundry: Fontsmith
Designer: Phil Garnham / Jason Smith
Designer Nationality: British
Date: 2009

FS Emeric

ABCDEFGHIJKLMNOPQRSTUVWXYZ
abcdefghijklmnopqrstuvwxyz
1234567890 !@#?:;"*&

FS Emeric presents a departure from the neutral, impersonal feel of many 20th-century sans serif typefaces. Created to demonstrate that utility within a sans serif design need not prevail over personality, its extensive family of weights and styles is both versatile and legible.

Foundry: Fontsmith
Designer: Phil Garnham
Designer Nationality: British
Date: 2013

FS Lucas

ABCDEFGHIJKLMNOPQRSTUVWXYZ
abcdefghijklmnopqrstuvwxyz
1234567890 !@#?:;"*&

In response to the trend for geometric, circular forms within typography and branding in the mid 2010s, Fontsmith (see p. 272) set out to develop its own optically balanced font family to offer brands a comprehensive typographic toolkit. FS Lucas, released in 2016, is the result.

Foundry: Fontsmith
Designer: Stuart de Rozario
Designer Nationality: British
Date: 2016

Futura

ABCDEFGHIJKLMNOPQRSTUVWXYZ
abcdefghijklmnopqrstuvwxyz
1234567890 !@#?:;"*&

Foundry: Linotype
Designer: Paul Renner
Designer Nationality: German
Date: 1928

German designer Paul Renner was a hugely influential graphic artist, type designer, writer, and teacher. He created the Futura typeface according to his Constructivist beliefs and to reflect Bauhaus principles, although he was never actually associated or affiliated to the famous German arts and crafts school.

Renner was commissioned to create the typeface by the Bauer Type Foundry based in Frankfurt am Main, Germany. His belief that a modern typeface should be based around the purest of geometric forms of the circle, square, and triangle was tempered by the foundry's need for a practical and usable product. Renner's earliest sketches were deemed to be extreme and unworkable, with characters losing their ability to be recognized clearly.

The foundry and Renner redrew and refined the designs, resulting in what is a timeless classic that was marketed by Bauer as capturing the spirit of modernity, using the slogan *die Schrift unserer Zeit* ("the typeface of our time.") In fact, Futura is as relevant and as popular today as it was when it first appeared in the early 20th century.

Futura's near constant stroke weight and crisp geometric forms have made it the most successful of these forms of type. It has had a great influence on sans serif types designed with a similar rationale because of the purity of its design. Efficient, elegant and versatile, Futura is employed from print to branding on a global scale. A wide variety of weights are available: its lighter weights suit text setting, while the typeface is ideal for display applications thanks to its Bold and Condensed styles.

Below left. Futura promotion and specimen from The Bauer Type Foundry's New York office.

Below right. Tourist map of Berlin for visitors to the 1936 Berlin Olympic Games.

Opposite. Barbican Arts Centre Identity and Interior. Identity guidelines by North with interior wayfinding by Cartlidge Levene with Studio Myerscough working with architects Allford Hall Monaghan Morris. The particular variant of Futura used for the wayfinding is Futura SH by Scangraphic, designed specifically for use at larger sizes.

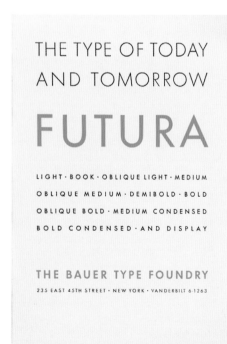

Typeface

Futura is our voice

We only use one font.

Futura is at the core of our visual identity and synonymous with our brand.

futura

41

42

all venues
lifts & stairs

Typeface

Three weights

The Barbican likes to be bold and strong in its communications, however with Futura we can also be quieter, more restrained and classical. Use a weight that best suits the message.

The version of Futura that we use belongs to the Scangraphic font library. Details about purchasing the font are at the back of this guide.

extra-
light
book
bold

43

44

Typeface

Three type sizes

Keeping things consistent and simple makes communication quicker and easier. When the audience is familiar with the hierarchy of information, it takes them just an instant to find what they're interested in.

Our system only utilises up to three sizes:

Size one for headlines or titles
Size two for descriptor/subheading
Size three for additional information

Our wordmark is not a typesize.

**one
two
three**

45

46

FS Sinclair

ABCDEFGHIJKLMNOPQRSTUVWXYZ
abcdefghijklmnopqrstuvwxyz
1234567890 !@#?:;"*&

Foundry: Fontsmith
Designer: Phil Garnham /
Jason Smith
Designer Nationality: British
Date: 2009

Phil Garnham and Jason Smith designed this modular, grid-based typeface in 2009, inspired by the blocky letterforms gracing the display of the ZX Spectrum home computer. Their careful refinements of each letterform have resulted in a technologically inspired typeface with a humanist touch.

Generica Condensed

ABCDEFGHIJKLMNOPQRSTUVWXYZ
abcdefghijklmnopqrstuvwxyz
1234567890!@#?:;"*&

Foundry: Monotype
Designer: Jim Parkinson
Designer Nationality: American
Date: 1994

Jim Parkinson worked as a lettering artist for Hallmark Cards before beginning his freelance type design career, and is well known for his design of editorial mastheads and logos for titles such as *Newsweek*, *Esquire*, and *Rolling Stone*. He designed this condensed sans for Monotype in 1994.

Generika

ABCDEFGHIJKLMNOPQRSTUVWXYZ
abcdefghijklmnopqrstuvwxyz
1234567890 !@#?:;"*&

Foundry: Milieu Grotesque
Designer: Alexander Colby
Designer Nationality: Swiss
Date: 2008

Generika is a geometric sans serif, inspired by the letterforms produced on an old Alder typewriter with an unreliable carbon ribbon and low-quality paper. The characters mimic the blurred aesthetics of the typewritten letters, seen primarily in Generika's rounded corners.

Geometric 212

ABCDEFGHIJKLMNOPQRSTUVWX
abcdefghijklmnopqrstuvwxyz
1234567890 !@#?:;"*&

Foundry: Bauer Type Foundry /
American Type Founders /
Linotype / Bitstream
Designer: Paul Renner /
ATF Staff
Designer Nationality: German /
American
Date: 1927 / 1936

This enigmatic Bitstream typeface is based on Linotype and American Type Founders' metal matrices for Spartan released in 1936, which was itself a version of Paul Renner's perennially popular Futura, first published by Bauer Type. It is available in four weights, including two condensed cuts.

Geometric 231

ABCDEFGHIJKLMNOPQRSTUVWXYZ
abcdefghijklmnopqrstuvwxyz
1234567890 !@#?:;"*&

Foundry: Klingspor / Bitstream
Designer: Rudolf Koch
Designer Nationality: German
Date: 1927

German designer Rudolf Koch created Kabel, on which this Bitstream digitization is based, for the Klingspor foundry in 1927. Stempel republished it later. The typeface features tall ascenders, a low x-height and geometric letters based on the interplay between circular forms and straight lines.

Geometric 415

ABCDEFGHIJKLMNOPQRSTUVWXYZ
abcdefghijklmnopqrstuvwxyz
1234567890 !@#?:;"*&

Foundry: Linotype / Bitstream
Designer: William A. Dwiggins
Designer Nationality: American
Date: 1937 / 1990

Geometric 415 is Bitstream's copy of Metro No. 2 by US designer William A. Dwiggins, originally published by Linotype in 1932. It was commissioned to compete with popular European sans serifs such as Futura. Dwiggins developed its lowercase letters to add further visual interest.

Geometric 706

ABCDEFGHIJKLMNOPQRSTUVWXYZ
abcdefghijklmnopqrstuvwxyz
1234567890 !@#?:;"*&

Foundry: Stempel / Bitstream
Designer: Wilhelm Pischner
Designer Nationality: German
Date: 1928 / 1990

Wilhelm Pischner's geometric Neuzeit Grotesk font has been the subject of several revivals, adaptations and digitizations since its release in 1928; it was selected by the German Standards Committee in 1970 for use on official and traffic signage. Bitstream's version was published in 1990.

Gotham Rounded

ABCDEFGHIJKLMNOPQRSTUVWXYZ
abcdefghijklmnopqrstuvwxyz
1234567890 !@#?:;"*&

Foundry: Hoefler & Frere-Jones
Designer: Tobias Frere-Jones
Designer Nationality: American
Date: 2005

Tobias Frere-Jones developed this cut of Gotham for the redesign of the US graphic-arts magazine *Print* in 2005; it was subsequently released as a retail typeface following the expiry of that exclusive license. Its rounded forms build upon the approachability and warmth of the original.

Gotham

ABCDEFGHIJKLMNOPQRSTUVWXYZ
abcdefghijklmnopqrstuvwxyz
1234567890 !@#?:;"*&

Foundry: Hoefler & Co
Designer: Tobias Frere-Jones
Designer Nationality: American
Date: 2000

Gotham started life as a commission for US men's magazine *GQ* to design a bespoke sans serif to be employed in its publication. Tobias Frere-Jones (see p. 80), the principal and type director of New York foundry Hoefler, Frere & Jones (now Hoefler & Co), used the project as a stepping stone to develop and design a typeface based on his interest and fascination with the architectural display lettering and signage seen around New York from the mid 20th century.

A key reference point in Frere-Jones's research was the letterforms found on "one of the city's most mundane buildings," the Port Authority Bus Terminal on Eighth Avenue in Manhattan. These vernacular letterforms, created and formed by engineers and draughtsmen from steel and bronze, were the inspiration for this highly popular geometric sans.

When *GQ*'s exclusive license ended in 2002, the foundry marketed Gotham as a commercial typeface. It gained in popularity and was nominated as "the font of the decade" by *USA Today*. Such was its success that it was used by Coca-Cola and on former President Barack Obama's presidential campaign in 2008; it has even been employed for the cornerstone of the One World Trade Center building.

Gotham is uniquely American in tone, and its clean lines, generous width and elegant forms mark a typeface that offers an honesty with clear readability no matter the application. Gotham offers an extremely large family of sixty-six styles with four widths, eight weights, separate fonts for screen use and a Rounded variant containing eight styles.

Below left. The iconic Barack Obama HOPE poster from 2008 by artist Shepard Fairey, which came to symbolize the future president's political campaign.

Below right. CD cover design for *Live 2002*, a recording of a concert near Newcastle, UK, by sound artist Carsten Nicolai (aka Alva Noto), and fellow musicians Ryoji Ikeda and the late Mika Vainio.

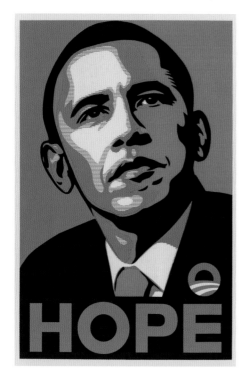

Left. Book cover for *Twice Upon A Time: Listening to New York* by Hari Kunzru, designed by award-winning New York graphic designer and writer Chip Kidd.

Below left. Wayfinding design using extruded Gotham Book by Cómo Design Studio, Barcelona for Biblioteca Camp de l'Arpa Caterina Albert.

Below. One of a series of posters for New York's Tribeca Film Festival by J. Walter Thompson.

GT Cinetype

ABCDEFGHIJKLMNOPQRSTUVWXYZ
abcdefghijklmnopqrstuvwxyz
1234567890 !@#?:;"*&

Foundry: Grilli Type
Designer: Mauro Paolozzi / Rafael Koch
Designer Nationality: Swiss
Date: 2015

Based on a design created for a now defunct cinema subtitling machine, GT Cinetype is a typeface that does not contain any curves. A laser that can only move in straight lines is used to erase the colored layer of the film, and small, brilliant white letters appear.

GT Eesti

ABCDEFGHIJKLMNOPQRSTUVWXYZ
abcdefghijklmnopqrstuvwxyz
1234567890 !@#?:;"*&

Foundry: Grilli Type
Designer: Reto Moser
Designer Nationality: Swiss
Date: 2016

Based on Anatoly Schukin's typeface Zhurnalnaya Roublennaya of 1947, and sourced from Estonian children's books, GT Eesti is described as "a free-spirited interpretation" of the geometric Soviet sans serif. It has two subfamilies, text and display, and Latin and Cyrillic versions.

GT Flexa

ABCDEFGHIJKLMNOPQRSTUVWXYZ
abcdefghijklmnopqrstuvwxyz
1234567890 !@#?:;"*&

Foundry: Grilli Type
Designer: Dominik Huber
Designer Nationality: Swiss
Date: 2019

This energetic sans serif started life as part of a branding project for a fashion label by Swiss agency Moiré. As its name implies, its curves flex from very narrow to very wide shapes. Its ink traps provide the glue that makes this family of extremes work so well together.

GT Walsheim

ABCDEFGHIJKLMNOPQRSTUVWXYZ
abcdefghijklmnopqrstuvwxyz
1234567890 !@#?:;"*&

Foundry: Grilli Type
Designer: Noël Leu
Designer Nationality: Swiss
Date: 2010

GT Walsheim is a geometric sans serif, informed by the lettering of Swiss designer Otto Baumberger. Drawing on poster designs from the 1930s, it revives a variety of Baumberger's hand-drawn idiosyncrasies, most notably the jovial uppercase "G" or the oversized counter of the uppercase "R."

Gubia

ABCDEFGHIJKLMNOPQRSTUVWXYZ
abcdefghijklmnopqrstuvwxyz
1234567890 !@#?;;"*&

Foundry: Graviton
Designer: Pablo Balcells
Designer Nationality:
Argentinian
Date: 2013

The rounded, rectangular forms of Pablo Balcells's Gubia typeface are well suited for display use, and its alternate characters offer the capacity to add further visual interest. Vertically extended tittles within the font's lowercase letterforms emphasize its condensed feel.

Harmonia Sans

ABCDEFGHIJKLMNOPQRSTUVWXYZ
abcdefghijklmnopqrstuvwxyz
1234567890 !@#?:;"*&

Foundry: Monotype
Designer: Jim Wasco
Designer Nationality: American
Date: 2010

Jim Wasco studied classic geometric designs such as Futura and Avant Garde when developing Harmonia Sans; the result is an evenly proportioned sans serif with its own distinct character. Details such as the single-storey "a" and "g" give the typeface a friendly, informal feel.

ITC Bauhaus

ABCDEFGHIJKLMNOPQRSTUVWXYZ
abcdefghijklmnopqrstuvwxyz
1234567890 !@#?:;"*&

Foundry: ITC
Designer: Herbert Bayer /
Ed Benguiat / Victor Caruso
Designer Nationality: German /
American / American
Date: 1925 / 1975

In 1975, Ed Benguiat (see p. 514) and Victor Caruso developed this ITC release from Herbert Bayer's typeface prototypes created at the Bauhaus in Dessau, Germany. Its unmistakably geometric, semi-stencilled design is available in five different weights, though it does not include italics.

ITC Conduit

ABCDEFGHIJKLMNOPQRSTUVWXYZ
abcdefghijklmnopqrstuvwxyz
1234567890 !@#?:;"*&

Foundry: ITC
Designer: Mark van Bronkhorst
Designer Nationality: American
Date: 1997

Conduit has long been regarded as something of an ugly duckling within the ITC roster—Erik Spiekermann (see p. 304) called it "wonderfully stupid," and designer Mark van Bronkhorst seems to agree. Nonetheless, its geometric, oversimplified forms have a certain inscrutable appeal.

ITC Avant Garde Gothic

ABCDEFGHIJKLMNOPQRSTUVWXYZ
abcdefghijklmnopqrstuvwxyz
1234567890 !@#?:;"*&

Foundry: ITC
Designer: Herb Lubalin /
Tom Carnase
Designer Nationality: American
Date: 1970

Graphic designer and lettering artist Herb Lubalin (see p. 62) drew up a logotype for the masthead of *Avant Garde* magazine, which was published in the United States in the late 1960s. Tom Carnase, fellow type designer and lettering artist, as well as partner at their agency Lubalin, Smith, Carnase, was charged with the task of creating the typeface from his sketches and workings. The result was an innovative and ever popular design that draws its appearance from past versions of geometric sans serifs, from the Bauhaus in Germany but also the first sans serif, all capitals design, produced in 1816 by the Caslon Foundry in London.

Its elegant construction from circular forms and straight lines masks the complexity of this elegant typeface. The typeface itself consists of monoline characters, overlapping characters, tightly set letters and the distinctive leaning uppercase "A"s. More often used for display work, it is also highly popular with branding and logotype applications, as seen with sports-equipment company Adidas.

The ITC Avant Garde Gothic family is made up of five weights and four condensed designs, all with matching italics. The later condensed designs were created in 1974 by a friend and peer of Lubalin's, Ed Benguiat (see p. 514), with obliques being designed by André Gürtler, Erich Gschwind and Christian Mengelt in 1977.

The most recent OpenType version, ITC Avant Garde Gothic Pro, includes a range of alternate upper- and lowercase characters and a collection of bitform characters (lowercase letters with capital proportions). A serif version exists where Lubalin and Benguiat added large rectangular slab serifs, which is called Lubalin Graph (see p. 55) and was released in 1974.

Below. ITC *Avant Garde* magazine covers for Issues No. 8, 1969 (the Picasso edition) and 13, 1971 (a photo essay of America by Alwyn Scott Turner).

Opposite. Adverts for the Audi Fox designed by renowned American art director Helmut Krone in 1975, employing Avant Garde Gothic in both headline and text applications.

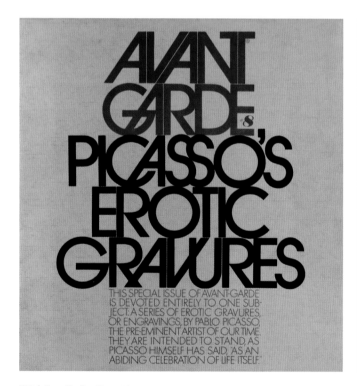

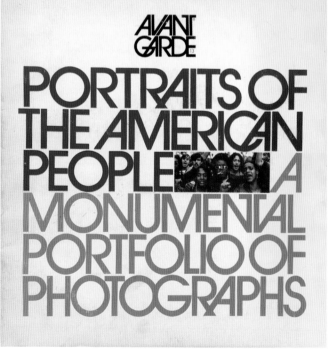

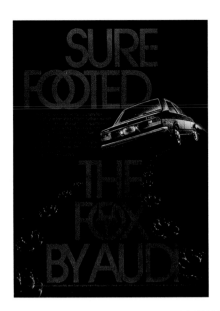
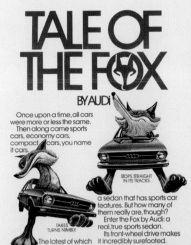

ITC Handel Gothic

ABCDEFGHIJKLMNOPQRSTUVWXYZ
abcdefghijklmnopqrstuvwxyz
1234567890 !@#?:;"*&

Foundry: Fotostar / ITC
Designer: Donald J. Handel /
Rod McDonald
Designer Nationality: American
Date: 2008

Designed by Donald J. Handel in the 1960s for phototypesetting, Handel Gothic will be familiar tto science-fiction fans thanks to its use on the *Star Trek* TV series. This ITC update adjusts the proportions of the original and expands its character set; Nadine Chahine designed its Arabic counterpart.

ITC Kabel

ABCDEFGHIJKLMNOPQRSTUVWXYZ
abcdefghijklmnopqrstuvwxyz
1234567890 !@#?:;"*&

Foundry: Klingspor / ITC
Designer: Rudolf Koch /
Victor Caruso
Designer Nationality: German /
American
Date: 1927 / 1975

Victor Caruso's revival of Kabel for ITC turned the design on its head, switching the diminutive x-height of the original for much shorter ascenders and descenders. Though extreme in this case, this approach, which can aid legibility, is characteristic of many ITC revivals.

ITC Octone

ABCDEFGHIJKLMNOPQRSTUVWXYZ
abcdefghijklmnopqrstuvwxyz
1234567890 !@#?:;"*&

Foundry: ITC
Designer: Éric de Berranger
Designer Nationality: French
Date: 1999

Alongside his typeface design work, Éric de Berranger has worked on brand identity and logotype design for corporations including Renault. This upright sans serif, designed by De Berranger for ITC in 1999, features flared letterforms reminiscent of stone-carved lettering.

Leroy

ABCDEFGHIJKLMNOPQRSTUVWXYZ
abcdefghijklmnopqrstuvwxyz
1234567890 !@#?:;"*&

Foundry: Colophon
Designer: Oscar & Ewan
Designer Nationality: British
Date: 2012

Leroy is a geometric sans serif inspired by a technical drawing found in a 1960s model car magazine. Despite being drawn with a lettering set from the same period, Leroy features several quirks, such as the angular cross stroke of the lowercase "e" and the uneven bowls of the uppercase "B."

Litera

ABCDEFGHIJKLMNOPQRSTUVWXYZ
abcdefghijklmnopqrstuvwxyz
1234567890 !@#?:;"*&

Foundry: Letraset
Designer: Michael Neugebauer
Designer Nationality: Austrian
Date: 1983

Originally designed for Letraset by Austrian Michael Neugebauer, Litera is a geometric sans serif, inspired by the Bauhaus and the purity of the circle, square and triangle. Distinctive features include the wide crossbar of the "G" and the stencil construction of the "e," "B," "P," and "R."

Mabry

ABCDEFGHIJKLMNOPQRSTUVWXYZ
abcdefghijklmnopqrstuvwxyz
1234567890 !@#?:;"*&

Foundry: Colophon
Designer: Benjamin Critton / Colophon Foundry
Designer Nationality: American
Date: 2018

First commissioned by fashion brand Nasty Gal in 2014, and initially titled NB Grotesque, Mabry is a simultaneously grotesque and geometric sans serif. Referencing and integrating features from each style, the letterforms draw inspiration from both 19th- and 20th-century faces.

Madera

ABCDEFGHIJKLMNOPQRSTUVWXYZ
abcdefghijklmnopqrstuvwxyz
1234567890 !@#?:;"*&

Foundry: Monotype
Designer: Malou Verlomme
Designer Nationality: French
Date: 2018

Designed in 2018 by Malou Verlomme, a French designer working for Monotype in London, Madera comes in eight weights with italics. A versatile, geometric sans serif, Madera was designed with graphic designers and corporate identities in mind. It has diamond-shaped tittles and full stops.

Mont

ABCDEFGHIJKLMNOPQRSTUVWXYZ
abcdefghijklmnopqrstuvwxyz
1234567890 !@#?:;"*&

Foundry: Fontfabric
Designer: Mirela Belova / Svet Simov
Designer Nationality: Bulgarian
Date: 2018

Designed by two of the six Bulgarian designers working for Sofia-based Fontfabric, Mont is a versatile, geometric sans with a large x-height and support for more than 130 languages thanks to Latin, Greek, and Cyrillic characters. Mont comes in ten weights; hairline to black, with italics.

Neo Sans

ABCDEFGHIJKLMNOPQRSTUVWXYZ
abcdefghijklmnopqrstuvwxyz
1234567890 !@#?:;"*&

Foundry: Monotype
Designer: Seb Lester
Designer Nationality: British
Date: 2004

Designed by British typographer Sebastian "Seb" Lester, now better known for his calligraphy, Neo Sans is a rounded, square sans with a technical, futuristic feel. It comes in six weights, light to ultra, with italics, and has been used by Intel, the British Labour Party, and car company Kia Motors.

Neo Tech

ABCDEFGHIJKLMNOPQRSTUVWXYZ
abcdefghijklmnopqrstuvwxyz
1234567890 !@#?:;"*&

Foundry: Monotype
Designer: Seb Lester
Designer Nationality: British
Date: 2004

A sister typeface to Neo Sans, Neo Tech is more minimal with some letters stripped of detail, a single-storey "g," and softer shapes in some places. Seb Lester, who worked at Monotype for nine years, has more than one million followers on Instagram where he shares calligraphy videos.

Neue Kabel

ABCDEFGHIJKLMNOPQRSTUVWXYZ
abcdefghijklmnopqrstuvwxyz
1234567890 !@#?:;"*&

Foundry: Monotype
Designer: Rudolf Koch / Marc Schütz
Designer Nationality: German
Date: 2016

An update of Kabel, the early geometric sans originally drawn by Rudolf Koch in 1927 for the Klingspor Foundry, Neue Kabel was designed by German typographer Marc Schütz, and came out of extensive archival research. Schütz reinstated italics and added new weights and missing characters.

Neue Plak

ABCDEFGHIJKLMNOPQRSTUVWXYZ
abcdefghijklmnopqrstuvwxyz
1234567890 !@#?:;"*&

Foundry: Monotype
Designer: Paul Renner / Linda Hintz / Toshi Omagari
Designer Nationality: German / German / Japanese
Date: 2018

Released by Stempel in 1928, Plak was overshadowed by Paul Renner's first font, also a geometric sans, Futura. Neue Plak, Linda Hintz and Toshi Omagari's update, is a versatile family of sixty styles. The oversized tittle and circle and rectangle construction of the "r" can be seen in the heavier cuts.

Noir Text

ABCDEFGHIJKLMNOPQRSTUVWXYZ
abcdefghijklmnopqrstuvwxyz
1234567890 !@#?:,"*&

Foundry: Playtype
Designer: Jonas Hecksher
Designer Nationality: Danish
Date: 2005

Noir Text is a geometric sans serif font family, designed in Light, Book, Regular, and Bold weights. The stroke contrast varies for individual joints, heavy on shoulders but minimal on bowls, and the hooks of letters such as "f" and "t" are flattened in order to balance the character widths.

November

ABCDEFGHIJKLMNOPQRSTUVWXYZ
abcdefghijklmnopqrstuvwxyz
1234567890 !@#?:,"*&

Foundry: Typotheque
Designer: Peter Biľak
Designer Nationality: Slovakian
Date: 2016

Peter Biľak described November as "a rational, utilitarian typeface inspired by street signage." It comes in nine weights with italics, and many travel-related signs, symbols, and directional arrows are included as glyphs. Slab, Stencil, Condensed, and Compressed versions also exist.

Objektiv

ABCDEFGHIJKLMNOPQRSTUVWXYZ
abcdefghijklmnopqrstuvwxyz
1234567890 !@#?:,"*&

Foundry: Dalton Maag
Designer: Bruno Mello
Designer Nationality: Brazilian
Date: 2015–19

Designed in three styles, Mk1 for display, Mk2, and Mk3 for text, the Objektiv family combines geometry with humanism. While the display style utilizes the severity of geometric forms for impact, the text styles are softer in their principles, enabling a greater legibility. Objektiv is also available as a variable font.

October

ABCDEFGHIJKLMNOPQRSTUVWXYZ
abcdefghijklmnopqrstuvwxyz
1234567890 !@#?:,"*&

Foundry: Typotheque
Designer: Peter Biľak
Designer Nationality: Slovakian
Date: 2016

A rounded sans serif, October was first carved in wood by the rotary cutters of a computer numerical control router, then optically corrected digitally. A large family, October comes in Latin, Hebrew, Cyrillic and Greek in nine weights with italics. Condensed and compressed versions are also available.

Orange

ABCDEFGHIJKLMNOPQRSTUVWXYZ
abcdefghijklmnopqrstuvwxyz
1234567890 !@#?:,"*&

Foundry: Neutura
Designer: Alexander McCracken
Designer Nationality: American
Date: 2006

Orange is a monoline geometric sans serif designed by Alexander McCracken and released in 2006 by his foundry Neutura (see p. 472). It is available in four weights; Light to Extra Bold, without italics. Neutura is the name of McCracken's foundry and design studio, whose clients include Nike and Sony.

Orange Round

ABCDEFGHIJKLMNOPQRSTUVWXYZ
abcdefghijklmnopqrstuvwxyz
1234567890 !@#?:,"*&

Foundry: Neutura
Designer: Alexander McCracken
Designer Nationality: American
Date: 2011

Released five years after Orange, Orange Round follows the exact same structure and comes in the same weights, but features rounded rather than flat terminals. Alexander McCracken's typefaces show interest in geometry, and he often uses them in work for his clients in the music industry.

Pembroke

ABCDEFGHIJKLMNOPQRSTUVWXYZ
abcdefghijklmnopqrstuvwxyz
1234567890 !@#?:,"*&

Foundry: Jeremy Tankard Typography
Designer: Jeremy Tankard
Designer Nationality: British
Date: 2014

Jeremy Tankard's Pembroke was inspired by the square proportions and geometry of Caslon Old Face and other early English types, as well as sans serif inscriptions from late 18th-century British buildings. It is a crisp, clean geometric sans serif available in regular and italic in eight weights.

Raisonné

ABCDEFGHIJKLMNOPQRSTUVWXYZ
abcdefghijklmnopqrstuvwxyz
1234567890 !@#?:,"*&

Foundry: Colophon
Designer: Benjamin Critton / Colophon Foundry
Designer Nationality: American
Date: 2018

First designed in a single Demibold weight in 2010, Raisonné was expanded in 2018 to add both Light and Regular weights. The geometric letterforms reference the aesthetic eccentricities of various 20th-century designs, including Avant Garde by Herb Lubalin (see p. 62) and Rudolf Koch's Kabel.

Refuel

ABCDEFGHIJKLMNOPQRSTUVWXYZ
abcdefghijklmnopqrstuvwxyz
1234567890 !@#?:;"*&

Foundry: Typodermic
Designer: Ray Larabie
Designer Nationality: Canadian
Date: 2016

An octagonal sans serif inspired by the type used on military aircraft, Refuel is a versatile family of six widths and six weights with italics, and support for Latin, Cyrillic, Greek, and Vietnamese. A clever feature is the capital "L," which gains serifs when set next to a lowercase "l."

Scene

ABCDEFGHIJKLMNOPQRSTUVWXYZ
abcdefghijklmnopqrstuvwxyz
1234567890 !@#?:;"*&

Foundry: Monotype
Designer: Seb Lester
Designer Nationality: British
Date: 2002

Seb Lester, who studied at Central Saint Martins College of Arts and Design and joined Monotype in 2000, was the designer of Scene, a versatile sans serif available in six weights with italics. Lester aimed to create a "clean, calm and highly legible" sans and developed Scene for over two years.

Styrene A

ABCDEFGHIJKLMNOPQRSTUVWXYZ
abcdefghijklmnopqrstuvwxyz
1234567890 !@#?:;"*&

Foundry: Commercial Type
Designer: Berton Hasebe
Designer Nationality: American
Date: 2016

Styrene A is geometric sans serif initially inspired by Breede Schreeflooze, a sans serif from a type specimen published by the Enschedé Typefoundry in 1932. Alongside its strict geometry, Styrene A is distinctive for its treatment of narrow forms, such as "f," "j," and "r," which are stretched and flattened.

Styrene B

ABCDEFGHIJKLMNOPQRSTUVWXYZ
abcdefghijklmnopqrstuvwxyz
1234567890 !@#?:;"*&

Foundry: Commercial Type
Designer: Berton Hasebe
Designer Nationality: American
Date: 2016

Styrene B is a narrower version of its sibling font Styrene A, designed for less spacious texts and environments. It is not truly condensed and the letterforms retain the guiding geometric principles, but with slightly more flexibility, and preserve the characteristic features of the design.

Foundry Profile

Colophon

Founded in 2009 by Edd Harrington and Anthony Sheret, Colophon is an international, award-winning independent type foundry based in London and Los Angeles, creating, publishing, and distributing high-quality retail and custom typefaces for analogue and digital media. It was initially formed as a design studio, The Entente, and Colophon Foundry was launched three months later.

Colophon's prominence within typeface design came to the fore when it released its grotesque sans serif Aperçu (see p. 186) in 2010. Adopted by organizations such as New York's Museum of Modern Art and a favored choice for contemporary editorial work, Aperçu soared in popularity, as did the foundry behind it.

Colophon's approach has been to task itself with producing fonts that are composed with aesthetic and technological care. Consequently, its reputable library of typefaces are considered modern classics that couple typographic history with contemporary sensibilities. In addition to its own designs, the foundry hosts and distributes original typefaces drawn by influential type designers and practitioners from varied design disciplines. The extensive catalogue offers graphic designers and typographers a wealth of opportunity with highly crafted considered fonts. As well as offering a diverse retail portfolio of more than thirty typefaces, Colophon takes on commissions for custom fonts, font families and logotypes, as well as tailoring bespoke versions of its existing typefaces, which include language extensions.

Colophon also provides an innovative and fun buying guide online, which enables the user to navigate the issues regarding licensing for different media and allowances for foreign-language versions incorporating Greek or Cyrillic fonts.

Founded: 2009
Countries: British / American
Website: colophon-foundry.org
Notable typefaces:
Aperçu (see p. 186)
Lisbon (see p. 554)

Below. A 24-page catalogue showcasing the concept and technical aspects of the Relative typeface family.

Opposite top and middle rows. Central Avenue typeface family specimen booklet. The unbound booklet also works as a series of four posters.

Opposite bottom row. Future II poster designed by Colophon Foundry.

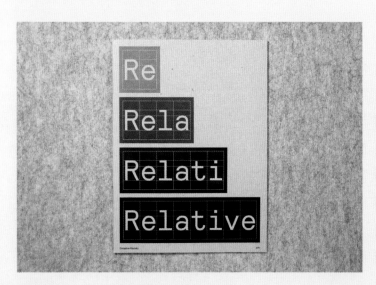

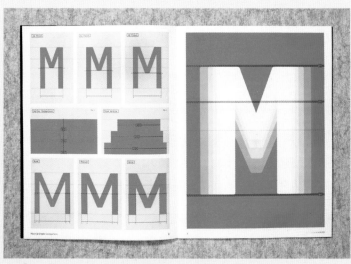

Twentieth Century

ABCDEFGHIJKLMNOPQRSTUVWXYZ
abcdefghijklmnopqrstuvwxyz
1234567890 !@#?:;"*&

Foundry: Monotype
Designer: Sol Hess
Designer Nationality: American
Date: 1936–47

Twentieth Century is a geometric sans serif, drawn between 1936 and 1947, and informed by the Bauhausian typefaces produced in Germany in the 1920s. Designed for function over form, the geometric shapes are disrupted only by the sharp, cutting junctures, which add distinction.

Ulissa

ABCDEFGHIJKLMNOPQRSTUVWXYZ
abcdefghijklmnopqrstuvwxyz
1234567890 !@#?:;"*&

Foundry: Monotype
Designer: Johannes Birkenbach
Designer Nationality: German
Date: 1993

Ulissa is a geometric sans serif, designed in Johannes Birkenbach's final year at Monotype before he returned to Germany to establish his own design studio, ABC Design. Ulissa's narrow, geometric frame is combined with acute joints and stroke endings to ensure legibility in all sizes.

Uni Grotesk

ABCDEFGHIJKLMNOPQRSTUVWXYZ
abcdefghijklmnopqrstuvwxyz
1234567890 !@#?:;"*&

Foundry: Typotheque
Designer: Peter Biľak / Nikola Djurek / Hrvoje Živčić
Designer Nationality: Slovakian / Croatian / Croatian
Date: 2016

Uni Grotesk is a modern adaptation of Universal Grotesk, a popular font from Communist Czechoslovakia, and is a geometric sans serif with the details of a 20th-century European grotesque. Unlike the original, Uni Grotesk also includes an italic version based upon the upright styles.

VAG Rounded

ABCDEFGHIJKLMNOPQRSTUVWXYZ
abcdefghijklmnopqrstuvwxyz
1234567890 !@#?:;"*&

Foundry: Linotype
Designer: Gerry Barney / David Bristow / Terence Griffin / Ian Hay / Kit Cooper
Designer Nationality: British
Date: 1979

Initially released as a corporate typeface for Volkswagen in 1979, VAG Rounded is a circular, geometric sans serif. The font family was released publicly in 1989 and alongside general release, it has been used by corporations such as Apple, Skype, and Myspace.

VAG Rounded Next

ABCDEFGHIJKLMNOPQRSTUVWXYZ
abcdefghijklmnopqrstuvwxyz
1234567890 !@#?:;"*&

Foundry: Linotype
Designer: Steve Matteson / Tom Grace
Designer Nationality: American
Date: 2018

VAG Rounded Next is an update and extension of the VAG Rounded font family. Maintaining its characteristically curved stroke endings and light informality, VAG Rounded Next includes the addition of two extra styles, Shine, and Rough, and much expanded European language support.

Value Sans

ABCDEFGHIJKLMNOPQRSTUVWXYZ
abcdefghijklmnopqrstuvwxyz
1234567890 !@#?:;"*&

Foundry: Colophon
Designer: The Entente
Designer Nationality: British
Date: 2012 / 2018

Value Sans is a geometric sans serif, designed in 2012 to contemplate the benefits of cultural and economic exchange. The design, which was expanded in 2018 to comprise four weights, finds inspiration in the style of typefaces such as the German Elegant Grotesk and the British Granby.

Visuelt

ABCDEFGHIJKLMNOPQRSTUVWXYZ
abcdefghijklmnopqrstuvwxyz
1234567890 !@#?:;"*&

Foundry: Colophon
Designer: The Entente
Designer Nationality: British
Date: 2013 / 2015 / 2016

Visuelt is a geometric sans serif, initially designed in 2013 for the National Norwegian Design Awards, commonly known as the "Visuelt." In 2015, the designers added light and black weights to the existing regular, while Medium and Bold weights were introduced in 2016.

Vita

ABCDEFGHIJKLMNOPQRSTUVWXYZ
abcdefghijklmnopqrstuvwxyz
1234567890 !@#?:;"*&

Foundry: Typotheque
Designer: Nikola Djurek
Designer Nationality: Croatian
Date: 2016

Vita is a 21st-century geometric sans serif, designed to perform effectively on both high- and low-resolution screens. Its modest yet distinctive characters, which feature minimalist serifs to distinguish between similar shapes, maintain its legibility at smaller sizes.

Akkurat Pro

ABCDEFGHIJKLMNOPQRSTUVWXYZ
abcdefghijklmnopqrstuvwxyz
1234567890 !@#?:;"*&

Foundry: Lineto
Designer: Laurenz Brunner
Designer Nationality: Swiss
Date: 2004

A contemporary take on the "pragmatic" traditions of Swiss typography, Akkurat, created by German type designer Laurenz Brunner, is an acclaimed modern-day classic of grotesque sans serif design. Sometimes referred to as a "Helvetica killer," it is available in three weights, with accompanying italics, and an alternate monospaced variation was made available in 2005. Ideal for a range of applications, the design allows for optimum readability for text set at nearly all sizes. Widely used in print because of its excellent legibility in editorial and publishing applications, Akkurat has become increasingly popular for web use in recent years. Its slightly widened letter spacing, more vertical forms and clean, simple character shapes improve on-screen readability greatly, even at reduced text sizes or on the poorest of displays.

Below. Part of a series of striking typographic poster designs by Portuguese studio Atelier Pedro Falcão employing Lineto's Akkurat Pro for the *Departamento de Arquitectura Universidade Autónoma de Lisboa.*

Aktiv Grotesk

ABCDEFGHIJKLMNOPQRSTUVWXYZ
abcdefghijklmnopqrstuvwxyz
1234567890 !@#?:;"*&

A typeface that goes all out to be a "Helvetica killer," Dalton Maag (see p. 594) first released Aktiv Grotesk in 2010 as a passion project for the studio founder and type designer Bruno Maag. Describing Helvetica as the "vanilla ice cream" of a designer's type library, Maag was determined to create an alternative grotesque to the most ubiquitous of Swiss grotesques, one that stayed true to the grotesque tradition—no humanist aspects, but remaining neutral and authoritative while retaining an element of "warmth" in its design with characters being simple, clear, and consistent.

Aktiv Grotesk is a hugely comprehensive and diverse design with twenty-four weights and matching italics, from Hairline to Black, with support for more than 130 languages. It can truly be described as a global grotesque and one that can be employed in every conceivable application across all media.

Foundry: Dalton Maag
Designer: Bruno Maag / Alex Blattmann / Pilar Cano / Fernando Caro / Kalapi Gajjar / Fabio Haag
Designer Nationality: Swiss / Swiss / Spanish / Brazilian / Indian / Brazilian
Date: 2010–18

Below. Example of weight scaling for Condensed, Standard and Extended styles and Dalton Maag promotional print to launch Aktiv Grotesk.

" So success for Aktiv would be to see Helvetica driven from the face of the earth?
BM Yes! When I do lectures I always have a little rant about Helvetica and at the end I say if everyone in the world used Univers instead from now on I'd happily retire, but it ain't going to happen.
PB When this is out can you let Helvetica go? Have you exorcised the demon?
BM Yes, it's catharsis. It's done now.

PB So let's talk about Aktiv, Dalt Maag's new Helvetica killer. Ca design a typeface in oppositic something? Is that what you s to do or were you just trying to as good a grotesk as you coul general use? BM Clearly, because we are competing against Uni Helvetica there are a lot of close similarities. The higher than Helvetica but the rounds have a little them that Helvetica's don't have. The differences are really subtle but give it just that bit of p pronged really. One was the fact that we were looking at our font library and felt that we were in a Univers style, purely as a commercial entity. It has been at the back of our minds to do th years now. We wanted to have a grotesk font positioned somewhere between Helvetica and as Univers but devoid of all the quirks of Helvetica. To have a font that is beautifully crafted, s chink in a curve or anything – perfectly drawn but hopefully with a bit of personality. We war

Albany

ABCDEFGHIJKLMNOPQRSTUVWXYZ
abcdefghijklmnopqrstuvwxyz
1234567890 !@#?:;"*&

Foundry: Monotype
Designer: Monotype Studio
Date: 2016

Possessing identical metrics to Robin Nicholas's ubiquitous Arial, this patriotic sans serif differs from both Arial and its arch rival Helvetica by having square dots over the letters "i" and "j." In contrast to its predecessors, it also has more open letterforms with larger apertures and counters.

Angro

ABCDEFGHIJKLMNOPQRSTUVWXYZ
abcdefghijklmnopqrstuvwxyz
1234567890 !@#?:;"*&

Foundry: Linotype
Designer: Erwin Koch
Designer Nationality: German
Date: 1989

Designed to be used with Hell typesetting machines, Angro has two weights, Light and Bold, and a distinctive lowercase "g." Based on a rectangular form, it has short "W"s and descenders and a high x-height, meaning that it can be set with very close line spacing.

Applied Sans

ABCDEFGHIJKLMNOPQRSTUVWXYZ
abcdefghijklmnopqrstuvwxyz
1234567890 !@#?:;"*&

Foundry: Monotype
Designer: Akira Kobayashi / Sandra Winter
Designer Nationality: Japanese / German
Date: 2016

Applied Sans was designed as a refined and more human version of early "jobbing" or "trade" grotesques from the late 19th and early 20th centuries. The typeface has open counters, large apertures, a generous x-height and terminals that are at 90° to the character strokes.

Arial

ABCDEFGHIJKLMNOPQRSTUVWXYZ
abcdefghijklmnopqrstuvwxyz
1234567890 !@#?:;"*&

Foundry: Monotype
Designer: Robin Nicholas / Patricia Saunders
Designer Nationality: British
Date: 1982

Allegedly commissioned by IBM because Microsoft did not want to license Helvetica—with which it shares the same metrics—Arial has appeared in Windows 3.1 onwards and also on the Mac operating systems. This generic sans serif comes in numerous weights and styles, including a rounded version.

Arial Nova

ABCDEFGHIJKLMNOPQRSTUVWXYZ
abcdefghijklmnopqrstuvwxyz
1234567890 !@#?:;"*&

Foundry: Monotype
Designer: Robin Nicholas / Patricia Saunders / Monotype Studio
Designer Nationality: British
Date: 1982 / 2014

Forever associated with the Windows operating system, Arial Nova is a reboot of Robin Nicholas's and Patricia Saunders's original version of Arial created for IBM laser printers in 1982. It features three weights of roman and three weights of condensed, all with matching italics.

Basic Commercial

ABCDEFGHIJKLMNOPQRSTUVWXYZ
abcdefghijklmnopqrstuvwxyz
1234567890 !@#?:;"*&

Foundry: Linotype
Designer: Linotype Design Studio
Date: 1900 / 1999

Basic Commercial is a type family based on sans serifs launched by the Berthold Foundry in Germany in 1898, as the Akzidenz Grotesk series. These typefaces were marketed as the Standard family elsewhere. Linotype made its version of Standard in 1957, and Basic Commercial follows those designs.

Basis

ABCDEFGHIJKLMNOPQRSTUVWXYZ
abcdefghijklmnopqrstuvwxyz
1234567890 !@#?:;"*&

Foundry: Colophon
Designer: The Entente
Designer Nationality: British
Date: 2015

Initially produced for the redesign of photography magazine *Hotshoe* in 2012, Basis is a sans serif font family with sixteen styles. Informed by early Monotype grotesques, but intentionally given more shape, Basis is defined by its tight apertures, curvy terminals, and refined counters.

Bell Centennial

ABCDEFGHIJKLMNOPQRSTUVWXYZ
abcdefghijklmnopqrstuvwxyz
1234567890 !@#?:;"*&

Foundry: Mergenthaler Linotype
Designer: Matthew Carter
Designer Nationality: British
Date: 1978

Commissioned by AT&T, this economical sans serif saved the telecoms company millions of dollars. Compared to the previously used Bell Gothic, it saved space and it also provided increased legibility under difficult printing conditions, which in turn reduced calls to the help desk.

Berthold Akzidenz Grotesk

ABCDEFGHIJKLMNOPQRSTUVWXYZ
abcdefghijklmnopqrstuvwxyz
1234567890 !@#?:;"*&

Foundry: Berthold
Designer: Günter Gerhard Lange
Designer Nationality: German
Date: 1958

Often referred to as the "original" sans serif, Akzidenz Grotesk has clean lines and forms that mean it is often mistaken for Helvetica (see p. 229) or Univers (see p. 248). However, its subtle varying stroke weights, more circular counters and bowls gives it a warmer and slightly softer appearance than its rivals.

Akzidenz Grotesk dates to a period of design much further back than the aforementioned 1950s' typefaces. The original design is believed to date to the 1880s, and understood to have been developed from Didone serif fonts such as the Walbaum and Didot typefaces. With their serifs removed, the proportions of the types are similar to a sans serif font resembling Akzidenz Grotesk.

As the years passed, Akzidenz Grotesk became a collection of differing grotesque types carrying the same name until the 1950s, when Günter Gerhard Lange, the art director for the renowned German type foundry Berthold, revised and improved upon the existing arrangment of designs to create the version of Akzidenz Grotesk of today. His efforts in increasing legibility and flexibility with a variety of weights led Akzidenz Grotesk to become one of the most widely used and successful typefaces in the world today as well as an instant classic.

Below left. *Fikkefuchs* movie poster by Johannes Stoll employing Akzidenz Grotesk and its condensed variant.

Below right. One of a series of posters, entitled *Swissted*, an ongoing project by US graphic designer Mike Joyce. Each poster is designed around lowercase Berthold Akzidenz Grotesk Medium and the designer's love of punk rock and Swiss Modernism.

Opposite. The School of Life special events poster designed by Tako Chabukiani.

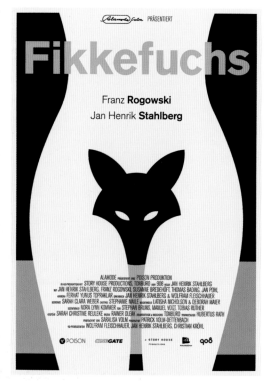

the school of life

2015

special events

18.40

5 February
Finding Your Voice
Caroline Goyder

12 February
A Romantic Take On Work
Tim Leberecht

19 February
Getting Perspective
Jack Fuller

26 February
Why Compassion Matters
Dr Chris Irons

To book visit:
theschooloflife.com
All events £55

The School of Life
70 Marchmont Street
London WC1N 1AB

Bell Gothic

ABCDEFGHIJKLMNOPQRSTUVWXYZ
abcdefghijklmnopqrstuvwxyz
1234567890 !@#?:;"*&

AT&T used Bell Gothic as its principal typeface for telephone books and other printed materials until 1978, when it became available for use by the public. Chauncey H. Griffith designed the typeface in 1938, when he was head of type development at Linotype. His experience with Excelsior, the highly successful newspaper typeface he created, earmarked him for the AT&T commission. The new typeface was required to be read at very small sizes and yet printed at very high speed, so the design had to overcome these challenging factors and ensure that legibility and readability were not compromised in any way. Griffith also had to optimize the restricted space it would be set within. The result, Bell Gothic, stood the test of time, and is still a popular choice within the design and publishing industries.

Foundry: Linotype
Designer: Chauncey H. Griffith
Designer Nationality: American
Date: 1938

Right. Promotional poster for director Alejandro G. Iñárritu's Oscar-winning film *Birdman*. Bell Gothic was the primary typeface for the marketing materials and also employed on the film's opening credits in an all capitals treatment.

Beret

ABCDEFGHIJKLMNOPQRSTUVWXYZ
abcdefghijklmnopqrstuvwxyz
1234567890 !@#?:;"*&

Foundry: Linotype
Designer: Eduardo Omine
Designer Nationality: Brazilian
Date: 2003

A jaunty sans serif, Beret has distinctive terminals at the ends of its vertical strokes which are slightly bent, suggesting a subtle flare and giving the impression that the letters are leaning. It comes with a set of obliques rather than traditional italics and is suitable for many applications, in both text and display sizes.

Between

ABCDEFGHIJKLMNOPQRSTUVWXYZ
abcdefghijklmnopqrstuvwxyz
1234567890 !@#?:;"*&

Foundry: Monotype
Designer: Akira Kobayashi
Designer Nationality: Japanese
Date: 2016

Between comprises one typeface with three different styles. Between 1, 2, and 3 have subtly different characteristics but share some of the same key characters, as well as caps and x-heights, which means that they have a harmonious feel when used together.

Brezel Grotesk

ABCDEFGHIJKLMNOPQRSTUVWXYZ
abcdefghijklmnopqrstuvwxyz
1234567890 !@#?:;"*&

Foundry: Milieu Grotesque
Designer: Stefanie Preis /
Milieu Grotesque
Designer Nationality: German /
Swiss
Date: 2011 / 2015

Brezel Grotesk, as its name implies, is informed by the character of traditional 19th-century sans serif grotesques and the looping shape of a Bavarian pretzel. Initially designed in 2011 by Stefanie Preis, Brezel Grotesk was revised and extended by Milieu Grotesque in 2015.

Bureau Grotesque

ABCDEFGHIJKLMNOPQRSTUVWXYZ
abcdefghijklmnopqrstuvwxyz
1234567890 !@#?:;"*&

Foundry: Font Bureau
Designer: David Berlow /
Jill Pichotta / Christian
Schwartz / Richard Lipton
Designer Nationality: American
Date: 1989–2006

Developed from original specimens of the grotesques made by the Stephenson, Blake & Co. foundry in Sheffield, Yorkshire, David Berlow added further weights to Bureau Grotesque. Jill Pichotta, Christian Schwartz and Richard Lipton expanded it further. It also goes under the name of 'Bureau Grot'.

CG Symphony

ABCDEFGHIJKLMNOPQRSTUVWXYZ
abcdefghijklmnopqrstuvwxyz
1234567890 !@#?:;"*&

Foundries: Stempel /
Compugraphic
Designer: Hans Eduard Meier /
Compugraphic Design Studio
Designer Nationality: German
Date: 1968 / 1988

Comprising Regular, Regular Italic, Bold and Black, CG Symphony is a restrained serif that started life as Hans Eduard Meier's Syntax (sometimes known as Syntax-Antiqua), and was one of the first one hundred PostScript faces released by Compugraphic in 1988.

Chiswick Grotesque

ABCDEFGHIJKLMNOPQRSTUVWXYZ
abcdefghijklmnopqrstuvwxyz
1234567890 !@#?:;"*&

Foundry: Commercial Type
Designer: Paul Barnes
Designer Nationality: British
Date: 2016

Chiswick Grotesque is a grotesque sans serif, the kind of style commonly seen in the early 19th century. The burly, industrial characters merge geometric frames with eccentric strokes, as seen in the loop of the lowercase "g" or the leg of the "k." It comes in eight weights plus italics.

Cisalpin

ABCDEFGHIJKLMNOPQRSTUVWXYZ
abcdefghijklmnopqrstuvwxyz
1234567890 !@#?:;"*&

Foundry: Linotype
Designer / Felix Arnold
Designer Nationality: Swiss
Date: 2004

A linear typeface designed specifically to be used for cartography Cisalpin is naturally very compact and legible at small sizes. Its letterforms have flattened curves, open interior forms and tall x-heights, with a capital height that almost reaches the tops of the ascenders.

Classic Grotesque

ABCDEFGHIJKLMNOPQRSTUVWXYZ
abcdefghijklmnopqrstuvwxyz
1234567890 !@#?:;"*&

Foundry: Monotype
Designer: Frank Hinman Pierpont / Rod McDonald
Designer Nationality: American / Canadian
Date: 1926 / 2008

This is a new take on the original Monotype Grotesque, with seven weights from Light to Extra Bold. A restrained sans serif, it bears the hallmark of a traditional grotesque but has some subtle variations in its uppercase letters, including bevelled terminals and curved descenders.

Compatil Fact

ABCDEFGHIJKLMNOPQRSTUVWXYZ
abcdefghijklmnopqrstuvwxyz
1234567890 !@#?:;"*&

Foundry: Linotype
Designer: Olaf Leu / Linotype Design Studio
Designer Nationality: German
Date: 2001

Compatil Fact is a refined sans serif forming part of the Compatil type system, created specifically for use in annual reports. This system comprises four compatible typefaces, each with four weights, making it possible to set any combination of different styles effortlessly.

Corinthian

ABCDEFGHIJKLMNOPQRSTUVWXYZ
abcdefghijklmnopqrstuvwxyz
1234567890 !@#?:;"*&

Foundry: ITC
Designer: Colin Brignall
Designer Nationality: British
Date: 1981

Colin Brignall designed Corinthian when he was type director of Letraset. It is an unassuming monolineal sans serif for text and display use, which takes inspiration from the typefaces of Edward Johnston and Eric Gill. Corinthian is available in four weights: Light, Medium, Bold, and Condensed.

Dialog

ABCDEFGHIJKLMNOPQRSTUVWXYZ
abcdefghijklmnopqrstuvwxyz
1234567890 !@#?:;"*&

Foundry: Omnibus
Designer: Franko Luin
Designer Nationality: Swedish
Date: 1993

Available in weights from Light to Extra Bold, all with a condensed and italic version, this is the first sans serif typeface designed by Franko Luin. After several false starts, and despite preferring serifs, he created Dialog—a confident sans serif suitable for multiple applications.

Divulge

ABCDEFGHIJKLMNOPQRSTUVWXYZ
abcdefghijklmnopqrstuvwxyz
1234567890 !@#?:;"*&

Foundry: Typodermic
Designer: Ray Larabie
Designer Nationality: Canadian
Date: 2008

Divulge is a modern grotesque inspired by metal type of the 19th and early 20th centuries. It is a handsome but restrained sans serif with some idiosyncratic features, which is available in three weights—Light, Medium, and Bold—with two widths and matching italics.

Elastik

ABCDEFGHIJKLMNOPQRSTUVWXYZ
abcdefghijklmnopqrstuvwxyz
1234567890 !@#?:;"*&

Foundry: BB-Bureau
Designer: Benoit Bedhuin
Designer Nationality: French
Date: 2017

Elastik is a grotesque sans serif with elasticated punctuation and diacritical marks, designed in four styles. The A style is small, B is regular, C is oversized, and D is extra-oversize. As the sizes increase, the mark's proportions stretch like elasticated materials.

Endurance

ABCDEFGHIJKLMNOPQRSTUVWXYZ
abcdefghijklmnopqrstuvwxyz
1234567890 !@#?:;"*&

Foundry: Ascender
Designer: Steve Matteson
Designer Nationality: American
Date: 2004

Created as a more refined, less industrial-looking Neo-grotesque sans serif, Endurance is designed to function well under challenging conditions, from mobile to billboard-sized applications. Optimized for on-screen legibility, it has careful detailing in order to give a refined appearance in large sizes.

Esseltube

ABCDEFGHIJKLMNOPQRSTUVWXYZ
abcdefghijklmnopqrstuvwxyz
1234567890 !@#?:;"'*&

Foundry: Linotype
Designer: Stig Åke Möller / Bo Berndal
Designer Nationality: Swedish
Date: 1955

Also known as "SL-Grotesk" and "Esseltub," the Esseltube sans serif typeface was originally created for the Stockholm underground system. It was designed by Stig Åke Möller and digitized by Bo Berndal. In the 1980s, it was replaced with black and white signs using Helvetica.

Folio

ABCDEFGHIJKLMNOPQRSTUVWXYZ
abcdefghijklmnopqrstuvwxyz
1234567890 !@#?:;"*&

Foundry: Bauer Type
Designer: Konrad F. Bauer / Walter Baum
Designer Nationality: German
Date: 1957

Released at the same time as Helvetica and Univers, Folio is a realist sans serif that is also modelled on Akzidenz Grotesk but follows its proportions more closely than Helvetica and Univers, which have larger x-heights. Extra Bold and Condensed versions were added in 1963.

FF Sizmo

ABCDEFGHIJKLMNOPQRSTUVWXYZ
abcdefghijklmnopqrstuvwxyz
1234567890 !@#?:;"*&

Foundry: FontFont
Designer: Verena Gerlach
Designer Nationality: German
Date: 2017

FF Sizmo is available in five weights from Light to Bold. It is unusual in that all its weights come in a separate "Line" version, in which a line runs along the bottom of the letterforms—with the exception of letters that drop below or are open to the baseline—and joins them up.

Foundry Context

ABCDEFGHIJKLMNOPQRSTUVWXYZ
abcdefghijklmnopqrstuvwxyz
1234567890 !@#?:;"*&

Foundry: The Foundry
Designer: David Quay
Designer Nationality: British
Date: 2005

Foundry Context is a grotesque sans serif designed for universal use and inspired by the utilitarian sans serifs of the 19th century. The letterforms are modest in stroke contrast and neutral in character, resisting the superfluous details usually found in terminals or joints.

FS Industrie

ABCDEFGHIJKLMNOPQRSTUVWXYZ
abcdefghijklmnopqrstuvwxyz
1234567890 !@?:;"*&

Foundry: Fonstmith
Designer: Phil Garnham /
Fernando Mello
Designer Nationality: British /
Brazilian
Date: 2018

FS Industrie is an incredibly versatile type system, with seventy variants within its family, consisting of five differing widths (Condensed, Narrow, Standard, Wide, and Extended) and seven different weights (ranging from Thin to Black). It was created by the type design director Phil Garnham and senior type designer Fernando Mello of London foundry Fontsmith (see p. 272). The key approach behind the design was to create a typeface that embraces "variable design," an inbuilt flexibility within the system that adapts to the changing needs of brands. As more communications go online, digital platforms evolve and in turn create new opportunities in how they present the written word.

The core design is based on fonts from Germany in the 1930s, whose origins emanate from manufacturing and signage applications. FS Industrie harnesses the clean and considered approach of these functional and highly legible fonts. The design adapts through the styles and the weights. Each character is hand drawn, and careful consideration has been given to the letterforms, with subtle changes in the terminals and angles according to the weight and style required. This creates a consistent visual design that evolves, as seen in the closed terminals of the Condensed version which gradually open up across the styles and form open terminals in the Extended version. Given its flexibility and functionality, FS Industrie is likely to be future-proof.

Below. Fontsmith launched FS Industrie with a limited-edition promotion of 1,000 printed specimen books, each design being unique. After a survey of hundreds of design professionals, each design had the recipient's name die-cut in the cover using a punched-card system. The content from the survey was then used inside to promote the typeface's abilities.

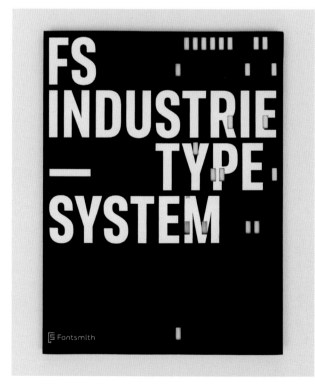

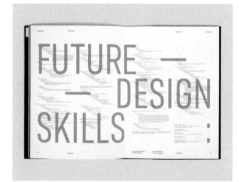

FS Jack

ABCDEFGHIJKLMNOPQRSTUVWXYZ
abcdefghijklmnopqrstuvwxyz
1234567890 !@#?:;"*&

Jason Smith and Fernando Mello designed FS Jack to include certain distinctive quirks within key letterforms, and it is particularly expressive in its heavier weights. In 2010, the typeface family won the Families category at the Tipos Latinos type design biennial in Mello's home country, Brazil.

Foundry: Fontsmith
Designer: Fernando Mello / Jason Smith
Designer Nationality: Brazilian / British
Date: 2010

FS Koopman

ABCDEFGHIJKLMNOPQRSTUVWXYZ
abcdefghijklmnopqrstuvwxyz
1234567890 !@#?:;"*&

The lighter cuts of FS Koopman display the influence of classic Swiss sans serif typography; its bold weights, however, feature details reminiscent of 20th-century British grotesques. Designers Andy Lethbridge and Stuart de Rozario also added an American Gothic flavour to the mix.

Foundry: Fontsmith
Designer: Andy Lethbridge / Stuart de Rozario
Designer Nationality: British
Date: 2018

Gerstner-Programm FSL

ABCDEFGHIJKLMNOPQRSTUVWXYZ
abcdefghijklmnopqrstuvwxyz
1234567890 !@#?:;"*&

Gerstner-Programm FSL is the digital reissue of an original type design by Karl Gerstner drawn between 1964 and 1967. Berthold first marketed the design with its Diatype phototypesetting system in 1967. Forgotten Shapes' published the reissue with Gerstner's permission

Foundry: Forgotten Shapes
Designer: Karl Gerstner / Stephan Müller
Designer Nationality: Swiss
Date: 1964–67 / 2007–17

GGX88

ABCDEFGHIJKLMNOPQRSTUVWXYZ
abcdefghijklmnopqrstuvwxyz
1234567890 !@#?:;"*&

Ray Larabie developed his Swiss-influenced design for GGX88 with screen use in mind. Its letterforms are optimized to be clear and legible in a range of digital contexts, such as TV screens, phones and watches. It includes seven weights with corresponding italics for each.

Foundry: Typodermic
Designer: Ray Larabie
Designer Nationality: Canadian
Date: 2010

Gothic 720

ABCDEFGHIJKLMNOPQRSTUVWXYZ
abcdefghijklmnopqrstuvwxyz
1234567890 !@#?:;"*&

Foundries: Monotype / Bitstream
Designer: Frank Hinman Pierpont
Designer Nationality: American
Date: 1926

This Bitstream font was modelled on the letterforms of Frank Hinman Pierpont's series of grotesque typefaces published by Monotype in the 1920s. The Monotype grotesques were themselves based on Berthold's Ideal Grotesk, and also referenced the Bauer type foundry's popular Venus typeface.

Graphik

ABCDEFGHIJKLMNOPQRSTUVWXYZ
abcdefghijklmnopqrstuvwxyz
1234567890 !@#?:;"*&

Foundry: Commercial Type
Designer: Christian Schwartz
Designer Nationality: American
Date: 2009

Graphik is a muted grotesque sans serif designed for efficacy across a variety of contexts and platforms. Instead of looking to the mainstays of utilitarian sans serifs, such as Helvetica or Univers, designer Christian Schwartz took inspiration from lesser known types such as Plak and Folio.

Graphik Compact

ABCDEFGHIJKLMNOPQRSTUVWXYZ
abcdefghijklmnopqrstuvwxyz
1234567890 !@#?:;"*&

Foundry: Commercial Type
Designer: Christian Schwartz
Designer Nationality: American
Date: 2017

Graphik Compact is a narrow alternative to the full-bodied Graphik and is intended for designs that require a strict economy of space, such as signage and user interfaces. While reduced in width, its letterforms retain a strong frame and open counters for maximum legibility.

Graphik Condensed

ABCDEFGHIJKLMNOPQRSTUVWXYZ
abcdefghijklmnopqrstuvwxyz
1234567890 !@#?:;"*&

Foundry: Commercial Type
Designer: Christian Schwartz
Designer Nationality: American
Date: 2017

Unlike Graphik Compact, which aims to maintain the physique of the original design, Graphik Condensed is closer to traditional condensed styles. While the vertical strokes are lengthened, the type's character is preserved in the curved upper and lower parts of the letterforms.

Graphik Wide

ABCDEFGHIJKLMNOPQRSTUVWXY
abcdefghijklmnopqrstuvwxyz
1234567890 !@#?:;"*&

Foundry: Commercial Type
Designer: Christian Schwartz
Designer Nationality: American
Date: 2018

Graphik Wide is a wide-set grotesque font family, inspired by the extended sans serifs that emerged in the 19th century, as well as those designed in the systematic tradition of the 20th century. The characters maintain a distinctly rounded shape, as per the original Graphik design.

GT America

ABCDEFGHIJKLMNOPQRSTUVWXYZ
abcdefghijklmnopqrstuvwxyz
1234567890 !@#?:;"*&

Foundry: Grilli Type
Designer: Noël Leu /
Seb McLauchlan
Designer Nationality: Swiss
Date: 2016

GT America is named after channelling the design origins of 20th-century European Neo-grotesques and 19th-century American Gothics, with a pragmatic, Swiss approach. The letterforms have tapered stems and angled spurs, with eighty-four styles available across six widths and seven weights.

GT Pressura

ABCDEFGHIJKLMNOPQRSTUVWXYZ
abcdefghijklmnopqrstuvwxyz
1234567890 !@#?:;"*&

Foundry: Grilli Type
Designer: Marc Kappeler /
Dominik Huber
Designer Nationality: Swiss
Date: 2012

Independent Swiss foundry Grilli Type (see p. 238) released GT Pressura in 2012. Inspired by the visual effect of ink spreading under pressure, Pressura is a robust sans available in regular and monospace, in three weights with italics. It was revised and extended with Cyrillic support in 2017.

GT Zirkon

ABCDEFGHIJKLMNOPQRSTUVWXYZ
abcdefghijklmnopqrstuvwxyz
1234567890 !@#?:;"*&

Foundry: Grilli Type
Designer: Tobias Rechsteiner
Designer Nationality: Swiss
Date: 2018

GT Zirkon is a grotesque sans serif that foregrounds the details typically found in small-scale body copy. Features such as ink traps, tapered curves and a high contrast between strokes are utilized as stylistic devices to enhance its character and utility.

Helvetica

ABCDEFGHIJKLMNOPQRSTUVWXYZ
abcdefghijklmnopqrstuvwxyz
1234567890 !@#?:;"*&

Foundry: Haas Type Foundry
Designer: Max Miedinger /
Eduard Hoffmann
Designer Nationality: Swiss
Date: 1957

Swiss typeface designer Max Miedinger, under the direction of Eduard Hoffmann, Haas director and fellow type designer, was responsible for designing perhaps the most widely used sans serif typeface, and possibly any typeface, of all time. Created in 1957 and originally titled Neue Haas Grotesk, it was renamed Helvetica in 1959 when released by Haas's new owners Stempel for the Linotype, which led to global success and domination in many quarters. At the Haas Type Foundry in Münchenstein, Switzerland, the two collaborated in creating a grotesque sans serif that would compete with the existing and popular Akzidenz Grotesk (see p. 218) released in 1898 by the Berthold Foundry of Berlin. Neither would envisage the phenomenal success that Helvetica would become once their work was done.

Miedinger trained as a typesetter from 1926, entering the School of Arts and Crafts, Abendkurse in Zurich. From 1947 to 1956, he worked at Haas before going freelance and picking up a commission from his now previous employer for the Neue Haas Grotesk project. The renaming of the typeface was undertaken by Haas's parent company Stempel and is a variation on the Latin word for Switzerland, Helvetia. Despite the designers expressing concern over the new name, it benefited from the positive attention the Swiss design movement had at the time of its release, and its universal appeal led to widespread usage. When Miedinger died in 1980 his legacy was the creation of one of the most specified and used typefaces of the 20th century. In 2007, US filmmaker Gary Hustwit directed the film *Helvetica* to celebrate its 50th anniversary.

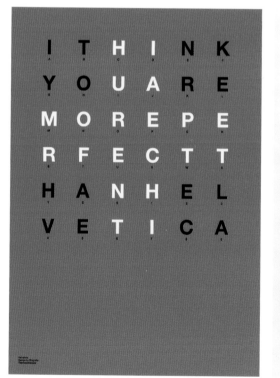

Far left. Poster design by Spanish studio Bisgràfic and their 2015 tribute to Helvetica.

Left. Taiwanese graphic designers Leslie Chan Wing Kei and Pei Lin share their feelings and the love for Miedinger and Hoffmann's sans serif, although Helvetica is not without its critics—in part due to its success. This is a typeface with a global reach.

Helvetica Neue

ABCDEFGHIJKLMNOPQRSTUVWXYZ
abcdefghijklmnopqrstuvwxyz
1234567890 !@#?:;"'*&

Foundry: Stempel / Linotype
Designer: Max Meidinger /
Linotype Design Studio
Designer Nationality: Swiss
Date: 1957 / 1983

Helvetica soon found global success after its release in 1957. Since then, a range of variations have been created, as well as derivative clones released, in an attempt to gain a share of the original's market. The variations that exist are wide and varied. Among them there are a number that are highly considered and which follow the principles of neutrality and aesthetic simplicity seen in the original designs.

Variations were not just created for commercial gain. As there were technological improvements in typesetting, from hot-metal composition through to digital fonts, so stresses were placed on the original designs that had in some ways been compromised by the technologies of the day. This meant the design warranted a revisit to embrace the opportunities and benefits that digital could bring to it.

The first digital version was Helvetica Neue, released by Linotype subsidiary Stempel. It is a complete reworking of the original Helvetica,

which, like Univers, follows a strict numerical classification system with a wider range of Condensed, Regular, and Extended families to convey width, weight or Roman / Italic for each of the fonts. Its design has also been refined with improved legibility, refined spacing, enhanced characters and a wider range of weights. The cap height is the same throughout the family and its improved legibility resulted in an incredibly popular typeface being more flexible than ever.

Truly global typefaces, both Helvetica and Helvetica Neue have been employed on every conceivable piece of graphic design: from corporate logos and identity programs through to signage and wayfinding, packaging, and publishing, film and TV, and even on the side of the now defunct Space Shuttle orbiters. Such overuse and domination means that there are many designers who are averse to using the typeface today. Nevertheless, it remains hugely popular and is one of the most successful typefaces ever created.

Below right. Postcard designs by Dutch studio Experimental Jetset for the De Theatercompagnie, now part of the MoMa New York collection.

Below left. Gold Award winner at the Graphis poster awards by Husmee Studio for their 60th anniversary poster design as part of the 60helvetica project.

Helvetica Now

ABCDEFGHIJKLMNOPQRSTUVWXYZ
abcdefghijklmnopqrstuvwxyz
1234567890 !@#?:;"*&

The first major revision of Helvetica in thirty-five years was released in 2019 by Monotype. The process spanned four years and was led by Jan Hendrik Weber and Charles Nix, and involved dozens of designers and engineers from the Monotype Studio. An exhaustive update of the most famous typeface of all time, the project has reinvigorated this classic sans serif for an evolving digital age. The redrawing resolves issues of legibility and readability at very small sizes (a perennial problem with Neue Helvetica)—and issues of spacing and style at large sizes.

Helvetica Now consists of forty-eight fonts in three optical sizes: Micro, Text, and Display. The twenty Helvetica Now Display fonts, in a weight range from Hairline to ExtraBlack, are ideal for

setting short amounts of text in sizes fourteen point and above. The sixteen Helvetica Now Text fonts, in a weight range from Thin to Black, are optimized for setting type in a range from eight to twelve point. The Helvetica Now Micro fonts, in ExtraLight to ExtraBold weights, are ideal for type in the micro-range of three to seven point and type in low-resolution environments. Within twenty-four hours of its release, Helvetica Now shot to number one in the sales charts—offering a new lease of life for a classic family.

Foundry: Monotype
Designer: Max Miedinger / Eduard Hoffmann / Jan Hendrik Weber / Charles Nix / Monotype Studio
Nationality: Swiss / Swiss / German / American / British
Date: 1957 / 2019

Below left. Promotional design conveying the three distinctive optical sizes, Display, Text, and Micro and ideal applications.

Opposite. The full range of characters (glyphs) in a single weight of Helvetica Now number 812, resulting in a total of 38,976 characters across the entire family. In addition, the new release also contains alternate characters (shown in red) and additional glyphs such as arrows and sets of circled and squared figures.

AÁĂÂÄÀĀĄÅǺÃÆǼBCĆČÇĈĊDĐĎÐEÉĚĔÊËĖÈĒ
ĘFGǴĞĜĢĠHĦĤIIJÍĬÎÏİÌĪĮĨĴJĴKĶĻĹĽĻĿMNŃŇŅŊÑ
OÓŎÔÖÒŐŌØǾÕŒPÞQRŔŘŖSŚŠŞŜŞßƏTŦŤŢŢU
ÚŬÛÜÙŰŪŲŮŨVWŃŴŴŴXYÝŶŸŶZŹŽŻ ÄĊËĖĢĞĨİ
ĶĻĿŅÖŖŞŢÜŴŸŻGǴĞĜĢĠĠRŔŘŖŖaáăâäàāąåǻ
ãæǽbcćčçĉċdðďđeéěĕêëėèēęəfgǵğĝġhħĥiıíĭî
ìïijīįĩjĵkķĸlĺľ'ļŀłmnń'ňņŋñoóŏôöòőōøǿõœpþqrŕř
ŗsśšşŝşßtŧťţţuúŭûüùűūųůũvwẃŵẅẁxyýŷÿỳzźžż
äċëėġĝiïıijĵĵķļŀ'nņöŗşţẅÿżaáăâäàāąåǻãäţüŧŧťţţ
üüúŭûüùűūųůũ ÿyýŷÿỳlĺľļĿłĻŀ fi fl fi fl ᵃ ᵒ ᵃ ʰ ⁿ ʳ ˢ † Δ Ω µ π
ᵈₙᵗ0123456789 ❶❷❸❹❺❻❼❽❾❿ ⓿➊➋➌➍➎
➏➐➑➒ ⓪①②③④⑤⑥⑦⑧⑨ ⓿❶❷❸❹❺❻❼❽❾ 0
0123456789 0123456789 0123456789 0123456789 / ½ ⅓ ⅔
¼ ¾ ⅕ ⅖ ⅗ ⅘ ⅙ ⅚ ⅛ ⅜ ⅝ ⅞ 0123456789 0 . , : ; … ! ¡ ? ¿
· • * ? ¿ # / \ . , : ; … ! ¡ ? ¿ · • ? ¿ ₍₎ ⁽⁾ { } [ ] ⁽⁾ ₍₎ { } [ ] - - - — - _ - - —
, „ " " ' ' « » ‹ › " ' « » ‹ › , „ " " ' ' - ₍₎ { } [ ] · , ⁻ ⁽⁾ { } [ ] · , · , ⁻ { } [ ]
· , - { } [ ] · , ₿ ¢ ¤ $ € ƒ ₤ ₥ ₮ £ ₸ ¥ ₠ ₹ ₣ ₳ ¥ · / + − × ÷ = ≠ > < ≥ ≤ ±
≈ ~ ¬ ∧ ∞ ∫ Ω Δ ∏ ∑ √ µ ∂ % ‰ ₌ ⁼ ₋ ⁻ ₊ ⁺ · ÷ ↑ ↗ → ↘ ↓ ↙ ← ↖ ↔ ↕
● ○ ◊ ■ □ ʰᵉˡᵛᵉᵗⁱᶜᵃ @ & ¶ § © ® ℗ ™ % ° | ¦ ℓ † ‡ ℮ № ¢ $ € + − = ¢ $ € + −
= ¢ $ € ¢ $ € · ` ´ ` ^ ˇ ˘ ˜ ¯ - / / ´ ` ¨ ˙ ˆ
- ˚ ˜ , ¸ ˝ " ^ ˇ ˘ · · · · , ,
' , ' , ' ,

Incised 901

ABCDEFGHIJKLMNOPQRSTUVWXYZ
abcdefghijklmnopqrstuvwxyz
1234567890 !@#?:;"*&

Foundry: Bitstream
Designer: Roger Excoffon
Designer Nationality: French
Date: 1962

This Bitstream typeface is based on Antique Olive, designed in 1962 by Roger Excoffon for Fonderie Olive in France. Although originally created to compete with other European grotesques such as Helvetica, this expressive design took the finished typeface in a much less neutral direction.

Interstate

ABCDEFGHIJKLMNOPQRSTUVWXYZ
abcdefghijklmnopqrstuvwxyz
1234567890 !@#?:;"*&

Foundry: Font Bureau
Designer: Tobias Frere-Jones
Designer Nationality: American
Date: 1993

Frere-Jones based the design of Interstate on the typeface created in 1949 by Ted Forbes and his team of J. E. Penton and E. E. Radek for the US Federal Highway Administration, Highway Gothic. Interstate's wide letter spacing and generous x-height make it particularly suitable for signage and display use.

Italian Plate No. 2 Expanded

ABCDEFGHIJKLMNOPQRSTUVWXYZ
abcdefghijklmnopqrstuvwxyz
1234567890 !@#?:;"*&

Foundry: Playtype
Designer: Jonas Hecksher
Designer Nationality: Danish
Date: 2014

Similar to Italian Plate No. 1, the characters of this font are informed by the Italian vehicle number plates of the 1960s. However, the design of Italian Plate No. 2 Expanded includes the addition of width and space in the letterforms, alongside sharper terminals, for greater readability.

ITC Franklin

ABCDEFGHIJKLMNOPQRSTUVWXYZ
abcdefghijklmnopqrstuvwxyz
1234567890 !@#?:;"*&

Foundry: American Type Founders / ITC
Designer: Morris Fuller Benton / David Berlow
Designer Nationality: American
Date: 1902–05 / 2008

Font Bureau founder David Berlow comprehensively reworked Franklin Gothic to marshal existing cuts of the font into a superfamily of forty-eight grotesque styles. This suite of typefaces built upon his work in the early 1990s to create condensed cuts of Franklin for ITC.

ITC Franklin Gothic

ABCDEFGHIJKLMNOPQRSTUVWXYZ
abcdefghijklmnopqrstuvwxyz
1234567890 !@#?:;"*&

Foundry: American Type Founders / ITC
Designer: Morris Fuller Benton / Victor Caruso
Designer Nationality: American
Date: 1902–05 / 1980

Franklin Gothic's expansion into a full font family from the first weight published by the American Type Founders in 1902 took several decades. This ITC version, created by Victor Caruso, adds lighter weights to the family while preserving the robust spirit of Morris Fuller Benton's original design.

La Fabrique

ABCDEFGHIJKLMNOPQRSTUVWXYZ
abcdefghijklmnopqrstuvwxyz
1234567890 !@#?:;"*&

Foundry: Colophon
Designer: The Entente
Designer Nationality: British
Date: 2017

This font was originally designed in 2012 as part of an installation for La Fabrique, an exhibition staged at the 23rd International Poster and Graphic Design Festival in Chaumont, France. The La Fabrique family was expanded in 2017 to include five weights, Italics and extended language support.

Linotype Gothic

ABCDEFGHIJKLMNOPQRSTUVWXYZ
abcdefghijklmnopqrstuvwxyz
1234567890 !@#?:;"*&

Foundry: Linotype
Designer: Linotype Design Studio
Date: 2005

Linotype Gothic is based on Morris Fuller Benton's News Gothic, which was first published in 1908 by American Type Founders, and on Stempel's digitization of the face in 1984, News Gothic 2. The Linotype in-house team designed a new Italic counterpart for this updated version.

Maison

ABCDEFGHIJKLMNOPQRSTUVWXYZ
abcdefghijklmnopqrstuvwxyz
1234567890 !@#?:;"*&

Foundry: Milieu Grotesque
Designer: Timo Gaessner
Designer Nationality: German
Date: 2018

Maison is a grotesque sans serif, designed to evoke an industrial aesthetic without an over-reliance on optical adjustments or symbolic elements. It was initially produced in 2010 as a monospaced font family and then expanded in 2018 to include a partnering standard alignment.

Maison Neue

ABCDEFGHIJKLMNOPQRSTUVWXYZ
abcdefghijklmnopqrstuvwxyz
1234567890 !@#?:;"*&

Foundry: Milieu Grotesque
Designer: Timo Gaessner
Designer Nationality: German
Date: 2017

Maison Neue is a revision of the initial Maison design. Unlike the original, Maison Neue's expanded font family, which includes forty styles, lessens its focus on geometry. Instead, Maison Neue favors an optical construction, producing a style closer to a traditional grotesque.

Monotype Grotesque

ABCDEFGHIJKLMNOPQRSTUVWXYZ
abcdefghijklmnopqrstuvwxyz
1234567890 !@#?:;"*&

Foundry: Monotype
Designer: Frank Hinman Pierpont
Designer Nationality: American
Date: 1926

Frank Hinman Pierpont supervised the designs of this family of numbered grotesques at Monotype in 1926, which were inspired by Berthold's Ideal Grotesk. Monotype Grotesque was digitized in 1992 and the numbering system was dropped in favor of descriptive names for the twelve styles in the family.

Monotype Lightline Gothic

ABCDEFGHIJKLMNOPQRSTUVWXYZ
abcdefghijklmnopqrstuvwxyz
1234567890 !@#?:;"*&

Foundry: Monotype
Designer: Morris Fuller Benton
Designer Nationality: American
Date: 1908

Morris Fuller Benton designed Lightline Gothic for the American Type Founders (ATF) in 1908. A thin sans serif with fairly narrow characters, it was conceived as a lighter alternative to his popular Franklin Gothic, which was released by ATF in 1904 but came in only one Bold weight.

Monotype News Gothic

ABCDEFGHIJKLMNOPQRSTUVWXYZ
abcdefghijklmnopqrstuvwxyz
1234567890 !@#?:;"*&

Foundry: Monotype
Designer: Morris Fuller Benton
Designer Nationality: American
Date: 1908

Morris Fuller Benton created News Gothic for the American Type Founders in 1908 to accompany his other sans serifs, the bolder Franklin Gothic and thinner Lightline Gothic. News Gothic became a popular choice for newspapers and magazines during the 20th century.

Mote

ABCDEFGHIJKLMNOPQRSTUVWXYZ
abcdefghijklmnopqrstuvwxyz
1234567890 !@#?:;"*&

Foundry: Typotheque
Designer: Hrvoje Živčić
Designer Nationality: Croatian
Date: 2013

Designed by Hrvoje Živčić, a Croatian designer educated on the Type and Media course at the Royal Academy of Arts in The Hague and now based in Zagreb, Mote is a utilitarian grotesque sans serif with low contrast. Mote comes in six weights with italics and many alternative characters.

Nationale

ABCDEFGHIJKLMNOPQRSTUVWXYZ
abcdefghijklmnopqrstuvwxyz
1234567890 !@#?:;"*&

Foundry: Playtype
Designer: Jonas Hecksher
Designer Nationality: Danish
Date: 2013

Jonas Hecksher designed Nationale as part of a new visual identity for the National Museum of Denmark. Informed by the timeless aesthetics of Futura, Avenir, and Gill Sans, the design of his streamlined grotesque sans serif resists stylistic details to transcend the periodization of history.

Neue Haas Grotesk Display

ABCDEFGHIJKLMNOPQRSTUVWXYZ
abcdefghijklmnopqrstuvwxyz
1234567890 !@#?:;"*&

Foundry: Linotype
Designer: Max Miedinger / Christian Schwartz / Berton Hasebe
Designer Nationality: Swiss / American / American
Date: 1957 / 2010

Christian Schwartz drew Neue Haas Grotesk Display for Richard Turley's redesign of *Bloomberg Businessweek* in 2010. It takes its name from Helvetica's first incarnation. Schwartz aimed to capture the spirit of Helvetica's original design, which he felt had been lost in digitizations.

Neue Haas Unica

ABCDEFGHIJKLMNOPQRSTUVWXYZ
abcdefghijklmnopqrstuvwxyz
1234567890 !@#?:;"*&

Foundry: Monotype
Designer: André Gürtler / Christian Mengelt / Erich Gschwind / Toshi Omagari
Designer Nationality: Swiss / Swiss / Swiss / Japanese
Date: 2014–15

Designed at Haas, Unica began as a Helvetica update for phototypesetting, but the rise of computers made this neutral Swiss sans redundant. Toshi Omagari based his Unica on files found in Linotype's archive. The Lineto foundry released its Unica digitization by Christian Mengelt in 2015.

Grilli Type

Grilli Type is an independent Swiss type foundry offering original retail and custom typefaces. Beautifully crafted, these are created in the Swiss tradition, marrying a classic design approach to a contemporary aesthetic. Based in Lucerne, the foundry was set up by Noël Leu and Thierry Blancpain in 2009. Today team Grilli also includes Reto Moser, Tobias Rechsteiner, and Anna Lind Haugaard. The foundry often collaborates with other designers, artists and developers, including Josh Schaub, Pieter Pelgrims, Refurnished+, XXIX, and David Elsener.

Notable releases include GT Sectra (see p. 30), a contemporary serif typeface combining the "calligraphy of the broad nib pen with the sharpness of the scalpel knife." The GT America sans serif bridges the American Gothic and European Grotesque typeface genres, combining design features from both traditions to unite them in a contemporary family. The versatile system consists of eighty-four styles across six widths and seven weights.

Founded: 2009
Country: Switzerland
Website: grillitype.com
Notable typefaces:
GT Sectra (see p. 30)

Below. NeoCon is the USA's largest contract design trade show. For its 50th edition, Maiarelli Studio created a new visual identity, using GT America as the main typeface across print and online materials.

Opposite top. Stereo Associates' catalogue for the Danish Architecture Center's opening exhibition for Politikens Forlag. The catalog is the first publication using their new visual identity, which prominently features GT Pressura.

Opposite, middle and bottom. Designed by Morphoria Design Collective in cooperation with Jazek Porallathe, GT Walsheim was employed within the new corporate design for the Museum Kunsthaus NRW.

Neutral

ABCDEFGHIJKLMNOPQRSTUVWXYZ
abcdefghijklmnopqrstuvwxyz
1234567890 !@#?:;"'*&

Foundry: Typotheque
Designer: Kai Bernau
Designer Nationality: German
Date: 2014

Neutral was designed by German Kai Bernau of Dutch design studio Atelier Carvalho Bernau. The typeface began as a graduate project on the Design & Typography course at the Royal Academy of Arts in The Hague. As its name implies, Neutral aims to be objective, free of connotations and character.

Neuzeit Office

ABCDEFGHIJKLMNOPQRSTUVWXYZ
abcdefghijklmnopqrstuvwxyz
1234567890 !@#?:;"'*&

Foundry: Linotype
Designer: Wilhelm Pischner / Akira Kobayashi
Designer Nationality: German / Japanese
Date: 1928 / 2006

Wilhelm Pischner designed the Neuzeit Grotesk geometric sans serif for the German foundry Stempel in 1928. It was then updated in 1959 and 1966. Akira Kobayashi created Neuzeit Office for Linotype in 2006, adding obliques and optimizing it for on-screen text usage.

Neuzeit Office Soft Rounded

ABCDEFGHIJKLMNOPQRSTUVWXYZ
abcdefghijklmnopqrstuvwxyz
1234567890 !@#?:;"'*&

Foundry: Linotype
Designer: Wilhelm Pischner / Akira Kobayashi
Designer Nationality: German / Japanese
Date: 1928 / 2006

Like many prominent sans serif typefaces, such as Arial and Helvetica, Neuzeit received a rounded version that softened it and made it appear friendlier. The Soft Rounded approach was applied to only two cuts of Neuzeit Office, Regular and Bold, without obliques.

Neuzeit S

ABCDEFGHIJKLMNOPQRSTUVWXYZ
abcdefghijklmnopqrstuvwxyz
1234567890 !@#?:;"'*&

Foundry: Linotype
Designer: Wilhelm Pischner / Arthur Ritzel
Designer Nationality: German
Date: 1928 / 1966

Neuzeit S is an update of Wilhelm Pischner's Neuzeit Grotesk of 1928 made by Arthur Ritzel at Linotype in 1966. "Neuzeit" is German for "new time" and the "S" in the name stands for "Siemens," which adopted a version as its corporate font. It comes in two weights, Book and Heavy.

News Gothic BT

ABCDEFGHIJKLMNOPQRSTUVWXYZ
abcdefghijklmnopqrstuvwxyz
1234567890 !@#?:;"*&

Foundry: Bitstream
Designer: Morris Fuller Benton
Designer Nationality: American
Date: 1908

Morris Fuller Benton designed News Gothic for the American Type Founders (ATF) in 1908. The ATF ceased to exist in 1993 and since then numerous foundries have created variants, among them Adobe, Monotype, and Linotype. Bitstream's version, News Gothic BT, is one of many variants of the original revived in digital font form. It comes in four weights and three widths—Regular, Condensed, and Extra Condensed.

As with Benton's other notable sans serif design Franklin Gothic, News Gothic shares the same proportions but is a lighter design with a slightly condensed appearance. It was originally developed as two lighter weight designs, with another, Lightline Gothic, being dropped. Dmitry Kirsanov of the Russian foundry Paratype created a Cyrillic version in 2005 and then a Greek glyphs variant in 2009.

News Gothic was a popular grotesque sans serif throughout the 20th century. The original design was widely used in newspaper and magazine publishing because of its availability on Monotype and similar machines employed for hot-metal typesetting. However, perhaps News Gothic's most notable use is for the opening crawl of scrolling text in the *Star Wars* films.

From left. A selection of cover designs for classical, jazz and pop albums, showing News Gothic's versatility as a display sans and demonstrating that it is ideal for a variety of text applications.

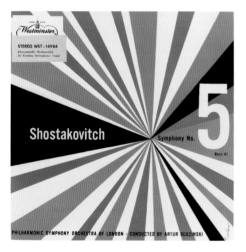

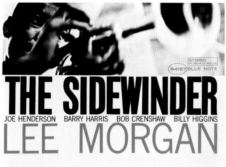

News Gothic No. 2

ABCDEFGHIJKLMNOPQRSTUVWXYZ
abcdefghijklmnopqrstuvwxyz
1234567890 !@#?:;"*&

Foundry: Stempel
Designer: Morris Fuller Benton / Stempel Design Studio
Designer Nationality: American / German
Date: 1908 / 1984

News Gothic No. 2 is an enhanced version of News Gothic created by German foundry Stempel in 1984. Stempel increased the number of weights to six, with matching italics, which is more than had previously been available, and helped encourage its use in contemporary design and communication.

Normal-Grotesk FSL

ABCDEFGHIJKLMNOPQRSTUVWXYZ
abcdefghijklmnopqrstuvwxyz
1234567890 !@#?:;"*&

Foundry: Forgotten Shapes
Designer: Haas Type Foundry / Stephan Müller
Designer Nationality: Swiss
Date: 1953 / 2008–18

Normal-Grotesk FSL is the digital reissue of Haas's Normal-Grotesk of 1953. Normal-Grotesk itself was based on Edel-Grotesk, released by the Ludwig Wagner foundry between c. 1912 and 1914. Haas redrew and substituted some of Edel-Grotesk's letters to give it a more modern appeal.

Oli Grotesk

ABCDEFGHIJKLMNOPQRSTUVWXYZ
abcdefghijklmnopqrstuvwxyz
1234567890 !#?:;"*&

Foundry: Typotheque
Designer: Shiva Nallaperumal / Aarya Purohit
Designer Nationality: Indian
Date: 2019

Oli by Shiva Nallaperumal and Aarya Purohit is available in Grotesk and Mono, with support for Latin, Cyrillic, Greek, Armenian, and Devanagari. The first use of Oli Grotesk, an appealing modern grotesque, was the identity for the Design Fabric design conference in India in 2018.

Parmigiano Sans

ABCDEFGHIJKLMNOPQRSTUVWXYZ
abcdefghijklmnopqrstuvwxyz
1234567890 !@#?:;"*&

Foundry: Typotheque
Designer: Riccardo Olocco / Jonathan Pierini
Designer Nationality: Italian
Date: 2014

Parmigiano Sans is part of a larger family inspired by the work of 18th-century Italian typographer Giambattista Bodoni and raises questions of how his design sensibilities may have been applied to a sans serif. It comes in eight styles, recalling early grotesques thanks to its contrasting thicks and thins.

Patron

ABCDEFGHIJKLMNOPQRSTUVWXYZ
abcdefghijklmnopqrstuvwxyz
1234567890 !@#?:;"*&

Foundry: Milieu Grotesque
Designer: Timo Gaessner
Designer Nationality: German
Date: 2014

Patron's grotesque design is a tribute to the conflicting styles of type designers Günter Gerhard Lange and Roger Excoffon. The font combines the craftsmanship of Lange, seen in the precision of shape and form, with the subversive strokes that are characteristic of Excoffon.

PL Brazilia

ABCDEFGHIJKLMNOPQRSTUVWXYZ
abcdefghijklmnopqrstuvwxyz
1234567890 !#?:;"*&

Foundry: Photo-Lettering
Designer: Albert Boton
Designer Nationality: French
Date: 1960

French designer Albert Boton created the elegant Brazilia font family for US company Photo-Lettering in 1960. The distinctive extended sans serif comes in two weights, numbered Three and Seven. The wide lowercase "r"is perhaps Brazilia's most characteristic letter.

Praxis

ABCDEFGHIJKLMNOPQRSTUVWXYZ
abcdefghijklmnopqrstuvwxyz
1234567890 !@#?:;"*&

Foundry: Hell
Designer: Gerard Unger
Designer Nationality: Dutch
Date: 1976

Dutch designer Gerard Unger created Praxis in 1976 for German company Hell. It is a legible, sans serif companion to his typeface Demos and both these early digital fonts have low contrast, a large x-height and fairly open counters. Praxis comes in five weights with matching obliques.

Praxis Next

ABCDEFGHIJKLMNOPQRSTUVWXYZ
abcdefghijklmnopqrstuvwxyz
1234567890 !@#?:;"*&

Foundry: Monotype
Designer: Gerard Unger / Linda Hintz
Designer Nationality: Dutch / Danish
Date: 2017

The German government adopted Praxis as an official typeface in the 1990s. In 2017, Linda Hintz at Monotype worked with its designer Gerard Unger on an update, Praxis Next, which added four new weights, as well as condensed versions, all with true italics rather than the original obliques.

Prima Sans

ABCDEFGHIJKLMNOPQRSTUVWXYZ
abcdefghijklmnopqrstuvwxyz
1234567890 !@#?:;"*&

Foundry: Bitstream
Designer: Jim Lyles
Designer Nationality: American
Date: 1998

Bitstream designer and font engineer Jim Lyles designed and released Prima Sans in 1998 as part of the Prima family, which also contained a serif and mono. Prima Sans was conceived to be easily read on-screen, even at lower resolutions. It is available in Roman and Bold with obliques.

Quitador Sans

ABCDEFGHIJKLMNOPQRSTUVWXYZ
abcdefghijklmnopqrstuvwxyz
1234567890 !@#?:;" * &

Foundry: Linotype
Designer: Arne Freytag
Designer Nationality: German
Date: 2016

Quitador Sans is a striking sibling of Arne Freytag's Quitador slab serif of 2014. It comes in seven weights with italics. Quitador Sans has many distinguishing features, such as the "Q" in two parts, and many glyphs feature fine, pointed terminals that do not join stems, giving an almost stencil feel.

Rather

ABCDEFGHIJKLMNOPQRSTUVWXYZ
abcdefghijklmnopqrstuvwxyz
1234567890 !@#?:;"*&

Foundry: Or Type
Designer: Mads Freund Brunse / Guðmundur Úlfarsson (GUNMAD)
Designer Nationality: Danish / Icelandic
Date: 2015

Rather is an unconventional grotesque sans serif that is designed in nine weights with italics. The variation between the expansive shapes found in the rounded characters and the shorter horizontal strokes in the narrower forms yield an irregular, yet highly legible, typographic rhythm.

Reader

ABCDEFGHIJKLMNOPQRSTUVWXYZ
abcdefghijklmnopqrstuvwxyz
1234567890 !@#?:;"*&

Foundry: Colophon
Designer: The Entente
Designer Nationality: British
Date: 2018

Reader is a grotesque sans serif based on an unknown typeface found in a Royal Society for the Protection of Birds letter from 1972. The Entente's design features slight changes to the original, such as a rebalancing of the proportions and the addition of further stroke contrast for enhanced legibility.

Relative

ABCDEFGHIJKLMNOPQRSTUVWXYZ
abcdefghijklmnopqrstuvwxyz
1234567890 !@#?:;"*&

Foundry: Colophon
Designer: The Entente
Designer Nationality: British
Date: 2011

Relative is a grotesque sans serif that was originally designed for Stephen Gill's photo book *Outside In* (2010). Released in 2011, the font was expanded to include ten styles, made up of proportional weights and pitched monospaced versions, alongside a hybrid Faux monospace design.

Similar

ABCDEFGHIJKLMNOPQRSTUVWXYZ
abcdefghijklmnopqrstuvwxyz
1234567890 !@#?:;"*&

Foundry: Or Type
Designer: Guðmundur Úlfarsson
Designer Nationality: Icelandic
Date: 2015

Similar is a grotesque sans serif that combines a traditional structure with several idiosyncratic details. Curves that bridge the stroke and the stem are flattened to create an angled interior joint, while the vertical strokes feature a slight bend toward the foot.

Spartan

ABCDEFGHIJKLMNOPQRSTUVWXYZ
abcdefghijklmnopqrstuvwxyz
1234567890 !@#?:;"*&

Foundry: Monotype
Designer: John L. Renshaw
Designer Nationality: American
Date: 1939

The success of the Bauer foundry's geometric Futura inspired many copies, such as Spartan, which was designed by a team at Mergenthaler Linotype. John L. "Bud" Renshaw later designed extra weights. Spartan is almost identical to Futura but has a flat-topped "1" and an alternate double-storey "a."

Surogat

ABCDEFGHIJKLMNOPQRSTUVWXYZ
abcdefghijklmnopqrstuvwxyz
1234567890 !@#?:;"*&

Foundry: Typotheque
Designer: Nikola Djurek
Designer Nationality: Croatian
Date: 2014

Nikola Djurek's Surogat is a versatile typeface family, comprised of three widths—Standard, Condensed and Compressed—in eight weights, all with italics. Dutch foundry Typotheque (see p. 90) markets it as a "raw, sturdy, industrial sans serif typeface with dominant horizontal strokes."

Swiss 721

ABCDEFGHIJKLMNOPQRSTUVWXYZ
abcdefghijklmnopqrstuvwxyz
1234567890 !@#?:;"*&

Foundry: Bitstream
Designer: Max Miedinger
Designer Nationality: Swiss
Date: 1957 / 1982

Swiss 721 is Bitstream's digitization of the legendary sans serif Helvetica, which it released in 1982. It comes in Roman and Italic in seven weights, Condensed in four weights with italics and extended in four weights without italics. There are outline versions of Bold, Black, and Bold Condensed.

Swiss 721 Rounded

ABCDEFGHIJKLMNOPQRSTUVWXYZ
abcdefghijklmnopqrstuvwxyz
1234567890 !@#?:;"*&

Foundry: Bitstream
Designer: Max Miedinger
Designer Nationality: Swiss
Date: 1957 / 1982

Bitstream created Swiss 721 Rounded in 1982, when there was a trend for rounded fonts. Available in Bold and Black, it is a version of Helvetica Rounded, which is a softened redesign of the popular typeface Helvetica created by the Haas Type Foundry in 1957.

Syntax

ABCDEFGHIJKLMNOPQRSTUVWXYZ
abcdefghijklmnopqrstuvwxyz
1234567890 !@#?:;" *&

Foundry: Stempel
Designer: Hans Eduard Meier
Designer Nationality: German
Date: 1968

Syntax, designed by Hans Eduard Meier in 1968, was the last hot-metal type family produced by the foundry Stempel. It is a distinctive, optically monoline sans serif with a humanistic, double-storey "a" and "g." The original cuts—four romans and an italic—were digitized in 1989.

Trade Gothic LT

ABCDEFGHIJKLMNOPQRSTUVWXYZ
abcdefghijklmnopqrstuvwxyz
1234567890 !@#?:;"*&

Foundry: Linotype
Designer: Jackson Burke
Designer Nationality: American
Date: 1948

Trade Gothic is an unorthodox, grotesque sans serif that was first cut in 1948 and then developed throughout Jackson Burke's time at Mergenthaler Linotype in the 1950s. Each of Trade Gothic's fourteen styles are designed with subtle variations in form and shape, unlike traditional font families. Originally released as "Gothic" with a numeral suffix, the variants soon became popular for everyday work thanks to the condensed designs, and eventually the term "Trade" was applied as they became the printers and typesetters' typeface of choice. Contemporary uses are in Amnesty International's logo and printed matter, and the branding of cycling-apparel company Rapha. The Bold Condensed weight is often chosen for impactful messaging and attention-grabbing designs.

AMNESTY
INTERNATIONAL

Trade Gothic Next

ABCDEFGHIJKLMNOPQRSTUVWXYZ
abcdefghijklmnopqrstuvwxyz
1234567890 !@#?:;"*&

Trade Gothic Next is both a revision and expansion of Jackson Burke's original design. Details such as the terminals, symbols, and spacing were revised to remedy the inconsistency of the original, while extra widths and weights have been added to provide more versatility.

Foundry: Linotype
Designer: Jackson Burke / Tom Grace / Akira Kobayashi
Designer Nationality: American / American / Japanese
Date: 2008

Trade Gothic Next Soft Rounded

ABCDEFGHIJKLMNOPQRSTUVWXYZ
abcdefghijklmnopqrstuvwxyz
1234567890 !@#?:;"*&

In addition to revising details and expanding weights, Tom Grace and Akira Kobayashi updated Trade Gothic in 2008 to include Trade Gothic Next Soft Rounded. Unlike the font's other versions, this design favours circular forms, seen especially in the stroke endings.

Foundry: Linotype
Designer: Jackson Burke / Tom Grace / Akira Kobayashi
Designer Nationality: American / American / Japanese
Date: 2008

Transcript

ABCDEFGHIJKLMNOPQRSTUVWXYZ
abcdefghijklmnopqrstuvwxyz
1234567890 !@#?:;"*&

Transcript is a grotesque sans serif that was originally designed in 2010 for issue 6 of *Centrefold Magazine* but was then released commercially as a single-weight font in 2011. In 2017, Transcript was expanded to include six weights and fourteen styles in proportional and monospaced versions.

Foundry: Colophon
Designer: The Entente
Designer Nationality: British
Date: 2017

Unitext

ABCDEFGHIJKLMNOPQRSTUVWXYZ
abcdefghijklmnopqrstuvwxyz
1234567890 !@#?:;"*&

Unitext is a versatile grotesque sans serif designed for 21st-century branding. The result of detailed research into the requirements of brand typography, Jan Hendrik Weber's design includes fourteen styles, and combines narrow spacing with open shapes for legibility across all platforms.

Foundry: Monotype
Designer: Jan Hendrik Weber
Designer Nationality: German
Date: 2018

Univers

ABCDEFGHIJKLMNOPQRSTUVWXYZ
abcdefghijklmnopqrstuvwxyz
1234567890 !@#?:;"*&

Foundry: Linotype
Designer: Adrian Frutiger
Designer Nationality: Swiss
Date: 1957

Univers is one of the most historically important typefaces to be designed in the 20th century. It possesses elegance, simplicity and purity within its modular forms, enabling it to become one of the most widely used typefaces of all time. Adrian Frutiger (see p. 290) designed the original twenty-one types that made up the family, which have a consistent and balanced structure throughout the differing weights. From the outset, a system was applied to the weights, widths, and slopes through an innovative numbering system, akin to a periodic table. He later adopted this system for his eponymously titled Frutiger typeface (see p. 268). Other foundries also employed the system such as for Helvetica Neue (see p. 230). Based on a two-digit system, each typeface's weight was described by the first number. For example, "5" was

Roman and "7" was Black. The second number described the style; "3" for Extended, "5" for Regular, "6" for Italic, "7" for Condensed, and so on.

Univers was based on Frutiger's earlier studies when he was a design student in Zurich, and from design principles and aesthetics established with the existing sans serif, Akzidenz Grotesk (see p. 248). He started designing Univers in 1954, when he was art director at the Parisian foundry Deberny & Peignot. The foundry required a linear sans serif as part of its offering. In 1957, the final design was released and was an instant success, and soon after Linotype produced it too. After Univers's launch, Frutiger worked on refinements and revisions to the design with the Linotype Design Studio and in 1997 released Linotype Univers, with a full revision to this family called Univers Next (see p. 250) in 2010.

Below. Konstantin Eremenko's award-winning packaging design for SRC Lab distinguishes their three product lines with a bold colour and numbering system.

Opposite. Otl Aicher's iconic Munich Olympic Games design from 1972 employs Univers across the entire range of printed and branded items.

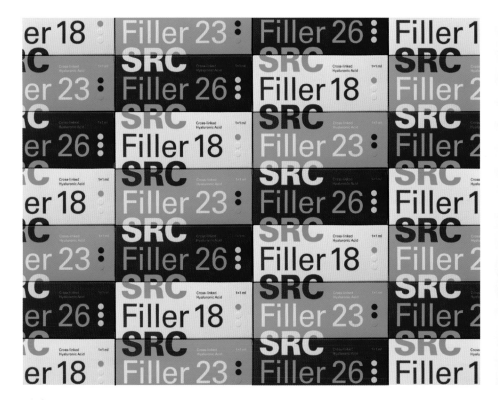

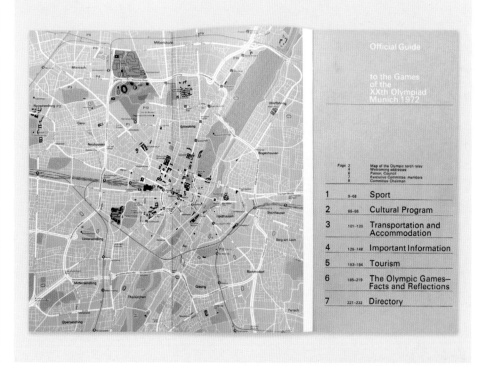

Univers Next

ABCDEFGHIJKLMNOPQRSTUVWXYZ
abcdefghijklmnopqrstuvwxyz
1234567890 !@#?:;"*&

Foundry: Linotype
Designer: Adrian Frutiger / Linotype Design Studio
Designer Nationality: Swiss
Date: 2010

Univers Next, originally titled Linotype Univers, is a detailed revision and expansion of the font family made in 1957 by Adrian Frutiger (see p. 290). Univers Next is collaboration between Frutiger and the design team at Linotype, and features redrawn strokes, revised weights, and 35 new styles.

Right. The identity and branding for Solothurn Literary Days is formed employing Univers Next across all materials print and online. Its logotype is formed around four languages (German, French, Italian, and Romansh). Design by Andrea Stebler, Thomas Berger and Thomas Hirter.

Vectora

ABCDEFGHIJKLMNOPQRSTUVWXYZ
abcdefghijklmnopqrstuvwxyz
1234567890 !@#?:;"*&

Foundry: Linotype
Designer: Adrian Frutiger
Designer Nationality: Swiss
Date: 1990

This grotesque sans serif was designed to enhance readability in small text sizes. Its design was influenced by the fonts of US type designer Morris Fuller Benton, such as News Gothic. Featuring tall x-heights and open counters, Vectora's precise forms are well suited to the demands of text typography.

Venus

ABCDEFGHIJKLMNOPQRSTUVWXYZ
abcdefghijklmnopqrstuvwxyz
1234567890 !@#?:;"*&

Foundry: Linotype
Designer: Bauersche Giesserei
Designer Nationality: German
Date: 1910

First produced by the Bauersche Giesserei foundry, but later digitized by Neufvill Digital and published by Linotype, Venus is a grotesque sans serif initially designed for use in German cartography. The family features distinctive left-leaning weights and a strict, taut frame.

Veto

ABCDEFGHIJKLMNOPQRSTUVWXYZ
abcdefghijklmnopqrstuvwxyz
1234567890 !@#?:;"*&

Foundry: Linotype
Designer: Marco Ganz
Designer Nationality: Swiss
Date: 1999

Veto is a functional, agile grotesque sans serif designed to reflect the dynamic mobility of the 21st century's digital culture. In each weight, from Light to Bold, letterforms are direct and utilitarian, seen in the single-sided cross-strokes and slanted stroke endings.

Vialog

ABCDEFGHIJKLMNOPQRSTUVWXYZ
abcdefghijklmnopqrstuvwxyz
1234567890 !@#?:;"*&

Foundry: Linotype
Designer: Werner Schneider / Helmut Ness
Designer Nationality: German
Date: 2002

Vialog is informed by Werner Schneider's previous work and extensive research on Euro Type, an unpublished design for the German Federal Transportation Ministry. It is a grotesque sans serif intended for transport information systems, which is legible at speed and distance.

Vialog 1450

ABCDEFGHIJKLMNOPQRSTUVWXYZ
abcdefghijklmnopqrstuvwxyz
1234567890 !@#?:;"*&

Foundry: Linotype
Designer: Werner Schneider / Helmut Ness
Designer Nationality: German
Date: 2016

Vialog 1450 is designed to conform to the German DIN 1450 regulations, a set of public standards issued by the Deutsches Institut für Normung that ensure readability in adverse conditions. Vialog 1450 features new proportions and stroke thicknesses, as well as redrawn characters that improve clarity.

Zurich

ABCDEFGHIJKLMNOPQRSTUVWXYZ
abcdefghijklmnopqrstuvwxyz
1234567890 !@#?:;"*&

Foundry: Bitstream
Designer: Adrian Frutiger
Designer Nationality: Swiss
Date: 1957

Zurich is Bitstream's digitization of the Univers grotesque sans serif. The font's title, Zurich, references the city in which designer Adrian Frutiger (see p. 290) made his first sketches for what would later become Univers, while a student at the School of Applied Arts.

Abadi

ABCDEFGHIJKLMNOPQRSTUVWXYZ
abcdefghijklmnopqrstuvwxyz
1234567890 !@#?:;"*&

Foundry: Monotype
Designer: Ong Chong Wah
Designer Nationality: Malaysian
Date: 1987

This friendly sans serif was inspired by Gill Sans and Helvetica, and blends humanist and Neo-grotesque styles. Its highly tapered strokes and generous x-height combine to give its curved letterforms an expanded look, and it is legible even at very small point sizes.

Adoquin

ABCDEFGHIJKLMNOPQRSTUVWXYZ
abcdefghijklmnopqrstuvwxyz
1234567890 !@#?:;"*&

Foundry: Huy!Fonts
Designer: Juanjo Lopez
Designer Nationality: Spanish
Date: 2013

Adoquin is described as a "semi serif" and is a playful combination of an Old Style calligraphic typeface with a modern geometric sans serif. It is suitable for display and text use, and features seven weights, as well as small caps, ligatures, Old Style figures, fractions, numerators, and denominators.

Adrianna

ABCDEFGHIJKLMNOPQRSTUVWXYZ
abcdefghijklmnopqrstuvwxyz
1234567890 !@#?:;"*&

Foundry: Chank
Designer: Chank Diesel
Designer Nationality: American
Date: 2015

Adrianna is a restrained sans serif with a sophisticated edge. It comes in five weights and three different widths: Regular (for general use), Extended (designed with HDTV and widescreens in mind), and Condensed, which is intended to look good on smartphones.

Aeris

ABCDEFGHIJKLMNOPQRSTUVWXYZ
abcdefghijklmnopqrstuvwxyz
1234567890 !@#?:;"*&

Foundry: Linotype
Designer: Tom Grace
Designer Nationality: American
Date: 2010

Aeris is a book face combining characteristics of both sans serif and script fonts, with open counters for optimal legibility. Each weight and style has two variants that should not be mixed. The A variant is for display use, while the B variant is best suited for use in text.

Agilita

ABCDEFGHIJKLMNOPQRSTUVWXYZ
abcdefghijklmnopqrstuvwxyz
1234567890 !@#?:;"*&

Foundry: Linotype
Designer: Jürgen Weltin
Designer Nationality: German
Date: 2006

Agilita is a humanist sans serif with classical proportions. It consists of thirty-two styles (including Italic and Condensed) and weights from Hairline to Black. With an emphasis on the horizontals, coupled with clear ascenders and descenders, the typeface looks solid and functional.

Antagométrica BT

ABCDEFGHIJKLMNOPQRSTUVWXYZ
abcdefghijklmnopqrstuvwxyz
1234567890 !@#?:;"*&

Foundry: Bitstream
Designer: Maximiliano Giungi
Designer Nationality: Argentinian
Date: 2006

Antagométrica is a condensed but curvy sans serif in the humanist tradition. It is the sole font available from Argentinian designer, Maximiliano Giungi, and is available in Light, Regular, and Bold. The font has a very distinctive lowercase "e", and is well suited for both display and text usage.

Antique Olive

ABCDEFGHIJKLMNOPQRSTUVWXYZ
abcdefghijklmnopqrstuvwxyz
1234567890 !@#?:;"*&

Foundry: Fonderie Olive
Designer: Roger Excoffon
Designer Nationality: French
Date: 1962

Antique Olive evolved from the lettering for the Air France logo, and is too eccentric to compete with Univers and Helvetica. Designer Roger Excoffon created the Nord and Nord italic versions, before completing the Bold, Compact, Black, Bold Condensed, Roman, and Italic.

Aptifer Sans

ABCDEFGHIJKLMNOPQRSTUVWXYZ
abcdefghijklmnopqrstuvwxyz
1234567890 !@#?:;"*&

Foundry: Linotype
Designer: Mårten Thavenius
Designer Nationality: Swedish
Date: 2006

This sans serif channels two quite different influences: the robust American Gothic and the more open humanist traditions. It shares many similarities, such as stroke contrast and vertical stress, with its sister typeface, Aptifer Slab, which was also created by Mårten Thavenius.

Ayita Pro

ABCDEFGHIJKLMNOPQRSTUVWXYZ
abcdefghijklmnopqrstuvwxyz
1234567890 !@#?:;"'*&

Foundry: Ascender
Designer: Jim Ford /
Steve Matteson
Designer Nationality: American
Date: 2010

Ayita Pro is a cheeky sans serif with a Cherokee name that means "first in dance." It is available in seven weights, from Thin to Fat. The typeface was conceived as an upright italic and has a distinctive bowed uppercase "A." It features a Latin character set and decorative patterns and ornaments.

Bariol

ABCDEFGHIJKLMNOPQRSTUVWXYZ
abcdefghijklmnopqrstuvwxyz
1234567890 !@#?:;"'*&

Foundry: Atipo
Designer: Raul Garcia del Pomar /
Ismael Gonzalez
Designer Nationality: Spanish
Date: 2010

This rounded, uncomplicated, and slightly condensed sans serif is free to download for Regular and Italic or whatever a user can afford for the full set. The typeface's pricing policy and accessibility has meant it has proved very popular with students and anyone who prefers not to pay for typefaces.

Berling Nova Sans

ABCDEFGHIJKLMNOPQRSTUVWXYZ
abcdefghijklmnopqrstuvwxyz
1234567890 !@#?:;"'*&

Foundry: Linotype
Designer: Karl-Erik Forsberg /
Örjan Nordling / Fredrik Andersson
Designer Nationality: Swedish
Date: c. 1950s / 2004

This redesign of Karl-Erik Forsberg's classic newspaper font from the 1950s was created using much of his original source material from Linotype. It is available in four weights, from Light to Extra Bold. It has an increased x-height, as well as the addition of small caps and Old Style figures.

Big Vesta

ABCDEFGHIJKLMNOPQRSTUVWXYZ
abcdefghijklmnopqrstuvwxyz
1234567890 !@#?:;"'*&

Foundry: Linotype
Designer: Gerard Unger
Designer Nationality: Dutch
Date: 2011

Gerard Unger designed this as a possible sans serif to mark the Jubilee of the Roman Catholic Church in 2000, then later expanded the family to create Big Vesta. A larger x-height than the original Vesta, shorter ascenders and descenders, and tighter letter spacing make it ideal for use at large sizes.

Bliss

ABCDEFGHIJKLMNOPQRSTUVWXYZ
abcdefghijklmnopqrstuvwxyz
1234567890 !@#?:;"*&

Name: Bliss
Foundry: Jeremy Tankard Typography
Designer: Jeremy Tankard
Designer Nationality: British
Date: 1996

Acclaimed independent British type designer Jeremy Tankard drew from the ideas of one of the founding fathers of modern calligraphy, Edward Johnston, to develop the sans serif humanist face Bliss. A Uruguayan-British craftsman, Johnston is an important figure who taught the British sculptor, typeface designer and printmaker Eric Gill.

In 1906, Johnston published his seminal book *Writing & Illuminating & Lettering*, which helped to revive the interest in calligraphy. One of his key ideas was the belief that a block sans serif form could be made more harmonious if it were derived from the proportions of the Roman square capitals that are the basis for modern capital letters. Johnston's concept of the "readableness, beauty and character" that constitute the "essential virtues of good lettering" underpins the structure of Bliss.

Bliss was launched in 1996 and since then has grown to be one of the most popular humanist sans. It has been widely employed in everything from publishing applications to identities for international organizations.

Its minimal stroke contrast, angled cuts on extenders such as uppercase "E" and "F," large apertures and open counters all work toward creating a highly legible and flexible typeface with a softness that makes it accessible and friendly to the reader.

Bliss's humanist appearance also carries a certain "Englishness" to it. This reflectis the influence of Johnston's own classic, the sans serif Johnston (see p. 278) that was first employed on the London Underground system in 1916, and to a degree, Gill's Gill Sans (see p. 276).

Below, clockwise from top left.
The many faces of Bliss in use: identity for the Royal National Lifeboat Institution; wayfinding at Cape Town Airport, South Africa; corporate identity for the UK's Bank of England.

Bosis

ABCDEFGHIJKLMNOPQRSTUVWXYZ
abcdefghijklmnopqrstuvwxyz
1234567890 !@#?:;"*&

Foundry: Monotype
Designer: Bo Berndal
Designer Nationality: Swedish
Date: 1991

Swedish master typographer Bo Berndal created this no-nonsense sans serif in 1991. Bosis comes in four weights, from Light to Semibold. Subtle details such as the sloping verticals on the uppercase "M" and the tail on the lowercase "l" give it a softer, humanist look.

Calmetta

ABCDEFGHIJKLMNOPQRSTUVWXYZ
abcdefghijklmnopqrstuvwxyz
1234567890 !@#?:;"*&

Foundry: Dalton Maag
Designer: Elí Castellanos / Marc Weymann
Designer Nationality: Mexican / British
Date: 2017

Calmetta is Elí Castellanos's revision of Pantograph, a custom wayfinding font initially designed by Marc Weymann for the Manchester Metrolink. Castellanos added further versatility to the family by designing two extra weights and more than an additional 180 icons.

Camphor

ABCDEFGHIJKLMNOPQRSTUVWXYZ
abcdefghijklmnopqrstuvwxyz
1234567890 !@#?:;"*&

Foundry: Monotype
Designer: Nick Job
Designer Nationality: British
Date: 2009

Nick Job's economical font is modern, uncluttered and quintessentially English. Camphor has its roots in the typefaces of Eric Gill, Edward Johnston and, to some extent, Adrian Frutiger (see p. 290), yet is more subtle than Gill Sans and narrower than Johnston's typeface for the London Underground.

Carter Sans

ABCDEFGHIJKLMNOPQRSTUVWXYZ
abcdefghijklmnopqrstuvwxyz
1234567890 !@#?:;"*&

Foundry: Monotype
Designer: Matthew Carter / Dan Reynolds
Designer Nationality: British / American
Date: 2011

Matthew Carter (see p. 616) has described Carter Sans as "a humanistic stressed sans." This refined, chiselled sans serif takes inspiration from Berthold Wolpe's Albertus typeface of the 1930s. Its slightly flared strokes and solid baseline terminals give even its lightest weight a powerful presence.

Castle

ABCDEFGHIJKLMNOPQRSTUVWXYZ
abcdefghijklmnopqrstuvwxyz
1234567890 !@#?:;"*&

Foundry: Linotype
Designer: Steve Jackaman
Designer Nationality: British
Date: 1975

Castle is a humanist, sans serif typeface that comes in four weights, ranging from Light to Ultra. It has an unusually high stroke contrast, as well as a large x-height. Although Castle is best used at twelve point and above for this reason, it is still very legible when used in text.

Charlotte Sans

ABCDEFGHIJKLMNOPQRSTUVWXYZ
abcdefghijklmnopqrstuvwxyz
1234567890 !@#?:;"*&

Foundry: Letraset
Designer: Michael Gills
Designer Nationality: British
Date: 1992

Charlotte is a modern roman typeface inspired by the designs of 18th-century punch-cutter Pierre-Simon Fournier and shares characteristics with Gill Sans, FF Scala Sans, and Syntax. It has a varied stroke width and its terminals on the vertical strokes are cut at an angle instead of parallel to the baseline.

Chiswick Sans

ABCDEFGHIJKLMNOPQRSTUVWXYZ
abcdefghijklmnopqrstuvwxyz
1234567890 !@#?:;"*&

Foundry: Commercial Type
Designer: Paul Barnes
Designer Nationality: British
Date: 2015

Chiswick Sans is a humanist typeface that integrates the utility of a sans serif with the formal flourishes of a serif. Intended primarily for headline use, it features seven weights which vary from Thin to Fat, each with an italic that enhances the font's distinctive details.

Chiswick Sans Poster

ABCDEFGHIJKLMNOPQRSTUVWXYZ
abcdefghijklmnopqrstuvwxyz
1234567890 !@#?:;"*&

Foundry: Commercial Type
Designer: Paul Barnes
Designer Nationality: British
Date: 2015

Chiswick Sans Poster is a high-contrast sans serif designed for the largest display sizes. It was first employed in *Document Journal*, a New York fashion and culture magazine. While sans serif in design, the letterforms have the elegance of a serif, seen in the expressive hooks and descenders.

Chiswick Sans Text

ABCDEFGHIJKLMNOPQRSTUVWXYZ
abcdefghijklmnopqrstuvwxyz
1234567890 !@#?:;"*&

Foundry: Commercial Type
Designer: Paul Barnes
Designer Nationality: British
Date: 2017

Unlike its siblings, Chiswick Sans and Chiswick Sans Poster, Chiswick Sans Text is designed to be most effective at smaller sizes. Its comparatively moderate stroke contrast allows the characters to provide legibility in denser texts while maintaining their expressive details.

Chong Modern

ABCDEFGHIJKLMNOPQRSTUVWXYZ
abcdefghijklmnopqrstuvwxyz
1234567890 !@#?:;"*&

Foundry: Monotype
Designer: Ong Chong Wah
Designer Nationality: Malaysian
Date: 2009

Along with its sister typeface Chong Old Style, this elegant Art Deco-inspired face mixes traditional and modern to great effect and has been likened to a Bodoni without serifs. Chong Modern has Light, Regular and Bold, Old Style figures, ligatures, and small caps; Chong Old Style also has an Extra Bold.

Chong Old Style

ABCDEFGHIJKLMNOPQRSTUVWXYZ
abcdefghijklmnopqrstuvwxyz
1234567890 !@#?:;"*&

Foundry: Monotype
Designer: Ong Chong Wah
Designer Nationality: Malaysian
Date: 2011

Chong Old Style is the sister typeface to Chong Modern. It has similarities to traditional Old Style designs such as Goudy Old Style, while avoiding pastiche. It lacks the serifs and inclined stroke axis customarily seen in the traditional Old Style faces but still retains the color and weight.

Clearface Gothic

ABCDEFGHIJKLMNOPQRSTUVWXYZ
abcdefghijklmnopqrstuvwxyz
1234567890 !@#?:;"*&

Foundry: ATF
Designer: Morris Fuller Benton / Linotype Studio
Designer Nationality: American
Date: 1910

Clearface Gothic is an informal sans serif by the designer of Franklin Gothic and Century Expanded, Morris Fuller Benton. It is notable for the upward-tilting horizontal stroke of its "e", its arched "k" and open forms. It is slightly condensed, making it legible when used at small sizes.

Daytona

ABCDEFGHIJKLMNOPQRSTUVWXYZ
abcdefghijklmnopqrstuvwxyz
1234567890 !@#?:;"*&

Foundry: Monotype
Designer: Jim Wasco
Designer Nationality: American
Date: 2015

Daytona was originally created to be used in televised sporting events but works well for any screen application. Its slightly condensed squared-off letterforms have humanist shapes and proportions. The typeface is available in seven weights from Thin to Fat.

Delvard

ABCDEFGHIJKLMNOPQRSTUVWXYZ
abcdefghijklmnopqrstuvwxyz
1234567890 !@#?:;"*&

Foundry: Typotheque
Designer: Nikola Djurek
Designer Nationality: Croatian
Date: 2010

Delvard is a low-contrast sans serif with four weights—Text, Condensed, Display, and an unusual Gradient version—as well as small caps and swashes. Its graceful curves, angled segments, and elevated crossbars are influenced by the lettering found on Art Nouveau posters.

Diurnal

ABCDEFGHIJKLMNOPQRSTUVWXYZ
abcdefghijklmnopqrstuvwxyz
1234567890 !@#?:;"*&

Foundry: Typotheque
Designer: Nikola Djurek
Designer Nationality: Croatian
Date: 2017

Diurnal is a companion font to Nocturno, which is available in both text and a more expressive display option. With a nod to Syntax and Legato, this humanist sans serif is designed for long, continuous reading, and its calligraphic rhythm and generous x-height both help legibility.

Diverda Sans

ABCDEFGHIJKLMNOPQRSTUVWXYZ
abcdefghijklmnopqrstuvwxyz
1234567890 !@#?:;"*&

Foundry: Linotype
Designer: Daniel Lanz
Designer Nationality: Swiss
Date: 2004

Diverda Sans stays true to the proportions of the Roman alphabet with its traditional round forms, low x-heights, heavier downward strokes and a clear contrast between its curved, square, and triangular elements. It is available in five weights plus matching italics.

Echo

ABCDEFGHIJKLMNOPQRSTUVWXYZ
abcdefghijklmnopqrstuvwxyz
1234567890 !@#?:;"*&

Foundry: Typotheque
Designer: Ross Milne
Designer Nationality: Canadian
Date: 2015

Echo is Ross Milne's counterpart to his serif Charlie from 2010 and it too takes its name from the International Radiotelephony Spelling Alphabet.

This no-nonsense sans serif is clear and direct, and also displays subtle influences of the broad nib pen. It features five weights from Regular to Black.

Effra

ABCDEFGHIJKLMNOPQRSTUVWXYZ
abcdefghijklmnopqrstuvwxyz
1234567890 !@#?:;"*&

Foundry: Dalton Maag
Designer: Jonas Schudel / Azza Alameddine / Fabio Haag
Designer Nationality: Swiss / Lebanese / Brazilian
Date: 2008–16

Effra was inspired by one of the first commercial sans serif designs, Caslon Junior. It is a sans serif that utilizes grotesque and humanist features. Effra is available in five weights, each with their own italic, and includes the characters for Latin, Cyrillic, Greek, and Arabic scripts.

Felbridge

ABCDEFGHIJKLMNOPQRSTUVWXYZ
abcdefghijklmnopqrstuvwxyz
1234567890 !@#?:;"*&

Foundry: Monotype
Designer: Robin Nicholas
Designer Nationality: British
Date: 2001

Felbridge is a clear, strong humanist sans serif with six weights from Light to Black. Created by British designer Robin Nicholas for on-screen use, it works equally well in print. It has distinctive italics that have lighter, "hooked" strokes instead of the traditional "sloped roman" style.

Fenland

ABCDEFGHIJKLMNOPQRSTUVWXYZ
abcdefghijklmnopqrstuvwxyz
1234567890 !@#?:;"*&

Foundry: Jeremy Tankard Typography
Designer: Jeremy Tankard
Designer Nationality: British
Date: 2012

Jeremy Tankard's bold design for Fenland evokes a modern, manufactured feel. Unlike most typefaces, it is not based on traditional handwritten forms; Tankard has shaped the letterforms according to their function, rather than how they would appear if created using a broad-nib pen.

Fedra Sans

ABCDEFGHIJKLMNOPQRSTUVWXYZ
abcdefghijklmnopqrstuvwxyz
1234567890 !@#?:;"*&

Foundry: Typotheque
Designer: Peter Biľak
Designer Nationality: Slovakian
Date: 2001

The creation of Fedra Sans came about as part of a rebrand of a German insurance company, Bayerische Rück. Paris-based studio Intégral Ruedi Baur was charged with the rebranding of the business and commissioned Dutch foundry Typotheque (see p. 90) to design a replacement for the company's existing typeface as a key component of the visual overhaul. The typeface in question was Univers, which had been employed since the 1970s when leading German graphic designer and typographer Otto "Otl" Aicher designed the original corporate identity.

The brief was to humanize the message but also to create a typeface that would work across paper and screen internationally in multiple languages. However, nearing completion the insurance company was bought out and the need for a new identity vanished. Typotheque decided to complete the typeface because it was so far advanced in design and digitization. This delay was of benefit because it allowed Typotheque's founder Peter Biľak to review the design and improve upon it before its general release.

Fedra Sans is a type that balances the need to work within the structure of a computer screen and retain the "handwritten," softer edge of a humanist sans. An OpenType Pro version was released in 2004 and Fedra Sans became Typotheque's most extensive offering with five weights, each accompanied by italics and small capitals. The font family supports Latin, Armenian, Bengali, Cyrillic, Devanagari, Greek, Hebrew, Inuktitut, and Tamil writing scripts. Now in its fourth incarnation, Fedra Sans is a typeface that improves with age.

Below left. Award-winning wayfinding system employing Fedra Sans across Vienna Airport. Design by French studio Intégral Ruedi Baur Paris.

Below right. Typotheque's Fedra Sans family is available in a huge variety of languages, increasing its international suitability for global design solutions.

FF Dax

ABCDEFGHIJKLMNOPQRSTUVWXYZ
abcdefghijklmnopqrstuvwxyz
1234567890 !@#?:;"＊&

Foundry: FontFont
Designer: Hans Reichel
Designer Nationality: German
Date: 1995

A humanist sans serif that also comes with a compact version, FF Dax is very popular. It was modified to make United Parcel Service's corporate typeface UPS Sans in 2005. The same year, David Cameron used the font in his campaign for leadership of the British Conservative Party.

FF Fago

ABCDEFGHIJKLMNOPQRSTUVWXYZ
abcdefghijklmnopqrstuvwxyz
1234567890 !@#?:;"*&

Foundry: FontFont
Designer: Ole Schäfer /
Andreas Eigendorf
Designer Nationality: German
Date: 2000

FF Fago is a straightforward sans serif that was created as a response to complex corporate design projects. It features thirty weights, including italics. It has an open structure and wide apertures that help legibility when viewed from a distance, making it suitable for information graphics and wayfinding.

FF Info Correspondence

ABCDEFGHIJKLMNOPQRSTUVWXYZ
abcdefghijklmnopqrstuvwxyz
1234567890 !@#?:;"*&

Foundry: FontFont
Designer: Erik Spiekermann /
Ole Schäfer
Designer Nationality: German
Date: 1998

FF Info Correspondence is part of the FF Info super family, which also includes FF Info Display and FF Info Text. A well-crafted sans serif, it is available in six weights from Regular to Bold. As its name suggests, it is perfect for information-design projects where clarity is essential.

FF Info Text

ABCDEFGHIJKLMNOPQRSTUVWXYZ
abcdefghijklmnopqrstuvwxyz
1234567890 !@#?:;"*&

Foundry: FontFont
Designer: Erik Spiekermann /
Ole Schäfer
Designer Nationality: German
Date: 1998

This finely tuned sans serif is part of the FF Info super family, which also includes FF Info Display and FF Info Correspondence. It was originally intended for use on traffic signage and is perfect for information-design projects where legibility is key and space is restricted.

FF Scala Sans

ABCDEFGHIJKLMNOPQRSTUVWXYZ
abcdefghijklmnopqrstuvwxyz
1234567890 !@#?:;"*&

Foundry: FontFont
Designer: Martin Majoor
Designer Nationality: Dutch
Date: 1993

This is a sister face to Martin Majoor's Old Style serif FF Scala from 1990. FF Scala Sans is a humanist sans serif typeface inspired by Gill Sans and Syntax. It was made for the Vredenburg music centre in Utrecht, the Netherlands and is used by the Los Angeles Metro Rail transportation system.

FF Unit

ABCDEFGHIJKLMNOPQRSTUVWXYZ
abcdefghijklmnopqrstuvwxyz
1234567890 !@#?:;"*&

Foundry: FontFont
Designer: Erik Spiekermann / Christian Schwartz
Designer Nationality: German / American
Date: 2003

FF Unit is more considered but equally as useable as its hugely popular predecessor, FF Meta. With greater contrast and simpler forms than Meta, it was first released in 2003, with the rounded version designed by New Zealand typeface designer Kris Sowersby. A slab serif was added later.

FF Unit Rounded

ABCDEFGHIJKLMNOPQRSTUVWXYZ
abcdefghijklmnopqrstuvwxyz
1234567890 !@#?:;"*&

Foundry: FontFont
Designer: Erik Spiekermann / Christian Schwartz
Designer Nationality: German / American
Date: 2008

FF Unit is a very considered typeface that irons out many of the idiosyncrasies of FF Meta by Erik Spiekermann (see p. 304). It was first released in 2003, with increased contrast and simplified forms. This rounded version was added in 2008, followed by a slab serif in 2009.

Foundry Sans

ABCDEFGHIJKLMNOPQRSTUVWXYZ
abcdefghijklmnopqrstuvwxyz
1234567890 !@#?:;"*&

Foundry: The Foundry
Designer: David Quay
Designer Nationality: British
Date: 1990

Foundry Sans is inspired by Hans Meier's design of the Syntax sans serif, which took its visual cues from the serif letterforms of Jan Tschichold's Sabon. Working in a similar manner, David Quay designed Foundry Sans by looking to the humanist serif characters of Stempel Garamond.

FF Meta

ABCDEFGHIJKLMNOPQRSTUVWXYZ
abcdefghijklmnopqrstuvwxyz
1234567890 !@#?:;"*&

Foundry: FontFont
Designer: Erik Spiekermann
Designer Nationality: German
Date: 1991

Renowned graphic and type designer Erik Spiekermann (see p. 304) created FF Meta typeface to be the "antithesis" of Helvetica, which he described as "boring and bland." FF Meta has gone on to become a hugely influential typeface since its release in 1991.

FF Meta started out as a commission in 1985 for British design agency Sedley Place to rebrand the German post office, Deutsche Bundespost, and part of the brief was to create a new sans serif corporate typeface family. The need to work at relatively small sizes on low-quality paper stocks was key to the design. One reason for this was that a lot of the organization's printing was done at a local level on laser printers, so economy and legibility was paramount for efficiency and readability. However, Spiekermann's and Sedley Place's design, entitled PT55, was never used by Deutsche Bundespost, which shied away from using such an innovative design.

Fortunately, all was not lost: FontFont, the independent type foundry that had been launched in 1990 by Spiekermann, along with Neville Brody and Spiekermann's then wife, Joan, completed the design, rebranding it FF Meta. It was one of the foundry's earliest releases and was soon a critical and commercial success. FF Meta was digitized by Just van Rossum and Erik van Blokland at Spiekermann's Berlin design practice, MetaDesign, from the original outlines. Over the years there have been a number of revisions, refinements and expansions to the family. Most notable was an accompanying serif design, FF Meta Serif, which was released in 2007.

Below left. FF Meta employed on the night network map of ZVV (Zurich's public transport system).

Below right. FF Meta's creator Erik Spiekermann designed this poster as part of a submission from a number of international designers on the theme of "public" for Public Bikes, Inc. The headline is set in the typeface Block, designed by Louis Oppenheim at the turn of the 20th century.

Opposite. The NYRB Classics series published by New York Review Books employs FF Meta consistently across its range of book covers.

PUBLIC

space | enemy | park | toilet | radio access | view | entrance | building baths | company | enterprise | deal transport | information | opinion money | private partnership | pool utility | relations | surplus | library storage | gardens | passage | vote performance | works | playground announcement | school | crossing grounds | beach | records | transit housing | data | declaration | issue parking | train | bicycles | persona institution | address | appearance

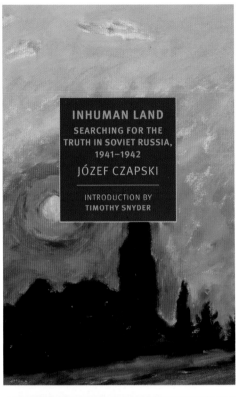

INHUMAN LAND

SEARCHING FOR THE
TRUTH IN SOVIET RUSSIA,
1941–1942

JÓZEF CZAPSKI

INTRODUCTION BY
TIMOTHY SNYDER

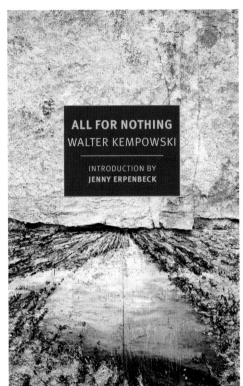

ALL FOR NOTHING
WALTER KEMPOWSKI

INTRODUCTION BY
JENNY ERPENBECK

ONCE AND FOREVER
THE TALES OF
KENJI MIYAZAWA

TRANSLATED BY
JOHN BESTER

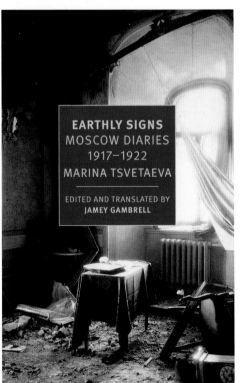

EARTHLY SIGNS
MOSCOW DIARIES
1917–1922
MARINA TSVETAEVA

EDITED AND TRANSLATED BY
JAMEY GAMBRELL

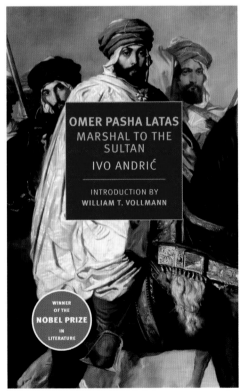

OMER PASHA LATAS
MARSHAL TO THE
SULTAN
IVO ANDRIĆ

INTRODUCTION BY
WILLIAM T. VOLLMANN

WINNER
OF THE
NOBEL PRIZE
IN
LITERATURE

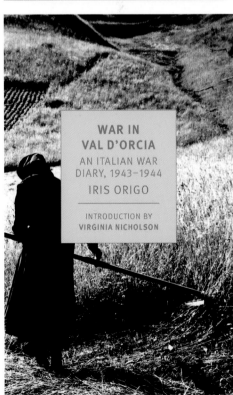

**WAR IN
VAL D'ORCIA**
AN ITALIAN WAR
DIARY, 1943–1944
IRIS ORIGO

INTRODUCTION BY
VIRGINIA NICHOLSON

Foundry Sterling

ABCDEFGHIJKLMNOPQRSTUVWXYZ
abcdefghijklmnopqrstuvwxyz
1234567890 !@#?:;"*&

Foundry: The Foundry
Designer: David Quay /
Freda Sack
Designer Nationality: British
Date: 2001

Foundry Sterling has been a consistently popular typeface since its inception and has gained the status of a modern classic. It also possesses a quintessentially English flavor for a modern sans serif type. Foundry Sterling's letterforms have been designed with particular attention to classical proportion and purity of form, yet its elegant and graceful appearance belies a flexibility and legibility that allow it to be incredibly versatile. It is a typeface that is as comfortable working in an editorial arena as in wayfinding and signage applications.

Designers David Quay and Freda Sack co-founded The Foundry (see p. 284) in 1989 and soon established an international reputation for original typefaces of a very high quality. The Foundry offers a diverse range of fonts, which combine traditional design approaches—thanks in great part to Quay and Sack's experience—and the latest digital OpenType technologies. Its typeface library includes collaborations with eminent designers such as Dutch typographer Wim Crouwel (see p. 540), and the Architype range of avant-garde typefaces derived mainly from the work of artists and designers of the interwar years.

Below. Foundry Sterling employed as wayfinding for the University of Applied Sciences Wildau, Germany where the type treatment also employed a cross-hatched infill for larger types describing building names.

Frisans

ABCDEFGHIJKLMNOPQRSTUVWXYZ
abcdefghijklmnopqrstuvwxyz
1234567890 !@#?:;"*&

Foundry: Monotype
Designer: Bo Berndal
Designer Nationality: Swedish
Date: 2005

Frisans was conceived as an experiment to combine the calligraphic forms of Warren Chappell's Lydian with 19th-century grotesque letterforms. Its regular weight shows similarities to Lydian's square-nib letters, while its slightly condensed proportions pay homage to faces like Franklin Gothic and Standard.

Frutiger Next

ABCDEFGHIJKLMNOPQRSTUVWXYZ
abcdefghijklmnopqrstuvwxyz
1234567890 !@#?:;"*&

Foundry: Linotype
Designer: Adrian Frutiger
Designer Nationality: Swiss
Date: 1976 / 1997

This is an updated cut of the sans designed in 1976. It was created for signage at Munich's Alte Pinakothek museum. Adrian Frutiger and the Linotype team optimized the forms of the original typeface to make them more consistent across the whole family, and created several sets of true italics.

FS Albert

ABCDEFGHIJKLMNOPQRSTUVWXYZ
abcdefghijklmnopqrstuvwxyz
1234567890 !@#?:;"*&

Foundry: Fontsmith
Designer: Jason Smith
Designer Nationality: British
Date: 2002

FS Albert features rounded edges to add warmth to its sans serif letterforms, helping make it solid and friendly, particularly in its heavier weights. The font is named after Jason Smith's son because of his chubbiness as a child, which is a dubious honor, although Smith says Albert has since forgiven him.

FS Aldrin

ABCDEFGHIJKLMNOPQRSTUVWXYZ
abcdefghijklmnopqrstuvwxyz
1234567890 !@#?:;"*&

Foundry: Fontsmith
Designer: Phil Garnham
Designer Nationality: British
Date: 2016

This approachable design by Fontsmith (see p. 272) includes an extensive icon set featuring symbols of space travel. Designer Phil Garnham felt its design was reminiscent of the space age, and gained approval from US astronaut Buzz Aldrin for the naming of the typeface.

Frutiger

ABCDEFGHIJKLMNOPQRSTUVWXYZ
abcdefghijklmnopqrstuvwxyz
1234567890 !@#?:;"*&

Foundry: Linotype / D. Stempel AG
Designer: Adrian Frutiger
Designer Nationality: Swiss
Date: 1976

Renowned Swiss type and graphic designer Adrian Frutiger (see p. 290) was commissioned in 1968 to create a new typeface for the wayfinding system for the soon to be constructed Charles de Gaulle Airport in France. Rather than adapt any of his existing types, Frutiger set about creating a new design, one that would become an instant classic when completed and installed in 1975 and released to the public in 1976.

The typeface was originally called "Roissy" and part of its design was to possess a modern yet friendly appearance, reflecting the architecture of its new home. Its success was also because of its outstanding ability to be read at varying distances, on the move at speed or at angles, and in low light—all of which helped recognition and navigation throughout the airport. The typeface's balanced letterforms and warm appearance also help to make

it easily legible in distinguishing characters and understanding directions.

Although created as a display typeface, Frutiger is highly adept working as a text face and is employed in publishing, corporate identities, and advertising applications across the globe. Its legibility has made it an incredibly versatile choice for designers and since its release a number of variations have been introduced, including Neue Frutiger World released by Monotype in 2018 and credited to Adrian Frutiger, Monotype type director Akira Kobayashi and the Monotype Studio. Neue Frutiger World covers more than 150 languages and scripts, providing a consistent voice and presentation to designs no matter where they are in the world.

Below left. Frutiger's wayfinding system in Charles de Gaulle Airport, Paris France, 1970.

Below right. Original drawing by Adrian Frutiger, showing his workings for the lowercase regular "a" complete with annotation.

Opposite. Striking wayfinding design by Metapur AG for Kantonsschule Obwalden (High School Obwalden).

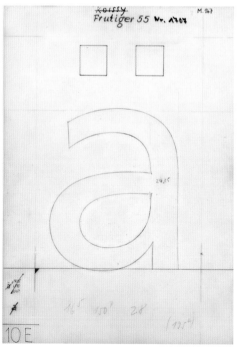

FS Blake

ABCDEFGHIJKLMNOPQRSTUVWXYZ
abcdefghijklmnopqrstuvwxyz
1234567890 !@#?:;"*&

Foundry: Fontsmith
Designer: Emanuela Conidi /
Jason Smith
Designer Nationality: Italian /
British
Date: 2010

Emanuela Conidi and Jason Smith's design for FS Blake wears its Art Deco influence lightly; the typeface's cool, contemporary appearance is tempered by a range of fine yet distinctive details within the design of each letterform. FS Blake is available in four weights, with corresponding italics.

FS Dillon

ABCDEFGHIJKLMNOPQRSTUVWXYZ
abcdefghijklmnopqrstuvwxyz
1234567890 !@#?:;"*&

Foundry: Fontsmith
Designer: Jason Smith
Designer Nationality: British
Date: 2009

FS Dillon was inspired by Bauhaus typography and features a strong vertical emphasis; its rounded, slightly condensed letterforms are built on a rectangular skeleton. The typeface was chosen for use on signage within the Queen Elizabeth Olympic Park in London for the Olympic Games in 2012.

FS Elliot

ABCDEFGHIJKLMNOPQRSTUVWXYZ
abcdefghijklmnopqrstuvwxyz
1234567890 !@#?:;"*&

Foundry: Fontsmith
Designer: Nick Job
Designer Nationality: British
Date: 2012

FS Elliot is the work of Nick Job, part of the team at Fontsmith (see p. 272). He designed it to follow in the footsteps of classic British Modernist typography, and it features clear, open letterforms with an even stroke weight throughout. The Pro edition also includes Greek and Cyrillic character sets.

FS Ingrid

ABCDEFGHIJKLMNOPQRSTUVWXYZ
abcdefghijklmnopqrstuvwxyz
1234567890 !@#?:;"*&

Foundry: Fontsmith
Designer: Jason Smith
Designer Nationality: British
Date: 2004

The sharp edges of this quietly authoritative sans serif by Jason Smith are softened by generous curves elsewhere within its letterforms. FS Ingrid was developed to perform well in screen-based contexts. The typeface is available in three weights plus italics.

FS Irwin

ABCDEFGHIJKLMNOPQRSTUVWXYZ
abcdefghijklmnopqrstuvwxyz
1234567890 !@#?:;"*&

FS Irwin was developed from calligraphic sketches, and retains a sense of movement within its letterforms; this liveliness is particularly apparent within the italics. Brazilian designer Fernando Mello took inspiration for the font from his studies at the Cooper Union in New York.

Foundry: Fontsmith
Designer: Fernando Mello
Designer Nationality: Brazilian
Date: 2017

FS Lola

ABCDEFGHIJKLMNOPQRSTUVWXYZ
abcdefghijklmnopqrstuvwxyz
1234567890 !@#?:;"*&

This semi-serif design by Phil Garnham, type director at Fontsmith (see p. 272), features lively curved spurs, wide open counters and a generous x-height. Leftward-facing single slab serifs on certain letterforms balance the soft femininity of other details within the typeface.

Foundry: Fontsmith
Designer: Phil Garnham
Designer Nationality: British
Date: 2005

FS Matthew

ABCDEFGHIJKLMNOPQRSTUVWXYZ
abcdefghijklmnopqrstuvwxyz
1234567890 !@#?:;"*&

Fontsmith (see p. 272) was commissioned to create FS Matthew for a UK terrestrial TV channel. The result is a curvaceous and legible sans serif typeface that features softened edges and slightly condensed letterforms, making it an economical choice for text typesetting.

Foundry: Fontsmith
Designer: Phil Garnham / Jason Smith
Designer Nationality: British
Date: 2013

FS Me

ABCDEFGHIJKLMNOPQRSTUVWXYZ
abcdefghijklmnopqrstuvwxyz
1234567890 !@#?:;"*&

FS Me began life as a commission from British charity Mencap to create a typeface with optimal legibility which would be accessible to readers with learning disabilities. A proportion of the proceeds from each FS Me license is donated to Mencap, which works with people with learning disabilities.

Foundry: Fontsmith
Designer: Jason Smith
Designer Nationality: British
Date: 2008

Fontsmith

Offering a complete font design and production service, Fontsmith is a world-class boutique-type foundry. Established in 1997 by Jason Smith, Fontsmith has designed an award-winning portfolio of typefaces, and the commercial commissions it has created have established a reputation for designing fonts with a "distinctively human character." Based in London, Fontsmith is made up of a team of international designers who believe passionately in the craft of type and pride themselves on their deep understanding of form and detailing when creating precision designs.

As well as offering an extensive collection of retail fonts, with more than forty designs ranging from Modern / Didone serifs to humanist sans, Fontsmith spends a significant amount of studio time designing bespoke fonts for organizations across a variety of sectors. The foundry allows for technological innovation so its types can be adaptable and flexible, which has been necessary in a number of its private commissions for the design of typefaces for UK and internationally based brands across a variety of sectors, including finance, retail, automotive, FMCG, sport, telecommunications, and luxury.

It designed the first-ever bespoke typeface for a digital television channel (E4) in 2001, and its credits also include the UK's BBC, Channel 4, ITV and Sky News, and Sweden's Kanal 5. Fontsmith aims to counter the challenges and limitations of television and similar platforms such as mobile media and computers, by designing typefaces that are consistently and clearly presented yet differentiate each brand, no matter the limitations of the presentation medium.

Founded: 1997
Country: UK
Website: fontsmith.com
Notable typefaces:
FS Benjamin (see p. 66)
FS Industrie (see p. 225)
Lost & Foundry (see p. 368)

Below. Fontsmith founder Jason Smith and team often start any new design by sketching ideas before translating to digital.

Opposite top. Spreads from Fontsmith's Brandfont book, showcasing a number of corporate typefaces.

Opposite below. Revisiting ampersand designs and reworking letterform designs by hand.

GOOD FOOD
DESERVES LURPAK

L'k

MARAMJAM
BACON
MASH
BREAKFAST
CRISTY WHITE
OMELETTE
POACHED
SCRAMBLED

A global Brandfont®

Ekgπஈक्ष

GARAGE DE LA PLACE
SAINT-GEORGES
RENAULT

00334 7243 6614

Renault
ASSISTANCE

ة
ش
ب

THE
ART
OF POURING
A DRAUGHT
BEER

¡Hola
Madrid!

Kaká

THE NEW F-TYPE.
YOUR TURN.

Reality
Reality

Dream
FIRE

FS Millbank

ABCDEFGHIJKLMNOPQRSTUVWXYZ
abcdefghijklmnopqrstuvwxyz
1234567890 !@#?:;"*&

Foundry: Fontsmith
Designer: Stuart de Rozario
Designer Nationality: British
Date: 2014

FS Millbank was designed by Stuart de Rozario to be clear and legible and to encourage speedy comprehension when used within signage. It incorporates an extensive set of wayfinding-specific icons and a special optically tailored cut for use in lighter colours on dark backgrounds.

FS Pimlico

ABCDEFGHIJKLMNOPQRSTUVWXYZ
abcdefghijklmnopqrstuvwxyz
1234567890 !@#?:;"*&

Foundry: Fontsmith
Designer: Fernando Mello
Designer Nationality: Brazilian
Date: 2011

The 1970s flavour of FS Pimlico reflects designer Fernando Mello's personal fondness for the era—he created the voluptuous Black weight of the typeface first, before moving on to develop Light and Bold versions. A set of swash caps and alternate characters are also included.

FS Siena

ABCDEFGHIJKLMNOPQRSTUVWXYZ
abcdefghijklmnopqrstuvwxyz
1234567890 !@#?:;"*&

Foundry: Fontsmith
Designer: Krista Radoeva / Jason Smith
Designer Nationality: Bulgarian / British
Date: 2016

Jason Smith drew his first sketches for FS Siena twenty-five years before its eventual release; its delicate and distinguished forms were developed into a fully functioning family by designer Krista Radoeva at Fontsmith (see p. 272). The original drawings were based on Optima by Hermann Zapf (see p. 574).

FS Silas Sans

ABCDEFGHIJKLMNOPQRSTUVWXYZ
abcdefghijklmnopqrstuvwxyz
1234567890 !@#?:;"*&

Foundry: Fontsmith
Designer: Phil Garnham
Designer Nationality: British
Date: 2015

This sans serif member of the Silas type system was designed with subtle angled cuts to the ascenders of its letterforms, adding a sense of consistency within body text. The typeface offers a functional, businesslike feel with a subtle touch of warmth and movement.

Generis Sans

ABCDEFGHIJKLMNOPQRSTUVWXYZ
abcdefghijklmnopqrstuvwxyz
1234567890 !@#?:,"*&

Foundry: Linotype
Designer: Erik Faulhaber
Designer Nationality: German
Date: 2006

Erik Faulhaber designed his extensive Generis type system to offer designers a cohesive family of styles that would serve a wide range of different typographic contexts and requirements. This slightly condensed sans serif version features wide open counters for maximum legibility.

Generis Simple

ABCDEFGHIJKLMNOPQRSTUVWXYZ
abcdefghijklmnopqrstuvwxyz
1234567890 !@#?:,"*&

Foundry: Linotype
Designer: Erik Faulhaber
Designer Nationality: German
Date: 2006

As its name suggests, this second sans serif member of the Generis family is a further refinement of Generis Sans. Working from the same formal skeleton, Erik Faulhaber removed the spurs from the original sans letterforms, simplifying their design for a more contemporary feel.

Gills Sans Nova

ABCDEFGHIJKLMNOPQRSTUVWXYZ
abcdefghijklmnopqrstuvwxyz
1234567890 !@#?:,"*&

Foundry: Monotype
Designer: Eric Gill / George Ryan
Designer Nationality: British / American
Date: 2015

Gill Sans Nova is part of Monotype's Eric Gill Series that builds upon the original Gill Sans (1931). Monotype designer George Ryan expanded its character set and added a range of weights, to create a fully fledged family that fulfils the diverse demands of contemporary typesetting.

Gordian

ABCDEFGHIJKLMNOPQRSTUVWXYZ
abcdefghijklmnopqrstuvwxyz
1234567890 !@#?:,"*&

Foundry: Typotheque
Designer: Nikola Djurek
Designer Nationality: Croatian
Date: 2018

Croatian type designer and winemaker Nikola Djurek has experience of stone-carving, which is evident within his design for Gordian, a Roman-influenced sans serif featuring subtle flared details. Alongside its four text weights are several handsome sets of display capitals.

Gill Sans

ABCDEFGHIJKLMNOPQRSTUVWXYZ
abcdefghijklmnopqrstuvwxyz
1234567890 !@#?:;'"*&

Foundry: Monotype
Designer: Eric Gill
Designer Nationality: British
Date: 1928

If any typeface offered itself as an English vernacular, then Gill Sans would take the crown. It was designed by engraver, calligrapher, and sculptor Eric Gill as a commission from Monotype's Stanley Morison, and was Gill's first typeface. Monotype released Gill Sans in 1928 as metal type to compete with the German sans serifs appearing at the time, such as Futura. Gill served as an apprentice under British type designer and calligrapher Edward Johnston, and Gill Sans owes much of its appearance to Johnston's sans serif typeface designs for the London Underground in 1916.

Gill Sans is more than just an elegant, classic and distinctive sans serif. The typeface was adopted by numerous companies that were integral to the UK's infrastructure and it evolved to become a part of the national identity, leading to the face being dubbed the "Helvetica of England." The London North Eastern Railway (LNER) adopted Gill Sans soon after its release in 1929. The railway operator employed Gill Sans on everything from timetables to locomotive name plates. When LNER and the other "Big Four" railways were nationalized in 1948 to form British Railways, Gill Sans was then used on all printed material and timetables. In addition, companies such as the Post Office, the BBC, Penguin Books, and Monotype have used Gill Sans as part of their identity over the years, meaning that Gill Sans has never been out of the public eye.

Gill Sans was not drawn up mechanically from a single design and is known for possessing inconsistencies in design between the weights ranging from Light to the overinflated Ultra Bold. Yet this variation contributes to its charm and humanity.

Below, from left. Gill Sans featuring in the guidelines for LNER; appearing on the name plate for the Mallard, an A4 Pacific Class Locomotive, holder of the world speed record for a steam locomotive; and a galley set of Gill Sans woodblock types held at Typoretum, a letterpress and vintage printing studio in Colchester, UK.

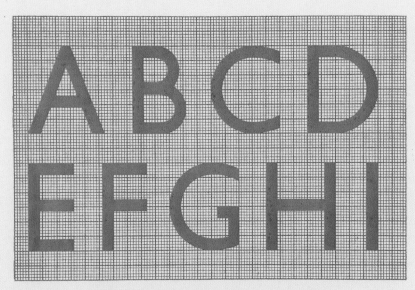

GILL SANS LIGHT SIGN LETTERS

Gill Sans Light Sign Letters and Figures (pages 6 to 10) are used only for
(i) notices requiring a considerable amount of lettering, where maximum legibility is not so important as economy in space
(ii) internally illuminated signs (anti-halation).

6

Greta Sans

ABCDEFGHIJKLMNOPQRSTUVWXYZ
abcdefghijklmnopqrstuvwxyz
1234567890 !@#?:;"*&

Foundry: Typotheque
Designer: Peter Biľak /
Nikola Djurek
Designer Nationality: Slovakian /
Croatian
Date: 2012

This sans serif member of Peter Biľak's innovative Greta type family was designed with the assistance of Nikola Djurek, his fellow designer at Typotheque (see p. 90). Its ten weights, four widths and distinctive, jaunty italics enable it to rise to even the most complex of editorial design challenges.

ITC Adderville

ABCDEFGHIJKLMNOPQRSTUVWXYZ
abcdefghijklmnopqrstuvwxyz
1234567890 !@#?:;"*&

Foundry: ITC
Designer: George Ryan
Designer Nationality: American
Date: 1999

When George Ryan of the Massachusetts-based Galapagos Design Group designed Adderville for ITC, he hoped to create a "truly original" sans serif. The result is a typeface that has an appealing irregularity and flared details, which make it a lively choice for display type.

ITC Bailey Sans

ABCDEFGHIJKLMNOPQRSTUVWXYZ
abcdefghijklmnopqrstuvwxyz
1234567890 !@#?:;"*&

Foundry: ITC
Designer: Kevin Bailey
Designer Nationality: American
Date: 1996

Kevin Bailey's first typeface, ITC Bailey Sans, was created for a project that required a restrained style of typeface he was unable to find elsewhere. In addition to the four weights of this sans, he also designed an accompanying serif display style, Bailey Quad Bold.

ITC Eras

ABCDEFGHIJKLMNOPQRSTUVWXYZ
abcdefghijklmnopqrstuvwxyz
1234567890 !@#?:;"*&

Foundry: ITC
Designer: Albert Boton /
Albert Hollenstein
Designer Nationality: French /
Swiss
Date: 1976

French designer Albert Boton and Swiss designer Albert Hollenstein collaborated on Eras for ITC in 1976. It upholds the French tradition for sans serif styles that favor idiosyncrasy and character over brisk neutrality. Eras' forward-leaning letterforms provide a distinctive sense of energy and purpose.

ITC Johnston

ABCDEFGHIJKLMNOPQRSTUVWXYZ
abcdefghijklmnopqrstuvwxyz
1234567890 !@#?:;"*&

Foundry: ITC
Designer: Edward Johnston / Richard Dawson / Dave Farey
Designer Nationality: British
Date: 1916 / 1999

Edward Johnston's humanist sans serif was originally created in a single weight and never intended for body text typesetting. Richard Dawson and Dave Farey's version of the font for ITC in 1999 referred to Johnston's original letterforms, preserving their carefully constructed proportions.

ITC Legacy Sans

ABCDEFGHIJKLMNOPQRSTUVWXYZ
abcdefghijklmnopqrstuvwxyz
1234567890 !@#?:;"*&

Foundry: ITC
Designer: Ronald Arnholm
Designer Nationality: American
Date: 1992

Ronald Arnholm developed this sans serif from the skeleton of his Legacy Serif typeface. The latter was inspired by the lettering in an edition of Eusebius's *De praeparatione evangelica* (*Preparation for the Gospel*) by French type designer and printer Nicolas Jenson in 1470.

ITC Migration Sans

ABCDEFGHIJKLMNOPQRSTUVWXYZ
abcdefghijklmnopqrstuvwxyz
1234567890 !@#?:;"*&

Foundry: ITC
Designer: André Simard
Designer Nationality: Canadian
Date: 2008

Québécois designer André Simard founded his own studio in 1980, and brought his experience within graphic-design practice to bear in the design of his first typeface, ITC Migration Sans. Reflecting his experience in newspaper design, the font works well at small point sizes.

ITC Mixage

ABCDEFGHIJKLMNOPQRSTUVWXYZ
abcdefghijklmnopqrstuvwxyz
1234567890 !@#?:;"*&

Foundry: ITC
Designer: Aldo Novarese
Designer Nationality: Italian
Date: 1985

True to its name, ITC Mixage is a hybrid typeface created by Italian type designer Aldo Novarese, within which he blended certain characteristics of Antique Olive and Syntax to create an affable new sans serif design. It is available in four weights with corresponding italics.

ITC Obliqua

ABCDEFGHIJKLMNOPQRSTUVWXYZ
abcdefghijklmnopqrstuvwxyz
1234567890 !@#?:;"*&

Foundry: ITC
Designer: César Puertas
Designer Nationality: Colombian
Date: 2009

Colombian designer César Puertas, who is type director at the Bogota-based Typograma type-design studio, designed Obliqua for ITC in 2009.

Its utilitarian design blends characteristics of traditional, industrial grotesques with a subtle sense of movement inspired by handwriting.

ITC Officina Sans

ABCDEFGHIJKLMNOPQRSTUVWXYZ
abcdefghijklmnopqrstuvwxyz
1234567890 !@#?:;"*&

Foundry: ITC
Designer: Ole Schäfer / Erik Spiekermann
Designer Nationality: German
Date: 1990

ITC Officina Sans was originally designed as a functional font for business correspondence, tailored to reproduce well on low-quality office printers. Its popularity upon release prompted Ole Schäfer and Erik Spiekermann (see p. 304) to expand the typeface into an extensive font family.

ITC Panache

ABCDEFGHIJKLMNOPQRSTUVWXYZ
abcdefghijklmnopqrstuvwxyz
1234567890 !@#?:;"*&

Foundry: ITC
Designer: Ed Benguiat
Designer Nationality: American
Date: 1988

Although Ed Benguiat (see p. 514) stated that legibility was his principal concern when designing ITC Panache, he also incorporated a number of stylistic flourishes that elevate the font from this straightforward foundation. The resulting typeface is well suited for both headlines and body text.

ITC Pino

ABCDEFGHIJKLMNOPQRSTUVWXYZ
abcdefghijklmnopqrstuvwxyz
1234567890 !@#?:;"*&

Foundry: ITC
Designer: Slobodan Jelesijevic
Designer Nationality: Serbian
Date: 2008

Serbian designer and illustrator Slobodan Jelesijevic developed ITC Pino to accompany illustrations he was working on for a children's magazine; unable to find a typeface that fulfilled his requirements, he decided to design his own. The font was licensed by ITC in 2008.

ITC Quay Sans

ABCDEFGHIJKLMNOPQRSTUVWXYZ
abcdefghijklmnopqrstuvwxyz
1234567890 !@#?:;"*&

Foundry: ITC
Designer: David Quay
Designer Nationality: British
Date: 1990

Alongside his work as a co-founder of London-based type studio The Foundry (see p. 284), David Quay has designed a range of typefaces for other foundries over the course of his career. This design for ITC adds subtle visual interest to its sans serif letterforms with slightly flared stroke ends.

ITC Stone Humanist

ABCDEFGHIJKLMNOPQRSTUVWXYZ
abcdefghijklmnopqrstuvwxyz
1234567890 !@#?:;"*&

Foundry: ITC
Designer: Sumner Stone
Designer Nationality: American
Date: 2005

A member of Sumner Stone's extensive, eponymous type system, ITC Stone Humanist was designed to incorporate characteristics of both sans and serif type styles. The typeface is a subtle development of the design of its predecessor, Stone Sans, with which it shares its italics.

ITC Stone Sans

ABCDEFGHIJKLMNOPQRSTUVWXYZ
abcdefghijklmnopqrstuvwxyz
1234567890 !@#?:;"*&

Foundry: ITC
Designer: Sumner Stone / Bob Ishi
Designer Nationality: American
Date: 1987

Designed by Sumner Stone with Adobe's Bob Ishi in 1987, Stone Sans is a humanist sans serif font that shares proportions with its Stone Serif counterpart. Alongside the Latin character set, a phonetic version by John Renner, and Cyrillic by Vladimir Yefimov, are also available.

ITC Stone Sans II

ABCDEFGHIJKLMNOPQRSTUVWXYZ
abcdefghijklmnopqrstuvwxyz
1234567890 !@#?:;"*&

Foundry: ITC
Designer: Sumner Stone / Jim Wasco / Delve Withrington
Designer Nationality: American
Date: 2010

Sumner Stone's original aim when updating Stone Sans was to add further weights and condensed styles to the existing family; upon revisiting the font, however, he decided a more extensive reworking was in order. Stone Sans II builds upon the impressive legibility of its predecessor.

Jeunesse

ABCDEFGHIJKLMNOPQRSTUVWXYZ
abcdefghijklmnopqrstuvwxyz
1234567890 !@#?:;"*&

Foundry: Monotype
Designer: Johannes Birkenbach
Designer Nationality: German
Date: 1993

This semi-serif typeface was created by German type designer Johannes Birkenbach at Monotype UK, shortly before he established his own foundry, ABC Design. Together with its serif and sans counterparts, it forms part of the versatile Jeunesse superfamily of typefaces.

Jeunesse Sans

ABCDEFGHIJKLMNOPQRSTUVWXYZ
abcdefghijklmnopqrstuvwxyz
1234567890 !@#?:;"*&

Foundry: Monotype
Designer: Johannes Birkenbach
Designer Nationality: German
Date: 1993

With a slightly heavier stroke weight and fewer serif details than Jeunesse, this sans member of the superfamily offers a slightly more businesslike feel than its counterparts. The high waist of certain uppercase letterforms is reminiscent of Venus, the Bauer grotesque released in 1907.

Joanna Sans Nova

ABCDEFGHIJKLMNOPQRSTUVWXYZ
abcdefghijklmnopqrstuvwxyz
1234567890 !@#?:;"*&

Foundry: Monotype
Designer: Terrance Weinzierl
Designer Nationality: American
Date: 2015

This design by Terrance Weinzierl is a member of Monotype's Eric Gill Series and was developed from Eric Gill's serif Joanna (1931). Less diverse in character across its range of weights than Gill Sans, Joanna Sans Nova is particularly well suited to digital applications.

L10

ABCDEFGHIJKLMNOPQRSTUVWXYZ
abcdefghijklmnopqrstuvwxyz
1234567890 !@#?:;"*&

Foundry: Or Type
Designer: Guðmundur Úlfarsson
Designer Nationality: Icelandic
Date: 2013 / 2015

L10 is a font family developed to revitalize the traditional form of a humanist sans serif. Its characters, designed in four weights, feature vigorous strokes and dynamic counters and are ideally suited to multiplatform environments, editorial and identity projects.

L15

ABCDEFGHIJKLMNOPQRSTUVWXYZ
abcdefghijklmnopqrstuvwxyz
1234567890 !@#?:;"*&

Foundry: Or Type
Designer: Guðmundur Úlfarsson
Designer Nationality: Icelandic
Date: 2015

L15 is a revision of the earlier L10 sans serif design from Icelandic foundry Or Type. L15 maintains the nature of the original and introduces several distinctive features, such as the widening of characters and the lengthening of curved terminals, as is visible on the lowercase 'a'.

Legal

ABCDEFGHIJKLMNOPQRSTUVWXYZ
abcdefghijklmnopqrstuvwxyz
1234567890 !@#?:;"*&

Foundry: Linotype
Designer: Hellmut G. Bomm
Designer Nationality: German
Date: 2004

Hellmut G. Bomm developed the design of Legal from his earlier experiments in simplified, grotesque sans serif type design during the 1970s. The typeface offers a legible neutrality at smaller point sizes, but conveys a more pronounced sense of personality within headlines.

Lemance

ABCDEFGHIJKLMNOPQRSTUVWXYZ
abcdefghijklmnopqrstuvwxyz
1234567890 !@#?:;"*&

Foundry: Dalton Maag
Designer: Damien Collot
Designer Nationality: French
Date: 2016

Lemance is a functional sans serif designed in the humanist style. It takes its name from the river that runs through the French town of Monsempron-Libos, Nouvelle-Aquitaine, where designer Damien Collot was born. Like the river, Lemance's letterforms are governed by their lively and organic curves.

Letraset Arta

ABCDEFGHIJKLMNOPQRSTUVWXYZ
abcdefghijklmnopqrstuvwxyz
1234567890 !@#?:;"*&

Foundry: Letraset
Designer: David Quay
Designer Nationality: British
Date: 1991

The slight forward tilt of Letraset Arta adds a jaunty vitality to both body text and headlines; unusually, its italics are not tilted at a more exaggerated angle, but are instead considerably condensed, providing a sense of contrast with the openness of Arta's roman styles.

Ligurino

ABCDEFGHIJKLMNOPQRSTUVWXYZ
abcdefghijklmnopqrstuvwxyz
1234567890 !@#?:;"*&

Foundry: Typodermic
Designer: Ray Larabie
Designer Nationality: Canadian
Date: 2005

This straightforward sans serif design by Canadian Ray Larabie of Typodermic was created with a deliberate lack of ornamentation, in order to function first and foremost as a readable text typeface. It is available in an array of weights and widths, with an all-caps outline counterpart.

Linex Sans

ABCDEFGHIJKLMNOPQRSTUVWXYZ
abcdefghijklmnopqrstuvwxyz
1234567890 !@#?:;"*&

Foundry: Monotype
Designer: Albert Boton
Designer Nationality: French
Date: 2002

Carpenter turned type designer Albert Boton developed Linex Sans from his earlier typeface Linex Sweet (1996). He sharpened Sweet's rounded edges while preserving the calligraphic contrast within its letterforms, to create an amiable and slightly unconventional sans serif design.

Linotype Aperto

ABCDEFGHIJKLMNOPQRSTUVWXYZ
abcdefghijklmnopqrstuvwxyz
1234567890 !@#?:;"*&

Foundries: Calligraphics / Linotype
Designer: Paul Veres
Designer Nationality: American
Date: 1996

Paul Veres created this transitional sans serif featuring a generous x-height for his one-man foundry Calligraphics in 1995; it was licensed by Linotype the following year. Aperto was Veres's first typeface design and was influenced by his experience in calligraphy.

Linotype Aroma No. 2

ABCDEFGHIJKLMNOPQRSTUVWXYZ
abcdefghijklmnopqrstuvwxyz
1234567890 !@#?:;"*&

Foundry: Linotype
Designer: Tim Ahrens
Designer Nationality: German
Date: 2007

Type designer and architect Tim Ahrens hoped to preserve a formal elegance he felt was missing from many neutral sans serif designs with Linotype Aroma (1999). He refined the design of many of its letterforms for this OpenType update to the font, which was published in 2007.

The Foundry

The Foundry was co-founded in London in 1989 by David Quay and Freda Sack, with just two typefaces (Foundry Sans and Foundry Old Style), but its typeface library has now grown into a range of font styles, covering a range of languages and formats. The founders bring a combination of traditional and modern approaches to font design and implementation, having worked in every technological development of type design since hot metal, including the beginnings of digital font technology.

Sack is a British type designer and typographer. Since the late 1970s, she has worked for various font manufacturers in all aspects of type design and font development, including Stempel, Linotype, Berthold, and the International Typeface Corporation (ITC), which still publishes many of her designs. Quay is a graphic designer, type designer, typographer,

and teacher from London, who now resides in the Netherlands. He has also designed fonts for Letraset, ITC and Berthold. He continues to work as a type and graphic designer, creating new typefaces for The Foundry as well as private commissions.

The Foundry's craft skills and predigital experience lend integrity and quality to its type design. Its involvement with design and typography gives the company a highly individual approach to its work as type designers. This is also motivated by personal dialogue with designers from all over the world. In 2013, the partners decided to work closely with Monotype towards a new era where all The Foundry typefaces would be available as web fonts and for use in e-publications, mobile apps, server-based applications, consumer devices, and other products, all to be licensed through Monotype.

Founded: 1989
Countries: UK
Website: foundrytypes.co.uk
Notable typefaces:
Foundry Sterling (see p. 266)
Foundry Gridnik (see p. 426)

Below. From a visual identity and brand direction developed by Swedish agency Kurppa Hosk, London / Croatian studio Bunch implemented a wide range of information and promotional materials employing Foundry Gridnik as the brand's core type.

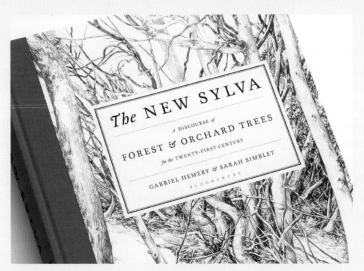

Above. *The New Sylva* book, designed by Grade Design in London, employs Foundry Wilson for titling and text setting across 400 pages. Foundry Wilson is a revival of a typeface originally cut in 1760 by Scottish type founder Alexander Wilson.

Below. Identity by UK designer and art director Patrick Myles for RIBA (Royal Institute of British Architects). The project employing Foundry Flek / Plek was applied online and in print, and as applied window graphics across London's Regent Street.

Linotype Authentic Sans

ABCDEFGHIJKLMNOPQRSTUVWXYZ
abcdefghijklmnopqrstuvwxyz
1234567890 !@#?:¡"*&

Foundry: Linotype
Designer: Karin Huschka
Designer Nationality: German
Date: 1999

This eccentric sans serif font is part of Linotype's TakeType Library, which was chosen from the entries of the International Digital Type Design Contest held in 1999. Slab serif, small serif and stencil versions of the typeface complete the Linotype Authentic family.

Linotype Projekt

ABCDEFGHIJKLMNOPQRSTUVWXYZ
abcdefghijklmnopqrstuvwxyz
1234567890 !@#?:;"*&

Foundry: Linotype
Designer: Andreas Koch
Designer Nationality: German
Date: 1999

Andreas Koch designed Linotype Projekt to capture some of the formal distortion that occurred from the process of printing metal type, which he felt resulted in a more robust and pleasing appearance. His humanist sans serif design also features slightly flared stroke ends.

Linotype Spitz

ABCDEFGHIJKLMNOPQRSTUVWXYZ
abcdefghijklmnopqrstuvwxyz
1234567890 !@#?:;"*&

Foundry: Linotype
Designer: Oliver Brentzel
Designer Nationality: German
Date: 1997

According to designer Oliver Brentzel, the pairing of pointed details and gentle semicircular curves within the letterforms of Linotype Spitz was inspired by the distinctive, decorative forms of the Chrysler Building in New York. The typeface is available in five weights.

Linotype Tetria

ABCDEFGHIJKLMNOPQRSTUVWXYZ
abcdefghijklmnopqrstuvwxyz
1234567890 !@#?:;"*&

Foundry: Linotype
Designer: Martin Jagodzinski
Designer Nationality: German
Date: 1999

Clear, legible and free from embellishment, Linotype Tetria shares some geometric characteristics with the German DIN typefaces, and its slightly condensed letterforms make it an economical choice for text typesetting. It was designed by Martin Jagodzinski for Linotype in 1999.

Linotype Textra

ABCDEFGHIJKLMNOPQRSTUVWXYZ
abcdefghijklmnopqrstuvwxyz
1234567890 !@#?:;"*&

Foundry: Linotype
Designer: Jörg Herz /
Jochen Schuss
Designer Nationality: German
Date: 2002

Linotype Textra is a versatile font featuring subtle idiosyncrasies within the design of its letterforms, which are difficult to discern when used for body text, but become more evident at larger point sizes. Its name is a portmanteau of "text" and "extra," which reflects that duality.

Luba

ABCDEFGHIJKLMNOPQRSTUVWXYZ
abcdefghijklmnopqrstuvwxyz
1234567890 !@#?:;"*&

Foundry: Linotype
Designer: Hendrik Möller
Designer Nationality: German
Date: 2009

German designer Hendrik Möller designed this friendly sans serif in 2009. Luba is a multi-script font that comes in four weights with Latin and Cyrillic support. Möller created it as part of a university project aiming to develop a typeface for people learning Cyrillic-based languages.

Lumin Sans

ABCDEFGHIJKLMNOPQRSTUVWXYZ
abcdefghijklmnopqrstuvwxyz
1234567890 !@#?:;"*&

Foundry: Typotheque
Designer: Nikola Djurek
Designer Nationality: Croatian
Date: 2013

Nikola Djurek's legible but distinctive Lumin Sans is part of the Lumin family. It is available in Regular and Condensed in six weights with italics. Lumin Sans has many distinguishing features; on heavier weights the stroke connections are chiselled and the "k" in the lighter weights is in two parts.

Mahsuri Sans

ABCDEFGHIJKLMNOPQRSTUVWXYZ
abcdefghijklmnopqrstuvwxyz
1234567890 !@#?:;"*&

Foundry: Monotype
Designer: Ong Chong Wah
Designer Nationality: Malaysian
Date: 2001

Mahsuri Sans is a legible, humanist sans serif available in four weights with italics. It was designed by Malaysian typographer Ong Chong Wah, who studied graphic design in England and worked in advertising before becoming a type designer and working in-house for Monotype in London.

Mallory

ABCDEFGHIJKLMNOPQRSTUVWXYZ
abcdefghijklmnopqrstuvwxyz
1234567890 !@#?:;"*&

Foundry: Frere-Jones Type
Designer: Tobias Frere-Jones
Designer Nationality: American
Date: 2015

Mallory was the first typeface released under Frere-Jones Type (see p. 80), the independent type design studio of Tobias Frere-Jones. It is a humanist design that combines British and US typographic traditions to fashion an unconventional, but novel, sans serif font family.

Mariposa Sans

ABCDEFGHIJKLMNOPQRSTUVWXYZ
abcdefghijklmnopqrstuvwxyz
1234567890 !@#?:;"*&

Foundry: ITC
Designer: Philip Bouwsma
Designer Nationality: American
Date: 1994

Mariposa Sans was released by ITC in 1994 as part of the Mariposa family. It is a distinctive, high-contrast sans serif with flared strokes. Philip Bouwsma's lifelong interest in calligraphy comes through in this face, which comes in four weights, of which only the book cut has an italic.

Massif

ABCDEFGHIJKLMNOPQRSTUVWXYZ
abcdefghijklmnopqrstuvwxyz
1234567890 !@#?:;"*&

Foundry: Monotype
Designer: Steve Matteson
Designer Nationality: American
Date: 2011

When Steve Matteson designed this rugged sans serif, he took inspiration from the many granite formations found in the Sierra Nevada mountains, particularly Yosemite National Park's Half Dome, which explains Massif's distinctive chiselled feel. It comes in six weights with italics.

Mentor Sans

ABCDEFGHIJKLMNOPQRSTUVWXYZ
abcdefghijklmnopqrstuvwxyz
1234567890 !@#?:;"*&

Foundry: Monotype
Designer: Michael Harvey
Designer Nationality: British
Date: 2005

British master typographer and book designer Michael Harvey designed Mentor Sans in 2005. It is a humanist sans serif with subtly flared strokes. The typeface is available from Monotype in four weights with italics. Harvey designed a serif partner, Mentor, the same year.

Metro Nova

ABCDEFGHIJKLMNOPQRSTUVWXYZ
abcdefghijklmnopqrstuvwxyz
1234567890 !@#?:;"*&

Foundry: Monotype
Designer: William A. Dwiggins / Toshi Omagari
Designer Nationality: American / Japanese
Date: 1928 / 2012

Metro is William A. Dwiggins's geometric, humanist sans; it came after he was critical of existing sans serifs in his book *Layout in Advertising* (1928), which lead to Mergenthaler Linotype asking him to create his own. Toshi Omagari's revival, Metro Nova, retains the spirit of the original in seven weights.

Metro Office

ABCDEFGHIJKLMNOPQRSTUVWXYZ
abcdefghijklmnopqrstuvwxyz
1234567890 !@#?:;"*&

Foundry: Linotype
Designer: William A. Dwiggins / Toshi Omagari
Designer Nationality: American / Japanese
Date: *c.* 1920s / 2006

Metro, which initially came in four weights, was William A. Dwiggins's first typeface, which he created at the age of forty-nine. Metro Office is an update by Linotype type director Akira Kobayashi which reinstates some lost features such as a double-storey "a" and "g" while enhancing legibility.

Metrolite #2

ABCDEFGHIJKLMNOPQRSTUVWXYZ
abcdefghijklmnopqrstuvwxyz
1234567890 !@#?:;"*&

Foundry: Linotype
Designer: William A. Dwiggins
Designer Nationality: American
Date: 1929–37

When William A. Dwiggins's geometric sans Metro was released in 1929, it was so successful that Mergenthaler Linotype was keen to expand it. The first addition was the heavier Metroblack, followed by Metromedium and Metrolite. They came in two styles: regular and #2. Only the latter has been digitized.

Metromedium #2

ABCDEFGHIJKLMNOPQRSTUVWXYZ
abcdefghijklmnopqrstuvwxyz
1234567890 !@#?:;"*&

Foundry: Linotype
Designer: William A. Dwiggins
Designer Nationality: American
Date: 1932–36

William A. Dwiggins updated Metro to Metro #2 in 1932, changing many glyphs to be more like its competitor Futura; characters such as "M," "N," "A," and "V" became sharp rather than flat. The additional weights added after 1932, such as Metromedium (1936), therefore had to be done in both versions.

Adrian Frutiger

Adrian Frutiger is considered to be the most important and influential type designers of the 20th century. His legacy pervades many aspects of everyday life, his craft being employed on everything from bus timetables to food packaging and airport wayfinding, shaping modern life.

Born in 1928, in Berne, Switzerland, Frutiger trained as a typesetter and then worked as a graphic designer before joining Paris-based type foundry Deberny & Peignot. In 1962, he formed his own design studio in Arcueil near Paris. His breakthrough typeface was Univers (see p. 248), which propelled him on to the world stage and became one of the most notable typeface designs of the 20th century. Univers had its roots in exercises Frutiger conducted at the age of twenty-one while studying at the School of Applied Arts, Zurich. Spending fifteen years to develop it, Frutiger devised a groundbreaking system in cataloguing the differing weights of type forms, making it an instant success upon release. Using a number system to indicate weight, width and slope, all set within a "periodic table," allowed the user to visualize the differing weights of the font family instantly. In Frutiger's system, the first digit represents the weight, the second the width; odd numbers define roman variants and even numbers obliques.

Following Univers's success, Frutiger was commissioned to develop the signage for the soon to be built Charles de Gaulle Airport in Paris. Although Univers was originally considered, Frutiger revisited a seven-year old sans serif design called Concorde, which he created in collaboration with Swiss typographer André Gürtler. The first bespoke airport alphabet was the result and upon the airport's inauguration, designers and typographers around the world clamoured to use it. Type foundries D. Stempel AG and Linotype eventually released the typeface renamed as Frutiger in 1976.

Frutiger designed more than twenty typeface families over sixty years. All of them were deemed revolutionary at the time of their release and the apex of perfection in legibility and form.

Date: 1928–2015
Nationality: Swiss
Notable typefaces:
Univers (see p. 248)
Frutiger (see p. 268)
Avenir (see p. 189)
Didot (see p. 96)

Below from left. Specimen card illustrating Univers's system of organizing weights and styles, 1955; promotional sample with Univers 53 highlighted from the Deberny et Peignot foundry, 1963; hand-lettered Univers bold "8" artwork, drawn for the Deberny et Peignot foundry, Paris, 1953.

Opposite, clockwise from left. Frutiger at work in his studio, 1996; presenting his Avenir typeface, September 1988; studying a type disc from a phototypesetting machine in his home studio, 1951.

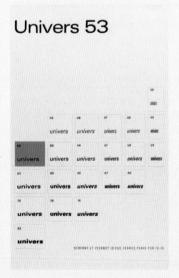

Miramonte

ABCDEFGHIJKLMNOPQRSTUVWXYZ
abcdefghijklmnopqrstuvwxyz
1234567890 !@#?:;"*&

Miramonte by Steve Matteson, co-founder of the Chicago-based foundry Ascender, is based on the Maršuv Grotesk humanist sans designed by Stanislav Maršo and released by Czech foundry Grafotechna in 1960. Miramonte, which means "behold the mountains" in Spanish, comes in two weights.

Foundry: Ascender
Designer: Steve Matteson / Stanislav Maršo
Designer Nationality: American / Czech Republic
Date: 1960 / 2006

Morandi

ABCDEFGHIJKLMNOPQRSTUVWXYZ
abcdefghijklmnopqrstuvwxyz
1234567890 !@#?:;"*&

Morandi was designed by Serbian typographer Jovica Veljović, a professor of type design at the Hamburg University of Applied Sciences, and was his first commercial sans serif release. It is a highly legible humanist sans serif available in three widths and eight weights with italics.

Foundry: Monotype
Designer: Jovica Veljović
Designer Nationality: Serbian
Date: 2018

Mosquito

ABCDEFGHIJKLMNOPQRSTUVWXYZ
abcdefghijklmnopqrstuvwxyz
1234567890 !@#?:;"*&

Mosquito's designer is French typographer Éric de Berranger, who has created corporate fonts for Martini, Renault, Hermès, and the French football governing body, Ligue de Football Professionnel. It is a jaunty but legible sans serif that comes in three weights—Regular, Bold, and Black—with italics.

Foundry: Linotype
Designer: Éric de Berranger
Designer Nationality: French
Date: 2002

Mosquito Formal

ABCDEFGHIJKLMNOPQRSTUVWXYZ
abcdefghijklmnopqrstuvwxyz
1234567890 !@#?:;"*&

Mosquito Formal was released a year after Éric de Berranger's Mosquito (2002). He took the original design and removed a lot of the quirks, while maintaining the same base and proportions, to increase its sophistication. De Berranger describes it as "Mosquito dressed in a tuxedo."

Foundry: Linotype
Designer: Éric de Berranger
Designer Nationality: French
Date: 2003

Mr Eaves XL Modern

ABCDEFGHIJKLMNOPQRSTUVWXYZ
abcdefghijklmnopqrstuvwxyz
1234567890 !@#?:;"*&

Foundry: Emigre
Designer: Zuzana Licko
Designer Nationality: Slovakian
Date: 2009

Mr Eaves XL Modern is based on the frame of Mrs Eaves, a serif family designed by Licko in 1996. As with the XL Sans version, Mr Eaves XL Modern couples taller x-heights with shorter ascenders and descenders, but unlike its siblings, also features defining geometric tendencies.

Mundo Sans

ABCDEFGHIJKLMNOPQRSTUVWXYZ
abcdefghijklmnopqrstuvwxyz
1234567890 !@#?:;"*&

Foundry: Monotype
Designer: Carl Crossgrove
Designer Nationality: Mexican
Date: 2002

Mundo Sans was begun by Mexican-born typographer Carl Crossgrove in 1991 and released by his employer Monotype in 2002. Mundo forms a family of sans serifs in seven weights with italics. It is a humanist sans serif, partly inspired by Futura, and is unpretentious, legible and easy to use.

Myriad Pro

ABCDEFGHIJKLMNOPQRSTUVWXYZ
abcdefghijklmnopqrstuvwxyz
1234567890 !@#?:;"*&

Foundry: Adobe
Designer: Carol Twombly / Robert Slimbach / Fred Brady / Christopher Slye
Designer Nationality: American
Date: 2002

Robert Slimbach and Carol Twombly of Adobe designed Myriad in 1992. A neutral, humanist sans serif typeface, it is similar in appearance to Frutiger, so much so that Adrian Frutiger (see p. 290) commented that the similarities had gone "a little bit too far." Myriad is notable for being adopted as Apple's corporate font from 2002 until 2017, replacing Apple Garamond. It is now a part of Adobe software, and the software company's programs default to Myriad when typefaces are missing. In 2000, Adobe released an OpenType update of Myriad, Myriad Pro, which added Greek and Cyrillic, Old Style figures, and better support for Latin-based languages. Myriad was discontinued at the release of Pro, which has Condensed, Normal, and Extended widths in five weights with italics.

Nara Sans

ABCDEFGHIJKLMNOPQRSTUVWXYZ
abcdefghijklmnopqrstuvwxyz
1234567890 !@#?:;"*&

Foundry: Typotheque
Designer: Andrej Krátky
Designer Nationality: Slovakian
Date: 2017

Nara Sans is a humanist sans partner to Andrej Krátky's serif face Nara (2017). It comes in five weights and like its serifed sibling has two types of italics—an upright cursive and a standard slanting italic. The cursive shares its uppercase with the regular, a reference to early Aldine italics.

Nautilus Monoline

ABCDEFGHIJKLMNOPQRSTUVWXYZ
abcdefghijklmnopqrstuvwxyz
1234567890 !@#?:;"*&

Foundry: Linotype
Designer: Hellmut G. Bomm
Designer Nationality: German
Date: 2008

German designer Hellmut G. Bomm released his sans serif typeface Linotype Nautilus in 1999. Less than ten years later, he added two new styles to the family, Nautilus Text and Nautilus Monoline. The monolinear Monoline shares the proportions of the text cut but lacks its calligraphic details.

Neue Frutiger

ABCDEFGHIJKLMNOPQRSTUVWXYZ
abcdefghijklmnopqrstuvwxyz
1234567890 !@#?:;"*&

Foundry: Linotype
Designer: Adrian Frutiger / Akira Kobayashi
Designer Nationality: Swiss / Japanese
Date: 1976 / 2009

Neue Frutiger is a revision and expansion of Frutiger (1976), made by Linotype type director Akira Kobayashi under the supervision of Adrian Frutiger (see p. 290). It comes in Regular and Condensed, in ten weights with italics. Frutiger was designed for wayfinding and is a highly legible face.

Neue Frutiger 1450

ABCDEFGHIJKLMNOPQRSTUVWXYZ
abcdefghijklmnopqrstuvwxyz
1234567890 !@#?:;"*&

Foundry: Linotype
Designer: Adrian Frutiger / Akira Kobayashi
Designer Nationality: Swiss / Japanese
Date: 1976 / 2013

Neue Frutiger 1450 is a slight update to Neue Frutiger. Akira Kobayashi designed it to be compliant with the German standard DIN 1450, a specification for barrier-free legibility. Neue Frutiger 1450 is a family of eight fonts in four weights—Book, Regular, Medium, and Bold—with obliques.

Neutura

ABCDEFGHIJKLMNOPQRSTUVWXYZ
abcdefghijklmnopqrstuvwxyz
1234567890 !@#?:;"*&

Foundry: Neutura
Designer: Alexander McCracken
Designer Nationality: American
Date: 2004

Neutura is the eponymous typeface of the San Francisco foundry of the same name (see p. 472) founded by designer Alexander McCracken in 2003.

It is a clean but distinctive geometric sans serif that comes in four weights, ranging from Light to ExBold, without italics.

Noa

ABCDEFGHIJKLMNOPQRSTUVWXYZ
abcdefghijklmnopqrstuvwxyz
1234567890 !@#?:;"*&

Foundry: Linotype
Designer: Nina Lee Storm
Designer Nationality: Korean
Date: 2004

Noa was designed for TV and computer screen use during the late 1990s by Korean-born designer Nina Lee Storm, who is now based in Denmark. It

has short ascenders and descenders and a large x-height. It was released in three weights with obliques, and a condensed version followed in 2009.

Nota

ABCDEFGHIJKLMNOPQRSTUVWXYZ
abcdefghijklmnopqrstuvwxyz
1234567890 !@#?:;"*&

Foundry: Typotheque
Designer: Nikola Djurek
Designer Nationality: Croatian
Date: 2009

This low-contrast humanist text sans serif was designed by Nikola Djurek, with a Cyrillic designed by Ilya Ruderman. It comes in four weights with

italics, though the non-italic versions are at a 2° slant rather than upright, which mimics handwriting and enhances readability.

Ocean Sans

ABCDEFGHIJKLMNOPQRSTUVWXYZ
abcdefghijklmnopqrstuvwxyz
1234567890 !@#?:;"*&

Foundry: Monotype
Designer: Ong Chong Wah
Designer Nationality: Malaysian
Date: 1993

Ong Chong Wah designed Ocean Sans at Monotype London in 1993. It is a grotesque sans serif with contrast between thick and thin rather than a

monoline. The typeface comes in five weights and three widths—Regular, Condensed, and Extended—all with cursive italics except for the Condensed.

Optima

ABCDEFGHIJKLMNOPQRSTUVWXYZ
abcdefghijklmnopqrstuvwxyz
1234567890 !@#?:;"*&

Foundry: Stempel
Designer: Hermann Zapf
Designer Nationality: German
Date: 1958

Optima is the most successful typeface created by Hermann Zapf (see p. 574). Inspired by the lettering at a church in Florence, it has the proportions of classical roman type but without serifs. Zapf designed the letterforms using the Golden Ratio, and its tapered stems were unique at the time.

Optima Nova

ABCDEFGHIJKLMNOPQRSTUVWXYZ
abcdefghijklmnopqrstuvwxyz
1234567890 !@#?:;"*&

Foundry: Linotype
Designer: Hermann Zapf / Akira Kobayashi
Designer Nationality: German / Japanese
Date: 2002

Hermann Zapf (see p. 574) collaborated closely with Linotype type director Akira Kobayashi to create a digital expansion and redesign of Optima more than fifty years after his first sketches at a church in Florence. Nova gave Optima real italics and added new weights, creating a family of forty fonts.

PL Westerveldt

ABCDEFGHIJKLMNOPQRSTUVWXYZ
abcdefghijklmnopqrstuvwxyz
1234567890 !©#?:;"*&

Foundry: Photo-Lettering
Date: 1965

Westerveldt was designed in-house at the Photo-Lettering foundry and first appeared in 1965 in its catalogue, *Alphabet Thesaurus Vol. 2*. Westerveldt is a sans serif with subtly flared strokes which was once part of a large family, including casual variants. Only the light weight has been digitized.

PMN Caecilia Sans

ABCDEFGHIJKLMNOPQRSTUVWXYZ
abcdefghijklmnopqrstuvwxyz
1234567890 !@#?:;"*&

Foundry: Linotype
Designer: Peter Matthias Noordzij
Designer Nationality: Dutch
Date: 2017

Dutch designer Peter Matthias Noordzij released his slab serif PMN Caecilia in 1991 after more than seven years of development; later it was adopted as the default typeface for Kindle e-readers. In 2017, it finally received a sans serif sibling, explicitly designed with on-screen use in mind.

Program

ABCDEFGHIJKLMNOPQRSTUVWXYZ
abcdefghijklmnopqrstuvwxyz
1234567890 !@#?:;"*&

Foundry: Emigre
Designer: Zuzana Licko
Designer Nationality: Slovakian
Date: 2013

Program is a sans serif designed to obscure traditional categorization, while maintaining the feel of a font family. The characters combine various structural features, terminals and proportions, alongside seemingly antithetical features, such as rounded edges and ink traps.

Quire Sans

ABCDEFGHIJKLMNOPQRSTUVWXYZ
abcdefghijklmnopqrstuvwxyz
1234567890 !@#?:;"*&

Foundry: Monotype
Designer: Jim Ford
Designer Nationality: American
Date: 2014

A type designer at Monotype USA, Jim Ford designed Quire Sans in 2014. It is a versatile, modern humanist sans serif with a double-storey "a" and "g," available in ten weights with italics. The name "Quire" comes from a printing term for a signature of printed pages ready to be bound.

Retina Standard

ABCDEFGHIJKLMNOPQRSTUVWXYZ
abcdefghijklmnopqrstuvwxyz
1234567890 !@#?:;"*&

Foundry: Frere-Jones Type
Designer: Tobias Frere-Jones
Designer Nationality: American
Date: 2000–16

Retina Standard is a humanist, low-contrast sans serif designed for headlines and portions of larger text. The characters, which range in weight from Thin to Black, utilize conventional proportions and features to maintain clarity and efficacy across a variety of platforms.

Retina Microplus

ABCDEFGHIJKLMNOPQRSTUVWXYZ
abcdefghijklmnopqrstuvwxyz
1234567890 !@#?:;"*&

Foundry: Frere-Jones Type
Designer: Tobias Frere-Jones
Designer Nationality: American
Date: 2000–16

Retina Microplus was initially commissioned by *The Wall Street Journal*. The title's tables of financial data require a typeface that remains legible in small sizes and condensed spaces. The font maintains clarity in such conditions through the accentuation of its details and proportions.

Milieu Grotesque

Established in 2010 and run by Timo Gaessner and Maiko Gubler, Milieu Grotesque is an independent type foundry located on the west coast of Portugal. The foundry offers not only an exclusive library of digital typefaces but a number of type-related products. Milieu Grotesque's portfolio may not be as extensive as some other foundries, but their type designs are beautifully executed and have the craft and attention to detail required of them. They have a contemporary edge to their forms, which not only makes them highly flexible in usage but also provides a timeless and clean aesthetic to any design. Their inspirations come from a wide variety of sources, including a letter by singer Johnny Cash, addressed to a former US. president, which went on to become their popular Chapeau typeface release.

Founded: 2010
Country: Portugal
Website: milieugrotesque.com
Notable typefaces:
Boutique (see p. 191)
Chapeau (see p. 192)
Maison (see p. 235)
Patron (see p. 242)

Right. Typeface library specimen, spreads showing Boutique (middle), which comes with an engraved version with hollow infill, and Maison, a monolined grotesque.

Opposite top. Chapeau specimen, loosely inspired by a letter that musician Johnny Cash wrote on an old IBM typewriter.

Opposite bottom. Detail from promotion for revised Maison typeface Maison Neue. Designed by Timo Gaessner and initially released in 2010, the new version is revised and extended and was published in April 2018.

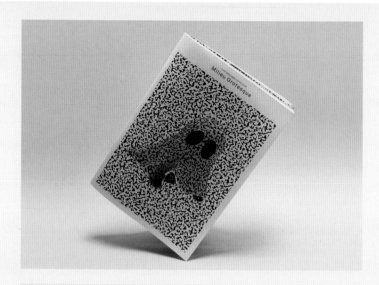

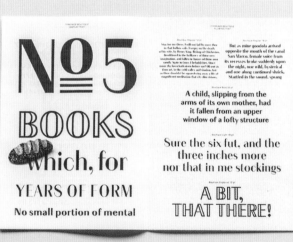

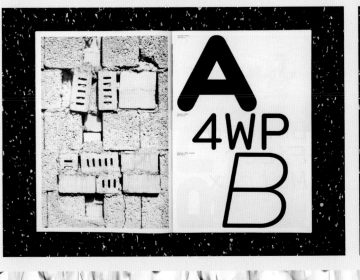

MaisonABCDE
FGHIJKLMNOPQ
RSTUVWXYZ&
MaisonABCDE
MonoFGHIJK
LMNOPQRSTUV

Robinson

ABCDEFGHIJKLMNOPQRSTUVWXYZ
abcdefghijklmnopqrstuvwxyz
1234567890 !@#?:;"*&

Foundry: Commercial Type
Designer: Greg Gazdowicz
Designer Nationality: American
Date: 2016

Robinson was Greg Gazdowicz's first release for Commercial Type (see p. 124). It is a humanist sans serif in the calligraphic style of typefaces such as Lydian and Samson. Grotesque frames combine with tapered stems, alongside the similarly calligraphic angling of the curves and stresses.

Saturday Sans

ABCDEFGHIJKLMNOPQRSTUVWXYZ
abcdefghijklmnopqrstuvwxyz
1234567890 !@#?:;"*&

Foundry: Image Club
Designer: Patricia Lillie
Designer Nationality: American
Date: 1996

Saturday Sans is an informal, rounded sans serif available in Regular and Bold weights. It was designed by US typographer and writer Patricia Lillie, a graduate of Parsons School of Design, in 1996 for the Image Club type library. Lillie has since drawn many dingbat fonts during her career.

Shaker

ABCDEFGHIJKLMNOPQRSTUVWXYZ
abcdefghijklmnopqrstuvwxyz
1234567890 !@#?:;"*&

Foundry: Jeremy Tankard Typography
Designer: Jeremy Tankard
Designer Nationality: British
Date: 2000

Jeremy Tankard, who worked at British brand consultancy Wolff Olins before leaving to start his type foundry in 1998, released Shaker in 2000. A companion to serif face Enigma, Shaker is a sans serif with small variations in stroke. It comes in three widths and five weights with italics.

Shannon

ABCDEFGHIJKLMNOPQRSTUVWXYZ
abcdefghijklmnopqrstuvwxyz
1234567890 !@#?:;"*&

Foundry: Compugraphic
Designer: Janice Prescott / Kris Holmes
Designer Nationality: American
Date: 1982

Janice Prescott and Kris Holmes designed Shannon for Compugraphic. It is a sans serif with slightly flared strokes that appear almost serif-like. It was inspired partly by 9th-century Irish calligraphy found in the *Book of Kells* illuminated manuscript and comes in Regular, Oblique, Bold, and Extra Bold.

Sinova

ABCDEFGHIJKLMNOPQRSTUVWXYZ
abcdefghijklmnopqrstuvwxyz
1234567890 !@#?:;"*&

Foundry: Linotype
Designer: Christian Mengelt
Designer Nationality: Swiss
Date: 2011

Sinova is a functional and highly legible humanist sans serif designed by Christian Mengelt, who previously worked with Karl Gerstner and later the design team creating Haas Unica. He developed Sinova in co-operation with Linotype from 2010 to 2011. It comes in five weights with italics.

Slate

ABCDEFGHIJKLMNOPQRSTUVWXYZ
abcdefghijklmnopqrstuvwxyz
1234567890 !@#?:;"*&

Foundry: Monotype
Designer: Rod McDonald
Designer Nationality: Canadian
Date: 2006

Slate is a neutral and highly legible sans serif family, designed by Canadian typographer Rod McDonald. It comes in eight weights and two widths—Regular, which has an italic, and condensed, which does not. Smartphone company BlackBerry used Slate Pro as a user-interface font from 2013.

Stellar

ABCDEFGHIJKLMNOPQRSTUVWXYZ
abcdefghijklmnopqrstuvwxyz
1234567890 !￼#?:;"*&

Foundry: Ludlow
Designer: Robert Hunter Middleton / Dave Farey
Designer Nationality: British
Date: 1929 / c. 1990

Stellar is a sans serif with roman proportions designed by Scottish-born typographer Robert Hunter Middleton, who immigrated to the United States and studied in Chicago before working for the Ludlow foundry. Dave Farey digitized Stellar in the 1990s, doubling the number of weights.

Tanseek Sans

ABCDEFGHIJKLMNOPQRSTUVWXYZ
abcdefghijklmnopqrstuvwxyz
1234567890 !@#?:;"*&

Foundry: Monotype
Designer: Dave Farey / Richard Dawson
Designer Nationality: British
Date: 2016

"Tanseek" is the Arabic word for "harmony." In keeping with its name, the Tanseek family of typefaces includes a serif and a sans that support Latin and Arabic. Tanseek Sans is a humanistic sans serif, which is based on the Latin typefaces in the family. It comes in five weights without italics.

TheMix

ABCDEFGHIJKLMNOPQRSTUVWXYZ
abcdefghijklmnopqrstuvwxyz
1234567890 !@#?:;"*&

Foundry: Lucas Fonts
Designer: Luc(as) de Groot
Designer Nationality: Dutch
Date: 1994

TheMix began life as an alphabet created by Luc(as) de Groot for the logotypes for Dutch governmental bodies while working at design agency BRS Premsela Vonk. TheMix is a sans with occasional asymmetric serifs and takes the middle ground between two other fonts, TheSans and TheSerif.

Tipperary eText

ABCDEFGHIJKLMNOPQRSTUVWXYZ
abcdefghijklmnopqrstuvwxyz
1234567890 !@#?:;"*&

Foundry: Monotype
Designer: Steve Matteson
Designer Nationality: American
Date: 2014

Tipperary eText is a humanist sans serif, designed to meet the demands of LCD and e-paper screens. The characters are spacious for legibility, and feature abrupt curves and keen corners, mimicking the routes on the Irish bike trail from which the font takes its name.

Trilogy Sans

ABCDEFGHIJKLMNOPQRSTUVWXYZ
abcdefghijklmnopqrstuvwxyz
1234567890 !@#?:;"*&

Foundry: Jeremy Tankard Typography
Designer: Jeremy Tankard
Designer Nationality: British
Date: 2009

Trilogy Sans is a humanist sans serif inspired by the early grotesques of the 17th century. Alongside the font's build and proportions, which reference the initial shapes of Caslon and Figgins, Trilogy Sans also features details such as shorter crossbars in the capital letters.

Typonine Sans

ABCDEFGHIJKLMNOPQRSTUVWXYZ
abcdefghijklmnopqrstuvwxyz
1234567890 !@#?:;"*&

Foundry: Typotheque
Designer: Nikola Djurek
Designer Nationality: Croatian
Date: 2008

Typonine Sans is a humanist sans serif with minimal contrast, which has been designed as a pragmatic and versatile font family. The letterforms combine spartan strokes with a slightly extended x-height, which maintains legibility in each weight and across both digital and printed surfaces.

Venn

ABCDEFGHIJKLMNOPQRSTUVWXYZ
abcdefghijklmnopqrstuvwxyz
1234567890 !@#?:;"*&

Foundry: Dalton Maag
Designer: Fernando Caro / Deiverson Ribeiro
Designer Nationality: Brazilian
Date: 2018

Venn is a humanist sans serif designed to meet the various demands of multiplatform brands. It features twenty-five styles, from Condensed Light to Extended Extra Bold, and is the first face by Dalton Maag (see p. 594) to have a Variable Font version, which contains every weight in a single file.

Verdana

ABCDEFGHIJKLMNOPQRSTUVWXYZ
abcdefghijklmnopqrstuvwxyz
1234567890 !@#?:;"*&

Foundry: Microsoft
Designer: Matthew Carter
Nationality: British
Date: 1996

Created by Matthew Carter (see p. 616) for the Microsoft Corporation, Verdana was created specifically to address the issues of on-screen legibility and readability with hand-hinting by leading expert Tom Rickner. Verdana's larger width and character spacing contributes to increased legibility.

Vista Sans

ABCDEFGHIJKLMNOPQRSTUVWXYZ
abcdefghijklmnopqrstuvwxyz
1234567890 !@#?:;"*&

Foundry: Emigre
Designer: Xavier Dupré
Designer Nationality: French
Date: 2004

As with Vista Slab, the design of Vista Sans was inspired by hand-lettered shop signs on the island of Sumatra. Unable to introduce calligraphic curves without serifs, Vista Sans features a slight bounce to the stroke endings, which soften the sturdy verticals and sharp joints.

Whitney

ABCDEFGHIJKLMNOPQRSTUVWXYZ
abcdefghijklmnopqrstuvwxyz
1234567890 !@#?:;"*&

Foundry: Hoefler & Co
Designer: Tobias Frere-Jones
Designer Nationality: American
Date: 1996–2004

Whitney was designed for the Whitney Museum in New York and developed to meet the distinct demands of editorial and signage typography. The design utilizes narrow forms and tall x-heights for compact spaces, while the vast counters maintain legibility at a distance.

Erik Spiekermann

German designer, author and professor Erik Spiekermann is one of the most prominent type designers and commentator on matters concerning typographic communications today. His work and contribution to the field have greatly influenced typeface and information design as well as how the industry operates. His impact in the arena of typography and communications is immeasurable.

In 1979, Spiekermann founded MetaDesign in Berlin, which became Germany's largest design company with overseas offices in London and San Francisco. It was at MetaDesign that Spiekermann's influence and reputation grew having designed corporate identity programs for multinational organizations including Audi, Volkswagen, and Bosch, along with wayfinding systems such as those at Dusseldorf Airport and BVG (Berlin Transport Company). In 1989, he founded an international manufacturer and distributor of digital typefaces, FontShop, with his then wife Joan Spiekermann and British designer Neville Brody. Soon after, they created FontFont, an independent type foundry to represent some of the most talented and interesting type designers in the world. Its first release was the FF Beowolf display serif font by Just Van Rossum and Erik Van Blokland. FontFont went on to become one of the largest libraries of contemporary fonts with more than 2,500 typefaces.

Spiekermann's own typefaces, such as FF Meta (see p. 264), ITC Officina, FF Info, and Berliner Grotesk have been hugely popular, and are widely used in everything from print applications to wayfinding and online usage. He is a board member of the German Design Council and past president of both the International Society of Typographic Designers and the International Institute for Information Design. In 2001, he left MetaDesign to run Edenspiekermann, which has offices in Berlin, Amsterdam, Los Angeles, Singapore, and San Francisco.

He has received numerous accolades in his career including an honorary professorship from the University of the Arts Bremen and an honorary doctorate from Pasadena Art Center. In 2007, the British Royal Society of Arts made him an Honorary Royal Designer for Industry and in 2009, the European Union made him Ambassador for the European Year of Creativity. In 2011, the German Design Council gave him the highest award in Germany, a Lifetime Achievement Award, and the same year he became the 25th recipient of the TDC Medal, awarded by the Type Directors Club New York.

Date: 1947–
Nationality: German
Notable typefaces:
ITC Officina Sans (see p. 279)
FF Meta (see pp. 264–65)
FF Meta Serif (see p. 264)

Below. Wayfinding system guidelines for BVG—*Berliner Verkehrsbetriebe* (Berlin Transport Company).

Opposite, clockwise from top left: Poster design by Spiekermann from his p98a experimental letterpress workshop in Berlin, dedicated to letters, printing, and paper. where he is a founder-member; Cover design to Spiekermann's best-selling book *Hallo, ich bin Erik* (Hello, my name is Erik); Printing at p98a a sample sheet of his FF Real typeface design (with Ralph du Carrois); Nokia corporate typeface, one of the many corporate typefaces he has created.

Don't work for assholes.
Don't work with assholes.

Hallo ich bin Erik

Erik Spiekermann:
Schriftgestalter
Designer
Unternehmer

Von Johannes Erler

gestalten

Erik Spiekermann | January 2002

A corporate type
A corporate typef
A corporate typefa
A corporate typefac
A corporate typeface
A corporate typeface f
A corporate typeface fo
A corporate typeface for
A corporate typeface for N
A corporate typeface for No
A corporate typeface for Nok
A corporate typeface for Noki

A corporate typeface for Nokia.

Xenois Sans

ABCDEFGHIJKLMNOPQRSTUVWXYZ
abcdefghijklmnopqrstuvwxyz
1234567890 !@#?:;"*&

Foundry: Linotype
Designer: Erik Faulhaber
Designer Nationality: German
Date: 2013

Xenois is a minimal humanist sans serif, designed to support the smooth rhythm of reading. Superfluous details, such as spurs or lengthy crossbars on the lowercase letters, are removed to maintain the reader's flow, while open counters and a tall x-height enhance legibility.

Xenois Semi

ABCDEFGHIJKLMNOPQRSTUVWXYZ
abcdefghijklmnopqrstuvwxyz
1234567890 !@#?:;"*&

Foundry: Linotype
Designer: Erik Faulhaber
Designer Nationality: German
Date: 2013

Much like Xenois Sans, Xenois Semi is a sans serif in the humanist style. The letterforms maintain the proportions and character of their siblings but feature a distinctly stronger stroke contrast, visible in both cases and especially in the shoulders, arcs and junctures.

Xenois Soft

ABCDEFGHIJKLMNOPQRSTUVWXYZ
abcdefghijklmnopqrstuvwxyz
1234567890 !@#?:;"*&

Foundry: Linotype
Designer: Erik Faulhaber
Designer Nationality: German
Date: 2013

Xenois Soft is distinguishable not only through its rounded terminals, but also its compliance with DIN 1450 requirements, a form of standardization that ensures readability in adverse conditions. This makes its design ideally suited to public signage and information systems.

Xenois Super

ABCDEFGHIJKLMNOPQRSTUVWXYZ
abcdefghijklmnopqrstuvwxyz
1234567890 !@#?:;"*&

Foundry: Linotype
Designer: Erik Faulhaber
Designer Nationality: German
Date: 2013

Xenois Super occupies the middle ground between its siblings Xenois Sans and Xenois Slab. Although designed with the characteristics of a humanist sans serif, Xenois Super introduces the occasional, muscular slab serif to several letters, spanning both upper- and lowercases.

Yalta Sans

ABCDEFGHIJKLMNOPQRSTUVWXYZ
abcdefghijklmnopqrstuvwxyz
1234567890 !@#?:;"*&

Foundry: Monotype
Designer: Stefan Claudius
Designer Nationality: German
Date: 2013

Yalta Sans is a humanist sans serif but draws on elements of both grotesque and square sans letterforms. It is also informed by the nature of Renaissance typefaces, designer Stefan Claudius combining calligraphic strokes with open counters, tapered verticals and gently squared curves.

Zapf Humanist 601

ABCDEFGHIJKLMNOPQRSTUVWXYZ
abcdefghijklmnopqrstuvwxyz
1234567890 !@#?:;"*&

Foundry: Bitstream
Designer: Hermann Zapf
Designer Nationality: German
Date: 1958

Zapf Humanist 601 is a humanist sans serif and Bitstream's digitization of the Optima typeface created in 1958 by Hermann Zapf (see p. 574). Bitstream's design mimics Optima's characteristically roman shapes and proportions, while also imitating the popular taper of its stems.

Zico Sans

ABCDEFGHIJKLMNOPQRSTUVWXYZ
abcdefghijklmnopqrstuvwxyz
1234567890 !@#?:;"*&

Foundry: Typotheque
Designer: Marko Hrastovec
Designer Nationality: Croatian
Date: 2017

Zico Sans was designed by Croatian type and graphic designer Marko Hrastovec and released by Dutch foundry Typotheque (see p. 90). It is a wide-set, humanist sans serif that was created to add versatility to the already established Zico typeface family, which has a beefy slab serif version with a corresponding Display design and Sans Condensed.

Much like the initial slab version, Zico Sans is informed by the aesthetics of sport, in particular the robust letterforms typically used in sport jerseys. Hrastovec attempted to convey their feel of "playful" boldness and warmth in his typeface. This is evident in the slightly squared shape of its curves and the low contrast of the strokes. Like all Typotheque fonts, Zico Sans includes small caps in all styles and possesses a wealth of OpenType features.

Italian Plate No. 1 Mono

ABCDEFGHIJKLMNOPQRSTUVWXYZ
abcdefghijklmnopqrstuvwxyz
1234567890 !@#?:;"*&

Foundry: Playtype
Designer: Jonas Hecksher
Designer Nationality: Danish
Date: 1998

Italian Plate No. 1 Mono is a grotesque, monospaced sans serif inspired by research into the rounded and condensed letterforms of Italian vehicle number plates from the 1960s. The characters, which are designed in ten weights, are distinguished by their equal stems and straight terminals.

Monospace 821

ABCDEFGHIJKLMNOPQRSTUVWXYZ
abcdefghijklmnopqrstuvwxyz
1234567890 !@#?:;"*&

Foundry: Bitstream
Designer: Max Miedinger
Designer Nationality: Swiss
Date: c. 1980s

This is Bitstream's version of Helvetica Monospaced, which was created using the original design by Max Miedinger (see p. 229) revamped by the Linotype Design Studio in 1983. It is available in Bold, Bold Italic and WGL Roman, as well as a Hebrew version.

Monosten

ABCDEFGHIJKLMNOPQRSTUVWXYZ
abcdefghijklmnopqrstuvwxyz
1234567890 !@#?:;"*&

Foundry: Colophon
Designer: The Entente
Designer Nationality: British
Date: 2017

Monosten combines the styles of monospaced and stencil type and takes its name from a combination of the two. After its initial release in 2010, Monosten was expanded in 2011 to encompass three weights and six styles, and then again in 2017 to include further language support.

OCR A Tribute

ABCDEFGHIJKLMNOPQRSTUVWXYZ
abcdefghijklmnopqrstuvwxyz
1234567890 !@#?:;"*&

Foundry: Linotype
Designer: Miriam Röttgers
Designer Nationality: German
Date: 2007

OCR A was designed at American Type Founders in 1968 as a monospaced font that could be read by machines using optical-character recognition. Miriam Röttgers designed OCR A Tribute to make a more versatile typeface that retained the spirit of the original, with mono and proportional spacing.

Olympia

ABCDEFGHIJKLMNOPQRSTUVWXYZ
abcdefghijklmnopqrstuvwxyz
1234567890 !@#?:;"*&

Olympia comes in one weight and is a monospaced typewriter font that shares its name with a now defunct typewriter brand. It was designed by the German foundry Hell, which merged with Linotype in 1990, and was available for the world's first digital typesetting system, Digiset, invented by Hell in 1965.

Foundry: Hell
Designer: Hell Design Studio
Date: *c.* 1960s

Orator

ABCDEFGHIJKLMNOPQRSTUVWXYZ
abcdefghijklmnopqrstuvwxyz
1234567890 !@#?:;"*&

Orator is a monospaced typewriter font that John Scheppler designed for technology company IBM in 1962. It comes in two styles, Medium and Slanted. The face features only capitals and small capitals because it was thought that uppercase was easier to read in typed-up speech notes, hence the name.

Foundry: Adobe
Designer: John Scheppler
Designer Nationality: American
Date: 1962

Prima Sans Mono

ABCDEFGHIJKLMNOPQRSTUVWXYZ
abcdefghijklmnopqrstuvwxyz
1234567890 !@#?:;"*&

Jim Lyles tasked one of his colleagues at Bitstream, Sue Zafarana, with creating the monospace, fixed-width version of Prima, having designed the serif and sans himself. During her spare time, she also designs fonts with her husband Steve as Tail Spin Studio in Boston.

Foundry: Bitstream
Designer: Sue Zafarana
Designer Nationality: American
Date: 1998

System85

ABCDEFGHIJKLMNOPQRSTUVWXYZ
abcdefghijklmnopqrstuvwxyz
1234567890 !@#?:;"*&

System85 is a monospaced sans serif that considers the vertical application of Latin type in Japan. Designed with uniform vertical-line spacing, irregular widths and short descenders, the design is also informed by the pan-Asian variants of Windows 3.1's grotesque system fonts.

Foundry: Colophon
Designer: The Entente
Designer Nationality: British
Date: 2018

Playtype

Created by Danish brand and design agency e-Types, Playtype is a foundry and online font shop that serves to showcase the e-Types type designs created over more than twenty years, from commissioned works to fonts created for pleasure. Typography has always been a focal point of e-Types' graphic design output. The decision to transform the e-Types typeface portfolio into an online foundry was taken so that others could benefit from its many years of crafting custom typefaces, as well as to promote Danish design.

Some of the fonts Playtype has released were custom-made for clients, and others come from sketches and doodles that gradually evolved into full-blown type families. There are others, such as Nouvel, which were inspired by a particular context—in this instance, the work of French architect Jean Nouvel for the Danish Broadcasting Corporation's Koncerthuset concert complex.

Playtype offers a comprehensive selection of differing styles with more than one hundred families and more than 1,000 different fonts. Playtype has over the years also been widely known for its concept store and use of type on design objects. These include limited-edition posters, notebooks, clothing, and ceramics highlighting singular letters, words or phrases.

Founded: 2010
Country: Denmark
Website: playtype.com

Below and opposite. Playtype built a range of elegant and stylish products around typeface releases over the years, from fashion accessories to iconic and minimal posters featuring singular letterforms.

PLAYTYPE™
TYPE FOUNDRY and CONCEPT STORE
typed in NOIR TEXT Bold

Aeonis

ABCDEFGHIJKLMNOPQRSTUVWXYZ
abcdefghijklmnopqrstuvwxyz
1234567890 !@#?:;"*&

Foundry: Linotype
Designer: Erik Faulhaber
Designer Nationality: German
Date: 2009

Aeonis mixes ancient and modern, and references Ancient Greek inscriptions and a lamp created by industrial designer Wilhelm Wagenfeld in 1952. It has a distinctive open uppercase "A" and all styles and weights share the same cap heights, x-heights, ascender heights and descender lengths.

Aguda

ABCDEFGHIJKLMNOPQRSTUVWXYZ
abcdefghijklmnopqrstuvwxyz
1234567890 !@#?:;"*&

Foundry: Graviton
Designer: Pablo Balcells
Designer Nationality: Argentinian
Date: 2014

Although Aguda is designed primarily to be used as a display face, this modular geometric typeface can also be used for short texts. Aguda is available in eight styles from Light to Bold, each containing small caps and several alternate characters, with Unicase and Stencil variants.

Akko

ABCDEFGHIJKLMNOPQRSTUVWXYZ
abcdefghijklmnopqrstuvwxyz
1234567890 !@#?:;"*&

Foundry: Linotype
Designer: Akira Kobayashi
Designer Nationality: Japanese
Date: 2011

Designer Akira Kobayashi describes Akko as a sans serif with a "soft-focus effect" that references German Textura type, and comprises the full-bodied sans serif Akko and the playful Akko Rounded. It has six weights from Thin to Black, along with small caps, ligatures and alternate characters.

Arian

ABCDEFGHIJKLMNOPQRSTUVWXYZ
abcdefghijklmnopqrstuvwxyz
1234567890 !@#?:;"*&

Foundry: Linotype
Designer: Naghi Naghashian
Designer Nationality: Iranian
Date: 2012

Arian is the debut typeface of Iranian designer Naghi Naghashian, who is now based in Germany. This Arabic typeface is designed for screen and electronic use, and combines a contemporary sans serif with calligraphic tradition. Its forms can be artificially obliqued in InDesign without any loss in quality.

Azbuka

ABCDEFGHIJKLMNOPQRSTUVWXYZ
abcdefghijklmnopqrstuvwxyz
1234567890 !@#?:;"*&

Foundry: Monotype
Designer: Richard Dawson /
Dave Farey
Designer Nationality: British
Date: 2008

This workmanlike sans serif was inspired by street signage from London and Prague and named after the Russian word for "alphabet." It has eight weights, ranging from Extra Light to Extra Black, with complementary italics on the five mid-weights, as well as seven condensed weights.

Biome

ABCDEFGHIJKLMNOPQRSTUVWXYZ
abcdefghijklmnopqrstuvwxyz
1234567890 !@#?:;"*&

Foundry: Monotype
Designer: Carl Crossgrove
Designer Nationality: American
Date: 2009

"Biome" means "ecosystem" and the Biome typeface reflects its name by being an amalgamation of many different influences. It has soft corners and a number of unusual character shapes, including a distinctive lowercase "g" with its two semi-open counters. Biome comes in forty-two styles.

Burlingame

ABCDEFGHIJKLMNOPQRSTUVWXYZ
abcdefghijklmnopqrstuvwxyz
1234567890 !@#?:;"*&

Foundry: Monotype
Designer: Carl Crossgrove
Designer Nationality: American
Date: 2014

Burlingame was originally intended for a game identity. Designer Carl Crossgrove then developed it for use as a dashboard display font. He increased the x-height, slimmed down the corners and loosened the spacing, improving clarity and making it suitable for a wide range of applications.

Cachet

ABCDEFGHIJKLMNOPQRSTUVWXYZ
abcdefghijklmnopqrstuvwxyz
1234567890 !@#?:;"*&

Foundry: Panache / Agfa
Designer: Dave Farey
Designer Nationality: American
Date: 1997

Cachet appears to be based on geometric shapes but in reality it is slightly condensed, with flared terminals on some letters and rounded stroke terminals. It comes in weights ranging from Thin to Heavy, and is precise, space efficient and more legible than the monospaced fonts it resembles.

Citadina

ABCDEFGHIJKLMNOPQRSTUVWXYZ
abcdefghijklmnopqrstuvwxyz
1234567890 !@#?:;"*&

Foundry: Graviton
Designer: Pablo Balcells
Designer Nationality:
Argentinian
Date: 2016

Citadina is a geometric sans serif with a cool, neutral look that is available in six weights from Thin to Black with matching italics. Its condensed design makes it a good choice when setting large blocks of text, but its heavier weights are equally effective as display fonts.

DIN 1451

ABCDEFGHIJKLMNOPQRSTUVWXYZ
abcdefghijklmnopqrstuvwxyz
1234567890 !@#?:;"*&

Foundry: Linotype
Designer: DIN / Linotype
Design Studio
Designer Nationality: German
Date: c. 1930 / 1990

"DIN" is an abbreviation of *Deutsches Institut für Normung* (German Institute for Industrial Standards) and DIN was the official typeface used on licence plates, trains and road signs across Germany from the 1930s. This is an updated version of the highly legible sans serif made by the Linotype Design Studio.

DIN Next

ABCDEFGHIJKLMNOPQRSTUVWXYZ
abcdefghijklmnopqrstuvwxyz
1234567890 !@#?:;"*&

Foundry: Linotype
Designer: Akira Kobayashi /
Sandra Winter
Designer Nationality:
Japanese / German
Date: 2009

DIN Next is the sister font to DIN Next Slab and DIN Next Rounded, designed by Akira Kobayashi. He created this as a more humanistic take on the classic 1930s DIN typeface. It features eight weights, ranging from Light to Black, as well as italics and a condensed version.

DIN Next Rounded

ABCDEFGHIJKLMNOPQRSTUVWXYZ
abcdefghijklmnopqrstuvwxyz
1234567890 !@#?:;"*&

Foundry: Linotype
Designer: Akira Kobayashi
Designer Nationality: Japanese
Date: 2009

This is a rounded version of Akira Kobayashi's more humanistic take on the typeface introduced in Germany for use in official signage and traffic directional systems by the *Deutsches Institut für Normung* (German Institute for Industrial Standards) in the 1930s.

Eurostile

ABCDEFGHIJKLMNOPQRSTUVWXYZ
abcdefghijklmnopqrstuvwxyz
1234567890 !@#?:;"*&

Foundry: Linotype
Designer: Aldo Novarese
Designer Nationality: Italian
Date: 1962

Eurostile was designed for the "future" in the early 1960s. Its release captured the zeitgeist of the science-fiction genre and intimated days to come through its clean lines, geometric square forms and rounded corners. The typeface is the creation of one of Italy's best-known and most prolific type designers, Aldo Novarese. He took his inspiration from Microgramma, an earlier design that he helped to create with his mentor Alessandro Butti, art director of the Nebiolo type foundry in Turin in 1952. A decade later, Novarese revisited the all-caps display face, designed a complementary lowercase—and Eurostile was born.

Ideally, Eurostile is best employed as a display face and its squared-up design appears to be influenced by old TV screens. Its distinctive appearance makes it stand out against many other sans serifs, thanks to its symmetry and the mathematical purity of its construction. It is used frequently in corporate identities and logos in everything from car to technology firms. The face is also highly visible in popular culture, appearing in film, video games, and music applications as well as the science-fiction genre.

In 2016, Linotype type director Akira Kobayashi created Eurostile Next based on the specimens of the original metal fonts. This new release was an optically rescaled and redesigned version of the original font family containing fifty variants from Ultra Light to Extended and matching italics for all.

Below. Eurostile has become an ever-popular choice for use in science-fiction films, whether it's seen on user-interfaces (UI) or for the branding and title credits. Clockwise from top left: David Cronenberg's *The Fly*, *Starship Troopers*, Disney's *Wall-E* (both Eurostile Bold Extended,) and *Johnny Mnemonic* (Eurostile Extended).

Estricta

ABCDEFGHIJKLMNOPQRSTUVWXYZ
abcdefghijklmnopqrstuvwxyz
1234567890 !@#?:;"*&

Foundry: Graviton
Designer: Pablo Balcells
Designer Nationality: Argentinian
Date: 2017

"Estricta" means "strict" in Spanish and this geometric sans is a very constrained, mechanical-looking typeface with sharp angles and edges. It is most suitable for short- and middle-length text blocks, and is available in six weights, from Light to Black, with complementary italics and small caps.

Eurostile LT

ABCDEFGHIJKLMNOPQRSTUVWXYZ
abcdefghijklmnopqrstuvwxyz
1234567890 !@#?:;"*&

Foundry: Nebiolo / Linotype
Designer: Aldo Novarese / Linotype Studio
Designer Nationality: Italian
Date: 1962 / 2009

Following on from his Microgramma typeface of 1952, this is Linotype's version of Aldo Novarese's popular and quintessentially 1960s design. It combines square shapes with rounded corners to give a modern, technological feel, and comes in eleven weights, including an outline version.

Eurostile Next

ABCDEFGHIJKLMNOPQRSTUVWXYZ
abcdefghijklmnopqrstuvwxyz
1234567890 !@#?:;"*&

Foundry: Linotype
Designer: Aldo Novarese / Akira Kobayashi / Terrance Weinzierl
Designer Nationality: Italian / Japanese / American
Date: 2016

This is a redrawn and expanded version of Aldo Novarese's design which references the original metal types and reinstates the subtle curves lost in previous digital cuts. There are five weights from Ultra Light to Bold, and all weights also have Condensed and Extended versions.

Fluctuation

ABCDEFGHIJKLMNOPQRSTUVWXYZ
abcdefghijklmnopqrstuvwxyz
1234567890 !@#?:;"*&

Foundry: Typodermic
Designer: Ray Larabie
Designer Nationality: Canadian
Date: 2013

Fluctuation takes inspiration from technology such as remote control devices, game controllers and synthesizers. Once, its square "M," "N," and "W" shapes were considered hard to read, but thanks to a generation raised on video games and low-res displays they now blend smoothly into a paragraph.

Foundry Monoline

ABCDEFGHIJKLMNOPQRSTUVWXYZ
abcdefghijklmnopqrstuvwxyz
1234567890 !@#?:;"*&

Designed for the various requirements of editorial and advertising design, Foundry Monoline is a squared sans serif produced in seven weights.

Quay's design combines a structured grid system with optical adjustments to create the look of linear, single-thickness strokes.

Foundry: The Foundry
Designer: David Quay
Designer Nationality: British
Date: 2000

Francker

ABCDEFGHIJKLMNOPQRSTUVWXYZ
abcdefghijklmnopqrstuvwxyz
1234567890 !@#?:;"*&

Francker's curves are based on the superellipse mathematical shape that is between an ellipse and a rectangle. The typeface is available in nine weights and two widths. Its lowercase letterforms "a," "b," "n," and "u" have no spurs, which serves to emphasize the simplicity of their construction.

Foundry: Linotype
Designer: Anders Francker
Designer Nationality: Danish
Date: 2010

From the Internet

ABCDEFGHIJKLMNOPQRSTUVWXYZ
abcdefghijklmnopqrstuvwxyz
1234567890 !@#?:;"*&

Canadian type designer Ray Larabie began his career in the video-game industry, and released freeware typefaces for several years before establishing his foundry, Typodermic, which is now based in Japan. From the Internet is a rectangular sans with a distinctly futuristic feel.

Foundry: Typodermic
Designer: Ray Larabie
Designer Nationality: Canadian
Date: 2011

From the Stars

ABCDEFGHIJKLMNOPQRSTUVWXYZ
abcdefghijklmnopqrstuvwxyz
1234567890 !@#?:;"*&

From the Stars is a departure from the more decorative, stylized display typefaces for which Ray Larabie is best known and he designed it in collaboration with his wife, Chikako. This square sans serif design is available in seven weights with corresponding italics.

Foundry: Typodermic
Designer: Ray Larabie / Chikako Larabie
Designer Nationality: Canadian / Japanese
Date: 2010

FS Hackney

ABCDEFGHIJKLMNOPQRSTUVWXYZ
abcdefghijklmnopqrstuvwxyz
1234567890 !@#?:;"*&

Foundry: Fontsmith
Designer: Nick Job / Jason Smith
Designer Nationality: British
Date: 2013

Built upon a super-elliptical foundation, this no-nonsense design by Nick Job achieves an effective balance of legibility, neutrality, and individuality. The font was named not for the notorious East London borough, but for the city's stalwart "Hackney Carriage" black cabs.

FS Joey

ABCDEFGHIJKLMNOPQRSTUVWXYZ
abcdefghijklmnopqrstuvwxyz
1234567890 !@#?:;"*&

Foundry: Fontsmith
Designer: Fernando Mello / Jason Smith
Designer Nationality: Brazilian / British
Date: 2009

FS Joey was designed for a TV streaming service from the BBC, ITV, and Channel 4 which was never released. However, Fernando Mello completed the font design and Fontsmith released it as a retail typeface. Fittingly, the project for which it was originally designed was codenamed "Kangaroo."

FS Truman

ABCDEFGHIJKLMNOPQRSTUVWXYZ
abcdefghijklmnopqrstuvwxyz
1234567890 !@#?:;"*&

Foundry: Fontsmith
Designer: Fernando Mello / Jason Smith
Designer Nationality: Brazilian / British
Date: 2002

This firm but friendly sans serif is designed for display on TV screens but is equally at home in print and on the web. It shares certain formal traits with the FS Dillon typeface by Fontsmith (see p. 272), and features a blend of geometric and cursive details, and irregular diagonal cuts.

FS Untitled

ABCDEFGHIJKLMNOPQRSTUVWXYZ
abcdefghijklmnopqrstuvwxyz
1234567890 !@#?:;"*&

Foundry: Fontsmith
Designer: Jason Smith
Designer Nationality: British
Date: 2016

FS Untitled is based on a design created by Fontsmith (see p. 272) for Channel 4 in 2005. Jason Smith modelled its letterforms according to the pixel structure of digital screens and developed two versions of each weight, offering designers fine control over the font's eventual appearance.

Great Escape

ABCDEFGHIJKLMNOPQRSTUVWXYZ
abcdefghijklmnopqrstuvwxyz
1234567890 !@#?:;"*&

Foundry: Typodermic
Designer: Ray Larabie
Designer Nationality: Canadian
Date: 2010

Great Escape is a super-elliptical sans serif from Ray Larabie's Typodermic foundry based in Japan. It has a slightly futuristic, technical feel and is available in a staggering twenty-eight different styles, including narrow and regular widths ranging from Hairline to Ultrabold.

Isonorm

ABCDEFGHIJKLMNOPQRSTUVWXYZ
abcdefghijklmnopqrstuvwxyz
1234567890 !@#?:;"*&

Foundries: Linotype / URW++
Designer: International Standard Organization
Designer Nationality: Swiss
Date: 1980

This typeface was developed by the International Standard Organization as a proposal for a standard typeface to be used on architectural drafts and technical drawings. Its simple, geometric letterforms were designed to be legible to machine readers as well as people.

ITC Tabula

ABCDEFGHIJKLMNOPQRSTUVWXYZ
abcdefghijklmnopqrstuvwxyz
1234567890 !@#?:;"*&

Foundry: ITC
Designer: Julien Janiszewski
Designer Nationality: French
Date: 2001

ITC Tabula was developed for use in subtitles; its clear, squared forms are designed to be legible both on TV displays and cinema screens. Although readability was a key concern for designer Julien Janiszewski, he worked hard to ensure his design also maintains a sense of visual interest.

Kairos Sans

ABCDEFGHIJKLMNOPQRSTUVWXYZ
abcdefghijklmnopqrstuvwxyz
1234567890 !@#?:;"*&

Foundry: Monotype
Designer: Terrance Weinzierl
Designer Nationality: American
Date: 2016

Kairos Sans is a wood-type-influenced design with a sporty feel. The typeface shares the octagonal skeleton of its slab serif predecessor published by Monotype in 2015. It is available in forty-eight styles, including three different widths, as well as Greek and Cyrillic character sets.

Klint

ABCDEFGHIJKLMNOPQRSTUVWXYZ
abcdefghijklmnopqrstuvwxyz
1234567890 !@#?:;"*&

Foundry: Linotype
Designer: Hannes von Döhren
Designer Nationality: German
Date: 2009

This versatile and assertive typeface from Linotype offers three different widths for each of its five weights. Hannes von Döhren's design features subtly curved details, and a comprehensive character set that caters to a broad range of typographic contexts.

Mensura

ABCDEFGHIJKLMNOPQRSTUVWXYZ
abcdefghijklmnopqrstuvwxyz
1234567890 !@#?:;"*&

Foundry: Graviton
Designer: Pablo Balcells
Designer Nationality: Argentinian
Date: 2012

Mensura was designed by Argentinian typographer Pablo Balcells, a graduate of the University of Buenos Aires. It is a modular, technical sans serif in eight styles, comprising four weights with italics. Balcells's foundry Graviton released Mensura in 2012 with a slab serif version too.

Milibus

ABCDEFGHIJKLMNOPQRSTUVWXYZ
abcdefghijklmnopqrstuvwxyz
1234567890 !@#?:;"*&

Foundry: Typodermic
Designer: Ray Larabie
Designer Nationality: Canadian
Date: 2006

Milibus was created by the prolific Canadian type designer Ray Larabie, and released by his foundry Typodermic. It is a non-traditional sans serif face with a futuristic, technical feel. Milibus comes in three weights with real italics and has a distinctive capital "A" with a low crossbar.

Order

ABCDEFGHIJKLMNOPQRSTUVWXYZ
abcdefghijklmnopqrstuvwxyz
1234567890 !@#?:;"*&

Foundry: Typodermic
Designer: Ray Larabie
Designer Nationality: Canadian
Date: 2006

Canadian Ray Larabie made this technical, angular sans serif in three weights. Larabie, who has drawn more than 1,000 fonts, once worked for Rockstar Games and his font Pricedown appears in the logo for the game *Grand Theft Auto*. In 2015, he devised a typeface, Canada 150, for Canada's 150th birthday.

Soho Gothic

ABCDEFGHIJKLMNOPQRSTUVWXYZ
abcdefghijklmnopqrstuvwxyz
1234567890 !@#?:;"*&

Foundry: Monotype
Designer: Seb Lester
Designer Nationality: British
Date: 2008

After the success of his Neo Sans and Neo Tech faces, Seb Lester worked for three years on the Soho family, which was released in 2008 and includes the slab serif Soho and sans Soho Gothic. The Gothic comes in nine weights and five widths with many alternate and semi-slab characters.

Square 721

ABCDEFGHIJKLMNOPQRSTUVWXYZ
abcdefghijklmnopqrstuvwxyz
1234567890 !@#?:;"*&

Foundry: Bitstream
Designer: Aldo Novarese
Designer Nationality: Italian
Date: 1962

Square 721 is a Bitstream version of Aldo Novarese's sans serif Eurostile (1962), which was an upper- and lowercase update of Alessandro Butti's Microgramma of ten years earlier. Square 721 is available in two weights—Roman and Bold—and evokes science fiction of the 1960s and 1970s.

Vellvé

ABCDEFGHIJKLMNOPQRSTUVWXYZ
abcdefghijklmnopqrstuvwxyz
1234567890 !@#?:;"*&

Foundry: ITC
Designer: Tomás Vellvé
Designer Nationality: Spanish
Date: 2006

Initially designed in 1971, Vellvé is a squared sans serif with numerous calligraphic flourishes and is the only one of Tomás Vellvé's designs produced in digital form. Now published by ITC, the updated font family includes three further weights and an italic for the Light version.

Venacti

ABCDEFGHIJKLMNOPQRSTUVWXYZ
abcdefghijklmnopqrstuvwxyz
1234567890 !@#?:;"*&

Foundry: Typodermic
Designer: Ray Larabie
Designer Nationality: Canadian
Date: 2005

Venacti is a squared sans serif with rounded features, inspired by the aesthetics of science fiction. Its characters combine dynamic counter shapes with clinical, spurless forms and avoid retro periodization by drawing from the full visual canon of science fiction.

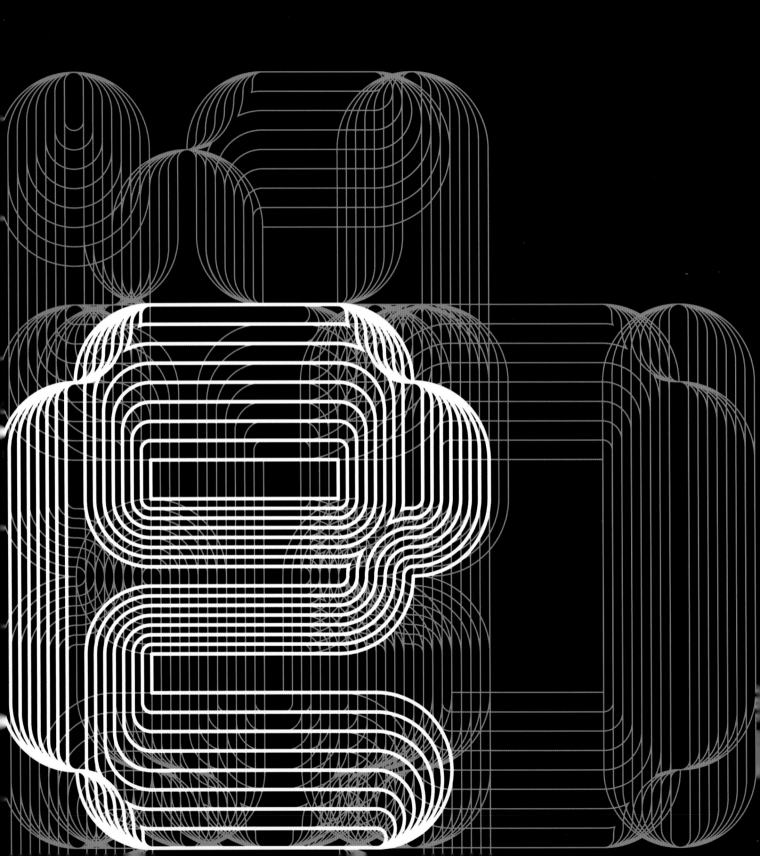

Display

Opposite. Detail showing the construction for the ThreeSix optical geomtretic type system by MuirMcNeil.

The very purpose of a display typeface is to catch the eye and provide an appropriate visual impact to a message, whether this be an advertisement in a magazine or a navigation sign by the side of a motorway. The distinguishing feature of display types over other typefaces is that they would never be appropriate to employ for lengthy pieces of text but are ideally suited for brief, attention-demanding titles or information that pull a reader's gaze towards their message, communicating in an instant. They not only help send a message but will evoke a mood or emotion. Display typefaces also intone historical reference points and styles in their presentation, providing all-important context quickly and clearly to a reader.

The earliest display types emerged in the early 19th century with an increasing use on posters, fliers (then known as handbills), and leaflets for commercial purposes as businesses sought to sell their goods and capture the attention of potential buyers. As such, and in order to aid distinction, mark themselves out from the competition and to deliver on the commercial demands required of their work, printers and typesetters looked for more innovative ways to present letterforms. Increasingly, they turned to elaborate and exaggerated type designs. With the advent and widespread use of woodblock types for printing, enlarged type styles such as heavy Clarendon serifs, emboldened grotesque sans serifs, and serif Fat Face designs became more commonplace for display usage of the period.

When metal type was introduced in the late 19th century, so the use of exaggerated display types cooled off. This is because the production and usage of large-sized letterforms was difficult on the mechanical systems employed for commercial use.

The advent of phototypesetting in the 1950s triggered a resurgence in the design of display types. The new technology could be used to create oversized texts. However, it was the invention of dry-transfer lettering in the 1970s that caused a boom in the creation of display types. Letraset was the market leader and pioneer of this transformative way of working for graphic designers, and the company created nearly 500 typeface designs over four decades. When digital technology arrived in the 1980s, the Letraset collection was digitized, making a wealth of typeface designs for almost every conceivable application available to all. The ease of typesetting on a digital system signalled the end of dry-transfer instant lettering as a commercially viable way to produce design work. Letraset continued to design and commission display typefaces until the mid 1990s. The majority of them are available online to purchase today via font marketing companies and so they are still widely used across many genres.

The digital design revolution, combined with the arrival of software to allow fonts to be created on a desktop system, triggered a great amount of experimentation and further typeface releases. Many designers and foundries invested their energies in experimental and innovative designs that could be achieved only through using a computer-aided system. For example, in 1991 the FontShop network began releasing the FUSE fonts. The first, a limited-edition package of four experimental PostScript typeface designs, contained Phil Baines's F Can You (read me)?, Neville Brody's F State, Malcolm Garrett's F Stealth, and Ian Swift's F Maze 91. All were highly experimental designs and all were achievable only with a computer. Around the same time, Zuzana Licko and Rudy VanderLans published their journal *Emigre*, which also acted as a catalyst for change. The title became a flagbearer for digital experimentation with adventurous layouts that employed digital typefaces from the duo's foundry for display and text purposes.

In recent years, the advancement and continuing sophistication of technology has allowed for increasingly complex designs with a number of display typefaces created as systems. These allow composite elements to be combined and integrated to create evermore interesting and exciting designs. Grid- and dot-based works, such as those envisaged and created by Dutch designer Wim Crouwel in the 1960s and 1970s with his *New Alphabet* manifesto, have provided inspiration and insight for contemporary designs as well as revivals by foundries including France's BB-Bureau, the United States' Neutura, and the United Kingdom's MuirMcNeil. All of them challenge the boundaries of legibility and readability through their innovative and unique deconstructed types and provide the designer with exciting ways to capture a reader's attention.

Acroyear

ABCDEFGHIJKLMNOPQRSTUVWXYZ
1234567890 !@#?:;"*&

Foundry: Typodermic
Designer: Ray Larabie
Designer Nationality: Canadian
Date: 2012

This distinctive display typeface, created by Nagoya-based Canadian type designer Ray Larabie, features an exaggerated forward slant that lends itself well to typesetting on an angled baseline. Irregular in form and irreverent in feel, it is available in uppercase only.

Adolescence

ABCDEFGHIJKLMNOPQRSTUVWXYZ
abcdefghijklmnopqrstuvwxyz
1234567890 !@*?:;"*&

Foundry: Lunchbox Studios
Designer: Adam Roe
Designer Nationality: American
Date: 1993

Type designer and former skateboarder Adam Roe established his Lunchbox Studios foundry in 1991, from which he created a range of postmodern and experimental typefaces. Adolescence, published in 1993, features distorted, grungy letterforms that vary wildly in weight and size.

Ammonia

ABCDEFGHIJKLMNOPQRSTUVWXYZ
a6cdefghijklmnopqrstuvwxyz.
1234S67890 !@*?:;"*&

Foundry: Chank Co.
Designer: Chank Diesel
Designer Nationality: American
Date: 1996

Chank Diesel established his Chank Co. foundry in 1996, and is renowned for his prolific output of playful, unpretentious display typefaces, influenced by his work in the music industry during the 1980s and 1990s. Available in one weight, Ammonia is a grungy, degraded sans serif.

Amorpheus

ABCDEFGHIJKLMNOPQRSTUVWXYZ
1234567890 !ATNo?:;""*&

Foundry: Device Type
Designer: Rian Hughes
Designer Nationality: British
Date: 1995

Multidisciplinary designer Rian Hughes has worked extensively in graphic design, illustration, type design, and comic art; he established Device Fonts in 1997 to distribute his own range of typefaces. Amorpheus displays the influence of his work in comics and illustration.

F2F Madame Butterfly

ABCDEFGHIJKLMNOPQRSTUVWXYZ
abcdefghijklmnopqrstuvwxyz
1234567890 !@#?:;"*&

Foundry: Face2Face
Designer: Alessio Leonardi
Designer Nationality: Italian
Date: 1995

Madame Butterfly is a distressed-looking experimental typeface that embodies the grunge style popular in mid 1990s. It was created by Italian designer Alessio Leonardi, who relocated to Berlin in 1990, where he worked at MetaDesign for two years with Erik Spiekermann (see p. 304).

FF Blur

ABCDEFGHIJKLMNOPQRSTUVWXYZ
abcdefghijklmnopqrstuvwxyz
1234567890 !@#?:;''*&

Foundry: FontFont
Designer: Neville Brody
Nationality: British
Date: 1992

FF Blur was designed by British typographer Neville Brody, who was one of the world's best-known graphic designers during the 1980s and 1990s. It is a postmodern sans serif typeface with contrast and irregular forms making it appear out of focus. It is available in light, medium, and bold weights.

ITC Binary

ABCDEFGHIJKLMNOPQRSTUVWXYZ
abcdefghijklmnopqrstuvwxyz
1234567890 !@#?:;"*&

Foundry: ITC
Designer: Mauricio Reyes
Nationality: American
Date: 1997

This semi-serif type was designed by Mexican-born Mauricio Reyes in 1997 and devised as a mash-up of elements from both Helvetica and Times. ITC Binary is available in light and bold without italics. It was selected as the official font for the Sydney 2000 Olympic Games in Australia.

Johnstemp

ABCDEFGHIJKLMNOPQRSTUVWXYZ
abcdefghijklmnopqrstuvwxyz
1234567890 !@#?:;"*&

Foundry: Linotype
Designer: Georg John
Nationality: German
Date: 2008

Available in four weights, Johnstemp is a distressed sans serif with bumpy edges that give it a stamped appearance. It features many alternate glyphs that break the monotony to give a more realistic stamped feel. Johnstemp Mix is a version with inbuilt stylistic and weight variety.

Linotype Araby Rafique

ABCDEFGHIJKLMNOPQRSTUVWXYZ
abcdefghijklmnopqrstuvwxyz
1234567890 !@#?:;"&*

Foundry: Linotype
Designer: Tehmina Rauf
Designer Nationality: British
Date: 1997

Created by British designer Tehmina Rauf in 1997, Linotype Araby Rafique is part of the TakeType Library, compiled from winners of the Linotype International Digital Type Design Contest. Legibility was clearly not an aim; letters are constructed from flowing, contrasting, curving shapes.

Linotype BioPlasm

ABCDEFGHIJKLMNOPQRSTUVWXYZ
abcdefghijklmnopqrstuvwxyz
1234567890 !@#?:;"*&

Foundry: Linotype
Designer: Mauro Carichini
Designer Nationality: Italian
Date: 2002

Linotype BioPlasm was designed by Mauro Carichini in 2002. It is an experimental sans serif with rounded features, short descenders and ascenders, and a tall x-height. Its distinguishing feature is that some letters are missing pieces as if it is a living organism, growing and morphing.

Linotype Mineru

ABCDEFGHIJKLMNOPQRSTUVWXYZ
abcdefghijklmnopqrstuvwxyz
1234567890 !@#?:;"*&

Foundry: Linotype
Designer: Ronny Edelstein
Designer Nationality: German
Date: 1997

Linotype Mineru is an amorphous display face produced in two weights, alongside an Outline style. The design's stroke weight fluctuates throughout, imitating the variability of a pen's nib, while the letters are restless in shape, and convey an eerie, volatile character.

Nowwhat

ABCDEFGHIJKLMNOPQRSTUVWXYZ
abcdefghijklmnopqrstuvwxyz
1234567890 !@#?:;"*&

Foundry: Monotype
Designer: Adam Roe
Designer Nationality: American
Date: 1993

Nowwhat is an amorphous display font designed in a single weight. The characters, in both upper and lowercases, have no coherent baseline and vary in shape, stroke width and angle, as if the designer roughly cut the letterforms from a piece of paper by hand.

Orange

ABCDEFGHIJKLMNOPQRSTUVWXYZ
abcdefghijklmnopqrstuvwxyz
1234567890 !?:;"*&

Foundry: ITC
Designer: Timothy Donaldson
Designer Nationality: British
Date: 1995

Orange is an amorphous display font conceived by the type designer and calligrapher Timothy Donaldson. Unlike those of a traditional sans serif, Orange's letterforms favor fluid joints over angled junctures and combine both flat and rounded terminals for an unorthodox outline.

Overprint ICG

ABCDEFGHIJKLMNOPQRSTUVWXYZ
abcdefghijklmnopqrstuvwxyz
1234567890 !@#?:;"*&

Foundry: Image Club Graphics
Date: 1996

Overprint is an amorphous display font designed in three weights, from Light to Heavy. Unlike conventional type designs, in which the designer may adjust the proportions from style to style, Overprint's characters differ only in thickness, as if repeatedly overprinted.

Seven Sans ICG

ABCDEFGHIJKLMNOPQRSTUVWXYZ
abcdefghijklmnopqrstuvwxyz
1234567890 !@#?:;"*&

Foundry: Image Club Graphics
Date: 1997

Seven Sans is an amorphous display face designed as part of the larger Seven typeface family that also includes the Seven Serif font. The letterforms, ranging from Regular to Black, combine a fluid outline with an erratic stroke width for a grungy appearance.

Surrogate

ABCDEFGHIJKLMNOPQRSTUVWXYZ
abcdefghijklmnopqrstuvwxyz
1234567890 !@#?:;"*&

Foundry: Lunchbox
Designer: Adam Roe
Designer Nationality: American
Date: 1995

A laid-back, ripple-effect display face, Surrogate was designed by the former actor and pro-skateboarder Adam Roe. He set up the experimental type foundry Lunchbox (part of Lunchbox Studios) in 1991 and went on to found the Zero Labs Group in Los Angeles during 2015.

Algol

ABCDEFGHIJKLMNOPQRSTUVWXYZ

abcdefghijklmnopqrstuvwxyz

1234567890 !@#?:;"*&

Foundry: Typodermic
Designer: Ray Larabie
Designer Nationality: Canadian
Date: 2005

Another layered design by Typodermic founder Ray Larabie, Algol is a technologically influenced typeface, whose three styles can be combined to create a range of effects. Its core letterforms have a blocky, pixellated structure similar to lettering on early digital displays.

Arkeo BT

ABCDEFGHIJKLMNOPQRSTUVWXYZ

abcdefghijklmnopqrstuvwxyz

1234567890 !@#?:;"*&

Foundry: Bitstream
Designer: Brian Sooy
Designer Nationality: American
Date: 2003

Arkeo BT, a pixel-based bitmap font by US type designer Brian Sooy, was published by Bitstream in 2003 in Regular, Condensed, and Extended styles. Despite its block-based skeleton, it remains legible at a range of sizes and is suitable for both print and screen-based use.

Bitmax

ABCDEFGHIJKLMNOPQRSTUVWXYZ

1234567890 !?:;"*&

Foundry: ITC
Designer: Alan Birch
Designer Nationality: British
Date: 1990

British typeface designer Alan Birch was inspired by the distortion created within fax-machine transmissions when creating Bitmax. Taking Helvetica Medium as his starting point, he developed an irregular, pixellated form for each character while preserving its essential shape.

Bubbledot ICG

ABCDEFGHIJKLMNOPQRSTUVWXYZ

abcdefghijklmnopqrstuvwxyz

1234567890 !@#?:;"*&

Foundry: Image Club Graphics
Designer: Noel Rubin
Designer Nationality: Canadian
Date: 1994

Noel Rubin designed Bubbledot for Image Club Graphics. It is offered in two styles: Coarse, which has its letterforms shrunk to the same overall height, and Fine, which features a more conventional range of ascenders and descenders. Negative versions of both styles are also available.

Elementar

ABCDEFGHIJKLMNOPQRSTUVWXYZ
abcdefghijklmnopqrstuvwxyz
1234567890 !@#?:;"*&

Foundry: Typotheque
Designer: Gustavo Ferreira
Designer Nationality: Brazilian
Date: 2011

A labor of love for its creator Gustavo Ferreira, Elementar is a parametric font system designed to bring flexibility to digital screens. Available in three styles—Sans A, Sans B, and Serif—it consists of thousands of individual fonts in a continuum of different styles, sizes, weights, and widths.

Facsimile

ABCDEFGHIJKLMNOPQRSTUVWXYZ
1234567890 !@#?:;"*&

Foundry: Linotype
Designer: Simon Wicker / Jenny Luigs
Designer Nationality: British
Date: 1994

One of the winners of Linotype's International Digital Type Design Contest, the bitmap face Facsimile is part of the TakeType Library. British designers Simon Wicker and Jenny Luigs created it in 1994, when the use of computers was increasing, to be used on electronic readers.

FF Moonbase Alpha

ABCDEFGHIJKLMNOPQRSTUVWXYZ
abcdefghijklmnopqrstuvwxyz
1234567890 !@◊?:;"*+

Foundry: FontFont
Designer: Cornel Windlin
Designer Nationality: Swiss
Date: 1991

Swiss designer Cornel Windlin created this display sans serif. FF Moonbase Alpha is a futuristic font created from connected, rounded blob shapes. It was initially released in 1991 with the debut issue of *FUSE*, a magazine of experimental type started by Jon Wozencroft and Neville Brody.

Indoo BT

ABCDEFGHIJKLMNOPQRSTUVWXYZ
abcdefghijklmnopqrstuvwxyz
1234567890 !@#?:;"*&

Foundry: Bitstream
Designer: Julien Janiszewski
Designer Nationality: French
Date: 2004

French typographer Julien Janiszewski designed Indoo BT in 2004; it is a blocky, bitmap sans serif created from small squares. It features a built-in underline that connects with every letter except for "o," "c," "O," "C," and "G." The Indoo BT family includes regular, italic, and ornaments.

Interact (02)

ABCDEFGHIJKLMNOPQRSTUVWXYZ
abcdefghijklmnopqrstuvwxyz
1234567890 !@#?;,"*&

ABCDEFGHIJKLMNOPQRSTUVWXYZ
abcdefghijklmnopqrstuvwxyz
1234567890 !@#?;,"*&

ABCDEFGHIJKLMNOPQRSTUVWXYZ
abcdefghijklmnopqrstuvwxyz
1234567890 !@#?;,"*&

Foundry: MuirMcNeil
Designer: Hamish Muir /
Paul McNeil
Designer Nationality: British
Date: 1994

Below. Promotional design by MuirMcNeil employing variable weights of Interact overlaid upon each other. The detail pictured shows the pixel junctions connecting the strokes.

British designer Hamish Muir created the Interact system of grid-based bitmap typefaces in 1994 as part of an invited submission to the *American Center for Design Journal* when he was a partner at London-based design studio 8vo. The design was originally created in lowercase only and purposed for screen use.

The starting point for the typeface was the optical characteristics of the stroke junctions in the lettering design used by Wim Crouwel (see p. 540) on his *Vormgevers* (*Designers*) poster for the Stedelijk Museum in Amsterdam in 1968. The lettering was built around horizontal and vertical strokes with 45° pixel steps forming the stroke junctions. By modulating these junctions, the effect was to round the letterforms. In Interact's grid system each weight follows a mathematical progression, which means the differing weights can be overlaid to create dynamic visual compositions.

MuirMcNeil (see p. 334) has expanded and revised Interact extensively to become a system of twenty-three typefaces in four scaleable groups or resolutions—02 (left), 03, 04, and 06—with a comprehensive range of twelve calibrated weights. MuirMcNeil has also added a complete set of capital letters, punctuation marks, and accented characters for Western European languages.

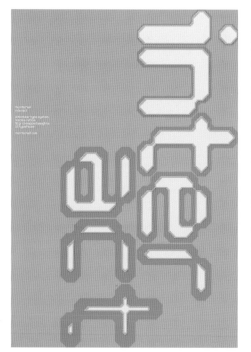

Intersect A

ABCDEFGHIJKLMNOPQRSTUVWXYZ
abcdefghijklmnopqrstuvwxyz
1234567890 !@#?:;'"*&

Foundry: MuirMcNeil
Designer: Hamish Muir / Paul McNeil
Designer Nationality: British
Date: 2013

In MuirMcNeil's words Intersect is a "type system which subverts typographic weight." Its two styles come in fifteen versions each. A, the regular weight, is a low-resolution sans serif made variously from stripes, both horizontal and vertical, and rectangular blocks of different sizes.

Intersect B

ABCDEFGHIJKLMNOPQRSTUVWXYZ
abcdefghijklmnopqrstuvwxyz
1234567890 !@#?:;'"*&

Foundry: MuirMcNeil
Designer: Hamish Muir / Paul McNeil
Designer Nationality: British
Date: 2013

Intersect B, which is of a far heavier weight than Intersect A, comes in fifteen numbered styles constructed using gridlike screen patterns. A and B are intended to be used in tandem and overlaid in their 256 possible combinations, and enhanced by the use of color, tint, and opacity.

Joystix

ABCDEFGHIJKLMNOPQRSTUVWXYZ
1234567890 /@#?:;"*&

Foundry: Typodermic
Designer: Ray Larabie
Designer Nationality: Canadian
Date: 2011

Designed by the prolific Canadian-born type designer Ray Larabie, who is based in Japan, Joystix is a single style, bold bitmap sans serif font. Its jagged look, the result of being constructed from large squares, mimics the early digital type found mainly in arcade games.

Linotype Leggodt

ABCDEFGHIJKLMNOPQRSTUVWXYZ
abcdefghijklmnopqrstuvwxyz
1234567890 !@#?:;'"*&

Foundry: Linotype
Designer: Gunter Schwarzmaier
Designer Nationality: German
Date: 1997

Linotype Leggodt is a bitmap display face based on early multimedia-inspired designs, such as OCR-B (1968) by Adrian Frutiger (see p. 290). The font's characters were designed in three styles, titled One, Two, and Three, and each proposes an alternative version of pixel-built letterforms.

Lomo

ABCDEFGHIJKLMNOPQRSTUV
abcdefghijklmnopqrstuvwxyz
1234567890 !@#?:;"*&

Foundry: Linotype
Designer: Fidel Peugeot
Designer Nationality: Swiss
Date: 2002

Designed by Fidel Peugeot, a Swiss designer based in Vienna, the Lomo family is named after an old Russian camera brand and was created for Lomography, a company selling modern reproductions of these fun cameras. Lomo, a lo-fi pixellated sans serif, comes in thirty-seven varied styles.

Nerdropol

ABCDEFGHIJKLMNOPQRSTUVWXY
abcdefghijklmnopqrstuvwxyz
1234567890 !@#?:;"*&

Foundry: Typodermic
Designer: Ray Larabie
Designer Nationality: Canadian
Date: 2012

Nerdropol, released by Typodermic in 2012, is a bitmap version of Neuropol X, a typeface designed by Larabie in 1997. It is a wide, low-resolution sans serif that comes in eight varied styles, including Nerdropol Screen, which mimics the distortions of an old cathode-ray tube monitor.

New Geneva Nine

ABCDEFGHIJKLMNOPQRSTUVWXYZ
abcdefghijklmnopqrstuvwxyz
1234567890 !@#?:;"*&

Foundry: Image Club Graphics
Designer: Grant Hutchinson
Designer Nationality: Canadian
Date: 1991

Canadian designer Grant Hutchinson created the New Geneva Nine pixellated typeface in 1991. In 2009, Hutchinson co-founded Veer, which sold stock photos, illustrations and fonts until the company closed in 2016. New Geneva Nine comes in two styles, Regular, and Point, which is condensed.

Pistol Shot

ABCDEFGHIJKLMNOPQRSTUVWXYZ
abcdefghijklmnopqrstuvwxyz
1234567890 !@#?:;"*&

Foundry: Linotype
Designer: Roselyne Besnard / Michel Besnard
Designer Nationality: French
Date: 2003

French couple Michel and Roselyne Besnard designed Pistol Shot, in 2003. The pixellated, blocky Western-style font was included in Linotype's TakeType 5 library, which comprised entries from the Linotype International Type Design Contest. It comes in two weights, Light and Normal.

Pixelar

ABCDEFGHIJKLMNOPQRSTUVWXYZ

abcdefghijklmnopqrstuvwxyz

1234567890 !@#?:;"*&

Pablo Balcells designed Pixelar for Graviton in 2014. The pixellated typeface comes in four styles; Regular, Outline, Textured (made from diagonal lines), and Textured Outline. An animated version, made in collaboration with Jeroen Krielaars, is available from Animography.

Foundry: Graviton
Designer: Pablo Balcells
Designer Nationality: Argentinian
Date: 2014

Rukyltronic

ABCDEFGHIJKLMNOPQRSTUVWXYZ

abcdefghijklmnopqrstuvwxyz

1234567890 !@#?:;"*&

Ray Larabie designed Rukyltronic in 2012. The typeface is an angular, simulated bitmap typeface that comes in eight different styles. It was inspired by the Sinclair ZX Spectrum, an early computer produced in Britain which was popular for video games.

Foundry: Typodermic
Designer: Ray Larabie
Designer Nationality: Canadian
Date: 2012

Zeitgeist

ABCDEFGHIJKLMNOPQRSTUVWXYZ

abcdefghijklmnopqrstuvwxyz

1234567890 !@#?:;"*&

Michael Johnson's only font, Zeitgeist is a low-resolution, pixellated condensed slab serif. It features alternate swashed letters and comes in six styles: Regular, Italic, Condensed, Bold, Cameo (white letters on black rectangles), and Crazy Paving, which has an eccentric lowercase.

Foundry: Monotype
Designer: Michael Johnson
Designer Nationality: British
Date: 1990

Zerbydoo

ABCDEFGHIJKLMNOPQRSTUVWXYZ

abcdefghijklmnopqrstuvwxyz

1234567890 !@#?::"*&

This eccentrically named face by Ray Larabie is a heavy, pixellated sans serif that is available in many styles; one is solid, one is constructed from circles, another from stars and three are made from different sized squares. Its kerning is restricted to full pixel increments.

Foundry: Typodermic
Designer: Ray Larabie
Designer Nationality: Canadian
Date: 2012

Foundry Profile

MuirMcNeil

Founded in 2010, MuirMcNeil focuses its activities on "exploring parametric design systems to generate appropriate solutions to visual communication problems." The founding partners are Paul McNeil and Hamish Muir. McNeil is a typographic designer with experience in brand and corporate communications. He is also a senior lecturer in typography at the London College of Communication, where he was course leader on the masters in contemporary typographic media from 2010–15. Muir co-founded the London-based graphic design studio 8vo in 1985 and was co-editor of *Octavo, International Journal of Typography* from 1986 to 1992. Since 2001, Muir has worked as a senior lecturer on the graphic and media design program at the London College of Communication.

The duo's unusual typefaces can be seen as challenging the notion of legibility and questioning letterforms in the traditional sense of the word. However, Muir and McNeil rigorously employ mathematics, grids and systems in their work to maintain readability. Their portfolio includes typefaces that are stunning—more pattern than texts—and their constructed appearance via overlays, alignments, contrasting stroke weights, and dot sizes communicate the beauty of the mathematics within. The intrinsic aesthetic beauty in the structure of their typefaces comes to the fore when using the fonts with a spirit of experimentation and exploration.

Founded: 2010
Country: UK
Website: muirmcneil.com
Notable typefaces:
ThreeSix (see p. 442)
TwoPoint (see p. 413)
TwoPlus (see p. 445)
TwoBit (see p. 444)
Cut (see p. 549)

Right. Limited-edition promotional poster of 100 for the TwoPoint typeface (top). Poster design for multi-disciplinary artist Russell Haswell's three-day festival held at Cafe Oto, London. The design is set in TwoPoint C in two weights (middle). Bisect poster typeface system (bottom).

Opposite. Detail from MuirMcNeil's limited-edition poster for their modular Intersect typeface system. All designs by MuirMcNeil.

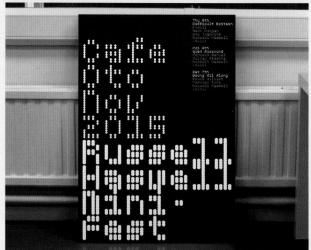

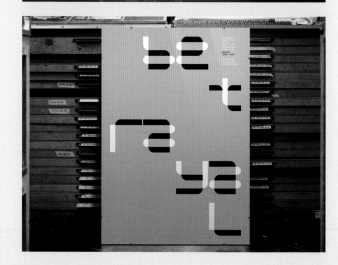

uirmcneil
tersect

modular type system:
 weights:
 grid-mapped
creen densities:
2 typefaces

uirmcneil.com

Ad Lib

ABCDEFGHIJKLMNOPQRSTUVWXYZ
abcdefghijklmnopqrstuvwxyz
1234567890 !@#?:;"*&

Foundry: American Type Founders
Designer: Freeman Craw
Designer Nationality: American
Date: 1961

Ad Lib's chunky forms and squared counters will be instantly recognizable to cartoon fans, thanks to its use in the credits of the *Looney Tunes* series and *The Pink Panther* films. Designer Freeman Craw went on to win the Type Director's Club Medal in 1988 for his contributions to typography.

Ambrose

ABCDEFGHIJKLMNOPQRSTUVWXYZ
1234567890 !?:;"*&

Foundry: ITC
Designer: Rudolf Koch / Alan Meeks
Designer Nationality: German / British
Date: 1914 / 1985

Designed by Alan Meeks shortly after he left Letraset to go freelance, Ambrose is based on Rudolf Koch's typeface Maximilian Antiqua, which was first published by the Klingspor foundry in Germany in 1914. Ambrose is a bold and characterful all-caps serif featuring engraved details.

Amherst

ABCDEFGHIJKLMNOPQRSTUVWXYZ
abcdefghijklmnopqrstuvwxyz
1234567890 !@#?:;"*&

Foundry: Linotype
Designer: Richard Yeend
Designer Nationality: British
Date: 2002

A member of Linotype's TakeType 5 Library, Amherst cleverly combines key formal features of Blackletter type with Art Deco details, to create a unique and contemporary sans serif. The family includes additional ornamental Gothic and Split styles alongside three standard weights.

Ampacity

ABCDEFGHIJKLMNOPQRSTUVWXYZ
1234567890 !@#?:;"*&

Foundry: Typodermic
Designer: Ray Larabie
Designer Nationality: Canadian
Date: 2012

Ampacity is a condensed display typeface available in uppercase only. Best set in larger point sizes to maximize legibility, each letterform within the font is made up of a single line of unwavering weight, folded and manipulated in much the same manner as neon lighting tubes.

Angle Bold

ABCDEFGHIJKLMNOPQRSTUVWXYZ
abcdefghijklmnopqrstuvwxyz
1234567890 !@#?:;"*&

Foundry: Monotype
Designer: Zavier Leslie Cabarga
Designer Nationality: American
Date: 2000

Illustrator, type designer and comic artist Zavier Cabarga started his career early—he sold his first comics at age fourteen and three years later he was developing his first font for phototypesetting. Angle, which is available in Bold and Inline styles, was first published in 2000.

Aquitaine Initials

ABCDEFGHIJKLMNOPQRSTUVWXYZ
ABCDEFGHIJKLMNOPQRSTUVWXYZ
1234567890 !@#?:;"*&

Foundry: Letraset
Designer: Steven Albert
Designer Nationality: American
Date: 1987

Displaying a distinctive Celtic influence throughout its letterforms, Aquitaine Initials was designed with two character sets: a basic uppercase alphabet, and a set of more decorative alternates that work particularly well at larger sizes. Both sets feature fine engraved details.

Arcadia

ABCDEFGHIJKLMNOPQRSTUVWXYZ
abcdefghijklmnopqrstuvwxyz
1234567890 !@#?:;"*&

Foundry: Linotype
Designer: Neville Brody
Designer Nationality: British
Date: 1990

This condensed, didone-influenced display font was designed by Neville Brody in 1986 for headline type within *Arena* magazine, which at the time was the first men's lifestyle title to be launched in Britain in two decades. Linotype published a retail version of the font in 1990.

Arnold Boecklin

ABCDEFGHIJKLMNOPQRSTUVWXYZ
abcdefghijklmnopqrstuvwxyz
1234567890 !@#?:;"*&

Foundry: Otto Weisert
Designer: Otto Weisert
Designer Nationality: German
Date: 1904

This archetypal Jungendstil font was designed in Stuttgart by Otto Weisert at the turn of the 20th century. Its swooping forms experienced a renaissance during the 1960s and 1970s, and it remains a popular if predictable choice to this day when an Art Nouveau look is required.

Artistik

ABCDEFGHIJKLMNOPQRSTUVWXYZ
abcdefghijklmnopqrstuvwxyz
1234567890 !@#?:;"* &

Foundry: Monotype
Designer: Monotype Studio
Date: 1897

Artistik was first published at the end of the 19th century. It features an irregularity influenced by brush-drawn calligraphy and Asian hand-lettering styles, and comes with a range of decorative alternate caps. Monotype published a digitization of the typeface in 1992.

Atomic

ABCDEFGHIJKLMNOPQRSTUVWXYZ
abcdefghijklmnopqrstuvwxyz
1234567890 !@#?:;"*¿

Foundry: Image Club Graphics
Designer: Lorne Maclean
Designer Nationality: Canadian
Date: 1997

Canadian typographer Lorne Maclean designed Atomic in 1997. It is available in both serif and sans serif styles and forms part of Linotype's NicePrice font collection, an array of decorative display typefaces intended for use outside of professional graphic design contexts.

Auriol

ABCDEFGHIJKLMNOPQRSTUVWXYZ
abcdefghijklmnopqrstuvwxyz
1234567890 !@#?:;"*&

Foundry: G. Peignot et Fils
Designer: George Auriol
Designer Nationality: French
Date: 1901

This stenciled typeface is based on the handwriting of Art Nouveau designer George Auriol, and displays the influence of brush-drawn calligraphy. It was used as the basis for the Paris Métro entrance signage. Linotype rereleased it with an additional bold cut in 1979.

Balega

ABCDEFGHIJKLMNOPQRSTUVWXYZ
abcdefghijklmnopqrstuvwxyz
1234567890 !@#?:;""*&

Foundry: Linotype
Designer: Jürgen Weltin
Designer Nationality: German
Date: 2003

German type designer Jürgen Weltin drew this stencil typeface, featuring a slight forward slant, for Linotype in 2003. It is based on Resolut, a font designed by H. Brünnel for the Turin-based foundry Nebiolo in 1937. It includes a range of new characters that were missing within the original.

Beluga LT

ABCDEFGHIJKLMNOPQRSTUVWXY
abcdefghijklmnopqrstuvwxyz
1234567890 !@#?:;"*&

Foundry: Linotype
Designer: Hans-Jürgen Ellenberger
Designer Nationality: German
Date: 1994

The German illustrator, type designer, and former science teacher Hans-Jürgen Ellenberger developed the medieval feel of this display typeface without direct reference to specific historic examples of calligraphy. Its forms nonetheless reflect the movement of the quill on the page.

Billsville

ABCDEFGHIJKLMNOPQRSTUVWXYZ
abcdefghijklmnopqrstuvwxyz
1234567890 !@#?:;"*&

Foundry: Chank Co.
Designer: Chank Diesel
Designer Nationality: American
Date: 1997

This display typeface was commissioned by the Tripod web-hosting company, one of the pioneers of user-generated content online. It is named for the town in which Tripod is based, Williamstown, Massachusetts. The font features irregular forms and star-shaped tittles.

Bomr

ABCDEFGHIJKLMNOPQRSTUVWXYZ
ABCDEFGHIJKLMNOPQRSTUVWXYZ
1234567890 !@#?:;"*&

Foundry: Typodermic
Designer: Ray Larabie
Designer Nationality: Canadian
Date: 2002

Ray Larabie's Bomr display typeface features exaggerated top serifs and an irreverent feel; its design was inspired by the graffiti tags seen on the side of freight trains. The typeface includes OpenType features that automatically substitute custom letter pairs for a remixed effect.

Bonehead

ABCDEFGHIJKLMNOPQRSTUVWXYZ
abcdefghijklmnopqrstuvwxyz
1234567890 !@#?:;"*&

Foundry: Chank Co.
Designer: Chank Diesel
Designer Nationality: American
Date: 1995

Chank Diesel designed this typeface for *Cake* magazine. It is one of a trio of typefaces created by Diesel as an experiment in type design without the use of curved lines, and is available in a package with its companion styles, Buckethead and Brainhead.

Boogie

ABCDEFGHIJKLMNOPQRST
UVWXYZ
1234567890 !@#?!@&...®©&

Foundry: Linotype
Designer: Ralf Weissmantel
Designer Nationality: German
Date: 2003

Ralf Weissmantel's playful and retro Boogie typeface was a winner in the Linotype International Digital Type Design Contest in 2003. It comprises several different styles intended to be layered over one another, allowing designers to control the impact and legibility of its appearance.

Boogie School Sans

ABCDEFGHIJKLMNOPQRSTUVWXYZ
abcdefghijklmnopqrstuvwxyz
1234567890 !@#?:;"*&

Foundry: Or Type
Designer: Mads Freund Brunse
Designer Nationality: Danish
Date: 2016

Or Type (see p. 498) was founded in 2013 by Guðmundur Úlfarsson and Mads Freund Brunse, who work between Reykjavik and London. They began development of this reverse contrast font in 2011, for use on a series of posters for a club night held in Freetown Christiania, Copenhagen.

Boogie School Serif

ABCDEFGHIJKLMNOPQRSTUVWXYZ
abcdefghijklmnopqrstuvwxyz
1234567890 !@#?:;"*&

Foundry: Or Type
Designer: Mads Freund Brunse
Designer Nationality: Danish
Date: 2016

This counterpart to Boogie School Sans features the addition of bulbous, rounded serifs, which heighten the appealing oddity of its predecessor—according to the foundry, its appearance was influenced by type found on old soul and funk record covers. It was published in 2016.

Breeze

ABCDEFGHIJKLMNOPQRSTUVWXYZ
abcdefghijklmnopqrstuvwxyz
1234567890 !@#?:;"*&

Foundry: Linotype
Designer: Frank Marciuliano
Designer Nationality: American
Date: 1997

US type designer Frank Marciuliano developed Breeze's letterforms to look like sails. Two versions of the typeface are available, each with its "sails" facing a different direction; the two can be combined to add a further sense of movement to display type.

Broadband

ABCDEFGHIJKLMNOPQRSTUVWXYZ
abcdefghijklmnopqrstuvwxyz
1234567890 !@#?:;"*&

Foundry: Image Club Graphics
Designer: Grant Hutchinson
Designer Nationality: Canadian
Date: 1991

This design by Veer co-founder Grant Hutchinson features rounded forms and geometric details. It remains legible even when set at smaller sizes— a somewhat unusual characteristic within display typefaces. First published by Image Club Graphics, it has since been licensed by Linotype.

Broadstreet

ABCDEFGHIJ K LWNOPQRSTUVWX YZ
abcdefghijklmnopqrstuvwxyz
1234567890 !@#?:;"*&

Foundry: Monotype
Designer: Richard Yeend
Designer Nationality: British
Date: 2001

Designer and cartoonist Richard Yeend has worked extensively in the editorial world, undertaking redesigns for newspapers including the *International Herald Tribune* and *Die Welt* over the course of his career. This stylized display serif design of his was published in 2001.

Broadway

ABCDEFGHIJKLMNOPQRSTUVWXYZ
abcdefghijklmnopqrstuvwxyz
1234567890 !@#?:;""*&

Foundry: American Type Founders
Designer: Morris Fuller Benton / Sol Hess
Designer Nationality: American
Date: 1927 / 1928

First designed by Morris Fuller Benton in uppercase only, this distinctive Art Deco font was quickly developed into a full typeface by Sol Hess following its release in 1928. He contributed an engraved cut the following year, alongside a condensed version designed by Fuller Benton.

Buckethead

ABCDEFGHIJKLMNOPQRSTUVWXYZ
abcdefghijklmnopqrstuvwxyz
1234567890 !@#?:;"*&

Foundry: Chank Co.
Designer: Chank Diesel
Designer Nationality: American
Date: 1995

The third of Chank Diesel's angular and jovial experiments in type design without the use of curves, Buckethead was designed for use in *Cake* magazine, which Diesel founded and worked on as creative director. The typeface has since been licensed for sale by Linotype.

Budmo

ABCDEFGHIJKLMNOPQRSTUVWXYZ
1234567890 !@#?:;''*&

Foundry: Typodermic
Designer: Ray Larabie
Designer Nationality: Canadian
Date: 1998

Budmo is a marquee signage-style typeface built on a geometric skeleton, and is available in a number of different variants that are designed to be layered to achieve a range of effects. Ray Larabie designed the typeface, which was published by his Typodermic foundry in 1998.

Burweed ICG

ABCDEFGHIJKLMNOPQRSTUVWXYZ
abcdefghijklmnopqrstuvwxyz
1234567890 !@#?:;"*&

Foundry: Image Club Graphics
Designer: Patricia Lillie
Designer Nationality: American
Date: 1996

Perhaps best known as a prolific producer of dingbat typefaces, US designer Patricia Lillie has also created a number of display typefaces, among them Burweed, which was published by Image Club Graphics in 1996. Tapered towards the bottom, it offers a jaunty and informal feel for headlines.

Buster

ABCDEFGHIJKLMNOPQRSTUVWXYZ
1234567890 !@#?:;"*&

Foundry: Letraset
Designer: Tony Wenman
Designer Nationality: British
Date: 1972

The letterforms of this shadowed display typeface by Letraset's Tony Wenman share similarities with those of traditional, industrial grotesques, but are presented here to appear three-dimensional. Buster, which has since been licensed by Linotype, is available in uppercase only.

Buxotic

ABCDEFGHIJKLMNOPQRSTUVWXYZ
1234567890 !?:;"*&

Foundry: Typodermic
Designer: Ray Larabie
Designer Nationality: Canadian
Date: 2006

The highly decorative and occasionally anthropomorphized forms of this display font by Ray Larabie feature a number of inclusions and embellishments. While legibility might not be its strength, the unconventional appearance of Buxotic rarely fails to make an impression.

Buzzer Three

ABCDEFGHIJKLMNOPQRSTUVWXYZ
1234567890 !?:;"*&

Foundry: Letraset
Designer: Paul Crome /
Tony Lyons
Designer Nationality: British
Date: 1993

Designed by Paul Crome and Tony Lyons at Letraset, this typeface is based on the appearance of early optical character recognition fonts, which were developed to be readable by the human eye and by computers. It features irregularly placed serif details and occasional curved forms throughout.

Candice

ABCDEFGHIJKLMNOPQRSTUV
abcdefghijklmnopqrstuvwxyz
1234567890 !@#?:;"*&

Foundry: Letraset
Designer: Alan Meeks
Designer Nationality: British
Date: 1976

Curvaceous and exuberant, Candice has become synonymous with the 1970s—instantly recognizable, it can be seen everywhere from The Carpenters' record covers to the logotype for the TV series *Cheers*. It shares similarities with Benguiat Charisma, published the previous decade.

Carouselambra

ABCDEFGHIJKLMNOPQRSTUVWXYZ
1234567890 !@#?:;"*&

Foundry: Typodermic
Designer: Ray Larabie
Nationality: Canadian
Date: 2008

Carouselambra was created in tribute to the type on the cover of Led Zeppelin's LP *Houses of the Holy* (1973). It shares certain similarities with ITC Willow (1990), including double crossbars and lifted letters, which were themselves influenced by the work of Scottish architect Charles Rennie Mackintosh.

Carver

ABCDEFGHIJKLMNOPQRSTUVWXYZ
abcdefghijklmnopqrstuvwxyz
1234567890 !@#?:;"*&

Foundry: Image Club Graphics
Designer: Grant Hutchinson /
Noel Rubin
Designer Nationality: Canadian
Date: 1994

Designed for Image Club Graphics in 1994, Carver is a blocky, angular sans serif font embellished with engraved strokes that provide both a slight sense of movement and the impression of crude tool marks. The details within its letterforms are best appreciated at larger point sizes.

Chic

ABCDEFGHIJKLMNOPQRSTUVWXYZ
1234567890 !@#?°°°"" * &

Foundry: American Type Founders
Designer: Morris Fuller Benton
Designer Nationality: American
Date: 1928

Morris Fuller Benton designed the Art Deco-influenced Chic typeface for American Type Founders in 1928. Linotype offers the font in digital form, and Nick Curtis's Odalisque NF (2008) is another contemporary interpretation, although this latter version lacks the striped details of the original.

Chilada ICG Uno

ABCDEFGHIJKLMNOPQRSTUVWXYZ
abcdefghijklmnopqrstuvwxyz
1234567890 !@#?:;"*&

Foundry: Image Club Graphics
Designer: Patricia Lillie
Designer Nationality: American
Date: 1994

Chilada is an angular font featuring zigzag emblems within the engraved outlines of its letterforms. It is unmistakably 1990s in style, its lowercase including some letters elevated from the baseline, encouraging playful typesetting. It was designed by Patricia Lillie for Image Club Graphics.

Chromium One

ABCDEFGHIJKLMNOPQRSTUVWXYZ
1234567890 !?:;"*&

Foundry: Letraset
Designer: David Harris
Designer Nationality: British
Date: 1983

This highly decorative font was designed by lettering artist and calligrapher David Harris for Letraset in 1983, and was later licensed by ITC and Linotype. Resembling hyper-glossy raised chrome type thanks to its intricate shaded details, it is available in uppercase only.

Chwast Buffalo

ABCDEFGHIJKLMNOPQRSTUVWXYZ
abcdefghijklmnopqrstuvwxyz
1234567890 !@#?:;"°&

Foundry: Linotype
Designer: Seymour Chwast
Designer Nationality: American
Date: 1978

Chwast Buffalo is a chunky semi-serif display typeface with rounded terminals and small counters, created by US designer Seymour Chwast in 1978 and published by Linotype three years later. Due to the font's heavy stroke weight, it is best used at large point sizes to maximize its legibility.

Clipwave

ABCDEFGHIJKLMNOPQRSTUVWXYZ
ABCDEFGHIJKLMNOPQRSTUVWXYZ
1234567890 !@#?:;"*&

Foundry: Typodermic
Designer: Ray Larabie
Nationality: Canadian
Date: 2011

Clipwave is a sans serif display typeface with an informal character; the design of its letterforms is angular but with rounded corners for added friendliness. As is characteristic of many Typodermic fonts, it offers a range of OpenType-enabled features and alternates.

Cosmic

ABCDEFGHIJKLMNOPQRSTUVWXYZ
abcdefghijklmnopqrstuvwxyz
1234567890 !@#?:;"*&

Foundry: Chank Co.
Designer: Chank Diesel
Designer Nationality: American
Date: 1995

Cosmic, designed by Chank Diesel for his Chank Co. foundry, is an ultra-heavy sans serif typeface with slim, open counters and a condensed appearance. In 1997, Swedish designer Claes Källarsson created an exaggerated version of the font, even bolder and more condensed than the original.

Creepy

ABCDEFGHIJKLMNOPQRSTUVWXYZ
ABCDEFGHIJKLMNOPQRSTUVWXYZ
1234567890 !@#?:;"*&

Foundry: Ascender
Designer: Carl Crossgrove / Steve Matteson
Designer Nationality: American
Date: 2001

Co-founder of the Ascender foundry and creative type director at Monotype, Steve Matteson designed the Creepy cartoonish typeface with its dripping details that suit a range of spooky scenarios. He created the font in collaboration with fellow US type designer Carl Crossgrove.

Croissant

ABCDEFGHIJKLMNOPQRSTUVWXYZ
abcdefghijklmnopqrstuvwxyz
1234567890 !@#?:;"*&

Foundry: Letraset
Designer: Philip Kelly
Designer Nationality: British
Date: 1978

Croissant is a pleasingly plump display typeface that appears to be formed from stylized and simplified brushstrokes. It was designed in 1978 by Philip Kelly, a prolific British type designer who worked at Letraset for twenty-five years. Croissant has since been licensed for sale by Linotype.

Curlz

ABCDEFGHIJKLMNOPQRSTUVWXYZ
abcdefghijklmnopqrstuvwxyz
1234567890 !@#?:;"*&

Foundry: Monotype
Designer: Carl Crossgrove /
Steve Matteson
Designer Nationality: American
Date: 1995

Curlz is ubiquitous thanks to its inclusion within a range of Microsoft programs and has been a popular choice for vernacular typesetting since its release by Agfa Monotype in 1995. It features a playful mix of straight serifs and curled stroke ends, with an uneven stress throughout.

Davida

ABCDEFGHIJKLMNOPQRSTUVWXYZ
1234567890 !@#?:;"*&

Foundry: VGC
Designer: Louis Minott
Designer Nationality: American
Date: 1965

Davida is a bold and highly decorative typeface, probably inspired by Victorian designs such as Central Type Foundry's Hogarth (1887). Also released as Silva and Darling, the original phototype font offered various alternates for "A," "E," and "F" and numbers 1 to 9, which digital versions lack.

Debusen

ABCDEFGHIJKLMNOPQRSTUVWXYZ
abcdefghijklmnopqrstuvwxyz
1234567890 !@#?:;"*&

Foundry: Typodermic
Designer: Ray Larabie
Nationality: Canadian
Date: 2008

Creator Ray Larabie has said the secret of this typeface is that it is "Soft like a kitten soaked in butter. That's what makes Debusen so friendly." The bulbous display typeface is completely devoid of any straight lines or angles, and in many ways it is similar to children's bubble writing.

Decorated 035

ABCDEFGHIJKLMNOP
QRSTUVWXYZ
1234567890 !@#?:;"*&

Foundry: Bitstream
Designer: Eugen Lenz /
Max Lenz
Designer Nationality: Swiss
Date: 1946 / c. 1980s

Formed from inclined rimmed capitals and numbers, Decorated 035 is Bitstream's version of Profil, which was designed by brothers Eugen and Max Lenz for the Swiss foundry Haas in 1946. Upright and Contour (without a shadow) versions were added by Photo-Lettering.

Desperate

ABCDEFGHIJKLMNOPQRSTUVWXYZ
1234567890 !@#?:;"*&

Foundry: Typodermic
Designer: Ray Larabie
Designer Nationality: Canadian
Date: 2009

Creator Ray Larabie has described Desperate as being "a punk, post-punk, new wave, Reagan-punk font." It is a visual cacophony of sharp points and angles—there are a few verticals to be found among the jagged edges, but not many, making it suitable for display purposes only.

Diamond Bodoni

Foundry: Monotype
Designer: Monotype Studio
Date: Unknown

Diamond comes in three styles: Bodoni, Negative and Positive. Bodoni has condensed Bodoni-style capitals and figures reversed on to the background. Positive and Negative offer capitals and figures in positive and negative form respectively. It is useful in labelling on certificates and advertising.

Digital

ABCDEFGHIJKLMNOPQRSTUVWXYZ
ABCDEFGHIJKLMNOPQRSTUVWXYZ
1234567890 !@#?:;"*&

Foundry: Image Club Graphics
Designer: Greg Kolodziejzyk
Designer Nationality: Canadian
Date: 1994

Canadian designer Greg Kolodziejzyk's typeface Digital was inspired by the very basic modular typefaces that first appeared on calculators and digital watches during the 1960s and 1970s. It scores very low on the legibility scale and is available in one uppercase weight.

DR Lineart

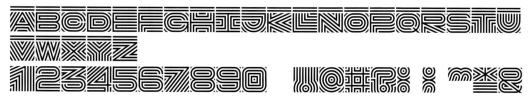

Foundry: Dmitry Rastvortsev
Designer: Dmitry Rastvortsev
Designer Nationality: Ukrainian
Date: 2017

This striking Op art display face by self-taught type designer Dmitry Rastvortsev can be tiled to create a grid format. In 2016, it won an award for the Best of Ukrainian Design in Typestyle and Typography. It contains five styles: Regular, Regular Alt, Skeleton, Background, and Ornament.

Ecliptica BT

ABCDEFGHIJKLMNOPQRSTUVWXYZ
abcdefghijklmnopqrstuvwxyz
1234567890 !@#?:;"*&

Foundry: Bitstream
Designer: Robert Bell
Designer Nationality: Australian
Date: 2004

An extended family of very condensed typefaces in a single bold weight, Ecliptica BT is available in Sans, Semi-Serif, Serif, Cursive, and Blackletter, all of which are designed to work well together. Both the Sans and Cursive versions contain some cap and lowercase alternatives.

Eirinn

ABCDEFGHIJKLMNOPQRSTUVWXYZ
abcdefghijklmnopqrstuvwxyz
1234567890 !@#?:;"*&

Foundry: Linotype
Designer: Norbert Reiners
Designer Nationality: German
Date: 1994

Eirinn's Celtic forms are based on Irish scripts of the 7th to 9th centuries, such as the *Book of Kells*. The typeface is characterized by its lowercase "f" with its short cross-stroke on baseline and long cross-stroke above, and the unusual form of the "g," and the "t," whose form is almost like that of a letter "c."

Eon Age ATT

ABCDEFGHIJKLMNOPQRSTUVWXYZ
1234567890 !@#?:;"*&

Foundry: ITC
Designer: Paul Prue
Designer Nationality: British
Date: 1994

Paul Prue designed this futuristic display typeface for the Agfa Compugraphic Creative Alliance in 1994. Eon Age features unusual characters with blocks that balance on the baseline. Prue also designed the similarly science-fiction influenced System X3, Galaxy Run, and Logan in the same year.

F2F Haakonsen

Foundry: Face2Face
Designer: Stefan Hauser
Designer Nationality: German
Date: 2003

An outline-based layered, experimental typeface, Haakonsen is part of the Face2Face series. It was created by German designer and educator Stefan Hauser. Many of Face2Face's typefaces featured in layouts for the leading 1990s German techno music magazine *Frontpage*.

F2F HogRoach

ABCDEFGHIJKLMNOPQRSTUVWXYZ
abcdefghijklmnopqrstuvwxyz
1234567890 !@#?;"*&

HogRoach is an experimental typeface that challenges conventional notions of legibility. It is part of the Face2Face series of unusual designs created by the collective formed by German designer and typographer Thomas Nagel and his friends. Many of Face2Face's typefaces featured in *Frontpage*.

Foundry: Face2Face
Designer: Thomas Nagel
Designer Nationality: German
Date: 1995

F2F Monako Stoned

ABCDEFGHIJKLMNOPQRSTUVWXYZ
abcdefghijklmnopqrstuvwxyz
1234567890 !@#?:;"*&

An Op art-inspired typeface created from half-tone textures, Monako Stoned is part of the Face2Face series that explored the design potential of type with experimental fonts and unconventional interfaces. Monako Stoned was created by German designers Alexander Branczyk and Heike Nehl.

Foundry: Face2Face
Designer: Alexander Branczyk / Heike Nehl
Designer Nationality: German
Date: 1995

Fajita Mild

ABCDEFGHIJKLMNOPQRSTUVWXYZ
ABCDEFGHIJKLMNOPQRSTUVWXYZ
1234567890 !@#?:;"*&

Fajita is named after the Tex-Mex dish. It is a woodcut-style display face with small caps for its lowercase and rough, textured random shapes around each glyph. The typeface is available in two styles, Mild and Picante, and the latter features accent lines above or below its small caps.

Foundry: Image Club Graphics
Designer: Noel Rubin
Designer Nationality: Canadian
Date: 1994

Fat Albert BT

ABCDEFGHIJKLMNOPQRSTUVWXYZ
abcdefghijklmnopqrstuvwxyz
1234567890 !@#?:;"*&

Fat Albert BT was inspired by 1970s pop-culture fonts and named after an animated cartoon starring Bill Cosby which debuted in 1972. It is a heavy display sans serif with circular- and oval-shaped counters and flat tops and bottoms. It comes in three styles: Solid, Outline, and Shadow.

Foundry: Bitstream
Designer: Ray Cruz
Designer Nationality: American
Date: 2004

Farset / Feirste

ABCDEFGHIJKLMNOPQRSTUVWXYZ
ABCDEFGHIJKLMNOPQRSTUVWXYZ
1234567890 !@#?:;"*&

ABCDEFGHIJKLMNOPQRSTUVWXYZ
abcdefghijklmnopqrstuvwxyz
1234567890 !@#?:;"*&

Foundry: MuirMcNeil
Designer: John McMillan
Designer Nationality: British / Irish
Date: 2019

From the streets of Northern Ireland's Belfast (literally) comes the typeface Farset (named after the river that flows to Belfast from the surrounding hills) and its Gaelic equivalent Feirste (from the city's Irish name Béal Feirste). The design of Farset / Feirste is based on Belfast's historic tiled street signage. These striking tiled signs were handmade during the late 19th and early 20th centuries and their distinctive white capital lettering on black tiles are familiar to residents and visitors alike.

The development of Latin and Gaelic typefaces was the brainchild of Belfast resident John McMillan, Emeritus Professor of Graphic Design at Ulster University. The project began in 2015 and was realized only in 2018, when McMillan approached foundry and design studio MuirMcNeil for help with the digitization. They interpreted his designs in both Latin and Gaelic variants with each available in the cameo format of the signs and in normal font format.

Below. The distinctive tiled street signage of Belfast was the inspiration behind Farset / Feirste. Its distinctive capital lettering has striking "G," "R," and "S" designs that provide a unique character to the letterforms.

Opposite. Examples and character sets of both typefaces.

SHANKILL ROAD
BURREN WAY
BROOMHILL PARK
FALLS ROAD
STRANMILLIS
CASTLEREACH
LECONIEL
SKECONEIL
MALONE

BÓTHAR NA SEANCHILLE
BEALACH NA BOIRNE
PÁIRC CHNOC NA SCUAB
BÓTHAR NA BHFÁL
AN SRUTHÁN MILIS
AN CAISLEÁN RIABHACH
LAS AN AOIL
SCEACHÓS AN IARLA
MASH LÓIN

ABCDEFCGHHIIJKLMM
NOPQRRSTTUVWWXYZ
abcdefgghijklm
nopqrstuvwxyz

0123456789

ÄÅÀÃÂÁÉÊÈËÍÎÏÌÖÕÓÔ
ÒØŒÚÛÙÜÇÑ¥Æáàâä
ãåæéèêëíîïìóòôöõø
œúùûüçñµÿ$&£§ß
ƒ@®©™aºoₒºₒₒ†‡
•*¶(){}/!?¿¡
'„""‚'‚
.,,,,.....;
--—‹‹›÷±¬~ ^˘°

ABCDEFShIJKLM
NOPQRSTUVWXYZ
abcdefShijklmn
opqrRsrtuvwxyz

0123456789

ÄÅÀÃÂÁBċÒÉÊÈËÈŕŠÍÏÌìm
ÖÕÓÒÔPŞŢÚÛÙÜÛẀẁẂẄ
ÄÅÀÃÂÁbċÒÉÊÈËÈŕŠÍÏÌìm
ÖÕÓÒÔPŞŕŢÚÛÙÜÛẀẁẂẄ
ØØŒœÇÑ¥Æñµÿ

$&7£§ßƒ@®©™aº
ºₒºₒₒ†‡•*¶(){}/!?¿¡
'„""‚'‚
.,,,,.....;
--—‹‹›÷±¬~ ^˘°

Faux Occident & Orient

A B C D E F G H I J K L M N O P Q R S T U V W X Y Z
1 2 3 4 5 6 7 8 9 0 ! Ⓐ # ? :; " * &

Foundry: Playtype
Designer: Jess Andersen / Andreas Peitersen / Stefan Friedli
Designer Nationality: Danish
Date: 2013

Developed by a team of Danish designers and published by Playtype (see p. 310), Faux is a three-dimensional, uppercase, sans serif display face.

It achieves an illusion of dimensionality through shadows; Faux Orient appears embossed while Faux Occident looks debossed.

FF CrashBangWallop

A B C D E F G H I J K L M N O P Q R S T U
a b c d e f g h i j k l m n o p q r s t u v w x y
1 2 3 4 5 6 7 8 9 0 ! @ @ ? :; " * @

Foundry: FontFont
Designer: Rian Hughes
Designer Nationality: British
Date: 1994

British graphic designer, illustrator and comic artist Rian Hughes designed FF CrashBangWallop. It is a quirky, angular display sans serif available in light and medium with italics, as well as in two decorative styles—Highlight, a three-dimensional version, and Contour, which features an outline.

FF Dolores

A B C D E F G H I J K L M N O P Q R S T U V W X Y Z
a b c d e f g h i j k l m n o p q r s t u v w x y z
1 2 3 4 5 6 7 8 9 0 ! @ # ? :; " * &

Foundry: FontFont
Designer: Tobias Frere-Jones
Designer Nationality: American
Date: 1991

An early font from the leading US typeface designer Tobias Frere-Jones, FF Dolores is a childlike, informal slab serif with many curls and quirks. It is available in five weights and has Cyrillic support. FF Dolores is the only typeface that Frere-Jones released with FontFont.

FF Dynamoe

A B C D E F G H I J K L M N O P Q R S T U V W X Y Z
1 2 3 4 5 6 7 8 9 0 ! ? : ; " * &

Foundry: FontFont
Designer: Just van Rossum
Designer Nationality: Dutch
Date: 1992

FF Dynamoe is a distressed, sans serif which is reversed out of a thick black band. It is based on the look of labels created with old Dymo handheld label makers that embossed letters into tape—a technique invented in 1958 which has been replaced by battery-powered printing.

FF Harlem

ABCDEFGHIJKLMNOPQRSTUVWXYZ
abcdefghijklmnopqrstuvwxyz
1234567890 !@#?:;"*&

Foundry: FontFont
Designer: Neville Brody
Designer Nationality: British
Date: 1993

Neville Brody's FF Harlem is named after the traditionally African-American neighbourhood of Harlem at the north end of Manhattan. It is a heavy, energetic sans serif with irregular counters that give it a vibrant feel. The typeface is available in two styles: Regular and a distressed version, Slang.

FF Klunder

ABCDEFGHIJKLMNOPQRSTUVWXYZ
abcdefghijkLMNopqrstuvwxyz
1234567890 !@# ?:;"*&

Foundry: FontFont
Designer: Barbara Klunder
Designer Nationality: Canadian
Date: 1994

This eponymous typeface by Canadian designer Barbara Klunder comes in regular and bold and was released by FontFont in 1994. Klunder Script is a quirky, irregular sans serif with a cheerful, festive mood. Letters alternate randomly between tilting left, upright and tilting right.

Fiesta

ABCDEFGHIJKLMNOPQRSTUVWXYZ
abcdefghijklmnopqrstuvwxyz
1234567890 !@#?:;""*&

Foundry: Aerotype
Designer: Stephen Miggas
Designer Nationality: American
Date: 1995

Fiesta is a decorative, display font in a woodcutlike style. It was released by Aerotype in 1995, the year that the foundry was established by Los Angeles-based graphic designer Stephen Miggas. Each letter features triangular inlaid details as well as small angular accenting just outside their outline.

Follies

ABCDEFGHIJKLMNOPQRSTUVWXYZ
1234567890 !?:;""*&

Foundry: Letraset
Designer: Alan Meeks
Designer Nationality: British
Date: 1991

Alan Meeks's Follies, released by Letraset in 1991, is a distinctive, display sans serif inspired by the 1940s and featuring a thin inline. The inline has small slab serifs on many letters. Follies is uppercase only and comes in a single style, which is heavy to allow for the inline.

Fruitygreen

ABCDEFGHIJKLMNOPQRSTUVWXYZ
abcdefghijklmnopqrstuvwxyz
1234567890 !@#?:;”*&

Foundry: Linotype
Designer: Andi AW. Masry
Designer Nationality: Indonesian
Date: 2012

Indonesian designer Andi AW. Masry created Fruitygreen, a distinctive soft sans serif inspired by the unique shapes of various fruits, in 2012. It is available in Regular, Bold, and Black weights with italics. Fruitygreen was Masry's second font release after his debut Coomeec the same year.

FS Erskine

ABCDEFGHIJKLMNOPQRSTUVWXYZ
1234567890 !@#?:;”*&

Foundry: Fontsmith
Designer: Jimmy Turrell
Designer Nationality: British
Date: 2017

FS Erskine by illustrator Jimmy Turrell was part of Local Characters, a collaboration between Fontsmith (see p. 272) and agency It's Nice That. The brief was to make a font inspired by a place. They chose the Byker Wall estate in Newcastle, his hometown, and used primary colors and geometric shapes.

FS Kitty

ABCDEFGHIJKLMNOPQRSTUVWXYZ
1234567890 !@#?:;”*&

Foundry: Fontsmith
Designer: Jason Smith / Phil Garnham
Designer Nationality: British
Date: 2009

FS Kitty, designed by Jason Smith and Phil Garnham, is a chunky, curvy, uppercase display sans serif. It comes in five styles: Light and Regular, which are outlined; Solid, which features hairline interior details; Headline, which is solid with a keyline; and Shadow, which has a 3D effect.

FS Sally Triestina

ABCDEFGHIJKLMNOPQRSTUVWXYZ
abcdefghijklmnopqrstuvwxyz
1234567890 !@#?:;”*&

Foundry: Fontsmith
Designer: Astrid Stavro
Designer Nationality: Italian
Date: 2017

Designed by Astrid Stavro and Fontsmith (see p. 272). Sally Triestina was inspired by Trieste, Italy, where Stavro was born. It is a splicing of a bold and regular serif, with the lower half heavier and offset. Stavro, then creative director of Atlas, is a partner at the international design studio, Pentagram.

Glowworm

ABCDEFGHIJKLMNOPQRSTUVWXYZ
abcdefghijklmnopqrstuvwxyz
1234567890 !@#?:;"*&

Foundry: Mecanorma
Designer: Bogdan Żochowski
Designer Nationality: Polish
Date: 1975

Glowworm was released by French dry-transfer lettering company Mecanorma in 1975 and designed by Polish typographer Bogdan Żochowski. It is a bold, round sans serif with small highlights that give it a shiny, 3D look. It is available in Regular and Compressed versions.

Goudy Ornate MT

ABCDEFGHIJKLMNOPQRSTUVWXY
1234567890 !@#?:;"*&

Foundry: Monotype
Designer: Frederic W. Goudy
Designer Nationality: American
Date: 1931

This decorative, titling serif display face by Frederic W. Goudy comes in a single weight with uppercase letters only. It is open and features many small curly details. Goudy described it as a "simple, decorative face that has been used by some good presses for use on title pages."

Gurkner

ABCDEFGHIJKLMNOPQRSTUVWXYZ
1234567890 !@#?:;"*&

Foundry: Typodermic
Designer: Ray Larabie
Nationality: Canadian
Date: 2007

Ray Larabie's typeface Gurkner is a rounded, top-heavy display sans serif. Its heavy, spooky forms bulge at the top. Released by Larabie's Typodermic foundry in 2007, Gurkner has capitals only. It is available in two styles, Regular and Jump, and the latter does not conform to a consistent baseline.

Harlow

ABCDEFGHIJKLMNOPQRSTUVWX
abcdefghijklmnopqrstuvwxyz
1234567890 !?:;"*&

Foundry: ITC / Letraset
Designer: Colin Brignall
Designer Nationality: British
Date: 1977

Colin Brignall's Harlow, released by both ITC and Letraset in 1977, is a retro, inclined display sans serif with exuberant swashed capitals and long ascenders. Harlow is available in two styles, Solid and Regular, and the latter is outlined with an offset shadow built-in to give a 3D look.

Hemi Head 426

ABCDEFGHIJKLMNOPQRSTUVWXYZ
abcdefghijklmnopqrstuvwxyz
1234567890 !@#?:;" *&

Foundry: Typodermic
Designer: Ray Larabie
Nationality: Canadian
Date: 1998

Hemi Head 426, named after an engine part, is a square, industrial sans serif available in a single heavy italic style. As with many of Ray Larabie's early fonts, it was available for free online. Larabie was inspired by the lettering on 1960s' Dodge cars and other muscle-car insignia.

Hobo

ABCDEFGHIJKLMNOPQRSTUVWXYZ
abcdefghijklmnopqrstuvwxyz
1234567890 !@#?:;"'*&

Foundry: American Type Founders
Designer: Morris Fuller Benton
Designer Nationality: American
Date: 1910

Hobo, an oft-derided sans serif, shares its name with the US term for a homeless drifter. It was designed by Morris Fuller Benton and released by American Type Founders in 1910 in one weight; a light cut followed in 1915. Inspired by Art Nouveau, it has no descenders and almost no straight lines.

Horndon

ABCDEFGHIJKLMNOPQRSTUVWXYZ
1234567890 !@#?:;"'*&

Foundry: Letraset
Designer: Martin Wait
Designer Nationality: British
Date: 1984

Martin Wait designed Horndon for Letraset in 1984, and named it after Horndon-on-the-Hill, the Essex village where he lives. It is an all uppercase display face with small serifs, high crossbars and a built-in drop shadow with uniform gaps between the shadow and type giving a 3D effect.

Ignatius

ABCDEFGHIJKLMNOPQRSTUVWXYZ
abcdefghijklmnopqrstuvwxyz
1234567890 !?:;"'*&

Foundry: Letraset
Designer: Freda Sack
Designer Nationality: British
Date: 1987

Freda Sack designed this elegant, two-line display serif face for Letraset in 1987. Ignatius comes in a single style with upper and lowercase. The two-line effect is extended even to the punctuation and tittles. Sack began her career at Letraset and then co-founded The Foundry in London.

ITC Aftershock

ABCDEFGHIJKLMNOPQRSTUVWXYZ
abcdefghijklmnopqrstuvwxyz
1234567890 !@#?:;"*&

Foundry: ITC
Designer: Bob Alonso
Designer Nationality: American
Date: 1996

US designer Bob Alonso worked at Photo-Lettering for many years and created Aftershock for the International Typeface Corporation (ITC) in 1996.

It is a robust and heavy display face whose irregular, square forms were intended to resemble lettering created through woodcut or linocut printing.

ITC Arecibo

ABCDEFGHIJKLMNOPQRSTUVWXYZ
ABCDEFGHIJKLMNOPQRSTUVWXYZ
1234567890 !@#?:;"*&

Foundry: ITC
Designer: Luis Siquot
Designer Nationality: Argentinian
Date: 2002

Luis Siquot designed ITC Arecibo for ITC in 2004. This typeface is a condensed display sans serif with a hairline shadow and high crossbars.

Available in one weight and two styles, Arecibo has uppercase and small caps only, and achieves an Art Deco feel.

ITC Batak

ABCDEFGHIJKLMNOPQRSTUVWXYZ
abcdefghijklmnopqrstuvwxyz
1234567890 !@#?:;"*&

Foundry: ITC
Designer: Charles Nix
Designer Nationality: American
Date: 2002

Charles Nix, US type designer and type director at Monotype, created ITC Batak in 2002 based on hand-painted lettering he saw in Northern Sumatra.

With the skeleton of a grotesque and hexagonal serifs, Batak is distinctive and comes in condensed and bold condensed versions.

ITC Belter

ABCDEFGHIJKLMNOPQRSTUVWXYZ
abcdefghijklmnopqrstuvwxyz
1234567890 !@#?:;"*&

Foundry: ITC
Designer: Andreu Balius
Designer Nationality: Spanish
Date: 1996

Barcelona-based Andreu Balius designed Belter in 1996. It is a distinctive, monoline display typeface with crosses at the ends of many of its strokes,

which act almost like serifs. It is available in two styles, Regular and Mega Outline, and the latter has dual outer keylines.

ITC Bottleneck

ABCDEFGHIJKLMNOPQRSTUVWXYZ

abcdefghijklmnopqrstuvwxyz

1234567890 !@#?:;"*&

Foundry: ITC
Designer: Tony Wenman
Designer Nationality: British
Date: 1972

ITC Bottleneck is a retro decorative serif that is characteristic of the groovy mood of the early 1970s. It has very thick and heavy lower serifs, which recall the platform shoes that were fashionable at the time. Bottleneck was also available as dry-transfer lettering from Letraset.

ITC Digital Woodcuts

ABCDEFGHIJKLMNOPQRSTUVWXYZ

1234567890 !@#?:;"*&

Foundry: ITC
Designer: Timothy Donaldson
Designer Nationality: British
Date: 1995

As its name implies, Timothy Donaldson's ITC Digital Woodcuts is inspired by traditional printing techniques but recreated on a computer. It is all caps and each letter is reversed out of a black, rough-edged square. An alternate with the squares outlined and black letters is also included.

ITC Einhorn

ABCDEFGHIJKLMNOPQRSTUVWXYZ

abcdefghijklmnopqrstuvwxyz

1234567890 !@#?:;"*&

Foundry: ITC
Designer: Alan Meeks
Designer Nationality: British
Date: 1980

Available in a single weight, which is very bold, ITC Einhorn is a distinctive semi-serif font by British designer Alan Meek. Many of its capital letters and all of the lowercase alphabet feature small upward flicks at their base which join them to the next letter, much like a connecting script.

ITC Florinda

ABCDEFGHIJKLMNOPQRSTUVWXYZ

ABCDEFGHIJKLMNOPQRSTUVWXYZ

1234567890 !@#?:;"*&

Foundry: ITC
Designer: Luis Siquot
Designer Nationality: Argentinian
Date: 1997

An interesting display face, Florinda by Luis Siquot has the basic form of an uppercase grotesque sans serif; however, it features rounded, ornamental knobs that jut out of the letters horizontally and vertically. It is available in one heavy weight, and has caps and small caps only.

ITC Jellybaby

ABCDEFGHIJKLMNOPQRSTUVWXYZ
abcdefghijklmnopqrstuvwxyz
1234567890 !@#?:;"*&

Foundry: ITC
Designer: Timothy Donaldson
Designer Nationality: British
Date: 1997

Available in a single style, and published in 1997, Timothy Donaldson's ITC Jellybaby is a curvy, fun, retro display sans serif with oval-shaped counters that are not placed centrally in the letters and ball terminals. It began life as a pumped-up version of another Donaldson font, Pink, published in 2001.

ITC Liverpool

ABCDEFGHIJKLMNOPQRSTUVWXYZ
abcdefghijklmnopqrstuvwxyz
1234567890 !@#?:;"*&

Foundry: ITC
Designer: Kevin Bailey
Designer Nationality: American
Date: 1999

ITC Liverpool, created by US typeface designer Kevin Bailey for the International Typeface Corporation (ITC) in 1999, is a bulbous, bold, display sans serif that brings to mind exuberant type from the 1960s and 1970s. It has wide letters and undersized counters that are not centrally placed.

ITC Magnifico

ABCDEFGHIJKLMNOPQ
RSTUVWXYZ
1234567890 !@#?:;"*&

Foundry: ITC
Designer: Akira Kobayashi
Designer Nationality: Japanese
Date: 1999

Inspired by 19th-century display types, Magnifico is an all-caps italic slab serif with built-in outlines and shadows. It comes in two styles: Daytime with white type and black shadows, and Nighttime with black type and white shadows. Akira Kobayashi was a freelance type designer in Japan at the time.

ITC Masquerade

ABCDEFGHIJKLMNOPQRSTUVWXYZ
ABCDEFGHIJKLMNOPQRSTUVWXYZ
1234567890 !@#?:;"*&

Foundry: ITC
Designer: Martin Wait
Designer Nationality: British
Date: 2009

Designed by Martin Wait, a British designer who worked in font production at Letraset for twenty-five years, ITC Masquerade is an all-caps, highly ornamented serif display face with a double outline and drop shadows. Included in the font are decorative capitals with elaborate curlicues.

ITC Minska

ΛBCDEFGHIJKLMNOPQRSTUVПXYZ
αBCDEFGHIJKLMNOPQRSTUVΨXYZ
1234567890 !@‡?:;"*℧

ITC Minska is a highly distinctive and unconventional typeface that blends upper and lowercase as well as curves and angles. Although legible, many of its characters do not conform to expected archetypes. It is available in three weights: Light, Medium, and Bold, without italics.

Foundry: ITC
Designer: Carl Crossgrove
Designer Nationality: American
Date: 1996

ITC Motter Sparta

ABCDEFGHIJKLMNOPQRSTUVWXYZ
abcdefghijklmnopqrstuvwxyz
1234567890 !@#?:;"*&

Austrian type designer Othmar Motter created ITC Motter Sparta in 1997. It is a heavy sans serif that mixes dynamic curves, points, and sharp angles in a unique way. The most distinctive characters are the pointy "o" and the "a," which is almost an upside-down "v" but still reads as an "a."

Foundry: ITC
Designer: Othmar Motter
Designer Nationality: Austrian
Date: 1997

ITC Pioneer

ABCDEFGHIJKLMNOPQRSTUVWXYZ
1234567890 !@#?:;"*&

Pioneer is one of a number of fonts designed for ITC by Ronne Bonder and Tom Carnase in 1970. It is an experimental, uppercase sans serif with angular forms, no curves, and a drop shadow. It was used on the film poster for *Shaft* (1971), the blaxploitation film with a soundtrack composed by Isaac Hayes.

Foundry: ITC
Designer: Ronne Bonder / Tom Carnase
Designer Nationality: American
Date: 1970

ITC Snap

ABCDEFGHIJKLMNOPQRSTUVWXY
abcdefghijklmnopqrstuvwxyz
1234567890 !@#?:;"*&

ITC Snap is the work of US designer David Sagorski, who created fonts for Letraset and the International Typeface Corporation (ITC) after changing his career as a worker in the oil industry. It is a curvy, bulbous font with small sharp serifs and a jaunty, humorous feel that evokes cartoons.

Foundry: ITC
Designer: David Sagorski
Designer Nationality: American
Date: 1995

ITC Talking Drum

ABCDEFGHIJKLMNOPQRSTUVWXYZ
abcdefghijklmnopqrstuvwxyz
1234567890 !@#?:;"'*&

Foundry: ITC
Designer: Timothy Donaldson
Designer Nationality: British
Date: 1999

ITC Talking Drum is a distinctive, angular, heavy sans serif font. Many elements—such as the crossbars of "F" and "H," the tail of "Q" and the arm of "r"—re constructed from a single square diamond. It reappears in unexpected places, such as the bottom of the "Y" and "L."

ITC Willow

ABCDEFGHIJKLMNOPQRSTUVWXYZ
1234567890 !@#?:;"'*&

Foundry: ITC
Designer: Tony Forster
Designer Nationality: British
Date: 1990

ITC Willow was designed by Tony Forster, a British lettering artist and designer who was based near Manchester and taught at Bolton College of Art. It is a condensed display sans serif inspired by Charles Rennie Mackintosh's style and features many decorative alternates and ligatures.

ITC Ziggy

ABCDEFGHIJKLMNOPQRSTUVWXYZ
abcdefghijklmnopqrstuvwxyz
1234567890 !@#?:;"'*&

Foundry: ITC
Designer: Bob Alonso
Designer Nationality: American
Date: 1997

Ziggy began as doodles made by Bob Alonso during the 1970s. When he later rediscovered some of these sketches, he was inspired to revive it as a full font. ITC Ziggy is a wild and curly display serif with bottom-heavy letters which is typical of the groovy, 1970s era in type design.

ITC Zinzinnati

ABCDEFGHIJKLMNOPQRSTUVWX
abcdefghijklmnopqrstuvwxyz
1234567890 !@#?:;"'*&

Foundry: ITC
Designer: Schriftguss Foundry / Nick Curtis
Designer Nationality: American
Date: 1924 / 2002

Nick Curtis based Zinzinnati on Ohio, an old German typeface released by the Schriftguss Foundry in Dresden in 1924. Ohio was a playful, curvy serif typical of the *Plakatstil* (poster style) type popular in Germany at the time. Curtis cleaned up its rough edges but kept Ohio's original spirit.

ITC Zipper

ABCDEFGHIJKLMNOPQRSTUUWXYZ
abcdefghijklmnopqrstuuwxyz
1234567890 !@#?:;"'*&

Foundry: ITC
Designer: Phillip Kelly
Designer Nationality: British
Date: 1970

ITC Zipper, designed by Letraset staff member Phillip Kelly, is a distinctive and heavy reverse-contrast condensed sans serif font available in a single weight. It has very wide horizontal strokes and thin verticals. It was used on the cover of David Bowie's album *Hunky Dory* (1971).

JMC Engraver

ABCDEFGHIJKLMNOPQRSTUVWXYZ
abcdefghijklmnopqrstuvwxyz
1234567890 !@#?:;"'*&

Foundry: Monotype
Designer: Terrance Weinzierl
Designer Nationality: American
Date: 2012

JMC Engraver was designed by Terrance Weinzierl, a US type designer and lettering artist who has worked at Monotype since 2008. It is a distinctive monoline sans serif that features an abundance of curls and kinks. It comes in a single style with upper and lowercases.

Jokerman

ABCDEFGHIJKLMNOPQRSTUVWXYZ
abcdefghijklmnopqrstuvwxyz
1234567890 !@#?:;"'*&

Foundry: ITC
Designer: Andrew Smith
Designer Nationality: British
Date: 1995

Jokerman is a jaunty decorative font, ornamented with dots, dashes and curls that stick out of its letters, float nearby, or are inlaid as negative space. It was once highly popular thanks to inclusion in many Microsoft programs, notably as one of the fonts bundled with Office.

Kalligraphia

ABCDEFGHIJKLMNOPQRSTUVWXYZ
abcdefghijklmnopqrstuvwxyz
1234567890 !@#?:;"'*&

Foundry: Berthold
Designer: Otto Weisert
Designer Nationality: German
Date: 1902

Kalligraphia was first cast in 1902 by Carl August Kloberg's eponymous type foundry that was acquired by Berthold in 1922. It is an exuberant, curvy Art Nouveau script in a single fairly heavy style. It was revived by Photo-Lettering in the 1960s when its style was suddenly back in fashion.

Karloff Negative

ABCDEFGHIJKLMNOPQRSTUVWXYZ
abcdefghijklmnopqrstuvwxyz
1234567890 !@#?:;"'*&

The Karloff family explores extreme contrast. It was conceived by Peter Biľak but designed by Pieter van Rosmalen with Nikola Djurek. Karloff Negative is a reverse-contrast serif inspired by the Italian styles of the 19th century which pioneered the switching of contrast, designed to attract readers' attention.

Foundry: Typotheque
Designer: Peter Biľak / Pieter van Rosmalen / Nikola Djurek
Designer Nationality: Slovakian / Dutch / Croatian
Date: 2015

Kelso

ABCDEFGHIJKLMNOPQRSTUVWXYZ
abcdefghijklmnopqrstuvwxyz
1234567890 !@#?:;""✿&

Kelso is a distinctive geometric sans serif where each letter is made from a continuous monoline, giving an outlined look. It was designed by British designer Adrian Talbot in 2014 and released by his independent foundry Talbot Type. Kelso comes in three weights: Light, Regular, and Bold.

Foundry: Talbot Type
Designer: Adrian Talbot
Designer Nationality: British
Date: 2014

Kino

ABCDEFGHIJKLMNOPQRSTUVWXYZ
abcdefghijklmnopqrstuvwxyz
1234567890 !@#?:;"'*&

Kino is an angular display sans serif with completely flat tops and bottoms that look to have been cleanly cut, leaving behind triangles in places such as the arm of the "r." Triangles are also found as the crossbars of "A," "E," and "H," and as the full point. The tittles are diamond shaped.

Foundry: Monotype
Designer: Martin Dovey
Designer Nationality: British
Date: 1930

La Pontaise Poster

ABCDEFGHIJKLMNOPQRSTUVWXYZ
abcdefghijklmnopqrstuvwxyz
1234567890 !@#?:;"'*&

La Pontaise Poster is a version of La Pontaise, a grotesque sans by Or Type (see p. 498), but with extreme contrast and more exaggerated forms.

Danish designer Mads Freund Brunse has been the head of the typography design program at La Cambre art school in Brussels since 2017.

Foundry: Or Type
Designer: Mads Freund Brunse
Designer Nationality: Danish
Date: 2013

Lazybones

ABCDEFGHIJKLMNOPQRSTUVWXYZ
abcdefghijklmnopqrstuvwxyz
1234567890 !@#?:;"*&

Foundry: URW
Designer: Letraset Design Studio
Date: 1972

Designed in 1972 at the Letraset design studio, and also available from ITC, Lazybones is a chunky, curvy and slightly inclined heavy display face with many exuberant swashed capitals, small counters, and an Art Nouveau feel, which became popular during the early 1970s.

LCD

ABCDEFGHIJKLMNOPQRSTUVWXYZ
1234567890!@#?:;"*&

Foundry: Letraset
Designer: Alan Birch
Designer Nationality: British
Date: 1981

An LCD (liquid crystal display) is a type of electronic screen and was first used on items such as digital watches and clock radios during the 1970s. These basic LCD screens led to a particular style of type, which British designer Alan Birch's LCD font replicates. It is an italic, all-caps stencil sans serif.

Linotype Albafire

ABCDEFGHIJKLMNOPQRSTUVWXYZ
abcdefghijklmnopqrstuvwxyz
1234567890 !@#?:;"*&

Foundry: Linotype
Designer: Hans-Jürgen Ellenberger
Designer Nationality: German
Date: 2002

Hans-Jürgen Ellenberger's Albafire is part of Linotype's Alba family, which also includes Albatross and Albawing, all from 2002. It is a decorative sans serif that features small jagged flame shapes sticking out of the right side of each letter like speed-lines, giving it a flaming, dynamic feel.

Linotype Albatross

ABCDEFGHIJKLMNOPQRSTUVWXYZ
abcdefghijklmnopqrstuvwxyz
1234567890 !@#?:;"*&

Foundry: Linotype
Designer: Hans-Jürgen Ellenberger
Designer Nationality: German
Date: 2002

Part of Linotype's Alba family, which also includes Albafire and Albawing, Albatross by German designer Hans-Jürgen Ellenberger is a decorative display font. Whereas Albafire has a standard base with flames jutting out, Albatross is made entirely from right-pointing flame shapes.

Linotype Alphabat

ABCDEFGHIJKLMNOPQRSTUVWXYZ
1234567890 !?¡;"&

Foundry: Linotype
Designer: Jan Tomás
Designer Nationality: Czech
Date: 1999

The Czech designer Jan Tomás, a graduate of the University of the Arts in Berlin's Visual Communication course, created Linotype Alphabat, a strange all-caps font that features distinctive batwing shapes and double counters. Many letters look doubled as if seen cross-eyed.

Linotype Atomatic

ABCDEFGHIJKLMNOPQRSTUVW
abcdefghijklmnopqrstuvwxyz
1234567890 !@#?:;"*¢

Foundry: Linotype
Designer: Johannes Plass
Designer Nationality: German
Date: 1997

Johannes Plass, a graduate of the Muthesius University of Fine Arts and Design in Kiel, Germany, designed Linotype Atomatic, a winner of the Linotype International Digital Type Design Contest. It comes in a single, wide, and bold style and leans to the right, giving a sense of dynamism and speed.

Linotype Barock

ABCDEFGHIJKLMNOPQRSTUVWXYZ
abcdefghijklmnopqrstuvwxyz
1234567890 !@#?:;"*&

Foundry: Linotype
Designer: Jean-Jacques Tachdjian
Designer Nationality: French
Date: 1999

Jean-Jacques Tachdjian's Barock is an experimental, postmodern font that challenges legibility. All of its characters are constructed from multiple versions of the same letter overlapping each other, some of which are smaller or reversed, or cause shapes to cut out of the black.

Linotype BlackWhite

Foundry: Linotype
Designer: Ferdinay Duman
Designer Nationality: German
Date: 1989

Linotype BlackWhite, the work of Ferdinay Duman, is an all-caps display sans in five styles. Its regular cut has no counters, a solid black lower half and an outlined. Other styles include entirely solid and outlined versions and Laser, which has a horizontal break in every capital.

Linotype Dharma

ABCDEFGHIJKLMNOPQRSTUD
abcdefghìjklmnopqrstuvwxyz
1234567890 !@#?:;"'*&

Foundry: Linotype
Designer: Gerd Sebastian Jakob / Joerg Ewald Meissner
Designer Nationality: German
Date: 1997

Linotype Dharma is a decorative display font, designed in a stand-alone Regular weight. The character set includes multiple ornamental details, such as the angled slashes that replace standard dots, the wedged serifs and the sicklelike curves found on vertical strokes.

Linotype Flamingo

ABCDEFGHIJKLMNOPQRSTUVWXYZ
abcdefghijklmnnopqrstuvwxyz
1234567890 !@#?:;"'*&

Foundry: Linotype
Designer: Michael Leonhard
Designer Nationality: German
Date: 1999

Linotype Flamingo is a decorative display face that tests the boundaries of reductionism. German font designer Michael Leonhard removed elements from each character, such as a curve, stroke ending or joint, thus forcing the reader to fill in the gaps for full legibility.

Linotype Funny Bones

ABCDEFGHIJKLMNOPQRSTUVWXYZ
abcdefghijklmnopqrstuvwxyz
1234567890 !@#?:;"'*&

Foundry: Linotype
Designer: Ingo Preuss
Designer Nationality: German
Date: 1997

Linotype Funny Bones is a decorative display face, produced in two distinct weights. The first, Linotype Funny Bones One, comprises a combination of eccentric all-capital letterforms. Alternatively, Linotype Funny Bones Two contains restrained, condensed lowercase characters.

Linotype Gotharda

ABCDEFGHIJKLMNOPQRSTUVWXYZ
abcdefghijklmnopqrstuvwxyz
1234567890 !@#?:;"'*et

Foundry: Linotype
Designer: Milo Dominik Ivir
Designer Nationality: Croatian
Date: 1997

Linotype Gotharda is a display font that combines the features of both gothic and sans serif type styles. The bullish characters exhibit the narrow width and bulky strokes, typical of gothic faces, alongside the clarity, standardization and economy of sans serif designs.

Linotype Konflikt

ABCDEFGHIJKLMNOPQRSTUVWXYZ
abcdefghijklmnopqrstuvwxyz
1234567890 !@#?:;"*&

Foundry: Linotype
Designer: Stefan Pott
Designer Nationality: German
Date: 1997

Linotype Konflikt is a decorative display face that addresses the aesthetic clash between print and digital type design. To bridge the gap, Linotype Konflikt blends calligraphic strokes, reminiscent of early print faces, and the pixelated forms of the computer screen.

Linotype Labyrinth

ABCDEFGHIJKLMNOPQRSTUVWXYZ
ABCDEFGHIJKLMNOPQRSTUVWXYZ
1234567890

Foundry: Linotype
Designer: Frank Marciuliano
Designer Nationality: American
Date: 2002

Linotype Labyrinth is a display face designed in a single style and is modelled on the complex blueprint of a maze. The characters share a single height, with no ascenders or descenders, and consist of concentric shapes that feature a single gap, or gateway, in their outer stroke.

Linotype Lindy

ABCDEFGHIJKLMNOPQRSTUVWXYZ
abcdefghijklmnopqrstuvwxyz
1234567890 !@#?:;"*&

Foundry: Linotype
Designer: Frank Marciuliano
Designer Nationality: American
Date: 1997

Frank Marciuliano's Linotype Lindy is a decorative display face designed for use at headline sizes, which is reminiscent of early digital lettering. The characters feature high-contrast, boxy outer strokes, and these in turn define the inner strokes through their creation of negative space.

Linotype MhaiThaipe

ABCDEFGHIJKLMNOPQRSTUVWXYZ
abcdefghijklmnopqrstuvwxyz
1234567890 !@#?:;"*&

Foundry: Linotype
Designer: Markus Remscheid
Designer Nationality: German
Date: 1997

Markus Remscheid's Linotype MhaiThaipe is a display font inspired by Arabic and Sanskrit letterforms. Features, such as the small circles that embellish the terminals and the calligraphic stroke styles, provide the design with a decorative approach similar to that of non-Latin alphabets.

Lost & Foundry

FS Berwick
ABCDEFGHIJKLMNOPQRSTUVWXYZ
1234567890 !@#?:;"*&

FS Cattle
ABCDEFGHIJKLMNOPQRSTUVWXYZ
1234567890 !@#?:;"*&

FS Century
ABCDEFGHIJKLMNOPQRSTUVWXYZ
1234567890 !@#?:;"*&

FS Charity
ABCDEFGHIJKLMNOPQRSTUVWXYZ
ABCDŁŀGHIJKLMNOPQRSTUVWXYZ
1234567890 !@#?:;"*&

FS Malborough
ABCDEFGHIJKLMNOPQRSTUVWXYZ
1234567890 !@#?:;"*&

FS Portland
ABCDEFGHIJKLMNOPQRSTUVWXYZ
1234567890 !@#?:;"*&

FS St James
ABCDEFGHIJKLMNOPQRSTUVWXYZ
ABCDEFGHIJKLMNOPQRSTUVWXYZ
1234567890 !@#?:;"*&

Lost & Foundry is a unique collection of seven typefaces that was created based on historic signage found within London's Soho, an area that is slowly disappearing because of the constant development of the city. London-based foundry Fontsmith (see p. 272) partnered with the House of St Barnabas, a private members' club in Soho Square to launch this innovative project in an effort to save the visual history of an area that is being redeveloped. Each sale of the fonts as a family pack comes with a month's membership to the club.

In addition, the project is helping break the cycle of homelessness in London. The House also works to tackle this social issue as charity, and its efforts have helped many individuals get off the streets. All the proceeds of the sale of the font family packs go toward the charity.

Each typeface has a remarkable story concerning its original source and is a document of times long past. Fontsmith's efforts have ensured that these characteristic and historical types are preserved for future use and admiration.

Foundry: Fontsmith
Designer: Jason Smith / Stuart de Rozario / Pedro Arilla
Designer Nationality: British / British / Spanish
Date: 2018

Opposite. Samples of the Lost & Foundry collection in use. A sign in an archway on Portland Mews (center) served as the inspiration for FS Cattle.

LOST &
FOUNDRY
··
TYPEFACES
INSPIRED BY THE
DISAPPEARING
SIGNS OF SOHO

ABCDEFGHIJK LOST&FO-
UNDRYMARLBOROUGH
NOPQRSTUVWXYZ?£!

TWENTIE
CENTUR
– HOUSE – SP
*CHISELL
†INSPIRE

R.N.CATTLE & S
PORTLAND WO

PORTLA
ESTMINS
*LONDO
D'ARB
STREE

ABCHARITYDE
GHIJK LOST&
FOUNDRY MNO
PQRSTUVWX
YZ123456789»

EXPRES
QUIRK
REDISCOV
¡BERW
†STRE

— 1864
– & 2018
*ST JAMES
SOHO CL
ONDONES

Linotype Mindline

Foundry: Linotype
Designer: Critzla
Designer Nationality: German
Date: 1997

Linotype Mindline was inspired by the aesthetics of 1920s advertising typefaces and Constructivist posters. It is a geometric display font, designed in two styles, Inside and Outside. The characters are comprised of rectangular frames, which each house a thin, inconspicuous letterform.

Linotype Minos

Foundry: Linotype
Designer: Christian Goetz
Designer Nationality: Swiss
Date: 1997

Linotype Minos is a decorative display font inspired by early Greek scripts and named after Crete's legendary King Minos. The design is informed by typical scripts found in the ornamental borders around the characters that embellished Cretan palaces such as Knossos, Phaistos, and Malia.

Linotype Paint It

Foundry: Linotype
Designer: Jochen Schuss
Designer Nationality: German
Date: 1997

Linotype Paint It is a playful face, designed in capitals and two styles. In the Empty style, the characters, which are at the center of a labyrinthine block, are visible only through dots on each stroke, whereas the letters in the Black style are discernible by color.

Linotype Tiger

Foundry: Linotype
Designer: Gerd Sebastian Jakob / Joerg Ewald Meissner
Designer Nationality: German
Date: 1997

Linotype Tiger is a display face designed entirely without curves, leaving the splintered strokes to meet at sharp angles. The font family consists of five weights, which range from Brave One, a heavy, outlined version, to Tame, comprised of light, single-stroke characters.

Logan

ABCDEFGHIJKLMNOPQRSTUVWXYZ
abcdefghijklmnopqrstuvwxyz
1234567890 !@#?:;"*&

Foundry: Monotype
Designer: Paul Prue
Designer Nationality: British
Date: 1994

Logan is a decorative display face designed to imitate the high-tech aesthetic of computing. The letterforms, released in a single Regular style, are high in contrast and squared in shape, while the strokes are reminiscent of the dynamic patterns found on computer chips.

Luncheonette

ABCDEFGHIJKLMNOPQRSTUVWXYZ
abcdefghijklmnopqrstuvwxyz
1234567890 !@#?:;"*&

Foundry: Chank Co.
Designer: Chank Diesel
Designer Nationality: American
Date: 2002

Luncheonette is a retro display face and is a horizontally scaled version of Laundrette, both of which, along with Lambrettista, comprise Chank's Laundry Fonts family. Unlike its sibling fonts, Luncheonette features slim strokes and narrow spacing for tighter compositions.

Macbeth

ABCDEFGHIJKLMNOPQRSTUVWXYZ
abcdefghijklmnopqrstuvwxyz
1234567890 !@#?:;"*&

Foundry: Linotype
Designer: Linotype Design Studio
Designer Nationality: American
Date: 1994

Macbeth is a burly, condensed display font that was inspired by posters for *Frankenstein* (1931) and other early films. Like much cinematic poster design at the start of the 20th century, Macbeth combines the sloping strokes of Art Deco with the gothic features of early horror films.

MAD Sans

ABCDEFGHIJKLMNOPQRSTUVWXYZ
abcdefghijklmnopqrstuvwxyz
1234567890 !@#?:;"*&

Foundry: Colophon
Designer: Dries Wiewauters
Designer Nationality: Belgian
Date: 2017

MAD Sans was designed by Dries Wiewauters, a Belgian graduate of the Werkplaats Typografie, a Dutch university in Arnhem. It is a distinctive sans serif inspired by computer-aided design and constructed without curves. It comes in four weights —Light to Black—with italics.

MAD Serif

ABCDEFGHIJKLMNOPQRSTUVWXYZ
abcdefghijklmnopqrstuvwxyz
1234567890 !@#?:;""*&

Foundry: Colophon
Designer: Dries Wiewauters
Designer Nationality: Belgian
Date: 2017

MAD Serif is an angular typeface with no curves, drawn using a plotter machine. It comes in roman and italic, and two styles, Fill and Outline, in four weights. With each higher weight, the Outline style gains a line, starting with the monoline Light. MAD stands for Machine Aided Design.

Maximus BT

ABCDEFGHIJKLMNOPQRSTUVWXYZ
1234567890 !@#?:;""*&

Foundry: Bitstream
Designer: Lou Scolnik
Designer Nationality: American
Date: 1973

Maximus BT is a decorative display face and is Bitstream's digital version of Lou Scolnik's Maximus font family, designed in 1973 for the Visual Graphics Corporation font foundry. The letterforms, produced in a single capitalized style, are characterized by their repeated horizontal strikethroughs.

Metropolitaines

ABCDEFGHIJKLMNOPQRSTUVWXYZ
1234567890 !@#?:;""*&

Foundry: URW
Designer: Hector Guimard
Designer Nationality: French
Date: c. 1905

Metropolitaines is a decorative display font that was produced by French architect Hector Guimard as signage lettering for Paris Métro stations, and then later published by German foundry URW. Like much of Guimard's architecture, Metropolitaines is designed in the Art Nouveau style.

Mexcellent

ABCDEFGHIJKLMNOPQRSTUVWXYZ
1234567890 !@#?:;"☆&

Foundry: Typodermic
Designer: Ray Larabie
Nationality: Canadian
Date: 2000

Mexcellent is a trilinear display face inspired by Lance Wyman's font for the Mexico City 1968 Olympic Games. Unlike traditional font families, Mexcellent's supporting styles are available as layers, as opposed to weights, which enables users to draft their own combinations.

Modern 735

ABCDEFGHIJKLMNOPQRSTUVWXYZ
abcdefghijklmnopqrstuvwxyz
1234567890 !@#?:,"*&

Foundry: Bitstream
Designer: Robert Hunter Middleton
Designer Nationality: British
Date: 1936

Modern 735 is Bitstream's version of Bodoni Campanile, a typeface originally designed by Robert Hunter Middleton for the US foundry Ludlow in 1936. Modern 735 is a heavy and compressed interpretation of the high-contrast serif face Bodoni and is available in a single weight.

Modernique

ABCDEFGHIJKLMNOPQRSTUVWXYZ
abcdefghijklmnopqrstuvwxyz
1234567890 !@#?:;""*&

Foundry: American Type Founders
Designer: Morris Fuller Benton
Designer Nationality: American
Date: 1928

Modernique is a decorative display face designed in the style of the early 20th century. The letterforms feature extreme contrasts, with the verticals often much thicker than the horizontal strokes, while smaller details, such as the lowercase tittles, are distinctive in shape.

Monotype Gallia

ABCDEFGHIJKLMNOPQRSTUVWXYZ
1234567890 !@#?:;""*&

Foundry: Monotype
Designer: Wadsworth A. Parker
Designer Nationality: American
Date: 1927 / 1928

Monotype Gallia is a decorative display face, initially designed by Wadsworth A. Parker for the American Type Founders foundry in 1927, before being republished by Monotype in 1928. The characters, with their high-contrast strokes and curled terminals, are typical of 1920s Art Deco lettering.

Mustang Sally

ABCDEFGHIJKLMNOPQRSTUVWXYZ
abcdefghijklmnopqrstuvwxyz
1234567890 !@#?:;"*&

Foundry: Monotype
Designer: Bo Berndal
Designer Nationality: Swedish
Date: 2001

Mustang Sally is a decorative display face that combines strict strokes with liberal outlines. The characters, designed in a single style, feature several quirks, such as the striped interiors and tittles, alongside the expressive ear of the lowercase 'g'.

Netherlands Dirty Numbers

Foundry: Typo Graphic Design
Designer: Manuel Viergutz
Designer Nationality: German
Date: 2017

Netherlands Dirty Numbers is a display face inspired by numeric forms, such as house numbers and graffiti, found by the designer in the Netherlands.

These numbers provided the basis for an alphabet, including upper- and lowercase characters alongside more than forty decorative glyphs.

Newtron ICG

Foundry: Image Club Graphics
Date: 1995

Newtron is an outlined sans serif display font comprising three distinct styles. While each design maintains a similar shape and character, certain

features express their slight variation, such as the alternative letterforms of Newtron Alt, or the open joints of Newtron Open.

Novecento Carved

Foundry: Synthview
Designer: Jan Tonellato
Designer Nationality: Polish
Date: 2016

Novecento Carved is a decorative display face designed as a complementary layer for Synthview's font of 2013, Novecento Sans. The minimal

letterforms, which imitate the shadowing of carved typography, were each manually adjusted to match the existing framework of Novecento Sans.

Nyxali

Foundry: Typodermic
Designer: Ray Larabie
Nationality: Canadian
Date: 2007

Nyxali is a decorative display font produced exclusively in capitals. Individual sans serif characters sit centrally within a squared, textured

oval which, along with the recess at the top of each outline, conjure a stamped design similar to that of military dog tags.

Odin

ABCDEFGHIJKLMNOPQRSTUVWXYZ
abcdefghijklmnopqrstuvwxyz
1234567890 !@#?:;"*&

Foundry: ITC
Designer: Bob Newman
Designer Nationality: British
Date: 1972

Odin is a decorative display face intended exclusively for headlines. Taking its name from the Norse god of war, Odin, the font features strong strokes and weighty serifs, while in the uppercase characters, the shoulder of each letterform is extended, forming a roof over the body.

Old Glory

ABCDEFGHIJKLMNOPQRSTUVWXYZ
ABCDEFGHIJKLMNOPQRSTUVWXYZ

Foundry: Monotype
Designer: Monotype Studio
Date: 2001

Old Glory is a display face designed in upper- and lowercase figures and inspired by the flag of the United States. Unlike conventional type designs, however, the cases of Old Glory are distinguished by pattern, the former being furnished with stars and the latter with stripes.

Owned

ABCDEFGHIJKLMNOPQRSTUVWXYZ
ABCDEFGHIJKLMNOPQRSTUVWXYZ
1234567890 !@#?:;"*&

Foundry: Typodermic
Designer: Ray Larabie
Nationality: Canadian
Date: 2005

Owned is a decorative display font designed to imitate the fast-paced scrawl of graffiti, hence its anti-authoritarian urgency. The font is comprised of two styles, Owned and Owned Concrete, the latter featuring a worn texture typical of fading spray paint.

Permanence

ABCDEFGHIJKLMNOPQRSTUVWXYZ
abcdefghijklmnopqrstuvwxyz
1234567890 !@#?:;"*&

Foundry: Typodermic
Designer: Ray Larabie
Nationality: Canadian
Date: 2012

Permanence is a decorative display font inspired by the lettering of S. Neil Fujita's cover for the book *Future Shock* (1970) written by sociologist and futurologist Alvin Toffler. The narrow shapes and liquid counters are, like Fujita's lettering, modelled on Stanley Davis's Amelia font designed in *c.* 1965.

Philco

ABCDEFGHIJKLMNOPQRSTUVWXYZ
1234567890 !@#?.:"*&

Foundry: Monotype
Designer: Jasper Manchipp
Designer Nationality: British
Date: 1994

The Philco decorative display face was inspired by the Art Deco movement. It comes in capitals only, in two distinct styles: Philco Regular is high in contrast with solid, angular strokes, while Philco Deco features a series of overlapping shapes that emphasize the font's geometry.

Phoebus

ABCDEFGHIJKLMNOPQRSTUVWXYZ
1234567890 !@#?:;"*&

Foundry: Linotype
Designer: Adrian Frutiger
Designer Nationality: Swiss
Date: 1953

Phoebus is a serif display face and one of the first designed by Adrian Frutiger (see p. 290) for the Deberny & Peignot foundry. Sharing its name with the Greek god of light, Phoebus is a shadowed font designed in italicized capitals, the style of which is emphasized by the sharp serifs.

Phosphor

ABCDEFGHIJKLMNOPQRSTUVWXYZ
1234567890 !@#?:;"*8

Foundry: Ludwig & Mayer
Designer: Jakob Erbar
Designer Nationality: German
Date: 1923

Phosphor is a display face based on the glowing letterforms of neon signage, which were first exhibited in 1910 at the Paris Motor Show. As with neon sign characters, Phosphor features a hairline stroke inside a bolder form, mimicking the appearance of the light tube inside its case.

Piercing

ABCDEFGHIJKLMNOPQRSTUVWXYZ
abcdefghijklmnopqrstuvwxyz
1234567890 !@#?:; *d

Foundry: Linotype
Designer: Michael Parson
Designer Nationality: Swiss
Date: 2003

Michael Parson's Piercing is a decorative display face constructed of single weight strokes and ball terminals that imitate the basic forms of a piercing bar. The font features three weights, including Regular, Bold, and an abstracted Code version with deconstructed letterforms.

Pierrot

ABCDEFGHIJKLMNOPQRSTUVWXYZ
abcdefghijklmnopqrstuvwxyz
1234567890 !@#?:;"'*&

Foundry: Linotype
Designer: Günter Jäntsch
Designer Nationality: German
Date: 1973

Inspired by the fluid designs of the 1960s and early 1970s, Pierrot is a decorative display face conceived for editorial headlines and posters. Unlike similar fonts, Pierrot is notable for its precise outlines and sharp stroke endings. Designer Günter Jäntsch also worked as an illustrator and sculptor.

Plotter Wave

ABCDEFGHIJKLMNOPQRSTUVWXYZ
1234567890 \.@#?:;"*&

Foundry: Typotheque
Designer: Nikola Djurek / Gustavo Ferreira
Designer Nationality: Croatian / Brazilian
Date: 2017

Plotter Wave is a sans serif display face inspired by the aesthetic of architectural drawings. The monolinear design utilizes a series of OpenType substitutions, specifically devised by designer Gustavo Ferreira, to order typed letterforms according to the angle of their sloping.

Porkshop

ABCDEFGHIJKLMNOPQRSTUVWXYZ
abcdefghijklmnopqrstuvwxyz
1234567890 !@#?:;"*&

Foundry: Chank Co.
Designer: Chank Diesel
Designer Nationality: American
Date: 2011

First designed in 1997, and expanded in 2011 to include Bold and Italic styles, Porkshop is a serif display face inspired by a vintage "Pork Shop" sign in New York. Mimicking a hand-rendered style, the letterforms combine upper- and lowercase letters into a single character set.

Promdate

ABCDEFGHIJKLMNOPQRSTUVWXYZ
ABCDEFGHIJKLMNOPQRSTUVWXYZ
1234567890 !@#?:;"*&

Foundry: Lunchbox
Designer: Adam Roe
Designer Nationality: American
Date: 1993

Promdate is a decorative display font designed in two styles, including a slightly heightened Tall version. The capitalized letterforms feature flat bases, even in the circular characters, and boast sharp angles in both the strokes and the serifs. The font's name evokes Americana, as does its styling.

Quartz

ABCDEFGHIJKLMNOPQRSTUVWXYZ
1234567890 !@#?;,"*&

Foundry: Letraset
Designer: Letraset Design Studio
Designer Nationality: British
Date: 1970

Quartz is a capitalized typeface based on the digital displays that began to proliferate in the 1960s and 1970s. The electronic letterforms, like those found on the faces of digital clocks, feature segmented strokes that imitate the construction of liquid-crystal display lettering.

Ragtime

ABCDEFGHIJKLMNOPQRSTUVWXYZ
1234567890 !?:,"*&

Foundry: ITC
Designer: Alan Meeks
Designer Nationality: British
Date: 1987

Ragtime is a sans serif display face designed in capitals for elegant yet eccentric headline use. Featuring both subtle shifts in stroke weight, seen particularly in the joints, and fine line shadowing, the letterforms are reminiscent of magazine headline styles from the 1940s.

Refracta

ABCDEFGHIJKLMNOPQRSTUVWXYZ
1234567890 !?:, "*&

Foundry: ITC
Designer: Martin Wait
Designer Nationality: British
Date: 1988

Designed in all caps, Refracta is a condensed display face intended for a variety of uses, from posters to editorials. The italicized sans serif characters, whose hairline strokes initially seem rather timid, are emboldened by a heavy shadow that adds an aesthetic authority.

Retro Bold

ABCDEFGHIJKLMNOPQRSTUVWXYZ
1234567890 !?:,"*&

Foundry: Letraset
Designer: Colin Brignall / Andrew Smith
Designer Nationality: British
Date: 1992

The Retro family, an uppercase slab serif in two weights—Bold and Bold Condensed—was designed for Letraset by Colin Brignall and Andrew Smith in 1992. As its name implies, it was inspired by old design movements, such as Constructivism, the Bauhaus, Art Deco, and Streamline.

Rundfunk

ABCDEFGHIJKLMNOPQRSTUVWXYZ

abcdefghijklmnopqrstuvwxyz

1234567890 !?.;"*&

Foundry: Berthold
Designer: Adolf Behrmann
Designer Nationality: Latvian
Date: 1928

Rundfunk was designed for the Berthold foundry in 1928 by Latvian-born designer Adolf Behrmann. It is a distinctive, heavy sans serif with a low x-height, short descenders and large, exaggerated ascenders. It was revived by Letraset in 1987 and comes in a single bold, roman style.

Salut

ABCDEFGHIJKLMNOPQRSTUVWXYZ

abcdefghijklmnopqrstuvwxyz

1234567890 !@#?:;"*&

Foundry: Klingspor
Designer: Heinrich Johannes Maehler
Designer Nationality: German
Date: 1931

Released by the Offenbach-based foundry Klingspor in 1931, Heinrich Johannes Maehler's Salut is an upright, calligraphic font that connects in a script-style. It is almost a sans serif but for a few of the capitals that have slabs, and comes in a single heavy style.

Samba

ABCDEFGHIJKLMNOPQRSTUVWXYZ

ABCDEFGHIJKLMNOPQRSTUVWXYZ

1234567890 !@#?:;"*&

Foundry: Linotype
Designer: Tony de Marco / Caio de Marco
Designer Nationality: Brazilian
Date: 2003

Samba comes in three styles: Regular, Expert, and Bold. It was designed by brothers Tony and Caio de Marco and inspired by the lettering of José Carlos de Brito e Cunha, a Brazilian illustrator working in the early 20th century. Samba is an exuberant, curly all-caps face with a monolinear regular cut.

Saphir

ABCDEFGHIJKLMNOPQRST

UVWXYZ

1234567890 !@#?:;"*&

Foundry: Stempel
Designer: Hermann Zapf
Designer Nationality: German
Date: 1952

Saphir, known as Sapphire in English-speaking countries, is an all-caps display serif with high-contrast and decorative patterns, made from a central diamond between flourishes, reversed out of the black. It was created by the prolific German designer Hermann Zapf (see p. 574).

Sarcophagus

ABCDEFGHIJKLMNOPQRSTUVWXYZ
abcdefghijklmnopqrstuvwxyz
1234561890 !@#?:;"*&

Foundry: T-26
Designer: Alexander McCracken
Designer Nationality: American
Date: 2004

Sarcophagus was designed by Alexander McCracken for the T-26 foundry and named after decorative stone coffins used in ancient Egypt. It is an intricate, Blackletter-inspired typeface with a spiky, gothic feel. It comes in Regular and Bold weights and has a monolinear construction.

Shaman

ABCDEFGHIJKLMNOPQRSTUVWXYZ
1234567890 !?:;""*&

Foundry: Letraset
Designer: Phill Grimshaw
Designer Nationality: British
Date: 1994

The work of British designer Phill Grimshaw, and released by Letraset and ITC, Shaman is an all-caps display font with a jagged inline. Grimshaw was aiming for a primitive feel, and the font also includes decorative borders and illustrative dingbats inspired by cave paintings.

Sharquefin

ABCDEFGHIJKLMNOPQRSTUVWXYZ
abcdefghijklmnopqrstuvwxyz
1234567890 !@#?:;"*&

Foundry: Linotype
Designer: Gary Tennant
Designer Nationality: British
Date: 2004

Sharquefin, by British type designer Gary Tennant, is one of two fonts he designed for Linotype. It is a postmodern display typeface that comes in two styles, Regular and Oblique. It features shapes that stick out of most of the letters like a shark's fin and was designed for fun use.

Shatter

ABCDEFGHIJKLMNOPQRSTUVWXYZ
abcdefghijklmnopqrstuvwxyz
1234567890 !?:;""*&

Foundry: Letraset
Designer: Vic Carless
Designer Nationality: British
Date: 1973

Shatter font was one of twenty winners of an international competition held by Letraset in 1973 and judged by leading designers Herb Lubalin (see p. 62), Derek Birdsall, Roger Excoffon, Colin Forbes, Armin Hofmann, and Marcello Minale. Shatter is a diagonally fractured, bold sans serif.

Siesta

ABCDEFGHIJKLMNOPQRSTUVWXYZ
abcdefghijklmnopqrstuvwxyz
1234567890 !@#?:;"'*&

Foundry: Aerotype
Designer: Steve Miggas
Designer Nationality: American
Date: 1995

US type designer Steve Miggas created Siesta for Aerotype in 1995. It is a single-style display font that is bold and inspired by lettering made using traditional printing techniques such as woodcut and linocut. It has upper- and lowercase letters, and rough, imperfect edges.

Sinah

ABCDEFGHIJKLMNOPQRSTUV
abcdefghijklmnopqrstuvwxyz
1234567890 !@#?:;"'*&

Foundry: Linotype
Designer: Peter Huschka
Designer Nationality: German
Date: 1994

A rounded ornamental font, created by artist Peter Huschka, Sinah has an Asian feel. Many of its strokes end in teardrop forms and none of its characters share a common baseline, meaning that it should be used with generous line spacing, and at sizes of 12 point or above.

Slipstream

ABCDEFGHIJKLMNOPQRSTUVWXYZ
1234567890 !?:;"'*&

Foundry: Letraset
Designer: Letraset Type Studio
Designer Nationality: British
Date: 1985

Slipstream, developed in-house by the Letraset Type Studio, is based on an italic sans serif. As the name suggests, its horizontal lines look like streaks left behind as the letters speed off to the right of the page. Characters can be slightly overlapped without losing the impression of movement.

Sprint

ABCDEFGHIJKLMNOPQRSTUVWXYZ
abcdefghijklmnopqrstuvwxyz
1234567890 !@#?:;"'*&

Foundry: VGC
Designer: Aldo Novarese
Designer Nationality: Italian
Date: 1974

A stylized forward-leaning display face created by the noted Italian type designer Aldo Novarese, Sprint was also the inspiration for the fonts Starlet and Star, both released in 2007 by Gestalten and created by the Berlin-based designer and VJ (video jockey) Critzla.

Syllogon

ABCDEFGHIJKLMNOPQRSTUVWXYZ
abcdefghijklmnopqrstuvwxyz
1234567890 !@#?:;"*&

Foundry: Image Club Graphics
Designer: Patricia Lillie
Designer Nationality: American
Date: 1995

Syllogon is just one of the many mainly display faces created by the prolific Ohio-based writer and type designer Patricia Lillie. This quirky, rectangular-based design is available in two weights: the very angular Syllogon Hard, and Syllogon Soft, which has more curves.

Syrup

abcdefghijklmnopqrstuvwxyz
1234567890 !@#?:;"*&

Foundry: Neutura
Designer: Alexander McCracken
Designer Nationality: American
Date: 2001

Syrup was created by the founder of Neutura (see p. 472), the San Francisco-based designer Alexander McCracken. The typeface is available in a single weight. Its very stylized and playful display face is based on the semi-abstract forms generated by bending paperclips.

System X3

ABCDEFGHIJKLMNOPQRSTUVWXYZ
1234567890 !@#?:;"*&

Foundry: Monotype
Designer: Paul Prue
Designer Nationality: British
Date: 1994

System X3 is a highly futuristic display typeface designed for the Agfa Type Creative Alliance by Paul Prue. He also designed the similarly science-fiction influenced Eon Age, Galaxy, Run and Logan in the same year. System X3 is available in a single weight and as uppercase only.

Tangerine

ABCDEFGHIJKLMNOPQRST
UVWXYZ
1234567890 !@#?:;"*&

Foundry: ITC
Designer: Tomi Haaparanta
Designer Nationality: Finnish
Date: 2001

A bulbous display face with many top-heavy characters, Tangerine is one of a number of display faces created by Finnish designer Tomi Haaparant. He began designing typefaces in 1990, founded the Suomi Type Foundry in 2005 and teaches type design at the University of Industrial Arts in Helsinki.

Tango

ABCDEFGHIJKLMNOPQRSTUVWXYZ
abcdefghijklmnopqrstuvwxyz
1234567890 !@#?:;”*&

Foundry: Letraset
Designer: Colin Brignall
Designer Nationality: British
Date: 1974

Tango was probably inspired by Joe Caroff's logo for the movie *Last Tango in Paris* (1972). Tango's playful curves and swashes made it a popular choice for many dance music LP covers from the 1970s. URW released a version that includes a second set of unswashed caps and is called Theia.

Tropica Script

ABCDEFGHIJKLMNOPQRSTUVWXYZ
abcdefghijklmnopqrstuvwxyz
1234567890 !?:;”*&

Foundry: Letraset
Designer: Vince Whitlock
Designer Nationality: British
Date: 1988

Tropica Script, created by British type designer Vince Whitlock for his employers Letraset in 1988, is an outlined italic connecting-script available in a single style. The thick outlines give Tropica Script the look of a retro neon sign. It was published by both Letraset and ITC.

Tugboat Annie

ABCDEFGHIJKLMNOPQRSTUVWXYZ
abcdefghijklmnopqrstuvwxyz
1234567890 !@#?:;”*&

Foundry: Monotype
Designer: Nick Curtis
Designer Nationality: American
Date: 2001

Tugboat Annie, named after a black and white comedy film released in 1933, was designed by Nick Curtis in 2001. It comes in a single heavy style and is a high-contrast, wide serif font with many quirky features, such as the small vertical strokes that stick out of some letters.

Umbra

ABCDEFGHIJKLMNOPQRSTUVWXYZ
1234567890 !@#?:;”*&

Foundry: Ludlow
Designer: Robert Hunter Middleton
Designer Nationality: British
Date: 1935

Umbra, designed for Ludlow in 1935, is an uppercase only sans serif whose letters were taken from an earlier Robert Hunter Middleton typeface, Tempo (1930), and are defined only by the existence of a drop shadow. Berthold released a shadow-only sans serif also called Umbra the same year.

University Roman

ABCDEFGHIJKLMNOPQRSTUVWXYZ
abcdefghijklmnopqrstuvwxyz
1234567890 !@#?:;"*&

University Roman, designed by Mike Daines in 1972, was inspired by Speedball-lettering. In 1984, it was updated by two Letraset staff; Phillip Kelly added swash alternatives and Freda Sack drew an italic. Available in regular, italic, and bold, it has small sharp serifs and a large x-height.

Foundry: Letraset
Designer: Mike Daines / Phillip Kelly / Freda Sack
Designer Nationality: British
Date: 1972

Vegas

ABCDEFGHIJKLMNOPQRSTUVWXYZ
abcdefghijklmnopqrstuvwxyz
1234567890 !?:;"*&

By the British designer David Quay, co-founder with Freda Sack of The Foundry (see p. 284), Vegas is a decorative italic script with a 3D effect created by outlines, highlights and shadows. Vegas, which suits its glitzy name, is non-connecting but its lowercase can be tightly set.

Foundry: Letraset
Designer: David Quay
Designer Nationality: British
Date: 1984

Victorian

ABCDEFGHIJKLMNOPQRSTUVWXYZ
abcdefghijklmnopqrstuvwxyz
1234567890 !@#?:;"*&

Victorian, developed by Letraset designer Freda Sack and directed by Colin Brignall, is a decorative, ornate serif inspired by the 19th-century font Victoria, which was released by the German foundry Schriftgiesserei Flinsch. Nick Belshaw later added an Inline Shaded display version.

Foundry: Letraset
Designer: Freda Sack / Nick Belshaw
Designer Nationality: British
Date: 1976

Warmer

ABCDEFGHIJKLMNOPQRSTUVWXYZ
ABCDEFGHIJKLMNOPQRSTUVWXYZ
1234567890 !@#?:;"*&

Ray Larabie's Warmer is a chunky, counter-less, all uppercase, sans serif display face, which looks like it was constructed by cutting paper with scissors. The family includes three fonts: a solid base version plus Check and Cross, both of which can be layered on top to give a plaid look.

Foundry: Typodermic
Designer: Ray Larabie
Designer Nationality: Canadian
Date: 2010

Wavy Rounded BT

ABCDEFGHIJKLMNOPQRSTUVWXYZ
abcdefghijklmnopqrstuvwxyz
1234567890 !@#?:;"*&

Foundry: Bitstream
Designer: Hajime Kawakami
Designer Nationality: Japan
Date: 2004

Japanese industrial designer turned graphic designer Hajime Kawakami created Wavy Rounded BT for Bitstream in 2004. It is an eccentric, rounded sans serif available in a single, extra-bold weight. Many letters feature small notches or steps that gives the font its wavy appearance.

Westwood

ABCDEFGHIJKLMNOPQRSTUVWXYZ
abcdefghijklmnopqrstuvwxyz
1234567890 !?::"*&

Foundry: Letraset
Designer: David Westwood
Designer Nationality: American
Date: 1991

David Westwood, a US designer based on the West Coast, designed this eponymous typeface for Letraset in 1991. Westwood is a bold, linocut-style display sans serif and is available in a single style. It features highlights and rough edges, which give it a hand-hewn look.

Whassis

ABCDEFGHIJKLMN©PQRSTUVWXYZ
abcdefghijklmn©pqrstuvwxyz
1234567890 !@#?:;"*&

Foundry: Image Club Graphics
Designer: Patricia Lillie
Designer Nationality: American
Date: 1995

Designed in 1995 for Image Club Graphics by Patricia Lillie, a US designer best known for her dingbat fonts, Whassis is a distinctive serif typeface with jagged edges and a spiral "O" and "o." It comes in two styles, Calm and Frantic, and the latter has dots and triangles floating around glyphs.

Wind

Foundry: Typotheque
Designer: Hansje van Halem / Peter Biľak
Designer Nationality: Dutch / Slovakian
Date: 2017

Wind, by Amsterdam-based designer Hansje van Halem, is an experimental typeface created from lines facing the same direction. Its four styles—NE, NW, SE, and SW—equate to the direction the strokes point. A variable font version allows the user total control over the angle the lines face.

BB-Bureau

The BB-Bureau foundry, based in Nantes, France, was established by the independent graphic and type designer Benoît Bodhuin, and offers an eclectic and highly innovative range of display types that challenge the conventions of legibility yet which are enthused with great wit and a dynamic playfulness.

Each is a typographical experiment, yet all have a high degree of mathematical integrity thanks to Bodhuin's passion for geometrical patterns developed from his earlier studies in mathematics ‖at university. He was subsequently able to channel these interests in a new direction at design school. His typefaces are developed from a range of ideas, from hand-drawn sketches to geometric shapes, and

his rigour and experimentation lead to typefaces of great distinction and integrity.

Typefaces of note include Elastik, a grotesk with elastic punctuation and diacritical mark in four styles: A (small), B (normal), C (big), and D (very too big). Other notable typefaces are Standard and Pickle Standard (see p. 436), both grid-inspired designs, and Brutal, a stencil calligraphic typeface designed in light, regular, and bold.

Founded: 2004
Country: France
Website: bb-bureau.fr
Notable typefaces:
Brutal (see p. 547)
Pickle Standard (see p. 436)
Standard (see p. 440)

Below. *Toulouse en vue[s]* exhibition branding, employing an extruded Mineral designed by Vif Design, Toulouse, France.

Below. bb-book B typeface specimen designed by Benoît Bodhuin.

Left. Poster design for Hellavision Television by US designer Peter Steineck employing BB Book.

Below. Marianne poster, a multi-layered titling typeface by BB-Bureau. Available in three styles (Inline, Solid and Outline).

Above. Large format BB-Bureau font catalogue, limited edition of 200 numbered copies. Design by Benoît Bodhuin.

Woodkit Print

ABCDEFGHIJKLMNOPQRSTUVWXYZ
1234567890 !@#?:;"*&

Foundry: Typotheque
Designer: Ondrej Jób
Designer Nationality: Slovakian
Date: 2014

Ondrej Jób's Woodkit Print is a worn version of Woodkit and collects four eclectic wood-type inspired fonts. Letterpress, the primary style, combines Tuscan, slab serif, reverse-contrast, and other type genres in the same font. There is also the more distressed Woodkit Reprint.

Zaragoza

ABCDEFGHIJKLMNOPQRSTUVW
abcdefghijklmnopqrstuvwxyz
1234567890 !?:;"*&

Foundry: Letraset
Designer: Phill Grimshaw
Designer Nationality: British
Date: 1995

Phill Grimshaw's font Zaragoza is named after the city in the Aragon region of Spain, and was designed for Letraset in 1995. It is a decorative, non-connecting serif script with inlaid zigzag decorations reversed out of the black. It has wide, swashed capitals and is best used at large sizes.

Zigzag

ABCDEFGHIJKLMNOPQRSTUVWXYZ
1234567890 !@#?:;"*&

Foundry: BB-Bureau
Designer: Benoît Bodhuin
Designer Nationality: French
Date: 2012

Benoît Bodhuin designed Zigzag for Le Vivat theatre near Lille in a single Rounded style. In 2012, it was originally published by Volcano Type with an additional Not Rounded version. Both fonts come with four forms of each letter; a simple uppercase sans serif, and three alternate distorted versions.

Zinjaro

ABCDEFGHIJKLMNOPQRSTUVWXYZ
1234567890 !?:;"*&

Foundry: Letraset
Designer: Carol Kemp
Designer Nationality: British
Date: 1994

Zinjaro, which was available from both Letraset and ITC, was created by British designer Carol Kemp in 1994. It is an uppercase display face with an exotic feel thanks to its inlaid patterns and ornaments. Zinjaro has slightly rough, bumpy edges and comes in a single heavy style.

Addlethorpe

ABCDEFGHIJKLMNOPQRSTUVWXYZ
abcdefghijklmnopqrstuvwxyz
1234567890 !@#?:;'"*&

Foundry: Typodermic
Designer: Ray Larabie
Designer Nationality: Canadian
Date: 2008

Addlethorpe is a layered typeface that allows designers to tailor its appearance in use. It is based on the physical appearance of metal type letters.

The letterforms themselves are based on Winthorpe, a more conventional design by Ray Larabie which he published the previous year.

Badoni

ABCDEFGHIJKLMNOPQRSTUVWXYZ
abcdefghijklmnopqrstuvwxyz
1234567890 !@#?:;'"*&

Foundry: Chank Co.
Designer: Chank Diesel
Designer Nationality: American
Date: 1993

Badoni was designed by Chank Diesel for *Cake*, a grunge music fanzine of which he was creative director at the time. As implied by its name, Badoni

is a heavily distorted and distressed typeface based on the forms of modern serifs such as Bodoni but set on an irregular baseline.

Blockade

ABCDEFGHIJKLMNOPQRSTUVWXYZ
1234567890 !@#?:;"*&

Foundry: Monotype
Designer: Hans Bacher
Designer Nationality: American
Date: 2001

Blockade was designed by Hans Bacher, a German animator based in California, who works for Disney and is a member of the Academy of Motion Picture

Arts and Sciences. This grungy display sans is one of several decorative typefaces produced by Bacher for Monotype.

Burnaby

ABCDEFGHIJKLMNOPQRSTUVWXYZ
abcdefghijklmnopqrstuvwxyz
1234567890 !@#?:;"*&

Foundry: Typodermic
Designer: Ray Larabie
Designer Nationality: Canadian
Date: 2007

This graffiti-inspired stencil typeface by Typodermic founder Ray Larabie features irregularities and imperfections reminiscent of the spray painting

process. An OpenType font, it offers a range of custom letter pairings to create a convincingly uneven and informal effect.

Ceroxa

ABCDEFGHIJKLMNOPQRSTUVWXYZ
abcdefghijklmnopqrstuvwxyz
1234567890 !@#?:,"*&

Foundry: Typodermic
Designer: Ray Larabie
Designer Nationality: Canadian
Date: 2006

Another stencil design by Typodermic founder Ray Larabie, Ceroxa features degraded details. The typeface makes use of OpenType features that allow for automatic ligatures, inserting custom letter pairings within text set in Ceroxa for a more random and irregular effect.

Chandler 42

ABCDEFGHIJKLMNOPQRSTUVWXYZ
abcdefghijklmnopqrstuvwxyz
1234567890 !@#?:;"*&

Foundry: Psy/Ops
Designer: Steve Mehallo
Designer Nationality: American
Date: 1994

This typewriter font was developed by US designer Steve Mehallo, and is based on the letters created by a portable typewriter from 1942. Mehallo's meticulous approach to the reproduction of its type resulted in a convincingly irregular font that is available in several weights.

Chinese Rocks

ABCDEFGHIJKLMNOPQRSTUVWXYZ
ABCDEFGHIJKLMNOPQRSTUVWXYZ
1234567890 !@#?:;"*+

Foundry: Typodermic
Designer: Ray Larabie
Designer Nationality: Canadian
Date: 1999

The design of this rough-hewn display typeface was based on the hand-cut lettering seen on shipping containers from China. Purposefully irregular, Chinese Rocks is available in a range of weights and styles, from Fine to Bold and Condensed to Fat, plus two shaded versions.

Chrysotile

ABCDEFGHIJKLMNOPQRSTUVWXYZ
ABCDEFGHIJKLMNOPQRSTUVWXYZ
1234567890 !@#?!;"*&

Foundry: Typodermic
Designer: Ray Larabie
Designer Nationality: Canadian
Date: 2008

Featuring sans serif uppercase letterforms reversed out of blocky tiles, this display font by Ray Larabie provides a tactile hand-printed effect for headlines. As with many Typodermic designs, it exploits OpenType functionality to swap in alternate characters as required.

Croteau

ABCDEFGHIJKLMNOPQRSTUVWXYZ
ABCDEFGHIJKLMNOPQRSTUVWXYZ
1234567890 !@#?:;"*&

Foundry: Typodermic
Designer: Ray Larabie
Designer Nationality: Canadian
Date: 1995

Reportedly based on old film posters, Croteau by Ray Larabie is a slightly distressed sans serif with a subtle forward incline. It features a range of ligatures, allowing letters to stack and sit closely within each other's space, adding a decorative element to headlines.

Crusti

ABCDEFGHIJKLMNOPQRSTUVWXYZ
abcdefghijklmnopqrstuvwxyz
1234567890 !@#?:;"*&

Foundry: Chank Co.
Designer: Chank Diesel
Designer Nationality: American
Date: 1993

Designed by Chank Diesel, the thoroughly distressed letterforms of Crusti were created by distorting type through a repeated process of photocopying. Diesel created two additional similar fonts, Crustier and Crustiest, with each providing an increase in weight and distortion.

Crustier

ABCDEFGHIJKLMNOPQRSTUVWXYZ
abcdefghijklmnopqrstuvwxyz
1234567890 !@#?:;"*&

Foundry: Chank Co.
Designer: Chank Diesel
Designer Nationality: American
Date: 1993

Chank Diesel's Crustier is part of a family that also contains Crusti, Crustiest and Crusti Wacky. It is a grungy, display serif with a large x-height and a distressed effect. It is bolder than Crusti, but lighter than Crustiest, and was made using a photocopier machine at a Kinko's store.

Crustiest

ABCDEFGHIJKLMNOPQRSTUVWXYZ
abcdefghijklmnopqrstuvwxyz
1234567890 !@#?:;"*&

Foundry: Chank Co.
Designer: Chank Diesel
Designer Nationality: American
Date: 1993

The Crusti family, of which Crustiest is the heaviest weight, was designed by Chank Diesel in 1993 for *Cake*, a fanzine celebrating grunge music. It was inspired by the rough DIY ethos that surrounded the grunge scene. Crustiest features lots of fine dirt and grime around its glyphs.

Dirtstorm

ABCDEFGHIJKLMNOPQRSTUVWXYZ
ABCDEFGHIJKLMNOPQRSTUVWXYZ
1234567890 !@#?:;"'*&

Foundry: Typodermic
Designer: Ray Larabie
Designer Nationality: Canadian
Date: 2007

A grungy, uneven spraypainted stencil font, and one of a number of stencil fonts designed by Typodermic's Ray Larabie, Dirtstorm is available in one weight and in uppercase. The font's legibility is deliberately low, making it suitable for display purposes only.

Ebenezer

ABCDEFGHIJKLMNOPQRSTUVWXYZ
ABCDEFGHIJKLMNOPQRSTUVWXYZ
1234567890 !@#?:;"*&

Foundry: Typodermic
Designer: Ray Larabie
Designer Nationality: Canadian
Date: 2008

Ray Larabie has described Ebenezer as "an eerie, detailed font." Its letterforms are based on another Typodermic font, Goldburg, which was inspired by the lettering found on Idaho's historical roadside markers. The marker scheme was launched in 1956, with lettering designed by George Bowditch.

Edifact

ABCDEFGHIJKLMNOPQRSTUVWXYZ
abcdefghijklmnopqrstuvwxyz
1234567890 !@#?:;"*&

Foundry: Typodermic
Designer: Ray Larabie
Designer Nationality: Canadian
Date: 2007

Edifact is a scratchy computer font that looks like it should belong on an obsolete computer from the 1960s. Its creator, Typodermic's Ray Larabie, has described it as being 'a severely damaged 1960s style techno font'. The font's poor legibility means it is suitable for display purposes only.

Emory

ABCDEFGHIJKLMNOPQRSTUVWXYZ
abcdefghijklmnopqrstuvwxyz
1234567890 !@#?:;"*&

Foundry: Typodermic
Designer: Ray Larabie
Designer Nationality: Canadian
Date: 2005

Emory is a typeface that looks like it has been torn from scraps of paper—there are no clean edges or right angles. Ray Larabie says his creation is "easy to grip and rather rough." The OpenType version offers class-based kerning and auto-ligatures. It is suitable for display purposes only.

Eroxion BT

ABCDEFGHIJKLMNOPQRSTUVWXYZ
abcdefghijklmnopqrstuvwxyz
1234567890 !@#?:;"'*&

Foundry: Bitstream
Designer: Eduardo Manso
Designer Nationality:
Argentinian
Date: 1997

This grunge font was created by Argentinian-born designer Eduardo Manso, who runs the EmType foundry in Barcelona. Eroxion channels degenerative typographic design, inspired by techniques first explored by designers such as Neville Brody and Erik van Blokland aka LettError.

F2F El Dee Cons

ABCDEFGHIJKLMNOPQRSTUVWX
abcdefghijklmnopqrstuvwxyz
1234567890 !@#?:;"'*&

Foundry: Face2Face
Designer: Thomas Nagel
Designer Nationality: German
Date: 1993

A layered, disjointed, and primarily experimental typeface, El Dee Cons is part of the Face2Face series created by the collective formed by Thomas Nagel and his friends. Many of the foundry's typefaces featured in layouts for *Frontpage*, the leading 1990s German techno magazine.

F2F Entebbe

ABCDEFGHIJKLMNOPQrsTUVWeX
aBcDefg#ijKLMnOPqrsTUVwxyz
1234567890 /\#?:;"'*&

Foundry: Face2Face
Designer: Alexander Branczyk
Designer Nationality: German
Date: 1995

Alexander Branczyk has designed a distressed ransom-note-style typeface, comprised of juxtaposed characters from different typefaces. Operation Entebbe was a successful counterterrorist hostage-rescue mission carried out by the Israel Defense Forces at Entebbe Airport, Uganda in 1976.

F2F OCRAlexczyk

ABCDEFGHIJKLMNOPQRSTUVWXYZ
abcdefghijklmnopqrstuvwxyz
1234567890 !@#?:;"'*&

Foundry: Face2Face
Designer: Alexander Branczyk
Designer Nationality: German
Date: 1995

This is Face2Face co-founder Alexander Branczyk's take on the classic OCR-A, designed by American Type Founders for the US National Bureau of Standards in 1968. OCRAlexczyk also has a sister typeface by the same designer for Face2Face, OCRAlexczyk Shake.

F2F Screen Scream

ABCDEFGHIJKLMNOPQRSTUVWXYZ
abcdefghijklmnopqrstuvwxyz
1234567890 !@#?:;"*&

Foundry: Face2Face
Designer: Thomas Nagel
Designer Nationality: German
Date: 1997

Screen Scream is an experimental typeface that is based on a textured screen aesthetic. It is part of the Face2Face series created by the collective formed by Thomas Nagel and his friends. Many of the foundry's typefaces featured in layouts for *Frontpage*, the leading German techno magazine.

F2F Tyrell Corp

ABCDEFGHIJKLMNOPQRSTUVWXY
abcdefghijklmnopqrstuvwxyz
1234567890 ! ?:;"*&

Foundry: Face2Face
Designer: Thomas Nagel
Designer Nationality: German
Date: 1997

This mechanical, layered font by Face2Face founder Thomas Nagel is named after a fictional biotechnology firm, Tyrell Corporation, which features in Ridley Scott's science-fiction epic *Blade Runner* (1982). In the film, the company manufactures androids, known as replicants.

FF Confidential

ABCDEFGHIJKLMNOPQRSTUVWXYZ
ABCDEFGHIJKLMNOPQRSTUVWXYZ
1234567890 !@#?:;"*&

Foundry: FontFont
Designer: Just van Rossum
Designer Nationality: Dutch
Date: 1992

FF Confidential is the work of Dutch designer and educator Just van Rossum. It is an uppercase, distressed sans serif available in a single style. The lowercase glyphs provide an alternate, rougher alphabet. The ghostly, thin lettering evokes the feel of documentation in spy films and thrillers.

Flyswim

ABCDEFGHIJKLMNOPQRSTUVWXYZ
abcdefghijklmnopqrstuvwxyz
1234567890 !@#?:;"*&

Foundry: Typodermic
Designer: Ray Larabie
Designer Nationality: Canadian
Date: 2007

Flyswim was created by prolific Canadian typeface designer Ray Larabie in 2007, and released by his foundry Typodermic. It is a single style, distressed san serif with built-in drop shadows. Its 3D effect and sketchy roughness means that Flyswim does not work well at smaller point sizes.

Gnuolane Grind

ABCDEFGHIJKLMNOPQRSTUVWXYZ
abcdefghijklmnopqrstuvwxyz
1234567890 !@#?:;"*&

Foundry: Typodermic
Designer: Ray Larabie
Designer Nationality: Canadian
Date: 2007

Gnuolane Grind is a distressed, rough-edged version of Ray Larabie's Gnuolane, a headline sans serif inspired by 19th-century grotesques but described by its creator as having a "superelliptical sixties sneer "Gnuolane Grind is available in two weights: Regular and Bold.

Goodies

ABCDEFGHIJKLMNOPQRSTUVWXYZ
ABCDEFGHIJKLMNOPQRST UVWXYZ.
1234567890 ! ?:;"*&

Foundry: Linotype
Designer: Anne Boskamp
Designer Nationality: German
Date: 2003

Goodies is a unique, illustrative typeface inspired by the work of Spanish artist Joan Miró. It comes in two styles: A and B. The typeface was the second font released by designer Anne Boskamp and her first, Merlin, had been a winner in the Linotype International Digital Type Design Contest in 1994.

Green

ABCDEFGHIJKLMNOPQRSTUVWXYZ
abcdefghijklmnopqrstuvwxyz
1234567890 !?:;"*G

Foundry: ITC / Letraset
Designer: Timothy Donaldson
Designer Nationality: British
Date: 1995

Timothy Donaldson's Green was released in 1995 by both ITC and Letraset. It is a single-weight postmodern, display sans serif with angular features and irregular contrast, which makes it better used at large sizes. Green is similar to Pink, another Donaldson font from a year earlier.

Hit

ABCDEFGHIJKLMNOPQRSTUVWXYZ
abcdefghijklmnopqrstuvwxyz
1234567890 !@#?:;"*&

Foundry: Typodermic
Designer: Ray Larabie
Designer Nationality: Canadian
Date: 2008

Described by its creator, the prolific Canadian type designer Ray Larabie, as "crunchy and primed for fun," Hit is a single-style, rough-edged informal sans serif. Its idiosyncratic forms are heavy, and its edges are bumpy. The legs of the "R," "K," "f," and "h" hang below the baseline.

Hot Plate

ABCDEFGHIJ-KLMNOPQRSTUVWXYZ
ffcdefghi-jklmnopqrstuvw.xyz
1934567890 !@ ?:, *&

Foundry: Linotype
Designer: Nico Hensel /
Timo Brauchle
Designer Nationality: German
Date: 2002

German designers Nico Hensel and Timo Brauchle created Hot Plate in 2002. It comes in ten variants and also includes a dingbat symbol font in the same style. Hot Plate is a distinctive, distressed typeface whose many versions can be mixed to create a effect akin to a ransom note.

ITC Coventry

ABCDEFGHIJKLMNOPQRSTUVWXYZ
abcdefghijklmnopqrstuvwxyz
1234567890 !@#?:;"*&

Foundry: ITC
Designer: Brian Sooy
Designer Nationality: American
Date: 1998

Brian Sooy's ITC Coventry is a distressed sans serif with the appearance of cheaply photocopied text. It comes in three weights and was named in honor of fliers found in Coventry Village, a bohemian suburb of Cleveland Heights, Ohio. Sooy now works under the name Altered Ego Fonts.

ITC Don't Panic

ABCDEFGHIJKLMNOPQRSTUVWXYZ
ABCDEFGHIJKLMNOPQRSTUVWXYZ
1234567890 !@#?:;"*&

Foundry: ITC
Designer: Wayne Thompson
Designer Nationality: Australian
Date: 1995

Wayne Thompson, an Australian designer, teacher and typographer, got the inspiration for ITC Don't Panic from the lettering stamped on envelopes. It is an uppercase, outlined and distressed sans serif that also features random square shapes alongside some letters, adding texture.

ITC Outback

ABCDEFGHIJKLMNOPQRSTUVWXYZ
abcdefghijklmnopqrstuvwxyz
1234567890 !@#?:;"*&

Foundry: ITC
Designer: Bob Alonso
Designer Nationality: American
Date: 1997

Bob Alonso's ITC Outback is a heavy, compact sans serif along the lines of Rudolph Koch's Neuland of 1923, yet with the rough, distressed-looking edges that were common during the 1990s. Alonso, who died in 2007, was a graduate of New York's School of Visual Arts, where he studied font design.

ITC Panic

ABCDEFGHIJKLMNOPQRSTUVWXYZ
ABCDEFGHIJKLMNOPQRSTUVWXYZ
1234567890 !@#?:;"*&

Foundry: ITC
Designer: Wayne Thompson
Designer Nationality: Australian
Date: 2000

Five years after Wayne Thompson designed ITC Don't Panic he decided to create ITC Panic, an even rougher and more distressed version of the uppercase outlined sans serif. He went on to found the Australian Type Foundry in 2002. Panic has alternate characters on a shifted baseline.

ITC Pious Henry

ABCDEFGHIJKLMNOPQRSTUVWXYZ
abcdefghijklmnopqrstuvwxyz
1234567890 !@#?:;"*&

Foundry: ITC
Designer: Eric Stevens
Designer Nationality: American
Date: 1997

ITC Pious Henry is a single-style distressed sans serif font whose letters have a random energy thanks to an inconsistent baseline and subtly different angles throughout. Its designer, the South Carolina-born Eric Stevens, describes it as evoking "a feeling of the rural South."

ITC Schizoid

ABCDEFGHIJKLMNOPQRSTUVWXYZ
abcdefghijklmnopqrstuvwxyz
1234567890 !@#?:;"*&

Foundry: ITC
Designer: Frank Marciuliano
Designer Nationality: American
Date: 1997

As the name implies, Frank Marciuliano's font ITC Schizoid is an eccentric, unbalanced and unconventional typeface. It is rough and angular with high contrast; its thin, fine strokes suddenly become wide and blocky, and small, spindly spikes that appear hand-drawn jut out at random.

Lavaman

ABCDEFGHIJKLMNOPQRSTUVWXYZ
abcdefghijklmnopqrstuvwxyz
1234567890 !@#?:;"*&

Foundry: Chank Co.
Designer: Chank Diesel
Designer Nationality: American
Date: 1995

Available in a single style, and published by Chank Diesel's foundry Chank Co., Lavaman is a craggy, rough-edged display sans serif. The single weight available is bold, and it has a high x-height, short ascenders and capitals that are barely taller than the lowercase letters.

Linotype Compendio

ABCDEFGHIJKLMNOPQRSTUVWXYZ
abcdefghijklmnopqrstuvwxyz
1234567890 !@#?:;"*&

Foundry: Linotype
Designer: Christian Bauer
Designer Nationality: German
Date: 1997

Linotype Compendio, by German designer Christian Bauer, is based on the forms of transitional serif faces of the 17th century and has rough, imperfect edges that give it an aged look. Available in regular and italic, it has Old Style numerals and large tittles, or dots, for "i" and "j."

Linotype Fluxus

ABCDEFGHIJKLMNOPQRSTUVWXYZ
abcdefghijklmnopqrstuvwxyz
1234567890 !@#?:;"*&

Foundry: Linotype
Designer: Andreas Karl
Designer Nationality: German
Date: 1997

Linotype Fluxus is a distressed display face, which was initially submitted by designer Andreas Karl for Linotype's International Digital Type Design Contest. Intended for headlines, Linotype Fluxus features erratic strokes, reminiscent of the inconsistency of ink, within a solid yet irregular structure.

Linotype Fresh Ewka

ABCDEFGHIJKLMNOPQRSTUVWXYZ
abcdefghijklmnopqrstuvwxyz
1234567890 !?:;"&

Foundry: Linotype
Designer: Dariusz Nowak-Nova
Designer Nationality: Polish
Date: 1997

Linotype Fresh Ewka is a display typeface designed to balance a variety of distinct stroke styles. The characters, in both Dry and Hot weights, feature a harmony of single hairlines, or triple hairlines in the thicker Hot version, squares and brushlike strokes. The typeface is part of Linotype's TakeType Library.

Linotype Invasion

ABCDEFGHIJKLMNOPQRSTUVWXYZ
ABCDEFGHIJKLMNOPQRSTUVWXYZ
1234567890 !@#?:;"*ET

Foundry: Linotype
Designer: Hellmut G. Bomm
Designer Nationality: German
Date: 2002

Linotype Invasion is a display typeface inspired by the letterforms found on Britain's Bayeux Tapestry, which recounts the Norman invasion of England in the 11th century. The font family comprises three versions—Harold, Wilhelm, and Rex—alongside a heraldic Animals style.

Linotype Laika

ABCDEFGHIJKLMNOPQRSTUVWXYZ
abcdefghijklmnopqrstuvwxyz
1234567890 !@?:;"*&

Foundry: Linotype
Designer: Mark van Wageningen
Designer Nationality: Dutch
Date: 1997

Linotype Laika is a display font that is informed by the design of a sans serif but with misshapen, wavy strokes. The undulation of the characters mimics the movement of water while the letters seem to drift independently in their own space when placed next to one another.

Linotype MMistel

ABCDEFGHIJKLMNOPQRSTUVWXYZ
1234567890 !#?:;"*&

Foundry: Linotype
Designer: Kerstin Fritsche
Designer Nationality: German
Date: 1997

Linotype MMistel is a display font that imitates the forms of the mistletoe plant and was acquired by Linotype after its entry into the company's International Digital Type Design Contest in 1999. Its letterforms combine separate, tapering stems with decorative dots like berries.

Linotype Not Painted

ABCDEFGHIJKLMNOPQRSTUVWXYZ
ABCDEFGHIJKLMNOPQRSTUVWXYZ
1234567890 !?:;" *&

Foundry: Linotype
Designer: Robert Bucan
Designer Nationality: American
Date: 1997

Linotype Not Painted is an energetic display font that combines multiple typographic layers. For the capitals, two uppercase styles sit on top of one another. The lowercase letters, alternately, layer one uppercase and one lowercase letterform in the same style.

Linotype Red Babe

ABCDEFGHIJKLMNOPQRSTUVWXYZ
abcdefghijklmnopqrstuvwxyz
1234567890 !@?:;"

Foundry: Linotype
Designer: Moritz Majce
Designer Nationality: Austrian
Date: 1997

Linotype Red Babe is a distressed display face, designed in a single weight for larger point sizes. Its letterforms are a composite of restless, jagged fragments, as if captured in the continual motion of a videotape playing on fast forward. The typeface is part of the Linotype TakeType Library.

Linotype Russisch Brot

ABCDEFGHIJKLMNOPQRSTUVWXYZ
abcdefghijklmnopqrstuvwxyz
1234567890 !@#?.;"*&

As its name suggests, Linotype Russisch Brot is modelled on the brittle form of *Russisch Brot*, (Russian bread), the dry biscuits produced in the style of letters. The font comprises six weights, each more eaten than the last, with the final weight mostly formed of crumbs.

Foundry: Linotype
Designer: Markus Remscheid / Helmut Ness
Designer Nationality: German
Date: 1997

Linotype Transis

ABCDEFGHIJKLMNOPQRSTUVWXYZ
abcdefghijpqrstuvwxyz
1234567890 !?.;"&

Linotype Transis is a distressed, restless display face that combines two stroke widths in a single character. Although using a similar vernacular of a painterly brushstroke, the letterforms feature a distinct contrast, with the right side a fuller, stronger version of the left.

Foundry: Linotype
Designer: Kelvin Tan Tec Loong
Designer Nationality: American
Date: 1999

Linotype Wildfont

ABCDEFGHIJKLMNOPQRSTUVWXYZ
1234567890 !?.;"*&

Linotype Wildfont is an unconventional display face, designed in all capitals, and constructed from the contorted figures of animals. The font features cats, alligators, and snakes, which are all rendered in the coarse texture of monoprint to enhance the design's animalistic character.

Foundry: Linotype
Designer: Meike Sander
Designer Nationality: German
Date: 1997

Linotype Zensur

ABCDEFGHIJKLMNOPQRSTUVWXYZ
abcdefghijklmnopqrstuvwxyz
1234567890 !@#?.;"*&

Linotype Zensur takes its name from the German word for "censorship." It is a distressed display font designed in a single weight. The rounded letterforms are sans serif in character, but the strokes are only partially complete, as if to abstract the true nature of each letter.

Foundry: Linotype
Designer: Gérald Alexandre
Designer Nationality: French
Date: 1997

Mallorca Dirty Numbers

AbcdEfGhIJkLMNOPqrStcv\WEH2
abcdefghijkLMn⊕pqrstuvwxy2
1234567890 ⚠@#2:; *ET

Foundry: Typo Graphic Design
Designer: Manuel Viergutz
Designer Nationality: German
Date: 2017

Mallorca Dirty Numbers is a display typeface inspired by numeric forms, such as house numbers and graffiti, found by the designer while in Mallorca. These numbers provided the basis for an alphabet, including upper- and lowercase characters alongside more than ninety-nine decorative glyphs.

Maychurch

ABCDEFGHIJKLMNOPQRSTUVWXYZ
ABCDEFGHIJKLMNOPQRSTUVWXYZ
1234567890 !@#?:;"*&

Foundry: Typodermic
Designer: Ray Larabie
Nationality: Canadian
Date: 2005

Maychurch is an architectural display face inspired by the drawings of a drafting technician. Its serif letterforms, which combine regular and small capitals in a single font, are complemented by extended rules, which overrun the regular stroke length in each character.

Merlin

ABCDEFGHIJKLMNOPQRSTUVWXYZ
1234567890 !?:;

Foundry: Linotype
Designer: Anne Boskamp
Designer Nationality: German
Date: 1994

Designed solely in capitals, Merlin is a distressed, historical display face. The strokes are trembling and irregular as if carved into paper with ink, or stone with flint. Meanwhile, the characters comprise several references to Stone Age pictograms, as seen in the "I" and "M."

Moonshine

ABCDEFGHIJKLMNOPQRSTUVWXYZ
abcdefghijklmnopqrstuvwxyz
1234567890 !@#?:;"*&

Foundry: Chank Co.
Designer: Chank Diesel
Designer Nationality: American
Date: 1993

Moonshine is a distressed display face, initially conceived for *Cake* magazine in the early 1990s. The unruly design, produced in a single Regular style, features distorted strokes and irregular shapes, and takes its name from the distilled spirit popularized in the southern United States.

Murkshine

ABCDEFGHIJKLMNOPQRSTUVWXYZ
abcdefghijklmnopqrstuvwxyz
1234567890 !@#?:;"'*&

Foundry: Chank Co.
Designer: Chank Diesel
Designer Nationality: American
Date: 1993

Like its quirky sibling typeface Moonshine, Murkshine is a distressed, grunge-serif display face. Chank Diesel designed Murkshine to complement Moonshine, and it features bolder versions of the initially disfigured letterforms to accentuate their buckled shapes.

Octin Spraypaint

ABCDEFGHIJKLMNOPQRSTUVWXYZ
ABCDEFGHIJKLMNOPQRSTUVWXYZ
1234567890 !@#?:;"'*&

Foundry: Typodermic
Designer: Ray Larabie
Designer Nationality: Canadian
Date: 2007

Octin Spraypaint is a stencil display font family designed in serif and sans serif styles and comprising three weights, from Regular to Black. The distressed letterforms imitate the visual effect of paint sprayed through a stencil and are reminiscent of military or institutional aesthetics.

Octin Vintage

ABCDEFGHIJKLMNOPQRSTUVWXYZ
ABCDEFGHIJKLMNOPQRSTUVWXYZ
1234567890 !@#?:;"'*&

Foundry: Typodermic
Designer: Ray Larabie
Designer Nationality: Canadian
Date: 2007

Ray Larabie's Octin Vintage is a distressed display font family designed in serif and sans serif styles. It consists of three weights, from Regular to Black. The font's forms exhibit inconsistencies in their surface and are reminiscent of analog printing methods such as stamps.

Octynaz

ABCDEFGHIJKLMNOPQRSTUVWXYZ
ABCDEFGHIJKLMNOPQRSTUVWXYZ
1234567890 !@#?:;"'*&

Foundry: Typodermic
Designer: Ray Larabie
Designer Nationality: Canadian
Date: 2006

Designed in a single style and all in capitals, Octynaz is a distressed display face intended for large headline sizes. The sans serif design includes several distinctions, such as filled counters, irregular alignment, and a textured surface that simulates the appearance of smudged ink.

Oxeran

ABCDEFGHIJKLMNOPQRSTUVWXYZ
abcdefghijklmnopqrstuvwxyz
1234567890 !@#?:;"*&

Foundry: Typodermic
Designer: Ray Larabie
Designer Nationality: Canadian
Date: 2007

Oxeran is a distressed display font comprised of two styles, Oxeran and Oxeran Z. While both character sets utilize worn slab serif letterforms set on an irregular baseline and feature upper and lowercases, Oxeran Z also includes a textured outline that encircles each letter.

Pitchfork

ABCDEFGHIJKLMNOPQRSTUVWXYZ
1234567890 !@#?:;"*&

Foundry: Monotype
Designer: Stephen Miggas
Designer Nationality: American
Date: 1995

Pitchfork is a distressed display face produced in all capitals and a single weight. The characters, modelled on the forms of an Old Style serif, feature a series of angular gouges and are reminiscent of those displayed in the publicity materials for early horror films such as *Frankenstein* (1931).

PRINTF

ABCDEFGHIJKLMNOPQRSTUVWXYZ
ABCDEFGHIJKLMNOPQRSTUVWXYZ
1234567890 !@#?:;"*&

Foundry: Typodermic
Designer: Ray Larabie
Designer Nationality: Canadian
Date: 2007

PRINTF is a distressed display face designed to mimic the appearance of typewriter characters. Although available in only a single style, PRINTF includes variable OpenType letter pairs, so that each form can be replaced by another to create more diverse and authentic combinations.

Raclette

ABCDEFGHIJKLMNOPQRSTUVWXYZ
abcdefghijklmnopqrstuvwxyz
1234567890 !@ ?:; &

Foundry: Linotype
Designer: Michael Parson
Designer Nationality: Swiss
Date: 2002

Raclette is a distressed display face inspired by a traditional Swiss grill designed to cook (and melt) raclette cheese. Its sans serif letterforms are irregular in shape and are similar in appearance to a raclette grill from which the individual cooking trays have been removed or replaced.

Raw Street Wall

ABCDEFGHIJKLMnoPQRStuVwXYZ
abcdefghijklmnopqrstuvwxyz
1234567890 !@#?:, "&

Foundry: Volcano Type
Designer: Manuel Viergutz
Designer Nationality: German
Date: 2016

Inspired by the playful lettering of graffiti art, Raw Street Wall is an eclectic display face comprised of a single style, more than 567 glyphs and contextual alternates. For authenticity, the blockish characters also imitate the texture of letters painted on a rough surface. It is best used in headlines.

Reagan

ABCDEFGHIJKLMNOPQRSTUVWXYZ
abcdefghijklmnopqrstuvwxyz
'1234567890 !@#?:;"*&

Foundry: Typodermic
Designer: Ray Larabie
Designer Nationality: Canadian
Date: 2007

Reagan is designed to symbolize the 1980s. It is based on a revival font, Pretorian, from the early 20th century which became an icon of T-shirt design in the 1980s. Reagan maintains the flamboyant style, but adds a layer of wear, as if the letters have been put repeatedly through the wash.

Rina BT

ABCDEFGHIJKLMNOPQRSTUVWXYZ
abcdefghijklmnopqrstuvwxyz
1234567890 !@#?:,"*&

Foundry: Bitstream
Designer: Eduardo Manso
Designer Nationality: Argentinian
Date: 2001

Rina BT is a distressed display font featuring two styles, Rina Regular and Rina Linea, the outline version. The serif figures, which designer Eduardo Manso inverted, cut and contorted at random, are chaotic yet refined and remain legible even at smaller display sizes.

Sabotage

ABCDEFGHIJKLMNOPQRSTUVWXYZ
abcdefghijklmnopqrstuvwxyz
1234567890 !@#?:,"*&

Foundry: PintassilgoPrints
Designer: Ricardo Marcin / Erica Jung
Designer Nationality: Brazilian
Date: 2013

Sabotage is a distressed display face inspired by the all-caps lettering of Saul Bass's seminal poster for the film *Vertigo* (1958). The design also includes a Sabotage Pictures version, which unlike Sabotage and Sabotage Solid, takes inspiration from the minimalist illustrations of Dutch artist Dick Bruna.

Schmutz

ABCDEFGHIJKLMNOPQRSTUVWXYZ
abcdefghijklmnopqrstuvwxyz
1234567890 !@#?:;""*&

Schmutz is a distressed display font produced in three versions. The characters, modelled on those of a typewriter, vary in clarity throughout the family, from the articulate appearance of the Cleansed face to the smudged and worn designs of the Clogged and Corroded styles.

Foundry: Image Club Graphics
Designer: Grant Hutchinson
Nationality: Canadian
Date: 1995

Shatterday

ABCDEFGHIJKLMNOPQRSTUVWXYZ
abcdefghijklmnopqrstuvwxyz
1234567890 !@#?:;"*&

Shatterday comprises three options—Shatterday Slice, Shatterday Dice and Shatterday Shred—all of which appear to be based on chopping up things.

These are just a handful of mainly display faces created by the prolific US writer and type designer Patricia Lillie.

Foundry: Image Club Graphics
Designer: Patricia Lillie
Designer Nationality: American
Date: 1996

Shnixgun

ABCDEFGHIJKLMNOPQRSTUVWXYZ
ABCDEFGHIJKLMNOPQRSTUVWXYZ
1234567890 !@Nº?:;"*&

Ray Larabie's Shnixgun is an all-caps copperplate-style serif font based on a an old metal type called Franklin Card Gothic. It has a distressed, grungy finish that looks like it has been printed from under-inked metal type. Some letters are slightly skewed or off the baseline.

Foundry: Typodermic
Designer: Ray Larabie
Designer Nationality: Canadian
Date: 2007

Spooky

ABCDEFGHIJKLMNOPQRSTUVWXYZ
abcdefghijklmnopqrstuvwxyz
1234567890 !@#?:;"*&

Spooky, by British educator and lettering artist Timothy Donaldson, is in the vampire-style genre of typefaces thanks to its eerie, tattered-looking letterforms, and "x" and "X" even resemble bats in flight. It is perfect for use in anything goth or related to Halloween.

Foundry: ITC
Designer: Timothy Donaldson
Designer Nationality: British
Date: 1995

Teeshirt

ABCDEFGHIJKLMNOPQRSTUVWXYZ
ABCDEFGHIJKLMNOPQRSTUVWXYZ
1234567890 !@#?:;'"*&

Foundry: Typodermic
Designer: Ray Larabie
Designer Nationality: Canadian
Date: 2008

Teeshirt is Ray Larabie's homage to ITC's typeface American Typewriter of 1974. Teeshirt is a heavier display face inspired by type found on vintage 1980s T-shirts. It is available in two weights: Teeshirt Regular has unevenly spaced characters and Teeshirt Pressed has letters sitting on the baseline.

Thumtax

ABCDEFGHIJKLMNOPQRS
TUVWXYZ
1234567890 !@#?:;"*&

Foundry: Image Club Graphics
Designer: Jeff Prybolsky
Designer Nationality: American
Date: 1996

Jeff Prybolsky designed Thumtax for Image Club Graphics. It comes in a single all-caps style and is a rough display typeface that has the appearance of being quickly scrawled with a heavy marker. Prybolsky designed type for various foundries as Disappearing Inc., from 1994–2000.

Wolfsblood

ABCDEFGHIJKLMNOPQRSTUVWXYZ
ABCDEFGHIJKLMNOPQRSTUVWXYZ
1234567890 !@#?:;'"*&

Foundry: Monotype
Designer: Jim Ford
Designer Nationality: American
Date: 2013

Jim Ford's Wolfsblood, an all-caps sans serif, is as its name suggests, horror-inspired, with rough wobbly edges. Wolfsblood's lowercase capitals are slightly smaller, and it also features a variety of ligatures and context-sensitive OpenType functions that help vary the style.

Woodcut Alpha

ABCDEFGHIJKLMNOPQRSTUVWXYZ
abcdefghijklmnopqrstuvwxyz
1234567890 !@#?:;"*&

Foundry: Monotype
Designer: Hans Bacher
Designer Nationality: American
Date: 2001

Woodcut Alpha is a rough, chaotic woodcut style sans serif, available in a single style, with imperfect shapes and textures that give a printed look. Its designer Hans Bacher was born in Germany but works in animation for Disney in California on films such as *The Lion King* (1994) and *Mulan* (1998).

DIN Next Shapes

ABCDEFGHIJKLMNOPQRSTUVWXYZ
abcdefghijklmnopqrstuvwxyz
1234567890 !@#?:;"*&

Designed to work in harmony with its sister typeface DIN Next (2009), Sabina Chipară has taken the outline of the German industrial classic and created four new and much more expressive versions using various shapes—dots, hearts, snowflakes and stars—to replace solid lines. Light Dots is shown here.

Foundry: Monotype
Designer: Sabina Chipară / Akira Kobayashi
Designer Nationality: Romanian / Japanese
Date: 2018

Foundry Flek/Plek

ABCDEFGHIJKLMNOPQRSTUVWXYZ
abcdefghijklmnopqrstuvwxyz
1234567890 !@#?;"*&

ABCDEFGHIJKLMNOPQRSTUVWXYZ
abcdefghijklmnopqrstuvwxyz
1234567890 !@#?;"*&

Foundry: The Foundry
Designer: Freda Sack / David Quay
Designer Nationality: British
Date: 2002

Below. Logo for online and print, leaflet, screen and window graphics by Patrick Myles for RIBA (Royal Institute of British Architects)

Foundry Flek was designed by David Quay and Freda Sack, the co-founders of The Foundry (see p. 284). It is a typeface created from circular forms on a consistent dot-matrix grid, which is visible in the background. It is available in four weights—Light, Regular, Medium and Bold—and includes a version with just the dot grid and no letters.

The sister type to Flek, Plek is built on the same dot-matrix grid. However, it just includes the letters without the gridded dot background. As with Flek, Plek is available in four weights and includes a font with only the dot-matrix grid that can then be built into a continuous background. With varying weights and the opportunity to overlay these weights, dynamic and involving designs can be created, with the resultant radiating circles forming letterforms as well as contrasting surrounding textures. This opportunity for experimentation allows for endless configurations and varying effects.

FourPoint (03)

Foundry: MuirMcNeil
Designer: Hamish Muir /
Paul McNeil
Designer Nationality: British
Date: 2014

MuirMcNeil (see p. 334) created this geometric typeface system as a playful response to the everyday lettering that can be seen on transportation light-emitting diode (LED) displays such as on train and road networks. The typeface system is formed around a varying dot size, stroke width and grid.

Designers Hamish Muir and Paul McNeil intended the FourPoint system to explore two specific typographic conditions. The first is resolution—"the proportionate relationship between scale and visual information." The second is weight—"the proportionate relationship between filled and negative space elements of letters and word forms." The resultant design has been built on a fixed grid at four resolutions. FourPoint 04 has a consistent stroke width of four dots; FourPoint 03, three dots (left;) FourPoint 02, two dots, and FourPoint 01, one dot. Every dot aligns consistently on the same grid and their weights are incremented without the dots altering position. The grid therefore dictates the letterform shapes, spacing, kerning and suchlike.

As with other MuirMcNeil typefaces, individual characters vary within the system. FourPoint is designed in four scaleable groups of five weights each. The five weights (or tonal densities) in each scale group are identified both by name—Light, Regular, Bold, Black, and Fat—and numerically. The number codes describe dot diameters in units as fractions of the 1,000-unit PostScript em square. "FourPoint 03 054 Regular," for example, indicates stroke width (3 dots) and dot diameter (54/1,000 units). Consequently, size and weight ratios can be accurately calculated in setting typographic compositions and overlays.

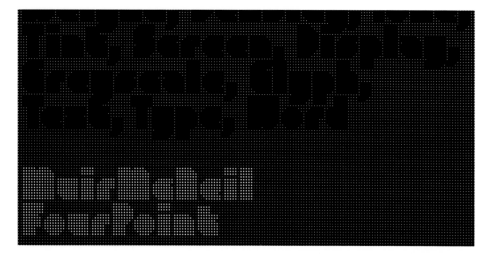

Left. FourPoint poster designed by MuirMcNeil (detail).

Led

ABCDEFGHIJKLMNOPQRSTUVWXYZ
abcdefghijklmnopqrstuvwxyz
1234567890 !@#?;,""*&

Foundry: Graviton
Designer: Pablo Balcells
Designer Nationality:
Argentinian
Date: 2012

Designed by Pablo Balcells, an Argentinian designer and a graduate of the University of Buenos Aires, Led is a display sans serif created from unconnected dots. It comes in two styles, Regular and Outline (whose dots are outlined rather than solid), and is published by Graviton.

Linotype Dot

ABCDEFGHIJKLMNOPQRSTUVWXYZ
abcdefghijklmnopqrstuvwxyz
1234567890 !?;""'

Foundry: Linotype
Designer: Lucy Davies
Designer Nationality: British
Date: 1997

Dot, by British designer Lucy Davies, was one of the winners in the display category of Linotype's second International Type Design Contest in 1997. It comes in two styles—Regular and Oblique—and is an intricate, ornamental display face made from interconnected white and black dots.

Linotype Punkt

abcdefghijklmnopqrstuvwxyz
1234567890 !e#?;,""*&

Foundry: Linotype
Designer: Mischa Leiner
Designer Nationality: Swiss
Date: 1999

Swiss typographer Mischa Leiner designed Linotype Punkt in 1999. It is an extended sans serif created from dots and is named after the German word for "dot," *punkt*. The font is available in three styles: Light, Regular and Bold. Leiner is a lecturer at the Basel School of Design.

Nebulae

ABCDEFGHIJKLMNOPQRSTUVWXYZ
abcdefghijklmnopqrstuvwxyz
1234567890 !@#?;,""&

Foundry: Lucas Fonts
Designer: Lucas de Groot
Designer Nationality: Dutch
Date: 1994

Nebulae is the work of Dutch designer Lucas de Groot and was released by his Lucas Fonts foundry in 1994. It is an experimental sans serif that comes in four styles; One, Two, Three, Three Dee, and Four. Each font is made from clouds of different-sized dots, and they can be layered together.

Perfin

A B C D E F G H I J K L M N O P Q R S T U V W X Y Z
1 2 3 4 5 6 7 8 9 0　! @ # ? : ; " " * &

Foundry: Colophon
Designer: Alison Haigh
Designer Nationality: British
Date: 2009

Created by Alison Haigh, a designer who has worked at DesignStudio and Wolff Olins, Perfin is short for "Perforated Initials," an old system whereby companies stamped letters or symbols into postage stamps as a protection against theft. It is an uppercase sans serif made from dots.

PIN

ABCDEFGHIJKLMNOPQRSTUVWXYZ
abcdefghijklmnopqrstuvwxyz
1234567890 !@#/?.,*&

Foundry: Colophon
Designer: Hoon Kim
Designer Nationality: Korean
Date: 2015

New York-based Korean designer Hoon Kim created PIN in three styles—Solid, Dot, and Stencil—and three roman weights—Light, Regular, and Medium. It is a friendly, geometric sans serif that is almost monoline and was initially constructed in its Dot style using a gridded dot matrix.

Synchro

ABCDEFGHIJKLMNOPQRSTUVWXYZ
1234567890 !@#?:;"*&

Foundry: Letraset
Designer: Alan Birch
Designer Nationality: British
Date: 1984

British designer Alan Birch created this pixellated typeface that simulates electronic display systems. Synchro is also available as Synchro Reversed, and in the non-pixellated versions as Synchro No. 1 and Synchro No. 2. It is suitable for instances where a high-tech appearance is required.

Telidon

ABCDEFGHIJKLMNOPQRSTUVWXYZ
abcdefghijklmnopqrstuvwxyz
1234567890　!@#?:;"*&

Foundry: Typodermic
Designer: Ray Larabie
Nationality: Canadian
Date: 2004

An adaptable dot-matrix display face, Telidon is available in a surprisingly wide range of weights: Regular, Bold, Heavy, Condensed, Condensed Bold, Condensed Heavy, Expanded, Expanded Bold, and Expanded Heavy. All of the weights come with matching italics.

TenPoint (08)

ABCDEFGHIJKLMNOPQRSTUVWXYZ
abcdefghijklmnopqrstuvwxyz
1234567890 !&#?:;""+&

TenPoint, by MuirMcNeil (see p. 334), is a modular type system built around a repeating single cell—a circular disc with an open counterform—all fixed to a consistent circular-based geometric grid. This experimental typeface pushes the barriers of legibility to the limit of what can be interpreted as a recognizable set of characters as well as creating a system of construction for the letterforms.

There are seven sizes of TenPoint: 01, 02, 03, 04, 05, 06, and 08 (above and below right). The numerical index refers to the vertical cell count repetitions that define the overall body height of each size. For example, TenPoint 08 is constructed from eight precisely positioned, partially overlapping circles on its vertical axis, allowing for ascenders and descenders.

Because of the nature of TenPoint's construction, it is challenging to identify individual characters when set at smaller sizes and readability is reduced, to the point of even disappearring. As such, it takes on a more geometric texture and the typeface creates rhythmic patterns. At larger settings, the letterforms' readability and shape become much clearer, allowing for legibility and communication.

Foundry: MuirMcNeil
Designer: Hamish Muir / Paul McNeil
Designer Nationality: British
Date: 2014

Below. A modular geometric type system in seven sizes. The repeating single cell construction is at the core of the typeface's design, with all points fixed to a geometric grid.

ThreePoint (A)

ThreePoint by MuirMcNeil (see p. 334) is based around four differing orthographic projections. It is a 3D display typeface formed of precisely placed and sized dots set on a standardized grid and is a development of MuirMcNeil's Panopticon typeface system (see p. 434). The four views making up ThreePoint are categorized as A: top right view (above), B: bottom left view, C: top left view and D: bottom right view.

The four viewpoints are each provided as four differing typefaces and with differing size dot patterns built on a consistent grid. They provide the illusion of three dimensions and depth to the letterforms. The variants for each of the projections are 01: Comp H, a two-tone composite that is darker in the horizontal plane; 02: Comp V, a two-tone composite that is darker in the vertical plane

(above); 03: Light, an even screen pattern of light dots; and 04: Bold, an even screen pattern of dark dots. Letterforms abut to each other with no interspacing between characters; so all dots may be aligned vertically and horizontally and therefore provide an evenly set placing for the dots making up the letterforms. The family comes in a Latin lowercase only and, for ease of use, the lowercase is duplicated in the uppercase family.

There are also a further four sub-variants for each projection, with variations supplied for Light and Bold weights in horizontal and vertical planes all designed to interact and link together as sharing the same grid construction. These additional types can be used to create textured patterns, overlays and offset types, and are intended for use for complex designs built around layered constructions.

Foundry: MuirMcNeil
Designer: Hamish Muir / Paul McNeil
Designer Nationality: British
Date: 2014

Below. A 3D type system in four orthographic projections. As such, the possibilities when combining the differing views are near infinite, when also adding in to the mix colour, transparency, outlining and the designers' experimentation and creativity.

TwoPoint (A)

ABCDEFGHIJKLMNOPQRSTUVWXYZ
abcdefghijklmnopqrstuvwxyz
1234567890 !&#?:;"'*$

TwoPoint was inspired by the earliest dot-matrix and light-emitting diode (LED) display letterforms. It is a monospaced geometric type system that explores how differing permutations can generate letterforms while maintaining legibility and readability. TwoPoint has been created around a consistent grid wherein placement of the centres of the dots that make up the letterform are always consistent at the intersections of horizontal and vertical lines of the grid behind the construction and placement of the dots.

TwoPoint has been created in four variant styles. A (above) is a two-dot stroke form that is consistent in both dimensions. B is a two-dot stroke form where alternate dot rows have been removed in order to emphasize the horizontal. C is a two-dot stroke form where alternate dot columns have been removed in

order to emphasize the vertical. D is a two-dot stroke form where alternate diagonal rows have been removed, thus creating a chequerboard effect.

Each of the four TwoPoint styles come in six weights, ranging from Light to Black. They are identified both by name and numerically in dot diameters. Their weight increases as the dot diameters increase in size in units as fractions of the 1,000-unit PostScript em square, while all the time never moving from their placed position on the grid. For example, the numerical value in "TwoPoint A 044 Regular" indicates the dot component diameter (44/1,000 units). Eventually, these dots scale up in size to touch and then overlap each other. This creates denser and bolder weights, and provides contrast and texture to longer set extents of text.

Foundry: MuirMcNeil
Designer: Hamish Muir / Paul McNeil
Designer Nationality: British
Date: 2014

Below. For the design, Paul McNeil and Hamish Muir of MuirMcNeil generated 8,000 uniquely different pieces of artwork using conditional design methods. The front cover of *Eye 94* employs their coordinated TwoPoint and TwoPlus typefaces.

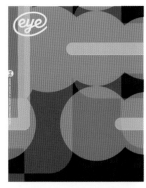

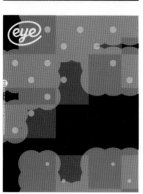
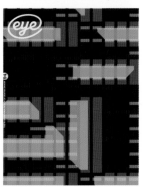

Blenny

ABCDEFGHIJKLMNOPQRSTUVWXYZ
abcdefghijklmnopqrstuvwxyz
1234567890 !@#?:;"*&

The curvaceous forms of this Fat Face display font are voluptuous and glorious, creating a truly individual and eye-catching display type. Blenny's dynamic character make it ideal for branding or product label applications or anywhere where a message needs to shout out. It is the work of US-born font developer Spike Spondike of Dalton Maag (see p. 594).

Spondike has created a number of ligatures with elegant hairlines and ball terminals to ensure the letter spacing is kept tight throughout and guarantee its solid appeal. A number of design features such as the ball terminals of the "A" provide letterforms that turn in to wrap itself up.

Unusually, the Blenny family is available in Thai as well as Latin. Indeed, the Latin design of Blenny was heavily influenced by Thai script and its diversity of character shapes. During the development of the Thai variant, refinements were made to the design of the Latin version, which brought the two language types closer together in appearance, and they share design characteristics. Bruno Maag, founder and chairman of Dalton Maag, loved the retro-feel design so much he said he was considering having a tattoo done in it. When the design was launched, a Blenny gin cocktail was invented to honour its arrival, which like its namesake is "bold, punchy and has a touch of class."

Foundry: Dalton Maag
Designer: Spike Spondike
Designer Nationality: American
Date: 2014

Below. Examples and workings for Dalton Maag's single weight Fat Face typeface Blenny, where the influence of Thai scripts can clearly be seen in the Latin version and vice versa.

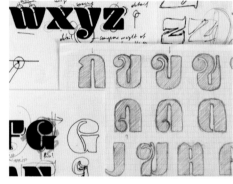

Bodoni Poster

ABCDEFGHIJKLMNOPQRSTUVWXYZ
abcdefghijklmnopqrstuvwxyz
1234567890 !@#?:;""*&

The archetypal "fat face," although not really a variant of Giambattista's eponymous typeface, this extreme cut was designed by Chauncey H. Griffith for Linotype in 1929 and resembles more of the fat face types that could be found in the 19th century. It was a popular choice for posters and advertisements in the mid 20th century and its generous presence, extremely heavy weighted strokes and curvaceous forms (as seen in the rounded ball terminals of letters such as "a," "c," and "r") still make it a popular choice today. Available in black, black italic and compressed, it can be seen used in film, musc and packaging applications. The logotype of American rock band Nirvana closely resembles the compressed cut of Bodoni Poster were it not for subtle differences in the terminals of the R and the shape of the serif on the V marking it as a revised variant.

Foundry: Linotype
Designer: Giambattista Bodoni /
Chauncey H. Griffith
Designer Nationality: Italian /
American
Date: 1929

Right. The cover for *123* by Màrius Sampere, one of a series of poetry titles published by Edicions del Buc and designed by Dídac Ballester.

Carousel

ABCDEFGHIJKLMNOPQRSTUVWXYZ
abcdefghijklmnopqrstuvw.xyz
1234567890 !@#?::""*&

Foundry: Letraset
Designer: Gary Gillot
Designer Nationality: British
Date: 1966

Carousel, by British type designer Gary Gillot, is a classic example of the Fat Face type style, which developed from earlier modern serifs such as Didot and Bodoni. It is a high-contrast typeface featuring generous curves and fine serifs, which is well-suited for display use.

Caslon Graphique

ABCDEFGHIJKLMNOPQRSTUVWXYZ
abcdefghijklmnopqrstuvwxyz
1234567890 !@#?:,"*&

Foundry: ITC
Designer: William Caslon / Leslie Usherwood
Designer Nationality: British
Date: 1980

Caslon Graphique was designed by the British-born and Toronto-based advertising designer, typographer and type designer Leslie Usherwood. This elegant display serif closely resembles the forms of the original Caslon yet possesses greatly contrasting stroke weights, from hairline to fat, along with incisor-like serifs, giving it an approachable appearance overall with precise, razor-sharp finishing details, making it ideal for headlines and titles in larger sizes.

Usherwood was a prolific type designer, who created 211 typefaces during his career. He created his first font design, Melure, in 1965 for Headliners International in New York and in 1968 he co-founded Typesettra in Toronto.

Right. Website interface for http://lesliink.com

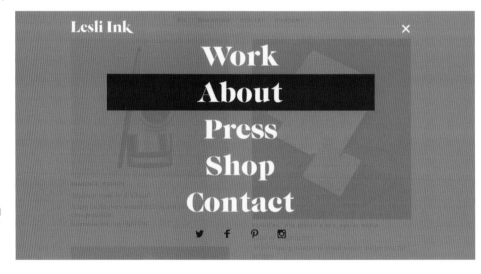

Falstaff

ABCDEFGHIJKLMNOPQRSTUV
abcdefghijklmnopqrstuvwxyz
1234567890 !@#?:,""*&

Foundry: Monotype
Designer: Monotype Studio
Date: 1931

Falstaff is named after the fictional character Sir John Falstaff, who appears in four plays by William Shakespeare. Monotype released the wide, bold, ultra-high-contrast antiqua serif in 1931, which was created in-house by an uncredited designer who took inspiration from 19th-century poster types.

ITC Scram Gravy

ABCDEFGHIJKLMNOPQRST
abcdefghijklmnopqrstuv
1234567890 !@#?:;"'*&

Foundry: ITC
Designer: Nick Curtis
Designer Nationality: American
Date: 2002

ITC Scram Gravy has extreme contrast, its thick strokes are broad, taking up two thirds or more of the width of most capitals, and its lowercase counters are very thin. Nick Curtis, who designed it in 2002, began this font after being inspired by the 1928 logotype for Sertal Toiletries.

Maisalle

ABCDEFGHIJKLMNOPQRSTUVWXYZ
abcdefghijklmnopqrstuvwxyz
1234567890 !@#?:;"'*&

Foundry: Neutura
Designer: Alexander McCracken
Designer Nationality: American
Date: 2012

US foundry Neutura (see p. 472) was inspired by the Fat Faces that were popular during the 1960s—especially in the fashion world—to create Maisalle. The foundry's faithful homage to this style of type design nevertheless possesses a refinement and sharpness that is its own. The high contrast between stroke weights and the near circular forms for its ball endings and exaggerated, incisor-like serifs combine to create a voluptous and flamboyant presentation to the design. Neutura has also created an accompanying italic.

Right. Poster designs by Neutura.

Normande

ABCDEFGHIJKLMNOPQRSTUVW
abcdefghijklmnopqrstuvwxyz
1234567890 !@#?:;"'*&

Foundry: Bitstream
Designer: Unknown
Date: 1860

Normande is Bitstream's digitization of a French Fat Face font, initially produced in 1860 and later acquired by the Berthold foundry in Berlin. As with the original design, Bitstream's Normande features two styles, Roman and Italic, and there are family-package options.

Royale

ABCDEFGHIJKLMNOPQRSTUVWXYZ
abcdefghijklmnopqrstuvwxyz
1234567890 !@#?:;"*&

Foundry: Neutura
Designer: Alexander McCracken
Designer Nationality: American
Date: 2009

Royale is an ultra-high-contrast didone serif typeface created by San Francisco-based designer Alexander McCracken and released by Neutura (see p. 472). It comes in a single style, Roman, and has a large x-height, chunky ball terminals and two attractive ampersands to choose between.

Stilla

ABCDEFGHIJKLMNOPQRSTUVWX
abcdefghijklmnopqrstuvwxyz
1234567890 !@#?:;"*&

Foundry: Letraset
Designer: François Boltana
Designer Nationality: French
Date: 1973

The prolific 20th-century French lettering artist François Boltana designed this voluptuous cursive Fat Face. It was inspired by the first large advertising and display faces that were produced following the successful launches of Bodoni, Didot, and Walbaum in the 19th century.

Thorowgood

ABCDEFGHIJKLMNOPQRSTUVWXYZ
abcdefghijklmnopqrstuvwxyz
1234567890 !@#?:;"*&

Foundry: Linotype
Designer: Robert Thorne
Designer Nationality: British
Date: 1836

This didone-style display face was created by English typefounder Robert Thorne, and named after his predecessor, the punch-cutter and typefounder William Thorowgood, who worked at the Fann Street foundry in London. Stephenson, Blake & Co. revived it in 1953. It is available in Regular and Italic weights.

Trilogy Fatface

ABCDEFGHIJKLMNOPQRSTUVWXYZ
abcdefghijklmnopqrstuvwxyz
1234567890 !@#?:;"*&

Foundry: Jeremy Tankard Typography
Designer: Jeremy Tankard
Designer Nationality: British
Date: 2009

Part of the Trilogy type family, Jeremy Tankard's Trilogy Fatface is a high-contrast serif that comes in a heavy weight in five widths: regular, wide, expanded, extra-expanded, and ultra-expanded. It is italic only and was inspired by the Fat Face poster types of the 19th century.

Amelia

ABCDEFGHIJKLMNOPQRSTUVWXYZ
abcdefghijklmnopqrstuvwxyz
1234567890 !@#?:;'"*&

Stan Davis designed Amelia for Visual Graphics Corporation in 1964. It was used in the titles artwork for the Beatles' film *Yellow Submarine* (1968).

Controversy surrounds the various digitizations of the font because Davis maintains they were created without his consent.

Foundry: Visual Graphics Corporation
Designer: Stan Davis
Designer Nationality: American
Date: 1964

Anlinear

ABCDEFGHIJKLMNOPQRSTUVWXYZ
abcdefghijklmnopqrstuvwxyz
1234567890 !@#?:;?•3

Anlinear is one of ten different designs by Michael Parson to be included in Linotype's TakeType 5 library. It is an experimental display typeface whose forms are composed of arrangements of straight lines set at right angles to one another. It is available in three weights.

Foundry: Linotype
Designer: Michael Parson
Designer Nationality: Swiss
Date: 2003

Architype Stedelijk

abcdefghijklmnopqrstuvwxyz
1234567890 ! ?:' +

In 1996, The Foundry, run by Freda Sack and David Quay, struck an agreement with Wim Crouwel (see p. 540) to create digital fonts based on lettering he had created. Stedelijk is based on his posters for the Stedelijk Museum in Amsterdam. It is a low-resolution sans serif created with a strict grid.

Foundry: The Foundry
Designer: Wim Crouwel / Freda Sack / David Quay
Designer Nationality: Dutch / British / British
Date: 1996

Armadura

ABCDEFGHIJKLMNOPQRSTUV
ƆBCDEƟFGHIJKLMNOPQRSTUV
1234567890 !@#?:;"*&

This geometric sans by Pablo Balcells features a distinctive diagonal tilt to its crossbars. It is available in a wide range of variants, including Inline, Outline, Stencil, and Double Line styles, with alternate lowercase characters to incorporate into its uppercase alphabet.

Foundry: Graviton
Designer: Pablo Balcells
Designer Nationality: Argentinian
Date: 2012

Belfast

ABCDEFGHIJKLMNOPQRSTUVWXYZ
1234567890 |A|#!"`* &

Foundry: Neutura
Designer: Alexander McCracken / Grant Dickson
Designer Nationality: American / British
Date: 2007

An early pre-Neutura (see p. 472) project, this collaboration with designer Grant Dickson and Neutura founder Alexander McCracken was produced while the latter worked at the renowned British design studio, Attik. Dickson had created letterforms but was struggling to work with them because they were still individual artworks. McCracken offered to make a working font from the design. Together, they revisited the characters that had been designed and went on to make them into a full working typeface with the addition of numbers, punctuation and alternate characters. The typeface gained its name after Dickson's home town in Northern Ireland, Belfast.

Belfast's minimal character forms use chamfered corners to create shape. Combined with its pared-back indentation for counters, this helps to create an aggressive and imposing font with high impact. An alternative set of characters features bold diagonal lines forming the characters, where shortening of the strokes and angled endings provide the shape of the characters.

Below and opposite. The octagonal-based Belfast typeface is available not only in solid form but also comes as a diagonal infill version. Designs by Neutura.

Betaphid

A futuristic font from prolific display typeface designer Ray Larabie, this sans serif features squat, extended square forms with floating details, and a distinctive diagonal slant to certain stroke ends. Betaphid is available in a single weight, in both upper and lowercase.

Foundry: Typodermic
Designer: Ray Larabie
Designer Nationality: Canadian
Date: 2006

Bisect A

A B C D E F G H I J K L M N O P Q R S T
a b c d e f g h i j k l m n o p q r s t
1 2 3 4 5 6 7 8 9 0   ! @ # ? : ; " ✿ +

The Bisect type system was begun by designer Natasha Lucas during her undergraduate studies, as a typographic response to the central conceit of Harold Pinter's so-called "memory plays." This modular typeface is built from sliced circular forms and rectangles, set on a geometric grid.

Foundry: MuirMcNeil
Designer: Natasha Lucas / Paul McNeil / Hamish Muir
Designer Nationality: British
Date: 2018

Bisect B

Natasha Lucas created this geometric modular font when she was a student at the London College of Communication, with help from her tutors Hamish Muir and Paul McNeil. Bisect B is made from the vertical elements of Bisect A and is illegible without being used in combination with Bisect C.

Foundry: MuirMcNeil
Designer: Natasha Lucas / Paul McNeil / Hamish Muir
Designer Nationality: British
Date: 2018

Bisect C

Natasha Lucas designed Bisect, an experimental type family, as an exploration into Harold Pinter's "memory plays," which feature the recollections of unreliable narrators. Bisect A is fully legible, while Bisect C features the horizontal strokes only and needs to be combined with Bisect B to be read.

Foundry: MuirMcNeil
Designer: Natasha Lucas / Paul McNeil / Hamish Muir
Designer Nationality: British
Date: 2018

Black Boton

ABCDEFGHIJKLMNOPQRSTUVWXYZ
1234567890 !@#?:;"'"*&

Foundry: Hollenstein
Designer: Albert Boton
Designer Nationality: French
Date: 1970

This solid geometric display face was originally created when Albert Boton was a director at the Delpire agency in Paris. Black Boton featured in a catalogue from the Hollenstein foundry in 1974 with Solid and Outline styles, and with lowercase. Monotype reissued this caps-only version in 1997.

Blippo

ABCDEFGHIJKLMNOPQRSTUVWXYZ
abcdefghijklmnopqrstuvwxyz
1234567890 !@#?::"'"*&

Foundry: Fotostar
Designer: Joe Taylor / Robert Trogman
Designer Nationality: American
Date: 1969

Joe Taylor designed Blippo as a photolettering font for FotoStar as part of its Facsimile Fonts range. It was inspired by a thinner, unfinished design developed by the Bauhaus. Blippo is available as a family that includes various Black, Stencil, Poster, and Outline versions.

Blocks

ABCDEFGHIJKLMNOPQRSTUVWXYZ
abcdefghijklmnopqrstuvwxyz
1234567890 !@#?:;"*&

Foundry: Keystrokes
Designer: Douglas Olena
Designer Nationality: American
Date: 1995

Blocks is a very black geometric face from Douglas Olena's Keystrokes foundry, which is similar in style to Albert Boton's display face Black Boton (1970). Blocks differs in that it has a lowercase option, but this scores relatively low on the legibility scale, even when used at large sizes.

Calcula

ABCDEFGHIJKLMNOPQRSTUVWXYZ
abcdefghijklmnopqrstuvwxyz
1234567890 !@#?:;"'"*&

Foundry: Typotheque
Designer: Shiva Nallaperumal
Designer Nationality: Indian
Date: 2017

Shiva Nallaperumal began Calcula during the final year of his Master of Fine Arts. This experimental font family was inspired by geometric Kufic lettering, a form of Arabic calligraphy. Exploiting OpenType functionality, its letters can stack, layer and tessellate to create myriad fascinating forms.

Children

abcdefghijklmnopqrstuvwxyz
1234567890 !@#?:;"*&

Foundry: Neutura / T-26
Designer: Alexander McCracken
Designer Nationality: American
Date: 2000

US designer Alexander McCracken constructed Children on a square skeleton. The typeface features letterforms built from a single folded line, as if bent into shape from a paper clip. It is available in two weights, and is published by McCracken's Neutura foundry (see p. 472) and the T-26 foundry.

Chilopod

ABCDEFGHIJKLMNOPQRSTUVWXYZ
1234567890 !@#?:;"*&

Foundry: Typodermic
Designer: Ray Larabie
Designer Nationality: Canadian
Date: 2006

This rounded linear design by Ray Larabie was inspired by the lettering within the logo of the arcade game Centipede, which was released by Atari in 1981. It deviates slightly from its source material, with forms such as the "E" opened up, and fewer letter ligatures throughout.

Circle

ABCDEFGHIJKLMNOPQRSTUVWXYZ
1234567890 !@№?:;"*&

Foundry: Neutura
Designer: Alexander McCracken
Designer Nationality: American
Date: 2006

Circle is an airy, sans serif display font featuring a blend of tall, narrow letterforms and open, circular forms, as its name implies. The typeface, which is available in four weights, includes a range of alternate characters and ligatures, and its numerals are particularly distinctive.

Cirkulus

abcdefghijklmnopqrstuvwxyz
1234567890 !@#:;"*&

Foundry: Letraset
Designer: Michael Neugebauer
Designer Nationality: Austrian
Date: 1970

This fine and airy typeface by Michael Neugebauer is composed of interconnected and bisected circles and straight strokes in a uniform hairline weight. Cirkulus is available in lowercase only. Originally published by Letraset, the typeface has since been licensed by Linotype.

Computechnodigitronic

ABCDEFGHIJKLMNOPQRSTUVWXYZ
1234567890 !@#?:;"*&

Foundry: Typodermic
Designer: Ray Larabie
Designer Nationality: Canadian
Date: 2010

The notched letterforms of Computechnodigitronic are designed to resemble those of simple light-emitting diode (LED) displays, but designer Ray Larabie has made them more solid by to aid legibility. The typeface is available in Regular and Oblique styles, and in uppercase only.

Countdown

ABCDEFGHIJKLMNOPQRSTUVWXYZ
abcdefghijklmnopqrstuvwxyz
1234567890 !@#?:;"*&

Foundry: Letraset
Designer: Colin Brignall
Designer Nationality: British
Date: 1965

The design of this early original Letraset font was influenced by digital displays, and it was frequently used in the initial years after its release to convey a science-fiction feel in display contexts. A Cyrillic version of the typeface was developed by Alexey Kustov in 1993.

Covent BT

ABCDEFGHIJKLMNOPQRSTUVWXYZ
abcdefghijklmnopqrstuvwxyz
1234567890 !@#?:;"*&

Foundry: Bitstream
Designer: Jochen Hasinger
Designer Nationality: German
Date: 2003

German type designer Jochen Hasinger studied under Wolfgang Weingart in Switzerland during the early 1990s, and has since started his own foundry, Typeimage, where he specializes in pictogram fonts. Hasinger designed Covent BT, a monolinear sans serif, for Bitstream in 2003.

Cuantica

ABCDEFGHIJKLMNOPQRSTUVWXYZ
ABCDEFGHIJKLMNOPQRSTUVWXYZ
1234567890 !@#?:;"*&

Foundry: Graviton
Designer: Pablo Balcells
Designer Nationality: Argentinian
Date: 2012

Pablo Balcells designed Cuantica for his Buenos Aires-based foundry Graviton. Geometric and monolinear, it features distinctive numerals and includes a slightly shorter set of small caps in place of lowercase characters. It comprises four styles—two solid and two outline.

Data 70

ABCDEFGHIJKLMNOPQRSTUVWXYZ
abcdefghijklmnopqrstuvwxyz
1234567890 !@#?:;"*&

Foundry: Letraset
Designer: Bob Newman
Designer Nationality: British
Date: 1970

Data 70, by British designer Bob Newman, and published by Letraset and ITC in 1970, is a sans serif with contrast inspired by early computer-readable type, specifically the MICR E13B font for bank checks, which had caps only. It was popular throughout the 1970s for giving a futuristic look.

Deuce

ABCDEFGHIJKLMNOPQRSTUVWXYZ
1234567890 !@#?:;"*&

Foundry: T-26
Designer: Alexander McCracken
Designer Nationality: American
Date: 2005

Alexander McCracken's Deuce is an uppercase, blocky sans serif typeface without counters and with characters that are all the same width. It comes in three styles: Solid, Outline, and Gradient. The Gradient style is made from horizontal stripes that get thicker as they travel up the letters.

Dujour

ABCDEFGHIJKLMNOPQRSTUVWXYZ
1234567890 !@#?:;"*&

Foundry: Ascender
Designer: Steve Matteson
Designer Nationality: American
Date: 2005

Dujour is an ultra-bold display sans serif with tiny circular counters and an Art Deco feel. It is a revival of Indépendant, a font designed by Jos Dufour and Joan Collette for the Belgian branch of the Amsterdam Foundry in 1931 to celebrate one hundred years of Belgian independence.

Frankfurter

ABCDEFGHIJKLMNOPQRSTUVWXYZ
1234567890 !@#?:;"*&

Foundry: Letraset
Designer: Bob Newman /
Alan Meeks / Nick Belshaw
Designer Nationality: British
Date: 1970 / 1978 / 1981

The chunky, round sans serif Frankfurter typeface was named after a sausage and created by Bob Newman in 1970. In 1978, Letraset released a Medium version, designed by Alan Meeks, and a Highlight version, designed by Nick Belshaw. The uncredited Inline version followed in 1981.

Foundry Gridnik

ABCDEFGHIJKLMNOPQRSTUVWXYZ
abcdefghijklmnopqrstuvwxyz
1234567890 !@#?:;"*&

Foundry: The Foundry
Designer: Wim Crouwel /
Freda Sack / David Quay
Designer Nationality: Dutch /
British / British
Date: 1960s / 1996

London type designers The Foundry (see p. 284) have a close working relationship with legendary Dutch designer Wim Crouwel (see p. 540). As part of this initiative, the company has worked to realize a digital version of his 1970s design of a single weight monospaced typewriter typeface, and Foundry Gridnik is the result.

Crouwel's original design was from a commission in 1974 by typewriter maker Olivetti, to create a typeface that could be used on its new electronic typewriters. The original design was called Politene, but the rapid decline in the use of typewriters with the advent of PC technology meant it was never used in the manner for which it was intended. However, it gained a new lease of life in 1976, when Crouwel used it on his range of postage stamps for the Dutch Post Office, PTT, where it was employed up to 2002.

Foundry Gridnik's geometric form, monoline stroke weight, and 45°-angled corners give a highly engineered appearance to its design, evoking a technical theme. Despite the consistent underlying grid approach to the typeface's creation, it has a humanist quality, so it is not entirely mechanical in tone. This reflects Crouwel's thoughts about his work; he oncáe said: "I am a functionalist troubled by aesthetics." The typeface was named after Crouwel's nickname "Mr Gridnik," a reference to his passion for grids and systems in his work. It extends Crouwel's single-weight design into a five-weight family, ranging from Light to Extra Bold plus italics.

Right. *5054* automative magazine employing Foundry Gridnik for its masthead and title typography. Design and art direction by Patrick Myles.

FS Conrad

ABCDEFGHIJKLMNOPQRSTUVWXYZ
abcdefghijklmnopqrstuvwxyz
1234567890 !@?:;"×+

FS Conrad is a display sans serif made from thin lines. The Regular weight is constructed from five lines, while Headline uses seven and is subsequently harder to use at small sizes. Conrad began as a commission to design a typeface to complement the sculptures of Conrad Shawcross.

Foundry: Fontsmith
Designer: Phil Garnham
Designer Nationality: British
Date: 2012

FS Pele

ABCDEFGHIJKLMNOPQRSTUVWXYZ
abcdefghijklmnopqrstuvwxyz
1234567890 !@?:;"*&

FS Pele is named after the legendary Brazilian footballer. Phil Garnham from Fontsmith (see p. 272) created the dynamic, retro typeface in 2009, inspired by "chunky typefaces from the late 1960s and early 1970s." It comes in two weights with italics and is best used at large headline sizes.

Foundry: Fontsmith
Designer: Phil Garnham
Designer Nationality: British
Date: 2009

Geometric 885

ABCDEFGHIJKLMNOPQRSTUVWXYZ
abcdefghijklmnopqrstuvwxyz
1234567890 !@#?:;"*&

Geometric 885 is Bitstream's version of Aldo Novarese's typeface Bloc (1974), which was originally released by Visual Graphics Corporation after Novarese left Italian foundry Nebiolo. Available in a single style, Geometric 885 is a heavy, outlined, geometric sans serif best used at large sizes.

Foundry: Bitstream
Designer: Aldo Novarese
Designer Nationality: Italian
Date: 1974

History 01

ABCDEFGHIJKLMNOPQRSTUVWXYZ
1234567890 !@#?:;"*&

History 01 is one of the twenty-one styles of Peter Biľak's History typeface. It is an elegant, hairline, geometric sans serif font. History's eclectic fonts are all inspired by the evolution of typography and can be layered together to create exciting and unexpected combinations.

Foundry: Typotheque
Designer: Peter Biľak
Designer Nationality: Slovakian
Date: 2008

Horatio

ABCDEFGHIJKLMNOPQRSTUVWXYZ
abcdefghijklmnopqrstuvwxyz
1234567890 !@#?:;"*&

Foundry: Letraset
Designer: Bob Newman
Designer Nationality: British
Date: 1971

Letraset typeface Horatio was created by British designer Bob Newman in 1971. It is a geometric sans serif inspired by the typographic experiments of early 20th-century modernist designers such as Herbert Bayer and Joost Schmidt. Horatio comes in three weights: Light, Medium, and Bold.

Industria

ABCDEFGHIJKLMNOPQRSTUVWXYZ
abcdefghijklmnopqrstuvwxyz
1234567890 !@#?:;"*&

Foundry: Linotype
Designer: Neville Brody
Designer Nationality: British
Date: 1990

Industria, by British designer Neville Brody, is a condensed geometric sans serif that mixes right-angles and curves. Linotype released it with three other fonts by Brody in 1990. It comes in two styles: Solid and Inline. *The X-Files* science-fiction TV series features Industria for intro titles.

Interpol

ABCDEFGHIJKLMNOPQRSTUVWXYZ
1234567890 !@#?:;"*&

Foundry: Neutura
Designer: Alexander McCracken
Designer Nationality: American
Date: 2008

Designed by Alexander McCracken and released by Neutura (see p. 472) in 2008, Interpol is an all-caps, geometric display sans serif that comes in eight styles, some of which are textured or include backgrounds. Interpol shares its name with a Fundición Tipográfica Nacional typeface from 1950.

ITC Ronda

ABCDEFGHIJKLMNOPQRSTUVWXYZ
abcdefghijklmnopqrstuvwxyz
1234567890 !@#?:;"*&

Foundry: ITC
Designer: Ronne Bonder / Tom Carnase
Designer Nationality: American
Date: 1970

Ronne Bonder and Tom Carnase created this modernist-inspired geometric, monoline sans serif in 1970. ITC Ronda is built around the forms of the circle, triangle and rectangle, clearly visible in the distinctive uppercase "Q." Originally, it was available in three weights, but ITC has digitized only one.

Julien

Foundry: Typotheque
Designer: Peter Biľak
Designer Nationality: Slovakian
Date: 2010–11

This wonderfully playful geometric typeface comes from Dutch foundry Typotheque (see p. 90) and its founder, Slovakian designer Peter Biľak. It was inspired by the simple, geometric forms of the 20th century avant-garde, in particular by art movements such as Dada and Futurism, as well as the Bauhaus school.

Key Bauhaus figures such as László Moholy-Nagy and Herbert Bayer considered typography primarily to be a medium of communication. They embraced 20th-century machine culture and favoured a highly functional approach to type, opting to employ simplified forms without ornamentation. As such, each of Julien's characters is formed from elementary geometric shapes, which simultaneously evoke and pay homage to this innovative period in the history of design.

Each of Julien's characters contain multiple glyphs so variation can be introduced when letters repeat themselves within words or in lengths of text. When the glyphs are partnered with intelligent OpenType scripts, they enhance the design process, since the user can choose the glyphs that make the best word shapes. Using software that is adept at handling OpenType substitutions, allows the Contextual Alternates feature to alter the characters and achieve a unique flow of letterforms. These can be overwritten and altered by replacing characters selected from the Glyphs palette.

Julien is a unicase typeface, which means upper- and lowercase letters are mixed together, giving the designer the opportunity to experiment. It is available in two weights; a light, thin-stroked version and a heavy black version.

Below left. Example setting of Julien showing variants.

Below right. With the Contextual Alternates feature switched on, Julien possesses a wide range of alternate characters. Here is shown in Light and Bold, both lower and uppercase.

Jillican

ABCDEFGHIJKLMNOPQRSTUVWXYZ
abcdefghijklmnopqrstuvwxyz
1234567890 !@#?:;"*&

Foundry: Typodermic
Designer: Ray Larabie
Designer Nationality: Canadian
Date: 2001

Inspired by a trip to London, Canadian designer Ray Larabie designed Jillican in 2001. He followed the proportions of Gill Sans to create an angular sans serif made from straight lines, not curves. It comes in eighteen styles, some of which are italic, stenciled, 3D or distressed.

Kairos

ABCDEFGHIJKLMNOPQRSTUVWXYZ
abcdefghijklmnopqrstuvwxyz
1234567890 !@#?:;"*&

Foundry: Monotype
Designer: Terrance Weinzierl
Designer Nationality: American
Date: 2015

Terrance Weinzierl of Monotype took inspiration from the forms and bevelled corners of 19th-century US wood types known as Grecians to design the Kairos geometric slab serif. It is available in regular, condensed, and extended, in eight weights, plus a display version with shadows and highlights.

Laundrette

ABCDEFGHIJKLMNOPQRSTUVWXYZ
abcdefghijklmnopqrstuvwxyz
1234567890 !@#?:;"*&

Foundry: Chank Co.
Designer: Chank Diesel
Designer Nationality: American
Date: 1993

Laundrette is the work of prolific US type designer Chank Diesel. It is an extended, angular, squat slab serif, which is constructed entirely without the use of curves. It has a particularly idiosyncratic lowercase "g." Laundrette has a low x-height and thin, rectangular tittles.

Linotype Carmen

ABCDEFGHIJKLMNOPQRSTUVWXYZ
abcdefghijklmnopqrstuvwxyz
1234567890 !@#?:;"&

Foundry: Linotype
Designer: Lutz Günther
Designer Nationality: German
Date: 2002

Lutz Günther's Carmen is part of the TakeType 4 library of winners from the Linotype International Digital Type Design Contest of 2002. It is a distinctive geometric stencil sans serif created from overlapping shapes in places. It has undersized, offset titles in the manner of Gill Kayo.

Linotype Fehrle Display

ABCDEFGHIJKLMNOPQRSTUVWXYZ
abcdefghijklmnopqrstuvwxyz
1234567890 !@#?;;""*&

Foundry: Linotype
Designer: Erich Fehrle
Designer Nationality: German
Date: 1976

Erich Fehrle's Linotype Fehrle Display is a geometric display face designed exclusively for headlines, which utilizes the structural forms of the rectangle.

The bold letterforms embrace a combination of sharp angles, rounded corners, slablike serifs, and narrowly opened joints.

Linotype Isilda

ABCDEFGHIJKLMNOPQRSTUVWXYZ
abcdefghijklmnopqrstuvwxyz
1234567890 !@#?:;""*&

Foundry: Linotype
Designer: Frank Marciuliano
Designer Nationality: American
Date: 1997

Linotype Isilda is a geometric display face with a focus on narrow vertical strokes. The characters are reminiscent of a sprawling skyline, a feature that

is emphasized by the slanted descender on the "y," which appears as a shadow extending beyond the letter's architectural stem.

Linotype Renee Display

ABCDEFGHIJKLMNOPQRSTUVWXY
abcdefghijklmnopqrstuvwxy
1234567890 !@#?:;""*&

Foundry: Linotype
Designer: Renee Ramsey-Passmore
Designer Nationality: American
Date: 1997

Linotype Renee Display is a geometric face designed on a strict, mathematical grid, which is made visible in the font's Lines weight. The

characters are seen more clearly in the Types weight, and are constructed from a combination of circles, triangles, and rectangles.

Linotype Vision

ABCDEFGHIJKLMNOPQRSTUVWXYZ
abcdefghijklmnopqrstuvwxyz
1234567890 !@#?:;""*&

Foundry: Linotype
Designer: Dan-André Niemeyer
Designer Nationality: German
Date: 1997

The Linotype Vision geometric display font was originally an entrant into the Linotype International Digital Type Design Contest, and Linotype published

it in 1997 as part of its TakeType Library. The letterforms, designed in five styles, are comprised of a single line, akin to an electrical circuit.

Matra

ABCDEFGHIJKLMNOPQRSTUVWXYZ
1234567890 !@#P:;"*&

Foundry: Monotype
Designer: Cassandre
Designer Nationality: French
Date: 1930

Matra is a modern, geometric display type, designed entirely in capitals and informed by the Art Deco style. Unlike similar designs, Matra tends to separate the thicker cross-strokes from the hairline verticals, as seen in the "E," "F," and "B." "Cassandre" was the pseudonym of Adolphe Jean-Marie Mouron.

Mineral

ABCDEFGHIJKLMNOPQRSTUVWXYZ
abcdefghijklmnopqrstuvwxyz
1234567890 !@#?:;"*&

Foundry: BB-Bureau
Designer: Benoît Bodhuin
Designer Nationality: French
Date: 2013

Mineral is the work of French type designer Benoît Bodhuin, who studied maths at university before switching to graphic design. He releases typefaces through his foundry BB-Bureau (see p. 386). It is a modular, experimental stencil sans serif in five varied styles: Solid, Blunt, Smooth, Outline, and Border.

Ned

ABCDEFGHIJKLMNOPQRSTUVWXY
abcdefghijklmnopqrstuvwxye
1234567890 !@#?:; *&

Foundry: Linotype
Designer: Michael Parson
Designer Nationality: Swiss
Date: 2002

Michael Parsons's Ned is a geometric display font designed using a broad hexagonal grid, similar in shape to the cells of a honeycomb. In both upper and lowercases, the characters are carefully regimented and employ interchangeable shapes alongside a uniform stroke width.

Neutrino

ABCDEFGHIJKLMNOPQRSTUVWXYZ
abcdefghijklmnopqrstuvwxyz
1234567890 !@#?:;"*&

Foundry: Neutura
Designer: Alexander McCracken
Designer Nationality: American
Date: 2004

Neutrino is a geometric display face designed in both Regular and Alternate styles. Unlike many heavy types, Neutrino's letterforms feature no counters and are a combination of shapely curves and sharp angles, evidenced in both the lower- and uppercase characters.

Nine Metric

ABCDEFGHIJKLMNOPQRSTUVWXYZ
abcdefghijklmnopqrstuvwxyz
1234567890 !@#?:;"*&

MuirMcNeil's Nine Metric, designed in 2013, is a rounded geometric sans serif constructed using a dot-matrix grid. It comes in nine weights—hence its name—each of which increase incrementally by eighteen units on the base grid. Weights go from the ultra-light 018 to extra-black 162.

Foundry: MuirMcNeil
Designer: Hamish Muir / Paul McNeil
Designer Nationality: British
Date: 2013

Nine Mono

ABCDEFGHIJKLMNOPQRSTUVWXYZ
abcdefghijklmnopqrstuvwxyz
1234567890 !@#?:;"*&

Nine Mono is designed by Hamish Muir and Paul McNeil. It is a monospaced version of Nine Metric which is also more angular, including right angles as well as added serifs in places to equalize letter widths. Muir and McNeil both teach at the London College of Communication.

Foundry: MuirMcNeil
Designer: Hamish Muir / Paul McNeil
Designer Nationality: British
Date: 2013

Oblong

ABCDEFGHIJKLMNOPQRSTUVWXYZ
abcdefghijklmnopqrstuvwxyz
1234567890 !@#?:;"*&

Oblong was designed by US-based couple Rudy VanderLans and Zuzana Licko, who also founded the digital type foundry and publisher Emigre (see p. 106) in 1984. Oblong is a square, monoline slab serif that comes in two roman weights. Its square forms point towards its construction from pixels.

Foundry: Emigre
Designer: Rudy VanderLans / Zuzana Licko
Designer Nationality: Dutch / Slovakian
Date: 1988

Oboe

ABCDEFGHIJKLMNOPQRSTU
VWXYZ
1234567890 ! ?:;"*&

Pablo Balcells designed Oboe for the Graviton foundry in 2012. It is a chunky, blocky, uppercase sans serif with rounded corners, fixed width and small counters. The typeface comes in six styles: Solid, Solid Wide, Solid Framed, Outline, Outline Wide, and Outline Framed.

Foundry: Graviton
Designer: Pablo Balcells
Designer Nationality: Argentinian
Date: 2012

Odessa

ABCDEFGHIJKLMNOPQRSTUVWXYZ
abcdefghijklmnopqrstuvwxyz
1234567890 !?:;"*&

Foundry: Letraset
Designer: Peter O'Donnell
Designer Nationality: British
Date: 1988

Odessa is a geometric sans serif with an inline that creates a fine line on the edge of the characters. Its forms, which come in a single roman style, are heavily influenced by Futura. Peter O'Donnell, Odessa's British designer, created a handful of other fonts for Letraset.

Panopticon

Panopticon A: 010 Perimeter

Panopticon A: 020 Interior

Panopticon A: 030 Horizontal

Panopticon A: 040 Vertical

Panopticon (left, Variation A) is a system of 3D display typefaces built in four orthographic projections by MuirMcNeil (see p. 334). It is named after a form of polygonal building developed in the 18th century by English philosopher and social reformer Jeremy Bentham to facilitate controlled and concealed viewpoints.

The Panopticon system challenges convention and legibility and has been implemented in four alternative viewpoints, or projections. A: is the top right view, B: is the bottom left view, C: is the top left view and D: is the bottom right view. Each of the four Panopticon projections is subdivided into four separate typeface layers: 10: Perimeter, 20: Interior, 30: Horizontal, and 40: Vertical.

Foundry: MuirMcNeil
Designer: Hamish Muir / Paul McNeil
Designer Nationality: British
Date: 2014

Right. Panopticon poster employing differing orthographic projections of the 3D display typeface. Design by MuirMcNeil.

Pump

ABCDEFGHIJKLMNOPQRSTUVWXYZ
abcdefghijklmnopqrstuvwxyz
1234567890 !@#?:;"*&

Foundry: ITC
Designer: Philip Kelly
Designer Nationality: British
Date: 1975

British designer Philip Kelly created Pump in 1975 while he was working at Letraset. The fun typeface is retro enough to create nostalgia for the 1970s, but can also look contemporary in the appropriate design setting. Its geometric curves and rounded forms share similar aesthetics to typefaces such as ITC Bauhaus, which was based around Herbert Bayer's designs of 1925 and revived by Ed Benguiat (see p. 514) and Victor Caruso for ITC in 1975, ITC Ronda designed in 1970 by Herb Lubalin (see p. 63) and Linotype's Blippo from 1992. Pump is available in Light, Medium, Demi, Bold and Triline versions. Triline is a bold design formed of three strokes in parallel, which is ideal for sport graphic applications.

Right. Album cover design for celebrated Brazilian guitarist and composer Baden Powell de Aquino, employing Pump and Pump Triline in its typography.

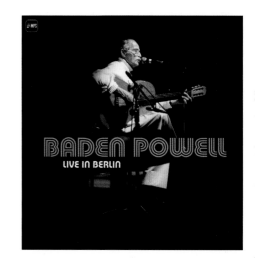

Rabbit

ABCDEFGHIJKLMNOPQRSTUVWXYZ
1234567890 !@#?:;"*&

Foundry: Neutura
Designer: Alexander McCracken
Designer Nationality: American
Date: 2000

Rabbit is one of Alexander McCracken's earliest font designs and was created three years before he founded the Neutura foundry (see p. 472). It is an all uppercase, geometric sans serif with a monoline construction, and rounded corners. It comes in four weights: Light, Regular, Bold, and Heavy.

Rimouski

ABCDEFGHIJKLMNOPQRSTUVWXYZ
abcdefghijklmnopqrstuvwxyz
1234567890 !@#?:;"*&

Foundry: Typodermic
Designer: Ray Larabie
Designer Nationality: Canadian
Date: 2005

Ray Larabie designed Rimouski in 2005. It is a rounded geometric type family that contains five weights, from ultra-light to bold. It has a large x-height and OpenType features such as automatic ligatures, class-based kerning and stylistic alternate slanted letters for "A," "V," and "W."

Pickle Standard

ABCDEFGHIJKLMNOPQRSTUVWXYZ
abcdefghijklmnopqrstuvwxyz
1234567890 !@#?:;""*&

Foundry: BB-Bureau
Designer: Benoît Bodhuin
Designer Nationality: French
Date: 2018

The Pickle Standard typeface is a grid-based design by French type and graphic designer Benoît Bodhuin (see p. 386). Its convoluted forms possess a logic and a simplicity as only a highly geometric typeface design can. Nevertheless, its resultant aesthetic is organic. On first impressions the typeface appears somewhat anarchic, with an almost runic quality to its forms. The letterform strokes kick back in 90° corners after flowing curves. Its deep-cut inset horizontal and vertical counters are even more exaggerated in the italic versions. Despite the abstract-shaped letterforms, this distinctive typeface is still highly legible.

Pickle Standard is based on Bodhuin's Standard typeface, which comes in six weights: 20, 40, 60, 80, 100, and 120. The Pickle Standard design comes in one weight and three styles: Regular, Italic, and a Reverse Italic.

Below and right. Launch material and specimen samples for the Pickle Standard grid-inspired typeface by BB-Bureau.

before touching
the ground
250

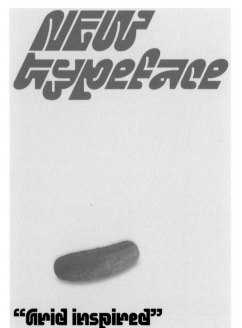

NEW
typeface

"Grid inspired"

Opening Night:

Lazer Notes

Good art is just
around the corner!
Scene of MoMaCaA

Museum of Modern
and Contemporary
and cool Art

We're very
excited, there
is a danger in
choice, in making
decisions and
sticking to
them!

Separat

ABCDEFGHIJKLMNOPQRSTUVWXYZ
abcdefghijklmnopqrstuvwxyz
1234567890 !@#?:;"*&

The Separat typeface comes from Or Type (see p. 498), the online type foundry of GUNMAD, the Iceland and Brussels-based design studio. It is based on the concept of separating the shapes of the letterforms. This gives the geometric sans serif display type an industrial feel. Built around short curves and straight lines, the design principle creates a number of striking letterforms. It is available in four styles: Regular, Medium, Bold, and Black. The lighter uppercase weights show the separate elements of the character construction, especially in letters such as "B," "K," and "R." Separat has fast become a popular choice for designers to use in branding and packaging applications. It has also been employed as display type for the British Council's *Ice Lab: New Architecture and Science in Antarctica* touring exhibition and the Europarque exhibition and conference centre in Portugal.

Foundry: Or Type
Designer: Mads Freund Brunse / Guðmundur Úlfarsson (GUNMAD)
Designer Nationality: Danish / Icelandic
Date: 2013

Below from left. Poster for *Learning from Japan* exhibition at the Designmuseum Denmark, design by Studio Claus Due; identity and branding for the London-based Redchurch Brewery (top), design by Bibliothèque; publication design *BAT: Bridging Art + Text* (bottom), design by Daniel Siim; poster design for British Council international touring exhibition *Ice Lab*, design by OK-RM.

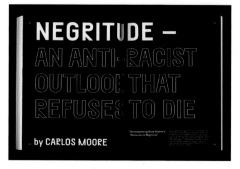

Sabre

ABCDEFGHIJKLMNOPQRSTUVWXYZ
1234567890 !@#?:;"*&

Foundry: Neutura
Designer: Alexander McCracken
Designer Nationality: American
Date: 2002

San Francisco-based designer Alexander McCracken created Sabre in 2002. It is a geometric sans serif with a monoline construction and rounded forms and corners. It comes in four weights: Thin, Light, Regular, and Bold. Sabre has uppercase roman letters only.

Shotgun

ABCDEFGHIJKLMNOPQRSTUVWXYZ
1234567890 !@#?:;"'*&

Foundry: Bitstream
Designer: J. Looney
Designer Nationality: American
Date: 1972

Bitstream's version of J. Looney's geometric Art Deco was originally designed for Visual Graphics Corporation in 1972, and comprises two options, the solid black Shotgun and the inline Shotgun Blanks. A Cyrillic version called Target was designed in 1997 by the Russian foundry Diai JS.

Sinaloa

ABCDEFGHIJKLMNOPQRSTUVWXYZ
1234567890 !?;"*&

Foundry: Letraset
Designer: Rosemarie Tissi
Designer Nationality: Swiss
Date: 1974

This very decorative display face with strong geometric forms and characters with distinctive striped strokes was one of a handful created by Swiss designer Rosemarie Tissi. She set up the renowned Zurich graphic design studio Odermatt & Tissi with Siegfried Odermatt in 1968.

Solida

ABCDEFGHIJKLMNOPQRSTUVWXYZ
1234567890 !O*?:;"*&

Foundry: Graviton
Designer: Pablo Balcells
Designer Nationality: Argentinian
Date: 2012

As its name suggests, Solida is a very solid, display-only block-based typeface with a geometric angular look and science-fiction overtones. Argentinian designer Pablo Balcells released Solida through Graviton, the small type foundry he established in Buenos Aires in 2013.

Slayer

ABCDEFGHIJKLMNOPQRSTUVWXYZ
1234567890 !@#?;;""*£

Never has a typeface been more appropriate for a Scandinavian death-metal record label in its appearance or by its name than the Slayer font family from Neutura (see p. 472). Slayer had its beginnings as a side project when Neutura's founder Alexander McCracken was working for Oslo design studio Bleed. Originally called Magma, Slayer comes in three weights: Regular, Bold, and Heavy. Its heavy, aggressive, angular strokes, combined with its dark and bold appearance, and diagonally slashed end strokes mark it out as one attention-seeking rocker of typeface.

Foundry: Neutura
Designer: Alexander McCracken
Designer Nationality: American
Date: 2005

Below and right. Promotional posters for Slayer. Design by Neutura.

Standard

ABCDEFGHIJKLMNOPQRSTUVWXYZ
abcdefghijklmnopqrstuvwxyz
1234567890 !@#?.;'"‡&

Foundry: BB-Bureau
Designer: Benoît Bodhuin
Designer Nationality: French
Date: 2018

Standard is a grid-based geometric display typeface from French type and graphic design guru Benoît Bodhuin and his foundry, BB-Bureau (see p. 386). It is available in six weights, described as 20, 40, 60, 80, 100, and 120, and the numbers denote percentage increases in stroke weight dictated by the underlying grid structure used for each weight. As with its accompanying typeface cousin, Pickle Standard, the letterforms are built over a grid structure. Bodhuin studied mathematics at university before starting design school, and his imagination, passion for mathematics and love of geometrical patterns has been let loose with the aid of the grid. He has used the grid to create exaggerated character shapes employing semicircular forms married with horizontal and vertical strokes. The resultant design possesses an industrial consistency to its letterforms, while distinctive and strikingly playful patterns run through extended lengths of text.

Far left. Identity and poster for French jazz festival *Sur le Grill*. Design by Brest Brest Brest, using both Standard and Pickle Standard along with Laurenz Brunner's Circular sans serif.

Left. Promotion designs for Standard by BB-Bureau. Design by Benoît Bodhuin.

Spade

ABCDEFGHIJKLMNOPQRSTUVWXYZ
abcdefghijklmnopqrstuvwxyz
1234567890 !@#?::;"'* &

Foundry: Neutura
Designer: Alexander McCracken
Designer Nationality: American
Date: 2008

Spade arrived on the scene during the early 21st century, when there was a trend in graphic design for contemporary, geometric, Fat Face typefaces. It struck first because Alexander McCracken, founder of Neutura (see p. 472), designed it as an all lowercase to accompany the uppercase.

Spade is an extremely heavy geometric display face that is available in three different styles. Ultralight possesses the thinnest of strokes tracing its outline, Regular is completely solid and is infilled, and Counter (above) possesses the smallest of counters.

Below. Posters for Spade display font by Neutura, designed by Alexander McCracken.

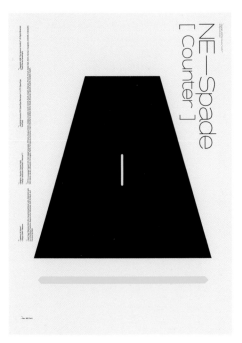

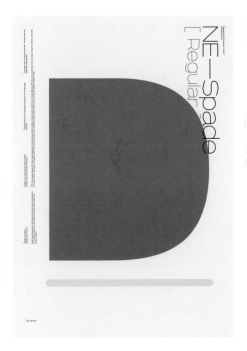

Ténica Slab

ABCDEFGHIJKLMNOPQRSTUVWXYZ
abcdefghijklmnopqrstuvwxyz
1234567890 !@#?:;"'*&

Foundry: Graviton
Designer: Pablo Balcells
Designer Nationality: Argentinian
Date: 2014

A slightly condensed, modular, geometric slab serif with subtle rounded angles, Pablo Balcells's Ténica Slab is available in Regular and Bold weights that give text a classic look. It is also available in Regular Alternate and Bold Alternate versions for text that requires a more playful apperance.

ThreeSix Typeface System

ABCDEFGHIJKLMNOPQRSTUVWXYZ
abcdefghijklmnopqrstuvwxyz
1234567890 !@#?:;"*&

Foundry: FontFont
Designer: Hamish Muir /
Paul McNeil
Designer Nationality: British
Date: 2011

The ThreeSix Typeface System from MuirMcNeil (see p. 334) is an optical / geometric type system consisting of six typefaces in eight weights. The system is the result of an exploration of the legibility and readability of geometric typeface design. MuirMcNeil researched issues relating to the design of geometric typefaces that could be used for extended lengths of text as opposed to display applications.

The ThreeSix system operates to a rigid grid system and works within strict geometric constraints. All of its typefaces are based on a grid of 36-unit squares subdivided into 9 units. All of the typefaces are constructed from a set of modules using vertical or horizontal straight lines and circular arcs. In each typeface group, the vertical strokes of all weights align on a central axis and weight is applied as an increase or decrease on the stroke axis in 18-unit

steps. In this way, all the letterform contours within each typeface group map on to each other exactly. This allows the designer to overlay differing weights precisely for varying effects because the cap-height, x-height, ascent and descent measurements are identical across all ThreeSix typefaces.

The optical and structural elements of ThreeSix operate on five key typographic functions: contour —the shape of individual letterforms; stroke modulation—the optical balance between horizontal strokes and vertical strokes; junctions—the optical effects at the intersections of strokes; weight—the progressive increase in density on the underlying structure of the letterforms; and spacing—the fit of the forms in sequences. Each typeface group has eight weights: 018 Ultra Light, 036 Extra Light, 054 Light, 072 Regular, 090 Medium, 108 Bold, 124 Heavy, and 144 Black.

Below from left. Design process workings for testing of weights; *Inside Out* poster design showing overlaying of decreasing weights in register to each other; *Wim Crouwel: A Graphic Odyssey* show poster by MuirMcNeil.

Opposite. 36 poster, design by MuirMcNeil.

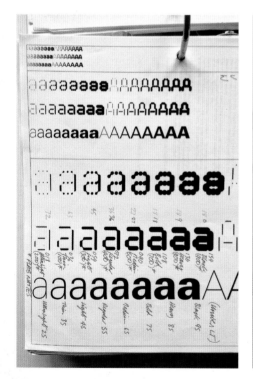

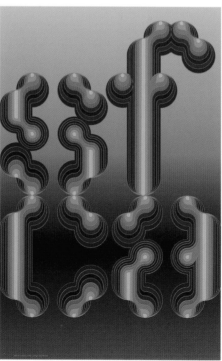

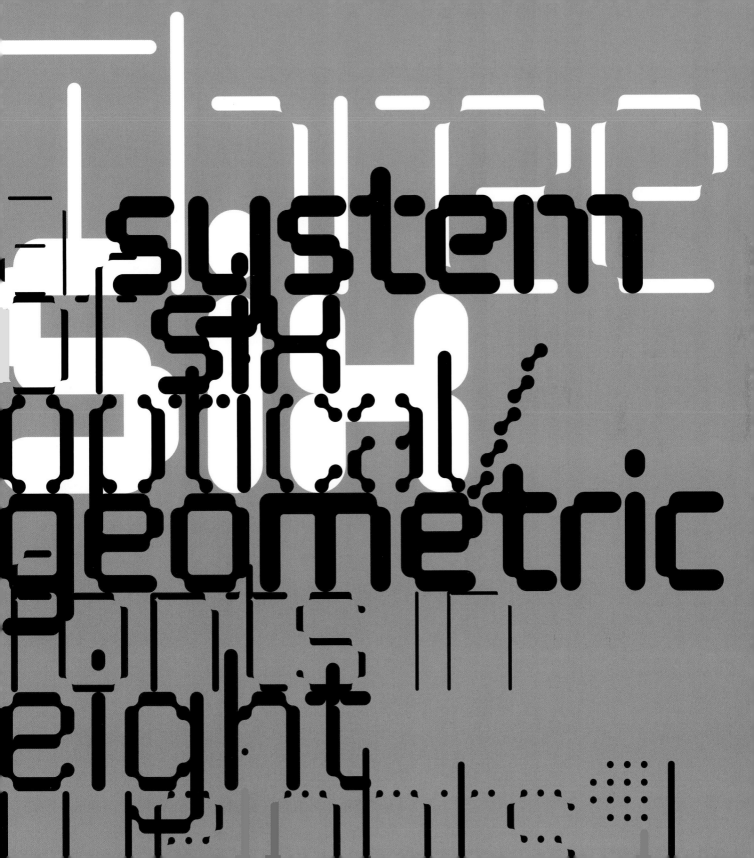

TwoBit

ABCDEFGHIJKLMNOPQRSTUVWXYZ
abcdefghijklmnopqrstuvwxyz
1234567890 !@#?:;"+&

Foundry: MuirMcNeil
Designer: Hamish Muir /
Paul McNeil
Designer Nationality: British
Date: 2018

TwoBit shares the same underlying grid as two other typefaces from MuirMcNeil (see p. 334), TwoPoint and TwoPlus. Also, as with a number of other typeface families from the foundry, individual characters are provided as segmented elements, which allows the designer free rein to experiment and build customized letterforms. The TwoBit family comes in five styles, each with seven weights. TwoBit A is a composite design. TwoBit B, C, D, and E are segmented elements of partial strokes and points. They can be combined in multiple overlays because they share the same underlying grid position so that matching, spacing and interlocking can be exact. When combined, the effect is reminiscent of electrical circuits and components linked together, with a visual connectivity linking the letterforms in a striking and dynamic presentation.

The ability for designers to create custom characters is not the only feature that makes TwoBit appealing. Overlaid in pairs, TwoBit's thirty-five fonts allow for 1,225 combinations and, when paired with any of the seventy-six MuirMcNeil TwoPoint and TwoPlus collections—a combined total of 111 fonts—a possible 12,321 combinations can be achieved. The designer's creative options are further increased as they can also use software to outline, tint and color type as well as apply textures, patterns and transparencies.

Below left. In TwoBit, one core (A) and four partial typefaces (B–E) comprise thirty-five fonts in matched ranges of seven numerically calibrated weights, all interlocking precisely when overlaid.

Below. Poster design for TwoBit by MuirMcNeil.

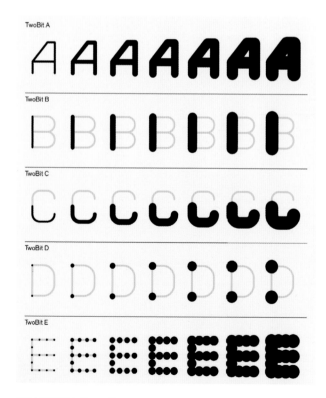

TwoBit A

TwoBit B

TwoBit C

TwoBit D

TwoBit E

TwoPlus

ABCDEFGHIJKLMNOPQRSTUVWXYZ
abcdefghijklmnopqrstuvwxyz
1234567890 !&#?:;"*&

Foundry: MuirMcNeil
Designer: Hamish Muir /
Paul McNeil
Designer Nationality: British
Date: 2016

TwoPlus began life in 2015 as a custom type design for the London College of Communication summer and postgraduate shows. MuirMcNeil (see p. 334) then refined, expanded and completed it to create a full typeface collection for TypeCon 2016, an annual convention of the American Society of Typographic Aficionados. TwoPlus was used as the identity for the event and in the supporting print and media.

The TwoPlus type system comprises seven monospaced type collections with a total of forty-eight typefaces. Each collection comes in matched ranges of calibrated weights and has a set of rectangular background panels in corresponding grid patterns to the letters. As with other MuirMcNeil designs, characters are supplied as component elements to allow the designer to combine and vary letterforms. All the elements match to an exact grid to permit precise layering, interlocking or even offsetting of the typeface components as well as inter-character spacing. It is possible to achieve 5,776 combinations when the seventy-six fonts across TwoPoint and TwoPlus are overlaid and used in pairs. The underlying precise grid structure means that the arrangement of characters and letter components can be set to exact positions. This makes TwoPlus and TwoPoint ideal for use in motion graphics, where precise placement of forms is vital when transitioning and animating, and in helping to create movement.

Below from left. Based on TwoPoint, TwoPlus is built around seven monospaced type groups, each font having a set of matching rectangular background panels with corresponding grid patterns; TwoPlus displayed at the LCC, London; TypeCon 2016 identity designed by MuirMcNeil.

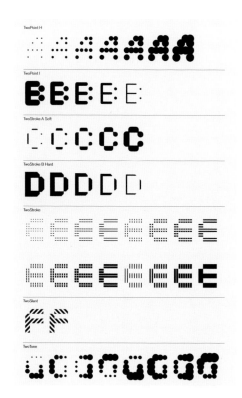

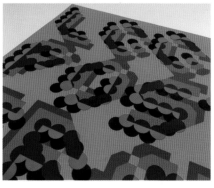

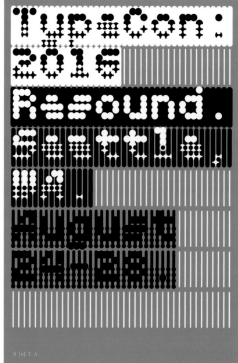

Cowhand

ABCDEFGHIJKLMNOPQRSTUVWXYZ
ABCDEFGHIJKLMNOPQRSTUVWXYZ
1234567890

Foundry: Monotype
Designer: Toshi Omagari
Designer Nationality: Japanese
Date: 2015

Toshi Omagari designed Cowhand as part of Monotype's first-ever Font Marathon, in which the foundry challenged designers to create a typeface from scratch in three days. Cowhand is a variable Western-style font, which allows all words set within it to share a single width.

DesperadoFLF

ABCDEFGHIJKLMNOPQRSTUVWXYZ
1234567890 !@#?:;"*&

Foundry: Casady & Greene
Designer: Richard Ware / Mike Wright
Designer Nationality: American
Date: 1993

The "FLF" in Desperado FLF stands for "Fluent Laser Fonts." It was published in 1993 by Casady & Greene, a software publisher started by Robin Casady and Mike Greene which released the world's first PostScript fonts and closed in 2003. Desperado is an all-caps, Western-style slab serif.

Figaro

ABCDEFGHIJKLMNOPQRSTUVWXYZ
abcdefghijklmnopqrstuvwxyz
1234567890 !@#?:;"*&

Foundry: Monotype
Designer: Monotype Studio
Date: 1940

Monotype developed Figaro in-house and it was initially released as Figaro 536. This heavy, condensed, slab serif font has thick horizontals that make it almost a reverse-contrast face. It is inspired by 19th-century advertising types, and was released as Showboat in the United States.

IFC Boothill

ABCDEFGHIJKLMNOPQRSTUVWXYZ
ABCDEFGHIJKLMNOPQRSTUVWXYZ
1234567890

Foundry: Ink Font Customs
Designer: Anton Krylov
Designer Nationality: Russian
Date: 2012

Ink Font Customs released IFC Boothill as a free font for personal use in 2012. It was created by Anton Krylov, a designer based in Chelyabinsk, Russia, close to the Ural Mountains. It is a wobbly, condensed, Western-style display font with fat slab serifs and uppercase and small caps only.

Italienne

ABCDEFGHIJKLMNOPQRSTUVWXYZ
abcdefghijklmnopqrstuvwxyz
1234567890 ! @ #?:;"'*&

Foundry: Linotype
Designer: Richard Yeend
Designer Nationality: British
Date: 2002

Italienne is a heavy, condensed display font with extreme contrast and thick serifs. British designer Richard Yeend created it for Linotype in 2002. The typeface was inspired by US wood type of the Wild West era and the reverse-contrast Italienne (or Italian) type style popular in the 19th century.

Old Towne No 536

ABCDEFGHIJKLMNOPQRSTUVWXYZ
abcdefghijklmnopqrstuvwxyz
1234567890 !@#?:;"*&

Foundry: Elsner+Flake
Designer: Elsner+Flake
Designer Nationality: German
Date: 1990

Old Towne No 356 is a robust, historical display face. It was inspired by old wood types, popularized in the United States through cinematic visions of the Wild West. The letterforms are notable for having serifs thicker than their strokes, which is a feature of Italienne-style reverse-contrast types.

Playbill

ABCDEFGHIJKLMNOPQRSTUVWXYZ
abcdefghijklmnopqrstuvwxyz
1234567890 !@#?:;"*&

Foundry: Stephenson, Blake & Co.
Designer: Robert Harling
Designer Nationality: British
Date: 1938

Playbill is an Italienne display font inspired by 19th-century wood types, later popularized in Hollywood westerns. The font contains a single style, which features bold, condensed shapes alongside serifs that are greater in weight than their corresponding strokes.

Rio Oro

ABCDEFGHIJKLMNOPQRSTUVWXYZ
ABCDEFGHIJKLMNOPQRSTUVWXYZ
1234567890 !@#?:;"*&

Foundry: Pixel Sagas
Designer: Neale Davidson
Designer Nationality: American
Date: 2012

Released in 2012, and later updated in 2015, Rio Oro is a Tuscan, Western-style, display slab serif with uppercase and small caps only. It was designed by Neale Davidson of Pixel Sagas and is available free for personal use. Rio Oro comes in Regular and Bold weights with italics.

Wainwright

ABCDEFGHIJKLMNOPQRSTUVWXYZ
1234567890 !@#?.:;"*&

Foundry: Image Club Graphics
Designer: Noel Rubin
Designer Nationality: Canadian
Date: 1995

Wainwright is an extremely condensed, uppercase slab serif with thick serifs. It comes in a single style, which is heavy with a Wild West feel. Noel Rubin designed many fonts for Image Club Graphics and later created interfaces shown in *Star Wars: Episode I* (1999) and *Star Wars: Episode III* (2005).

Wanted

ABCDEFGHIJKLMNOPQRSTUVWXYZ
abcdefghijklmnopqrstuvwxyz
1234567890 !@#?.:;"*&

Foundry: Letraset
Designer: Letraset Design Studio
Date: 1995

Designed by an unnamed staffer at Letraset in 1996, Wanted is a distressed, condensed slab serif in the Italienne style that emerged in the 19th century. As the name suggests, it would suit a wanted poster in the old West, thanks to its thick serifs and under-inked appearance.

Westside

ABCDEFGHIJKLMNOPQRSTUVWXYZ
abcdefghijklmnopqrstuvwxyz
1234567890 !@#?.:;"*&

Foundry: Linotype
Designer: Adrian Frutiger
Designer Nationality: Swiss
Date: 1989

Westside, which is perhaps one of the most surprising of the typeface designs by Adrian Frutiger (see p. 290), is a wood-type-inspired Italienne slab serif with thick serifs and reverse-contrast. Westside is best used at large sizes and comes in one style. As the name implies, it has a Wild West feel.

Winslett

ABCDEFGHIJKLMNOPQRSTUVWXYZ
ABCDEFGHIJKLMNOPQRSTUVWXYZ
1234567890 !@#?.:;"*&

Foundry: Pixel Sagas
Designer: Neale Davidson
Designer Nationality: American
Date: 2012

Winslett is a decorative Western-style typeface with thick slab serifs and central diamond ornaments on most letters. It was designed by Neale Davidson and has caps and small caps only. It comes in two weights, with a further outline version, all of which have matching italics.

Academy Engraved

ABCDEFGHIJKLMNOPQRSTUVWXYZ
abcdefghijklmnopqrstuvwxyz
1234567890 !@#?:;"*&

Foundry: Letraset
Designer: Vince Whitlock
Designer Nationality: British
Date: 1989

Vince Whitlock designed this distinguished serif typeface for Esselte Letraset in 1989. It was based on the forms of 18th-century Roman fonts such as Caslon, which were a popular source of inspiration for designers of similar engraved typefaces in the early 20th century.

Augustea Open

ABCDEFGHIJKLMNOPQRSTUVWXYZ
1234567890 !@#9:;"*&

Foundry: Nebiolo
Designer: Alessandro Butti / Aldo Novarese
Designer Nationality: Italian
Date: 1951

Augustea Open is a classical uppercase serif typeface with distinctive details influenced by Roman stone carved type. It was originally published under the name Augustea Filettato, and digital versions of the font were later developed by Letraset, ITC, and Elsner+Flake.

Boca Raton

ABCDEFGHIJKLMNOPQRSTUVWXYZ
abcdefghijklmnopqrstuvwxyz
1234567890 !@#?:;""*&

Foundry: Image Club Graphics
Designer: Grant Hutchinson
Designer Nationality: Canadian
Date: 1993

Grant Hutchinson designed Boca Raton during his years working the night shift at Image Club, which he worked around his day job as a high school assistant. Hutchinson and his co-workers went on to found the visual-content library Veer, which has since been bought by Getty Images.

Burlington

ABCDEFGHIJKLMNOPQRSTUVWXYZ
abcdefghijklmnopqrstuvwxyz
1234567890 !@#?:;"*&

Foundry: ITC
Designer: Alan Meeks
Designer Nationality: British
Date: 1985

Burlington is an engraved typeface designed by Alan Meeks in 1985, shortly after he departed from his role at Letraset to go freelance. Its tall ascenders and sharp serifs lend it a delicate, retro feel, and elongated tittles on the lowercase "i" and "j" add further interest.

Cabaret

ABCDEFGHIJKLMNOPQRSTUVWXYZ
abcdefghijklmnopqrstuvwxyz
1234567890 !?:;""*&

Foundry: Letraset
Designer: Alan Meeks
Designer Nationality: British
Date: 1980

This typeface shares certain similarities with the rounded letter forms of George Auriol's Robur Noir, which was published by Peignot in 1909 and in turn is said to have influenced the design of Cooper Black. Cabaret features additional engraved details and shaded embellishments.

Caslon Open Face

ABCDEFGHIJKLMNOPQRSTUVWXYZ
abcdefghijklmnopqrstuvwxyz
1234567890 !@#?:;""*&

Foundry: Bitstream
Designer: William Caslon / Unknown
Designer Nationality: British
Date: 1915

The first engraved typeface to be published under the name "Caslon Open Face" was released by Barnhart Brothers & Spindler in 1915; it features a lower x-height than many other Caslon-style fonts. This later digitization, created by Bitstream, is slightly heavier than its predecessor.

Castellar

ABCDEFGHIJKLMNOPQRSTUVWXYZ
1234567890 !@#?:;""*&

Foundry: Monotype
Designer: John Peters
Designer Nationality: British
Date: 1957

British type designer John Peters based his design of Castellar on ancient Roman square capitals; the typeface was first published by Monotype in 1957, relatively early in the phototypesetting era. Its finely chiselled serifs and engraved details suit larger point sizes.

Chevalier

ABCDEFGHIJKLMNOPQRSTUV
ABCDEFGHIJKLMNOPQRSTUVWXY
1234567890 !@#?:;""*&

Foundry: Haas
Designer: Emil A. Neukomm
Designer Nationality: Swiss
Date: 1946

Chevalier is an all-caps serif typeface with distinctive striped engraving, and was first released by Haas as metal type in 1946. Based on a style of lettering popular within 19th-century stationery and documents, it has since been expanded to include a full set of small caps.

Chisel

ABCDEFGHIJKLMNOPQRSTUVWXYZ
abcdefghijklmnopqrstuvwxyz
1234567890 !@#?:;"*&

Robert Harling created this inline font for Stephenson, Blake & Co. based on the earlier Latin Bold Condensed. Harling was an interesting figure in the type world; he co-founded the journal *Typography* and the Shenval Press, and was also typographic advisor to London Transport.

Foundry: Stephenson Blake
Designer: Robert Harling
Designer Nationality: British
Date: 1939

Citation

ABCDEFGHIJKLMNOPQRSTUVWXYZ
1234567890 !@#?:;"*&

Citation is a Copperplate-influenced display font designed by Trevor Loane for Letraset; it was one of the company's later releases and was published in 1990. The typeface features engraving, adding dimension and lending a sense of quiet authority to its uppercase letter forms.

Foundry: Letraset
Designer: Trevor Loane
Designer Nationality: British
Date: 1990

Cloister Open Face

ABCDEFGHIJKLMNOPQRSTUVWXYZ
abcdefghijklmnopqrstuvwxyz
1234567890 !@#?:;"*&

Originally part of the Cloister Old Style family, this engraved Open Face version was first designed by Morris Fuller Benton for American Type Founders, and would later be revived for digital type by Bitstream. Benton's original design was heavily influenced by the work of Nicolas Jenson.

Foundry: American Type Founders
Designer: Morris Fuller Benton
Designer Nationality: American
Date: 1929

Commerce Gothic

ABCDEFGHIJKLMNOPQRSTUVWXYZ
1234567890 !@#?:;"*&

Type and logo designer Jim Parkinson developed this shadowed headline font in 1998 for the AgfaType Creative Alliance, one year after Monotype joined forces with Agfa to expand the Alliance's growing library of typefaces. Commerce Gothic is available in uppercase only.

Foundry: Monotype
Designer: Jim Parkinson
Designer Nationality: American
Date: 1998

Fashion

ABCDEFGHIJKLMNOPQRSTUVWXYZ
abcdefghijklmnopqrstuvwxyz
1234567890 !?.:;"'*&

Foundry: Letraset
Designer: Alan Meeks
Designer Nationality: British
Date: 1986 / 1991

This font was first released as Fashion Compressed No. 3 in 1986. Alan Meeks updated it in 1991, when he added an extra style, Fashion Engraved. Fashion is a condensed but elegant high-contrast modern, roman, serif typeface with fine serifs, ball terminals, and hairline contrast in places.

Festival

ABCDEFGHIJKLMNOPQRSTUVWXYZ
1234567890 !@#?.:;"'*&

Foundry: Monotype
Designer: Phillip Boydell
Designer Nationality: British
Date: 1950

Festival, cut by Monotype in 1950 and used as the official type of the Festival of Britain in 1951, then released to the public in 1952, comes in a single Titling style. Festival Titling, designed by Phillip Boydell, is a distinctive uppercase, angular, shaded display sans serif.

ITC Abaton

ABCDEFGHIJKLMNOPQRSTUVWXYZ
ABCDEFGHIJKLMNOPQRSTUVWXYZ
1234567890 !@#?.:;"'*&

Foundry: ITC
Designer: Luis Siquot
Designer Nationality: Argentinian
Date: 1997

The work of Argentine designer Luis Siquot, ITC Abaton is a shaded display typeface with a thick outline, horizontal stripes within, and small wedge-shaped serifs. It includes only uppercase and small-cap letters. Siquot studied in Germany, worked in Spain, and then moved back to Argentina.

Jazz

ABCDEFGHIJKLMNOPQRSTUVWXYZ
abcdefghijklmnopqrstuvwxyz
1234567890 !?.:;"'*&

Foundry: Letraset
Designer: Alan Meeks
Designer Nationality: British
Date: 1992

Alan Meeks's Jazz, designed for Letraset and ITC in 1992, is a bold, wide headline font that has an Art Deco look thanks to thin stripes inlaid into its characters. These black and white horizontals also give it an elegant energy, much like the music from which it takes its name.

Modernistic

ABCDEFGHIJKLMNOPQRSTUVWXYZ
1234567890 !@#?¿¡""*&

Foundry: Monotype
Designer: Wadsworth A. Parker
Designer Nationality: American
Date: 1928

Wadsworth A. Parker's Modernistic is an open-face display font designed in the Art Deco style. The characters, which were drawn solely in uppercase, are defined by their high contrast, ornamental patterned interiors and short, keen serifs. It is ideal for posters and packaging.

PL Torino

ABCDEFGHIJKLMNOPQRSTUVWXYZ
abcdefghijklmnopqrstuvwxyz
1234567890 !©#?¿¡""*&

Foundry: Photo-Lettering
Designer: Ed Benguiat
Designer Nationality: American
Date: 1960

PL Torino is an open display typeface based on Alessandro Butti's Torino font, designed in 1908 for the Nebiolo foundry in Turin. While preserving the modern style of Butti's design, PL Torino introduces hollow, outlined strokes, which are accommodated by wider character widths.

Princetown

ABCDEFGHIJKLMNOPQRSTUVWXYZ
1234567890 !@#?¿""*&

Foundry: ITC
Designer: Richard Jones
Designer Nationality: British
Date: 1981

Princetown is an open display typeface based on the lettering commonly found on college and university sports garments. The geometric characters, designed in all-capitals, utilize squared curves, monoweight strokes, and muscular slab serifs to convey an athletic style.

Smaragd

ABCDEFGHIJKLMNOPQRSTU
VWXYZ
1234567890 !@#?:;"*&

Foundry: Stempel
Designer: Gudrun Zapf von Hesse
Designer Nationality: German
Date: 1952

Smaragd is named after the German word for "emerald." A light and elegant font, it is ideally suited for formal situations, and is Gudrun Zapf von Hesse's interpretation of Baroque adornment engravings. Originally produced as metal type, it was later digitized by Linotype.

Advertisers Gothic

ABCDEFGHIJKLMNOPQRSTUVWXYZ
abcdefghijklmnopqrstuvwxyz
1234567890 !@#?:;"*&

German-born type designer Robert Wiebking built
an impressive career as a type cutter in Chicago at
the turn of the 20th century, using a pantographic

punch-cutting device he designed himself.
This assertive sans serif design of his from
1917 proved very popular upon its release.

Foundry: Western Type
Designer: Robert Wiebking
Designer Nationality: German
Date: 1917

AG Book Rounded

ABCDEFGHIJKLMNOPQRSTUVWXYZ
abcdefghijklmnopqrstuvwxyz
1234567890 ! ?:;"*&

A friendlier counterpart to Berthold's Book font
family, designed by Günter Gerhard Lange, this
rounded typeface is well-suited to a wide range

of informal display contexts. AG Book Rounded is
available in six weights, with accompanying italics
and an outline version.

Foundry: Berthold
Designer: Günter Gerhard
Lange
Designer Nationality: German
Date: 1980

Aldous

ABCDEFGHIJKLMNOPQRSTUVWXYZ
1234567890 !@#?:;"*&

Walter Huxley created this condensed monoline
typeface in 1935, and it was originally published by
American Type Founders as Huxley Vertical. Subject

to several subsequent digitizations, the typeface
is now also known as Aldous Vertical, and is
published by Monotype.

Foundry: American Type
Founders / Monotype
Designer: Walter Huxley
Designer Nationality: American
Date: 1935

Alternate Gothic

ABCDEFGHIJKLMNOPQRSTUVWXYZ
abcdefghijklmnopqrstuvwxyz
1234567890 !@#?:;"*&

Alternate Gothic shares several formal traits with
Franklin Gothic and News Gothic, both of which it
was designed to pair with well. The typeface was

expanded in 2015, when it was republished as
American Type Founders Alternate Gothic, to
include a much wider range of weights and widths.

Foundry: American Type
Founders
Designer: Morris Fuller Benton
Designer Nationality: American
Date: 1903

Anzeigen Grotesk

ABCDEFGHIJKLMNOPQRSTUVWXYZ
abcdefghijklmnopqrstuvwxyz
1234567890 !@#?:;"*&

Foundry: Haas Type Foundry
Designer: Haas Studio
Designer Nationality: Swiss
Date: 1943

A heavy sans serif typeface featuring an extremely large x-height, Anzeigen Grotesk was developed by the Swiss foundry Haas in 1943 for display use in advertising. Its influence can be seen in the design of later heavyweight condensed display typefaces such as Impact (1965).

Aura

ABCDEFGHIJKLMNOPQRSTUVWXYZ
abcdefghijklmnopqrstuvwxyz
1234567890 !@#?:;"*&

Foundry: Linotype
Designer: Jackson Burke
Designer Nationality: American
Date: 1960

This authoritative display sans was designed by Jackson Burke, then director of typographic development at Linotype, who was also responsible for the design of the popular Trade Gothic typeface. Aura remains a steadfast choice for headline type in an array of contexts.

Aurora

ABCDEFGHIJKLMNOPQRSTUVWXYZ
abcdefghijklmnopqrstuvwxyz
1234567890 !@#?:;"*&

Foundry: Linotype
Designer: Jackson Burke
Designer Nationality: American
Date: 1960

Based on the earlier heavy sans serif Corona and designed by Jackson Burke for newspaper use, Aurora is a German-influenced grotesque typeface, with distinctive curved diagonal details within certain uppercase letter forms. It has been the subject of numerous digitizations.

Avenida

ABCDEFGHIJKLMNOPQRSTUVWXYZ
ABCDEFGHIJKLMNOPQRSTUVWXYZ
1234567890 !@#?:;"*&

Foundry: ITC
Designer: John Chippindale
Designer Nationality: American
Date: 1994

John Chippindale designed Avenida in 1994, influenced by the type styles found on buildings in Andalusia around the time of World War II. Available in uppercase only, it features a mix of low-slung and raised crossbars, and high vertices within the "M" and "N."

Balkan

ABCDEFGHIJKLMNOPQRSTUVWXYZ
АБЦДЕФГХИJКЛМНОПQРСТУВWXУЗ

ABCDEFGHIJKLMNOPQRSTUVWXYZ
АБЦДЕФГХИJКЛМНОПQРСТУВWXУЗ

1234567890 !@#?:;"*&

Created by Croatian designers Nikola Djurek and Mrija Juza, this bi-script display typeface features Cyrillic and Latin characters in tandem. Highlighting the letter forms shared between alphabets frequently used within the Balkan states, it is intended to promote unity and communication.

Foundry: Typotheque
Design: Nikola Djurek / Marija Juza
Designer Nationality: Croatian
Date: 2012

Bernhard Fashion

ABCDEFGHIJKLMNOPQRSTUVWXYZ
abcdefghijklmnopqrstuvwxyz
1234567890 !@#?:;"*&

Developed by the German-born designer Lucian Bernhard for American Type Founders, this fine and airy typeface captures the blithe spirit of the 1920s, with its balance of exaggerated capitals, low x-height, and comparatively short descenders. It has since been digitized by URW and Bitstream.

Foundry: American Type Founders
Designer: Lucian Bernhard
Designer Nationality: German
Date: 1929

Bigband

ABCDEFGHIJKLMNOPQRSTUVWXYZ
abcdefghijklmnopqrstuvwxyz
1234567890 !@#?:;"*&

This heavyweight sans serif typeface was originally issued by German foundry Ludwig & Mayer in 1974, featuring open and shaded styles; its later reissue by Linotype did away with the open Light cut and replaced it with Bigband Terrazo, a fractured version of the typeface.

Foundry: Ludwig & Mayer
Designer: Karlgeorg Hoefer
Designer Nationality: German
Date: 1974

Biondi Sans

ABCDEFGHIJKLMNOPQRSTUVWXYZ
ABCDEFGHIJKLMNOPQRSTUVWXYZ
1234567890 !@#?:;"*&

Biondi Sans is a Copperplate-influenced uppercase sans serif with a subtly extended feel; it is also more formally restrained than many of Ray Larabie's other display typeface designs. It is available in a range of six weights, from Ultra Fine to Bold, with corresponding italics for each.

Foundry: Typodermic
Designer: Ray Larabie / Chikako Larabie
Designer Nationality: Canadian / Japanese
Date: 2010

Brda

ABCDEFGHIJKLMNOPQRSTUVWXYZ
abcdefghijklmnopqrstuvwxyz
1234567890 !@#?:;"*&

Foundry: Linotype
Designer: Franciszek Otto
Designer Nationality: Polish
Date: 2003

Brda was a winner of Linotype's International Type Design Contest in 2003. The heavy grotesque typeface features distinctive notched details. It was originally designed by Franciszek Otto for the Polish weekly newspaper *Powiat*, and is available in three weights, plus italics.

Camulogen

ABCDEFGHIJKLMNOPQRSTUVWXYZ
1234567890 !@#?:;"*&

Foundry: Typodermic
Designer: Ray Larabie
Designer Nationality: Canadian
Date: 2012

This condensed sans serif typeface features geometric details and a subtly irregular stress within its stroke weight, making it an impactful yet distinctive choice for typesetting at a larger scale. Inspired by 19th-century poster type, Camulogen is available in uppercase only.

Carbon

ABCDEFGHIJKLMNOPQRSTUVWXYZ
1234567890 !@#?:;"*&

Foundry: Typodermic
Designer: Ray Larabie
Designer Nationality: Canadian
Date: 1999

Carbon, designed by Ray Larabie in 1999, is a unicase, rounded geometric sans serif that comes in seven weights with italics. There are also two textured display versions: Fence which has a diagonal grid cut into it, and Phyber, with a hexagonal pattern inspired by carbon fibre.

Central Avenue

ABCDEFGHIJKLMNOPQRSTUVWXYZ
ABCDEFGHIJKLMNOPQRSTUVWXYZ
1234567890 !@#?:;"*&

Foundry: Colophon
Designer: Studio Makgill
Designer Nationality: British
Date: 2011

Central Avenue was created for the identity of a show *Made in Birmingham: The Exhibition of Local Manufactures and Natural History 1886*. It is based on the exhibition's Victorian hand-painted type. This simple sans serif also has a superscripted alternative that enables users to create their own word logos.

Conductor

ABCDEFGHIJKLMNOPQRSTUVWXYZ
abcdefghijklmnopqrstuvwxyz
1234567890 !@#?:;"*&

Conductor was inspired by the blocky numerals appearing on vintage Bulgarian lottery tickets. The imposing sans serif display is a release from the foundry of esteemed US typeface designer Tobias Frere-Jones. As with many of Frere-Jones's type designs, there are a myriad of influences at play in the structure of these elegant letter forms. The chance for Bulgarians to become millionaires was not the only influence to play a part in the design; vernacular shopfront lettering and mid-century type designs, such as Eurostile, all contributed to the aesthetic.

Frere-Jones designed Conductor with Nina Stössinger, aided by contributions from colleague Fred Shallcrass. The intention was always that Conductor would be a display typeface, a change from the foundry's previous releases of text typefaces Exchange, Mallory, and Retina. Conductor is available in four widths—wide, normal, narrow and condensed—with just bold and bold italic variants of each. Its roman construction is based around rectangular forms whereas the italic style is triangular forms, which is evident in the dramatic three-sided bowls and counters, and the vibrant movement and rhythm of its lowercase.

Foundry: Frere-Jones Type
Designer: Tobias Frere-Jones / Nina Stössinger
Designer Nationality: American / Swiss
Date: 2017

Below and opposite. Conductor is a commanding display family, which references among its various sources of inspiration delicate, blocky numerals from vintage Bulgarian lottery tickets.

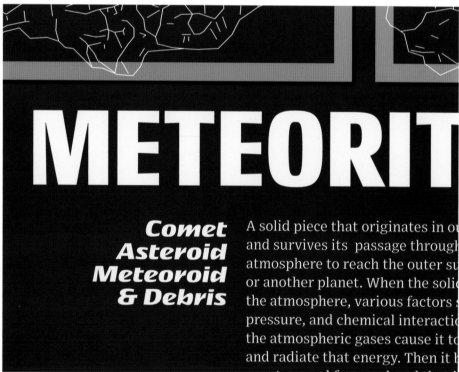

Conductor
Conductor
Conductor
Conductor
Conductor
Conductor
Conductor
Conductor

Cable
Inertia
23 Volts
Semitone

CUBS
GLOVE
DINKUM
PALISADE

CONDUCTOR

Wide	*Wide Italic*
Normal	*Normal Italic*
Narrow	*Narrow Italic*
Condensed	*Condensed Italic*

CONDUCTOR

Chervonec Uzkj BT

ABCDEFGHIJKLMNOPQRSTUVWXYZ
abcdefghijklmnopqrstuvwxyz
1234567890 !@#?:;"*&

Foundry: Bitstream
Designer: Oleg Karpinsky
Designer Nationality: Ukrainian
Date: 2002

A hybrid semi-serif design, this condensed typeface with irregular serif details was created by Ukrainian type designer Oleg Karpinsky in three weights, each with a corresponding italic. A versatile and legible display typeface, it was published by Bitstream in 2002.

Compacta

ABCDEFGHIJKLMNOPQRSTUVWXYZ
abcdefghijklmnopqrstuvwxyz
1234567890 !@#?:;"*&

Foundry: Letraset
Designer: Fred Lambert
Designer Nationality: British
Date: 1963

Letraset's first original typeface design, Compacta was published in 1963 and went on to become widely used throughout the 1960s and beyond. Heavy and condensed, its rectangular forms are softened by rounded corners; two outline versions and a black cut are also available.

Conference

ABCDEFGHIJKLMNOPQRSTUVWXYZ
abcdefghijklmnopqrstuvwxyz
1234567890 !@#?:;"*&

Foundry: Letraset
Designer: Martin Wait
Designer Nationality: British
Date: 1978

British designer Martin Wait created Conference for Letraset. Wait is also known for the logos he designed for household brands, including Tetley Tea and the *Radio Times* TV listings magazine. Conference is a friendly and bold display font featuring a minuscule flare on some stroke ends.

Cruz Cantera BT

ABCDEFGHIJKLMNOPQRSTUVWXYZ
abcdefghijklmnopqrstuvwxyz
1234567890 !@#?:;"*&

Foundry: Bitstream
Designer: Ray Cruz
Designer Nationality: American
Date: 2002

Cruz Cantera is a narrow font featuring rounded stroke ends and a high contrast within its letter forms. It was designed by US type designer Ray Cruz, who founded his own Cruz Fonts foundry in New Jersey in 2004 and has created typefaces for a range of other distributors.

Decotura

ABCDEFGHIJKLMNOPQRSTUVWXYZ
ABCDEFGHIJKLMNOPQRSTUVWXYZ
1234567890 !@#?:,"*&

Foundry: Image Club Graphics
Designer: Greg Kolodziejzyk
Designer Nationality: Canadian
Date: 1995

Also available as an inline version, Decotura is an uppercase-only, geometric, Art Deco-inspired display typeface designed by Greg Kolodziejzyk, who was the founder of Image Club Graphics. A successful Canadian type foundry and distributor, Image Club Graphics was sold to Adobe in 1994.

Diablo

ABCDEFGHIJKLMNOPQRSTUVWXYZ
ABCDEFGHIJKLMNOPQRSTUVWXYZ
1234567890 !@#?:,"*&

Foundry: Monotype
Designer: Jim Parkinson
Designer Nationality: American
Date: 2002

Diablo is named after the Spanish word for "devil." The chunky geometric display font was inspired by the type found in early 20th-century sample books and hand-drawn poster lettering, and the aesthetic of the Arts and Craft movement. It has no lowercase, but there is a set of alternative characters.

Doric

ABCDEFGHIJKLMNOPQRST
abcdefghijklmnopqrstuvwxyz
1234567890 !@#?:;" *&

Foundry: Linotype
Designer: Walter Tracy
Designer Nationality: British
Date: 1973

Doric was originally released by the Stephenson, Blake & Co. foundry. It is modeled on one of William Caslon IV's popular sans serifs and was designed by Walter Tracy, who was head of the type development department at Linotype for thirty years, as well as typographic advisor to *The Times*.

Dynamo

ABCDEFGHIJKLMNOPQRSTUVWXYZ
abcdefghijklmnopqrstuvwxyz
1234567890 !@#?:,"*&

Foundry: Ludwig & Mayer
Designer: Karl Sommer
Designer Nationality: German
Date: 1930

Karl Sommer designed Dynamo in 1930 for Ludwig & Mayer. It is a bold typeface with the structure of a sans serif but with small angular notches and serifs. Letraset updated the typeface in the 1970s, with Colin Brignall creating a Medium weight and Alan Meeks adding a shadow version.

Druk

Druk

ABCDEFGHIJKLMNOPQRSTUVWXYZ
abcdefghijklmnopqrstuvwxyz
1234567890 !@#?:;"*&

Druk Text

ABCDEFGHIJKLMNOPQRSTUVWXYZ
abcdefghijklmnopqrstuvwxyz
1234567890 !@#?:;"*&

Druk Text Wide

ABCDEFGHIJKLMNOPQRSTUVWX
abcdefghijklmnopqrstuvwxyz
1234567890 !@#?:;"*&

Druk Wide

ABCDEFGHIJKLMNOPQRSTUVW
abcdefghijklmnopqrstuvwxyz
1234567890 !@#?:;"*&

Druk Cond

ABCDEFGHIJKLMNOPQRSTUVWXYZ
abcdefghijklmnopqrstuvwxyz
1234567890 !@#?:;"*&

Druk XCond

ABCDEFGHIJKLMNOPQRSTU
abcdefghijklmnopqrstuvwxyz
1234567890 !@#?:;"*&

Druk XXCond

ABCDEFGHIJKLMNOPQRSTU
abcdefghijklmnopqrstuvwxyz
1234567890 !@#?:;"*&

The extensive and uncompromising Druk typeface family by Independent US type designer Berton Hasebe is influenced by the sans serif types created in the 19th century for display purposes. The condensed styles established in Britain in the 1830s were soon widespread across Europe; their condensed and expanded forms with flat sides allowed for tight letter spacing, which made them ideal for eye-catching headline typography.

The Druk typeface came about in response to a commission in 2013 from Richard Turley, when he was creative director at *Bloomberg Businessweek*, to create a typeface for use in the style and culture section of the journal. Hasebe's research led him to investigate titles such as *Twen*, a 1960s German style magazine designed and art directed by influential post war German graphic designer Willy Fleckhaus. Hasebe also examined the work of Dutch typographer Willem Sandberg and his catalogue designs for the Stedelijk Museum in Amsterdam. Druk contemporizes the historic condensed sans serifs that Hasebe researched.

It possesses no regular width and aims to be heavy and condensed or heavy and wide. Mixing the differing styles together, the designer can achieve the effect of woodblock compositions as contrasting lettershapes interlock with each other for dramatic effect.

Druk is available in twenty-two styles in four distinct families: Text, Text Wide, Wide, and Condensed. Both Text and Text Wide are ideal for using the texts at smaller sizes. Condensed is the most extreme in design ranging from a Condensed Super, which is recommended for 40 point and above, to a Condensed XX Super, which is ideal for 72 point and above.

Foundry: Commercial Type
Designer: Berton Hasebe
Designer Nationality: American
Date: 2014 / 2015

Below left. *Bloomberg Businessweek* cover. Illustration by Tracy Ma, creative director Richard Turley.

Below right. Promotional print for Skate Agora, a stand-out typography system for the largest skate park in Europe in Barcelona. Design by Solo design studio, Madrid. Druk's variable styles employed to create design reminiscent of woodblock composition.

Eagle

ABCDEFGHIJKLMNOPQRSTUVWXYZ
1234567890 !@#?:;"* &

Foundry: American Type Founders
Designer: Morris Fuller Benton
Designer Nationality: American
Date: 1933

Morris Fuller Benton designed Eagle in 1933 for the National Recovery Administration established by President Franklin D. Roosevelt, and it was released by American Type Founders. It is an uppercase only, geometric sans serif in a single bold weight. The "G" and "Q" have angular spurs.

Engravers Gothic BT

ABCDEFGHIJKLMNOPQRSTUVWXYZ
ABCDEFGHIJKLMNOPQRSTUVWXYZ
1234567890 !@#?:;"*&

Foundry: Bitstream
Designer: Frederic W. Goudy
Designer Nationality: American
Date: 1990

Engravers Gothic BT is an extended sans serif font that has caps and small caps only. It is essentially Frederic W. Goudy's Copperplate Gothic but with the sharp little serifs removed, and comes in a regular weight only. Isabella Chaeva added a bold weight and Cyrillic for ParaType in 2003.

F2F Czykago

ABCDEFGHIJKLMNOPQRSTUVWXYZ
abcdefghijklmnopqrstuvwxyz
1234567890 !@#?:;"*&

Foundry: Linotype
Designer: Alexander Branczyk
Designer Nationality: German
Date: 1995

F2F Czykago was inspired by the Apple font Chicago. It comes in three distinct styles; a light sans serif, a bolder semi serif, and the extended, experimental Trans. Its designer Alexander Branczyk worked at MetaDesign in Berlin and teaches typography at the Bauhaus-Universität Weimar.

FF Info Display

ABCDEFGHIJKLMNOPQRSTUVWXYZ
abcdefghijklmnopqrstuvwxyz
1234567890 !@#?:;"*&

Foundry: FontFont
Design: Erik Spiekermann / Ole Schäfer
Designer Nationality: German
Date: 2000

Erik Spiekermann (see p. 304) and Ole Schäfer began FF Info Display at agency Meta in 1996. The soft, highly legible sans serif typeface is part of a superfamily that also includes Info Correspondence and Info Text. It comes in eighteen styles and nine weights with italics.

FF Marten

ABCDEFGHIJKLMNOPQRSTUVWXYZ
abcdefghijklmnopqrstuvwxyz
1234567890 !@#?:;"*&

Foundry: FontFont
Designer: Martin Wenzel
Designer Nationality: German
Date: 1991

FF Marten is a condensed display sans in two styles: Regular and the less-rounded Grotesque. Its creator, German designer Martin Wenzel, releases fonts with the Supertype foundry he co-founded with Jürgen Huber, a fellow typography teacher at the HTW Berlin.

Francis

ABCDEFGHIJKLMNOPQRSTUVWXYZ
abcdefghijklmnopqrstuvwxyz
1234567890 !@#?:;"*&

Foundry: Typotheque
Designer: Nikola Djurek
Designer Nationality: Croatian
Date: 2016

Francis is a narrow sans serif in five weights with italics, and as the weight increases so does overall width. There is also Francis Gradient, four capital-only display versions, which each contain 2,690 glyphs that are selected automatically using OpenType's contextual alternates feature.

Gill Display Compressed

ABCDEFGHIJKLMNOPQRSTUVWXYZ
abcdefghijklmnopqrstuvwxyz
1234567890 !?:;"*&

Foundry: ITC / Letraset
Designer: Eric Gill /
Alan Meeks
Designer Nationality: British
Date: 1987

Alan Meeks designed this additional version of Gill Sans in 1987. Meeks stuck firmly to Eric Gill's design vision, creating a new cut that was heavy and compressed, filling a gap in Gill's initial range of weights and styles. It was released by International Typeface Corporation (ITC) and Letraset.

Gill Kayo Condensed

ABCDEFGHIJKLMNOPQRSTUVWXYZ
abcdefghijklmnopqrstuvwxyz
1234567890 !?:;"*&

Foundry: Letraset
Designer: Eric Gill
Designer Nationality: British
Date: 1980

Gill Kayo, the ultra-bold version of Gill Sans drawn in 1932, received a condensed version from Letraset in 1980. Its extreme forms are far removed from the regular cut of Gill Sans. Eric Gill originally wanted to call Kayo (derived from "KO," boxing slang for "knockout") Double Elefans.

Good Times

ABCDEFGHIJKLMNOPQRSTU VWXYZ
1234567890 !@#?:;"*&

Foundry: Typodermic
Designer: Ray Larabie
Designer Nationality: Canadian
Date: 2005

Good Times is a futuristic, extended, uppercase display sans serif created by Canadian designer Ray Larabie. It is available in seven weights with italics. Also included in the family is Bad Times, which is a distressed version of the heavy cut. Larabie was inspired by lettering on Pontiac cars.

Gothic 13

ABCDEFGHIJKLMNOPQRSTUVWXYZ
abcdefghijklmnopqrstuvwxyz
1234567890 !@#?:;"*&

Foundry: Adobe
Designer: Unknown
Date: *c.* 1800s

Gothic 13 is a single-style Bitstream sans serif. It is a digitization of an anonymous grotesque typeface called simply "Gothic Condensed," which dates to the 19th century. It is heavy, compact, and utilitarian, and is well-suited to use at large sizes such as headlines and poster type.

Gothic 821

ABCDEFGHIJKLMNOPQRSTUVWXYZ
abcdefghijklmnopqrstuvwxyz
1234567890 !@#?:;"*&

Foundry: Bitstream
Designer: Heinz Hoffmann
Designer Nationality: German
Date: 1921

Gothic 821 is a Bitstream version of Block, the heavy, rough sans serif released by Berthold in 1908. Block was first released in Bold only, but many weights followed in the two following decades. Gothic 821 is based on Block Condensed, known in German as *Schmale Block*.

Graphik XCond

ABCDEFGHIJKLMNOPQRSTUVWXYZ
abcdefghijklmnopqrstuvwxyz
1234567890 !@#?:;"*&

Foundry: Commercial Type
Designer: Christian Schwartz
Designer Nationality: American
Date: 2017

Christian Schwartz designed Graphik XCond with production assistance from Croatian type designer Hrvoje Živčić. It is an extra-condensed version of the earlier typeface Graphik, released in 2009 by Commercial Type (see p. 124). It comes in nine weights with italics and has been used by *Esquire*.

Graphik XXCond

ABCDEFGHIJKLMNOPQRSTUVWXYZ
abcdefghijklmnopqrstuvwxyz
1234567890 !@#?:;"*&

Foundry: Commercial Type
Designer: Christian Schwartz
Designer Nationality: American
Date: 2017

Christian Schwartz, the US co-founder of Commercial Type (see p. 124) who runs the foundry's New York office, designed Graphik XXCond in 2017. It is a very condensed grotesque sans serif type family that contains a large range of styles and comes in nine weights—Thin to Super—with matching italics.

Graphik XXXCond

ABCDEFGHIJKLMNOPQRSTUVWXYZ
abcdefghijklmnopqrstuvwxyz
1234567890 !@#?:;"*&

Foundry: Commercial Type
Designer: Christian Schwartz
Designer Nationality: American
Date: 2017

Graphik XXXCond, the third most condensed version of Schwartz's Graphik, has a large x-height and small ascenders and descenders. Commercial Type (see p. 124) explains that its open terminals create "breathing room in the white spaces within the characters" and "an inviting openness in the text."

Graphik XXXXCond

ABCDEFGHIJKLMNOPQRSTUVWXYZ
abcdefghijklmnopqrstuvwxyz
1234567890 !@#?:;"*&

Foundry: Commercial Type
Designer: Christian Schwartz
Designer Nationality: American
Date: 2017

This is the most extreme of the Graphik condensed family and comes in eighteen styles. It was created while Christian Schwartz was working on what he thought would be the narrowest possible variant of Graphik when fellow designer Abi Huynh challenged him to try making it twice as narrow.

Halte

ABCDEFGHIJKLMNOPQRSTUVWXYZ
abcdefghijklmnopqrstuvwxyz
1234567890 !@#?:;"*&

Foundry: Typotheque
Designer: Hrvoje Živčić
Designer Nationality: Croatian
Date: 2018

Hrvoje Živčić's Halte is a distinctive and blocky condensed sans serif that was inspired by type used on transport signage in the streets of Zagreb. It is available in five weights with italics and small caps, and includes many alternate letters and transport-related pictograms.

Headline

ABCDEFGHIJKLMNOPQRSTUVWXYZ
abcdefghijklmnopqrstuvwxyz
1234567890 !@#?:;"'*&

Foundry: Monotype
Designer: Eleisha Pechey
Designer Nationality: British
Date: 1906

Headline is a compact grotesque sans serif available in bold only. It is a Monotype copy of Grotesque No. 9, which was designed by Eleisha Pechey for the Stephenson, Blake & Co. foundry in 1906 but based on 19th-century type styles. Headline, as the name implies, is best used large.

Helvetica Compressed

ABCDEFGHIJKLMNOPQRSTUVWXYZ
abcdefghijklmnopqrstuvwxyz
1234567890 !@#?:;"'*&

Foundry: Linotype
Designer: Matthew Carter
Designer Nationality: British
Date: 1966

Matthew Carter (see p. 616) designed Helvetica Compressed, a heavy condensed sans serif, for the Linofilm phototypesetter in 1966. Although by name it is part of the Helvetica family, this was mainly for marketing reasons; it has more in common with an earlier sans serif, Schmalfette Grotesk.

Horizon

ABCDEFGHIJKLMNOPQRSTUVWXYZ
abcdefghijklmnopqrstuvwxyz
1234567890 !@#?:;"'*&

Foundry: Bitstream
Designer: Bitstream Design Studio
Designer Nationality: American
Date: 1992

Horizon is an uncredited font designed in-house at digital foundry Bitstream in 1992. It was supposedly inspired by lettering used in the early series of the science-fiction TV show *Star Trek*. Available in one style, it is a heavy, sharp sans serif with angled crossbars and diamond tittles.

Huxley Vertical

ABCDEFGHIJKLMNOPQRSTUVWXYZ
1234567890 !@ #?:;"'*&

Foundry: American Type Founders
Designer: Walter Huxley
Designer Nationality: American
Date: 1935

An uppercase, monoline condensed sans serif released in 1935, Walter Huxley's Huxley Vertical has an Art Deco feel. It originally came in one style, which is fairly thin, with alternate versions of "A," "K," "M," "N," "W," and "Y." There have been many digitizations, some of which added weights.

Impact

ABCDEFGHIJKLMNOPQRSTUVWXYZ
abcdefghijklmnopqrstuvwxyz
1234567890 !@#?:,"*&

Foundry: Stephenson Blake & Co.
Designer: Geoffrey Lee
Designer Nationality: British
Date: 1965

This compact heavy sans serif is ubiquitous thanks to its inclusion in Microsoft software. It was originally designed by Geoffrey Lee for Stephenson, Blake & Co. in 1965. Two extra styles, Condensed and Outline, were added in 1967. It has a large x-height and short ascenders and descenders.

Impacta

ABCDEFGHIJKLMNOPQRSTUVWXYZ
abcdefghijklmnopqrstuvwxyz
1234567890 !@#?:,"*⊕

Foundry: Linotype
Designer: Marc Lubbers
Designer Nationality: Dutch
Date: 1994

Impacta was created by Dutch typographer Marc Lubbers of GraphicMix in 1994 and was a winner in Linotype's first International Digital Type Design Contest. It is a heavy sans serif with angular details and sloped strokes. The typeface is available in a single style, which is very black.

Industrial Gothic

ABCDEFGHIJKLMNOPQRSTUVWXYZ
ABCDEFGHIJKLMNOPQRSTUVWXYZ
1234567890 !@#?:,"*&

Foundry: Agfa
Designer: Jim Parkinson
Designer Nationality: American
Date: 1997

Industrial Gothic is a heavy, condensed all-caps sans serif. It comes in three styles, each of which has different lowercases. In Single Line, these letters are smaller and float above a line; Double Line has lines above and below; and Banner has lines and a gap through the middle.

Ingram BT

ABCDEFGHIJKLMNOPQRSTUVWXYZ
abcdefghijklmnopqrstuvwxyz
1234567890 !@#?:,"*&

Foundry: Bitstream
Designer: Alexander Marshall
Designer Nationality: Scottish
Date: 2004

Ingram BT was created by Scottish-born designer Alexander Marshall, who trained in London before moving to California in 1980. The typeface is a tall, thin, decorative sans with Arts and Crafts details such as the dots on "A," "E," "F," "H," and "Q," which replace crossbars. It has a slightly rough finish.

Insignia

ABCDEFGHIJKLMNOPQRSTUVWXYZ
abcdefghijklmnopqrstuvwxyz
1234567890 !@#?:;"*&

Foundry: Linotype
Designer: Neville Brody
Designer Nationality: British
Date: 1989

Linotype released Insignia under the name 'Stadia' in 1989. Insignia began life as lettering used by Neville Brody on *Arena*, the British men's magazine, for which he designed the debut issue in 1986. It is a geometric sans serif with eye-catching, extended strokes on many capitals.

Integral

ABCDEFGHIJKLMNOPQRSTUVWXYZ
abcdefghijklmnopqrstuvwxyz
1234567890!@#?:;"*&

Foundry: Monotype
Designer: Jim Marcus
Designer Nationality: American
Date: Unknown

Integral was designed by Jim Marcus, a US designer who created many fonts while working in-house at the T-26 foundry. It is a distinctive, rounded sans serif with letters that look like they have been squeezed horizontally. Available in a single weight, it has a large x-height.

ITC Blair

ABCDEFGHIJKLMNOPQRSTUV
ABCDEFGHIJKLMNOPQRSTUVWXYZ
1234567890 !@#?:;"*&

Foundry: ITC
Designer: Jim Spiece
Designer Nationality: American
Date: 1997

ITC Blair is a revival made by Jim Spiece in 1997 of Blair, an extended serif-less take on the Copperplate style released in 1900 by the St Louis-based Inland Type Foundry. ITC Blair originally came in three styles, but after input from Monotype in 2016, this was expanded to twelve.

ITC Flatiron

ABCDEFGHIJKLMNO
PQRSTUVWXYZ
1234567890 !@#?:;"*&

Foundry: ITC
Designer: Unknown
Date: 1997

Flatiron is an extremely wide, monoline, uppercase only sans serif typeface, which the International Typeface Corporation (ITC) released in 1997. It was based on an earlier design from Photo-Lettering, whose co-founder Ed Rondthaler also co-founded ITC, so the two foundries shared many fonts.

ITC Freddo

ABCDEFGHIJKLMNOPQRSTUV
abcdefghijklmnopqrstuvw
1234567890 !@#?:;"'*&

Foundry: ITC
Designer: James Montalbano
Designer Nationality: American
Date: 1996

US type designer James Montalbano trained under Ed Benguiat (see p. 514). He designed Freddo for the International Typeface Corporation (ITC) in 1996.

It is a wide sans serif with rounded forms and an informal feel. Available in one style with upper and lowercase, it is suited to large use only.

ITC Grapefruit

ABCDEFGHIJKLMNOPQRSTUVWXYZ
abcdefghijklmnopqrstuvwxyz
1234567890 !@#?:;"'*&

Foundry: ITC
Designer: Györi Attila
Designer Nationality: Hungarian
Date: 1997

ITC Grapefruit is the only font release from Hungarian designer Györi Attila. Informal and energetic, this angular geometric sans serif has a slightly retro feel. The typeface is available in a single weight—Bold, with upper and lowercases— and is suitable for a wide variety of uses.

ITC Migrate

ABCDEFGHIJKLMNOPQRSTUVWXYZ
abcdefghijklmnopqrstuvwxyz
1234567890 !@#?:;"'*&

Foundry: ITC
Designer: George Ryan
Designer Nationality: American
Date: 1999

ITC Migrate is a condensed display sans serif. It is an update of the Oz Handicraft typeface George Ryan designed for Bitstream in 1991, based on drawing samples found by type designer Oswald Bruce Cooper in the *Book of Oz Cooper* (1949), published by the Society of Typographic Arts in Chicago.

ITC New Rennie Mackintosh

ABCDEFGHIJKLMNOPQRSTUVWXYZ
abcdefghijklmnopqrstuvwxyz
1234567890 !@#?:;"'*&

Foundry: ITC
Designer: Phill Grimshaw
Designer Nationality: British
Date: 2017

ITC Rennie Mackintosh was the result of a collaboration between the International Typeface Corporation (ITC) and the Glasgow School of Art in 1996 based on the work of architect Charles Rennie Mackintosh. The update improved on the original two styles, expanding it to four weights with italics.

Neutura

Neutura, the San Francisco-based foundry and design studio established by Alexander McCracken in 2003, offers a concise portfolio of fine display typefaces. Design styles include modern, antique, and classical, as well as a range of illustrative, contemporary block and stencil types. Neutura offers bespoke font-design services as well as customization of its existing types, and its types can be seen in commissions for high-profile clients including Nike, Electronic Arts, and *Wired* magazine. In addition, the studio specializes in producing visual identities and print design for creative, design-led clients. A number of typefaces in the Neutura portfolio were created specifically for design commissions and later developed to be available to the public.

Founded: 2003
Country: USA
Website: neutura.org
Notable typefaces:
Maisalle (see p. 417)
Spade (see p. 441)

Below and right. Neutura promotional designs for a selection of its crafted display types—from left, Royale (ampersand detail), Royale, Neutrino, and Interpol (top).

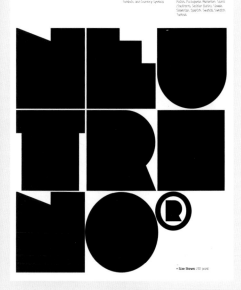

Below. Geometric sans serif
Orange Round.

Bottom. Decorative display type
Cérie available in Regular and
Outline styles.

Below. A sans serif design
with humanist traits, Aperture
is available in thin, regular, and
heavy weights.

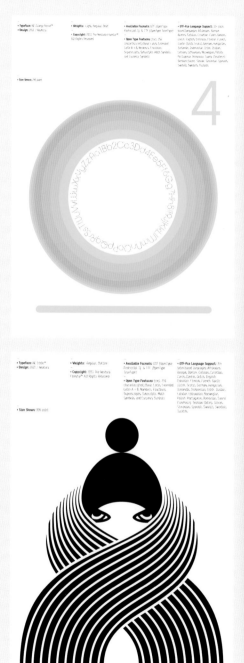

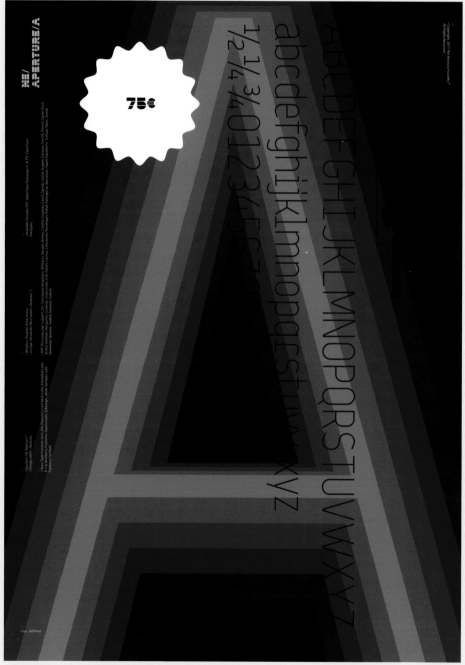

ITC Odyssée

ABCDEFGHIJKLMNOPQRSTUVWXYZ
abcdefghijklmnopqrstuvwxyz
1234567890 !@#?:;"*&

Foundry: ITC
Designer: Roselyne Besnard / Michel Besnard
Designer Nationality: French
Date: 1996

ITC Odyssée is a sans serif display typeface, inspired by the illusionary aesthetics of digital media. The font, designed in four weights from Light to Ultra, replicates the dynamic lines created by a TV screen's optical residue to fashion a series of electric letter forms.

ITC Verkehr

ABCDEFGHIJKLMNOPQRSTUVWXYZ
abcdefghijklmnopqrstuvwxyz
1234567890 !@#?:;"*&

Foundry: ITC
Designer: Mott Jordan
Designer Nationality: American
Date: 1996

Available in one bold weight, ITC Verkehr is a heavy, condensed grotesque sans serif. It was created by Mott Jordan, a freelance designer from California, who reversed the usual convention of a grotesque by making the top halves of letters slightly heavier than their bottoms.

Kadeworth

ABCDEFGHIJKLMNOPQRSTUVWXYZ
abcdefghijklmnopqrstuvwxyz
1234567890 !@#?:;"*&

Foundry: Typodermic
Designer: Ray Larabie
Designer Nationality: Canadian
Date: 2010

Kadeworth is a bold, rounded condensed sans serif in a single style designed with headline usage in mind. It manages to achieve an authoritative feel while remaining friendly. According to its designer, Ray Larabie, Kadeworth was "specifically designed for use on the web."

Kleptocracy

ABCDEFGHIJKLMNOPQRSTUVWXYZ
abcdefghijklmnopqrstuvwxyz
1234567890 !@#?:;"*&

Foundry: Larabie Fonts
Designer: Ray Larabie
Designer Nationality: Canadian
Date: 1999

Before he started commercial foundry Typodermic in 2001, Canadian designer Ray Larabie released fonts on his Larabie Fonts website, publishing some 250 free fonts from 1996 to 2001. Kleptocracy is a curvy sans serif that comes in three weights and three widths—Condensed, Regular, and Extended.

Koala

ABCDEFGHIJKLMNOPQRSTUVWXYZ
abcdefghijklmnopqrstuvwxyz
1234567890 !@#?:;"'*&

Foundry: Linotype
Designer: Éric de Berranger
Designer Nationality: French
Date: 2003

Koala was created by French type designer Éric de Berranger, a former student of Jean-François Porchez and co-founder of La Fonderie. The display sans serif was first published by Linotype in three weights. It has a large x-height, short descenders, and broad strokes.

Kobalt

ABCDEFGHIJKLMNOPQRSTUVWXYZ
abcdefghijklmnopqrstuvwxyz
1234567890 !@#?:;"'*&

Foundry: ITC
Designer: Leslie Cabarga
Designer Nationality: American
Date: 1998

US illustrator, writer, and designer Leslie Cabarga created Kobalt for the International Typeface Corporation (ITC). It is a heavy geometric sans serif that pays homage to fonts of the 1920s and 1930s. Kobalt is available in two weights—Bold and Black—and has an all-caps, shadowed version, Kartoon.

Koloss

ABCDEFGHIJKLMNOPQRSTUVWXYZ
abcdefghijklmnopqrstuvwxyz
1234567890 !@#?:;"'*&

Foundry: Ludwig & Mayer
Designer: Jakob Erbar
Designer Nationality: German
Date: 1923

German foundry Ludwig & Mayer released Koloss in 1923 as an extra-bold companion to Feder-Grotesk, a sans serif family designed by Jakob Erbar in 1909. Koloss is a heavy and wide upright sans serif with broad strokes, small counters, a large x-height, and short descenders.

La Pontaise

ABCDEFGHIJKLMNOPQRSTUVWXYZ
abcdefghijklmnopqrstuvwxyz
1234567890 !@#?:;"'*&

Foundry: Or Type
Designer: Mads Freund Brunse
Designer Nationality: Danish
Date: 2013

La Pontaise is a high-contrast, elegant grotesque sans serif designed by Mads Freund Brunse, the Danish co-founder of foundry Or Type (see p. 498). It was first used on opening invitations to the Saint-Valentin gallery in Lausanne, Switzerland. It comes in four roman weights from Light to Semibold.

Lexikos

ABCDEFGHIJKLMNOPQRSTUVWXYZ

abcdefghijklmnopqrstuvwxyz

1234567890 !?:;"*&

Foundry: ITC
Designer: Vince Whitlock
Designer Nationality: British
Date: 1990

British designer Vince Whitlock designed Lexikos for the International Typeface Corporation (ITC) in 1990. It is a condensed sans serif, which seems squished thanks to narrow letters and horizontal strokes heavier than the vertical. Colin Brignall's typeface Corinthian provided Whitlock's base.

Linotype Freytag

ABCDEFGHIJKLMNOPQRSTUVWXYZ

abcdefghijklmnopqrstuvwxyz

1234567890 !@#?:;"*&

Foundry: Linotype
Designer: Arne Freytag
Designer Nationality: German
Date: 2012

Linotype Freytag is a geometric display typeface comprised of four weights and corresponding italics. The condensed sans serif characters combine rounded strokes with spur-less stems, as seen in the "a" or "n," alongside distinguishing stroke endings, notable in the uppercase "T."

Linotype Rory

ABCDEFGHIJKLMNOPQRSTUVWXYZ

abcdefghijklmnopqrstuvwxyz

1234567890 !@#?:;"*&

Foundry: Linotype
Designer: Tad Biernot
Designer Nationality: Canadian
Date: 1997

Linotype Rory is a dynamic display typeface, initially submitted to Linotype's International Digital Type Design Contest and later published as part of Linotype's TakeType Library. The font's oblique forms are reminiscent of mechanical precision, strength, and speed.

Loft

ABCDEFGHIJKLMNOPQRSTUVWXYZ

abcdefghijklmnopqrstuvwxyz

1234567890 !@#?:;"*&

Foundry: Monotype
Designer: Julien Janiszewski
Designer Nationality: French
Date: 2007

Loft is a sans serif display typeface inspired by 19th-century wood types and *défense d'afficher* (post no bills) signs, commonly found across France. The font features seven weights, which expand only in stroke thickness, with counter size remaining the same throughout.

Marché Super

ABCDEFGHIJKLMNOPQRSTUVWXYZ
abcdefghijklmnopqrstuvwxyz
1234567890 !@#?:;""*&

Foundry: Colophon
Designer: The Entente
Designer Nationality: British
Date: 2014

Marché Super was designed by The Entente—the graphic design agency linked to the independent London-based foundry Colophon (see p. 210)—for issue 186 of the photography magazine *Hotshoe*. It is a heavy, utilitarian sans serif inspired by Eurostile, which is available in a single bold, roman style.

Metroblack 2

ABCDEFGHIJKLMNOPQRSTUVWXYZ
abcdefghijklmnopqrstuvwxyz
1234567890 !@#?:;"*&

Foundry: Linotype
Designer: William A. Dwiggins
Designer Nationality: American
Date: 1932

In 1929, pioneering US graphic designer William A. Dwiggins was commissioned to create a sans serif, which he named Metro. Linotype wanted a competitor to Bauer's Futura, so in 1932 Dwiggins made revisions, creating the more geometric Metro No. 2 starting with the black weight.

Modified Gothic

ABCDEFGHIJKLMNOPQRSTUVWXYZ
ABCDEFGHIJKLMNOPQRSTUVWXYZ
1234567890 !@#?:;"*&

Foundry: Linotype
Designer: Linotype Design Studio
Date: 2002

Modified Gothic is a 1920's style Art Deco-inspired titling sans serif typeface designed in-house by Linotype. It has uppercase and small caps only and a monoline geometric construction. It comes in a single weight and was included in Linotype's TakeType 4 Library released in 2002.

Monotype Clearface Gothic

ABCDEFGHIJKLMNOPQRSTUVWXYZ
abcdefghijklmnopqrstuvwxyz
1234567890 !@#?:;"*&

Foundry: Monotype
Designer: Morris Fuller Benton
Designer Nationality: American
Date: 1910

US type designer Morris Fuller Benton created Clearface Gothic, a slightly flared sans serif companion to his serifed Clearface, for the American Type Founders in 1910. Monotype's digitization, one of many foundries' versions, comes in two roman weights, Bold and Demi Bold.

Montefiore

ABCDEFGHIJKLMNOPQRSTUVWXYZ
abcdefghijklmnopqrstuvwxyz
1234567890 !@#?:;"*&

Foundry: Colophon
Designer: The Entente
Designer Nationality: British
Date: 2009

Montefiore, a condensed utilitarian sans serif, was initially released by Colophon (see p. 210) in 2009 in two weights. In 2017, it was revamped and comes in six condensed weights—Thin to Extra Bold. It was inspired by lettering on a Victorian street nameplate on Montefiore Road in Hove, East Sussex, England.

Moon Cresta

ABCDEFGHIJKLMNOPQRSTUVWXYZ
abcdefghijklmnopqrstuvwxyz
1234567890 !@#?:;"*&

Foundry: Typodermic
Designer: Ray Larabie
Designer Nationality: Canadian
Date: 2010

Ray Larabie, the prolific Canadian type designer based in Japan, designed Moon Cresta in 2010. It is a friendly, bold rounded sans serif font that was built using the same proportions as Goudy Sans. Moon Cresta comes in a single roman weight and is intended for contemporary headline usage.

Neographik

ABCDEFGHIJKLMNOPQRSTUVWXYZ
abcdefghijklmnopqrstuvwxyz
1234567890 !@#?:;"*&

Foundry: Monotype
Designer: Robert Barbour
Designer Nationality: British
Date: 1970

Neographik by British designer Robert Barbour was one of Monotype's first photolettering fonts. It is a heavy sans serif with a large x-height and short ascenders and descenders. It was released in 1970 and appeared on the cover of *Monotype Newsletter 88* in February 1971.

Pantograph

ABCDEFGHIJKLMNOPQRSTUVWXYZ
abcdefghijklmnopqrstuvwxyz
1234567890 !@#?:;"*&

Foundry: Colophon
Designer: Studio Makgill
Designer Nationality: British
Date: 2009

Designed by the Brighton-based creative agency Studio Makgill in 2009, Pantograph is a quirky, narrow, rounded sans serif typeface that replicates the lettering used in the British pantograph etching process, mostly for technical signs on buildings and streets. It is available in a single roman style.

PDU

ABCDEFGHIJKLMNOPQRSTUVWXYZ
abcdefghijklmnopqrstuvwxyz
1234567890 !@#?:;"*&

Foundry: Colophon
Designer: Dries Wiewauters
Designer Nationality: Belgian
Date: 2011

Dries Wiewauters designed PDU; its name refers to the *Plaque Découpée Universelle* stencil-based signwriting system patented by Joseph A. David in 1876. It is a bold sans serif and comes in Solid, Stencil and Outline versions, with many ornament glyphs for making patterns.

Peignot

ABCDEFGHIJKLMNOPQRSTUVWXYZ
abcdefghijklmnopqrstuvwxyz
1234567890 !@#?:;"*&

Foundry: Deberny & Peignot
Designer: Cassandre / Charles Peignot
Designer Nationality: French
Date: 1937

Peignot was created in 1937 by leading French designer Cassandre and Charles Peignot of the foundry Deberny & Peignot. It is a sans serif with contrast, which mixes the styles of upper- and lowercase letters. It was released in two weights, with a third—the Bold—added in 1938.

Placard

ABCDEFGHIJKLMNOPQRSTUVWXYZ
abcdefghijklmnopqrstuvwxyz
1234567890 !@#?:;"*&

Foundry: Monotype
Designer: Monotype Studio
Date: 1937

Placard is a heavy, condensed poster sans serif designed by an unnamed staff member at Monotype. It was released in a single weight in 1937 and four extra styles followed in 1939. In 2018, Monotype's Malou Verlomme designed Placard Next, expanding the family to four widths with six weights each.

Plaza

ABCDEFGHIJKLMNOPQRSTUVWXYZ
1234567890 !@#?:;"*&

Foundry: Letraset
Designer: Alan Meeks
Designer Nationality: British
Date: 1975

Plaza—originally named Playboy until magazine publisher Hugh Hefner threatened legal action—was designed by Letraset type designer Alan Meeks in 1975. It was released in three styles—Plaza, Plaza Ultra, and Plaza Inline—and is an uppercase, geometric sans serif with swashed alternates.

Posterama

ABCDEFGHIJKLMNOPQRSTUVWXYZ
abcdefghijklmnopqrstuvwxyz
1234567890 !@#?:;"*&

Foundry: Monotype
Designer: Jim Ford
Designer Nationality: American
Date: 2016

The Posterama typeface has been described "as a journey through space and type." Its creator Jim Ford, a US visual artist and type designer for Monotype, has said it is "the typeface of the future… only yesterday." Posterama's subtle but distinctive varying styles have been influenced by reference points in art, typography, science fiction, architecture, science, and culture of the 20th century.

Each year referred to in the Posterama typeface names has a variation in its construction reflecting the time period after which it is named, as well as themes from the time and 20th-century depictions of the future. At its core is Posterama 1927, referring to the year Paul Renner created the Futura typeface. However, 1927 is also the year that the groundbreaking science-fiction drama *Metropolis* by Expressionist film director Fritz Lang was released.

Other typefaces in the family include Posterama 1901, which pays homage to the Art Nouveau and Art and Crafts movement that arose at the turn of the 20th century. Posterama 1913 is a tribute to the "International Exhibition of Modern Art" (aka "Armory Show") of 1913, where the work of revolutionary artists such as Pablo Picasso, Marcel Duchamp, and Wassily Kandinsky were first shown in the United States. Posterama 1919 recalls the founding of the Bauhaus and its ensuing influence on the design of European typography. Posterama 1933 includes Art Deco elements. Posterama 1945's Cyrillic characters signify the end of World War II, and the start of the Cold War and the nuclear arms race. Posterama 1984 alludes to George Orwell's novel and the science-fiction movies of the 1980s such as *Blade Runner* (1982) and *Terminator* (1984), along with the

advent of arcades games such as Pac-Man. Finally, Posterama 2001 was inspired by director Stanley Kubrick's space epic *2001: A Space Odyssey* (1968) as well as influences from the National Aeronautics and Space Administration's logotype. Each of the eight typefaces in the Posterama collection are available in seven weights, ranging from Thin through to Ultra.

Below. With multiple cultural reference points from the 20th century, Posterama is a comprehensive and diverse portfolio of display types.

Railroad Gothic

ABCDEFGHIJKLMNOPQRSTUVWXYZ
1234567890 !@#?:;"*&

Foundry: American Type Founders
Date: 1906

Railroad Gothic—a heavy, condensed, uppercase grotesque sans serif—was released by the American Type Founders in 1906 and was a popular choice for headline use thanks to its no-nonsense, industrial feel. Derek Birdsall used it on his series of book covers for Penguin Education.

Regatta Condensed

ABCDEFGHIJKLMNOPQRSTUVWXYZ
abcdefghijklmnopqrstuvwxyz
1234567890 !?:;"*&

Foundry: Letraset
Designer: Alan Meeks
Designer Nationality: British
Date: 1987

Regatta Condensed was designed by former Letraset in-house type designer Alan Meeks in 1987. It comes in a single roman weight, which is black and narrow. The typeface is a quirky sans serif with diamond-shaped dots, a large x-height, and angled terminals.

Republik Sans

ABCDEFGHIJKLMNOPQRSTUVWXYZ
1234567890 !@#?:;"*&

Foundry: Image Club Graphics
Designer: Jackson Mahr / Noel Rubin
Designer Nationality: British / Canadian
Date: 1994

British designer Jackson Mahr and US designer Noel Rubin created Republik Sans for Image Club Graphics in 1994. It is an angular all-caps sans serif that comes in four styles: 01, which is the regular weight; 02, which is bold; 03, which is outlined; and 03 Alt, which is inlined.

Revue

ABCDEFGHIJKLMNOPQRSTUVWXYZ
abcdefghijklmnopqrstuvwxyz
1234567890 !@#?:;"*&

Foundry: Letraset
Designer: Colin Brignall
Designer Nationality: British
Date: 1968

Letraset designer Colin Brignall created Revue in 1968, inspired by poster lettering from the early 20th century. It is a heavy, quirky sans serif font with many distinguishing features, such as the angled lower terminals of "F," "H," and "Y," which hang below the baseline.

Rubino Sans

ABCDEFGHIJKLMNOPQRSTUVWXYZ
abcdefghijklmnopqrstuvwxyz
1234567890 !@#?:;"'*&

Foundry: Image Club Graphics
Designer: Noel Rubin
Designer Nationality: Canadian
Date: 1994

Noel Rubin created Rubino Sans for Image Club Graphics in 1994. It is a humanist sans serif with contrast. The typeface comes in five styles that are the same weight: the conventional Fill and Outline, as well as three versions—Regular, Solid, and Guides—which features construction lines and grids.

Rumori

ABCDEFGHIJKLMNOPQRSTUVWXYZ
abcdefghijklmnopqrstuvwxyz
1234567890 !@#?:;"'*&

Foundry: Type Brut
Designer: Paul McNeil
Designer Nationality: British
Date: 2014

Rumori was designed for a reprint of Luigi Russolo's Futurist manifesto *L'Arte dei rumori* (*The Art of Noise*, 1913). Paul McNeil found inspiration for the heavy grotesque sans serif from lettering on the cover of a 1916 edition. It comes in one weight in two versions: Chiari (sharp) and Morbidi (soft).

Sackers Gothic

ABCDEFGHIJKLMNOPQRSTUVWX
ABCDEFGHIJKLMNOPQRSTUVWXYZ
1234567890 !@#?:;"'*&

Foundry: Compugraphic
Designer: Gary Sackers
Designer Nationality: American
Date: 1975

Sackers Gothic is part of a series of typefaces designed by Gary Sackers for Compugraphic in 1974 and 1975 based on old engraving types. It is an uppercase and small caps-only extended sans serif, which comes in three roman weights: Light, Medium, and Heavy. A square version is also available.

Smart Sans

ABCDEFGHIJKLMNOPQRSTUVWXYZ
abcdefghijklmnopqrstuvwxyz
1234567890 !@#?:;"'*&

Foundry: Monotype
Designer: Rod McDonald
Designer Nationality: Canadian
Date: 2000

Smart Sans is a tribute to Canada's design pioneer Leslie "Sam" Smart, and this is Rod McDonald's second typeface. He was inspired by Fred Lambert's Compacta designed in 1963 for Letraset and the Helvetica Compressed series designed by Matthew Carter (see p. 616) for Linotype in 1966.

Shire Types

ABCDEFGHIJKLMNOPQRSTUVWXYZ
ABCDEFGHIJKLMNOPQRSTUVWXYZ
1234567890 !@#?:;"*&

Foundry: Jeremy Tankard Typography
Designer: Jeremy Tankard
Designer Nationality: British
Date: 1998

Shire Types, by British type designer Jeremy Tankard, is a heavy, Blackletter design that was inspired by idiosyncratic 19th-century grotesque and Egyptian-style vernacular lettering from around the British Isles. The playful and characterful family is designed in an Ultra Heavy style, with a mix of eye-catching sans and serif characters whose chunky and rounded forms make an impact.

Shire Types is available in six fonts, each named after English counties grouped around the Black Country, which formed the industrial heartland of the UK. The fonts have design variations to create variety when used separately, yet have a unified appearance when mixed together. The block sans of Derbyshire and Staffordshire are capitals only and reflect the industrial strength of the areas. The Cheshire and Shropshire designs have a more

uncial feel to their appearance, based on historical ideas of mixing uppercase and lowercase letters. The fonts named after the counties of Warwickshire and Worcestershire possess a more rounded, scriptlike design to reflect the rolling hills of the English countryside.

The Shire Types family features a number of highly crafted design details. For example, there are no ascenders or descenders so all the characters fit to the same height, allowing lowercase and capital letters to be mixed with a uniform setting. Some letters are constant across the designs—for instance, the "O" and "S." Cyrillic and Greek variants were released in 2011 in addition to the Roman. In 2012, Mourad Boutros, one of the world's leading Arabic calligraphers, designers, and typographers, helped to create an Arabic version, Shire Arabic.

Below. From snappy hairdresser store fronts to bicycle liveries, Shire Types' mix of upper and lowercase and sans and serif letter forms make for playful and impactful designs.

Steelfish

ABCDEFGHIJKLMNOPQRSTUVWXYZ
abcdefghijklmnopqrstuvwxyz
1234567890 !@#?:,"*&

Foundry: Typodermic
Designer: Ray Larabie
Designer Nationality: Canadian
Date: 2005

Steelfish is a gritty display typeface with an authoritative tone that was inspired by newspaper headlines from the mid 20th century. It has been updated and expanded since its release in 2001 and comprises fifteen weights, from ExtraLight to ExtraBold, with matching italics and an inline version.

Storm Sans

ABCDEFGHIJKLMNOPQRSTUVWXYZ
abcdefghijklmnopqrstuvwxyz
1234567890 !@#?:,"*&

Foundry: Agfa / Monotype
Designer: Nina Lee Storm
Designer Nationality: Danish
Date: 1999

Storm Sans was the first commercially available typeface from Korean-born, Denmark-based designer Nina Lee Storm. A neutral, fairly condensed sans serif display typeface, it is available in two weights, Regular and Bold. Storm's next creation was for Linotype in 2004, Noa.

Swiss 911

ABCDEFGHIJKLMNOPQRSTUVWXYZ
abcdefghijklmnopqrstuvwxyz
1234567890 !@#?:,"*&

Foundry: Bitstream
Designer: Max Miedinger /
Hans-Jörg Hunziker /
Matthew Carter
Designer Nationality: Swiss /
Swiss / British
Date: 1957 / 1966

Bitstream's version of Helvetica Compressed was developed in 1966 by Hans-Jörg Hunziker and Matthew Carter (see p. 616) from the original Neue Haas Grotesk design created for the Haas foundry in Switzerland by Max Miedinger (see p. 229) in 1957 and renamed Helvetica in 1960.

Swiss 921

ABCDEFGHIJKLMNOPQRSTUVWXYZ
abcdefghijklmnopqrstuvwxyz
1234567890 !@#?:,"*&

Foundry: Bitstream
Designer: Max Miedinger
Designer Nationality: Swiss
Date: 1957

Swiss 921 is Bitstream's version of Helvetica Inserat (1957) by Max Miedinger (see p. 229), renamed to avoid copyright infringement. It is a grotesque sans serif with short ascenders and descenders and comes in a bold condensed roman style that is well suited to advertising and headline use.

Tempo

ABCDEFGHIJKLMNOPQRSTUVWXYZ
abcdefghijklmnopqrstuvwxyz
1234567890 !@#?:;"*&

Foundry: Ludlow Typograph
Designer: R. Hunter Middleton
Designer Nationality: British
Date: 1930–31

This headline typeface was created for use in newspapers and produced as a response to the instant success of Paul Renner's Futura. Tempo is a heavy, condensed font that is also based on a geometric design, but with a number of more humanistic traits.

THD Sentient

ABCDEFGHIJKLMNOPQRSTUVWXYZ
1234567890 !@#?:;"*&

Foundry: MuirMcNeil
Designer: Tim Hutchinson / Hamish Muir / Paul McNeil
Designer Nationality: British
Date: 2017

THD Sentient is an all-caps monolinear sans serif designed for the *Beyond 2001: New Horizons* exhibition at the London College of Communication to celebrate ten years of the Stanley Kubrick Archive. It was inspired by type used on the screen of HAL 9000 in *2001: A Space Odyssey* (1968).

Trotzkopf

ABCDEFGHIJKLMNOPQRSTUVWXYZ
abcdefghijklmnopqrstuvwxyz
1234567890 !@#?:;"*&

Foundry: Agfa
Designer: Bo Berndal
Designer Nationality: Swedish
Date: 1997

Bo Berndal designed Trotzkopf in 1997 for Agfa and was one of Sweden's leading graphic designers and typographers up until his death in 2013. It is a decorative sans serif that comes in two weights, Regular and Bold. Trotzkopf blends rounded corners with wider, swooping curves.

Valter

ABCDEFGHIJKLMNOPQRSTUVWXYZ
abcdefghijklmnopqrstuvwxyz
1234567890 !@#?:;"*&

Foundry: Typotheque
Designer: Nikola Djurek
Designer Nationality: Croatian
Date: 2014

Nikola Djurek's Valter is a distinctive, elegant high-contrast sans serif that comes in seven weights—Hairline to Bold—with matching cursive italics. It was published by Typotheque (see p. 90) in 2014 and the Type Directors Club awarded it a Certificate of Typographic Excellence a year later.

Vendela

ABCDEFGHIJKLMNOPQRSTUVWXYZ
1234567890 !@#?:;"*&

Neutura, the San Francisco-based foundry and studio of Alexander McCracken, published the Vendela heavy rounded sans serif in 2011. It is available in a single weight, without italics or lowercase, and has a futuristic, technical feel thanks to its geometric construction.

Foundry: Neutura
Designer: Alexander McCracken
Designer Nationality: American
Date: 2011

Vienna Extended

ABCDEFGHIJKLMNO
PQRSTUVWXYZ
1234567890 !@#?:;"*&

Foundry: Letraset
Designer: Anthony De Meester
Designer Nationality: Canadian
Date: 1989

The work of Canadian designer Anthony De Meester, Vienna Extended is a very wide, monoline uppercase sans serif that was released by Letraset in 1989. It is available in a single weight, which is Light, and it has high crossbars. Vienna is most effective where a look of regal elegance is desired.

Windpower

ABCDEFGHIJKLMNOPQRSTUVWXYZ
ABCDEFGHIJKLMNOPQRSTUVWXYZ
1234567890 !@#?:;'"&*

Foundry: Typodermic
Designer: Ray Larabie
Designer Nationality: Canadian
Date: 2005

Windpower, released by Typodermic in 2005, is a heavy sans serif display font in a single style. Both its upper and lowercase are capitals only, but the uppercase capitals feature triangular wings facing left—which, according to designer Ray Larabie, "give them extra aerodynamic thrust."

Algerian

ABCDEFGHIJKLMNOPQRSTUVWXYZ
1234567890 !@#?:;"*&

Algerian was first released in c. 1907 by Stephenson, Blake & Co. and then experienced a revival during the 1980s when several digitizations of the typeface were developed. Algerian has been included with Microsoft Office products since 1993, and has earned a certain notoriety as a result.

Foundry: Stephenson, Blake & Co.
Designer: Alan Carr / Philip Kelly / Alan Meeks
Designer Nationality: British
Date: 1907

Arsis

ABCDEFGHIJKLMNOPQRSTUVWXYZ
abcdefghijklmnopqrstuvwxyz
1234567890 !@#?:;"*&

Credited to former American Type Founders director Gerry Powell, this neoclassical typeface is said to have been released by two foundries simultaneously: as Arsis in the Netherlands and as Onyx in the United States. Whatever its origin, it remains an elegant and robust choice for display typesetting.

Foundry: American Type Founders / Amsterdam Type
Designer: Gerry Powell
Designer Nationality: American
Date: 1937

BB-book A

ABCDEFGHIJKLMNOPQRSTUVWXYZ
abcdefghijklmnopqrstuvwxyz
1234567890 !@#?:;"*&

BB-book A is part of Benoît Bodhuin's playful BB-book font family. It is a characterful display typeface featuring a mix of jaunty curves, diagonal forms, and triangular semi-serif details. It is available in four distinctive styles, from an ultra-extended Bold to a super-condensed Light.

Foundry: BB-Bureau
Designer: Benoît Bodhuin
Designer Nationality: French
Date: 2016

BB-book B

ABCDEFGHIJKLMNOPQRSTUVWXYZ
abcdefghijklmnopqrstuvwxyz
1234567890 !@#?:;"*&

BB-book B continues the ideas Benoît Bodhuin explored within BB-book A (2016), and features increased contrast and more open characters throughout. Its distinctive wedge details are more pronounced than in the previous version, and its line weight grows finer within its expanded weights.

Foundry: BB-Bureau
Designer: Benoît Bodhuin
Designer Nationality: French
Date: 2016

BB-book Contrasted

ABCDEFGHIJKLMNOP
abcdefghijklmnopqrs
1234567890 !@#?:;"*&

Foundry: BB-Bureau
Designer: Benoît Bodhuin
Designer Nationality: French
Date: 2016

This font is based on the bold cut of Bodhuin's earlier typeface BB-book A (2016). It was developed with increased contrast and a deliberate sense of awkwardness within its characters. The extended forms and exaggerated curves offer a distinctly contemporary feel within display contexts.

BB-book Monospaced

ABCDEFGHIJKLMNOPQRSTUVWXYZ
abcdefghijklmnopqrstuvwxyz
1234567890 !@#?:;"*&

Foundry: BB-Bureau
Designer: Benoît Bodhuin
Designer Nationality: French
Date: 2018

This addition to the BB-book family features monospaced characters based on those of its predecessors, BB-book A and BB-book B (both 2016). Unifying the widths of the entire alphabet means the unconventional proportions and irregular details of Bodhuin's earlier designs are amplified.

BB-book Text

ABCDEFGHIJKLMNOPQRSTUVWX
abcdefghijklmnopqrstuvwxyz
1234567890 !@#?:;"*&

Foundry: BB-Bureau
Designer: Benoît Bodhuin
Designer Nationality: French
Date: 2018

Bodhuin developed BB-book Text from his earlier designs for BB-book A and BB-book B (both 2016), translating their unexpected angular details and reversed contrast into a typeface more suitable for the setting of longer passages of text. BB-book Text retains the distinctiveness of its predecessors.

Belshaw

ABCDEFGHIJKLMNOPQRSTUVWXYZ
abcdefghijklmnopqrstuvwxyz
1234567890 !@#?:;"*&

Foundry: ITC
Designer: Nick Belshaw
Designer Nationality: British
Date: 1980

Nick Belshaw's eponymous display font exhibits the influence of Art Nouveau typefaces, featuring generous curves and rounded corners throughout. A heavy typeface with comparatively small counters, it is best used at larger point sizes for headline type to remain legible.

Bernhard Modern

ABCDEFGHIJKLMNOPQRSTUVWXYZ
abcdefghijklmnopqrstuvwxyz
1234567890 !@#?:;"*&

Foundry: American Type Founders
Designer: Lucian Bernhard
Designer Nationality: German
Date: 1937

German typographer and creative polymath Lucian Bernhard designed this high-contrast modern serif font for American Type Founders in 1937. A versatile design with a low x-height, it features a subtle softness and slight irregularity within its fine serifs, appearing crisp yet approachable.

Bodebeck

ABCDEFGHIJKLMNOPQRSTUVWXYZ
abcdefghijklmnopqrstuvwxyz
1234567890 !@#?:;"*&

Foundry: Linotype
Designer: Anders Bodebeck
Designer Nationality: Swedish
Date: 2002

This neo-transitional roman type family by Swedish designer Anders Bodebeck is a clean, elegant choice for display typesetting, featuring sinuous curves and wide open counters. Published by Linotype in 2002, it is available in three weights with two accompanying italics.

Bodoni Unique

ABCDEFGHIJKLMNOPQRSTUVWXYZ
ABCDEFGHIJKLMNOPQRSTUVWXYZ
1234567890 !@#?:;"*&

Foundry: Panache Typography
Designer: Giambattista Bodoni / David Farey
Designer Nationality: Italian / British
Date: 1995

Based on Giambattista Bodoni's eponymous design, this contemporary interpretation by British type designer David Farey is extreme in terms of distortion and is the result of an experiment to see how far the original Bodoni could be condensed. It is available in uppercase only.

Bordeaux

ABCDEFGHIJKLMNOPQRSTUVWXYZ
abcdefghijklmnopqrstuvwxyz
1234567890 !@#?:;"*&

Foundry: Letraset
Designer: David Quay
Designer Nationality: British
Date: 1987

David Quay, the co-founder of The Foundry (see p. 284), designed this didone display typeface for Letraset in 1987. Condensed and romantic in style, it has subsequently been licensed by several other distributors, and both script and shadowed counterparts to the original are also available.

Brothers

ABCDEFGHIJKLMNOPQRSTUVWXYZ
abcdefghijklmnopqrstuvwxyz
1234567890 !@#?:;"'*&

Foundry: Emigre
Designer: John Downer
Designer Nationality: American
Date: 1999

Brothers was inspired by lettering found on the stationery of a travelling-circus company from the turn of the 20th century. It is a robust and angular display typeface featuring flared serifs and octagonal forms, which is available in Regular and Bold styles with a Super Slant oblique.

Burgstaedt Antiqua

ABCDEFGHIJKLMNOPQRSTUVWXYZ
abcdefghijklmnopqrstuvwxyz
1234567890 !@#?:;"'*&

Foundry: Linotype
Designer: Richard Yeend
Designer Nationality: British
Date: 2002

Burgstaedt Antiqua is part of Linotype's TakeType 5 collection. It features a mix of different serif styles within its character set. Irregularities and asymmetric forms appear throughout the design, creating a sense of character that becomes more pronounced upon closer inspection.

Burin

ABCDEFGHIJKLMNOPQRSTUVWXYZ
abcdefghijklmnopqrstuvwxyz
1234567890 !@#?:;"*&

Foundry: Monotype
Designer: Monotype Studio
Date: 1994

Burin is a quirky serif designed in 1994 by an unnamed member of Monotype's type design team. It is part of a two-font family that contains its sans serif sibling Burin Sans. Burin, which comes in one regular roman weight, is a Clarendon-esque serif with contrast and ball terminals.

Cajoun

ABCDEFGHIJKLMNOPQRSTUVWXYZ
abcdefghijklmnopqrstuvwxyz
1234567890 !@#?:;"*&

Foundry: Linotype
Designer: Hans-Jürgen Ellenberger
Designer Nationality: German
Date: 2002

The curves of Cajoun's distinctive letter forms have a distribution of weight similar to Old Style typefaces. This, coupled with a low x-height, causes the letter forms to pull the eye in a downward direction, meaning that the typeface is most effective when used at larger sizes.

Canela

ABCDEFGHIJKLMNOPQRSTUVWXYZ
abcdefghijklmnopqrstuvwxyz
1234567890 !@#?:;"*&

Foundry: Commercial Type
Designer: Miguel Reyes
Designer Nationality: Mexican
Date: 2016

Miguel Reyes took Caslon as his starting point for the design of Canela, developing an elegant font with a contemporary feel that offers a new perspective on this traditional type style. Canela made its debut in Issue No. 5 of the US arts and fashion magazine *Document Journal*.

Canela Condensed

ABCDEFGHIJKLMNOPQRSTUVWXYZ
abcdefghijklmnopqrstuvwxyz
1234567890 !@#?:;"*&

Foundry: Commercial Type
Designer: Miguel Reyes
Designer Nationality: Mexican
Date: 2018

This condensed cut of Canela was created by Mexican designer Miguel Reyes. It was developed to emphasize the verticality of the original, while preserving the fluid balance of its forms. Like its predecessor, its details are best appreciated within large-scale display and headline applications.

Carlton

ABCDEFGHIJKLMNOPQRSTUVWXYZ
abcdefghijklmnopqrstuvwxyz
1234567890 !@#?:;"*&

Foundry: Letraset
Designer: Letraset Design Studio
Date: 1983

Digitized by Letraset in 1983, this graceful and refined serif font was based on an earlier Stephenson, Blake & Co. typeface of the same name, which itself was copied from Fritz Helmuth Ehmcke's Ehmcke Antiqua from 1909. It has since been licensed by ITC and Linotype.

Caslon Antique

ABCDEFGHIJKLMNOPQRSTUVWXYZ
abcdefghijklmnopqrstuvwxyz
1234567890 !@#?:;"*&

Foundry: Barnhart Brothers & Spindler / American Type Founders
Designer: Berne Nadall
Designer Nationality: American
Date: 1898

Originally called Fifteenth Century, this was acquired by American Type Founders and renamed Caslon Antique. However, it is not a true Caslon type, having been designed to imitate 15th-century types created for the Venetian master printers. The first digital version was made by URW in 1990.

Caslon Black

ABCDEFGHIJKLMNOPQRSTUVWXYZ
abcdefghijklmnopqrstuvwxyz
1234567890 !@#?:;"*&

Foundry: ITC
Designer: William Caslon /
Dave Farey
Designer Nationality: British
Date: 1725 / 1982

Caslon Black is one of the many variations of William Caslon's 18th-century original and is intended exclusively for display use. It retains a hint of the original design but has taken on its own robust character. Designer Dave Farey has described his work as being that of a "letter repairer."

Caslon Titling

ABCDEFGHIJKLMNOPQRSTUVWXYZ
1234567890 !@#?:;"*&

Foundry: Monotype
Designer: William Caslon /
Monotype Studio
Designer Nationality: British
Date: 1932

This is one of many versions of William Caslon's 18th-century classic and one of three revivals by the British Monotype company. Caslon Titling's letters were based on those from the British foundry Stephenson, Blake & Co., giving it a distinctive style, with generous proportions.

Central Station

ABCDEFGHIJKLMNOPQRSTUVWXYZ
abcdefghijklmnopqrstuvwxyz
1234567890 !@#?:;"*&

Foundry: Monotype
Designer: Leslie Cabarga
Designer Nationality: American
Date: 1999

The multitalented US author, illustrator, cartoonist, animator, publication, and typeface designer Leslie Cabarga took part in the underground comix movement in the early 1970s. His refined Central Station font is available in Standard Regular and Bold, as well as Pro Regular and Bold.

Chesterfield

ABCDEFGHIJKLMNOPQRSTUVWXYZ
abcdefghijklmnopqrstuvwxyz
1234567890 !@#?:;"*&

Foundry: Linotype
Designer: Alan Meeks
Designer Nationality: British
Date: 2004

Chesterfield is a retro-inspired type referencing decorative design from the turn of the 19th century, with many subtle Art Nouveau traits and curves, and a nod to Frederic W. Goudy. It is available in two styles, Chesterfield and Chesterfield Antique; the latter has characters that appear corroded.

Chiswick Headline

ABCDEFGHIJKLMNOPQRSTUVWXYZ
abcdefghijklmnopqrstuvwxyz
1234567890 !@#?:;"*&

Foundry: Commercial Type
Designer: Paul Barnes
Designer Nationality: British
Date: 2010

This is part of Paul Barnes's Chiswick family and was designed for situations where Chiswick Deck is too heavy and Chiswick Poster is too delicate. Chiswick Headline is perfect for use at sizes from 30 to 60 point and is available in five weights from Extralight to Bold with matching italics, plus small caps.

Chiswick Poster

ABCDEFGHIJKLMNOPQRSTUVWXYZ
abcdefghijklmnopqrstuvwxyz
1234567890 !@#?:;"*&

Foundry: Commercial Type
Designer: Paul Barnes
Designer Nationality: British
Date: 2010

Chiswick Poster is designed to be used at 80 point and above. Paul Barnes's expertly crafted design was the primary display typeface in the redesign of O, The Oprah Magazine in 2010 and is available in five weights from Extralight to Bold with matching italics, plus small caps and swashes.

Classic Roman

ABCDEFGHIJKLMNOPQRSTUVWXYZ
ABCDEFGHIJKLMNOPQRSTUVWXYZ
1234567890 !@#?:;"*&

Foundry: Monotype
Designer: Monotype Studio
Date: 1998

Classic Roman is an elegant all-caps headline typeface that was created in-house at Monotype. It shares similarities with Carol Twombly's font Trajan of 1989, which is one of many typefaces inspired by the letter forms used on the inscription on the base of Trajan's Column in Rome.

Cocaine

ABCDEFGHIJKLMNOPQRSTUVWXYZ
abcdefghijklmnopqrstuvwxyz
1234567890 !@#?:;"*&

Foundry: Chank Co.
Designer: Chank Diesel / Josh Eshbach
Designer Nationality: American
Date: 2000

Cocaine was created by prolific US typeface designer Chank Diesel in 2000 with help from Josh Eshbach, an intern from the Minneapolis College of Art and Design. It is a single-style, informal display typeface inspired by Speedball type designs of the 1920s and 1930s.

Columna

ABCDEFGHIJKLMNOPQRSTUVWXYZ
1234567890 !@#?:;"'*&

Foundry: Bauer
Designer: Max Caflisch
Designer Nationality: Swiss
Date: 1952

Columna by Swiss typographer Max Caflisch is an uppercase titling serif inspired by classical Roman inscriptions. The original type of 1952 was outlined, a solid version was created decades later, and it is this that has been variously digitized by Linotype, URW, and Elsner+Flake.

Cooper BT

ABCDEFGHIJKLMNOPQRSTUVWXYZ
abcdefghijklmnopqrstuvwxyz
1234567890 !@#?:;"'*&

Foundry: Bitstream
Designer: Oswald Cooper
Designer Nationality: American
Date: 1922

Oswald Cooper's famous chunky display serif Cooper Black was released by US foundry Barnhart Brothers & Spindler in 1922. Cooper Black originally came in a single weight, but an italic soon followed. Bitstream's expansion and update, Cooper BT, added three weights with italics.

Delphian

ABCDEFGHIJKLMNOPQRSTUVWXYZ
1234567890 !©?:;"'*&

Foundry: Ludlow
Designer: Robert Hunter Middleton
Designer Nationality: Scottish
Date: 1928

Robert Hunter Middleton's Delphian, designed for Ludlow Typograph in 1928, is an elegant uppercase titling serif with classical proportions. Known on its release as Delphian Open Titling, it features small serifs and a fine inline. Middleton worked at Ludlow from 1923 to 1971.

Edwardian

ABCDEFGHIJKLMNOPQRSTUVWXYZ
abcdefghijklmnopqrstuvwxyz
1234567890 !@#?:;"'*&

Foundry: Letraset
Designer: Colin Brignall
Designer Nationality: British
Date: 1983

British designer Colin Brignall made use of Letraset's Ikarus font-design software to create this playful, rather decorative serif with early 20th-century charm, which proved to be very popular on release. Edwardian features a true italic as opposed to a sloped Roman.

Engravers

ABCDEFGHIJKLMNOPQRSTUVWXYZ
ABCDEFGHIJKLMNOPQRSTUVWXYZ
1234567890 !@#?:;"*&

Engravers was designed by Robert Wiebking for the Chicago-based type foundry Barnhart Brothers & Spindler in 1899. An elegant, extended high-contrast serif typeface with small caps, it was based on lettering used by copperplate engravers of the time for luxury applications.

Foundry: Barnhart Brothers & Spindler
Designer: Robert Wiebking
Designer Nationality: German
Date: 1899

Engravers 2

ABCDEFGHIJKLMNOPQRSTUV
ABCDEFGHIJKLMNOPQRSTUVWXYZ
1234567890 !@#?:;"*&

Engravers 2 is one of the types made by Robert Wiebking in 1899 based on traditional engraving alphabets. It is available in Regular and Bold, with uppercase and small caps only. The "2" is in the name because American Type Founders' Engravers Roman came in three numbered styles.

Foundry: Barnhart Brothers & Spindler
Designer: Robert Wiebking
Designer Nationality: German
Date: 1899

Engravers Roman BT

ABCDEFGHIJKLMNOPQRSTUVWXYZ
ABCDEFGHIJKLMNOPQRSTUVWXYZ
1234567890 !@#?:;"*&

This is Bitstream's version of Engravers Roman, which was originally designed by Robert Wiebking for US foundry Barnhart Brothers & Spindler in 1899. It is available in two styles, Regular and Bold. An extended copperplate-style serif, it features small caps rather than a lowercase.

Foundry: Bitstream
Designer: Robert Wiebking
Designer Nationality: German
Date: 1899

Engravure

ABCDEFGHIJKLMNOPQRSTUVWX
ABCDEFGHIJKLMNOPQRSTUVWXYZ
1234567890 !@#?:;"*&

Engravure is one of Robert Wiebking's typefaces based on traditional engraving lettering designed for American Type Founders at the turn of the 19th century. It is an elegant extended, high-contrast serif typeface with uppercase and small caps in a single weight. The "R" is distinctive with a notched leg.

Foundry: American Type Founders
Designer: Robert Wiebking
Designer Nationality: German
Date: 1903

Façade

ABCDEFGHIJKLMNOPQRSTUVWXYZ
abcdefghijklmnopqrstuvwxyz
1234567890 !@#?:.,"'*&

Foundry: Boston Type Foundry / Monotype
Designer: Steve Matteson
Designer Nationality: American
Date: c. 1890 / 2001

Façade is a revival, by Monotype's American typeface designer Steve Matteson, of display type Facade No. 2 created by the Boston Type Foundry in the late 19th century. It is a tall, condensed display font with small serifs, a very high x-height, and short ascenders and descenders.

Felix Titling

ABCDEFGHIJKLMNOPQRSTUVWXYZ
1234567890 !@#?:,"'*&

Foundry: Monotype
Designer: Felice Feliciano
Designer Nationality: Italian
Date: 1463

Felix Titling is based on an alphabet included in a treatise on Roman inscriptions by the Italian calligrapher Felice Feliciano, written in 1463. It is a single-style, uppercase serif in the tradition of inscriptional lettering. The typeface has small angular serifs, wide curves, and high contrast.

FF Trixie

ABCDEFGHIJKLMNOPQRSTUVWXYZ
abcdefghijklmnopqrstuvwxyz
1234567890 ! #?:;"'*&

Foundry: FontFont
Designer: Erik van Blokland
Designer Nationality: Dutch
Date: 1991

Dutch designer Erik van Blokland, who works under the name "LettError," designed Trixie for FontFont in 1991. It is a grungy typewriter face initially available in five styles: Light, Plain, Text, Extra, and Cameo. In 200, Van Blokland released an update with additional styles and features.

FS Rome

ABCDEFGHIJKLMNOPQRSTUVWXYZ
"
..

Foundry: Fontsmith
Designer: Jason Smith
Designer Nationality: British
Date: 1996

FS Rome was created by Jason Smith, the British typeface designer and founder of Fontsmith (see p. 272). It is a classical, titling serif in uppercase only. It was inspired by the lettering inscribed on Trajan's Column (AD 106–113). FS Rome is available in a single style only.

Gill Facia

ABCDEFGHIJKLMNOPQRSTUVWXYZ
abcdefghijklmnopqrstuvwxyz
1234567890 !@#?:;"*&

Foundry: Monotype
Designer: Eric Gill / Colin Banks
Designer Nationality: British
Date: 1996

Colin Banks's Gill Facia is a typeface based on lettering created by Eric Gill for the British book retailer WHSmith, and first used in 1903 for its Paris branch. It is a distinctive typeface with small, sharp serifs and a double storey "a" and "g." It is available in regular, italic, and titling styles.

Ginkgo

ABCDEFGHIJKLMNOPQRSTUVWXYZ
abcdefghijklmnopqrstuvwxyz
1234567890 !@#?:;"*&

Foundry: Linotype
Designer: Alex Rütten
Designer Nationality: German
Date: 2008

Ginkgo was the first published font by German type designer Alex Rütten, and it won him a Certificate of Excellence in Type Design at the Type Directors Club Awards in 2009. It is designed for use in long passages of text, and its open counters offer enhanced legibility at smaller point sizes.

Goudy Handtooled

ABCDEFGHIJKLMNOPQRSTUVWXYZ
abcdefghijklmnopqrstuvwxyz
1234567890 !@#?:;"*&

Foundry: American Type Founders
Designer: Frederic W. Goudy / Morris Fuller Benton
Designer Nationality: American
Date: c. 1915

Goudy Handtooled is a decorative, display version of Frederic W. Goudy's serif typeface Goudy; it has thin white lines on the left side of every letter, which look like highlights, creating a 3D effect. Unlike the standard Goudy, it comes in only one weight without italics.

GT Super

ABCDEFGHIJKLMNOPQRSTUVWXYZ
abcdefghijklmnopqrstuvwxyz
1234567890 !@#?:;"*&

Foundry: Grilli Type
Designer: Noël Leu
Designer Nationality: Swiss
Date: 2018

Grilli Type's GT Super is a versatile typeface family inspired by various high-contrast titling serifs that were popular in the 1970s and 1908s, such as Times Modern, Trooper Roman, and Perpetua Bold. It is available in text and display styles, each in five weights with italics.

Or Type

Or Type is an Icelandic type foundry established by Guðmundur Úlfarsson and Mads Freund Brunse in 2013 to publish typefaces designed by the Reykjavík/Brussels-based design studio GUNMAD, whose primary work is typographically focused.

Or Type's works aim to challenge the conventions found in typographic traditions and contemporary values. The company placed the typefaces it developed as research or designed for specific projects on its online type foundry to display and sell. It works with local references and from intrinsic ideas, designing its typefaces to have their own reason for being, rather than filling a gap in the font market. Through its growing library of alphabets, new ideas are being developed and existing typefaces are refined and revised in order to "create a new take on previous ideas."

The foundry offers ten typefaces. These include Lemmen, a decorative serif reminiscent of Victorian period; Separat (see p. 437); L10, a geometric sans serif; Boogie School Sans, a contrasting stroke sans serif display face; and Landnáma and variant Landnáma Nýja (see p. 506) an elegant display serif that incorporates a number of quirks within its strokes and counters, such as missing serifs or incomplete strokes.

Founded: 2013
Country: Iceland / Belgium
Website: ortype.is
Notable typefaces:
Landnáma / Landnáma Nýja
(see p. 506)
Separat (see p. 437)

Below. Various exhibitions featuring Or Type's creations on show.

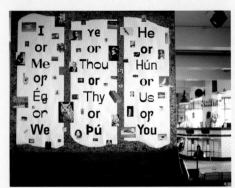

Right. Various type specimens.

Below. Poster for the Most Beautiful Swiss Books exhibition in Copenhagen in 2011. Design by GUNMAD.

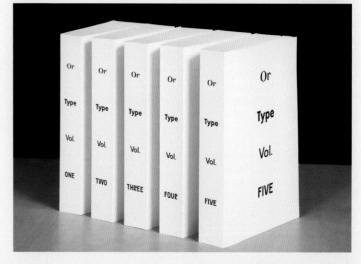

Handle Oldstyle

ABCDEFGHIJKLMNOPQRSTUVWXYZ
ABCDEFGHIJKLMNOPQRSTUVWXYZ
1234567890 !@#?:;"*&

Handle Oldstyle is one of Monotype's Engravers series of types released at the turn of the 20th century based on lettering styles traditionally used by engravers for stationery. It is an uppercase and small caps only, broad serif typeface that comes in a relatively heavy, single style.

Foundry: Monotype
Designer: Monotype Studio
Date: Unknown

Hawthorn

ABCDEFGHIJKLMNOPQRSTUVWXYZ
abcdefghijklmnopqrstuvwxyz
1234567890 !@#?:;"*&

Based on DeVinne, which originated at the Central Type Foundry (St Louis) *c.* 1892 (and was hugely popular at the time), Hawthorn was revived by Mike Daines and is a heavy compact serif, often used for book covers in the 1970s. It has a mixture of features, both sharp and bulbous, and has a slightly gothic feel.

Foundry: Letraset
Designer: Mike Daines
Designer Nationality: British
Date: 1968

Homeland BT

ABCDEFGHIJKLMNOPQRSTUVWXYZ
abcdefghijklmnopqrstuvwxyz
1234567890 !@#?:;"*&

Ray Cruz began his career in the phototypesetting industry, and has since worked extensively on custom lettering and type design for corporate clients, advertising agencies, and publishers. Open counters and bracketed serifs make his Homeland BT font family characterful and readable.

Foundry: Bitstream
Designer: Ray Cruz
Designer Nationality: American
Date: 2004

Isis

ABCDEFGHIJKLMNOPQRSTUVWXYZ
1234567890 !?:;"*&

Named after the ancient Egyptian goddess, Isis is an uppercase, classical titling, roman-style serif font with an open engraved effect. Michael Gills, who designed Isis in 1990, worked at the Letraset Type Studio under Colin Brignall after studying design at Suffolk College, Ipswich.

Foundry: Letraset
Designer: Michael Gills
Designer Nationality: British
Date: 1990

Italia

ABCDEFGHIJKLMNOPQRSTUVWXYZ
abcdefghijklmnopqrstuvwxyz
1234567890 !@#?:;"*&

Foundry: Letraset
Designer: Colin Brignall
Designer Nationality: British
Date: 1974

British type designer and photographer Colin Brignall joined Letraset in 1964, and was promoted to UK type director at the foundry in 1980. Italia is his revival of Joseph W. Phinney's Jenson Oldstyle released by American Type Founders in 1893, which was based on William Morris's Golden Type of 1890.

ITC Benguiat

ABCDEFGHIJKLMNOPQRSTUVWXYZ
abcdefghijklmnopqrstuvwxyz
1234567890 !@#?:;"*&

Foundry: ITC
Designer: Ed Benguiat
Designer Nationality: American
Date: 1977

This robust, Art Nouveau-influenced font was a popular choice for display type in the decades following its release; it is particularly well known for its appearance on the covers of novels by Stephen King and those of the *Choose Your Own Adventure* children's book series (1979–98).

ITC Cheltenham Handtooled

ABCDEFGHIJKLMNOPQRSTUVWXYZ
abcdefghijklmnopqrstuvwxyz
1234567890 !@#?:;"*&

Foundry: ITC
Designer: Ed Benguiat
Designer Nationality: American
Date: 1993

ITC Cheltenham was designed in 1975 by Tony Stan, and based on the typeface first designed by architect Bertram Goodhue and later expanded by Morris Fuller Benton. In 1993 Ed Benguiat (see p. 514) created a Handtooled style, adding a highlight to the Bold and Bold Italic cuts.

ITC Clearface

ABCDEFGHIJKLMNOPQRSTUVWXYZ
abcdefghijklmnopqrstuvwxyz
1234567890 !@#?:;"*&

Foundry: ITC
Designer: Linton Boyd Benton / Morris Fuller Benton / Victor Caruso
Designer Nationality: American
Date: 1978

Clearface was designed by Morris Fuller Benton in 1907 with assistance from his father. Victor Caruso updated it for the International Typeface Corporation (ITC) in 1978, removing some of the more unusual details from within the font's letter forms, achieving a more consistent feel across four weights.

ITC Elan

ABCDEFGHIJKLMNOPQRSTUVWXYZ
abcdefghijklmnopqrstuvwxyz
1234567890 !@#?:;"*&

Foundry: ITC
Designer: Albert Boton
Designer Nationality: French
Date: 1985

The low contrast and open counters of Albert Boton's design for Elan create a stable, legible impression in both body text and display contexts.

Boton worked under Adrian Frutiger (see p. 290) at Deberny & Peignot during the 1950s, and has taught type design since the late 1960s.

ITC Garamond Handtooled

ABCDEFGHIJKLMNOPQRSTUVWXYZ
abcdefghijklmnopqrstuvwxyz
1234567890 !@#?:;"*&

Foundry: ITC
Designer: Ed Benguiat
Designer Nationality: American
Date: 1993

ITC's Garamond was developed in 1977 by Tony Stan, and based on the serif type designed by Claude Garamond in the 16th century, but with tighter spacing and a taller x-height. In 1993, Ed Benguiat (see p. 514) created a Handtooled style, adding a highlight to the Bold and Bold Italic cuts.

ITC Golden Type

ABCDEFGHIJKLMNOPQRSTUVWXYZ
abcdefghijklmnopqrstuvwxyz
1234567890 !@#?:;"*&

Foundry: ITC
Designer: Sigrid Engelmann / Helga Jörgenson / Andrew Newton
Designer Nationality: German / German / British
Date: 1989

Sigrid Engelmann, Helga Jörgenson, and Andrew Newton designed ITC Golden Type. It is a revival of a classical serif by British designer William Morris, which was used by the Kelmscott Press to print its edition of *The Golden Legend* (1846) in 1892 and was itself based on type designs by Nicolas Jenson.

ITC Isbell

ABCDEFGHIJKLMNOPQRSTUVWXYZ
abcdefghijklmnopqrstuvwxyz
1234567890 !@#?:;"*&

Foundry: ITC
Designer: Jerry Campbell / Richard Isbell
Designer Nationality: American
Date: 1981

Designed in 1981 by Jerry Campbell and Richard Isbell, ITC Isbell is a distinctive, stylized roman serif typeface with a large x-height, stencil-style gaps in the joins of many lowercase letters, and short ascenders and descenders. It comes in four styles— Book and Bold with italics.

ITC Korinna

ABCDEFGHIJKLMNOPQRSTUVWXYZ
abcdefghijklmnopqrstuvwxyz
1234567890 !@#?:;"*&

Foundry: Berthold / ITC
Designer: Ed Benguiat /
Victor Caruso
Designer Nationality: American
Date: 1904 / 1974

The contemporary redrawing by Ed Benguiat (see p. 514) and Victor Caruso of this German Art Nouveau design made its debut for the International Typeface Corporation (ITC) in the second issue of *U&lc*, the foundry's free quarterly type magazine, art directed by Herb Lubalin (see p. 62).

ITC Newtext

ABCDEFGHIJKLMNOPQRSTUVWXYZ
abcdefghijklmnopqrstuvwxyz
1234567890 !@#?:;"*&

Foundry: ITC
Designer: Ray Baker
Designer Nationality: American
Date: 1974

Ray Baker designed the extended letter forms of ITC Newtext, with their flared serifs and consistent stroke weight, for optimal legibility when used for body text. Its squat proportions permit more lines of type to be set on a page, which is useful where economy is a key concern.

ITC Quorum

ABCDEFGHIJKLMNOPQRSTUVWXYZ
abcdefghijklmnopqrstuvwxyz
1234567890 !@#?:;"*&

Foundry: ITC
Designer: Ray Baker
Designer Nationality: American
Date: 1977

Ray Baker's design for ITC Quorum borrows several formal characteristics from sans serif type design, with its subtle flared serifs adding a sense of historic detail. The slightly condensed letter forms of this ovoid typeface make it an economical choice for text typesetting.

ITC Serif Gothic

ABCDEFGHIJKLMNOPQRSTUVWXYZ
abcdefghijklmnopqrstuvwxyz
1234567890 !@#?:;"*&

Foundry: ITC
Designer: Antonio DiSpigna /
Herb Lubalin
Designer Nationality: Italian /
American
Date: 1972

Herb Lubalin (see p. 62) and Antonio DiSpigna collaborated on the design of ITC Serif Gothic, resulting in an unusual, display-friendly font, which was widely used on film posters, album artwork, and book covers following its release. Its tiny serifs give it the appearance of a sans at smaller sizes.

ITC Stepp

ABCDEFGHIJKLMNOPQRSTUVWXYZ
abcdefghijklmnopqrstuvwxyz
1234567890 !@#?:;"*&

Foundry: ITC
Designer: Hal Taylor
Designer Nationality: American
Date: 2005

Hand-lettering artist and illustrator Hal Taylor began his career in phototypesetting, and went on to design typefaces. He developed his design for ITC Stepp from uppercase lettering found within an Art Deco logo for the Stetson Shoe Company of Weymouth, Massachusetts from 1930.

ITC Tiffany

ABCDEFGHIJKLMNOPQRSTUVWXYZ
abcdefghijklmnopqrstuvwxyz
1234567890 !@#?:;"*&

Foundry: ITC
Designer: Ed Benguiat
Designer Nationality: American
Date: 1974

An early release from the International Typeface Corporation (ITC), Tiffany has a sturdy, voluptuous design incorporating formal details taken by Ed Benguiat (see p. 514) from two earlier typefaces, Caxton and Ronaldson. ITC published a true italic version of the typeface, also cut by Benguiat, in 1981.

Jenson Old Style

ABCDEFGHIJKLMNOPQRSTUVWXYZ
abcdefghijklmnopqrstuvwxyz
1234567890 !@#?:;"*&

Foundry: Letraset
Designer: Freda Sack /
Colin Brignall
Designer Nationality: British
Date: 1982

Jenson Old Style is a display serif based on the work of Nicolas Jenson, a French printer who made his name in 13th-century Italy. While many have optimized Jenson's designs for text purposes, the broad characters of Jenson Old Style are better suited to headline typography.

Juliana Text

ABCDEFGHIJKLMNOPQRSTUVWXYZ
ABCDEFGHIJKLMNOPQRSTUVWXYZ
1234567890 !@#?:;"*&

Foundry: Linotype
Designer: Sem Hartz /
Sam Berlow
Designer Nationality: Dutch /
American
Date: 1958 / 2009

Dutch typographer Sem Hartz was commissioned by Walter Tracy at Linotype to design Juliana, which is a classical serif reminiscent of the Roman typefaces designed in 16th-century Italy. Juliana has diamond-shaped dots and is available in roman, italic, and small capitals.

Kelvingrove

ABCDEFGHIJKLMNOPQRSTUVWXYZ

ABCDEFGHIJKLMNOPQRSTUVWXYZ

1234567890 !@#?:;"*&

Foundry: Typodermic
Designer: Ray Larabie
Designer Nationality: Canadian
Date: 2007

Kelvingrove is a copperplate display typeface designed in regular and small capitals, including alternative swash characters for the "k," "q" and "r." Intended for headlines and short runs of text, Kelvingrove features two sets of balanced numerals to match both capital styles.

Latin

ABCDEFGHIJKLMNOPQRSTUVWXYZ

abcdefghijklmnopqrstuvwxyz

1234567890 !@#?:;"*&

Foundry: Monotype
Designer: Monotype Studio
Date: 1890

Latin is a condensed serif display typeface design in the Latin type style popularized in the 19th century. Like those that preceded it, Monotype's Latin font features structured strokes, glyphic serifs, and keen terminals. The foundry was set up in Philadelphia in 1887 and this was one of its first fonts.

Latin #2

ABCDEFGHIJKLMNOPQRSTUVWXYZ

1234567890 !@#?:;"*&

Foundry: Stephenson, Blake & Co
Designer: Stephenson, Blake & Co
Date: 1884

Similar to Monotype's Latin, the Latin #2 font is a structured, glyphic serif designed for headline purposes. Unlike the former, Stephenson, Blake & Co.'s Latin #2 offers two styles, Compressed and Wide, both in a single weight, to cater for a variety of layouts and compositions.

Latin Extra Condensed

ABCDEFGHIJKLMNOPQRSTUVWXYZ

1234567890 !@#?:;"*&

Foundry: Bitstream
Designer: M. Jean Rochaix
Designer Nationality: French
Date: 1873

Latin Extra Condensed is a Bitstream revival of M. Jean Rochaix's Elongated Latin, a typeface released by Stephenson, Blake & Co. in 1873. A tall, stout, triangular-serifed typeface, Latin Extra Condensed is available in one weight and, unlike Monotype's version Latin Condensed, has only an uppercase.

Landnáma / Landnáma Nýja

ABCDEFGHIJKLMNOPQRSTUVWXYZ
abcdefghijklmnopqrstuvwxyz
1234567890 !@#?:;"*&

ABCDEFGHIJKLMNOPQRSTUVWXYZ
abcdefghijklmnopqrstuvwxyz
1234567890 !@#?:;"*&

Foundry: Or Type
Designer: Guðmundur Úlfarsson
Designer Nationality: Icelandic
Date: 2015

Landnáma and Landnáma Nýja were designed by Guðmundur Úlfarsson of the Danish / Icelandic foundry Or Type (see p. 498). He based his design on embossed lettering on a plaque on a public sculpture in Reykjavik. The tightly set letter forms have partially melted counters and strokes, as is visible in the "a," which has a ball ending on a part of the bowl beneath. There are also omissions to certain strokes, which aim to reflect the inaccuracies created when lettering has been blind-embossed through a metal surface. Available in the one weight with no italic, the Landnáma pairing is ideal when looking for a serif display type with a part-weathered appearance or unusual, distressed quirk.

Below. *Competing Temporalities* and *The World For Less* are artist publications by Lloyd Corporation (artists Ali Eisa and Sebastian Lloyd Rees). Design by GUNMAD.

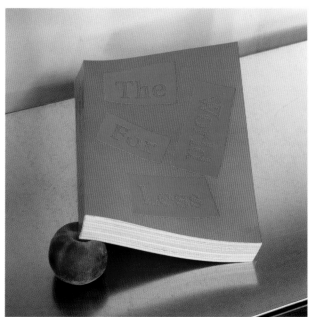

Lemmen

ABCDEFGHIJKLMNOPQRSTUVWXYZ
abcdefghijklmnopqrstuvwxyz
1234567890 !@#?:;"'*&

Lemmen is modeled on the typeface Antiqua, designed by the Belgian painter Georges Lemmen in the early 20th century. It is a serif display font comprised of six styles. Informed by the original specimen, the characters feature incised junctures alongside high-contrast strokes.

Foundry: Or Type
Designer: Mads Freund Brunse / Guðmundur Úlfarsson (GUNMAD)
Designer Nationality: Danish / Icelandic
Date: 2018

Letraset Romic

ABCDEFGHIJKLMNOPQRSTUVWXYZ
abcdefghijklmnopqrstuvwxyz
1234567890 !@#?:;"*&

Letraset Romic is a quirky, chunky calligraphic serif created by Colin Brignall, an in-house designer at Letraset. It features distinctive notches cut out of various letters, which leave the dots of the "i" and "j" shaped like speech bubbles, as are the counters of the "e," "P," "R," and "B."

Foundry: Letraset
Designer: Colin Brignall
Designer Nationality: British
Date: 1979

Light Roman

ABCDEFGHIJKLMNOPQRSTUVWX
ABCDEFGHIJKLMNOPQRSTUVWXYZ
1234567890 !@#?:;"'*&

Light Roman is an all-capitals serif display typeface intended to bestow a delicate elegance to printed materials, such as invitations and stationery. Inspired by classical engraved lettering, Light Roman utilizes both high-contrast strokes and its angled joints and brackets.

Foundry: Monotype
Designer: Monotype Studio
Date: 1998

Linotype Venezia

ABCDEFGHIJKLMNOPQRSTUVWXYZ

Linotype Venezia is modeled on the classical style of Roman writing, found in the architecture of the 1st and 2nd centuries. It is a historical serif display face that combines positive and negative space to imitate the chiseled aesthetic of carved letter forms. Linotype Venezia is part of the TakeType Library.

Foundry: Linotype
Designer: Robert Kolben
Designer Nationality: German
Date: 1997

Lucian

ABCDEFGHIJKLMNOPQRSTUVWXYZ
abcdefghijklmnopqrstuvwxyz
1234567890 !@#?:;"*&

Foundry: Bitstream
Designer: Lucian Bernhard
Designer Nationality: German
Date: 1928 / 1990

Lucian was drawn by the leading German designer of the early 20th century for the Bauer foundry. Bitstream digitized it in two weights—Bold and Roman—and initially renamed it "Kuenstler 185." A chunky serif, Lucian has large dots and ball terminals, most obvious on top of the quirky "g."

LuMarc

ABCDEFGHIJKLMNOPQRSTUVWXYZ
abcdefghijklmnopqrstuvwxyz
1234567890 !@#?:;"*&

Foundry: Monotype
Designer: Marc Lubbers
Designer Nationality: Dutch
Date: 1994

With squat, wide letters and tiny angular serifs, LuMarc is almost a sans serif. It is available in Roman and Bold. Utrecht-based designer Marc Lubbers began many of his fonts while still a student and switched his focus to web design by the late 1990s.

Marco Polo

ABCDEFGHIJKLMNOPQRSTUVWXYZ
abcdefghijklmnopqrstuvwxyz
1234567890 !@#?:;"*&

Foundry: Omnibus Typografi
Designer: Franko Luin
Designer Nationality: Swedish
Date: 1993

Franko Luin of Omnibus Typografi designed Marco Polo and named it after the famous Venetian explorer. It is an Old Style serif with fairly rounded serifs that has been designed with imperfect rough edges to give an antique, old world feel; it comes in roman, italic, and small caps.

Maximus

ABCDEFGHIJKLMNOPQRST
abcdefghijklmnopqrstuvwxyz
1234567890 !@#?:;" *&

Foundry: Linotype
Designer: Walter Tracy
Designer Nationality: American
Date: 1967

Maximus was designed for the Linotype foundry in 1967 by Walter Tracy, the renowned English type designer, typographer, and writer. It is a horizontally striped, all-caps sans serif, with bold, condensed forms and was specifically designed for use at very small sizes on newsprint.

Medium Roman

ABCDEFGHIJKLMNOPQRSTUVWX
ABCDEFGHIJKLMNOPQRSTUVWXYZ
1234567890 !@#?:;"*&

Foundry: Monotype
Designer: Monotype Studio
Date: Unknown

Monotype's Medium Roman is one of many fonts based on lettering used historically by engravers. It is an extended, high-contrast serif in a single weight and style with caps and small caps. The font has many quirks, such as the spurs on "J" and "U," the tail of the "Q" and the unconnected leg of "R."

Monotype Clearface

ABCDEFGHIJKLMNOPQRSTUVWXYZ
abcdefghijklmnopqrstuvwxyz
1234567890 !@#?:;"*&

Foundry: Monotype
Designer: Morris Fuller Benton
Designer Nationality: American
Date: 1907

As its name implies, Morris Benton designed Clearface for American Type Founders to be easy to read, even at smaller sizes. Letters are relatively condensed and heavy, with short ascenders and descenders. Monotype's version, one of many, comes in the original Bold.

Monotype Engravers

ABCDEFGHIJKLMNOPQRSTUV
WXYZ
1234567890 !@#?:;"*&

Foundry: Monotype
Designer: Robert Wiebking / Morris Fuller Benton / Monotype Studio
Designer Nationality: German / American
Date: 1902

Monotype Engravers is an all-caps display typeface inspired by the copper- and steel-plate designs of the 19th century. Robert Wiebking designed the initial Regular version, while Morris Fuller Benton added the Bold style in 1902 before they were both packaged by Monotype.

Monotype Modern Display

ABCDEFGHIJKLMNOPQRSTUVWXYZ
abcdefghijklmnopqrstuvwxyz
1234567890 !@#?:;"*&

Foundry: Monotype
Designer: Dan Rhatigan
Designer Nationality: American
Date: 2013

US typographer Dan Rhatigan designed Modern Display when he was UK type director at Monotype. It is a single-weight headline font intended to supplement the Monotype Modern family. A beautiful serif, with extreme contrast, it was initially a custom font for fashion title *Centrefold Magazine*.

Musketeer

ABCDEFGHIJKLMNOPQRSTUVWXYZ
abcdefghijklmnopqrstuvwxyz
1234567890 !@#?:;"*&

Foundry: Compugraphic
Designer: Tony Geddes
Designer Nationality: British
Date: 1968

Musketeer was designed for Quick Brown Fox by Tony Geddes, who later co-founded the Panache Graphics foundry. It is a quirky, Art Nouveau-inspired display serif now available from Monotype in four weights: Light, Regular, Demi Bold, and Extra Bold. The lowercase has large, open counters.

Onyx

ABCDEFGHIJKLMNOPQRSTUVWXYZ
abcdefghijklmnopqrstuvwxyz
1234567890 !@#?:;"*&

Foundry: American Type Founders
Designer: Gerry Powell
Designer Nationality: American
Date: 1937

Onyx is a serif display typeface created by Gerry Powell, former director of typographic design for the American Type Founders. It was designed in the style of a modern serif but optimized for display, and the refined impact of its characters made Onyx a popular choice for advertising in the 1940s.

Origami

ABCDEFGHIJKLMNOPQRSTUVWXYZ
abcdefghijklmnopqrstuvwxyz
1234567890 !@#?:;"*&

Foundry: Monotype
Designer: Carl Crossgrove
Designer Nationality: American
Date: 1998

The Origami typeface is named after the ancient Japanese art of paper folding. It is a low-contrast, angular typeface with virtually no curves and fairly minimal serifs, especially on the regular cut. Origami is available in four weights, with a chancery italic, and is best suited to headline use.

Paddington

ABCDEFGHIJKLMNOPQRSTUVWXYZ
abcdefghijklmnopqrstuvwxyz
1234567890 !@#?:;"*&

Foundry: Letraset
Designer: Freda Sack
Designer Nationality: British
Date: 1977

Adrian Williams commissioned Freda Sack, the co-founder of The Foundry (see p. 284), to design Paddington. Sack also designed the popular types Proteus, Stratford, and Victorian. Paddington is a soft-serifed roman in the classic style, which is reminiscent of Frederic W. Goudy's types.

PL Latin

ABCDEFGHIJKLMNOPQRSTUVWXYZ
abcdefghijklmnopqrstuvwxyz
1234567890 !©#?:;"*&

With enunciated details found in the serifs and terminals, PL Latin is a glyphic style typeface intended for headline typography. The PL Latin font family features only two styles, Elongated and Bold, which were both designed for maximum impact at larger sizes.

Foundry: Monotype
Designer: David Quay
Designer Nationality: British
Date: 1988

PL Modern

ABCDEFGHIJKLMNOPQRSTUVWXYZ
abcdefghijklmnopqrstuvwxyz
1234567890 !©#?:;"*&

PL Modern (also known as PL Modern Heavy Condensed) is based on a design done in 1936 by Robert Hunter Middleton, the Scottish book designer, painter, and type designer. Created at Photo-Lettering in New York, it has classic Bodoni-style letter forms, typical of modern serif faces.

Foundry: Photo-Lettering
Designer: Robert Hunter Middleton
Designer Nationality: British
Date: 1936

Plate Gothic

ABCDEFGHIJKLMNOPQRSTUVWXYZ
ABCDEFGHIJKLMNOPQRSTUVWXYZ
1234567890 !@#?:;"*&

Plate Gothic, which was designed by the Monotype team in 1921 and inspired by Goudy's Copperplate, is an extended, engraving-style typeface. It is essentially a sans serif with added thin, straight serifs, and it comes in fifteen styles. Five of these are italic, with caps and small caps.

Foundry: Monotype
Designer: Monotype Studio
Date: 1921

Pompeii

ABCDEFGHIJKLMNOPQRSTUVWXYZ
ABCDEFGHIJKLMNOPQRSTUVWXYZ
1234567890 !@#?:;"*&

Philip Bouwsma designed Pompeii Capitals for the International Typeface Corporation (ITC) in 1994. It is a calligraphic titling serif typeface with uppercase and small caps only. It takes its name from the Roman city outside Naples destroyed by the eruption of the Mount Vesuvius volcano in AD 79.

Foundry: ITC
Designer: Philip Bouwsma
Designer Nationality: American
Date: 1994

Portrait Inline

ABCDEFGHIJKLMNOPQRSTUVWXYZ
ABCDEFGHIJKLMNOPQRSTUVWXYZ
1234567890 !@#?:;”’*&

Foundry: Commercial Type
Designer: Berton Hasebe
Designer Nationality: American
Date: 2013

Portrait Inline was designed by Hawaiian-born designer Berton Hasebe, who worked in the New York office of Commercial Type (see p. 124) from 2008 to 2013 before starting his own studio. It is a classical, inlined titling serif with capitals and small caps only. A sans serif version is also available.

President

ABCDEFGHIJKLMNOPQRSTUVWXY
ABCDEFGHIJKLMNOPQRSTUVWXYZ
1234567890 !@#?:;”*&

Foundry: Deberny & Peignot
Designer: Adrian Frutiger
Designer Nationality: Swiss
Date: 1954

President (also known as Initiales Président) is one of the first typefaces produced by legendary Swiss designer Adrian Frutiger (see p. 290) for Deberny & Peignot. It is an uppercase, Latin titling font with low contrast and small, sharp serifs. The addition of small caps came after its initial release in 1954.

Ragnar

ABCDEFGHIJKLMNOPQRSTUVWXYZ
abcdefghijklmnopqrstuvwxyz
1234567890 !@#?:;”*&

Foundry: Omnibus Typografi
Designer: Franko Luin
Designer Nationality: Swedish
Date: 1993

Swedish type designer Franko Luin named the Ragnar typeface after "Ragnarök," which is an apocalyptic event predicted in Norse mythology. Ragnar is an angular text serif with a large x-height; it comes in three weights with italics and one weight of small caps.

Rameau

ABCDEFGHIJKLMNOPQRSTUVWXYZ
abcdefghijklmnopqrstuvwxyz
1234567890 !@#?:;”*&

Foundry: Linotype
Designer: Sarah Lazarevic
Designer Nationality: French
Date: 2011

French typographer, teacher, designer, and engraver Sarah Lazarevic designed Rameau in 2011. It began as an italic font inspired by engraved text found on a manuscript of music composed by Jean-Philippe Rameau in 1747 for an opera. It is a sharp text serif in three weights with italics.

Rosella

ABCDEFGHIJKLMNOPQRSTU
VWXYZ
1234567890 !@#?:;"*&

Foundry: Monotype
Designer: Sabina Chipară
Designer Nationality: Romanian
Date: 2017

Sabina Chipară, a Romanian designer based in the Netherlands, designed Rosella in 2017. It is an uppercase and small caps only high-contrast serif inspired by majuscule engraving fonts. Rosella comes in a single weight with five display versions: Inline, Engraved, Hatched, Deco, and Flourish.

Rundfunk Antiqua

ABCDEFGHIJKLMNOPQRSTUVWXYZ
abcdefghijklmnopqrstuvwxyz
1234567890 !@#?:;"*&

Foundry: Linotype
Designer: Linotype Design Studio
Date: 1933–35

An unknown member of Linotype's studio drew Rundfunk Antiqua in the 1930s. It is a text serif with a large x-height and short ascenders and descenders. Rundfunk Antiqua comes in a single roman weight and was designed with a sans serif, Rundfunk Grotesk, but neither evolved beyond one style.

Sackers Classic Roman

ABCDEFGHIJKLMNOPQRSTUVWXYZ
ABCDEFGHIJKLMNOPQRSTUVWXYZ
1234567890 !@#?:;"*&

Foundry: Agfa Compugraphic
Designer: Gary Sackers
Designer Nationality: American
Date: 1975

Sackers Classic Roman was one of a series of fonts designed by Gary Sackers between 1974 and 1975, based on old engraving masterplates for Agfa Compugraphic. It is a thin, classical titling serif with caps and small caps only, and it is available from Monotype in a single light weight.

Sackers Roman

ABCDEFGHIJKLMNOPQRSTUV
ABCDEFGHIJKLMNOPQRSTUVWX
1234567890 !@#?:;"*&

Foundry: Agfa Compugraphic
Designer: Gary Sackers
Designer Nationality: American
Date: 1975

Between 1974 and 1975, Gary Sackers created a range of fonts for Agfa Compugraphic based on historic engraving masterplates, including Sackers Roman, a wide high-contrast serif available in light and heavy weights with caps and small caps only. It has an especially distinctive "U."

Designer Profile

Ed Benguiat

Typographer and lettering artist Ed Benguiat is one of the most prolific US type designers of all time and a legendary character. He has crafted and been involved in the creation of more than 600 typefaces, and is recognized as one of the leading logotype designers, who has created a wealth of iconic marques.

Born in New York in the 1920s, Benguiat's first job was as a jazz percussionist—and as an accomplished one, playing in several big bands, and with some of the jazz greats of the day. With a young family, he became concerned that his musical career did not have long-term work prospects and having drawn since a boy, he decided to become an illustrator. After his change in direction, he studied at the Workshop School of Advertising Art, New York where he experimented with his first typeface. In 1962, he joined Photo-Lettering Inc (PLINC) as a type designer. The company was one of the first and most successful foundries to utilize photo technology in the production of typography and lettering. From 1936 to 1997, it served the design and advertising studios of New York, providing typesetting and designs.

In 1971, he joined fellow designers Aaron Burns, Herb Lubalin, and Edward Rondthaler, who had founded International Typeface Corporation (ITC) as the first independent licensing company for type designers. He also worked on ITC's typographic in-house magazine *U&lc* with his contemporary and great collaborator Lubalin (see p. 62–63). Benguiat has created many notable fonts over his long and incredibly productive career, including ITC Bookman, ITC Souvenir, ITC Tiffany, and the eponymously titled ITC Benguiat.

He has also produced logotypes for institutions such as *The New York Times, Playboy, Sports Illustrated*, and *Esquire*, and for brands such as Coca-Cola, Ford, AT&T, and Estée Lauder, as well as film titles including the original *Planet of the Apes* (1968) and *The Guns of Navarone* (1961). Benguiat was lauded in 1989, when he was awarded the New York Type Directors Club Medal, citing for those "who have made significant contributions to the life, art and craft of typography."

In 2002, US foundry House Industries released the Ed Benguiat Font Collection. House Industries type designer Ken Barber collaborated with Benguiat to redraw a collection of five of Benguiat's PLINC display typefaces along with a fun dingbats font entitled Bengbats. As further tribute, House Industries made a documentary film about him, honoring his contribution and influence on US type design and craft. ITC Benguiat has enjoyed a resurgence in the 21st century and is used for the main titles on the Netflix hit show *Stranger Things* (2016).

Date: 1927–
Nationality: American
Notable typefaces:
ITC Bookman (see p. 42)
ITC Benguiat (see p. 501)
ITC Edwardian Script (see p. 611)
ITC Souvenir (see p. 129)
ITC Tiffany (see p. 501)

Below. Benguiat's iconic logotypes for *Esquire* magazine and *Planet of the Apes*. In recent years his ITC Benguiat typeface was modified and employed for the main logo on hit Netflix show *Stranger Things*, design by Jacob Boghosian.

Left. Promotion for ITC Benguiat Condensed by Photo-Lettering Inc. (top) and specimen page for ITC Benguiat Book (bottom). An Art Nouveau-influenced design, it was a popular choice for display type for many years after its release, being particularly well known for its use on the covers of novels by Stephen King.

Above. Hand-lettered and colored artwork by Ed Benguiat for a New York television network.

Below left. Legendary type designer and lettering artist Ed Benguiat at work.

Below. Cover for Photo-Lettering Inc.'s catalogue of *Psychedelitypes*. A collection of typeface designs built around the visual properties of Psychedelia sub-culture. The ornate circular typographic kaleidoscope motif and design were created by Ed Benguiat, employing Dave Davison's Arabesque typeface for the headlines.

26 good reasons to use ITC Benguiat Book

Schnyder M

ABCDEFGHIJKLMNOPQRSTUVWXYZ
abcdefghijklmnopqrstuvwxyz
1234567890 !@#?:;"*&

Foundry: Commercial Type
Designer: Berton Hasebe /
Christian Schwartz
Designer Nationality: American
Date: 2018

Schnyder is a vast family by Christian Schwartz and Berton Hasebe of Commercial Type (see p. 124). It was released in 2018 but designed in 2013 for *T: The New York Times Style Magazine*. Schnyder, the regular width, comes in four optical sizes: Schnyder M, the medium is available in three weights with italics.

Schnyder Cond M

ABCDEFGHIJKLMNOPQRSTUVWXYZ
abcdefghijklmnopqrstuvwxyz
1234567890 !@#?:;"*&

Foundry: Commercial Type
Designer: Berton Hasebe /
Christian Schwartz
Designer Nationality: American
Date: 2018

Schnyder was inspired by Beaux Arts serifs from the late 19th century and the lettering of Swiss artist Jean-Frédéric Schnyder (from whom it got its name). It comes in four widths. The condensed style comes in four optical sizes and three weights: Light, Demi, and Bold (without italics).

Schnyder Wide M

ABCDEFGHIJKLMNOPQRSTUVWXYZ
abcdefghijklmnopqrstuvwxyz
1234567890 !@#?:;"*&

Foundry: Commercial Type
Designer: Berton Hasebe /
Christian Schwartz
Designer Nationality: American
Date: 2018

Schnyder has one expanded style, Schnyder Wide. It was first created in 2014 when *T: The New York Times Style Magazine* wanted more versatility from the serif it had commissioned a year earlier. Schnyder Wide comes in four optical sizes and three weights: Light, Demi, and Bold.

Schnyder Xcond XL

ABCDEFGHIJKLMNOPQRSTUVWXYZ
abcdefghijklmnopqrstuvwxyz
1234567890 !@#?:;"*&

Foundry: Commercial Type
Designer: Berton Hasebe /
Christian Schwartz
Designer Nationality: American
Date: 2018

The creative director of *T: The New York Times Style Magazine*, Patrick Li, often worked with Christian Schwartz and Berton Hasebe. Apart from Schnyder, they also created Pialat, Karl, and Graphik Titling for the magazine. Schnyder Xcond comes in only two optical sizes, L and XL.

Schnyder XL

ABCDEFGHIJKLMNOPQRSTUVWXYZ
abcdefghijklmnopqrstuvwxyz
1234567890 !@#?:;"*&

Foundry: Commercial Type
Designer: Berton Hasebe / Christian Schwartz
Designer Nationality: American
Date: 2018

Schnyder is an elegant, high-contrast display serif; the XL cut is the version optically optimized for larger use such as headlines. It comes in three weights with italics drawn by Miguel Reyes, which are unique to the regular width. Hrvoje Živčić provided production assistance.

Serlio

ABCDEFGHIJKLMNOPQRSTUVWXYZ
ABCDEFGHIJKLMNOPQRSTUVWXYZ
1234567890 !@#?:;"*&

Foundry: Linotype
Designer: Sebastiano Serlio
Designer Nationality: Italian
Date: 1990

Linotype's font Serlio, designed in-house in 1990, is based on lettering created by the 16th-century Italian architect, engraver, and painter Sebastiano Serlio. It is an uppercase and small caps only inscriptional titling typeface, with classical proportions and small, fine serifs.

SG Cheltenham Old Style SB

ABCDEFGHIJKLMNOPQRSTUVWXYZ
abcdefghijklmnopqrstuvwxyz
1234567890 !@#?:;"*&

Foundry: Scangraphic
Designer: Bertram Grosvenor Goodhue / Morris Fuller Benton
Designer Nationality: American
Date: 1902

Cheltenham Old Style SB is a Scangraphic version of Cheltenham Old Style, the quirky serif designed by architect Bertram Grosvenor Goodhue and refined by Morris Fuller Benton in 1902. The "SB" in the name references a Scangraphic convention and indicates it was created to set text or body type.

SG Copperplate SB

ABCDEFGHIJKLMNOPQRSTUVWXYZ
ABCDEFGHIJKLMNOPQRSTUVWXYZ
1234567890 !@#?:;"*&

Foundry: Scangraphic
Designer: Frederic W. Goudy
Designer Nationality: American
Date: 1901

Copperplate SB is Scangraphic's version of Copperplate, an extended uppercase and small caps only typeface designed by Frederic W. Goudy. It comes in Light, Regular, and Bold weights in two widths and has blunt, straight serifs on otherwise sans serif-style letters.

SPQR

ABCDEFGHIJKLMNOPQRSTUVWXYZ
ABCDEFGHIJKLMNOPQRSTUVWXYZ
1234567890 !@#?:;"*&

Foundry: Munch Fonts
Designer: Gary Munch
Designer Nationality: American
Date: 1993

SPQR is named after the Latin abbreviation of *Senatus Populusque Romanus* (the Roman Senate and People). US font designer Gary Munch created the classical, uppercase titling serif for his foundry Munch Fonts. It is heavy and comes in roman and italic styles.

Stevens Titling

ABCDEFGHIJKLMNOPQRSTUVWXYZ
ABCDEFGHIJKLMNOPQRSTUVWXYZ
1234567890 !@#?:;"*&

Foundry: Linotype
Designer: John Stevens / Ryuichi Tateno
Designer Nationality: American / Japanese
Date: 2011

Calligraphers John Stevens and Ryuichi Tateno created Stevens Titling in 2011. It is a collection of four classical uppercase serif fonts. Three variants— Badger Brush, Boar Brush, and Wolf Brush—have visible brushstroke textures, while Sable Brush is solid and also has small caps.

Throhand

ABCDEFGHIJKLMNOPQRSTUVWXYZ
abcdefghijklmnopqrstuvwxyz
1234567890 !@#?:;"*&

Foundry: Font Bureau
Designer: David Berlow
Designer Nationality: American
Date: 1995

David Berlow worked at Linotype and Bitstream before co-founding the Font Bureau in 1989. His design for Throhand was inspired by the 16th-century types of Claude Garamond and Hendrik van den Keere. It is a sharp, elegant high-contrast serif in three weights with italics.

Titus

ABCDEFGHIJKLMNOPQRSTUVWXYZ
abcdefghijklmnopqrstuvwxyz
1234567890 !@#?:;"*&

Foundry: Linotype
Designer: David Quay
Designer Nationality: British
Date: 1984

Titus is a serif text typeface with subtly calligraphic features, a tall x-height, and large counters. It comes in Light Roman only. British type designer David Quay created Titus for Linotype in 1984. He went on to co-found The Foundry (see p. 284) in 1990 with fellow British type designer Freda Sack.

Trajan

ABCDEFGHIJKLMNOPQRSTUVWXYZ
1234567890 ! ?:;"*&

Foundry: Adobe
Designer: Carol Twombly
Designer Nationality: American
Date: 1989

Carol Twombly designed Trajan in 1989. It is a classical, inscriptional titling serif typeface with uppercase and small caps only in Regular and Bold roman weights. It was based on the lettering inscribed on Trajan's Column (106–113 AD) in Rome and is a popular choice for film-poster text.

Ultramarina

ABCDEFGHIJKLMNOPQRSTUVWXYZ
abcdefghijklmnopqrstuvwxyz
1234567890 !@#?:;"*&

Foundry: Huy!Fonts
Designer: Juanjo Lopez
Designer Nationality: Spanish
Date: 2011

Huy!Fonts, the Madrid-based foundry of Spanish designer Juanjo Lopez, released Ultramarina in 2011. It is a quirky, condensed bold serif in a single style with ball terminals and a large x-height. Lopez is also involved in lettering, letterpress printing, calligraphy, and teaching.

Value Serif

ABCDEFGHIJKLMNOPQRSTUVWXYZ
abcdefghijklmnopqrstuvwxyz
1234567890 !@#?:;"*&

Foundry: Colophon
Designer: Benjamin Critton
Designer Nationality: American
Date: 2013

Benjamin Critton's Value Serif, which comes in a single style, was designed in 2013 to pair with the Value Sans font designed by The Entente's Edd Harrington and Anthony Sheret. Value Serif is a chunky, quirky typeface with a tall x-height. Plantin Infant was an influence on Value Serif.

VeraCruz BT

ABCDEFGHIJKLMNOPQRSTUVWXYZ
abcdefghijklmnopqrstuvwxyz
1234567890 !@#?:;"*&

Foundry: Bitstream
Designer: Ray Cruz
Designer Nationality: American
Date: 2003

US lettering artist and typeface designer Ray Cruz began his career at the Headliners photolettering firm in New York. His VeraCruz is a sharp, angular flared serif font in a bold weight. It features contextual alternates that sit off the baseline, thus giving any text a bouncy feel.

Volta

ABCDEFGHIJKLMNOPQRSTUVWXY
abcdefghijklmnopqrstuvwxyz
1234567890 !@#?:;"*&

Foundry: Bauer
Designer: Konrad F. Bauer / Walter Baum
Designer Nationality: German
Date: 1956

Volta is a Clarendon-esque slab serif released by the Bauer foundry in 1956, and designed by Konrad F. Bauer and Walter Baum. It comes in three weights: Regular, Medium, and Bold. In the United States, Volta was renamed Fortune and it is sometimes known as Fortuna.

Windsor

ABCDEFGHIJKLMNOPQRSTUVWXYZ
abcdefghijklmnopqrstuvwxyz
1234567890 !@#?:;"*&

Foundry: Stephenson Blake & Co
Designer: Eleisha Pechey
Designer Nationality: British
Date: 1905

Eleisha Pechey designed Windsor for Stephenson, Blake & Co., and the typeface was released three years after his death. It is a quirky, Old Style serif with many distinctive features. It is Woody Allen's favorite typeface; the director has used it on his film titles and credits since *Annie Hall* (1977).

Woodblock

ABCDEFGHIJKLMNOPQRSTUVWXYZ
1234567890 !@#?:;"*&

Foundry: Monotype
Designer: Monotype Studio
Date: 1999

Woodblock was designed in 1999 by Monotype's in-house design team, inspired by old, wood type styles. It is an uppercase only, heavy condensed font with small, sharp triangular serifs, angled terminals, and mainly diagonal crossbars. Woodblock is constructed from exclusively straight lines.

Woodley Park

ABCDEFGHIJKLMNOPQRSTUVWXYZ
abcdefghijklmnopqrstuvwxyz
1234567890 !@#?:;"*&

Foundry: Monotype
Designer: Nick Curtis
Designer Nationality: American
Date: 2001

Nick Curtis's Woodley Park was a winner in the Type Directors Club's Typeface Design competition in 2002. It is a double-stroked, medieval-style display serif inspired by the Naudin Champlevé uppercase serif released by Deberny & Peignot in 1924, which was known as Sylvan in the United States.

Affichen-Schriften FSL

ABCDEFGHIJKLMNOPQRSTUVWXYZ
abcdefghijklmnopqrstuvwxyz
1234567890 !@#?:;"*&

In the 1830s, German typefounder Eduard Haenel was inspired by the new, large, eye-catching type designs found in England and France, and he became one of the first to introduce such types to the German printing trade. The Affichen-Schriften series revives four distinctive and brutal display styles, covering a spectrum of the peculiar shapes common to that era.

Doppel-Mittel Egyptienne is based on an Egyptian that Haenel imported and advertised in 1833. British typographer William Thorowgood orginally showed it as Two Lines English Egyptian No. 1, in London in 1821. Schmale Egyptienne No. 12 is another reissue of a Haenel typeface. With a cap height of 11.7 cm (4⅝ in.), it is the largest font shown in his specimen from 1841. Antiques originated at E. Tarbé & Cie in Paris and hints at

the splendor found in French poster typefaces. Advertised in 1839, it represents an early sans serif adaption of a condensed Egyptian. Breite-Fette Antiqua FSL is the digital reissue of an unidentified display typeface that was part of the type case in Oskar Leiner's printing workshop in Leipzig from c. 1850. It is unknown whether it was a custom-made design or if the typeface was distributed commercially by a foundry.

Type designer Pierre Pané-Farré, the co-founder of Forgotten Shapes, translated the historical shapes into digital fonts for contemporary use. Pané-Farré extended the language support and added subscript and superscript figures. He also included various font-specific OpenType features like a second set of numerals, alternate glyphs, and case-sensitive punctuation.

Foundry: Forgotten Shapes
Designer: William Thorowgood / Eduard Haenel / E. Tarbé & Cie / Pierre Pané-Farré
Designer Nationality: British / German / French
Date: c. 1821–50 / 2011–17

Below from left. Overview of the different styles within the Affichen-Schriften family; *Soirée Fantastique* book design using Schmale Egyptienne FSL for the headline; posters from 1848 and 1849 from two Leipzig printing houses.

Plakate der Druckerei **OSKAR LEINER** in Leipzig. Mit Fotografien von **ALEXANDER SEITZ.**

Institut für Buchkunst Leipzig

Soirée FAN-TAS TIQUE.

Urversammlung der ganzen Einwohnerschaft LEIPZIGS heute Mittag 1 Uhr im Hofe der I. Bürgerschule.

Deutscher Verein. Heute Donnerstag den 13. April Abends 7½ Uhr Versammlung im ODEON.

Aachen

ABCDEFGHIJKLMNOPQRSTUVWXYZ
abcdefghijklmnopqrstuvwxyz
1234567890 !@#?:;"*&

Foundry: Letraset
Designer: Colin Brignall
Designer Nationality: British
Date: 1969

Aachen was originally designed in a Bold weight by Colin Brignall in 1969, and another British Letraset designer, Alan Meeks, created a Medium weight eight years later. Aachen is a strong, heavy slab serif ideally suited to use at large point sizes, such as posters and headlines.

Claire News

ABCDEFGHIJKLMNOPQRSTUVW
abcdefghijklmnopqrstuvwxyz
1234567890 !@#?:;"*&

Foundry: Monotype
Designer: Unknown
Date: Unknown

Claire News is a robust and slightly extended slab serif typeface that shares certain proportions and design details with Clarendon and its ilk, though it displays a higher contrast within its letter forms. Its tall x-height and pronounced serifs make it a legible choice for headlines.

Epokha

ABCDEFGHIJKLMNOPQRSTUVWXYZ
1234567890 !@#?:;"*&

Foundry: Letraset
Designer: Colin Brignall
Designer Nationality: British
Date: 1992

Letraset and the International Typeface Corporation (ITC) released Colin Brignall's Ephoka in 1992. It is a very heavy, uppercase only slab serif font that comes in a single weight. It features many alternate letters that add variety and was inspired by early 20th-century geometric poster typefaces.

Goudy Heavyface

ABCDEFGHIJKLMNOPQRSTUVWXYZ
abcdefghijklmnopqrstuvwxyz
1234567890 !@#?:;"*&

Foundry: Monotype
Designer: Frederic W. Goudy
Designer Nationality: American
Date: 1925

Following the success of Cooper Black from a rival foundry, Lanston Monotype had Frederic W. Goudy design a heavy, rounder serif typeface of his own. The result, Goudy Heavyface, was released in 1925 in roman and italic styles. Sol Hess added condensed and outlined versions in 1926 and 1927.

Impakt

ABCDEFGHIJKLMNOPQRSTUVWXYZ
abcdefghijklmnopqrstuvwxyz
1234567890 !?:;"*&

Foundry: Linotype
Designer: Leonard Currie
Designer Nationality: British
Date: 1995

Created by British designer Leonard Currie for Letraset in 1995, and also sold by the International Typeface Corporation (ITC), Impakt is a quirky, bold slab serif available in a single weight. The Russian Constructivist movement of the 1920s inspired its condensed, geometric forms.

ITC Bailey Quad

ABCDEFGHIJKLMNOPQRSTUVWXYZ
abcdefghijklmnopqrstuvwxyz
1234567890 !@#?:;"*&

Foundry: ITC
Designer: Kevin Bailey
Designer Nationality: American
Date: 1994

ITC Bailey Quad, an eponymous typeface by Texas-born graphic designer Kevin Bailey, is a semi-serif font; it has slab-style serifs on some letters but not others and does not always follow the conventions of serif placement, giving a modern look. It is available in Bold only.

Kegger

ABCDEFGHIJKLMNOPQRSTUVWXYZ
abcdefghijklmnopqrstuvwxyz
1234567890 !@#?:;"*&

Foundry: Chank Co.
Designer: Chank Diesel
Designer Nationality: American
Date: 2007

Kegger is named after a US college term for a party with kegs of beer. It was designed in 2007 by Canadian-born, Florida-based type designer Chank Diesel. It is a bold slab serif that comes in two styles, a solid Regular and alternate Collegiate, which is outlined and shadowed.

Kengwin

ABCDEFGHIJKLMNOPQRSTUVWXYZ
abcdefghijklmnopqrstuvwxyz
1234567890 !@#?:;"*&

Foundry: Typodermic Fonts
Designer: Ray Larabie
Designer Nationality: Canadian
Date: 2010

The Kengwin typeface was created by prolific type designer Ray Larabie and published by his foundry Typodermic Fonts in 2010. It is a display slab serif that is available in a single style, which is bold and softly rounded, giving it a friendly, childish appeal despite its overall heaviness.

Letraset Bramley

ABCDEFGHIJKLMNOPQRSTUVWXYZ
abcdefghijklmnopqrstuvwxyz
1234567890 !@#?:;"" * &

Foundry: Letraset
Designer: Alan Meeks
Designer Nationality: British
Date: 1979

Bramley was created by Alan Meeks, a type designer at the British dry-transfer lettering company Letraset, whose fonts are all now held by Monotype. A key feature is a gap between the base of the bowl and stem on "a," "d," and "q." It recalls Morris Fuller Benton's Souvenir designed in 1914.

Linotype Authentic Serif

ABCDEFGHIJKLMNOPQRSTUVWXYZ
abcdefghijklmnopqrstuvwxyz
1234567890 !@#?:¡"*&

Foundry: Linotype
Designer: Karin Huschka
Designer Nationality: German
Date: 1999

The Authentic type family was acquired by Linotype when it was chosen from the entries of the foundry's International Digital Type Design Contest in 1999. Authentic Serif is a quirky, distinctive text typeface with many distinctive shapes and is typical of the postmodern, experimental fonts of the era.

Linotype Authentic Small Serif

ABCDEFGHIJKLMNOPQRSTUVWXYZ
abcdefghijklmnopqrstuvwxyz
1234567890 !@#?:¡"*&

Foundry: Linotype
Designer: Karin Huschka
Designer Nationality: German
Date: 1999

German designer Karin Huschka's widely spaced Authentic family is a member of the TakeType Library, which was created from the winners of Linotype's International Type Design Contest. Small Serif has thinner serifs than Authentic Serif, making it even more idiosyncratic.

Magnus

ABCDEFGHIJKLMNOPQRSTUVWXYZ
abcdefghijklmnopqrstuvwxyz
1234567890 !@#?:;"*&

Foundry: ITC
Designer: Bruno Grasswill
Designer Nationality: American
Date: 1981

Magnus is a titling display font designed in the style of a slab serif. Its characters are narrow but sturdy, with low-contrast strokes and serifs that swap between rectangular blocks and curved stroke endings, which are often combined, as seen in several lowercase figures.

Melina BT

ABCDEFGHIJKLMNOPQRSTUVWXYZ
abcdefghijklmnopqrstuvwxyz
1234567890 !@#?:;"*&

Foundry: Bitstream
Designer: Nick Curtis
Designer Nationality: American
Date: 2003

Melina BT is an eloquent display serif designed in two styles, Plain and Fancy. It is modeled on two typefaces, Greco Adornado and Greco Bold, which were produced by the Imprenta y Fundición Tipográfica Richard Gans type foundry in Madrid during the 1920s.

Mensura Slab

ABCDEFGHIJKLMNOPQRSTUVWXYZ
abcdefghijklmnopqrstuvwxyz
1234567890 !@#?:;"*&

Foundry: Graviton Font Foundry
Designer: Pablo Balcells
Designer Nationality: Argentinian
Date: 2013

A modular, geometric slab serif, Mensura Slab has a technical feel and is versatile thanks to many alternate letters, which are curved rather than angular. Argentinian typographer Pablo Balcells also designed a sans version, called Mensura; both come in four weights with italics.

Monotype Bernard

ABCDEFGHIJKLMNOPQRSTUVWXYZ
abcdefghijklmnopqrstuvwxyz
1234567890 !@#?:;"*&

Foundry: Monotype
Designer: Monotype Studio
Date: 1926

Monotype Bernard is a serif display font, closely associated with the Art Nouveau movement of the early 20th century. The design's trademarks include bold strokes, moderate contrast, rounded edges, and bulbous terminals. It is typical of romans evolving at the time with a soft, scriptlike quality.

Monotype Egyptian 72 Extended

ABCDEFGHIJKLMNOPQRSTUVWXYZ
abcdefghijklmnopqrstuvwxyz
1234567890 !@#?:;"*&

Foundry: Monotype
Designer: Monotype Studio
Date: c. 1930s

Available in one weight, Egyptian 72 Extended is a characterful slab serif that was designed in-house by the Monotype Studio, and is a revival of a French style from the late 19th century, adapted by Monotype before World War II. It has large, square serifs and is suited to display use only.

Forgotten Shapes

Forgotten Shapes was formed in 2018 by Stephan Müller (founding partner of Lineto), Pierre Pané-Farré, and Reymund Schröder to publish digital reconstructions of typefaces that have vanished from existence. The foundry revives such typefaces according to its guiding principle of *werktreue*—meaning in a form as faithful to the original as possible. To do this, they extensively research from archive material, sketches, and drawings and, in several instances, have worked with the original type designers such as Karl Gerstner and Gert Wunderlich. As most of the source designs were created post war, in the 1950s and 1960s, they were never digitized and so remain in predigital formats. Through the efforts of Forgotten Shapes, past design processes can be examined and explored, providing insight into current methodologies.

The first of the four releases are an unpublished design for a Clarendon-type serif Kleukens-Egyptienne, created in 1929 by German designer Friedrich Wilhelm Kleukens. The source material was part of a collection of digital materials by Hans Reichardt, a former Stempel employee who had been maintaining the archives of the D. Stempel AG foundry since its dissolution in 1985. The second family, Affichen-Schriften, is a collection of woodblock poster types used in German-speaking countries in the mid 19th century. Third in the suite is Gerstner-Programm, a sans serif Grotesque by Gerstner, who was one of the key figures in Swiss graphic design. Finally, Lector is an elegant serif type design Wunderlich created in the 1960s in East Germany.

To create an "historical" atmosphere and more general associations in regards to each typeface published, every individual type specimen by Forgotten Shapes introduces the typeface with a specific and curated image collage. For the *The Essential Type Directory* in order to represent the approach of the Forgotten Shapes foundry and its collection, the foundry created this bespoke collage based on the different photographs they have used so far, with each image representing one typeface.

Founded: 2018
Country: Germany
Website: forgotten-shapes.com
Notable typefaces:
Affichen-Schriften FSL
(see p. 521)
Gerstner-Programm FSL
(see p. 226)
Kleukens-Egyptienne FSL
(see p. 46)
Lector FSL (see p. 167)
Normal-Grotesk FSL (see p. 242)

Above. Stonehenge. Inger
Schulstad, 1963.

Left. Ether Dome Daguerreotype
No. 1. A. Southworth & J. Hawes,
c. 1847.

Right top. Painters Jindrich
Štyrský a Toyen in masks during
work with 'Deka' colors. n/a,
before 4 May 1929.

Right middle. Maclyn McCarty
with Francis Crick and James D.
Watson. Marjorie McCarty, 1953.

Right below. People on
the steps of Konserthuset,
Stockholm. Andy Eick, 1965.

Neo Contact

ABCDEFGHIJKLMNOPQRSTUVWXYZ
abcdefghijklmnopqrstuvwxyz
1234567890 !@#?:;"*&

Foundry: American Type Founders / Linotype
Designer: Frank H. Riley
Designer Nationality: American
Date: 1948 / 1955

Originally called Contact when released by ATF, this bold, condensed Egyptian display typeface is recognizable as being used on Marlboro cigarette packs. The design combines strong, moderately contrasted strokes, as seen in the stems and curves, alongside thinner, sharper serifs and crossbars.

Octin Sports

ABCDEFGHIJKLMNOPQRSTUVWXYZ
1234567890 !@#?:;"*&

Foundry: Typodermic
Designer: Ray Larabie
Designer Nationality: Canadian
Date: 2007

Octin Sports is a slab serif display font and comprises seven weights, including Light, Semibold, and Black. Like the letter forms often found on the back of sporting jerseys, Octin Sports is designed entirely in capitals, and features squared curves and mono-weighted strokes.

PL Barnum Block

ABCDEFGHIJKLMNOPQRSTUVWXYZ
abcdefghijklmnopqrstuvwxyz
1234567890 !© #?:;"*&

Foundry: Monotype
Designer: Dave West
Designer Nationality: American
Date: 1960

Named after P. T. Barnum, the US traveling showman, PL Barnum Block is a slab serif display typeface inspired by 19th-century woodcut lettering. Intended for posters, signage, and packaging, the heavy strokes and minimal apertures ensure impact in both upper and lowercases.

PL Behemoth

ABCDEFGHIJKLMNOPQRSTUVWXYZ
abcdefghijklmnopqrstuvwxyz
1234567890 !© #?:;"*&

Foundry: Photo-Lettering
Designer: Dave West
Designer Nationality: American
Date: 1960

PL Behemoth is a slab serif display typeface inspired by 19th-century woodcut lettering. In comparison to similar typefaces designed by Dave West for Photo-Lettering in the 1960s, such as PL Barnum Block, PL Behemoth features narrower forms as well as stricter strokes and serifs.

PL Tower Condensed

ABCDEFGHIJKLMNOPQRSTUVWXYZ
abcdefghijklmnopqrstuvwxyz
1234567890 ! © #?:;"*&

PL Tower is a light slab serif display font based around an earlier, heavier design by Morris Fuller Benton. Published originally by the Photo-Lettering type foundry, the condensed characters contain a wealth of white space and pronounced serifs, and are intended for use in narrow headlines.

Foundry: Photo-Lettering / Monotype
Designer: Morris Fuller Benton
Designer Nationality: American
Date: 1934

Pokerface

abcdefghijklmnopqrstuvwxyz
abcdefghijklmnopqrstuvwxyz
1234567890 !@#?:;"*&

Jim Ford's Pokerface is a slab serif display font inspired by the randomness of drawing playing cards. The letter forms are grouped in either pairs or fours, similar to traditional poker hands, and are shuffled upon their use to generate serendipitous style combinations.

Foundry: Ascender
Designer: Jim Ford
Designer Nationality: American
Date: 2009

P.T. Barnum

ABCDEFGHIJKLMNOPQRSTUVWXYZ
abcdefghijklmnopqrstuvwxyz
1234567890 !@#?:;"*&

P.T. Barnum is Bitstream's revival of a 19th-century type produced at the Barnhart Brothers & Spindler foundry in c. 1880 and subsequently published by the American Type Founders. In contrast to the majority of wood type designs, P.T. Barnum includes a number of bracketed serifs.

Foundry: Bitstream
Designer: Unknown
Date: Unknown

Pueblo

ABCDEFGHIJKLMNOPQRSTUVWXYZ
abcdefghijklmnopqrstuvwxyz
1234567890 !@#?:;"*&

Pueblo is a display typeface that draws upon a variety of influences, from Speedball lettering to fin-de-siècle sign painting. The distinctive forms feature bold strokes and gently rounded stroke endings, which reference the softness of the Speedball pen while retaining legibility.

Foundry: Monotype
Designer: Jim Parkinson
Designer Nationality: American
Date: 1998

Robotik

ABCDEFGHIJKLMNOPQRSTUVWXYZ
abcdefghijklmnopqrstuvwxyz
1234567890 !?:;"*&

Foundry: ITC
Designer: David Quay
Designer Nationality: British
Date: 1989

David Quay's Robotik is a slab serif display font informed by the mechanic precision of Russian Constructivism after World War I. The font, designed in regular and italic styles, features condensed, squared letter forms. Robotik is best used for headlines in large point sizes.

Scriptek

ABCDEFGHIJKLMNOPQRSTUVWXYZ
abcdefghijklmnopqrstuvwxyz
1234567890 !?:;"*&

Foundry: Letraset / ITC
Designer: David Quay
Designer Nationality: British
Date: 1992

British type designer David Quay designed Scriptek for Letraset; it was also released by the International Typeface Corporation. It is a compact, angular slab serif that comes in a single bold weight in roman and italic styles. It was inspired by early Constructivist typefaces popular in interwar Europe.

Special Forces

ABCDEFGHIJKLMNOPQRSTUVWXYZ
abcdefghijklmnopqrstuvwxyz
1234567890 !@#?:;"*&

Foundry: Typodermic
Designer: Ray Larabie
Designer Nationality: Canadian
Date: 2010

Special Forces is a robust, slab serif headline font designed especially for screen use by the Typodermic founder, Canadian designer Ray Larabie. It is available in upper and lowercase, and in two styles, Special Forces Regular and Special Forces Italic. Its name and appearance evoke the military.

Stratford

ABCDEFGHIJKLMNOPQRSTUVWXYZ
abcdefghijklmnopqrstuvwxyz
1234567890 !@#?:;"*&

Foundry: Fonts
Designer: Freda Sack
Designer Nationality: British
Date: 1977

Stratford is an idiosyncratic slab serif display font, with an Arts and Crafts overtone, skilfully crafted to facilitate the close letterspacing in 1970s fashion. Its creator Freda Sack co-founded The Foundry (see p. 284) and together with Colin Brignall designed popular faces such as Proteus and Paddington.

Teknik

ABCDEFGHIJKLMNOPQRSTUVWXYZ
abcdefghijklmnopqrstuvwxyz
1234567890 !@#?:;"*&

David Quay's Teknik is an impactful and stylized display typeface that is often categorized as an Egyptian due to its slab serifs. It is similar to his Robotik design of 1989, and both typefaces are inspired by the geometric designs of the 1920s Soviet Constructivist movement.

Foundry: Letraset
Designer: David Quay
Designer Nationality: British
Date: 1990

Tesla Caps

ABCDEFGHIJKLMNOPQRSTUVWXYZ
1234567890 !@#?:;"*&

The Tesla family is named after the inventor, physicist and engineer Nikola Tesla. It consists of Tesla Slab, Stencil, Caps, and Mono. Tesla Caps is a constructed slab serif typeface with monolinear and inverted contrast, which is available in three weights from the lightweight A, to the super black weight C.

Foundry: Typotheque
Designer: Nikola Djurek
Designer Nationality: Croatian
Date: 2015

Waterloo Bold

ABCDEFGHIJKLMNOPQRSTUVWXYZ
abcdefghijklmnopqrstuvwxyz
1234567890 !?:;"*&

British designer Alan Meeks joined the studio at Letraset in 1975. He created Waterloo Bold in 1987. It is a heavy slab serif with a large x-height, high crossbars, and a subtle slant. It comes in a single bold weight only and is suited best to display and headline usage.

Foundry: Letraset
Designer: Alan Meeks
Designer Nationality: British
Date: 1987

Yearbook

ABCDEFGHIJKLMNOPQRSTUVWXYZ
1234567890 !@#?:;"*&

Yearbook is an uppercase, angular, heavy slab serif constructed without curves. It comes in three styles, which are all the same weight: Filler, Outline, and Solid. The first two of these faces are designed to be superimposed. Yearbook has a US collegiate feel, reminiscent of the type on letterman jackets.

Foundry: Monotype
Designer: Monotype Studio
Date: Unknown

Aerion

ABCDEFGHIJKLMNOPQRSTUVWXYZ
1234567890 !@#?;;"*&

In 2003, US designer Alexander McCracken established his San Francisco-based foundry Neutura, which specializes in display typeface design. Aerion is a square sans serif typeface with extended letter forms and a slightly futuristic feel, and is available in four weights.

Foundry: Neutura
Designer: Alexander McCracken
Designer Nationality: American
Date: 2012

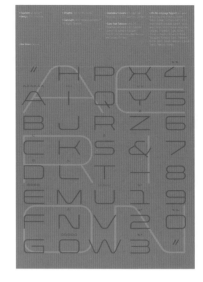

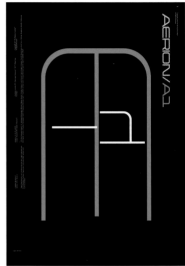

Ambule BT

ABCDEFGHIJKLMNOPQRSTUVWXYZ
abcdefghijklmnopqrstuvwxyz
1234567890 !@#?:;"⁑&

Foundry: Bitstream
Designer: Julien Janiszewski
Designer Nationality: French
Date: 2002

Julien Janiszewski designed Ambule BT for Bitstream in 2002. It is a hybrid typeface featuring letter forms from both upper and lowercase within its single character set. The font combines several stylistic flourishes found within Huxley Vertical (1935) and Peignot (1937).

Board of Directors

ABCDEFGHIJKLMNOPQRSTUVWXYZ
abcdefghijklmnopqrstuvwxyz
1234567890 !@#?:;"*&

Foundry: Typodermic
Designer: Ray Larabie
Designer Nationality: Canadian
Date: 2010

Board of Directors was influenced by early plotter typefaces and has a distinct science-fiction feel. It is a display sans serif typeface available in a broad range of weights, from fine Ultralight through to Black. It was designed by Ray Larabie for his foundry Typodermic in 2010.

Bank Gothic

ABCDEFGHIJKLMNOPQRSTUVWXYZ

ABCDEFGHIJKLMNOPQRSTUVWXYZ

1234567890 !@#?:;"*&

Foundry: Bitstream
Designer: Morris Fuller Benton
Nationality: American
Date: 1930–33

Despite being widely used to reflect technological and science-fiction themed genres, Bank Gothic has lasted the test of time. It remains as popular in the 21st century as when it was created in the early 1930s by the esteemed and influential type designer Morris Fuller Benton. Bank Gothic has become firmly established as the typeface *de rigueur* for science-fiction film posters, while films such as *I, Robot* (2004), *Source Code* (2011), and *The Hunger Games* (2012) have all employed its geometric, squared-up forms that are indicative of technology.

Bank Gothic's monoline stroke weight and rectilinear construction provide a no-nonsense appearance. The typeface's slightly extended character width makes it ideal for titling purposes where a sense of gravitas is required. Benton designed Bank Gothic in capitals only, and the suite of characters comes in uppercase and small caps. There have been a number of versions since the original cut by Benton for American Type Founders, with the most popular being offered by Linotype and Bitstream. Fonthaus created an extended family in 2010 with Bank Gothic Pro, which included lowercase and three weights—Light, Medium, and Bold.

Below. Bank Gothic features heavily in and around Arsenal Football Club's Emirates Stadium in North London. Here it is seen set in concrete at the start of one of the pedestrian approaches.

Bullet

ABCDEFGHIJKLMNOPQRSTUVWXYZ
abcdefghijklmnopqrstuvwxyz
1234567890 !@#?:;"*&

Foundry: House Industries
Designer: Tal Leming
Designer Nationality: American
Date: 2000

Tal Leming designed Bullet for House Industries before he started his own foundry in 2005, Type Supply. It began as lettering by Ken Barber on House Industries' *Pop Art* catalogue. Bullet is a heavy, italic sans serif and also comes in a script style with a joined, underlined lowercase.

Cintra

ABCDEFGHIJKLMNOPQRSTUVWXYZ
ABCDEFGHIJKLMNOPQRSTUVWXYZ
1234567890 !⓪#?:;"*&

Foundry: Graviton
Designer: Pablo Balcells
Designer Nationality: Argentinian
Date: 2014

Pablo Balcells's Graviton foundry published Cintra in 2014. It is a square sans serif font with a friendly appearance. The font includes two character sets of uppercase letter forms, one featuring a range of rounded details. A slab serif counterpart, Cintra Slab, is also available.

Conthrax

ABCDEFGHIJKLMNOPQRSTUVW
abcdefghijklmnopqrstuvwxyz
1234567890 !@#?:;"*&

Foundry: Typodermic
Designer: Ray Larabie
Designer Nationality: Canadian
Date: 2016

This futuristic and slightly extended display font by Typodermic's Ray Larabie offers an extensive character set, and supports languages including Greek, Cyrillic, and Vietnamese alongside the Latin. The foundry offers a desktop licence for the semi-bold cut free of charge.

Eurostile Candy

ABCDEFGHIJKLMNOPQRSTUV
abcdefghijklmnopqrstuvwxyz
1234567890 !@#?:;"*&

Foundry: Linotype
Designer: Aldo Novarese / Akira Kobayashi
Designer Nationality: Italian / Japanese
Date: 2008

Eurostile Candy is based on Akira Kobayashi's Eurostile Next, which is part of the Eurostile Next superfamily. Eurostile Candy's extra strokes have been removed and its corners and joints have been rounded off, giving a friendlier, softer feel than the original Eurostile created by Aldo Novarese in 1962.

Eurostile Unicase

ABCDEFGHIJKLMNOPQRSTU
abcdefghijklmnopqrstu
1234567890 !@#?:;"'*&

Foundry: Linotype
Designer: Aldo Novarese / Akira Kobayashi
Designer Nationality: Italian / Japanese
Date: 2008

Eurostile Unicase is an adaption of Akira Kobayashi's Eurostile Next design. Here, Kobayashi has created a quirky unicase version that does away with ascenders and descenders to create letters which are the same height, such as a raised lowercase "y," and modified lowercase "a," and "e."

Hemi Head

ABCDEFGHIJKLMNOPQRSTUVWXYZ
abcdefghijklmnopqrstuvwxyz
1234567890 !@#?:;"'*&

Foundry: Typodermic
Designer: Ray Larabie
Designer Nationality: Canadian
Date: 2009

In 1998, Canadian designer Ray Larabie created the original Hemi Head 426, inspired by the old Dodge logo. The square, industrial sans serif came in one bold, italic style. Eleven years later, he released an extensive update that included eight weights with italics.

Injekuta

ABCDEFGHIJKLNOPQRSTUV
WXYZ
1234567890 !@#?:;"'*&

Foundry: Typodermic
Designer: Ray Larabie
Designer Nationality: Canadian
Date: 2007

Ray Larabie designed Injekuta for Typodermic in 2007. It is an extended, uppercase only, geometric sans serif. Like many of Ray Larabie's fonts, the overall feel is technical, futuristic, and sleek. Injekuta comes in four weights—Light to Black—without italics or lowercase.

ITC Black Tulip

ABCDEFGHIJKLMNOPQRSTUVWXYZ
abcdefghijklmnopqrstuvwxyz
1234567890 !@#?:;"'*&

Foundry: ITC
Designer: Dudley Rees
Designer Nationality: British
Date: 1997

Black Tulip is a heavy, compact sans serif with distinctive open counters on many lowercase glyphs. Designer Dudley Rees was inspired by the Greek fret band, which is a repeating pattern formed by tracing a line at right angles between two horizontal rules to form an interlocking motif.

ITC Bolt

ABCDEFGHIJKLMNOPQRSTUVWXYZ
abcdefghijklmnopqrstuvwxyz
1234567890 !☐☐?:;"* &

Foundry: ITC
Designer: Ronne Bonder /
Tom Carnase
Designer Nationality: American
Date: 1970

ITC Bolt is a heavy, squat modular sans serif font designed by Ronne Bonder and Tom Carnase. The US duo had worked together as the Bonder & Carnase studio in New York during the 1960s before Carnase left to join Herb Lubalin and Ernie Smith as a partner in Lubalin, Smith, Carnase (see p. 62).

ITC CuppaJoe

ABCDEFGHIJKLMNOPQRSTUVWXYZ
ABCDEFGHIJKLMNOPQRSTUVWXYZ
1234567890 !@#?:;"*&

Foundry: ITC
Designer: Nick Curtis
Designer Nationality: American
Date: 2001

Nick Curtis's ITC CuppaJoe is a bold, Art Deco-inspired sans serif. It gained its name because it was based on lettering found on Bokar Coffee packaging from the 1930s. Curtis also released fonts from his own foundry, Nick's Fonts, and most of its designs were based on authentic historical sources.

ITC Deli

ABCDEFGHIJKLMNOPQRSTUVWXYZ
ABCDEFGHIJKLMNOPQRSTUVWXYZ
1234567890 !@#?:;"*&

Foundry: ITC
Designer: Jim Spiece
Designer Nationality: American
Date: 1999

ITC Deli is a retro, extended sans serif designed by Jim Spiece in 1999. It is evocative of mid-century ideas of futuristic type. ITC Deli comes in two styles: Deluxe is square with rounded corners and small caps, while Supreme has a lowercase that joins together as a script style.

ITC Machine

ABCDEFGHIJKLMNOPQRSTUVWXYZ
1234567890 !@#?:;"*&

Foundry: ITC
Designer: Ronne Bonder /
Tom Carnase
Designer Nationality: American
Date: 1970

ITC Machine is a dense, all-caps sans serif available in Bold and Medium. It has a very utilitarian feel, achieved through the lack of curves; letters are constructed using straight lines alone and often 45° angles. The Blockbuster video-rental service used the face for its company logo.

ITC Stenberg

ABCDEFGHIJKLMNOPQRSTUVWXYZ

ABCDEFGHIJKLMNOPQRSTUVWXYZ

1234567890 !@#?:;"*&

Foundry: ITC
Designer: Tagir Safayev
Designer Nationality: Russian
Date: 1997

Moscow-based designer Tagir Safayev drew inspiration from the Constructivist movement, especially the work of the brothers Vladimir and Georgii Stenberg, to create this typeface. Available in regular and inline, Stenberg is a heavy, curveless, geometric sans serif with caps and small caps only.

ITC Tetra

ABCDEFGHIJKLMNOPQRSTUVWXYZ

abcdefghijklmnopqrstuvwxyz

1234567890 !@№?:;"*&

Foundry: ITC
Designer: Tomi Haaparanta
Designer Nationality: Finnish
Date: 2005

ITC Tetra is the work of Finnish designer Tomi Haaparanta, who studied graphic design at the University of Industrial Arts in Helsinki and founded the Suomi Type Foundry in 2004. It is a simple geometric sans serif with mostly square letters and rounded corners. ITC Tetra comes in three weights.

Just Square

ABCDEFGHIJKLMNOPQRSTUVWXYZ

abcdefghijklmnopqrstuvwxyz

1234567890 !@#?:;"*&

Foundry: Linotype
Designer: Zoran Kostic
Designer Nationality: Serbian
Date: 2004

Zoran Kostic began Just Square during the Kosovo War in 1999; he based it on a logo drawn by his son. It is a part of a family that started with Why Square (2004), and both are sans serifs constructed from squares. Just Square comes in eight weights with Latin and Cyrillic support.

Korataki

ABCDEFGHIJKLMNOPQ

abcdefghijklmnopqrstuvwxyz

1234567890 !@#?:;"*&

Foundry: Typodermic
Designer: Ray Larabie
Designer Nationality: Canadian
Date: 2006

Typodermic published Korataki in 2006. It was inspired by China, a futuristic font designed by M. Mitchell in 1975. Korataki is an extended sans serif typeface available in fourteen styles—seven weights with italics—and features alternate versions of "A," "G," "Q," and "4."

Las Vegas

ABCDEFGHIJKLMNOPQRSTUVWXYZ
abcdefghijklmnopqrstuvwxyz
1234567890 !@#?:;"*&

Foundry: Or Type
Designer: Guðmundur Úlfarsson
Designer Nationality: Icelandic
Date: 2015

Las Vegas is an unreleased design by Guðmundur Úlfarsson of Or Type (see p. 498), which debuted in *Conveyor* magazine in 2015. It is an angular sans serif with multiple alternate letters, some of which were inspired by New Alphabet (1967) by Wim Crouwel (see p. 540).

Lineavec

ABCDEFGHIJKLMNOPQRST
abcdefghijklmnopqrstuvwxyz
1234567890 !@#?:;"*&

Foundry: Typodermic
Designer: Ray Larabie
Designer Nationality: Canadian
Date: 2006

Ray Larabie's Lineavec, designed in 2006, is a wide, monoline, futuristic sans serif available from Typodermic in a single style, Light. As with many of Larabie's fonts it achieves a science-fiction, high-tech feel thanks to its angular construction and subtly rounded corners.

Linotype Kaliber

ABCDEFGHIJKLMNOPQRSTUVWXYZ
abcdefghijklmnopqrstuvwxyz
1234567890 !@#?:;"*&

Foundry: Linotype
Designer: Lutz Baar
Designer Nationality: German
Date: 1999

Linotype Kaliber is an exacting display font designed in four styles, including Regular, Italic, Bold, and Black. The rigid, monoline strokes and stiff curves characterizing the letter forms give the impression of steel pipes that have been carefully bent into shape.

Linotype Lichtwerk

ABCDEFGHIJKLMNOPQRSTUVWXYZ
abcdefghijklmnopqrstuvwxyz
1234567890 !@#?:;"*&

Foundry: Linotype
Designer: Bernd Pfannkuchen
Designer Nationality: German
Date: 1999

Linotype Lichtwerk is a headline typeface designed in three styles—Regular, Italic, and Bold—and inspired by the mechanical forms of 1920s Constructivism. The characters contain extended x-heights, narrow forms, and rounded strokes, and convey both precision and approachability.

Linotype Spacera

ABCDEFGHIJKLMNOPQRSTUVW
ABCDEFGHIJKLMNOPQRSTUVW
1234567890 !@#?:;"*&

Foundry: Linotype
Designer: Louis Lemoine
Designer Nationality: American
Date: 2002

Linotype Spacera is a squared display font, conceived to embody a futuristic sensibility. The characters, which are designed exclusively in capitals, feature several distinguishing details, such as cubic serifs, extended cross-strokes, and central dots in the "c" and the "d."

Liquorstore

ABCDEFGHIJKLMNOPQRSTUVWXYZ
abcdefghijklmnopqrstuvwxyz
1234567890 !@#?:;"*&

Foundry: Chank Co.
Designer: Chank Diesel
Designer Nationality: American
Date: 1997

Liquorstore is a sans serif display font informed by the hand-rendered liquor-store signage around Minneapolis, Minnesota. The squared letter forms, also inspired by Constructivist posters and vintage magazine logos, were designed in four weights, including Jazz and 3D.

Mesotone BT

ABCDEFGHIJKLMNOPQRSTUVWXYZ
abcdefghijklmnopqrstuvwxyz
1234567890 !@#?:;"*&

Foundry: Bitstream
Designer: Matt Desmond
Designer Nationality: American
Date: 2006

Matt Desmond's Mesotone BT is a computer-style display typeface, conceived in a single weight. The font's unicase characters feature monoweight strokes, a relatively standardized width, and an accompanying glyph set that incorporates Baltic, Turkish, and European languages.

Morris Sans

ABCDEFGHIJKLMNOPQRSTU
abcdefghijklmnopqrstuvwxyz
1234567890 !@#?:;"*&

Foundry: Linotype
Designer: Morris Fuller Benton / Dan Reynolds
Designer Nationality: American
Date: 2006

Designed by Dan Reynolds, Morris Sans is a revision and extension of Bank Gothic designed by Morris Fuller Benton for the American Type Founders in 1930. In addition to redrawing the uppercase characters, Reynolds also introduced a lowercase character set and six new figure styles.

Wim Crouwel

Designer Wim Crouwel was a leading exponent of the International Style that came to prominence in the 1950s and 1960s. His underlying use of grids in all aspects of his work signified a distinctive and revolutionary approach to type development as well as his own graphic design output.

In the late 1940s, Crouwel studied Fine Art at Academie Minerva in Groningen, the Netherlands and typography at what is now the Gerrit Rietveld Academie in Amsterdam. In 1963, he co-founded the design studio Total Design (now Total Identity). He earned an international reputation for brilliance and radical design just a year later, when he created the designs for the posters, catalogues, and exhibitions of the Stedelijk Museum, Amsterdam. This was a relationship that would last over two decades, Crouwel the sole-appointed designer. His grid-based design systems offered flexibility and creativity, all the while providing the museum with a recognizable visual language. The wealth of work created during this period stands up to be some of the most innovative and striking designs created.

In 1967, he wrote and designed a short book presenting his experimental *New Alphabet* design. A personal project, it was a typeface design that adopted the limitations of the cathode-ray tube technology of the time, being constructed in grid form with only horizontal and vertical strokes making up its characters. Other significant designs were his Fodor and Gridnik types. The latter was originally called Politene and was commissioned by Olivetti in 1974 as a typewriter typeface but was later renamed after a nickname given to Crouwel by his friends. Digital versions of these highly constructed and experimental types were created by London-based The Foundry (see p. 284) in close collaboration with Crouwel as part of its Architype 3 Crouwel Collection in 1996.

In later life, Crouwel was active in education, teaching at a number of top design schools. In 1985, he was appointed a director at the Museum Boijmans van Beuningen in Rotterdam, commissioning London design studio 8vo to meet the design requirements for the site. He retired from the museum in 1993. Crouwel continues to design on a range of print and exhibition projects.

In July 2019, Wim Crouwel was given the highest honor from the internationally renowned Type Directors Club, the award of its 32nd TDC Medal. This is only given out to "the the most influential and inspiring practitioners and thinkers in typography."

Date: 1928–
Nationality: Dutch
Notable typefaces:
Foundry Gridnik (see p. 426)
Foundry Stedelijk (see p. 419)

Below. Crouwel's book *New Alphabet*, released in 1967, documenting his proposals for "programmed typography."

Opposite top. Wim Crouwel, not only designing, but dressing for the future, 1969 (left). *Visuele Communicatie Nederland*, Stedelijk Museum, 1969 (right).

Opposite bottom. A selection of Crouwel's iconic designs for the Stedelijk Museum. From left: Poster *Elmar Berkovich*, Stedelijk van Abbemuseum, 1962; Poster *Vormgevers*, Stedelijk Museum Amsterdam, 1968; Catalogue cover *Werkgroep Plakat Prag politieke affiches uit Tsjechoslowakije*, Stedelijk Museum Amsterdam, 1966.

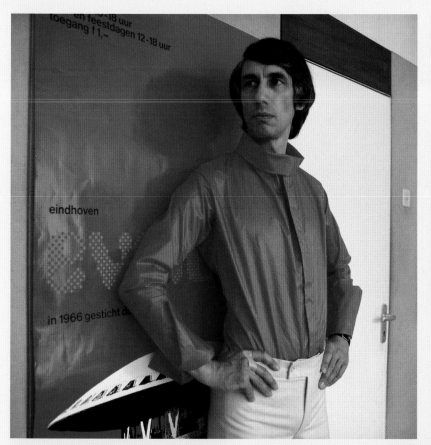

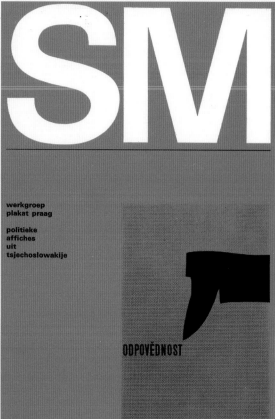

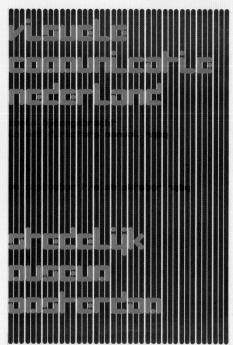

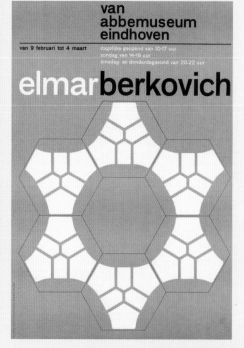

Necia

ABCDEFGHIJKLMNOPQRSTUVWXYZ
abcdefghijklmnopqrstuvwxyz
1234567890 !@#?:;"*&

Foundry: Graviton
Designer: Pablo Balcells
Designer Nationality:
Argentinian
Date: 2014

Necia is a geometric display typeface that combines sharply angled joints and terminals with softly rounded corners. Designed in the style of a squared sans serif, the Necia font family includes four weights, from Light to Black, each with corresponding unicase versions.

Nicotine

ABCDEFGHIJKLMNOPQRSTUVWXYZ
abcdefghijklmnopqrstuvwxyz
1234567890 !@#?:;"*&

Foundry: Chank Co.
Designer: Chank Diesel
Designer Nationality: American
Date: 1998

Nicotine is a squared sans serif display font comprising five styles, including the unicase Nicotine Jazz. The condensed characters, most notably the "I," which takes the silhouette of a filtered cigarette, were designed to exert a strong influence in tight compositions.

Pacifica

ABCDEFGHIJKLMNOPQRSTUVWXYZ
1234567890 !@#?:;"*&

Foundry: Solotype
Designer: Dan X. Solo
Designer Nationality: American
Date: 2005

Pacifica is a display typeface designed in a single style. It was based on the Congo font produced by the US foundry Barnhart Brothers & Spindler c. 1895 and is almost identical to the original. Solotype conceived Pacifica in an effort to smooth Congo's curves and refine the font's shape.

PL Fiedler Gothic

ABCDEFGHIJKLMNOPQRSTUVWXYZ
abcdefghijklmnopqrstuvwxyz
1234567890 !©#?:;"*&

Foundry: Monotype
Designer: Hal Fiedler
Designer Nationality: American
Date: Unknown

Hal Fiedler's PL Fiedler Gothic is a sans serif display typeface designed in a single style. The squared letter forms, which are in many ways typical of a gothic sans, feature several quirks, such as the short tail on the lowercase "q" or the dented stem on the "t."

Quartan

ABCDEFGHIJKLMNOPQRSTUVWXYZ
ABCDEFGHIJKLMNOPQRStUVWXYZ
1234567890 !@#?:;"*&

Foundry: Linotype
Designer: Maria Martina Schmitt
Designer Nationality: Austrian
Date: 2004

Maria Martina Schmitt's Quartan is a display font comprised of three weights, from Light to Bold. The industrial characters, which feature unicase forms that resist the use of ascenders and descenders, act like building blocks that allow the designer to render the text in stylish stacks.

Sackers Square Gothic

ABCDEFGHIJKLMNOPQRSTUVWXY
ABCDEFGHIJKLMNOPQRSTUVWXYZ
1234567890 !@#?:;"*&

Foundry: Compugraphic
Designer: Gary Sackers
Designer Nationality: American
Date: 1975

Sackers Square Gothic is part of a collection of faces designed by Gary Sackers for Compugraphic between 1974 and 1975, based on old engraving type masterplates. It is a caps and small caps only extended sans serif with square edges that comes in three roman weights: Light, Medium, and Heavy.

Serpentine

ABCDEFGHIJKLMNOPQRSTUVWXYZ
abcdefghijklmnopqrstuvwxyz
1234567890 !@#?:;"*&

Foundry: VGC
Designer: Dick Jensen
Designer Nationality: American
Date: 1972

Dick Jensen's Serpentine is a wide, slightly flared semi serif with a blocky feel and large x-height. The Visual Graphics Corporation released it in 1972 in Light, Medium, Bold, and Bold Italic styles. The typeface was used in the posters and titles for the James Bond film *Tomorrow Never Dies* (1997).

Superstar

ABCDEFGHIJKLMNOPQRSTUVWXYZ
1234567890 !@#?:;"*&

Foundry: Letraset
Designer: Colin Brignall
Designer Nationality: British
Date: 1970

Letraset type director Colin Brignall was inspired by US sportswear graphics—in particular the lettering found on baseball and soccer shirts—when he designed Superstar. It is an inline sans serif with wedgelike cutouts taking the place of curves, and is the perfect choice for sports-related designs.

Tank

ABCDEFGHIJKLMNOPQRSTUVWXYZ
1234567890 !@#?:;"*&

Foundry: Typodermic
Designer: Ray Larabie
Designer Nationality: Canadian
Date: 2004

Available in two weights, Tank and Tank Lite, this sturdy display typeface has a heavy mechanical look and tight spacing. Tank is supplied with a set of alternate characters with no counters, whereas Tank Lite is designed for smaller spaces and sizes, when Tank Regular's narrow counters are likely to vanish.

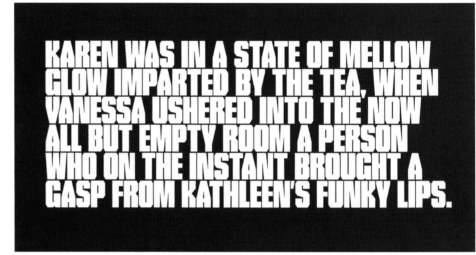

Titanium

ABCDEFGHIJKLMNOPQRSTUVWXYZ
abcdefghijklmnopqrstuvwxyz
1234567890 !@#?:;"*&

Foundry: Ascender
Designer: Steve Matteson
Designer Nationality: American
Date: 2006

Titanium is a rounded monoline sans serif with a futuristic feel available in a single weight. Steve Matteson designed it for the Chicago-based Ascender foundry in 2006. Matteson co-founded Ascender in 2004, and it was purchased by his former employer, Monotype, in 2010

Titanium Motors

ABCDEFGHIJKLMNOPQRSTUVW
XYZ
1234567890 !@#?:;"*&

Foundry: Monotype
Designer: Steve Matteson
Designer Nationality: American
Date: 2012

Steve Matteson became Monotype's creative type director when the company subsumed his foundry Ascender in 2010. He designed Titanium Motors two years later; this bold, rounded all-caps sans serif is available in regular and italic, conveying a dynamic sense of speed, especially when used in italic.

Violenta

ABCDEFGHIJKLMNOPQRSTUVWXYZ
ABCDEFGHIJKLMNOPQRSTUVWXYZ
1234567890 !@#?:;"*&

Foundry: Graviton
Designer: Pablo Balcells
Designer Nationality: Argentinian
Date: 2015

Pablo Balcells, the Argentinian designer and graduate of the University of Buenos Aires, created this condensed, bold, geometric sans serif. Violenta comes in uppercase and unicase in four styles: Solid, Outline, Inline, and Stencil. The Graviton type foundry published Violenta in 2015.

Why Square

abcdefghijklmnopqrstuvwxyz
1234567890 !@#?:;"*&

Foundry: Linotype
Designer: Zoran Kostic
Designer Nationality: Serbian
Date: 1999

Zoran Kostic drew Why Square in 1999 during the Kosovo War; it was the start of a type family that also includes Just Square and began as lettering by Kostic's son. It is a narrow, square sans serif and comes in five weights with Cyrillic support and alternate ultra-wide capitals.

Zekton

ABCDEFGHIJKLMNOPQRSTUVWXYZ
abcdefghijklmnopqrstuvwxyz
1234567890 !@#?:;"*&

Foundry: Typodermic
Designer: Ray Larabie
Designer Nationality: Canadian
Date: 1998

Zekton, designed by the prolific font maker Ray Larabie, is a geometric sans serif with round corners and even line widths. It comes in many styles, with three widths and seven weights, all of which have matching italics. Like many of Larabie's fonts, it has a futuristic atmosphere.

Zosma

ABCDEFGHIJKLMNOPQRSTUV
WXYZ
1234567890 !@#?:;"*&

Foundry: Typodermic
Designer: Ray Larabie
Designer Nationality: Canadian
Date: 2005

Zosma, designed by Ray Larabie and released by his foundry Typodermic in 2005, is an uppercase, geometric sans serif that is constructed with straight lines and subtle curves. Zosma conveys a technical feel and comes in three weights—Light to Bold—with matching italics.

AG Book Stencil

ABCDEFGHIJKLMNOPQRSTUVWXYZ
abcdefghijklmnopqrstuvwxyz
1234567890 ! ?:;"*&

Günter Gerhard Lange added this stencil design to his AG Book family in 1985. It is sold by Berthold as part of a package with several other display typefaces, including AG Old Face Shaded, Barmeno Extra Bold, and Formata Outline, offering designers a range of impactful fonts from which to choose.

Foundry: Berthold
Designer: Günter Gerhard Lange
Designer Nationality: German
Date: 1985

Aguda Stencil

ABCDEFGHIJKLMNOPQRSTUVWXYZ
ABCDEFGHIJKLMNOPQRSTUVWXYZ
1234567890 !@#?:;"*&

Aguda Stencil is published by Graviton, a foundry established by Pablo Balcells in 2013 to focus on the design of geometric fonts suitable for technical and digital use. Two versions of the typeface are available, with one tailored for display use and the other for smaller text.

Foundry: Graviton
Designer: Pablo Balcells
Designer Nationality: Argentinian
Date: 2014

Ammo

ABCDEFGHIJKLMNOPQRSTUVWXYZ
1234567890 !@#?:;"*&

This extremely heavyweight sans serif typeface was designed by Alexander McCracken, founder of the independent foundry Neutura (see p. 546), who also publishes typefaces through T26. A stencil design, the font features an unconventional approach to divisions within its letter forms.

Foundry: Neutura
Designer: Alexander McCracken
Designer Nationality: American
Date: 2010

Audree

ABCDEFGHIJKLMNOPQRSTUVWXYZ
abcdefghijklmnopqrstuvwxyz
1234567890 !@#?:;"*&

Published in 2013 by Typotheque (see p. 90), this comprehensive type system is staggering in its scope, offering designers the ability to create hundreds of potential type styles from its selection of components. *Typographica* review featured Audree as one of the best releases of 2013.

Foundry: Typotheque
Designer: Nikola Djurek / Marko Hrastovec
Designer Nationality: Croatian
Date: 2013

Brutal

ABCDEFGHIJKLMNOPQRSTUVWXYZ
abcdefghijklmnopqrstuvwxyz
1234567890 !ct#?:;"* et

Foundry: BB-Bureau
Designer: Benoît Bodhuin
Designer Nationality: French
Date: 2017

Brutal's distinctive features and highly deconstructed look mark it out as truly unique. An anarchic and fun stencil design from the furtive imagination of French designer Benoît Bodhuin and his foundry BB-Bureau (see p. 386), the typeface is available in Light, Regular, and Bold weights.

With a varying contrast in stroke weight, Brutal possesses a calligraphic quality. Its non-aligning characters provide fluidity and rhythm as the letters bounce to one another. The use of verticals and horizontal-only strokes, with the curved connections made in a broad-nib manner, help make for a striking appearance.

A mathematical design principle underpins all the characters, which share the same construction. This rigor is visible in the separated strokes, 90° angles, and consistently matching bowls.

Below left. *Oripeau* by Benoît Bodhuin.

Below. Art directed by Yu Qiongjie and designed by Transwhite Studio, an exhibition catalogue celebrating the first decade of the Inna Art Space, based in New York and Huangzhou, China, which features the work of thirteen contemporary artists.

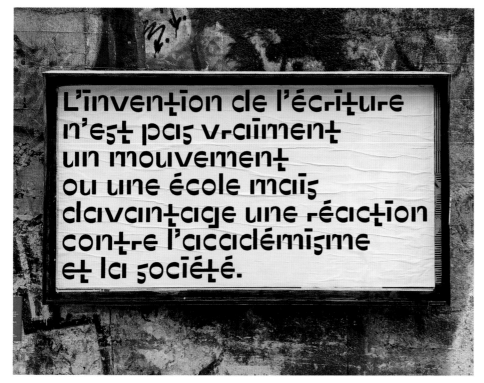

Braggadocio

ABCDEFGHIJKLMNOPQRSTUV
abcdefghijklmnopqrstuvwxyz
1234567890 !@#?:;"'*&

Foundry: Monotype
Designer: William A. Woolley
Designer Nationality: American
Date: 1930

Influenced by the design of Futura Black, this geometric stencil font was created by US type designer William A. Woolley for Monotype in 1930. Its heavy letter forms offer relatively poor legibility, but give a strong and characterful impression in display contexts.

Campaign

ABCDEFGHIJKLMNOPQRSTUVWXYZ
1234567890 !@#?:;"'*&

Foundry: ITC
Designer: Alan Meeks
Designer Nationality: British
Date: 1987

Campaign is a stencil typeface designed by Alan Meeks in 1987, featuring a uniform stroke weight and distinctive diagonal details within its uppercase-only letter forms. It is available in a single weight, and works best when set at larger point sizes and in headline contexts.

Densmore

Foundry: Typodermic
Designer: Ray Larabie
Designer Nationality: Canadian
Date: 2009

A solidly built and blocky stencil typeface, Densmore consists of three styles: Regular, Blue, and Pink. Blue and Pink are designed to be used together to create a layered effect by using different colors, with the double lowercase "o" combination automatically replaced by a mirrored "o o."

DIN Next Stencil

ABCDEFGHIJKLMNOPQRSTUVWXYZ
abcdefghijklmnopqrstuvwxyz
1234567890 !@#?:;"'*&

Foundry: Linotype
Designer: Akira Kobayashi / Sabina Chipară
Designer Nationality: Romanian / Japanese
Date: 2017

DIN Next Stencil is based on DIN Next, Akira Kobayshi's 2009 version of the classic 1930s typeface DIN by Deutsches Institut für Normung (German Institute for Standardization). The commanding stencil font was customized by Romanian designer Sabina Chipară. It is available in seven weights.

Cut

ABCDEFGHIJKLMNOPQRSTUVWXYZ
abcdefghijklmnopqrstuvwxyz
1234567890 !@#?:;"*&

Foundry: MuirMcNeil
Designer: Hamish Muir /
Paul McNeil
Designer Nationality: British
Date: 2016

The Cut typeface was inspired by two distinct typographical periods from history, and draws it design and proportions from the work of leading designers who shaped type design and construction. It is available in three weights.

Cut's proportions are based on those of neoclassical typefaces from the early 19th century, created by innovative type designers such as Firmin Didot and Giambattista Bodoni. Cut takes the contrast seen in the strokes of their typefaces to such an extreme that the hairline strokes connecting the components of the letter forms disappear, leaving just geometric shapes.

Cut also refers to the early 20th century and typographers such as Herbert Bayer, Josef Albers, and Jan Tschichold, who worked with type elements often as simple geometric elements. Their work informs the system construction behind Cut.

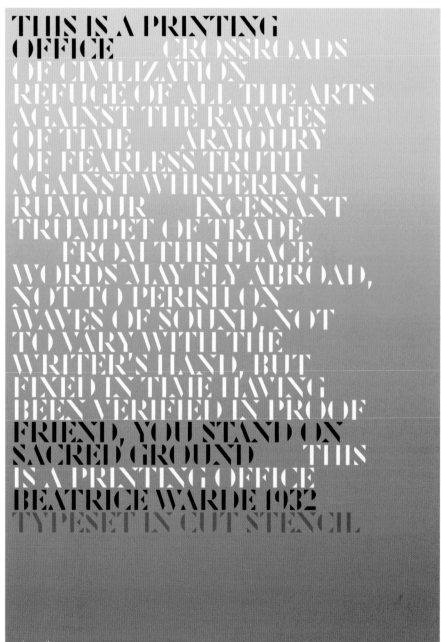

THIS IS A PRINTING OFFICE CROSSROADS OF CIVILIZATION REFUGE OF ALL THE ARTS AGAINST THE RAVAGES OF TIME ARMOURY OF FEARLESS TRUTH AGAINST WHISPERING RUMOUR INCESSANT TRUMPET OF TRADE FROM THIS PLACE WORDS MAY FLY ABROAD, NOT TO PERISH ON WAVES OF SOUND, NOT TO VARY WITH THE WRITER'S HAND, BUT FIXED IN TIME HAVING BEEN VERIFIED IN PROOF FRIEND, YOU STAND ON SACRED GROUND THIS IS A PRINTING OFFICE BEATRICE WARDE 1932 TYPESET IN CUT STENCIL

Dirty Baker's Dozen

ABCDEFGHIJKLMNOPQRSTUVWXYZ
1234567890 !@#?:;"★&

Foundry: Typodermic
Designer: Ray Larabie
Designer Nationality: Canadian
Date: 1998

A solid stencil font with lots of deliberate imperfections, Dirty Baker's Dozen by Ray Larabie comes with plenty of symbols, fractions, and accents. Two new styles were introduced in 2009: Scorch, which has a burnt-out effect, and Spraypaint, which has a rough-edged look.

DR Zhek

ABCDEFGHIJKLMNOPQRSTUVWXYZ
ABCDEFGHIJKLMNOPQRSTUVWXYZ
1234567890 !@#?:;"*&

Foundry: Dmitry Rastvortsev
Designer: Dmitry Rastvortsev
Designer Nationality: Ukrainian
Date: 2017

Ukrainian designer Dmitry Rastvortsev released DR Zhek through his eponymous foundry in 2017. It is a single-style, condensed stencil sans serif with a utilitarian feel and uppercase and small caps only. DR Zhek is a multilingual font with support for Cyrillic, Greek, and Latin alphabets.

Five 01

ABCDEFGHIJKLMNOPQRSTUVWXYZ
abcdefghijklmnopqrstuvwxyz
1234567890 !@#?:;"*&

Foundry: MuirMcNeil
Designer: Hamish Muir / Paul McNeil
Designer Nationality: British
Date: 2017

The Five geometric stencil family was designed and released by the MuirMcNeil foundry (see p. 334) in 2017. It comes in three styles. The first, Five 01, is angular and curve-less and has four weights: the counter-less 330; and 290, 250, and 210, each of which has progressively wider counters.

Five 02

ABCDEFGHIJKLMNOPQRSTUVWXYZ
abcdefghijklmnopqrstuvwxyz
1234567890 !@#?:;"*&

Foundry: MuirMcNeil
Designer: Hamish Muir / Paul McNeil
Designer Nationality: British
Date: 2017

The Five family was inspired by a variety of typefaces such as Schmalfette Grotesk, Compacta, and Josef Albers's Kombinations-Schrift, as well as Walter Ballmer's lettering for Olivetti. Five 02 has soft rounded corners and comes in four numbered weights: 330, 290, 250, and 210.

Five 03

ABCDEFGHIJKLMNOPQRSTUVWXYZ
abcdefghijklmnopqrstuvwxyz
1234567890 !@#?:;"*&

Foundry: MuirMcNeil
Designer: Hamish Muir /
Paul McNeil
Designer Nationality: British
Date: 2017

Five 03 is the most geometric and curved of the Five family from MuirMcNeil (see p. 334), and has many details constructed from half or quarter circles.

It comes in four, bold, numbered weights: the totally solid 330; and 290, 250, and 210, each of which has progressively wider counters and more white space.

Foundry Fabriek

ABCDEFGHIJKLMNOPQRSTUVWXYZ
abcdefghijklmnopqrstuvwxyz
1234567890 !@#?:;"*&

Foundry: The Foundry
Designer: David Quay /
Wim Crouwel
Designer Nationality: British /
Dutch
Date: 2016

Foundry Fabriek began as a commission when Dutch designer Wim Crouwel (see p. 540) recommended The Foundry (see p. 284) to interior-

design consultant Kho Liang Ie, who wanted a stencil version of the Gridnik typeface to laser cut in steel for a building-signage project.

Frank

ABCDEFGHIJKLMNOPQRSTUVW
XYZ
1234567890 !@#?:;"*&

Foundry: Neutura
Designer: Alexander McCracken
Designer Nationality: American
Date: 2005

Alexander McCracken released his typeface Frank through Neutura, the foundry he runs in San Francisco. It is a heavy slab serif in three numbered

styles: 1 and 2 are solid and counter-less, while 3 is a stencil version with extremely fine gaps. All three styles are the same weight.

Gendouki

ABCDEFGHIJKLMN
abcdefghijklmnopqrst
1234567890 !@#?:;"*&

Foundry: Typodermic
Designer: Ray Larabie
Designer Nationality: Canadian
Date: 2006

A wide, geometric stencil sans serif typeface, Gendouki was designed by prolific Canadian type designer Ray Larabie in 2006 and released by his

foundry Typodermic. Gendouki has a futuristic feel and is angular, with "filament stencil lines inspired by spaceship access panels."

Glaser Stencil

ABCDEFGHIJKLMNOPQRSTUVWXYZ
123-4567890 !@#?:;"*&

Foundry: Photo-Lettering
Designer: Milton Glaser
Designer Nationality: American
Date: 1969

Glaser Stencil was first used as lettering on a Carnegie Hall poster by the legendary illustrator and designer Milton Glaser in 1967. Photo-Lettering debuted Glaser Stencil in its yearbook for 1969. It was available in three weights—Light, Regular, and Bold—but many digital versions only include Bold.

Gunplay

ABCDEFGHIJKLMNOPQRSTUVWXYZ
abcdefghijklmnopqrstuvwxyz
1234567890 !@#?:;"'&

Foundry: Typodermic
Designer: Ray Larabie
Designer Nationality: Canadian
Date: 2000

Gunplay was inspired by lettering on posters for the Steve McQueen film *The Getaway* (1972). It is a bold, no-nonsense stencil sans serif available in four styles: Regular; 3D, which has drop shadows; Damage, which is distressed but mostly solid edged; and Spraypaint, which is rough edged.

Interrogator Stencil

ABCDEFGHIJKLMNOPQRSTUVWXYZ
1234567890 !@#?:;"*&

Foundry: Typodermic
Designer: Ray Larabie
Designer Nationality: Canadian
Date: 2014

Interrogator Stencil was created by the prolific Japan-based designer Ray Larabie. It is a tall, condensed sans serif stencil typeface from the Typodermic foundry. The stencilling details include a thin horizontal gap that runs through the center of all letters. It is available in one weight.

ITC Portago

ABCDEFGHIJKLMNOPQRSTUVWXYZ
ABCDEFGHIJKLMNOPQRSTUVWXYZ
1234567890 !@#?:;"*&

Foundry: ITC
Designer: Luis Siquot
Designer Nationality: Argentinian
Date: 1997

Luis Siquot's ITC Portago, published in 1997, is a heavy, uppercase only, stencil sans serif with rough edges and small caps. It was inspired by the lettering spray-painted on crates and luggage. Siquot was born in Argentina and educated at the University of Fine Arts Hamburg.

Iwan Stencil

ABCDEFGHIJKLMNOPQRSTUVWXYZ
abcdefghijklmnopqrstuvwxyz
1234567890 !@#?:;"*&

German designer Klaus Sutter, a former Linotype employee, specializes in creating digital revivals of metal type. For Iwan Stencil he focused on a font created by German designer Jan Tschichold in 1929, adding new characters and language support to this high-contrast, stencilled semi serif.

Foundry: Linotype
Designer: Klaus Sutter
Designer Nationality: German
Date: 2007

Jigsaw Stencil

ABCDEFGHIJKLMNOPQRSTUVWXYZ
abcdefghijklmnopqrstuvwxyz
1234567890 !@#?:;"*&

Johanna Biľak designed the Jigsaw type family for Typotheque (see p. 90), the foundry she runs with Peter Biľak and Nikola Djurek. Jigsaw is a geometric sans serif and was neatly turned into an attractive stencil version. Both faces are available in twelve styles, six weights with italics.

Foundry: Typotheque
Designer: Johanna Biľak
Designer Nationality: Slovakian
Date: 1999

Linotype Authentic Stencil

ABCDEFGHIJKLMNOPQRSTUVWXYZ
abcdefghijklmnopqrstuvwxyz
1234567890 !@#?:;"*&

Linotype Authentic Stencil is a stencil display font and is part of the Linotype Authentic typeface family, which also includes Sans, Serif, and Small Serif versions. The characters feature small slab serifs, gently squared curves, and three weights with corresponding italics.

Foundry: Linotype
Designer: Karin Huschka
Designer Nationality: German
Date: 1999

Linotype Element

ABCDEFGHIJKLMNOPQRSTUVWXY
abcdefghijklmnopqrstuvwxyz
1234567890 !!?:;"&

Linotype Element is an abstract display typeface inspired by the emergent technology of the 1990s. Its characters blur the typical structure of letter forms by introducing concentric forms, which generate an aesthetic of hypnotic motion when displayed in large point sizes.

Foundry: Linotype
Designer: Jan Tomás
Designer Nationality: Czech
Date: 1999

Lisbon

ABCDEFGHIJKLMNOPQRSTUVWXYZ
abcdefghijklmnopqrstuvwxyz
1234567890 !@#?:;"*&

Lisbon is a geometric stencil typeface from acclaimed graphic artist, printmaker, and designer Anthony Burrill, developed and marketed by the Colophon foundry (see p. 210). The typeface's source of inspiration was a metal stencil that Burrill discovered in a signmaker's shop in Lisbon, Portugal. Digitized by Colophon, Lisbon was first used in a series of Burrill's posters commissioned by the British Council for the ExperimentaDesign cultural biennale in the Portuguese capital in 2010. Lisbon was originally an all-caps design, and a lowercase set and punctuation has been added using the same geometric elements as the original.

Foundry: Colophon
Designer: Anthony Burrill
Designer Nationality: British
Date: 2013

Below. Global design group Pentagram created the identity, signage and website design for Mediterranean restaurant Gato in New York. Burrill's stencil design is perfectly suited for the architecture of the site as well as or being printed. It is also stencilled on its restroom walls.

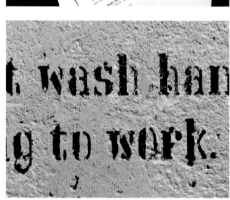

Octin Prison

ABCDEFGHIJKLMNOPQRSTUVWXYZ
1234567890 !@#?:;"*&

Foundry: Typodermic
Designer: Ray Larabie
Designer Nationality: Canadian
Date: 2007

Octin Prison is part of Typodermic's Octin type family, which also contains Octin College, Octin Sports, Octin Stencil, Octin Spraypaint, and Octin Vintage. It is a tough, uppercase, stencil slab serif that comes in seven roman weights: Light, Book, Regular, Semi-bold, Heavy, and Black.

Octin Stencil

ABCDEFGHIJKLMNOPQRSTUVWXYZ
1234567890 !@#?:;"*&

Foundry: Typodermic
Designer: Ray Larabie
Designer Nationality: Canadian
Date: 2007

Octin Stencil was created by Canadian type designer Ray Larabie. It is an angular, curve-less, authoritative, stencil sans serif typeface with uppercase letters only. Octin Stencil comes in seven weights: Light, Book, Regular, Semi-bold, Heavy, and Black.

Plotter Display

ABCDEFGHIJKLMNOPQRSTUVWXYZ
abcdefghijklmnopqrstuvwxyz
1234567890 !@#?:;"*&

Foundry: Typotheque
Designer: Nikola Djurek
Designer Nationality: Croatian
Date: 2017

According to Typotheque (see p. 90), Plotter "explores the world of technical drawings and architectural plans." Plotter Display is the most experimental of the family. It comes in five styles of the same weight which can be layered: Bold, Layer A, Layer B, Layer C, and Layer D.

Rubber Stamp

ABCDEFGHIJKLMNOPQRSTUVWXYZ
1234567890 !@#?:;"*&

Foundry: Letraset
Designer: Alan Birch
Designer Nationality: British
Date: 1983

Created by Alan Birch for Letraset in 1983, and also released by the International Typeface Corporation, Rubber Stamp is a bold, uppercase only, stencil serif font with corroded, imperfect edges and a distressed texture that mimics the effect of text printed with a worn rubber stamp and ink.

Rumori Stencil

ABCDEFGHIJKLMNOPQRSTUVWXYZ
abcdefghijklmnopqrstuvwxyz
1234567890 !@#?:;"*&

Foundry: MuirMcNeil
Designer: Hamish Muir /
Paul McNeil
Designer Nationality: British
Date: 2017

Three years after designing Rumori, Paul McNeil refined it, adding a stencil version and releasing the updated family through MuirMcNeil, the foundry and studio he runs with Hamish Muir. The stencil cut comes in roman and italic, in two styles: the rounded Morbidi and angular Chiari.

Stem

ABCDEFGHIJKLMNOPQRSTUVWXYZ
abcdefghijklmnopqrstuvwxyz
1234567890 !@#?:;"*&

Foundry: MuirMcNeil
Designer: Hamish Muir /
Paul McNeil
Designer Nationality: British
Date: 2016

MuirMcNeil (see p. 334) designed Stem, a stencil typeface with contrast, in 2016 as an evolution of its earlier typeface, Cut. In 2018, MuirMcNeil expanded it to include two styles in five weights. Style A is squarer with hairline flat serifs, while B is more rounded with floating circular terminals.

Stencil

ABCDEFGHIJKLMNOPQRSTUVWXYZ
1234567890 !@#?:;"*&

Foundry: Linotype
Designer: Gerry Powell
Designer Nationality: American
Date: 1938

Gerry Powell designed Stencil for American Type Founders in 1938. It has rounded edges and thick strokes and is inspired by the traditional stencilled letters found on packaging and crates. It is used in the TV series *M*A*S*H*. Alexei Chekulaev designed a Cyrillic version of Stencil in 1997.

Stencil Moonlight

ABCDEFGHIJKLMNOPQRSTUVWXYZ
ABCDEFGHIJKLMNOPQRSTUVWXYZ
1234567890 !@#?:;"*&

Foundry: Linotype
Designer: Gustav Andrejs
Grinbergs
Designer Nationality: Latvian
Date: 2003

Gustav Andrejs Grinbergs's Stencil Moonlight was a runner-up in the Display category in Linotype's International Type Design Contest in 2003. It is a fresh take on Gerry Powell's classic Stencil typeface and shares many of its characteristics, but has an added lowercase.

Stop

ABCDEFGHJKLMNOPQRSTUVWXYZ
1234567890 !@#?:;"*&

Foundry: URW
Designer: Aldo Novarese
Designer Nationality: Italian
Date: 1971

This stylized and very heavy display typeface with a number of abstract characters is one of Aldo Novarese's many futuristic-looking fonts. Stop's strong horizontal lines give it a distinct look, and its influence can clearly be seen on the font used for the *Blade Runner* (1982) film poster.

Ténica Slab Stencil

ABCDEFGHIJKLMNOPQRSTUVWXYZ
abcdefghijklmnopqrstuvwxyz
1234567890 !@#?:;"*&

Foundry: Graviton
Designer: Pablo Balcells
Designer Nationality: Argentinian
Date: 2014

The stencil version of Ténica Slab is available in eight styles. Stencil 1 consists of four styles with a narrow stem, suitable for larger-sized text and printing on rigid materials. Stencil 2 consists of four styles with a wider stem, suitable for larger-sized text and printing on lighter materials.

Ténica Stencil

ABCDEFGHIJKLMNOPQRSTUVWXYZ
abcdefghijklmnopqrstuvwxyz
1234567890 !@#?:;"*&

Foundry: Graviton
Designer: Pablo Balcells
Designer Nationality: Argentinian
Date: 2014

Designed for the Graviton Font Foundry by Pablo Balcells in 2014, the stencil version of the Ténica font family is available in eight styles. With two stem widths (Stencil 1 and Stencil 2), each variant consists of four styles, each with Regular and Bold weights and each having an alternate variant.

Threefortysixbarrel

ABCDEFGHIJKLMNOPQRSTUVWXYZ
ABCDEFGHIJKLMNOPQRSTUVWXYZ
1234567890 !@#?:;"*&

Foundry: Typodermic
Designer: Ray Larabie
Designer Nationality: Canadian
Date: 2004

Ray Larabie's Threefortysixbarrel is a slightly condensed stencil font inspired by lettering found sprayed on to the air filter of a 1970 Plymouth Barracuda, and which he describes as "the ultimate, barely street legal font." It is available in three weights: Regular, Intake, and Exhaust.

Buffalo Gal

ABCDEFGHIJKLMNOPQRSTUVWXYZ
abcdefghijklmnopqrstuvwxyz
1234567890 !@#?:;"'*&

This Wild West-inspired font was designed by Tom Rickner following his two-year tenure as lead typographer for Apple, where he supervised the production of the company's first TrueType releases. Buffalo Gal is one of the first of a generation of variable GX fonts released during the 1990s.

Foundry: Rickner Type
Designer: Tom Rickner
Designer Nationality: American
Date: 1994

Circus Poster Shadow

ABCDEFGHIJKLMNOPQRSTUVWXYZ
abcdefghijklmnopqrstuvwxyz
1234567890 !@#?:;"'*&

Ascender co-founder Tom Rickner designed Circus Poster. The typeface was influenced by the forms of wood type used within 19th-century advertising, which have become synonymous with depictions of the Wild West in popular culture. It features shadow details for further weight and impact.

Foundry: Ascender
Designer: Tom Rickner
Designer Nationality: American
Date: 2005

ITC Buckeroo

ABCDEFGHIJKLMNOPQRSTUV
ABCDEFGHIJKLMNOPQRSTUVWXYZ
1234567890 !@#?:;"'*&

Buckeroo is credited to US type designer Richard William Mueller. It is a heavy, Wild West-inspired display typeface with distinctive notched slab serifs. Mueller digitized an earlier typeface Frontier, which was released by Photo-Lettering, and then improved it by adding small caps.

Foundry: ITC
Designer: Richard William Mueller
Designer Nationality: American
Date: 1997

Madame

ABCDEFGHIJKLMNOPQRSTUVWXYZ
1234567890 !@#?:;"'*&

Madame is a display typeface designed to add flamboyance to titles, headlines or initials, and initially appeared in a sample with a variety of other similar types. Its letter forms are defined by their expressive Tuscan aesthetic, seen in the ornate serifs and embellished strokes.

Foundry: Fonderie Typographique Française
Designer: Joseph Gillé
Designer Nationality: French
Date: 1820

PL Davison Americana

ABCDEFGHIJKLMNOPQRSTUVW
abcdefghijklmnopqrstuvwxyz
1234567890 !©#?:;"'*&

Foundry: Photo-Lettering
Designer: M. M. Davison
Designer Nationality: American
Date: 1965

Designer M. M. Davison created fonts for Photo-Lettering during the 1950s and 1960s, often based on historical models. Monotype has digitized two of these fonts: PL Davison Americana, a bold, spurred, Wild West-style titling slab serif; and PL Davison Zip, a chunky uppercase handwritten script.

Rosewood

ABCDEFGHIJKLMNOPQRSTUVWXYZ
1234567890 !@#?:;"'*&

Foundry: Adobe
Designer: William Page / Carl Crossgrove / Carol Twombly / Kim Buker Chansler
Nationality: American
Date: 1874 / 1994

Rosewood is a Tuscan display typeface based on a chromatic design by William Page dating to 1874. Rosewood includes two styles, Regular and Fill, with the latter designed to overlay the first. Like original overprinting methods, it uses layers to add multiple colors to a single character.

Thunderbird Extra Condensed

ABCDEFGHIJKLMNOPQRSTUVWXYZ
1234567890 !@#?:;"'*&

Foundry: Linotype
Designer: American Type Founders Studio
Date: 1920

Thunderbird is an ornate Tuscan serif in all caps, which was released by the American Type Founders in 1920. Its anonymous designer was clearly inspired by Wild West-era wood type. Many foundries have digitized Thunderbird; Linotype's version includes the extra-condensed style.

Zebrawood

ABCDEFGHIJKLMNOPQRSTUVWXYZ
1234567890 !@#?:;"'*&

Foundry: Adobe
Designer: Carl Crossgrove / Carol Twombly / Kim Buker Chansler
Designer Nationality: American
Date: 1994

The Zebrawood uppercase Tuscan serif was created by a team of designers at Adobe. It is based on lettering found in a Wells & Webb type catalogue dating to 1854, which was often used in circus posters and advertisements. Zebrawood comes in two styles: the decorated Regular and solid Fill.

DALTON MAAG LTD.
SINCE 1991 · LONDON

Script

Opposite. Design detail showing Volina typeface by London typeface design studio Dalton Maag.

Based on the principles of handwriting, Script typefaces possess fluid forms, varying strokes, and a rhythm to their appearance when set as if they were drawn by hand. Script typefaces can be categorized into two main areas: "Formal" are predominantly based around actual writing, often nibbed or quill-penned from the 17th and 18th centuries, and did not actually become typefaces until the 18th / 19th centuries; and "Casual" scripts, whose style is much looser, more brushlike in appearance, mostly emerged from the early 20th century. To aid visual comparison and construction, the two groupings have been divided further with the addition of Calligraphic and Handwriting. There are inevitably always many shared design elements across the styles.

The earliest form of script is Blackletter, also referred to as Gothic Script. Blackletter types were developed and predominantly used across Europe in the Middle Ages, starting from around the 1100s until around the 17th century. The generic term *blackletter* comes from their heavy and dominant presence on the page, with condensed letterforms, tightly spaced setting, and heavy, evenly spaced vertical strokes. There are, however, a number of variations in construction and appearance for these Gothic types. Textualis (Textura) is a style associated with northern parts of Europe, and was used by German printer and pioneer Johannes

Gutenberg when he printed his 42-line Bible (one of the first books printed using metal movable type in the 1450s); it is the most calligraphic in terms of appearance. By contrast, the Italian Rotunda from Europe used a less angular approach. Further variations appeared around the 15th century, such as Bastarda from France (an amalgamation of differing styles), and in the 16th century came Fraktur from Germany, which was widely used there until the middle of the 20th century.

Calligraphic scripts connect closely to a cursive process, with their classical, angular appearance informing their creation from a broad-edged nib or brush and their inclined letterforms denoting a rhythm and movement from the writer which provides a dynamism to the letterforms. Decorative elements are often employed, such as extended descenders with flourishes and swashes to provide a more extrovert and flamboyant tone. Casual scripts are increasingly playful and relaxed in appearance, as if rendered by an active and impatient hand. Their immediacy, whether seemingly created by brush or marker pen or more precisely drawn, brings a softer appearance and their informal aesthetic invariably commands less authority.

Often seen as the perfect typeface for a wedding invitation or similar, Formal script typefaces have in recent years been enjoying a comeback as their usage increases and diversifies. Even so,

not many smaller contemporary foundries take on the challenge of creating new formal scripts. This is probably based on commercial and financial considerations when creating any new typeface but also on the designer's preference and interest (or lack of interest). A number of the formal typefaces that have been created owe much to the hand-drawn letters from English writing masters such as George Bickham and George Shelley. These fluid and elegant letterforms often have connecting strokes so that they appear joined when typeset. They are a demanding technical challenge to replicate when many historical reference points were originally created as Copperplate engravings (letters incised into copper plates using the intaglio method of printing). This progressed into hot metal type in later years, and with the advent of phototypesetting; the process became easier as technological advances such as OpenType meant that the letter pairing permutations were realized with less effort.

To conclude; from childish playfulness to anarchic and quirky scribblings, the digital technologies today allow any Handwriting styles to be captured. What is more, they can convey not only any individual's handwriting but also the personality that lay behind them, for others to use and enjoy.

Agincourt

𝔄𝔅𝔠𝔇𝔢𝔉𝔊𝔥𝔍𝔍𝔎𝔏𝔐𝔫𝔬𝔭𝔔𝔕𝔖𝔗𝔘𝔙𝔚𝔛𝔜𝔷
abcdefghijklmnopqrstuvwxyz
1234567890 !@#?:;"*&

Foundry: ITC
Designer: David Quay
Designer Nationality: British
Date: 1983

Agincourt is a beautifully crafted Old English script featuring intricate capitals and a more reserved, condensed lowercase. It was inspired by the age of chivalry and King Henry V, who was the first English monarch to send a letter (announcing his victory at Agincourt in 1415) written in the English language.

Beneta

ABCDEFGHIJKLMNOPQRSTUVWXYZ
abcdefghijklmnopqrstuvwxyz
1234567890 !@#?:;"*&

Foundry: Linotype
Designer: Karlgeorg Hoefer
Designer Nationality: German
Date: 1995

Beneta is a French bastarda, which is a blackletter script that was used in France, Germany, and the Burgundian Netherlands during the 14th and 15th centuries. It was inspired by the *littera Beneventana* (Beneventan script) Latin script used by Benedictine scribes from the 8th to the 16th centuries.

Blackletter 686 BT

𝔄𝔅𝔠𝔇𝔈𝔉𝔊𝔥𝔍𝔍𝔎𝔏𝔐𝔫𝔒𝔭𝔔𝔕𝔖𝔗𝔘𝔙𝔚𝔛𝔜𝔷
abcdefghijklmnopqrstuvwxyz
1234567890 !?:;"*&

Foundry: Bitstream
Designer: Unknown
Date: 1998

Bitstream's version of a classic blackletter is based on Linotype's London Text, which emulates scripts created using a quill pen in the Middle Ages, and its clean, traditional letterforms give it an engraved appearance. Blackletter 686 is available in a single regular weight.

Blackmoor

ABCDEFGHIJKLMNOPQRSTUVWXYZ
abcdefghijklmnopqrstuvwxyz
1234567890 !@#?:;"*&

Foundry: ITC
Designer: David Quay
Designer Nationality: British
Date: 1983

Blackmoor is a textura-style blackletter based on an Old English letter style. It is unusual in that it mixes gothic lowercase with Lombardic capitals. Its rough, distressed features and medieval influences give it a very distinctive character, making it perfect for anything related to horror.

Bollatica

ABCDEFGHIJKLMNOPQRSTUVWXYZ
abcdefghijklmnopqrstuvwxyz
1234567890 !@#?:;"*&

Foundry: Monotype
Designer: Philip Bouwsma
Designer Nationality: American
Date: 2012

Bollatica is one of Philip Bouwsma's many fonts based on broad pen calligraphy. It is a modern interpretation of the *scrittura bollatica* historical script, which was used from the 16th to 19th centuries for papal bulls and had no punctuation, and was virtually indecipherable by ordinary readers.

Clairvaux

ABCDEFGHIJKLMNOPQRSTUVWXYZ
abcdefghijklmnopqrstuvwxyz
1234567890 !@#?:;"*&

Foundry: Linotype
Designer: Herbert Maring
Designer Nationality: German
Date: 1990

Clairvaux is named after Clairvaux Abbey, a Cistercian monastery in northeastern France. It is based on the early gothic typefaces used by Cistercian monks. Available in a single weight, it is closer than any other bastarda to the forms of the Caroline minuscule, making it more legible.

Clemente Rotunda

ABCDEFGHIJKLMNOPQRSTUVWXY
abcdefghijklmnopqrstuvwxyz
1234567890 !@#?:;"*&

Foundry: Monotype
Designer: Philip Bouwsma
Designer Nationality: American
Date: 1997

One of Philip Bouwsma's many fonts based on broad pen calligraphy and inspired by classic manuscripts, this robust typeface is a rotunda—the medieval Italian version of blackletter type, less angular than those created in northern Europe and characterized by several unique abbreviations.

Cloister Black

ABCDEFGHIJKLMNOPQRSTUVWXYZ
abcdefghijklmnopqrstuvwxyz
1234567890 !@#?:;"*&

Foundry: Bitstream
Designer: Morris Fuller Benton / Joseph Warren Phinney
Designer Nationality: American
Date: 1904

Bitstream's version of American Type Founders' original version, Cloister Black was an adaptation of Priory Text, itself a version of Caslon Text from the 1870s. Morris Fuller Benton and Joseph Warren Phinney streamlined it, making it a popular version of Old English.

Duc De Berry

ABCDEFGHIJKLMNOPQRSTUVWXYZ
abcdefghijklmnopqrstuvwxyz
1234567890 !@#?:;"'*♂

Foundry: Linotype
Designer: Gottfried Pott
Designer Nationality: German
Date: 1990

German designer Gottfried Pott created Duc De Berry as part of the Type Before Gutenberg program, for which Linotype invited lettering artists to create typefaces based on historical handwriting styles. It is a decorative, blackletter font in the style of medieval bastarda scripts.

Engravers Old English BT

ABCDEFGHIJKLMNOPQRSTUVWXYZ
abcdefghijklmnopqrstuvwxyz
1234567890 !@#?:;"'*&

Foundry: Bitstream
Designer: Morris Fuller Benton
Designer Nationality: American
Date: 1901

Morris Fuller Benton created this archetypal blackletter typeface for American Type Founders at the turn of the 20th century; it was designed as a development upon his earlier Wedding Text font, which is very similar in style. This version is a contemporary digitization by Bitstream.

Fette Fraktur

ABCDEFGHIJKLMNOPQRSTUVWXYZ
abcdefghijklmnopqrstuvwxyz
1234567890 !@#?:;"'*&

Foundry: Weber
Designer: Johann Christian Bauer
Designer Nationality: German
Date: 1850

Johann Christian Bauer designed this heavy blackletter typeface in 1850. Fette Fraktur was first published by the Weber foundry in 1875; many subsequent versions have since been released by numerous foundries worldwide. Its bold weight and complex letterforms are best suited for display use.

Fette Gotisch

ABCDEFGHIJKLMNOPQRSTUVWXYZ
abcdefghijklmnopqrstuvwxyz
1234567890 !@#?:;"'*&

Foundry: Bauer
Designer: Friedrich Wilhelm Bauer
Designer Nationality: German
Date: c. 875

Published by a variety of foundries since its creation, Fette Gotisch was first cut in c. 1975 by Friedrich Wilhelm Bauer. Son of the founder of the Bauer type foundry, he went on to establish Bauer & Co in 1880 and designed several other blackletter fonts during his career.

Frakto

𝔄𝔅𝔆𝔇𝔈𝔉𝔊𝔥𝔍𝔍𝔎𝔏𝔐𝔑𝔒𝔓𝔔𝔕𝔖𝔗𝔘𝔙𝔚𝔛𝔜𝔝
abcdefghijklmnopqrstuvwxyz
1234567890 !@#?:;"*&

This contemporary interpretation of the Fraktur type tradition, which originated in 16th-century Germany, was created by Dutch designer Julius de Goede

for Linotype in 2003. Featuring slightly condensed and upright letterforms, Frakto displays a clear calligraphic influence throughout.

Foundry: Linotype
Designer: Julius de Goede
Designer Nationality: Dutch
Date: 2003

Fraktur

𝔄𝔅𝔆𝔇𝔈𝔉𝔊𝔥𝔍𝔍𝔎𝔏𝔐𝔑𝔒𝔓𝔔𝔕𝔖𝔗𝔘𝔙𝔚𝔛𝔜𝔝
abcdefghijklmnopqrstuvwxyz
1234567890 !@#?:;"*&

This Bitstream interpretation of Fraktur is based on Linotype Luthersche Fraktur, probably created in the design studio at Stempel, Germany, which was

itself a revival of a typeface designed by Erasmus Luther in 1708. It is more legible than other examples of Fraktur but is still best suited for display use.

Foundry: Bitstream
Designer: Unknown
Date: 1708 / 1990–93

Goudy Text

𝔄𝔅𝔆𝔇𝔈𝔉𝔊𝔥𝔍𝔍𝔎𝔏𝔐𝔑𝔒𝔓𝔔𝔕𝔖𝔗𝔘𝔙𝔚𝔜𝔝
abcdefghijklmnopqrstuvwxyz
1234567890 !@#?:;"*&

Goudy Text is based on the forty-two-line Gutenberg Bible. Frederic W. Goudy first employed the blackletter type in 1928 in a Christmas card, using

type cast at his foundry. It was originally known as Goudy Black, but Monotype sought permission to copy the face and to change its name to Goudy Text.

Foundry: Monotype
Designer: Frederic W. Goudy
Designer Nationality: American
Date: 1928

ITC Honda

ABCDEFGHIJKLMNOPQRSTUVWXYZ
abcdefghijklmnopqrstuvwxyz
1234567890 !?:;"*&

US typeface designers Ronne Bonder and Tom Carnase designed this distinctive, Fraktur-inspired sans serif blackletter face in 1970. Carnase often

worked closely with Herb Lubalin (see p. 62), one of the founders of the International Typeface Corporation (ITC). ITC Honda has a single weight.

Foundry: ITC
Designer: Ronne Bonder / Tom Carnase
Designer Nationality: American
Date: 1970

Linotext

ABCDEFGHIJKLMNOPQRSTUVWXYZ
abcdefghijklmnopqrstuvwxyz
1234567890 !@#?:;”’*&

American Type Founders initially released this heavy, ornamental blackletter script font in 1901 under the name "Wedding Text." It was renamed "Linotext" when it was adapted to work with Linotype machines; many other foundries also released metal versions copied from the original designs.

Foundry: American Type Founders
Designer: Morris Fuller Benton
Designer Nationality: American
Date: 1901 / 1924

Linotype Dala

ABCDEFGHIJKLMNOPQRSTUVWXYZ
abcdefghijklmnopqrstuvwxyz
1234567890 !@#?:;”’*&

Swedish designer Bo Berndal created this quirky, Fraktur-inspired blackletter script influenced by Scandinavian folktales in 1999. Many of Dala's letters feature distinctive double kinks, such as the "T," "w," "z," and "y." It comes with an ornamental frame typeface and dingbats.

Foundry: Linotype
Designer: Bo Berndal
Designer Nationality: Swedish
Date: 1999

Linotype Richmond

ABCDEFGHIJKLMNOPQRSTUVWXY
abcdefghijklmnopqrstuvwxyz
1234567890 !@#?:;”*&

The newspaper art director, type designer, and caricaturist Richard Yeend has designed more than twenty typefaces—mostly for Linotype—including this gothic, medieval-style blackletter. Richmond is available in two styles: a solid version, Fraktur, and an inlaid version, Zierschrift.

Foundry: Linotype
Designer: Richard Yeend
Designer Nationality: British
Date: 2002

Linotype Textur

ABCDEFGHIJKLMNOPQRSTUVWXYZ
abcdefghijklmnopqrstuvwxyz
1234567890 !@#?:;”*&

Textur is an extremely heavy ornate and intricate blackletter typeface by British designer Roland John Goulsbra. It comes in two styles: Gotisch, the regular, and Lombardisch, which has wider, more decorative capitals, including a "J" whose tail more than doubles the standard cap height.

Foundry: Linotype
Designer: Roland John Goulsbra
Designer Nationality: British
Date: 2002

Luthersche Fraktur

𝕬𝕭𝕮𝕯𝕰𝕱𝕲𝕳𝕴𝕵𝕶𝕷𝕸𝕹𝕺𝕻𝕼𝕽𝕾𝕿𝖀𝖁𝖂𝖃𝖄𝖅
abcdefghijklmnopqrstuvwxyz
1234567890 !@#?:;"*&

Foundry: Linotype
Designer: Erasmus Luther / Linotype Design Studio
Designer Nationality: German
Date: 1708 / 1996

Luthersche Fraktur is an ornate blackletter designed by the Linotype Design Studio and based on type drawn by Erasmus Luther in 1708. Linotype's version is lighter and crisper than Luther's original and is available in a single weight. Many other foundries have their own versions.

Mariage

𝔄𝔅ℭ𝔇𝔈𝔉𝔊𝔥𝔍𝔍𝔎𝔏𝔐𝔑𝔒𝔓𝔔𝔕𝔖𝔗𝔘𝔙𝔚𝔛𝔜ℨ
abcdefghijklmnopqrstuvwxyz
1234567890 !@#?:;"*&

Foundry: American Type Founders
Designer: Morris Fuller Benton
Designer Nationality: American
Date: 1907

Mariage, Morris Fuller Benton's Old English blackletter typeface designed for American Type Founders in 1901, was also released under the name "Wedding Text." The Old English style, which dates to the work of Wynken de Worde in 1498, was a popular choice for 20th-century newspaper mastheads.

Monotype Engravers Old English

𝔄𝔅ℭ𝔇𝔈𝔉𝔊𝔥𝔍𝔍𝔎𝔏𝔐𝔑𝔒𝔓𝔔𝔕𝔖𝔗𝔘𝔙𝔚𝔛𝔜ℨ
abcdefghijklmnopqrstuvwxyz
1234567890 !@#?:;"*&

Foundry: Monotype
Designer: Morris Fuller Benton / Monotype Studio
Designer Nationality: American
Date: 1901 / c. 1910

Part of Monotype's Engravers collection, this Old English was first designed by Morris Fuller Benton in 1901 for American Type Founders and was based on steel plate engravers lettering. It is a heavy blackletter font, available in a single weight, and evocative of gothic, medieval writing styles.

Monotype Old English Text

𝔄𝔅ℭ𝔇𝔈𝔉𝔊𝔥𝔍𝔍𝔎𝔏𝔐𝔑𝔒𝔓𝔔𝔕𝔖𝔗𝔘𝔙𝔚𝔛𝔜ℨ
abcdefghijklmnopqrstuvwxyz
1234567890 !@#?:;"*&

Foundry: Monotype
Designer: William Caslon / Monotype Studio
Designer Nationality: British
Date: c. 1760 / 1935

Caslon Black, a blackletter designed by William Caslon c. 1760, was the source material for Monotype's Old English, which was first released in 1935 and digitized in the 1990s. American Type Founders' Cloister Black (1904) was an earlier interpretation of the same Caslon face, one of many.

Neudoerffer Fraktur

ABCDEFGHIJKLMNOPQRSTUVWXYZ
abcdefghijklmnopqrstuvwxyz
1234567890 !@#?:;"*&

Foundry: Linotype
Designer: Hellmut G. Bomm
Designer Nationality: German
Date: 2009

Neudoerffer Fraktur is a blackletter script based on Johan Neudörffer the Elder's writing manual of 1538 and his design of the Fraktur type style he created with Albrecht Dürer and Hieronymus Andreä. Hellmut G. Bomm's adaptation includes four versions, which each feature a variation on the initial flourish.

Notre Dame

ABCDEFGHIJKLMNOPQRSTUVWXYZ
abcdefghijklmnopqrstuvwxyz
1234567890 !@#?:;"*&

Foundry: Linotype
Designer: Karlgeorg Hoefer
Designer Nationality: German
Date: 1993

Notre Dame is a blackletter script informed by the shapes found in traditional liturgical writings. It was designed as part of Linotype's Type Before Gutenberg program, which invited contemporary calligraphers to revise historical handwriting styles for digital publication.

Old English

ABCDEFGHIJKLMNOPQRSTUVWXYZ
abcdefghijklmnopqrstuvwxyz
1234567890 !@#?:;"*&

Foundry: Monotype
Designer: Monotype Studio
Date: 1935

Old English is a blackletter script inspired by the textura forms of Europe's early printed manuscripts. Unlike most blackletter revivals, Old English features a long "s," a prominent vertical figure that fell out of favor at the start of the 18th century. It is ideal for use in certificates and diplomas.

Old English (Let)

ABCDEFGHIJKLMNOPQRSTUVWXYZ
abcdefghijklmnopqrstuvwxyz
1234567890 !@#?:;"*&

Foundry: Monotype
Designer: Monotype Studio
Date: c. 1990

Old English (Let) is a digital revival of Caslon Black, a blackletter font cast by William Caslon's foundry in the middle of the 18th century, which remained popular for centuries. The letterforms, designed in the textura style, feature spacious counters and high-contrast strokes for optimum readability.

Rockner

ABCDEFGHIJKLMNOPQRSTUVWXYZ
abcdefghijklmnopqrstuvwxyz
1234567890 !@s?:;ßäG

Rockner is a script designed in the Fraktur style, the most popular blackletter style that emerged from the manuscript traditions of northern Europe in the medieval period. The blackletter lines are broken up. Unlike the majority of Fraktur fonts, Rockner includes Regular, Medium, and Bold weights.

Foundry: Linotype
Designer: Julius de Goede
Designer Nationality: Dutch
Date: 2003

Rudolph

ABCDEFGHIJKLMNOPQRSTUVWXYZ
abcdefghijklmnopqrstuvwxyz
1234567890 !@#?:;"*ß

Rudolph is a blackletter script inspired by the Fraktur style of the 16th and 17th centuries. The structured lowercase forms feature thick, calligraphic terminals and high-contrast joints, while the uppercase characters exhibit embellishment typical of manuscript initials.

Foundry: Monotype
Designer: Julius de Goede
Designer Nationality: Dutch
Date: 1999

Sachsenwald

ABCDEFGHIJKLMNOPQRSTUVWXYZ
abcdefghijklmnopqrstuvwxyz
1234567890 !@#?:;"*&

Monotype's Sachsenwald is a revival and digitization of Berthold Wolpe's 20th-century decorative blackletter script of the same name. Revised by Toshi Omagari, as part of Monotype's Wolpe Collection, the updated design includes the addition of both Regular and Light weights.

Foundry: Monotype
Designer: Berthold Wolpe / Toshi Omagari
Designer Nationality: German / Japanese
Date: 1937 / 2017

San Marco

ABCDEFGHIJKLMNOPQRSTUVWXYZ
abcdefghijklmnopqrstuvwxyz
1234567890 !@#?:;"*&

San Marco is a blackletter script designed for Linotype's Type Before Gutenberg program, for which a series of designers revived historical type styles. San Marco's gothic letterforms were inspired by those found on the facade of St Mark's Basilica in Venice, Italy.

Foundry: Linotype
Designer: Karlgeorg Hoefer
Designer Nationality: German
Date: 1990

Walbaum Fraktur

𝕬𝕭𝕮𝕯𝕰𝕱𝕲𝕳𝕴𝕵𝕶𝕷𝕸𝕹𝕺𝕻𝕼𝕽𝕾𝕿𝖀𝖁𝖂𝖃𝖄3
abcdefghijklmnopqrstuvwxyz
1234567890 !@§?.:;"*&

Foundry: Berthold
Designer: Justus Erich Walbaum
Designer Nationality: German
Date: *c.* 1800 / 1918

Walbaum Fraktur is a blackletter script designed by prominent punchcutter Justus Erich Walbaum at the start of the 19th century. The font, cast by Berthold more than a century later, features the extreme stroke contrasts and decorative capitals typical of the Fraktur style.

Wedding Text

𝔄𝔅ℭ𝔇𝔈𝔉𝔊ℌ𝔍𝔍𝔎𝔏𝔐𝔑𝔒𝔓𝔔ℜ𝔖𝔗𝔘𝔙𝔚𝔛𝔜ℨ
abcdefghijklmnopqrstuvwxyz
1234567890 !@#?.:;"*&

Foundry: American Type Founders
Designer: Morris Fuller Benton
Designer Nationality: American
Date: 1901

Wedding Text is a blackletter script designed in a single style and intended, as its name suggests, for formal occasions. Intensely popular and widely imitated, Morris Fuller Benton's letterforms combine formal structure in the lowercase with decorative flourishes in the capitals.

Wilhelm Klingspor Gotisch

𝔄𝔅ℭ𝔇𝔈𝔉𝔊ℌ𝔍𝔍𝔎𝔏𝔐𝔑𝔒𝔓𝔔ℜ𝔖𝔗𝔘𝔙𝔚𝔛𝔜ℨ
abcdefghijklmnopqrstuvwxyz
1234567890 !@#?.:;"*&

Foundry: Klingspor
Designer: Rudolf Koch
Designer Nationality: German
Date: 1925

Wilhelm Klingspor Gotisch is a blackletter script designed in the textura style. It is named after the co-owner of the type foundry for which Rudolph Koch produced the font. The design, one of the most significant of its kind, is notable for its refined forms and meticulous spacing.

Wittenberger Fraktur

𝔄𝔅ℭ𝔇𝔈𝔉𝔊ℌ𝔍𝔍𝔎𝔏𝔐𝔑𝔒𝔓𝔔ℜ𝔖𝔗𝔘𝔙𝔚𝔛𝔜3
abcdefghijklmnopqrstuvwxyz
1234567890 !@#?.:;"*&

Foundry: Monotype
Designer: Monotype Studio
Date: 1906

An adaptation of Schul-Fraktur, released by the Schelter & Giesecke foundry in the late 19th century, Wittenberger Fraktur is a blackletter script designed in two weights, Regular and Semibold, and is one of the earliest typefaces Monotype produced. There are two "s" versions: a long "s" and a round, or final, "s."

Alfie

ABCDEFGHIJKLMNOPQRSTUVWXYZ
abcdefghijklmnopqrstuvwxyz
1234567890 !@#?:;"*&

Foundry: Monotype
Designer: Jim Ford
Designer Nationality: American
Date: 2018

Alfie is a jaunty, curvaceous face with a decidedly 1950s' vibe, which takes inspiration from Emil J. Klumpp's font Murray Hill (1956). Alfie is a connecting script that is available in four variations: Casual (regular and small caps), Script (regular), and Informal (regular).

Amanda

ABCDEFGHIJKLMNOPQRSTUVWXYZ
abcdefghijklmnopqrstuvwxyz
1234567890 !@#?:;"*&

Foundry: Monotype
Designer: Tom Rickner
Designer Nationality: American
Date: 1996

Amanda is a well-crafted calligraphic script that is one of a handful of fonts designed by Tom Rickner. A co-founder of Ascender, he oversaw the development of the first TrueType fonts that were shipped with Apple Computer's System 7 operating system in 1991. Amanda is available in two weights.

Angeletta

ABCDEFGHIJKLMNOPQRSTUV
abcdefghijklmnopqrstuvwxyz
1234567890 !@#?:;"*&

Foundry: Monotype
Designer: Robert E. Leuschke
Designer Nationality: American
Date: 2018

The former Hallmark Cards lettering artist and prolific designer Robert E. Leuschke created Angeletta. It is an exuberant semiconnecting script available in a single weight with briskly drawn loops and dashes reminiscent of hand-lettered forms, and is ideal for greeting cards, menus, packaging, or posters.

Arioso

ABCDEFGHIJKLMNOPQRSTUVWXYZ
abcdefghijklmnopqrstuvwxyz
1234567890 !@#?:;"*&

Foundry: Linotype
Designer: Gottfried Pott
Designer Nationality: German
Date: 1995

Arioso's combination of Roman square capitals and Carolingian lowercase make it similar to other Italic Chancery typefaces, such as ITC Zapf Chancery by Hermann Zapf (see p. 574). Its calligraphic style originates from an early form of old face developed in Italy during the 14th and 15th centuries.

Augusta

ABCDEFGHIJKLMNOPQRSTUVWXYZ
abcdefghijklmnopqrstuvwxyz
1234567890 !@#?.;"*&

Foundry: Monotype
Designer: Julius de Goede
Designer Nationality: Dutch
Date: 1999

Augusta is based on the chancery style, which is a cursive Italian hand originating from 15th- and 16th-century Italian writing masters such as

Giambattista Palatino and Giovanantonio Tagliente. It is available in three variations: Augusta Regular, Augusta Cancellaresca, and Augusta Schnurkl.

Basilica

ABCDEFGHIJKLMNOPQRSTUVWXYZ
abcdefghijklmnopqrstuvwxyz
1234567890 !@#?:;"*&

Foundry: Monotype
Designer: Monotype Studio
Date: 1990

This calligraphic script with ecclesiastical influences bridges the gap between historical and contemporary. Basilica takes its name from a

rectangular building with double colonnades and a semicircular apse. St Peter's Basilica in Rome is often considered to be the largest church in the world.

Belltrap

ABCDEFGHIJKLMNOPQRSTUVWXYZ
abcdefghijklmnopqrstuvwxyz
1234567890 !@#?:;"*&

Foundry: ITC
Designer: Bo Berndal
Designer Nationality: Swedish
Date: 2006

Belltrap is one of the lesser known designs by Bo Berndal, Sweden's master typographer and founder of the design and advertising agency Berndal,

Ingemarsson, Günther & Günther (BIGG). It is a low-key but beautifully crafted calligraphic script available in a single weight.

Bendigo

ABCDEFGHIJKLMNOPQRSTUVWXYZ
abcdefghijklmnopqrstu wxyz
1234567890 !@#?:;"*&

Foundry: Letraset
Designer: Phill Grimshaw
Designer Nationality: British
Date: 1993

Bendigo is an energetic script font with generous uppercase characters that fit well with the more reserved lowercase characters, both of which slant

to the right, emphasizing its dynamic nature. The typeface is best suited to headline use, and it is advisable to use it at a size of 14 point or more.

Bernhard Tango

ABCDEFGHIJKLMNOPQRSTUVWXYZ
abcdefghijklmnopqrstuvwxyz
1234567890 !@#?:;"'*&

Foundry: American Type Founders
Designer: Lucian Bernhard
Designer Nationality: German
Date: 1931

Bernhard Tango is a very open and delicate non-connected script face that is available in a single regular weight. It was designed in 1931 but not cut until *c.* 1933. The typeface has a companion set of swash capitals that was issued in 1939 by Lettergieterij Amsterdam as the font Aigrette.

Bernhardt Standard

ABCDEFGHIJKLMNOPQRSTUVWXYZ
abcdefghijklmnopqrstuvwxyz
1234567890 !@#?:;"'*&

Foundry: Linotype
Designer: Julius de Goede
Designer Nationality: Dutch
Date: 2003

One of the subcategories of blackletter, this is a flowing Bastarda script face with elements of the wide-nibbed pen stroke within its forms. Bernhardt Standard is available in two weights—its highly calligraphic style makes it most suitable for formal applications.

Bible Script

ABCDEFGHIJKLMNOPQRSTUVWXYZ
abcdefghijklmnopqrstuvwxyz
1234567890 !@#?:;"'*&

Foundry: Letraset
Designer: Richard Bradley
Designer Nationality: British
Date: 1979

Richard Bradley created Bible Script in close conjunction with Letraset's Colin Brignall. It is a modest, no-frills calligraphic script face that is enhanced by a textured edge, swash alternate characters, and additional flourishes. The typeface is available in a single regular weight.

Bickley Script

ABCDEFGHIJKLMNOPQRSTUVW
abcdefghijklmnopqrstuvwxyz
1234567890 !@#?:;"'*&

Foundry: Letraset
Designer: Alan Meeks
Designer Nationality: British
Date: 1986

Bickley Script is a poised and elegant, flowing script that resembles handwriting. It combines expressive uppercase characters with a more reserved lowercase. The font was created by ex-Letraset senior designer Alan Meeks, and was released by the new company formed when Letraset and ITC merged.

Hermann Zapf

The prolific career of German type designer and calligrapher Hermann Zapf spanned more than five decades and the creation of more than 200 typefaces, including classics such as Palatino, Optima, Zapf Chancery, and Zapfino.

Zapf started designing typefaces in the 1930s, creating his first printed font—a fraktur type called Gilgengart—at the age of twenty. During World War II, he served as a cartographer in the German army. Afterwards he joined the esteemed D. Stempel AG type foundry, and as art director there he gained international attention for the first time for his Palatino typeface released in 1950. Published within a limited-edition journal *Feder und Stichel* (*Pen and Graver*), it had an immediate impact and because of demand was soon reprinted in German and English, impressing the typographic community in his native Germany and overseas. An exhibition of his work was held soon after Palatino's release at the Cooper Union in New York in 1951, where his outstanding skills were celebrated.

Zapf continued to work at Stempel, where he also created the elegant sans serif Optima (see p. 296). Released in 1958, this refined humanist sans serif with elegant flared details is widely used and was inspired by etched grave plates he saw on the floor of Florence's Santa Croce church while on a trip to Italy.

In the 1950s, Zapf turned his skills to book design, working on several titles that enhanced his reputation even further. In the 1960s, he was one of the first designers to explore the nature of computerized typefaces and typesetting. Although the norm today, this was then in its infancy and seen as radical. In the early 1970s, he designed one of the first typefaces for computer-based typesetting. In 1976, Zapf took up a professorship at the Rochester Institute of Technology, New York to teach the principles of the subject. In later life, he created digital typefaces for computer programs for companies such as IBM and Xerox, and worked with Aaron Burns and Herb Lubalin in the mid 1970s creating typographical computer software.

Date: 1928–2015
Nationality: German
Notable typefaces:
Palatino (see p. 138)
Optima (see p. 296)
Zapf Chancery (see p. 581)
Zapfino Extra (see p. 586)

Below. Sketched on the back of bank notes, Zapf's initial designs of letterforms from etched graved plates in Florence's Santa Croce church would lead to the creation of his hugely successful Optima sans serif typeface.

Opposite, middle left. Optima employed on a German Deutsche Bundepost stamp, 1976.

Opposite, bottom left. Hermann Zapf, designer of more than 200 typefaces including the ever popular Palatino and Optima designs.

abcdefghijklmnopqrstuvwxyz
abcdefghijklmnopqrstuvwxyz
abcdefghijklmnopqrstuvwxyz

yz

ABCDEFGHIJKLMNOPQRSTUVWXYZ
ABCDEFGHIJKLMNOPQRSTUVWXYZ
ABCDEFGHIJKLMNOPQRSTUVWXYZ

Printed in Germany. Our type designs are fully protected by international copyright

Above. Specimen page for Hermann Zapf's Palatino Old Style serif by the Stempel Foundry, *c.* 1960, amed after the 16th-century Italian calligrapher Giovanni Battista Palatino.

Below. Advert by Herb Lubalin for Zapf's iconic ITC Zapf Dingbats typeface appearing in volume 5 of *U&lc journal*, 1978.

Above. Page detail from Hermann Zapf's 1968 book *Manuale Typographicum*, consisting of 100 typographical arrangements by Zapf and essays on type, typography and printing.

Blado

ABCDEFGHIJKLMNOPQRSTUVWXYZ
abcdefghijklmnopqrstuvwxyz
1234567890 !@#?:;"*&

Foundry: Monotype
Designer: Ludovico degli Arrighi / Stanley Morison
Designer Nationality: Italian / British
Date: 1539 / 1923

The italic companion to Poliphilus (1499), Blado is based on the italic created by the calligrapher Ludovico degli Arrighi for Aldus Manutius in 1526.

Despite not being considered good enough at the time, the well-crafted Old Style italic was revived by Stanley Morison for Monotype in 1923.

Boscribe

ABCDEFGHIJKLMNOPQRSTUVWXYZ
abcdefghijklmnopqrstuvwxyz
1234567890 !@#?:;"*&

Foundry: Monotype
Designer: Bo Berndal
Designer Nationality: Swedish
Date: 1989

When Bo Berndal worked as an apprentice in a printing shop, he spent time copying Garamond Italic to improve his terrible handwriting. Later, he created Boscribe inspired by Paul Standard, the US calligrapher, and Alfred Fairbank, the British calligrapher and advocate of handwriting reform.

Brigida

ABCDEFGHIJKLMNOPQRSTUVWXYZ
abcdefghijklmnopqrstuvwxyz
1234567890 !@#?:;"*&

Foundry: Monotype
Designer: Bo Berndal
Designer Nationality: Swedish
Date: 1995

Brigida is named after one of the six patron saints of Europe, St Bridget of Sweden, who was famed for her visions. Swedish designer Bo Berndal's modest, single-weight calligraphic script was influenced by a European letterform that was commonly used in Sweden between 1350 and 1500.

Cancellaresca Script

ABCDEFGHIJKLMNOPQRSTUVWXYZ
abcdefghijklmnopqrstuvwxyz
1234567890 !@#?:;" *&

Foundry: ITC
Designer: Alan Meeks
Designer Nationality: British
Date: 1982

Letraset stalwart Alan Meeks designed this graceful, finely crafted, and rather decorative calligraphic script face. Cancellaresca Script has some unusual detailing, along with flowing uppercase letterforms that are combined with a more reserved lowercase.

Captain Quill

ABCDEFGHIJKLMNOPQRSTUVWXYZ
abcdefghijklmnopqrstuvwxyz
1234567890 !@#?:;"*&

Foundry: Ascender
Designer: Jim Ford
Designer Nationality: American
Date: 2008

This jaunty calligraphic script font is based on the handwriting of a fictional pirate figure Paul Pierce—aka Captain Quill, the forgotten son of Blackbeard, and his 12th wife—as dreamed up by Ascender's Jim Ford. Suitably swashbuckling, it has an authentic rough texture and an old-world feel.

Carmela

ABCDEFGHIJKLMNOPQRSTUVWXYZ
abcdefghijklmnopqrstuvwxyz
1234567890 !@#?:;"*&

Foundry: Monotype
Designer: Philip Bouwsma
Designer Nationality: American
Date: 2006

The US type designer and calligrapher Philip Bouwsma has an enduring love of traditional broad-pen calligraphy found in historic scripts. This inspired Carmela, a calligraphic low-key connecting script with very open counters, which is available in a single weight.

Cataneo BT

ABCDEFGHIJKLMNOPQRSTUVWXYZ
abcdefghijklmnopqrstuvwxyz
1234567890 !@#?:;"*&

Foundry: Bitstream
Designer: Richard Lipton / Jacqueline Sakwa
Designer Nationality: American
Date: 1993

This elegant cursive serif was inspired by the work of 16th-century Italian writing master Bennardino Cataneo, who is best known for his single manuscript copybook of twenty leaves. It has three weights—Light, Regular, and Bold—as well as complimentary swash characters and extensions.

Codex

ABCDEFGHIJKLMNOPQRSTUVWXYZ
abcdefghijklmnopqrstuvwxyz
1234567890 !@#?:;"*&

Foundry: Weber
Designer: Georg Trump
Designer Nationality: German
Date: 1954

The Codex handwriting font is based on 13th-century German gothic script and its uppercase letters are extremely large compared to the lowercase characters, making it ideal for contrast in short pieces of text. Bitstream released a digitized version in the 1990s called Calligraphic 421.

Coptek

ABCDEFGHIJKLMNOPQRSTUVWXYZ
abcdefghijklmnopqrstuvwxyz
1234567890 !?:; "*&

Foundry: Letraset
Designer: David Quay
Designer Nationality: British
Date: 1992

Coptek derives its name from its combination of a high-tech, computer-generated look and the flowing lines of a traditional copperplate script. The uppercase characters fit well with its lowercase characters, whose letters are joined together in the style of handwriting.

Delphin

ABCDEFGHIJKLMNOPQRSTUVWXYZ
abcdefghijklmnopqrstuvwxyz
1234567890 !@#?:; "*&

Foundry: Weber
Designer: Georg Trump
Designer Nationality: German
Date: 1951

The German type designer and educator Georg Trump designed Delphin for Weber in 1951. It is unusual in its pairing of upright capitals with slanted calligraphic lowercase letterforms. The typeface was originally developed for hot-metal typesetting, and has since been digitized.

Diskus

ABCDEFGHIJKLMNOPQRSTUV
abcdefghijklmnopqrstuvwxyz
1234567890 !@#?:; "*&

Foundry: Stempel
Designer: Martin Wilke
Designer Nationality: German
Date: 1938

Diskus is a high-contrast, ribbon-style script typeface available in two weights, Mager (lean) and Halbfett (medium-fat). Its creator, German type designer Martin Wilke, created a varied range of attractive script fonts for several foundries during his long career.

Elegy

ABCDEFGHIJKLMNOPQRST
abcdefghijklmnopqrstuvwxyz
1234567890 !@#?:; "*&

Foundry: Monotype
Designer: Ed Benguiat / Jim Wasco
Designer Nationality: American
Date: 2010

This elaborate typeface is based on a hand-lettered logotype created for ITC by Ed Benguiat (see p. 514). It was requested regularly by the foundry's customers as a usable typeface, and Jim Wasco of Monotype worked for two years to develop its complex design into a fully functioning font.

Fairbank

ABCDEFGHIJKLMNOPQRSTUVWXYZ
abcdefghijklmnopqrstuvwxyz
1234567890 !@#?:;"'*&

Foundry: Monotype
Designer: Alfred Fairbank / Carl Crossgrove / Robin Nicholas
Designer Nationality: British
Date: 2004

Fairbank is a revival of a font commissioned by Stanley Morison from Alfred Fairbank in the early 20th century—it was intended as an italic for Bembo, but was never used. Robin Nicholas and Carl Crossgrove breathed new life into its letterforms with this respectful digitization.

Gravura

ABCDEFGHIJKLMNOPQRSTUV
abcdefghijklmnopqrstuvwxyz
1234567890 !@# ?:;"'*&

Foundry: Letraset
Designer: Phill Grimshaw
Designer Nationality: British
Date: 1995

Gravura is a classic copperplate script with perfect strokes and proportions. It has intricate capitals and an elegant and perfectly linked lowercase. Gravura is one of many typefaces created for Letraset by Phill Grimshaw under the watchful eye of the foundry's type director Colin Brignall.

Hamada

ABCDEFGHIJKLMNOPQRSTUV
abcdefghijklmnopqrstuvwxyz
1234567890 !@#?:;"'*&

Foundry: Linotype
Designer: Gaynor Goffe
Designer Nationality: British
Date: 2007

An elegant script typeface based on the work of English calligrapher Gaynor Goffe, Hamada captures the unmistakable irregularities of the pen marks on the page, allowing the ink to edge out from the contours. Most of the characters have alternate versions, including ligatures and ending swashes.

ITC Braganza

ABCDEFGHIJKLMNOPQRSTUVWXYZ
abcdefghijklmnopqrstuvwxyz
1234567890 !@#?:;"'*&

Foundry: ITC
Designer: Phill Grimshaw
Designer Nationality: British
Date: 1995

This refined, upright script is inspired by handwritten manuscript styles of the 16th century, and is available in Light and Regular weights. ITC Braganza takes its name from Catherine, Duchess of Braganza, who was a prominent figure in Portuguese society and wife of King Charles II of England.

ITC Cali

ABCDEFGHIJKLMNOPQRSTUVWXYZ
abcdefghijklmnopqrstuvwxyz
1234567890 !@#?:;"*&

Luis Siquot based ITC Cali on his own handwriting using a pen designed for left-handed calligraphers, and decided to leave in some of the imperfections to avoid an overtly mechanical look. The unusual notches in the strokes are intended to imitate the texture of writing on a rough cotton paper stock.

Foundry: ITC
Designer: Luis Siquot
Designer Nationality: Argentinian
Date: 2004

ITC Chivalry

ABCDEFGHIJKLMNOPQRSTUVWXYZ
abcdefghijklmnopqrstuvwxyz
1234567890 !@#?:;"*&

ITC Chivalry is a very legible calligraphic hybrid combining roman capitals with italic lowercase letters. It was created by digitizing drawings made using a flat-nib pen on textured watercolor paper. Designer Rob Leuschke added a companion set of more decorative blackletter caps for display use.

Foundry: ITC
Designer: Rob Leuschke
Designer Nationality: American
Date: 2003

ITC Freemouse

ABCDEFGHIJKLMNOPQRSTUVWXYZ
abcdefghijklmnopqrstuvwxyz
1234567890 !@#?:;"*&

Serbian font designer Slobodan Miladinov captures the expressiveness of calligraphic writing with ITC Freemouse, which is named after the freehand technique he used to create it. The result is a lively script with a contrast of stroke and curve similar to that of a chancery italic.

Foundry: ITC
Designer: Slobodan Miladinov
Designer Nationality: Serbian
Date: 1998

ITC Grimshaw Hand

ABCDEFGHIJKLMNOPQRSTUVWXYZ
abcdefghijklmnopqrstuvwxyz
1234567890 !@#?:;"*&

This lively script typeface has lots of personality and is based on Phill Grimshaw's own handwriting. Grimshaw designed it at a time when he was playing the guitar and mandolin, and it is easy to detect the musical influences in the typeface's enthusiastic strokes.

Foundry: ITC
Designer: Phill Grimshaw
Designer Nationality: British
Date: 1995

ITC Hedera

ABCDEFGHIJKLMNOPQRSTUVWXYZ
abcdefghijklmnopqrstuvwxyz
1234567890 !@#?:;"*&

Foundry: ITC
Designer: Olivera Stojadinovic
Designer Nationality: Serbian
Date: 2002

ITC Hedera by Serbian designer Olivera Stojadinovic began as a set of initials drawn with a makeshift pen (a pair of flexible metal strips tied to some wood) as part of a book design project. The finished font, a rough exuberant calligraphic script, is available in one weight.

ITC Rastko

ABCDEFGHIJKLMNOPQRSTUVWXYZ
abcdefghijklmnopqrstuvwxyz
1234567890 !@#?:;"*&

Foundry: ITC
Designer: Olivera Stojadinovic
Designer Nationality: Serbian
Date: 2001

Named after the Serbian poet Rastko Petrović, ITC Rastko started out as capital letters drawn for a book. An elegant, calligraphic script, it features wide capitals with flourishes and many fine details that give a spontaneous feel and are the result of forms drawn with a pointed pen.

ITC Regallia

ABCDEFGHIJKLMNOPQRSTUVWXY
abcdefghijklmnopqrstuvwxyz
1234567890 !@#?:;"*&

Foundry: ITC
Designer: Phill Grimshaw
Designer Nationality: British
Date: 1998

ITC Regallia is a calligraphic script drawn by the British designer Phill Grimshaw, a graduate of the Royal College of Art. It features many ligatures, decorative capitals, and more reserved, yet elegant lowercase letters. Available in a single regular weight, Regallia is graceful and legible.

ITC Zapf Chancery

ABCDEFGHIJKLMNOPQRSTUVWXYZ
abcdefghijklmnopqrstuvwxyz
1234567890 !@#?:;"*&

Foundry: ITC
Designer: Hermann Zapf
Designer Nationality: German
Date: 1979

Zapf Chancery comes in four weights with italics and debuted in the June 1979 issue of ITC's publication *U&lc*. For Zapf Chancery, Hermann Zapf (see p. 574) put his calligraphy skills to use and took inspiration from Renaissance scripts. The Medium Italic is a system font on most computers.

Klang

ABCDEFGHIJKLMNOPQRSTUVWXYZ
abcdefghijklmnopqrstuvwxyz
1234567890 !@#?:;"'*&

Foundry: Monotype
Designer: Will Carter
Designer Nationality: British
Date: 1955

British typographer and printer Will Carter designed Klang for Monotype in 1955. It is a slightly inclined, heavy calligraphic sans serif available in a single weight. In 1960, British type foundry Stephenson, Blake & Co. released a bold cut, but unlike the regular, it has not been digitized.

Laser

ABCDEFGHIJKLMNOPQRSTUVWXYZ
abcdefghijklmnopqrstuvwxyz
1234567890 !?:;"'*&

Foundry: Letraset
Designer: Martin Wait
Designer Nationality: British
Date: 1987

Martin Wait designed Laser for Letraset in 1987. It is an energetic, inclined connecting script in a single, fairly heavy weight. Wait, who was born in Forest Gate, London in 1942, designed many typefaces for Letraset, including a decorative, display version of Laser called Laser Chrome.

Le Griffe

ABCDEFGHIJKLMNOPQRSTUVWXYZ
abcdefghijklmnopqrstuvwxyz
1234567890 !?:;"'*&

Foundry: Letraset
Designer: André-Michel Lubac
Designer Nationality: French
Date: 1973

French designer André-Michel Lubac created Le Griffe for Letraset in 1973. It is a classical, angular calligraphic script in a single weight. Digital versions are available from ITC and Elsner+Flake. Le Griffe has many alternate swash letters and is Lubac's sole font credit.

Lightnin'

ABCDEFGHIJKLMNOPQRSTUVWXYZ
abcdefghijklmnopqrstuvwxyz
1234567890 !?:;"'*&

Foundry: ITC
Designer: Alan Meeks
Designer Nationality: British
Date: 1994

Lightnin' is an angular, heavy script designed by former Letraset designer Alan Meeks. It is slightly inclined and features diagonal terminals, which give it a dynamic, energetic feel that is in keeping its name. Available in one weight, Lightnin' is best suited to display and headline usage.

Linotype Gaius

ABCDEFGHIJKLMNOPQRSTUVWXYZ
abcdefghijklmnopqrstuvwxyz
1234567890 !@#?:;"*&

Foundry: Linotype
Designer: Julius de Goede
Designer Nationality: Dutch
Date: 2002

Julius de Goede's Gaius is a versatile typeface. This attractive, calligraphic script offers the contrast that comes from being drawn with a broad-edged pen nib. It comes in two weights—Regular and Bold—each of which have alternate versions with beginning and ending swashes, and ligatures.

Linotype Gneisenauette

ABCDEFGHIJKLMNOPQRSTUVWXYZ
abcdefghijklmnopqrstuvwxyz
1234567890 !@#?:;"*&

Foundry: Linotype
Designer: Gustavs Andrejs Grinbergs
Designer Nationality: Latvian
Date: 1997

Heavy, angular, and condensed, Gneisenautte is a distinctive, connecting sans serif script available in four weights, from Light to Black, although the Light is of a color that would be considered Bold in most scripts. Each weight has an alternate cut with more exuberant letterforms.

Ludovico

ABCDEFGHIJKLMNOPQRSTUVWXYZ
abcdefghijklmnopqrstuvwxyz
1234567890 !@#?:;"*&

Foundry: Linotype
Designer: Philip Bouwsma
Designer Nationality: American
Date: 2007

US designer Philip Bouwsma's Ludovico is an angular, old-fashioned calligraphic script, which features elongated ascenders and descenders, a high x-height and capitals that are predominantly swashed. Ludovico comes in two styles: Smooth and the much rougher Woodcut.

Mantegna

ABCDEFGHIJKLMNOPQRSTUVWXYZ
abcdefghijklmnopqrstuvwxyz
1234567890 !@#?:;"*&

Foundry: Agfa
Designer: Philip Bouwsma
Designer Nationality: American
Date: 1994

Philip Bouwsma designed the single-weight, spiky calligraphic script Mantegna in 1994. It is available in italic only; however, it is an almost upright italic. The "e" features a distinctive horizontal line under its bowl. Since 2005, Bouwsma has released exclusively with Toronto-based Canada Type studio.

Medici Script

ABCDEFGHIJKLMNOPQRSTUVWXYZ
abcdefghijklmnopqrstuvwxyz
1234567890 !@#?:;"*&

Foundry: Linotype
Designer: Hermann Zapf
Designer Nationality: German
Date: 1971

Medici is a calligraphic script that takes its name from the prominent Medici family of Renaissance Florence. The refined letterforms, designed in a single style, imitate the strokes of a broad-edged pen and exhibit many of the details later featured in ITC Zapf Chancery.

Nuptial Script

ABCDEFGHIJKLMNOPQRSTUVWXYZ
abcdefghijklmnopqrstuvwxyz
1234567890 !@#?:;"*&

Foundry: Linotype
Designer: Edwin W. Shaar
Designer Nationality: American
Date: 1952

Nuptial Script is, as its name suggests, a calligraphic script designed exclusively for wedding invitations. Combining the shape of English copperplate types with Italian swash capitals, Edwin W. Shaar's design conveys opulence while maintaining maximum legibility in all sizes.

Ondine

ABCDEFGHIJKLMNOPQRSTUVWXYZ
abcdefghijklmnopqrstuvwxyz
1234567890 !@#?:;"*&

Foundry: Linotype
Designer: Adrian Frutiger
Designer Nationality: Swiss
Date: 1954

Ondine is a calligraphic script designed primarily for use in headlines, and is evocative of the humanist letterforms of 15th-century Florence. It is seemingly drawn with the broad nib of a pen, though Swiss designer Adrian Frutiger (see p. 290) actually cut the distinctive letterforms from paper with scissors.

Pristina

ABCDEFGHIJKLMNOPQRSTUVWXYZ
abcdefghijklmnopqrstuvwxyz
1234567890 !@#?:;"*&

Foundry: ITC
Designer: Phill Grimshaw
Designer Nationality: British
Date: 1994

Pristina is a calligraphic script designed to imitate the refined characteristics of calligraphic artistry. The font features expressive terminals and exaggerated strokes in upper- and lowercase forms and is designed to meet the demands of both text and display sizes.

Pyes Pa

ABCDEFGHIJKLMNOPQRSTUVWXYZ
abcdefghijklmnopqrstuvwxyz
1234567890 !@#?:;"*&

Foundry: The Suburbs
Designer: Tim Donaldson
Designer Nationality: New Zealander
Date: 2010

Pyes Pa is a script font that combines the dynamic stroke contrast of late 19th-century modern faces, such as Bodoni or Modern Didot, with the eloquent forms of calligraphy. Designed for display use, the Pyes Pa font family includes Headline, Poster, and Billboard styles.

Quill

ABCDEFGHIJKLMNOPQRSTUVWXYZ
abcdefghijklmnopqrstuvwxyz
1234567890 !@#?:;"*&

Foundry: Monotype
Designer: Monotype Design Studio
Date: 2005

Quill is a script face informed by the practice of broad-pen calligraphy during the Renaissance. The figures feature strong strokes, high-contrast junctures, sharp terminals, and angled stresses, mimicking the visual quality of forms drawn with the nib of a quill.

Sho

ABCDEFGHIJKLMNOPQRSTUVWXYZ
abcdefghijklmnopqrstuvwxyz
1234567890 !@#?:;"*&

Foundry: Linotype
Designer: Karlgeorg Hoefer
Designer Nationality: German
Date: 1992

Released as part of Linotype's Calligraphy for Print package, Sho is a script face designed in a single style and reminiscent of the thick, rounded brushstrokes of Japanese calligraphy. Its distinctive characters are intended for display uses, such as posters and headlines.

Supernova

ABCDEFGHIJKLMNOPQRSTUVWXYZ
abcdefghijklmnopqrstuvwxyz
1234567890 !@#?:;"*&

Foundry: Typotheque
Designer: Martina Flor
Designer Nationality: Argentinian
Date: 2013

Supernova is a script font family comprised of five weights, from Light to Black, alongside an expressive Poster version. The design, partly inspired by brush calligraphy, was conceived to combine the energy of a script with the adaptability and legibility of a Roman text face.

Tiranti Solid

ABCDEFGHIJKLMNOPQRSTUVWXYZ
abcdefghijklmnopqrstuvwxyz
1234567890 !@#?:;"&*

Foundry: ITC
Designer: Tony Forster
Designer Nationality: British
Date: 1993

Tiranti Solid is a calligraphic script and Tony Forster's revision of his earlier Tiranti font. Unlike the original design, in which the strokes were gently textured, Tiranti Solid is more substantial in its structure, and thus better suited to the demands of digital displays.

Veljovic Script

ABCDEFGHIJKLMNOPQRSTUVWXYZ
abcdefghijklmnopqrstuvwxyz
1234567890 !@#?:;"'&*

Foundry: Linotype
Designer: Jovica Veljović
Designer Nationality: Serbian
Date: 2009

Veljovic Script is a brush-style calligraphic font family that includes four weights, from Light to Bold, in both Latin and Cyrillic alphabets. Alongside its multiple styles, the font also includes a variety of alternates and more than 2,000 glyphs in each character set.

Vivaldi

ABCDEFGHIJKLMNOPQR
abcdefghijklmnopqrstuvwxyz
1234567890 !@#?:;"&*

Foundry: VGC
Designer: Friedrich Peter
Designer Nationality: German
Date: 1966

Vivaldi is a calligraphic script conceived for formal applications, such as invitations or certificates. The font's characters combine traditional calligraphic details, seen in the rhythmic strokes and flourishes, with the keen terminals that are commonly found in copperplate types.

Zapfino Extra

ABCDEFGHIJKLMNOPQRSTUVWXYZ
abcdefghijklmnopqrstuvwxyz
1234567890 !@#?:;"'&*

Foundry: Linotype
Designer: Hermann Zapf / Akira Kobayashi
Designer Nationality: German / Japanese
Date: 1998 / 2003

Zapfino Extra is an expansion of the Zapfino script created by Hermann Zapf (see p. 574) in 1998. Designed in collaboration with Akira Kobayashi, Zapfino Extra is comprised of eleven styles, in contrast to the original four, and features a range of alternative characters ligatures, and flourishes.

Volina

ABCDEFGHIJKLMNOPQRST
abcdefghijklmnopqrstuvwxyz
1234567890 !@#?.;"*&

Volina is a contemporary interpretation of 19th-century pointed pen calligraphy by Francesca Bolognini and Sebastian Losch. The face draws its inspiration from Bolognini's childhood ambition to become an Olympic gymnast. She played for hours twirling a ribbon wand, fascinated by the patterns it created in the air. The flowing forms of a ribbon in movement are echoed throughout Volina's exquisite forms, and its many detailed design features mark it as a remarkably innovative and highly crafted script.

The three-dimensional effect of an undulating ribbon is ingeniously built into the character strokes. An everchanging stroke direction varies the line thickness, while the designers' passion for flowing copperplate calligraphy and the stroke modulation of a nib under pressure are reflected in the lines broken by negative space like a ribbon turning

over. Bolognini photographed moving ribbons to understand how light plays upon them, and then translated these transitions between light and dark into various copperplate styles. Extensive development went into each character and some of them, such as the lowercase "f" had more than fifty exploratory versions. This helped ensure a correct rhythm was maintained across the characters when set. The diagonal emphasis to the character forms also reflect that of handwriting and provide further flourishes to this most elegant of typefaces.

Volina is available in a single weight. Like most classically proportioned script fonts, it possesses extended ascenders and descenders, and oversized flowing capitals. It includes a wide range of playful symbols and dingbats, from pointing hands and arrows to ribbons and flying birds.

Foundry: Dalton Maag
Designer: Francesca Bolognini / Sebastian Losch
Designer Nationality: Italian / German
Date: 2017

Below. Drawing inspiration from flowing ribbons and copperplate calligraphy, Volina's elegant forms are also accompanied by a range of illustrated symbols and dingbats.

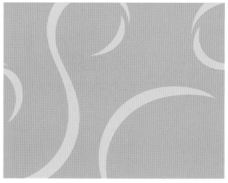

Amazone

ABCDEFGHIJKLMNOPQRSTUV
abcdefghijklmnopqrstuvwxyz
1234567890 !@#?:;"*&

Foundry: Lettergieterij Amsterdam
Designer: Leonard H. D. Smit
Designer Nationality: Dutch
Date: 1958

Leonard H. D. Smit's first typeface was created to compete with Günter Gerhard Lange's font Boulevard (1955). It is a graceful script designed to be connected without kerning. This made it much easier to cast and handle than other connected scripts, with no effect on how the characters joined.

Amienne

ABCDEFGHIJKLMNOPQRSTUVWXYZ
abcdefghijklmnopqrstuvwxyz
1234567890 !@#?:;"*&

Foundry: Typodermic
Designer: Ray Larabie
Designer Nationality: Canadian
Date: 2004

Ray Larabie's Amienne is a lively and very informal brush script font with an open, airy feel and a distinctive rhythm. It is available in Regular and Bold weights in full upper and lowercase, with regular numerals, accents, and punctuation as well as a set of arrows.

Arriba

ABCDEFGHIJKLMNOPQRSTUVWXYZ
abcdefghijklmnopqrstuvwxyz
1234567890 !@#?:;"*&

Foundry: Letraset
Designer: Phill Grimshaw
Designer Nationality: British
Date: 1993

Arriba is an energetic Latin-American influenced font with angular forms and a simulated broad-brush style, which works best when its characters are set close together. It has two variants: Arriba Plain and Arriba Arriba, an even more decorative version of the original.

Banco

ABCDEFGHIJKLMNOPQRSTUVWXYZ
abcdefghijklmnopqrstuvwxyz
1234567890 !@#?:;"*&

Foundry: Fonderie Olive
Designer: Roger Excoffon / Phill Grimshaw
Designer Nationality: French / British
Date: 1951

Roger Excoffon's first typeface, Banco, was designed as an uppercase font with strong forms and upright, tapering strokes; lowercase and Light versions were added in 1997 by Phill Grimshaw. Banco is often associated with musician Bob Marley and the skateboarding magazine *Thrasher*.

Barrista

ABCDEFGHIJKLMNOPQRSTUVWXYZ
abcdefghijklmnopqrstuvwxyz
1234567890 !@#?:;"*&

Foundry: Typodermic
Designer: Ray Larabie
Designer Nationality: Canadian
Date: 2005

This casual, retro-inspired curly script, reminiscent of the swirling curls of steam from a hot cup of coffee, is available in a single weight. Barrista is not the only caffeine-inspired font from Ray Larabie. In 1999 he designed the seven-weight, sans serif typeface Kenyan Coffee.

Becka Script

ABCDEFGHIJKLMNOPQRSTUVWXY
abcdefghijklmnopqrstuvwxyz
1234567890 !@#?:;"*a

Foundry: ITC
Designer: David Harris
Designer Nationality: British
Date: 1985

Becka Script is a bold, single-weight font that looks like it could have been created with a marker pen. It is one of only a handful of typefaces created by British lettering artist David Harris, who specializes in cadels, which are the large, patterned capitals used in medieval manuscripts

Brody

ABCDEFGHIJKLMNOPQRSTUVWXYZ
abcdefghijklmnopqrstuvwxyz
1234567890 !@#?:;"*&

Foundry: American Type Founders
Designer: Harold Broderson
Designer Nationality: American
Date: 1953

This nostalgic-looking, cursive-style brush script echoes the showcard style of lettering popular in the United States during the first half of the 20th century. Its characters look like they were drawn with a wide, flat brush, giving it a feeling of fun and spontaneity.

Bronx

ABCDEFGHIJKLMNOPQRSTUVWXYZ
abcdefghijklmnopqrstuvwxyz
1234567890 !@#?:;"*&

Foundry: Letraset
Designer: David Quay
Designer Nationality: British
Date: 1986

With its deliberate imperfections and rough edges, this very stylized and dynamic script resembles quickly rendered (but very neat) brush lettering. Quintessentially 1980s, Bronx has uppercase letters that can be joined with the lowercase to look like handwriting.

Brophy Script

ABCDEFGH99KLMNOPQRSTUVWXY3
abcdefghijklmnopqrstuvwxyz
1234567890 !@#?:;"*&

Foundry: Monotype
Designer: Harold Broderson / Carolyn Gibbs
Designer Nationality: American
Date: 1953

Brophy Script is a very close interpretation of Harold Broderson's nostalgic, showcard-influenced Brody typeface from 1953 but with more handwritten letters. It features different versions of the uppercase characters "Y," "E," "I," and "J," as well as a new, double-story lowercase "z."

Brush 455

ABCDEFGHIJKLMNOPQRSTUVWX
abcdefghijklmnopqrstuvwxyz
1234567890 !@#?:;"*&

Foundry: Bitstream
Designer: Martin Wilke
Designer Nationality: German
Date: 1950 / 1990

This is Bitstream's digitized version of Palette, a lively, single-weight brush script that was originally created by German designer Martin Wilke for the Berthold type foundry in 1950. Wilke's other typefaces of note are Diskus, New Berolina, and the eponymous Wilke.

Brush 738

ABCDEFGHIJKLMNOPQRSTUVWXYZ
abcdefghijklmnopqrstuvwxyz
1234567890 !@#?:;"*&

Foundry: Bitstream
Designer: Julius Kirn
Designer Nationality: German
Date: 1938 / 1990

This is Bitstream's version of Bison, the font designed by Julius Kirn in 1938 for the Stuttgart-based foundry, Weber. The foundry shared some designs with Altona-based J. D. Trennert, which released Bison as Blizzard. URW++'s digitized version is more tightly spaced than Brush 738.

Brush Script

ABCDEFGHIJKLMNOP2RSTUVWXYZ
abcdefghijklmnopqrstuvwxyz
1234567890 !@#?:;"*&

Foundry: American Type Founders
Designer: Robert E. Smith
Designer Nationality: American
Date: 1942

The classic and much-copied Brush Script was designed by Robert E. Smith for the American Type Founders with the intention of replacing similar designs from the early part of the 20th century. It has a pleasing hand-lettered look and carefully joined letters that give it a seamless appearance.

Cascade Script

ABCDEFGHIJKLMNOPQRSTUVWXYZ
abcdefghijklmnopqrstuvwxyz
1234567890 !@#?:;"*&

Foundry: Mergenthaler
Designer: Matthew Carter
Designer Nationality: British
Date: 1965

Matthew Carter (see p. 616) designed this reserved but very balanced calligraphic script face when he was in his twenties. Cascade Script evokes the fonts used in the advertising agencies of the 1940s, with its angular outlines and appearance as if drawn using a broad-tipped pen.

Challenge

ABCDEFGHIJKLMNOPQRSTUVWXYZ
abcdefghijklmnopqrstuvwxyz
1234567890 !@#?:;"*&

Foundry: Letraset
Designer: Martin Wait
Designer Nationality: British
Date: 1982

Challenge is a jaunty, non-connecting, brush-lettering face that looks like it was created with a marker pen. It is one of more than thirty typefaces created for Letraset by British type designer Martin Wait. Challenge is available in two weights—Bold and Extra Bold.

Challenger

ABCDEFGHIJKLMNOPQRSTUVW
abcdefghijklmnopqrstuvwxyz
1234567890 !@#?:;"*&

Foundry: Linotype
Designer: Manfred Kloppert
Designer Nationality: German
Date: 2011

This dynamic and expressive single weight handwriting font was the first digital typeface developed by German graphic designer and calligrapher Manfred Kloppert. It is well suited for use in advertisement texts, on packaging, invitations, and greetings cards.

Chaplin

ABCDEFGHIJKLMNOPQRSTUVWXYZ
abcdefghijklmnopqrstuvwxyz
1234567890 !@#?:;"*&

Foundry: Monotype
Designer: Monotype Studio
Date: Unknown

Chaplin is a light-hearted script created for display purposes. It leans slightly to the right, evoking the Tramp, the silent film character made famous by actor Charlie Chaplin. Available as a single regular weight, the script has a relaxed charm that makes it ideal for everything from packaging to posters.

Choc

ABCDEFGHIJKLMNOPQRSTUVWXYZ
abcdefghijklmnopqrstuvwxyz
1234567890 !@?:;"*&

Foundry: Fonderie Olive
Designer: Roger Excoffon
Designer Nationality: French
Date: 1955

This brush script was created as a result of Roger Excoffon's repeated efforts to make a bold version of his typeface Mistral of 1953, which is based on his own handwriting. It is supplied with CorelDraw as Bitstream's Staccato 555, and is very popular with Asian-themed restaurants in New York.

Chunder

ABCDEFGHIJKLMNOPQRSTUVWXYZ
abcdefghijklmnopqrstuvwxyz
1234567890 !@#?:;"*&

Foundry: Chank Co.
Designer: Chank Diesel
Designer Nationality: American
Date: 1996

Chunder was inspired by hand-painted vernacular signage where the sign writing is less than perfect. US designer Chank Diesel said of his clunky yet flowery script: "It's not pretty, but it's mine." The quirky looking—and named—Chunder is available in a single weight.

Comedia

ABCDEFGHIJKLMNOPQRSTUVWXYZ
abcdefghijklmnopqrstuvwxyz
1234567890 !@#?:;" *&

Foundry: Monotype
Designer: Olivier Nineuil
Designer Nationality: French
Date: 1996

A simplified single-weight typeface with some unexpected angles and quirky additions, Comedia was created by the self-taught French designer, lecturer and "magician of letters" Olivier Nineuil. He is also co-founder of the Paris-based foundry and publisher Typofacto.

Coomeec

ABCDEFGHIJKLMNOPQRSTUVWXYZ
abcdefghijklmnopqrstuvwxyz
1234567890 !@#?:;"*&

Foundry: Linotype
Designer: Andi AW. Masry
Designer Nationality: Indonesian
Date: 2012

Although Indonesian designer Andi AW. Masry is a big fan of comics, Coomeec has more in common with a calligraphic brush typeface than a conventional cartoon font. It has several distinct characters, such as the lowercase "g" and "s" and uppercase "Y." It is available in regular and bold with matching italics.

Crestwood

ABCDEFGHIJKLMNOPQRSTUVWXYZ
abcdefghijklmnopqrstuvwxyz
1234567890 !@#?:;"'&*

Foundry: Ascender
Designer: Robert Hunter Middleton / Steve Matteson
Designer Nationality: American
Date: 1937 / 2006

Crestwood is an elegant semiformal script typeface that was first released by the US foundry Ludlow Typograph in 1937 and titled Coronet. The typeface is best used at larger sizes, and it is often found on greeting cards and invitations. Matteson, who created the revival, is now type director at Monotype.

Demian

ABCDEFGHIJKLMNOPQRSTUVWXYZ
abcdefghijklmnopqrstuvwxyz
1234567890 !?:;"'&*

Foundry: Letraset
Designer: Peter O'Donnell / Jan van Dijk
Designer Nationality: British / Dutch
Date: 1984 / 1987

This informal script font features narrow letterforms with a pronounced forward slant, angular details, and horizontal tittles on the lowercase "i" and "j." It was designed for Letraset by Jan van Dijk in 1984, with Peter O'Donnell contributing the bold cut three years later.

DR Agu Script

ABCDEFGHIJKLMNOPQRSTUVWXYZ
abcdefghijklmnopqrstuvwxyz
1234567890 !@#?:;"'*&

Foundry: Dmitry Rastvortsev
Designer: Dmitry Rastvortsev
Designer Nationality: Ukrainian
Date: 2016

This font is part of Dmitry Rastvortsev's DR Agu family. It supports a wide range of languages, including Latin and Cyrillic alphabets with stylistic subsets for Baltic and Serbian Cyrillic. It features an extensive set of contextual ligatures, alternate letterforms, and numerals.

Éclat

ABCDEFGHIJKLMNOPQRST
abcdefghijklmnopqrstuvwxyz
1234567890 !@#?:;"'&*

Foundry: Letraset
Designer: Doyald Young
Designer Nationality: American
Date: 1984

Doyald Young, an ccomplished logo designer once mentored by Hermann Zapf (see p. 574), created this highly decorative fat face font replete with loops, curls, and flourishes. It was initially published by Letraset and subsequently digitized by ICG; Monotype released its own version in 2015.

Dalton Maag

Dalton Maag is a London-based typeface design studio founded in 1991 by Swiss designer Bruno Maag. The studio works with designers, advertising agencies, and brands in their visual communications. With an international team of over forty staff, spanning twenty nationalities and twelve languages, it is truly an international studio, working with clients from around the world.

As well as the creation of small to large custom font families, Dalton Maag works on any number of type-related projects, including type modifications and logotype refinements. It is this level of assistance and broad range of services that have endeared it to global organizations such as Amazon, Intel, Nokia, Airbnb, Ubuntu, and the USA Today network, which all require multilingual typeface systems that can communicate in separate languages across platforms, often in completely different writing systems.

Dalton Maag has a library of almost forty retail fonts and a number of these have been recognized in awards by the New York Type Directors Club, London's Design Museum and D&AD. Its portfolio crosses a wide array of styles, from its best-selling fonts Effra and Aktiv Grotesk (see p. 215) to its elegant ribbon-inspired script design Volina (see p. 587.)

Founded: 1991
Country: UK
Website: daltonmaag.com
Notable typefaces:
Aktiv Grotesk (see p. 215)
Blenny (see p. 414)
Volina (see p. 587)

Below. Lush Handwritten for Lush Cosmetics and AT&T Aleck for communications giant.

Opposite. Typefaces for Airbnb (Airbnb Cereal), the BBC (BBC Reith) and branding for cyclist Sir Bradley Wiggins in conjunction with cycling brand Rapha.

Airbnb Cereal · **Welcon**
ommunity · Sans serif
ide · **playful & friendly**
Six styles · Superhost ·
belong anywhere · com

BBC Reith
The new face of the BBC
Inform, educate & entertain
fit for all Audiences
LEGIBLE & FUNCTIONAL
Broadcasting

WIGGINS ◎

Enamel Brush

ABCDEFGHIJKLMNOPQRSTUVWXYZ
abcdefghijklmnopqrstuvwxyz3
1234567890 !@#?:;"*&

Enamel Brush is a contemporary digitization of Catalina, an earlier typeface published in 1955 and created by Emil J. Klumpp, the former American Type Founders type design director. It is a jaunty brush script font, its appearance characteristic of the more informal type styles popular during that decade.

Foundry: Typodermic
Designer: Emil J. Klumpp / Ray Larabie
Designer Nationality: American / Canadian
Date: 1955 / 2009

Excritura

ABCDEFGHIJKLMNOPQRSTUVWXYZ
abcdefghijklmnopqrstuvwxyz
1234567890 !@#?:;"*&

This calligraphic typeface by Spanish designer Alex Camacho features connected letterforms and a characterful irregularity in its stroke weight. Slightly condensed and upright, Excritura captures a dynamic sense of the movement of the pen within its forms and flourishes.

Foundry: Linotype
Designer: Alex Camacho
Designer Nationality: Spanish
Date: 2013

Expectation

ABCDEFGHIJKLMNOPQRSTUVWXYZ
abcdefghijklmnopqrstuvwxyz
1234567890 !@#?:;"*&

Expectation is a script typeface based on the handwriting of German type designer Guido Bittner, who developed the font from scans of his own lettering. Its irregular forms, available in a single weight, capture the texture of the paper on which the originals were written.

Foundry: Linotype
Designer: Guido Bittner
Designer Nationality: German
Date: 2003

Flash

ABCDEFGHIJKLMNOPQRSTUVWXYZ
abcdefghijklmnopqrstuvwxyz
1234567890 !@#?:;"*&

US type designer Edwin W. Shaar designed this cartoonish typeface for Monotype in 1939; a bold cut, also by Shaar, was published the following year. Flash was a popular choice for title typesetting on the pulp-fiction novels popular during that era, and is still widely used to this day.

Foundry: Monotype
Designer: Edwin W. Shaar
Designer Nationality: American
Date: 1939

Forte

ABCDEFGHIJKLMNOPQRSTUVWXYZ
abcdefghijklmnopqrstuvwxyz
1234567890 !@#?:;"*&

Foundry: Monotype
Designer: Carl Reissberger
Designer Nationality: Austrian
Date: 1962

Bold yet soft, Forte was created by Austrian type designer Carl Reissberger for Monotype and published in 1962. Its rounded letterforms and heavy appearance make this script typeface well-suited to large-scale display use, as its legibility is rather limited at smaller point sizes.

Freestyle Script

ABCDEFGHIJKLMNOPQRSTUVWXYZ
abcdefghijklmnopqrstuvwxyz
1234567890 !@# ?:;"*&

Foundry: Letraset
Designer: Martin Wait
Designer Nationality: British
Date: 1981

The even stroke weight and linked letterforms of Freestyle Script make it an elegant yet informal choice for typesetting where a handwritten look is required. The typeface was created by British designer Martin Wait for Letraset in 1981; he added a bold weight five years later.

FS Shepton

ABCDEFGHIJKLMNOPQRSTUVWXYZ
abcdefghijklmnopqrstuvwxyz
1234567890 !@#?:;"*&

Foundry: Fontsmith
Designer: Andy Lethbridge
Designer Nationality: British
Date: 2015

The three versions of FS Shepton were created as a collection of alphabets with similar characters but different styles and textures. Inspired by the organic shapes and textures of market stall signs, Regular was drawn with a wet brush pen, Light with a dry brush, and Bold with a wider, looser dry brush pen.

Glastonbury

ABCDEFGHIJKLMNOPQRSTUVWXYZ
abcdefghijklmnopqrstuvwxyz
1234567890 !?:;" *&

Foundry: Letraset
Designer: Alan Meeks
Designer Nationality: British
Date: 1979

Glastonbury is a soft, monolinear script typeface with an intricate set of free-flowing initial capitals. It is one of more than forty typefaces developed by British font designer Alan Meeks during his time as senior type designer and studio manager at Letraset from 1975 to 1984.

Greyhound

ABCDEFGHIJKLMNOPQRSTUVWXYZ
abcdefghijklmnopqrstuvwxyz
1234567890 !&#?.;,"*&

Foundry: Panache Typography
Designer: Dave Farey
Designer Nationality: British
Date: 1998

Greyhound is a delicate single-weight script with connecting lowercase and plenty of pleasing curls. It is published by British foundry Panache Typography, which is run by Richard Dawson and self-confessed "letter-repairer" Dave Farey. Panache has issued many revivals of the classics.

Impuls

ABCDEFGHIJKLMNOPQRSTUVWXYZ
abcdefghijklmnopqrstuvwxyz
1234567890 !@#?.;,"*&

Foundry: Ludwig Wagner
Designer: Paul Zimmermann
Designer Nationality: German
Date: 1945

German designer Paul Zimmermann's vigorous brush-stroke font Impuls was originally released in 1945. Bitstream revived and digitized it in 1993 (where it also appears as Brush 439). Leading German type designer Ralph M. Unger revived it in 2010 as Impuls Pro.

ITC Arid

ABCDEFGHIJKLMNOPQRSTUVW
abcdefghijklmnopqrstuvwxyz
1234567890 !@#?.;,"*&

Foundry: ITC
Designer: Rob Leuschke
Designer Nationality: American
Date: 1997

This sparky calligraphy font looks as though it was drawn with a piece of charcoal but was actually drawn using a camel-hair bristle brush on cold-press Strathmore Watercolor paper. ITC Arid's forward slanting letterforms give it a dynamic feel. It is best used at sizes of 12 point and above.

ITC Blaze

ABCDEFGHIJKLMNOPQRSTUVWXYZ
abcdefghijklmnopqrstuvwxyz
1234567890 !@#?.;,"*&

Foundry: ITC
Designer: Patty King
Designer Nationality: American
Date: 1995

The ITC Blaze script font looks as though it were written by hand with a broad-tipped pen on rough paper. It has a dynamic feel, thanks to the pointed ends of its characters and their leaning to the right. Blaze is influenced by the typography of the late 1940s and is best suited for headlines.

ITC Kick

ABCDEFGHIJKLMNOPQRSTUVWXYZ
abcdefghijklmnopqrstuvwxyz
1234567890 !@#?:;"*&

Available in a single italic weight, ITC Kick by Californian designer Patty King is a rough, bold, and dynamic brush script. King designed five calligraphic faces for ITC before her death in 2002, including her final font ITC Bette, which was completed in 2002 and released posthumously.

Foundry: ITC
Designer: Patty King
Designer Nationality: American
Date: 1995

ITC True Grit

ABCDEFGHIJKLMNOPQRSTUVWXYZ
abcdefghijklmnopqrstuvwxyz
1234567890 !@#?:;"*&

US designer Michael Stacey is a keen collector of vintage graphics and ephemera. His single-weight ITC True Grit was inspired by lettering from the 1930s and he describes the typeface as "a hybrid design, a cross between German Blackletter and brush script with a hint of Jugendstil thrown in."

Foundry: ITC
Designer: Michael Stacey
Designer Nationality: American
Date: 1995

ITC Wisteria

ABCDEFGHIJKLMNOPQRSTUVWXYZ
abcdefghijklmnopqrstuvwxyz
1234567890 !@#?:;"*&

Michael Stacey's ITC Wisteria is a distinctive, heavy double-stroke script font that mimics the effects of drawing with a broad split-tip pen. The energetic and robust typeface entered into the ITC library in 1995. Stacey based it on an alphabet by the inventor of the Speedball pen, type designer Ross F. George.

Foundry: ITC
Designer: Michael Stacey
Designer Nationality: American
Date: 1995

Jiffy

ABCDEFGHIJKLMNOPQR
abcdefghijklmnopqrstuvwxyz
1234567890 !@#?:;"*&

An exuberant, wispy connecting script, Jiffy is available in one weight and was digitized by the Linotype Design Studio in 2003, based on a phototype released by Filmotype in the 1960s. Garrett Boge's Wendy (1998) from LetterPerfect is based on the same source and has two extra weights.

Foundry: Linotype
Designer: Unknown / Linotype Design Studio
Date: c. 1960 / 2003

Kaufmann

ABCDEFGHIJKLMNOPQRSTUVWXYZ
abcdefghijklmnopqrstuvwxyz
1234567890 !@#?:;"*&

Foundry: American Type Founders
Designer: Max R. Kaufmann
Designer Nationality: American
Date: 1936

Max R. Kaufmann, US typographer and art director of *McCall's* magazine, drew the Kaufmann monoline connecting script for American Type Founders in 1936. It comes in a single bold weight and has relatively short descenders. Many different foundries have digitized Kaufmann.

Limehouse Script

ABCDEFGHIJKLMNOPQRSTUVWXYZ
abcdefghijklmnopqrstuvwxyz
1234567890 !@#?:;"*&

Foundry: ITC
Designer: Alan Meeks
Designer Nationality: British
Date: 1986

Limehouse Script is an informal, upright monoline handwriting font designed by Alan Meeks for ITC in 1986. It is named after a neighbourhood in the East End of London. The lowercase "o," the most distinctive character, features a horizontal terminal above its bowl.

Mantika Informal

ABCDEFGHIJKLMNOPQRSTUVWXYZ
abcdefghijklmnopqrstuvwxyz
1234567890 !@#?:;"*&

Foundry: Linotype
Designer: Jürgen Weltin
Designer Nationality: German
Date: 2010

Mantika Informal is part of the Mantika superfamily, which also includes another sans serif and two serifs. It is a soft, slightly cursive sans serif with humanist influences, and German designer Jürgen Weltin created it with children's books in mind. It is available in two weights—Regular and Bold.

Marnie

ABCDEFGHIJKLMNOPQRSTUVWXYZ
abcdefghijklmnopqrstuvwxyz
1234567890 !@#?:;"*&

Foundry: Agfa
Designer: Gérard Mariscalchi
Designer Nationality: Canadian
Date: 1997

Marnie, Gérard Mariscalchi's elegant connecting script, was inspired by early 20th-century Art Nouveau calligraphic hand-lettering. It is highly legible, thanks to a high x-height and low contrast, and features large curlicued capitals that often wrap around the next letter.

Mercurius Script

ABCDEFGHIJKLMNOPQRSTUVWXYZ
abcdefghijklmnopqrstuvwxyz
1234567890 !@#?:;"'*&

Foundry: Monotype
Designer: Imre Reiner
Designer Nationality: Hungarian
Date: 1957

Hungarian-born graphic artist and typographer Imre Reiner designed Mercurius in 1957, when he was living in the Swiss town of Ruvigliana near Lugano.

It is a bold, inclined script font with angular features. Reiner achieved its distinct look through the use of a bamboo pen.

Monoline Script

ABCDEFGHIJKLMNOPQRSTUVWXYZ
abcdefghijklmnopqrstuvwxyz
1234567890 !@#?:;"'*&

Foundry: Monotype
Designer: Monotype Studio
Date: 1933

A fun, optimistic connecting script with a consistent stroke width, Monoline Script is available in a single weight (roughly a medium). It was designed

in-house at Monotype in 1933 and is slightly inclined with many curling, looping features, especially on capitals and ascenders.

Monterey BT

ABCDEFGHIJKLMNOPQRSTUVWXYZ
abcdefghijklmnopqrstuvwxyz
1234567890 !@#?.:;"'*&

Foundry: Bitstream
Designer: Rand Holub
Designer Nationality: American
Date: 1958 / 1987

Monterey BT is a Bitstream digitization of Monterey Script, designed by Rand Holub for Intertype in 1958 as a response to Emil J. Klumpp's Murray Hill font

published by American Type Founders two years earlier. The casual characters feature a moderate contrast and include a single, regular style.

Morris Freestyle

ABCDEFGHIJKLMNOPQRSTUVWXYZ
abcdefghijklmnopqrstuvwxyz
1234567890 !@#?:;"'*&

Foundry: Monotype
Designer: Keith Morris
Designer Nationality: Australian
Date: 2006

Morris Freestyle is a casual script designed in a single style. The font, which features upper- and lowercase forms, combines spacious character

widths, broad strokes, and open counters with shortened ascenders and descenders for an approachable and articulate appearance.

New Berolina

ABCDEFGHIJKLMNOPQRSTUVWXY
abcdefghijklmnopqrstuvwxyz
1234567890 !@#?:;"*&

Foundry: Monotype
Designer: Martin Wilke
Designer Nationality: German
Date: 1965

New Berolina is a casual script designed in a single weight and intended for careful use in body text. The lowercase letterforms feature sharp, calligraphic strokes, which, combined with a relatively low x-height and expressive capitals, comprise a dynamic, spirited typeface.

Okay

ABCDEFGHIJKLMNOPQRSTUVWXYZ
abcdefghijklmnopqrstuvwxyz
1234567890 !@#?:;"*&

Foundry: Linotype
Designer: Edwin W. Shaar
Designer Nationality: American
Date: 1939

Okay is a casual script designed in a single style. Like other script faces designed by Edwin W. Shaar in this period, such as Flash, Okay's characters are narrow, italicized, and comprised of thick, brushlike strokes with irregular terminals that render them both soft and dynamic.

Park Avenue

ABCDEFGHIJKLMNOPQRSTUVWXYZ
abcdefghijklmnopqrstuvwxyz
1234567890 !@#?:;"*&

Foundry: American Type Founders
Designer: Robert E. Smith
Designer Nationality: American
Date: 1933

Park Avenue is a casual script, designed in a single style, which combines decoration and readability. The calligraphic letterforms feature a low x-height and long, swirling strokes, alongside brushlike terminals that provide the sturdy shapes with a formal elegance.

Pendry Script

ABCDEFGHIJKLMNOPQRSTUVWXYZ
abcdefghijklmnopqrstuvwxyz
1234567890 !?:;"*&

Foundry: ITC
Designer: Martin Wait
Designer Nationality: British
Date: 1981

Pendry Script is a casual script that imitates the idiosyncrasies of calligraphic lettering. Alongside the organic and high-contrast strokes, the design also features a smeared outline that mimics the effect of ink smudging, as if a hand is dragging across the page as it writes.

Pepita

ABCDEFGHIJKLMNOPQRSTUVWXY
abcdefghijklmnopqrstuvwxyz
1234567890 ! @ #?:;"*&

Foundry: Monotype
Designer: Imre Reiner
Designer Nationality: Hungarian
Date: 1959

Inspired by the stylish sweep of the artist's brush stroke, Pepita is a casual script designed for display purposes, such as advertising, menus or book covers. The characters, with their oblique forms and irregular baseline, combine elegance with a measured flamboyance.

Rapier

ABCDEFGHIJKLMNOPQRSTUVWXYZ
abcdefghijklmnopqrstuvwxyz
1234567890 ! @# ?:; "*&

Foundry: ITC
Designer: Martin Wait
Designer Nationality: British
Date: 1989

Rapier is a casual script designed in a single style and inspired by the brush-style fonts found in advertising of the 1940s. The cursive characters, which assert their energy through vigorous adjoining strokes and sweeping terminals, were conceived for dynamic headline texts.

Reporter No. 2

ABCDEFGHJJKLMNOPQRSTUVWXYZ
abcdefghijklmnopqrstuvwxyz
1234567890 !@#?:;"*&

Foundry: Linotype
Designer: Carlos Winkow
Designer Nationality: Spanish
Date: 1938

Reporter No. 2 is a casual script and a revision by German type designer Carlos Winkow of his own Reporter font, initially designed for the Wagner foundry in 1938. In an effort to simplify the design, Reporter No. 2 includes fewer aesthetic details, while also removing various alternative characters.

Ribjoint

ABCDEFGHIJKLMNOPQRSTUVWXYZ
abcdefghijklmnopqrstuvwxyz
1234567890 !@#?:;"*&

Foundry: Chank Co.
Designer: Chank Diesel
Designer Nationality: American
Date: 1992

Ribjoint is a casual script designed in the Egyptian style. The font's lowercase letterforms, in which the rigid curves and robust strokes combine to induce a distinctly muscular character, represent Chank Diesel's first experiment in the design of computerized cursive.

Romany

ABCDEFGHIJKLMNOPQRSTUVWXYZ
abcdefghijklmnopqrstuvwxyz
1234567890 !@#?:;"*&

Foundry: Ascender
Designer: A. R. Bosco / Terrance Weinzierl
Designer Nationality: American
Date: 1934 / 2009

Romany is a digitization of A. R. Bosco's design of 1934 with the same name, produced in a single weight for American Type Founders. Terrance Weinzierl's revival, and expansion into a family of four styles, was conceived to revitalize Romany as a flexible script across all platforms.

Sagrantino

ABCDEFGHIJKLMNOPQRSTUVWXYZ
abcdefghijklmnopqrstuvwxyz
1234567890 !@#?:;"*&

Foundry: Monotype
Designer: Carl Crossgrove / Karl Leuthold / Juan Villanueva
Designer Nationality: American
Date: 2017

Sagrantino is a vivacious, casual script designed for use at large sizes, from packaging to banners. The font comprises three styles, including Regular, Highlight, and Shadow, alongside a variety of OpenType features, such as decorative ligatures and alternate characters.

Salsbury

ABCDEFGHIJKLMNOPQRSTUVWXYZ
abcdefghijklmnopqrstuvwxyz
1234567890 !@#?:;"*&

Foundry: Typodermic
Designer: Ray Larabie
Designer Nationality: Canadian
Date: 2006

Salsbury is a casual script inspired by the 20th-century brush fonts Dom Casual and Flash, by Peter Dom and Edwin W. Shaar respectively. The letterforms, which feature rounded strokes and terminals, were optimized for television graphics such as DVD menus and video games.

Santa Fe

ABCDEFGHIJKLMNOPQRSTUVWXYZ
abcdefghijklmnopqrstuvwxyz
1234567890 !@#?:;"*&

Foundry: Letraset
Designer: David Quay
Designer Nationality: British
Date: 1983

David Quay's Santa Fe is a casual script font that is evocative of lettering found in American popular culture of the 1960s. The font combines rodlike verticals with inflated curves and rounded terminals and features several distinctive forms in both the upper- and lowercases.

Saussa

ABCDEFGHIJKLMNOPQRSTUVWXYZ
abcdefghijklmnopqrstuvwxyz
1234567890 !@#?:;"*&

Foundry: Linotype
Designer: Patricia Roesch-Pothin
Designer Nationality: French
Date: 2009

Saussa is a casual script initially designed for the packaging of a French brand of fruit salad. The brushlike strokes, which were first painted by hand before being refined digitally, and the lowercase styling of the capitals ensure an informality throughout the font.

Shamrock

ABCDEFGHIJKLMNOPQRSTUVWXYZ
abcdefghijklmnopqrstuvwxyz
1234567890 !@#?:;"*&

Foundry: Letraset
Designer: Alan Withers
Designer Nationality: British
Date: 1978

Shamrock is a casual, hand-drawn script designed in a single style. It takes its name from the three-leafed clover that serves as the symbol for Ireland. The letterforms share many characteristics with traditional Irish type, such as the angled stress and looping strokes.

Stempel Elan

ABCDEFGHIJKLMNOPQRSTUVWX
abcdefghijklmnopqrstuvwxyz
1234567890 !@#?:;"*&

Foundry: Linotype
Designer: Hans Karl Gustav Möhring / Frank Griesshammer
Designer Nationality: German
Date: 2010

Stempel Elan is a casual script and Frank Griesshammer's digital revival of Stempel's Elan font, designed by Hans Möhring in 1937. While remaining faithful to the original, Stempel Elan increases flexibility with a variety of OpenType features, such as alternative characters.

Sunetta

ABCDEFGHIJKLMNOPQRSTUVWXYZ
abcdefghijklmnopqrstuvwxyz
1234567890 !@#?:;"*&

Foundry: Linotype
Designer: Werner Schneider
Designer Nationality: German
Date: 2005

Sunetta is a casual script drawn using an inkstone, ink, a brush, and paper, known in the Chinese calligraphic tradition as the Four Treasures of the Study. The font's three styles—Sunetta Flair, Sunetta Charme, and Sunetta Magic—range from relatively moderate to expressive.

Swing

ABCDEFGHIJKLMNOPQRSTUVWXYZ
abcdefghijklmnopqrstuvwxyz
1234567890 !@#?:;"*&

Foundry: Monotype
Designer: Max R. Kaufmann / Monotype Studio
Designer Nationality: American
Date: 1936

Swing is a casual script and Monotype's revival of Kaufmann, a rhythmic script originally created by US font designer Max R. Kaufmann for American Type Founders in 1936. Unlike the majority of cursive script designs, Swing's characters feature minimal stroke contrast.

Time Script

ABCDEFGHIJKLMNOPQRSTUVWXYZ
abcdefghijklmnopqrstuvwxyz
1234567890 !@#?:;"*&

Foundry: Weber
Designer: Georg Trump
Designer Nationality: German
Date: 1956

Time Script is a casual script designed in three weights, including Light, Medium, and Bold. The characters are distinctive in their blending of calligraphic detail with the zealous strokes of handwriting, notable in both the capital and lowercase letterforms.

WilliamLucas

ABCDEFGHIJKLMNOPQRSTUVWXYZ
abcdefghijklmnopqrstuvwxyz
1234567890 !@#?.;"*&

Foundry: ITC
Designer: Martin Wait
Designer Nationality: British
Date: 2010

WilliamLucas is a casual script designed to replicate the versatility of hand-lettering. The font utilizes OpenType software to provide a variety of alternative characters and glyphs, such as initials, swashes, capitals, and terminals, which add both flexibility and balance.

Zennor

ABCDEFGHIJKLMNOPQRSTUVWXYZ
abcdefghijklmnopqrstuvwxyz
1234567890 !?:;"*&

Foundry: ITC
Designer: Phill Grimshaw
Designer Nationality: British
Date: 1935

Zennor is a casual script designed for display uses in a single bold style. The brushlike figures, which appear to have been painted at speed, provide a muscular dynamism in the lowercase, while the capitals, which can also serve as initials, exhibit a more placid authority.

Aristocrat

ABCDEFGHIJKLMNOPQRSTUVWX
abcdefghijklmnopqrstuvwxyz
1234567890 .!@# ?:; ¨&*

Foundry: Letraset
Designer: Donald Stevens
Designer Nationality: British
Date: 1978

Aristocrat, the typeface by British designer Donald Stevens, combines intricately crafted uppercase characters with a more reserved lowercase. It is a very refined single-weight script face, which makes a good choice for use on certificates, greeting cards, and invitations.

Balmoral

ABCDEFGHIJKLMNOPQRS
abcdefghijklmnopqrstuvwxyz
1234567890 !@#?:; "&*

Foundry: Letraset
Designer: Martin Wait
Designer Nationality: British
Date: 1978

Available as a single weight, Martin Wait's Balmoral is an elegant and free-flowing copperplate-script style typeface. It has elaborate initial capitals that complement the more restrained lowercase characters, which join for more balanced letter spacing in word settings.

Carl Beck

ABCDEFGHIJKLMNOPQRSTUVWXYZ
abcdefghijklmnopqrstuvwxyz
1234567890 !@ ?:;"&*

Foundry: Monotype
Designer: Carolyn Gibbs
Designer Nationality: American
Date: 1992

This modest script was inspired by the cartographer Carl Beckman. He published an instruction and pattern book showing four different styles (including Cursiv Skriften No. 1, upon which this font is based) in Stockholm in 1794, as a response to the poor standard of lettering in Sweden at the time.

Carmine Tango

ABCDEFGHIJKLMNOPQRSTUVWXYZ
abcdefghijklmnopqrstuvwxyz
*1234567890 !#?:;" * &*

Foundry: Bitstream
Designer: Lucian Bernhard
Designer Nationality: American
Date: 1931

This is Bitstream's version of Lucian Bernhard's original script face Bernhard Tango of 1931, an open and delicate non-connected script face. A companion set of swash capitals to Bernhard's design was issued in 1939 by Lettergieterij Amsterdam as the font Aigrette.

Citadel Script

ABCDEFGHIJKLMNOPQRSTUV
abcdefghijklmnopqrstuvwxyz
1234567890 !@#?.:; " * &

Foundry: Monotype
Designer: Monotype Studio
Date: 1994

This delicate, flowing script is based on the handwriting and engraving traditionally found in formal announcements and invitations. While Flemish Script, Florentine Script, and Old Fashion Script have similar lowercase letters, Citadel Script has unique flourished capitals.

Commercial Script

ABCDEFGHIJKLMNOPQRSTUVWXYZ
abcdefghijklmnopqrstuvwxyz
1234567890 !@#?.:; " * &

Foundry: American Type Founders
Designer: Morris Fuller Benton
Designer Nationality: American
Date: 1906

Also known as Spencerian, this very popular copperplate connected script is similar to Bank Script but slightly heavier and without so many flourishes. It was influenced by a similar face by Barnhart Brothers & Spindler from 1895. Digitized versions have been released by Letraset, Bitstream, and ITC.

Coronet

ABCDEFGHIJKLMNOPQRSTUVWXYZ
abcdefghijklmnopqrstuvwxyz
1234567890 !@# ?.:; " * &

Foundry: Ludlow Typograph
Designer: Robert Hunter Middleton
Designer Nationality: American
Date: 1937

Coronet is a stylized retro-looking script originally designed for the Ludlow hot-metal typesetting system used in letterpress printing. It was digitized by Bitstream (as Ribbon 131) and later by Steve Jackaman. The script is used on the cover of the LP *The Velvet Underground & Nico* (1967).

Dorchester Script

ABCDEFGHIJKLMNOPQRSTUVWXYZ
abcdefghijklmnopqrstuvwxyz
1234567890 !@#?.:;" * &

Foundry: Monotype
Designer: Monotype Studio
Date: 1939

This elegant typeface with a slight forward slant was widely used to provide a high-society feel within correspondence and invitations following its release by Monotype in 1939. No specific designer is credited for the font, which was probably created by the foundry's in-house team.

Embassy

ABCDEFGHIJKLMNOPQRSTUVWXYZ
abcdefghijklmnopqrstuvwxyz
1234567890 !@# ?.:; "&*

Foundry: Bitstream
Designer: Studio of H. W. Caslon
Designer Nationality: British
Date: 1923 / c. 1955

Embassy is based on the rounded script styles popular with engravers at the turn of the 20th century. It was designed at the Caslon works in London in 1923 as a rival to Stephenson, Blake & Co.'s Palace Script (1923). It was converted for phototypesetting c. 1955; Bitstream's version was likely published in the 1990s.

English 111

ABCDEFGHIJKLMNOPQRSTU
abcdefghijklmnopqrstuvwxyz
1234567890 !@#?.:; "&*

Foundry: Bitstream
Designer: George Shelley
Designer Nationality: British
Date: c. 1990s

This Bitstream digitization stems from the work of the 18th-century British writing master George Shelley. It is based on the Shelley Script typeface developed by British designer Matthew Carter (see p. 616) for Linotype in 1972, in reference to Shelley's distinctive lettering style.

English 157

ABCDEFGHIJKLMNOPQRSTUVWXYZ
abcdefghijklmnopqrstuvwxyz
1234567890 !@#?.:; "&*

Foundry: Bitstream
Designer: Günther Gerhard Lange
Designer Nationality: German
Date: c. 1990s

English 157 is a digital revival of Englische Schreibschrift, originally published by Berthold. It is an example of the Spencerian style popular in the United States in the latter half of the 19th century. English 157 features unlinked letterforms, which is unusual for script fonts of its kind.

English Script

ABCDEFGHIJKLMNOPQRSTUVWXYZ
abcdefghijklmnopqrstuvwxyz
1234567890 !@#?.:; "&*

Foundry: Linotype
Designer: Günther Gerhard Lange
Designer Nationality: German
Date: 2006

This is Linotype's version of Englische Schreibschrift. It is available in three weights, including an appealingly robust bold cut. The typeface features a heavy slant to its letterforms, and its distinctive horizontal stroke ends are emphasized within the Demi and Bold styles.

Flemish Script

ABCDEFGHIJKLMNOPQRSTUVWXYZ
abcdefghijklmnopqrstuvwxyz
1234567890 !@#?.;"&*

Foundry: Bitstream
Date: 1998

The origins of this ornamental Roundhand script typeface are difficult to discern; it is said to have originated at the Photon foundry in Wilmington, as a font for phototypesetting, and was subsequently digitized by Bitstream. Featuring complex curlicues, it is best used at larger point sizes.

Fluidum

ABCDEFGHIJKLMNOPQRSTUVWXYZ
abcdefghijklmnopqrstuvwxyz
1234567890 !@#?.;"&*

Foundry: Nebiolo
Designer: Alessandro Butti / Aldo Novarese
Designer Nationality: Italian
Date: 1951

Fluidum is a high-contrast script font, whose uniformity provides a linear and regular appearance. It was originally published in two weights, though only the heavier was digitized by Monotype. In 2011, Ralph Unger's foundry RMU released an alternative revival of Fluidum, Butti, which also includes the lighter cut.

French Script

ABCDEFGHIJKLMNOPQRSTUVWXYZ
abcdefghijklmnopqrstuvwxyz
1234567890 !@#?.;"&*

Foundry: Monotype
Designer: Morris Fuller Benton / Monotype Studio
Designer Nationality: American
Date: 1905 / 1989

French Script is based on script handwriting and engraving used for invitations and announcements and on the Typo Upright script created by Morris Fuller Benton for American Type Founders in 1905. It is an elegant, upright script with flourished capitals and joining lowercase characters.

Gavotte

ABCDEFGHIJKLMNOPQRSTUVWXYZ
abcdefghijklmnopqrstuvwxyz
1234567890 !@#?.;"&*

Foundry: Klingspor
Designer: Rudo Spemann
Designer Nationality: German
Date: 1940

Rudo Spemann's decorative script is named after an 18th-century French dance. The script shows off his expert calligraphic skills. Spemann was much respected as an educator and since 1954 the city of Offenbach has awarded the Rudo Spemann Prize every two years in memory of his work.

ITC Edwardian Script

ABCDEFGHIJKLMNOPQRSTUVWXY

abcdefghijklmnopqrstuvwxyz

1234567890 !@#?:; "©*

ITC Edwardian Script is one of more than 600 typefaces created by US type designer Ed Benguiat (see p. 514). It is a sophisticated, connected script with delicate letterforms, inspired by the strong stroke contrasts created when writing with a steel pointed pen.

Foundry: ITC
Designer: Ed Benguiat
Designer Nationality: American
Date: 1994

ITC Isadora

ABCDEFGHIJKLMNOPQRSTUVWXYZ

abcdefghijklmnopqrstuvwxyz

1234567890 !@#?:;"&*

US type designer Kris Holmes founded the Bigelow & Holmes studio with Charles Bigelow in 1976. She designed the ITC Isadora elegant calligraphic script, which is available in Regular and Bold weights. The US ballet dancer Isadora Duncan inspired the type's forms and its name.

Foundry: ITC
Designer: Kris Holmes
Designer Nationality: American
Date: 1989

ITC Redonda

ABCDEFGHIJKLMNOPQRSTUVWX

abcdefghijklmnopqrstuvwxyz

1234567890 !@#?:;"&*

French-born designer Gérard Mariscalchi created this elegant single-weight script inspired by 19th-century French handwriting in 1998. ITC Redonda has two sets of flourished, swashed capitals to add variety. Mariscalchi lives in Canada and has designed everything from fonts to stamps.

Foundry: ITC
Designer: Gérard Mariscalchi
Designer Nationality: French
Date: 1998

Kuenstler Script

ABCDEFGHIJKLMNOPQRSTUVWXYZ

abcdefghijklmnopqrstuvwxyz

1234567890 !@#?:; "&*

Hans Bohn designed Kuenstler Script for Linotype in 1957. It is based on Künstlerschreibschrift, an elegant script released by Stempel in 1902. Kuenstler Script comes in three weights; the Medium and Bold are based on the two original Stempel weights and the Black was Bohn's addition in 1957.

Foundry: Linotype
Designer: Stempel Studio / Hans Bohn
Designer Nationality: German
Date: 1902 / 1957

Libelle

ABCDEFGHIJKLMNOPQRSTUVWXYZ
abcdefghijklmnopqrstuvwxyz
1234567890 !@#?.:;""&*

Foundry: Linotype
Designer: Jovica Veljović
Designer Nationality: Serbian
Date: 2009

Experienced Serbian calligrapher and designer Jovica Veljović created Libelle. It is an elegant, modern take on the copperplate script style.

Although only available in a single weight, Libelle is highly versatile with many ligatures, ornaments, alternates, and swash options.

Liberty Script

ABCDEFGHIJKLMNOPQRSTUVWXYZ
abcdefghijklmnopqrstuvwxyz
1234567890 !@#?.:; "&*

Foundry: American Type Founders
Designer: Willard T. Sniffin
Designer Nationality: American
Date: 1927

Willard T. Sniffin designed this delicate, non-connecting script released by American Type Founders. Sniffin designed many typefaces for the trust from 1927 to 1933. Liberty Script features large, flourish-heavy capitals and a slightly more understated lowercase with a very small x-height.

Linoscript

ABCDEFGHIJKLMNOPQRSTUVWXYZ
abcdefghijklmnopqrstuvwxyz
1234567890 !@#?.:;""&*

Foundry: American Type Founders
Designer: Morris Fuller Benton
Designer Nationality: American
Date: 1905 / 1926

American Type Founders released this upright, connecting script as Typo Upright in 1905. It was renamed "Linoscript" in 1926 when it was launched on the Linotype machine. It was inspired by the French script style and features large, flourished capitals. Many lowercase letters have flourishes too.

Lucia

ABCDEFGHIJKLMNOPQRSTUVWXYZ
abcdefghijklmnopqrstuvwxyz
1234567890 !@#?.:; "&*

Foundry: Bitstream
Date: c. 1990

Bitstream's Lucia is an elegant, delicate roundhand script with a small x-height and swashed capitals. It is a digitization of a font that was first transferred from an engravers' master plate (where it was named Italian Script) to the Intertype Fotosetter system by Compugraphic in 1955.

Old Fashion Script

ABCDEFGHI JKLMNOPQRSTUVWXYZ

abcdefghijklmnopqrstuvwxyz

1234567890 !@#.?.;' " &*

Foundry: Monotype
Designer: Monotype Studio
Date: 1920

Old Fashion Script is a formal script inspired by antiquated handwriting styles. The decorous letterforms, while featuring extravagant flourishes and high-contrast strokes, alongside cursive characters in the lowercase, are suitable for both text and headline sizes.

Original Script

ABCDEFGHIJKLMNOPQRSTUVWXYZ

abcdefghijklmnopqrstuvwxyz

1234567890 !@#?.;' " &*

Foundry: Monotype
Designer: Monotype Studio
Date: 1999

Original Script is a hand-lettered font designed as part of Monotype's script collection. The elegant characters, which are linked together through a series of cursive strokes, are intended for formal occasions, such as wedding invitations, and for items such as certificates and stationery.

Palace Script

ABCDEFGHIJKLMNOPQRSTUVWXYZ

abcdefghijklmnopqrstuvwxyz

1234567890 !@#?.;' " &*

Foundry: Monotype
Designer: Monotype Studio
Date: 1936

Palace Script is a formal script inspired by English copperplate engravings from the 18th and 19th centuries. The font, designed in both Regular and Semibold weights, features high-contrast, cursive strokes, alongside a low x-height for optimum legibility.

Phyllis

ABCDEFGHIJKLMNOPQRSTUVWXYZ

abcdefghijklmnopqrstuvwxyz

1234567890 !@#?.;' " &*

Foundry: Linotype
Designer: Heinrich Wieynck
Designer Nationality: German
Date: 1911

Linotype's Phyllis, which was also released by the Schriftgiesserei Bauer foundry under the name of Wieynck Cursive, is a formal script that merges calligraphic strokes, seen in the flourished uppercase, with sturdy serifs, demonstrated in the reserved lowercase.

Sackers Script

ABCDEFGHIJKLMNOPQRSTUVWXYZ
abcdefghijklmnopqrstuvwxyz
*1234567890 !@#?.:;" *&*

Foundry: Monotype
Designer: Monotype Studio
Date: 1900

Sackers Script is a formal script designed in two styles, Sackers English Script and Sackers Italian Script, both conceived primarily for invitations and stationery. The two styles are discernible in weight, the English font being slightly heavier, as well as stroke detail.

Shelley Script

ABCDEFGHIJKLMNOPQRSTUVWXYZ
abcdefghijklmnopqrstuvwxyz
*1234567890 !@#?.:;" *&*

Foundry: Linotype
Designer: George Shelley / Matthew Carter
Designer Nationality: British
Date: 1972

Shelley Script is a formal script face and a revival of the handwriting style of the 18th-century writing master George Shelley. This design from Matthew Carter (see p. 616) includes three versions—Allegro, Andante, and Volante—in which only the flourishes of the capitals differ.

Snell Roundhand

ABCDEFGHIJKLMNOPQRSTUVWXYZ
abcdefghijklmnopqrstuvwxyz
*1234567890 !@#?.:;" *&*

Foundry: Linotype
Designer: Charles Snell / Matthew Carter
Designer Nationality: British
Date: 1966

Snell Roundhand is a formal script and a revival of a 17th-century roundhand by English writing master Charles Snell, who avoided all flourishes in keeping with Puritan tradition. While retaining the distinctive details of the original, Snell Roundhand includes the addition of two new weights, Bold and Black.

Young Baroque

ABCDEFGHIJKLMNOPQRSTU
abcdefghijklmnopqrstuvwxyz
*1234567890 !@#?.:;" *&*

Foundry: ITC
Designer: Doyald Young
Designer Nationality: American
Date: 1984

Young Baroque is a formal script inspired by the decorative forms of 17th-century baroque lettering. The font integrates gentle cursive strokes in the lowercase with ostentatious flourishes in the capitals and is intended for formal correspondence, such as invitations.

Amadeo

ABCDEFGHIJKLMNOPQRSTUVWXYZ
abcdefghijklmnopqrstuvwxyz
1234567890 !@#?;,"*&

Foundry: Monotype
Designer: Julius de Goede
Designer Nationality: Dutch
Date: 1999

This informal handwriting script is by Dutch designer, typographer, and teacher Julius de Goede. He is the author of several books on type and calligraphy including *Kalligraphie Lehrbuch* (*Calligraphy Manual*, 2003). Amadeo is available in Regular and Bold weights, both with small caps.

Ambiance BT

ABCDEFGHIJKLMNOPQRSTUVWXYZ
abcdefghijklmnopqrstuvwxyz
1234567890 !@#?;,"*&

Foundry: Bitstream
Designer: Rob Leuschke
Designer Nationality: American
Date: 2004

This fine, expressive calligraphic script is the first typeface created for Bitstream by US designer Rob Leuschke, a former lettering artist at Hallmark Cards. Ambiance BT is available in a single weight. It also includes a swash alternate for each upper- and lowercase letter.

Andy

ABCDEFGHIJKLMNOPQRSTUVWXYZ
abcdefghijklmnopqrstuvwxyz
1234567890 !@#?;,"*&

Foundry: Monotype
Designer: Steve Matteson
Designer Nationality: American
Date: 1993

Andy was originally known as "Mead" because designer Steve Matteson loosely based the font on the handwriting of his friend Andy Mead. It is a childish looking, slightly slanted handwriting script that is available in Regular and Bold weights, with corresponding italics.

Ashley Script

ABCDEFGHIJKLMNOPQRSTUVWXYZ
abcdefghijklmnopqrstuvwxyz
1234567890 !@#?;,"*&

Foundry: Monotype
Designer: Ashley Havinden
Designer Nationality: British
Date: 1955

A relatively plain brush script, Ashley Script is based on Ashley Havinden's own handwriting. He was a key figure in the British design industry during the post war years, and worked at the top British advertising agency W. S. Crawford. In 1947, he was appointed a Royal Designer for Industry.

Matthew Carter

British designer Matthew Carter is one of the foremost type creatives of the last sixty years. His contribution to type design is inestimable: his typefaces are employed across the globe every day.

He was born in London in 1937, the son of Harry Carter, a book designer and in later years a print historian. His early forays in the world of print and type began with an apprenticeship at the esteemed Joh. Enschedé type foundry and printers in the Netherlands. There he studied the craft of traditional punchcutting, the process of creating the physical designs to cast hot-metal type. Inspired, he moved into a graphic design and printing career.

Returning to London, Carter set up as a freelance type designer and was soon a consultant to Crosfield Electronics, a British electronic-imaging company. In 1965, he moved to New York and began a long relationship designing typefaces for Mergenthaler Linotype. Among them are his well-known script designs Snell Roundhand (see p. 614) and Bell Centennial (see p. 217), the revolutionary design commissioned by the US Bell Telephone Company for its telephone directories to mark the company's centenary. In 1971, he moved back to England, where he continued to work for Mergenthaler Linotype. Later for the International Typeface Corporation he created among others, the serif ITC Galliard as a tribute to 16th-century master letter-cutter Robert Granjon, and ITC Charter.

In 1981, Carter and Mike Parker, a former director of Mergenthaler Linotype, co-founded Bitstream, a digital type design studio, in Marlborough, Massachusetts. A highly successful and well-timed venture, Bitstream developed a library of digital type where anyone could license a font. As the advancement of desktop publishing and personal computer use became widespread, so did the distribution of their typefaces.

In 1991, Carter left Bitstream and a year later he founded the Carter & Cone Type foundry with Cherie Cone. Clients included *Time, Newsweek, Wired* and *The New York Times*. There he began his work for Microsoft by creating a series of screen fonts such as Verdana and Georgia, recognized as two of the most successful designs created for monitor use thanks to their remarkable legibility even at small sizes. Carter has won numerous accolades: the British Royal Society of Arts made him a Royal Designer for Industry in 1981, the Type Directors Club gave him the TDC Medal in 1997 and in 2011 he received the Lifetime Achievement Award at the Cooper-Hewitt National Design Awards. Carter is one of the craftspeople who has experienced the transitions from physical type to photosetting to digital type creation, and his career has transcended the technological advances of type development and printing.

Date: 1937–
Nationality: British
Notable typefaces:
ITC Galliard (see p.127)
Verdana (see p. 303)
Bell Centennial (see p. 217)
Snell Roundhand (see p. 614)

Below. Carter's Verdana typeface was adopted in 2009 by Swedish furniture giant IKEA for all print and media use, creating a wave of controversy over the decision to change from Futura.

Opposite top. Carter's Georgia typeface showing the bitmapping (hinting) process at work (left); Bell Centennial for the Bell Telephone Company used in directories across the USA (right).

Opposite middle and far right. MoMa Gothic, house font to the Museum of Modern Art, New York.

Opposite bottom left. Matthew Carter's contribution to the field of type design is inestimable.

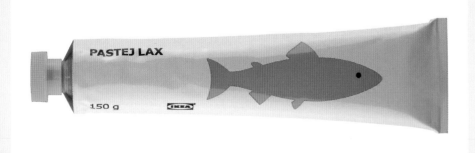

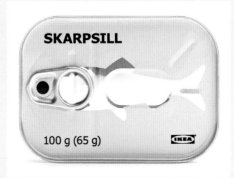

Georgia
Georgia

Bell Centennial
Name & Number

ABCDEFGHIJK
LMNOPQRSTU
VWXYZ&1234
567890abncdef
ghijklmnopqrst
uvwxyz.-,:;$?!

Commissioned by AT&T and released in 1978.

MoMA

NEW
PHOTOGRAPHY
2012

MICHELE ABELES, BIRDHEAD,
ANNE COLLIER, ZOE CROSHER,
SHIRANA SHAHBAZI

Polaroid

Bazar

ABCDEFGHIJKLMNOPQRSTUVWXYZ
abcdefghijklmnopqrstuvwxyz
1234567890 !@#?:;"*&

Foundry: Stempel
Designer: Imre Reiner
Designer Nationality: Hungarian
Date: 1956

Hungarian emigré Imre Reiner designed this 1950s painterly and very expressive script typeface. Bazar was digitized later by German designer Klaus Sutter. It was then revived in 2005 by Patrick Griffin for Toronto-based Canada Type, and released under the name "Boondock."

Bradley Texting

ABCDEFGHIJKLMNOPQRSTUVWXYZ
abcdefghijklmnopqrstuvwxyz
1234567890 !@#?:;"*&

Foundry: Monotype
Designer: Richard Bradley
Designer Nationality: British
Date: 2016

Richard Bradley designed Bradley Texting in the same vein as his previous fonts Bradley Hand (1995) and Bradley Type (2010). Its open counters and a large x-height make this friendly, marker-pen font very legible, particularly when used at small sizes, and on screens and devices.

Bradley Type

ABCDEFGHIJKLMNOPQRSTUVWXYZ
abcdefghijklmnopqrstuvwxyz
1234567890 !@#?:;"*&

Foundry: Monotype
Designer: Richard Bradley
Designer Nationality: British
Date: 2010

Bradley Type is designed to be used as a complement or counterpart to Richard Bradley's casual handwriting font Bradley Hand (1995). Bradley Type is more refined and slightly more condensed, making it better suited to text usage. It is available in three weights.

Bruno JB

ABCDEFGHIJKLMNOPQRSTUVWXYZ
abcdefghijklmnopqrstuvwxyz
1234567890 !@#?:;"*&

Foundry: Adobe
Designer: Jill Bell
Designer Nationality: American
Date: 1999

Los Angeles-based lettering artist Jill Bell named Bruno after the biggest of her three cats. She was inspired by a note that she had written to remind herself to buy cat food. It is an informal handwriting script with an unusual lowercase "a," which is available in Regular and Bold weights.

Cariola Script

ABCDEFGHIJKLMNOPQRSTUVWXYZ
abcdefghijklmnopqrstuvwxyz
1234567890 !@#?:;"*&

Foundry: Image Club Graphics
Designer: James West
Designer Nationality: American
Date: 1882 / 1993

This is one of a number of revivals of Carpenter Script, designed by Scottish-American punchcutter and type designer James West and originally published by Cleveland Type Foundry in 1882. Cariola Script has the same elegant swashes and fine detailing as the original.

Cavolini

ABCDEFGHIJKLMNOPQRSTUVWXYZ
abcdefghijklmnopqrstuvwxyz
1234567890 !@#?:;"*&

Foundry: Monotype
Designer: Carl Crossgrove
Designer Nationality: American
Date: 2017

This casual handwriting font (not dissimilar to Comic Sans) has been developed for use on small screens. Cavolini is available in roman, bold, and italic in regular and condensed, its large x-height, clearly defined apertures and open character spacing make it very legible at small sizes.

Chauncy

ABCDEFGHIJKLMNOPQRSTUVWXYZ
abcdefghijklmnopqrstuvwxyz
1234567890 !@#?:;"*&

Foundry: Chank Co.
Designer: Chank Diesel
Designer Nationality: American
Date: 1996

Chank Diesel's Chauncy is available in two weights: Deluxxe is the medium and Fatty is the bold. It is a playful font based on the left-handed penmanship of an artist to resemble children's handwriting. Chauncy Pro was released in 2012, in two weights plus matching italics.

Comic Sans

ABCDEFGHIJKLMNOPQRSTUVWXYZ
abcdefghijklmnopqrstuvwxyz
1234567890 !@#?:;"*&

Foundry: Microsoft
Designer: Vincent Connare
Designer Nationality: American
Date: 1994

An informal comic-book script, Comic Sans has been supplied with Microsoft Windows since the introduction of Windows 95. It is perhaps the most-talked-about typeface ever, its widespread use—often in situations for which it was not intended—having made it the subject of discussion.

Dom

ABCDEFGHIJKLMNOPQRSTUVWXYZ
abcdefghijklmnopqrstuvwxyz
1234567890 !@#?:;"*&

Peter Dombrezian's approachable type family is comprised of three styles: the upright Dom Casual and slanted Dom Diagonal, plus Dom Bold.

The fonts were a popular choice for TV-show titles during the mid 20th century, appearing everywhere from *Looney Tunes* to *Sesame Street*.

Foundry: American Type Founders
Designer: Peter Dombrezian
Designer Nationality: American
Date: 1951

Enviro

ABCDEFGHIJKLMNOPQRSTUVWXYZ
abcdefghijklmnopqrstuvwxyz
1234567890 !@#?:;"*&

Enviro is a sans serif display font similar to the Tekton family released in 1989, with fine strokes, rounded terminals, and an architectural feel, but

it is slightly more geometric in structure. Certain letterforms are unusual in their construction; the uppercase "S" and "W" are particularly distinctive.

Foundry: Letraset
Designer: F. Scott Garland
Designer Nationality: American
Date: 1982

Escript

ABCDEFGHIJKLMNOPQRSTUVWXYZ
abcdefghijklmnopqrstuvwxyz
1234567890 !@#?:;"*&

This handwriting-inspired font was designed by Hans-Jürgen Ellenberger and was a winner in Linotype's International Digital Type Design Contest

2003; it was included in the TakeType 4 Collection of typefaces the following year as a result. Escript is best suited to informal display use.

Foundry: Linotype
Designer: Hans-Jürgen Ellenberger
Designer Nationality: German
Date: 1994

FF Erikrighthand

ABCDEFGHIJKLMNOPQRSTUVWXYZ
abcdefghijklmnopqrstuvwxyz
1234567890 !@)#?:;"*&

FF Erikrighthand was developed by Dutch type designer Erik van Blokland in 1990. Working with Just van Rossum, he created the typeface from

examples of his own handwriting, pioneering a new, naturalistic style of font made possible by developments in type-design technology.

Foundry: FontFont
Designer: Erik van Blokland
Designer Nationality: Dutch
Date: 1990

FF Providence

ABCDEFGHIJKLMNOPQRSTUVWXYZ
abcdefghijklmnopqrstuvwxyz
1234567890 !@#?:;"*&

FF Providence was first designed in 1987 for use within a comic, with its serif and sans serif styles being used for narrative and dialogue respectively.

The typeface was expanded by designer Guy Jeffrey Nelson for release by FontFont in 1994, creating a family of four styles.

Foundry: FontFont
Designer: Panos (Panagiotis) Haratzopoulos / Guy Jeffrey Nelson
Designer Nationality: Greek / American
Date: 1987 / 1994

Fine Hand

ABCDEFGHIJKLMNOPQRSTUVWXYZ
abcdefghijklmnopqrstuvwxyz
1234567890 !@#?:;"*&

British calligrapher and lettering artist Richard Bradley designed Fine Hand based on his own handwriting. It includes a range of alternate characters, which provide scope for a varied approach to typesetting. First published by Letraset, the font has since been digitized.

Foundry: Letraset
Designer: Richard Bradley
Designer Nationality: British
Date: 1987

Fineprint

ABCDEFGHIJKLMNOPQRSTUVWXYZ
abcdefghijklmnopqrstuvwxyz
1234567890 !@#?:;"*&

Fineprint includes a number of swash characters and alternates, reflecting the irregularity of designer Steve Matteson's handwriting, on which it is based.

The axis on which its letterforms are set varies slightly throughout. It is included in the Monotype Library OpenType Edition.

Foundry: Monotype
Designer: Steve Matteson
Designer Nationality: American
Date: 1999

Flight

ABCDEFGHIJKLMNOPQRSTUVWXYZ
abcdefghijklmnopqrstuvwxyz
1234567890 !@#?:;"*&

Tim Donaldson designed Flight for Letraset and it was published in the mid 1990s, when new type design technology enabled the design of fonts that mimicked the irregularity of informal handwriting. Its stroke junctions are thickened throughout, giving the appearance of pooling ink.

Foundry: Letraset
Designer: Timothy Donaldson
Designer Nationality: British
Date: 1995

Ford's Folly

ABCDEFGHIJKLMNOPQRSTUVWXYZ
abcdefghijklmnopqrstuvwxyz
1234567890 !@#?:;'"*&

Foundry: Ascender
Designer: Jim Ford
Designer Nationality: American
Date: 2009

Based on forms written in Sharpie marker by designer Jim Ford, Ford's Folly is an amiable handwriting font available in two weights with corresponding italics. Ford developed an extensive character set for the typeface, which includes Latin, Greek, and Cyrillic alphabets.

FS Sammy

ABCDEFGHIJKLMNOPQRSTUVWXYZ
abcdefghijklmnopqrstuvwxyz
1234567890 !@#?:;"*&

Foundry: Fontsmith
Designer: Phil Garnham / Satwinder Sehmi
Designer Nationality: British / Kenyan
Date: 2009

A hand-drawn script with a chalky texture, FS Sammy was originally drawn for a drinks manufacturer. It was made by creating handwritten impressions on textured watercolor paper with a soft pencil, with the aim of having the breezy, spontaneous air of real handwriting.

Full Moon BT

ABCDEFGHIJKLMNOPQRSTUVWXYZ
abcdefghijklmnopqrstuvwxyz
1234567890 !@#?:;"*&

Foundry: Bitstream
Designer: Mary Trafton / Charles Gibbons
Designer Nationality: American
Date: 2001

This casual script is a collaboration based on lettering by illustrator Mary Trafton and designer Charles Gibbons. Its weights are named after folk names for the Moon. The family members include Falling Leaves and Black Cherry. It won the Type Directors Club Type Design Competition in 2003.

GFY Kersti

ABCDEFGHIJKLMNOPQRSTUVWXYZ
abcdεfghijklmnopqrstuvwxyz
1234567890 !@#?:;"*3

Foundry: Chank Co.
Designer: Chank Diesel
Designer Nationality: American
Date: 2002

GFY Kersti is part of Chank Co. foundry's GFY (Go Font Yourself) Handwriting Fontpak, which is a collection of twenty-one handwritten alphabets digitized by Chank Diesel. It falls into the "unusual and quirky" category along with GFY Aunt Susan, GFY Kimberly, and GFY Michael.

GFY Loopy

ABCDEFGHIJKLMNOPQRSTUVWXYZ
abcdefghijklmnopqrstuvwxyz
1234567890 !@#?;;"*&

Forming part of Chank Co. foundry's GFY (Go Font Yourself) Handwriting Fontpak, a collection of twenty-one handwritten alphabets drawn by real people and digitized by Chank Diesel, GFY Loopy falls into the "girly bubble letters" category.

Foundry: Chank Co.
Designer: Chank Diesel
Designer Nationality: American
Date: 2002

GFY Marcie

ABCDEFGHIJKLMNOPQRSTUVWXYZ
abcdefghijklmnopqrstuvwxyz
1234567890 !@#?;;"*&

Falling in to the "mature woman's penmanship" category in Chank Co. foundry's irreverent collection of handwritten typefaces, GFY Marcie has a more connected appearance in its lowercase with a looser irregular structure to the capital letterforms, and little consistency in the bowls and counters.

Foundry: Chank Co.
Designer: Chank Diesel
Designer Nationality: American
Date: 2002

GFY Palmer

ABCDEFGHIJKLMNOPQRSTUVWXYZ
abcdefghijklmnopqrstuvwxyz
1234567890 !@#?;;"*&

The GFY Palmer font is one of twenty-one handwritten alphabets that make up the GFY (Go Font Yourself) Handwriting Fontpak from the Chank Co. foundry digitized by Chank Diesel. It is part of the "loose casual" category alongside GFY Brutus, GFY Hey Steve, and GFY Josie.

Foundry: Chank Co.
Designer: Chank Diesel
Designer Nationality: American
Date: 2002

Gillies Gothic

ABCDEFGHIJKLMNOPQRSTUVWXYZ
abcdefghijklmnopqrstuvwxyz
1234567890 !@#?;;"*&

William S. Gillies created Gillies Gothic in 1935 for Bauer. It is known as Flott in Germany, Bolide in France, and Vigor in Spain. It comes in four weights: Light, Bold, Extra Bold, and Extra Bold Shaded. Freda Sack designed the Extra Bold for Letraset in 1980, and Phillip Kelly the Extra Bold Shaded in 1982.

Foundry: Bauer
Designer: William S. Gillies
Designer Nationality: American
Date: 1935

Indy Italic

ABCDEFGHIJKLMNOPQRSTUVWXYZ
abcdefghijklmnopqrstuvwxyz
1234567890 !@#?:; ”*&

Foundry: Letraset
Designer: Charles E. Hughes
Designer Nationality: American
Date: 1990

Indy Italic is a stylized lightweight script, whose lowercase letters are linked to imitate handwriting. Lettering designer Charles E. Hughes also designed Century Nova for American Type Founders in 1966, a variation on Century Expanded (1900), one of the last metal typefaces.

ITC Arnova

ABCDEFGHIJKLMNOPQRSTUVWXYZ
abcdefghijklmnopqrstuvwxyz
1234567890 !@#?:;”*&

Foundry: ITC
Designer: Genevieve Cerasoli
Designer Nationality: American
Date: 1997

ITC Arnova is a calligraphic script with pronounced stroke contrast and rough contours. The script is inspired by the distinctive brush style of Japanese sign-painting. Its characters have pointed strokes and lean both towards and away from one another, giving the typeface a dynamic and energetic feel.

ITC Ballerino

ABCDEFGHIJKLMNOPQRSTUVWXYZ
abcdefghijklmnopqrstuvwxyz
1234567890 !@#?:; ”*&

Foundry: ITC
Designer: Viktor Solt-Bittner
Designer Nationality: Austrian
Date: 1990

Although inspired by various 18th-century calligraphic styles, Ballerino is not based on any specific typeface. The rough texture of its edges combines with its lowercase swash ascenders and descenders to give it a distinct handwritten feel. The swash caps should be used with the lowercase characters only.

ITC Berranger Hand

ABCDEFGHIJKLMNOPQRSTUVWXYZ
abcdefghijklmnopqrstuvwxyz
1234567890 !@#?:;”*&

Foundry: ITC
Designer: Éric de Berranger
Designer Nationality: French
Date: 1999

Although it has roots in chancery calligraphy, Berranger Hand resembles contemporary handwriting, written quickly with a felt-tip pen on absorbent paper. Some of the lowercase counters are narrow or filled in completely, and the uppercase letters are made without swashes, so they can be combined.

ITC Blackadder

ABCDEFGHIJKLMNOPQRSTUVWX

abcdefghijklmnopqrstuvwxyz

1234567890 !@#?:; "*&

Foundry: ITC
Designer: Bob Anderton
Designer Nationality: British
Date: 1996

Popular in the late 1990s, this so-called "vampire" script is based on the signature of the orchestrator of the Gunpowder Plot of 1605, Guy Fawkes, after he had been tortured. Bob Anderton captures the scrolls and curlicues of his 16th-century handwriting, and added the sinister tremble.

ITC Coconino

ABCDEFGHIJKLMNOPQRSTUVWXYZ

abcdefghijklmnopqrstuvwxyz

1234567890 !@#?:;"*&

Foundry: ITC
Designer: Slobodan Miladinov
Designer Nationality: Serbian
Date: 1998

Serbian font designer Slobodan Miladinov created ITC Coconino using a freemouse technique, inspired by the "surprising and confusing" music of Serbian hip-hop artist Voodoo Popeye. It is an unconventional script with strokes that have a deliberate irregularity and rather chaotic feel.

ITC Coolman

ABCDEFGHIJKLMNOPQRSTUVWXYZ

abcdefghijklmnopqrstuvwxyz

1234567890 !@#?:;"*&

Foundry: ITC
Designer: Per Ellstrøm
Designer Nationality: Swedish
Date: 1999

This quirky, informal font is the work of the Swedish font designer Per Ellstrøm, an accomplished musician as well as a typographer, who goes by the stage name of Pelle Piano. It is inspired by lettering styles of the 1950s found on B-movie posters, pocketbooks and cartoons.

ITC Cyberkugel

ABCDEFGHIJKLMNOPQRSTUVWXYZ

abcdefghijklmnopqrstuvwxyz

1234567890 !@#?:;"*&

Foundry: ITC
Designer: Timothy Donaldson
Designer Nationality: British
Date: 1997

Although it looks very organic and takes inspiration from his love of writing with an extra-fine ballpoint pen, ITC Cyberkugel was created by Timothy Donaldson entirely digitally, using a Wacom tablet. The name originates from a combination of cyberspace and *Kugelschreiber*, the German word for "ballpoint pen."

ITC Dartangnon

ABCDEFGHIJKLMNOPQRSTUVWXYZ
abcdefghijklmnopqrstuvwxyz
1234567890 !@#?.;"*&

Foundry: ITC
Designer: Nick Cooke
Designer Nationality: British
Date: 1998

Nick Cooke started his design for ITC Dartangnon by doodling using a chunky pencil. The resulting typeface is a spontaneous and swashbuckling script that retains many of the quirks and idiosyncrasies present in handwriting. The energetic script is surprisingly legible even at small point sizes.

ITC Django

ABCDEFGHIJKLMNOPQRSTUVWXYZ
abcdefghijklmnopqrstuvwxyz
1234567890 !@#?.;"*&

Foundry: ITC
Designer: Wayne Thompson
Designer Nationality: Australian
Date: 2000

Wayne Thompson based ITC Django on the handwriting of an acquaintance who called himself Django, after jazz guitarist Django Reinhardt. Thompson said the lively script has a split personality, with the looseness of the lowercase contrasting with the edginess of the uppercase characters.

ITC Humana Script

ABCDEFGHIJKLMNOPQRSTUVWXYZ
abcdefghijklmnopqrstuvwxyz
1234567890 !@#?.;"*&

Foundry: ITC
Designer: Timothy Donaldson
Designer Nationality: British
Date: 1995

British typographer Timothy Donaldson designed Humana Script for ITC in 1995. It was digitized from lettering first drawn on paper with a broad-tipped pen. It comes in Light, Medium, and Bold weights, and is part of the ITC Humana family that also contains sans serif and serif typefaces.

ITC Kloegirl

ABCDEFGHIJKLMNOPQRSTUVWXYZ
abcdefghijklmnopqrstuvwxyz
1234567890 !@#?.;"*&

Foundry: ITC
Designer: Scott Carslake
Designer Nationality: Australian
Date: 2006

Australian fashion designer Chloé Papazahariakis commissioned Scott Carslake, co-founder of Australian agency Voice Design, to create an identity for her brand. He created ITC Kloegirl inspired by her handwriting. It comes in two versions: Lotus and New York.

ITC Kulukundis

ABCDEFGHIJKLMNOPQRSTUVWX
abcdefghijklmnopqrstuvwxyz
1234567890 !@#?:;"*&

Foundry: ITC
Designer: Daniel Pelavin
Designer Nationality: American
Date: 1997

US designer Daniel Pelavin's ITC Kulukundis is a single-weight connecting script whose lowercase letters all connect in the same way via a diagonal join creating a continuous line. It was inspired by French upright scripts and the chrome lettering found on old cars.

ITC Mattia

ABCDEFGHIJKLMNOPQRSTUVWXYZ
abcdefghijklmnopqrstuvwxyz
1234567890 !@#?:;"*&

Foundry: ITC
Designer: Giuseppe Errico
Designer Nationality: Italian
Date: 2007

Giuseppe Errico's Mattia, released by ITC in 2007, is a distinctive, informal handwriting font that is somewhat scrawled but highly legible. Its lack of a consistent baseline gives the feel of real handwriting. Errico, who was born in Italy, has designed three typefaces for ITC.

ITC Musclehead

ABCDEFGHIJKLMNOPQRSTUVWXYZ
abcdefghijklmnopqrstuvwxyz
1234567890 !@#?:;"*&

Foundry: ITC
Designer: Timothy Donaldson
Designer Nationality: British
Date: 1997

British type designer, calligrapher, and author Timothy Donaldson designed the single-weight, heavy handwriting font ITC Musclehead in 1997. It was drawn using a ruling pen because Donaldson wanted to show that this tool could be used on something robust rather than skinny.

ITC Out Of The Fridge

ABCDEFGHIJKLMNOPQRSTUVWXYZ
abcdefghijklmnopqrstuvwxyz
1234567890 !@#?:;"*&

Foundry: ITC
Designer: Jochen Schuss
Designer Nationality: German
Date: 1996

Jochen Schuss drew ITC Out Of The Fridge in 1996. It is a single-weight, imperfect sans serif script with a scratchy feel and slight drips visible in places, most notably inside the capital "O." Schuss, who was born in Marburg, Germany, has released with ITC, Linotype, and Typic.

ITC Samuel

ABCDEFGHIJKLMNOPQRSTUVWXYZ
abcdefghijklmnopqrstuvwxyz
1234567890 !@#?:;"'"* &

Foundry: ITC
Designer: Phill Grimshaw
Designer Nationality: British
Date: 1998

Phill Grimshaw entered type design thanks to Tony Forster, his teacher at Bolton College of Art. When Grimshaw died in 1998, he had released forty-four typefaces through Letraset and ITC, including ITC Samuel, which was one of his last. It is a light, delicate brush script in one weight.

ITC Santangeli

ABCDEFGHIJKLMNOPQRSTUVWXYZ
abcdefghijklmnopqrstuvwxyz
1234567890 !@#?:;"'"* &

Foundry: ITC
Designer: Guiseppe Errico
Designer Nationality: Italian
Date: 2007

Guiseppe Errico based this face on 18th-century manuscripts written by the Italian calligraphy master Benedetto Santangeli. ITC Santangeli is a baroque, decorative script font in a single weight. It features long, curvaceous ascenders and descenders and many alternate characters.

ITC Studio Script

ABCDEFGHIJKLMNOPQRSTUVWXYZ
abcdefghijklmnopqrstuvwxyz
1234567890 !@#?:;"'"* &

Foundry: ITC
Designer: Robert Evans
Designer Nationality: British
Date: 1991

A retro, friendly monoline script face, ITC Studio Script was developed by British type designer Robert Evans in 1991. It was initially released by ITC, and there is also a version by the foundry Elsner+Flake. It comes in one weight and features a wide range of extra alternate characters.

ITC Viner Hand

ABCDEFGHIJKLMNOPQRSTUVWXYZ
abcdefghijklmnopqrstuvwxyz
1234567890 !@#?:;"'"* &

Foundry: ITC
Designer: John Viner
Designer Nationality: British
Date: 1995

This eponymous typeface by British designer John Viner is, as the name suggests, based on his own handwriting. Viner worked as a font designer for Letraset but also released fonts with ITC, such as Viner Hand, which is a single-weight, informal script that adds a personal touch to any application.

ITC Zemke Hand

ABCDEFGHIJKLMNOPQRSTUVWXYZ
abcdefghijklmnopqrstuvwxyz
1234567890 !@#?.;"*&

Foundry: ITC
Designer: Deborah Zemke
Designer Nationality: American
Date: 1997

US illustrator Deborah Zemke designed Zemke Hand in 1997. The monoline handwriting font is friendly and highly legible. Zemke is primarily an author and illustrator of children's books. However, she has developed two other fonts for ITC, both of which are cartoon dingbats.

John Handy

ABCDEFGHIJKLMNOPQRSTUVWXYZ
abcdefghijklmnopqrstuvwxyz
1234567890 !?:;"*&

Foundry: Letraset
Designer: Timothy Donaldson
Designer Nationality: British
Date: 1995

British designer Timothy Donaldson created John Handy for Letraset in 1995. It is an informal, slightly rough but elegant script based on the designer's own handwriting. It is an apt choice for letters, greeting cards and menus. Donaldson started a foundry called Shapes for Cash in 2018.

JP2

ABCDEFGHIJKLMNOPQRSTUVWXYZ
abcdefghijklmnopqrstuvwxyz
1234567890 !@#?.;"*&

Foundry: ITC
Designer: Franciszek Otto
Designer Nationality: Polish
Date: 2008

JP2 by Polish designer Franciszek Otto takes its name from a fellow Pole, Pope John Paul II, and Otto based it on the pontiff's handwriting. Available in one weight, JP2 is a lively, realistic script that features an inconsistent baseline, long ascenders and a low x-height.

Jump

ABCDEFGHIJKLMNOPQRSTUVWXYZ
abcdefghijklmnopqrstuvwxyz
1234567890 !@#?:;"*&

Foundry: Linotype
Designer: Sine Bergmann / Lenore Poth
Designer Nationality: German
Date: 2008

Jump by German designers Sine Bergmann and Lenore Poth is a single-weight, light-hearted handwriting typeface initially released by Linotype. It is based on the kind of informal notes written quickly by hand. Jump takes its name from the effect of letters having different baselines.

Katfish

ABCDEFGHIJKLMNOPQRSTUVWXYZ
abcdefghijklmnopqrstuvwxyz
1234567890 !?:;"*&

Foundry: Letraset
Designer: Michael Gills
Designer Nationality: British
Date: 1994

Michael Gills's Katfish is a quirky script that features sharp letters—some of which incorporate a pair of dots—a variety of ligatures, many alternate characters, and three illustrated dingbats of a cat face, a fish, and a dolphin. Gills worked at Letraset from 1988 to 1995.

Kloi BT

ABCDEFGHIJKLMNOPQRSTUVWXYZ
abcdefghijklmnopqrstuvwxyz
1234567890 !@#?:;"*&

Foundry: Bitstream
Designer: Boris Mahovac
Designer Nationality: Croatian
Date: 2004

Kloi BT, released by Bitstream in 2004, is the work of Boris Mahovac, the founder of Alphabet Design based in Ontario. It is a chunky, friendly, and somewhat naive monoline handwriting font. Kloi BT has varied capital sizes and the appearance of writing drawn with a felt-tip pen.

Leon Kinder

ABCDEFGHIJKLMNOPQRSTUVWXYZ
abcdefghijklmnopqrstuvwxyz
1234567890 !@#?:;"*&

Foundry: Dmitry Rastvortsev
Designer: Dmitry Rastvortsev /
Lev Rastvortsev
Designer Nationality: Ukrainian
Date: 2014

Leon Kinder is a friendly, childlike handwriting font. It was designed by Ukrainian typographer and designer Dmitry Rastvortsev (with assistance from his relative Lev) and released by his eponymous foundry in 2014. It is available in a single weight and features many ligatures.

Linotype Cadavre Exquis

ABCDEFGHIJKLMNOPQRSTUVWXYZ
abcdefghijklmnopqrstuvwxyz
1234567890 /?:;"&

Foundry: Linotype
Designer: Wiebke Hoeljes
Designer Nationality: German
Date: 1997

Wiebke Hoeljes's Cadavre Exquis font is included in Linotype's Halloween Value Pack of thirty-three spooky fonts. The font was picked up by Linotype in 1997 when it was an entry in the company's International Digital Type Design Contest. It features spindly letters of different weights and styles.

Linotype Colibri

ABCDEFGHIJKLMNOPQRSTUVWXYZ
abcdefghijklmnopqrstuvwxyz
1234567890 !@#?:;"*&

Available in light and regular, Hans-Jürgen Ellenberger's Linotype Colibri is a light-hearted, informal script with an inconsistent baseline and a chunky monoline, which gives the effect of writing done with a thick, felt-tip pen. It has a childlike feel due to its quirks and imperfections.

Foundry: Linotype
Designer: Hans-Jürgen Ellenberger
Designer Nationality: German
Date: 1999

Linotype Ego

ABCDEFGHIJKLHNOPQRSTUVWXYZ
abcdefghijklmnopqrstuvwxyz
1234567890 !@#?:;"*&

German creative Jörn Rings, who also goes by Jörn Lehnhoff, designed Linotype Ego in 1999. It is a sharp, imperfect handwriting font with contrast, available in a single weight. Rings, who is based in Düsseldorf, founded an agency called Zellteilung and an art gallery.

Foundry: Linotype
Designer: Jörn Rings
Designer Nationality: German
Date: 1999

Linotype Elisa

ABCDEFGHIJKL MNOPQRSTUV
abcdefghijklmnopqrstuv wxyz
12345 67890 !@#?:;"*&

Elisa, designed by the New Zealand-born Christopher Young in 1999, is a delicate, refined handwriting typeface with wide capitals and long ascenders and descenders. It comes in two weights; Regular and Bold. Young moved to Germany in 1996 and then relocated to Perth, Australia in 2002.

Foundry: Linotype
Designer: Christopher Young
Designer Nationality: New Zealander
Date: 1999

Linotype Notec

ABCDEFGHIJKLMNOPQRSTUVWXYZ
abcdefghijklmnopqrstuvwxyz
1234567890 !@#?:;"*&

An attractive, connecting handwriting script, Notec mimics the spontaneity and inconsistent nature of scribbled writing and has a non-uniform stroke width. By Franciszek Otto, Notec came second in the display category of Linotype's 3rd International Digital Type Design Contest in 2000.

Foundry: Linotype
Designer: Franciszek Otto
Designer Nationality: Polish
Date: 1999

Linotype Sallwey Script

ABCDEFGHJJKLMNOPQRSTUVWXYZ
abcdefghijklmnopqrstuvwxyz
1234567890 !@#?:;"*&

Foundry: Linotype
Designer: Friedrich Karl Sallwey
Designer Nationality: German
Date: 1980

Linotype released German designer Friedrich Karl Sallwey's eponymous script in 1980; it is a distinctive, slightly inclined non-connecting script in a single weight with diamond-shaped tittles. Sallwey began his career as an assistant to Heinrich Jost, art director of the Bauer type foundry.

Linotype Tapeside

ABCDEFGHIJKLMNOPQRSTUVWXYZ
abcdefghijklmnopqrstuvwxyz
1234567890 !@#?:;"*&

Foundry: Linotype
Designer: Stephan B. Murphy
Designer Nationality: British
Date: 1997

Tapeside, which was selected by Linotype at its International Digital Type Design Contest in 1997, is a childlike sans serif with inconsistent stroke widths. Available in Light, Regular, and Bold weights, all of which have obliques, it is the only typeface Stephan B. Murphy has released.

Liorah BT

ABCDEFGHIJKLMNOP2RST
abcdefghijklmnopqrstuvwxyz
1234567890 !@#?:;"*&

Foundry: Bitstream
Designer: Holly Goldsmith
Designer Nationality: American
Date: 2000

A wide and curly connecting script, Liorah was released by Bitstream in 2000. This elegant typeface by Holly Goldsmith is slightly oblique and comes in a single regular weight. Goldsmith worked for Mergenthaler Linotype and Xerox before starting her studio called Small Cap Graphics.

Malibu

ABCDEFGHIJKLMNOPQRSTUVWXYZ
abcdefghijklmnopqrstuvwxyz
1234567890 !?:;"*&

Foundry: ITC
Designer: Alan Meeks
Designer Nationality: British
Date: 1992

Alan Meeks's Malibu, named after the famous beach city just outside Los Angeles, California, is a chunky, inclined non-connecting script. The typeface has an energetic, angular feel and manages to evoke the atmosphere of the beach with which it shares its name.

Manu

ABCDEFGHIJKLMNOPQRSTUVWXYZ
abcdefghijklmnopqrstuvwxyz
1234567890 !@#?:; "*&

Foundry: Typotheque
Designer: Peter Biľak
Designer Nationality: Slovakian
Date: 2016

Manu is based on Peter Biľak's handwriting. It is available in four styles: a hand-drawn sans, Formal; a connecting script, Informal; a bold, handwritten uppercase, Emphasis; and a dingbat font, Symbol. Formal and Informal were drawn with a 0.7 mm pen and Emphasis with a chunky marker.

Markerfield

ABCDEFGHIJKLMNOPQRSTUVWXYZ
abcdefghijklmnopqrstuvwxyz
1234567890 !@#?:;"*&

Foundry: Typodermic
Designer: Ray Larabie
Designer Nationality: Canadian
Date: 2010

Ray Larabie's Markerfield, released by Typodermic in 2010, is a single-weight handwritten script that achieves the texture and thickness of lettering drawn with a heavy, black marker pen. Larabie included many ligature options, which help produce a more realistic handwriting feel.

Matthia

ABCDEFGHIJKLMNOPQRSTUVWXYZ
abcdefghijklmnopqrstuvwxyz
1234567890 !@#?:;"*&

Foundry: Linotype
Designer: Dieter Kurz
Designer Nationality: German
Date: 1994

German designer Dieter Kurz's Matthia is a reasonably compact brush script inspired by lettering used in advertising in the 1950s. Linotype inducted it into its TakeType Library when it was a category winner in the company's first International Digital Type Design Contest in 1994.

Missy BT

ABCDEFGHIJKLMNOPQRSTUVWXYZ
abcdefghijklmnopqrstuvwxyz
1234567890 !@#?:;"*&

Foundry: Bitstream
Designer: Holly Goldsmith
Designer Nationality: American
Date: 2000

Holly Goldsmith designed Missy for Bitstream in 2000. It is a single-style, informal handwritten sans serif, which has a naive, childlike energy. Its vertical strokes all begin below the baseline. Missy is one of six fonts Goldsmith released with Bitstream between 2000 and 2001.

Mistral

ABCDEFGHIJKLMNOPQRSTUVWXYZ
abcdefghijklmnopqrstuvwxyz
1234567890 !@#?:;"*&

Foundry: Fonderie Olive
Designer: Roger Excoffon
Designer Nationality: French
Date: 1957

Mistral, one of the world's most popular script typefaces, was designed for the French Fonderie Olive in 1957. A loose joined-up script, Mistral is based on Roger Excoffon's handwriting and has the texture of brush or felt-tip pen lettering. It comes in Light and Regular weights.

Nevison Casual

ABCDEFGHIJKLMNOPQRSTUVWXYZ
abcdefghijklmnopqrstuvwxyz
1234567890 !@#?:;"*&

Foundry: VGC
Designer: Thomas J. Nevison
Designer Nationality: American
Date: 1965

Nevison Casual, designed for the Visual Graphics Corporation (VGC), is a script in the style of informal handwriting. The uppercase characters are typically open and bountiful, while the lowercases are narrower and more reserved, giving the font a dynamic contrast when set in text.

One Stroke Script

ABCDEFGHIJKLMNOPQRSTUVWXYZ
abcdefghijklmnopqrstuvwxyz
1234567890 !@#?:;"*&

Foundry: ITC
Designer: Paul Clarke
Designer Nationality: British
Date: 1991

One Stroke Script is a casual script in which the letterforms imitate the broad strokes of a brush. The font family, which includes Regular, Bold, and Shaded styles, resists a formal structure and instead favors the loose curves often associated with hand-lettering.

Papyrus

ABCDEFGHIJKLMNOPQRSTUVWXYZ
abcdefghijklmnopqrstuvwxyz
1234567890 !@#?:;"*&

Foundry: Letraset
Designer: Chris Costello
Designer Nationality: American
Date: 1983

Papyrus was drawn over six months, using a calligraphy pen on textured paper. It is a script designed to imitate the appearance of ancient handwriting. The distinctive characters feature rough outlines, tall ascenders, and a combination of roman and calligraphic styles.

PL Trophy

ABCDEFGHIJKLMNOPQRSTUVWXYZ
abcdefghijklmnopqrstuvwxyz
1234567890 !© #?:; "*&

Foundry: Monotype
Designer: Frank Bartuska
Designer Nationality: American
Date: 1950

PL Trophy is Monotype's digital revival of Frank Bartuska's Trophy Oblique, a script designed in 1950 for the Photo-Lettering foundry. Unlike most scripts, which reference calligraphic forms, these handwritten characters are informal in shape and low in stroke contrast.

Rage Italic

ABCDEFGHIJKLMNOPQRSTUVWXYZ
abcdefghijklmnopqrstuvwxyz
1234567890 !@# ?:; "*&

Foundry: ITC
Designer: Ron M. W. Zwingelberg
Designer Nationality: American
Date: 1984

Rage Italic is a handwritten script font, and one of the first designs to purposely feature a rugged outline that imitates the texture of ink on parchment. The cursive letterforms also utilize a low x-height and looping ascenders and descenders for clarity at small sizes.

Ru'ach

ABCDEFGHIJKLMNOPQRSTUVWXYZ
abcdefghijklmnopqrstuvwxyz
1234567890 !?:;"*&

Foundry: ITC
Designer: Timothy Donaldson
Designer Nationality: British
Date: 1990

Ru'ach is a script font designed in the style of handwriting. The letterforms, which are distinctive in their dry brush texture, are the result of Timothy Donaldson's numerous investigations into the effects of using different writing instruments on a variety of surfaces.

Scooter

ABCDEFGHIJKLMNOPQRSTUVW
abcdefghijklmnopqrstuvwxyz
1234567890 !@#?:;"*&

Foundry: Ascender
Designer: Steve Matteson
Designer Nationality: American
Date: 2009

Scooter is a script designed in the style of colloquial handwriting. The font shares its name with a "bashful but lovable" Labrador Retriever and intends to convey friendliness in objects, such as badges, T-shirts, or even a personalized dog's bed, or in communications via cards and memos.

Skippy Sharp

ABCDEFGHIJKLMNOPQRSTUVWXYZ
abcdefghijklmnopqrstuvwxyz
1234567890 !@#?:;"*¿

Foundry: Chank Co.
Designer: Skippy McFadden / Chank Diesel
Designer Nationality: American
Date: 1995

Skippy Sharp is a script designed to imitate the appearance of writing by hand with a marker. The characters were initially drawn by Skippy McFadden, who later sent them by fax to designer Chank Diesel, who then adjusted the kerning and filled the gaps in the font's character set.

Staehle Graphia

ABCDEFGHIJKLMNOPQRSTUVWXYZ
abcdefghijklmnopqrstuvwxyz
1234567890 !@#?:;"*&

Foundry: Linotype
Designer: Walter Stähle
Designer Nationality: German
Date: *c.* 1960

Staehle Graphia is a script face modeled on correspondences produced on private printing presses in the 19th century. The letterforms combine calligraphic flourishes, which are seen primarily in the capitals, with the direct vertical strokes found in the lowercase forms.

Teebrush Paint

ABCDEFGHIJKLMNOPQRSTUVWXYZ
abcdefghijklmnopqrstuvwxyz
1234567890 !@№?:;"*&

Foundry: Linotype
Designer: Tomi Haaparanta
Designer Nationality: Finnish
Date: 2002

Designed to imitate the quirks of hand-painted lettering, Teebrush Paint is a script designed in two versions, Teebrush Paint, and Teebrush Paint Alternate. When combined, the two styles, which feature only slight differences in design, mitigate inauthentic character repetition

---

Terry Junior

ABCDEFGHIJKLMNOPQRSTUVWXYZ
abcdefghijklmnopqrstuvwxyz
1234567890 !@#?:;'"*&

Foundry: Monotype
Designer: Terrance Weinzierl
Designer Nationality: American
Date: 2018

Terry Junior is a handwritten script designed to convey a childish playfulness. Initially, Terrance Weinzierl drew the letterforms as part of a Monotype Font Marathon before expanding them digitally to comprise a family of five fonts, including Deluxe, Inline, and Rotalic versions

Trackpad

ABCDEFGHIJKLMNOPQRSTUVWXYZ
abcdefghijklmnopqrstuvwxyz
1234567890 !?:;"*&

Foundry: ITC
Designer: Timothy Donaldson
Designer Nationality: British
Date: 1995

Trackpad is a handwritten script that combines an informal character with a functional shape. The colloquial letterforms, which feature large x-heights, upright strokes, and varying slants, were designed to maintain both readability and personality in the smallest of text sizes.

Wiesbaden Swing

ABCDEFGHIJKLMNOPQRSTUVWXY
abcdefghijklmnopqrstuvwxyz
1234567890 !@#?:;"*&

Foundry: Linotype
Designer: Rosemarie Kloos-Rau
Designer Nationality: German
Date: 1992

Based on the style of the designer's own handwriting, Wiesbaden Swing is an informal script designed in Regular and Bold weights. The letterforms, which remain resolute and legible in either display or text sizes, are complemented by a full set of convivial dingbats.

Wola

ABCDEFGHIJKLMNOPQRSTUVWXYZ
abcdefghijklmnopqrstuvwxyz
1234567890 !@#?:;"*&

Foundry: Monotype
Designer: Franciszek Otto
Designer Nationality: Polish
Date: 2017

Wola is a handwritten script designed for digital and printed headlines. The letterforms integrate the high-contrast stroke style of Bodoni with the vigour of hand-painted figures, which engenders a structured yet informal appearance in both the upper and lowercases.

Yellabelly

ABCDEFGHIJKLMNOPQRSTUVWXYZ
abcdefghijklmnopqrstuvwxyz
1234567890 !@#?:;"*&

Foundry: Chank Co.
Designer: Chank Diesel
Designer Nationality: American
Date: 1998

Chank Diesel's Yellabelly is a handwritten script that simulates the effects of writing cursive left-handed. For right-handed writing, the pen trails across the page; by contrast, a left-handed writer is forced to push the pen, which can result in irregular, stuttering, letterforms.

Index of Typefaces

Index of Designers

Index of Foundries

Picture Credits

About the Author

Peter Dawson worked as a designer and then creative director at a number of design studios after studying graphic design at Kingston University. He went on to found Grade Design in 2000, a London-based graphic design studio specializing in typography, editorial, and book design, corporate identity and art direction for the art, commercial, charitable, and publishing sectors.

He has designed for a diverse and extensive range of clients over the years, including the British Museum, Historic Royal Palaces, The National Museum of Qatar, Rolex, Royal Mail, Thames & Hudson, the V&A, and Yale University Press.

Peter has designed a number of best-selling and recognized illustrated book titles, and his awards include British D&AD annual inclusion, several ISTD Certificates of Excellence and a Premiere Award, and, in recent years, "Best Jacket," "Best Book Series," and "Best Trade Illustrated" in the British Book Design and Production Awards.

A Fellow of the ISTD, and a former Chair and board member, he has been a visiting typography and design lecturer at a number of universities in the UK and overseas.

Peter is co-author of the book *Graphic Design Rules* (Frances Lincoln) and author of *The Field Guide to Typography* (Thames & Hudson), and has written articles on design and typography for several industry journals.

www.gradedesign.com

Acknowledgments

Writing and creating a book of this extent and complexity has been without doubt, a team effort and I could not have done it without the contributions, hard work and generosity of many dedicated and skilled individuals and organizations. My deepest gratitude goes to my publisher Philip Cooper of White Lion Press, who commissioned me for such an undertaking. He, together with my managing editor Jennifer Barr, provided valuable guidance and support throughout the challenge of creating the *The Essential Type Directory*. Thank you also for the efforts of my editor Carol King, whose dedication and diligence in checking facts when historical references were unclear or contradictory went beyond the norm in helping us make sense of it all.

My thanks also go to my team of contributing writers for the quarter-page typeface profiles: the ever-patient Caroline Roberts, writer, editor, and founder of *Grafik* magazine, who headed up the team; freelance graphic designer and writer Theo Inglis; design writer, editor, and lecturer Anna Lisa Reynolds and design historian Alex J. Todd. They collaborated in a seamless manner while under pressure to meet deadlines, despite having a proverbial typographic mountain to climb. Thanks also to Mike Daines at eLexicons for his assistance with historical research.

My special thanks go to my colleagues at Grade Design, who worked so hard to help research, compile, design, and build the book. My everlasting thanks go to both Katie Holmes and to Alice Kennedy-Owen. Their unwavering enthusiasm, patience, insight, and dedication— with never a complaint—over the year it took to create the *The Essential Type Directory* has been immeasurable.

Thank you to Luped Limited for their assistance and aid in the never-ending quest for images and permissions.

Very special thanks go to Tobias Frere-Jones for very kindly providing time, insight, and advice in writing the Foreword to the *The Essential Type Directory* and advising on other areas of the book's content. Thanks also go to Christine Bateup in organizing the Frere-Jones Type contributions to feature within the *The Essential Type Directory*.

Of course, a book on typefaces could not come to fruition without the generous contribution, time and expertise given by the type designers and foundries who have very kindly provided content for the book. My heartfelt thanks go to (in no preference of order): Benoît Bodhuin of BB-Bureau; Anthony Sheret and Edd Harrington of Colophon Foundry; Paul Barnes, Christian Schwartz, and Emil Martirosian of Commercial Type; Bruno Maag, Kathrin Heimel, Katy Smith, and Beatrix Fletcher at Dalton Maag; Rudy VanderLans and Zuzana Licko of Emigre; Jason Smith, Tamasin Handley, and Stuart de Rozario of Fontsmith; Stephan Müller of Forgotten Shapes / Lineto; David Quay and Freda Sack of The Foundry; Noël Leu and Thierry Blancpain of Grilli Type; Charles Nix, Andy Rodgers, and Jim Ford of Monotype; Jeremy Tankard of Jeremy Tankard Typography; Timo Gaessner and Maiko Gubler of Milieu Grotesque; Paul McNeil and Hamish Muir of MuirMcNeil; Alexander McCracken of Neutura; Guðmundur Úlfarsson and Mads Freund Brunse of Or Type; Mathias Jespersen and Annemarie Friislund of Playtype Foundry; and Peter Bil'ak of Typotheque.

A big thank you for the generosity and expertise of Alexander Tochilovsky at The Herb Lubalin Study Center of Design and Typography, who went out of his way checking and suggesting images and to his colleague Laura Mircik-Sellers.

I also want to pay a debt of gratitude to those graphic designers, studios and organizations who have allowed us to showcase their work within the book as examples of particular typefaces: Pedro Falcão of Atelier Pedro Falcão; Professor John McMillan, Emeritus Professor of Graphic Design at Ulster University; Clare Playne at the International Society of Typographic Designers (www.istd.org.uk;) Patrick Myles; Konstantin Eremenko of Eremenko Visual Communication, Russia; Margus Tamm; Tako Chabukiani of Pragmatika Design, Georgia; Chantal Manella of Metapur AG, Germany; Solo, Spain; Mikhail Rul; Blok Design, Canada; Trüf Creative, United States; Sacred Bones Records; The Martin Agency, United States; Bisgràfic, Spain; Leslie Chan Wing Kei, Taiwan; Maiarelli Studio, United States; Stereo Associates, Denmark; Morphoria Design Collective, Germany; Intégral Ruedi Baur Paris, France; Erik Spiekermann; Nick Kapica, SV Associates; Typoretum, United Kingdom; Bunch Design, United Kingdom.

Finally, I would like to pay tribute to Freda Sack, my close friend, colleague, and mentor, who passed away during the writing of this book. I had the great pleasure and privilege of working with Freda for many years while we were members of the board for the International Society of Typographic Designers (ISTD). However, we first met many years before, just after I left college, and I was always impressed and inspired by her enthusiasm, generous spirit and immense talent. Freda was not only a highly skilled and accomplished type designer and typographer but also contributed inestimably to typographic and design education through her long-standing commitment to the ISTD. She will be greatly missed by all who knew her and this book is in small part a humble tribute to her.

Peter Dawson
London, 2019

For Frederick

Black Dog & Leventhal Publishers
Hachette Book Group
1290 Avenue of the Americas
New York, NY 10104

www.hachettebookgroup.com
www.blackdogandleventhal.com

Simultaneously published in the UK by Thames & Hudson.

First US Edition: December 2019

Black Dog & Leventhal Publishers is an imprint of Perseus Books, LLC, a subsidiary of Hachette Book Group, Inc. The Black Dog & Leventhal Publishers name and logo are trademarks of Hachette Book Group, Inc.

The publisher is not responsible for websites (or their content) that are not owned by the publisher.

The Hachette Speakers Bureau provides a wide range of authors for speaking events. To find out more, go to www.HachetteSpeakersBureau.com or call (866) 376-6591.

LCCN: 2019940029
ISBNs: 978-0-7624-6817-1 (hardcover); 978-0-7624-6851-5 (ebook), 978-0-7624-7043-3 (ebook), 978-0-7624-7042-6 (ebook)

Printed in China

QRT
10 9 8 7 6 5 4 3 2 1

T = top; B = bottom; M = middle, L = left; R = right; BL = bottom left; BR = bottom right; TL = top left, TR = top right.

Page 2. T: Bespoke typeface for Umbro by Commercial Type for the England football team kit; BL: Promotional print for Skate Agora, using Druk by Commercial Type, design by Solo Design Studio, Madrid; BR: Editorial design by Yevgeniy Anfalov using Mineral by BB-Bureau.

Page 3. T: Identity and branding for the London-based Redchurch Brewery, employing Separat by Or-Type, design by Bibliothèque; B: Poster series by Design by Atlas for Museu del Disseny using Graphik by Commercial Type.

Page 4. Optical/geometric type system Nine by MuirMcNeil.

Page 5. TL: Albertus as used by Barnbrook studio in the book *David Bowie Is*; TR: Program promotional design by Emigre; BL: Lost & Foundry typeface collection by Fontsmith; BR: BB-Bureau's ZigZag in use for Antigel Festival 2014, design by Pablo Lavalley.

Page 6. T: Preparatory workings for Dalton Maag's Blenny font; BL: Pembroke serif by Jeremy Tankard Typography; BR: Empirica by Frere-Jones Type.

Page 7. TL: FS Benjamin by Fontsmith; TR: The innovative History type system by Typotheque employed in shop window display, design by Pentagram NYC; BL: Berthold Akzidenz Grotesk employed on architect's Tim Mein's website, design by Sons & Co. / Timothy Kelleher; BR: Chapeau type specimen by Milieu Grotesque.

Page 8. T: Wayfinding and information graphics by Design by Atlas for Museu del Disseny using Graphik by Commercial Type; BL: Detail showing *DieseWoche* poster employing Univers, designed by Otl Aicher for the 1972 Munich Olympics; BR: *Habitar* poster by Atelier Pedro Falcão using Akkurat Pro.